P9-CAG-643

Critical Survey of Mystery and Detective Fiction

Critical Survey of Mystery and Detective Fiction

Revised Edition

Volume 4

Ellis Peters – Israel Zangwill

Editor, Revised Edition
Carl Rollyson
Baruch College, City University of New York

Editor, First Edition
Frank N. Magill

SALEM PRESS, INC.
Pasadena, California   Hackensack, New Jersey

Editor in Chief: Dawn P. Dawson

Editorial Director: Christina J. Moose
Developmental Editor: R. Kent Rasmussen
Project Editor: Rowena Wildin Dehanke
Editorial Assistant: Dana Garey
Research Supervisor: Jeffry Jensen
Research Assistant: Keli Trousdale
Acquisitions Editor: Mark Rehn
Photo Editor: Cynthia Breslin Beres
Production Editor: Joyce I. Buchea
Design and Graphics: James Hutson

Cover image: *Love Story Magazine*, Mar. 9, 1929/
(*Love Story Magazine* is the property of Condé Nast)

Some of the essays in this work, which have been updated, originally appeared in the following Salem Press sets: *Critical Survey of Mystery and Detective Fiction* (1988, edited by Frank N. Magill) and *One Hundred Masters of Mystery and Detective Fiction* (2001, edited by Fiona Kelleghan). New material has been added.

∞ The paper used in these volumes conforms to the American National Standard for Permanence of Paper for Printed Library Materials, Z39.48-1992(R1997).

Library of Congress Cataloging-in-Publication Data

Critical survey of mystery and detective fiction. — Rev. ed. / editor, Carl Rollyson.
p. cm.
ISBN 978-1-58765-397-1 (set : alk. paper) — ISBN 978-1-58765-398-8 (vol. 1 : alk. paper) —
ISBN 978-1-58765-399-5 (vol. 2 : alk. paper) — ISBN 978-1-58765-400-8 (vol. 3 : alk. paper) —
ISBN 978-1-58765-401-5 (vol. 4 : alk. paper) — ISBN 978-1-58765-402-2 (vol. 5 : alk. paper)
1. Detective and mystery stories—History and criticism. 2. Detective and mystery stories—Bio-bibliography.
3. Detective and mystery stories—Stories, plots, etc. I. Rollyson, Carl E. (Carl Edmund)

PN3448.D4C75 2008
809.3'872—dc22

2007040208

First Printing
PRINTED IN THE UNITED STATES OF AMERICA

CONTENTS

VOLUME 4

COMPLETE LIST OF CONTENTS

VOLUME 1

VOLUME 2

VOLUME 3

VOLUME 4

VOLUME 5

PAST AND PRESENT MYSTERY AND DETECTIVE FICTION

MYSTERY FICTION AROUND THE WORLD

SUBGENRES OF MYSTERY FICTION

THE DETECTIVES

OTHER MEDIA

RESOURCES

INDEXES

Authors

ELLIS PETERS

Edith Mary Pargeter

Born: Horsehay, Shropshire, England; September 28, 1913
Died: Shropshire, England; October 14, 1995
Also wrote as Jolyon Carr
Types of plot: Amateur sleuth; historical; police procedural; thriller; cozy

PRINCIPAL SERIES

Felse family, 1951-1978
Brother Cadfael, 1977-1995

PRINCIPAL SERIES CHARACTERS

GEORGE FELSE is detective sergeant and later detective chief inspector of the Criminal Investigation Department in Comerford, a provincial town in central England. Felse, is a highly professional and honest police officer. A middle-aged family man, Felse is deeply in love with his wife and devoted to their son. He is dependable, mature, understanding, and reasonable.

BERNARDA "BUNTY" ELLIOT FELSE, the wife of George Felse, was a concert contralto before she married George. Bunty is a loyal and devoted wife and mother. Intelligent, sensitive, and thoughtful, she proves to be shrewd and fearless when she accidentally becomes involved in detection.

DOMINIC FELSE, the son of George and Bunty Felse, matures in the course of the series from a thirteen-year-old boy who discovers the corpse in his father's first murder case to a young Oxford University graduate. Engaging, adventurous, and aware, Dominic figures directly as an amateur detective in several of the novels, and peripherally in the others.

BROTHER CADFAEL, a twelfth century Benedictine monk, is a Welshman in his early sixties. Cadfael fought in the Crusades and had several amatory adventures as a young man before retiring to Shrewsbury Abbey. His youthful experiences gave him an understanding of human nature, and his present work as gardener and medicinal herbalist figures in his detection of criminals.

PRIOR ROBERT, a monk of Shrewsbury Abbey, is around fifty years of age. He is handsome, aristocratic, authoritative, and ambitious. His scheming for power in the abbey sets him at odds with Brother Cadfael and makes him that character's principal foil.

HUGH BERINGAR, sheriff of Shrewsbury, is a bold and keenly intelligent man in his early twenties. He is the friend and principal secular ally of Brother Cadfael and aids him in solving several of his cases.

CONTRIBUTION

Ellis Peters's Felse family series and her chronicles of Brother Cadfael are in the British tradition of detective-fiction writers such as P. D. James and Ruth Rendell. These writers' works, while displaying the careful and suspenseful plotting characteristic of the detective genre, frequently transcend the effect of pure entertainment and share with the traditional "literary" novel the aims of engaging in complex examinations of human character and psychology and achieving thematic depth and moral vision.

Peters herself expressed her dislike for the distinction between detective fiction and serious novels and succeeded in interweaving traditional novelistic materials—love interests, the study of human growth and maturation, the depiction of communities and their politics—with the activity of crime solving. The Brother Cadfael chronicles are her most popular as well as her most impressive achievements, locating universal human situations in the meticulously particularized context of twelfth century England. These novels are masterpieces of historical reconstruction; they present a memorable and likable hero, Brother Cadfael, and a vivid picture of medieval life, in and out of the monastery, in its religious, familial, social, political, and cultural dimensions.

BIOGRAPHY

Ellis Peters was born Edith Mary Pargeter on September 28, 1913, in Horsehay, Shropshire, England, the daughter of Edmund Valentine Pargeter and Edith

Hordley Pargeter. (Ellis Peters is a pen name that she adopted in 1959 after having published numerous books.) She attended Dawley Church of England Elementary School in Shropshire and Coalbrookdale High School for Girls and earned an Oxford School Certificate. She worked as a pharmacist's assistant and dispenser in Dawley from 1933 to 1940. During this time, she also began writing novels on a wide range of historical and contemporary subjects; the first was *Hortensius, Friend of Nero* (1936). From 1940 to 1945, she served as a petty officer in the Women's Royal Naval Service, receiving the British Empire Medal in 1944. During World War II she developed an interest in Czechoslovakia because she was haunted by the Western powers' betrayal of that country at Munich. After the war, she translated many volumes of prose and poetry from the Czech and Slovak and continued writing her own fiction.

Her first detective novel, which she published as Edith Pargeter in 1951, was *Fallen into the Pit*. It initiated a series of thirteen novels featuring the Felse family, a series that continued until 1978. Peters wrote five other detective novels and numerous detective short stories during this period as well. Her interests in music, theater, and art are reflected in several of these works. In 1977, she began publishing the Brother Cadfael novels.

Ellis Peters in 1995. (AP/Wide World Photos)

As both Edith Pargeter and Ellis Peters, this writer received much recognition for her work, including the Mystery Writers of America's Edgar Allan Poe Award in 1963 for *Death and the Joyful Woman* (1961), which was cited as the best mystery novel of the year; the Czechoslovak Society for International Relations Gold Medal in 1968; and the Crime Writers' Association's Silver Dagger in 1980 for *Monk's-Hood* (1980). She was awarded the Crime Writers' Association's Cartier Diamond Dagger for lifetime achievement in 1993. Peters died on October 14, 1995.

Analysis

Ellis Peters came to detective fiction after many years of novel writing. Disliking the frequently made distinction between detective novels, or "thrillers," as she called them, and serious novels, she stressed that "the thriller *is a novel*. . . . The pure puzzle, with a cast of characters kept deliberately two-dimensional and all equally expendable at the end, has no attraction for me." Her detective novels bear witness both to her life experiences and to her statements about her art.

Peters was essentially a social novelist. Murder serves as her occasion to dramatize a wide variety of human interactions and motivations in settings that are vividly realized. One might think of an Ellis Peters mystery in terms of a set of concentric circles. At the center is the detective character, usually preoccupied at the beginning of the novel with something other than crime. Frequently, he or she is an amateur who assumes the role of detective only circumstantially. The amateur status of several of her detectives allows Peters to move the narrative comfortably beyond crime into other areas such as love relationships, family interactions, and the struggles of adolescents maturing toward self-discovery. Except for *Death Mask* (1959), Peters's detective novels are narrated from a third-person point of view through an anonymous persona. Peters is able to narrow or broaden her perspective with ease, and therefore to present the inner workings of her central characters' minds and to focus on external matters—landscapes, social or historical background, local customs—with equal skill.

The central character is generally carefully placed within the circle of a close family or community that is described in depth. The earlier mysteries often focus on Central Intelligence Division detective sergeant George Felse of Comerford, his wife, Bunty, and their son Dominic. Although George and Dominic are the most actively involved in detection, Bunty too becomes accidentally involved in solving a murder in *The Grass-Widow's Tale* (1968). Peters's later series places its central character, Brother Cadfael, within the twelfth century Benedictine community of monks at the Abbey of St. Peter and St. Paul in Shrewsbury, England. Although the Felse family series ranges in locale from central England to such places as the Cornish coast, Scotland, Czechoslovakia, Austria, and India, the Brother Cadfael novels usually stay within the vicinity of Shrewsbury, allowing Peters to develop her picture of medieval life in great depth.

Beyond these family and community circles, there are larger milieus. For the Felse family, these include a variety of worlds—for example, those of concert musicians, of diplomats, and of professional thieves. Brother Cadfael and his fellow monks live in the Shropshire of the late 1130's and earlier 1140's and frequently find themselves caught in the political strife between Empress Maud and her cousin King Stephen, who contend for the British crown. At other times, the political feuds are more local if not less complex and bitter.

The Grass-Widow's Tale

Typically, Peters's detective novels begin at a fairly leisurely pace. In *The Grass-Widow's Tale*, for example, Bunty Felse at the outset is feeling frustrated that her husband and son are going to be absent on her forty-first birthday, doubtful about her identity and accomplishments, and gloomy as she ponders "age, infirmity, and death." The plot of this novel takes many surprising twists and turns before focusing on the solution of a murder and robbery case, a case that becomes the occasion for Bunty to find renewed meaning in her life and to discover some precious truths about the nature of human love.

A Morbid Taste for Bones

In *A Morbid Taste for Bones: A Mediaeval Whodunnit* (1977), the first chronicle of Brother Cadfael, Peters begins with the background for the Shrewsbury monks' mission to Wales to obtain the bones of Saint Winifred and proceeds to dramatize the initial results of that mission and to establish the novel's major characters and subplots. It is only on page 91 of this 256-page novel that a murder case surfaces.

Once the scenes have been set and the characters established, Peters's detective novels become absorbingly suspenseful and often contain exciting action scenes. *The Grass-Widow's Tale* includes a terrifying episode in which Bunty and her companion, Luke, must fight their way out of a cottage in which they are being held by a gang of ruthless professional criminals who are planning to murder them. *Saint Peter's Fair* (1981), one of the most suspenseful of the Brother Cadfael chronicles, features a remarkable chase-and-rescue sequence.

A highly skillful creator of suspense, Peters proves to be at least as gifted as a student of human character. She has explained her interest in crime novels thus:

> The paradoxical puzzle, the impossible struggle to create a cast of genuine, rounded, knowable characters caught in conditions of stress, to let readers know everything about them, feel with them, like or dislike them, and still to try to preserve to the end the secret of which of these is a murderer—this is the attraction for me.

Brother Cadfael

The most successfully realized of Peters's characters is Brother Cadfael, who combines worldly wisdom and experience with moral and spiritual insight. He is a middle-aged man who entered monastic life after fighting for many years in the Crusades. His experiences and travels to such places as Venice, Cyprus, and the Holy Land afforded him a knowledge of human nature unusual in a monk and developed in him courage and a liking for adventure. He came to know not only the ways of men but also those of women; he has been a lover as well as a warrior, and he readily acknowledges that he committed a fair share of "mischief" as a younger man.

This "mischief" is to be distinguished, however, from evil. Brother Cadfael is essentially a good man. It was the desire to develop his spiritual side that led him to retire to the Benedictine abbey at Shrewsbury, where he has been living as a monk for fifteen years when the chronicles begin.

Cadfael's experiences of a life of action set him apart from most of the other monks; his experiences as a monk, in turn, set him apart from people living a worldly life. Even his birthplace sets him apart: He is a Welshman in an English monastery. Like many other famous detective heroes, Cadfael is unique in his milieu, a more complete person than his contemporaries. As a man of action, moreover, he shares the abilities, though never the ruthlessness, of hard-boiled detectives, while as a participant in the contemplative life, he bears some resemblance to armchair detectives.

Monk's-Hood

At the abbey, Brother Cadfael is in charge of a flourishing garden. He specializes in herbs used for seasoning and medicine. Some of these herbs can be dangerous, and, to Cadfael's horror, malefactors sometimes steal them from the garden to use them as poisons. Cadfael becomes involved in several of his cases through such circumstances. In *Monk's-Hood*, for example, he commits himself to solve the murder of Master Bonel, who died after being served a dinner sent from the monastery. The dish proved to be laced with liniment prepared by Cadfael himself and containing monkshood (wolfsbane), a deadly poison.

Cadfael's garden is a living symbol of the hero himself as well as of the human world around him. Growth takes place there, as it does in human life, growth of things either healthful and nourishing or harmful. Just as Brother Cadfael cultivates, nurtures, and controls his plants, so too does he foster the proper kinds of growth in his community. In a number of the chronicles, Cadfael has a young assistant, a novice monk whom he lovingly guides toward psychological and spiritual maturity. Sometimes this guidance takes the form of transplanting. In *A Morbid Taste for Bones*, Cadfael recognizes that Brother John lacks a vocation for the monastery and eventually helps him to begin a new life with the woman with whom he falls in love in Wales.

The Devil's Novice

In *The Devil's Novice* (1983), Cadfael obtains justice for Brother Meriet, a "green boy" who has been banished to the monastery for a crime he did not commit. Cadfael's detective activities extend the gardening metaphor further—he weeds out undesirable elements in his community and distinguishes the poisonous from the harmless. Cadfael's herbs are most beneficial as medicinal aids, and he himself is, ultimately, not merely an amateur detective but also a healer of physical, moral, and spiritual maladies.

In his role as healer, Brother Cadfael exemplifies Peters's principal concerns as a novelist. She has commented, "It is probably true that I am not very good at villains. The good interest me so much more." Her villains are typically motivated by ambition or greed, dehumanizing vices that lead them to murder and treachery. The element of treachery makes Cadfael's cases something more than simply puzzles to be solved; it invests them with an enhanced moral dimension. Peters declares that she has "one sacred rule" about her detective fiction, apart from treating her characters "with the same respect as in any other form of novel":

> It is, it ought to be, it must be, a morality. If it strays from the side of the angels, provokes total despair, wilfully destroys—without pressing need in the plot—the innocent and the good, takes pleasure in evil, that is unforgivable sin. I use the word deliberately and gravely.

The villains in the Brother Cadfael series characteristically attempt to destroy "the innocent and the good." Brother Cadfael repeatedly becomes involved in his cases when a young person is unjustly accused of murder. In *A Morbid Taste for Bones*, for example, Engelard, an exiled Englishman in love with the Welsh squire Rhisiart's daughter, is wrongly thought to have killed Rhisiart, who had opposed Engelard's suit. The murderer proves instead to be a fanatically ambitious young monk. Brother Cadfael works to prove the innocence of Master Bonel's stepson Edwin when Bonel dies of poisoning in *Monk's-Hood*. A complicating motivational force in this novel is the fact that Edwin is the son of Richildis, Cadfael's sweetheart of long ago, whom he has not seen in forty-two years.

The Leper of Saint Giles and The Sanctuary Sparrow

In *The Leper of Saint Giles* (1981), the lovely Iveta is about to be married by her ambitious and greedy guardians to a man she does not love. When that man's mangled body is found in a forest, the man she loves is accused of the murder, and Brother Cadfael steps in to prove that he is innocent. Cadfael saves Liliwin, a traveling performer who seeks sanctuary at the abbey, and proves his innocence of robbery and murder in *The Sanctuary Sparrow* (1983).

One Corpse Too Many and Saint Peter's Fair

Although threats to innocent young men in the Brother Cadfael chronicles usually take the form of false accusations of crime, threats to innocent young women tend to involve actual or potential entrapments requiring their rescue, as in *One Corpse Too Many* (1979) and *Saint Peter's Fair*. Peters's young female characters are not passive victims, however, but intelligent, persistent, and courageous, and they frequently work with Brother Cadfael in solving his cases. In doing so, these young women are motivated not only by the desire for justice but also by love. Young love, at first thwarted and then fulfilled, is omnipresent in these novels, and Brother Cadfael is its chief facilitator. As surely and steadily as he brings murderers to the bar of justice, he brings lovers to the altar of marriage. The chronicles of Brother Cadfael follow the literary tradition of social comedy: affirming love; thwarting whatever blocks it; reestablishing the social order that has been upset by ambition, greed, and murder; and promoting the continuity of that order in future generations.

Although Edith Pargeter will ever be better known as her alter ego, Ellis Peters, the success of the Brother Cadfael series brought recognition to all of her writings. In 1991 Mysterious Press began reissuing the Felse novels, and these were followed in 1993 by *The Heaven Tree* (1960), *The Green Branch* (1962), and *The Scarlet Seed* (1963) bound as a set and rechristened the *Heaven Tree* trilogy. Though these historical novels did not enjoy the acclaim of the Brother Cadfael series, they were created with the same eye for detail and filled with the lively atmosphere of medieval Britain.

Brother Cadfael's Penance

The last Brother Cadfael novel, *Brother Cadfael's Penance* (1994) was published a year before the author's death. The venerable series attained even greater fame when the BBC produced several television installments starring Derek Jacobi as Brother Cadfael. The books have also been recorded, and an entire line of Brother Cadfael paraphernalia, including maps, handbooks, needlework, glassware, and numerous trinkets, is available in the United Kingdom and the United States.

To Peters this was all icing on the cake; her goals were purely literary when she was writing her historical characters, "to demonstrate," as Rosemary Herbert wrote in *Publishers Weekly* in 1991, "that people from distant ages can be portrayed with vitality and intimacy." In this, Peters more than succeeded—millions mourned her death at the age of eighty-two and the loss of her extraordinary creations.

Eileen Tess Tyler
Updated by Fiona Kelleghan

Principal mystery and detective fiction

Felse family series: *Fallen into the Pit*, 1951 (as Pargeter); *Death and the Joyful Woman*, 1961; *Flight of a Witch*, 1964; *A Nice Derangement of Epitaphs*, 1965 (also known as *Who Lies Here?*); *The Piper on the Mountain*, 1966; *Black Is the Colour of My True-Love's Heart*, 1967; *The Grass-Widow's Tale*, 1968; *Mourning Raga*, 1969; *The House of Green Turf*, 1969; *The Knocker on Death's Door*, 1970; *Death to the Landlords!*, 1972; *City of Gold and Shadows*, 1973; *Rainbow's End*, 1978

Brother Cadfael series: *A Morbid Taste for Bones: A Mediaeval Whodunnit*, 1977; *One Corpse Too Many*, 1979; *Monk's-Hood*, 1980; *Saint Peter's Fair*, 1981; *The Leper of Saint Giles*, 1981; *The Virgin in the Ice*, 1982; *The Devil's Novice*, 1983; *The Sanctuary Sparrow*, 1983; *Dead Man's Ransom*, 1984; *The Pilgrim of Hate*, 1984; *An Excellent Mystery*, 1985;

The Raven in the Foregate, 1986; *The Rose Rent*, 1986; *The Confession of Brother Haluin*, 1988; *The Hermit of Eyton Forest*, 1987; *The Heretic's Apprentice*, 1989; *The Potter's Field*, 1990; *The Summer of the Danes*, 1991; *The Holy Thief*, 1992; *Brother Cadfael's Penance*, 1994

Nonseries novels: *Death Mask*, 1959; *The Will and the Deed*, 1960 (also known as *Where There's a Will*); *Funeral of Figaro*, 1962; *The Horn of Roland*, 1974; *Never Pick Up Hitch-Hikers!*, 1976

Other short fiction: *The Assize of the Dying*, 1958 (as Pargeter)

Other major works

Novels (as Pargeter): 1936-1950 • *Hortensius, Friend of Nero*, 1936; *Iron-Bound*, 1936; *The City Lies Foursquare*, 1939; *Ordinary People*, 1941 (also known as *People of My Own*); *She Goes to War*, 1942; *The Eighth Champion of Christendom*, 1945; *Reluctant Odyssey*, 1946; *Warfare Accomplished*, 1947; *By Firelight*, 1948 (also known as *By This Strange Fire*); *The Fair Young Phoenix*, 1948

1951-1970 • *Lost Children*, 1951; *Holiday with Violence*, 1952; *Most Loving Mere Folly*, 1953; *This Rough Magic*, 1953; *The Soldier at the Door*, 1954; *A Means of Grace*, 1956; *The Heaven Tree*, 1960; *The Green Branch*, 1962; *The Scarlet Seed*, 1963

1971-1979 • *A Bloody Field by Shrewsbury*, 1972; *Sunrise in the West*, 1974; *The Dragon at Noonday*, 1975; *The Hounds of Sunset*, 1976; *Afterglow and Nightfall*, 1977; *The Marriage of Meggotta*, 1979

Short fiction: *The Lily Hand, and Other Stories*, 1965 (as Pargeter); *A Rare Benedictine*, 1988; *Feline Felonies*, 1993 (with others)

Radio play: *The Heaven Tree*, pb. 1973 (as Pargeter)

Nonfiction: *The Coast of Bohemia*, 1950 (as Pargeter); *Shropshire*, 1992 (with Roy Morgan; also known as *Ellis Peter's Shropshire*); *Strongholds and Sanctuaries: The Borderland of England and Wales*, 1993 (with Morgan)

Translations (as Pargeter): *Tales of the Little Quarter*, 1957 (by Jan Neruda); *A Handful of Linden Leaves: An Anthology of Czech Poetry*, 1958; *Don Juan*, 1958 (by Josef Toman); *The Sorrowful and Heroic Life of John Amos Comenius*, 1958 (by Frantisek Kosík); *The Abortionists*, 1961 (by Valja Stýblová); *Granny*, 1962 (by Bozena Nemcová); *The Linden Tree*, 1962 (with others); *Legends of Old Bohemia*, 1963 (by Alois Jirásek); *The Terezin Requiem*, 1963 (by Josef Bor); *May*, 1965 (by Karel Hynek Mácha); *The End of the Old Times*, 1965 (by Vladislav Vancura); *A Close Watch on the Trains*, 1968 (by Bohumil Hrabal; also known as *Closely Watched Trains*); *Report on My Husband*, 1969 (by Josefa Slánská); *A Ship Named Hope*, 1970 (by Ivan Klíma); *Mozart in Prague*, 1970 (by Jaroslav Seifert)

Bibliography

Ellis, Margaret. *Edith Pargeter—Ellis Peters*. Reprint. Bridgend, Mid Glamorgan, Wales: Seren, 2003. Literary biography of Peters covering all her works, including the Cadfael series, the Felse family series, and her historical novels.

Greeley, Andrew M. "Ellis Peters: Another Umberto Eco?" *The Armchair Detective* 18 (Summer, 1985): 238-245. Compares Peters's Brother Cadfael to Umbero Eco's William of Baskerville.

Kaler, Anne K., ed. *Cordially Yours, Brother Cadfael*. Bowling Green, Ohio: Bowling Green State University Press, 1998. Compilation of scholarly criticism of the Cadfael novels, including discussions of religion, philosophy, and the study of herbs.

Klein, Kathleen Gregory, ed. *Great Women Mystery Writers: Classic to Contemporary*. Westport, Conn.: Greenwood Press, 1994. Places Peters within a coherent lineage of great women mystery writers, discussing her relationship to her forebears and followers.

Reynolds, Moira Davison. *Women Authors of Detective Series: Twenty-one American and British Authors, 1900-2000*. Jefferson, N.C.: McFarland, 2001. Examines the life and work of major female mystery writers, including Peters.

Riley, Edward J. "Ellis Peters: Brother Cadfael." In *The Detective as Historian: History and Art in Historical Crime Fiction*, edited by Ray B. Browne and Lawrence A. Kreiser, Jr. Bowling Green, Ohio: Bowling Green State University Popular Press, 2000. Examination of the function and representation of history in Peters's Cadfael novels. Bibliographic references.

Whiteman, Robin. *The Cadfael Companion: The World of Brother Cadfael*. Rev. ed. London: Little, Brown, 1995. An encyclopedia of the world represented by the Cadfael stories. Includes entries on the herbs grown and used by the monk-cum-sleuth, as well as on the major characters, locations, and properties of the novels.

EDEN PHILLPOTTS

Born: Mount Abu, India; November 4, 1862
Died: Broadclyst, Exeter, England; December 29, 1960
Also wrote as Harrington Hext
Types of plot: Amateur sleuth; police procedural

PRINCIPAL SERIES

John Ringrose, 1925-1926
Avis Bryden, 1932-1933

PRINCIPAL SERIES CHARACTERS

JOHN RINGROSE, recently retired from the Criminal Investigation Department of Scotland Yard, first appears as a central character in *A Voice from the Dark* (1925). Made wiser and cynical by his years with the yard, Ringrose relies on hard-nosed investigation and careful analysis based on fact.

AVIS BRYDEN, born Avis Ullathorne, is a young woman reared in humble surroundings who becomes the mistress of a Devonshire farmer, Peter Bryden, and bears his child.

CONTRIBUTION

Eden Phillpotts's significance in the history of mystery and detective fiction derives largely from his occasional inventiveness in the matter of how fictional crimes are committed and, more important, from his highly detailed and carefully crafted descriptions of southwest England, the setting for most of his work. This area, which includes Dartmoor National Park, contains hundreds of square miles of rolling moorland, within which are mysterious mists, fierce winds, and peaceful villages. His careful evocation of the spirit of this region informs almost all of his fiction. Phillpotts also achieved some standing in the English literary community for his novels about the moors, and his forays into detective fiction certainly helped to legitimize the genre for many in the English-reading public.

BIOGRAPHY

Eden Phillpotts was born in Mount Abu, India, on November 4, 1862, to Captain Henry Phillpotts, an Indian army officer, and Adelaide Matilda Sophia Waters, whose father worked for the Indian civil service. When he was three years old, his father died, and his mother, barely twenty-one years old, returned to Devonshire, England, taking Eden and his two brothers with her. He was educated at public school in Plymouth, which he left at the age of seventeen for a clerk's job in an insurance firm in London. Phillpotts studied acting for several years in his spare time but decided that he was not suited to it and began trying his hand at writing. By 1890, he had become somewhat successful at marketing some of his writing, and he left his job with the insurance company to become an assistant editor for *Black and White*, a minor periodical. Practice and an enormous creative energy enabled Phillpotts to give up his editorial work and devote himself full-time to writing. He moved from London to Devon, settling first at Torquay, where he spent thirty years. In 1929, he moved to Broadclyst, a town near Exeter, and not far from the Dartmoor National Park. He remained at Broadclyst until his death in 1960.

In 1892, while still in London, Phillpotts was married to Emily Topham. Together they had a son, Henry Eden, born in 1895, and a daughter, Mary Adelaide, born in 1896. Soon after his wife died in 1928, Phillpotts was married to Lucy Robina Joyce Webb, the daughter of a physician.

During his long life, Phillpotts wrote more than one hundred novels, of which nineteen were tales of mystery and detection. He also wrote some forty-five plays, numerous short stories, verse, and children's literature. In addition, he published essays, travel writing, and memoirs. At his death he also left behind some six thousand letters written during his lifetime.

Analysis

Eden Phillpotts began his novel-writing career with a work of detective fiction—*The End of Life* (1891)—and produced many other detective novels and short stories over the course of the next sixty years. Of the twenty-some works in the detective genre, only *The Grey Room* (1921), "*Found Drowned*" (1931), and *The Red Redmaynes* (1922) have earned much positive critical attention. Never an innovator, Phillpotts brought a solid knowledge of craft and a fine eye for detail to his detective fiction. While some of the plot complications and their resulting denouements stretch credibility to the breaking point, his painstaking delineations of the people and places of the Moorlands give his work a ring of authenticity. In fact, Phillpotts's detective novels are, for the most part, examples of the work of a local colorist whose story lines are really subservient to his celebration of the region.

Southwest England was the area to which Phillpotts's mother brought him from India in 1865, and southwest England, specifically Devon and Cornwall and the area known as Dartmoor, is the place to which he returned when his writing gave him independence. For sixty years, he wrote about the place and its people. Agatha Christie, whose work Phillpotts encouraged when she was very young, dedicated *Peril at End House* (1932) to Phillpotts, whom she called "the Hardy of the Moors."

The use of setting as a major element in mystery and detective fiction was certainly not a new idea; in the work of writers such as Raymond Chandler, for example, setting can play a major part in shaping the motivation of characters and in establishing tone. In Phillpotts's fiction, however, setting has little impact on the characters. Instead, it is often the subject of long, slow passages in which the writer rhapsodizes about the physical beauty of a particular place or geographic feature. These passages seldom have anything to do with driving the narrative or complicating the plot. It is as if the writer pauses in mid-story to comment on a matter unrelated to the action. That these passages are carefully written, providing accurate pictures of the region Phillpotts knew so well, does not mitigate their deadening effect on the story itself.

The Thing at Their Heels

The detectives with whom Phillpotts peopled his novels fall into two rather general categories: those who are inexperienced and given to a number of false starts and those who are much older and much less naïve about the potential for wrongdoing that lies just beneath the surface of many an innocent-looking person. The writer's worldview as evidenced by these creations seems not to differ significantly from the standard values of early twentieth century English society. Villains are villains primarily because of flaws in their characters and not because of flaws in their social environment. Persons whose views differ markedly from those of the majority are suspect. For example, in *The Thing at Their Heels* (1923), which Phillpotts wrote under the pseudonym Harrington Hext, four people are murdered by a clergyman who is a social-reform zealot. The reader soon realizes that the clergyman's views are so far afield from those of his community that he is suspect. Further, Phillpotts's world is one in which hard work, honesty, and thrift are rewarded. Greed of any kind—but particularly the lust for money—is the soil in which evil grows.

The Marylebone Miser

Solving crimes is not always easy for Phillpotts's detectives. He strews endless numbers of red herrings in their paths, confusing them and many of his readers in the process. Moreover, Phillpotts tries out most of the then-standard conventions in the genre, appearing in the process to be more interested in whether he can use the convention than in its applicability to the tale he is telling. In *The Marylebone Miser* (1926), for example, a Scotland Yard detective named Ambrose and the retired Central Investigations Department man John Ringrose are involved in a locked-room mystery. Yet the focus of the action in this lumbering story is on murders that occur elsewhere, and the mystery of who killed an old miser in the locked room is left largely unresolved at the end of the novel.

The Grey Room and They Were Seven

Another characteristic of Phillpotts's detective novels is his penchant for inventing bizarre means for committing crimes. In one of his best-known novels, *The Grey Room*, persons who spend the night in a particular bedroom are found dead in the morning. After endless peregrinations and exhaustive analyses of possibilities, Phillpotts finally reveals to his readers that the bed belonged to members of the Borgia family, who used it to murder their enemies by an ingenious method of causing poison to be emitted from the bed covers whenever anyone lay on it for a period of time. Other novels, for example, "*Found Drowned*" and *Monkshood* (1939), feature murderers who use rare and almost impossible-to-detect poisons. In *They Were Seven* (1944), seven people, all cousins, conspire in an unlikely fashion to murder an uncle, but they bungle the attempt. A Scotland Yard detective, no less a bungler, muddles through in the end, but the book contains one improbability after another.

"Found Drowned"

On a few occasions, Phillpotts managed to get most things right and produced work that serious students of the genre have admired. One such example is "*Found Drowned*." Two friends, a small-town police officer and a retired physician, are given depth of character rarely seen in Phillpotts's detective fiction. They exude a certain warmth, and they are not without wit. Phillpotts mixes in popular notions about politics, and he introduces a private investigator to aid the two friends in the resolution of the single murder that occurs in the novel. Shorter than many of his other novels, "*Found Drowned*" is more tightly constructed and is mercifully freer of long-winded passages describing the landscape. His use of rural dialect in contrast with the somewhat stilted speech of the central characters gives the tale another nice touch.

The Red Redmaynes

The Red Redmaynes is another Phillpotts novel that, though extraordinarily long, is well controlled. It features an American private detective, Peter Ganns. He is full of idiosyncrasies, but he is equal to the task at hand: tracking down a villain who is the murderer of the brothers Redmayne. Though the novel is primarily set in Cornwall, the action ranges as far away as Italy, and the suspense is well maintained.

Bred in the Bone

Three of Phillpotts's mystery novels featured Avis Bryden, born Avis Ullathorne, who first appears in *Bred in the Bone* (1932). The young woman, the wife of farmer Peter Bryden, meets a police inspector, Victor Midwinter, who is in the area to investigate a murder in which her husband appears to be involved. By the novel's end, Avis has become the instrument of her deranged husband's death, but she has earned the respect of Inspector Midwinter.

Serious students of the genre should be familiar with Phillpotts's fiction because it provides some indication of the wide variety of the sort of detective writing that was being produced in the United States and England during the 1920's and 1930's. For the most part, however, his mystery and detective fiction is unremarkable, and few of his characters remain long with the reader.

Dale H. Ross

Principal mystery and detective fiction

John Ringrose series: *A Voice from the Dark*, 1925; *The Marylebone Miser*, 1926 (also known as *Jig-Saw*)

Avis Bryden series: *Bred in the Bone*, 1932; *Witch's Cauldron*, 1933; *A Shadow Passes*, 1933

Nonseries novels: 1891-1920 • *The End of Life*, 1891; *A Tiger's Club*, 1892; *Doubloons*, 1906 (also known as *The Sinew of War*); *The Statue*, 1908; *The Three Knaves*, 1912; *The Master of Merripit*, 1914; *Miser's Money*, 1920

1921-1930 • *The Grey Room*, 1921; *Number Eighty-seven*, 1922; *The Red Redmaynes*, 1922; *The Thing at Their Heels*, 1923 (as Hext); *Who Killed Diana?*, 1924; *The Monster*, 1925; *Peacock House*, 1926; *The Jury*, 1927

1931-1940 • *"Found Drowned*,*"* 1931; *A Clue from the Stars*, 1932; *The Captain's Curio*, 1933; *Mr. Digweed and Mr. Lumb*, 1934; *Physician, Heal Thyself*, 1935 (also known as *The Anniversary Murder*); *The Wife of Elias*, 1935; *A Close Call*, 1936; *Lycanthrope:*

The Mystery of Sir William Wolf, 1937; *Portrait of a Scoundrel*, 1938; *Monkshood*, 1939; *Awake Deborah!*, 1940

1941-1959 • *A Deed Without a Name*, 1941; *Ghostwater*, 1941; *Flower of the Gods*, 1942; *The Changeling*, 1944; *They Were Seven*, 1944; *There Was an Old Woman*, 1947; *Address Unknown*, 1949; *Dilemma*, 1949; *George and Georgina*, 1952; *The Hidden Hand*, 1952; *There Was an Old Man*, 1959

OTHER SHORT FICTION: *Loup-Garou!* 1899; *Fancy Free*, 1901; *The Transit of the Red Dragon, and Other Tales*, 1903; *My Adventure in the Flying Scotsman: A Romance of London and North-Western Railway Shares*, 1888; *The Unlucky Number*, 1906; *Tales of the Tenements*, 1910; *The Judge's Chair*, 1914; *Black, White, and Brindled*, 1923; *Peacock House, and Other Mysteries*, 1926; *It Happened Like That*, 1928; *Once upon a Time*, 1936

OTHER MAJOR WORKS

NOVELS: 1891-1900 • *Folly and Fresh Air*, 1891; *Some Every-Day Folks*, 1894; *A Deal with the Devil*, 1895; *Lying Prophets*, 1896; *Children of the Mist*, 1898; *The Human Boy*, 1899; *Sons of Morning*, 1900

1901-1910 • *The Good Red Earth*, 1901 (also known as *Johnny Fortnight*); *The River*, 1902; *The American Prisoner*, 1903; *The Golden Fetich*, 1903; *The Farm of the Dagger*, 1904; *The Secret Woman*, 1905; *The Poacher's Wife*, 1906 (also known as *Daniel Sweetland*); *The Portreeve*, 1906; *The Virgin in Judgment*, 1907 (revised as *A Fight to the Finish*, 1911); *The Whirlwind*, 1907; *The Human Boy Again*, 1908; *The Mother*, 1908; *The Haven*, 1909; *The Three Brothers*, 1909; *The Flint Heart: A Fairy Story*, 1910 (revised 1922); *The Thief of Virtue*, 1910

1911-1920 • *Demeter's Daughter*, 1911; *The Beacon*, 1911; *From the Angle of Seventeen*, 1912; *The Forest on the Hill*, 1912; *The Lovers: A Romance*, 1912; *The Joy of Youth*, 1913; *Widecombe Fair*, 1913; *Faith Tresillion*, 1914; *Brunel's Tower*, 1915; *Old Delabole*, 1915; *The Girl and the Faun*, 1916; *The Green Alleys*, 1916; *The Human Boy and the War*, 1916; *The Chronicles of St. Tid*, 1917; *The Nursery (Banks of Colne)*, 1917 (also known as *The Banks of Colne*); *The Spinners*, 1918; *Evander*, 1919; *Storm in a Teacup*, 1919; *Orphan Dinah*, 1920

1921-1930 • *Eudocia*, 1921; *The Bronze Venus*, 1921; *Pan and the Twins*, 1922; *Children of Men*, 1923; *The Lavender Dragon*, 1923; *Cheat-the-Boys*, 1924; *Redcliff*, 1924; *The Human Boy's Diary*, 1924; *The Treasurers of Typhon*, 1924; *George Westover*, 1925; *A Cornish Droll*, 1926; *Circé's Island, and The Girl and the Faun*, 1926; *The Miniature*, 1926; *Arachne*, 1927; *Dartmoor Novels*, 1927-1928; *The Ring Fence*, 1928; *The Apes*, 1929; *Tryphena*, 1929; *Alcyone: A Fairy Story*, 1930; *The Three Maidens*, 1930

1931-1940 • *Stormbury*, 1931; *The Broom Squires*, 1932; *Nancy Owlett*, 1933; *Minions of the Moon*, 1934; *Portrait of a Gentleman*, 1934; *The Oldest Inhabitant*, 1934; *Ned of the Caribbees*, 1935; *The Owl of Athene*, 1936; *Wood-Nymph*, 1936; *Farce in Three Acts*, 1937; *Dark Horses*, 1938; *Saurus*, 1938; *Tabletop*, 1939; *Thorn in Her Flesh*, 1939; *Chorus of Clowns*, 1940; *Goldcross*, 1940

1941-1957 • *Pilgrims of the Night*, 1942; *A Museum Piece*, 1943; *The Drums of Dombali*, 1945; *Quartet*, 1946; *Fall of the House of Heron*, 1948; *The Waters of Walla*, 1950; *Through a Glass Darkly*, 1951; *His Brother's Keeper*, 1953; *The Widow Garland*, 1955; *Connie Woodland*, 1956; *Giglet Market*, 1957

SHORT FICTION: *Summer Clouds, and Other Stories*, 1893; *Down Dartmoor War*, 1895; *The Striking Hours*, 1901; *Knock at a Venture*, 1905; *The Folk Afield*, 1907; *The Fun of the Fair*, 1909; *The Old Time Before Them*, 1913 (also known as *Told at the Plume*); *Up Hill, Down Dale*, 1925; *The Torch, and Other Tales*, 1929; *Cherry Gambol, and Other Stories*, 1930; *They Could Do No Other*, 1933; *The King of Kanga, and The Alliance*, 1943

PLAYS: 1887-1910 • *The Policeman*, pr. 1887 (with Walter Helmore); *A Platonic Attachment*, pr. 1889; *A Breezy Morning*, pr. 1891; *Allendale*, pr. 1893 (with G. B. Burgin); *The Prude's Progress*, pr. 1895 (revised 1900, with Jerome K. Jerome); *The MacHaggis*, pr. 1897 (with Jerome); *A Golden Wedding*, pr. 1898; *A Pair of Knickerbockers*, pr. 1899; *For Love of Prim*, pr. 1899

1911-1920 • *Curtain Raisers*, pb. 1912; *The Secret Woman*, pb. 1912 (revised 1935); *Hiatus*, pr. 1913; *The*

Carrier-Pigeon, pr. 1913; *The Mother*, pb. 1913; *The Point of View*, pr. 1913; *The Shadow*, pb. 1913; *The Angel in the House*, pr. 1915 (with Basil Macdonald Hastings); *Bed Rock*, pr. 1916 (with Hastings); *The Farmer's Wife*, pb. 1916; *St. George and the Dragons*, pb. 1918 (also known as *The Bishop's Night Off*)

1921-1930 • *The Market-Money*, pb. 1923; *Devonshire Cream*, pr. 1924; *A Comedy Royal*, pb. 1925 (revised 1932); *Jane's Legacy: A Folk Play*, pr. 1925; *The Blue Comet*, pb. 1927; *The Purple Bedroom*, pr. 1926; *Yellow Sands*, pb. 1926 (with Adelaide Eden Phillpotts); *Devonshire Plays*, pb. 1927; *Something to Talk About*, pr. 1927; *My Lady's Mill*, pr. 1928 (with Adelaide Eden Phillpotts); *The Runaways*, pb. 1928; *Three Short Plays*, pb. 1928; *Buy a Broom*, pb. 1929

1931-1949 • *A Cup of Happiness*, pb. 1932; *Bert*, pb. 1932; *The Good Old Days*, pb. 1932 (with Adelaide Eden Phillpotts); *At the 'Bus Stop: A Duologue for Two Women*, pb. 1943; *The Orange Orchard*, pr. 1949 (with Nancy Price)

Radio plays: *Old Bannerman*, 1938; *Witch's Cauldron*, 1940; *The Tiger's Tail*, 1941; *The Gentle Hangman*, 1942; *Honest to Goodness Noah*, 1943; *Brownberry*, 1944; *The Poetical Gentleman*, 1944; *Hey-Diddle-Diddle*, 1946; *On the Night of the Fair*, 1947; *The Master Plumber*, 1947; *Hunter's Moon*, 1948; *The Orange Orchard*, 1949; *On Parole*, 1951; *Kitty Brown of Bristol*, 1953; *Quoth the Raven*, 1953; *The Laughing Widow*, 1954; *Aunt Betsey's Birthday*, 1955; *The Outward Show*, 1958; *The Red Dragon*, 1959; *Between the Deep Sea and the Devil*, 1960

Poetry: *Up-Along and Down-Along*, 1905; *Wild Fruit*, 1911; *The Iscariot*, 1912; *Delight*, 1916; *Plain Song, 1914-1916*, 1917; *As the Wind Blows*, 1920; *A Dish of Apples*, 1921; *Pixies' Plot*, 1922; *Cherry-Stones*, 1923; *A Harvesting*, 1924; *Brother Man*, 1926; *Brother Beast*, 1928; *Goodwill*, 1928; *A Hundred Sonnets*, 1929; *For Remembrance*, 1929; *A Hundred Lyrics*, 1930; *Becoming*, 1932; *Song of a Sailor Man: Narrative Poem*, 1933; *Sonnets from Nature*, 1935; *A Dartmoor Village*, 1937; *Miniatures*, 1942; *The Enchanted Wood*, 1948

Children's literature: *The White Camel*, 1936; *Golden Island*, 1938

Nonfiction: *In Sugar-Cane Land*, 1893; *My Laughing Philosopher*, 1896; *Little Silver Chronicles*, 1900; *My Devon Year*, 1903; *My Garden*, 1906; *The Mount by the Way*, 1908; *Dance of the Months*, 1911; *My Shrubs*, 1915; *The Eden Phillpotts Calendar*, 1915; *A Shadow Passes*, 1918; *One Hundred Pictures from Eden Phillpotts*, 1919; *A West Country Pilgrimage*, 1920; *Thoughts in Prose and Verse*, 1924; *A West Country Sketch Book*, 1928; *Essays in Little*, 1931; *A Year with Bisshe-Bantam*, 1934; *A Mixed Grill*, 1940; *From the Angle of 88*, 1951; *One Thing and Another*, 1954

Bibliography

Barzun, Jacques, and Wendell Hertig Taylor. "Preface to '*Found Drowned*.'" In *A Book of Prefaces to Fifty Classics of Crime Fiction, 1900-1950*. New York: Garland, 1976. Preface by two preeminent scholars of mystery and detective fiction, arguing for Phillpott's novel's place in the annals of the genre.

Day, Kenneth F. *Eden Phillpotts on Dartmoor*. North Pomfret, Vt.: David & Charles, 1981. Study of Phillpotts's home and haunts, as well as of his fictionalized representation of them in his novels.

Dayananda, James Y., ed. *Eden Phillpotts (1862-1960): Selected Letters*. Lanham, Md.: University Press of America, 1984. Collected personal and professional correspondence of Phillpotts; provides invaluable insights into his life and work.

Girvan, Waveney, ed. *Eden Phillpotts: An Assessment and a Tribute*. London: Hutchinson, 1953. Collection of homages to Philpotts by his professional admirers.

Hanson, Gillian Mary. *City and Shore: The Function of Setting in the British Mystery*. Jefferson, N.C.: McFarland, 2004. A useful work for contextualizing Phillpotts's distinctive use of the moors of England in his fiction. Bibliographic references and index.

Horsley, Lee. *Twentieth-Century Crime Fiction*. New York: Oxford University Press, 2005. Looks at the history of detective fiction and contains a chapter on classic detective fiction and how it changed that sheds light on Phillpotts's work.

NANCY PICKARD

Born: Kansas City, Missouri; September 19, 1945
Types of plot: Amateur sleuth; cozy

Principal series

Jenny Cain, 1984-
Eugenia Potter, 1993-
Marie Lightfoot, 2000-

Principal series characters

Jennifer "Jenny" Cain is the daughter of Massachusetts clam entrepreneurs, James Damon Cain III and his first wife, Margaret. She earned a master's degree in business administration from the Wharton School of the University of Pennsylvania. A trust fund supplements the income she earns as Port Frederick Civic Foundation director. In her thirties, she balances the complex dynamics presented by her younger sister, parents, friends, coworkers, enemies, husband Geof Bushfield, and his son David Mayer. Although Jenny is from the upper class, she is concerned about the welfare of people in her community. She seeks answers to family secrets that perplex and frustrate her.

Eugenia "Genia" Potter is a widowed chef in her sixties. Originally from Iowa, she lives on a vast Arizona ranch that her husband had bought. Genia's property also includes a house in Maine, and she often visits family in Rhode Island. She collects and tests recipes, which she shares with friends. An amateur sleuth, she investigates deaths and crimes that occur among relatives and acquaintances or occur at locations where she travels.

Marie Lightfoot is the pseudonym of a true-crime author who was born in northwestern Alabama and lives in Bahia Beach, Florida. Born to social activists Michael Folletino and Lyda Folletino, Marie was raised by her aunt and uncle with her cousin Nathan after her parents allegedly abandoned her. A journalist, she writes fact-based crime books, earning significant income and fame. Residing in a gated community near the shore, Marie prefers her solitude, although she pursues a relationship with divorced African American state attorney Franklin DeWeese, which often complicates her life because of their sometimes conflicting professional and personal interests.

Contribution

Nancy Pickard was one of the first female mystery writers to introduce feminist elements to traditional cozy mysteries in the early 1980's, depicting a female amateur sleuth with a career unlike previous female protagonists, who solved mysteries without professional commitments interfering with or benefitting their efforts. In her later works, Pickard has continued creating affluent, savvy protagonists and supporting characters who are educated and experienced in their fields, earn incomes, and contribute to their communities economically and intellectually.

Pickard's versatile sleuths enable her to incorporate diverse elements to portray autonomous, competent women who can tackle crooks using new resources, such as computing skills, to investigate financial fraud and white-collar crimes. Pickard's novels preceded mysteries by such authors as Linda Grant, Carolyn Hart, and Joan Hess, who featured corporate or entrepreneurial women sleuths.

Most critics and peers consider Pickard an exemplary mystery author, and her talents have been recognized with numerous awards. In 1986, Pickard's second novel, *Say No to Murder* (1985), received the initial Anthony Award for best paperback original at the Bouchercon Mystery Convention. Malice Domestic Mystery Convention attendees voted for Pickard's novel *I.O.U.* (1991) to receive an Agatha Award. That mystery also won a Shamus Award from the Private Eye Writers of America and was a Mystery Writers of America's Edgar Allan Poe Award nominee. Pickard's mystery, *The Virgin of Small Plains* (2006), was nominated in 2007 for both Edgar and Agatha best novel awards.

Biography

Nancy Pickard was born Nancy J. Wolfe on September 19, 1945, in Kansas City, Missouri, to Clint Wolfe and Mary Wolfe. As a child, she enjoyed reading Nancy Drew books. After high school graduation in 1963, she enrolled in journalism school at the University of Missouri. When she was a senior, Pickard took a creative writing class. The teacher mocked aloud to the class a short story she had written, inhibiting Pickard from writing additional fiction. She completed a bachelor's degree in 1967.

Pickard reported for *The Squire* in Overland Park, Kansas, then wrote training programs for Western Auto at Kansas City, Missouri, through 1972, before seeking freelance writing assignments. In 1976, she married Guy Pickard and lived on a Flint Hills, Kansas, ranch. By 1981, Pickard had stopped writing freelance articles and turned to fiction. An avid reader, especially of mysteries, she relied on her reading experiences and writing guides rather than formal instruction to create mysteries. She soon sold a short story, "A Man Around the House," to *Ellery Queen's Mystery Magazine*.

During the early 1980's, an editor rejected Pickard's initial novel, saying the manuscript confused her as to whether it was a mystery or romance with suspense. She considered those comments and focused on mystery, resulting in her first published novel, *Generous Death* (1984).

Pickard's son, Nicholas, was born in 1983 (she and her husband later divorced). That year, Pickard read Virginia Rich's mystery, *The Cooking School Murders* (1982), and wrote Rich, who responded, telling Pickard she had a fourth book in progress. After Rich's death in 1985, her husband asked Pickard to complete that author's fourth Eugenia Potter book, *The Twenty-seven-Ingredient Chili Con Carne Murders* (1993), and allowed her to continue the series.

Throughout the 1980's, Pickard wrote mystery novels prolifically. Despite her success with novels and her initial success in the short-story form, she was unable to sell other short stories. At a writer's conference, a speaker emphasized that short stories must include epiphanies. Pickard began applying that revelation to her stories, publishing her work in *Alfred Hitchcock's Mystery Magazine*, *Mystery Scene*, *Armchair Detective*, and numerous anthologies. She studied peers' books, especially Sue Grafton's mysteries, to improve her writing techniques. Pickard edited several mystery anthologies and contributed a chapter to the serial novel *Naked Came the Phoenix* (2001).

In 1986, Pickard helped establish Sisters in Crime (SIC) and served on that organization's first steering committee. From 1988 to 1989, Pickard presided as SIC president. She also was active in the Mystery Writers of America (MWA), becoming a member of that group's national board. Pickard's experiences on the MWA committee choosing an Edgar Allan Poe Award true-crime book winner resulted in her analyzing those books' structure. Her contemplation served as a catalyst for her trilogy featuring true-crime author Marie Lightfoot.

In 1990, Pickard's favorite Jenny Cain mystery, *Bum Steer*, set on a Kansas ranch, was published. The Kansas City, Kansas, public library presented Pickard its Edgar Wolfe Award in 1997. Pickard collaborated with psychologist Lynn Lott to write *Seven Steps on the Writer's Path: The Journey from Frustration to Fulfillment* (2003), describing her struggles as a writer. Tired of series writing, Pickard wrote *The Virgin of Small Plains*, published in 2006. Pickard has spoken at writers' conferences. She has served on panels at Boucheron, and has led workshops at SIC meetings.

Analysis

Nancy Pickard depicts resourceful, independent female protagonists in her mysteries, emphasizing their intelligence, bravery, and competence. Her characters and plots represent many of the qualities found in innovative mysteries featuring female sleuths and detectives written by female authors including Margaret Maron and Sue Grafton in the 1980's. Pickard's sleuths exemplified similar traits of strength, resilience, and perseverance. Creating appealing narrators, she sought to provide readers with entertainment as well as to offer protagonists with whom they could identify.

Although the structures of Pickard's series varied, her writing style exhibited constants, especially strong voice, effective use of setting, and intricate layers of seemingly unrelated characters and events to hide clues and enable plot twists revealing connections. Her characterizations were strengthened with humor, often dark. Although criticisms of her writing have noted that her narratives often include too much explanation and that some of her character development is implausible or flat, many reviewers have praised Pickard's ingenious plots and pacing.

Pickard focuses on the theme of family in most of her mysteries. Characters feel compelled to support their relatives emotionally despite deceptions and other wrongdoings inflicted on them. Family is equated with other themes, particularly power and prestige. The absence of strong family ties can be detrimental to characters who lack supporters to defend and protect them. Without an intact family structure, characters struggle against outsiders' biases, often negative or incorrect, which shape public opinion. Varying forms of family, offered by lovers and friends, bolster characters. Family can paradoxically provide characters with safety or weaken them. The theme of disintegration, represented by people falling apart financially or emotionally, intensifies the somber tones of such Pickard novels as *Marriage Is Murder* (1987).

Social issues are important aspects of Pickard's mysteries, often enhancing characterizations and strengthening plots. Pickard became aware of such concerns, particularly mental health, because her grandmother died in a state mental hospital, similar to Jenny's mother dying in a private facility. Coming of age during the 1960's, she witnessed social movements demanding improvements. Her friends participated in assisting abused spouses and indigent people, increasing Pickard's knowledge of how bureaucracy and politics affect services, which provided her details to improve the authenticity of her characters' conflicts. Altruism is present as some characters strive to help people, despite their flaws, reinforcing character development within her novels and throughout her series.

Pickard's settings help reflect her characters' moods and establish tones to alert readers to potentially dangerous situations and people capable of inflicting pain and anguish. Her small communities, in New England and the Midwest, both nurture and stifle characters. The seemingly pleasant ocean community of Port Frederick deceivingly contains vengeful residents. The prairie's bleak territory intensifies characters' fears and sense of isolation. Fog rolls across scenes and in people's minds to convey sinister elements and distortion. Twilight in her novels blinds and confuses people. Snow proves deadly and conceals crimes. Storms and fires obliterate evidence necessary to determine the truth and expose secrets.

I.O.U.

In *I.O.U.*, commitment to duty and truth guide Jenny Cain, whom Pickard introduced in *Generous Death*, as she grieves after her mother Margaret Cain's death and is confronted by physical and emotional threats. At the cemetery, someone shoves Jenny and murmurs a request for forgiveness. Unsure who spoke to her, she initiates inquiries in an attempt to comprehend what happened to her mother to cause her to become mentally ill and institutionalized in a psychiatric facility. Her mother's emotional collapse occurred just as Jenny's family's business, Cain Clams, declared bankruptcy, terminating the employment on which many Port Frederick residents relied.

Jenny starts with research at the library, applying her business knowledge in her investigation. She interviews her family, including her aloof father, unaware of the impact he has had on the community; colleagues; and friends. Jenny feels accountable to her mother and the community, feeling she owes them a debt that must be repaid through her deeds. As she boldly pushes to determine the truth, Jenny risks agitating enemies and encounters perils, including becoming exhausted and almost suffocating on carbon monoxide in her car. Some people think she has tried to commit suicide, which causes Jenny to question her mental well-being and consider leaving her professional position. Themes of wealth and greed and tones of despair interplay as Jenny reassesses her assumptions regarding familial and community relations, revealing that trusted relatives and friends can be liars and foes.

TWILIGHT

Clarity and transition are the underlying themes of *Twilight* (1995), the tenth Jenny Cain mystery, which resolves many issues present throughout the series. As the Judy Foundation's director, Jenny is planning a fall festival; however, she despairs as she is unable to obtain the necessary insurance coverage and fears that she will run out of time to do so. Antagonists, particularly Peter Falwell, a former employer, enjoy taunting Jenny, saying that the festival will be canceled.

Additionally, Jenny becomes involved in a controversy debating whether a nature trail should be closed because several people, including a young girl, have died at a highway crossing. Enduring angry fundamentalists and environmental protestors who burn her in effigy, Jenny finds comfort in runes that her delivery woman Cleo Talbot interprets for her. Devastating fires and physical attacks, including a brutal assault on David Mayer, Jenny's stepson, and the unresolved insurance dilemma intensify suspense.

Child characters and several adults who interact with Jenny emphasize themes of innocence and vulnerability, while pride and opportunism set the tone for others' hostile actions and deceptions for monetary and egotistical gain. Jenny's family and friendship ties are reinforced, and enemies' true intentions are exposed as transparency and serenity replace the confusion Jenny associates with twilight.

The Truth Hurts

The third volume of Pickard's Marie Lightfoot series, *The Truth Hurts* (2002), explores Marie's past, which the previous books, *The Whole Truth* (2000) and *Ring of Truth* (2001), foreshadowed. Confronted by a tabloid's claim that her parents were racists, Marie is shaken. She is unsure of the truth because her parents abandoned her in 1963 when she was a baby. When she receives threatening e-mails from a man named Paulie Barnes, Marie fearfully submits to his requests to write a book that will feature her murder. Suspense builds as Barnes sends Marie a copy of John MacDonald's *The Executioners* (1958) and mails her an airplane ticket to Birmingham, Alabama, near her hometown of Sebastion. Marie's cousin Nathan arrives in Sebastion, lured there by Barnes, whom Marie desperately is seeking to identify. She questions residents who knew her parents in 1963, gaining self-knowledge and revising her perceptions of civil rights and family history. She discovers and embraces some truths.

The theme of truth resonates in these three books. Structurally, chapters present Marie's published account of a true crime, often manipulating facts to protect people, in past tense; she narrates present-tense sections, divulging her thoughts and what she perceives is true. Characters' misperceptions and paradoxes contribute to plots twists, exposing truths.

The Virgin of Small Plains

In *The Virgin of Small Plains*, which takes place in 2004, Abby Reynolds slides into a ditch while driving on an icy road because she had been startled by the sight of her former boyfriend Mitch Newquist's elderly mother wandering through a snowy cemetery near Small Plains, Kansas. Flashing back to 1987, when she was in high school, Abby recalls when her relationship with Mitch abruptly ended. Alternating characters' perspectives reveal what each person experienced seventeen years before: Mitch was at Abby's house when he watched, horrified, while Abby's physician father and the sheriff disfigured a woman's corpse. When Abby went to Mitch's house the next day, he was gone and his parents refused to tell her where he went.

In the Small Plains cemetery where Abby saw Mitch's mother, an unknown girl was buried. Credited with miracles, she has been dubbed the Virgin of Small Plains, and people flock to her grave desiring her help. Abby is determined to identify the girl and mark her grave properly. Shifting between 1987 and 2004, Pickard presents clues about both past and present events. Themes of memory, betrayal, and lost innocence strengthen the plot as Abby deals with Mitch's return. The Kansas prairie personifies this mystery's suspense, enhancing elements of solitude and foreboding. Weather represents perils the characters endure as they encounter deception and violence from people they trust. Like most of Pickard's fiction, fear and terror boil underneath the surface of seemingly innocuous people and places.

Elizabeth D. Schafer

Principal mystery and detective fiction

Jenny Cain series: *Generous Death*, 1984; *Say No to Murder*, 1985; *No Body*, 1986; *Marriage Is Murder*, 1987; *Dead Crazy*, 1988; *Bum Steer*, 1990; *I.O.U.*, 1991; *But I Wouldn't Want to Die There*, 1993; *Confession*, 1994; *Twilight*, 1995

Eugenia Potter series: *The Twenty-seven-Ingredient Chili Con Carne Murders*, 1993; *The Blue Corn Murders*, 1998; *The Secret Ingredient Murders*, 2001

Marie Lightfoot series: *The Whole Truth*, 2000; *Ring of Truth*, 2001; *The Truth Hurts*, 2002

Nonseries novels: *Naked Came the Phoenix*, 2001 (with others); *The Virgin of Small Plains*, 2006

Other major works

Short fiction: *Storm Warnings*, 1999

Nonfiction: *Seven Steps on the Writer's Path: The Journey from Frustration to Fulfillment*, 2003 (with Lynn Lott)

Edited texts: *Nancy Pickard Presents Malice Domestic Three: An Anthology of Original Traditional Mystery Stories*, 1994; *The First Lady Murders*, 1999; *Mom, Apple Pie, and Murder*, 1999

Bibliography

Dyer, Carolyn Stewart, and Nancy Tillman Romalov, eds. *Rediscovering Nancy Drew.* Iowa City: University of Iowa Press, 1995. Includes Pickard's essay telling how Nancy Drew books influenced her to write mysteries and her remarks at a conference, describing her experiences writing in the mystery genre.

Hall, Melissa Mia. "Small Miracles." *Publishers Weekly* 253, no. 13 (March 27, 2006): 61. Focusing on *The Virgin of Small Plains*, Pickard answers questions explaining why she wrote that mystery and how the Midwest shaped that novel's imagery and themes.

Klein, Kathleen Gregory, ed. *Great Women Mystery Writers: Classic to Contemporary.* Westport, Conn.: Greenwood Press, 1994. An essay featuring Pickard provides brief novel analyses through *But I Wouldn't Want to Die There* and compares her work to mysteries depicting career women.

Marks, Jeffrey. "An Interview with Nancy Pickard." *The Armchair Detective* 26, no. 2 (Spring, 1993): 84-88. Pickard describes how she became a mystery writer, her work habits, social issues concerns, and how her protagonist has changed from her first novel through *I.O.U.*

Shindler, Dorman T. "Nancy Pickard: The Third Stage of Evolution." *Publishers Weekly* 249, no. 31 (August 5, 2002): 48-49. Based on an interview with Pickard, reveals how she perceives her writing changed during three phases of her career, undergoing doubt then confidence to alter and enhance her style and techniques.

EDGAR ALLAN POE

Born: Boston, Massachusetts; January 19, 1809
Died: Baltimore, Maryland; October 7, 1849
Types of plot: Amateur sleuth; psychological

Principal series

C. Auguste Dupin, 1841-1844

Principal series character

C. Auguste Dupin is a young French gentleman of an illustrious family who has been reduced to living on a modest inheritance in Paris. Extremely well-read, highly imaginative, and master of a keen analytical ability, Dupin is the original armchair detective, the progenitor of every amateur sleuth in detective fiction from Sherlock Holmes to the present.

Contribution

Although Edgar Allan Poe's career was relatively short, he was the leading figure in the mid-nineteenth century transformation of the legendary tale into the form now known as the short story. Experimenting with many different styles and genres—the gothic tale, science fiction, occult fantasies, satire—Poe gained great recognition in the early 1840's for his creation of a genre that has grown in popularity ever since—the tale of ratiocination, or detective story, which features an amateur sleuth who by his superior deductive abilities outsmarts criminals and outclasses the police.

"The Murders in the Rue Morgue" and "The Mystery of Marie Rogêt," the first works in the Dupin series, created a small sensation in the United States when they were first published. Following fast on these works was "The Gold Bug," which, although not featuring Dupin, focused on analytical detection; it was so popular that it was immediately reprinted three times. "The Purloined Letter," the third and final story in the Dupin series, has been the subject of much critical analysis.

Biography

Edgar Allan Poe was born in Boston, Massachusetts, on January 19, 1809. When his parents, David Poe, Jr., and Elizabeth Arnold Poe, indigent actors, died when he was two years old, Poe was taken in by a wealthy tobacco exporter, John Allan. In 1826, Poe entered the University of Virginia but withdrew after less than a year because of debts Allan would not pay. After a brief term in the Army, Poe entered West Point Academy, argued further with Allan about financial support, and then purposely got himself discharged. In 1831, he moved to Baltimore, where he lived with his aunt, Maria Clemm, and her daughter Virginia.

After winning a short-story contest sponsored by a Philadelphia newspaper, Poe was given his first job as an editor on the *Southern Literary Messenger* in Richmond, Virginia. During his two-year tenure, he gained considerable public attention with his stories. With the end of that job, Poe, who had by this time both a new wife (his cousin Virginia) and his aunt to support, took his small family to Philadelphia, where he published some of his best-known works—*The Narrative of Arthur Gordon Pym* (1838), "Ligeia," "The Fall of the House of Usher," and "William Wilson."

At this point, Poe discovered a new way to capitalize on his popularity as a critic, writer, and generally respected man of letters. He joined the lecture circuit, delivering talks on poetry and criticism in various American cities. Poe continued to present lectures on literature for the last five years of his life, with varying degrees of acclaim and success, but never with enough financial reward to make his life comfortable. Even the immediate sensation created by his poem "The Raven," which was reprinted throughout the country and which made Poe an instant celebrity, still could not satisfy the need for enough funds to support his family.

On a trip from Richmond to New York, Poe, a man who could not tolerate alcohol, stopped in Baltimore and began drinking. After he was missing for several days, he was found on the street, drunk and disheveled. Three days later, he died of what was diagnosed as delirium tremens.

Analysis

Although Edgar Allan Poe is credited as the creator of the detective story and the character type known as the amateur sleuth, C. Auguste Dupin and his ratiocinative ability were clearly influenced by other sources. Two probable sources are Voltaire's *Zadig: Ou, La Destinée, Histoire orientale* (1748; *Zadig: Or, The Book of Fate*, 1749) and François-Eugène Vidocq's *Mémoires de Vidocq, chef de la police de Sûreté jusqu'en 1827* (1828-1829; *Memoirs of Vidocq, Principal Agent of the French Police Until 1827*, 1828-1829). Poe mentions Zadig in "Hop-Frog" and thus most likely knew the story of Zadig's ability to deduce the description of the king's horse and the queen's dog by examining tracks on the ground and hair left on bushes. He also mentions Vidocq, the first real-life detective, in "The Murders of the Rue Morgue" as a "good guesser," but one who could not see clearly because he held the object of investigation too close.

Poe's creation of the ratiocinative story also derives from broader and more basic interests and sources. First, there was his interest in the aesthetic theory of Samuel Taylor Coleridge, heavily indebted to nineteenth century German Romanticism. In several of Poe's most famous critical essays, such as his 1842 review of Nathaniel Hawthorne's *Twice-Told Tales* (1837) and his theoretical articles, "Philosophy of Composition" in 1846 and "The Poetic Principle" in 1848, Poe develops his own version of the theory of the artwork as a form in which every detail contributes to the overall effect. This organic aesthetic theory clearly influenced Poe's creation of the detective genre, in which every detail, even the most minor, may be a clue to the solution of the story's central mystery.

Edgar Allan Poe. (Library of Congress)

The development of the mystery and detective genre also reflected the influence of gothic fiction. The gothic novel, based on the concept of hidden sin and filled with mysterious and unexplained events, had, like the detective story, to move inexorably toward a denouement that would explain all the previous puzzles. The first gothic novel, Horace Walpole's *The Castle of Otranto* (1765), with its secret guilt and cryptic clues, was thus an early source of the detective story.

A third source was Poe's fascination with cryptograms, riddles, codes, and other conundrums and puzzles. In an article in a weekly magazine in 1839, he offered to solve any and all cryptograms submitted; in a follow-up article in 1841, he said that he had indeed solved most of them. Although Poe demonstrated his skill as a solver of puzzles in many magazine articles, the most famous fictional depiction of his skill as a cryptographer is his story "The Gold Bug."

"The Gold Bug"

William Legrand, the central character in "The Gold Bug," shares some characteristics with Poe's famous amateur sleuth, Dupin. Legrand is of an illustrious family, but because of financial misfortunes, he has been reduced to near poverty. Although he is of French ancestry from New Orleans, he lives alone on an island near Charleston, South Carolina. In addition, like Dupin, he alternates between melancholia and enthusiasm, which leads the narrator (also like the narrator in the Dupin stories) to suspect that he is the victim of a species of madness.

The basic premise of the story is that Legrand is figuratively bitten by the gold bug after discovering a piece of parchment on which he finds a cryptogram with directions to the buried treasure of the pirate Captain Kidd. As with the more influential Dupin stories,

"The Gold Bug" focuses less on action than on the explanation of the steps toward the solution of its mystery. To solve the puzzle of the cryptogram, Legrand demonstrates the essential qualities of the amateur detective: close attention to minute detail, extensive information about language and mathematics, far-reaching knowledge about his opponent (in this case Captain Kidd), and, most important, a perceptive intuition as well as a methodical reasoning ability.

Poe's famous gothic stories of psychological obsession, such as "The Black Cat," "The Tell-Tale Heart," "The Fall of the House of Usher," and "Ligeia," seem at first glance quite different from his ratiocinative stories of detection. In many ways, however, they are very similar: Both types depend on some secret guilt that must be exposed; in both, the central character is an eccentric whose mind seems distant from the minds of ordinary men; and both types are elaborate puzzles filled with clues that must be tied together before the reader can understand their overall effect.

"The Oblong Box"

"The Oblong Box" and "Thou Art the Man," both written in 1844, are often cited as combining the gothic and the ratiocinative thrusts of Poe's genius. The narrator of "The Oblong Box," while on a packet-ship journey from Charleston, South Carolina, to New York City, becomes unusually curious about an oblong pine box that is kept in the state room of an old school acquaintance, Cornelius Wyatt. In the course of the story, the narrator uses deductive processes to arrive at the conclusion that Wyatt, an artist, is smuggling to New York a copy of Leonardo da Vinci's "The Last Supper" done by a famous Florentine painter.

When a storm threatens to sink the ship, Wyatt ties himself to the mysterious box and, to the horror of the survivors, sinks into the sea with it. Not until a month after the event does the narrator learn that the box contained Wyatt's wife embalmed in salt. Although earlier in the story the narrator prided himself on his superior acumen in guessing that the box contained a painting, at the conclusion he admits that his mistakes were the result of both his carelessness and his impulsiveness. The persistent deductive efforts of the narrator to explain the mystery of the oblong box, combined with the sense of horror that arises from the image of the artist's plunging to his death with the corpse of his beautiful young wife, qualifies this story, although a minor tale in the Poe canon, as a unique combination of the gothic and the ratiocinative.

"Thou Art the Man"

"Thou Art the Man," although often characterized as a satire of small-town life and manners, is also an interesting but minor contribution to the genre. The story is told in an ironic tone by a narrator who proposes to account for the disappearance of Mr. Barnabus Shuttleworthy, one of the town's wealthiest and most respected citizens. When Shuttleworthy's nephew is accused of murdering his uncle, Charley Goodfellow, a close friend of Shuttleworthy, makes every effort to defend the young man. Every word he utters to exalt and support the suspected nephew, however, serves only to deepen the townspeople's suspicion of him.

Throughout the story, Goodfellow is referred to as "Old Charley" and is praised as a man who is generous, open, frank, and honest. At the story's conclusion, he receives a huge box supposedly containing wine promised him by the murdered man before his death. When the box is opened, however, the partially decomposed corpse of Shuttleworthy sits up in the box, points his finger at Goodfellow, and says, "Thou art the man!" Goodfellow, not surprisingly, confesses to the murder.

Although the basic ironies of Charley's not being such a "good fellow" after all and of his efforts to have the nephew convicted even as he pretended to have him exonerated are central to the story's plot, the final irony focuses on the means by which Goodfellow is made to confess. It is Goodfellow's frankness and honesty that causes the narrator to distrust him from the beginning and thus find the corpse, stick a piece of whale bone down its throat to cause it to sit up in the box, and use ventriloquism to make it seem as if the corpse utters the words of the title. The tale introduces such typical detective-story conventions as the creation of false clues by the criminal and the discovery of the criminal as the least likely suspect.

"The Murders in the Rue Morgue"

It is in the C. Auguste Dupin stories, however, that Poe develops most of the conventions of the detective story, devices that have been used by other writers ever since. The first of the three stories, "The Murders in the Rue Morgue," is the most popular because it combines horrifying, seemingly inexplicable events with astonishing feats of deductive reasoning. The narrator, the forerunner of Dr. Watson of the Sherlock Holmes stories, meets Dupin in this story and very early recognizes that he has a double personality, for he is both wildly imaginative and coldly analytical. The reader's first encounter with Dupin's deductive ability takes place even before the murders occur, when he seems to read his companion's mind by responding to something that the narrator had only been thinking. When Dupin explains the elaborate method by which he followed the narrator's thought processes by noticing small details and associating them, the reader has the beginning of a long history of fictional detectives taking great pleasure in recounting the means by which they solved a mystery.

Dupin's knowledge of the brutal murder of a mother and daughter on the Rue Morgue is acquired by the same means that any ordinary citizen might learn of a murder—the newspapers. As was to become common in the amateur-sleuth genre, Dupin scorns the methods of the professional investigators as being insufficient. He argues that the police find the mystery insoluble for the very reason that it should be regarded as easy to solve, that is, its bizarre nature; thus, the facility with which Dupin solves the case is in direct proportion to its apparent insolubility by the police.

This first illustration of Auguste Dupin appeared in an English edition of Edgar Allan Poe's works published in London in 1851. Here, Dupin listens to the prefect of police explaining the case of the missing Marie Rogêt.

The heart of the story focuses on Dupin's extended explanation of how he solved the crime rather than on the action of the crime itself. The points about the murder that stump the police—the contradiction of several neighbors who describe hearing a voice in several foreign languages, and the fact that there seems to be no possible means of entering or exiting the room where the murders took place—actually enable Dupin to master the case. He accounts for the foreign-sounding voice by deducing that the criminal must have been an animal; he explains the second point by following a mode of reasoning based on a process of elimination to determine that apparent impossibilities are in fact possible. When Dupin reveals that an escaped orangutan did the killing, the Paris prefect of police complains that Dupin should mind his own business. Dupin is nevertheless content to have beaten the prefect in his own realm; descendants of Dupin have been beating police inspectors ever since.

"The Mystery of Marie Rogêt"

"The Mystery of Marie Rogêt," although it also focuses on Dupin's solving of a crime primarily from newspaper reports, is actually based on the murder of a young girl, Mary Cecilia Rogers, near New York City. Because the crime had not been solved when Poe wrote the story, he made use of the facts of the case to tell a story of the murder of a young Parisian girl, Marie Rogêt, as a means of demonstrating his superior deductive ability.

The story ostensibly begins two years after the events of "The Murders in the Rue Morgue," when the prefect of police, having failed to solve the Marie Rogêt case himself, worries about his reputation and asks Dupin for help. Dupin's method is that of the classic armchair detective; he gathers all the copies of the newspapers that have accounts of the crime and sets about methodically examining each one. He declares the case more intricate than that of the Rue Morgue because, ironically, it seems so simple.

One of the elements of the story that makes it less popular than the other two Dupin tales is the extensive analysis of the newspaper articles in which Dupin engages—an analysis that makes the story read more like an article critical of newspaper techniques than a narrative story. In fact, what makes Poe able to propose a solution to the crime is not so much his knowledge of crime as his knowledge of the conventions of newspaper writing. In a similar manner, it was his knowledge of the conventions of novel writing that made it possible for him to deduce the correct conclusion of Charles Dickens's novel *Barnaby Rudge: A Tale of the Riots of '80* (1841) the previous year when he had read only one or two of the first installments.

Another aspect of "The Mystery of Marie Rogêt" that reflects Dupin's deductive genius and that has been used by subsequent detective writers is his conviction that the usual error of the police is to pay too much attention to the immediate events while ignoring the peripheral evidence. Both experience and true philosophy, says Dupin, show that truth arises more often from the seemingly irrelevant than from the so-called strictly relevant. By this means, Dupin eliminates the various hypotheses for the crime proposed by the newspapers and proposes his own hypothesis, which is confirmed by the confession of the murderer.

Although "The Mystery of Marie Rogêt" contains some of the primary conventions that find their way into later detective stories, it is the least popular of the Dupin narratives not only because it contains much reasoning and exposition and very little narrative but also because it is so long and convoluted. Of the many experts of detective fiction who have commented on Poe's contribution to the genre, only Dorothy L. Sayers has praised "The Mystery of Marie Rogêt," calling it a story especially for connoisseurs, a serious intellectual exercise rather than a sensational thriller such as "The Murders in the Rue Morgue."

"The Purloined Letter"

Professional literary critics, however, if not professional detective writers, have singled out "The Purloined Letter" as the most brilliant of Poe's ratiocinative works. This time, the crime is much more subtle than murder, for it focuses on political intrigue and manipulation. Although the crime is quite simple—the theft of a letter from an exalted and noble personage—its effects are quite complex. The story depends on several ironies: First, the identity of the criminal is known, for he stole the letter in plain sight of the noble lady; second, the letter is a threat to the lady from whom he stole it only as long as he does nothing with it; and third, the Paris Police cannot find the letter, even though they use the most sophisticated and exhaustive methods, precisely because, as Dupin deduces, it is in plain sight.

Also distinguishing the story from the other two is Dupin's extended discussion of the important relationship between the seemingly disparate talents of the mathematician and the poet. The minister who has stolen the letter is successful, says Dupin, for he is both a poet and a mathematician. In turn, Dupin's method of discovering the location of the letter is to take on the identity of a poet and mathematician, thus allowing him to identify with the mind of the criminal. The method follows the same principle used by a young boy Dupin knows of who is an expert at the game of "even and odd," a variation of the old game of holding an object behind one's back and asking someone to guess which hand holds the prize. The boy always wins, not because he is a good guesser but because he fashions the expression on his face to match the face of the one holding the object and then tries to see which thoughts correspond with that expression.

The various techniques of deduction developed by Poe in the Dupin stories are so familiar to readers of detective fiction that to read his stories is to be reminded that very few essential conventions of the genre have been invented since Poe. Indeed, with the publication of the Dupin stories, Poe truly can be said to have single-handedly brought the detective story into being.

Charles E. May

Principal mystery and detective fiction

Short fiction: *Tales of the Grotesque and Arabesque*, 1840; *The Prose Romances of Edgar Allan Poe*, 1843; *Tales*, 1845; *The Short Fiction of Edgar Allan Poe*, 1976 (Stuart Levine and Susan Levine, editors)

Other major works

Novel: *The Narrative of Arthur Gordon Pym*, 1838

Play: *Politian*, pb. 1835-1836

Poetry: *Tamerlane, and Other Poems*, 1827; *Al Aaraaf, Tamerlane, and Minor Poems*, 1829; *Poems*, 1831; *The Raven, and Other Poems*, 1845; *Eureka: A Prose Poem*, 1848; *Poe: Complete Poems*, 1959; *Poems*, 1969 (volume 1 of *Collected Works*)

Nonfiction: *The Letters of Edgar Allan Poe*, 1948; *Literary Criticism of Edgar Allan Poe*, 1965; *Essays and Reviews*, 1984

Miscellaneous: *The Complete Works of Edgar Allan Poe*, 1902 (17 volumes); *Collected Works of Edgar Allan Poe*, 1969, 1978 (3 volumes)

Bibliography

Bloom, Harold, ed. *Edgar Allan Poe*. New York: Chelsea House, 2006. Compilation of essays by leading Poe scholars on various aspects of the author's work, including the boundaries of the detective-fiction genre and its relationship to psychoanalysis. Bibliographic references and index.

Irwin, John T. *The Mystery to a Solution: Poe, Borges, and the Analytical Detective Story*. Baltimore: The Johns Hopkins University Press, 1994. An analytical/theoretical discussion of Poe and Jorge Luis Borges's contribution to the detective story. Argues that Borges echoes Poe's three most famous detective stories—"The Murders in the Rue Morgue," "The Purloined Letter," and "The Mystery of Marie Rogêt"—in three of his own stories.

Kennedy, J. Gerald. *A Historical Guide to Edgar Allan Poe*. New York: Oxford University Press, 2001. Considers the tensions between Poe's otherworldly settings and his representations of violence, delivers a capsule biography situating Poe in his historical context, and addresses topics such as Poe and the American publishing industry, Poe's sensationalism, his relationships to gender constructions, and Poe and American privacy. Includes bibliographic essay, chronology of Poe's life, bibliography, illustrations, and index.

Martin, Terry J. *Rhetorical Deception in the Short Fiction of Hawthorne, Poe, and Melville*. Lewiston, N.Y.: Edwin Mellen Press, 1998. An original reading of "The Murders in the Rue Morgue." Martin seeks to identify this story and those by Hawthorne and Melville as "a significant sub-genre of the modern short story."

May, Charles E. *Edgar Allan Poe: A Study of the Short Fiction*. Boston: Twayne, 1991. An introduction to

Poe's short stories that attempts to place them within the nineteenth century short narrative tradition and within the context of Poe's aesthetic theory. Suggests Poe's contributions to the short story in terms of his development of detective fiction, fantasy, satire, and self-reflexivity.

Peeples, Scott. *Edgar Allan Poe Revisited.* New York: Twayne, 1998. An introductory critical study of selected works and a short biography of Poe. Includes bibliographical references and index.

Perry, Dennis R. *Hitchcock and Poe: The Legacy of Delight and Terror.* Lanham, Md.: Scarecrow Press, 2003. This work discusses the thematic and stylistic parallels between Alfred Hitchcock's film and Poe's writing, both in general terms and through comparisons of specific works. Bibliographic references and index.

Quinn, Arthur Hobson. *Edgar Allan Poe: A Critical Biography.* Baltimore: The John Hopkins University Press, 1998. A comprehensive biography of Poe, with a new introduction by Shawn Rosenheim, is devoted to fact and describes how Poe's life and legend were misconstrued by other biographers.

Sova, Dawn B. *Edgar Allan Poe, A to Z: The Essential Reference to His Life and Work.* New York: Facts On File, 2001. A thorough guide to the life and works of Poe.

JOYCE PORTER

Born: Marple, Cheshire, England; March 28, 1924
Died: On a flight to England from China; December 9, 1990
Types of plot: Police procedural; espionage; thriller; private investigator

Principal series

Inspector Wilfred Dover, 1964-1980
Eddie Brown, 1966-1971
Constance Morrison-Burke, 1970-1979

Principal series characters

Wilfred Dover, detective chief inspector of Scotland Yard, is a grotesque caricature of the yard stereotype. This inept detective is obese, stupid, and petty.

Sergeant MacGregor, dapper and competent, serves as Dover's foil.

Edmund "Eddie" Brown, a secret agent, is as much a threat to the British intelligence service as he is to Soviet intelligence. Ineffectual and unattractive, his efforts to penetrate Soviet security are laughable at best.

The Honourable Constance Ethel Morrison-Burke, or the Hon-Con, a private investigator, became a detective because nothing else satisfied her desire to be active. As a gentlewoman of independent means, the Hon-Con has the time and money to pursue her hobby. Her tactlessness and incompetence, however, short-circuit her achievements.

Miss Jones is the Hon-Con's patient and long-suffering confidant.

Contribution

Joyce Porter's ten Inspector Dover novels, four Eddie Brown novels, and five Morrison-Burke novels lampoon the genres of police procedural, international thriller, and private investigator. Although the books generally follow the rules of each genre, the main character in each series is a spoof of the usual hero. Porter delighted in ridiculing pompous human behavior, and she excelled at poking fun at various elements in society as well as at august public institutions. Porter's novels utilize straightforward crime/spy stories as their backdrop, but her humorous jabs at officiousness provide the reader with an alternative to the standard offerings of the genres.

Biography

Joyce Porter was born on March 28, 1924, in Marple, Cheshire, England, the daughter of Joshua Porter and Bessie Evelyn (née Earlam) Porter. She was educated at the High School for Girls in Macclesfield, Cheshire, and at King's College in London, where she received a bachelor of arts degree with honors in 1945. She served in the Women's Royal Air Force between 1949 and 1963, attaining the rank of flight officer. While in the air force, Porter learned Russian, as she had a special interest in Russian history, especially the czarist period. She toured the Soviet Union by car in 1964.

In 1963, Porter became a full-time writer. She once said that she "began writing in order to be able to retire from [the] Air Force," and that she continued to write "because it is easier than work." She later commented that she tried "to write books that will while away a couple of hours for the reader—and make as much money as possible for me." In her writing, she used outrageously humorous "heroes" who are the very antithesis of the protagonists of such crime and mystery novelists as Frederick Forsyth, Ian Fleming, or P. D. James. Porter's series characters are all unimaginative, bumbling, and unattractive people who, if they solve their cases, do so despite themselves, not because of their insight and abilities. In addition to her novels, Porter wrote many short stories for magazines such as *Ellery Queen's Mystery Magazine* and *Alfred Hitchcock's Mystery Magazine*. She died on a flight home from China in 1990.

Analysis

The novels of Joyce Porter are humorous jabs at three of the most popular genres of modern fiction: the police procedural, the international thriller, and the private-investigator novel. In her work, the common thread is human behavior reduced to absurdity. Her heroes are ludicrous antitheses of what the reader has come to expect in these genres.

Porter's most infamous character is Wilfred Dover, detective chief inspector of Scotland Yard. Dover is described in the following fashion:

> His six-foot-two frame was draped, none too elegantly, in seventeen and a quarter stone [241 pounds] of flabby flesh. . . . Round his thick, policeman's neck . . . a thin, cheap tie was knotted under the lowest of his double chins. . . . Dover's face . . . was large and flabby like the rest of him. Only the details—nose, mouth and eyes—seemed out of scale. They were so tiny as to be almost lost in the wide expanse of flesh. . . . His hair was thin and black and he had a small black moustache of the type that the late Adolf Hitler did so much to depopularize.

Dover Three

In *Dover Three* (1965), when it is suggested that Dover be given a case, the assistant commissioner of New Scotland Yard says, "I thought I told you to get rid of that fat, stupid swine months ago!" "I've tried, sir," replies his subordinate unhappily, "but nobody'll have him." With a primary character such as this, the reader knows immediately that Scotland Yard's reputation is in dire straits.

Dover's career, as chronicled by Porter, is always set in wretched locales far from metropolitan London. New Scotland Yard wants Dover as far away as he can be sent. He is assigned missions no one else would want. Once on the scene of the crime, Dover invariably finds miserable weather and terrain. When unattractive characters and bizarre crimes are added to the plot, the reader is quite aware that little good can possibly come from such a situation. Throughout the series, Dover's assistant, Sergeant MacGregor, provides the obligatory straight character, but MacGregor's solid procedures are always sacrificed to Dover's animalistic behavior. Inevitably, Dover's bowels or personal pique interrupt reasoned efforts to solve crimes. While on a case, Dover meets characters who are driven by the same passions that drive him—greed, petty revenge, or hatred. He does usually solve his cases, though in unorthodox and malevolent fashion.

Porter frequently twists her endings to absurd degrees. Dover may solve a case but ignore justice, for example, because of his prejudices. In *Dover Three*, while far from home, Dover dawdles in solving a case until after his hated sister-in-law has finished her visit to his home, for he knows that an early resolution to the crime would result in another confrontation at home. He selects as his culprit an aggressive upper-class woman to whom he has taken an immediate and intense dislike. During his train trip home, the real culprit confesses to Dover and then commits suicide. Dover chooses to ignore the confession. In *Dover Goes to*

Pott (1968), Dover decides that an individual whom he despises must be the guilty party. As events transpire, the suspect is indeed found to be guilty, but Dover's handling of the case virtually ensures his going free.

DOVER ONE

Most of the characters in Porter's novels are easy-to-dislike caricatures. In *Dover One* (1964), it is not only the detective who is obnoxious but also the victim, whom the reader meets only through the descriptions by other characters in the novel. A less likable victim cannot be imagined: fat, ugly, promiscuous, stupid, and an extortionist. Yet Dover solves the case, in his usual unorthodox fashion. In a typical Porter twist, the victim is discovered dismembered in the murderer's freezer. In this first novel, Dover, through a mighty leap of the imagination, chooses a suspect who is actually guilty. Other Dover novels have the detective confronted with bizarre murder and mutilation cases; a simple, uncomplicated murder is not for Dover. Porter indulges herself in long digressions on Dover's unhygienic habits and internal disorders, evidently preferring such comic essays to tightly reasoned unravelings of crimes.

NEITHER A CANDLE NOR A PITCHFORK

Porter's other characters, while not as well known, are just as ludicrous. Secret Agent Eddie Brown is sent by the British intelligence service on assignments to dangerous foreign locales, but he is a foil and a dupe rather than a superspy. One comic scene in *Neither a Candle Nor a Pitchfork* (1969) has Eddie in female disguise warding off amorous advances by a lesbian Russian official. Later, Eddie's attempt to attack a prison—a scene that might have constituted the climax of a conventional spy novel—degenerates into a pathetic joke. Indeed, the Eddie Brown novels leave the reader believing that Soviet officialdom is roughly equivalent to English officialdom. Porter hopes that the reader will ask, if that be true, how many other parallels might be drawn.

Heroines are also given an opportunity to perform in Porter's novels. Her third series character is the Honourable Constance Ethel Morrison-Burke (the Hon-Con), a gentlewoman of independent means. She becomes a detective because she is bored, her boundless energy unsatisfied by "usual" feminine activities such as calisthenics. The Hon-Con is tactless, shortsighted, and quite naïve. Although she is frequently foolish, she is shown to be not quite the fool that most people believe her to be. Her shortcomings, however, do leave her frustrated and unsatisfied.

Porter's statement that her work is designed to "while away a couple of hours for the reader" certainly defines her style. She did not intend for her work to be incisive or insightful. Rather, she made use of the simplest form of satire: caricature. She was not interested in character development, and her characters are little more than line drawings (fat and bumbling though they may be). Her plots are also simple, and the humor usually focuses on the overtly crude and grotesque rather than on subtleties. Thus, her work is ideal for those who wish to escape for a few hours. In this regard, Porter accomplished her stated purpose.

William S. Brockington, Jr.

PRINCIPAL MYSTERY AND DETECTIVE FICTION

INSPECTOR WILFRED DOVER SERIES: *Dover One*, 1964; *Dover Three*, 1965; *Dover Two*, 1965; *Dover and the Unkindest Cut of All*, 1967; *Dover Goes to Pott*, 1968; *Dover Strikes Again*, 1970; *It's Murder with Dover*, 1973; *Dover and the Claret Tappers*, 1977; *Dead Easy for Dover*, 1978; *Dover Beats the Band*, 1980

EDDIE BROWN SERIES: *Sour Cream with Everything*, 1966; *The Chinks in the Curtain*, 1967; *Neither a Candle Nor a Pitchfork*, 1969; *Only with a Bargepole*, 1971

CONSTANCE MORRISON-BURKE SERIES: *Rather a Common Sort of Crime*, 1970; *A Meddler and Her Murder*, 1972; *The Package Included Murder*, 1975; *Who the Heck Is Sylvia*, 1977; *The Cart Before the Crime*, 1979

OTHER MAJOR WORK

NOVEL: *No Easy Answers*, 1987

BIBLIOGRAPHY

Barzun, Jacques, and Wendell Hertig Taylor. *A Catalogue of Crime*. Rev. ed. New York: Harper & Row, 1989. List, with commentary, of the authors' choices for the best or most influential examples of crime fiction. Porter's work is included and evaluated.

Huang, Jim, ed. *They Died in Vain: Overlooked, Underappreciated, and Forgotten Mystery Novels*. Carmel, Ind.: Crum Creek Press, 2002. Porter is among the authors discussed in this book about mystery novels that never found the audience they deserved.

Kemp, Simon. *Defective Inspectors: Crime Fiction Pastiche in Late-Twentieth-Century French Literature*. London: LEGENDA, 2006. Although devoted to French examples of parodic mystery stories, this study is instructive as to the general methods and strategies employed in Porter's rather specialized subgenre.

Klein, Kathleen Gregory, ed. *Great Women Mystery Writers: Classic to Contemporary*. Westport, Conn.: Greenwood Press, 1994. Contains an essay on the life and works of Porter.

Melling, John Kennedy. *Murder Done to Death: Parody and Pastiche in Detective Fiction*. Lanham, Md.: Scarecrow Press, 1996. Study of British and American detective-fiction parodies, concentrating especially on the intertextual pastiche. Sheds light on Porter's works.

Norris, Luther. "Crime with a Smile." *The Mystery Readers/Lovers Newsletter* 3 (December, 1969): 19-22. Brief overview of Porter's spoof mysteries discussing their ability to function simultaneously as detective fiction and as parody.

Winn, Dilys. *Murder Ink: The Mystery Reader's Companion*. Rev. ed. New York: Workman, 1984. Study of all things relating to the murder mystery, from a reading of specific famous works to a nonfictional history of Scotland Yard to general comments on the conventions of the mystery genre. Contains some discussion of Porter's work and an essay on professional jealousy by Porter.

MELVILLE DAVISSON POST

Born: Romines Mills, West Virginia; April 19, 1869
Died: Clarksburg, West Virginia; June 23, 1930
Types of plot: Amateur sleuth; historical; espionage; police procedural; thriller

Principal series

Randolph Mason, 1896-1908
Uncle Abner, 1911-1918
M. Jonquelle, 1913-1923
Sir Henry Marquis, 1915-1920
Captain Walker, 1920-1929
Colonel Braxton, 1926-1930

Principal series characters

Randolph Mason is an aristocratic New York City lawyer and omniscient, shadowy force. A recluse, he serves only clients who come to him as a last resort; they receive counsel that, taking advantage of legal loopholes, urges them to unethical if not criminal acts. Later, mellowing, he restricts his practice to unfortunate victims of the legal system.

Uncle Abner, a cattle rancher and outdoorsman on the old Virginia frontier, is a middle-aged, fatherly protector and wise philosopher. He involves himself directly in the resolution of rural crime and mystery. His analyses rest solidly on superior ratiocination, biblical ethics, and the law and spirit of the American constitution.

M. Jonquelle, the préfect of police in Paris and an international cop, travels to London, Washington, D.C., and other locales to uncover acts of crime or espionage that imperil international security.

Sir Henry Marquis, the chief of the Criminal Investigation Department at Scotland Yard, is a renowned criminologist and master of abstruse knowledge. He wins battles of wits with archcriminals whose espionage or criminal activities might otherwise have international consequences.

Captain Walker, the chief of the United States Secret Service, as a youth pursued a life of crime. As chief, he records or resolves cases renowned because of the bizarre, unforeseen ends to which evil comes.

Colonel Braxton is a mature Virginia lawyer whose country-town wisdom, gained from life and knowledge of the law, leads him successfully through courthouse dramas that unravel criminal acts.

Contribution

Melville Davisson Post's crime and detective fiction followed basic conventions of the puzzle mystery. Like Edgar Allan Poe's C. Auguste Dupin and Arthur Conan Doyle's Sherlock Holmes, Post's series characters generally repudiate tough-guy violence in favor of detached, superior rationality to pierce the mystery and restore social order. Post wrote short fiction for a variety of popular magazines. Although often using the inflated language of melodrama, his stories nevertheless evoked horror and suspense and convincingly used surprise endings. Through the use of series characters, he sought to give novelistic continuity and organic form to published collections of stories, which first appeared separately in family magazines; most of his fiction underwent that transformation. A superlative entertainer, Post would have been quite comfortable writing scripts for presentation on radio, film, or television.

Biography

Melville Davisson Post was born on April 19, 1869, into a prosperous landed family that took pride in its participation in the American Revolution and the development of West Virginia. Post grew up knowing horses, cattle, the outdoors, frontier character, folklore, and traditional values. This knowledge provided him with literary matter and the youth's perspective he used in many of his narratives.

After completing a law degree at the University of West Virginia in 1892, Post started a short-lived career in law and politics; this activity gave him the knowledge of legal subtleties on which his first series depended. The success of his series encouraged him to move away from the law and to continue the development of series detective stories. He developed six different series protagonists between 1896 and 1930; during that time, his fiction appeared in such magazines as *Pearson's*, *The Saturday Evening Post*, *Metropolitan*, *Hearst's*, and *Ladies' Home Journal*.

Post and his wife, Ann, lived fashionably, enjoying the activities of resort life at Bar Harbor and Newport and their frequent European travels. Their lifestyle engendered the international perspective and flair for the exotic that appears in the Sir Henry Marquis and M. Jonquelle series, as well as the nostalgic return to the past of the West Virginia hill country in the Uncle Abner and Colonel Braxton series.

World War I saw the Posts return to live outside Clarksburg, West Virginia, in a house called The Chalet, built in the design of Swiss Alpine houses and furnished with pieces from their European travels. There, Post maintained a polo ground and ponies. After the death of his wife in 1919, Post traveled less but continued to write fiction. He died in Clarksburg on June 23, 1930, from injuries sustained in a fall from a horse.

Analysis

In the introduction to his first series collection, *The Strange Schemes of Randolph Mason* (1896), Melville Davisson Post established his fiction's fundamental characteristics. There he pointed out the writer's obligation as an entertaining "magician" to relieve the audience from the tedium of the commonplace. Post saw little contradiction between that charge and adherence to the puzzle-mystery convention as established by Poe and Doyle, for the puzzle is the universal paradigm of the human encounter with experience: "The human mind loves best the problem." Every new generation has a fresh experience of the puzzle of meaning lying beneath the surface.

Post found novelty variously. He adapted puzzle-mystery conventions to the new generation of American readers who, as he did, remembered the agrarian past and looked forward to the future. Often, the narrative point of view belongs to an adolescent male who seeks meaning by observing the mature male (the detective); Post's fiction often synthesizes the initiation story and the mystery plot. The author also sought novelty by finding ever more ingenious ways to move toward unsuspected and satisfying resolutions.

The Strange Schemes of Randolph Mason

In *The Strange Schemes of Randolph Mason*, Post collected stories marked by novel changes on the

Post's unethical attorney, Randolph Mason.

puzzle-mystery conventions. The series character lives an aristocratic, solitary existence in private apartments, tended only by his man-of-all-work, Courtland Parks. Although Mason's grossness of feature may suggest (to those who do not know him) craftiness, cynicism, and even brutality, seen truly, it is a face of "unusual power"—of mind, not body, for Mason suffers from an enervating illness that makes him unfit for ordinary life and forces his withdrawal from the world (as Poe's Dupin and Doyle's Holmes are monkish intellectuals). Yet as a lawyer of extraordinary intellect, Mason's shadowy influence on New York City society is felt. All Post's series detectives are variations on such characters of remote mental power.

Further reflecting convention, Mason's relation to his man Parks is like that between the rationally superior detective and his inferior confidant. Parks becomes the physical agency of Mason's mind; he communicates the lawyer's advice to clients and checks on the progress of events. Unlike Dupin's nameless confidant and Holmes's Watson, however, Parks is not of the same social class as Mason. Nor does he engage in familiarities with his master as Bunter does with Lord Peter Wimsey in Dorothy L. Sayers's detective fiction. Finally, he is not in the muscular mode of Rex Stout's Archie Goodwin, who with detective Nero Wolfe is a later variation on the mind-body division of labor.

Beyond these developments, Post served the principle of variety by introducing a shocking deviation in *The Strange Schemes of Randolph Mason*, for his Mason becomes the mastermind behind shady if not criminal conspiracies. As a preface, each story cites case law, with brief explanations, showing how justice may be evaded, and the stories serve as dramatic illustrations. The author's justification for writing stories that seem to condone corruption of the law is artful and complex as well as (one suspects) an unsubtle defense of sensationalism. Post's own legal experience had shown him that moral law and statute law were not synonymous and that the war of life generated battles in the courts between equally bad men who corrupted the law in self-interest. It is therefore the writer's obligation, according to Post, to warn "the friends of law and order" through such instructive narratives as those in *The Strange Schemes of Randolph Mason*.

The Man of Last Resort and The Corrector of Destinies

Despite Post's stated purpose, the Mason stories fail to rise above the flatness of stereotype and the turgidity of melodrama. The second Mason collection,

The Man of Last Resort: Or, The Clients of Randolph Mason (1897), continues in much the same vein as *The Strange Schemes of Randolph Mason*. In *The Corrector of Destinies* (1908), Post rehabilitates Mason. He recovers "from his attack of acute mania" and now works "to find within the law a means by which to even up and correct every manner of injustice." Despite their weaknesses, the stories gained an audience for Post, encouraging him to write full time. The stories possess strengths: the persuasive evocation of terror and suspense and an economy of style that moves plot toward direct resolutions.

Ten years separated the last Mason collection and the first Uncle Abner collection. During the interim, Post wrote two novels about the West Virginia hill country that do not belong to the detective genre, *Dwellers in the Hills* (1901) and *The Gilded Chair* (1910); a novel of mystery fantasy, *The Nameless Thing* (1912); and short detective fiction for *The Saturday Evening Post*, *Metropolitan*, *Pictorial Review*, *Illustrated Sunday Magazine*, and *Redbook*. These stories were later collected and published as *Uncle Abner, Master of Mysteries* (1918).

UNCLE ABNER, MASTER OF MYSTERIES

As Charles A. Norton has shown, *Uncle Abner, Master of Mysteries* received critical praise on its publication and has continued to do so. The series represents Post's most successful writing in the detective-fiction genre, for it unites themes and characters about which the writer felt deeply with tightly controlled and persuasive narrative techniques. Separately, the stories possess the inner vitality of this organic unity; together, they achieve the effect of novelistic continuity—the effect for which Post always worked when he collected his various short-fiction series into single volumes. Nowhere did he achieve that end so well as in *Uncle Abner, Master of Mysteries*.

A single narrative point of view helps unify the stories. The adolescent Martin observes and reports on the events in which his Uncle Abner (a self-designated detective) and his confidant Squire Randolph are central. In the boys' adventure novel *Dwellers in the Hills*, Post had developed a similar character in its protagonist, Quiller. Because his older brother is bedridden, the child Quiller is given the task of herding cattle to market to fulfill a contract, despite the forestalling violence of rival herdsmen. Quiller is knowledgeable about horses and cattle but feels threatened by the opaqueness of the natural and human worlds. He is attracted to the perception of physical nature as mystery (Post tellingly introduces the folklore of powerful creatures who control the forests and rivers) and is kept from knowledge of human nature because the adults of his world do not explain the tensions lying beneath the surface (rivalries between and within families over wealth, passion, and violence; the weakness of law on the frontier; the secrets of human sexuality).

Melville Davisson Post's cattle rancher and amateur detective Uncle Abner of the antebellum South.

Like Quiller, young Martin of *Uncle Abner, Master of Mysteries* seeks understanding and lives in an anxiety born of ignorance. The physical positions Post assigns to Martin further suggest the character's fear and longing: He peeps from lofts and through windows and overhears from porches and behind hedgerows the deeds and words of Uncle Abner.

Although his character may derive from the superdetective of remote intellectual superiority, Abner's fullness of character comes from the way in which Post defines the cattleman-detective in the complex matrix of his culture. Abner believes in personal courage, the demystification of experience through common sense, the providential ordering of history, adherence to the Judeo-Christian ethic, and the progress of the American system toward justice. Post's success in showing rather than telling about Uncle Abner is largely a product of the narrative viewpoint; the boy Martin looks, listens, and records but does not explain beyond his understanding.

Yet the stories also benefit richly from the control of style. The writing is simple, direct, without Post's habitual excess of melodramatic language. Nevertheless, it is poetic and redolent of atmosphere, the product of complexly related, antithetical images: supernaturalism and naturalism, mystery and knowledge, terror and safety The narratives move surely, economically from the firmly established snarl of complication to the snap of release.

The relation of ideal to real justice seems central to the detective's work. In the service of the ideal, he may sacrifice the real, as in "An Act of God," which tells of the revenge exacted by a circus performer whose daughter has been impregnated and abandoned by a cattle shipper named Blackford. The circus artist carries out Blackford's murder, making it seem accidental, and it is legally adjudged "an act of God." Seeing through the ruse, Uncle Abner confronts the performer and analyzes the crime. In view of Blackford's evil and the fact that the performer's granddaughter would be left alone and impoverished if he were charged, however, Abner chooses to leave the case in God's hands.

Nevertheless, Abner always works to unite the ideal with the real, as "The Wrong Hand" shows. Martin has been sent on an errand from which he is returning late because his horse has broken a shoe. He meets Uncle Abner, on his own private mission; because of the deepening winter night and threatening weather, Abner takes his nephew in charge. They enter the house of a man named Gaul, widely known because of his hunchback and bitterness. One wife went mad; another was found by Abner's drovers "on a summer morning[,] swinging to the limb of a great elm that stood before the door, a bridle-rein knotted around her throat and her bare feet scattering the yellow pollen of the ragweed."

Post shades in details masterfully. The unnatural Gaul sits before the fireplace with a cane that has a gold piece in its head so his "fingers might be always on the thing he loved." The grotesque recognizes Martin's fear but reassures him by asserting that he has no wish to frighten children, that it was "Abner's God" who twisted his body. Gaul and Abner talk about the marketing of cattle, a seemingly ordinary conversation, but one in which the hunchback's hate, self-pity, paranoia, and greed are revealed. The storm grows more severe, the rain turning into "a kind of sleet that rattled on the window-glass like shot," while the wind "whooped and spat into the chimney." When the conversation turns to religion and Gaul begins to blaspheme, Abner tells Martin that he must go to sleep. The boy is wrapped in his uncle's greatcoat; feigning obedience, Martin watches and listens from his hiding place. He senses his uncle's grave intention.

A terrible death has recently occurred in Gaul's house. His brother was found dead, having apparently killed himself with a knife. Gaul, rather than the victim's own children, has received the inheritance. Having examined the body of evidence the judicial committee used to make the finding of suicide, Abner knows that Gaul has murdered his own brother.

In the subtle interrogation Martin overhears from the greatcoat, Uncle Abner seeks a confession from Gaul through innocent, circular, philosophical questioning. It is the pattern Post assigns to Uncle Abner in other of the series stories. Abner intends to right Gaul's injustice to his brother's children as well as see that the man is charged with murder. Outlining the clues, he comes at last to the fact that a bloody handprint on the dead brother's right hand came from a right hand, a clear impossibility, unless a murderous second party was present. His resistance broken, Gaul confesses to the murder and agrees to sign over the deed of inheritance to his brother's children. At dawn, uncle and nephew ride away,

> with the hunchback's promise that he would come that afternoon before a notary and acknowledge what he had signed; but he did not come—neither on that day nor on any day after that.
>
> When Abner went to fetch him he found him swinging from his elm tree.

Later works

In some individual stories that followed this series, Post achieved again the superiority of the Uncle Abner stories, though never with consistency. One reason for his lack is that he did not often work again with the synthesis of boy's adventure, detective story, and regional history that sparked *Uncle Abner, Master of Mysteries*. In the magazine fiction and collections that followed, the author introduced four series detectives (Sir Henry Marquis, M. Jonquelle, Captain Walker, and Colonel Braxton) and continued to enjoy a success based on his control of suspenseful narrative. Yet all the detectives are really only one character: the intelligent, remote, resourceful, highly placed police official. The arena is national and international life. The detective works behind the scenes through disguise and secret conspiracy. In "The House by the Loch" (a Sir Henry Marquis story), Post achieved the richness of the Uncle Abner stories, largely by resorting again to a child narrator. In *Walker of the Secret Service* (1924), the opening six stories return to the point of view of a boy, a naïve narrator who recounts his abortive criminal career under the guidance of two failed train robbers. Seeking unity, Post makes an improbable biographical connection between the boy of these stories and the Captain Walker of the remainder. Despite such lapses, however, as an entertainer, Post rarely failed.

Bill Brubaker

Principal mystery and detective fiction

Randolph Mason series: *The Strange Schemes of Randolph Mason*, 1896; *The Man of Last Resort: Or, The Clients of Randolph Mason*, 1897; *The Corrector of Destinies*, 1908

Uncle Abner series: *Uncle Abner, Master of Mysteries*, 1918; *The Methods of Uncle Abner*, 1974

M. Jonquelle series: *Monsieur Jonquelle, Prefect of Police of Paris*, 1923

Sir Henry Marquis series: *The Sleuth of St. James's Square*, 1920; *The Bradmoor Murders*, 1929 (also known as *The Garden in Asia*)

Captain Walker series: *Walker of the Secret Service*, 1924

Colonel Braxton series: *The Silent Witness*, 1930

Nonseries novels: *The Nameless Thing*, 1912; *The Mystery at the Blue Villa*, 1919; *The Revolt of the Birds*, 1927

Other major works

Novels: *The Gilded Chair*, 1910; *The Mountain School-Teacher*, 1922

Children's literature: *Dwellers in the Hills*, 1901

Nonfiction: *The Man Hunters*, 1926

Bibliography

Hubin, Allen J. Introduction to *The Complete Uncle Abner*. San Diego: University of California, 1977. Hubin provides both the critical introduction and an annotated bibliography to this collection of the Uncle Abner mysteries.

Norton, Charles A. *Melville Davisson Post: Man of Many Mysteries*. Bowling Green, Ohio: Bowling Green University Popular Press, 1974. Study of Post's life and work. Includes extensive bibliography of Post's writing, as well as of writing about him.

_______. "The Randolph Mason Stories." *The Armchair Detective* 6 (October, 1972): 86-96. Overview of Post's tales of an unethical attorney manipulating the law.

Panek, LeRoy Lad. *The Origins of the American Detective Story*. Jefferson, N.C.: McFarland, 2006. Study of the beginnings and establishment of American detective-fiction conventions, focusing especially on the replacement of the police by the private detective and the place of forensic science in the genre. Sheds light on Post's work.

Peters, Ellis. Foreword to *Historical Whodunits*, edited by Mike Ashley. New York: Barnes & Noble, 1997. The well-known practitioner of historical crime fiction comments on Post's entry in the subgenre.

Van Dover, J. K., and John F. Jebb. *Isn't Justice Always Unfair? The Detective in Southern Literature.* Bowling Green, Ohio: Bowling Green State University Popular Press, 1996. Critical examination of the narrow tradition of southern detective fiction and the distinctive contributions of southern authors to the mystery genre. Includes a chapter on Post and Irvin S. Cobb.

Williams, Blanche Colton. "Melville Davisson Post." In *Our Short Story Writers*. Reprint. Freeport, N.Y.: Books for Libraries Press, 1969. Profile of Post emphasizing his prowess as a crafter of short fiction.

JEAN POTTS

Born: St. Paul, Nebraska; November 17, 1910
Died: New York, New York; November 10, 1999
Type of plot: Psychological

Contribution

Between 1943 and 1975, Jean Potts published fifteen novels, fourteen of which are within the realm of mystery and detective fiction. Few of them even remotely resemble the classic whodunit. Potts started writing crime novels at a time when the general style of the genre was undergoing a transformation toward a more realistic approach. Instead of dealing with police procedure, courtroom trials, or private investigators, Potts found her brand of realism by focusing on a close-knit band of characters face to face with a murder—real, imaginary, or impending.

Curiously, the physical act of the crime itself and how it is committed is incidental to almost all the plots. More than one "mystery" unfolds without a murdered victim. Vital to the plots, on the other hand, is the psychology of the characters and their interactions. There is no omniscient narrator, no one point of view, no hero or villain. Several points of view, each one justifiable, are presented simultaneously. The denouement is almost a studied anticlimax. Any of the characters may end up guilty without eliciting the reader's surprise. In Potts's novels, both judgment and punishment come from within the guilty; the judicial system is given no role.

Biography

Jean Catherine Potts spent most of her early life in her home state, completing her education at Nebraska Wesleyan University in Lincoln, then starting her career as a journalist in Nebraska. The lure of freelance writing took her to New York, where she made her home. Little of her private life is known.

Potts's first novel was *Someone to Remember*, published by Westminster Press in Philadelphia in 1943. It was eleven years before her second novel, *Go, Lovely Rose* (1954), was published. A crime novel, *Go, Lovely Rose* won for her the Mystery Writers of America's Edgar Allan Poe Award in 1955. After 1954 she published a novel every year until 1958. Her mystery-writing career of twenty-one years yielded fourteen novels and three short stories published in magazines.

In June, 1988, admitting that her literary career "seems to have run out of steam," Potts said that her only output after 1975 was two stories in *Ellery Queen's Mystery Magazine*—"In the Absence of Proof" in July, 1985, and "Two on the Isle" in January, 1987. An English firm, Chivers Press, accepted two of her books, *Go, Lovely Rose* and *Home Is the Prisoner* (1960), for reprinting in 1988. Potts died in New York in 1999.

Analysis

Go, Lovely Rose started Jean Potts's career as a mystery writer with an Edgar Allan Poe Award. It is, perhaps, the only novel in her corpus that has all the ingredients of a conventional whodunit. A murder begins the plot, a range of suspects are introduced and brought together, and a police officer and detective are on the chase, taking statements, asking questions, and "going by the book of police procedure." Still, even in this first effort, almost all the ideas and innovations that made her contribution to the genre so distinctive are present in embryonic form.

The Diehard

Straying more than slightly from the rules in that first crime novel, Potts achieved that special voice writers strive for surprisingly early in her career. By the time her third crime novel, *The Diehard* (1956)—a murder mystery without an actual murder—was published, she had discarded even the pretense of following the prescribed rules that made a mystery novel in the eyes of purist readers and writers. The question in *The Diehard* is not who did it but who could have done it—and nobody does it. Thus, *The Diehard* constitutes an outworking of one of Potts's theories on her genre: that the thought is the crime and that a murder committed in the mind alone often has consequences as serious as those of an actual killing. The intention or even the desire to do away with someone makes a character as culpable as the hand that fires a gun.

Like *The Diehard, Home Is the Prisoner* pursues another angle of the idea of a mystery without a murder to precipitate it. *The Man with the Cane* (1957) differs from the concept in a minor way: The victim is almost a total stranger who is introduced to most of the characters only after his murder. *The Evil Wish* (1962), another variation on the same theme, develops a concept that was casually introduced in *Go, Lovely Rose* and *The Diehard*—what Potts christened a "left-over murder."

Other devices and motifs link the novels written between 1965 and 1975. Career connections replace the lifelong small-town bonds of the earlier plots. Anonymous parts of New York City or a strange resort environment become the backdrop, replacing the familiarity of a suburban hamlet where everybody knows everybody else. A faceless, impersonal voice of an unnamed detective replaces the identifiable "friendly neighborhood policeman," though these official characters are equally unimportant to the real working of the plot. There is murder committed toward the beginning of these later novels, and the murderer is almost invariably a woman with an obsessive, irrational love for her husband (*The Footsteps on the Stairs*, 1966, and *An Affair of the Heart*, 1970) or her son (*The Only Good Secretary*, 1965, and *The Troublemaker*, 1972).

All fourteen novels have some things in common. There is always a small community of people, with each individual inextricably tied to the crime in one way or another, each contributing to and being affected by the psychological anguish caused by the crime (regardless of whether it has been committed), each having to shoulder his or her share of the total guilt even as collectively they piece together fragmentary clues and pronounce judgment on the actual act. In itself, the act is not important, and neither is justice by law. Suicide, insanity, and a total indifference to any punishment the legal system can impose on them are the only way Potts's criminals can react to the crimes they commit, because justice does not come down on them impersonally: It originates in the crime itself and in the very motive behind it.

Psychologically, the novels become progressively more complicated and introspective in both characterization and action. The private worlds within the minds of the people Potts creates become the real focus of the novels. It is the internal world of a character that causes the normally mundane external world of a community to disintegrate. Shorn of this psychological complexity, her plots would seem bare and inadequate. *Home Is the Prisoner*, for example, is the story of an ex-convict who returns home to avid speculation on the part of the people who have known him all of his life, while in *The Man with the Cane* the corpse of a stranger triggers the curiosity of a normally apathetic community. All physical acts of aggression are either catalyst or solution and fade into inconsequence. Physical violence, if there is any, is restricted to the crime, its gruesome details glossed, and sometimes a suicide in the end (also underplayed and generally out of sight), or as in several novels, a small fistfight at some point.

The Evil Wish

Mental violence, on the other hand, abounds, kept a malicious, malevolent secret under the gentlest or the most sensible exterior. Potts points out, time and again, that even ordinary people with the most uneventful existences are capable of heinous crimes. Doll-like, docile women who chatter away inconsequentially throughout their sheltered lives—Lucy Knapp in *The Evil Wish*, Barbara in *The Man with the Cane*, Thelma Holm in *The Footsteps on the Stairs*—are found to possess hidden reserves of the most uncompromising determination and capacity for cruelty. Lovable, responsible men, pillars of small-town goodness, are driven to murder because of emotional pressure. Everybody, Potts seems to say, every face in the world, can harbor a criminal. Her novels' action and drama stem from the psychological complexities of the minds of her characters, all very human, very flawed, and totally credible. In one of her most intriguing psychological studies, *The Evil Wish*, two sisters wish their father dead and plan his murder meticulously, only to have their plans thwarted but their wish fulfilled when their father, Dr. Knapp, obligingly dies in an accident. The consciences of the sisters are then burdened with a "left-over murder," their guilt growing while the desire to see their plan through is left unsatisfied. They are killers without a crime to justify the guilt they feel, and the mental state resulting from this turmoil destroys their lives and eventually forces them to become each other's murderer.

Although her characters are trapped into facing the consequences they bring on themselves, Potts is not beyond playing occasional psychological games with her readers. Readers of *The Diehard*, for example, find themselves waiting almost impatiently for the unnatural death of Lew Morgan to occur, for they are privy to the information that all but one of the major characters are out to kill him. In the end, Lew dies in an accident caused, ironically, by the only person who wished him alive, and the reader is left burdened with the uncomfortable weight of an impossibly ambiguous truth: No one in the novel kills Lew Morgan, yet everyone does.

This kind of mental realism, this internalized action and characterization, became Potts's hallmark and is perhaps the most important factor in the literary success of her novels, lending them a several-layered, multifaceted psychological depth that is rare in crime fiction. Potts has the brilliant talent of revealing both appearance and reality with simple, economical strokes. There are no extensive descriptions, explanations, or justifications, only the characters revealed through their own thought processes. There are no "good" or "bad" characters; rather, Potts's protagonists are fully fleshed-out human beings with weaknesses and strengths. Marcia Knapp in *The Evil Wish*, an otherwise intelligent and pragmatic woman, has a tendency toward alcoholism; Judge McVey (*Home Is the Prisoner*), an upright, honest man, is revealed to be a coward; Fern Villard (*The Only Good Secretary*), efficient and charming, is driven by pathological avarice.

Potts's characters indulge in trivial eccentricities, petty secrets and obsessions, gossiping, blackmailing, pathetic attempts to seem younger, lying—behavior that shows them to be less than wholesome but makes them wholly credible. Her novels are full of people who are simultaneously attractive and repulsive. The reader cannot help but understand them, think their thoughts with them, pity and forgive them; nevertheless, an emotional distance is always maintained between reader and character. There is never any question of self-identification or empathy with a Potts character on the part of the reader. Potts achieves this distance simply by presenting several points of view, with different characters picking up the telling of the tale at irregular intervals, sharing their personal points of view, introspections, and interactions. Each character has firm convictions and an individual set of questions and answers. The reader is thus involved with several different opinions and people and is forced to change his own mind several times. Eventually, a process of elimination leaves only two or three central characters whose accounts can be tentatively accepted—a far cry from a consistent, omniscient narrative voice presenting a single, authoritative version of an event.

Though each character in a Jean Potts novel is undeniably an individual, there is a limited range of types to which most of them conform. Her women fall for the most part under three categories. There is the matter-of-fact, likable, do-gooder type with a sensible head on her shoulders—Mary Walsh in *An Affair of the Heart*, Rachel Buckmaster or Myra Graves in *Go, Lovely Rose*, Margaret Robinson in *The Troublemaker*, and "Hen" in *The Man with the Cane*. Then there are Barbara (*The Man with the Cane*), Lucy Knapp (*The Evil Wish*), and Thelma Holm (*The Footsteps on the Stairs*)—fragile, nervous, sheltered escapists who refuse to face reality and prefer to drown all ugliness in bright chatter. Finally, Potts creates worldlywise career women who can absorb and accept all aspects of life with the indifference that comes with jaded knowledge. Marcia in *The Evil Wish*, Fern in *The Only Good Secretary*, and Enid Baxter in *The Footsteps on the Stairs* can outdrink and outphilander any man.

The men, similarly, could be divided into three classifications, starting with responsible, upright, honest men such as Hugh in *Go, Lovely Rose*, "Mack" in *Home Is the Prisoner*, and Val Bryant in *The Man with the Cane*. Another type would be the charming, arrogant, superficial character who remains likable despite his blatant flaws—Gordon Llewellyn in *The Evil Wish*, Dr. Craig in *Go, Lovely Rose*, Kirk Banning in *An Affair of the Heart*, and Lew Morgan in *The Diehard*. Finally, there is the man who is a failure, despite unusual intelligence, because of a lack of motivation or a fondness for alcohol: Archie O'Brien in *The Only Good Secretary* and Martin Shipley and Vic Holm in *The Footsteps on the Stairs*.

Apart from these identifiable types, Potts liberally peppered her novels with colorful eccentrics such as Gladys Popejoy (*The Only Good Secretary*), who is sure that germs that spread "Diseases" are waiting to catch her unprepared in a bus or at the office, or the homosexual Teddy (*An Affair of the Heart*), who flutters around nervously and cannot resist malicious digs at others, even his friends.

Any one of these characters might be the victim and anyone the killer. They are all suspects and sleuths by turn. Their interactions make for remarkably lifelike unlikelihoods. Friendship and hostility between Potts's characters are marked by the strange complexity of reality. Antagonists in a Potts novel often cannot help liking each other. Martin Shipley and Vic Holm understand each other instinctively, just as Marcia Knapp and Chuck Llewellyn do. Each can see the other's unsavory side and identify with it. Suspicion and trust go hand in hand where these pairs are concerned, because though a bond of affection and concern ties them together they can never give up the individual convictions that created the original antagonism.

The narrow, humdrum existences of Potts's characters are inevitably and irreparably distorted by crimes of emotion, misdeeds motivated by an obsessive, misguided love for father, spouse, or child. Potts always focused on the elemental emotion of love, which, in her opinion, is more treacherous than any hatred or selfish need could be.

Potts's awareness of love's pitfalls creates a distinctive kind of crime fiction. In her novels, life does not simply return to normal after the crime is solved and justice served. The reason for that lies in the motivation for the crime and the deep emotions it stirs in each of the characters. Those who had wanted to kill but could not are racked by guilt. Even the relatively innocent will forever carry painful memories. As for the murderers, once they have accomplished the deed to which their tortured desires drove them, the only thing left to desire is death.

Ravinder Kaur

Principal mystery and detective fiction

Novels: *Go, Lovely Rose*, 1954; *Death of a Stray Cat*, 1955 (also known as *Dark Destination*); *The Diehard*, 1956; *The Man with the Cane*, 1957; *Lightning Strikes Twice*, 1958 (also known as *Blood Will Tell*); *Home Is the Prisoner*, 1960; *The Evil Wish*, 1962; *The Only Good Secretary*, 1965; *The Footsteps on the Stairs*, 1966; *The Little Lie*, 1968; *The Trash Stealer*, 1968; *An Affair of the Heart*, 1970; *The Troublemaker*, 1972; *My Brother's Killer*, 1975

Other major work

Novel: *Someone to Remember*, 1943

Bibliography

Boucher, Anthony. Review of *The Footsteps on the Stairs*, by Jean Potts. *The New York Times Book Review* 71 (July 25, 1966): 20. A famous detective-fiction author and critic reviews one of Potts's novels.

_______. Review of *The Trash Stealer*, by Jean Potts. *The New York Times Book Review* 73 (February 4, 1968): 43. A celebrated detective-fiction author and critic reviews Potts's novels about an attempt to atone for an accidental killing.

"Jean Potts, Eighty-eight, Author of Prize-Winning Mystery." *The New York Times*, November 17, 1999, p. C29. Obituary of Potts looks at her life and career, noting that her strong point was characterization.

Klein, Kathleen Gregory, ed. *Women Times Three: Writers, Detectives, Readers*. Bowling Green, Ohio: Bowling Green State University Popular Press, 1995. Study of female detective writers, fictional sleuths, and consumers of detective fiction provides perspective on Potts's fiction.

Scaggs, John. *Crime Fiction*. New York: Routlege, 2005. Study of the cultural import of crime fiction and its conventions; helps elucidate the significance of unconventional approaches such as Potts's.

DOUGLAS PRESTON and LINCOLN CHILD

Douglas Preston
Born: Cambridge, Massachusetts; May 20, 1956

Lincoln Child
Born: Westport, Connecticut; October 13, 1957
Types of plot: Master sleuth; psychological; thriller

Principal series

Special Agent Pendergast, 1995-

Principal series characters

Aloysius Pendergast is a mysterious Federal Bureau of Investigation (FBI) agent originally from New Orleans who suddenly appears on the scene knowing more than he should know and refusing to take no for an answer. Tall, extremely thin, but muscular, he has whitish blond hair, pale blue eyes, and an extremely pale complexion that make him easily noticed. He always wears well-tailored, black wool suits. His fund of general knowledge is no less than encyclopedic, and his ability to disguise himself is phenomenal. He possess an undeniable charisma that appeals to most of the characters with whom he comes in contact, but he is vulnerable and haunted by the mental and emotional instability that is his legacy from both sides of his family.

Vincent D'Agosto is a dedicated police officer. A hard worker, he has total belief and faith in Pendergast, even though that faith costs him a relationship with a woman who is extremely important to him. Vincent is middle-aged and is just getting back into shape after a period of letting himself go physically. For a while he left police work to write detective novels, but he is reestablishing himself in police work. Basically a good person, he is a good police officer and detective.

Bill Smithback, a writer-journalist, is a perpetually loose cannon. If there is somewhere he should not be, he will be there. If there is a wrong time to approach a subject, Smithback will find it. He is brash, abrasive, and somewhat uncouth, but he still possess a kind of naïve charm. However, expensive Italian suits cannot make a silk purse of a sow's ear, and Smithback has a way to go before he becomes generally acceptable. He is, though, thoroughly dedicated and devoted to Pendergast. Smithback seems to be nearly killed every time he appears in a book.

Contribution

Douglas Preston and Lincoln Child have written more than ten books as a team and are enjoying great success in the process. Even though they claim not to have seen each other face to face for ten years, their perfection of the collaboratory process is an inspiration to other aspiring collaborators, especially because each author also writes individually. Although these solo novels have some of the trademark action and suspense of the collaborations, there does not seem to be quite as much richness and layering as there is when the two minds are applied to a project. Preston has explained that phenomenon by saying that their minds just happen to be "twisted" in the same way. That may be, but the two men still experience differences and disagreements while working on a project.

Preston and Child both bring ideas and suggestions for books to the table and collaborate on projects that appeal to both of them equally strongly. Preston's *The Codex* (2004) and Child's *Utopia* (2002) were both projects rejected by the other partner. After a thorough discussion of concepts, Child makes a chapter outline. Preston takes the outline and writes the book. Child edits and rewrites. Then, Preston takes that draft and works through it again. This is the pattern that the two of them have followed since the beginning of their partnership.

In the course of their collaboration, Preston and Child are creating a mythology based on character exchanges within their various novels. William Smithback, in addition to the Pendergast books, is also a character in *Thunderhead* (1999). A character in *The Ice Limit* (2000) also appears in *Book of the Dead* (2006). Interesting characters reappear from novel to novel in both series and nonseries novels. Like Special Agent Aloysius Pendergast, Preston and Child have a great fund of general knowledge and many special interests to draw on for their books. They can write with authority about many subjects and have practical experience in most areas of science and technology. This special knowledge results in the production of some outstanding techno-thrillers grounded in detective fiction. Working in the arena of classic imagery and plot, the two men are strongly influenced by Sir Arthur Conan Doyle, Charles Dickens, and Edgar Allan Poe.

Biography

Douglas J. Preston was born in Cambridge, Massachusetts, in 1956 and grew up in Wellesley. Douglas and his two brothers, Richard and David, lived a rough-and-tumble boy's life, losing fingertips and teeth with joyous abandon and entertaining various friends and neighbors. Douglas attended Pomona College in Claremont, California, and studied a wide range of subjects before he eventually settled on a major in English literature. After graduation, Preston worked with the Museum of Natural History in New York City as editor, writer, and director of special events. He also freelanced, writing articles about the progress of the museum, and taught writing at Princeton.

Luckily, he gave in to an invitation to write about the museum in *Dinosaurs in the Attic: An Excursion into the American Museum of Natural History* (1985). The invitation to write was extended by a young editor at St. Martin's Press named Lincoln Child. Preston took Child for a midnight tour of the museum, and that experience became the basis for *Relic* (1995). In 1986, Preston moved to Santa Fe, where after a period of time, he wrote *Cities of Gold: A Journey Across the American Southwest in Pursuit of Coronado* (1992) and became interested in the history and legends of the southwest. Preston later moved to the coast of Maine. He and his wife, Christine, have three children. Like Agent Pendergast, Preston claims kinship with a number of famous and infamous relatives.

Lincoln B. Child was born in Westport, Connecticut, in 1957. Although his family moved away before he reached his first birthday, he still regards it as his hometown. He acquired an interest in writing early on and majored in English in college. After graduation he secured a job as an editorial assistant at St. Martin's Press, where he worked his way up to full editor. He worked on more than a hundred books and collected several anthologies of ghost tales that more or less established a horror division at the press. In 1987, Child left St. Martin's and went to work doing highly technical computer jobs. After *Relic* was a success, he quit his job. He settled in New Jersey with his wife and daughter. A list of his interests would parallel those of Agent Pendergast—probably because Lincoln firmly believes in that bit of writer's advice to write about what one knows.

Analysis

Neither Douglas Preston nor Lincoln Child likes to categorize their work. They feel that literature is too "genrecized" already and that what is important is for them to enjoy what they write and try to introduce readers to new jobs, places, and disciplines. Their novels combine so many elements and influences that they are nearly impossible to classify.

In *Relic*, Preston and Child introduced the notion of a museum as a bizarre microcosm of the world at large. Given the erudition of the New York Natural Museum of History, the nature of its exhibits, its labyrinthine passages, and its scientific equipment, the potential for a tale of horror and mad scientists as in the 1953 film *House of Wax* not only existed but also virtually begged to be brought to life. At the same time that Preston and Child were thinking about a museum mystery, a Holmesian figure presented himself to the authors in the person of Special Agent Aloysius Pendergast. According to Preston and Child, he sprang, Athena-like, fully formed into their minds. Within the Diogenes trilogy (*Brimstone*, 2004, *Dance of Death*, 2005, and *Book of the Dead*, 2006) there seems to be a Sherlock Holmes/Moriarty—Holmes/Mycroft reference at work. The rivalry between Special Agent Pendergast and his criminal brother Diogenes Pendergast is so intense that readers begin to think about their own familial relationships. Diogenes Pendergast is a totally evil literary character who reminds readers that, undoubtedly, several criminal masterminds like Diogenes have existed in real life.

Although the authors have suggested that *The Cabinet of Curiosities* (2002), a Pendergast novel, could be considered a nonseries novel, in actuality, it is *Still Life with Crows* (2003) that might fit in that category, as it takes place in the Midwest and away from New York and the museum. *Relic* and its successor, *Reliquary* (1997), are obviously related, a fact denoted by the titles: A reliquary is a place or thing designed to hold and protect relics, and what is a museum but a very large reliquary? In that sense, a cabinet of curiosities—holding a collection of rare and valuable things as it does—is also a reliquary. In some of the books, the museum is never far away from the consciousness of the characters, and in others the scene changes and becomes worldwide, offering the solution of one riddle while presenting the detective with another in the style of Dan Brown's books about ancient mysteries. The mysteries of Preston and Child are, however, not that ancient, even if they sometimes seem to be. Their books are immediate life-or-death mysteries on behalf of characters that readers have come to know and to like.

Preston and Child have developed complex plots in which they leave the actions of one character to begin another chapter dealing with the progress of a different character whose actions seem to have nothing to do with the plot. In this way, the suspense is advanced, only to come to a jarring halt when a dead end appears or a promising lead fails to pay off. Nothing is ever simple in a Preston and Child book, and always, as the book develops, a psychological element begins to surface.

Relic

Without a doubt, the major character of *Relic* is the museum, in all of its aspects: as a building, as an organization, as an institution. Shirley Jackson used the device of place as character to devastating advantage in *The Haunting of Hill House* (1959) and so have Preston and Child in *Relic*. From the first murder, the whole impetus of the book becomes an imperative to save the museum.

The coincidence of the emergence of a monster with the creation of the new Superstition exhibit is so stunning in its visual, emotional, and intellectual content and so technically cutting-edge in its presentation that it is literally calculated to shock museum patrons into reaching for their checkbooks to help fund the museum. In the course of touring the museum and seeing the behind-the-scenes work that goes into mounting new exhibits and keeping the institution meaningful and vital to a changing society, the readers also learn some unfortunate truths about the personalities involved. Even doctors of various sciences, the best and brightest of their kind, are not above cheap, petty competition for grants to back up or extend their own research interests, and in most cases, those research projects have less to do with improving the world than they do with advancing the career and reputation of the individual. To catch the monster, the combined talents of Smithback, Margo Green, Agent Pendergast, and Vincent D'Agosto are required. Although Pendergast plays a small role, he did capture some attention in this book, and D'Agosto and Smithback made their own impressions. Green returns to the museum in later books.

The Cabinet of Curiosities

The Cabinet of Curiosities, part of the Pendergast series, focuses on gruesome discoveries in the basement of a New York building that once housed a col-

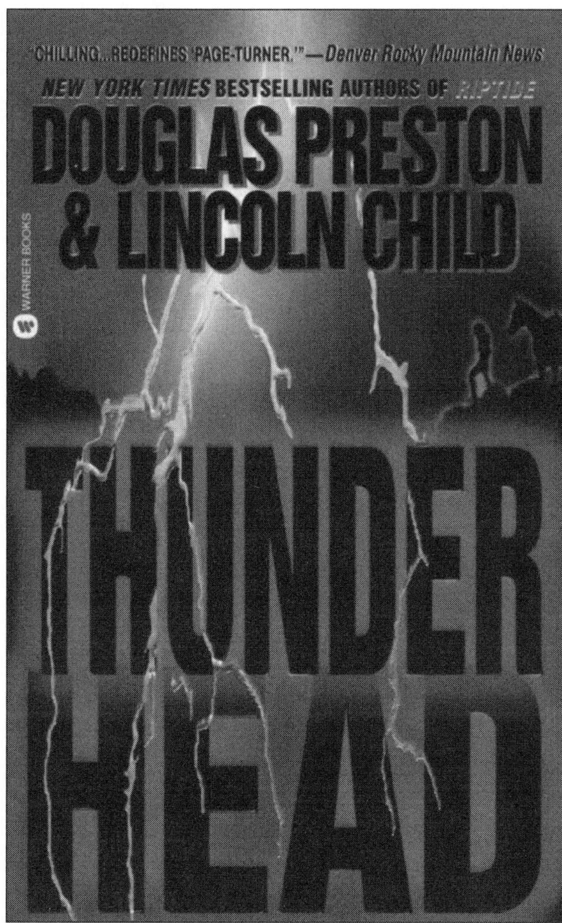

lection of curiosities. In this work, Preston and Child unravel a bit more of the mystery surrounding the Pendergast family. It seems that Special Agent Pendergast is the family oddball, a lawman in a family in which criminal lunacy is prevalent. He entered his profession because of his need to combat his family, especially his younger brother, Diogenes.

In this novel, the demolition of an old building opens an underground charnel house: catacombs where the skeletons of numerous young people from the beginning of the twentieth century are found. Readers are reminded that the Museum of Natural History is also a charnel house: a place where the remains of both animal and human dead are kept and exhibited. The concepts of the museum, the charnel house, and the cabinet of curiosities all relate to the mysterious mansion on Riverside Drive, which houses a cabinet of curiosities, but the cabinet is only one of many. Actually, the entire mansion is an extended cabinet of curiosities and a charnel house as well, entombing a living person in the house for nearly a hundred years. The extension of the museum metaphor throughout this work is a brilliant concept on the part of the authors.

Thunderhead

In *Thunderhead*, a nonseries novel, Nora Kelly is leading an expedition in search for the origins of the Anasazi, and journalist Bill Smithback is traveling along to record her findings. In later novels, both of these characters are absorbed into the museum framework of the Pendergast series. Perhaps one of the most outstanding aspects of the novels of Preston and Child is the research that goes into their work. Preston has written several *New Yorker* articles on the subject and has followed some of the trails and passages that Kelly and Smithback travel in the work. Within the works of Preston and Child, there is almost always a breathtaking array of facts that are illumined by the imagination of these two men.

H. Alan Pickrell

Principal mystery and detective fiction

Agent Pendergast series: *Relic*, 1995; *Reliquary*, 1997; *The Cabinet of Curiosities*, 2002; *Still Life with Crows*, 2003; *Brimstone*, 2004; *Dance of Death*, 2005; *Book of the Dead*, 2006; *Wheel of Darkness*, 2007

Nonseries novels: *Mount Dragon*, 1996; *Riptide*, 1998; *Thunderhead*, 1999; *Ice Limit*, 2000

Nonseries novels (by Preston): *The Codex*, 2004; *Tyrannosaur Canyon*, 2005

Nonseries novels (by Child): *Utopia*, 2002; *Death Match*, 2004; *Deep Storm*, 2007

Other major works

Novel (by Preston): *Jennie*, 1994

Nonfiction (by Preston): *Dinosaurs in the Attic: An Excursion into the American Museum of Natural History*, 1986; *Cities of Gold: A Journey Across the American Southwest in Pursuit of Coronado*, 1992; *Talking to the Ground: One Family's Journey on Horseback Across the Sacred Land of the Navajo*, 1995; *The Royal Road: El Camino Real from Mexico*

City to Santa Fe, 1998 (with Christine Preston and Jose Antonio Esquibel)

EDITED TEXTS (BY CHILD): *Dark Company: The Ten Greatest Ghost Stories*, 1983; *Dark Banquet: A Feast of Twelve Great Ghost Stories*, 1985; *Tales of the Dark*, 1987 (3 volumes)

BIBLIOGRAPHY

Preston, Douglas, and Lincoln Child. *The Book of the Dead*. New York: Warner Books, 2006. In a "Note to the Reader," Preston and Child offer suggestions about in what order their books should be read.

_______. "Duo Keeps the Suspense Building." Interview by Jeff Ayers. *Writer* 119, no. 7 (July, 2006): 18-22. Interview examines how the writers came to be collaborators, the process of writing together, their plot development, and characterization.

_______. Official Web site: Douglas Preston and Lincoln Child. http://www.prestonchild.com. On their official Web site, Preston and Child offer biographies, future plans, selections from their works, reviews, comments, and answers to fans' questions about their work and their viewpoints.

_______. "*PW* Talks with Douglas Preston and Lincoln Child: The Joys of Fictional Collaboration." Interview by Leonard Picker. *Publishers Weekly* 253, no. 10 (May 15, 2006): 46. Short interview concentrates on the development of the character Aloysius Pendergast.

Stableford, Brian. "Introduction." In *Cyclopedia of Literary Places*, edited by Kent Rasmussen. Pasadena, Calif.: Salem Press, 2003. Stableford discusses purposes and uses of setting within literary works. Settings are especially important to the work of Preston and Child in that their settings nearly become characters. This introduction informs the reader of why the authors are so very setting-specific.

J. B. PRIESTLEY

Born: Bradford, Yorkshire, England; September 13, 1894
Died: Stratford-upon-Avon, Warwickshire, England; August 14, 1984
Also wrote as Peter Goldsmith
Types of plot: Amateur sleuth; espionage

CONTRIBUTION

J. B. Priestley's seven crime novels, including one written with Gerald Bullett, are, compared to the bulk of his published work, a minute part of the Priestley canon. Each of the novels exists independently of the others, and each is an unrepeated foray into crime fiction. The central characters are not detectives or professional police officers; they are medical doctors, artists, newspapermen, and trained professional people who are very good at their chosen work. Something piques their interest—a patient goes missing, a scientist disappears, an experiment is stolen—and they turn their obvious mental powers to the task. The books themselves, as might be expected from one of the twentieth century's most prolific dramatists, read like scripts for stage and screen, and their visual impact is strong. Priestley's sly wit, his socialistic philosophy, and his stagecraft mark the novels and give them the easy progress of well-written works. At the same time, in all of his crime novels, Priestley takes a cold and dispassionate look at his society and finds it less than perfect.

BIOGRAPHY

John Boynton Priestley was born on September 13, 1894, in Bradford, Yorkshire, England, the son of a schoolmaster. He was educated in the Bradford schools and at Trinity College of the University of Cambridge. He served with the Duke of Wellington's and Devon regiments from 1914 to 1919. He was graduated from Trinity College with honors in English literature, political science, and modern history. He married Patricia Tempest, with whom he had two daughters, in 1919;

J. B. Priestley in 1958. (Hulton Archive/Getty Images)

Mary Wyndham Lewis, with whom he had three more daughters and a son, in 1926; and Jacquetta Hawkes, the writer and his sometime collaborator, in 1953.

He began his writing career at sixteen, contributing articles to London and provincial newspapers. He went to London in 1922 and established himself as a reviewer, critic, and essayist; in addition, he published two or three books a year, including studies of the work of George Meredith and Thomas Love Peacock for the English Men of Letters series, a history of the English novel, and other works. By 1930, he had established a strong reputation both in England and the United States through his novels, including *Angel Pavement* (1930), which falls loosely into the category of crime fiction. His work during this period was a mixture of personal history and social criticism.

In 1932, he wrote *Dangerous Corner*, a highly successful drama that launched him on a new career, one that occupied much of his time from then on. Among other activities, he served as the director of Mask Theatre in London; the United Kingdom delegate and chairman to the United Nations Educational, Scientific, and Cultural Organization's International Theater Conferences in Paris (1947) and Prague (1948); the chairman of the British Theatre Conferences; the president of the International Theatre Institute; and on the National Theatre Board. He was a regular contributor to *New Statesman* and broadcast uplifting commentaries for the British Broadcasting Corporation during World War II; these broadcasts were published as *Britain Speaks* (1940) and *Postscripts* (1940) and earned for him the unofficial title "the voice of the common people of Great Britain."

Priestley traveled extensively in the United States and spent two winters in Arizona. Despite his criticism—and he freely criticized everything—Priestley was fond of the United States and probably knew as much about its history and literature as did any modern English novelist.

Priestley was awarded the James Tait Black Memorial Prize in 1930, the Ellen Terry Award in 1948, and honorary degrees from the University of St. Andrews, the University of Birmingham, the University of Bradford, and Trinity College. He was awarded the Order of Merit in 1977. In 1978, he moved, appropriately, to Stratford-upon-Avon. He died on August 14, 1984, one month short of his ninetieth birthday.

ANALYSIS

J. B. Priestley's early novel *Benighted* (1927), published in the United States as *The Old Dark House* (1928), was more of a gothic horror story than a detective story, and *I'll Tell You Everything* (1932), written with Gerald Bullett, was an early spoof of the cloak-and-dagger tale then gaining in popularity. It was with his last three crime novels, *Saturn over the Water: An Account of His Adventures in London, South America, and Australia by Tim Bedford, Painter* (1961), *The Shapes of Sleep: A Topical Tale* (1962), and *Salt Is Leaving* (1966), that Priestley hit his peak as a detective-fiction writer.

SATURN OVER THE WATER

Saturn over the Water is a good book and much more of a mystery than the earlier novels. It owes something to Nevil Shute's *On the Beach* (1957) and has delicious reflections of John Buchan's *The Power-House* (1916), *The Thirty-nine Steps* (1915), and his neglected *The Courts of the Morning* (1929). Tim Bedford, a successful painter, promises his dying cousin Isabel Frame that he will find her estranged and missing husband, Joe, and tell him that she still loves him. It is a soap-opera opening to a nicely constructed and skillfully plotted novel of intrigue, travel, and involvement with a secret organization. This group is busily plotting to force the Northern Hemisphere to destroy itself through biological and atomic warfare, leaving the cabal, whose sign is Saturn over the water, free to create a new and better world in their own image in South America, Australia, and Africa.

Bedford's only clue to the whereabouts of the missing scientist, Joe Frame, is the hastily scribbled list of names, places, and things in his last letter, posted from Chile. He is intrigued by the mystery, especially when he identifies one of the names as that of another English scientist, Frank Semple. Semple had worked with Frame at the Arnaldos Institute in Peru and had returned home psychotic and had committed suicide. Bedford travels from London to New York, then to Peru, Chile, and Australia, each stop identifying more of Frame's list and bringing him into contact with shadowy people who will ultimately play major roles in the solution of the mystery. Bedford, unknown to himself, is in reality a pawn in a power struggle, the catalyst the opponents of the cabal have needed to bring the global plot to an unsuccessful conclusion.

Similar to Richard Hannay's foes in *The Thirty-nine Steps* and *The Power-House*, the opponents in *Saturn over the Water* are men with superhuman intellects, men capable of exerting powerful influence over lesser minds. Using the concept of the astrological changing of the ages, Priestley matches the Saturnians against those under the sign of Uranus, the peaceful ones.

As Bedford makes his journey, Priestley makes use of his stops to comment on the neo-Nazi mentality, the threat of communism, the misuse of technology, and the strange world of the arts. Although Priestley himself espoused Fabian socialism, he despised Marxist principles, instead identifying himself as anticonservative politically.

The characters here are not as exhaustively drawn as those in *Angel Pavement*, but the reader does get to know them well enough for their motivations to be acceptable, at least for the more realistic of them. Other characters, especially as the novel nears its end, seem fantastic: Mrs. Biro, the clairvoyant; Major Jorvis, the Australian police officer through whose form the Saturn superintellect works; and Pat Daily, an apparent drunken junk dealer who is in fact the Old Astrologer of the Mountain and the "force" representing the Uranian side of the new age. As the novel ends, the reader is pleased to find that Tim Bedford and Rosalia Arnaldos, the granddaughter of the founder of the institute and the Saturn cabal, have married. She has inherited the institute and Arnaldos's vast fortune, and together they dedicate their resources to the betterment of humankind. Still, the reader is left with the uneasy feeling that although a battle has been won, the war is far from over.

The Shapes of Sleep

The Shapes of Sleep is considered by many to be Priestley's best work in the genre, although *Salt Is Leaving* has its champions. Ben Sterndale, a forty-two-year-old freelance journalist, is hired by a friend, an advertising executive, to locate and recover a mysterious piece of green paper that has been stolen. Sterndale has only a list of names of those who visited the office the day the paper disappeared with which to work. He begins his search, unaware of the import of the missing paper, which is part of an experiment in subliminal mind altering, designed for use not only in marketing but also, and more important for the story, in political propaganda.

Sterndale's search takes him to the Continent; in and out of the clutches of Eastern and Western espionage agents; through late-night forays in breaking and entering, into romantic trysts with secret agents; and on journeys by car, train, and boat to arrive somewhere and do something before someone else arrives and does something less pleasant. His role is that of an amateur James Bond, and he falls into and somehow escapes from one dangerous situation after another until everything falls into place. Priestley's usual concerns are present. He uses the book to poke fun at the deadly serious espionage services of both sides, at the ultrajingoism of people involved in that type of activity, at the social situations that give rise to "sides" competing for the minds of humankind, and at the powers that control the political machines on both sides of the Iron Curtain.

The Shapes of Sleep is a suspenseful, rapidly moving book with realistic action (so far as the secret services are concerned), enough danger to whet the reader's interest, and a surprise ending that justifies the novel's existence. The characters and their actions are presented in a typically strong Priestley dramatic form. It would make a fine film.

Salt Is Leaving

Salt Is Leaving would also make a satisfactory film or even a stage play. Lionel Humphrey Salt ("Call me Salt when you're tired of doctoring me") has given up his medical practice in the depressed and depressing town of Birkden after seven years. He yearns to move on, to the south of France and then possibly to Africa or India, where he apparently lived for some time. He delays his departure out of concern for a patient, Noreen Wilks, who has been missing for three weeks. Salt's concern is centered on his interest in kidney diseases, Noreen's rare chronic nephritis, and her failure to renew the prescription needed to keep her alive. His search involves him with the world of Sir Arnold Donnington—the industrialist who owns United Fabrics and, through his company, the town of Birkden—and with Maggie Culworth, whose father has also disappeared. Maggie works in her father's bookstore in nearby Henton, her place of refuge after several years and a disastrous romance in London. All she knows is that her father took the 1:35 bus to Birkden and that a letter from a Peggy Pearson, written on stationery from the Lyceum Cinema in Birkden, has come to her father. Maggie goes to Birkden and meets Salt.

Because there is no obvious crime, the police are not eager to help Salt in his search for Noreen, who is described by Superintendent Hurst as "just another of these little fly-by-nights." As the story develops, the reader learns that Noreen knows Culworth; that Noreen has been having an affair with Sir Arnold's son, Derek; that Derek has accidentally killed himself while cleaning a gun at five in the morning; that Worsley Place, next to the United Fabrics Club, has been used as a romantic trysting place by Noreen and Derek; that Noreen is Culworth's child from a romance during World War II; that Sir Arnold is desperately trying to cover up everything that concerns his son; and that Culworth has suffered a concussion at Worsley Place and is under sedation at a private home. As the story progresses, the relationship between Salt and Maggie, at first an uneasy truce, begins to develop into a romance, culminating in their planning to leave together at the end to find whatever happiness the world has to offer elsewhere.

Two other characters contribute to prolonging the

mystery: Sir Arnold's daughter Erin, full of barbiturates, alcohol, and misplaced sexual drives, and Jill Frinton, a "hostess" at the United Fabrics Club. At the end, Salt, Maggie, her brother Alan, and Jill confront Sir Arnold with the truth, and the mystery is solved. Salt and company agree to keep silent about the truth in return for Sir Arnold's agreement to their terms.

The story is a good one and well written. The characters are believable and realistically motivated. Priestley here, as elsewhere, uses his novel as a means of looking askance at social problems and conditions he does not like. The high-handed industrialist who controls a town through his wealth and power is revealed in a most unfavorable light. The plight of those who must work under less than desirable conditions comes under scrutiny. Even those who seem to have some power within the structure are belittled, because they do nothing without the approval of Sir Arnold. The everyday lives of Salt's patients, mostly drawn from the lower and depressed side of Birkden, are given in such a way as to elicit sympathy.

Priestley's work in the detective-fiction genre is short on bulk, but his political theories and beliefs, his socialistic leanings, his practical but utopian ideals, are easily found in his novels. As a technician, Priestley is sharp, oriented toward the stageability of his product, and a careful constructor of plot and character. His novels read easily and command the respect and attention of the reader.

William H. Holland, Jr.

Principal mystery and detective fiction

Novels: *Benighted*, 1927 (also known as *The Old Dark House*); *I'll Tell You Everything*, 1933 (with Gerald Bullett); *The Doomsday Men: An Adventure*, 1938; *Blackout in Gretley: A Story of—and for—Wartime*, 1942; *Saturn over the Water: An Account of His Adventures in London, South America, and Australia by Tim Bedford, Painter*, 1961; *The Shapes of Sleep: A Topical Tale*, 1962; *Salt Is Leaving*, 1966

Other major works

Novels: *Adam in Moonshine*, 1927; *Farthing Hall*, 1929 (with Hugh Walpole); *The Good Companions*, 1929; *Angel Pavement*, 1930; *Faraway*, 1932; *Wonder Hero*, 1933; *They Walk in the City: The Lovers in the Stone Forest*, 1936; *Let the People Sing*, 1939; *Daylight on Saturday; A Novel About an Aircraft Factory*, 1943; *Three Men in New Suits*, 1945; *Bright Day*, 1946; *Jenny Villiers: A Story of the Theatre*, 1947; *Festival at Farbridge*, 1951 (also known as *Festival*); *Low Notes on a High Level: A Frolic*, 1954; *The Magicians*, 1954; *The Thirty-first of June: A Tale of True Love, Enterprise, and Progress in the Arthurian and Ad-Atomic Ages*, 1961; *Sir Michael and Sir George: A Tale of COMSA and DISCUS and the New Elizabethans*, 1964 (also known as *Sir Michael and Sir George: A Comedy of New Elizabethans*); *Lost Empires: Being Richard Herncastle's Account of His Life on the Variety Stage from November, 1913, to August, 1914, Together with a Prologue and Epilogue*, 1965; *It's an Old Country*, 1967; *The Image Men: "Out of Town" and "London End,"* 1968; *The Carfitt Crisis*, 1975; *Found, Lost, Found: Or, The English Way of Life*, 1976; *My Three Favorite Novels*, 1978

Short fiction: *The Town Major of Miraucourt*, 1930; *Going Up: Stories and Sketches*, 1950; *The Other Place, and Other Stories of the Same Sort*, 1953; *The Carfitt Crisis, and Two Other Stories*, 1975

Plays: 1931-1940 • *The Good Companions*, pr. 1931, pb. 1935 (adaptation of his novel; with Edward Knoblock); *Dangerous Corner*, pr., pb. 1932; *The Roundabout*, pr. 1932, pb. 1933; *Laburnum Grove*, pr. 1933, pb. 1934; *Eden End*, pr., pb. 1934; *Cornelius*, pr., pb. 1935; *Duet in Floodlight*, pr., pb. 1935; *Bees on the Boat Deck*, pr., pb. 1936; *Spring Tide*, pr., pb. 1936 (with George Billam); *I Have Been Here Before*, pr., pb. 1937; *People at Sea*, pr., pb. 1937; *Time and the Conways*, pr., pb. 1937; *Music at Night*, pr. 1938, pb. 1947; *Mystery at Greenfingers*, pr., pb. 1938; *When We Are Married*, pr., pb. 1938; *Johnson over Jordan*, pr., pb. 1939; *The Long Mirror*, pr., pb. 1940

1941-1950 • *Goodnight, Children*, pr., pb. 1942; *They Came to a City*, pr. 1943, pb. 1944; *Desert Highway*, pr., pb. 1944; *How Are They at Home?*, pr., pb. 1944; *The Golden Fleece*, pr. 1944, pb. 1948; *An Inspector Calls*, pr. 1946, pb. 1947; *Ever Since Paradise*, pr. 1946, pb. 1950; *The Linden Tree*, pr. 1947, pb. 1948; *The Rose and Crown*, pb. 1947 (one act); *Home Is Tomorrow*, pr. 1948, pb. 1949; *The High*

Toby, pb. 1948 (for puppet theater); *The Plays of J. B. Priestley*, pb. 1948-1950 (3 volumes); *Summer Day's Dream*, pr. 1949, pb. 1950; *Bright Shadow*, pr., pb. 1950; *Seven Plays of J. B. Priestley*, pb. 1950

1951-2001 • *Dragon's Mouth*, pr., pb. 1952 (with Jacquetta Hawkes); *Treasure on Pelican*, pr. 1952, pb. 1953; *Mother's Day*, pb. 1953 (one act); *Private Rooms*, pb. 1953 (one act); *Try It Again*, pb. 1953 (one act); *A Glass of Bitter*, pb. 1954 (one act); *The White Countess*, pr. 1954 (with Hawkes); *The Scandalous Affair of Mr. Kettle and Mrs. Moon*, pr., pb. 1955; *These Our Actors*, pr. 1956; *The Glass Cage*, pr. 1957, pb. 1958; *A Severed Head*, pr. 1963, pb. 1964 (with Iris Murdoch; adaptation of Murdoch's novel); *The Pavilion of Masks*, pr. 1963; *An Inspector Calls, and Other Plays*, pb. 2001

SCREENPLAY: *Last Holiday*, 1950

POETRY: *The Chapman of Rhymes*, 1918

CHILDREN'S LITERATURE: *Snoggle*, 1972

NONFICTION: 1922-1930 • *Brief Diversions: Being Tales, Travesties, and Epigrams*, 1922; *Papers from Lilliput*, 1922; *I for One*, 1923; *Figures in Modern Literature*, 1924; *Fools and Philosophers: A Gallery of Comic Figures from English Literature*, 1925 (also known as *The English Comic Characters*); *George Meredith*, 1926; *Talking: An Essay*, 1926; *Open House: A Book of Essays*, 1927; *The English Novel*, 1927, 1935, 1974; *Thomas Love Peacock*, 1927; *Apes and Angels: A Book of Essays*, 1928; *Too Many People, and Other Reflections*, 1928; *English Humour*, 1929, 1976; *The Balconinny, and Other Essays*, 1929 (also known as *The Balconinny*, 1931)

1931-1940 • *Self-Selected Essays*, 1932; *The Lost Generation: An Armistice Day Article*, 1932; *Albert Goes Through*, 1933; *English Journey: Being a Rambling but Truthful Account of What One Man Saw and Heard and Felt and Thought During a Journey Through England During the Autumn of the Year 1933*, 1934; *Four-in-Hand*, 1934; *Midnight on the Desert: A Chapter of Autobiography*, 1937 (also known as *Midnight on the Desert: Being an Excursion into Autobiography During a Winter in America, 1935-1936*, 1937); *Rain upon Godshill: A Further Chapter of Autobiography*, 1939; *Britain Speaks*, 1940; *Postscripts*, 1940 (radio talks)

1941-1950 • *Out of the People*, 1941; *Britain at War*, 1942; *British Women Go to War*, 1943; *The Man-Power Story*, 1943; *Here Are Your Answers*, 1944; *The New Citizen*, 1944; *Letter to a Returning Serviceman*, 1945; *Russian Journey*, 1946; *The Secret Dream: An Essay on Britain, America, and Russia*, 1946; *The Arts Under Socialism: Being a Lecture Given to the Fabian Society, with a Postscript on What Government Should Do for the Arts Here and Now*, 1947; *Theatre Outlook*, 1947; *Delight*, 1949

1951-1960 • *Journey Down a Rainbow*, 1955 (with Jacquetta Hawkes); *All About Ourselves, and Other Essays*, 1956; *The Writer in a Changing Society*, 1956; *The Art of the Dramatist: A Lecture Together with Appendices and Discursive Notes*, 1957; *The Bodley Head Leacock*, 1957; *Thoughts in the Wilderness*, 1957; *Topside: Or, The Future of England, a Dialogue*, 1958; *The Story of Theatre*, 1959; *Literature and Western Man*, 1960; *William Hazlitt*, 1960

1961-1970 • *Charles Dickens: A Pictorial Biography*, 1962; *Margin Released: A Writer's Reminiscences and Reflections*, 1962; *The English Comic Characters*, 1963; *Man and Time*, 1964; *The Moments and Other Pieces*, 1966; *All England Listened: J. B. Priestley's Wartime Broadcasts*, 1968; *Essays of Five Decades*, 1968 (Susan Cooper, editor); *Trumpets over the Sea: Being a Rambling and Egotistical Account of the London Symphony Orchestra's Engagement at Daytona Beach, Florida, in July-August, 1967*, 1968; *The Prince of Pleasure and His Regency, 1811-1820*, 1969; *Anton Chekhov*, 1970; *The Edwardians*, 1970

1971- 1977 • *Over the Long High Wall: Some Reflections and Speculations on Life, Death, and Time*, 1972; *Victoria's Heyday*, 1972; *The English*, 1973; *A Visit to New Zealand, Particular Pleasures: Being a Personal Record of Some Varied Arts and Many Different Artists*, 1974; *Outcries and Asides*, 1974; *The Happy Dream: An Essay*, 1976; *Instead of the Trees*, 1977 (autobiography)

EDITED TEXTS: *Essayist Past and Present: A Selection of English Essays*, 1925; *Tom Moore's Diary: A Selection*, 1925; *The Book of Bodley Head Verse*, 1926; *The Female Spectator: Selections from Mrs. Eliza Heywood's Periodical, 1744-1746*, 1929; *Our Nation's Heritage*, 1939; *Scenes of London Life, from*

"Sketches by Boz" by Charles Dickens, 1947; *The Best of Leacock*, 1957; *Four English Novels*, 1960; *Four English Biographies*, 1961; *Adventures in English Literature*, 1963; *An Everyman Anthology*, 1966

Bibliography

Atkins, John. *J. B. Priestley: The Last of the Sages*. New York: Riverrun Press, 1981. Describes Priestley's development as essayist, critic, novelist, dramatist, autobiographer, social commentator, historian, and travel writer. The book is most useful on the political, social, and economic background of the late 1920's and 1930's, the period of Priestley's first three mystery novels.

Brome, Vincent. *J. B. Priestley*. London: Hamish Hamilton, 1988. Brome offers an affectionate but candid portrait of the writer in public and private life. Argues that the prolific writer has been denied his proper niche by critics who do not deal fairly with those who write for a wide, general audience.

Cook, Judith. *Priestley*. London: Bloomsbury, 1997. Cook provides a biography of Priestley, examining both his prose and dramatic works. Includes a bibliography and an index.

DeVitis, A. A., and Albert E. Kalson. *J. B. Priestley*. Boston: Twayne, 1980. After a biographical chapter that includes a discussion of Priestley's time theories, the book divides into two sections, the first half dealing with Priestley as novelist, the second half dealing with Priestley as dramatist. All Priestley's works in the two genres are discussed, the more significant ones in some detail. Includes a chronology of the important events in Priestley's life and a useful bibliography.

Gray, Dulcie. *J. B. Priestley*. Stroud, Gloustershire, England: Sutton, 2000. This volume in the Sutton Pocket Biographies series provides a concise look at Priestley's life and many works. Includes a bibliography.

Klein, Holger. *J. B. Priestley's Fiction*. New York: P. Lang, 2002. Massive, eight-hundred-page study of Priestley's entire fictional output, including all of his mystery novels. Bibliographic references and index.

BILL PRONZINI

Born: Petaluma, California; April 13, 1943
Also wrote as Russell Dancer; Robert Hart Davis; Jack Foxx; Romer Zane Grey; William Jeffrey; Rick Renault; Alex Saxon
Types of plot: Hard-boiled; private investigator

Principal series

Nameless Detective, 1969-
Carmody, 1970-
Quincannon and Carpenter, 1985-

Principal series characters

The Nameless Detective is a private eye who was with the San Francisco Police Department for fifteen years. About forty-seven years old at the start of the series, Nameless has aged through the years, and, by 1988, is actively considering retirement. He is sloppy, moderately overweight, unmarried, and concerned both with his health and with being loved. By 2006, he is husband and father and mentor to two protégés. His real obsessions, however, are collecting pulp magazines and trying to make the world a better place.

Lieutenant "Eb" Eberhardt, a detective for the San Francisco Police Department at the outset of the series, is Nameless's closest friend and has appeared in all the series' novels and most of the stories. The two met as trainees at the police academy. Nameless turns to Eb for help, whether working on a case or working through a personal problem. Eb eventually joins Nameless as a partner in his agency after retiring from the police department.

CARMODY is an international dealer in "legal and extralegal services and material" who occasionally does detective work. An American, he lives in isolation on the Spanish island of Majorca. He is the flinty, silent type, with a good tan and green eyes; he smokes thin black cigars and drives a 911-T Porsche Targa.

JOHN FREDERICK QUINCANNON, a former Secret Service agent and reformed alcoholic, works as a detective in San Francisco of the 1890's. He would like to form a sexual relationship with his partner, Sabina Carpenter, but she dodges his advances.

SABINA CARPENTER is a widow and a former Pinkerton Agency detective. Equal to Quincannon's witty banter, she teams up with him to solve a variety of "impossible" crimes.

CONTRIBUTION

Bill Pronzini's Nameless detective novels move the hard-boiled detective genre toward a new kind of authenticity. To the unsentimental realism of Dashiell Hammett, the descriptive power of Raymond Chandler, and the psychological depth of Ross Macdonald, all meant to transcend the artificial atmosphere of the traditional English detective story, Pronzini adds attention to everyday human problems—emotional as well as physical. Nameless struggles with health concerns of varying seriousness and also spends a modest but significant portion of his narrative seeking stable female companionship. He ages and on occasion gets depressed. In short, Nameless is revealed in a way that would be utterly foreign to a character such as Hammett's Sam Spade or Chandler's Philip Marlowe.

Pronzini also seeks heightened authenticity, largely shedding the tough-guy image associated with the hard-boiled genre. To be sure, Nameless is tough. He doggedly seeks the truth and unhesitatingly puts himself into risky situations. Nameless eschews violence and sarcasm, however, and he is willing, at least occasionally, to wear his heart on his sleeve. Indeed, Nameless does nothing to hide the fact that he cares about people and is generally sympathetic. He cultivates a good working relationship with the police and with few exceptions stays on the right side of the law. Pronzini also occasionally works in some of the banality and drudgery involved with real-life private investigation.

All this is mixed in with some of the more classic hard-boiled elements: twisting plots, sparsely furnished offices, feverish pace, compelling descriptions of California settings (though Nameless does occasionally leave the state, pursuing one case in Europe), and a hero so dedicated to his vocation that he will often go without sleep and will sometimes work without fee. In addition, the very namelessness of Pronzini's detective harks back to Hammett's Continental Op. It is, in fact, the blend of old with new that makes Pronzini's series unique.

Pronzini does not merely build on the work of Hammett, Chandler, and Macdonald. Through Nameless's love of the pulps, the reader is reminded that many fine writers have helped shape and promote the hard-boiled genre—a significant bibliographic contribution on Pronzini's part.

Pronzini is also a widely read author of Westerns. As one of the industry's busiest anthologists, Pronzini has promoted short-fiction writers in several genres. He has edited more than one hundred collections and written extensively about Westerns and crime fiction.

BIOGRAPHY

William John Pronzini was born on April 13, 1943, in Petaluma, a small town north of San Francisco, to Joseph Pronzini and Helen Gruder Pronzini. Joseph Pronzini was a farmworker. The younger of two children, Bill was reared in Petaluma, where he attended the local schools. He wrote his first novel at the age of twelve. In high school, he began collecting pulp magazines. It was at this point that Pronzini did his first professional writing, working as a reporter for the Petaluma *Argus Courier* from 1957 to 1960. After attending Santa Rosa Junior College for two years, Bill refused a journalism scholarship to Stanford University, choosing instead to become a freelance fiction writer. During the early years of his writing career, Bill supplemented his income by working at various times as a newsstand clerk, warehouseman, typist, salesperson, and civilian guard with the marshal's office.

Pronzini married Laura Patricia Adolphson in May, 1965. The following year, he sold his first story, "You Don't Know What It's Like," to the *Shell Scott Mys-*

tery Magazine. Pronzini was divorced in 1967. His writing career flourished, however, and he had short stories published in a variety of pulp magazines. One product of this period was his unnamed detective: *The Snatch*, published in 1971, was Pronzini's first novel featuring Nameless. Pronzini moved to Majorca in 1971. There he met Brunhilde Schier, whom he married in 1972. They lived in West Germany before moving to San Francisco in 1974. Their marriage ended, and in 1992 Pronzini married author Marcia Muller.

Pronzini has become one of the most prolific authors of his time, producing more than seventy-five novels and hundreds of stories in a variety of genres: detective, Western, and science fiction. In addition to those works published under his own name, Pronzini has written novels and short stories using the pseudonyms Jack Foxx, Alex Saxon, and Russell Dancer. He has also been a prolific collaborator, working with such authors as Barry N. Malzberg, Jeffrey M. Wallman, Michael Kurland, Collin Wilcox, and Marcia Muller. In addition to his writing, Pronzini has edited a number of books in the mystery, Western, and science-fiction fields.

Pronzini's quantitative achievements have been augmented by qualitative ones. Although he has yet to achieve the high literary acclaim accorded Hammett, Chandler, and Macdonald, he is greatly respected by his fellow writers of mysteries. His novels *The Stalker* (1971) and *A Wasteland of Strangers* (1997) were nominated for Edgar Awards, as were his short stories "Strangers in the Fog" and "Incident in a Neighborhood Tavern" and two nonfictional works, *Gun in Cheek: A Study of "Alternative: Crime Fiction* (1982) and *1001 Midnights: The Aficionado's Guide to Mystery and Detective Fiction* (1986, with Marcia Muller). *A Wasteland of Strangers* was nominated for the best crime novel of 1997 by the International Association of Crime Writers. He received the Grand Prix de la Littérature Policière in 1989 for *Snowbound* (1974) and Shamus Awards from the Private Eye Writers of America for his novels *Hoodwink* (1981) and *Boobytrap* (1998) and his short story "Cat's Paw." The Private Eye Writers of America awarded Pronzini with the Eye, a lifetime achievement award, in 1987, and in 2005, he and Marcia Muller received a lifetime achievement award from the Bouchercon World Mystery Convention.

Analysis

Although Bill Pronzini has produced stories and novels at a truly enviable pace, both he and his critics have accorded the Nameless series a special status. First, it is clear that Pronzini identifies strongly with the Nameless detective. Indeed, this is one reason his hero has remained without a name. Second, the Nameless series has been recognized as marking the literary high point of Pronzini's career. It is this body of work for which Pronzini will probably be remembered, for the Nameless series has staying power derived both from its faithfulness to the well-hallowed tradition of the hard-boiled detective story and from its innovations and freshness within that tradition.

The hard-boiled detective story goes back to the 1920's, when Hammett, taking advantage of the flourishing trade in pulp magazines and the stylistic trends of the times, almost single-handedly established a new subgenre of popular fiction. Drawing on his experience as a Pinkerton's detective, Hammett brought a new realism and depth to crime fiction while holding to the constraints of the pulp market. These constraints dictated plenty of action and consummate directness of expression. The result was a hybrid literary form with elements of both high and low art—something roughly akin, both conceptually and chronologically, to the Marx brothers' *A Night at the Opera* (1935). The hard-boiled genre expanded quickly and profusely. As Pronzini and others have remarked, numerous authors, some well known, others relatively obscure, though often talented, went on to produce notable works within it. In addition, the genre was a natural for films and later for television. The action-oriented, economic prose and crisp dialogue of hard-boiled stories translated readily to both the large and the small screen, resulting in classic films such as *The Maltese Falcon* (1941) and popular television programs such as *Peter Gunn* (1958-1961), *The Rockford Files* (1974-1980), and *Spenser: For Hire* (1985-1988). In short, the hard-boiled detective became a significant mythic figure in American culture, one that, for all its very considerable international appeal, remains as distinctly American as jazz.

Why has the hard-boiled detective had so broad and lasting an appeal? This type of detective has been likened to a modern-day knight, defending the weak, seeking truth, and striving for justice in ways that legal authorities cannot or will not duplicate. Put another way, the hard-boiled detective is an independent agent who acts as he does because it is right, not for material gain or out of blind allegiance to a cause, and who is willing to face stiff opposition in the name of principle. The hard-boiled detective is a person of action, a doer, living up to the dictates of a demanding personal code; therefore, this type of detective must not only pass up wealth and other modern measures of "success" but also risk grave personal danger. It is this precarious existence that dictates that the detective be a loner; privation and danger are the crosses to bear and are not readily transferable to loved ones and other intimates.

The Nameless detective

Pronzini's Nameless series consciously carries on this tradition both stylistically and substantively. Using the genre's classic, first-person narrative, lean prose, and crisp dialogue, Pronzini portrays Nameless as being nearly everything the detective as modern-day knight is supposed to be. Nameless helps the weak, at times working without pay to do so. For example, in the early stories "It's a Lousy World" and "Death of a Nobody," Nameless takes up the causes of a former convict and a derelict, both of whom have been killed. There are no wealthy relatives footing the bill, thus no hope for a paycheck. Yet Nameless follows through, simply because he cares about the sanctity of every human life, not merely those for whom a fee can be collected. He also cares about the quality of each life, a characteristic that leads his friend Eb to call him a social worker. Beyond this universal compassion lies a hunger for truth in all of its complexity (as opposed to mere appearances) and for thoroughgoing justice (rather than the rough equivalent provided by law). To pursue these goals, Nameless must devote himself single-mindedly to his investigations, wading through a sea of lies, warding off threats, and ignoring weariness to the point of exhaustion. Nameless does all this and more in the name of a higher code, a modern form of chivalry aimed at making the world a better place in which to live.

Nevertheless, the Nameless series does more than simply pay homage to the hard-boiled genre; it adds a new twist or two to the tradition. Drawing on the model of Thomas B. Dewey's detective, "Mac," Pronzini has aimed for a new kind of authenticity, eschewing the more superficial and fantastic elements of the genre. Nameless starts off his literary existence middle-aged and paunchy, anything but the romanticized figure often presented, particularly in screen variations of the hard-boiled tradition. Nor is Nameless always wildly successful in his endeavors: He is sometimes mistaken about things and sometimes used.

In a more conspicuous break with the hard-boiled tradition, Nameless is far less private about the details of his life and his needs than are most of the classic hard-boiled characters. Nameless has a long-running, close friendship with a San Francisco cop named Eberhardt. He also has had two enduring relationships with women—first with Erica Coates, who turns down Nameless's proposal because of his line of work, and later with Kerry Wade, although a bad first marriage keeps Kerry from marrying Nameless. In addition, the reader is given details of Nameless's state of physical well-being that the Continental Op or Sam Spade would never have dreamed of sharing. These run the gamut from Nameless's bouts with heartburn to a tumor and the possibility of lung cancer. (It is the later that induces Nameless to quit smoking.)

In addition to these very human insights, Pronzini's hero is much less prone to play the tough guy. Nameless rarely breaks the law or engages in violence. Indeed, he almost always refuses to carry a gun, especially later in the series, and he throws the only gun he owns into the ocean in *Dragonfire* (1982).

Pronzini's quest for heightened authenticity (or what one pair of critics has called "unromanticized realism") has been additionally enhanced in three specific ways that deserve to be noted. First, by making Nameless a collector of pulp magazines and an expert on the hard-boiled genre in particular, Pronzini has not merely been autobiographical. He has also moved his hero one step away from the fictional world toward the world of the reader. The pulps are real. Though the stories in the pulps are fictional , these fictions are read and collected by real people. Nameless reads and collects these works. Therefore, Nameless is (or, at least, seems) more real.

Second, Pronzini has preserved continuity between the stories and novels of the series, leaving situations hanging and having Nameless and Eb age somewhat realistically from work to work. Both characters have changing relationships with the opposite sex and both experience career shifts. Like everyone, Nameless and his friend must deal with the trials, tribulations, and occasional comforts of the human life-cycle.

Third, Pronzini twice has collaborated with other authors of detective fiction to produce works that provide mutual validation for the main characters involved. Nameless does not exist merely in the minds of Pronzini and his readers. He also cohabits San Francisco with Collin Wilcox's Lieutenant Frank Hastings and Marcia Muller's Sharon McCone. In something akin to the way governments extend or deny one another diplomatic recognition, these authors have brought their fictional characters closer to life through these collaborations, making them more authentic in the process. The result has been the creation of a unique character and series in the hard-boiled tradition as well as the emergence of a significant audience for Pronzini's Nameless stories and novels.

A final comment or two should be added regarding the anonymity of Pronzini's best-known character, particularly since it may seem difficult to find a connection between this aspect of Pronzini's series and his quest for authenticity. It could be argued that the reality of Pronzini's character is best preserved by not tying him down to a name that can easily be proved fictional. Yet Nameless apparently owes his condition to two factors largely separate from the quest for authenticity: serendipity and the close identification of Pronzini with his character.

Pronzini claims no profound goal in leaving his hero nameless—merely that no name suited the man: "Big, sort of sloppy Italian guy who guzzles beer, smokes too much and collects pulp magazines. What name fits a character like that? Sam Spadini, Philip Marlozzi?" Additionally, Pronzini admits that his character is autobiographical, reflecting his own perceptions and reactions:

> Nameless and I are the same person; or, rather, he is an extrapolation of me. His view of life, his hang-ups and weaknesses, his pulp collecting hobby—all are essentially mine. . . . So, even though I can't use it, his name is Bill Pronzini.

Indeed, when Pronzini's hero is referred to in one of the sections of *Twospot* (1978), a collaborative effort with Collin Wilcox, he is called "Bill." Thus, while the situation does not handicap the series—some readers are even intrigued by it—the precise meaning of the hero's anonymity is unclear and possibly not very important. Indeed, it seems ironic to be told the details of Nameless's life, where he lives (the upstairs apartment of a Victorian house in Pacific Heights), whom he sees, how he amuses himself, and yet never learn his name. Whether this irony is intended is left unclear.

The Nameless Detective series is arguably the longest currently running series in the genre. Noted from the beginning for its signature tone of sadness, Pronzini's alter ego has aged along with him. By 2006's *Mourners*, Nameless has a wife named Kerry (who is holding somewhat aloof) and an adopted daughter, Emily. He has two junior associates, Tamara and Jake, with troubles of their own and no lack of clients.

In the mid-1980's, Pronzini allowed his love of the Western genre—he has edited dozens of Western anthologies and collections—to spill over into his mystery writing with the invention of two new series characters. John Quincannon and his partner (and unrequited love interest) Sarah Carpenter are detectives working in San Francisco of the 1890's. Chiefly they solve locked-room mysteries and other "impossible" crimes, although they do encounter the occasional six-gun or thrown punch. Though the series has not progressed very far, it has achieved critical acclaim. One critic wrote that the historical setting contains "some of the most elaborate landscapes since those of Arthur Morrison in the 1890's," adding of the Delta region of the Sacramento River east of San Francisco that "this watery region is marked as being peculiarly Pronzini's own. J. G. Ballard has suggested that delta regions represent the unconscious, a sort of living map of the interior landscape of part of the human mind." The story "Burgade's Crossing," for example, involves a search of the landscape for the possible site of a premeditated murder, so that the setting itself almost acts as a character.

Whether this series will be developed to the extent of the Nameless Detective series remains to be seen. With or without a name, Pronzini's detective does achieve a significant level of authenticity and freshness. Joining the ranks of today's liberated men, Nameless is unafraid to cry or communicate his emotional needs, fears, and concerns. He is willing to confess his desire to be loved and to have at least a few close friends. Nameless provides an alternative to the tough-guy private eyes of old.

Ira Smolensky and Marjorie Smolensky
Updated by Fiona Kelleghan and Janet Alice Long

PRINCIPAL MYSTERY AND DETECTIVE FICTION

NAMELESS DETECTIVE SERIES: 1971-1980 • *The Snatch*, 1971; *The Vanished*, 1973; *Undercurrent*, 1973; *Blowback*, 1977; *Twospot*, 1978 (with Collin Wilcox); *Labyrinth*, 1979

1981-1990 • *Hoodwink*, 1981; *Dragonfire*, 1982; *Scattershot*, 1982; *Bindlestiff*, 1983; *Casefile*, 1983; *Double*, 1984 (with Marcia Muller); *Nightshades*, 1984; *Quicksilver*, 1984; *Bones*, 1985; *Deadfall*, 1986; *Shackles*, 1988; *Jackpot*, 1990

1991-2006 • *Breakdown*, 1991; *Epitaphs*, 1992; *Quarry*, 1992; *Demons*, 1993; *Hardcase*, 1995; *Sentinels*, 1996; *Spadework: A Collection of "Nameless Detective" Stories*, 1996; *Illusions*, 1997; *Boobytrap*, 1998; *Crazybone*, 2000; *Bleeders*, 2002; *Scenarios: The "Nameless Detective" Casebook*, 2003; *Spook*, 2003; *Nightcrawlers*, 2005; *Mourners*, 2006

CARMODY SERIES: *A Run in Diamonds*, 1973; *Carmody's Run*, 1992

QUINCANNON AND CARPENTER SERIES: *Quincannon*, 1985; *Carpenter and Quincannon, Professional Detective Services*, 1998; *Quincannon's Game*, 2005

NONSERIES NOVELS: 1971-1980 • *The Stalker*, 1971; *Panic!*, 1972; *The Jade Figurine*, 1972 (as Foxx); *Snowbound*, 1974; *Dead Run*, 1975 (as Foxx); *Freebooty*, 1976 (as Foxx); *Games*, 1976; *The Running of Beasts*, 1976 (with Barry N. Malzberg); *Acts of Mercy*, 1977 (with Malzberg); *Wildfire*, 1978 (as Foxx); *Night Screams*, 1979 (with Malzberg)

1981-1990 • *Masques*, 1981; *Gun in Cheek*, 1982; *Day of the Moon*, 1983; *The Eye*, 1984 (with John Lutz); *Son of Gun in Cheek*, 1987; *The Lighthouse*, 1987 (with Muller); *Firewind*, 1989; *The Hangings*, 1989

1991-2004 • *Stacked Deck*, 1991; *The Tormentor*, 1994; *With an Extreme Burning*, 1994; *Blue Lonesome*, 1995; *A Wasteland of Strangers*, 1997; *Nothing but the Night*, 1999; *In an Evil Time*, 2001; *The Alias Man*, 2004

SHORT FICTION: *A Killing in Xanadu*, 1980; *Graveyard Plots: The Best Short Stories of Bill Pronzini*, 1985; *Small Felonies: Fifty Mystery Short Shorts*, 1988; *Criminal Intent I: All New Stories*, 1993 (with Muller and Ed Gorman); *Duo*, 1998 (with Muller); *Sleuths*, 1999; *Night Freight*, 2000; *Oddments: A Short Story Collection*, 2000

OTHER MAJOR WORKS

NOVELS: *Prose Bowl*, 1980 (with Malzberg); *The Cambodia File*, 1980 (with Jack Anderson); *The Gallows Land*, 1983; *Starvation Camp*, 1984; *Prime Suspects*, 1987 (with Martin H. Greenberg); *Suspicious Characters*, 1987 (with Greenberg); *The Horse Soldiers*, 1987 (with Greenberg); *The Last Days of Horse-Shy Halloran*, 1987; *The Gunfighters*, 1988 (with Greenberg); *The Dying Time*, 1999 (as Saxon); *The Crimes of Jordan Wise*, 2006

SHORT FICTION: *The Best Western Stories of Bill Pronzini*, 1990; *All the Long Years: Western Stories*, 2001; *Coyote and Quarter-Moon*, 2006

NONFICTION: *Gun in Cheek: A Study of "Alternative" Crime Fiction*, 1982; *San Francisco*, 1985 (with Larry Lee, Mark Stephenson, and West Light); *1001 Midnights: The Aficionado's Guide to Mystery and Detective Fiction*, 1986 (with Marcia Muller); *Son of Gun in Cheek*, 1987; *Six-Gun in Cheek: An Affectionate Guide to the "Worst" in Western Fiction*, 1997

EDITED TEXTS: 1976-1980 • *Tricks and Treats*, 1976 (with Joe Gores; also as *Mystery Writers Choice*); *Dark Sins, Dark Dreams*, 1977 (with Malzberg); *Midnight Specials*, 1977; *Shared Tomorrows: Collaboration in SF*, 1979 (with Malzberg); *Werewolf*, 1979; *Bug-Eyed Monsters*, 1980 (with Malzberg); *Mummy!*, 1980; *The Edgar Winners*, 1980; *Voodoo!*, 1980

1981-1985 • *Creature!*, 1981; *The Arbor House Necropolis*, 1981; *The Arbor House Treasury of Horror and the Supernatural*, 1981 (with Malzberg and Greenberg); *Specter!*, 1982; *The Arbor House Treasury of Great Western Stories*, 1982 (with Greenberg); *The Arbor House Treasury of Detective and Mystery Stories from the Great Pulps*, 1983; *The Web She Weaves*, 1983 (with Muller); *Child's Ploy*, 1984 (with Muller); *The Best Western Stories of Wayne D. Overholser*, 1984 (with Greenberg); *The Best Western Stories of Steve Frazer*, 1984 (with Greenberg); *The Lawmen*, 1984 (with Greenberg); *The Mystery Hall of Fame*, 1984 (with Charles G. Waugh and Greenberg); *The Outlaws*, 1984 (with Greenberg); *The Western Hall of Fame*, 1984 (with Greenberg); *Witches' Brew*, 1984 (with Muller); *A Treasury of Civil War Stories*, 1985 (with Greenberg); *A Treasury of World War II Stories*, 1985 (with Greenberg); *Baker's Dozen: Thirteen Short Espionage Novels*, 1985 (with Greenberg); *Chapter and Hearse: Suspense Stories about the World of Books*, 1985 (with Muller); *Dark Lessons: Crime and Detection on Campus*, 1985 (with Muller); *Kill or Cure: Suspense Stories about the World of Medicine*, 1985 (with Muller); *Murder in the First Reel*, 1985 (with Waugh and Greenberg); *Police Procedurals*, 1985 (with Greenberg); *She Won the West: An Anthology of Western and Frontier Stories by Women*, 1985 (with Muller); *The Cowboys*, 1985 (with Greenberg); *The Deadly Arts*, 1985 (with Muller); *The Ethnic Detectives: Masterpieces of Mystery Fiction*, 1985 (with Greenberg); *The Second Reel West*, 1985 (with Greenberg); *The Warriors*, 1985 (with Greenberg); *The Wickedest Show on Earth: A Carnival of Circus Suspense*, 1985 (with Muller); *Woman Sleuths*, 1985 (with Greenberg)

1986-1990 • *101 Mystery Stories*, 1986 (with Greenberg); *Best of the West: Stories That Inspired Classic Western Films*, 1986-1988 (3 volumes; with Greenberg); *Great Modern Police Stories*, 1986 (with Greenberg); *Locked Room Puzzles*, 1986 (with Greenberg); *Mystery in the Mainstream: An Anthology of Literary Crimes*, 1986 (with Greenberg and Malzberg; also known as *Crime and Crime Again: Mystery Stories by the World's Greatest Writers*); *The Railroaders*, 1986 (with Greenberg); *The Steamboaters*, 1986 (with Greenberg); *The Third Reel West*, 1986 (with Greenberg); *Wild Westerns: Stories from Grand Old Pulps*, 1986; *Manhattan Mysteries*, 1987 (with Carol-Lynn Rössel Waugh and Greenberg); *Prime Suspects*, 1987 (with Greenberg); *The Best Western Stories of Lewis B. Patten*, 1987 (with Greenberg); *The Cattlemen*, 1987 (with Greenberg); *The Gunfighters*, 1987 (with Greenberg); *The Horse Soldiers*, 1987 (with Greenberg); *Uncollected Crimes*, 1987 (with Greenberg); *Cloak and Dagger: A Treasury of Thirty-five Great Espionage Stories*, 1988 (with Greenberg); *Criminal Elements*, 1988 (with Greenberg); *Homicidal Acts*, 1988 (with Greenberg); *Lady on the Case*, 1988 (with Muller and Greenberg); *The Mammoth Book of Private Eye Stories*, 1988 (with Greenberg); *The Texans*, 1988 (with Greenberg); *Felonious Assaults*, 1989 (with Greenberg); *More Wild Westerns*, 1989; *The Arizonans*, 1989 (with Greenberg); *The Best Western Stories of Frank Bonham*, 1989 (with Greenberg); *The Best Western Stories of Loren D. Estelman*, 1989 (with Greenberg); *The Californians*, 1989 (with Greenberg); *The Mammoth Book of World War II Stories*, 1989; *Christmas Out West*, 1990 (with Greenberg); *New Frontiers*, 1990 (with Greenberg); *The Best Western Stories of Ryerson Johnson*, 1990 (with Greenberg); *The Northerners*, 1990 (with Greenberg)

1991-2001 • *The Best Western Stories of Les Savage, Jr.*, 1991; *The Montanans*, 1991 (with Greenberg); *Combat!: Great Tales of World War II*, 1992 (with Greenberg); *The Best Western Stories of Ed Gorman*, 1992 (with Greenberg); *In the Big Country: The Best Western Stories of John Jakes*, 1993 (with Greenberg); *The Mammoth Book of Short Crime Novels*, 1996 (with Greenberg); *American Pulp*, 1997 (with Gorman and Greenberg); *Detective Duos*, 1997 (with Muller); *Hard-Boiled: An Anthology of American Crime Stories*, 1997 (with Jack Adrian); *Under the Burning Sun: Western Stories by H. A. DeRosso*, 1997; *Renegade River: Western Stories by Giff Cheshire*, 1998; *The Best of the American West: Outstanding Frontier Fiction*, 1998 (with Greenberg); *Heading West: Western Stories by Noel M. Loomis*, 1999; *Pure Pulp*, 1999 (with Gorman and Greenberg); *Riders of the Shadowlands*, 1999; *War Stories*, 1999 (with Greenberg); *Tracks in the Sand*, 2001

Bibliography

Gorman, Ed, Lee Server, and Martin H. Greenberg, eds. *The Big Book of Noir*. New York: Carroll & Graf, 1998. Pronzini's contribution to this work reveals his personal relationship to this subgenre.

Landrum, Larry. *American Mystery and Detective Novels*. Westport, Conn.: Greenwood, 1999. A prolific author and critic, Pronzini pops up in many contexts throughout this work.

Lauer, George. "Murder They Wrote: Husband and Wife Bill Pronzini and Marcia Muller Are Major Characters in the Mystery-Writing Genre." *The Press Democrat*, March 21, 2005, p. D1. This profile of the authors describes their separate histories and paths to writing, their writing lives together, and their future aspirations. Contains lists of their publications and considerable biographic information.

Muller, Marcia, and Bill Pronzini. "Q&A: Marcia Muller and Bill Pronzini." Interview by Andi Schecter. *Library Journal* 131, no. 12 (July, 2006): 54. Interview with the married couple discusses their collaborative work with Nameless-McCone books. They discuss the creative opportunities presented by writing nonseries novels.

Pronzini, Bill. *Gun in Cheeck: A Study of "Alternative" Crime Fiction*. New York: The Mysterious Press, 1982. Humorous look at the worst in crime fiction. Shows what Pronzini considers good and bad writing.

_______. Introduction to *Private Eyes: One Hundred and One Knights, A Survey of American Detective Fiction, 1922-1984*, by Robert A. Baker and Michael T. Nietzel. Bowling Green, Ohio: Bowling Green State University Popular Press, 1985. In his introduction to this work, Pronzini provides insights into what he believes a private eye should be and how a detective should function in a novel.

Scaggs, John. *Crime Fiction*. New York: Routledge, 2005. While Pronzini's work is not directly discussed, this fascinating source has a valuable chapter, "The Hard-Boiled Mode," that provides context for the study of Pronzini's Nameless detective.

MANUEL PUIG

Juan Manuel Puig

Born: General Villegas, Argentina; December 28, 1932
Died: Cuernavaca, Mexico; July 22, 1990
Type of plot: Psychological

Contribution

Manuel Puig's contribution to the mystery and detective genre is limited to a single novel, *The Buenos Aires Affair: Novela policial* (1973; *The Buenos Aires Affair: A Detective Novel*, 1976). A member of the literary avant-garde as well as a pop novelist, Puig mixed high and low culture in his fiction and rejected the dismissal of popular literature, such as detective fiction, as subliterature.

Each of Puig's novels can be identified with one or more genres of popular writing: serial melodrama, science fiction, screenplay, and detective fiction. His use of these various genres shifted between parody and emulation. *The Buenos Aires Affair*, for example, combines a playful attitude toward the conventions of the detective novel with an earnest desire to present a spectacle and to communicate directly with a mass audience. In adapting the detective novel to his use, Puig commented that it was the ideal form for his proposed theme of contained violence. Nevertheless, his use of the genre was decidedly self-critical and experimental in the manner of Jorge Luis Borges or Alain Robbe-Grillet.

Biography

Manuel Puig was born on December 28, 1932, in the small town of General Villegas in the Argentine

Pampas. According to his own account, the provincial elevation of machismo and authority made his daily existence extremely unpleasant in his youth, so that he sought escape by going to the movie theater. Puig's childhood immersion in the Hollywood superproductions of the 1930's and 1940's became a powerful influence in his life and work.

In 1951, Puig left the provinces to begin his studies at the university in Buenos Aires, expecting the big city to resemble Hollywood. Disappointed by reality, he left Argentina for Italy on a grant to study cinematography in 1956. In Italy he pursued his dream of working in the film industry, acting as an assistant director at Cinecittà in Rome until 1962. During this time, however, he became disillusioned with life on the set and began his first novel, *La traición de Rita Hayworth* (1968; *Betrayed by Rita Hayworth*, 1971), in part to express his disenchantment. As Puig later explained, that novel was an attempt to discover why he suddenly found himself at the age of thirty without a career or money and with the knowledge that his life's vocation was a sham. From that time onward, the betrayal of reality by illusion and the seduction of the individual by popular culture would be constant themes in his writing.

Manuel Puig. (© Jerry Bauer)

From 1964 until 1967, Puig worked as a clerk at Kennedy Airport in New York while he finished *Betrayed by Rita Hayworth*. Following its publication, he returned to Buenos Aires and began a second novel, *Boquitas pintadas* (1969; *Heartbreak Tango*, 1973). His return to his home country was short-lived. Following the banning in Argentina of his third novel, *The Buenos Aires Affair*, Puig spent three years in exile in Mexico and then returned to New York in 1976. At that time he published what is perhaps his best-known work, *El beso de la mujer araña* (1976; *Kiss of the Spider Woman*, 1979). He later collaborated with director Hector Babenco on a film adaptation that premiered in 1985. He remained in exile for the rest of his life. Puig continued to write novels, plays, and screenplays, and his work has been translated into fourteen languages.

In 1989, Puig moved to Cuernavaca, Mexico. The following summer he underwent emergency surgery for an inflamed gallbladder and died shortly afterward.

Analysis

Manuel Puig was not, strictly speaking, a mystery and detective novelist. His modus operandi was consistently more or less to usurp some popular genre for each of his novels. In *Heartbreak Tango*, he used the serialized melodrama, in *Kiss of the Spider Woman*, the screenplay. Even as he plundered the artifacts of mass culture, Puig's attitude toward popular culture was deeply ironic. It is this obvious ambivalence that made him one of the most self-conscious of twentieth century writers.

The Buenos Aires Affair

Consequently, Puig's use of the police-novel format for *The Buenos Aires Affair*, his third novel, reflects a sincere interest in the genre yet simultaneously permits him to parody its conventions. The result is an interesting amalgamation of pop fiction and the avant-garde. In reviewing the novel for *The New York Times Book Review*, Robert Alter called it a "sustained bravura performance by a writer keenly conscious of how both the novel as a literary form and the kinds of people who are its best subjects have been caught up in the clichés of popular culture."

Puig initially chose to write the book as a detective novel because he had already selected the themes he wanted to treat—repressed sexuality and contained violence. He believed that the narrative structure typical of detective literature would facilitate his project. In fact, the conventions of detective writing were particularly well suited to his undertaking. First, the rules of the genre are very well defined. Puig had only to subtitle his book "detective novel" to activate an entire set of expectations in readers. Second, the detective novel appeals to those who read critically and enjoy filling in missing details and information. Puig's narrative technique has always required such readers.

Puig's critics have often compared his technique to the neorealism of the French New Novelists. Puig was generally quick to deny any literary influence and to insist that the cinema had a greater impact on his work. Specifically, he mentioned Alfred Hitchcock as a major influence on *The Buenos Aires Affair.* The majority of Puig's novels are attempts to render in prose reality as it might be seen by a camera's eye—that is, with distortions, omissions, and plenty of room for an audience to draw false conclusions. This coincides with the efforts of the New Novelists to record reality in an objective fashion, without commentary or interpretation in the text, much as a camera would. It is the same nonintrusive style of writing that French critic Roland Barthes has called "zero degree writing." The technique in itself creates mystery, and Puig's fiction has much in common with works by New Novelists Robbe-Grillet and Michel Butor that have been classified as detective fiction.

The classic detective story has well-defined rules of functioning. Generally, the whodunit begins with a crime, preferably a murder. The story, then, involves a detective's reconstruction of the event from available clues to unmask the perpetrator of the crime. The text moves toward a solution while at the same time postponing that solution through a series of false leads and delays. It is this process of discovery, rather than the answer to the problem or the identity of the criminal, that forms the body of the book. The detective, not being omniscient, must piece together his solution through careful observation of evidence found at the scene of the crime as well as from eyewitness accounts that are necessarily fragmented and sometimes unreliable. Puig's fiction works in a similar manner, often requiring readers to supply connections and interpretations.

In *The Buenos Aires Affair,* Puig uses a variety of narrative techniques. There is no consistent narrative voice or point of view, and there is no detective other than the reader. Sometimes a dispassionate third-person narrator catalogs objects in a room, listing, for example, the sharpest object, the most expensive objects, metal objects, and the like. At other times, an omniscient narrator lays bare the hearts and minds of the characters, revealing their dreams and sexual fantasies. The novel is itself a process of investigation and a constant reminder of the ambiguity of life, the complexity of character, the ultimate inaccessibility of reality. This philosophy of fiction is central to Puig's work and has its origins, for him, in film technique. The notion that some points of view are more privileged than others, just as some witnesses are more reliable than others, is also implicit in detective fiction.

As a master of the occluded narrative, Puig conceals and withholds information throughout the novel. In one chapter, he records one side (all that a casual observer would realistically hear) of a phone conversation in a police station, and he includes fragments of the newspaper articles the character is reading. He also offers a shorthand transcription of another telephone conversation. While the message of the transcription seems apparent, the missing words create ambiguity.

Thus, the importance of point of view is demonstrated: Reality is fragmented and open to interpretation. Reading a novel by Puig is essentially detective work. He presents information in a manner that requires readers to piece together the truth from the available clues, and this process often leads them to mistaken conclusions. Puig has used this technique consistently in his fiction. It also commonly occurs in detective fiction: In the process of discovering the solution to the problem, the readers and the detective pursue a number of false leads as they uncover the missing links that will allow all the clues to make sense. Puig, too, lures the readers into erroneous conclusions.

Clearly, in its very nature, the detective-story format lends itself to Puig's project. Its conventions are helpful to him; in fact, they provide a justification, more or less, for his customarily inventive method of telling a story. However, Puig goes beyond using the rules of the genre: He draws readers' attention to the fact that there are elaborate rules dictating how they read. By revealing to readers their own reading processes, Puig shows them how much they can be deceived by all manner of fictions. By the end of the novel, readers discover that the murder they thought they were witnessing at the start did not take place.

The Buenos Aires Affair begins with what can easily be construed as a crime. A mother discovers her daughter's absence from the house they are sharing and notes certain signs of intrusion. In the subsequent chapter, Puig describes an ominous scene in which a woman—gagged, very still and pale, and missing an eye—is lying on a bed. A man dressed in a towel is standing over her. Although the details are vague, and the narrator does note that there is no sign of violence, readers will construe this scene as typical of the scene of the crime in the whodunit. Having shown readers the anticipated "crime," the narrator then predictably flashes back to reconstruct the events leading up to it and re-create the lives of the presumed female victim and male perpetrator.

At this point, the novel shifts to a style that has been called pop Freudianism. In an exercise in psychoanalysis at once serious and parodic, it relates how both "victim" and "criminal" suffer from sexual disorders originating in a missing parent and exacerbated by a damaging sexual experience. The woman appears to enjoy abusive sex; the man needs to be the abuser. The characters are ideally cast for their respective roles. Clearly, this is a crime waiting to happen.

There is an element of the thriller here too, as Tzvetan Todorov defines it. The man has committed a previous, undiscovered murder (or so he thinks, although the victim's death is not verified). In this case, just the right set of circumstances combine with his psychosis to produce violent results—violence that suggests the possibility of a future episode. The novel is sustained by the readers' suspense as they await the eruption of the projected violence that will fully explain the mysterious scene at the beginning.

As Puig leads up to the reenactment of the murder the readers believe has occurred, he endeavors to justify it in psychoanalytical terms. When at length the narrative returns to the scene with which it began, the perspective is much more informed. As it turns out, the man has lured the woman to his apartment to pretend to another woman that he is going to murder her to displace her suspicion that he murdered the original victim (who may or may not be dead), as he has partially confessed to her.

Unlike the typical whodunit, the novel returns to its starting point not so that the detective can disclose his ingenious solution to the crime but so that Puig can reveal to readers how they have been duped. Anticipating a murder, readers create one from the textual fragments supplied, or from the gaps within the text. They then proceed to read the psychological case histories as means of discovering how or why the crime occurred. In the process, they discover instead the conventions by which they read detective fiction (or any fiction, for that matter). As the scene of the supposed murder comes to a close, the proposed victim sleeps, while the would-be criminal departs and kills himself by driving too fast. His case history concludes with a clinical, pseudoscientific autopsy report.

Finally, and typically, it is the relationship between the text and the reader, together with the reading activity itself, that becomes the focus of the novel. By tricking readers into misreading a series of textual clues and activating a set of extratextual expectations, Puig managed to reveal the betraying power of fictions. This was the central theme in *Betrayed by Rita Hayworth*, in which he explored his personal sense of having been a victim of cinematic illusions. Present in all Puig's work, this theme is echoed in *The Buenos Aires Affair*. The characters, as their lives are depicted, fall prey to the illusions perpetrated by popular culture. Lest readers judge them too harshly for their weakness, however, Puig showed how easily the readers themselves are deceived by a fictional construct and fall for all the clichés of the detective novel. In doing so, Puig criticized yet affirmed the value of popular culture.

Barbara L. Hussey
Updated by Janet Alice Long

Principal mystery and detective fiction

Novel: *The Buenos Aires Affair: Novela policial*, 1973 (*The Buenos Aires Affair: A Detective Novel*, 1976)

Other major works

Novels: *La traición de Rita Hayworth*, 1968 (*Betrayed by Rita Hayworth*, 1971); *Boquitas pintadas*, 1969 (*Heartbreak Tango*, 1973); *El beso de la mujer araña*, 1976 (*Kiss of the Spider Woman*, 1979); *Pubis angelical*, 1979 (English translation, 1986); *Maldición eterna a quien lea estas páginas*, 1980 (*Eternal Curse on the Reader of These Pages*, 1982); *Sangre de amor correspondido*, 1982 (*Blood of Requited Love*, 1984); *Cae la noche tropical*, 1988 (*Tropical Night Falling*, 1991)

Plays: *Bajo un manto de estrellas*, pb. 1983 (*Under a Mantle of Stars*, 1985); *El beso de la mujer araña*, pb. 1983 (*Kiss of the Spider Woman*, 1986; adaptation of his novel); *Misterio del ramo de rosas*, pb. 1987 (*Mystery of the Rose Bouquet*, 1988)

Screenplays: *Boquitas pintadas*, 1974 (adaptation of his novel); *El lugar sin límites*, 1978 (adaptation of José Donoso's novel)

Bibliography

Bacarisse, Pamela. *The Necessary Dream: A Study of the Novels of Manuel Puig*. Totowa, N.J.: Barnes & Noble Books, 1988. Chapters on the major novels. The introduction provides a useful overview of Puig's career and themes. Includes notes and bibliography.

Levine, Suzanne Jill. *Manuel Puig and the Spider Woman: His Life and Fictions*. Madison: University of Wisconsin Press, 2001. A full-length biography by one of Puig's translators, focusing on the intersections between his life and his art.

Puig, Manuel. "The Art of Fiction: Manuel Puig." Interview by Kathleen Wheaton. *The Paris Review* 31 (Winter, 1989): 129-147. An intensive exploration of Puig's themes and techniques.

Tittler, Jonathan. *Manuel Puig*. New York: Twayne, 1993. The best introduction to Puig. Tittler provides a useful survey of Puig's career in his introduction and devotes separate chapters to the novels. Includes detailed notes and an annotated bibliography.

Q

QIU XIAOLONG

Born: Shanghai, China; 1953
Type of plot: Police procedural

Principal series

Chief Inspector Chen, 2000-

Principal series character

Chief Inspector Chen Cao is in charge of investigating politically sensitive cases for the Shanghai Police Bureau. In his mid-thirties and already an important cadre, he has an understated manner, discretion, and integrity. These help him solve difficult cases without upsetting the Communist Party, which rules China. He is also a celebrated poet and translator with an interest in American literature. His dedication to work leaves him with little time for his personal life and romance, much to the annoyance of his mother, who expects him to marry and start a family.

Contribution

Literary reviewers greeted Qiu Xiaolong's Chief Inspector Chen novels with warmth, albeit more for their setting and literary texture than for their plots. Before the first in the series, *Death of a Red Heroine*, appeared in 2000, relatively few novels in English dealt with the changes taking place in the People's Republic of China in the 1990's from a Chinese point of view. Accordingly, Qiu's descriptions of his native Shanghai piqued the interest of critics and readers alike. The novels reveal a exuberant nation in transition from a largely closed, state-controlled economy and society to a much more open, capitalistic society. They also portray the conflicts between the Communist Party and the new openness and between traditional Chinese values and the modern mania for material wealth.

Although some reviewers found Qiu's English prose style somewhat stilted and his text burdened with explanations of Chinese culture, many cited the freshness of his writing. It was said to bring an engaging realism to his characters and convey much vivid information about such matters as Chinese cuisine and architecture. Moreover, critics considered his inclusion of Chinese and English poetry as innovative, moving, and evocative in establishing the intellectual milieu of Shanghai. *Death of a Red Heroine* was awarded the 2001 Anthony Award for Best First Mystery and named one of the year's best five political novels by *The Wall Street Journal* and one of the ten best books by National Public Radio in 2000.

Biography

Qiu Xiaolong was born in the Chinese port city of Shanghai in 1953, just four years after the Communist Party led by Mao Zedong established the People's Republic of China. A shop owner, Qiu's father was classified as a capitalist during China's massive internal restructuring, the Cultural Revolution (1969-1976), and forced to write a "confession." Because his father had undergone eye surgery and was temporarily unable to see, Qiu wrote the confession for him, joking later that it was the beginning of his writing career. At the age of sixteen, Qiu suffered a serious case of bronchitis. It kept him bedridden at home while most of his classmates were sent away for re-education under the Educated Youths Going to the Countryside program. While reading to amuse himself, he developed a serious interest in writing. In 1977 he began studying English and entered the East Chinese Normal University. He subsequently studied at the Chinese Academy of Social Science, earning a master's degree in Western literature.

In the early 1980's Qiu became an assistant research professor at the Shanghai Academy of Social Science. He began writing poetry and stories in Chinese and translated English and American literature, including the works of T. S. Eliot, William Butler Yeats, Joseph Conrad, William Faulkner, James Joyce, and Ezra Pound. After winning awards for both his translations and his own poetry, he became a member of the Chinese Writers' Association. In 1986 he traveled to the United States for the first time, attending the third Chinese American Writers' Conference. He returned in 1988 to study for a doctorate at Washington University in St. Louis, Missouri, on a Ford Foundation grant. The next year the Chinese government suppressed a student rebellion in Tiananmen Square in Beijing, an act that profoundly disturbed Qiu. He decided to defect and remained in St. Louis, where he was joined by his wife, Wang Lijun; they have a daughter, Julia.

Qiu became a college instructor, teaching Chinese language and literature, and a writer. He also translated Western crime fiction into Chinese and Chinese poetry into English. He published *Treasury of Chinese Love Poems: In Chinese and English* in 2003. The same year his first book of English poetry, *Lines Around China* (2003), appeared and earned for him a Missouri Arts Council Writers' Biennial Award. He told an interviewer that he began writing fiction about his homeland to explore the changing conditions in Shanghai during the 1990's. It was not his initial intention to write a mystery story. That it turned into one, sold well, was translated into ten languages, and resulted in demands for sequels from his publisher astonished him. He continues to write poetry and fiction. Known for his self-deprecating manner and sense of humor, Qiu has maintained contact with China, periodically returning to Shanghai to renew his acquaintance with its food, literary culture, and evolving society.

Analysis

Qiu Xiaolong's mystery novels are set and thematically centered in Shanghai in the 1990's, when the nation was making a swift transition from a centrally planned economy to an open marketplace based on capitalism. Although the novels are not told exclusively from the point of view of Chief Inspector Chen Cao, he is the primary means by which Qiu exposes the deep turmoil of that transition. The fictional detective serves as a alter ego for the author, whose concern for his hometown informs nearly all of his writing. However, as Qiu insisted to interviewers, Chen differs markedly in character from him. In fact, Qiu remarked that he does not much care for his protagonist. Chen is loosely based on a friend of Qiu, a literature student who became a police officer. Like modern China, Chen makes his uncertain way in life by struggling with fundamental contradictions. From these contradictions emerge the specific themes of the Chen series.

Chen is dutiful and loyal. He values his relations to those around him, especially his partner, Detective Yu Guangming; Yu's father, Old Hunter; and Yu's wife, Peiqin. Accordingly, he is modest and generous, but his high rank means he must often keep information from them and expose them to dangers during the course of his investigations for the special cases squad of the Shanghai Police Bureau. In that position he is a Communist Party member, and his first loyalty requires him always to act in the "interest of the party." His job is politically delicate in that he must solve cases even when the solutions might expose the party to internal or international criticism, and yet he must prevent such exposure. Moreover, Chen's dedication to his job brings him into unintentional conflict with his mother, for whom he maintains a deep devotion, as Chinese traditional values require. His mother wants him to marry and produce grandchildren, but he lacks both the time for romance and the inclination to dwell on his own desires.

Nowhere does the conflict between traditional values and modern life become more evident than in Chen's dealings with corruption. Corruption permeates Qiu's novels, reflecting the widespread pursuit of selfish interest by government leaders, bureaucrats, and businesspeople at all levels in China. In *A Case of Two Cities* (2006), in the course of investigating a scandal involving Xing Xing, a businessman made wealthy through his connections to high-ranking party members, Chen discovers that the Communist Party wishes to make the businessman a scapegoat, punishing him but not changing the underlying corruption. He finds that corruption goes beyond the party, being ingrained in Chinese society. The characters in *A Case of Two Cities* speak of a "white way" and a "black way" to accomplish nearly every public action—the officially approved or legal means in contrast with the underground, black-market way, often involving bribery. Chen himself engages in corrupt practices because of his loyalty to friends. For example, he uses his clout as a chief inspector to get a job as a traffic monitor for his partner's father, Old Hunter, a retired police officer who cannot survive on his pension. He also does favors for several businessmen who help him, at least one of whom has connections to organized crime.

As Qiu vividly shows, the white-way and black-way conflict arises from the rapid economic and social change in China. The oldest generation, represented by Old Hunter, spent their lives with an "iron rice bowl" economy, guaranteed a job and health care from cradle to grave. The Communist Party taught them to believe that everyone should receive equal treatment. The liberalizing economic policies of Deng Xiaoping changed that. Proclaiming that it is "glorious to be wealthy," Deng encouraged entrepreneurship and capitalism. It bewildered the older generation, but many of those who grew up during and after the Cultural Revolution, like Chen, seized on any opportunity to grow rich. Many became wealthy, and their free spending drove up prices in urban China so that those dependent on the old system could not handle the cost of living in Shanghai. They sank into poverty, and an economic gap was created between young and old and between country people and city people. As one character bitterly quips in *A Case of Two Cities*, "The gap between rich and poor is really like that between cloud and clod." Just to survive, many poor must resort to the black way to get the food and services they need.

Qiu finds a spiritual vacuum in post-Maoist China. The values of loyalty to the state, mass political action, and contentment with an equal share are obsolete. Partly it is the lingering trauma from the Cultural Revolution that is responsible. The deprivations and turmoil of that era left the young, like Qiu, longing for security and liberties. The moribund efforts to sustain the old communist values are symbolized in *Death of a Red Heroine* by a young woman who is named a National Model Worker at a time when the distinction no longer means much. In the place of the communist values, Qiu writes, have come rampant materialism and the scramble for money and social advantages. This covetousness disillusions Chen and many like him, who still owe their careers to the autocratic but increasingly venal one-party system. Moreover, many Chinese grew increasingly enamored of Western culture and material goods in the 1990's. Chen is among them. Not only does he like American poetry, but he moves, albeit slowly, toward a romance with an American U.S. marshal, Katherine Rohn, his occasional partner in *A Loyal Character Dancer* (2002) and *A Case of Two Cities*.

Chen follows the advice of his father, a Confucian scholar, to negotiate among his conflicting interests: A man must recognize what he can do and what he cannot do. Chen resolves to persevere in trying to bring as much justice for the poor and victimized as the party will allow, whatever the personal cost to him.

Death of a Red Heroine

Death of a Red Heroine focuses on a beautiful young clerk, honored as a National Model Worker, who is found murdered in Shanghai in 1990. Chief Inspector Chen investigates her murder, following an elaborate sequence of shadowy clues and revelations until he discovers that the culprit appears to be the pampered son of a high-ranking Communist Party official and therefore untouchable for political reasons. Chen sees the case as the slaying of a proletariat hero by a corrupt member of the oligarchy. Despite the pressure on Chen to end the investigation, he arrests the young man, who is tried and executed the same day. The scandal besmirches but does not damage the party, and Chen earns a reputation as a trustworthy law enforcement official.

A Loyal Character Dancer

In *A Loyal Character Dancer*, Chief Inspector Chen teams with Inspector Catherine Rohn of the U.S. Marshal Service to track down the missing wife of a witness in an important international case involving the smuggling of illegal workers to the United States. Their investigation uncovers unsettling connivance between police officers and gangsters, witnesses the aftermath of injustices wrought by the Cultural Revolution, and reveals a government both reluctant to expose its own corruption but eager to appear cooperative in international affairs. Chen and Rohn become close friends and are on the verge of an affair when she must return to the United States as the fugitive has been located because of Chen's spectacular hunches and imperturbable diligence.

When Red Is Black

When an internationally known dissident writer, Yin Lige, is murdered in her shabby apartment in *When Red Is Black* (2004), people suspect that the murder was politically motivated. Chief Inspector Chen's squad is called in to catch the murderer without embarrassing the party. While Chen is on leave (to translate a business brochure to make money to pay for his mother's medical care), Detective Yu does the footwork, but Chen remains the strategist of the investigation. The team not only finds the murderer but also discovers that Yin's reputation is based on plagiarism from a book by her teacher and lover, a famous but denounced professor who died during the Cultural Revolution. The case highlights a scar left by the fanatical Red Guard that dominated the era, the government's continued suppression of literature for tenuous political reasons, and the entanglement of quid pro quo friendships that Chen needs to solve the mystery.

A Case of Two Cities

In *A Case of Two Cities*, Chief Inspector Chen pursues a fugitive from a corruption scandal, Xing Xing, a wealthy businessman whose political connections reach to the Politburo itself. Chen can conduct his investigation only when he is given carte blanche by the head of the Party Central Committee for Discipline. As he closes in on the solution, however, some people in the party hierarchy become alarmed. They deflect Chen by sending him to the United States as the head of a writers' delegation. Detective Yu continues the investigation in China while Chen manages to track down Xing in Los Angeles with the help of his friend Catherine Rohn of the U.S. Marshal Service. Chen arrests Xing, but at a high cost: Two people close to Chen are murdered, and he himself is targeted. Xing is punished, but high-level corruption appears untouched. The party wants the appearance of battling corruption, but nothing more—a source of self-doubt and chagrin to Chen. The novel ends with several themes unresolved, including the reignited love interest with Rohn. Despite his uneasiness in his job and the danger to him, Chen resolves to persevere.

Roger Smith

Principal mystery and detective fiction

Chief Inspector Chen series: *Death of a Red Heroine*, 2000; *A Loyal Character Dancer*, 2002; *When Red Is Black*, 2004; *A Case of Two Cities*, 2006

Other major works

Poetry: *Lines around China*, 2003

Translations: *Shu qing shi ren Yezhi shi xuan*, 1986 (of the lyric poetry of William Buter Yeats); *Lida yu tian e*, 1987 (of "Leda and the Swan" and other poems by William Butler Yeats); *Treasury of Chinese Love Poems: In Chinese and English*, 2003; *Evoking Tang: An Anthology of Classical Chinese Poetry*, 2007

Bibliography

Chi, Pang-Yuan, and David Der-Wei Wang. *Chinese Literature in the Second Half of a Modern Century:*

A Critical Survey. Bloomington: Indiana University Press, 2000. Fifteen essays on modern literature in Taiwan and mainland China, including an examination of the post-Maoist literature frequently referred to in Qiu's novels.

Cummins, Caroline. "Qiu Xiaolong and the Chinese Enigma." *January Magazine* (November, 2002). This article discusses Qiu's background and attitudes about China, the origin and character of Inspector Chen, and Qiu's purposes in writing.

French, Howard. "For Creator of Inspector Chen, China Is a Tough Case to Crack." *The New York Times*, April 7, 2007, p. A4. In this profile of Qiu, the author describes his upbringing and reflects on China and his work.

Kinkley, Jeffrey C. "Chinese Crime Fiction." *Society* 30, no. 4 (May-June, 1993): 51-62. An overview article about the origin of Chinese mystery narratives, the difficulties of writing them in China, and typical themes. Sheds light on Qiu's work.

_______. *Chinese Justice, the Fiction: Law and Literature in Modern China*. Stanford, Calif.: Stanford University Press, 2000. Kinkley recounts the rise of crime fiction in China following the death of Mao Zedong in 1976, tracing both its native forebears and its borrowings from Western literature. Helps place Qiu's fiction.

Zhao, Henry Y. H. "The River Fans Out: Chinese Fiction Since the Late 1970's." *European Review* 11, no. 2 (May, 2003): 193-209. A review of post-Mao fiction in general, arguing that the utilitarian, political nature of fiction before 1989 changed during the 1990's to an appreciation of literature for its own sake. Provides context for Qiu's work.

ELLERY QUEEN

Authors

Frederic Dannay (Daniel Nathan; 1905-1982) and Manfred B. Lee (Manford Lepofsky; 1905-1971); Avram Davidson (1923-1993); Richard Deming (1915-1983); Edward D. Hoch (1930-); Stephen Marlowe (Milton Lesser; 1928-); Talmage Powell (1920-2000); Theodore Sturgeon (Edward Hamilton Waldo; 1918-1985); Jack Vance (John Holbrook Vance; 1916-)

Also wrote as Barnaby Ross

Type of plot: Amateur sleuth

Principal series

Ellery Queen, 1929-1971
Drury Lane, 1932-1933
Tim Corrigan, 1966-1968
Mike McCall, 1969-1972

Principal series characters

Ellery Queen, a mystery writer and an amateur sleuth, is single and lives with his father in New York City. In his mid-twenties when the series begins, he is middle-aged by its close and has lost much of the effete brittleness of character that marked his earliest appearances. Brilliant and well-read, he has a restless energy and a sharp grasp of nuance and detail that he brings to bear on the crimes he investigates—and later records in murder mystery form. He is sometimes deeply affected by the cases on which he works and often blames himself for failing to arrive at a quicker solution.

Inspector Richard Queen, Ellery's father, is a respected member of the New York Police Department. A longtime widower, fond of snuff, he lives with his adored son, whom he often consults on particularly difficult cases. A kindly man who is nevertheless tough and persistent in his pursuit of the truth, he enjoys an affectionate, bantering relationship with Ellery.

Djuna, the Queens' young houseboy and cook, appears regularly throughout the earlier books in the series. A street waif when he is first taken in by Inspector Queen, he takes charge of the two men's Upper West Side apartment while still a teenager. Bright, slight of build, and possibly a Gypsy by birth, he is tutored and trained by Ellery and his father and greatly admires them both.

Contribution

The novels and short stories of Ellery Queen span four decades and have sold more than 150 million copies worldwide, making Queen one of the mystery genre's most popular authors. (For the sake of clarity and simplicity, "Ellery Queen" will be referred to throughout this article as an individual, although the name is actually the pseudonym of two writers, Frederic Dannay and Manfred B. Lee, and several other writers who worked with them.) Queen is both the author and the leading character in his novels.

Queen's early novels are elaborate puzzles, carefully plotted and solved with almost mathematical logic and precision. They represent a style of detective fiction that flourished in the 1920's, and Queen's contributions have become classics of the form. As the series progressed and Queen developed as a character, the books improved in depth and content, sometimes incorporating sociological, political, or philosophical themes. Their settings range from New York to Hollywood to small-town America, and each is examined with perceptive intelligence. In several of the series' later books, Queen abandons outward reality for the sake of what Dannay termed "fun and games," letting a mystery unfold in a setting that is deliberately farfetched or farcical.

Queen's novels and stories are also famed for several key plot devices that have become trademarks of his style. Among them are the dying message (a clue left by the victim to the killer's identity), the negative clue (a piece of information that should be present and is notable by its absence), the challenge to the reader (a point in the story at which Queen addresses the reader directly and challenges him to provide the solution), and the double solution (in which one, entirely plausible solution is presented and is then followed by a second, which offers a surprising twist on the first).

Queen's contributions to the field of mystery and detection are not limited to his novels and short stories. *Ellery Queen's Mystery Magazine*, begun in 1941, remains one of the world's leading mystery publications, printing stories by a wide range of authors, while Queen the detective has also been the hero of a long-running radio series, *The Adventures of Ellery Queen* (1939-1948), and several television series, the first of which aired in 1950. In addition, Queen founded the Mystery Writers of America and edited dozens of mystery anthologies and short-story collections.

Biography

The two men who together invented the Ellery Queen persona were Brooklyn-born cousins, Frederic Dannay and Manfred B. Lee. In reality, their famous alter ego is a pseudonym for two pseudonyms: Dannay was born Daniel Nathan, while Lee's real name was Manford Lepofsky. Both were born in 1905, and both attended Boys' High School in Brooklyn. Lee went on to receive a degree from New York University in 1925,

Frederic Dannay. (Library of Congress)

where he pursued what was to be a lifelong interest in music. In 1942, Lee married actress Kaye Brinker, his second wife, with whom he had eight children—four daughters and four sons. Dannay was married three times: in 1926 to Mary Beck (who later died), with whom he had two sons, in 1947 to Hilda Wisenthal (who died in 1972), with whom he had one son, and in 1975 to Rose Koppel.

During the 1920's, Dannay worked as a writer and art director for a New York advertising agency, while Lee was employed, also in New York, as a publicity writer for several film studios. In 1928, the two cousins began collaborating on a murder mystery, spurred on by a generous prize offered in a magazine detective-fiction contest. The two won the contest, but the magazine was bought by a competitor before the results were announced. The following year, however, Frederick A. Stokes Company, the publishing house cosponsoring the contest, published the cousins' novel, *The Roman Hat Mystery* (1929), and Ellery Queen was born.

By 1931, Dannay and Lee were able to quit their jobs and devote themselves completely to their writing, producing one or two books a year throughout the 1930's. During this period, the pair also wrote briefly under the name Barnaby Ross, publishing the four books that make up the Drury Lane series, *The Tragedy of X* (1932), *The Tragedy of Y* (1932), *The Tragedy of Z* (1933), and *Drury Lane's Last Case* (1933). The bulk of their energy, however, was directed toward Queen, and the series flourished. Queen's stories were a regular feature in many magazines of the period, and their popularity brought Dannay and Lee to Hollywood, which would later serve as the setting for several of their books.

It was also during the 1930's that Queen began making appearances on the lecture circuit, and Dannay and Lee's background in advertising and publicity came into play. It was virtually unknown in the early stages of their career that Queen was actually two men, and the cousins perpetuated their readers' ignorance by sending only Dannay, clad in a black mask, to give the lectures. Later, Lee would also appear, as Barnaby Ross, and the pair would treat audiences to a carefully planned "literary argument" between their two fictional creations. It was not until the cousins first went to Hollywood that the world learned that Ellery Queen was actually Dannay and Lee.

During the 1940's, Dannay and Lee produced fewer books and stories, choosing instead to devote themselves to their weekly radio show, *The Adventures of Ellery Queen*, which ran until 1948. In 1941, the pair also created *Ellery Queen's Mystery Magazine*, with Dannay serving as the principal editor. Their collaboration continued throughout the 1950's and 1960's as they produced more Queen novels and stories, edited numerous anthologies and short-story collections, and cofounded the Mystery Writers of America. Dannay also wrote an autobiographical novel, *The Golden Summer* (1953), under the name Daniel Nathan. In 1958, they published *The Finishing Stroke*, a book intended as the last Queen mystery, but they returned to their detective five years later and eventually produced seven more Queen novels, the last of which, *A Fine and Private Place*, appeared in 1971, the year of Lee's death. Dannay continued his work with the magazine until his own death eleven years later.

Among the critical acclaim and wide array of awards Dannay and Lee received were numerous Edgar Allan Poe awards and a Grand Master Award from the Mystery Writers of America in 1961 and a place on a 1951 international list of the ten best active mystery writers. Throughout their long partnership, the pair, who bore a remarkable resemblance to each other and often finished each other's sentences in conversations, steadfastly refused to discuss the details of their collaboration. The division of labor between them, in terms of plotting, characterization, and editing, remains unknown.

It is known, however, that during Lee and Dannay's lifetimes, their pseudonym became a household name, and numerous mystery novels by Ellery Queen were published by other writers under Lee's or Dannay's supervision. This type of collaboration began in the early 1940's with novelizations of filmscripts. Eventually, two new series characters were introduced under Queen's name: Tim Corrigan and Mike McCall. Some of the authors who wrote as Ellery Queen have been identified: Avram Davidson, Richard Deming, Edward D. Hoch, Stephen Marlowe, Talmage Powell, Theodore Sturgeon, and Jack Vance.

Analysis

Like Agatha Christie, Ellery Queen was a master of intricate plotting. From the very first of the Queen novels, *The Roman Hat Mystery*, his cases are cunningly devised puzzles that the reader must work to assemble along with Queen. Unlike some practitioners of the art, Queen is a believer in fair play; all the pieces to his puzzles are present, if the reader is observant enough to spot them. One of the features of many of the books is Queen's famous "challenge to the reader," in which the narrator notes that all the clues have now been presented and diligent mystery lovers are invited to offer their own solutions before reading on to learn Queen's. The mysteries abound with misdirections and red herrings, but no vital clue is ever omitted or withheld—although arcane bits of knowledge are sometimes required to reach the proper solution.

The early Queen books

In Queen's earliest books, all of which sport "nationality" titles such as *The Egyptian Cross Mystery* (1932) or *The Chinese Orange Mystery* (1934), the clever plotting is often at the expense of character development (as is also true of Christie). The Ellery Queen featured in these novels is a rather cool, bloodless character—an assessment shared by at least one half of the writing partnership that created him. According to Francis M. Nevins, Jr., in his later years, Lee was fond of referring to the early Queen as "the biggest prig that ever came down the pike." It is an accurate description, and one that the Queen sought to change later in his career.

Queen appears in the early books as a brilliant, self-absorbed gentleman sleuth, complete with pince-nez and a passion for rare books. As the series progressed, he slowly grew into a character of some depth and feeling, although he never reached the level of three-dimensional humanity achieved by Dorothy L. Sayers in her development of Lord Peter Wimsey. Indeed, Wimsey is an apt comparison for Queen; both are gentleman sleuths with scholarly interests who begin their fictional careers more as caricatures than characters. Yet Sayers fleshed out her detective so successfully in the following decade and a half that Wimsey's emotional life becomes a central feature in several of her later novels. Queen, on the other hand, is humanized and sketched in without ever becoming a truly compelling figure apart from his dazzling crime-solving talents.

Character development aside, however, Queen's mysteries employ several ingenious recurring plot devices that have become trademarks of the series. Chief among these is the "dying message," in which the victim somehow provides a vital clue to his killer's identity, a ploy that would play an important part in many of the series' later books. It first appeared in *The Tragedy of X*, a Drury Lane novel originally written under the name Barnaby Ross and later reissued with Ellery Queen listed as the author. *The Scarlet Letters* (1953) features one of the most gripping examples of the device, as a dying man leaves a clue for Ellery by writing on the wall in his own blood. *The Roman Hat Mystery* contains another important trademark, the "negative clue," in this case a top hat that should have been found with the victim's body but is missing. The negative clue exemplifies Queen's skills as a detective: He is able to spot not only important evidence at the scene but also details that should have been present and are not.

The Finishing Stroke

Another familiar motif in Queen's stories is a carefully designed pattern of clues, sometimes left deliberately by the murderer, which point the way to the crime's solution. *The Finishing Stroke* contains a superb example of the technique in its description of a series of odd gifts left on the twelve days of Christmas for the murderer's intended victim (although the fact that a knowledge of the Phoenician alphabet is necessary to arrive at the solution may strike some readers as unfair). Several of the plots, including those of four back-to-back novels, *Ten Days' Wonder* (1948), *Cat of Many Tails* (1949), *Double, Double* (1950), and *The Origin of Evil* (1951), hinge on a series of seemingly unrelated events, with the murderer's identity hidden within the secret pattern that connects them.

Cat of Many Tails

Several of Queen's books also contain "double solutions," with Queen providing an initial, plausible solution and then delving deeper and arriving at a second, correct conclusion. This device brings added suspense to the stories, as well as opening the door to the realm of psychological detection into which Queen sometimes ventures. In *Cat of Many Tails*, Queen's initial conclusion, plausible except for one small detail, is forced on him by a guilt-stricken suspect who is attempting to shield the true murderer. A similar situation arises in *And on the Eighth Day* (1964), when Queen is deliberately misled—this time by a suspect with noble motives—into providing an incorrect solution that leads to a man's death.

The psychological motivations of his characters play an increasingly important part in Queen's books as the series progresses. One of the author's favorite ploys is the criminal who uses other characters to carry out his plans, a situation that occurs in *Ten Days' Wonder, The Origin of Evil*, and *The Scarlet Letters*. In these cases, Queen is forced to look beyond the physical details of the crime and search for insight into the mind of the murderer. Often the quarry he seeks is toying with him, taking advantage of the knowledge that Queen is his adversary to tease him with clues or lead him astray. At the close of both *Ten Days' Wonder* and *Cat of Many Tails*, Queen is overcome with guilt, blaming himself for not solving the cases more quickly and possibly preventing further deaths. Indeed, *Cat of Many Tails* opens with Queen so shattered by his confrontation with Diedrich Van Horn, the villain of *Ten Days' Wonder*, that he has given up sleuthing altogether—until his father's pleas draw him into a suspenseful serial killer case.

The filial relationship between Ellery Queen and Inspector Richard Queen plays a far greater part in the series' earlier books than it does in later ones. Queen and his father share a Manhattan apartment located on West Eighty-seventh Street (the site of New York's famous Murder Ink bookstore), and Inspector Queen's long career with the police force provides an entrée for Ellery Queen to many of his cases. The two are devoted to each other, and the inspector's admiration for his son's brilliant detective powers knows no bounds. Eventually, however, Queen the author may have believed that he had exhausted the possibilities of the father-son crime-solving team, for Ellery's later cases tend to occur away from home.

Calamity Town

A wider variety of settings for his books also gave Queen the opportunity to work a thread of sociological observations throughout his later stories. *Calamity Town* (1942) is set in the small community of Wrightsville (also the setting for *Double, Double*), and Queen colors his story with details of small-town life. Queen knew that there is a particular horror inherent in crimes that shatter an apparently tranquil and unspoiled community. Yet urban crimes have their own form of terror, one that Queen examines in *Cat of Many Tails* as the serial killer strikes seemingly random victims and brings New York City to the brink of panic and chaos. The action shifts from Greenwich Village and Times Square to Harlem and the Upper East Side as Queen searches for the thread that links the victims' lives. In other Queen novels, Hollywood comes under close scrutiny, sometimes with bemused humor and amazement (*The Four of Hearts*, 1938) or contempt for its greed and power-seeking (*The Origin of Evil*).

The Origin of Evil

The Origin of Evil is also representative of the forays into philosophy and religion that Queen undertakes on occasion. This story, whose title is a play on Charles Darwin's *On the Origin of Species* (1859), explores humankind's innate capacity for evil. Religious philosophy is given an interesting twist in *And on the Eighth Day*, in which Ellery stumbles on a lost desert community and is taken by its inhabitants to be a prophet whose coming had been foretold to them. Although he believes that their reaction to him is based on a series of misunderstandings and coincidences, he finds that his presence among them has indeed come at a crucial time, and the fulfillment of their ancient prophecy unfolds before his eyes. One chapter, in a clear biblical reference, consists simply of the sentence "And Ellery wept."

Ellery Queen's novels and stories are mysteries with classic components: a murder, a set of clues, a group of suspects, and a gifted detective capable of assembling a revealing picture out of seemingly unrelated facts. Queen's long career as a writer gave him the opportunity to play with the mystery genre, exploring a wide range of settings and themes as he took his character from a "priggish" youth to a more satisfyingly three-dimensional middle age. Yet Queen's enduring popularity remains grounded in those classic elements, and his work stands as proof that there are few things that will delight a reader like a baffling, carefully plotted mystery.

Janet E. Lorenz

Principal mystery and detective fiction

Ellery Queen series: 1929-1940 • *The Roman Hat Mystery*, 1929; *The French Powder Mystery*, 1930; *The Dutch Shoe Mystery*, 1931; *The Egyptian Cross Mystery*, 1932; *The Greek Coffin Mystery*, 1932; *The American Gun Mystery*, 1933 (also known as *Death at the Rodeo*, 1951); *The Siamese Twin Mystery*, 1933; *The Adventures of Ellery Queen*, 1934; *The Chinese Orange Mystery*, 1934; *The Spanish Cape Mystery*, 1935; *Halfway House*, 1936; *The Door Between*, 1937; *The Devil to Pay*, 1938; *The Four of Hearts*, 1938; *The Dragon's Teeth*, 1939 (also known as *The Virgin Heiresses*, 1954); *The New Adventures of Ellery Queen*, 1940

1941-1960 • *Calamity Town*, 1942; *There Was an Old Woman*, 1943 (also known as *The Quick and the Dead*, 1956); *The Case Book of Ellery Queen*, 1945; *The Murderer Is a Fox*, 1945; *Ten Days' Wonder*, 1948; *Cat of Many Tails*, 1949; *Double, Double*, 1950 (also known as *The Case of the Seven Murders*, 1958); *The Origin of Evil*, 1951; *Calendar of Crime*, 1952; *The King Is Dead*, 1952; *The Scarlet Letters*, 1953; *QBI: Queen's Bureau of Investigation*, 1954; *Inspector Queen's Own Case*, 1956; *The Finishing Stroke*, 1958

1961-1971 • *The Player on the Other Side*, 1963 (wr. by Sturgeon based on a detailed outline by Dannay); *And on the Eighth Day*, 1964 (wr. by Davidson based on a detailed outline by Dannay); *Queens Full*, 1965; *The Fourth Side of the Triangle*, 1965 (wr. by Davidson based on a detailed outline by Dannay); *A Study in Terror*, 1966 (novelization of the screenplay; also known as *Sherlock Holmes vs. Jack the Ripper*, 1967); *Face to Face*, 1967; *QED: Queen's Experiments in Detection*, 1968; *The House of Brass*, 1968 (wr. by Davidson based on a detailed outline by Dannay); *The Last Woman in His Life*, 1970; *A Fine and Private Place*, 1971

Ellery Queen series (edited and supervised by Lee): *Ellery Queen, Master Detective*, 1941 (novelization of the screenplay by Eric Taylor; also known as *The Vanishing Corpse*); *The Penthouse Mystery*, 1941 (novelization of a screenplay by Taylor); *The Murdered Millionaire*, 1942 (novelization of the radio play); *The Perfect Crime*, 1942 (novelization of a screenplay by Taylor); *Beware the Young Stranger*, 1965 (by Powell)

Drury Lane series (as Barnaby Ross): *The Tragedy of X*, 1932; *The Tragedy of Y*, 1932; *The Tragedy of Z*, 1933; *Drury Lane's Last Case*, 1933; *The XYZ Murders*, 1961 (omnibus)

Tim Corrigan series (edited and supervised by Lee): *Where Is Bianca?*, 1966 (by Powell); *Who Spies, Who Kills?*, 1966 (by Powell); *Why So Dead?*, 1966 (by Deming); *How Goes the Murder?*, 1967 (by Deming); *Which Way to Die?*, 1967 (by Deming); *What's in the Dark?*, 1968 (by Deming; also known as *When Fell the Night*)

Mike McCall series (edited and supervised by Lee): *The Campus Murders*, 1969 (by Gil Brewer); *The Black Hearts Murder*, 1970 (by Deming); *The Blue Movie Murders*, 1972 (by Hoch; edited and supervised by Dannay)

Nonseries novels (edited and supervised by Lee): *The Last Man Club*, 1940 (novelization of radio show); *Dead Man's Tale*, 1961 (by Stephen Marlowe); *Death Spins the Platter*, 1962 (by Deming); *Kill as Directed*, 1963; *Murder with a Past*, 1963 (by Powell); *Wife or Death*, 1963 (by Deming); *Blow Hot, Blow Cold*, 1964; *The Four Johns*, 1964 (by Vance; also known as *Four Men Called John*); *The Golden Goose*, 1964; *The Last Score*, 1964; *A Room to Die In*, 1965 (by Vance); *The Copper Frame*, 1965 (by Deming); *The Killer Touch*, 1965; *Losers, Weepers*, 1966 (by Deming); *Shoot the Scene*, 1966 (by Deming); *The Devil's Cook*, 1966; *The Madman Theory*, 1966 (by Vance); *Guess Who's Coming to Kill You?*, 1968

Other nonseries novels: *The Golden Summer*, 1953 (as Nathan); *The Glass Village*, 1954; *Cop Out*, 1969 (by Dannay and Lee); *Kiss and Kill*, 1969

Other major works

Play: *Danger, Men Working*, c. 1936 (with Lowell Brentano)

Radio play: *The Adventures of Ellery Queen*, 1939-1948

Screenplay: *Ellery Queen, Master Detective*, 1940 (with Taylor)

Children's literature (as Ellery Queen, Jr.): *The Black Dog Mystery*, 1941; *The Green Turtle Mystery*, 1941; *The Golden Eagle Mystery*, 1942; *The Red Chipmunk Mystery*, 1946; *The Brown Fox Mystery*, 1948; *The White Elephant Mystery*, 1950; *The Yellow Cat Mystery*, 1952; *The Blue Herring Mystery*, 1954; *The Mystery of the Merry Magician*, 1961; *The Mystery of the Vanished Victim*, 1962; *The Purple Bird Mystery*, 1965; *The Silver Llama Mystery*, 1966

Nonfiction: *The Detective Short Story: A Bibliography*, 1942; *Queen's Quorum: A History of the Detective-Crime Short Story As Revealed by the 106 Most Important Books Published in This Field Since 1845*, 1951 (revised 1969); *In the Queen's Parlor, and Other Leaves from the Editors' Notebook*, 1957; *Ellery Queen's International Case Book*, 1964; *The Woman in the Case*, 1966 (also known as *Deadlier than the Male*, 1967)

Edited texts: 1938-1950 • *Challenge to the Reader*, 1938; *101 Years' Entertainment: The Great Detective Stories, 1841-1941*, 1941 (revised 1946); *Sporting Blood: The Great Sports Detective Stories*, 1942 (also known as *Sporting Detective Stories*); *The Female of the Species: The Great Women Detectives and Criminals*, 1943 (also known as *Ladies in Crime: A Collection of Detective Stories by English and American Writers*); *Best Stories from "Ellery Queen's Mystery Magazine,"* 1944; *The Adventures of Sam Spade, and Other Stories*, 1944 (by Dashiell Hammett; also known as *They Can Only Hang You Once*); *The Misadventures of Sherlock Holmes*, 1944; *Rogues' Gallery: The Great Criminals of Modern Fiction*, 1945; *The Continental Op*, 1945 (by Hammett); *The Return of the Continental Op*, 1945 (by Hammett); *Hammett Homicides*, 1946 (by Hammett); *The Queen's Awards*, 1946-1959; *To the Queen's Taste: The First Supplement to "101 Years' Entertainment," Consisting of the Best Stories Published in the First Five Years of "Ellery Queen's Mystery Magazine,"* 1946; *Dead Yellow Women*, 1947 (by Hammett); *Dr. Fell, Detective*, 1947 (by John Dickson Carr); *Murder by Experts*, 1947; *The Case Book of Mr. Campion*, 1947 (by Margery Allingham); *The Department of Dead Ends*, 1947 (by Roy Vickers); *The Riddles of Hildegarde Withers*, 1947 (by Stuart Palmer); *Cops and Robbers*, 1948 (by O. Henry); *Nightmare Town*, 1948 (by Hammett); *Twentieth Century Detective Stories*, 1948 (revised 1964); *The Creeping Siamese*, 1950 (by Hammett); *The Literature of Crime: Stories by World-Famous Authors*, 1950 (also known as *Ellery Queen's Book of Mystery Stories*); *The Monkey Murder, and Other Hildegarde Withers Stories*, 1950 (by Palmer)

1951-1970 • *Woman in the Dark*, 1952 (by Hammett); *Mystery Annals*, 1958-1962; *Ellery Queen's Anthology*, 1959-1973; *A Man Named Thin, and Other Stories*, 1962 (by Hammett); *To Be Read Before Midnight*, 1962; *Mystery Mix*, 1963; *Double Dozen*, 1964; *Twelve*, 1964; *Lethal Black Book*, 1965; *Twentieth Anniversary Annual*, 1965; *All-Star Lineup*, 1966; *Crime Carousel*, 1966; *Poetic Justice: Twenty-three Stories of Crime, Mystery, and Detection by World-Famous Poets from Geoffrey Chaucer to Dylan Thomas*, 1967; *Mystery Parade*, 1968; *Minimysteries: Seventy Short-Short Stories of Crime, Mystery, and Detection*, 1969; *Murder Menu*, 1969; *Murder—In Spades!*, 1969; *Shoot the Works!*, 1969; *The Case of the Murderer's Bride, and Other Stories*, 1969 (by Erle Stanley Gardner); *Grand Slam*, 1970; *Mystery Jackpot*, 1970; *P as in Police*, 1970 (by Lawrence Treat)

1971-1980 • *Headliners*, 1971; *The Golden Thirteen: Thirteen First Prize Winners from "Ellery Queen's Mystery Magazine,"* 1971; *The Spy and the Thief*, 1971 (by Hoch); *Ellery Queen's Best Bets*, 1972; *Mystery Bag*, 1972; *Amateur in Violence*, 1973 (by Michael Gilbert); *Christmas Hamper*, 1974; *Crookbook*, 1974; *Aces of Mystery*, 1975; *Kindly Dig Your Grave, and Other Stories*, 1975 (by Stanley Ellin); *Masters of Mystery*, 1975; *Murdercade*, 1975; *Crime Wave*, 1976; *Giants of Mystery*, 1976; *Magicians of Mystery*, 1976; *Champions of Mystery*, 1977; *Faces of Mystery*, 1977; *How to Trap a Crook and Twelve Other Mysteries*, 1977 (by Julian Symons); *Masks of Mystery*, 1977; *Searches and Seizures*, 1977; *Who's Who of Whodunits*, 1977; *A Multitude of Sins*, 1978; *Japanese Golden Dozen: The Detective Story World in Japan*, 1978; *Napoleons of Mystery*, 1978; *The Supersleuths*, 1978; *Scenes of the Crime*,

1979; *Secrets of Mystery*, 1979; *Wings of Mystery*, 1979; *Circumstantial Evidence*, 1980; *Veils of Mystery*, 1980; *Windows of Mystery*, 1980

1981-1984 • *Crime Cruise Round the World*, 1981; *Doors to Mystery*, 1981; *Eyes of Mystery*, 1981; *Eyewitnesses*, 1981; *Book of First Appearances*, 1982 (with Eleanor Sullivan); *Maze of Mysteries*, 1982; *Lost Ladies*, 1983 (with Sullivan); *Lost Men*, 1983 (with Sullivan); *The Best of Ellery Queen*, 1983; *Prime Crimes*, 1984 (with Sullivan)

Bibliography

Breen, Jon L. "The Ellery Queen Mystery." *The Weekly Standard* 11, no. 4 (October 10, 2005): 41-43. A profile of Lee and Dannay that looks at their rise to fame and then at the decline of the popularity of their works and the reasons behind the drop.

Dove, George N. *The Reader and the Detective Story.* Bowling Green, Ohio: Bowling Green State University Popular Press, 1997. This examination of the conventions of the detective stories discusses Ellery Queen.

"Ellery Queen." In *Modern Mystery Writers*, edited by Harold Bloom. New York: Chelsea House, 1995. Scholarly essay on Queen placing the works produced under that name in the context of mystery and detective fiction generally and discussing their place in the canon.

Harmon, Jim. *The Great Radio Heroes*. Rev. ed. Jefferson, N.C.: McFarland, 2001. Includes a chapter on radio detectives comparing Queen to Sherlock Holmes, Sam Spade, and others. Bibliographic references and index.

Keating, H. R. F., ed. *Whodunit? A Guide to Crime, Suspense, and Spy Fiction.* London: Windward, 1982. Keating's short entry on Ellery Queen contains some useful biographical information but has little in the way of literary criticism.

Malmgren, Carl D. *Anatomy of Murder: Mystery, Detective, and Crime Fiction.* Bowling Green, Ohio: Bowling Green State University Popular Press, 2001. Malmgren discusses Queen's *Halfway House* and *The House of Brass*, alongside many other entries in the mystery and detective genre. Bibliographic references and index.

Symons, Julian. *Bloody Murder: From the Detective Story to the Crime Novel, a History.* London: Faber and Faber, 1972. Symons's history of the detective story includes several pages on Ellery Queen in the chapter entitled "The Golden Age: The Thirties."

PATRICK QUENTIN

Richard Webb and Hugh Wheeler

Richard Webb

Born: England; 1901

Died: Place unknown; probably 1965 or 1970

Also wrote as Q. Patrick (with Mary Louise Aswell, Martha Mott Kelley, and Wheeler); Jonathon Stagge (with Wheeler)

Hugh Wheeler

Born: London, England; March 19, 1912

Died: Pittsfield, Massachusettes; July 27, 1987

Also wrote as Q. Patrick (with Webb); Jonathan Stagge (with Webb)

Types of plot: Amateur sleuth; police procedural

Principal series

Peter Duluth, 1936-1954

Lieutenant Timothy Trant, 1937-1959

Principal series characters

Peter Duluth is a theatrical producer who solves crimes to straighten out his own life. In the first book of the series, he is in an asylum because of alcoholism brought on by the death of his first wife. He meets his future wife at the asylum and investigates a murder there.

Lieutenant Timothy Trant, on two occasions involved in cases with Duluth, is an elegantly dressed police detective. The son of a physicist, he was graduated from Princeton University and became a lawyer. He abandoned that profession to become a detective because "murderers, while fascinating at any stage of their careers, were particularly fascinating while they were still at large."

Contribution

The authors who used the pseudonyms Patrick Quentin, Q. Patrick, and Jonathan Stagge moved the fair-play, challenge-to-the-reader tradition away from the chess-problem story. In many of their novels, the focal character is not a detective solving the crime for intellectual or professional satisfaction but rather someone caught in the mesh of circumstance who must discover the guilty party to save himself or someone he loves. In some of the stories, especially those of the middle and later 1930's, the challenge is to discover not only who committed the crime but also who will eventually solve it. Few other authors dared to try a "least-likely detective" gambit.

Biography

Unfortunately, little is known of the life of one of the authors who contributed to the books published under the pseudonym Patrick Quentin. The main figure in the early books of the collaboration was Richard Wilson Webb, who had been born in England in 1901. He later moved to the United States and became an executive in a pharmaceutical company. In 1931, with Martha Mott Kelley, he wrote a mystery novel titled *Cottage Sinister.* They choose the nom de plume Q. Patrick because, Webb explained, *Q* is "the most intriguing letter of the alphabet" and "Patrick" combined their nicknames, "Patsy" and "Rickie." After the next book, Kelley left the collaboration, and Webb used the Q. Patrick name himself for *Murder at Cambridge.* Webb then found a new collaborator in Mary Louise Aswell. Aswell worked with Webb on two succeeding Q. Patrick detective novels.

In 1936, Webb found a third coauthor in Hugh Callingham Wheeler. Born in London in 1912, Wheeler had been educated at Clayesmere in Dorset, and in 1932 he received a bachelor's degree from the University of London. Together, Webb and Wheeler produced a detective novel with a public-school background, *Death Goes to School* (1936). Although continuing to write as Q. Patrick, they began to write books under two additional pseudonyms, Patrick Quentin and Jonathan Stagge.

Around 1952, Webb retired from the collaboration because of ill health, and Wheeler retained the Patrick Quentin name. In 1961, he began a new career as a dramatist. After 1965, when his final mystery novel was published, he concentrated solely on his stage work, often in association with Stephen Sondheim and Hal Prince, and with his Tony-winning scripts for such musical successes as *A Little Night Music* (pr. 1973), *Candide* (pr. 1973), and *Sweeney Todd: The Demon Barber of Fleet Street* (pr., pb. 1979), he became one of the most successful figures in the American theater. He died on July 27, 1987, at the age of seventy-five.

Analysis

The first five Q. Patrick novels, written by Richard Webb either alone or with Martha Mott Kelley or Mary Louise Aswell, are typical Golden Age mysteries of the 1930's, with intricate plots and fair-play clueing. Nevertheless, some of the Q. Patrick books—most notably, the first Webb-Wheeler collaboration, *Death Goes to School*—feature a gimmick that had been rarely used by earlier writers. Not only do the books unmask the least likely suspect, but also they frequently are constructed around trying to identify the least likely detective. In the usual detective novel, the reader knows quite early which character is the detective, whether amateur or professional. In a Q. Patrick story of this period, and in some of the early Patrick Quentin and Jonathan Stagge tales as well, the sleuth can turn out to be almost anybody. At times, the reader is fooled when the person who seems to be investigating the crime is identified at the end of the story as the guilty person; occasionally, the chief suspect turns out to be the detective. Indeed, because Webb and his coauthors so frequently hid the genuine roles of their characters, readers familiar with these works almost automatically distrust anyone who seems to be a detective or is helping the narrator unravel the mystery.

A Puzzle for Fools

With the publication of *A Puzzle for Fools* in 1936 under the new pseudonym of Patrick Quentin, Webb and Wheeler began their most important and popular series of detective novels. Eventually, the series protagonist, theatrical producer Peter Duluth, would be featured in nine novels and one short story, and two of the novels would be adapted as feature-length films. The first Duluth book is notable for its imaginative setting, an asylum for wealthy patients suffering from relatively minor mental disorders. When murder occurs, however, it seems obvious that one of the patients has a problem that is not so minor. Peter Duluth, who has lost his wife in a fire, is in the sanatorium recovering from alcoholism. Questions of what is real and what is imagined, of who is sane and who is mad, make this novel a memorable opening for the Duluth series.

For both *A Puzzle for Fools* and its notable successor, *Puzzle for Players*, published two years later, Quentin borrowed a technique from the hard-boiled private-eye writers: The story is told in breezy, colloquial prose by the narrator-detective, and the events are sordid. Unlike such detectives as Raymond Chandler's Philip Marlowe, however, Duluth cannot remain a detached investigator. In almost all the Duluth novels, Peter has to stay one step ahead of the police to save himself or someone he loves. Clear examples of Quentin's approach to the mystery novel can be found in *Puzzle for Players*.

Puzzle for Players

Puzzle for Players is a carefully constructed murder mystery aimed at fooling both neophyte mystery fans and jaded readers who believe that they can always identify the murderer. Quentin provides clues (involving brothers and plastic surgery) that allow expert mystery fans to identify, wrongly, an unlikely suspect as the killer. The real murderer is an even less likely suspect. Duluth, who narrates the story, looks on the murders not as crimes to be solved but as threats to his happiness. After the events in *A Puzzle for Fools*, Duluth has begun to revive his career by producing a new play, *Troubled Waters*. He is in love with Iris Pattison, one of the characters in the earlier book, who is beginning her career as an actress in Duluth's play. His psychoanalyst, Dr. Lenz, has forbidden him to wed her until he has proved for six months that he has regained his emotional stability. Thus, when a series of strange events occur at the Dagonet Theater, they threaten Duluth's comeback as well as his marriage plans.

The Dagonet is a decrepit, rat-filled theater, watched over by an ancient caretaker whose wife hanged herself in a dressing room there almost forty years earlier. One of the actors in Duluth's play claims to see a ghost, and another actor dies of a heart attack after announcing that the same ghost walked out of a mirror toward him. Though Duluth suspects foul play, he refuses to call in the police because he does not want the opening of the play to be delayed. The cast is dominated by emotional crosscurrents. The playwright is being blackmailed by his own uncle. An aging character actress is in love with the leading man, an Austrian refugee, but he does not notice her. To make matters worse, the leading lady hates the Austrian. Meanwhile, the leading lady's former husband, whom she has divorced because he abused her, blackmails Duluth into allowing him to join the cast by threatening to tell the police about the strange events at the Dagonet.

Even when one of the actors is murdered inside a coffin that is an important prop in the play, Duluth's sole concern is to make the play a success. He tortures himself by making a list of "REASONS WHY TROUBLED WATERS CAN'T CONCEIVABLY SEE THE LIGHT OF DAY." When the police arrive on the scene, he does his best to convince Inspector Clarke that the murder is merely an accidental death. The cast generally supports Duluth; one of the characters complains that the play is not getting a "very even break. . . . How about the policeman, Clarke? I didn't trust him. He's too bright. He suspects something, doesn't he?" Two-thirds of the way through the book, the production is near collapse, and Duluth laments, "I'm not directing a Broadway production. I'm directing the Sino-Japanese war." Finally, he succumbs to the temptation he has been fighting through most of the novel: He goes out and gets drunk. He is dragged back to the show just in time for the denouement. Iris, meanwhile, has taken advantage of his condition to trick him into a marriage ceremony, and his psychoanalyst, Dr. Lenz, kindly assures him that one drunken episode is acceptable. Even at the conclusion, Duluth is more interested in the success of *Troubled Waters* than in the mundane problem of whodunit. Indeed, he has to be reminded that it makes a difference "which member of your company is going to be arrested."

The plot elements given above are typical of the Peter Duluth series. Quentin usually tries to create an unusual or self-contained world, such as that of the theater, as the milieu for the murder. Whatever the setting, Peter Duluth is normally faced with threats to his happiness. Almost never does he have the same goals as the police, and often he is engaged in outright obstruction of justice. Occasionally, the reader may sympathize with the official police: "Of course I see your point," Inspector Clarke says to Duluth in exasperation. "You're scared we'll close the show if we find out too much. Even so, are you sure you're being smart? You'd look pretty funny if you had a third accidental death around here, wouldn't you?"

Puzzle for Puppets and Puzzle for Wantons

The contrast between the manner of telling and the grimness of the events, which plays a part in *Puzzle for Players*, is even more obvious in Duluth's next adventures, *Puzzle for Puppets* (1944) and *Puzzle for Wantons* (1945). Reviewers praised the novels for their wacky comedy and witty dialogue, yet the stories themselves involve such unamusing matters as serial murder. The relationship between Peter and Iris Duluth was clearly influenced by the Mr. and Mrs. North novels by Frances Lockridge and Richard Lockridge, although Iris is not a scatterbrain like Pamela North (Gracie Allen played Mrs. North in a 1941 motion picture). In these books and all the later Quentin novels, there is a strong undercurrent of sexual tension, not only between Peter and Iris but also among many of the other characters. It is this tension that, despite Quentin's wisecracking style, gives the books their drive.

Puzzle for Fiends

In the succeeding Quentin books, Duluth is faced with crises in his relationships with Iris and other women. In *Puzzle for Fiends* (1946), he suffers from amnesia and is attracted to one of the female characters—but in spite of his mental state, he is still able to tell the story in the first person. In *Puzzle for Pilgrims* (1947) and *Run to Death* (1948)—the latter probably the best of the later novels in the series with its combination of hunter-and-hunted with fair-play clueing—the Duluths try to deal with their collapsing marriage.

Black Widow and My Son, the Murderer

Quentin let Duluth catch his breath for four years before having him face another crisis in *Black Widow* (1952); in that novel, Peter becomes the chief suspect when the body of a pregnant woman is found in his apartment. Fortunately, Lieutenant Timothy Trant, who has solved cases in earlier books published under the pseudonym Q. Patrick, helps Duluth extricate himself from the situation. In the final novel of the series, *My Son, the Murderer* (1954), written by Wheeler alone, the protagonist is Peter's brother, Jake, who faces a crisis typical of the Duluth family: He tries to prove that, in spite of all appearances, his son is innocent of murder. To do so, he must outwit Lieutenant Trant.

This outline of the Duluth novels makes the series sound like a soap opera, and when the books are read in quick succession, it does seem difficult to believe that one family could have been faced with so many disasters connected with so many murders. This may be the reason that Wheeler's later books, also published under the Quentin pseudonym, do not have a series character as the protagonist, although three of the novels enlist Lieutenant Trant to help solve the mystery. Nevertheless, all these books continue the Duluth tradition in which the main character struggles to free himself from a web of circumstances. Sometimes, as in *The Man with Two Wives* (1955), the hero—if he can be called that—helps to create the situation by his own actions. At other times, in an almost Hardyesque way, the gods of chance seem to have decided capriciously to lay traps for the main characters.

Douglas G. Greene

Principal mystery and detective fiction

Peter Duluth series: *A Puzzle for Fools*, 1936; *Puzzle for Players*, 1938; *Puzzle for Puppets*, 1944; *Puzzle for Wantons*, 1945 (also known as *Slay the Loose Ladies*); *Puzzle for Fiends*, 1946 (also known as *Love Is a Deadly Weapon*); *Puzzle for Pilgrims*, 1947 (also known as *The Fate of the Immodest*

Blonde); *Run to Death*, 1948; *Black Widow*, 1952 (also known as *Fatal Woman*)

DR. HUGH WESTLAKE SERIES (AS STAGGE): *Murder Gone to Earth*, 1936 (also known as *The Dogs Do Bark*); *Murder or Mercy*, 1937 (also known as *Murder by Prescription*); *The Stars Spell Death*, 1939 (also known as *Murder in the Stars*, 1940); *Turn of the Table*, 1940 (also known as *Funeral for Five*); *The Yellow Taxi*, 1942 (also known as *Call a Hearse*); *The Scarlet Circle*, 1943 (also known as *Light from a Lantern*); *Death My Darling Daughters*, 1945 (also known as *Death and the Dear Girls*, 1946); *Death's Old Sweet Song*, 1946; *The Three Fears*, 1949

LIEUTENANT TIMOTHY TRANT SERIES: *Death for Dear Clara*, 1937 (as Patrick); *Death and the Maiden*, 1939 (as Patrick); *My Son, the Murderer*, 1954 (by Wheeler as Quentin; also known as *The Wife of Ronald Sheldon*); *The Man with Two Wives*, 1955; *Shadow of Guilt*, 1959; *Family Skeletons*, 1965

NONSERIES NOVELS: *Cottage Sinister*, 1931 (Webb with Martha Mott Kelley as Patrick); *Murder at the Women's City Club*, 1932 (Webb with Mary Louise Aswell as Patrick; also known as *Death in the Dovecote*, 1934); *Murder at Cambridge*, 1933 (Webb as Patrick; also known as *Murder at the Varsity*); *S. S. Murder*, 1933 (Webb with Aswell as Patrick); *The Grindle Nightmare*, 1935 (Webb with Aswell as Patrick; also known as *Darker Grows the Valley*, 1936); *Death Goes to School*, 1936 (as Patrick); *File on Claudia Cragge*, 1937 (as Patrick); *The File on Fenton and Farr*, 1937 (as Patrick); *Return to the Scene*, 1941 (as Patrick; also known as *Death in Bermuda*); *The Follower*, 1950; *Danger Next Door*, 1951 (as Patrick); *The Man in the Net*, 1956; *Suspicious Circumstances*, 1957; *The Green-Eyed Monster*, 1960

OTHER SHORT FICTION: *The Ordeal of Mrs. Snow, and Other Stories*, 1961

OTHER MAJOR WORKS (WHEELER)

NOVEL: *The Crippled Muse*, 1951

PLAYS: *Big Fish, Little Fish*, pr., pb. 1961; *Look! We've Come Through!*, pr. 1961, pb. 1963; *Rich Little Rich Girl*, pr. 1966, pb. 1967 (adaptation of the play by Miguel Mihura and Alvaro de Laiglesia); *We Have Always Lived in the Castle*, pr. 1966, pb. 1967 (adaptation of the novel by Shirley Jackson); *A Little Night Music*, pr. 1973 (music and lyrics by Stephen Sondheim; adaptation of the film by Ingmar Bergman); *Candide*, pr. 1973 (music by Leonard Bernstein, lyrics by Richard Wilbur; adaptation of the novel by Voltaire); *Irene*, pr. 1973 (with Joseph Stein; music by Harry Tierney, lyrics by Joseph McCarthy; adaptation of the play by James Montgomery); *Truckload*, pr. 1975 (music by Louis St. Louis, lyrics by Wes Harris); *Pacific Overtures*, pr. 1976 (with John Weidmann; music and lyrics by Stephen Sondheim); *Sweeney Todd, the Demon Barber of Fleet Street*, pr., pb. 1979 (music and lyrics by Stephen Sondheim; adaptation of the play by C. G. Bond); *Silverlake*, pr. 1980 (music by Kurt Weill; adaptation of a libretto by Georg Kaiser); *The Student Prince*, pr. 1980 (music by Sigmund Romberg; adaptation of a libretto by Dorothy Donelly)

SCREENPLAYS: *Five Miles to Midnight*, 1962 (with Peter Viertel); *Something for Everyone*, 1969; *Caberet*, 1972; *Travels with My Aunt*, 1973 (with Jay Presson Allen); *A Little Night Music*, 1977; *Nijinsky*, 1980

TELEPLAY: *The Snoop Sisters*, 1972 (with Leonard B. Stern)

BIBLIOGRAPHY

Endrebe, Maurice. "Patrick Quentin." *Enigmatika* 19 (June, 1981): 47-49. Brief profile of the pseudonymous collective author and "his" works.

Horsley, Lee. *Twentieth-Century Crime Fiction*. New York: Oxford University Press, 2005. Comprehensive overview of the development of crime fiction in the twentieth century helps place the nature and importance of Quentin's contributions.

Shibuk, Charles. Review of *Puzzle for Fiends*. *The Armchair Detective* 13 (Winter, 1980): 75. Review of a Peter Duluth book in which the main character has amnesia. This look back at an earlier work allows for an examination of its staying power.

_______. Review of *Puzzle for Pilgrims*. *The Armchair Detective* 13 (Spring, 1980): 135. A review of a Peter Duluth series book in which the Duluths struggle in their marriage. Shibuk assesses the work's ability to withstand the "test of time" and its enjoyability for later audiences.

R

ANN RADCLIFFE
Ann Ward

Born: London, England; July 9, 1764
Died: London, England; February 7, 1823
Types of plot: Psychological; thriller

Contribution

Ann Radcliffe, who created a readership for moralizing tales of terror and horror, influenced not only a host of forgotten imitators but also several great writers of the Romantic period and a number of later nineteenth century novelists. Radcliffe refined the crude sensationalism of the gothic novel so that it became a vehicle for sensibility, the sublime, and the picturesque. In place of fast-paced and blood-spattered action, Radcliffean gothic characteristically created psychological tension and suspense, while avoiding the incredible. Though retaining many conventional props of the gothic novel, Radcliffe minimized their significance, being more concerned with moral tests for her heroines. She also enriched her narratives with landscape descriptions.

Biography

Little is known for certain about Ann Radcliffe's life. She was born Ann Ward on July 9, 1764, in London, the daughter of a successful haberdasher. In 1772, her family moved to Bath, where she may have attended a school for young ladies operated by the novelist Sophia Lee.

In 1787 she married William Radcliffe, a parliamentary reporter and later the owner-editor of the *English Chronicle*. Though childless, the marriage appears to have been happy, and William encouraged her writing. In 1794, the couple made a tour of the Continent, and she published a report of their travels in 1795.

By the time Radcliffe's third novel was published, in 1791, she had attained a vast popularity, but although she was the leading modern novelist, she lived out of the public eye. At the height of her career, she decided to publish no more novels, possibly because she objected to the resulting notoriety. In addition, her imitators had added a strain of sensuality to their fiction antipathetic to her. Having by now received a legacy that made her financially independent, she could afford to stop writing. In 1816, however, she published a volume of poems. Radcliffe died on February 7, 1823.

Analysis

The novel was a young genre, not yet a century old, when Ann Radcliffe began writing. She modified both its structure and its themes and established the gothic novel (the novel with a quasi-medieval setting) as a popular form. The first gothic novel, Hugh Walpole's *The Castle of Otranto* (1764), had fused medieval chivalry and the ghost story, creating a fast-paced, incredible tale that drips with blood as it piles shock on shock. In Radcliffe's more leisurely novels, which blend the gothic with the sentimental, the psychological effects of incidents take precedence over action. Her own distinctive version of the gothic novel, moralistic and rationalist, requires that sensitive heroines show their worth by their behavior during suspenseful ordeals whose mysteries prove to be rationally explicable. Radcliffe considerably developed the principle of suspense, adapting the techniques of drama to fiction more completely than had yet been achieved in the novel. Moreover, a precursor to the Romantics, she laced her prose with poetry, her own and others', and she transformed the natural landscape into an appropriate setting for her tales.

The Castles of Athlin and Dunbayne

In Radcliffe's first novel, *The Castles of Athlin and Dunbayne* (1789), an unsuccessful, amateurishly plot-

Ann Radcliffe.

ted tale centered on a hero in the sixteenth century Scottish Highlands, she had not yet found her distinctive style, though she had found her favorite, if not invariable, time setting: the sixteenth century. More important, the book's conclusion, exalting the eventual triumph of virtue in a universe ruled by divine goodness, anticipated the characteristic moral tone of her mature fiction. In the typical Radcliffe novel, a beautiful but solitary and eminently virtuous maiden undergoes persecutions amid picturesque and usually gothic surroundings, whether castle, abbey, or convent. Each time this heroine is about to reach safety, she is thrust back into danger by new ordeals. Finally, wiser for her experiences, she is rescued and marries the man she loves.

Not only does virtue, like love, triumph, but reason does as well. In the final pages of the novel, mysteries are solved—though many have already resolved themselves along the way. As one critic has aptly remarked, the appeal of Radcliffe's books is

> not intellectual but emotional. The reader is not invited to unpick a knot, but to enjoy the emotion of mystery; the knot, indeed, is not unpicked at all; at the appointed hour an incantation is breathed over it, and it dissolves.

Gaston de Blondeville

Only in Radcliffe's posthumously published *Gaston de Blondeville* (1826) does an unexplained knightly ghost, returned to bring his murderer to justice, form the pivot of the plot. With its twelfth century setting, this story is told as a medieval legend rather than as a gothic fiction of supernatural terror and suspense.

A Sicilian Romance

A Sicilian Romance (1790), the first of the novels written in her characteristic mode, illustrates Radcliffe's typical plotline. The heroine, Julia, kept secluded in a castle where mysterious lights are seen in a deserted wing, is burdened with not only a licentious stepmother but also a tyrannical marquess of a father. The marquess proposes to marry her to an evil duke instead of to her beloved. Persuaded by her brother Ferdinand and her lover Hippolitus to flee, after a desperate midnight flight through secret, underground chambers, Julia is overtaken and imprisoned; she manages to flee again to a nunnery, which the marquess besieges. In the ensuing complications, Ferdinand and Hippolitus rescue and re-rescue Julia. Finally, Julia finds her mother, supposedly dead but in fact imprisoned by her father, in a subterranean dungeon (hence the apparently supernatural lights). When her stepmother poisons the marquess and commits suicide, Julia and Hippolitus finally wed.

Radcliffe's plotting would become more polished in later novels, inviting a readier suspension of disbelief. Even in this early novel, however, emphasis falls not on events but on their effects on characters, on the psychological torments created, especially the fear of what may happen next. Having discovered certain valuable techniques, she would perfect them in subsequent novels.

Characteristically, Radcliffe arouses fear by making use of suggestion: the sound of haunting music on the midnight air, a vanishing light, the shadow of a figure, a pregnant sigh, and the like. Night, desolation, and gloom proliferate. Versed in the aesthetic theories of her time, such as Edmund Burke's *Philosophical Inquiry into the Origin of Our Ideas of the Sublime and Beautiful* (1757), she assumes that terror, not horror, expands the soul toward the sublime, and she combines terror with beauty. This combination is achieved partly through scene painting—besides crumbling gothic castles, she delights in natural landscapes, a delight rare in the eighteenth century novel. In her books, pastoral scenes, towering mountaintops touched with moonlight, the distant surge of the sea, gusts of wind, and moving clouds are everywhere. An index to the characters' moral status is their responsiveness to the natural scene. The wicked are impervious to its sublime beauties; the good are immediately responsive.

Radcliffe also makes terror more agreeable by refracting her tales through the mind of a young girl, one who is not only hypersensitive to the atmosphere of her surroundings but also subject to imagining that she has witnessed supernatural events. Thus, the reader participates in the action only indirectly, through the heroine, instead of being exposed directly to any horrors. (Servants and male characters are also used to articulate superstitious fancies, though ordinarily figuring much less prominently.) The irrationality of such imagination is exposed and censured.

The Romance of the Forest

Although Radcliffe insisted that her heroines—and readers—ultimately remain rational beings, there is nevertheless some fascination with the twilight side of human nature as well. Thus, in her third novel, *The Romance of the Forest* (1791), the persecuted and lonely heroine, Adeline, discovers her true identity while living in a ruined abbey, where she dreams of being pursued through darkened corridors and finding a dying man in a coffin. Her dream becomes reality when the secret door that she finds leads her deeper into the building and down into a chamber. Here a prisoner who expected to be murdered had composed a manuscript, which she reads with pity and terror. Later, the writer proves to have been Adeline's real father. Like Julia's discovery of her lost mother in *A Sicilian Romance*, such situations resonate with unconscious parental images, though Radcliffe chooses not to explore the psychological implications of her imagery.

The Mysteries of Udolpho

Most of the supernatural effects in Radcliffe's novels prove to be mere fancies created by the heroine's own trembling sensibilities or else deliberate impostures staged by villains for their own benefit; the actually horrible is a rare event that occurs offstage, if at all. Thus, the reader is perpetually being titillated and then reassured. In Radcliffe's fourth and most famous novel, *The Mysteries of Udolpho* (1794), for example, when heroine Emily St. Aubert is taken to the grim castle of Udolpho in the Italian Apennines by her aunt's new husband, the villainous Montoni, she is soon affrighted by the worm-eaten corpse she sees there—but the corpse proves to be only a wax image. When Montoni locks up his shrewish wife in a tower because she refuses to sign over her property to him, Emily assumes after finding a trail of blood that he has had her killed; in reality, her aunt dies of natural causes, though her death is brought on by Montoni's harsh treatment. Emily also assumes that the scheming Montoni murdered the previous owner of the castle, a woman who disappeared mysteriously many years before. Later, Emily discovers that the woman is living in a convent in France under an assumed name—and was herself a murderess.

Emily is in constant terror for her life and her honor while held captive in Udolpho, but she is never injured (no Radcliffe heroine is ever raped). She even escapes with two servants for another round of adventures in France. When one of these servants mysteriously disappears from a locked chamber that supposedly harbors a ghost, it turns out that he was only carried away through a secret door by robbers who had been using that wing of the castle to store their loot. Moreover, when members of the castle family accidentally fall into the robbers' hands, the servant is conveniently present to help them escape.

Radcliffe's techniques answer to her sense of existence: Her universe is a rational one presided over by a benevolent God. As Radcliffe states in the penultimate paragraph of *The Mysteries of Udolpho*, "though the vicious can sometimes pour affliction upon the good, their power is transient and their punishment certain; and . . . innocence, though oppressed by injustice, shall, supported by patience, finally triumph over misfortune!" According to her philosophy, the reader enjoys shivers of suspense and touches of terror but should carry away no disquieting thoughts from her books.

Radcliffe is inventive in her mysteries and resourceful in resolving them, but the heart of her mature novels lies elsewhere. *The Mysteries of Udolpho* also illustrates her thematic concerns. Amid its gothic trappings, it is a *bildungsroman*, portraying three stages in the growth of its heroine and three corresponding settings in France and Italy.

Emily has been reared by her father at an idyllic estate in southern France to have high ideals and active and generous sensibilities. She is cast out of her Eden and into the world of evil and self-interest, first in sophisticated Venice and then at the gloomy castle of Udolpho. Though her aunt has torn the orphaned Emily away from her true love and callously subjected her to Montoni's villainies at Udolpho, Emily refuses to harden her heart; she tries at some risk to succor her aunt. Strong-minded like all Radcliffe heroines, she never collapses into self-pity or misanthropy under her own trials. Nevertheless, Emily errs not only in imagining ghosts but also in attributing to Montoni a more sinister personality than he actually has; he is not the monster her imagination creates.

Having escaped his clutches and returned to France for the final stage of her education, Emily discovers certain important family secrets, although some have an unexpected twist. For example, plentiful hints lead the reader to assume that Emily will discover her true mother to have been her father's mysterious lover; in fact, the miniature her father has preserved proves only to have been of Emily's aunt. More important thematically, Emily overcomes her severest trial not in contending with any mystery but in acknowledging the moral shortcomings of her lover (who has impetuously gambled away his good name during her absence) without losing her love for him. Recognizing that he is only rash and generous rather than dissolute, she marries him. She has learned through her experiences to maintain her ideals but temper them to the reality of the fallen world, relegating evil to its ordinary human manifestations.

THE ITALIAN

The Mysteries of Udolpho is generally considered Radcliffe's best novel, despite its diffuseness and repetitious incidents, but her fifth novel, *The Italian: Or, The Confessional of the Black Penitents* (1797), contains her most interesting characterization of a villain. Schedoni is a morose monk, taciturn, enigmatic, and with a secret sin in his past. Unlike other Radcliffe characters, who are free of inner conflict, this ambitious and murderous Iago, whose malignity seems assured and who reputedly can see only evil in human nature, falls prey to his conscience on the point of the murder that would have realized his worldly desires. When he afterward recognizes the intended victim as his long-lost daughter (though later he will be proved wrong), he displays inchoate but touching paternal feelings. The allegedly supernatural also plays very little part in this book, which contains far more dialogue than earlier novels, though the superstitious dread of Catholicism that pervades its imaginative scenes of the Inquisition yields an atmosphere just as foreboding. In this last of the novels published during her lifetime, Radcliffe demonstrated anew her versatility for turning suggestive terror into pleasurable, suspenseful fiction.

Harriet Blodgett

PRINCIPAL MYSTERY AND DETECTIVE FICTION

NOVELS: *The Castles of Athlin and Dunbayne*, 1789; *A Sicilian Romance*, 1790; *The Romance of the Forest*, 1791; *The Mysteries of Udolpho*, 1794; *The Italian: Or, The Confessional of the Black Penitents*, 1797; *Gaston de Blondeville*, 1826

OTHER MAJOR WORKS

POETRY: *The Poems of Ann Radcliffe*, 1816; *St. Alban's Abbey*, 1826

NONFICTION: *A Journey Made in the Summer of 1794 Through Holland and the Western Frontier of Germany*, 1795

Bibliography

Dekker, George G. *The Fictions of Romantic Tourism: Radcliffe, Scott, and Mary Shelley.* Stanford, Calif.: Stanford University Press, 2005. Discusses the importance of British Romanticism to Radcliffe's work and argues that her fiction represents a sort of "spiritual tourism."

McIntyre, Clara Frances. *Ann Radcliffe in Relation to Her Time.* New Haven, Conn.: Yale University Press, 1920. Reprint. New York: Archon Books, 1970. Useful study of Radcliffe that reviews the facts of her life and surveys her work. Presents contemporary estimates of her novels, considers the novels' sources, and lists their translations and dramatizations.

Miles, Robert. *Ann Radcliffe: The Great Enchantress.* Manchester, England: Manchester University Press, 1995. Explores the historical and aesthetic context of Radcliffe's fiction, with separate chapters on her early works and mature novels. Miles also considers Radcliffe's role as a woman writer and her place in society. Includes notes and bibliography.

Murray, E. B. *Ann Radcliffe.* New York: Twayne, 1972. Surveys Radcliffe's life, drawing from her *A Journey Made in the Summer of 1794 Through Holland and the Western Frontier of Germany* to illustrate her novels' geography. Examines the background of the gothic, with its supernatural elements, sentiment and sensibility, and sense of the sublime and the picturesque. Includes notes, a selected annotated bibliography, and an index.

Norton, Rictor. *The Mistress of Udolpho: The Life of Ann Radcliffe.* New York: Leicester University Press, 1999. An important scholarly study of Radcliffe's life, attempting to fill in the many gaps in previous biographies.

Rogers, Deborah D., ed. *The Critical Response to Ann Radcliffe.* Westport, Conn.: Greenwood Press, 1994. A good selection of critical essays on Radcliffe. Includes bibliographical references and an index.

Smith, Nelson C. *The Art of the Gothic: Ann Radcliffe's Major Novels.* New York: Arno Press, 1980. Contains a valuable introduction which reviews the scholarship on Radcliffe between 1967 and 1980. Analyzes the narrative techniques used to craft the gothic tale, and surveys the gothic writers who followed Radcliffe. Includes end notes for each chapter and a bibliography.

IAN RANKIN

Born: Cardenden, Fife, Scotland; April 28, 1960
Also wrote as Jack Harvey
Types of plot: Police procedural; thriller

Principal series

Inspector Rebus, 1987-

Principal series characters

Inspector Rebus is a tough-guy loner who smokes and drinks too much. He has a family but rarely leads a family life. However, like the traditional detective, Rebus will not rest until he has solved the crime, which often means coming into conflict with Edinburgh's power class and his superiors at work. He does not care who he offends, and his dogged pursuit of truth establishes his integrity.

Contribution

Although Ian Rankin's Inspector John Rebus owes something to the detectives in the hard-boiled school of mystery fiction, he has none of the romantic aura that imbues characters like Dashiell Hammett's Sam Spade or Raymond Chandler's Philip Marlowe. Rebus is the epitome of the detective as demotic hero. He is an ordinary man whose humor is his saving grace. Rankin's emphasis on the Edinburgh locale, attention to the city's class structure, and willingness to develop several plot strands at once are a deviation from the melodrama of most mystery and detective fiction. Rankin's aim is not so much to create mysteries per se but to use the genre of detective fiction as a vehicle for a realistic appraisal of society and modern manners. Like Colin Dexter's Inspector Morse, Rankin's Inspector Rebus is an odd man out, although the Oxford-educated Morse has none of Rebus's working-class alienation.

Ian Rankin. (Courtesy, Little Brown and Company)

Rankin does not like neatly tied up plots—a hallmark of mystery and detective fiction. Crimes are solved but only up to a point; in other words, not all the guilty parties are punished or even exposed. Indeed, the solution of one crime in a Rebus mystery often leads to the discovery of crimes elsewhere. Old cases get opened, which often means that the detective has to confront the mistakes of his past. The sociology and psychology of crime intersect in ways that Rebus can hardly apprehend.

Rankin's *Black and Blue* (1997) was nominated for an Edgar and won a Gold Dagger Award from the Crime Writers' Association (CWA). He won a Macallan Award (now CWA Short Story Award) in 1996 for "Herbert in Motion" and received the Edgar Award for *Resurrection Men* (2002) in 2004. In 2005 Rankin received the Grand Prix de Littérature Policière for *Dead Souls* (1999) and the Cartier Diamond Dagger for lifetime achievement from the Crime Writers' Association.

Biography

Ian Rankin grew up in Cardenden, Fife, Scotland, where he attended the local comprehensive school. He describes a rather bleak town in the midst of an economic downturn when the coal mines closed. As a young boy, Rankin developed his own imaginative world in compensation for the grim reality of his immediate surroundings. He majored in English and earned a master of arts degree with honors at the University of Edinburgh. When he began writing fiction, he abandoned his plans to attain a doctorate in the modern Scottish novel.

Rankin began by writing comic books, then poetry and short stories while working as a journalist and book reviewer in London. After a period of living in the French countryside, which included employment as a swineherd, he turned a long story into a novel, *The Flood* (1986), the story of a young man growing up in Fife but dreaming of moving to Edinburgh.

Rankin's lifelong love of American fiction and film

led him to crime stories. Inspector Rebus appears in Rankin's second novel, *Knots and Crosses* (1987). Rankin learned police procedure by interviewing and accompanying Edinburgh detectives. However, he emphasizes that his main interest is in modern Scotland, not in the mystery genre itself. Clearly his novels acquire their authenticity through his evocative descriptions of the city and countryside. Rankin regards Edinburgh, with its dour Calvinist history, as a wonderful setting for crime novels. He calls it a perfect place for conspiracies because of its much darker view of the world than that of other Scottish cities.

Rankin's interest in music is evident is many of his novels. As a young boy he wrote song lyrics, and he briefly played in a punk band, the Dancing Pigs, in the 1970's. Songs from the period are often referred to in his novels and become a way of characterizing Rebus as a man somewhat out of place in contemporary Edinburgh, where although the nature of police work is changing, it remains basically the same for the nuts-and-bolts detective.

Rebus reflects Rankin's working-class background, and Rebus's friends, like Rankin's early ones, tend to go into occupations like law enforcement or the army when the closing of the mines damaged the local economy.

The first Rebus novel was not a success, and Rankin turned to the spy story, publishing *The Watchman* (1988), set in London. After trying other kinds of novels, Rankin took a friend's advice and returned to writing about Rebus. However, he found he needed another outlet and, using the name Jack Harvey, began producing novels that he describes as "airport thrillers." *Blood Hunt* (1995), for example, deals with a transnational corporation that is poisoning the food supply. Such thrillers, Rankin has said, demand more research because readers want to know far more details than he has to supply in the Rebus novels, which focus more on character than on forensics.

Analysis

Inspector John Rebus is a relentless detective with no time for police department politics or respect for the power types he encounters. He pursues crime, and that means he is rarely tactful—indeed he is sometimes barely polite when he confronts complacency, cover-ups, and other forms of resistance to his investigations.

Rebus is in his mid-thirties when he first appears in *Knots and Crosses* and ages over the course of the series. Retirement age for Edinburgh police is fifty-five, and Rankin has said that means the series will have to end in another three to five novels. The ending of the series is important because it points to Rankin's achievement: He has not created a fantasy figure, a character that could go on in some timeless fashion solving crimes. Rebus is aware that he is aging, and by his mid-forties he is already considering whether he should give up the job, which for him is all-consuming.

Words such as "poetic prose" and "gritty realism" have been used to describe Rankin's work, but there is also Rebus's sly sense of humor, which emerges in the later novels. Rebus gets better at repartee as the man becomes the job, so to speak. Regardless of whom Rebus is interviewing, he remains the same man, refusing to be unduly deferential to authority figures or diplomatic with his colleagues.

Knots and Crosses

In *Knots and Crosses*, Rebus is introduced as a former army man, divorced and recovering from a nervous breakdown, trying to rebuild his life while serving on the Edinburgh police force. The army had seemed a good solution for a young man who did not want to go to college but felt he had no future in a small Scottish town devastated by the closing of the coal mines. These basic details of Rebus's life figure in several of Rankin's novels, serving as a key to the detective's character. Detective work is as close to a métier as he is ever likely to get. It is also an escape from army regimentation, although working in a city police force inevitably means he will have to deal with bureaucrats and careerists. He does so grudgingly.

When several young girls are murdered in Edinburgh, Rebus calls on newspaper reporter Jim Stevens and another friend. The murders remind Rebus of a childhood trauma he has repressed. The novel's plot becomes an intricate puzzle (Rebus, as Rankin has pointed out, means picture puzzle).

Hide and Seek

In *Hide and Seek* (1991), male prostitutes are the victims. Reminiscent of Robert Louis Stevenson's *The*

Strange Case of Dr. Jekyll and Mr. Hyde (1886), this mystery calls on Rankin's considerable knowledge of literature. Some kind of satanic cult seems to be involved in a complex interplay of milieus that includes Edinburgh drug culture. Complicating Rebus's investigation is a cast of two-faced characters. Their duplicity emphasizes the good/evil, Jekyll/Hyde axis on which this novel rotates. As is often the case in the Rebus novels, crimes are not viewed in isolation but rather as symptoms of a corrupt society, not to mention a sickness that strikes deeply into the human soul.

Black and Blue

In *Black and Blue*, a serial killer is at large, although he seems to be a copycat, duplicating murders committed thirty years earlier in Edinburgh. Rebus, however, is preoccupied with another old case: Did Rebus's partner frame Lenny Spaven for a murder he did not commit? Even worse, on assignment in Aberdeen while attempting to determine whether Spaven's claim of innocence is credible, Rebus runs afoul of police who not only thwart his investigation but also begin to treat him as a suspect when the copycat killer strikes again. Rebus's penchant for going off on his own is partly what makes him a target, but his independence is precisely what allows him to find clues that other conventional cops are in no position to detect. Complicating Rebus's investigation is the original serial killer, who is out to snuff his imitator.

Rankin's handling of police and criminals at cross purposes with each other and the rest of the world reaches a crescendo in this novel. Its scope and depth mark an advance over earlier novels in the series.

Dead Souls

The title of the tenth Inspector Rebus novel, *Dead Souls*, suggests the cumulative impact of the crimes and corruption the inspector has investigated. The toll on him has been tremendous. His daughter Sammy is in a wheelchair, run down in connection with a crime Rebus investigated. He is drinking heavily, and the romance in his life has been soured by his surly, brooding behavior.

In a dark mood already, Rebus is stunned when a fellow police officer, Jim Margolies, apparently commits suicide. Margolies seemed Rebus's opposite: an officer who got along with everyone and was superb at his job as well. Why would this man throw himself off a cliff? No one seems to have a clue, not even Margolies's wife, who just wants Rebus to stop asking questions.

Rebus makes matters even worse for himself when he leaks to the press that a pedophile has been released and placed in an Edinburgh housing project. The subsequent uproar has made Rebus's boss angry and in no mood to follow the inspector's lead in investigating a child abuse case at the Sheillion children's home.

Next, a former high school sweetheart, Janice Mee, contacts Rebus about her missing son. She arouses romantic feelings at a time when he already seems unable to cope with his shaky career and personal problems. However, finding Janice's son helps him to focus, and her obvious romantic interest in Rebus buoys him, even though she is married to one of Rebus's high school friends—clearly Janice's second choice.

The frustrating cases pile up, and then Cary Oakes, a devilishly clever serial killer, returns to Edinburgh after serving a fifteen-year sentence in an American prison. Oakes taunts Rebus and the Edinburgh police force, teases a journalist who thinks he can turn Oakes's story into a best-selling book, and continues a killing spree that has its roots in his own childhood abuse.

The crossing plotlines emphasize Rankin's continuing view that crime does not exist in a vacuum and that the nature of crime is not only individual but also communal—a problem for society to solve that goes far beyond apprehending criminals.

The Naming of the Dead

The seventeenth Rebus novel, *The Naming of the Dead* (2007), is set in Scotland during the Group of Eight (G8) world summit. In this overtly political novel, Rebus collides with the aptly named Commander Steelforth, in charge of G8 security. Rebus is called to Edinburgh Castle, where Ben Webster, a Scottish member of Parliament, has fallen over a wall to his death. Is it an accident, suicide, or murder? Steelforth treats the matter as merely a security problem and refuses to cooperate with Rebus, who finds his access to information (such as security camera tapes) blocked. Rebus refuses to consider the political implications of this shocking incident and has to find ways to work around Steelforth.

Even Rebus's boss wants to delay an investigation

until the summit is over. However, Rebus, a stickler for police procedure, pursues the case and eventually has a showdown with Steelforth that illuminates the nature of a world in which the detective can be only partially effective. Rather than diminishing Rebus's stature, this novel enhances it because he pursues his cases even though the punishment may not fit the crime and the establishment will not honor his mission. Rebus the realist does the best job he can, leaving open at least a quest for the truth that the higher-ups have attempted to quash.

Carl Rollyson

Principal mystery and detective fiction

Inspector Rebus series: *Knots and Crosses*, 1987; *Hide and Seek*, 1991; *Strip Jack*, 1992; *Wolfman*, 1992 (also known as *Tooth and Nail*, 1996); *The Black Book*, 1993; *Mortal Causes*, 1994; *Let It Bleed*, 1995; *Black and Blue*, 1997; *The Hanging Garden*, 1998; *Death Is Not the End*, 1998; *Dead Souls*, 1999; *Set in Darkness*, 2000; *The Falls*, 2001; *Resurrection Men*, 2002; *A Question of Blood*, 2004; *Fleshmarket Close*, 2004 (also known as *Fleshmarket Alley*, 2005); *The Naming of the Dead*, 2007

Nonseries novels: *The Flood*, 1986; *Watchman*, 1988; *Westwind*, 1990; *Witch Hunt*, 1993 (as Harvey); *Bleeding Hearts*, 1994 (as Harvey); *Blood Hunt*, 1995 (as Harvey); *The Beggar's Banquet*, 2002

Short fiction: *A Good Hanging, and Other Stories*, 1992

Bibliography

Bradford, Richard. *The Novel Now: Contemporary British Fiction*. Malden, Mass.: Blackwell Publishing, 2007. Discusses the Rebus novels as one of the mainstays of contemporary British fiction along with those of P. D. James, Colin Dexter, and Ruth Rendell, among others. Bradford notes Rebus's depressive personality and his penchant for heavy drinking but also Rankin's superb evocation of the seedy side of Edinburgh life.

Mullan, John. *How Novels Work*. New York: Oxford University Press, 2006. Contains illuminating, if brief, comments on Rankin's novels. Rankin's use of literary epigraphs, for example, is a witty way for his more sophisticated readers to puzzle through the solutions to the crimes Rebus is investigating.

Rankin, Ian. Ian Rankin. http://www.ianrankin.net. This author's Web site includes news items (such as exhibitions of his work), new audio editions of his books, dramatic (television) adaptations of his work, and an interview of the author.

_______. *Rebus's Scotland: A Personal Journey*. London: Orion Publishing, 2005. Evocative black-and-white photographs of buildings and places by Trish Malley and Ross Gillespie are accompanied by Rankin's text detailing Rebus's history, the origins of other fictional characters, and Rankin's biography. Part memoir, part travel guide, this volume is a good introduction to the Rebus series.

Scaggs, John. *Crime Fiction*. New York: Routledge, 2005. Explores Rebus's antiauthoritarian attitudes, comparing him to other detectives such as James Lee Burke's Dave Robicheaux, even as Rebus "serves the interests of the dominant social order." Even though Rebus's interests in politics are marginal, his actions help restore the political balance of society.

ARTHUR B. REEVE

Born: Patchogue, New York; October 15, 1880
Died: Trenton, New Jersey; August 9, 1936
Type of plot: Amateur sleuth

Principal series

Craig Kennedy, 1910-1936

Principal series characters

Craig Kennedy, a professor of chemistry at an unnamed New York City university, uses the tools of science to solve mysteries and confront crimes committed with scientific devices. He treats most of his clients, as he treats his cases, with scientific detachment.

Walter Jameson, a journalist with the New York *Star*, narrates most of the Kennedy stories. He and Kennedy were college roommates and still share an apartment. His air of perpetual astonishment at his colleague's ability makes him the perfect foil.

Inspector Barney O'Connor, who rises to the rank of first deputy commissioner of the New York Police Department as a result of Kennedy's successes, consults the professor on a regular basis.

Contribution

The twenty-six books about scientific detective Craig Kennedy were once among the most popular detective stories by an American writer, with sales of two million copies in the United States alone. Arthur B. Reeve was popular primarily because of his emphasis on the use of the latest scientific devices to solve mysteries. Reeve was not one to waste time on deeply etched characters; he focused instead on an imaginative rendition of a scientific marvel—the Maxim silencer, an oxyacetylene blowtorch, the Dictaphone, the seismograph, liquid rubber to conceal fingerprints—with which the crime was committed or by means of which Kennedy could solve the mystery. The very reason for Reeve's popularity in the years before World War I, his topicality, dates the stories and makes him a largely forgotten author.

Reeve's straightforward, journalistic style, combined with a lively imagination and an ability to tell a good story in spite of his cardboard characters, makes the earliest episodes readable and entertaining, despite his scientific marvels having become commonplace. The emphasis on topicality makes them documents for the social scientist rather than the literary critic.

Biography

Arthur Benjamin Reeve was born in Patchogue, New York, on October 15, 1880, the son of Walter Franklin Reeve and Jennie Henderson Reeve. Having been graduated from Princeton University in 1903, he attended New York Law School but never finished, preferring journalism instead.

Reeve became assistant editor of the magazine *Public Opinion*, contributing articles on science. On January 31, 1906, he married Margaret Allen Wilson of Trenton, New Jersey; they had three children, two sons and a daughter. He continued writing articles on topics such as politics, crime, science, farming, social conditions, and sports. In later years, he became a specialist in growing dahlias.

Reeve's first Kennedy story was rejected by several magazines before being accepted by the editor of *Cosmopolitan*, where it appeared in the December, 1910, issue; this publication marked the beginning of a long series of monthly appearances of Kennedy stories in the Hearst magazines.

Fascinated with the technology of the motion picture, Reeve wrote a series of fourteen interconnected stories that became one of the most successful early silent film serials, *The Exploits of Elaine* (1914). It resulted in two sequels, for a total of thirty-six episodes. Reeve wrote screenplays for several other serials and features, including three starring Harry Houdini.

Although Kennedy was not as popular after the war, Reeve continued to find a market for him in the pulp magazines. In 1926, he published a Kennedy novel entitled *Pandora*, then turned his typewriter to the service of society with articles on crime prevention and a radio series on the topic in 1930-1931. In 1935, he covered the Lindbergh kidnapping trial for a Philadelphia newspaper.

Encouraged by the renewed interest in his character and a film serial based on his 1934 novel *The Clutching Hand*, Reeve wrote another Kennedy novel, *The Stars Scream Murder* (1936). It was Kennedy's last case. Reeve died in Trenton, New Jersey, of complications brought on by an asthmatic and bronchial condition, on August 9, 1936.

Analysis

Arthur B. Reeve may have borrowed the idea of using a word-association test in "The Scientific Cracksman" (in *The Silent Bullet*, 1912) from "The Man in the Room" (in *The Achievements of Luther Trant*, 1910, by Edwin Balmer and William MacHarg), but the emphasis differs. Reeve's success with Craig Kennedy went far beyond anything his predecessors had achieved. Within a few months, Kennedy the scientific detective was a household name, and his creator was hard put to keep up with the demand for his adventures.

In less than a decade, Reeve turned out enough material to make a twelve-volume collected edition of his books not only feasible but a marketable commodity as well. A few decades later, Craig Kennedy would be forgotten, but during the years between 1910 and 1920, he was the best-selling fictional detective in the United States, considered by his publisher (especially for advertising purposes) the American Sherlock Holmes.

The secret of Reeve's success lay in his timing; his emphasis on the latest scientific discoveries in an age that took pride in progress; and the appearance of the stories in one of the most popular magazines of the day, one part of the publishing empire of William Randolph Hearst. Although Reeve wrote ten novels about Kennedy, it is in the short form that the writer's skill as a storyteller lies. Although the series spanned two and a half decades in publication, it is the earlier stories that retain the greatest interest—as reflections of a vanished period in American society as well as examples of an earlier mode of detective fiction.

To keep up with the demand for stories about Kennedy, Reeve often reused ideas and even recycled actual episodes that had appeared in earlier stories. Short stories were often expanded to fit a longer format, and stories that had appeared in magazines were often rewritten for book publication with characters altered and situations reversed. Some of this recycling was the

Arthur B. Reeve. (Library of Congress)

result of contractual obligations, but some was simply a matter of expedience. Reeve was a one-man fiction factory with insufficient raw materials.

Reeve may not have described Kennedy's physical appearance, but there was no doubt in anyone's mind what he looked like. Will Foster's illustrations made it obvious that the professor of chemistry at an unnamed university (apparently intended to be Columbia) was clean-cut, square jawed, and stocky. Walter Jameson, his reporter friend who narrated the stories, was slight of build with fine features. Beyond that, it was up to the readers to form their own images.

In the early period, a Craig Kennedy story was as ritualistic as any in the Holmes canon. Each story opens in Kennedy's laboratory in the chemistry building on the campus of the university or in the apartment he shares with Jameson. Enter the client or Inspector Barney O'Connor to present a problem to Kennedy and ask for his help. Kennedy may suggest that the case should be easy to solve simply because it seems so extraordinary. This is quite in keeping with one of Holmes's own patterns of reasoning.

The crime is usually murder committed in unusual circumstances. A young couple is found dead with no discernible means or motive to be found. There are so few suspects that the focus is not so much on who did it as on how the crime was committed and the motive. The motive is often apparent, since there is only one logical individual who benefits. Each story contains two scientific devices, one used to commit the crime and one to solve the mystery. Kennedy discovers the first through his own wide knowledge of scientific matters, but he creates the second in his laboratory, often concealing its nature and significance until the end of the story.

It was this element, the scientific device, which was responsible for Reeve's great popularity. Kennedy's basic theory was that science could be applied to the detection of crime just as it could trace the presence of a chemical or locate a germ. Ballistics, voiceprints, the use of film cameras to record crimes in progress, the identification of the typewriter used by comparing the alignment of the letters, and Dictaphones are only some of the devices that Kennedy uses to combat crime. Yet the novelty wore off, much of it quickly became outdated, and even more novel devices had to be described in subsequent stories. Some of this is sufficiently representative of the period for the stories to have acquired a significance as social history.

If some of the descriptions of the scientific principles and marvels seem vague and insubstantial, verisimilitude is nevertheless established by the offhand references to authorities who have performed similar experiments or published papers on the same topic. Occasionally, Kennedy will read aloud from an account in a newspaper that supports his own thesis. The press's well-known reputation for objectivity adds the required substance to this hitherto unfamiliar scientific theory.

The series' decline in quality is easy to follow. Reeve's popularity was often in inverse ratio to the quality of his writing and his ingenuity. Eventually, his popularity waned, the response of a fickle public that always demanded the new and novel. Reeve was able to ring the changes on his own formula with success only for a decade.

Reeve's best stories were produced between 1910 and 1918 for *Cosmopolitan* and *Hearst's International Magazine*. Not uniform in quality, they nevertheless convey an inventiveness and an ability to tell a good story, no matter how improbable the premise, producing in the reader that necessary and traditional willing suspension of disbelief.

The decline began even before this era was ended, with the novelizations of the film serials that starred Pearl White. It continued into the novels, which replaced science with psychoanalysis. (Reeve did utilize psychology in the short stories as well, but not to the extent that he did in his novels.) The decline continued in the thematic groups of short stories in the 1920's, through his stories for a juvenile audience (*The Boy Scouts' Craig Kennedy*, 1925; *The Radio Detective*, 1926), and ended in his attempts to rekindle an interest in his hero shortly before his own death. The ideas and their execution are weak and lack the ingenuity of the early years.

Although Reeve's first two Kennedy books are clearly collections of short stories, subsequent titles are more subtle about their content. Not only has the original magazine sequence been altered, but also Reeve edited the original texts so that the collection appeared to be a novel in appearance if not in fact. *The Dream Doctor* (1914) consists of twelve short stories, but they are divided into twenty-four chapters, with the second story beginning a few pages before the end of the second chapter, thus leading into the third chapter. A similar subterfuge occurs in *The War Terror* (1915), although the twelve stories are divided into thirty-six chapters—roughly three chapters to one episode, with a few sentences added where necessary to accomplish the transition. *The Social Gangster* (1916) was the last group of short stories collected in this manner.

The Dream Doctor

The Dream Doctor was the first of Reeve's attempts to group his stories thematically. As with the others—*The Fourteen Points: Tales of Craig Kennedy, Master of Mystery* (1925) and *Craig Kennedy on the Farm* (1925), for example—the premise is promising, but the results are unsatisfactory. The idea in *The Dream Doctor* of having Jameson assigned by his editor to report on Kennedy's activities for a month is stronger than the theme of *The War Terror*, in which the war plays a part in only one of the episodes.

Elaine Dodge trilogy

The episodes in the trilogy about Elaine Dodge—*The Exploits of Elaine* (1915), *The Romance of Elaine* (1916), and *The Triumph of Elaine* (1916)—seem embarrassingly melodramatic beside the earlier stories. The difference between the two groups may be one of degree, but the Elaine sequence seems more blatantly exaggerated. Written to promote three Pathé film serials, these are not cliffhangers, in which the audience awaits the next episode to learn the resolution of the previous one, but a series of interconnected episodes, each complete in itself, designed to advance the overall story line. (The American edition of *The Romance of Elaine* contains a truncated version of the second and third serials; the British edition contains the complete serial. The third serial was also published complete only in the British edition.) Craig Kennedy's encounters with a masked archvillain, an Asian mastermind, a foreign spy, and a romantic alliance contrast strangely with his earlier dealings with financiers, Russian émigrés, and debutantes. Yet this film version, with the great detective portrayed on the screen by Arnold Daly, is the one many people recall when the name Craig Kennedy is mentioned.

A close reading of the text reveals that Reeve borrowed from himself in preparing these episodes for the screen. The termite that eats through the top of the safe in the initial episode of *The Exploits of Elaine* ("The Clutching Hand") came from "The Diamond Maker"; the discussion of tire tracks and fingerprints as means of identification in the third episode ("The Vanishing Jewels") is taken from "The Scientific Cracksman." Both of these earlier stories are in *The Silent Bullet* (1912).

The Film Mystery

Reeve's interest in motion pictures continued beyond these serial adventures of his hero. He wrote screenplays for several other films and based a 1918 pulp magazine serial ("Craig Kennedy and the Film Tragedy") on his own experiences in the film world. Published as a book three years later (*The Film Mystery*, 1921), it is more interesting for its portrayal of the methods of making silent films than as a detective story.

Following a period of decline in the quality of his work as well as in the popularity of Kennedy, Reeve was persuaded by Leo Margulies, a pulp magazine editor, to let another writer adapt some of his old, unsold Kennedy stories for the pulp market of the 1930's. As a result, four novellas by Ashley T. Locke appeared in *Popular Detective* from 1934 to 1935 and were collected under the title *Enter Craig Kennedy* in 1935. Reeve had hopes for Kennedy's renewed success, if only the right format could be found.

Nostalgia for the golden age of the serials made him revive his archvillain, the Clutching Hand (who had not died in 1915), for a 1934 novel. A new film serial followed in 1936.

Having retained creative control, Reeve wrote a new Kennedy novel in which the detective tried to determine the value of astrology in solving the mystery. The results were inconclusive, and the contest between science and pseudoscience was ruled a draw. Readers of 1936 were more sophisticated than those of 1910, and the novel was not a success.

Reeve's real contribution to the detective story lies

in his portraits of the scientific marvels of his day, the social settings, and the relationships between rich and poor, banker and burglar, society matron and ingenue, which live in his simple prose. Craig Kennedy still represents the science of detection as it was understood in a less sophisticated world.

J. Randolph Cox

Principal mystery and detective fiction

Craig Kennedy series: 1911-1920 • *The Poisoned Pen*, 1911; *The Silent Bullet*, 1912 (also known as *The Black Hand*); *The Dream Doctor*, 1914; *The Exploits of Elaine*, 1915; *The Gold of the Gods*, 1915; *The War Terror*, 1915 (also known as *Craig Kennedy, Detective*); *The Ear in the Wall*, 1916; *The Romance of Elaine*, 1916; *The Social Gangster*, 1916 (also known as *The Diamond Queen*); *The Triumph of Elaine*, 1916; *The Adventuress*, 1917; *The Treasure Train*, 1917; *The Panama Plot*, 1918; *The Soul Scar*, 1919

1921-1936 • *The Film Mystery*, 1921; *Craig Kennedy Listens In*, 1923; *Atavar: The Dream Dancer*, 1924; *Craig Kennedy on the Farm*, 1925; *The Boy Scouts' Craig Kennedy*, 1925; *The Fourteen Points: Tales of Craig Kennedy, Master of Mystery*, 1925; *Pandora*, 1926; *The Radio Detective*, 1926; *The Kidnap Club*, 1932; *The Clutching Hand*, 1934; *Enter Craig Kennedy*, 1935; *The Stars Scream Murder*, 1936

Nonseries novels: *Constance Dunlap, Woman Detective*, 1913; *Guy Garrick*, 1914; *The Master Mystery*, 1919; *The Mystery Mind*, 1921

Other major works

Novel: *Tarzan the Mighty*, 1928 (serial)

Screenplays: *The Exploits of Elaine*, 1914 (with Charles William Goddard); *The New Exploits of Elaine*, 1915; *The Romance of Elaine*, 1915; *The Hidden Hand*, 1917 (with Charles A. Logue); *The House of Hate*, 1918 (with Logue); *The Carter Case*, 1919 (with John W. Grey); *The Grim Game*, 1919 (with Grey); *The Master Mystery*, 1919 (with Logue); *The Tiger's Trail*, 1919 (with Logue); *One Million Dollars Reward*, 1920 (with Grey); *Terror Island*, 1920 (with Grey); *The Mystery Mind*, 1920 (with Grey); *The Clutching Hand*, 1926; *The Radio Detective*, 1926; *The Return of the Riddle Rider*, 1927; *Unmasked*, 1929 (with others)

Nonfiction: *The Golden Age of Crime*, 1931

Edited text: *The Best Ghost Stories*, 1930

Bibliography

Cox, J. Randolph. "A Reading of Reeve: Some Thoughts on the Creator of Craig Kennedy." *The Armchair Detective* 11 (January, 1978): 28-33. A critical examination of Reeve and his crime-solving chemistry professor.

Frank, Lawrence. *Victorian Detective Fiction and the Nature of Evidence: The Scientific Investigations of Poe, Dickens, and Doyle*. New York: Palgrave Macmillan, 2003. Study of Reeve's immediate precursors and influences in the representative of science being used to solve crimes.

Harwood, John. "Arthur B. Reeve and the American Sherlock Holmes." *The Armchair Detective* 10 (October, 1977): 354-357. Brief reading of Craig Kennedy's use of science in relation to Sherlock Holmes's own forensic scientific method.

Moskowitz, Sam. "Crime: From Sherlock to Spaceships." In *Strange Horizons: The Spectrum of Science Fiction*. New York: Scribner, 1976. Looks at Reeve's work at the intersection of mystery and science fiction.

Panek, LeRoy Lad. *The Origins of the American Detective Story*. Jefferson, N.C.: McFarland, 2006. Study of the beginnings and establishment of American detective-fiction conventions that focuses on the replacement of the police by the private detective and the place of forensic science in the genre; provides perspective for understanding Reeve's work.

Thomas, Ronald R. *Detective Fiction and the Rise of Forensic Science*. New York: Cambridge University Press, 1999. Study of the mutual influence of mystery authors and forensic scientists on each other that sheds light on Reeve's work. Bibliographic references and index.

KATHY REICHS

Born: Chicago, Illinois; 1950
Also wrote as K. J. Reichs; Kathleen J. Reichs
Types of plot: Police procedural; thriller

Principal series

Temperance Brennan, 1997-

Principal series character

Temperance "Tempe" Brennan, a forensic anthropologist, is single-minded in her pursuit of answers and unapologetically matter of fact, which often puts her in harm's way. Like her creator, Tempe divides her time between the United States and Canada, teaching and consulting on forensic anthropology. Her character, immediately appealing, develops in the series as details of her background are revealed. The reader gradually learns that Tempe is a recovering alcoholic; is estranged from her husband; worries about her winsome daughter Katy, who is in college; has a quirky sister, "Harry," whose son is troubled; and has a growing (and mutual) affection for Andrew Ryan. Tempe is driven and professional, sympathetic to the victims, unconventional in her social interactions, lacking in political savvy (and with no desire to acquire any), and all too oblivious of the danger in which she immerses herself when she takes her inquiries out of the forensics lab.

Contribution

Sometimes dubbed the "next Patricia Cornwell," Kathy Reichs writes books that are as much about the science of forensics as the fiction of mystery. Her efforts as a mystery writer are an extension of her successful career as a forensic anthropologist. The immediate popular appeal of her first novel, *Déjà Dead* (1997), was based on a fascinating character being placed in menacing, primitive situations. There is no doubt that timing was also a factor—the successes of mystery writer Patricia Cornwell and later *CSI* (began in 2000) and other mystery and television series dealing with forensic science showed a growing interest in this subject among members of the public.

Reichs had written extensively before penning *Déjà Dead*, but only articles in scientific journals and forensic science textbooks. Her first serious venture into fiction, *Déjà Dead* was immediately recognized by the publishing community as a success, earning a $1.2 million two-book deal with Scribner after a bidding war at the Frankfurt Book Fair and later winning the Arthur Ellis Award for best first novel.

USA Today suggested that Reichs was making more money writing about what she did as a forensic anthropologist than actually doing her job. Two years later, her second novel was also well received, and she began writing books at the rate of one per year. Her books have been translated into more than thirty languages and consistently make *The New York Times* best-seller list.

Biography

Kathleen Joan Reichs was born in 1950 in Chicago. Because Reichs writes about what she knows, it is likely that her character, Tempe Brennan, draws largely from the personality and experiences of her creator, but little is known about Reich's personal life. Reichs makes a concerted effort to keep the details of her life private, bristling at questions about her age and about her family and displaying a determination to keep her husband and three grown children out of the public eye. She may have developed this attitude for security reasons before becoming a popular author, when her work as a forensic anthropologist could have made her the focus of unwanted attention from the media or criminals while working on highly controversial and dangerous cases.

Reichs was one of four daughters. Her mother was a musician with the Chicago Symphony Orchestra and her father was a manager in the food industry. As a child, Reichs was always interested in science, although she did try her hand at writing when she was nine, authoring two books, according to the *Independent*: "One was a mystery and one was a romance and both were hideous."

At the age of nineteen, she married an attorney, Paul A. Reichs, while pursuing a bachelor's degree in

Kathy Reichs. (AP/Wide World Photos)

anthropology from American University. She graduated in 1971 and went on to Northwestern University, where she received her master's degree in 1972 and her doctorate in 1975, both in physical anthropology with an emphasis on bio-archaeology, and wrote a dissertation titled "Biological Variability and the Hopewell Phenomenon: An Interregional Approach."

Reichs began her career as an academician in the study and examination of very old remains, teaching at Northern Illinois University, University of Pittsburgh, and Concordia University. Ultimately, while teaching at the University of North Carolina at Charlotte, she found herself drawn to a more real-world application of her knowledge when the police showed up with bones. She continued to teach full-time and investigate as many as eighty cases per year. She began consulting as a forensic anthropologist for the Office of the Chief Medical Examiner in North Carolina in 1985, receiving her Diplomate American Board of Forensic Anthropology the following year.

In 1989, Reichs went to Montreal on the National Faculty Exchange to teach at Concordia and McGill and consult for the Laboratoire de Sciences Judiciaires et de Médecine Légale for the province of Quebec. She has kept this appointment, dividing her time between Quebec and North Carolina.

Reichs has appeared as an expert witness in multiple trials and testified before the United Nations Tribunal on Genocide in Rwanda. She has assisted Clive Snow in an exhumation in the area of Lake Atitlán in the highlands of southwest Guatemala. She was also a member of the Disaster Mortuary Operational Response Team assigned to assist at the World Trade Center disaster in 2001. She was engaged to identify the remains of dead soldiers from World War II, including the remains from the Tomb of the Unknown Soldier. She has also weighed in on controversial cases covered by the media, appearing on a panel of experts on *Larry King Live* (began in 1985) discussing the disappearance of Natalee Holloway. In addition, she has published in numerous scientific journals and monographic collections.

Analysis

In Kathy Reichs's mystery novels, it is undeniably true that art imitates life: Science and fiction are inextricably intertwined, just as they are in the author's life, and details in the novels come from cases in which she was involved or ones that caught her attention through the media. Reichs's writing graphically reveals the very elemental and gruesome elements of her real-life work as a forensic anthropologist, pairing an engaging and unselfconscious character with an expertise in the science and technological methods that are critical to finding the answers and solving the mystery. Reichs was quoted as saying that the appeal of forensic anthropology was that it bought the science and the mystery together.

Reichs's work is as much defined by her choice of

venue as by her lead characters, graphic descriptions, and twisted plots: Montreal and North Carolina provide dynamic backdrops for the twists of plot and escapades of Tempe Brennan. Reichs peppers the text with French and regional idioms to set the scene, an effort that is fairly effective for an audience ignorant of the language and culture but somewhat annoying to those who may be more familiar with them. Tempe's fictional résumé reads like a duplicate of Reichs's own experience, and the character's attributes come from the author herself. In fact, it is difficult to separate where the personality of Tempe ends and that of Reichs begins. Reichs says that her friends tell her that Tempe talks like her and that her abrasiveness and tendency to be a smart aleck are traits that the author possesses. However, the author says that Tempe's personal life is not like her own.

Reichs often focuses on the scientific details, emphasizing the process in a clinical way. The grotesque, gory detail in some forensic novels is muted in those of Reichs; however, she includes a lot of scientific details regarding bone measurement, analysis of blood spatter, cut marks, bite marks, the life cycle of bugs and carrion, degradation of body tissue and fatty acids, and DNA (deoxyribonucleic acid).

Déjà Dead

In her first novel, *Déjà Dead*, Reichs introduces Temperance Brennan, a self-contained, smart, and well-connected forensic anthropologist. Tempe's initial involvement in a seemingly straightforward case becomes much more, through Tempe's own tenacity and extreme coincidence (both of which come to be signatures in Reichs's novels). Tempe meets her match in a couple of police detectives: Andrew Ryan, to whom she is strongly attracted, and Claudel, whom she finds as annoying as Andrew is appealing.

Tempe immediately identifies the victim and, within days, stumbles on three other victims that she contends were all killed by the same person. Where others might be content to contain their involvement to the lab, she plays an active part in the investigation. She even goes with police to a suspect's residence and participates in chasing him through the city; however, the suspect gets away.

The story comes to a climax when she discovers that the man whom the police have in custody could not be the killer because his bite marks do not match the killer's and she is attacked by the real killer. A fight ensues, and she disables the killer but not before he fairly incapacitates her as well.

As with most of Reichs's novels, the plot for *Déjà Dead* was taken from a real-life case: Serge Archambault killed two women, then used one of his victim's bank cards, which enabled the police to track the transaction and arrest him. He later confessed to killing a third victim, dismembering her, and burying the parts in five different locations. Reichs described the case in an interview with the Home Box Office (HBO), relating the details of the dismemberment and how she helped with the identification of the suspect:

> It [the dismemberment] was quite unique and showed a lot of skill going directly into the joints. I was able to say you're looking for someone who knows something about anatomy—an orthopedic surgeon or butcher. And it turned out he was a butcher.

Death du Jour and Deadly Decisions

Death du Jour (1999) was also based on reality, using a number of details from deaths surrounding the Solar Temple cult. Reichs interweaves this plotline with an account of the research into a woman recommended for sainthood, an investigation taken from Reichs's own experience when the Catholic Archdiocese of Quebec asked Reichs to help confirm that the remains interred as Jeanne Le Ber were actually her. *Deadly Decisions* (2000) unveiled the world of gang wars, biker culture, and violence committed for profit, a criminal activity then gaining notoriety in the news.

Fatal Voyage

Fatal Voyage (2001) borrowed another story from the headlines, introducing the story of a college soccer team killed in the mysterious crash of a plane. Tempe is distraught when she arrives at the scene and discovers that her daughter might have been on the plane. She quickly discovers that her daughter is safe and sound with a friend, but her peace of mind is soon disturbed when Andrew Ryan turns up at the scene and informs her that his partner was on the plane, escorting a witness. When sorting out the wreckage and the body parts from that disaster, Tempe unearths an anomaly, a foot near the crash site that does not belong to anyone on the plane.

When the foot mysteriously disappears, Tempe is suddenly under fire and her competence is questioned. As she pursues her inquiry about the missing foot, she comes across some sort of lair with mysterious images and names of ancient bloodthirsty figures from myth and folklore. When one of her colleagues is killed, she becomes more determined to find out what it all means.

Ultimately, Tempe learns that there is a perversion of a gentleman's club, modeled on a Hellfire Club, operating in the area. They are responsible for a number of disappearances over the years as part of their sacrificial rituals. In an effort to bring the details to light, Tempe faces off with a murderer who has no compunction about killing to keep this secret society safe.

Grave Secrets

Human rights is the main theme in *Grave Secrets* (2002), making it obvious that Reichs puts a lot of herself into her work and a lot of her work into her art, not just the situations that Tempe is embroiled in but also the emotional reaction to these situations and the commitment to find answers to put the dead to rest and to ease the pain of the living. This is evident in the dedication: "For the innocents: Guatemala, 1962-1996; New York, New York; Arlington, Virginia; Shanksville, Pennsylvania; September 11, 2001. I have touched their bones. I mourn for them."

Tempe is sifting through remains in Guatemala, assisting the Fundación de Antropología Forense de Guatemala with the recovery and identification of remains of those who "disappeared" during the civil war from 1962 to 1996. The plot then takes a turn when remains are found in a septic tank; police suspect the remains are connected with a serial killer and may belong to one of four missing young women, among them the Canadian ambassador's daughter. Then a colleague, mistaken for Tempe, is shot and injured. Tempe fights bureaucracy, corruption, ego, and a bout of food poisoning to get at the truth.

Other works

Bare Bones (2003) looks at the victims of drug smuggling and animal poaching, and although it follows the same formula as Reichs's other works, it is more mundane. *Monday Mourning* (2004) also is a little tepid in comparison with Reich's other novels. Tempe unearths the bodies of three murdered women buried in the basement of a pizza parlor. *Cross Bones* (2005) was a bit of a departure from the previous Temperance Brennan novels, as it took place in the Middle East. It has been likened to Dan Brown's *The Da Vinci Code* (2003), no doubt because of the secondary plot revolving around the family of Jesus. The novel has an entirely different ambience, probably because Reichs has attempted to create a sense of place, much as she does with her settings in Montreal and North Carolina. *Break No Bones* (2006) is set in North Carolina, where a televangelist is a major contributor to a free clinic whose patients are turning up dead, missing organs.

The popularity of Reichs's work has led to a television series, *Bones* (began in 2005), based on the character of Temperance Brennan as well as the work and experiences of the author herself. Reichs consults for the series, in which Tempe works by day as a forensic anthropologist and writes novels as Kathy Reichs. The characters in the television show, however, bear little resemblance to the characters in her books other than sometimes having the same names.

Wendi Arant Kaspar

Principal mystery and detective fiction

Temperance Brennan series: *Déjà Dead*, 1997; *Death du Jour*, 1999; *Deadly Decisions*, 2000; *Fatal Voyage*, 2001; *Grave Secrets*, 2002; *Bare Bones*, 2003; *Monday Mourning*, 2004; *Cross Bones*, 2005; *Break No Bones*, 2006; *Bones to Ashes*, 2007

Other major works

Nonfiction: *Hominid Origins: Inquiries Past and Present*, 1983; *Forensic Osteology: Advances in the Identification of Human Remains*, 1986

Bibliography

Firrincili, Dan. "Kathy Reichs." *Current Biography* 67, no. 10 (October, 2006): 42-48. Contains an extensive analysis of the body of Reichs's novels. Also examines her work as a forensic anthropologist, including the more sensational aspects, and its impact on her writing.

Genge, Ngaire. *The Forensic Casebook: The Science*

of Crime Scene Investigation. New York: Ballantine Books, 2002. Deals with all aspects of forensic science as it pertains to investigation crime. Draws on interviews with forensic experts and police and contains many true-crime stories. Helps put Reichs's writings in context.

Houde, John. *Crime Lab: A Guide for Nonscientists*. 2d ed. Rollingbay, Wash.: Calico Press, 2006. A guide to forensics designed to be understood by the average nonscientist. Provides insight into Reichs's real-life world and that of her fictional character Tempe.

Reichs, Kathy. "Reichs's Literary Skullduggery: Forensic Anthropologist Digs into Mysteries with *Déjà Dead*." Interview by Bob Minzesheimer. *USA Today*, August 28, 1997, p. 06D. Interview with the author on her first novel and how her work informs her writing.

_______. The World of Kathy Reichs. http://www.kathyreichs.com Author's Web site includes brief biographical information, a curriculum vitae, a list of her fiction (with plot summaries and first chapters), and an overview of forensic science.

Stanford, Peter. "Ice Queen of Crime." *The Independent*, July 21, 2006, p. 20. A comparison and discussion of Kathy Reichs and Patricia Cornwell.

Wayman, E. R. "Forensic Anthropology." *Current Anthropology* 47, no. 4 (August, 2006): 567. Profile of Reichs that looks at her career and how she uses her knowledge in her writing.

Wecht, Cyril H., and John T. Rago, eds. *Forensic Science and Law: Investigative Applications in Criminal, Civil, and Family Justice*. Boca Raton, La.: CRC/Taylor & Francis, 2006. An explanation by a leading forensic expert of how the science is used in the legal system. Provides a perspective on the real-life world of forensic science and also on Reichs's work.

HELEN REILLY

Helen Kieran

Born: New York, New York; 1891
Died: Albuquerque, New Mexico; January 11, 1962
Also wrote as Kieran Abbey
Type of plot: Police procedural

Principal series

Inspector McKee, 1930-1962

Principal series character

Christopher McKee, a Scot who heads the Manhattan Homicide Squad, relies on his intuitive powers, keen observation, and ability to reason logically to solve his cases. He is a tough but fair person who if necessary will use bullying tactics to get information from a suspect. He admires attractive women but does not ignore them in his search for the guilty.

Contribution

When Helen Reilly began writing detective stories in the 1930's, most female writers followed the Had-I-But-Known style. In this type of plot, a young woman unwittingly becomes involved in a romance with a handsome but evil man. The author usually tells the story from the woman's point of view. Reilly wanted none of this. Instead, she wrote police procedurals, giving a detailed and realistic picture of a homicide squad in operation. Her female characters are not "flighty young things" but rather mature, competent persons. Reilly has been recognized by Howard Haycroft, an authority on the detective story, as one of the most important mystery writers of the 1930's.

Biography

Helen Reilly was born in New York City in 1891. Her father was John Michael Kieran, the president of

Hunter College, and her brother, John Kieran, produced the famous *Information Please* series, a radio program that showcased his encyclopedic learning. Helen married Paul Reilly, an artist and cartoonist, in 1914, before she completed her degree from Hunter. The couple had four daughters, two of whom, Ursula Curtiss and Mary McMullen, followed in their mother's footsteps as mystery writers. (Her brother also wrote a mystery.)

At the urging of her lifelong friend, William McFee, an eminent author, Reilly began writing detective stories. Almost all of her stories feature Inspector McKee and follow the formula of a detailed presentation of a homicide investigation, told from the point of view of the police. It is easy to understand Reilly's reason for writing this way—her stories were major successes. She wrote thirty-three mysteries in her thirty-year career, as well as three others under the pen name Kieran Abbey. The leading magazines of the time that published popular fiction, such as *The Saturday Evening Post* and *Collier's*, often featured her work. She served as president of the Mystery Writers of America in 1953.

She lived in Connecticut for a number of years; this state is the setting of *Certain Sleep* (1961). After her husband died in 1944, she returned to New York. Although she eventually moved from New York City to Santa Fe, New Mexico, to live with her daughter Ursula Curtiss and the latter's family, she always considered herself a native New Yorker. She died on January 11, 1962, continuing to write almost to the end of her life.

ANALYSIS

According to Ursula Curtiss, Helen Reilly was formed by her early life in New York City. It is in fact her knowledge of the city that lay behind two of the main features of her novels. First, she displayed a thorough understanding of the Manhattan Homicide Squad. It was her expertise in this area that enabled her to achieve success as an author of police procedurals. Her acquaintance with the city, however, was by no means confined to its seamy side. Her background was upper class, and her novels often display her insider's grasp of the workings of New York high society. Although her style lacked the unusual qualities of her plots, it nevertheless was brisk and efficient.

Modern popular mystery writers such as Elmore Leonard and John D. MacDonald are often tough and hard-boiled. In contrast with Victorian figures such as Arthur Conan Doyle, whose "scientific" detection carefully avoided much contact with actual criminals, these writers stress the sordid; in the modern school, there is no battle of the giants in the style of Sherlock Holmes against Professor Moriarty.

Readers of Dashiell Hammett will not need to be told that detective fiction's change from romance to realism began early. Although Hammett is the most famous of all writers of realistic detective fiction, he was not the only pioneer of this genre. Reilly, though she lacked the master touch of Hammett, exercised great influence on subsequent detective fiction through her extensive knowledge of police methods of investigation.

How carefully Reilly studied police procedure is obvious from an examination of her early novel *File on Rufus Ray* (1937). Here photographs of the actual evidence found by the police and used as exhibits are included in the book. Included are telegrams, a button inadvertently left at the murder scene, photographs of suspects, and a small packet of cigarette ashes. The reader is invited to follow along with the police as they proceed to the solution.

Reilly was not the only writer of the 1930's who did things like this: Several "crime kits," for example, were issued by the popular British writer Dennis Wheatley at roughly the same time. Reilly's police stories, however, differed entirely from Wheatley's. He was a "classic" writer, stressing pure deduction and bizarre details in the commission of the crime.

Reilly, on the other hand, was grimly realistic. Her Inspector McKee operates not through inspired hunches and supernatural powers of deduction but through hard work and persistent intelligence. Unlike detectives such as Agatha Christie's Hercule Poirot, whose "little grey cells" operate in sovereign indifference to those of anyone else, McKee does not do the job alone.

Quite the contrary, one of the realistic features of Reilly's stories is her constant emphasis on teamwork. McKee, though clearly first among equals, does not

solve his cases by himself. He discusses his solutions with Dr. Fernandez, the assistant medical examiner. On McKee's staff are Lucy Sturm, a nurse and undercover agent, and Officer Pierson, an accurate observer. Probably the most significant of McKee's assistants is Detective Todhunter, an unassuming person who is nevertheless a skilled detective.

Each of these persons is characterized briefly in a few bold strokes: Anyone who has read several of Reilly's McKee series novels will get a good picture of the team in action. Although her portrayal of these characters aided her in the factual approach to crime solving she was trying to achieve, she sometimes took a good thing too far. All of her McKee novels feature the same cast of police characters—they sometimes appear mere formulas repeated by rote.

Police work as Reilly describes it differs in many more ways from the methods of the great intuitive detectives such as Poirot and Holmes. On more than one occasion, force as well as intelligence is required to solve the case. Reilly's novels were written long before the *Miranda* decision and the modern emphasis on the rights of accused criminals. A key aspect of police work as Reilly tells the tale involves rousting the suspects and subjecting them to persistent, third-degree questioning. In *Certain Sleep*, for example, McKee does not let the fact that a suspect lies wounded in a hospital bed stop him from securing a confession. Although some of McKee's methods would probably get him into trouble with the modern United States Supreme Court, he does not employ brutality and is presented as a very sympathetic character.

Reilly's knowledge of police procedure was acquired in the same way she presented crimes as being solved: through detailed study. She was on excellent terms with the Manhattan Homicide Squad about which she wrote, and she was one of the few people not employed in police work who had access to its files. A number of her stories were in fact based on real cases. Regardless of whether a novel followed the details of an actual case, it always adhered to true-to-life police methods. *File on Rufus Ray* was unusual in the extent to which Reilly was prepared to go to give her readers a taste of an actual case. Her later novels did not offer a grasp of the evidence in so literal a way, because the expense involved proved too much for her publishers. This setback did not stop her from continuing her production of police procedurals; she wrote twenty-five more after *File on Rufus Ray.*

Lament for the Bride

The fact that Reilly emphasized the grinding, day-to-day character of a police investigation, avoiding its glamour, did not at all imply that her work avoided the upper classes. Quite the contrary, most of her novels involved crimes committed by the rich or socially prominent. As one might anticipate from her attitude to police work, her perception of these people was grimly realistic. Often, as with the business executive Howard Fescue in *Lament for the Bride* (1951), members of this class are presented as ruthlessly grasping for money and power. Reilly here relied once more on personal knowledge. She came from an upper-class family herself and was the daughter of the president of Hunter College. She does not, like Edith Wharton, describe the intricacies of New York society with full attention to every nuance. She nevertheless writes from real knowledge, and her treatment of the rich accordingly avoids the error of many popular novelists, who present them as virtual dwellers on a different planet.

Realism rather than fantasy has so far been claimed to be the leitmotif of Reilly's way of writing mysteries. This thesis receives reinforcement from another basic building block of her stories—her portrayal of women. Her heroines are not gossamer creatures who fall in love with the first handsome man to bestow a smile on them. Like Reilly herself, these women are fully competent. In *Lament for the Bride*, Judith Fescue is genuinely in love with Horace Fescue. She is far from unmindful, however, of his great wealth, and the reader quickly gathers that financial security was a reason for her marriage.

Reilly was well aware that in contrast to storybook romances, women as well as men frequently are capable of attraction to more than one person. As Judith Fescue attempts to deal with the kidnapping of her husband, she finds herself becoming increasingly interested in Charles Darlington, a family friend. When, at the novel's close, she is compelled to face some unpleasant truths about her husband, she does not collapse into hysterics or fall into a faint, as a Christie heroine would do. She calmly faces facts and departs with Charles.

Certain Sleep

Reilly's attitude toward her female characters remained constant to the end. In *Certain Sleep*, one of her last two novels, Jo Dobenny, a young career woman, finds herself involved in a complicated plot. An heiress has died through carbon-monoxide poisoning; a chief suspect turns out to be her former fiancé. Once more, the heroine does not become hysterical and leave the solution of her troubles to her friends of the opposite sex. She ably assists in her vindication and that of her one-time fiancé as well. At the book's close, it is strongly implied that the two of them will resume their relationship.

The weaknesses of Reilly's approach are also in evidence in this novel. "Realistic" plots, with their stress on detail, carry with them the danger of overemphasis on items of minor importance. In *Certain Sleep*, the plot turns on a complicated will, the provisions of which are presented in tedious fullness. No doubt realistic, but also more than slightly wearying.

Further, Reilly sometimes went to extreme lengths in her repetition of a winning recipe. One of the clues that enables McKee to discover the culprit in *Certain Sleep* is a cigarette left at the scene of the heiress's demise. As one recalls *File on Rufus Ray*, one cannot help wondering whether Reilly had a "thing" about ashes. Again, one of Jo Dobenny's romantic interests is named Charles; this time, however, unlike the Charles of *Lament for the Bride*, the heroine does not select him. Reilly's proved record of success led her to repeat detailed clues and names from book to book—surely a mistake.

More important than her minor failings, however, is the fact that Reilly's fiction, however much it followed a formula, gained justifiable attention. Her style, while not remarkable, was a good instrument for her purposes. She spent little time on description of anything other than evidence relevant to the case. She devoted scant attention to detailed characterization, except for her female leads. Even here, her view of character comes through the action presented rather than through descriptive passages or interior monologue. Much of the normal Reilly mystery takes place in dialogue: Her characters tend to speak in short exclamations.

All in all, Helen Reilly, though not a major writer, contributed significantly to the evolution of the detective story. Her early use of the police procedural has established for her a secure reputation.

Bill Delaney

Principal mystery and detective fiction

Inspector McKee series: 1930-1940 • *The Diamond Feather*, 1930; *Murder in the Mews*, 1931; *McKee of Centre Street*, 1934; *The Line-Up*, 1934; *Dead Man Control*, 1936; *Mr. Smith's Hat*, 1936; *All Concerned Notified*, 1939; *Dead for a Ducat*, 1939; *Death Demands an Audience*, 1940; *Murder in Shinbone Alley*, 1940; *The Dead Can Tell*, 1940

1941-1950 • *Mourned on Sunday*, 1941; *Three Women in Black*, 1941; *Name Your Poison*, 1942; *The Opening Door*, 1944; *Murder on Angler's Island*,

1945; *The Silver Leopard*, 1946; *The Farmhouse*, 1947; *Staircase 4*, 1949; *Murder at Arroways*, 1950

1951-1962 • *Lament for the Bride*, 1951; *The Double Man*, 1952; *The Velvet Hand*, 1953; *Tell Her It's Murder*, 1954; *Compartment K*, 1955 (also known as *Murder Rides the Express*); *The Canvas Dagger*, 1956; *Ding, Dong, Bell*, 1958; *Not Me, Inspector*, 1959; *Follow Me*, 1960; *Certain Sleep*, 1961; *The Day She Died*, 1962

Nonseries novels: *The Thirty-first Bullfinch*, 1930; *Man with the Painted Head*, 1931; *The Doll's Trunk Murder*, 1932; *File on Rufus Ray*, 1937; *Run with the Hare*, 1941 (as Abbey); *And Let the Coffin Pass*, 1942 (as Abbey); *Beyond the Dark*, 1944 (as Abbey)

Bibliography

DuBose, Martha Hailey, with Margaret Caldwell Thomas. *Women of Mystery: The Lives and Works of Notable Women Crime Novelists*. New York: St. Martin's Minotaur, 2000. Briefly mentions Reilly but elaborates on other Americans writing in the Golden Age of mysteries and thereby places her in the genre.

Haycraft, Howard. *Murder for Pleasure: The Life and Times of the Detective Story*. 1941. Rev. ed. New York: Carroll & Graf, 1984. Discusses the aesthetic appeal of tales of murder and intrigue; provides background for understanding Reilly.

Huang, Jim, ed. *They Died In Vain: Overlooked, Underappreciated, and Forgotten Mystery Novels*. Carmel, Ind.: Crum Creek Press, 2002. Reilly is among the authors discussed in this book about mystery novels that never found the audience they deserved.

Reynolds, William. "Seven 'Crimefiles' of the 1930's: The Purest Puzzles of the Golden Age." *Clues: A Journal of Detection* 1 (Fall/Winter, 1980): 42-53. Includes Inspector McKee in a list of Golden Age genre-defining puzzles and the detectives who solved them.

RUTH RENDELL

Born: London, England; February 17, 1930
Also wrote as Barbara Vine
Types of plot: Police procedural; psychological; inverted

Principal series

Inspector Wexford, 1964-

Principal series characters

Reginald Wexford is a middle-aged family man with two grown-up daughters. Despite his stolid appearance, he is an intuitive police inspector who works as much by empathy and by understanding the reasons behind a crime as by reason and procedure. His intuition often leads him to persevere with a case despite false leads or no evidence. He is well-read and often finds clues in the literature he reads.

Michael Burden, Wexford's assistant detective, by contrast, dresses neatly and tries to follow police procedure. He lacks Wexford's culture, but learns to be more sympathetic to the human follies and foibles that he encounters on a regular basis.

Contribution

Ruth Rendell moved both the detective and suspense genres toward serious fiction, as did Wilkie Collins in the nineteenth century. She does this not only with her well-crafted style but also with her concern for psychological analysis of both the criminal mind and the investigator's mind, often also encompassing the victim's mind. She structures her plots and subplots using a sophisticated parallelism, and there is a keen awareness of the context of literature within the plotting. There is, in other words, a conscious literariness as well as a conscious crafting in her fiction. Her awareness of contemporary British culture and its

Ruth Rendell. (Courtesy, Random House)

crosscurrents melds strongly with concrete description and accurate characterization. In achieving this, Rendell has shown younger writers the demands of the genre and how it can be developed.

Biography

Ruth Barbara Rendell was born Ruth Barbara Grasemann, the only daughter of two teachers, Arthur Grasemann, and his Swedish wife, Ebba Elise Kruse Grasemann. Although her parents shared an interest in literature and the arts, their relationship was fraught, causing their lonely daughter to escape into an imaginative world. She had been born in an outer suburb of London, then moved farther out to Loughton, Essex, at the age of seven. She attended the local high school and, after graduating, decided to pursue journalism rather than attend a university.

Rendell worked for some years on local newspapers but felt increasingly restricted by the medium. When she had to report on an after-dinner speech at a local tennis club, she wrote up the whole speech without attending, only to find later that the speaker had dropped dead half way through it. Needless to say, she resigned. She met a fellow journalist, Don Rendell, and they married in 1950. She left journalism altogether in 1953 to raise her son, Simon. She then began writing fiction, as much for her own amusement as anything, also extending her own education. She unsuccessfully submitted several short stories for publication. When she submitted a comic novel, an editor responded, asking her to turn it into a detective novel. Thus, in 1964, emerged Inspector Wexford.

Rendell immediately began developing Inspector Wexford as a series, but at the same time began writing suspense novels about ordinary people caught up in extraordinary inner compulsions and situations, the first one of which was published in 1965 as *To Fear a Painted Devil.* She wrote, and has continued to write, prolifically, alternating detective and suspense novels. In 1975, her marriage fell apart, and she and her husband were divorced; however, by 1977 they had reconciled and remarried. Rendell received an Edgar Award from the Mystery Writers of America for the short story "The Fallen Curtain" in 1975 and for "The New Girlfriend" in 1984, the 1976 Gold Dagger for fiction for *A Demon in My View* (1976), and the 1981 Arts Council National Book Award for genre fiction for *The Lake of Darkness* (1980). About this time, she and her husband purchased a fifteenth century cottage in Suffolk. This became her preferred place to write, though she also retained a place in London.

As Rendell's reputation grew on both sides of the Atlantic, she decided to start a third group of novels under the pen name of Barbara Vine, being her middle name plus the family name of a grandmother. These novels were also suspense novels but more historical, more exploratory of the tensions between culture and heredity, the past and the present—and also somewhat longer and a more demanding read. The first of these, *A Dark-Adapted Eye*, appeared in 1986. At this time, the Inspector Wexford novels were becoming somewhat of a chore for Rendell, written for popular demand. The novels became the basis for a successful television series starring George Barker.

Further recognition came in a series of literary awards. From the Crime Writers' Association, Rendell received Gold Daggers in 1987 for *A Fatal Inversion* and in 1991 for *King Solomon's Carpet* and a Cartier Diamond Dagger for lifetime achievement in 1991. She was also awarded a Companion of the British Empire (CBE) in 1996, and the next year was created Baroness Rendell of Babergh, partly through her political involvement in a number of causes, to sit as a Labour peer in the House of Lords. She was named a Grand Master by the Mystery Writers of America in 1997.

Analysis

The novels by which Ruth Rendell is best known are the Inspector Wexford series. These are set in the fictional town of Kingsmarkham, in the south of England. Wexford lives with his wife, Dora, and has two grown-up daughters. The elder of the daughters, Sylvia, along with her two daughters, moves back home after separating from her husband. Inspector Wexford is assisted by Michael Burden. Over the course of the series, both men earn promotions. The series develops the characters of the two men and their relationship with each other. At times, their families become involved in the plots.

One of the features of all Ruth Rendell's fiction is the use of parallel plots. At first, the plots appear unrelated, but gradually similarities emerge, and at certain crucial points, the plots actually cross. Sometimes both plots involve murder, but sometimes one plot centers on personal happenings in the lives of the two police officers in the Wexford series or other happenings in the victim's family. There is a marked degree of literary allusion, too, and sometimes the parallelism comes from literature. For this, Wexford needs to be a well-read man, which he is.

Later Wexford novels take on more social and political issues, overlaying the psychological and personal ones. Rendell deals with racism (*Simisola*, 1994), feminism (*An Unkindness of Ravens*, 1985), and ecological issues (*Road Rage*, 1997), though never taking a strong political stance in any of her novels. In fact, Rendell has been labeled antifeminist by some critics. Wexford himself goes through changes, suffering a heart attack, disillusionment, and an attempted seduction. His own experiences make him more understanding of the perpetrators' motives.

In the suspense novels, written both as Rendell and as Vine, a somewhat different scenario emerges. The police novels have a sense of order and a return to normality at their conclusions; the suspense novels have no such normative presence. Instead, perfectly normal people on the outside commit crimes of great passion and violence, often out of sexual obsessions. The novels develop an understanding of why they committed such apparently out-of-character crimes. The point of view varies, there being no central organizing police consciousness: Sometimes it is of the perpetrator, sometimes objective, sometimes multiple. Rendell is willing to leave many of her novels open-ended; others have a circular form.

From Doon with Death

From Doon with Death (1964) was the first of Rendell's novels to be published and the first of more than twenty Inspector Wexford books. The murder victim is a very ordinary former schoolteacher, Margaret ("Minna") Parsons, married to an equally ordinary husband. Rendell shows that in the past of even the most ordinary person can lie great passion, here revealed as the lesbian passion of "Doon," a former schoolfriend, now apparently well-married, though the marriage turns out to be sexless. At first Inspector Wexford cannot see that Doon could be a woman and gets caught up in the various adulterous relationships of the characters. Finally the discovery of old photos and letters and the correct interpretation of various literary clues and allusions lead to the correct solution. Wexford emerges as an interesting central character, though it took Rendell several more books to develop Burden and the two men's relationship.

A Sleeping Life

In *A Sleeping Life* (1978), the victim is in some ways quite similar to Margaret Parsons. Rhoda Comfrey is middle-aged, unmarried, and plain. Why should anyone want to murder her? Her only acquaintance appears to be an unlikely one, a successful novelist called Grenville West. The arrival of Sylvia, Wexford's older daughter and somewhat of a feminist, leads to a number of arguments, during one of which Wexford has to think of the possibility of women being truly successful only when disguised as men. He realizes Parsons and West are one and the same person. He goes on to find out that someone else who had fallen in love with West has made the same discovery. The murder is the result of thwarted passion, after all. Themes of appearance and reality, as well as feminist themes, mark the novel, as does Wexford's sympathy with both the victim and the perpetrator.

The Bridesmaid

The Bridesmaid (1989) is one of Rendell's suspense thrillers. The central characters are Philip Wardman and Senta, a beautiful schizophrenic woman. Wardman seems to be the model of respectability, living in an unmarried household composed of mother and sisters. However, Senta, in the form of a statue, becomes an embodiment of the ideal female with whom Wardman is obsessed. Senta herself is mentally sick and has already killed a former lover. She enters into a murder pact with Wardman, her part of which she fulfils. The novel closes as he realizes just what Senta has done and what he, too, has done, as they wait for their arrest. The novel explores, as do many others by Rendell, the powers of the subconscious that can no longer be contained by the outer forms of respectability.

The Keys to the Street

To some, *The Keys to the Street* (1996) is unsatisfactory and incomplete. To others, it is one of her most complex works, with the lack of completion a deliberate postmodern statement. It is symbolic in a Dickensian sense, in that an area of London, Regent's Park, is taken and its various aspects symbolized as aspects of modern urban life. The interweaving paths represent the plotlines of the characters' lives; the iron railings and gates, the exclusion and boundaries between one social class and another. The serial killing of a number of homeless men on these railings is less important than the hidden lives of those who frequent the park. One of these is Roman, who has "killed off" his former life and chosen to be a vagrant but then protects a young woman being stalked by a former abusive lover. Only the reader is aware of their real interconnectedness, again, as in a Charles Dickens novel.

A Dark-Adapted Eye

A Dark-Adapted Eye is the first of the Barbara Vine novels. It shows Rendell's thesis that the past often is much more powerful than the present in determining people's perceptions. A woman has been hanged for murdering her niece. Thirty-five years later, another niece tries to reconstruct the story as a piece of journalism. She has eyewitness statements and faded photos from which to work. The only way reality can be reconstructed is in a sort of jigsaw puzzle, as the reconstruction needs multiple viewpoints and interpretations.

David Barratt

Principal mystery and detective fiction

Inspector Wexford series: *From Doon with Death*, 1964; *A New Lease of Death*, 1967 (also known as *Sins of the Fathers*, 1970); *Wolf to the Slaughter*, 1967; *The Best Man to Die*, 1969; *A Guilty Thing Surprised*, 1970; *No More Dying Then*, 1971; *Murder Being Once Done*, 1972; *Some Lie and Some Die*, 1973; *Shake Hands Forever*, 1975; *A Sleeping Life*, 1978; *Means of Evil*, 1979; *Put On by Cunning*, 1981 (also known as *Death Notes*, 1981); *The Speaker of Mandarin*, 1983; *An Unkindness of Ravens*, 1985; *The Veiled One*, 1988; *Kissing the Gunner's Daughter*, 1992; *Simisola*, 1995; *Road Rage*, 1997; *Harm Done*, 1999; *The Babes in the Wood*, 2002; *End in Tears*, 2005

Nonseries novels: *To Fear a Painted Devil*, 1965; *Vanity Dies Hard*, 1966 (also known as *In Sickness and in Health*); *The Secret House of Death*, 1968; *One Across, Two Down*, 1971; *The Face of Trespass*, 1974; *A Demon in My View*, 1976; *A Judgement in Stone*, 1977; *Make Death Love Me*, 1979; *The Lake of Darkness*, 1980; *Master of the Moor*, 1982; *The Killing Doll*, 1984; *The Tree of Hands*, 1984; *Live Flesh*, 1986; *Talking to Strange Men*, 1987; *Heartstones*, 1987; *The Bridesmaid*, 1989; *Going Wrong*, 1990; *The Crocodile Bird*, 1993; *The Keys to the Street*, 1996; *A Sight for Sore Eyes*, 1998; *Thornapple*, 1998; *Adam and Eve and Pinch Me*, 2001; *The Rottweiler*, 2003; *Thirteen Steps Down*, 2004; *The Water's Lovely*, 2006; *The Thief*, 2006

Nonseries novels (as Vine): *A Dark-Adapted Eye*, 1986; *A Fatal Inversion*, 1987; *The House of Stairs*, 1988; *Gallowglass*, 1990; *King Solomon's Carpet*, 1991; *Asta's Book*, 1993 (also known as *Anna's Book*); *No Night Is Too Long*, 1994; *The Brimstone Wedding*, 1995; *In the Time of His Prosperity*,

1995; *The Chimney-sweeper's Boy*, 1998; *Grasshopper*, 2000; *The Blood Doctor*, 2002; *The Minotaur*, 2005

Short fiction: *The Fallen Curtain, and Other Stories*, 1976; *The Fever Tree, and Other Stories*, 1982; *The New Girlfriend, and Other Stories of Suspense*, 1985; *Collected Short Stories*, 1987; *The Copper Peacock, and Other Stories*, 1991; *Blood Lines: Long and Short Stories*, 1996; *Piranha to Scurfy, and Other Stories*, 2000

Other major works

Nonfiction: *Ruth Rendell's Suffolk*, 1989 (with Paul Bowden); *Undermining the Central Line*, 1989

Edited texts: *Dr. Thorne*, 1991 (by Anthony Trollope); *The Reason Why: An Anthology of the Murderous Mind*, 1995

Bibliography

Bakerman, Jane S. "Ruth Rendell." In *Ten Women of Mystery*, edited by Earl Bargainnier. Bowling Green, Ohio: Bowling Green University Press, 1981. A sound assessment of Rendell's work, set against a number of other female writers.

Dubose, Martha Hailey, with Margaret Caldwell Thomas. *Women of Mystery: The Lives and Works of Notable Women Crime Novelists*. New York: St. Martin's Minotaur, 2000. A look at female mystery writers from Mary Roberts Rinehart to cozy writers such as Agatha Christie to modern writers such as Ruth Rendell. Essay on Rendell calls her "a writer for our paranoid times." Contains list of works through 1999.

Lindsay, Elizabeth Blakesley, ed. *Great Women Mystery Writers*. 2d ed. Westport, Conn.: Greenwood Press, 2007. Contains an essay that discusses Rendell's work and her life and their interactions.

Munt, Sally R. *Murder by the Book? Feminism and the Crime Novel*. London: Routledge, 1994. Tries to place Rendell in the feminist debate over this genre. Munt poses a number of crucial questions about the genre as a whole and why it has been so much used in antiestablishment writing.

Reynolds, Moira Davison. *Women Authors of Detective Series: Twenty-one American and British Authors, 1900-2000*. Jefferson, N.C.: McFarland, 2001. Examines the life and work of major female mystery writers, including Rendell.

Rowland, Susan. *From Agatha Christie to Ruth Rendell: British Women Writers in Detective and Crime Fiction*. London: Palgrave, 2001. This is the best introduction to Rendell. Rowland covers forty-two novels by various crime writers, putting them within the context of their lives and culture. She examines the drift toward the gothic as well as toward feminist stances. An interview with Rendell is included.

Symons, Julian. *Bloody Murder: From the Detective Story to the Crime Novel*. London: Viking, 1985. An overall survey of the genre, but pp. 177-180 give a detailed critique of Rendell's place in the wider picture.

JOHN RHODE

Cecil John Charles Street

Born: Place unknown; 1884

Died: Eastbourne, Sussex, England; December 8, 1964

Also wrote as Miles Burton; F.O.O.; I.O.; Cecil Waye

Types of plot: Amateur sleuth; private investigator; thriller

PRINCIPAL SERIES

Lancelot Priestley, 1925-1961

Desmond Merrion and Henry Arnold, 1930-1960

PRINCIPAL SERIES CHARACTERS

DR. LANCELOT PRIESTLEY, a great ratiocinator in the tradition of Sherlock Holmes, solves his cases by analysis rather than investigation and relies on others to bring him the facts for analysis. An academic chemist by training, he is retired from the academic life before the series begins. No wife is mentioned in the series, although a daughter, April, appears in the first book, *The Paddington Mystery* (1925).

JIMMY WAGHORN, honest, easygoing, and fair, rises rapidly through the ranks of the Criminal Investigation Department at Scotland Yard, eventually becoming a superintendent. Only once (in *Twice Dead*, 1960) does he solve a case without being given at least a strong hint from Priestley, but he is far from being the sort of official bungler encountered by Sherlock Holmes or Philo Vance.

DESMOND MERRION is a private detective and a more active participant in his cases than is Priestley. In Miles Burton's World War II novels, Merrion becomes an intelligence agent. Although married, Merrion spends long periods away from home investigating crimes. Mrs. Merrion has an active role in some of the novels of this series (for example, *Heir to Murder*, 1953, *Murder in Absence*, 1954, and *Found Drowned*, 1956), but like Superintendent Waghorn's wife, Diana, in the later books of the Priestley series, she is all talk without insight.

INSPECTOR HENRY ARNOLD is a more active police detective than either of Priestley's superintendents, and he and Merrion are more active partners in unmasking criminals. Merrion and Arnold have an engaging relationship that involves constant bickering and differences of opinion but with an underlying mutual respect.

CONTRIBUTION

The detective novels written by Cecil John Charles Street under the pseudonym John Rhode are books of detective reasoning almost to the exclusion of action. The murder has usually been committed before the book begins. Dr. Lancelot Priestley solves the crime by deductive logic on the basis of information brought to him by his friends at Scotland Yard. He frequently gives Scotland Yard hints that open the appropriate lines of investigation. In his day, Rhode was often cited as one of the leading figures of British detective fiction, but he has not retained his popularity from the Golden Age quite so well as some of the others. His greatest achievement is in meticulously observing the rules of fair play even in the most complex situations involving arcane knowledge.

The books that Street wrote under the name Miles Burton are in general regarded as weaker than those he wrote as Rhode. Jacques Barzun and Wendell Hertig Taylor suggest, however, that the Burton books "tend to be wittier and less dependent on mechanical devices, as well as more concerned with scenery and character. They are often less solid, too, the outcome being sometimes pulled out of a hat rather than demonstrated." Another difference is that Merrion and Arnold operate in the country, while Priestley is an urbane Londoner.

BIOGRAPHY

John Rhode, born as Cecil John Charles Street and also known as John Street, was extremely reticent about his private life. He refused to be listed in *Who's Who*, and many reference works do not give the exact date of his birth or death (several are in error about the year of his death). An indication of how secretive a person Street was and how carefully he separated his various personalities is the fact that he used the title *Up the Garden Path* for both a Burton book published in 1941 and a Rhode book published in 1949. He even invented a fictitious year of birth for Burton, whose books he never admitted were his. He is said to have been a career officer, a major, in the British army and a field officer in both World War I and World War II. Awarded the Order of the British Empire, he also received a Military Cross, a fairly high distinction. Street's firsthand experience of war may perhaps even be credited with directing him to literary pursuits because his first few books were studies of gunnery and a war novel (*The Worldly Hope*, 1917) published under the pseudonym F.O.O. (for Forward Observation Officer) while World War I was still being fought. Curiously, no trace of Street appears in *Quarterly Army List* of this period or of later periods. Immediately after the war, he tried his hand at thrillers before launching his two highly successful series. Between the wars, Street was stationed in Ireland and Central Europe, and while maintaining a steady production of two novels a year in each of his series, he also published a number of political works that grew out of his firsthand experience. His intelligence experience during World War II was put to use in such Desmond Merrion novels of the war years as *Up the Garden Path* and *Situation Vacant* (1946). He continued to write at a steady pace into his seventies and died at a hospital near his Seaford home in Sussex.

Analysis

The John Rhode novels are essentially locked-room mysteries. Rhode did not practice the hermetically sealed locked-room mystery of John Dickson Carr, however, so the device is primarily useful for circumscribing the incidents of the story. Understanding how the murderer had access to the victim is usually less the focus of interest than is the cause of death. Rhode was a master at finding unusual causes of death and was particularly adept at developing new variations on poisoning. Rhode is also justly famous for the atmospheric presentation of special settings such as the antique car rally of *The Motor Rally Mystery* (1933) and the séances of *The Claverton Mystery* (1933).

The Murders in Praed Street

Both Ellery Queen and Melvyn Barnes have singled out *The Murders in Praed Street* (1928) as one of Rhode's best books because it shows how the story of serial killings can avoid monotony. Barzun and Taylor, on the other hand, criticize the book because Priestley blunders conspicuously into the action of the case, getting himself nearly gassed in the process. If not necessarily better, Priestley is certainly more characteristic (and Rhode is more comfortable) when he has ceased such active participation in cases.

Death in Harley Street

A good example of Rhode at his best and an excellent illustration of his method of fair play is *Death in Harley Street* (1946). The death mentioned in the title has already occurred before the story opens. The police have dismissed as a rather bizarre accident the death of Dr. Richard Knapp Mawsley, who seems to have injected himself with a fatal dose of strychnine. Someone might have entered the consulting room after hours, but it is hardly credible that Mawsley would have accepted an injection of strychnine without putting up a struggle. From the police description of the scene and of the events leading up to Mawsley's death, Priestley is able to posit the existence of a missing letter and hypothesize (accurately, as it develops) its contents. This dazzling demonstration of his reasoning powers is a red herring, however, for it supports the theory of suicide, which is no more accurate than the official coroner's verdict of accidental death. Early in the book, Priestley theorizes that this case must be a special instance of a violent death that cannot be explained as suicide, as accident, or as murder. While the police are pursuing missing wills and the whereabouts of the butler on his night out, Priestley uncovers a secret relationship based on facts and attitudes from Mawsley's past that are clearly indicated to the reader. Priestley's theory of the special nature of this death is vindicated at last when he administers a poison to himself to prove how the death occurred. Most readers will be less fastidious about terminology than Priestley and will count the final explanation as indicating murder, however subtle the guise.

THE DR. LANCELOT PRIESTLEY SERIES

The Priestley series evolves in several ways over its thirty-six-year span. Superintendent Hanslet of the earlier novels retires, and the younger, more energetic, and somewhat more naïve Jimmy Waghorn replaces him and later rises to the rank of superintendent himself. On the other hand, this change of personnel does not alter Priestley's working procedures. In addition, his Saturday dinners continue to be attended by Hanslet and Waghorn. These dinners are also attended by Dr. Mortimer Oldland in the later books. The primary way the books change is that Priestley becomes a more sedentary person over time. Like Nero Wolfe, he seldom leaves home in these later books. Because he was already elderly at the start of the series, this is hardly surprising, but he reveals his true character when he ceases pursuing facts entirely and participates in the cases only as a disinterested analyst. A third way in which the books in this series change is, unfortunately, that after World War II they become somewhat more mechanical and less imaginative.

It is often remarked that Rhode had no gift for characterization; Nicholas Blake has called Rhode's characters ciphers. Although Priestley is allowed as a grand exception to the generalization, there are problems of two sorts with this appraisal. The type of mystery that Rhode wrote is concerned primarily with an intellectual puzzle. Well-rounded characterization is not merely unnecessary, it is inappropriate. The unimportance of characterization to the form in which Rhode was working is perhaps indicated by the inconsistencies in the names of some of his major continuing characters. Dr. Oldland witnesses a will as Sidney Oldland in *The Claverton Mystery*, but his given name appears to be Mortimer in *Death at Breakfast* (1936). Even Priestley himself absentmindedly initials a note to his secretary with "J. P." in *The Ellerby Case* (1926). Although the character of Superintendent Hanslet appears throughout the series, his given name is never revealed. Within the limitations of his genre, however, Rhode's characterizations are more than competent. Except for a few later books in which he is clearly not writing up to his best standard (for example, *The Fourth Bomb*, 1942; *By Registered Post*, 1953; and *The Fatal Pool*, 1960), the characterizations are various and have a realistic probability in context. No murderer is ever, for example, revealed as having committed his crime because of secret passions about which the reader could not have known anything.

On the other hand, the characterization of Priestley is not well rounded, nor could it have been. Priestley is not so much a character as a symbol for rational deduction. What seem at first glance to be quirks of character prove on analysis to be part of the theory of detection embodied by the books. For example, Priestley's cavalier willingness to let some criminals get away with murder is really Street's comment on the art of John Rhode rather than Rhode's comment on the morals of Lancelot Priestley. Street does not mean that it ought to be possible to get away with murder, but in fact it is often possible to do so in the real world. When Priestley dismisses the murderer at the end of *Death in Harley Street* with the bland advice that he "not carry [his] experiments in toxicology any further," Rhode is acknowledging that it would be extremely difficult to convict the guilty party in this case, and Street is allowing the reader the pleasure of being an aesthetic observer of the ethical dilemma. No comment on the real world is intended.

Priestley's occasional regret at the passing of the old order is, like his willingness to allow an artful murderer to get away with his crime, less personal characterization than a necessary part of the nostalgia of the puzzle mystery as a genre. As David I. Grossvogel has said of Agatha Christie's first readers, Rhode's first readers wished to "purchase at the cost of a minor and passing disturbance the comfort of knowing that the disturbance was *contained*, and that at the end of the story the world they imagined would be continued in its innocence and familiarity." As with Christie, this tenuous keeping of sordid realities at arm's length could not survive the devastations of World War II, as Rhode's uncertain tone and inconsistent performance in the novels of the 1950's testify.

When the setting is outside London, Priestley can receive only occasional reports on the progress of a case. When this is so, as in *Death of a Godmother* (1955), the fact that the brief scenes in which he appears are intrusive also helps rebut the familiar understanding of Priestley as a triumph of characterization.

Priestley is a brilliant idea, but he is a triumph of plot and point of view, not of characterization.

In addition to the more than six dozen novels about Priestley, there are three short stories, "The Elusive Bullet," "The Vanishing Diamond," and "The Purple Line," the first two written for original anthologies. "The Elusive Bullet" is the only work in which Priestley gets kissed (he does offer a deathbed kiss of peace in *Tragedy on the Line*, 1931), and even here he is only being thanked for resolving a case.

The Secret of High Eldersham

The Desmond Merrion and Henry Arnold series by Miles Burton was an attempt by Rhode to be more lighthearted. Although for the most part he succeeded, the general standard of the series falls somewhat behind that of the Priestley books. One of the best novels in this series is the first, *The Secret of High Eldersham* (1930). This tale of witchcraft, murder, and smuggling shows a nice balance of action and analysis. Merrion meets his wife in this story, but Inspector Arnold has yet to appear.

Other works

Despite Rhode's association with puzzle mysteries both as Rhode and as Burton, he began his career in detective fiction as Street with a number of thrillers, *A.S.F.: The Story of a Great Conspiracy* (1924), *The Double Florin* (1924), and *The Alarm* (1925). Barzun and Taylor note *A.S.F.* as a particularly effective 1920's thriller in its depiction of the cocaine traffic. Rhode's reticence about his personal life extended to his craft as a writer. The appendix to *The Floating Admiral* (1931), which was written a section at a time by the members of the Detection Club, includes the solution each writer had in mind at the time he wrote his section, but Rhode gives a straightforward summary of his solution without theoretical asides. His book-length study of a real murder in *The Case of Constance Kent* (1928) is highly regarded for its elucidation of the case, but it offers no insight into Rhode's workings as a mystery writer. He did, however, provide a useful history of the Detection Club in the introduction to an anthology called *Detective Medley* (1939).

Only one mystery novel by Rhode or Burton has been made into a film. In 1936, *The Murders in Praed Street* became *Twelve Good Men* under the direction of Ralph Ince. The film stars Henry Kendall, Nancy O'Neil, Joyce Kennedy, and Percy Parsons. The writers Frank Launder and Sidney Gilliat did an excellent job of providing a clear and suspenseful screenplay, yet Priestley does not appear, a testament perhaps to the extent to which he is an observer of rather than a participant in the main action of the novels in which he appears.

Edmund Miller

Principal mystery and detective fiction

Lancelot Priestley series: 1925-1930 • *The Paddington Mystery*, 1925; *Dr. Priestley's Quest*, 1926; *The Ellerby Case*, 1926; *The Murders in Praed Street*, 1928; *Tragedy at the Unicorn*, 1928; *The Davidson Case*, 1929 (also known as *Murder at Bratton Grange*); *The House on Tollard Ridge*, 1929; *Peril at Cranbury Hall*, 1930; *Pinehurst*, 1930 (also known as *Dr. Priestley Investigates*)

1931-1940 • *The Hanging Woman*, 1931; *Tragedy on the Line*, 1931; *Dead Men at the Folly*, 1932; *Mystery at Greycombe Farm*, 1932 (also known as *The Fire at Greycombe Farm*); *The Claverton Mystery*, 1933 (also known as *The Claverton Affair*); *The Motor Rally Mystery*, 1933 (also known as *Dr. Priestley Lays a Trap*); *The Venner Crime*, 1933; *Poison for One*, 1934; *Shot at Dawn*, 1934; *The Robthorne Mystery*, 1934; *Hendon's First Case*, 1935; *Mystery at Olympia*, 1935 (also known as *Murder at the Motor Show*); *The Corpse in the Car*, 1935; *Death at Breakfast*, 1936; *In Face of the Verdict*, 1936; *Death in the Hop Fields*, 1937 (also known as *The Harvest Murder*); *Death on the Board*, 1937 (also known as *Death Sits on the Board*); *Proceed with Caution*, 1937 (also known as *Body Unidentified*); *Invisible Weapons*, 1938; *The Bloody Tower*, 1938 (also known as *Tower of Evil*); *Death on Sunday*, 1939 (also known as *The Elm Tree Murder*); *Death Pays a Dividend*, 1939; *Death on the Boat-Train*, 1940; *Murder at Lilac Cottage*, 1940

1941-1950 • *Death at the Helm*, 1941; *They Watched by Night*, 1941 (also known as *Signal for Death*); *The Fourth Bomb*, 1942; *Dead on the Track*, 1943; *Men Die at Cyprus Lodge*, 1943; *Death Invades the Meeting*, 1944; *Vegetable Duck*, 1944 (also known as *Too Many Suspects*); *The Bricklayer's Arms*, 1945 (also known as *Shadow of a Crime*); *Death in Harley Street*, 1946; *The Lake House*, 1946 (also known as *The Secret of the Lake House*); *Death of an Author*, 1947; *Nothing but the Truth*, 1947 (also known as *Experiment in Crime*); *The Paper Bag*, 1948 (also known as *The Links in the Chain*); *The Telephone Call*, 1948 (also known as *Shadow of an Alibi*); *Blackthorn House*, 1949; *Up the Garden Path*, 1949 (also known as *The Fatal Garden*); *Family Affairs*, 1950 (also known as *The Last Suspect*); *The Two Graphs*, 1950 (also known as *Double Identities*)

1951-1961 • *Dr. Goodwood's Locum*, 1951 (also known as *The Affair of the Substitute Doctor*); *The Secret Meeting*, 1951; *Death at the Dance*, 1952; *Death in Wellington Road*, 1952; *By Registered Post*, 1953 (also known as *The Mysterious Suspect*); *Death at the Inn*, 1953 (also known as *The Case of the Forty Thieves*); *Death on the Lawn*, 1954; *The Dovebury Murders*, 1954; *Death of a Godmother*, 1955 (also known as *Delayed Payment*); *The Domestic Agency*, 1955 (also known as *Grave Matters*); *An Artist Dies*, 1956 (also known as *Death of an Artist*); *Open Verdict*, 1956; *Death of a Bridegroom*, 1957; *Robbery with Violence*, 1957; *Death Takes a Partner*, 1958; *Licensed for Murder*, 1958; *Murder at Derivale*, 1958; *Three Cousins Die*, 1959; *The Fatal Pool*, 1960; *Twice Dead*, 1960; *The Vanishing Diary*, 1961

Desmond Merrion and Inspector Henry Arnold series (as Burton): 1930-1940 • *The Secret of High Eldersham*, 1930 (also known as *The Mystery of High Eldersham*); *The Menace on the Downs*, 1931; *The Three Crimes*, 1931; *Death of Mr. Gantley*, 1932; *Death at the Cross-Roads*, 1933; *Fate at the Fair*, 1933; *Tragedy at the Thirteenth Hole*, 1933; *The Charabanc Mystery*, 1934; *To Catch a Thief*, 1934; *The Devereaux Court Mystery*, 1935; *The Milk-Churn Murders*, 1935 (also known as *The Clue of the Silver Brush*); *Death in the Tunnel*, 1936 (also known as *Dark Is the Tunnel*); *Murder of a Chemist*, 1936; *Where Is Barbara Prentice?*, 1936 (also known as *The Clue of the Silver Cellar*); *Death at the Club*, 1937 (also known as *The Clue of the Fourteen Keys*); *Murder in Crown Passage*, 1937 (also known as *The Man with the Tattooed Face*); *Death at Low Tide*, 1938; *The Platinum Cat*, 1938; *Death Leaves No Card*, 1939; *Mr. Babbacombe Dies*, 1939; *Death Takes a Flat*, 1940 (also known as *Vacancy with Corpse*); *Mr. Westerby Missing*, 1940; *Murder in the Coalhole*, 1940 (also known as *Written in Dust*)

1941-1950 • *Death of Two Brothers*, 1941; *Up the Garden Path*, 1941 (also known as *Death Visits Downspring*); *This Undesirable Residence*, 1942 (also known as *Death at Ash House*); *Dead Stop*, 1943; *Murder, M.D.*, 1943 (also known as *Who Killed the Doctor?*); *Four-Ply Yarn*, 1944 (also known as *The Shadow on the Cliff*); *The Three-Corpse Trick*, 1944; *Early Morning Murder*, 1945 (also known as *Accidents Do Happen*); *Not a Leg to Stand On*, 1945; *Situation Vacant*, 1946; *The Cat Jumps*, 1946; *A Will in the Way*, 1947; *Heir to Lucifer*, 1947; *Death in Shallow Water*, 1948; *Devil's Reckoning*, 1948; *Death Takes the Living*, 1949 (also known as *The Disappearing Parson*); *Look Alive!*, 1949; *A Village Afraid*, 1950; *Ground for Suspicion*, 1950

1951-1960 • *Beware Your Neighbor*, 1951; *Murder Out of School*, 1951; *Murder on Duty*, 1952; *Heir to Murder*, 1953; *Something to Hide*, 1953; *Murder in Absence*, 1954; *Unwanted Corpse*, 1954; *A Crime in Time*, 1955; *Murder Unrecognized*, 1955; *Death in a Duffle Coat*, 1956; *Found Drowned*, 1956; *The Chinese Puzzle*, 1957; *The Moth-Watch Murder*, 1957; *Bones in the Brickfield*, 1958; *Death Takes a Detour*, 1958; *A Smell of Smoke*, 1959; *Return from the Dead*, 1959; *Death Paints a Picture*, 1960; *Legacy of Death*, 1960

Nonseries novels: *A.S.F.: The Story of a Great Conspiracy*, 1924 (also known as *The White Menace*); *The Double Florin*, 1924; *The Alarm*, 1925; *Mademoiselle from Armentières*, 1927; *The Hardway Diamonds Mystery*, 1930 (as Burton); *The Floating Admiral*, 1931 (with others); *Murder at the Moorings*, 1932 (as Burton); *Ask a Policeman*, 1933 (with others); *Drop to His Death*, 1939 (with Carter Dickson; also known as *Fatal Descent*); *Night Exercise*, 1942 (also known as *Dead of the Night*)

Other major works

Novel: *The Worldly Hope*, 1917 (as F.O.O.)

Nonfiction: *The Making of a Gunner*, 1916 (as F.O.O.); *With the Guns*, 1916 (as F.O.O.); *The Admin-*

istration of Ireland, 1921 (as I.O.); *Ireland in 1921*, 1922 (as Street); *Hungary and Democracy*, 1923 (as Street); *Rhineland and Ruhr*, 1923 (as Street); *East of Prague*, 1924 (as Street); *The Treachery of France*, 1924 (as Street); *A Hundred Years of Printing: 1795-1895*, 1927 (as Street); *Lord Reading*, 1928 (as Street); *Slovakia Past and Present*, 1928 (as Street); *The Case of Constance Kent*, 1928 (as Street); *President Masaryk*, 1930 (as Street; also known as *Thomas Masaryk of Czechoslovakia*)

Edited texts: *Detective Medley*, 1939 (as Street; also known as *Line-Up: A Collection of Crime Stories by Famous Mystery Writers*)

Translations (as Street): *French Headquarters: 1915-1918*, 1924 (by Jean de Pierrefeu); *Vauban: Builder of Fortresses*, 1924 (by Daniel Halévy); *The Life and Voyages of Captain Cook*, 1929 (by Maurice Thiéry; also known as *Captain Cook: Navigator and Discoverer*)

Bibliography

Barnes, Melvyn. "John Rhode." In *Twentieth Century Crime and Mystery Writers*, edited by John M. Reilly. 2d ed. New York: St. Martin's Press, 1985. Combined biography, bibliography, and criticism of Rhode and his works.

Barzun, Jacques, and Wendell Hertig Taylor. *A Catalogue of Crime*. Rev. ed. New York: Harper & Row, 1989. List, with commentary, of the authors' choices for the best or most influential examples of crime fiction; provides perspective on Rhode's works.

Cuppy, Will. Introduction to *World's Great Detective Stories: American and English Masterpieces*, edited by Will Cuppy. Cleveland: World, 1943. Rhode is included in this anthology of detective fiction by recognized masters in the genre, and the introduction justifies his inclusion in their rarefied company.

Knight, Stephen Thomas. *Crime Fiction, 1800-2000: Detection, Death, Diversity*. New York: Palgrave Macmillan, 2004. This work looks at the history of the detective novel, containing a chapter on club-puzzle forms, which includes locked-room mysteries such as those of Rhode.

Routley, Erik. *The Puritan Pleasures of the Detective Story: A Personal Monograph*. London: Gollancz, 1972. Idiosyncratic but useful discussion of crime fiction in terms of nominally puritanical ideology; sheds light on Rhode's work.

Steinbrunner, Chris, and Otto Penzler, eds. "John Rhode." In *Encyclopedia of Mystery and Detection*. New York: McGraw-Hill, 1976. Examines Rhode's distinctive contribution to genre fiction.

CRAIG RICE

Georgiana Ann Randolph

Born: Chicago, Illinois; June 5, 1908

Died: Los Angeles, California; August 28, 1957

Also wrote as Ruth Malone; Daphne Sanders; Michael Venning

Types of plot: Hard-boiled; amateur sleuth; psychological; comedy caper; cozy

Principal series

John J. Malone, 1939-1967
Melville Fairr, 1942-1944
Bingo Riggs and Handsome Kusak, 1943-1958

Principal series characters

John Joseph Malone is a Chicago criminal lawyer whose idea of dressing up involves changing his necktie and brushing the cigar ashes from his suit front. When not in his office, he may be found in Joe the Angel's City Hall Bar, drinking rye with a beer chaser.

Jake Justus, a press agent turned saloon owner (having won it on a bet), stays barely sober and barely free of the law in spite of (or because of) his friendship with Malone.

HELENE BRAND JUSTUS, Jake's wife, is a wealthy heiress, a stunning blonde with a patrician beauty, who has an ability to drive men mad with her driving—and a knack for keeping her husband and Malone one step ahead of the law.

DANIEL VON FLANAGAN is an Irish cop who is only trying to do his duty. He has two goals in life: not to be stereotyped as an Irish cop (the "von" was added to his name legally) and to retire "next year" so that he will never have to deal with Malone and the Justuses again.

BINGO RIGGS, who works as a street photographer, is short and skinny, with sandy hair, a sharp, thin face, and a gleam in his eye that no one notices.

HANDSOME KUSAK, Bingo's partner and a professional photographer, is six feet, one inch tall with wavy, dark hair. He never forgets a fact, and he recites his knowledge frequently. Kusak and Bingo become detectives in spite of themselves and with no professional training whatsoever.

CONTRIBUTION

In less than two decades, Craig Rice successfully overturned many of the time-honored traditions of the detective story in most of her twenty-eight books. (The number is an estimate because some may have been ghostwritten for her.) In a genre in which death can be a game of men walking down mean streets unafraid to meet their doom, she wrote of men whose fearlessness came from a bottle—from several bottles, in fact—and made it seem comical. At heart, the drinking in her books is the social drinking of Mr. and Mrs. North or Topper.

Rice's blend of humor with homicide and mirth with mayhem works because her stories have a foundation in a realistic crime situation. Eventually the situation reaches a point at which readers must laugh or lose their minds. Crime, Rice insists, is not funny, but her characters are funny by contrast because of their reactions and because they closely resemble characters in the screwball comedies of the 1930's. Eternally optimistic, they never take themselves any more seriously than is called for. Her style allies her more with Damon Runyon than with Dashiell Hammett. A unique and original writer, Rice has never been imitated successfully.

BIOGRAPHY

Georgiana Ann Randolph was born in Chicago on June 5, 1908, the daughter of Harry Moschiem "Bosco" Craig and Mary Randolph Craig. Her father was an itinerant artist, her mother the daughter of a Chicago physician. Accounts differ on her correct surname. Her most famous pen name combines her father's last name and the last name of his brother-in-law and sister with whom she lived, Mr. and Mrs. Elton Rice.

Educated by her uncle and in a Jesuit missionary school, Rice developed a dislike of conformity and at the age of eighteen began earning a precarious living in the Chicago literary world. She succeeded because of her versatility; she took on jobs as a crime reporter, a radio and motion-picture script writer, and publicity manager for Gypsy Rose Lee and a group of traveling wrestlers, as well as working as a general freelance writer.

Rice was married at least four times, to Arthur John Follows, a newspaperman named Arthur Ferguson, H. W. DeMott, Jr., and a writer named Lawrence Lipton, not necessarily in that order. Her children, Nancy, Iris, and David, appear as characters in her semiautobiographical novel, *Home Sweet Homicide* (1944). The children spent much of their time in boarding schools while their mother wrote at home in Santa Monica, California. Her husband at the time, Lawrence Lipton, worked in an office in Los Angeles.

Rice's first detective novel, *Eight Faces at Three* (1939), took her nearly two years to write. The first chapter was easy enough, but she had trouble getting beyond its intriguing problem. She claimed that she never understood how she did it, but the character of the hard-drinking, womanizing John J. Malone succeeded with the public and appeared in several subsequent novels.

Reportedly an expert marksman, cook, and grower of prize gardenias, Rice enjoyed life enormously. Nevertheless, in spite of fame and financial rewards (she was the first mystery writer to appear on the cover of *Time*), she found meeting deadlines increasingly difficult. The drinking that she made amusing in print was not amusing in her own life. On August 28, 1957, she died of an overdose of barbiturates and alcohol.

Analysis

Craig Rice used a number of pseudonyms in her career as a mystery writer. As Michael Venning or Daphne Sanders, she could produce certain types of stories unlike those the public came to associate with the name Craig Rice. Less light-hearted, these stories constitute serious character portrayals accompanied by psychological insight.

Even the titles she ghosted for Gypsy Rose Lee (*The G-String Murders*, 1941; *Mother Finds a Body*, 1942) and George Sanders (*Crime on My Hands*, 1944) were written to satisfy reader expectation of the public persona of those entertainers. In each instance, the author on the title page serves as the detective in the story as well.

With few exceptions (principally *Telefair*, 1942, also published as *Yesterday's Murder*), the "Craig Rice" style is unmistakable, with its light and clean prose. There is an underlying seriousness (the situation is always a serious matter to her characters), but the story is told in a manner that reveals the comic side of life.

Rice claimed not to be aware of what she was doing in the detective novel or of how she was doing it. In two pieces on the craft of mystery writing ("It's a Mystery to Me" and "Murder Makes Merry"), she contends that if she really did know what made her mystery novels funny or how to find the solution to an intriguing problem she would be wealthy. She appears to have followed the system of putting a clean sheet of paper in the typewriter and typing until she reached the end of the manuscript, making it all up as she went—no outlines, no list of characters with thumbnail descriptions next to the names, not even a note about the solution. Some writers, she admits, begin with the ending and then write what leads up to it, but she never found this method to work for her.

Actually, Rice probably knew very well what she was doing, but the subconscious, creative method worked so well for her that she decided not to tamper with it by analyzing it. This casual approach to discussing her craft fit the type of novel she wrote; she had been a public relations manager, after all, and her instincts served her well.

The situations in her best works are unusual enough to attract the attention of the reader from the first and to remain in the memory afterward. The victim is found in a room in which the clocks have all stopped at three o'clock; a murder committed on a crowded street corner goes unnoticed; a murder victim's clothes vanish on the way to the morgue; a murderess on death row threatens to haunt the people who had sent her to jail.

Still, a clever situation or plot device is not enough to hold the reader through a series of books without interesting characters. It is in the portrayal of memorable characters, particularly that of John J. Malone, that Rice excels. Take one criminal lawyer, dress him in expensive suits, give him a thirst for good liquor and an appreciation for women and good cigars, and mix well. In the process, make him careless about money and where he leaves the ashes from his cigars. To top it off, give him the instinct of a gambler without his luck. The result is a description of John J. Malone of Chicago, Illinois.

In many ways Craig Rice's method was to take the traditional stereotypes and clichés of the mystery field and reverse them or hold them up to ridicule. Malone becomes a parody of the hard-boiled detective, with his penchant for rye, his habit of keeping a bottle in his filing cabinet under such imaginative categories as "Confidential" and "Unsolved Cases," and the frequency with which he finds himself in a strange place with no memory of how he arrived there. His invariable solution is to repair to the nearest bar or other watering hole, perhaps his favorite, Joe the Angel's City Hall Bar, and drink until he reconstructs the general condition he was in at the time.

Malone is chronically broke or in search of his retaining fee, playing poker to recoup his losses from the last game, and getting Joe diAngelo to extend him credit for drinks, even to the point of advancing him cash. Maggie O'Leary, his secretary, knows that any expenses on a case will come out of her pocket, assuming that she has been paid that month.

The Fourth Postman

Rice's 1948 novel, *The Fourth Postman*, rings the changes on a number of detective-fiction traditions, from the upper-class family of eccentrics to the serial murders. The novel opens with a brief chapter from the point of view of the unknown murderer that sets a

tone of tragic suspense. The victim is not identified as a postal carrier (unless the description of his brisk walk and cheerful whistle makes his identity clear). The sudden cut to a dialogue between John J. Malone and Captain Daniel von Flanagan, who never wanted to be a police officer and so resents being a stereotypical Irish cop that he changed his name, alters the mood but continues the suspense. It is this juxtaposition of moods—from murder to farce—that keeps the reader engrossed.

Why would anyone want to kill a postman? Malone offers his answer: to avoid getting bills in the mail—a simple, direct, human reason with which anyone can identify. Still, three postal carriers? In the same alleyway, near the Fairfaxx mansion? There must be a connection.

The chief suspect is the gentle, wealthy, and eccentric Rodney Fairfaxx. (The Fairfaxx family added the extra *x* to their name to avoid being confused with a notorious individual of the same name.) Rodney is still waiting for a letter from his sweetheart, Annie Kendall, who went to England on the *Titanic* thirty years earlier and never returned; he labors under the illusion that she is still in England. Rodney is so obviously not guilty that von Flanagan is certain of his guilt, and the family retains Malone to defend him (though they forget to pay his retaining fee).

There are members of the Fairfaxx family who have better motives for the crime than Rodney. Malone sets out to sort them out and in so doing meets his friends from earlier stories, Jake and Helene Justus. The Justuses do not play as large a role in *The Fourth Postman* as they do in some of the other books, but they are appropriate to the situation nevertheless.

Jake is soon relegated to the sidelines by a case of the chickenpox. His discovery of his ailment and the confusion over the proper way of applying cocoa butter is related in as hilarious a scene as one could wish. (The stray dog Malone acquires and insists on referring to as a rare Australian beer hound has a preference for having it spread on toast.)

Jake's dazed condition as a result of his illness makes it plausible that he should stumble out of bed, disguise himself as a masked bandit to conceal his identifying facial spots, call a cab, and find the hammer that served as the murder weapon. Given that premise, it becomes equally plausible (and humorous) that at a dramatic climax Helene should find him back in bed, clutching the hammer.

It is determined that this is the real murder weapon and not the hammer wielded by the sinister Karloffian butler Huntleigh when he nailed Malone by his Capper and Capper suit to the cellar wall. The "real" hammer becomes a vital piece of evidence and as useful as the information Malone and Helene gather when they visit Uncle Ernie Fairfaxx in the hospital. Uncle Ernie has been hit by a brick wall (he says) in the same alley where the postal carriers were killed. It is impossible to paraphrase adequately Rice's depiction of the scene in which Malone, Helene, and Uncle Ernie share the bottle of Bushmill's Irish whiskey that came in the bottom of the traditional basket of hospital fruit. It would be an equal disservice to the author's inventiveness to say too much about the disappearance and reappearance of Jake Justus.

As is to be expected in a Craig Rice novel, the clues are distributed fairly throughout the story, and short-range deductions carry the reader along until the final solution is achieved. Throughout, along with running gags such as the questions Malone is asked about the breed of his dog, are gentle philosophical statements, such as Uncle Ernie's comments about the differences among the rich, the poor, and those in between. Meanwhile, the mysteries, large and small—who killed whom, and who is really whom—are sorted out as well.

Malone receives a check for ten thousand dollars, so that for once in his life he is able to pay his bill at Joe the Angel's City Hall Bar. Ironically, no one, not even gambling chief Max the Hook, will cash the check or even advance him any money on it, for it is signed by Rodney Fairfaxx, and anyone can attest that Rodney Fairfaxx is crazy.

When Craig Rice died in 1957 she left a legacy of detective fiction that has seldom been equaled. At least three writers made the attempt to continue her principal series. In 1960, Laurence Mark Janifer published a novel about John J. Malone titled *The Pickled Poodles: A Novel Based on the Characters Created by Craig Rice*. It is possible that he was responsible also for the posthumous *But the Doctor Died* (1967), which was copyrighted by "Followes, Atwill and Ferguson" (names suggestive of at least two of Rice's former husbands).

People vs. Withers and Malone

More straightforward are the admitted collaborations between Craig Rice and Stuart Palmer, in which Rice supplied the ideas and Palmer polished the final manuscripts: six short stories written for *Ellery Queen's Mystery Magazine* in which Palmer's character, Hildegarde Withers, meets Rice's John J. Malone. Two of the six were written entirely by Palmer following Rice's death, with plots based on suggestions in her letters. Allowed complete freedom with the character, Palmer framed each story from Malone's point of view to the extent that Miss Withers's contribution seems almost secondary. Published over a period of thirteen years, from 1950 to 1963, the stories were collected as *People vs. Withers and Malone* in 1963.

The April Robin Murders (1958), left unfinished at Rice's death, was completed by Ed McBain to make the Bingo Riggs and Handsome Kusak series into a trilogy. Stylistically, there is no indication of where Craig Rice left off and Ed McBain began.

After her death, it was revealed that she had served as a ghostwriter for burlesque queen Gypsy Rose Lee and (in collaboration with Cleve Cartmill) for George Sanders. There have been other suggestions that, pressed to meet deadlines that continued to elude her, she employed ghostwriters herself on some of her own work, in particular for the short fiction for *Manhunt*, *The Saint Detective Magazine*, and *Mike Shayne Mystery Magazine* that appeared in the 1950's.

That she may have left behind mysteries of misattributed authorship is of less significance than the legacy of solid work signed Craig Rice. She may have claimed not to understand her own craft, but the series of novels and short stories (*The Name Is Malone*, 1958) about her Chicago lawyer give the lie to that. In successfully blending humor and detection she created much memorable entertainment that can withstand repeated readings.

J. Randolph Cox

Principal mystery and detective fiction

John J. Malone series: *Eight Faces at Three*, 1939 (also known as *Death at Three*); *The Corpse Steps Out*, 1940; *The Wrong Murder*, 1940; *The Right Murder*, 1941; *Trail by Fury*, 1941; *The Big Midget Murders*, 1942; *Having Wonderful Crime*, 1943; *The Lucky Stiff*, 1945; *The Fourth Postman*, 1948; *Mrs. O'Malley and Mr. Malone*, 1951; *Knocked for a Loop*, 1957 (also known as *The Double Frame*); *My Kingdom for a Hearse*, 1957; *The Name Is Malone*, 1958; *People vs. Withers and Malone*, 1963 (with Stuart Palmer); *But the Doctor Died*, 1967

Melville Fairr series (as Venning): *The Man Who Slept All Day*, 1942; *Murder Through the Looking Glass*, 1943; *Jethro Hammer*, 1944

Bingo Riggs and Handsome Kusak series: *The Sunday Pigeon Murders*, 1942; *The Thursday Turkey Murders*, 1943; *The April Robin Murders*, 1958 (with Ed McBain)

Nonseries novels: *The G-String Murders*, 1941 (ghostwritten for Gypsy Rose Lee; also known as *Lady of Burlesque* and *The Strip-Tease Murders*); *Mother Finds a Body*, 1942 (ghostwritten for Gypsy Rose Lee); *Telefair*, 1942 (also known as *Yesterday's Murder*); *To Catch a Thief*, 1943 (as Sanders); *Crime on My Hands*, 1944 (with Cleve Cartmill; ghostwritten for George Sanders); *Home Sweet Homicide*, 1944; *Innocent Bystander*, 1949

Other short fiction: *Once upon a Time, and Other Stories*, 1981 (with Stuart Palmer)

Other major works

Radio play: *Miracle at Midnight*, n.d.

Screenplays: *The Falcon's Brother*, 1942 (with Stuart Palmer); *The Falcon in Danger*, 1943 (with Fred Niblo, Jr.)

Nonfiction: *Forty-five Murderers: A Collection of True Crime Stories*, 1952

Edited text: *Los Angeles Murders*, 1947

Bibliography

Dubose, Martha Hailey, with Margaret Caldwell Thomas. *Women of Mystery: The Lives and Works of Notable Women Crime Novelists*. New York: St. Martin's Minotaur, 2000. Contains a short biography and an analysis of Rice's work. Notes the alcohol that permeated her work and her life.

Dueren, Fred. "John J. Malone (and Cohorts)." *The Armchair Detective* 8 (1974/1975): 44-47. Profile of several of Rice's most famous characters.

Grochowski, Mary Ann. "Craig Rice: Merry Mistress of Mystery and Mayhem." *The Armchair Detective* 13 (1980): 265-267. Celebration of Rice's use of humor in her crime fiction.

Klein, Kathleen Gregory, ed. *Great Women Mystery Writers: Classic to Contemporary*. Westport, Conn.: Greenwood Press, 1994. Contains an essay on the life and works of Rice.

Marks, Jeffrey A. *Who Was That Lady? Craig Rice: The Queen of the Screwball Mystery*. Lee's Summit, Mo.: Delphi Books, 2001. Primarily a biography of the novelist, delving into her rather dark life, which contrasts notably with the tone of her fiction; secondary attention is paid to the fiction itself.

Moran, Peggy. "Craig Rice." In *And Then There Were Nine: More Women of Mystery*, edited by Jane S. Bakerman. Bowling Green, Ohio: Bowling Green State University Popular Press, 1985. Study of the life and work of Rice, who is discussed alongside Margery Allingham and Patricia Highsmith, among other famous "women of mystery."

"Mulled Murder, with Spice." *Time* 47 (January 28, 1946): 84, 86, 88, 90. Rice is featured on the cover of this issue of *Time*—the first mystery author ever to receive a cover story in the magazine.

PHIL RICKMAN

Born: Lancashire, England; date unknown
Also wrote as Will Kingdom; Thom Madley
Types of plot: Thriller; psychological; amateur sleuth

Principal series

Reverend Merrily Watkins, 1998-

Principal series characters

Merrily Watkins is an Anglican priest who comes to the small village of Ledwardine as parish priest and later becomes a "deliverance consultant," or exorcist, for the diocese of Hereford. A single mother, widowed at a young age, Merrily struggles to prove herself as an attractive woman in a traditionally male domain. Merrily is an unabashed nicotine addict who often questions herself as a priest, mother, and woman, lending her character an appealing realism and vulnerability.

Jane Watkins, Merrily's resourceful, independent, and often rebellious teenage daughter, is initially skeptical about church matters and her mother's decision to enter the priesthood, but she discovers a spiritual sensitivity in herself, a quality her mother shares. Her adolescent growing pains are rendered without apology, making Jane a strong character some readers love but others hate.

Lol Robinson is a melancholy, sensitive songwriter and musician, the former head of a briefly popular rock band, Hazey Jane. Lol came to Ledwardine to escape his past; deeply depressed after his girlfriend leaves him for the local squire, he begins a tentative relationship with Merrily.

Contribution

Phil Rickman began his career as a novelist with *Candlenight* (1991) and *Crybbe* (1993), novels that mixed Celtic and British mythology with supernatural elements and a strong regional flavor. His effective use of supernatural suspense led him to be typed as a horror writer, a label he has worked to change. Although his early work was sometimes compared to that of Stephen King and ghost-story writer M. R. James, Rickman told interviewer David Mathew that he did not identify himself as a horror writer nor did he feel that he really fit into any other category, genre, or subgenre. His first five novels, from *Candlenight* to *The Chalice* (1997), mixed folklore, history, and mysticism, providing subtle chills rather than the fantastic events and outright gore that had come to dominate the horror genre. Although these novels were moderately successful, most critics agree that with *The Wine of Angels* (1998), his first Merrily Watkins mystery, Rickman found his true voice.

The Merrily Watkins books can be classified as crime novels because the investigation of a crime, usually murder, features prominently in most of the novels, but they also allow Rickman to explore mythology, religion, gender and sexuality, rural life, and the conflicts between natives and outsiders and between tradition and change in modern-day Britain. In *The Wine of Angels*, the persecution for witchcraft of a seventeenth century vicar who may or may not have been gay leads to conflicts and resentments within present-day Ledwardine. *A Crown of Lights* (2001) finds Merrily caught in the middle of a conflict between neopagans and Christians, while *The Smile of a Ghost* (2005) uses medieval Ludlow Castle, a real-life castle on the Welsh border, as the setting for mysterious suicides and a possible haunting. In *The Prayer of the Night Shepherd* (2004), Merrily's daughter Jane takes a job at Stanner Hall, a hotel on the Welsh border in a village that may have been the model for Sir Arthur Conan Doyle's *The Hound of the Baskervilles* (1902-1902). Despite the presence of ghosts and other mysterious forces, Rickman's novels achieve a strong sense of realism through their lifelike and vivid depictions of landscape and people along the rural border of England and Wales.

Biography

Philip Rickman was born in Lancashire, England, a county infamous for its seventeenth century witch trials. His interest in writing began as a child, with "mysteries, spy stories—whatever I was into at the time." At the age of eighteen, he managed to get a job at a newspaper and began a successful career in journalism, eventually writing and producing pieces for Radio Wales and the British Broadcasting Corporation's (BBC's) Radio 4. A documentary he wrote and presented, *Aliens*, won the Wales Current Event Affairs Reporter of the Year award in 1987. The program, about the rise in English people moving to Wales, drawn by cheap land, and their not always warm reception by Welsh natives, was the inspiration for Rickman's first novel, *Candlenight*, published in 1991 after several publishers rejected it for not fitting their template of a horror novel. In an interview originally published in *The New Writer*, Rickman said that one publisher turned the book down because of its humorous passages: horror novels were not supposed to be funny. With the encouragement of writer and editor Alice Thomas Ellis, Rickman published *Candlenight* to mostly good reviews.

Crybbe, Rickman's first novel to be released in the United States (as *Curfew*), was a more explicitly spooky work that took a satirical look at New Age devotees who come to a sleepy village determined to unlock its ancient magic, not understanding that some elemental forces are best left contained. His second novel was successful enough for Rickman to devote most of his time to fiction, and three more supernatural novels followed: *The Man in the Moss* (1994), inspired when Rickman's wife, Carol, suggested he do a book about bog bodies; *December* (1994), a ghost story involving the murder of John Lennon; and *The Chalice* (1997), which drew on some of Rickman's earlier research on the search for the Holy Grail.

Tired of having his complex works classed as horror, Rickman began work on a story he thought would be closer to one of Agatha Christie's Miss Marple books than to a novel by Anne Rice. Rickman's the Reverend Merrily Watkins was originally conceived as a supporting character, but she soon took over his imagination and his new novel, *The Wine of Angels*. Rickman told *Counterculture* magazine that he conceived of a plot that contained supernatural elements but could also be resolved in the real world. As he wrote, Rickman realized that he had created something unique.

Although other authors such as Ellis Peters had used the device of a clerical sleuth, no character quite like Merrily Watkins—a woman vicar and professional exorcist who also investigates crimes—had ever been seen before. Both critics and readers gave Merrily a warm welcome, and Rickman found himself the creator of a successful mystery series, turning out books at the rate of about one per year. Rickman has said he plans to stay with the Merrily character, but at the same time is experimenting with other genres of fiction. He has written two mystery novels under the Will Kingdom pseudonym, both featuring a police detective, and in 2006 he published his first young-adult novel, *Marco's Pendulum*, as Thom Madley.

Rickman has said that while fiction writing is his main avocation, he never formally quit journalism and still produces radio programs and the occasional newspaper piece. Most notably, he has worked as writer and presenter of *Phil the Shelf*, a book program for BBC Radio Wales. The author's Web site describes it as an irreverent and sometimes controversial program with author interviews and discussions of popular and genre fiction.

Analysis

Phil Rickman's novels create a fictional world that might, in another writer's hands, be called cozy. His stories are set in rural villages where everybody knows everybody else and in quaint old towns rich in history, with castles and cathedrals and humorously gruff local characters. The author subverts this pretty picture, however, sometimes with murder and supernatural dread and sometimes by a realistic depiction of the animosity between the romantic views of visitors and newcomers and the more practical attitude of the local people. His use of detail to build a credible, fully imagined background makes the intrusion of the supernatural more disturbing because what happens does not take place in some fantasy world but in a real place. Rickman's journalism background is evident in the research he does for each book; as a whole, his work provides a wealth of information about paranormal phenomena, traditional English and Welsh folklore, pagan beliefs, the workings of the Anglican church, and what Rickman calls "earth-mysteries," formations such as Stonehenge.

In an interview, Rickman discussed his approach to the occult as simply another aspect of real life. When he writes about the paranormal, he does not treat it as fantasy or even horror. He uses a basis of documentary realism to write about the work of exorcist-priest Merrily and the politics involved with her job, although he admits that Merrily's real-life equivalent would not be involved in as many criminal investigations as she is.

Crybbe

Crybbe is probably the most successful of Rickman's early novels and was the first to be released in the United States. According to the author, his American publishers renamed the novel *Curfew* because they thought Americans would not know how to pronounce the original title. In retrospect, he said, he felt that *Curfew* was a better title. In many ways, this nonseries novel is a precursor to the Merrily Watkins series: It is set in a village not far from Ledwardine, features a clerical hero, and marks the first appearance of Gomer Parry, local contractor.

Crybbe, an isolated village between England and Wales, has been left to itself for centuries, and most who live there follow the old traditions, such as the nightly ringing of the church bell marking curfew, without question. When a millionaire record producer, inspired by the writings of a local paranormal investigator, comes to town with a plan to make Crybbe a New Age mecca, ancient forces begin to stir. Faye Morrison, a reporter stranded with her vicar father in

Crybbe, does some digging into the sinister origins of village traditions. Rickman uses real folklore elements—"ley-lines" around the town, marked by ancient, Stonehenge-like rock formations—and creates a convincing sense of enclosure and paranoia. *Publishers Weekly* praised *Curfew* for its stylish treatment of occult themes.

The Wine of Angels

The Wine of Angels marks the first appearance of Merrily Watkins. In this novel, she is not yet a diocesan deliverance consultant and is still finding her way as a priest, struggling with a crisis of faith, a rebellious daughter, and a seemingly haunted house. It does not help that within her first few weeks as priest in charge of Ledwardine, an old village that some newer residents are trying to develop as a tourist site, she witnesses a gruesome apparent suicide and faces sexism from parishioners and outright hostility from James Bull-Davies, heir to the local manor. While Merrily struggles with nightmares and horrific visions, her fifteen-year-old daughter Jane has a mystical experience in the apple orchard and takes up with Lucy Devenish, an eccentric shopkeeper rumored to be a bit of a witch. Then Colette Cassidy, the wild daughter of a newcomer family, goes missing, and Merrily finds herself in the midst of murder and mysteries both ancient and modern.

The novel draws on traditional folklore regarding fairies, apples, and cider but places these topics in a modern setting, with a satirical subplot about the appropriation of the past. Controversy erupts when a gay playwright champions the cause of a seventeenth century cleric charged with witchcraft, deciding, on no particular evidence, that homophobia was the true reason for his persecution. Gomer Parry, a "digger-driver" and contractor in Ledwardine, muses on the sanitizing of the village, with art galleries where slaughterhouses once stood and gourmet restaurants instead of rough-and-tumble pubs.

The Wine of Angels, named for Ledwardine's famous apple cider, introduces Lol Robinson, a troubled singer-songwriter (his idol is suicidal musician Nick Drake) trying to escape his past. He becomes a romantic interest for Merrily as the series develops. Jane, though sometimes a trial to her mother, emerges as a strong and sensible character who helps Merrily unravel the town's mysteries. Gomer, transplanted from Crybbe, offers his unique perspective on local goings-on. Merrily spends much of the novel racked by self-doubt, but she emerges as a compassionate and determined woman, a spiritual leader strong enough to face the challenges her future position as exorcist will demand.

The Prayer of the Night Shepherd

At some point, every mystery writer must address the long shadow of Sir Arthur Conan Doyle, and *The Prayer of the Night Shepherd* is Rickman's nod to Sherlock Holmes. In this novel, Merrily Watkins's sixth outing, Rickman explores the possibility that the origin for Doyle's *The Hound of the Baskervilles* was not Dartmoor but Herefordshire on the Welsh border. Ben Foley, a television producer, hosts murder-mystery weekends at Stanner Hall, an old mansion turned hotel. Proving his theory that Doyle's hound was based on a local legend of a black dog that presaged death will be a sure path to profit, Foley thinks, but others are not so sure of his methods.

When Jane Watkins, now seventeen, gets her first job at Stanner Hall, Merrily becomes drawn into a real-life mystery involving an ancient family curse, a medieval exorcism, and the potentially dangerous Sebbie Dacre, an alcoholic landowner with a bad temper and a worse family history.

In an afterword, Rickman describes how his research for a BBC radio program called *The Return of the Hound* led to the writing of *The Prayer of the Night Shepherd*. The setting details and the legends of the hound are drawn from his reading and interviews with area residents. Adding to the novel's sense of realism are photos of Herefordshire landmarks and quotations from Ella Mary Leather's *The Folk-Lore of Herefordshire* (1912) interspersed with the text. The various plot threads are woven together seamlessly, and many reviewers called *The Prayer of the Night Shepherd* Rickman's best work yet.

Kathryn Kulpa

Principal mystery and detective fiction

Reverend Merrily Watkins series: *The Wine of Angels*, 1998; *Midwinter of the Spirit*, 1999;

A Crown of Lights, 2001; *The Cure of Souls*, 2001; *The Lamp of the Wicked*, 2003; *The Prayer of the Night Shepherd*, 2004; *The Smile of a Ghost*, 2005; *The Remains of an Altar*, 2006; *The Fabric of Sin*, 2007

Nonseries novels: *Candlenight*, 1991; *Crybbe*, 1993 (also known as *Curfew*); *The Man in the Moss*, 1994; *December*, 1994; *The Chalice*, 1997; *The Cold Calling*, 1998 (as Will Kingdom); *Mean Spirit*, 2001 (as Kingdom)

Children's literature: *Marco's Pendulum*, 2006 (as Madley)

Bibliography

Counterculture. "Phil Rickman: Exorcising Crime with Merrily Watkins." Interview. http://www.counterculture.co.uk/interview/phil-Rickman.html. An interview with the author, including a detailed discussion of the origins of the Merrily Watkins series and Rickman's thoughts on genre writing.

Humphreys, Simon. Review of *The Remains of an Altar*, by Phil Rickman. *Mail on Sunday*, December 31, 2006, p. 60. Review of a Merrily Watkins book that praises the work, although the reviewer would have preferred the action to be centered on Merrily rather than on her daughter.

Rickman, Phil. Phil Rickman: Mystery upon Mystery. http://www.philRickman.co.uk. Phil Rickman's official Web site contains a biography, descriptions and reviews of all his books, and information on the *Phil the Shelf* radio program. Especially useful are the author's comments on the background of his works.

Savill, Richard. "The Dubious Pedigree of the Baskerville Hound." *The Daily Telegraph*, June 1, 2004, p. 5. Savill looks at Rickman's claim that Sherlock's hound may have originated in a local legend concerning Black Vaughn of Kington and his dog.

Scaggs, John. *Crime Fiction*. New York: Routledge, 2005. Provides chapters on mystery and detective fiction and on the crime thriller that enable the reader to place Rickman's works within the genre and see where they differ.

MARY ROBERTS RINEHART

Mary Roberts

Born: Pittsburgh, Pennsylvania; August 12, 1876
Died: New York, New York; September 22, 1958
Types of plot: Amateur sleuth; cozy

Principal series

Miss Pinkerton, 1914-1942

Principal series characters

Hilda "Miss Pinkerton" Adams, is a trained nurse, who is single, sensible, intelligent, and strong-willed. Twenty-nine in her first appearance and thirty-eight by the last, she often attends the bedside of prominent citizens who suffer illness or nervous collapse after a robbery, murder, or family crisis.

Detective Inspector Patton, the police detective who gave Miss Pinkerton her nickname, depends on her keen ability to observe.

Contribution

In a 1952 radio interview, Mary Roberts Rinehart said that she had helped the mystery story grow up by adding flesh and muscle to the skeleton of plot. Beginning at the height of the Sherlock Holmes craze, Rinehart introduced humor and romance and created protagonists with whom readers identified. Thus, the emotions of fear, laughter, love, and suspense were added to the intellectual pleasure of puzzle tales. *The Circular Staircase* (1908) was immediately hailed as something new, an American detective story that owed little to European influences and concerned characteristically American social conditions.

Rinehart's typical novel has two lines of inquiry, often at cross purposes, by a female amateur and by a police detective. The woman, lacking the resources and scientific laboratories to gather and interpret physical evidence, observes human nature, watches for unexpected reactions, and delves for motive. The necessary enrichment of background and characterization forced the short tale (which was typical at the turn of the century) to grow into the detective novel. Critics sometimes patronize Rinehart as inventor of the Had-I-But-Known school of female narrators who withhold clues and stupidly prowl around dark attics. Her techniques, however, were admirably suited to magazine serialization. In addition to its influence on detective fiction, Rinehart's work led to the genre of romantic suspense.

Biography

Mary Roberts Rinehart, born Mary Roberts, was reared in Pittsburgh. Her father was an unsuccessful salesman, and her mother took in roomers. At fifteen, Mary was editing her high school newspaper and writing stories for *Pittsburgh Press* contests. In 1893 she entered nurse's training at a hospital whose public wards teemed with immigrants, industrial workers, and local prostitutes. In 1895 her father committed suicide. Mary Roberts completed her training and, in April, 1896, married a young physician, Stanley Rinehart.

In the next six years she had three sons, helped with her husband's medical practice, and looked for a means of self-expression. By 1904 she was selling short stories to *Munsey's Magazine*, *Argosy*, and other magazines. *The Circular Staircase* was published, and

Mary Roberts Rinehart. (Library of Congress)

The Man in Lower Ten (1909) became the first detective story ever to make the annual best-seller list.

In 1910-1911, the Rineharts traveled to Vienna so that Stanley Rinehart could study a medical specialty. During the next few years, Rinehart wrote books with medical and political themes. When war broke out, she urged *The Saturday Evening Post* to make her a correspondent. In 1915 reporters were not allowed to visit the Allied lines, but Rinehart used her nurse's training to earn Red Cross credentials. She examined hospitals, toured "No Man's Land," and interviewed both the king of Belgium and the queen of England.

Her war articles made Rinehart a public figure as well as a best-selling novelist. She covered the political conventions of 1916 (taking time out to march in a women's suffrage parade) and turned down an offer to edit *Ladies' Home Journal*. In 1920 two plays written with Avery Hopwood were on Broadway. *The Bat* had an initial run of 878 performances and eventually brought in more than nine million dollars. Rinehart lived in Washington, D.C., during the early 1920's. In 1929 two of her sons set up a publishing firm in partnership with John Farrar. Annual books by Mary Roberts Rinehart provided dependable titles for the Farrar and Rinehart list.

Rinehart moved to New York in 1935, following her husband's death in 1932, and continued an active life. Eleven of her books made best-seller lists between 1909 and 1936. The comic adventures of her dauntless never-married heroine Tish had been appearing in *The Saturday Evening Post* since 1910. During the 1930's, she also produced an autobiography, wrote the somber short fiction collected in *Married People* (1937), and underwent a mastectomy. In 1946 Rinehart went public with the story of her breast cancer and urged women to have examinations. Her last novel was published in 1952, although a story in *Ellery Queen's Mystery Magazine* in 1954 neatly rounded out the half century of detective writing since her poem "The Detective Story"—a spoof of the Sherlock Holmes craze—appeared in *Munsey's Magazine* in 1904. She died in 1958.

ANALYSIS

Mary Roberts Rinehart significantly changed the form of the mystery story in the early years of the twentieth century by adding humor, romance, and the spine-chilling terror experienced by readers who identify with the amateur detective narrator. Borrowing devices from gothic novels of the late eighteenth and early nineteenth centuries and from sensational fiction of the 1860's, Rinehart infused emotion into the intellectual puzzles that dominated late nineteenth and early twentieth century magazines. By securing identification with the central character, she made readers share the perplexity, anxiety, suspense, and terror of crime and detection. Because she did not deal in static cases brought to a master detective for solution but rather with stories of ongoing crime, in which the need for concealment escalates as exposure approaches, the narrator almost inevitably becomes a target and potential victim.

Rinehart's typical mystery has two investigators. One is a professional detective and the other a female amateur who narrates the story. All the important characters must be sufficiently developed so that the amateur can make deductions by watching their emotional responses and penetrating their motives. Rinehart's books also include both romance (sometimes between the two detectives) and humor. *The Man in Lower Ten*, her first full-length mystery, was intended as a spoof of the pompous self-importance with which Great Detectives analyzed clues.

Like many readers, Rinehart used mysteries for escape; the "logical crime story," she wrote, "provided sufficient interest in the troubles of others to distract the mind from its own." On the wards of a busy urban hospital she had seen "human relations at their most naked." In writing, however, she "wanted escape from remembering" and therefore chose "romance, adventure, crime, . . . where the criminal is always punished and virtue triumphant."

She saw the mystery as "a battle of wits between reader and writer," which consists of two stories. One is known only to the criminal and to the author; the other is enacted by the detective. These two stories run concurrently. The reader follows one, while "the other story, submerged in the author's mind [rises] to the surface here and there to form those baffling clews." In "The Repute of the Crime Story" (*Publishers Weekly*, February 1, 1930), Rinehart outlined the "ethics" of crime writing. The criminal

> should figure in the story as fully as possible; he must not be dragged in at the end. There must be no false clues. . . . Plausibility is important, or the story may become merely a "shocker." The various clues which have emerged throughout the tale should be true indices to the buried story, forming when assembled at the conclusion a picture of that story itself.

In most of Rinehart's mysteries the "buried story" is not simply the concealment of a single crime. Also hidden—and explaining the criminal's motives—are family secrets such as illegitimacy, unsuitable marriages, or public disgrace. This material reflects the sexual repression and social hypocrisy embodied in Victorian culture's effort to present an outward appearance of perfect respectability and moral rectitude. Rinehart forms a bridge between the sensational novels of the 1860's, which had used similar secrets, and the twentieth century psychological tale. Clues locked in character's minds appear in fragments of dream, slips of the tongue, or inexplicable aversions and compulsions. In a late novel, *The Swimming Pool* (1952), the amateur detective enlists a psychiatrist to help retrieve the repressed knowledge. Even in her earliest books Rinehart used Freudian terminology to describe the unconscious.

Rinehart's stories typically take place in a large house or isolated wealthy community. In British mysteries of the interwar years, a similar setting provided social stability; in Rinehart, however, the house is often crumbling and the family, by the end of the tale, disintegrated. The secret rooms, unused attics, and hidden passageways not only promote suspense but also symbolize the futile attempt of wealthy people to protect their status by concealing secrets even from one another. These settings also allow for people to hide important information from motives of privacy, loyalty to friends, and distaste for the police. In the Miss Pinkerton series (two stories published in *The Saturday Evening Post* in 1914, a collection of short fiction published in 1925, novels dated 1932 and 1942, and an omnibus volume published under the title *Miss Pinkerton* in 1959), Inspector Patton uses nurse Hilda Adams as an agent because when any prominent family is upset by crime, "somebody goes to bed, with a trained nurse in attendance."

Relations between the professional detective and the female amateur—who is generally an intelligent and spirited single woman in her late twenties or early thirties—are marked by mutual respect and friendly sparring. Rinehart was not ignorant of scientific methods; her medical training made her perfectly comfortable with physiological evidence and the terminology of coroners' reports. The official detective discovers physical clues and uses police resources to interview witnesses and tail suspects. Yet, as the narrator of *The Circular Staircase* says, "both footprints and thumbmarks are more useful in fiction than in fact." The unofficial detective accumulates a separate—and often contradictory—fund of evidence by observing people's reactions, analyzing unexpected moments of reticence, understanding changes in household routine, and exploring emotional states. The official detective enlists her aid, but she may conceal some information because she senses that he will laugh at it or because she is afraid that it implicates someone about whom she cares. She ventures into danger to conduct investigations on her own partly because she wants to prove the detective wrong and partly because of her own joy in the chase.

Although she wrote several essays on the importance to women of home and family life, Rinehart was an active suffragist and proud of having been a "pioneer" who went into a hospital for professional training at a time "when young women of my class were leading their helpless protected lives." In her work, Rinehart used women's "helplessness" and repression as a convincing psychological explanation for failure to act, for deviousness, and even for crime. In *The Circular Staircase*, a young woman complains of the humiliation of being surrounded by "every indulgence" but never having any money of her own to use without having to answer questions. The sexual repression and social propriety of women forced to depend on relatives for support because class mores prohibit their employment breed bitterness and hatred. Rinehart's explicit yet empathetic exploration of motives for crime among women of the middle and upper classes is a marked contrast to the misogyny of the hard-boiled school.

The Circular Staircase

The innovations of Rinehart's formula were almost fully developed in her first published book, *The Circular Staircase*. The wry tone, the narrator's personality, the setting, and the foreshadowing are established in the opening sentence:

> This is the story of how a middle-aged spinster lost her mind, deserted her domestic gods in the city, took a furnished house for the summer out of town, and found herself involved in one of those mysterious crimes that keep our newspapers and detective agencies happy and prosperous.

Rachel Innes shares certain traits with Anna Katharine Green's Amelia Butterworth—both are inquisitive single women of good social standing—but Rinehart's humor, her economical and spirited narration, and her ability to manage multiple threads of a complex plot made an instant impact on reviewers.

The house that Rachel Innes rents is a typical Rinehart setting with its twenty-two rooms, five baths, multiple doors, French windows, unused attics, and a circular staircase off the billiard room that was installed apparently so licentious young men could get up to bed without waking anyone. In addition, the electric company that serves the remote locale regularly shuts down at midnight. Before many days have passed, Rachel Innes is awakened by a gunshot at three o'clock in the morning and discovers, lying at the bottom of the circular staircase, the body of a well-dressed gentleman whom she has never seen before.

The romantic complications that shortly ensue confound the mystery. Rachel Innes's nephew and niece (Halsey and Gertrude) are both secretly engaged, and each has some possible provocation for having murdered the intruder. Fear that her nephew or niece might be involved gives Rachel Innes a reason to conceal information from the detective, Jamieson. At the same time, some of the evidence that seems to point toward Halsey or Gertrude arises from their attempts to preserve the secrecy of their romantic attachments.

There are actually two "buried stories" in *The Circular Staircase*, although both Jamieson and Innes believe that they are on the track of a single criminal. The "outcroppings" that provide clues toward the solution of one mystery therefore lay false trails for the other. One involves a secret marriage, an abandoned child, and a vengeful woman; the other is a banker's scheme to stage a fake death so that he can escape with the proceeds of an embezzlement. The ongoing efforts to conceal the second crime lead to further murders, and then to Halsey's disappearance. That is a significant emotional shift; the tale now concerns not only the process of detection but also the threat of danger to characters about whom the reader cares. Rinehart orchestrates the suspense with additional gothic elements, a midnight disinterment, and a climax in which Innes is trapped in the dark with an unknown villain in a secret chamber that no one knows how to enter. The identification of reader with detective and the sure-handed manipulation of suspense and terror are hallmarks of the Rinehart style (and of a great many subsequent thrillers).

Illustration by artist Henry Raleigh for the Saturday Evening Post *publication of Rinehart's "Amazing Interlude" in 1918.* (Library of Congress)

The competition between the female amateur and the male professional is to some degree a conflict between intuitive and rational thinking. While Jamieson accumulates physical evidence and investigates public records, Innes listens to the tones that indicate concealment, understands when people are acting against their will, and believes her senses even when they seem to perceive the impossible. At one point her nephew says, "Trust a woman to add two and two together, and make six." She responds,

> If two and two plus X make six, then to discover the unknown quantity is the simplest thing in the world. That a household of detectives missed it entirely was because they were busy trying to prove that two and two make four.

Both the suspense and the humor are heightened by Rinehart's facility with language. Her use of a middle-aged never-married woman's genteel vocabulary to describe crime, murder, and terror is amusing, and her ease with other dialects and with the small linguistic slips that mar a banker's disguise in the role of a gardener show the range of her verbal resources.

An influential writer

In a later generation, when some of Rinehart's innovations had been incorporated in most crime fiction and others had given rise to the separate genre of romantic suspense, critics of the detective story frequently wrote condescendingly of her as the progenitor of the Had-I-But-Known school of narration. The device grew from the demands of magazine writing; only two of Rinehart's mysteries had their initial publication in book form. When writing serials, she pointed out, each installment "must end so as to send the reader to the news stand a week before the next installment is out." The narrator's veiled reference to coming events arouses suspense and maintains the reader's anxious mood.

Rinehart began writing mysteries two years after *The Hound of the Baskervilles* (1901-1902) was published; she was already well established by the heyday of British classical detection, published throughout the hard-boiled era, and was still writing when Ian Fleming started work on the James Bond books. By the time Rinehart died, her books had sold more than eleven million copies in hardcover and another nine million in paperback. The bibliographical record pre sents some problems. Rinehart identified seventeen books as crime novels; in these, the central action is an attempt to discover the causes of a murder. Almost all of her fiction, however, combines romance, humor, violence, and buried secrets, and paperback reprints often use the "mystery" label for books that Rinehart would not have put into that category. There are also variant British titles for some books and a number of omnibus volumes that collect novels and short stories in various overlapping configurations.

Sally Mitchell

Principal mystery and detective fiction

Miss Pinkerton series: *Mary Roberts Rinehart's Crime Book*, 1925; *Miss Pinkerton*, 1932 (also known as *Double Alibi*); *Haunted Lady*, 1942; *Miss Pinkerton*, 1959

Nonseries novels: *The Circular Staircase*, 1908; *The Man in Lower Ten*, 1909; *The Window at the White Cat*, 1910; *Where There's a Will*, 1912; *The Case of Jennie Brice*, 1913; *The After House*, 1914; *Sight Unseen, and The Confession*, 1921; *The Red Lamp*, 1925 (also known as *The Mystery Lamp*); *The Bat*, 1926 (with Avery Hopwood); *Two Flights Up*, 1928; *The Door*, 1930; *The Album*, 1933; *The Wall*, 1938; *The Great Mistake*, 1940; *The Yellow Room*, 1945; *The Swimming Pool*, 1952 (also known as *The Pool*)

Other short fiction: *Alibi for Isabel, and Other Stories*, 1944; *Episode of the Wandering Knife: Three Mystery Tales*, 1950 (also known as *The Wandering Knife*); *The Frightened Wife, and Other Murder Stories*, 1953

Other major works

Novels: *When a Man Marries*, 1909; *The Secret of Seven Stars*, 1914; *K*, 1915; *Long Live the King!*, 1917; *The Amazing Interlude*, 1918; *Twenty-three and a Half Hours' Leave*, 1918; *Dangerous Days*, 1919; *A Poor Wise Man*, 1920; *The Truce of God*, 1920; *The Breaking Point*, 1921; *Lost Ecstasy*, 1927 (also known as *I Take This Woman*); *The Trumpet Sounds*, 1927; *This Strange Adventure*, 1929; *Mr. Cohen Takes a Walk*, 1933; *The State Versus Elinor*

Norton, 1933 (also known as *The Case of Elinor Norton*); *The Doctor*, 1936; *The Curve of the Catenary*, 1945; *A Light in the Window*, 1948

Short fiction: *The Amazing Adventures of Letitia Carberry*, 1911; *Tish*, 1916; *Bab: A Sub-Deb*, 1917; *Love Stories*, 1919; *Affinities, and Other Stories*, 1920; *More Tish*, 1921; *Temperamental People*, 1924; *Tish Plays the Game*, 1926; *The Romantics*, 1929; *Married People*, 1937; *Tish Marches On*, 1937; *Familiar Faces: Stories of People You Know*, 1941; *The Best of Tish*, 1955

Plays: *A Double Life*, pr. 1906; *Seven Days*, pr. 1907 (with Avery Hopwood); *Cheer Up*, pr. 1912; *Spanish Love*, pr. 1920 (with Hopwood); *The Bat*, pr. 1920 (with Hopwood); *The Breaking Point*, pb. 1922

Screenplay: *Aflame in the Sky*, 1927 (with Ewart Anderson)

Nonfiction: *Kings, Queens, and Pawns: An American Woman at the Front*, 1915; *Through Glacier Park: Seeing America First with Howard Eaton*, 1916; *The Altar of Freedom*, 1917; *Tenting Tonight: A Chronicle of Sport and Adventure in Glacier Park and the Cascade Mountains*, 1918; *Isn't That Just like a Man!*, 1920; *The Out Trail*, 1923; *Nomad's Land*, 1926; *My Story*, 1931 (revised as *My Story: A New Edition and Seventeen New Years*, 1948); *Writing Is Work*, 1939

Bibliography

Bachelder, Frances H. *Mary Roberts Rinehart: Mistress of Mystery*. San Bernardino, Calif.: Brownstone Books, 1993. Monograph examining Rinehart's work and her place in the pantheon of mystery writers.

Bargainnier, Earl F., ed. *Ten Women of Mystery*. Bowling Green, Ohio: Bowling Green State University Popular Press, 1981. Compares Rinehart's work to that of nine of her fellow female mystery writers.

Cohn, Jan. *Improbable Fiction: The Life of Mary Roberts Rinehart*. Rev. ed. Pittsburgh, Pa.: University of Pittsburgh Press, 2006. Detailed biographical study of Rinehart, focusing on her unusual situation as a famous and influential woman at a time when few women enjoyed such a position in American culture.

Doran, George H. *Chronicles of Barabbas, 1884-1934*. New York: Harcourt, Brace, 1935. Written by Rinehart's publisher, this detailed account of the business of publishing provides insight into the practical considerations of marketing Rinehart's work.

Downing, Sybil, and Jane Valentine Barker. *Crown of Life: The Story of Mary Roberts Rinehart*. Niwot, Colo.: Roberts Rinehart, 1992. An authorized biography of Rinehart, focusing on her development from nurse to successful author.

DuBose, Martha Hailey, with Margaret Caldwell Thomas. *Women of Mystery: The Lives and Works of Notable Women Crime Novelists*. New York: St. Martin's Minotaur, 2000. Describes the life of Rinehart and provides critical comment on her work.

Fleenor, Julian E., ed. *The Female Gothic*. Montreal: Eden Press, 1983. Places Rinehart's work within the centuries-old gothic tradition.

Huang, Jim, ed. *They Died In Vain: Overlooked, Underappreciated, and Forgotten Mystery Novels*. Carmel, Ind.: Crum Creek Press, 2002. Rinehart is among the authors discussed in this book about mystery novels that never found the audience they deserved.

MacLeod, Charlotte. *Had She But Known: A Biography of Mary Roberts Rinehart*. New York: Mysterious Press, 1994. This biography of Rinehart concentrates on the extent to which her later career as an influential author was an unpredictable swerve in the road of what began as a fairly conventional life.

ALAIN ROBBE-GRILLET

Born: Brest, Finistère, France; August 18, 1922
Types of plot: Metaphysical and metafictional parody; espionage; thriller

Contribution

Alain Robbe-Grillet enjoyed immediate success in the French literary community. He received a literary prize for each of his first two novels and was referred to as one of the most talented and interesting of the young novelists who were experimenting with the novel form. However, his novels were not praised by everyone. The traditionalist literary critics, who insisted that novels should contain all the elements that made a work a novel in the nineteenth century, had little praise for his work. For them, the novel structure (plot, character, description, and narrative chronology), had been well defined by the realist writers, and contemporary novelists had only to follow the model. Although the jury for the Prix des Critiques awarded Robbe-Grillet their prize for *Le Voyeur* (1955; *The Voyeur*, 1958), some members of the jury expressed reservations about calling the work a novel. The critics employed by the newspapers and the reading public found his novels difficult and unreadable.

Robbe-Grillet published a number of articles in newspapers and magazines in an attempt to convince his detractors that his works were readable novels. The articles changed few opinions but placed him at the head of the movement for the creation of the New Novel (*le nouveau roman*). Although he had no intention of setting forth a theory of the novel, the articles that contained his ideas about the novel form did precisely that in the eyes of the literary critics, whether they were favorable to him or not. Thus he disseminated not only the theoretical basis for the New Novel but a definition of the novel as a genre.

Because many of Robbe-Grillet's novels contain elements of the mystery and detective genre, particularly espionage, murders, and murder investigations, Robbe-Grillet in reinventing the novel has enlarged the scope of mystery and detective fiction by adding greater complexity to it and by creating multilayered, multifaceted texts that are themselves mysteries to be solved.

Biography

Alain Robbe-Grillet was born on August 18, 1922, in Brest, Finistère, France. He received his early education at the lycée Buffon in Paris, the lycée in Brest, and the lycée Saint Louis in Paris. Growing up in a family of scientists and engineers, he chose to study mathematics and biology. In 1944 he graduated from the Institut National d'Agronomique with a degree in agricultural engineering. During World War II, he was sent to Germany to work in a tank factory. He was an engineer at the Institut National de la Statistique in Paris from 1945 to 1948. Then from 1949 to 1951 he was an agronomist with the Institut des Fruits et Agrumes Coloniaux in Morocco, in French Guyana, in Martinique, and in Guadeloupe, where he was involved in the supervision of banana plantations.

In 1951, Robbe-Grillet suffered from ill health. While recuperating, he wrote *Les Gommes* (1953; *The Erasers*, 1964). With the publication of this novel, he began a new career as a writer. Although *The Erasers* was his first published novel, it was not the first novel that he had written. In 1949, while working in his sister's biology laboratory, he had written *Un Régicide* (1978; a regicide). This novel was not published until 1978. *The Erasers* brought him considerable attention from the literary community and recognition as one of the major new authors whose works were referred to as the New Novel. In 1954, *The Erasers* received the Prix Fénélon. The following year, Robbe-Grillet published *The Voyeur*, for which he received the Prix des Critiques, and became a literary consultant for the French publishing house Les Editions de Minuit. He remained in this capacity through 1985. On October 23, 1957, he married Catherine Rstakian, a film and theater actress.

In spite of Robbe-Grillet's insistance that he was a writer and not a theoretician of the novel, he came to play an ever more important role in the controversy between the traditionalists, who insisted that novels must use the conventions established by the novelists of the nineteenth century, and the New Novel writers who believed the novel must be reinvented or die from stagnation. Robbe-Grillet continued to write novels, publishing *La Jalousie* (*Jealousy*, 1960) in 1957 and *Dans le Labyrinthe* (*In the Labyrinth*, 1960) in 1959.

In 1961, Robbe-Grillet embarked on yet another career when he was asked to write the screenplay for a film to be directed by Alain Renais. The result of their collaboration was the film *L'Année dernière à Marienbad* (1961; *Last Year at Marienbad*). Robbe-Grillet, fascinated by film as an art form, felt compelled to direct a film as well as write the screenplay for it. Between 1963 and 1968, he wrote and directed three black-and-white films: *L'Immortelle* (1963; *The Immortal One*), *Trans-Europ-Express* (1966), and *L'Homme qui ment* (1968; *The Man Who Lies*).

In 1963, still insisting that he did not have a theory of the novel, Robbe-Grillet published *Pour un nouveau roman* (*For a New Novel*, 1965), a collection of essays exploring his own view of the novel and critically applying these ideas to several contemporary novels. In 1965, he published *La Maison de rendez-vous* (English translation, 1966), a novel influenced by his work in film. From 1966 to 1968, he served as a member of the Haut-Comité pour la Défense et l'Expansion de la Langue Française.

Alain Robbe-Grillet in 1966. (AP/Wide World Photos)

During the 1970's, Robbe-Grillet was primarily involved in filmmaking. He spent 1980 to 1988 as the director of the Centre de la Sociologie de la Littérature at the University of Brussels. At this time, he began writing a three-volume imaginary autobiography, which he did not finish until 1994. He also taught and lectured at several university campuses, among them New York University and Washington University. In 1981, working with Yvonne Lenard, he wrote a mystery story for use in teaching intermediate French entitled "Le Rendez-vous" (the meeting). Robbe-Grillet considers this work, which he had to create while respecting the restriction of a progressive presentation of French grammar, a significant part of his work and an excellent introduction to his writing. *Djinns* (English translation, 1982) a novel written the same year and similar in plot and narrative, received the Prix Mondello. Some twenty years passed before the publication of his next novel, *La Reprise* (2001; *Repetition*, 2003).

On March 25, 2004, Robbe-Grillet was elected to the Académie Française. He has also been awarded the honorific titles of officer of the Legion of Honor, officer of the Ordre National du Mérite, and officer of the Ordre des Arts et des Lettres. He has been recognized for his innovative work in film writing and directing and as the major author in the New Novel genre.

Analysis

Alain Robbe-Grillet's writing is best described as experimental narrative. Believing that the novel as a genre was doomed to die from stagnation, he set about reinventing the novel. To achieve this goal, he rejected the conventions of traditional realism and permitted himself to subvert the narrative structure.

The traditional novel relies heavily on plots that, although they may digress or lead to surprise endings, are logical. Robbe-Grillet's plots not only lack logic but often evaporate as the novel unfolds. A murder is mentioned, or the possibility that a murder was committed is suggested, but it may be simply left at that, or a number of conclusions may be proposed, or the character who is dead or is not really dead may appear again. This occurs in slightly different fashion in both *The Erasers* and *La Maison de Rendez-vous*.

The characters in novels traditionally have pasts and usually futures. The author provides the reader with psychological insights into the characters' behavior. Robbe-Grillet's characters exist only within the immediate reality of the novel. He portrays his characters through their perception of objects and events that they see. The characters may have multiple names such as the spy in *Repetition*, or may be identified by only an initial.

Traditional narrators are for the most part reliable, although they may be biased or opinionated. Robbe-Grillet's narrators are not reliable. Robbe-Grillet moves at times from one narrator to another without indicating the change. He shifts his narrative from first person to third or from third person to first without any identifiable transition. By doing this, he leaves the reader unsure if there is one narrator or multiple narrators.

In the traditional novel, description creates a cultural, social, or historical milieu in which the story unfolds. Objects often add an emotive aspect to the story; for example, an old abandoned house may have a sinister appearance. Robbe-Grillet insists on the elimination of all descriptions of objects that invest them with human characteristics or attributes or any mythic symbolism. He uses description only to describe exactly what is perceived. Meticulous, repetitive, at times even tedious, descriptions of objects create the reality of the novel, which is a reality of things.

In the traditional novel, the story unfolds in a chronological order. It may contain flashbacks or dream sequences, but they are presented in such a way that the reader does not lose track of the chronology of the story. Robbe-Grillet totally subverts chronological order in his novels as he folds his story back on itself, shifts the narrative from the past to the present to dreams, and changes how the story happens or may have happened. The mystery and detective genre, which traditionally has relied so very much on plot and characters as well as other traditional elements of narrative structure, provides an excellent opportunity for the subversion of that structure.

Jealousy

In *Jealousy*, Robbe-Grillet fully explores the subversion of characterization. Set on a banana plantation in the tropics, it is a story of suspicion and jealousy. A husband suspects his wife of being involved in a love affair with their neighbor.

There are three characters in the novel. The jealous husband has no name, no physical description, and no physical presence except for that indicated by the description of the number of chairs on the verandah or the number of place settings on the table. The wife is referred to only by the initial A. She is frightened of centipedes. The description of the centipede on the wall is constantly repeated in the novel. The description of the neighbor, Franck, killing the centipede is also repeated with minor variations. It is this centipede, not the characters, that remains in the reader's mind.

The husband, in the manner of a detective, observes A and Franck through the window blinds (in French *jalousie*). Robbe-Grillet uses the double meaning of the word to confuse the sense of the novel. Is it the story of jealousy caused by knowledge of a real love affair and observed through the window blinds? Or is it the story of a man's jealousy based on his perception of events observed through a window blind? Is the story real or is it a fantasy? The story itself remains an unsolved mystery.

La Maison de Rendez-vous

La Maison de Rendez-vous opens with a first-person narration about women's flesh and its importance in the narrator's dreams. Moving through a number of sadomasochistic-erotic images, the narrative becomes a description of the events, places, and characters who will be involved in the murder of Edouard Manneret or in the play about the death of Edouard Manneret. Set in Hong Kong, the novel shifts back and forth from images of a Eurasian girl in a clinging satin dress leading or being led by a large black dog, to images of the city's filthy streets and the illiterate sweepers who clean them, to images of the garden statuary, the buffet, and the clientele at the Blue Villa owned by Lady Ava.

The novel contains what could be termed multiple plots except none of the so-called plots continue to a logical conclusion. They rather remain descriptions repeated over and over again, sometimes in exactly the same way, sometimes with minor changes. Many of the characters have a multiplicity of names or means of identity. Sir Ralph is also referred to as the American, as Johnson, as the tall man talking to the red-faced man, and as Jonstone. The happenings that make up the events of the novel are also the fictional events of the plays presented by Lady Ava at the Blue Villa.

With its repeated descriptions of characters, events, objects, and places, the "story" of the novel continually folds back on itself to start off in a different direction, only to once again fold back and begin again. Near the end of the book, Lady Ava and Sir Ralph discuss the murder of Edouard Manneret. At first the reader believes that they will explain and solve the murder, but as the discussion continues it becomes obvious that what is taking place is a discussion of numerous ways that a writer might create a story about a murder.

By distorting the components of the narrative structure of the novel, particularly of the mystery novel, Robbe-Grillet denies the reader entry into an orderly prefabricated reality. The reader is led into an interactive participation with the author in the creation of the reality of the novel.

Shawncey Webb

PRINCIPAL MYSTERY AND DETECTIVE FICTION

NOVELS: *Les Gommes*, 1953 (*The Erasers*, 1964); *Le Voyeur*, 1955 (*The Voyeur*, 1958); *La Jalousie*, 1957 (*Jealousy*, 1960); *Dans le Labyrinthe*, 1959 (*In the Labyrinth*, 1960); *La Maison de Rendez-vous*, 1965 (English translation, 1966); *Projet pour une révolution à New York*, 1970 (*Project for a Revolution in New York*, 1972); *Un Régicide*, 1978; *Djinns*, 1981 (English translation, 1982); *La Reprise*, 2001 (*Repetition*, 2003)

OTHER MAJOR WORKS

NOVELS: *La Belle Captive*, 1983 (*The Beautiful Captive*, 1983); *Topologie d'une cité fantôme*, 1976 (*Topology of a Phantom City*, 1977); *Souvenirs du triangle d'or*, 1978 (*Memories of the Golden Triangle*, 1984); *Le Miroir qui revient*, 1984 (*Ghosts in the Mirror*, 1988); *Angélique ou l'Enchantement*, 1987; *Les Derniers jours de Corinthe*, 1994

SHORT FICTION: *Instantanés*, 1962 (*Snapshots*, 1965)

SCREENPLAYS: *L'Année dernière à Marienbad* 1961 (*Last Year at Marienbad* 1962); *L'Immortelle* 1963 (*The Immortal One*, 1971); *Trans-Europ-Express*, 1966; *L'Homme qui ment*, 1968 (*The Man Who Lies*, 1968); *L'Eden et après*, 1970 (*Eden and Afterwards*, 1970); *N a pris des dés*, 1971; *Glissements progressifs du plaisir*, 1973 (*The Successive Slidings of Pleasure*, 1974); *Le Jeu avec le feu*, 1975 (*Playing with Fire*, 1975); *La Belle Captive*, 1983 (*The Beautiful Prisoner*, 1983); *Taxandria*, 1994; *Un bruit qui rend fou*, 1995 (*The Blue Villa*, 1995); *C'est Gradiva qui vous appelle*, 2002 (*It's Gradiva Who Is Calling You*, 2006)

NONFICTION: *Pour un nouveau roman*, 1963 (*For a New Novel*, 1965); *Rêves des jeunes filles*, 1971 (*Dreams of a Young Girl*, 1971); *Construction d'un temple en ruines ála Désse Vanadé*, 1975; *Le Rendez-vous*, 1981; *Le Voyageur, essais et entretiens*, 2001

BIBLIOGRAPHY

Fragola, Anthony N., and Roch C. Smith. *The Erotic Dream Machine: Interviews with Alain Robbe-Grillet on His Films*. Carbondale: Southern Illinois University Press, 1995. Presents Robbe-Grillet's ideas on film techniques and their similarities and differences from the elements of the novel.

Hellerstein, Marjorie H. *Inventing the Real World: The Art of Alain Robbe-Grillet*. Selinsgrove, Penn.: Susquehanna University Press, 1998. Discusses the real world as defined by Robbe-Grillet and how he creates it.

Robbe-Grillet, Alain. *Two Novels: "Jealousy" and "In the Labyrinth."* Translated by Richard Howard. Introductions by Roland Barthes, Bruce Morrissette, and Anne Minor. New York: Grove Press, 1965. The three introductory essays discuss Robbe-Grillet's work in regard to theory of the novel and to development of the New Novel.

Smith, Roch Charles. *Understanding Robbe-Grillet*. Columbia: University of South Carolina Press,

2000. Excellent introduction and guide for the reader new to Robbe-Grillet's fiction. Contains in-depth analysis of major novels. Selected bibliography. Indexed.

Unwin, Timothy, ed. *Cambridge Companion to the French Novel.* New York: Cambridge University Press, 2003. Contains a chapter on reality and its representation in the nineteenth century novel as well as theoretical discussions of the novel and its changes from nineteenth century to New Novel. Chronology, guide to further reading, and index included.

PETER ROBINSON

Born: Castleford, Yorkshire, England; March 17, 1950

Type of plot: Police procedural

Principal series

Chief Inspector Alan Banks, 1987-

Principal series character

Chief Inspector Alan Banks is somewhat of an anachronism on the London police force. He is an outsider and a rebel, more leftist than the typical officer. He cuts corners and defies authority but gets the job done. When he is reassigned to a more bucolic part of the country, Yorkshire, he brings his peccadilloes with him, falling into the same patterns of stress while continuing methodically and patiently to solve the puzzle of who did what to whom. He is intelligent, insightful, sometimes moody, grumpy, and even melancholic. He can be hard to work for, but few have serious complaints. He understands the frailties of both the victims and victimizers because he himself can be weak. He enjoys spending hours in the pub with his favored single malt scotch, smoking the cigarettes he is trying so hard to give up. His other constant comfort is music. His shaky marriage eventually ends in divorce; although he is uncomfortable in relationships, women love him.

Contribution

Nearly every published work by Peter Robinson has been on a best-seller list or earned some sort of recognition. Robinson received an Arthur Ellis Award for best short story in 1990 for "Innocence"; Arthur Ellis awards in 1990 and 1991 for *The Hanging Valley* (1989) and *Past Reason Hated* (1991); an Author's Award from the Foundation for the Advancement of Canadian Letters in 1995 for *Final Account* (1994); an Arthur Ellis Award in 1996 for *Innocent Graves* (1996); and the Barry Award in 1999, the Anthony Award in 2000, Sweden's Martin Beck Award in 2001, and the Grand Prix de Littérature Policière in 2001 for *In a Dry Season* (1999). His novel *Cold Is the Grave* (2000) won an Arthur Ellis Award in 2000 as well as the Palle Rosen Krantz Award for the Danish edition. His short stories have won the Ellis, the Edgar, the Macavity, and other honors. He has been translated into more than fifteen languages. He creates dignified yet riveting, mostly gore-free tales with a concentration on both the key characters and the intriguing landscape, in the manner of his inspiration, writer Ruth Rendell. He wanted, he says, to write social and psychological crime novels to gain insight into society and individuals and to investigate crimes in a particular region, in his case, Yorkshire, which he adds, is actually the main character of his series.

Biography

Peter Eliot Robinson was born in Castleford, Yorkshire, England, on March 17, 1950, to Clifford Robinson, a photographer, and Miriam Jarvis Robinson. There were not many books in his boyhood home, reading being a luxury for hard-working people, but he was encouraged to use the library. The family did not have a television set until Robinson was the age of twelve, so he turned to radio and films to find wonderful adventure stories. One of his earliest memories is of his mother reading *Black Beauty: The Autobiography of a Horse* (1877) to him at bedtime. He also remembers filling his notebooks with illustrations drawn from the tales of Robin Hood, William Tell, and King Arthur. He began writing poetry while still young, liking its structure and form, but grew bored and began experimenting with longer narrative works. The transition to fiction was easy.

In 1974, after earning his bachelor's degree with honors in English literature from the University of Leeds, Robinson moved to Canada in hopes of studying creative writing under Joyce Carol Oates at the University of Windsor. His short-story and poetry submissions apparently did not impress Oates sufficiently, and he failed to gain admittance into her creative writing classes. However, two months into the semester, after hearing Robinson read some of his latest works, Oates asked why he was not studying with her. He explained and she declared him ready. Her tutelage was key in Robinson's development as a writer. She gave direction but not too much, pointing out weaknesses as well as strengths, always expecting her students to fix the problems themselves, while being true to their own voices. He earned his master's degree in 1975.

Teaching positions were not readily available in England, jobs having grown even more scarce after Margaret Thatcher became prime minister in 1979, so Robinson returned to Ontario and entered the doctoral program at York University, earning his doctorate in 1983. By that time, he and his lawyer wife, Sheila Halladay, had settled into permanent residence in the Beaches area of Toronto, and he had begun teaching college composition and literature classes. By the late 1990's, he was able to devote full time to his writing.

Robinson's interest in the mystery genre came as a surprise because he had never read, much less written, in that form. However, during a summer visit in Yorkshire, Robinson picked up one of the many books his father had been enjoying in his retirement, and he was fascinated, recognizing the potential for his own writing. He devoured works by Raymond Chandler and Georges Simenon, then published his first Chief Inspector Alan Banks novel, *Gallow's View*, in 1987.

Although all of Robinson's works are set in Yorkshire, he finds it difficult to write about the area while he resides there. He suspects that this difficulty stems from the fact that as a young writer he lacked the confidence to enter the world of letters in a country with a prevailing class distinction, one that was more prevalent then. At the time, members of the working class simply were not expected to assume themselves capable of entering into a higher station in life, and they mostly stayed within the confines of what had been handed to them. Rather than try to buck the traditional system, the young Robinson decided he needed the aesthetic distance of Canada for his writing. He began spending his time divided between the two countries, returning to Yorkshire to reacquaint himself with the sounds, the smells, and the people who populate his novels. Although Canadians also tend to dismiss genre fiction, Robinson has been able to adopt a bemused attitude. Though he seldom makes the best-seller listings of major prestigious publications, he has a broad audience and has gained the respect of Italians, Americans, and Germans. However, he admits to still harboring a fear that one day he will be found out and will wind up "working at the yeast factory or the frozen food plant in Leeds."

Analysis

Most of Peter Robinson's novels are set in the fictional market town of Eastvale, in Yorkshire. His detective, Chief Inspector Alan Banks, formerly of the Metropolitan Police Service in London, has taken a job in a presumably quieter place with less prevalent and dramatic crime. Banks learns immediately that the job pressures are just as great despite the tranquil setting. Instead of having time to reflect on his life and to recoup from the hectic, fast-paced existence that threatened to unnerve him, he finds himself again at the core of turbulence and in the midst of bad people who do bad things as well as essentially good people who are driven to commit criminal acts.

Robinson's stories usually start with a corpse found in some distinctive part of the Yorkshire countryside or its environs. Then Inspector Banks goes to work, using his journalistic approach to crime solving, which seeks the answers to the five *w*'s and an *h*: who, what, when, where, why, and how. Banks methodically delves into the dead person's past, learning all he can about friends, family, neighbors, and the tenor of the times. He walks the streets, visits homes, confers with colleagues, and frequents the pubs with the locals. Many a clue emerges from a night of sampling local brews and old favorites. Banks's cases are solved—although not all the criminals are always brought to justice—in jigsaw fashion, with starts and misses until the final pieces fit together.

Robinson says that he used to think quite a bit of his personality was reflected in Alan Banks until he began a closer examination of the inspector. Although, for example, they share the same interests in music, they went on separate paths in their late teens. In one of many revealing interviews, Robinson makes it clear that Banks has become a living entity. The author says that, in contrast to Banks, he is not as "temperamentally suited to deal with the officiousness" of such people as Bank's superior Detective Chief Inspector Jeremiah Riddle. If Robinson were involved in a conflict with his supervisor, he would most likely quit the job. He concedes that Banks is "more physically astute, . . . [a] little scrapper, . . . not afraid of getting down and dirty."

Robinson admits that he hates violence and gore, which perhaps accounts for his declining of invitations to sit in on autopsies to add greater authority to his writing. Most of the novels' despicable acts occur offstage. He does not believe that a graphic accounting of bloody acts is always necessary; however, when he feels that it is essential for the plot, he does not spare the details.

The Hanging Valley

In *The Hanging Valley*, Robinson describes a gruesome scene involving the discovery of the body of a murder victim, hidden by rocks, with the head smashed beyond recognition, infested with maggots, and surrounded by flies. Robinson describes the corpse's face gone but moving, the "flesh . . . literally crawling," the maggots "wriggling under his clothes [making] it look as if the body were rippling like water in the breeze." Robinson felt that these details were integral to the plot and used his narrative skills to bring the moment to disgusting life. In a less repulsive passage, one very telling of the essence of British life, he describes the typical English breakfast, consisting of "two fried eggs, two thick rashers of Yorkshire bacon, Cumberland sausage, grilled mushrooms and tomato, with two slices of fried bread to mop it all up." This repast was preceded by grapefruit juice and cereal and followed by toast and marmalade.

In a Dry Season

In the novel *In a Dry Season*, Robinson excels in conveying the stunning bucolic environs while uncovering nasty little secrets. He also delves deeply into his protagonist's personality and his recurrent bouts of depression. This time, Inspector Banks is going through a serious midlife crisis: His wife has divorced him for a younger man, his son is dropping out of college to become a rock musician, his antagonistic superior Detective Chief Inspector Riddle has taken him off the active force and assigned him a desk job in the equivalent of police Siberia. As Banks struggles to understand his deep depression, he gains a kind of self-awareness that may not significantly alter his bouts of melancholia but will help him regain the confidence to go on to new tasks. He is asked to lead an investigation with another police force outcast, Detective Sergeant Annie Cabbot, in a case that the London division thinks of as a joke. His nemesis, Chief Inspector Riddle, hopes that an ages-old crime in the remote Yorkshire Dales, which took place in a period when few murders and no missing persons were reported, will herald the end of Banks's career and will show him that, at fifty, he is too old. The assignment will intrigue any mystery lover—to identify the bones uncovered when a drained reservoir reveals the remains of an old village. A critic credits Robinson with a work that "stands out for its psychological and moral complexity, its startling evocation of pastoral England, and its gritty compassionate portrayal of modern sleuthing." Robinson nicely interweaves two periods—wartime and modern Yorkshire.

Piece of My Heart

Each novel in the series brings new personal and professional challenges for Inspector Banks. *Piece of My Heart* (2006) opens the day after Britain's first outdoor rock concert in 1969, featuring the wildly popular Mad Hatters. During the cleanup of the grounds, a dead woman is discovered bundled up in a sleeping bag. An investigation fails to yield the identity of her killer. Thirty-five years later, Banks is called on to investigate another, presumably unrelated murder, of a journalist writing a piece on the Mad Hatters. Similarities soon become apparent as the detective's work begins spanning the decades. Again Robinson uses the compelling device of exploring one period in history and another in recent times and bringing both together in a logical, believable resolution. Here Robinson is able to indulge his love of rock music, re-creating the mood of the past and the tenor of the present without a hint of bifurcation.

Alan Banks

The character of Alan Banks has evolved over the years. Each new case takes more of a toll on him. He has become more introspective and allows the reader glimpses into his past that help explain why he is the way he is. In later novels, he has a darker view of the world. Unlike Agatha Christie's Hercule Poirot and Arthur Conan Doyle's Sherlock Holmes, static protagonists who can be relied on to systematically solve crimes without any substantial changes to their personae, Banks is a modern detective and develops as an ordinary person would do. Banks's evolving personality appears to appeal to the readers of the series, as the correspondence Robinson receives generally asks what will happen to Banks rather than questions about his plots.

When readers ask if Banks will ever settle down and find happiness, Robinson says he doubts that it is in Banks's nature to embrace the day, but who knows? He likes to throw situations at Banks to see how he will handle them. He claims to have even been surprised by the divorce, especially with the twist of his wife leaving for someone younger. He says that he is writing about a man who just "happens to work as a policeman, and about the things that happen to him as he grows older." He gets an idea and begins writing, not knowing where the story will go. He puts the character first and lets the plot develop because he believes that the plot stems from the main character. Possibly the key to the success of the series is that Banks is a kind of Everyman, with the same temptations, subject to the vagaries of life, which include losing power as he ages and having to settle for less.

Robinson does not want to be viewed as anything other than a writer of crime fiction. He says that when a work of crime fiction is described as a "literary thriller" or being a novel that "transcends the genre," he feels that such language is condescending, as if being crime fiction were not enough.

Gay Pitman Zieger

Principal mystery and detective fiction

Inspector Banks series: *Gallow's View*, 1987; *A Dedicated Man*, 1988; *A Necessary End*, 1989; *The Hanging Valley*, 1989; *Past Reason Hated*, 1991; *Wednesday's Child*, 1992; *Final Account*, 1994; *Innocent Graves*, 1996; *Dead Right*, 1997 (also known as *Blood at the Root*); *In a Dry Season*, 1999; *Cold Is the Grave*, 2000; *Aftermath*, 2001; *The Summer that Never Was*, 2003 (also known as *Close to Home*); *Playing with Fire*, 2004; *The First Cut*, 2004; *Strange Affair*, 2005; *Piece of My Heart*, 2006; *Friend of the Devil*, 2007

Nonseries novels: *Caedmon's Song*, 1991; *No Cure for Love*, 1995

Short fiction: *Not Safe After Dark, and Other Stories*, 1998

Other major works

Poetry: *With Equal Eye*, 1979; *Nosferatu*, 1981

Bibliography

Bethune, Brian. "Working-Class Boys Made Good." *McLean's* 117, no. 8 (February 23, 2004): 48-49. Discusses Canadian crime fiction and Robinson's domination of the field.

Hanson, Gillian Mary. *City and Shore: The Function of Setting in the British Mystery*. Jefferson, N.C.: McFarland, 2004. A discussion of the importance of setting in British crime fiction. Sheds light on Robinson's use of Yorkshire for his settings although it does not deal with him in particular.

Priestman, Martin, ed. *The Cambridge Companion to Crime Fiction*. New York: Cambridge University Press, 2003. Contains a chapter on postwar British fiction that provides perspective on Robinson's work.

Robinson, Peter. "Peter Robinson." Interview. *Writer*

116, no. 9 (September, 2003): 66. Short biography of the writer, plus answers to questions regarding how he writes and why.

_______. Peter Robinson: Author of the Inspector Banks novels. http://www.peterrobinsonbooks.com. The author's Web site provides information on the author's life, his books, and upcoming events.

Windolf, Jim. "Soundtrack for Murder." Review of *Piece of My Heart*, by Peter Robinson. *The New York Times Review of Books*, July 2, 2006, p. 9. Reviewer praises *Piece of My Heart* and notes how Inspector Banks's personal life is developed with each work in the series. Briefly discusses the series and its development.

SAX ROHMER

Arthur Henry Sarsfield Ward

Born: Birmingham, Warwickshire, England; February 15, 1883
Died: London, England; June 1, 1959
Also wrote as Michael Furey
Type of plot: Thriller

Principal series

Fu Manchu, 1912-1959
Gaston Max, 1915-1943
Morris Klaw, 1918-1919
Daniel "Red" Kerry, 1919-1925
Paul Harley, 1921-1922
Sumuru, 1950-1956

Principal series character

Fu Manchu, a brilliant Mandarin Chinese who used his criminal organization, the Si-Fan, in various attempts to conquer the world, was to millions of readers the symbol of the "Yellow Peril" that faced the Western world. Instead of hordes of Asiatic invaders, however, Rohmer utilized exotic locations, devices, and people to create an atmosphere of fear, dread, and doom. Fu Manchu was always defeated, but always just barely.

Contribution

Although only one-quarter of Sax Rohmer's mystery novels and collected stories feature the insidious Fu Manchu, it is that character who guaranteed Rohmer's fame and success as a mystery writer. Although he neither invented the genre of the thriller nor created the "Yellow Peril" plot, it was he who combined the two aspects most successfully during the first half of the twentieth century. The stories of Fu Manchu appeared over the course of five decades, which is strong evidence that Rohmer's creation was popular throughout most of his writing career. Fu Manchu himself underwent a gradual metamorphosis, changing from, in 1912, a self-serving villain to, by the late 1940's, an anticommunist. The character appeared on radio, in film, and on television. Fu Manchu was also the pattern for many other evil Asian geniuses in popular culture.

Although Rohmer's major contribution to the writing of mystery fiction is a villain, his detectives do deserve some mention. Fu Manchu's worthy adversary was usually Sir Denis Nayland Smith or a similar type who had lived in the East and had studied the techniques of Asia. The stories themselves are in the tradition of Sherlock Holmes, wherein the brilliant Holmes/Smith matches wits with the equally brilliant Moriarty/Fu Manchu. Similarly, the stories are recorded by an associate, Dr. Petrie, who plays the role of the bumbling Dr. Watson. Over his long writing career Rohmer used many other detectives and villains. None, however, is as memorable as Fu Manchu.

Biography

Sax Rohmer was born Arthur Henry Ward on February 15, 1883, in Birmingham, England. He was the only child of William Ward, an office clerk, and Margaret Furey Ward, an alcoholic homemaker. With his father working long hours and his mother usually in an alcoholic daze, the young Ward was left to develop in his own way. Fortunately, he became a voracious reader, although his reading was chiefly confined to popular novels and to works on the bizarre and foreign. His formal schooling began at the age of nine; he was an unremarkable student, leaving school sometime in the early 1900's. That he was different from other students is evidenced by his decision, in his late teens, to drop his middle name and to adopt the name of Sarsfield (from an ancestor) in its stead. His interests left him ill prepared for bureaucratic work, and he failed the British civil service examination. He then became a bank clerk.

It was soon obvious that Ward had little interest in the mundane world of finance, and his career in banking was quite brief. He was far more interested in hypnotism, the occult, and archaeology. He turned to writing, becoming a reporter for a weekly newspaper. He also submitted short stories to various popular journals of the day and had his first stories accepted in 1903. Ward soon adopted the pen name Sax (Saxon for blade) Rohmer (for roamer). At first he used it only as his byline; later he used it in his personal life as well. Rohmer met and was married to Rose Elizabeth Knox in 1909; they were to have no children.

As a journalist, Rohmer was assigned to cover the Limehouse area of London, a section notorious for its criminal activities. It was this contact that led to his writing several episodic short stories that he published in 1912 and 1913 in *The Story-Teller*, a cheap British thriller magazine. These were soon collected and published as *The Mystery of Dr. Fu-Manchu* (1913). Further serializations resulted in two more novels, and Rohmer's popularity soared. Rohmer was read on both sides of the Atlantic, as his books were, from the beginning, published both in Great Britain and in the United States. He was soon able to retire from his reporting career and become a full-time writer.

For the next forty-odd years, Rohmer published prolifically, averaging a novel and several short stories per year. He spent most of his writing life in London and New York City, finally moving to New York City after World War II. He also traveled extensively to provide himself with details for his novels and stories. Sadly, Rohmer was never an astute businessman. He was often cheated on contracts, but he rarely chose to enter into litigation. Indeed, on one occasion in the early 1950's, Rohmer actually signed away the rights to all of his work—past, present, and future. Only after an extensive legal battle, and at enormous cost, was he able to regain his own property. In 1959, he became ill with influenza, which was followed by complications. He was determined to return to England. There he died on June 1, 1959.

Analysis

The London of 1900 was the trading center of the world and the capital of a large empire focused on Asia. East London, an area composed primarily of docks, wharves, sailors' bars, and working-class slums, was where this international community was centered. It was there that Sax Rohmer's writing career began. His job was to report on the criminal elements in the Limehouse area of East London. There he had the opportunity to meet the prototypes of the characters who were to populate his novels. He also witnessed, at first hand, the frightening settings for many of his novels. What set Rohmer apart was his ability to blend his reportorial observations with his skill as a thriller writer.

The Mystery of Dr. Fu-Manchu

Although Rohmer's first published short story appeared in 1903, it was not until 1912 that his archvillain was introduced. "The Zayat Kiss," published in October, 1912, in *The Story-Teller*, introduced Dr. Fu Manchu, the evil Asian genius, to the British thriller-reading public. Over the next ten issues a series of adventures pitted Fu Manchu against the forces of good, each adventure ending with the Chinese villain on the verge of victory. Finally, in the tenth episode, the sinister Mandarin was vanquished. In 1913, the serialized adventures were collected into a book, *The Mystery of Dr. Fu-Manchu*, and published in both Great Britain and the United States.

Over the next four years two more episodic thrillers were serialized, then published in book form. Rohmer grew weary of the doctor and had the archfiend killed at the end of *The Si-Fan Mysteries* (1917). Thirteen years later, however, Rohmer resurrected his villain; using the same formula as before, he published seven new Fu Manchu novels in eleven years. It was during this period that Rohmer was most popular. These later novels differed from the earlier ones in several ways; in particular, they dealt less with the Yellow Peril and more with the themes of the 1930's. Following World War II, Rohmer published three more Fu Manchu novels, the last of which appeared in the year of his death, 1959.

The Asian menace, vividly described

Sax Rohmer's success may be attributed, at least in part, to his very simple formula for writing. First, his plots were never too complex for the average reader. The English-language reading public of that day feared that Asians, through numbers alone, could someday overwhelm Western civilization. If those hordes ever acquired Western technological superiority, it was thought, they would swarm over the West even sooner. As a journalist in an era of sensational journalism, Rohmer was well aware of the success of Yellow Peril stories. Hordes of Asians, however, would make for complicated stories. Rohmer chose instead to use one man to symbolize the Asian menace.

> Imagine a person, tall, lean and feline, high-shouldered, with a brow like [William] Shakespeare and a face like Satan . . . Invest him with all the cruel cunning of an entire Eastern race, accumulated in one giant intellect, with all the resources of science past and present . . . Imagine that awful being, and you have a mental picture of Dr. Fu Manchu, the yellow peril incarnate in one man.

Rohmer endowed this embodiment of Asian evil with a brilliant mind, one capable not only of using Eastern cunning but also of understanding Western science. This was an easily understandable threat. Rohmer was to change this villain's interests, but the villain was a constant.

A second part of the formula was vivid description. Rohmer's extensive reading provided him with numerous exotic curiosities for his background detail. His lifelong interest in and study of the Far East gave him an intimate knowledge of Asian exotica. He filled secret rooms with incense, low teakwood tables, and lacquered cabinets. His work as a journalist in London had introduced him to the threatening locales of so many of his works. Fog-shrouded streets, rat-infested wharves, seedy bars, and opium dens provided the backdrop for many of Rohmer's plots. The characters who populated these environs were also drawn from his study. He once declared, "I made my name on Fu Manchu because I know nothing about the Chinese," adding "I know something about Chinatown." Although the first statement may have been true (he filled his stories with racial stereotypes), Rohmer did know how to create colorful characters. In his stories, sailors and thugs jostle one another with a polyglot array of Asian threats. Taken as a whole, Rohmer's works provided his readers with access to places about which they could only

The fifth novel in Sax Rohmer's Fu Manchu series, The Mask of Fu Manchu, *concerns the Chinese criminal mastermind's acquisition of relics, including an armor mask, that had belonged to the thirteenth century Mongol emperor Genghis Khan.*

dream. He painted pictures for his readers.

Rohmer's success also rested on thrilling action. Although his plots are rarely plausible, the action never ceases. Strange drugs, venomous animals, Burmese dacoits, and other dastardly things appear in rapid succession. Death or narrow escape occurs on almost every page. Only through skill, much luck, and many adventures are the schemes of Dr. Fu Manchu foiled. Rohmer himself did not create the thriller genre; Sir Arthur Conan Doyle pioneered it in the late nineteenth century. Rohmer simply added a few twists of his own. Rohmer's sleuths were less intelligent but more dogged than Holmes. More important, his sleuths underwent far more exciting chases and adventures than did Holmes.

In another way, Rohmer reversed the formula, shifting emphasis to the villain: Although rarely seen in the books, Dr. Fu Manchu is always the focal point. Furthermore, Fu Manchu usually failed because of the ineptitude of his minions, especially his female (usually beautiful) operatives who fell in love with the wrong person. (This is yet another difference; Rohmer used a love element to titillate his audience.) Rohmer's formula was used with great success by many other authors throughout the first half of the twentieth century. One need only note the success of the Flash Gordon series character Ming the Merciless for a parallel.

President Fu Manchu and Emperor Fu Manchu

Rohmer's plots reflected his times. He was never so tightly bound by a formula that he could not meet the interests of his readers. When Dr. Fu Manchu was first introduced, he was evil incarnate. The early novels reflected the nationalism, the xenophobia, and the white man's racism of the immediate pre-World War I era. The novels of the 1930's were different, dealing with political activities of that turbulent era. *President Fu Manchu* (1936) portrayed the Chinese menace as the power behind a demagogic American presidential candidate. *The Drums of Fu Manchu* (1939) had him fighting Fascism and deposing Rudolf Adlon (Adolf Hitler). Also in the 1930's, Fu Manchu, while still Asian, became more of a supercriminal than the personification of the Yellow Peril. Fascism was more to be feared than the Chinese, who, after all, were fighting the Japanese. After World War II Fu Manchu returned as an anticommunist. In *Emperor Fu Manchu* (1959) he strived to rid his homeland of the communists who were destroying "his" China. Although these plots date the stories, it can be seen that Rohmer's Fu Manchu novels are a barometer of certain public opinions during the twentieth century. His popularity was a measure of what the public wanted to read.

Other series

In addition to the highly successful Fu Manchu series, Rohmer utilized many other characters. A series of five Sumuru novels (1950-1956) featured a female villain. Although the Sumuru books were mildly popular, Rohmer dropped her to return to Fu Manchu. Earlier in his career, he had written several books featuring the psychic detective Morris Klaw. In *Brood of the Witch Queen* (1918), *The Quest of the Sacred Slipper* (1919), and *The Dream-Detective* (1920), Klaw solved bizarre cases by using his psychic powers. Another detective used by Rohmer was Gaston Max, who fought supercriminals in *The Yellow Claw* (1915), *The Golden Scorpion* (1919), and *The Day the World Ended* (1930) or Axis agents in *Seven Sins* (1943). Paul Harley appeared in *Bat-Wing* (1921) and *Fire-Tongue* (1922), and Chief Inspector Daniel "Red" Kerry was featured in *Dope* (1919) and *Yellow Shadows* (1925).

Rohmer is best remembered for a villain, Fu Manchu. His plots were simple, full of action, and thrilling. He cannot be considered a great or innovative writer, but he was a good teller of tales. His stories reflected his times, and his work was popular because his audience, which was by no means intellectual, identified with what it read.

William S. Brockington, Jr.

Principal mystery and detective fiction

Fu Manchu series: *The Mystery of Dr. Fu-Manchu*, 1913 (also known as *The Insidious Fu-Manchu*); *The Devil Doctor*, 1916 (also known as *The Return of Dr. Fu-Manchu*); *The Si-Fan Mysteries*, 1917 (also known as *The Hand of Fu-Manchu*); *Daughter of Fu Manchu*, 1931; *The Mask of Fu Manchu*, 1932; *Fu Manchu's Bride*, 1933 (also known as *The Bride of Fu Manchu*); *The Trail of Fu Manchu*,

1934; *President Fu Manchu*, 1936; *The Drums of Fu Manchu*, 1939; *The Island of Fu Manchu*, 1941; *Shadow of Fu Manchu*, 1948; *Re-Enter Fu Manchu*, 1957; *Emperor Fu Manchu*, 1959; *The Wrath of Fu Manchu, and Other Stories*, 1973

Gaston Max series: *The Yellow Claw*, 1915; *The Golden Scorpion*, 1919; *The Day the World Ended*, 1930; *Seven Sins*, 1943

Morris Klaw series: *Brood of the Witch Queen*, 1918; *The Quest of the Sacred Slipper*, 1919; *The Dream-Detective*, 1920

Daniel "Red" Kerry series: *Dope*, 1919; *Yellow Shadows*, 1925

Paul Harley series: *Bat-Wing*, 1921; *Fire-Tongue*, 1922

Sumuru series: *Nude in Mink*, 1950 (also known as *Sins of Sumuru*); *Sumuru*, 1951 (also known as *Slaves of Sumuru*); *The Fire Goddess*, 1952 (also known as *Virgin in Flames*); *Return of Sumuru*, 1954 (also known as *Sand and Satin*); *Sinister Madonna*, 1956

Nonseries novels: *The Sins of Séverac Bablon*, 1914; *The Green Eyes of Bâst*, 1920; *Grey Face*, 1924; *Moon of Madness*, 1927; *She Who Sleeps*, 1928; *The Emperor of America*, 1929; *Yu'an Hee See Laughs*, 1932; *The Bat Flies Low*, 1935; *White Velvet*, 1936; *Egyptian Nights*, 1944; *Hangover House*, 1949; *Wulfheim*, 1950; *The Moon Is Red*, 1954

Other short fiction: *The Exploits of Captain O'Hagan*, 1916; *Tales of Secret Egypt*, 1918; *The Haunting of Low Fennel*, 1920; *Tales of Chinatown*, 1922; *Tales of East and West*, 1932; *Salute to Bazarada, and Other Stories*, 1939; *Bimbâshi Barûk of Egypt*, 1944; *The Secret of Holm Peel, and Other Strange Stories*, 1970

Other major works

Novel: *The Orchard of Tears*, 1918

Plays: *Round in Fifty*, pr. 1922 (with Julian and Lauri Wylie); *The Eye of Siva*, pr. 1923; *Secret Egypt*, pr. 1928; *The Nightingale*, pr. 1947 (with Michael Martin-Harvey)

Nonfiction: *Pause!*, 1910; *The Romance of Sorcery*, 1914

Bibliography

Chan, Jachinson. *Chinese American Masculinities: From Fu Manchu to Bruce Lee*. New York: Routledge, 2001. Study of the gendering of iconic Chinese American male characters, including Fu Manchu, in film and fiction.

Chen, Tina. "Dissecting the 'Devil Doctor': Stereotype and Sensationalism in Sax Rohmer's Fu Manchu." In *Double Agency: Acts of Impersonation in Asian American Literature and Culture*. Stanford, Calif.: Stanford University Press, 2005. Discussion of the intersection of the conventions of racial stereotype and sensationalist fiction in the figure of Fu Manchu.

Christensen, Peter. "Political Appeal of Dr. Fu Manchu." In *The Devil Himself: Villainy in Detective Fiction and Film*, edited by Stacy Gillis and Philippa Gates. Westport, Conn.: Greenwood Press, 2002. Examines the ideologies of race and nation that lie behind the popularity of the Fu Manchu character.

Clegg, Jenny. *Fu Manchu and the Yellow Peril: The Making of a Racist Myth*. Stoke-on-Trent, Staffordshire, England: Trentham Books, 1994. Brief but focused study of the nationalist and racist agendas behind Rohmer's characterization of Fu Manchu.

Frayling, Christopher. "Criminal Tendencies: Sax Rohmer and the Devil Doctor." *London Magazine* 13 (June/July, 1973): 65-80. Extended discussion of Rohmer and Fu Manchu, his most famous creation.

Kingsbury, Karen. "Yellow Peril, Dark Hero: Fu Manchu and the 'Gothic Bedevilment' of Racist Intent." In *The Gothic Other: Racial and Social Constructions in the Literary Imagination*, edited by Ruth Bienstock Anolik and Douglas L. Howard. Jefferson, N.C.: McFarland, 2004. Argues that Rohmer's works represent a version of gothic fiction and that his specific methods of representing racial otherness employ gothic modes of othering.

Van Ash, Cay, and Elizabeth Sax Rohmer. *Master of Villainy: A Biography of Sax Rohmer*, edited by Robert E. Briney. Bowling Green, Ohio: Bowling Green University Popular Press, 1972. Extended study of the life and fiction of Sax Rohmer.

LAURA JOH ROWLAND

Born: Harper Woods, Michigan; 1953
Type of plot: Historical

Principal series

Sano Ichirō and Lady Reiko, 1994-

Principal series characters

Sano Ichirō begins as a thirty-year-old *yoriki*, or senior police commander, in the service of Shogun Tokugawa Tsunayoshi in 1689. His unconventional, intelligent, and ethical approach to solving crimes earns him promotion to *sōsakan-sama*, most honorable investigator of events, situations, and people. In this position he solves eight more cases until he is promoted (ahistorically) to the position of *sobayōnin*, or grand chamberlain, in 1694. Operating at the highest level of government, he remains an independent-minded detective.

Ueda Reiko marries Sano at the beginning of his fourth case. The daughter of a judge, Reiko rejects a traditional female role. Moved by a strong desire for justice, especially for women, she deeply involves herself in her husband's cases and, in many instances, proves instrumental in solving them. Her complex character and ongoing development threaten to eclipse Sano in more than one case.

Contribution

In Sano Ichirō and his wife, Lady Reiko, Laura Joh Rowland has created a multidimensional detective couple who have propelled her series to a long and sustained life. Rowland attracts readers who savor both historical mysteries and good old-fashioned detective work. Her mysteries live off her meticulous historical research, which brings to life Japan's seventeenth century Genroku era, and her keen understanding of humanity's weaknesses and its penchant for crime and political intrigue, which are mediated by the desire of a few good persons to see justice prevail. One of Rowland's key achievements is that she makes her characters, from a geographically and chronologically remote past, become so familiar and feel so real that critics enthused that Sano has more in common with Philip Marlowe or Sam Spade than with a costumed warrior of times past.

Throughout her crime series, Rowland carefully develops her central cast of characters, beginning with Sano and Reiko. By having Sano move up the ranks, she is able to create mysteries with ever larger social and political ramifications. Similarly, the amazing development of Lady Reiko has fascinated Rowland's appreciative and steadily growing readership.

The existence of the magical in Rowland's world, with villains felling their opponents through arcane mystic martial arts skills, does not distract from the reality of her crime-solving characters, who are caught in the nets and restraints of a deeply stratified society where a false step may mean instant death. In each novel, the stakes are raised to the utmost for Sano and Reiko, yet they have been able to extricate themselves, often at a price, from all the traps laid for them by their nefarious adversaries.

Biography

Laura Joh Rowland was born in Michigan, the third generation of Chinese and Korean immigrants. Initially, she followed her family's tradition of studying for a career in education or the sciences, earning a bachelor's in microbiology and a master's degree in public health from the University of Michigan and working almost twenty years in her field. When she and her husband, Marty Rowland, an environmental scientist and political activist, moved to New Orleans in 1981, she began yearning for a creative outlet while working for the city's public health office and later for Lockheed Martin at a National Aeronautics and Space Administration facility as a quality engineer. Her fondness for her father's classic English and American mysteries propelled her to start writing. To make her mark in the mystery market and to realize her Asian heritage, Rowland decided to set her crime fiction in seventeenth century Japan. The period appealed for its combination of social tension and individual aspirations, its distance from modern scientific crime solving (which would favor a classical detective approach), and its thoroughly Asian setting.

After abandoning two projects, Rowland got a break when an editor at Random House showed interest in her novel *Shinjū* (1994). The manuscript and its sequel were auctioned off for a hundred thousand dollars, going to Random House. Both *Shinjū* and its sequel, *Bundori* (1996), captured American readers, who took to samurai detective Sano Ichirō and his fight to defend justice within the military dictatorship of early Tokugawa Japan. This success enabled Rowland to continue her long-running series.

In *The Concubine's Tattoo* (1998) Rowland decided to put a female partner at Sano's side, his loyal wife, Lady Reiko. Earlier hints that a high-class prostitute or a mysterious female Ninja might win Sano's affections were stilled.

Rowland's next four mysteries put the detective couple through an amazing array of complex crime situations. Her fiction explored male-female relations both in Tokugawa Japan and in the timeless realm of psychological realism, probing issues of trust, dependency, and mutual love. With *The Samurai's Wife* (2000), Rowland proved to be at the height of her craft.

Perhaps to give Sano room for growth, Rowland decided on the historically inaccurate move of having his long-time adversary, *sobayōnin* (grand chancellor) Yanagisawa, exiled in 1694. Sano is appointed to the office vacated by Yanagisawa at the end of his ninth adventure, *The Perfumed Sleeve* (2004).

As the series progressed, Rowland's fictional universe of Japan's Genroku era became so familiar to her readers that she spent less time on explanatory passages. In the murder case in *Red Chrysanthemum* (2006), as Sano and Reiko rush to save their lives by proving their own innocence, seventeenth century Edo (Tokyo) is described as matter of factly as if it were modern Washington, D.C., or Los Angeles. The focus in this novel is on the crime, not the background. Rowland's characters ring true, and her setting adds to, rather than detracts from, the compelling crimes of passion at the heart of her mysteries.

Analysis

When Laura Joh Rowland decided to write mysteries, she deliberately chose a historical period. Driven to write novels in the style of classical detective stories where good sleuthing makes all the difference and looking for an exciting setting where both crime and justice could flourish, she settled on late seventeenth century Japan. It was a time of strictly set and enforced social standards, in some ways similar to Victorian England, and gave rise to imaginative criminals and colorful renegades.

In creating her hero, Sano Ichirō, Rowland took advantage of the period's emphasis on an active police force to ensure the peace of the Tokugawa shogunate. Rowland's mysteries take on a unique dimension from the precarious balance between actual police work, in the modern sense of upholding order in a burgeoning metropolis where citizens of many classes compete and private desires clash, and the political dimension of police as upholders of an authoritarian regime.

Beginning with her debut novel, *Shinjū*, Rowland successfully overcame key challenges of the historical mystery genre. She escaped the temptation to bog down the plot with too many historical details and managed to create a sympathetic yet still believable historical protagonist. An utterly historically correct rendering of the actual thoughts, actions, and beliefs of a bygone era in a foreign country always risks alienating, if not offending, modern American readers. Examples of historically accurate details that might offend in Rowland's case include a samurai's explicit permission to strike down any offending peasant and then-prevailing attitudes toward women and the less privileged.

It is to Rowland's credit that she has managed to bridge successfully the gap between the mind-set of the past and the present and, in her protagonists, has developed characters who gain and maintain the sympathy of her readers. In her second novel, *Bundori*, Rowland presents readers with the samurai code, which because of emphasis on the samurai's absolute, unquestioning loyalty and obedience to his lord is likely to strike modern American readers as questionable if not absurd, but she endows Sano with sufficient iconoclastic characteristics to gain readers' sympathy and an understanding for his culturally prescribed position.

In *The Concubine's Tattoo*, Rowland took the inspired step of placing at Sano's side his young wife, Lady Reiko. An exceptional and utterly unconventional woman who defies traditional historical restraints on a noble woman of the Genroku era, Reiko almost steals the show from Sano in *Black Lotus* (2001) and *The Dragon King's Palace* (2003). Readers may get the impression that Reiko's character is the more dynamic of the two. Her independence is unusual for the period, yet within the realm of the possible.

What distinguishes Rowland's series is that the prime characters develop in time, create a family, and advance in their careers. They are not the timeless detectives of American crime classics whose lives change little from case to case. Soon after their marriage, Sano and Lady Reiko have a son.

Just as her series appeared to lose steam, Rowland decided on the bold stroke of changing history: Sano and Reiko's longtime adversary, Grand Chamberlain Yanagisawa, is exiled, and Sano occupies his office at the end of *The Perfumed Sleeve.* Although this may be as odd as having Philip Marlowe replace a disgraced J. Edgar Hoover as the director of the Federal Bureau of Investigation, it gave Rowland's series a fresh impetus.

Stylistically, Rowland's Sano Ichirō and Lady Reiko mysteries follow a set pattern. All the novels open with a decisive account of the crime that sets the investigation in motion. Reiko favors investigations regarding women and Sano pursues villains in his official position. The time line for solving the crime is generally shortened by political ploys on the part of Sano and Reiko's adversaries intended to cause the shogun to disgrace the idiosyncratic couple, raising the personal stakes at every turn of their inquiries. Rowland's mysteries often incorporate supernatural beliefs of the era and treat them as real, such as an acolyte's power to kill by will alone. There is also a strong emphasis on physical combat at the end of the story, when Rowland's mysteries enter the realm of a martial arts novel. Sexuality, particularly deviant sexuality such as pederasty, forced sex, and exotic sexual predilections, feature strongly and are described in rather explicit terms.

Solving a case often brings more of an ominous foreboding to Sano and Reiko than a final resolution. This is, of course, what propels the series forward. Another trademark of Rowland is her successful creation of strong secondary characters such as Sano's loyal assistant Hirata. These characters are consistently developed throughout the series and given a genuine life, for example, having a wife and children of their own. A persistent figure serving as lodestar is the historical, homosexual shogun Tokugawa Tsunayoshi, whom Sano serves and who has always rewarded him in the end.

Shinjū

Rowland's acclaimed first mystery, *Shinjū*, begins with the discovery of a dead couple, an apparent double love suicide, or *shinjū*, the subject of many Japanese plays and novels. Young Sano Ichirō, who has just been appointed a senior police commander through the patron of his family, refuses to stop investigating the case as is expected of him. His dogged pursuit of the truth, which points at murder, quickly

makes him run afoul of his police superiors as well as his bemused patron and father.

Indicative of his unconventional thinking and his dedication to finding the truth, Sano takes recourse in the forensic wisdom of Dr. Ito Genboku, who has been demoted to work at Edo jail for taking an interest in the forbidden Western medical sciences. When Sano learns that the couple was murdered as he suspected, he launches an inquiry that points to a plot by twenty-one nobles, including the brother of the murdered woman.

Saving the shogun after a dramatic sword battle with the insurgents earns Sano his new position of *sōsakan-sama*, most honorable investigator of events, situations, and people.

Bundori

In *Bundori*, Sano's case features a deranged man who kills his victims so that he can sever their skulls and nail them to a wooden board in the fashion that samurai used to prepare their war trophies. This ancient custom, described, for example, in the Japanese classic *Heike monogatari* (wr. thirteenth century C.E.; *The Tale of the Heike*, 1918-1921) and featured in Jun'ichirō Tanizaki's novel *Bushōkō hiwa* (1931-1932 serial; 1935; *The Secret History of the Lord of Musashi*, 1982) is an odd anachronism in Sano's seventeenth century.

Great tension derives from Sano's psychological grappling with the samurai warrior code, or Bushido. The code requires unquestioning obedience to one's superior, even if that person is despicable. Thus at the climax of the novel, Sano saves his sworn arch-enemy, jealous Grand Chancellor Yanagisawa, during the climactic battle with the deranged murderer aboard a seagoing vessel.

Red Chrysanthemum

Red Chrysanthemum, Rowland's eleventh mystery, reveals her storytelling at its finest and challenges her detective duo to the utmost. After Sano's marriage to Lady Reiko in *The Concubine's Tattoo*, which delves into the realm of forbidden love and establishes Yanagisawa as a moral monster who survives by virtue of his political power, Reiko's crime-solving skills are tested further in *The Samurai's Wife*. Out of sympathy for a woman suspect, Reiko commits a serious error of judgment in *Black Lotus* that nearly gets her killed at the hands of a vicious cult leader. *The Red Chrysanthemum* places Sano and Reiko in deepest peril. At the beginning, five-months pregnant Reiko is discovered naked, atop the castrated and murdered body of Lord Mori, lying in his own blood with a blood-drenched chrysanthemum. The question as to how she got there is answered in the fashion of multiple, contradictory narratives consciously modeled after Akutagawa Ryūnosuke's short story "Yabu no naka" (1922; "In a Grove," 1952) that was made into Akira Kurosawa's famous film *Rashōmon* (1950).

Even though the mysterious circumstances of the crime cause each character to distrust each other, in the end, Sano and Reiko's love and their dedication to justice solve the case. The case leaves Sano a much more cynical character than ever before. Rowland hints at future complications born out of political intrigues, ending this novel, as she does others, with suggestions of future adventures.

R. C. Lutz

Principal mystery and detective fiction

Sano Ichirō and Lady Reiko series: *Shinjū*, 1994; *Bundori*, 1996; *The Way of the Traitor*, 1997; *The Concubine's Tattoo*, 1998; *The Samurai's Wife*, 2000; *Black Lotus*, 2001; *The Pillow Book of Lady Wisteria*, 2002; *The Dragon King's Palace*, 2003; *The Perfumed Sleeve*, 2004; *The Assassin's Touch*, 2005; *Red Chrysanthemum*, 2006; *The Snow Empress*, 2007

Bibliography

Cannon, Peter. Review of *The Dragon King's Palace*, by Laura Joh Rowland. *Publishers Weekly* 250, no. 5 (February 3, 2003): 57. Reviewer is impressed by author's ability to combine rich period detail with universal human emotions and dark obsessions that make for an original mystery.

Drabelle, Dennis. "Bundori: Going Great Shoguns." Review of *Bundori*, by Laura Joh Rowland. *The Washington Post*, March 4, 1996, p. D2. Discusses Sano's difficulties as a detective embedded in an authoritarian society and beset by jealous enemies. Emphasizes Sano's traditional beliefs, which he augments with real human cunning and insight, and lauds Rowland's re-creation of her historical setting.

Klett, Rex. Review of *Black Lotus*, by Laura Joh Rowland. *Library Journal* 126, no. 4 (March 1, 2001): 133. Focuses on the novel's intricate plot and the threat to Sano and Reiko's marriage; stresses Rowland's display of class interest and political intrigue and depiction of daily life in a remote era.

Needham, George. Review of *The Samurai's Wife*, by Laura Joh Rowland. *Booklist* 96, no. 13 (March 1, 2000): 1199. Describes premises of the novel challenging Sano and Reiko to cooperate with their adversary Yanagisawa to mediate between the shogun and emperor.

Pitt, David. Review of *Red Chrysanthemum*, by Laura Joh Rowland. *Booklist* 103, no. 3 (October 1, 2006): 42. Positive review; praises Rowland for bringing her series back on track with entertaining new ideas and vibrant plots in her last three novels.

Rowland, Laura Joh. Laura Joh Rowland: Home of the Sano Ichiro Mystery Series. http://www.laurajohrowland.com. Author's Web site features introductions and critical blurbs for her most recent novels, interviews with photographs, news, and dates of speaking engagements. Her latest novel is always presented.

J. K. ROWLING

Joanne Kathleen Rowling

Born: Yate, South Gloucestershire, England; July 31, 1965
Also wrote as Newt Scamander; Kennelworthy Whisp
Types of plot: Amateur sleuth; horror; psychological

Principal series

Harry Potter, 1997-2007

Principal series characters

Harry Potter, the central character in all seven novels, is a powerful wizard who was orphaned in infancy and raised by nonmagical relatives who never told him the truth about his origins. After reaching the age of eleven, he enters a school for wizards and gradually learns about his powers and his destiny to fight the immensely powerful and evil Lord Voldemort. Most of the series' storylines revolve around his quests to answer questions about himself and Voldemort.

Ron Weasley is Harry's classmate and best friend. A member of a large wizarding family and the son of a Ministry of Magic official, he helps introduce Harry to the world of magic and assists him in his struggles against Voldemort.

Hermione Granger, another of Harry's classmates and close friends, is a brainy and studious girl who repeatedly uses her book learning and intelligence to help Harry in his quests.

Albus Dumbledore is the grandfatherly and good-humored headmaster of Hogwarts School of Witchcraft and Wizardry and the only wizard whom Voldemort fears. He serves as Harry's mentor throughout the series but occasionally behaves in ways that Harry cannot fully understand and makes serious mistakes. One of the many mysteries in the series is the full extent of Dumbledore's knowledge about Harry and Voldemort.

Lord Voldemort, originally named Tom Riddle and also known as the Dark Lord, is Harry's archenemy and the principal villain throughout the series. Harry's central mission is to combat Voldemort's quest to rule the wizarding world and use his great magical powers for evil. Voldemort's powers appear to be limitless, but he is eventually defeated by gaps in his knowledge.

Contribution

J. K. Rowling became an internationally known writer after the 1997 release of her first book, *Harry Potter and the Philosopher's Stone* (also known as *Harry Potter and the Sorcerer's Stone*). The Cinderella-like tale of an ordinary boy who discovers he has magical powers captured the imagination of adults as well as children, and the book soared to the top of international best-seller lists. Rowling was credited by teachers, parents, and librarians with motivating even the most reluctant students to read. Six more titles followed: *Harry Potter and the Chamber of Secrets* (1998), *Harry Potter and the Prisoner of Azkaban* (1999), *Harry Potter and the Goblet of Fire* (2000), *Harry Potter and the Order of the Phoenix* (2003), *Harry Potter and the Half-Blood Prince* (2005), and *Harry Potter and the Deathly Hallows* (2007). Each successive book became more popular than the previous one in the seven-book series.

Although Rowling's novels take place in the parallel world of Hogwarts and other magical locations, her young characters are similar to contemporary teenagers. They study, flirt, play sports, gossip, and date. They also wield considerable power that can transform reality in an instant. Following the arc of the hero's journey, Harry struggles to come of age as a wizard and an adult. In each novel, he must solve a mystery, which leads him to a deeper understanding of his mission to vanquish the evil Lord Voldemort.

Biography

Joanne Kathleen Rowling was born in Yate, South Gloucestershire, England, on a July 31, the same date on which her fictional Harry Potter was born. Her father, Peter Rowling, worked on airplane engines for Rolls Royce. Her mother, Ann, died in 1990 of multiple sclerosis.

From an early age, Rowling loved to write stories. When she was six, she wrote her first book, *Rabbit*, a story about a sick rabbit and the visitors who came to cheer him up. When her family moved to Tutshill in South Wales, she attended Wyedean School and College. She then attended the University of Exeter, where she studied French and the classics. She also spent a year studying in Paris. After graduating, she worked as a researcher and secretary for Amnesty International. During this period she commuted by train between Manchester and London and began formulating a story about a young boy who discovers that he has magical powers. When she was twenty-six, she quit her job and went to Portugal to teach English as a second language. In 1992, she married journalist Jorge Arantes; they had a daughter, Jessica, the following year. Their marriage was troubled and was dissolved that same year.

Rowling returned to Great Britain and settled near Edinburgh, Scotland. She completed her first Harry Potter book in 1994 while she was unemployed and living on welfare. She sent the manuscript of *Harry Potter and the Philosopher's Stone* to several publishers, who rejected the work. Finally in 1997, Bloomsbury published the book in England to rave reviews. A year later, the book was published in the United States by Scholastic under the title *Harry Potter and the Sorcerer's Stone.* The novel became an international publishing sensation and won several awards, including the Nestlé Smarties Book Prize and the British Book Award for Children's Book of the Year. In 1999,

J. K. Rowling. (Richard Young/ Courtesy, Allen & Unwin)

Harry Potter and the Prisoner of Azkaban, the third book in the series, again received the Nestlé Smarties Prize, as well as the Whitbread Children's Book of the Year award in 2000. *Harry Potter and the Order of the Phoenix* earned the W. H. Smith People's Choice Award in 2003, and *Harry Potter and the Half-Blood Prince* was named British Book Awards Book of the Year in 2006. The much-anticipated final installment, *Harry Potter and the Deathly Hallows*, was released in 2007.

Many of the books in the series have been adapted to film. Rowling has also published two spin-off volumes based on books mentioned in the Potter novels, *Fantastic Beasts and Where to Find Them* (2001) and *Quidditch Through the Ages* (2001).

In addition to the awards her books have garnered, Rowling herself has been the recipient of many honors. She holds honorary degrees from Dartmouth College in the United States, and the University of Exeter, University of St. Andrews, Napier University, and University of Edinburgh in Great Britain. In 2001, she was awarded the Order of the British Empire by Queen Elizabeth for her contributions to children's literature, and in 2002, she became a fellow of the Royal Society of Edinburgh.

Rowling settled in Scotland with her second husband, Dr. Neil Murray, whom she married in 2001, along with her children, Jessica, David, and MacKenzie.

Analysis

J. K. Rowling's *Harry Potter* novels are similar in construction to Sir Arthur Conan Doyle's Sherlock Holmes stories. To solve the mysteries at the heart of each story, Harry, Ron, and Hermione, the three principal characters, act as amateur sleuths who sift through clues and puzzles to eliminate suspects and identify actual wrongdoers. The books require careful reading, as seemingly insignificant phrases and sentences often turn out to be major clues. Throughout each narrative, Rowling presents several possible solutions to the mystery, which frequently lead the characters to draw false conclusions based on circumstantial evidence. When Harry, Ron, and Hermione act on their incorrect assumptions, they discover that things are rarely as they seem and that their mistaken conclusions have blinded them to the truth.

In general, each Potter novel follows a set formula. At the beginning of each book, Harry is living with his nonmagical ("muggle") aunt, uncle, and cousin, the Dursleys, during his summer vacations. In the fall, Harry returns to Hogwarts School of Witchcraft and Wizardry. There he, Ron, and Hermione become involved in increasingly dangerous adventures that lead them to new revelations concerning the series' central villain, Lord Voldemort, and his plans to dominate the wizarding and muggle worlds. The climax of each story occurs when Harry and Voldemort—or one of the latter's Death Eaters—engage in a dramatic confrontation. Following Harry and Voldemort's altercations, the school's headmaster, Albus Dumbledore, reveals to Harry more about his family history, as well as the possible outcome of his inevitable final battle with Voldemort. When the school year ends, Harry returns to the home of his muggle relatives until the next term begins.

The overall story arc does not change from book to book, and plots of the individual novels are intricate and multilayered. Magical objects, characters, and places mentioned only briefly in one book may play a major role in another. As the characters mature, the plots become more weighty. Over the course of the series, the children deal with life and death issues, the ups and downs of adolescence, and the pain of loss.

The final chapters of traditional mysteries tie up loose ends. Although Rowling follows that custom in each of her novels, she also leaves important questions unanswered or poses new ones that she addresses in later books. Volumes in the series as a whole can be viewed as individual chapters in a larger story that poses a number of central questions: What is the true relationship between Harry and Voldemort? Which of them will be victorious? Are certain major characters truly what they seem? Interconnections among the novels maintain suspense from book to book until the final resolution is reached in the seventh novel.

Harry Potter and the Philosopher's Stone

Laying the intricate groundwork for the succeeding six books, the first novel, *Harry Potter and the Philospher's Stone*, introduces Harry as an eleven-year-old orphan who does not realize he is a wizard. Although a nonentity in the muggle world that he shares with his nasty aunt, uncle, and cousin, he is famous in the parallel wizarding world because he survived Lord Voldemort's murderous attack that killed his mother and father when he was an infant. During that attack, Voldemort's curse left a lightning-bolt scar on Harry's forehead. The battle also robs Voldemort of his body and most of his power. A wraith of his former self, he goes into hiding for years. It is unclear why Harry did not perish with his parents, and the mystery surrounding his survival is explored in subsequent books.

The philosopher's stone, a magical object that bestows immortality on its owner, leads Harry to his second encounter with Lord Voldemort ten years after his parents' deaths. When Harry arrives at Hogwarts, he and his new friends, Ron and Hermione, learn that the stone is hidden somewhere on school grounds and that Voldemort's followers need it to restore Voldemort to his full power. When Harry overhears Professors Snape and Quirrell discussing how to get past a giant three-headed dog guarding the entry to a subterranean room, he concludes that Snape wants Quirrell to steal the stone for Voldemort. To stop Quirrell, Harry, Ron, and Hermione must decipher various clues and puzzles and play their way across a huge chessboard populated by living pieces. Their quest ultimately leads Harry to Quirrell, whose own body hosts the disembodied Voldemort. Harry learns that Snape was actually trying to talk Quirrell out of stealing the stone. Snape remains an ambiguous character throughout the series; it appears that he hates Harry for reasons left unexplained until later volumes; however, he shields him from harm.

Harry Potter and the Chamber of Secrets

In the second volume, *Harry Potter and the Chamber of Secrets*, Rowling reveals more about Lord Voldemort's background and how he and Harry are connected. When Harry returns to Hogwarts, he hears sinister voices announcing that someone will be killed. He also sees a message scrawled across a wall proclaiming that the Chamber of Secrets has been opened and witnesses the results of attacks that leave some students in a petrified state. The Chamber of Secrets can only be opened by the heir of Salazar Slytherin, one of the four founders of Hogwarts. Suspicion for the attacks falls on Harry because he can speak to snakes, a dark arts trait he shares with Voldemort. His classmates wonder if he is a dark wizard in disguise.

Meanwhile, Harry finds an enchanted diary written by Tom Riddle, a student at Hogwarts fifty years earlier. The diary reveals that the Chamber of Secrets was opened when Riddle attended the school. In the diary, Riddle vows to catch the person who opened the chamber and accuses a large boy who is raising a huge spider. Harry recognizes that that boy is his friend Hagrid, the good-natured but simple-minded Hogwarts game keeper. The picture Riddle paints of Hagrid's supposed transgression is deliberately deceptive, portraying Hagrid as the villain and Riddle as the conscientious student. Harry, Ron, and Hermione cannot believe that Hagrid would practice dark magic.

After Hermione goes to the library to seek information, she is found petrified. Ron and Harry later discover that her stiff hand holds a piece of paper with information on a basilisk, a giant serpent that can kill by gazing into its victim's eyes. This information enables Harry and Ron to gain entrance to the chamber to look for Ginny, Ron's younger sister. Harry finds her on the floor with the ghostly image of Tom Riddle beside her. Riddle admits that he, not Hagrid, opened the chamber fifty years earlier and that he has possessed Ginny to open the chamber again. He also reveals that he is the heir of Slytherin and will become Lord Voldemort. When Harry kills the basilisk and destroys the diary, Riddle's apparition fades away. The narrative culminates with the destruction of the diary, but it plays an important part in solving a mystery of a later book.

Harry Potter and the Prisoner of Azkaban

The primary mystery of the third novel, *Harry Potter and the Prisoner of Azkaban*, is the identity of a man named Sirius Black, whom Harry and the Dursley family learn from television news has escaped from prison. When Harry leaves the Dursleys' house, he sees a large black dog. The animal seems to be a portent of death. Eventually, Harry discovers that Sirius Black escaped from Azkaban, the wizard prison, and may have been responsible for betraying Harry's par-

Emma Watson (left) has played Hermione Granger, Daniel Radcliffe (center) has played Harry Potter, and Rupert Grint (right) has played Ron Weasley in all the films adapted from J. K. Rowling's Harry Potter novels. (Courtesy, Warner Bros.)

ents to Voldemort. Sirius's name is significant because Rowling's ingenious choice of names is one way she inserts clues into her narratives. Drawing on Greco-Roman myth, as well as the Anglo-Saxon and French languages, she creates names that hint of the characters' secret traits, identities, and motivations. For example, the last name of Draco Malfoy, Harry's archenemy classmate at Hogwarts, means "bad faith." "Voldemort" means "flight of death" in French, an evident allusion to Voldemort's quest for immortality. Black's first name derives from the name of the double star known as the Dog Star in the constellation Sirius. Black is eventually revealed to be an animagus, a wizard who can transform himself into an animal, in this case a large black dog.

Remus Lupin, the seemingly even-tempered defense against the dark arts teacher in the third novel, provides a counterpoint to Black's threatening presence. Lupin's name also reflects a secret aspect to his personality. He is a werewolf, which makes him an outcast even within the wizarding community. He takes a fatherly interest in Harry, however, and acts as his protector and mentor.

As the story progresses, Harry eventually has an opportunity to kill Black and avenge his parents. However, Lupin intercedes and explains that Black, Harry's father, and a boy named Peter Pettigrew—all animagi—were his best friends in school and roamed with him when he became a wolf during the full moon. The surprising revelation that Sirius Black was actually the best friend of Harry's father, James, and is Harry's godfather casts the frightening appearances of the black dog in a new light. Black was trying to protect Harry, not kill him. Another shocking disclosure is that Peter Pettigrew has been masquerading as Ron's rat, Scabbers, to spy on the trio for Voldemort.

Harry Potter and the Goblet of Fire

In *Harry Potter and the Goblet of Fire*, when Harry, Ron, and Hermione return to school for their fourth year, Dumbledore announces that a contest among three schools of magic—the Triwizard Tournament—will be held at Hogwarts. An object called the Goblet of Fire selects one champion from each school to compete in the tournament's three highly dangerous tasks. Contestants must be seventeen, the age at which witches and wizards are considered adults. After the goblet selects Cedric Diggory as the Hogwarts champion, Fleur Delacour as the Beauxbatons Academy champion, and Victor Krum as the Durmstrang Institute champion, it unexpectedly spits out a fourth name—that of the underage Harry Potter. The primary mystery in the novel centers on who entered Harry's name in the goblet.

As Harry prepares for the tournament, he is helped by Mad Eye Moody, the new defense against the dark arts teacher, who frequently sips something from a mysterious hip flask. The first task requires the champions to capture golden eggs from dragons. The second task requires the champions to rescue persons they love from the bottom of a deep lake. Harry does well at both tasks. The third task requires the champions to make their way through a booby-trapped maze to reach the Triwizard Cup. When Harry and Cedric reach the cup at the same time, they agree to seize it together. The cup turns out to be a portkey that magically transports them to a graveyard. There they are met by Peter Pettigrew, who carries a deformed infant that is actually Voldemort. Voldemort has Diggory killed immediately; Pettigrew binds Harry and bleeds him and cuts off his own hand. In a frightening resurrection scene involving Harry's blood and Pettigrew's blood, Voldemort rises from a large cauldron in possession of his full powers.

In a dramatic confrontation scene, Voldemort and Harry duel, but their wands lock in an unyielding connection neither of them understands. When Harry breaks the link, he grabs Cedric's body and uses the portkey to return to Hogwarts. There, Mad Eye Moody takes him to his office and reveals that he is actually a servant of Voldemort impersonating the real Moody by sipping a potion that has transformed his appearance. He also admits putting Harry's name in the goblet and helping to engineer Harry's path to the portkey and Voldemort.

Harry Potter and the Goblet of Fire is a pivotal book in the series. This novel, more than the previous three, points to a deep link between Voldemort and Harry, raises new questions about their connections, and foreshadows the deaths of major characters.

Harry Potter and the Order of the Phoenix

At the end of *Harry Potter and the Goblet of Fire*, Dumbledore reassembles the Order of the Phoenix, a group of witches and wizards who fought Voldemort the first time he rose to power. In the fifth book, *Harry Potter and the Order of the Phoenix*, Sirius Black offers his home at 12 Grimmauld Place in London to the order for its headquarters, while the Ministry of Magic publicly denies that Voldemort is alive and silences all those who insist that he has returned. Because Dumbledore refuses to follow the ministry's orders, a senior ministry official, Delores Jane Umbridge, is made the new defense against the dark arts teacher at Hogwarts, where she spies for the ministry. Umbridge's instruction is so inadequate that Hermione persuades Harry to teach his classmates how to repel attacks by dark wizards. About thirty students, calling themselves Dumbledore's Army, meet in the school's Room of Requirement, despite Umbridge's ban on students meeting in groups without her authorization.

Meanwhile, Harry experiences severe pain in his scar and suffers from recurring nightmares. In one disturbing dream, he enters a snake's body and attacks Ron's father near the entrance to the ministry's Department of Mysteries. In another dream, Harry sees Sirius being tortured at the ministry. Harry, Ron, Hermione, and three other students fly to the ministry to rescue Sirius. However, Voldemort, who is finally aware of the mental connection he shares with Harry, has tricked Harry into thinking Sirius is in danger, and his Death Eaters await in ambush. Voldemort seeks a particular prophecy in the Department of Mysteries, and Harry is the only one who can retrieve it for him. When Harry and his friends engage the Death Eaters in battle, other members of the Order of the Phoenix join the fray, and Sirius is killed in the fighting. Dumbledore and Voldemort duel, but Voldemort flees.

After Dumbledore and Harry return to Hogwarts, Dumbledore apologizes to Harry for having kept information from him. He also tells Harry that the prophecy Voldemort sought foretold the birth of a boy who would vanquish him, and that neither Voldemort nor the unnamed boy could live while the other survived. Furthermore, Dumbledore tells Harry that the reason he must stay with the Dursleys during the summer is because his aunt is a blood relative. The family relationship draws on deep magic that protects Harry from Voldemort's attacks.

Harry Potter and the Half-Blood Prince

After Voldemort's assault on the ministry, both the wizarding and muggle worlds are turned upside down. In *Harry Potter and the Half-Blood Prince*, dementors, the spectral guardians of Azkaban that are now under Voldemort's control, roam freely, while Death Eaters wreak havoc in both worlds. The situation at Hogwarts has also changed. Severus Snape has finally become professor of defense against the dark arts. Dumbledore is often away from the school, strong spells protect the grounds, and aurors trained to combat dark magic stand watch. An ominous tone pervades the book, but it is the first in which Voldemort himself does not appear. The novel does, however, offer more of Voldemort's history, exploring the psychology of evil that motivates him.

Through pensieve sessions with Dumbledore, Harry learns that he and Tom Riddle share similar backgrounds. Both are of muggle and wizard ancestry, both were orphaned at an early age, and both possessed magical skills beyond their years at similar ages. Their major difference is that Harry's parents loved him, and his mother's love still shields him from Voldemort's attacks. Because Voldemort never experienced love, he cannot understand the reason for Harry's continued survival.

Dumbledore is ever ready to give people a second chance, but his trust in Snape is puzzling. Snape was once a Death Eater, and his loyalty to Dumbledore is suspect throughout the series. At the end of *Harry Potter and the Half-Blood Prince*, Snape kills Dumbledore. His apparent betrayal seems firmly to place him among Voldemort's cadre of loyal followers. However, the murder scene contains hints that he is acting in concert with Dumbledore: Dumbledore's plea, "Please, Severus," is ambiguous and is an example of Rowling's propensity for narrative misdirection. If Snape is truly Dumbledore's man, does he really kill him, or will Dumbledore rise again?

Another central mystery in the novel concerns horcruxes, magical storage receptacles in which dark wizards hide part of their souls to attain immortality. If a horcrux is destroyed, its dark wizard dies. Voldemort has created seven horcruxes—one of which remains unknown even to him—leaving an eighth piece of his soul in his newly formed body. By the end of *Harry Potter and the Half-Blood Prince*, two horcruxes have been destroyed—Tom Riddle's diary, which first appeared in the second book, and Marvolo Gaunt's ring, which appears in the sixth book. After the publication of this sixth book, speculation was rife among readers arguing that Harry's scar is a sign that Voldemort unintentionally made Harry himself into a horcrux when he was a baby. The quest to discover which objects are horcruxes and how to destroy them continues in the seventh and final novel.

Harry Potter and the Deathly Hallows

During the interval between publication of *Harry Potter and the Half-Blood Prince* and *Harry Potter and the Deathly Hallows*, fans and critics alike were consumed with curiosity about several questions raised in the previous books. Which characters will die and which will survive? Is Snape good or evil? Where are the horcruxes? What are the "deathly hallows"? Is Harry a horcrux? Will Voldemort ultimately be defeated?

The plot of the seventh novel revolves around two quests: Harry, Ron, and Hermione's search for the missing horcruxes and their search for three magical objects known as the deathly hallows. The latter comprise the stone of resurrection, the cloak of invisibility, and the elder wand, which together are believed to conquer death. Originally belonging to the Peverell brothers, the hallows were passed down as family heirlooms. Harry's father left him the invisibility cloak, which originally belonged to Ignotus Peverell. Marvolo Gaunt's ring, inherited by Voldemort through Cadmus Peverell, qualifies not only as a horcrux but also as one of the hallows because it is set with the stone of resurrection. At the beginning of the seventh novel, Harry is in possession of the invisibility cloak, and the ring has been destroyed (although its stone is missing), but the whereabouts of the elder wand is a mystery.

The book opens with Harry's departure from the Dursleys' home with an Order of the Phoenix guard. Shortly after they take flight, they are attacked by Death Eaters, who kill Mad Eye Moody and Harry's pet owl, Hedwig. After spending the rest of the summer with Ron Weasley's family, Harry begins his journey with Ron and Hermione to find the horcruxes and the deathly hallows. Their search takes them to Sirius's Grimmauld Place house, whose house elf helps them retrieve the third horcrux, which is later destroyed by Ron. After the three friends are captured by Bellatrix Lestrange, Sirius's Death Eater cousin, Lestrange's behavior leads them to believe that the fourth horcrux is hidden in her vault in Gringott's bank. The trio breaks into the bank and steals the cup. Meanwhile, Voldemort momentarily drops his mental guard and inadvertently reveals to Harry that a fifth horcrux is at Hogwarts.

Alberforth Dumbledore, the brother of the dead

headmaster, helps Harry and his friends sneak into the school, where a monumental battle between Voldemort's forces and those of the Order of the Phoenix and Dumbledore's Army commences. As the battle rages, Harry, Ron, and Hermione find the next object, Rowena Ravenclaw's diadem, in the Room of Requirement. However, Draco Malfoy and his henchmen, Crabbe and Goyle, are there to oppose them. During a scuffle, Crabbe botches a powerful spell, killing himself and destroying the diadem.

Harry again connects to Voldemort's mind and sees Voldemort and Snape at the Shrieking Shack. When the three friends reach the shack, Voldemort is gone after attacking Snape, who lies dying on the floor. Snape gives Harry his memories, which answer many important questions raised throughout the series. For example, Snape loved Harry's mother throughout his life, and Dumbledore trusted him because of his ability to love. Also, Gaunt's ring infected Dumbledore with a slow-working but fatal curse, and Dumbledore arranged for Snape to kill him to prevent Draco Malfoy from killing him under Voldemort's orders. Finally, Harry himself is indeed a horcrux and Voldemort cannot die while Harry remains alive.

These facts make it appear that both Voldemort and Harry would have to die. However, in the first of two battles between Voldemort and Harry, one of Voldemort's curses stuns Harry so severely that it rids him of the piece of Voldemort's soul that had resided in him since he was an infant. Harry feigns death until he meets Voldemort again in the great hall of Hogwarts. In a dramatic confrontation, Voldemort is vanquished and Harry survives.

Pegge Bochynski

Principal mystery and detective fiction

Harry Potter series: *Harry Potter and the Philosopher's Stone*, 1997 (also known as *Harry Potter and the Sorcerer's Stone*, 1998); *Harry Potter and the Chamber of Secrets*, 1998; *Harry Potter and the Prisoner of Azkaban*, 1999; *Harry Potter and the Goblet of Fire*, 2000; *Harry Potter and the Order of the Phoenix*, 2003; *Harry Potter and the Half-Blood Prince*, 2005; *Harry Potter and the Deathly Hallows*, 2007

Other major works

children's literature: *Fantastic Beasts and Where to Find Them*, 2001 (as Scamander); *Quidditch Through the Ages*, 2001 (as Whisp)

Bibliography

Anatol, Giselle Liza, ed. *Reading Harry Potter: Critical Essays.* Westport, Conn.: Praeger, 2003. Engaging collection of scholarly essays treating the literary influences, moral and social values, and historical contexts of Rowling's first four novels.

Bochynski, Pegge. "Harry Potter and the Half-Blood Prince." In *Magill's Literary Annual*, edited by John D. Wilson and Steven G. Kellman. Pasadena, Calif.: Salem Press, 2006. Review of the penultimate novel in the series that explores questions concerning the relationship between Harry and Voldemort and Snape's true loyalties.

Granger, John. *Unlocking Harry Potter: Five Keys for the Serious Reader.* Wayne, Pa.: Zossima Press, 2007. Meticulous examination of Rowling's first six books that includes chapters on narrative misdirection and predictions on what might happen in the final book based on clues appearing throughout the series.

_______, ed. *Who Killed Albus Dumbledore?* Wayne, Pa.: Zossima Press, 2006. Collection of essays from fan-theorists who attempt to unravel clues presented in *Harry Potter and the Half-Blood Prince* to predict the outcome of the seventh novel.

Hallet, Cynthia Whitney, ed. *Scholarly Studies in Harry Potter: Applying Academic Methods to a Popular Text.* Lewiston, N.Y.: Edwin Mellen Press, 2005. Critical analysis of Rowling's books for teachers, scholars, and college students. Includes chapters on the geography, chronology, and mythology of Rowling's wizarding world.

Langford, David. *The End of Harry Potter?* New York: Tor Books, 2007. Thought-provoking analysis of the entire series that addresses questions left unanswered in the first six Potter books.

Lovett, Charles. *J. K. Rowling: Her Life and Works.* New York: Spark Publishing, 2003. Guide to the early Potter books that features chapter-by-chapter synopses, followed by brief interpretive sections with comments about the mysteries in each book.

Nel, Philip. *J. K. Rowling's Harry Potter Novels: A Reader's Guide.* New York: Continuum, 2001. Thoughtful and well-researched overview of the first four books written for adults that places the novels in their literary context.

Rasmussen, R. Kent. "Harry Potter and the Order of the Phoenix." In *Magill's Literary Annual*, edited by John D. Wilson and Steven G. Kellman. Pasadena, Calif.: Salem Press, 2004. Comprehensive review of the fifth book that includes an informative overview of the series, a detailed plot synopsis, and a shrewd analysis of characters and events.

Schafer, Elizabeth D. *Exploring Harry Potter.* Osprey, Fla.: Beachham, 2000. Written for teachers and librarians, this sourcebook offers a chapter on the linguistic and mythological origins of characters' names.

S

SAKI

Hector Hugh Munro

Born: Akyab, Burma (now Myanmar); December 18, 1870
Died: Beaumont Hamel, France; November 14, 1916
Types of plot: Inverted; psychological; horror

Contribution

Hardly any of Saki's short stories, which fill five volumes, can be regarded as works of detective fiction in the more limited sense of the term. Many of his brilliantly crafted, deeply sarcastic pieces, however, deal with the criminal impulse of humankind. In direct contrast to the classic hero of detective fiction, who tries to restore order by abolishing the chaos let loose by antisocial impulses, Saki's mischievous protagonists arrive on the scene to wreak havoc on victims who have invited their tormentors out of folly or a streak of viciousness of their own. Nevertheless, Saki's insistence on a masterfully prepared surprise ending demonstrates the closeness in form of his short stories to detective fiction as this genre was understood by its fathers, preeminently Edgar Allan Poe. Moreover, as powerful elements in a poignant satire on society, Saki's criminal protagonists can claim descent from the heroes of Restoration playwrights William Congreve and William Wycherley and precede some of the post-hard-boiled detectives such as Douglas Adams's Dirk Gently.

Biography

Saki was born Hector Hugh Munro on December 18, 1870, in Akyab, Burma, the third child of Major Charles Augustus Munro and his wife, Mary (née Mercer) Frances. Saki's mother would die in pregnancy two years later. Brought to Great Britain by their father, Hector and his siblings were reared by two rather repressive aunts until Major Munro resigned his commission and took his children on extended tours through Europe to further their education; this period marked the end of Hector's time at one of Great Britain's upper-class public schools.

During this time, the Munros liked to stay in Davos, Switzerland; it was there that the boy made the acquaintance of the writer John Addington Symonds, a man whose homosexual orientation the adult Munro would share. At twenty-three, Munro served for a short time as a military police officer in Burma before malaria brought him back to Great Britain, where he set up bachelor's quarters in London.

Munro published his first book, *The Rise of the Russian Empire*, in 1900, yet readers delighted much more in his political satires, which featured an Alice in Wonderland who encountered modern political figures. Accompanied by the drawings of F. Carruthers Gould, *The Westminster Alice* (collected in 1902) made famous its creator, who took the pen name of Saki from the boyish cupbearer to the gods of Edward FitzGerald's *The Rubáiyát of Omar Khayyám* (1859) and would continue to write all of his fiction under this pseudonym.

In 1902, Saki served as correspondent for the conservative London newspaper *Morning Post* and saw the Balkans, Russia, and France before he retired to London after the death of his father in 1908. As Saki, he steadily wrote his short stories for publication in British magazines and enjoyed such a success among his exclusive readership that his stories were collected in book form in 1910 and 1911. A year later, Saki's novel *The Unbearable Bassington* (1912) appeared, and another novel followed, *When William Came* (1913).

At the height of his fame for his short fiction and while he was working on a play, World War I broke

H. H. Munro, better known as Saki, a name he borrowed from the cupbearer to the gods in Edward FitzGerald's The Rubáiyát of Omar Khayyám (1859).

out. Saki volunteered for military service. Refusing an officer's commission or a "safe" position, Munro fought in France and was killed in action during the Beaumont-Hamel offensive on November 14, 1916.

Two further collections of Saki's criminous short stories and other works were posthumously published; one, *The Square Egg* (1924), contains work written in the trenches on the Western Front. A revival of Saki's work took place in the 1920's, and stories such as "Sredni Vashtar" have been continuously in print.

Analysis

Saki came to the short story as a satirist and never averted his eye from the darker side of human nature, a place where not only social ineptness, pomposity, and foolishness are rooted but criminality as well. Saki's first works of fiction, collected in *Reginald* (1904), are short sketches featuring a rakish but keen observer of the follies of his upper-middle-class London society. As a prototype of later narrator-protagonists, Reginald is something like a witty and caustic Socrates of the salon, whose passion to expose the foibles of his dim-witted and obnoxiously stupid contemporaries is reflected in much of Saki's fiction.

Reginald in Russia

Saki's criminous short stories—the first collection of which, *Reginald in Russia* (1910), plays off the fame of the early protagonist—follow suit. In their aim to ridicule, and often to punish, self-imposing and occasionally tyrannical victims, Saki's stories exploit plots crafted by a masterful imagination; they often read like gigantic, fiendishly designed practical jokes, with varying degrees of realism.

"Sredni Vashtar"

"Sredni Vashtar" (in *The Chronicles of Clovis*, 1911) features one such cruel and fantastic scheme. The boy Conradin is afflicted with a forbidding aunt who gets perverse pleasure from closing off all avenues of play from her ward. His only undisturbed space is a small shed in which he keeps a hen and a caged "polecatferret" named Sredni Vashtar, for an Asian deity. The boy has devised a cult around Sredni Vashtar. After his aunt breaks into the shed and removes the hen, Conradin prays to his other playmate: "Do one thing for me, Sredni Vashtar." The wish is never made explicit, but after the aunt breaks in a second time, Conradin chants to his deity until the ferret emerges, "a long, low, yellow-and-brown beast, with eyes a-blink at the waning daylight, and dark wet stains around the fur of jaws and throat." When the aunt is discovered dead, the boy calmly prepares some toast for himself in obvious satisfaction.

"Tobermory"

As in this tale, in which the divine ferret acts out the boy's fantasy of revenge, Saki gives animals uncanny power, and they act to expose the worst in their human counterparts. In "Tobermory," also in *The Chronicles of Clovis*, a dignified tomcat is taught human language and, to the horror of a house party, freely divulges compromising personal information that he had overheard. The humans' response is instant and malicious: Tobermory is to be poisoned. Their decision is described as if the guests were plotting the murder of a human. By a typical quirk of fate, Saki saves Tobermory from poison by having him die in dignified battle with another tomcat; his owners demand recompense from his adversary's masters.

Because his fiction always succeeds in bringing forth the worst in people, be it greed, tyranny, or selfishness, Saki has himself been accused of inhumanity. A more intent look at the reasons for his deep sarcasm cannot fail to establish that the cruelty of his stories is the cruelty of the well-to-do society around him, the greed and vice of which stir his disgust and in turn impel him to put much of what he sees and feels on paper in ironic form, adding a dash of the exotic and supernatural to his often-murderous fiction. As to Saki's motives for presenting his society with his work, one might echo Clovis Sangrail on his ideas for "The Feast of Nemesis" (in *Beasts and Super-Beasts*, 1914): "There is no outlet for demonstrating your feelings towards people whom you simply loathe. That is really the crying need of our modern civilization."

In a society where a faux pas could literally annihilate a person's social position, leaving him a choice only of internal or external exile, a man such as Saki (excolonial, homosexual) must have felt some of the shady morality, hypocrisy, and bigotry behind the façades of respectability. Yet Saki never outwardly shocks or lectures his audience. His wit is so fine and his irony so subtle that he always remains the gentleman in his fiction. Sexuality is never really exposed, and social or political radicalism is absent from the work of the staunch conservative Saki. Yet he triumphs by giving his readers an exquisitely crafted inside view of members of a social class who stood on top of their world before the war destroyed everything forever.

"THE PEACE OF MOWSLE BARTON"

It is appropriate that an author who could write the story "Birds on the Western Front" (in *The Square Egg*), in which the horror of trench warfare is brought home via a tranquil description of how the feathery folk have adjusted to "lyddite and shrapnel and machine-gun fire," should use a pond in a forest to evoke the most chilling scene of horror in his fiction. In "The Peace of Mowsle Barton" (in *The Chronicles of Clovis*), city-weary Crefton Lockyer has retired to a remote spot in the country only to discover himself at the center of a feud between witches. Gazing at a small pool, he witnesses the evil effect of a spell of one of the rival hags. Saki's description of the drowning ducks is terrifyingly uncanny; the reader is captured in a pastoral world gone to hell, where the most basic and thus most trusted assumptions about the world have so suddenly disappeared that one can only feel the silent terror of a perversely defamiliarized universe:

> The duck flung itself confidently forward into the water, and rolled immediately under the surface. Its head appeared for a moment and went under again, leaving a train of bubbles in its wake, while wings and legs churned the water in a helpless swirl of flapping and kicking.

If such a scene captures the essence of witchcraft—the sudden and magic performance of a practical joke on the beliefs of humankind about what can and what cannot happen in the world—then Saki has just demonstrated another aspect of his fascination with "what if" and "how to get back at" something or somebody.

In its exploration of the art of cynically humorous revenge, Saki's fiction delights in the idea of negative endings triggered by quirks of fate. Unlike traditional detective stories, in which the master sleuth comes up with an idea at the eleventh hour or cracks the case on the final page, Saki's stories often thrive on the prevention of exactly such a fortunate occurrence.

"LOST SANJAK"

The jailed protagonist of "Lost Sanjak" (in *Reginald in Russia*) is one such butt of a murderous joke by the forces of fate. On the eve of his execution, this slighted Don Juan confesses the bizarre story of his life to a chaplain. Rejected by a married woman and determined to disappear from the known world, the narrator exchanges clothes with a major of the Salvation Army, whom a road accident has left an unidentifiable corpse. In a turn of fate that is characteristic of Saki's world, the corpse is mistaken for the young gentleman's, and the hunt is on for the Salvationist, who has been observed at the scene of the "crime." The relations of the Salvationist attest his "depraved youth," and when captured, the man fails an absurd test to prove his identity by trapping himself in his own designs: Having tried to impress his love by posing as an expert on the Balkans, he cannot locate the city of Novibazar and is duly condemned. Guardedly, the chaplain looks up the city after the execution, and his reason for doing so not only compromises this man of God as a potential adulterer but also betrays the text's general feeling toward the morals of humankind: "A thing like that," he observed, "might happen to any one."

There is a strong undercurrent of feeling in Saki's fiction that certain behavior on the part of the victim justifies criminal action by the clever ones who seize the opportunity for a trick. In "Mrs. Packletide's Tiger" and "The Secret Sin of Septimus Brode" (both in *The Chronicles of Clovis*), the pompous characters of the titles have to pay off the person who gets behind their schemes. Thus, blackmail appears to be the correct social behavior toward vain people who cannot bear that ignominious facts about themselves should be made known.

"The Unrest-Cure"

The complacent who dare to complain stupidly about their lot without really desiring change, and who will fail bitterly when tested, are another butt of criminal jokes. In "The Unrest-Cure" (in *The Chronicles of Clovis*), Clovis Sangrail challenges a man bored by his tranquil life. Impersonating a bishop's secretary, he arrives at J. P. Huddle's house supposedly a few hours ahead of his master. He tricks the oafish Huddle into believing that the bishop has set up quarters in Huddle's library and is planning a massacre; the man falls for the outlandish lie and spends a frightful night, definitely "cured" of his restlessness.

"The Sheep" and "The Gala Programme"

Saki's fascination with the idea of revenge has led some critics to label him a misanthrope whose thirst for vengeance ignores the lessons humanity has learned since William Shakespeare's *Hamlet, Prince of Denmark* (pr. c. 1600-1601); indeed, critics have had trouble with stories such as "The Sheep" (in *The Toys of Peace*, 1919), in which a dog involuntarily prevents the rescue of an obnoxious blunderer and, for that feat, becomes the narrator's most cherished friend. Nevertheless, in a turn of fate that Saki would have appreciated, critics have generally failed to bewail the uncensored atrocity in "The Gala Programme" (in *The Square Egg*), in which a fictitious Roman emperor finds out that the best way to hold chariot races at his coronation ceremony without interference from female protesters (*suffragetae*) is to feed them to the wild beasts that were supposed to be the second part of the festivities.

"Gabriel-Ernest," "The She-Wolf," and "Laura"

The supernatural is an integral part of Saki's imagination. It is most powerfully used as part of a clever revenge or joke plot, and it is indicative of the quality and range of Saki's mind that his stories vary in the degree to which the reader is to take the unreal as real. In "Gabriel-Ernest" (in *Reginald in Russia*), a landlord encounters a real werewolf on his territory; his foolhardiness in wanting to believe in the rational reasons for the disappearance of a miller's baby only leads to the death of another infant by the fangs of the boy-werewolf. "The She-Wolf" (in *Beasts and Super-Beasts*), however, mirrors the theme when party guests play an elaborate joke on a braggart who professes knowledge of magical powers yet is quite unable to change a wolf (supposedly the hostess) "back" into her human shape. "Laura" (from the same collection) is the synthesis of Saki's treatment of the unreal. Days before her death, Laura confides her wish to be reborn as an otter; when this comes true, she is hunted to death after wreaking havoc on her old human opponents. Yet she is again reincarnated as a Nubian boy to continue her pranks on the adversaries, who have gone to Egypt to relax after the mischief she has caused. Again, the joke, with all of its nasty effects, is on the self-satisfied.

"Louis"

Saki's short fiction succeeds thanks to its unique mixture of satire, high comedy of manners, mystery and horror, and psychological insight into the minds and world of the bygone Edwardian era. As cynical antidetective fiction, it reverses the quest to reinstate order; Saki is more impressive in his portraiture of humans than many of the classic authors of the genre, who give their readers a fair share of the horrible in human nature yet insist on a conformist and pacifying "happy ending." Saki does not allow his reader to settle back into the armchair with the sense that once again virtue has triumphed; instead, one is shown the underlying forces that motivate people to evil, and one is coaxed into admiration for Saki's clever doers of mischief. Like the protagonist of "Louis" (in *The Toys of Peace*), whose sister finally delivers him from his wife's schemes, the reader might come to admire those clever perpetrators, as does the husband here: "'Novels have been written about women like you,' said Strudwarden; 'you have a perfectly criminal mind.'" This, however, is too sinister a response to such a gift as Lena Strudwarden's.

R. C. Lutz

Principal mystery and detective fiction

Short fiction: *Reginald in Russia*, 1910; *The Chronicles of Clovis*, 1911; *Beasts and Super-Beasts*, 1914; *The Toys of Peace*, 1919; *The Square Egg*, 1924

Other major works

Novels: *The Unbearable Bassington*, 1912; *When William Came*, 1913

Short fiction: *Reginald*, 1904; *The Short Stories of Saki (H. H. Munro) Complete*, 1930

Plays: *Karl-Ludwig's Window*, pb. 1924; *The Death-Trap*, pb. 1924; *The Square Egg, and Other Sketches, with Three Plays*, pb. 1924; *The Watched Pot*, pr., pb. 1924 (with Cyril Maude)

Nonfiction: *The Rise of the Russian Empire*, 1900; *The Westminster Alice*, 1902

Bibliography

Birden, Lorene M. "Saki's 'A Matter of Sentiment.'" *Explicator* 5 (Summer, 1998): 201- 204. Discusses the Anglo-German relations in the story "A Matter of Sentiment" and argues that the story reflects a shift in Saki's image of Germans.

Byrne, Sandie. "Saki." In *British Writers: Supplement VI*, edited by Jay Parini. New York: Charles Scribner's Sons, 2001. Includes discussion of Saki's short fiction, its influence, and its historical and cultural importance.

Gillen, Charles H. *H. H. Munro (Saki)*. New York: Twayne, 1969. A comprehensive presentation of the life and work of Saki, with a critical discussion of his literary output in all of its forms. Balanced and readable, Gillen's work also contains an annotated bibliography.

Lambert, J. W. Introduction to *The Bodley Head Saki*. London: Bodley Head, 1963. A perceptive, concise, and persuasive review of Saki's work. Written by a biographer who enjoyed a special and productive working relationship with Saki's estate.

Langguth, A. J. *Saki*. New York: Simon and Schuster, 1981. Probably the best biography, enriching an informed, analytical presentation of its subject with a fine understanding of Saki's artistic achievement. Eight pages of photos help bring Saki and his world to life.

Munro, Ethel M. "Biography of Saki." In *The Square Egg and Other Sketches, with Three Plays*. New York: Viking, 1929. A warm account of the author by his beloved sister, who shows herself deeply appreciative of his work. Valuable for its glimpses of the inner workings of Saki's world and as a basis for late twentieth century evaluations.

Queenan, Joe, ed. *The Malcontents: The Best Bitter, Cynical, and Satirical Writing in the World*. Philadelphia: Running Press, 2002. This anthology of cynicism and satire includes the editor's commentaries on each author; five of Saki's stories are featured.

Salemi, Joseph S. "An Asp Lurking in an Apple-Charlotte: Animal Violence in Saki's *The Chronicles of Clovis*." *Studies in Short Fiction* 26 (Fall, 1989): 423-430. Discusses the animal imagery in the collection, suggesting reasons for Saki's obsessive interest in animals and analyzing the role animals play in a number of Saki's major stories.

Spears, George J. *The Satire of Saki*. New York: Exposition Press, 1963. An interesting, in-depth study of Saki's wit, which combines careful textual analysis with a clear interest in modern psychoanalysis. The appendix includes four letters by Ethel M. Munro to the author, and the bibliography lists many works that help place Saki in the context of the satirical tradition.

JAMES SALLIS

Born: Helena, Arkansas; December 21, 1944
Types of plot: Hard-boiled; private investigator

Principal series

Lew Griffin, 1992-2001
John Turner, 2003-

Principal series characters

Lewis "Lew" Griffin is an African American man from rural Arkansas who left for New Orleans at the age of sixteen. Sometimes employed as a detective, he usually becomes involved in investigations, such as finding a missing person, through the network of people he knows or has helped before. Griffin is physically tough but has some psychological flaws. He has trouble maintaining relationships with women and is an alcoholic, although he mostly controls his drinking. He is highly literate, a part-time writer with a strong interest in classical music and the blues.

John Turner is a country boy from Crowley's Ridge, which lies in eastern Arkansas. He fought in Vietnam and later became a police officer in Memphis. He was involved in a shooting and was sent to prison, where he earned a master's in psychology. After serving almost ten years, he was released and became a therapist. Although successful, he burned out after six years and retired to the country near his childhood home.

Contribution

One of James Sallis's major contributions has been his ability to combine hard-boiled and noir elements with literary-quality characterizations and elegant prose. Although often identified as mysteries, Sallis's intensely introspective novels are only loosely plotted around some puzzle and are primarily explorations of character and the meaning of experience.

Sallis is also notable for being one of the first white authors to explore in depth the life of an African American protagonist (Lew Griffin). On occasion, Sallis has been criticized for writing so intimately of the African American experience, but he grew up in an area that was 70 percent African American and learned at firsthand about the lives of poor and rural blacks in the South. He has also made a long-term study of Chester Himes (1909-1984), the African American author of nine detective novels and an influence on Sallis's hard-boiled fiction. In Sallis's books, Griffin is treated neither stereotypically nor overly sympathetically, but with absolute realism as a complex, flawed individual. The character was initially modeled on the life of Himes but has developed to include aspects of many men that Sallis has known, from blues musicians to intellectuals, from family men to petty criminals.

Biography

James Sallis was born December 21, 1944, in Helena, Arkansas, which sits on Crowley's Ridge on the banks of the Mississippi River. The nearest big city is Memphis, about seventy miles away. Helena, a river port, lies in mostly rural Phillips County, one of the poorest areas in the United States. Sallis protects his privacy, but some sources list his parents as Chappelle Horace Sallis and Mildred C. Liming Sallis. He has an older brother, John Sallis, who has a doctorate in philosophy and is widely published in his field.

When Sallis was growing up in Helena, the city was 70 percent African American and had a reputation as a gathering place for delta blues musicians such as Sonny Boy Williamson and Roosevelt Sykes. It was also a highly conservative town, however, noted for the dramatic contrast between the abject poverty of many inhabitants and the wealth of others. Sallis used his childhood experiences to develop the Lew Griffin character.

As a child, Sallis was a voracious reader and knew that he wanted to write. His first love was poetry, although he also was interested in music. Helena was not easy to escape, but Sallis earned a scholarship to Tulane University in New Orleans, where he had his first success as a writer of short stories. New Orleans also became a spiritual home for Sallis, and he has returned several times to live there for brief periods.

Sallis left Tulane without finishing his degree, then

attended the University of Iowa for a short time before leaving to write on his own. He met Michael Moorcock, who invited him at the age of twenty-one to move to London and become fiction editor for *New Worlds*, a seminal science-fiction magazine of the period. While in England, Sallis's first book was published, a short-story collection entitled *A Few Last Words* (1970).

After *New Worlds* folded, Sallis returned to the United States. With markets for short fiction hard to find, he turned to nonfictional works about music, writing *The Guitar Players: One Instrument and Its Masters in American Music* (1982) and editing *Jazz Guitars: An Anthology* (1984). He also gave guitar-playing lessons and played string instruments with various club bands while living in such cities as New Orleans, New York, Boston, and Fort Worth, Texas. In 1992, Sallis's first novel, *The Long-Legged Fly*, was published. This, the first Lew Griffin book, earned Sallis critical acclaim and spawned a series. Sallis has averaged less than one novel a year since 1992, but he has also released several collections of his stories and poetry and has written a number of nonfictional works.

In addition to his roles as musician, music teacher, and writer, Sallis has taught creative writing, worked as a screenwriter and translator, and even served as a respiratory therapist. His writing spans just as wide a range. Besides literary, mystery, and science-fiction novels, he has published poetry, essays, book reviews, biographies, musicologies, and French translations. He has been nominated for the Nebula Award for one of his short stories and for the Anthony, Edgar, Shamus, and Gold Dagger awards in mystery. Sallis has been married three times. He moved to Phoenix, Arizona, with his third wife, Karyn, in 1999.

Analysis

James Sallis has carved a niche for himself as a literary novelist with the ability to cross over to genre writing, especially mysteries. His books work consistently as entertainment, yet are filled with word play and complex characters that even the most sophisticated reader can appreciate. A lifelong lover of music, Sallis writes with a spontaneous and inventive style similar to the playing styles of his favorite jazz and blues musicians. His plots are minimal and his stories are almost always told in nonlinear form. It seems clear that Sallis believes this to reflect the realistic, if meandering, course of actual life. Sallis's essay "Where I Live," from the collection *Gently into the Land of the Meateaters* (2000), expresses the writer's attitude perfectly. He is little interested in plot and traditional forms of narration but is much more drawn toward works that have a unique voice.

Physical location also plays an exceptionally important role in Sallis's work, especially in his two series. Both Griffin and Turner are from rural Arkansas, specifically from the Helena area, which is where Sallis grew up. Griffin flees that world for New Orleans, and it is clear from *Gently into the Land of the Meateaters*, especially an essay entitled "Gone So Long," that Sallis did the same thing in leaving Helena for Tulane University. Sallis hated the casual racism and abject poverty that he saw growing up, and leaving Helena for cosmopolitan New Orleans was his way of both escaping and protesting those inequities. His Lew

James Sallis. (© Ingrid Shults/Courtesy, Walker & Company)

Griffin mysteries were certainly a way of dealing with such experiences and were best told through the point of view of an African American protagonist. It is notable that John Turner, the white protagonist of his second series, also leaves the rural South for the city—Memphis—but then returns to the same country that he once fled. Through Turner, Sallis is, at least metaphorically, returning home.

Another characteristic of Sallis's writing is his frequent and playful use of literary and musical references. In one sentence he may reference a European poet who is obscure to most readers in the United States; in another he alludes to hard-boiled American writers such as Jim Thompson or David Goodis. He mixes quotes from blues musicians with those from country stars. This reflects the enormous range of Sallis's reading and musical experiences and his ability to make meaningful connections between diverse lives and viewpoints.

Some critics dislike the relentless connectivity of Sallis's work, perhaps because many of the allusions are not familiar to them. For many readers, however, the allusions create a fleeting familiarity, a feeling of near revelation, as if they have just made a connection that deepens their understanding of the world. The Lew Griffin series is particularly rich with such connections, but it reflects perfectly the character of the narrator, Griffin. Griffin is much like Sallis. He is a self-taught writer with a huge interest in music. The references come naturally to Griffin because they reflect how he understands his world. This is a near-seamless meld of character and author.

Sallis's improvisational style, especially his nonlinear storytelling, also draws occasional criticism. This style of presentation does require work from the reader, but there is always a logical pattern in the way the story proceeds. For example, in *Cypress Grove* (2003), the first John Turner mystery, the chapters alternate. Turner is shown in real time in chapter 1; chapter 2 explores the past. In *Ghost of a Flea* (2001), the sixth Griffin novel, the nonlinear portion of the work "bookends" the rest. The first chapter and last two chapters are told by Griffin's son, David, out of sequence to the remainder of the tale.

Like the best literary fiction, Sallis's work can be read on two levels. On the first level, he tells an interesting story, albeit focused more on character than plot. The second level requires effort from the reader. There is meaning, but it must be extracted through critical reading. Perhaps it is best to read each Sallis work twice, once for story and mood, and again for the deeper meaning.

Ghost of a Flea

Ghost of a Flea is the sixth and final Lew Griffin mystery. It begins with Griffin's death, although the reader does not know this until the last two chapters, when the opening scene is revisited to show that Griffin's son, David, is narrating. It is unusual for mystery writers to kill their main characters, but little about the Griffin series is typical. Even the way Griffin dies defies the conventions of the hard-boiled genre. Sallis's hero does not go out with guns blazing; he dies in his bed, from the aftermath of a stroke. It is a fitting end, however, for a series that consistently shaped the genre into new forms.

The Turner mysteries

Cypress Grove is the first John Turner mystery, published two years after Sallis ended the Lew Griffin series. It was not clear even to Sallis whether Cypress Grove would begin a new series, or whether it would be another nonseries novel like those he had been writing since the mid-1990's. Something in the character caught the interest of both Sallis and his readers, however, and a second Turner book, *Cripple Creek*, appeared in 2006. The ending of the second book seems to cement Sallis's plans for a series.

John Turner—though his first name is almost never used and appears only on the last page of the second book of the series—is similar to Lew Griffin in some important ways and different in others. Turner is white but comes from the same part of rural Arkansas as Griffin does. Like Griffin, Turner listens to classical and blues music, but he does not appear to know as much about those forms. Turner is widely read but not interested in writing and not as engulfed in literature as Griffin. Accordingly, the Turner books are not as saturated with literary allusions. This makes them more accessible to general readers but may disappoint those who enjoyed wrestling with Sallis's literary references in the Griffin books. Finally, Turner is not as driven by internal anger as was Griffin. This is probably meant to reflect the different childhood experiences of blacks and whites in the rural South.

DRIVE

Drive (2005) may well be Sallis's most accessible novel, although it is more a novella in length. It was named one of the top ten books of the year by *Entertainment Weekly* and has generated considerable Internet discussion. *Drive* is a noir thriller featuring a character known only as Driver. As a child, Driver watches his mother cut his criminal father's throat with a knife. At the age of sixteen, Driver leaves a thank-you note to his foster parents, takes the family car, and heads to California. He becomes a stunt driver, and his skill behind the wheel leads to a second life driving getaway cars in robberies. A robbery goes wrong and some mobsters come after Driver.

Drive is different in many ways from Sallis's previous novels. The pace is faster, the plot tighter, although it is certainly not a plot-driven novel. The character Driver is also a departure for Sallis. Driver is uneducated and not much of a reader or music buff. He is certainly street wise and very tough. Staying true to the character, Sallis uses few literary allusions in *Drive*, but in keeping with his attitude toward traditional narrative, he still employs nonlinear storytelling techniques as he moves between present and past.

Charles A. Gramlich

PRINCIPAL MYSTERY AND DETECTIVE FICTION

LEWIS "LEW" GRIFFIN SERIES: *The Long-legged Fly*, 1992; *Moth*, 1993; *Black Hornet*, 1994; *Eye of the Cricket*, 1997; *Bluebottle*, 1999; *Ghost of a Flea*, 2001

JOHN TURNER SERIES: *Cypress Grove*, 2003; *Cripple Creek*, 2006

NONSERIES NOVELS: *Death Will Have Your Eyes*, 1997; *Drive*, 2005

OTHER MAJOR WORKS

NOVEL: *Renderings*, 1995

SHORT FICTION: *A Few Last Words*, 1970; *Limits of the Sensible World*, 1994; *Time's Hammers: Collected Stories*, 2000; *A City Equal to My Desire*, 2004; *Potato Tree*, 2007

POETRY: *Sorrow's Kitchen*, 2000; *Black Night's Gonna Catch Me Here: Selected Poems, 1968-1998*, 2001

NONFICTION: *The Guitar Players: One Instrument and Its Masters in American Music*, 1982; rev. ed., 1994; *Difficult Lives: Jim Thompson, David Goodis, Chester Himes*, 1993; rev. ed., 2000; *Gently into the Land of the Meateaters*, 2000; *Chester Himes: A Life*, 2000

TRANSLATIONS: *Saint Glinglin*, 1993 (by Raymond Queneau); *My Tongue in Other Cheeks: A Selection of Translations*, 2003

EDITED TEXTS: *The War Book*, 1969; *The Shores Beneath*, 1971; *Jazz Guitars: An Anthology*, 1984; *The Guitar in Jazz: An Anthology*, 1996; *Ash of Stars: On the Writings of Samuel R. Delany*, 1996

BIBLIOGRAPHY

Duncan, Paul. "Professional Liar." In *The Long-legged Fly/Moth Omnibus Edition*. Harpenden, England: No Exit Press, 2000. An in-depth interview with Sallis about his writing habits and themes.

Haut, Woody. *Neon Noir: Contemporary American Crime Fiction*. New York: Serpent's Tail, 1999. Devotes an entire chapter to Sallis, covering mainly the Lew Griffin series.

Sallis, James. *Gently into the Land of the Meateaters*. Seattle: Black Heron Press, 2000. Essays by Sallis describe his life philosophy, his history, and his writing.

_______. The James Sallis Web Pages. http://www.jamessallis.com. Sallis's official Web site is a very good resource with a lot of information on his life and works and numerous links to other sources.

Silet, Charles L. P. *Talking Murder: Interviews with Twenty Mystery Writers*. Princeton, N.J.: Ontario Review Press, 1999. Contains a Sallis interview entitled "To New Orleans with Love." Concerns mostly his New Orleans period.

LAWRENCE SANDERS

Born: Brooklyn, New York; March 15, 1920
Died: Pompano Beach, Florida; February 7, 1998
Also wrote as Lesley Andress
Types of plot: Police procedural; private investigator; espionage; amateur sleuth; hard-boiled

Principal series

Edward X. Delaney, 1970-1978
Peter Tangent, 1976-1978
Commandment, 1978-1991
Archy McNally, 1992-1997

Principal series characters

Edward X. Delaney is a retired chief of detectives of the New York City Police Department. Known as "Iron Balls" among longtime departmental members, he is in his mid-fifties. A man of uncompromising integrity who revels in the smallest investigative details, Delaney is well-read, enjoys food enormously, possesses a sardonic sense of humor, and can laugh at himself. He insists that reason must prevail and maintains that his work as a police detective helps to restore a moral order quickly falling into ruins.

Peter Tangent is a quasi investigator in West Africa for an American oil company. Although not heroic himself, he is capable of recognizing and admiring heroism in others. Initially he comes to West Africa as an exploiter of the political chaos there, but by coming to know a genuine native hero, he loses some of his cynicism.

Contribution

The range of Lawrence Sanders's novels covers the classic police procedural, the private investigator, the amateur sleuth, the hard-boiled, and the espionage genres. He made some distinctive contributions to detective fiction by crossing and combining the conventions of the police procedural with those associated with the private investigator and/or the amateur sleuth. By synthesizing these genres, he was able to expand his areas of interest and inquiry, blending the seasoned perceptions of the professional with the original perceptions of the amateur. While working within the tradition of both Raymond Chandler and Dashiell Hammett, Sanders added technical innovations of his own, notably in *The Anderson Tapes* (1970), an entire novel created out of a Joycean montage gleaned from police reports, wiretaps, and listening devices.

Sanders became a best-selling novelist with this first book and remained so with each subsequent novel. Most important, however, is the complexity of the characters he added to detective fiction. They are mature, multifaceted, and perplexing. His heroes probe their criminals with a Dostoevskian level of insight rare in popular crime fiction. Unlike any other practitioner of the genre, Sanders unashamedly took as the principal content in his two major series the most basic ethical and moral precepts of a Judeo-Christian society: the deadly sins and the commandments. He also explored in great depth the qualities that the pursued and the pursuer secretly share.

Biography

Lawrence Sanders was born in Brooklyn, New York, in 1920, and was reared and educated in the Midwest, specifically Michigan, Minnesota, and Indiana. He was graduated from Wabash College in Crawfordsville, Indiana, earning a bachelor's degree in literature in 1940. The literary allusions in Sanders's works attest his formal education. It was the encouragement of a ninth-grade English teacher, however, that caused him to entertain seriously the notion of becoming a professional writer. The English teacher published in the school paper a book review written by the young Sanders; once he saw his byline in print, he knew that he wanted to be a writer.

After four years in the United States Marine Corps, from 1943 to 1946, Sanders returned to New York City and began working in the field of publishing. He worked for several magazines as an editor and as a writer of war stories, men's adventure stories, and detective fiction. He eventually became feature editor of *Mechanix Illustrated* and editor of *Science and Mechanics*. Utilizing information that he had gained in the course of editing articles on surveillance devices, Sanders wrote *The Anderson Tapes*, an audaciously innovative first novel for a fifty-year-old man—and one that foreshadowed the Watergate break-in.

Since 1970, the year in which *The Anderson Tapes* was published, Sanders produced novels at the rate of one or more per year. His first novel made him wealthy enough to devote himself full-time to his own writing. Most of his crime novels were best sellers, and several of them were made into successful films. Sanders died in Florida in 1998; however, the Archy McNally series continues under the authorship of Vincent Lardo.

Analysis

Some of Lawrence Sanders's early works were collected in a book titled *Tales of the Wolf* (1986). These stories were originally published in detective and men's magazines in 1968 and 1969 and concern the adventures of Wolf Lannihan, an investigator for International Insurance Investigators, or Triple-I. Wolf Lannihan is a hard-boiled detective who describes women in terms of their sexual lure ("She was a big bosomy Swede with hips that bulged her white uniform") and criminals by their odor ("He was a greasy little crumb who wore elevator shoes and smelled of sardines"). Like Chandler's Philip Marlowe, he keeps a pint of Jim Beam in the bottom drawer of his desk for emergencies. These stories follow the pattern of the classic hard-boiled, hard-drinking, irreverent loner who punches his way out of tight spots. While weak on originality, they do have their witty moments and can be read today as parodies of the hard-boiled style of writing popular in the 1930's.

The Anderson Tapes

It was, however, the first novel that Sanders wrote, *The Anderson Tapes*, that brought him success as a writer of detective fiction. He had blue-penciled other writers for twenty-odd years as an editor for pulp and science magazines and churned out adventure stories at night during that time. In despair over the abominable writing he was editing, he determined to write an innovative detective novel. *The Anderson Tapes* became an immediate best seller and was made into a film starring Sean Connery.

Sanders talked about his method of composition in several articles, and the outstanding characteristic of his comments and advice is utter simplicity. Having started out in the 1960's writing gag lines for cheesecake magazines and fast-paced formula fiction for men's adventure magazines, war magazines, and mystery pulps, he became adept at writing tight, well-plotted stories to hold the reader's attention:

> When you're freelancing at seventy-five dollars a story, you have to turn the stuff out fast, and you can't afford to rewrite. You aren't getting paid to rewrite. You can't afford to be clever, either. Forget about how clever you are. Tell the damn story and get on with it. I know a guy who kept rewriting and took eighteen years to finish a novel. What a shame! It was probably better in the first version.

Sanders's views about the writer's vocation were refreshingly democratic and pragmatic. He insisted that anyone who can write a postcard can write a novel:

> Don't laugh. That's true. If you wrote a postcard every day for a year, you'd have 365 postcards. If you wrote a page every day, you'd have a novel. Is that so difficult? If you have something to say and a vocabulary, all you need is a strict routine.

The First Deadly Sin

Sanders's next novel was *The First Deadly Sin* (1973), and it was an even bigger success than *The Anderson Tapes*. Some critics believe it to be his masterpiece because it possesses in rich and varied abundance all the literary devices, techniques, and characters that his readers have come to expect. Although Captain Edward X. Delaney was first seen in the second half of *The Anderson Tapes*, as he took absolute charge of an invading police force, in *The First Deadly Sin*, the reader sees him as a complete character in his home territory. A commanding presence, he is a mature, complex man who understands clearly the viper's tangle of administrative and political infighting. He has operated within the labyrinthine organization of the police force for many years and become a captain, though not without making some uncomfortable compromises.

The key to understanding Edward X. Delaney is the quotation from Fyodor Dostoevski's *Besy* (1871-1872; *The Possessed*, 1913) that Sanders plants in *The*

First Deadly Sin: "If there was no God, how could I be a captain?" Delaney is tortured by the possibility of a world without meaning, and he yearns for an earlier, innocent world that has deteriorated into a miasma of demolished orders and become an existential nightmare in which no authority exists except the law itself. He views himself as a principal agent of this last remaining order, the law. The fallen world he inhabits is very much a wasteland, fragmented by corruption, chaos, and evil. For Delaney, evil exists and is embodied in criminals who break the law. He lives next door to his own precinct on the Upper East Side of Manhattan. He cannot separate his integrity from his life as an officer of the law: They are one. Without a god or an order outside himself, Delaney cannot be a captain because the order necessary to create and enforce such hierarchical categories no longer exists. In an earlier time, he might have become a priest, but he realizes that the Church too has fallen victim to bureaucratic chaos and corruption.

Delaney must attend to the smallest details because they may become the keys to solving the mystery, to revealing its order. Delaney possesses an essentially eighteenth century mind; he believes that when one accumulates enough details and facts, they will compose themselves into a total meaningful pattern: Everything must cohere. His work provides the facts and, therefore, controls and determines the outcome. It is that control that gives his life and work meaning. Without it, his world remains an existential void.

Edward X. Delaney is not, however, a dreary thinking machine; he possesses an incisive sense of humor about others and himself. He can be refreshingly sardonic, especially when his wife, Monica, points out his little quirks. A firm believer in women's intuition, Delaney asks her advice when he finds himself hopelessly mired in the complications of a particularly elaborate series of crimes, such as the serial murders of both *The First Deadly Sin* and *The Third Deadly Sin* (1981). It is both the human and the professional Chief Delaney that Gregory Mcdonald parodies in several of his crime novels. In these parodies, he takes the form of Inspector Francis Xavier Flynn of the Boston Police Department, a resourceful, civilized, and impudent supercop.

First Deputy Commissioner Ivar Thorsen, known as the Admiral, appears in all the Deadly Sin novels, serving to call Delaney to adventure. Perpetually beleaguered, he furnishes, as he sips Delaney's Glenfiddich, three key ingredients to assure Delaney's success: a description of the complexities of the crime, an analysis of the political pressures deriving from the inability of the New York City Police Department to solve the crime, and protection for Delaney so that he may bring his peculiar and sometimes questionable procedures into play (thus circumventing the bureaucratic barriers that hamper the investigation). Abner Boone, Delaney's psychologically wounded protégé, appears in most of the Deadly Sin novels. He is described as horse-faced, with a gentle and overly sensitive temperament. He can sympathize with Delaney because they are both disillusioned romantics (Delaney lost his innocence when he saw a German concentration camp in 1945). Delaney trusts Boone because he is without cynicism, and there is nothing he detests more than cynicism and its source, self-pity.

Many of the women in Sanders's novels are either castrating bitch goddesses or nourishing mother types. Celia Montfort, in *The First Deadly Sin*, provides the narcissistic Daniel Gideon Blank with what he perceives as a conduit to the primal, amoral energies of primitive man; through Celia, Daniel, who has become a Nietzschean superman, is relieved of any guilt for his actions. Bella Sarazen, whose name embodies her pragmatic and warlike sexuality, performs any act if the price is right in *The Second Deadly Sin* (1977). The promiscuously alcoholic but loving Millie Goodfellow in *The Sixth Commandment* (1978) helps the equally alcoholic but clever field investigator Samuel Todd uncover the rotten secrets of Coburn, New York, a dying upstate hamlet steeped in paranoia and guilt.

The Third Deadly Sin and The Fourth Deadly Sin

Of the four major villains in these novels, two are women. Zoe Kohler's first name, which is derived from the Greek word meaning "life," ironically defines her function throughout *The Third Deadly Sin*. Although a victim of Addison's disease, she moves throughout the novel as the castrating goddess par excellence, luring her victims to hotel rooms, exciting them with the promise of sexual ecstasy, and then slashing their sexual organs to pieces with a knife. She, like Daniel Blank, is one of Sanders's Midwest monsters, victims of the kind of sexual and emotional repression that only the Puritan Midwest can produce. Zoe Kohler's psychological and physical illnesses have produced in her a maniacal lust turned upside down, a classic form of sexual repression whose cause is rejection and whose manifestation is vengeful behavior of the most violent kind. The other female villain, the psychologist of *The Fourth Deadly Sin* (1985), suffers no physical illness that exacerbates her emotional condition. Rather, her anger, which is the fourth deadly sin, is a response to her husband's extramarital affair. She is a privileged, wealthy, highly educated woman who knows exactly what she is doing; her crime is all the more heinous because it is premeditated.

The most frightening villain in all Sanders's crime novels, however, is Daniel Gideon Blank; he is also the author's most complex, believable, and magnificently malignant character. He is taken directly from the Old Testament and Dante's *Inferno*. His first name, Daniel, comes from the Hebrew word meaning "God is my judge," certainly an ironic choice of name because Daniel Blank commits numerous murders throughout the novel. Blank's middle name, Gideon, refers to a famous Hebrew judge and literally means "a warrior who hews or cuts down his enemies." The last name of Sanders's antihero suggests the empty, impotent, and gratuitous nature of the murders he commits.

Blank is an Antichrist figure, Christ become Narcissus—not the Man for Others who sacrifices himself for the salvation of humankind, but the man who sacrifices others for his own salvation, to fill in the Blank, as it were. He identifies himself as "God's will" and calls himself "God on earth," particularly at the orgasmic moment of the actual sinking of his weapon into a hapless victim's skull. He identifies himself with the computer he brings with him to his new job and states, "I am AMROK II." A true narcissist, Daniel Blank, by identifying himself as AMROK II, sets himself up as both the founder of a church, Jesus Christ, and Peter, whose name means "rock" and who was designated by Christ to be the Church's first leader.

The key to Delaney's genius as an investigator can be found in examining his relationship with the criminals themselves. It is a complex relationship that entails serious psychological risks for him because the pursued and the pursuer secretly share some key characteristics. Toward the end of *The First Deadly Sin*, Delaney writes an article on this Dostoevskian theme:

> It was an abstruse examination of the sensual . . . affinity between hunter and hunted, of how, in certain cases, it was necessary for the detective to penetrate and assume the physical body, spirit and soul of the criminal in order to bring him to justice.

Needless to say, Delaney's wife gently persuades him not to publish it, because he, like Daniel Blank, has been tempted into the destructive element and risks losing himself in it.

Sanders is one of the finest American writers of detective fiction. His style resonates not only with the snappy dialogue of Raymond Chandler and Dashiell Hammett but also with the long, balanced sentences of the most accomplished American and British classic writers, such as Henry James, Nathaniel Hawthorne, F. Scott Fitzgerald, and William Faulkner. His moral enigmas evoke the persistently tormenting conflicts of a Charles Dickens or a Fyodor Dostoevski. Like all serious writers, Sanders was disturbed by important questions. He could evoke and sustain, as few modern writers can, a deeply disturbing sense of sin and courageously plunged into an exploration of the lines between guilt and innocence, responsibility and victimization, heredity and environment. He resisted easy answers to complex situations, entering fully into each case. In trying to determine when human beings become morally responsible and, therefore, guilty of crimes, he struggled alongside his characters. Sanders was one of the most important and innovative writers of crime fiction in the twentieth century.

Patrick Meanor

Principal mystery and detective fiction

Edward X. Delaney series: *The Anderson Tapes*, 1970; *The First Deadly Sin*, 1973; *The Second Deadly Sin*, 1977; *The Third Deadly Sin*, 1981; *The Fourth Deadly Sin*, 1985

Peter Tangent series: *The Tangent Objective*, 1976; *The Tangent Factor*, 1978

Commandment series: *The Sixth Commandment*, 1978; *The Tenth Commandment*, 1980; *The Eighth Commandment*, 1986; *The Seventh Commandment*, 1991

Timothy Cone series: *The Timothy Files*, 1987; *Timothy's Game*, 1988

Archy McNally series: *McNally's Luck*, 1992; *McNally's Secret*, 1992; *McNally's Risk*, 1993; *McNally's Caper*, 1994; *McNally's Trial*, 1995; *McNally's Puzzle*, 1996; *McNally's Gamble*, 1997; *McNally's Dilemma*, 1999 (with Vincent Lardo); *McNally's Folly*, 2000 (with Lardo); *McNally's Chance*, 2001 (with Lardo); *McNally's Dare*, 2003 (with Lardo); *McNally's Bluff*, 2004 (with Lardo)

Other short fiction: *Tales of the Wolf*, 1986

Other major works

Novels: *Pleasures of Helen*, 1971; *Love Songs*, 1972; *The Tomorrow File*, 1975; *The Marlow Chronicles*, 1977; *Caper*, 1980 (as Andress); *The Case of Lucy Bending*, 1982; *The Seduction of Peter S.*, 1983; *The Passion of Molly T.*, 1984; *The Loves of Harry Dancer*, 1986; *Capital Crimes*, 1989; *Dark Summer*, 1989; *Stolen Blessings*, 1989; *Sullivan's Sting*, 1990; *Private Pleasures*, 1994; *The Adventures of Chauncey Alcock*, 1997 (with others); *Guilty Pleasures*, 1998; *Guilty Secrets*, 1998

Nonfiction: *Handbook of Creative Crafts*, 1968 (with Richard Carol)

Edited text: *Thus Be Loved*, 1966

Bibliography

Anderson, Patrick. *The Triumph of the Thriller: How Cops, Crooks, and Cannibals Captured Popular Fiction*. New York: Random House, 2007. Section on Sanders hails the originality of *The First Deadly Sin*, which Anderson says is one of the first modern thrillers.

Bertens, Hans, and Theo D'haen. *Contemporary American Crime Fiction*. New York: Palgrave, 2001. Wide-ranging study of the contemporary scene in American crime fiction; helps place Sanders's varied body of work within its larger milieu.

Kuhne, David. *African Settings in Contemporary American Novels*. Westport, Conn.: Greenwood Press, 1999. Work discusses the use of Africa as a setting in American novels and examines *The Tangent Objective* and *The Tangent Factor*.

Nelson, William. "Expiatory Symbolism in Lawrence Sanders' *The First Deadly Sin*." *Clues: A Journal of Detection* 1 (Fall/Winter, 1980): 71-76. Discusses the nature of redemption, both as plot device and as thematic consideration, in Sanders's novel.

Nelson, William, and Nancy Avery. "Art Where You Least Expect It: Myth and Ritual in the Detective Series." *Modern Fiction Studies* 19 (Autumn, 1983): 463-474. Scholarly study of Sanders's use of mythological and ritualistic elements in his fiction.

Weeks, Linton. "Ghost Writers in the Sky: A Popular Author's Death No Longer Means the End of a Career." *Washington Post*, August 6, 1999, p. C01. Weeks looks at *McNally's Dilemma*, which was written after Sanders's death, and discusses the trend in which publishers continue to release ghostwritten books after the death of a popular author such as V. C. Andrews.

SAPPER

Herman Cyril McNeile

Born: Bodmin, Cornwall, England; September 28, 1888
Died: West Chiltington, Sussex, England; August 14, 1937
Also wrote as H. C. McNeile
Type of plot: Amateur sleuth

Principal series

Bulldog Drummond, 1920-1937

Principal series character

Captain Hugh "Bulldog" Drummond, formerly an officer in the British army who served in World War I, finds himself at loose ends after the war and begins taking on investigative cases. Drummond typifies the kind of gentleman sleuth so popular in England at the beginning of the twentieth century. Educated at the right schools and connected with the right people.

Contribution

Although Sapper's character Bulldog Drummond was extremely popular in novels and on the stage in the 1920's, in the 1930's and 1940's Drummond was best known through film and radio. In the transition from novels to radio and film, Drummond was transformed from a somewhat snobbish retired British officer to a suave gentleman. Indeed, most Americans who remember Bulldog Drummond will not remember him from the novels, which were read primarily in England.

Bulldog Drummond was a continuation of the tradition of the gentleman sleuth, called in by clients or friends to solve a murder, disappearance, or robbery—all in the tradition of Sherlock Holmes. In fact, Sapper's fiction was a mainstay of *The Strand* magazine, the same magazine where the Holmes stories regularly appeared. Fast-paced and well-plotted, Sapper's novels were aimed at the same public that took to the Holmes series. Today this kind of entertainment seems tame, and the social prejudices of those days, very prominent in the Drummond novels, are judged unacceptable by many critics.

Biography

Sapper was born Herman Cyril McNeile in Bodmin, Cornwall, England, on September 28, 1888. He was the son of a naval officer, Captain Malcolm McNeile, who was once governor of the Royal Naval Prison at Lewes. His mother was Christiana Mary Sloggett. Educated at Cheltenham College, McNeile went on to officer school at the Royal Military Academy in Woolwich. In 1907, he joined the Royal Engineers (from which he adopted the pen name Sapper, a slang word for a military engineer). Promoted to captain in 1914, McNeile served in World War I from 1914 to 1918 and was awarded the Military Cross.

In 1919, McNeile retired from the service with the rank of lieutenant colonel. Not wanting to take up a mundane profession, he began writing for a living. He had already published several books and articles on the war, but it was not until 1920, when *Bull-Dog Drummond: The Adventures of a Demobilized Officer Who Found Peace Dull* appeared, that he had his first success. This success was so great that a dramatized version of the book quickly went on the boards the following year (with Gerald du Maurier playing Drummond) and later played in New York.

McNeile reaped the rewards of his lucrative invention, and new Drummond books appeared almost annually. When the first film with the Drummond character was released in the early 1920's, another source of income was opened, and it proved to be a rich one. Some twenty films later, Drummond had been played by Ronald Colman, Ralph Richardson, John Howard, Tom Conway, Ron Randell, and even Walter Pidgeon. As a result of these films, and the books, McNeile became a wealthy man.

McNeile was married to Violet Baird, the daughter of Scottish boxing patron Arthur Sholto Douglas, and had two sons. Aside from his very successful career as a writer, McNeile lived a quiet life. However, he had not escaped from his experiences in the Great War: He died, from complications resulting from his war injuries, on August 14, 1937.

Analysis

British adventure fiction is full of retired captains and colonels, but the most successful of them all was Bulldog Drummond, the former captain who returns from World War I to find a new career as a private sleuth. Sapper, who had written several fictional works based on his experiences in the trenches, patterned Drummond partly on himself and partly on his friend Gerard Fairlie, who in fact carried on the series after 1937. (The new series continued until 1954; most of the seven novels written by Fairlie were not published in the United States.)

Challenge

Sapper wrote a brisk, accomplished prose, with few frills. He had no pretensions as an author, and there are those who believe that his first Drummond novel is his best. Nevertheless, his last novel, *Challenge* (1937), contains the standard ingredients of plot and style and may serve as a model. There is fast-paced dialogue, very little descriptive prose, and a wide range of characters. Sapper's plots are lively, and there is very little cogitating over a cup of tea. Although his prose was close to that of the pulp writers, it was definitely a notch above it. The style is clean and strongly influenced by American popular fiction. Note this dialogue from *Challenge*:

> "Come on, Captain Talbot," cried Molly. "If we stop here talking all night, their meeting will be over."
>
> "Dash it, Molly," said Algy. "I *don't* like it."
>
> "Dry up," she laughed. "Now what are you going to do?" She turned to the soldier.
>
> "Go with you and show you the room. Then lurk round a corner out of sight, but within hearing. And if anything happens, just give a call and I'll be with you."

This dialogue from Sapper's last Drummond novel shows a strong American influence ("Dry up") as well as a traditional British touch ("Dash it"). To some readers, the mixture seems odd; to others, who do not take their detective fiction so seriously, it adds interest. At any rate, Sapper tried to blend modern American slang with traditional British expressions. Indeed, Sapper could not and did not want to escape the British tradition of good schools, good breeding, and decent behavior.

Bulldog Drummond

Above all, one must understand that Sapper was writing for a British audience, for whom the gentleman sleuth was a beloved figure. From Sherlock Holmes to Sexton Blake and Lord Peter Wimsey, the detective with a "good background" has always been popular. This detective often has a sidekick, a Dr. Watson; in Bulldog Drummond's case, it was Ronald Standish—whom Sapper featured in several novels—as well as Algy Longworth and James Denny. His sidekick serves, in most cases, as an admirer and supporter. In *Challenge*, Standish tells another character, "You can take it from me that there is generally a reason for everything that Drummond does."

Perhaps one reason for Bulldog Drummond's popularity was that the detective did not flaunt his background, except to show a fondness for the military and

Ronald Colman played Bulldog Drummond in a 1929 film adaptation of Sapper's novel and reprised the role five years later in Bulldog Drummond Strikes Back.

officers (honorable British officers, that is). Drummond's business was to solve the crimes put before him, and he wasted little time with salon chitchat. Sapper learned this lesson from *The Strand*, where the editors insisted on straightforward fiction.

Another aspect of Bulldog Drummond that appealed to his fans was his steely determination to get the job done. He had little patience for the slowness of the police, because he generally believed that they did little more than get in his way. Drummond cut through red tape and solved mysteries. It was this perhaps more than any other quality that made Drummond so attractive.

Yet one must never forget that, as Colin Watson maintains in his book *Snobbery with Violence* (1972), "Bulldog Drummond was a melodramatic creation workable only within a setting of melodrama." Many of the novels have pulpish plots featuring international conspiracies and fiendish villains. These are the materials of a bygone fiction, a fiction that championed such figures as the Shadow, Fu Manchu, and Charlie Chan, to name a few. Thus, Drummond ceased to have much appeal after World War II, save as a film detective who was clearly too suave to be pursuing mad scientists and international criminals.

There is yet another feature of the Drummond novels of the 1920's and 1930's that dates them badly. Captain Drummond reflected the prejudices of his age. In Sapper's novels and stories, foreigners are always comic characters—or sinister ones. Derogatory terms such as "wops" and "dagoes" appear in the novels. The French are excitable and cry out "*Mon dieu!*" and the Germans are swinish and dull ("a heavy-jowled German looked up sullenly").

Again, the difference between the Drummond of films and radio and the Drummond of fiction is instructive. As played by Tom Conway and Walter Pidgeon in films, Drummond is more at home in the salon than on a fast car chase after a sinister villain. He is sophisticated and intelligent—not at all like the Drummond of fiction, who resembles a hearty kind of hero, a Captain Midnight or Doc Savage. The Drummond of fiction, who talks of "wogs" and "Frogs," is remarkably different from the suave Drummond of the films, who is more comfortable in a tuxedo than in tweed.

Many critics have tried to deal with the social implications of detective fiction, especially how it reveals the psychology of the audience. George Orwell, in his essay "Raffles and Miss Blandish," sought to relate the modern crime novel, with its sex and sadism, to the change in public mores. He found that the character Raffles (created by E. W. Hornung) reflected an old-fashioned admiration of British readers for the "better classes." Colin Watson goes as far as to say that the readers of gentleman-sleuth novels are inherently snobs, at least in their secret hearts. Why else would one want to read about an improbable gentleman detective who outwits master criminals every time?

The Bulldog Drummond of fiction is less of a snob than others of his kind. He is happy to deliver a left hook to a deserving villain, rather than, in the manner of Holmes, to deliver him to the police. He is far more ready to take on a gang of criminals bare-handed, as in *Challenge*, where he taunts his attackers, "Come on, you spawn. . . . Or are you still afraid?"

It is primarily Drummond's determination, his decency, his sense of devotion to law and order, that made him appealing to a broad audience. His honesty and courage were always contrasted with the qualities of the villains he faced, international criminals such as Carl Peterson. Peterson is unscrupulous, Drummond is honorable; Peterson is a cold-blooded murderer, Drummond prefers a left to the jaw; Peterson has a gang of criminals, Drummond has only his sidekicks, good men but men who are often bested by the villains. In short, Drummond is a man who can be admired by those from ages ten to seventy.

No one can possibly take the Bulldog Drummond novels as anything more than popular entertainment. While the hero's long reign in print can be called a success of sorts, the social importance of the Drummond saga is no weightier than that of the Shadow or Charlie Chan. The transformation that took place when the character of Drummond was transmuted in films and on the radio is another story.

Philip M. Brantingham

Principal mystery and detective fiction

Bulldog Drummond series: *Bull-Dog Drummond: The Adventures of a Demobilized Officer Who*

Found Peace Dull, 1920; *Bulldog Drummond*, 1921 (with Gerald du Maurier); *The Black Gang*, 1922; *The Third Round*, 1924 (also known as *Bulldog Drummond's Third Round*); *The Final Count*, 1926; *The Female of the Species*, 1928 (also known as *Bulldog Drummond Meets the Female of the Species*); *Temple Tower*, 1929; *The Return of Bulldog Drummond*, 1932 (also known as *Bulldog Drummond Returns*); *Knockout*, 1933 (also known as *Bulldog Drummond Strikes Back*); *Bulldog Drummond at Bay*, 1935; *Bulldog Jack (Alias Bulldog Drummond)*, 1935 (with J. O. C. Orton and Gerard Fairlie); *Bulldog Hits Out*, 1937 (with Fairlie); *Challenge*, 1937

Nonseries novels: *Mufti*, 1919; *Jim Maitland*, 1923; *Jim Brent*, 1926; *Tiny Carteret*, 1930; *The Island of Terror*, 1931 (also known as *Guardians of the Treasure*); *Ronald Standish*, 1933

Other short fiction: *The Lieutenant and Others*, 1915; *Sergeant Michael Cassidy, R.E.*, 1915 (also known as *Michael Cassidy, Sergeant* as H.C. McNeile); *Men, Women, and Guns*, 1916; *No Man's Land*, 1917; *The Human Touch*, 1918; *The Man in Ratcatcher, and Other Stories*, 1921; *The Dinner Club*, 1923; *Out of the Blue*, 1925; *Word of Honour*, 1926; *The Saving Clause*, 1927; *When Caruthers Laughed*, 1927; *Sapper's War Stories*, 1930; *The Finger of Fate*, 1930; *Fifty-one Stories*, 1934; *Ask for Ronald Standish*, 1936; *"Sapper": The Best Short Stories*, 1984

Other major works

Short fiction: 1916-1925 • *The Fatal Second*, 1916; *The Motor-Gun*, 1916; *The Truce of the Bear*, 1918; *Mark Danver's Sin, and The Madman of Coral Reef Lighthouse*, 1923; *Molly's Aunt at Angmering*, 1923; *Peter Cornish's Revenge*, 1923; *A Scrap of Paper*, 1924; *Bulton's Revenge*, 1924; *That Bullet Hole Has a History!*, 1924; *The Ducking of Herbert Polton, and Coincidence*, 1924; *The Valley of the Shadow*, 1924; *A Native Superstition*, 1925; *A Question of Identity*, 1925; *The Other Side of the Wall*, 1925; *The Professor's Christmas Party, and A Student of the Obvious*, 1925; *Who Was This Woman?, Two Photographs, and The Queen of Hearts*, 1925

1926-1930 • *The Eleventh Hour*, 1926; *The Loyalty of Peter Drayton and Mrs. Skeffington's Revenge*, 1926; *The Message*, 1926; *The Rout of the Oliver Samuelsons*, 1926; *The Rubber Stamp, and A Matter of Voice*, 1926; *The Taming of Sydney Marsham*, 1926; *Three of a Kind, and The Haunting of Jack Burnham*, 1926; *A Hundred Per Cent*, 1927; *An Act of Providence*, 1927; *Billie Finds an Answer*, 1927; *Dilemma*, 1927; *Once Bit, Twice Hit*, 1927; *Relative Values*, 1927; *The Diamond Hair Slide*, 1927; *The Undoing of Mrs. Cransby*, 1928; *A Question of Mud*, 1929; *The Hidden Witness*, 1929

1931-1933 • *The Great Magor Diamond, and The Creaking Door*, 1931; *The Haunted Rectory*, 1931; *The Missing Chauffeur*, 1931; *The Brides of Mertonbridge Hall*, 1932; *Uncle James's Golf Match*, 1932; *The Man in Yellow, and The Empty House*, 1933

Play: *The Way Out*, pr. 1930

Edited text: *The Best of O. Henry: One Hundred of His Stories*, 1929

Bibliography

Panek, LeRoy. "Sapper." In *The Special Branch: The British Spy Novel, 1890-1980*. Bowling Green, Ohio: Bowling Green University Popular Press, 1981. Scholarly study of British espionage thrillers written by a major critic in the academic study of mystery and detective fiction contains an essay on Sapper.

Treadwell, Lawrence P., Jr. *The Bulldog Drummond Encyclopedia*. Jefferson, N.C.: McFarland, 2001. Reference work entirely devoted to Drummond, his adventures, and his fictional world.

Usborne, Richard. *Clubland Heroes: A Nostalgic Study of Some Recurrent Characters in the Romantic Fiction of Dornford Yates, John Buchan and Sapper.* 3d ed. London: Hutchinson, 1983. Study of Drummond, comparing him to such other fictional characters as Dickson Mc'Cunn and Richard Hannay.

_______. Introduction to *Bulldog Drummond*. London: J. M. Dent & Sons, 1983. Overview of Sapper's most famous character and his fictional adventures.

Watson, Colin. "The Bulldog Breed." In *Snobbery with Violence: Crime Stories and Their Audience*. London: Eyre and Spottiswoode, 1979. Study of the representation of snobbery within crime fiction. Provides perspective for Sapper's writing.

DOROTHY L. SAYERS

Born: Oxford, England; June 13, 1893
Died: Witham, Essex, England; December 17, 1957
Types of plot: Master sleuth; cozy

Principal series

Lord Peter Wimsey, 1923-1937

Principal series characters

Lord Peter Wimsey, a wealthy aristocrat, is an Oxford graduate, book collector, wine connoisseur, and lover of fast cars, cricket, and crime. Though he gives the appearance, particularly in the early novels, of being a foppish playboy, his flippancy masks intelligence, conscience, and sensitivity.

Bunter, an imperturbable, supremely competent manservant, served under Wimsey in World War I, then became his valet, bringing his master through a war-induced breakdown. His skills range from photographing corpses and cooking superb meals to extracting crucial evidence from cooks and housemaids over tea in the servants' quarters.

Chief Inspector Charles Parker, a Scotland Yard detective, is Lord Peter's friend and later his brother-in-law. He provides a calm, rational balance to Wimsey's flamboyant personality.

Harriet Vane, the detective novelist with whom Lord Peter falls in love as he saves her from the gallows in *Strong Poison* (1930). Independent, capable, and proud, she refuses to marry him until she is convinced that their marriage can be an equal partnership.

Contribution

Dorothy L. Sayers never considered her detective novels and short stories to be truly serious literature, and once Lord Peter Wimsey had provided a substantial income for her, she turned her attention to religious drama, theology, and a translation of Dante's *La divina commedia* (c. 1320; *The Divine Comedy*, 1802). Yet she wrote these popular works with the same thoroughness, commitment to quality, and attention to detail that infuse her more scholarly writings. Her mystery novels set a high standard for writers who followed her—and there have been many. Her plots are carefully constructed, and she was willing to spend months, even years, in researching background details. What gives her works their lasting appeal, however, is not the nature of the crimes or the cleverness of their solutions. Readers return to the novels for the pleasure of savoring Sayers's wit, her literary allusions, the rich settings, the deftly developed characters, and, above all, her multitalented aristocratic sleuth, Lord Peter Wimsey. Blending the conventions of detective fiction with social satire and unobtrusively interweaving serious themes, she fulfilled her goal of making the detective story "once more a novel of manners instead of a pure crossword puzzle."

Biography

Dorothy Leigh Sayers was born in Oxford, England, on June 13, 1893, the only child of the Reverend Henry Sayers, headmaster of the Christ Church Choir School, and his talented wife, Helen Leigh Sayers. When Dorothy was four, the family moved to the fen country immortalized in *The Nine Tailors* (1934), and there she was educated by her parents and governesses. By the time she entered the Godolphin School in Salisbury in 1909, she was fluent in French and German and an avid reader and writer. Her life as a pampered only child did not, however, prepare her well to fit in with her contemporaries, and she found real friends only when she entered Somerville College, Oxford, in 1912. There she participated enthusiastically in musical, dramatic, and social activities and won first-class honors in French. She was among the first group of women granted degrees in 1920.

After leaving Oxford in 1915, she held a variety of jobs, finally settling at Benson's Advertising Agency in London as a copywriter. Shortly after she joined Benson's, she began work on her first detective novel, *Whose Body?* (1923). Following its publication, she took a leave of absence from her work, ostensibly to work on a second book but in reality to give birth to a son out of wedlock. One of her biographers, James Brabazon, has identified her child's father as a

Dorothy L. Sayers. (Library of Congress)

working-class man to whom she may have turned in reaction to a painful affair with the writer John Cournos.

She placed her son in the care of a cousin, returned to work, and two years later married Captain Oswald Arthur "Mac" Fleming, another man who shared almost none of her intellectual interests. Fleming, a divorced journalist, suffered throughout most of their married life from physical and psychological damage resulting from his service in World War I. She and Fleming informally adopted her son in 1934, but the boy continued to live with her cousin, and she never told him that he was her own child.

In this decade of personal stress, Sayers's career as a detective novelist was taking shape. By 1937 she had published more than a dozen books and was recognized as one of England's best mystery writers. In the last twenty years of her life, she devoted her energies to becoming an articulate spokeswoman for the Church of England and a respected Dante scholar. She did not quite abandon her earlier pursuits, maintaining a strong interest in the Detection Club, which she had helped found in 1930. She died in 1957.

Analysis

In her introduction to *Great Short Stories of Detection, Mystery, and Horror* (1928-1934), Dorothy L. Sayers writes that the detective story "does not, and by hypothesis never can, attain the loftiest level of literary achievement. . . . It rarely touches the heights and depths of human passion." It is, she adds,

> part of the literature of escape, and not of expression. We read tales of domestic unhappiness because that is the kind of thing which happens to us; but when these things gall too close to the sore, we fly to mystery and adventure because they do not, as a rule, happen to us.

Clearly, she cherished no ambition of finding literary immortality in the adventures of Lord Peter Wimsey. Nevertheless, she brought to the craft of writing detective fiction a scholar's mind and a conviction that any work undertaken is worth doing well, qualities that have won acclaim for her as one of the best mystery writers of the twentieth century.

Her biographers have suggested that the impetus for her writing of mystery stories was economic. Still financially dependent on her parents in her late twenties, she began work on *Whose Body?* in 1921 as one last effort to support herself as a writer. In a letter to her parents, she promised that if this effort were unsuccessful, she would give up her ambitions and take a teaching position—not a career she coveted. Her choice of this genre was a sensible one for her purposes. Mysteries were enormously popular in England and America in the 1920's and 1930's, and by 1937, when Lord Peter Wimsey made his last major appearance, her twelve detective novels and numerous short stories had guaranteed her a substantial income for the rest of her life.

Having chosen her form, Sayers entered on her task with diligence, studying the work of the best of her predecessors, particularly Edgar Allan Poe, Sir Arthur Conan Doyle, and Wilkie Collins. She applied her academic training to the genre, its history, its structures, and its compacts with its readers. Her efforts were so successful that only a few years after the publication of her first novel she was asked to edit a major anthology of detective stories and to write an introduction that is both a short history of the genre and an analysis of its major characteristics.

Sayers's work is not, on the surface, especially innovative. Particularly in her early work, she used the popular conventions of the form—mysterious methods of murder, amoral villains, and the clever amateur detective in the tradition of C. Auguste Dupin, Sherlock Holmes, and E. C. Bentley's Philip Trent. From the beginning, however, she lifted the quality of the mystery novel. First, as critic and detective novelist Carolyn Heilbrun (Amanda Cross) notes, "Miss Sayers wrote superbly well." A reader can open her books to almost any page and find lines that reflect her pleasure in a well-turned phrase. She enjoyed experimenting with different types of styles, even imitating Wilkie Collins's *The Moonstone* (1868) by using letters to tell the story in *The Documents in the Case* (1930; with Robert Eustace).

Sayers was a skillful creator of plots, adhering firmly to the "fair play" she describes in her introduction to *Great Short Stories of Detection, Mystery, and Horror*: "The reader must be given every clue—but he must not be told, surely, all the detective's deductions, lest he should see the solution too far ahead." Her adherence to this principle is especially clear in her short stories, both those featuring Wimsey and those involving her second amateur detective hero, Montague Egg. Egg, a traveling salesman of wine and spirits, is a master interpreter of the hidden clue and another delightful character, though the stories about him tend to be more formulaic than the Wimsey tales.

Sayer's full-length novels are unusual in the variety of crimes and solutions they depict. She never fell into a single pattern of plot development, and in fact she argued that a successful mystery writer cannot do that, for each work arises out of a different idea, and each idea demands its own plot: "To get the central idea is one thing: to surround it with a suitable framework of interlocking parts is quite another. . . . idea and plot are two quite different things." The challenge is to flesh out the idea in a suitable sequence of events and to develop characters in ways that make these events plausible.

The character most crucial to the effectiveness of the mystery novel is, naturally, that of the detective. Sayers developed Lord Peter Wimsey gradually over the fifteen years in which she wrote about him. In his first appearances he is a rather stereotypical figure, comprising elements of Trent, Holmes, and P. G. Wodehouse's Bertie Wooster, the quintessential "silly-ass-about-town." In his first case, he greets the discovery of a body in a bathtub, clad only in a pair of gold-rimmed eyeglasses, with gleeful enthusiasm. Sayers herself might later have considered him too gleeful; as she wrote in her introduction to *Great Short Stories of Detection, Mystery, and Horror*, "The sprightly amateur must not be sprightly all the time, lest at some point we should be reminded that this is, after all, a question of somebody's being foully murdered, and that flippancy is indecent."

At the beginning of his career, Wimsey is distinguished chiefly by superficial attributes—wealth; an aristocratic upbringing; interest in rare books, wine, and music; skill in languages; arcane knowledge in a variety of fields; and the services of the unflappable Bunter. Although the early Wimsey is, in Margaret

The first illustration of Lord Peter Wimsey, drawn by John Campbell for Pearson's Magazine *in 1926.*

Hannay's words, something of a "cardboard detective," nevertheless there are in him elements that allowed Sayers to "humanize him" in her later works. He is shown in *Whose Body?* and *Unnatural Death* (1927) to have moments of self-doubt as he contemplates his responsibility for actions that follow on his intervention into the crimes. His moral sensitivity is also revealed in his sympathetic response to the irritating but understandable war victim George Fentiman in *The Unpleasantness at the Bellona Club* (1928), who so bitterly resents his dependence on his wife. The later Lord Peter retains the ability to "talk piffle" as a mask to cover his intelligence, but his detecting is now seen not as an amateur's game but as work in service of truth. His stature is also increased by his work for the Foreign Office, which sends him out to exercise his conversational skills as a diplomat.

Strong Poison

As Sayers acknowledges in her essay "Gaudy Night," in which she discusses the composition of the novel of the same name, Peter's growth came largely in response to the creation of Harriet Vane in *Strong Poison*. Sayers invented Harriet, she confessed, with the idea of marrying him off before he consumed her whole existence. When she came to the end of the novel, however, her plan would not work. "When I looked at the situation I saw that it was in every respect false and degrading; and the puppets had somehow got just so much flesh and blood in them that I could not force them to accept it without shocking myself." The only solution, she decided, was to make Peter "a complete human being, with a past and a future, with a consistent family and social history, with a complicated psychology and even the rudiments of a religious outlook." In the novels written after 1930, Wimsey becomes wiser, more conscious of the complexities of human feelings, less certain of the boundaries of good and evil. As he becomes a more complex figure, the novels in which he appears begin to cross the border between the whodunit and the novel of manners.

Another major factor in Sayers's success as a mystery writer was her ability to create authentic, richly detailed settings for her work. "Readers," she says in "Gaudy Night,"

> seem to like books which tell them how other people live—any people, advertisers, bell-ringers, women dons, butchers, bakers or candlestick-makers—so long as the detail is full and accurate and the object of the work is not overt propaganda.

She alludes here to the three novels many readers consider her best—*Murder Must Advertise* (1933), *The Nine Tailors*, and *Gaudy Night* (1935). In each she drew on places and people she knew well to create worlds that her readers would find appealing.

Murder Must Advertise

From her nine years as copywriter with Benson's, Sayers created Pym's Publicity in *Murder Must Advertise*. There is an aura of verisimilitude in every detail, from the office politics to the absurd advertisements for "Nutrax for Nerves" to the Pym's-Brotherhood annual cricket match. Sayers even borrowed Benson's spiral iron staircase as the scene of Victor Dean's murder, and she drew on her own successful "Mustard Club" campaign for Wimsey's brilliant cigarette-advertising scheme, "Whiffle your way around Britain."

The Nine Tailors

Sayers set *The Nine Tailors* in a village in the fen country much like the parish in which her father served for most of her childhood and adolescence. The plot depends heavily on the practice of bell ringing, which Sayers studied for two years before she completed her novel. Her account of the mechanics of draining the fen country and the attendant dangers of flooding shows equally careful research. Many of the greatest delights of the book, however, lie in the evocation of village life, epitomized in the final scene, in which the inhabitants of Fenchurch St. Paul have taken refuge from the floodwaters in the huge church:

> A curious kind of desert-island life was carried on in and about the church, which, in course of time, assumed a rhythm of its own. Each morning was ushered in by a short and cheerful flourish of bells, which rang the milkers out to the cowsheds in the graveyard. Hot water for washing was brought in wheeled waterbutts from the Rectory copper. Bedding was shaken and rolled under the pews for the day. . . . Daily school was carried on in the south aisle; games and drill were organized in the Rectory garden by Lord Peter Wimsey; farmers attended to their cattle; owners of poultry brought the eggs to a

> communal basket; Mrs. Venables presided over sewing-parties in the Rectory.

The mystery plot is here grounded in a world of rich and poor, old and young, that seems to go on beyond the confines of the novel.

Gaudy Night

For some readers the most interesting community of all those that Sayers depicted is Shrewsbury College, the setting for *Gaudy Night*—one of the first works of a still-popular type of detective fiction, the university mystery. Shrewsbury is closely modeled on Somerville, where the author spent three of the most personally rewarding years of her life. Although her picture of life in the Senior Common Room did not win universal approval from her Somerville acquaintances, she captured brilliantly the camaraderie and rivalries of the educational institution, the dedication of committed teachers to their students and their scholarly disciplines, and the undergraduates' struggle to deal with academic and social pressures.

The characters

Sayers's settings come to life chiefly through their inhabitants, many of whom have little do with the solution to the mystery but much to do with the lasting appeal of the works. Every reader has favorite characters: old Hezekiah Lavender, who tolls the passing of human life on the venerable bell Tailor Paul; Tom Puffett, the loquacious chimney sweep in *Busman's Honeymoon* (1937); Ginger Joe, the young fan of fictional detective Sexton Blake who provides Wimsey with an important clue in Murder Must Advertise; Miss Lydgate, the kindly scholar in *Gaudy Night*. These characters are often seen most vividly through their own words. Lord Peter's delightful mother, the Dowager Duchess of Denver, is instantly recognizable for her stream-of-consciousness conversation, dotted with malapropisms that cover underlying good sense. Wimsey's indefatigable never-married investigator, Miss Climpson, is best known through her self-revelatory letters, which are as full of italics as Queen Victoria's diaries:

> My train got in quite late on Monday night, after a *most dreary* journey, with a *lugubrious* wait at *Preston*, though thanks to your kindness in insisting that I should travel *First-class*, I was not really at all tired! Nobody can realise what a *great* difference these extra comforts make, especially when one is *getting on* in years, and after the *uncomfortable* traveling which I had to endure in my days of poverty, I feel that I am living in almost *sinful* luxury!

Of Wimsey himself, Carolyn Heilbrun wrote, "Lord Peter's audience, if they engage in any fantasy at all about that sprig of the peerage, dream of having him to tea. They don't want to *be* Lord Peter, only to know him, for the sake of hearing him talk." It might even be said that good conversation finally brings Peter and Harriet Vane together, for it is talk that establishes their mutual respect, allowing them to reveal their shared commitment to intellectual honesty and their mutual conviction that husband and wife should be equal partners.

Taken as a whole, the conversations of Sayers's characters dazzle readers with the skill and erudition of their author, who reproduces the voices from many levels of English society while keeping up a steady stream of allusion to works as diverse as Dante's *The Divine Comedy*, Robert Burton's *The Anatomy of Melancholy* (1621), the operettas of Gilbert and Sullivan, and the adventures of fictional character Sexton Blake.

Women and work

Although Sayers's brilliant handling of plot, character, setting, and dialogue would probably have made her novels classics in the genre without additional elements, these works are also enriched by serious themes that preoccupied her throughout her career: the place of women in society, the importance of work, and the nature of guilt and innocence.

The works show a recurrent concern with the problems of the professional woman searching for dignity and independence in a man's world. Sayers embodies these concerns in such characters as Ann Dorland in *The Unpleasantness at the Bellona Club*, Marjorie Phelps, Sylvia Marriott, and Eiluned Price in *Strong Poison*, Miss Meteyard in *Murder Must Advertise*, and especially Harriet Vane, the character who most resembles her author. Wimsey is attractive to all these women not so much for his undeniable sex appeal as for his taking them seriously as human beings. If Sayers can be said to have fallen in love with her detective, as many have suggested, it is surely this quality that she found most appealing. She argues passionately in her lecture *Are Women Human?* (1971) that women should be treated as individuals, not as members of an inferior species:

> "What," men have asked distractedly from the beginning of time, "what on earth do women want?" I do not know that women, *as* women, want anything in particular, but as human beings they want, my good men, exactly what you want yourselves: interesting occupation, reasonable freedom for their pleasures, and a sufficient emotional outlet. What form the occupation, the pleasures and the emotion may take, depends entirely on the individual.

As this quotation suggests, Sayers's concern with the place of women in society is closely related to her belief that each person needs to find his or her own proper work and do it well. This idea, later to be the major theme of her religious drama *The Zeal of Thy House* (pr. 1937) and her theological volume *The Mind of the Maker* (1941), is central to the action of *Gaudy Night* and to the development of Peter and Harriet's relationship. The plot of this novel arises out of a young scholar's suppression of evidence that would invalidate the argument of his master's thesis, an action whose discovery led to his professional disgrace and eventually to his suicide. His wife sets out to avenge his death on the female scholar who discovered his fraud. Although Sayers does not deny the moral ambiguities in the situation, she makes it clear that fraudulent scholarship is no minor matter. One must do one's work with integrity, regardless of personal considerations.

Acting on this conviction, Lord Peter urges Harriet to "abandon the jig-saw kind of story and write a book about human beings for a change," even if it means confronting painful episodes from her past. When she responds, "It would hurt like hell," he replies, "What would that matter, if it made a good book?" She interprets his respect for her work as respect for her integrity as a human being and moves a step closer to accepting his proposal of marriage.

Good and evil

The issue of guilt and innocence—more fundamentally, of good and evil—is handled more obliquely. As R. D. Stock and Barbara Stock note in their essay "The Agents of Evil and Justice in the Novels of Dorothy L. Sayers," the nature of the criminals changes during the course of the author's career. In most of the early novels the criminal is a cold, heartless villain, quite willing to sacrifice others for his or her own goals. In the later works, however, the author shows her readers a world in which guilt and innocence are less clear-cut. The victims, such as Campbell in *The Five Red Herrings* (1931) and Deacon in *The Nine Tailors*, are thoroughly unsympathetic figures. Their killers are seen not as monsters but as human beings caught in circumstances they are not strong enough to surmount. In *The Nine Tailors* the murderers are the bells, inanimate objects controlled by individuals who share in the guilt of all humanity. This novel reflects Sayers's conviction, stated in *The Mind of the Maker*, that "human situations are subject to the law of human nature, whose evil is at all times rooted in its good, and whose good can only redeem, but not abolish, its evil."

By moving away from "the jig-saw kind of story" to deal with issues of moral and intellectual complexity, Sayers was enlarging the scope of her genre but also testing its limits. One of the great appeals of detective stories, she once wrote, is that they provide readers who live in a world full of insoluble problems with problems that unfailingly have solutions. Her last works still provide answers to the questions around which her plots revolve: Who killed the man whose body was found in Lady Thorpe's grave? Who was disrupting Shrewsbury College? Who murdered Mr. Noakes? These solutions do not, however, answer all the questions raised: What are one's obligations to other human beings, even if they are wrongdoers? When does one become a contributor to the development of another's guilt? What are the moral consequences of solving crimes? It is not surprising that she felt the need to move on to literary forms that would allow her to deal more directly with these issues, though there are many readers who wish she had continued to let Lord Peter and Harriet explore them.

By the time Sayers ended Wimsey's career with several short stories written in the late 1930's and early 1940's, she had left an indelible mark on the twentieth century detective story. Her world of aristocrats and manservants, country vicars, and villages in which everyone had a place and stayed in it, was vanishing even as she wrote about it; Wimsey tells Harriet at one point, "Our kind of show is dead and done for." Yet her works continue to appeal to large numbers of readers. Why? Some readers simply desire to escape the problems of the present—but the secret of Sayers's popularity surely goes beyond that. Her reputation rests partly on her superb handling of language, her attention to details of plot and setting, her humor, and her memorable characters. Yet it is ultimately those elements that push at the boundaries of the detective stories that have kept her works alive when those of many of her popular contemporaries have vanished. She left her successors a challenge to view the mystery novel not simply as entertainment (though it must always be that) but also as a vehicle for both literary excellence and reflection on serious, far-reaching questions.

Elizabeth Johnston Lipscomb

Principal mystery and detective fiction

Lord Peter Wimsey series: *Whose Body?*, 1923; *Clouds of Witness*, 1926; *Unnatural Death*, 1927 (also known as *The Dawson Pedigree*); *The Unpleasantness at the Bellona Club*, 1928; *Lord Peter Views the Body*, 1928; *Strong Poison*, 1930; *The Five Red Herrings*, 1931 (also known as *Suspicious Characters*); *Have His Carcase*, 1932; *Murder Must Advertise*, 1933; *Hangman's Holiday*, 1933; *The Nine Tailors*, 1934; *Gaudy Night*, 1935; *Busman's Honeymoon*, 1937; *In the Teeth of the Evidence, and Other Stories*, 1939; *Striding Folly*, 1972; *Lord Peter*, 1972 (James Sandoe, editor)

Nonseries novels: *The Documents in the Case*, 1930 (with Robert Eustace); *The Floating Admiral*, 1931 (with others); *Ask a Policeman*, 1933 (with others); *Six Against the Yard*, 1936 (with others; also known as *Six Against Scotland Yard*); *Double Death: A Murder Story*, 1939 (with others); *The Scoop, and Behind the Scenes*, 1983 (with others); *Crime on the Coast, and No Flowers by Request*, 1984 (with others)

Other major works

Plays: *Busman's Honeymoon*, pr. 1937 (with Muriel St. Clare Byrne); *The Zeal of Thy House*, pr., pb. 1937; *The Devil to Pay, Being the Famous Play of John Faustus*, pr., pb. 1939; *Love All*, pr. 1940; *The Just Vengeance*, pr., pb. 1946; *The Emperor Constantine*, pr. 1951 (revised as *Christ's Emperor*, 1952)

Radio play: *The Man Born to Be King: A Play-Cycle on the Life of Our Lord and Saviour Jesus Christ*, 1941-1942

Poetry: *Op 1*, 1916; *Catholic Tales and Christian Songs*, 1918; *Lord, I Thank Thee—*, 1943; *The Story of Adam and Christ*, 1955

Children's literature: *Even the Parrot: Exemplary Conversations for Enlightened Children*, 1944

Nonfiction: *The Greatest Drama Ever Staged*, 1938; *Strong Meat*, 1939; *Begin Here: A War-Time Essay*, 1940; *Creed or Chaos?*, 1940; *The Mind of the Maker*, 1941; *The Mysterious English*, 1941; *Why Work?*, 1942; *The Other Six Deadly Sins*, 1943; *Making Sense of the Universe*, 1946; *Unpopular Opinions*, 1946; *Creed or Chaos?, and Other Essays in Popular Theology*, 1947; *The Lost Tools of Learning*, 1948; *The Days of Christ's Coming*, 1953 (revised 1960); *The Story of Easter*, 1955; *The Story of Noah's Ark*, 1955; *Further Papers on Dante*, 1957; *Introductory Papers on Dante*, 1957; *The Poetry of Search and the Poetry of Statement, and Other Posthumous Essays on Literature, Religion, and Language*, 1963; *Christian Letters to a Post-Christian World*, 1969; *Are Women Human?*, 1971; *A Matter of Eternity*, 1973; *Wilkie Collins: A Critical and Biographical Study*, 1977 (E. R. Gregory, editor); *The Letters of Dorothy L. Sayers, 1937-1943*, 1998

Edited texts: *Oxford Poetry 1917*, 1918 (with Wilfred R. Childe and Thomas W. Earp); *Oxford Poetry 1918*, 1918 (with Earp and E. F. A. Geach); *Oxford Poetry 1919*, 1919 (with Earp and Siegfried Sassoon); *Great Short Stories of Detection, Mystery, and Horror*, 1928-1934 (also known as *The Omnibus of Crime*); *Tales of Detection*, 1936

Translations: *Tristan in Brittany*, 1929 (Thomas the Troubadour); *The Heart of Stone, Being the Four Canzoni of the "Pietra" Group*, 1946 (Dante); *The Comedy of Dante Alighieri the Florentine*, 1949-1962 (Cantica III with Barbara Reynolds); *The Song of Roland*, 1957

Bibliography

Brown, Janice. *The Seven Deadly Sins in the Work of Dorothy L. Sayers*. Kent, Ohio: Kent State University Press, 1998. Links Sayers's literary and religious works by analyzing her representation of the seven deadly sins in her mystery fiction.

Coomes, David. *Dorothy L. Sayers: A Careless Rage for Life*. New York: Lion, 1992. Coomes concentrates on reconciling the author of religious tracts with the detective novelist, thereby providing a portrayal of a more complex Sayers. He draws heavily on her papers at Wheaton College. Brief notes.

Dale, Alzina, ed. *Dorothy L. Sayers: The Centenary Celebration*. New York: Walker, 1993. Memoirs and essays situating Sayers in the history of detective fiction. Includes a brief biography and annotated bibliography.

Downing, Crystal. *Writing Performances: The Stages of Dorothy L. Sayers*. New York: Palgrave Macmillan, 2004. This study discusses Sayers's popular detective fiction and later dramatic works in the context of the modernist disdain for such forms. It argues that despite the negative judgment of her contemporaries in the academy, Sayers actually holds an important position with relation both to literary modernism and to postmodern dramatic works.

Hall, Trevor H. *Dorothy L. Sayers: Nine Literary Studies*. Hamden, Conn.: Archon Books, 1980. Hall discusses the connection between Sayers's creation, Lord Peter Wimsey, and Arthur Conan Doyle's creation, Sherlock Holmes. Hall also speculates in some detail on the influence of Sayers's husband, Atherton Fleming, on her writing.

Lewis, Terance L. *Dorothy L. Sayers's Peter Wimsey and British Interwar Society*. Lewiston, N.Y.: Edwin Mellen Press, 1994. Analyzes Sayers's detective and her mysteries as they reflect and comment on British society in the 1920's and 1930's.

McGregor, Robert Kuhn, and Ethan Lewis. *Conundrums for the Long Week-End: England, Dorothy L. Sayers, and Lord Peter Wimsey*. Kent, Ohio: Kent State, 2000. A cultural study of interwar England through the lens of Sayers's Wimsey books.

Pitt, Valerie. "Dorothy Sayers: The Masks of Lord Peter." In *Twentieth-Century Suspense: The Thriller Comes of Age*, edited by Clive Bloom. New York: St. Martin's Press, 1990. Analysis of Sayers's use of masquerade and disguise in the Lord Peter Wimsey mysteries.

Reynolds, Moira Davison. *Women Authors of Detective Series: Twenty-one American and British Authors, 1900-2000*. Jefferson, N.C.: McFarland, 2001. Examines the life and work of major female mystery writers, including Sayers.

STEVEN SAYLOR

Born: Port Lavaca, Texas; March 23, 1956
Also wrote as Aaron Travis
Type of plot: Historical

Principal series

Roma Sub Rosa (Secret Rome), 1991-

Principal series character

Gordianus the Finder is a citizen of the ancient Roman Republic with a knack for solving puzzles. Relentless in his pursuit of the truth, he often puts his own personal quest for answers above his clients' objectives.

Contribution

Along with British novelist Lindsey Davis, who first introduced her comic detective, Marcus Didius Falco, in 1989, and John Maddox Roberts, whose investigator, Decius Caecilius Matellus the Younger, made his first appearance in print in 1990, Steven Saylor is part of a small cadre of modern mystery writers who have chosen to set their narratives in the world of ancient Rome. Unlike the work of Davis and Roberts, however, the novels and short stories of Saylor are perhaps less dependent on the clever sleuthing of their fictional protagonist and more focused on the recovery of a palpable, visitable past.

Saylor asserts that his work is dominated not by Gordianus the Finder but by the historical figures who populate his narratives. Critics seem to agree that the author's greatest strength is his successful evocation of the tumultuous years of the last century B.C.E. In recreating the ancient world, however, Saylor is not content to adopt, without question, generally accepted interpretations of historical events; on the contrary, he is adept at exploring plausible alternative explanations for why some larger-than-life personages, such as Catilina or Julius Caesar, made some of their pivotal decisions. In so doing, Saylor often draws parallels to the social and political forces operative in modern times.

Saylor's fiction has been translated into more than a dozen languages, and his novels have been shortlisted for prestigious literary prizes, including the Ellis Peters Historical Dagger Award from the Crime Writers' Association.

Biography

Steven Warren Saylor was born in Port Lavaca, Texas, on March 23, 1956, and grew up in the small town of Goldthwaite. His parents divorced when he was quite young; his two siblings, Gwyn and Ronny, and he were raised by their mother, who did secretarial work to make ends meet. Saylor credits his mother, Lucy, with instilling in the family a solid sense of self-worth. In particular, she emphasized academic achievement. As a consequence, by the time that they graduated from high school, all three Saylor children earned grants and loans to attend college.

During Saylor's formative years in the hill country of Texas, he strove to conform to external expectations. He got good grades, played trumpet in the school band, got a part-time job at the local supermarket, and dated girls. All the while, however, he harbored a secret that he was not willing to divulge until he moved one hundred miles away from home to attend the University of Texas in Austin in 1974. In Austin, which Saylor has described as an oasis in a desert of intolerance, Saylor felt comfortable enough to embrace his sexuality. At the age of nineteen, he found his life partner, Richard Solomon; the two moved in together as a gay couple.

In 1978, Saylor graduated from the University of Texas with a bachelor's degree in history with honors, and in 1980, he and Solomon moved to San Francisco. For more than ten years thereafter, he worked as a freelance writer and magazine and newspaper editor. It was during this period that he began writing erotic fiction under the pseudonym of Aaron Travis. Saylor credits his first visit to Italy in 1987 with re-igniting his longstanding interest in the ancient world. When he returned to San Francisco after this trip, he decided to write a murder mystery set in Rome before the days of the empire.

The success of Saylor's first novel, *Roman Blood*, in 1991 allowed him to devote himself to writing fiction. The Roma Sub Rosa (secret Rome) series of historical mysteries that evolved from the publication of that first novel permitted Saylor and Solomon to buy a house in Berkeley, California. The series also solidified his credentials as a classicist, and Saylor has been called on to speak to academic audiences and appear on television documentaries (History Channel) to offer expert commentary on topics related to the classical world.

In addition to his mysteries set in ancient Rome, Saylor has published two books with Texas settings: *A Twist at the End: A Novel of O. Henry* (2000), set partially in Austin in 1885 when the city was rocked by a series of serial murders, and *Have You Seen Dawn?* (2003), a contemporary suspense novel set in a small town like the one in which he was raised.

Analysis

Gordianus the Finder, characterized by one of his enemies as a man of "no ancestry at all, a dubious career, and most irregular family," would appear, at first blush, to be an odd choice for the protagonist of a historical novel. This choice seems particularly odd for Steven Saylor because of his decision to focus on the last three decades of the Roman Republic when various politicians, often representatives of the noblest families, vied for supremacy. However, by virtue of the fact that he has no pedigree and hence no class loyalties, Gordianus can move freely among competing parties in search of the answers to problems that vex some of the key figures of his time.

Gordianus's "dubious career"—finding the truth without prejudice—is made possible because ancient Rome had no police force by modern standards. Thus, his career as a private detective often involves Gordianus in matters of considerable public import, from the moment in *Roman Blood* when he is hired by Cicero to investigate matters related to the great orator's first court case to the time in *The Judgment of Caesar: A Novel of Ancient Rome* (2004) when he is charged by Caesar to discover who might have tried to poison him at a key moment in his Egyptian campaign. By virtue of his unusual profession, Gordianus, an ordinary citizen during extraordinary times, can move easily across social strata and bear witness, from more than one perspective, to some of the key events in a momentous period in world history.

The reader's interest in Gordianus transcends his roles as detective and reader's stand-in. Over multiple volumes, Gordianus accumulates an "irregular family" that calls into question standard definitions of the term. His half-Egyptian, half-Jewish wife, Bethesda, was once his slave and concubine; his son and junior partner, Eco, was once a street orphan abandoned by his mother as a consequence of her witnessing a brutal murder. In conservative circles in ancient Rome and in modern times, family values have often been used as a justification for intolerance of domestic arrangements that do not match some rigid prescription. Set against the often dark consequences of the real-life blood ties that figure so prominently in many of the novels—the feuding, blue-blooded Claudii in *Catilina's Riddle* (1993) or the treacherous royal siblings of the House of Ptolemy in *The Judgment of Caesar*—Gordianus's hand-selected family shines.

The three elements of Saylor's formula for success are creating a character that serves as an eyewitness to history, giving that character an interesting puzzle to solve, and allowing that character to make a family of his own choosing. All three elements engage the reader's interest and sustain that interest from book to book.

Roman Blood

In *Roman Blood*, the first novel of the Roma Sub Rosa series, Steven Saylor establishes the formula that he successfully applies to each book. He provides his fictional protagonist with a mystery to unravel and, in so doing, makes him a convincing player at a critical point in the history of ancient Rome. Inspired by his reading of Michael Grant's book *Murder Trials* (1975), a translation of selected speeches by Marcus Tullius Cicero, Saylor involves Gordianus the Finder in the real-life public defense by Cicero, the famous orator and statesman, of the patrician Sextus Roscius, who stands accused of hiring someone to kill his father.

As the novel begins, Gordianus is thirty, and he has already established his investigative credentials and his reputation for integrity. Hoping to make his mark on the public stage, Cicero hires Gordianus to help him find the evidence that he needs to turn an appar-

ently hopeless case of parricide into a judicial victory. During the course of his investigation, Gordianus turns up some interesting facts, some of which shed light on political corruption during the last days of the constitutional dictatorship of the Roman general Sulla. The latter figure makes a brief but memorable appearance near the end of the novel when he passes judgment on Gordianus's chosen profession and the sometimes unsavory consequences of his inquiries. Sulla refers to Gordianus as a dog, the "kind that goes about digging up bones that other dogs have buried."

Gordianus also expands his unorthodox family when he gives shelter to the orphaned Eco, whose mother witnessed the murder that sets the plot in motion. This simple act of kindness toward a stranger stands in sharp contrast to the larcenous and even murderous practices that characterize the relations of those connected by blood.

Catilina's Riddle

The riddle referred to in the title of *Catilina's Riddle*, the longest novel in the series, involves the truth behind one of the most interesting figures in the history of early Rome, the populist politician Lucius Sergius Catilina. Was he the principal conspirator behind a plan to overthrow the Roman government by force or was he a man driven to desperate measures by a calculated campaign to defame his reputation and subvert his democratic motives?

Propositioned once again by Cicero, this time to offer his newly acquired farm as a place of sanctuary to Catilina and to report back anything that might be useful, Gordianus reluctantly finds himself attracted to the charismatic, if not seductive, figure. Gordianus also finds that he and his family reside at the epicenter of another crisis, both personal and public. On the local level, he must discover the source of a series of headless bodies found on his land and contend with the animosity of yet another patrician family who will stop at nothing in their maintenance of privilege. On a larger scale, he bears witness to history, from the moment of Catilina's electoral defeat in 64 B.C.E. to the fateful Battle of Pistoria in 62 B.C.E.

Like most of the other Roma Sub Rosa narratives, this novel gives Gordianus the opportunity to act on two stages. There is the private mystery centered on the farm that he has inherited from a wealthy friend and confidant; the key to untying the knots of this conundrum is a classic device of mystery fiction: The villain is most likely to be the least suspected person. There is also Cicero's very public campaign to expose Catilina's conspiracy. It is the fictional linkage between Gordianus and Catilina during this fateful moment in the life of the Roman Republic that may very well be the heart of the book, for it affords Saylor the opportunity to ponder the motivation of one of the most controversial figures in ancient history. Many critics consider this novel to be a high point in the series.

The Judgment of Caesar

In *The Judgment of Caesar*, Gordianus escorts his wife, Bethesda, to her native Egypt in his quest for a cure for her at yet another critical turning point in world history, the first meeting of Caesar and Cleopatra. Because of his role as inadvertent witness to the assassination of Pompey the Great, Caesar's great rival for domination of the Mediterranean, Gordianus becomes an involuntary guest at the royal palace in Alexandria, where he soon finds himself embroiled in the deadly rivalry between the queen of Egypt and her royal brother, Ptolemy XIII, as they contend for Caesar's political alliance and personal affection.

Once again Gordianus's private life and the course of history intersect as he must solve the mystery of who tried to poison Caesar, who has just arrived in Egypt, a once great power that has now become little more than a protectorate of Rome. Because one of the suspects is Meto, the adopted son of Gordianus, his family loyalties are engaged; and once again, the Finder's familial devotion stands in sharp contrast to that of those with royal blood, especially the contentious members of the Ptolemaic dynasty. Yet, despite his misgivings that with the passage of time he has lost his edge, Gordianus solves the puzzle, thanks to his characteristically open mind and open heart.

In this novel, as in *Catilina's Riddle*, much of the interest in the narrative comes from Saylor's decision to recreate a pivotal point in history from the perspective of someone who did not carry the day. Like Catilina, Ptolemy XIII remains a figure of scholarly conjecture because his early death gave his rivals free rein to spin the tale of his failure. Saylor, on the other hand, tries to give voice to history's losers in order to paint a more complete picture of their place in history. Therefore, in *The Judgment of Caesar*, the author devotes as much attention to Ptolemy as he does to his sister Cleopatra, and he tries to flesh out the triangle of ambition and seduction of which Caesar and the two royal siblings form the three points.

S. Thomas Mack

Principal mystery and detective fiction

Roma Sub Rosa series: *Roman Blood*, 1991; *Arms of Nemesis*, 1992; *Catilina's Riddle*, 1993; *The Venus Throw*, 1995; *A Murder on the Appian Way*, 1996; *The House of the Vestals: The Investigations of Gordianus the Finder*, 1997; *Rubicon*, 1998; *Last Seen in Massilia*, 2000; *A Mist of Prophecies*, 2002; *The Judgment of Caesar: A Novel of Ancient Rome*, 2004; *A Gladiator Dies Only Once: The Further Adventures of Gordianus the Finder*, 2005

Other major works

Novels: *Beast of Burden*, 1993 (as Travis); *Big Shots*, 1993 (as Travis); *Slaves of the Empire*, 1996 (as Travis); *A Twist at the End: A Novel of O. Henry*, 2000; *Have You Seen Dawn?*, 2003; *Roma: A Novel of Ancient Rome*, 2007

Bibliography

Fletcher, Connie. Review of *A Gladiator Dies Only Once*, by Steven Saylor. *Booklist* 101, no. 15 (April 1, 2005): 1348. Review praises Saylor's collection of short stories for their ability to evoke the Roman Repulic.

Lewis, Terrance L. "John Maddox Roberts and Steven Saylor: Detecting in the Final Decades of the Roman Republic." In *The Detective as Historian: History and Art in Historical Crime Fiction*, edited by Ray Broadus Browne and Lawrence Kreiser. Bowling Green, Ohio: Bowling Green University Popular Press, 2000. A comparative analysis of the works of Roberts and Saylor with an emphasis on their respective accuracy of historical detail, particularly their incorporation of historical figures and events in their fictional plots.

Saylor, Steven. Steven Saylor. http://www.steven saylor .com. The author's own Web site, which offers up-to-date, visually appealing information on his life and work, including reviews of books, personal interviews, and links to sites related to mystery fiction and classical studies.

Sikov, Ed. "Gordianus Redux." *James White Review* (Summer/Fall, 2004). An attempt to place Saylor's Roman mysteries in the context of gay literature and, in so doing, define what is meant by the genre.

Sonntag, Claire. "*Pudd'nhead Wilson* and *Arms of Nemesis*: Two Portraits of Slavery." In *Prentice Hall Reference Guide*, edited by Muriel Harris. Upper Saddle River, N.J.: Pearson Prentice Hall, 2006. A comparative analysis of Mark Twain's depiction of slavery in nineteenth century America and Saylor's portrait of slavery in ancient Rome.

ANTHONY SHAFFER

Born: Liverpool, England; May 15, 1926
Died: London, England; November 6, 2001
Also wrote as Peter Anthony (joint pseudonym with Peter Shaffer)
Types of plot: Amateur sleuth; cozy; private investigator; psychological; thriller

Contribution

A longtime admirer of the classical mystery story in the tradition of Agatha Christie, John Dickson Carr, and Dorothy L. Sayers, Anthony Shaffer won lasting fame for his popular and wildly successful satirical send-up of the cozy genre, *Sleuth* (pr., pb. 1970). The play, which ran for more than twenty-three hundred performances in London's West End, and for more than two thousand performances on Broadway, garnered a Tony Award and an Edgar Award for the best play of 1970. The film of the play, for which Shaffer wrote the screenplay, also won an Edgar Award and secured Oscar nominations for both principal actors Michael Caine and Laurence Olivier (Olivier won a New York Critics' award for his role). *Sleuth* has been called one of the best examples of the comedy-thriller ever written.

Shaffer, who despite the enthusiastic reception of *Sleuth* never achieved quite the level of name recognition as his twin brother Peter Shaffer (author of such works as *Amadeus*, 1980; *The Royal Hunt of the Sun*, 1964; and *Equus*, 1973), nonetheless became quite respected for his film work with director Alfred Hitchcock. He won Edgar Awards for his screenplays of *Frenzy* (1972) and *Death on the Nile* (1978). Shaffer also won the Grand Prix from the Oxford and from the Miami film festivals for the screenplay of his own play *Absolution* (1978), and won the Grand Prix for his film script of the critically acclaimed play he cowrote with Robin Hardy, *The Wicker Man* (1973).

Biography

Anthony Joshua Shaffer was born the twin brother of fellow writer (later Sir) Peter Levin Shaffer on May 15, 1926, in Liverpool, England. They were the sons of Jewish estate agent Jack Shaffer and Reka Fredman Shaffer. The family moved to London in 1936, where the twins won scholarships to St. Paul's school, which, following the German blitz of World War II, was moved to Berkhamsted. For three years late in the war and in the early postwar period (1944-1947), both brothers, in lieu of military service, worked as Bevin Boys (essential workers in service to the country, named for the program organizer, Ernest Bevin, minister of labor under Prime Minister Winston Churchill), as coal-mine conscripts in Kent and Yorkshire.

After finishing their national obligation, Anthony and his brother both attended Trinity College, Cambridge, where they coedited the student publication *Grantha* and cowrote detective stories for publication in various periodicals. Both graduated in 1950, Anthony majoring in law, Peter in history. Anthony Shaffer was married for the second of three times to former model Carolyn Soley, with whom he had two daughters. In 1951 he began practicing as a barrister, specializing in divorce work. That same year, he and his brother collaborated on the first of three mystery novels in the classical tradition, published under the joint pseudonym Peter Anthony: *Woman in the Wardrobe* (1951), *How Doth the Little Crocodile?* (1952), and *Withered Murder* (1955). For some six years, beginning in the mid-1950's, Anthony Shaffer served as book reviewer for *London Mystery Magazine*.

Dissatisfied with the income he earned as a lawyer, Shaffer left the legal profession to become an advertising copywriter with Pearl & Dean, a firm that produced most of the film trailers in the United Kingdom. In 1960 Shaffer established his own production company, Hardy Shaffer Associates, which focused on television commercials. Encouraged by his brother, who was already achieving success as a playwright, Shaffer wrote his first play, *The Savage Parade* (pr. 1963), based on the kidnap from Argentina and trial in Israel of Nazi war criminal Adolph Eichmann. Produced in 1963, the play closed after one night.

During the late 1960's, Shaffer experimented with LSD (lysergic acid diethylamide), an experience that inspired him to quit advertising in favor of writing plays full time. His next effort was the Tony and Edgar Award-winning work with which his name has been indelibly linked: the clever thriller *Sleuth*. Though Shaffer wrote other plays that are still produced to this day—including *Murderer* (pr. 1975), and *The Case of the Oily Levantine* (pr. 1977; revised as *Whodunnit*, pb. 1983)—after the success of *Sleuth*, he became associated with Alfred Hitchcock. For the renowned director, he wrote screenplays for such films as *Frenzy* (1972), *Death on the Nile* (1978), and *Evil Under the Sun* (1982). Shaffer also wrote screenplays for *The Wicker Man* (1973), *Masada* (1974), and *The Moonstone* (1975). Shaffer's only other novel, *Absolution* (1979), was an adaptation of his earlier screenplay of the same name.

After the early 1980's, Shaffer's output diminished. He cowrote the screenplay for *Appointment with Death* (1988) and developed the story for *Sommersby* (1993), an update of *The Return of Martin Guerre* (1982). His last published work was a memoir, *So What Did You Expect?* (2001).

Shaffer, who was married since 1985 to his third wife, actress Diane Cilento, died at the age of seventy-five on November 6, 2001.

ANALYSIS

From the beginning of his writing career, in collaboration with his twin brother Peter Shaffer, Anthony Shaffer was known for his keen ear for dialogue. The brothers' three out-of-print mystery novels (*How Doth the Little Crocodile?*, *Woman in the Wardrobe*, and *Withered Murder*), written between 1951 and 1955 under the joint pseudonym Peter Anthony, were all standard entries in the cozy genre: typical drawing-room mysteries with intriguing character types put through their paces in the course of a convoluted plot. The protagonist in the first two novels, an abbreviated series called Murder Revisited, was gifted amateur detective Mr. Verity, who assisted the police with unusual cases. The hero of the third novel, *Withered Murder*, was another flamboyant, eccentric master detective, Mr. Fathom. Although the books are otherwise nothing special, it is the characters' speeches that make the novels stand out: wry, sardonic, and urbanely acerbic. His facility for putting witty words into the mouths of characters marks all of Anthony Shaffer's later work.

Shaffer's first published play, *The Savage Parade* (pr. 1963, revived as *This Savage Parade*, pr. 1982), like much of his work, deals with issues beneath the surface of the story. A controversial thriller in which Rudolf Bauer, a Nazi officer, is captured in South America and transported to Tel Aviv to face trial, *The Savage Parade* dramatically examines the concepts of faith, justice, and morality while making the case that Israel has fascist leanings similar to the Third Reich.

The smash hit *Sleuth* is at its core a study of the experience of age versus the enthusiasm of youth. A revenge comedy-tragedy, the play also deals with the competitive nature of players who turn games into deadly serious business, with the disparity between the aristocracy and common folk, with the bitterness of the pure-blood native-born toward ethnic immigrants, and with the difference between appearance and reality.

The latter theme, naturally enough, crops up frequently in Shaffer's plays and screenplays for Hitchcock: without deception and misdirection there would be little mystery in his crime stories. In the film *Frenzy*, for example, the hot-tempered Richard Blaney appears to be a vicious psychosexual serial killer. In the play *Murderer*, main character Norman has apparently killed his girlfriend Millie—but is she really dead? In *Absolution*, Catholic schoolboy Benjie Stanfield falsely confesses to the murder of Blakey, a wanderer he has befriended. In Shaffer's four adaptations for Hitchcock—*Murder on the Orient Express*, 1974; *Death on the Nile*; *Evil Under the Sun*; and *Appointment with Death*)—he worked from material provided by the mistress of deception, Agatha Christie.

Sexuality, of a normal or abnormal mature, also factors in much of Shaffer's work. It provides the tension between the two characters in *Sleuth*, who were both involved with the same woman. It is a driving force in *The Wicker Man*, and it permeates the psychosexual thriller *Frenzy*.

Though not a prolific writer by modern standards, Shaffer's theatrical output is a triumph of quality over quantity.

SLEUTH

Shaffer's acknowledged masterpiece, *Sleuth*, made into a critically acclaimed film in 1972 starring Sir Laurence Olivier and Michael Caine, in two acts details a battle of wits between aging aristocrat Andrew Wyke, a successful cozy mystery writer, and a youthful commoner, the half-Italian, half-Jew Milo Tindle—originally Tindolini—who owns a modest travel agency (he is transformed into a hairdresser in the film). The game-loving Wyke invites Tindle to his country manor ostensibly for a conference regarding his spendthrift wife, Marguerite, with whom Milo is having a torrid affair. Outwardly, Wkye, who has a Finnish mistress, Tea, is concerned that Tindle will be unable to provide for Marguerite's ostentatious lifestyle, and that he will be stuck with her once the romance has run its course.

The battle lines are drawn early: to Wyke, everything is a game, ripe for humorous riposte, while Tindle is in deadly earnest. Wyke is scornful of the younger man's background and profession. Tindle is likewise scornful of Wyke's occupation and proves himself capable of puncturing the writer's inflated ego.

Andrew: (Speaking of his alleged sexual prowess) . . . I'm pretty much of a sexual athlete.
Milo: I suppose these days you're concentrating on the sprints rather than the long distance stuff.

Once the preliminaries are out of the way, Wyke convinces Tindle to steal a box of valuable jewelry that can be fenced on the European continent to produce the wherewithal to provide for Marguerite; Wyke meanwhile will collect the insurance. Andrew concocts an elaborate scheme supposedly for the benefit of investigators, which entails Milo dressing in a clown's costume to carry out the break-in. At the crucial moment, Andrew reveals a game within a game: he produces a pistol and tells Milo that he is going to kill him; as a homeowner preventing a burglary, he will get away with murder. When Milo asks why he is doing it, Andrew bursts out viciously:

Andrew: I hate you. I hate your smarmy, good-looking Latin face and your easy manner. . . . I hate you because you are a culling spick. A wop—a not one-of-me . . .

This humiliating complication sets off a series of increasingly elaborate twists, turns, and one-upmanship as the plot winds relentlessly to its surprising and suspenseful conclusion. Toward the end of the play, Milo, the put-upon dupe, makes the following observation, which forms the thesis of the work:

Milo: Take a look at yourself, Andrew, and ask yourself a few simple questions about your attachment to the English detective story. Perhaps you might come to realize that the only place you can inhabit is a dead world—a country house world where peers and colonels died in their studies; where butlers steal the port, and pert parlor maids cringe, weeping malapropisms behind green baize doors. It's a world of coldness and class hatred, and two-dimensional characters who are not expected to communicate; it's a world where only the amateurs win, and where foreigners are automatically figures of fun. To be *puzzled* is all. . . . To put it shortly, the detective story is the normal recreation of snobbish, outdated, life-hating, ignoble minds . . .

The Wicker Man

Cowritten with Robin Hardy (who directed the film), *The Wicker Man* is a thriller with erotic and mythical undertones. The plot concerns protagonist Neil Howie (played in the film by Edward Woodward), a police sergeant of the make-believe West Highland constabulary in Scotland, who receives a message telling him that a girl, Rowan Morrison—whose snapshot is enclosed—has disappeared on Summerisle, an obscure island beyond the Outer Hebrides. When Howie travels to the island to investigate the claim, he discovers a community of modern pagans (led on celluloid by Christopher Lee). The cult members believe in reincarnation, worship the sun, and perform sexual rituals to appease nature. These practices contrast sharply with the beliefs of Howie, a devout Christian, who is both shocked at the pagans' uninhibited behavior and simultaneously drawn to one of the earthy and attractive female practitioners of the cult.

During his investigation, Howie receives conflicting accounts of the missing girl: Some deny knowledge of her while others affirm she was there but has died. Howie uncovers evidence that suggests Rowan was, or is to be, a human sacrifice intended to ensure fertile crops. He dresses in disguise to attend a pagan May Day celebration but finds too late that the letter he received was the opening gambit in an elaborate ploy to bring him to the island for the cult's nefarious purposes.

A chilling, suspenseful, yet plausible examination of age-old Celtic beliefs flourishing in modern society, *The Wicker Man* and its horrific, yet inevitable, finale linger long in the memory. A 2006 remake of the film—though considerably different in a number of key aspects—starred Nicolas Cage.

Jack Ewing

Principal mystery and detective fiction

Novels: *Woman in the Wardrobe*, 1951 (as Anthony); *How Doth the Little Crocodile?*, 1952 (as Anthony); *Withered Murder*, 1955 (as Anthony); *The Wicker Man*, 1978 (with Robin Hardy; novelization of screenplay); *Absolution*, 1979 (novelization of screenplay)

Other major works

Plays: *The Savage Parade*, pr. 1963 (revised as *This Savage Parade*, pr. 1982); *Sleuth*, pr., pb. 1970; *Murderer*, pr. 1975; *The Case of the Oily Levantine*, pr. 1977 (revised as *Whodunnit*, pb. 1983); *Widow's Weeds: Or, For Years I Couldn't Wear My Black*, pr. 1977

Screenplays: *Play with a Gypsy*, 1970; *Black Comedy*, 1970 (adapted from the play by Peter Shaffer); *Cry of the Penguins*, 1971 (adapted from a Graham Billing story, re-released as *Mr. Forbush and the Penguins*, 1971); *Frenzy*, 1972 (adapted from the Arthur La Bern novel *Goodbye Piccadilly, Farewell Leicester Square*); *Sleuth*, 1973 (adapted from the author's play); *The Wicker Man*, 1973; *The Goshawk Squadron*, 1973; *Masada*, 1974; *Murder on the Orient Express*, 1974 (adapted from the novel by Agatha Christie); *The Moonstone*, 1975; *Death on the Nile*, 1978 (adapted from the novel by Agatha Christie); *Absolution*, 1978; *Evil Under the Sun*, 1982 (adapted from the novel by Agatha Christie); *Appointment with Death*, 1988 (co-written with Peter Buckman and Michael Winner, adapted from the novel by Agatha Christie); *Sommersby*, 1993 (co-writer of story, adapted from the 1982 French film *The Return of Martin Guerre*)

Nonfiction: *So What Did You Expect?*, 2001

Bibliography

Carlson, Marvin A. *Deathtraps: The Postmodern Comedy Thriller*. Bloomington: Indiana University Press, 1993. This volume examines mystery and detective comedic plays, including *Sleuth* by Shaffer.

Hewes, Henry. "The Theater: Two Can Play at a Game." *Saturday Review* 53, no. 48 (November 28, 1970): 6. A highly favorable review of the production of *Sleuth*, starring Anthony Quayle and Keith Baxter, which points out the "cat-and-mouse byplay in which comedy and terror fluctuate," and which notes the author's clever criticisms of a number of British institutions.

Kalem, T. E. Review of *Sleuth*, by Anthony Shaffer. *Time*, November 23, 1970, 100. A highly favorable review of the stage version of *Sleuth*, which points out its satirical nature in which the author gives vent to anti-British sentiments, and calls the work one of the best plays of its genre.

Kerr, Walter. Review of *Whodunnit*, by Anthony Shaffer. "Stage View: A Parody That Fizzles, a Drama That Baffles." *The New York Times*, January 9, 1983, p. H5. This is an unfavorable review of Shaffer's *Whodunnit*, which is deemed "flat and stale," a condition that is blamed more on the producer than the author.

Lewis, Paul. "Anthony Shaffer, Seventy-five, Author of Long-Running 'Sleuth' Dies." *New York Times*, November 12, 2001, p. F7. Obituary of Shaffer notes his greatest hit, *Sleuth*, and describes his background and relationship to Peter Shaffer.

Newsweek, 66, no. 12 (September 21, 1970): 104-105. This is a brief recap of the forthcoming theatrical season, mentioning Anthony Quayle's re-creation of his London role in Shaffer's *Sleuth*, opening at the Music Box.

Shaffer, Anthony. *So What Did You Expect?* London: Picador, 2001. Shaffer's memoir takes him from childhood through his days as a lawyer to his success with *Sleuth* and beyond.

GEORGES SIMENON

Born: Liège, Belgium; February 13, 1903
Died: Lausanne, Switzerland; September 4, 1989
Also wrote as Christian Brulls; Georges Sim
Types of plot: Police procedural; psychological

Principal series

Inspector Maigret, 1930-1972

Principal series character

Jules Maigret is chief inspector of the Police Judiciaire (the French equivalent of Scotland Yard). He is about forty-five in most of the stories, although there are a few that look forward to his retirement or backward to his first cases. He and his self-effacing, intuitively understanding wife have no children, their one daughter having died in infancy. His approach is to penetrate the particular world of each event, getting to know the causative factors and interrelationships among those involved; he often feels a strong bond with the criminals, so that when he brings them to justice he is left with ambivalent feelings.

Contribution

Georges Simenon's extremely prolific writing career provided fans of the *roman policier* with a number of unrelated crime novels marked by extreme fidelity to detail and with the series featuring Inspector Maigret. The novels featuring Maigret represent a fusion of the American detective story tradition with French realism. The stories are somewhat reminiscent of the American hard-boiled school, particularly the works of Ross Macdonald, in the lack of sentimental justice and in the often-fatalistic plots in which "old sins cast long shadows" and bring about current tragedies. The psychological realism of the more tightly drawn Maigret characters, however, is more reminiscent of François Mauriac or Julien Green. Moreover, the conclusions are usually less devastating than those of the hard-boiled mysteries, and there is often an element of muted optimism in the Maigret novel.

Critical circles have long argued whether Simenon's detective stories are more than genre pieces and approach literature. His many other novels use the same devices and express the same themes as his Maigret stories: the desire for home and the impossibility of finding it, the destructive potency of the past, the futility of flight, and the fatal seductiveness of illusion. His major contribution consists of the vividly drawn, almost symbiotic relationship between criminal and inspector—and the portrait of Maigret himself as he enters into the scene of each event pertaining to the crime, his vision informed by the French maxim *tout comprendre, c'est tout pardonner* (to understand all is to forgive all).

Biography

Georges Joseph Christian Simenon was born on February 13, 1903, in Liège, Belgium. His father, Désiré Simenon, was an accountant from a solid petit bourgeois background; his mother, Henriette Brull, came from a family known for financial instability and social snobbery. The contrast between his paternal and maternal families preoccupied Simenon and often figures in his stories, which tend to idealize the petit bourgeois life and cruelly satirize the pretentious social climbers of the upper-middle class.

Simenon's family was never well-off, and his education was interrupted by the need to earn money when he learned (at the age of sixteen) that his father was seriously ill. After failing at two menial jobs, he became a cub reporter, at which he was an immediate success. While working at a newspaper and frequenting a group of young artists and poets, he wrote his first novel, *Au pont des arches* (1921), at the age of seventeen. In 1920 he became engaged to Regine Renchon and enlisted in the army; in 1922 he went to Paris, and he was married the following year. At this time he was writing short stories for Paris journals with amazing rapidity; he wrote more than one thousand stories over the next few years. For two years he was secretary to two young aristocrats, and through them, especially the second, the marquess de Tracy, he made literary connections. In 1924 he began writing popular novels at an incredible rate. The first, a romance titled *Le Roman d'une dactylo* (1924; the novel of a secretary), was written in a single morning. Simenon ordinarily spent three to five days writing a novel; he was once hired to write a novel in three days before the public in a glass cage, but the publisher who set up the stunt went bankrupt before the event. In 1929 he wrote his first Maigret, *Pietr-le-Letton* (1931; *The Strange Case of Peter the Lett*, 1933; also known as *Maigret and the Enigmatic Lett*, 1963); Maigret was an instant success.

In 1939 Simenon's son Marc was born, but his marriage was already in trouble, partly because of his rapacious womanizing (in later life, in a typical Simenon embellishment, he claimed to have had sexual relations with ten thousand women). In the 1940's he traveled to the United States, where he lived for ten years in relative contentment, adding to his repertoire of atmospheres. In 1949 he was divorced from Regine; the day after the divorce was finalized he married Denyse Ouimet, with whom the couple had been traveling. That year his second son, Johnny, was born to Denyse. He and Denyse had two more children, Marie-Georges (born in 1953) and Pierre (born in 1959, after their return to Europe). He received the Grand Master Award from the Mystery Writers of America in 1966.

Georges Simenon in 1981. (AP/Wide World Photos)

Denyse's alcoholism led to their separation and a bitter literary attack on Simenon in her memoirs, *Un Oiseau pour le chat* (1978). Because it vilified the father adored by Marie-Georges, the book contributed to her depression and suicide in 1978. After her death, Simenon was wracked by guilt and memorialized his daughter in *Mémoires intimes* (1981; *Intimate Memoirs*, 1984), "including Marie-Jo's book," drawing in part on notes, diaries, letters, and voice recordings that Marie-Georges left behind. Though scandal resulted from the revelation that her suppressed incestuous love for her father may have led to her death, a potentially greater scandal was itself suppressed by Denyse's lawyers, who recalled the books to censor the story of Marie-Jo's sexual abuse by her mother at the age of eleven. Unable to reconcile with Denyse, Simenon would live out the rest of his days with his Italian companion Teresa Sburelin.

For most of Simenon's writing life he produced from one to seven novels a year, writing both Maigrets and serious novels. In 1973 he decided to stop producing novels, and after that time he wrote only autobiographical works, including the controversial *Intimate Memoirs*.

ANALYSIS

Georges Simenon began his writing career with romances, envisioning an audience of secretaries and shop girls, but he soon began to imagine another kind of mass audience and another genre. He began writing short thrillers in his early twenties, and one of these, *Train de nuit* (1930), featured a police officer named Maigret, although this Maigret was only a shadow character. The full embodiment of Maigret came to Simenon all at once after three glasses of gin on a summer afternoon:

> As Simenon walked, a picture of his principal character came to him: a big man, powerful, a massive presence rather than an individual. He smoked his pipe, wore a

bowler hat and a thick winter coat with a velvet collar (both later abandoned as fashions in police clothing changed). But he did not see his face. *Simenon has never seen the face of Jules Maigret.* "I still do not know what his face looks like," he says. "I only see the man and his presence."

The Strange Case of Peter the Lett

The first Maigret, *The Strange Case of Peter the Lett*, was begun the next day, finished within a few more days, and promptly sent to Fayard, Simenon's publisher. Yet it was not the first Maigret to appear; Simenon rapidly wrote four more, so that five Maigret novels appeared almost simultaneously and established this popular new detective firmly in the French mind.

Inspector Maigret of the Police Judiciaire is the idealized father figure whose life in many ways reflects that of Désiré Simenon. Born into a petit bourgeois household, he has the close tie to the land and the contentment in small pleasures of the senses associated with petit bourgeois life. He enjoys his pipe and the air on a clear Paris day and the meals prepared for him by his wife, a self-effacing woman whose almost wordless sympathy is equaled in detective fiction only by that of Jenny Maitland. Saddened by his intuitive understanding of the underside of life (and also by the death of his only child—which puts him in the class of the wounded detective), he desires to bring about healing more than to bring criminals to justice. Because his personal desires do not always merge with his professional duties, he is sometimes unhappy about the results of his investigations.

Maigret's method is intuitive rather than ratiocinative, which places him outside the locked-room armchair-detective school. Indeed, Maigret often says, "I never think." He means that he feels and senses instead of figuring, and he arrives at his intuitions by immersing himself completely in the milieu of the crime. As he becomes more and more involved with the figures of the incident, he learns to think as they do, and the truth emerges. It is ironic that although the Maigret books followed one another with such astonishing rapidity, there is no classic Maigret plot. Although usually the criminal is caught and brought to justice, occasionally he escapes. Now and then he is punished despite Maigret's deep regrets, and at least once the wrong man is executed. The stories do not provide the archetypal pleasure of the Agatha Christie type of plot, in which the villain is caught and the society thus purged. Rather, there is often a sense of the relativity of innocence and guilt, and the inescapability of evil. Moreover, it is somewhat misleading to think of the novels as police novels, for Maigret is often fighting the system as well as the criminals. Hampered by bureaucratic shackles and a superior (Judge Comeliau) who represents reason over intuition and head over heart, Maigret is pressed from both sides in his effort to provide some healing for the fractured human beings he encounters.

Maigret Returns

What makes the Maigrets a momentous departure from the traditional realm of the detective story, though, is not the characterization of Maigret, however intriguing he may be. It is their realism, built on intensely observed detail and grounded in a rich variety of settings, from the locks along the Seine to the countryside of the Loire valley. The stories enter into particular trades and professions, always describing by feel as well as by sight, so that the reader has a sense of having been given an intimate glimpse into a closed world. Even in *Maigret* (1934; *Maigret Returns*, 1941), the novel that was intended to conclude the series, the details of the retirement cottage are so subtly and lovingly sketched that readers automatically make the comparison between the country life and the Paris to which Maigret is driven to return by the pressure of events. Simenon was a newspaperman par excellence and his powers of observation and description are his genius. In the context of the novels, the details of weather, dress, and furniture acquire symbolic significance. It is this evocative use of the concrete that raises the Maigrets from the genre and makes them, like Graham Greene's thrillers, literature.

The first batch of Maigrets consisted of nineteen novels written over four years, from 1930 to 1934, and ending with *Maigret Returns*, which is atypically set in Maigret's retirement years. It would seem that Simenon had decided to leave Maigret to cultivate his garden. Simenon then wrote a number of other novels, some of which received critical acclaim. André Gide was one of the writer's greatest fans, especially appreciating the nondetective novels; what he found to be Simenon's most compelling quality applies to the Maigrets as well as the other novels. Gide credited Simenon with "a striking, haunting vision of the lives of others in creating living, gasping, panting beings." Other fans bemoaned the lack of new Maigrets; one even sent a cable to the Police Judiciaire reporting that Maigret was missing. Indeed, Simenon was publicly so involved with Maigret that he could not leave him long in his garden; in 1939, the writer began the second series of novels concerning the popular detective. He continued writing Maigrets along with his other stories until he finally stopped writing novels altogether in the early 1970's.

The non-Maigret novels with which he interspersed the Maigrets had many of the characteristics of the detective story, except that usually there was little (if any) focus on detection. These are psychological crime novels somewhat similar to the non-Inspector Wexford novels of Ruth Rendell: The character of the criminal is dissected, his effect on others is analyzed, and an ironic discrepancy develops between his self-image and the way he is perceived. The atmosphere tends to be colder and more clinical because of the absence of the father figure, Maigret. Ironically, the theme in these stories is often the need for warmth, identification, and family.

THE LODGER

Perhaps typical of the non-Maigret is *Le Locataire* (1934; *The Lodger*, 1943), a story of a homeless Jew who impulsively commits a casual and brutal murder and then finds a home in a boardinghouse. The atmosphere of the boardinghouse—its standard decor, its trivial and yet telling conversations—is so perfectly portrayed that it is easy to connect this pension with Simenon's mother's experience taking in roomers. The focus of the story is the myth of home with which the exiled Elie comforts himself, a myth that has a dimension of truth. Even when caught (the police are in the background, and readers barely encounter them but do see the results of their investigations), Elie is followed by the dream of home he has invented, as the owner of the boardinghouse goes to see Elie off on the convict ship.

Criminals notwithstanding, these novels are not fully realized detective stories, because the discovering or unraveling aspect is missing (as well as the complementary balance between investigator and culprit, who in the Maigrets are often something like father and errant son). These other novels are more like case studies that underscore the unpredictability of the human animal in the most extreme circumstances. The Maigret addict who is also a general detective-story fan may be unable to make the transition.

The second Maigrets did not begin appearing until 1942, when four of them appeared in rapid succession to launch the new series. Many of these new Maigrets do not contain the detective's name in the title, causing some confusion among Maigret fans and those who would choose only Simenon's non-Maigret novels. Much critical discussion has focused on the differences between the new and the old series, but in fact the later Maigrets are not substantially different from the early ones, although it might be argued that they show more careful attention to plot and that they have a higher proportion of main characters who are *ratés*—failures—of one sort or another. One unarguable difference, too, is that they reflect Simenon's American experience, even going so far as to introduce an American police officer who serves as foil and apprentice to Maigret.

SIMENON AND GRAHAM GREENE

Considering the mixture of detective novels and other novels, as well as the characteristic Simenon plots and themes in both, it is worth comparing the French novelist with Graham Greene, who also wrote a mixture of thrillers and literary novels and dealt with the same materials in both. The French failures in the Maigrets correspond with Greene's seedy British types. The themes of flight, of the need to escape self, of intuitive penetration of the darkness of human existence are parallel. Both authors use precise, concrete details to communicate a moral ambience. An important difference is that Greene's Catholic underpinnings are not present in Simenon's novels, or at least are not immediately evident. Some critics have claimed to see them, and Simenon, who claimed agnosticism, has conceded that there may be something to the religious claims made for his work.

The reliable character of Maigret carries Simenon's detective novels even when their plots fail. Fatherly, reflective, Maigret makes the reader believe that justice will be done if it is humanly possible—a qualification that sets these novels apart from the Golden Age detective stories by such writers as Agatha Christie and Dorothy L. Sayers, in which justice is always done. In the typical Maigret, the detective is filling his pipe at the beginning of the story and looking out his office window at some unpleasant manifestation of Paris weather when the case begins. He consults his officers, the same characters briefly but effectively sketched in novel after novel: the young Lapointe, whom Maigret fathers (and calls by the familiar *tu*); the Inspector's old friend Janvier; the miserable Lognon who is like Eeyore in *Winnie-the-Pooh* (1926), always feeling abused and neglected; and others. (Sometimes the inspector is at home, asleep, when the call comes—and his wife has everything ready for his departure before he hangs up.) Throughout the investigation, he orders some characteristic drink (different drinks for different cases) at various cafés, while Mme Maigret's cassoulets or tripes go cold at home. (Some of Maigret's favorite dishes make the American reader's hair stand on end.) When the criminal is finally apprehended and his confession recorded, Maigret often goes home to eat and to restore himself in the comfort of his wife's silent sympathy. The reader is always Maigret for Maigret's little idiosyncrasies and for those of the other recurrent characters; thus, the ritual is enacted successfully even if there is some standard deviation from the typical plot, such as the escape of the criminal or a final sense that justice was not quite done.

Despite the pleasant familiarity of the characters and the archetypal paternalism of the inspector, style and theme give the Maigret novels depth. The smallest observations—how a prostitute's face looks when dawn comes in the course of questioning, what is in an aggressively house-proud bourgeoise's kitchen, what the nightclub owner's wife does each night to prepare for the club's opening—are so convincingly portrayed that the reader feels that he too is penetrating into the mystery. The mystery is the secret of the human heart, as it is in Graham Greene's novels. Simenon's style is not hard-boiled, nor is it overly descriptive. It is evocative and direct—a few words, a detail, a snatch of dialogue carry multiple suggestions. A half sentence may intimate an entire complex relationship between a husband and wife. The recurrent weather details make the reader gain a sense of the atmosphere. Simenon's details not only are visual but also appeal to the other senses, particularly the tactile. The reader feels on his own skin the fog that is blurring Maigret's vision; he too glories in the occasional clear day. Simenon's use of the concrete is not unlike Colette's; indeed, this famous celebrant of the sensual was Simenon's adviser and friend.

As has been suggested, the flaw in the Maigret story is most often the plot; Simenon claimed to give little attention to plotting, and even not to know how a story would end until he had finished it. Nevertheless, his best plots are psychological tours de force. The unveiling of character is steady throughout the series of events; readers sense the intuitive rightness of Maigret's insights, and, at the end, they find that the motive meshes with the deed.

MAIGRET IN MONTMARTRE

Not all of his stories, however, afford this sense of closure. *Maigret au "Picratt's"* (1951; *Maigret in Montmartre*, 1963) is a case in point. In this story the focus is on the victim, a twenty-year-old nightclub stripper who becomes after her death a fully realized character, through the course of the investigation. She is given a subtle case-study history and a network of believable motivations, and through analysis of her life Maigret is able to identify her killer. Yet this killer remains a shadow character himself, and therefore the final scenes in which the police track him down are somewhat anticlimactic. One expects some final revelation, some unveiling of the killer's nature, but none is forthcoming.

Other stories, such as *Maigret et Monieur Charles* (1972; *Maigret and Monsieur Charles*, 1973), focus on both criminal and victim, so that the conclusion has no (or at least fewer) loose ends. It is indeed rare that the plot of any Maigret is itself particularly compelling. Plot is a function of character in Simenon's works, and the success or failure of plot hinges on the adequate development and believable motivation of the people involved. The early Maigrets, such as *Le*

Charretier de la "Providence" (1931; *The Crime at Lock 14*, 1934; also known as *Maigret Meets a Milord*, 1963), are particularly susceptible to weakness in plot. This story gives an intriguing, provocative picture of a criminal in whom the reader somehow cannot quite believe.

No one, however, reads Maigrets for the plot. They are read for character, for atmosphere, for the ritual of detection, for the more subtle benefits of this genre of literature, including no doubt the values Aristotle found in tragedy: the purging of pity and fear. Simenon's true genius lay in his merging of French realism with the traditional detective story, with the effect that the detective-story understanding of justice is modified to an ideal that is appropriate for life in the real world. Justice in the Maigret stories is not a negative, fatalistic force, as it usually is in the stories of the hard-boiled school (some of which have no winners in the end except the investigator, and all he has gained is the sad truth). Nor is justice the inexorable working out of divine retribution as it is in the Golden Age stories, in which evil is purged and the innocent are left ready to begin new lives. Rather, Simenon's world is a complex and ambiguous place where evil and good are closely related and cannot always be separated. There is still, however, a chance for purgation and rededication, usually supplied by the intuitive researches of that archetypal father figure, Inspector Maigret.

Maigret and Monsieur Charles

The last Maigret, *Maigret and Monsieur Charles*, appeared in 1972; after that, Simenon announced that he would write no more novels. *Maigret and Monsieur Charles* is a subtle psychological study of an unhealthy relationship. This story, satisfying on levels of plot, character, and theme, makes an appropriate farewell to Maigret. The hundreds of Maigret novels and short stories Simenon wrote over a period of forty years will continue to appeal not only to detective-story fans but also to those readers attracted to evocative description and intrigued by the darker side of human experience.

Janet McCann
Updated by C. A. Gardner

Principal mystery and detective fiction

Inspector Maigret series: 1931-1940 • *Pietr-le-Letton*, 1931 (*The Strange Case of Peter the Lett*, 1933; also known as *Maigret and the Enigmatic Lett*, 1963); *M. Gallet, décédé*, 1931 (*The Death of Monsieur Gallet*, 1932; also known as *Maigret Stonewalled*, 1963); *Le Pendu de Saint-Pholien*, 1931 (*The Crime of Inspector Maigret*, 1933; also known as *Maigret and the Hundred Gibbets*, 1963); *Le Charretier de la "Providence,"* 1931 (*The Crime at Lock 14*, 1934; also known as *Maigret Meets a Milord*, 1963); *La Tête d'un homme*, 1931 (*A Battle of Nerves*, 1939); *Le Chien jaune*, 1931 (*A Face for a Clue*, 1939; also known as *Maigret and the Yellow Dog*, 1987; also known as *The Yellow Dog*, 1940); *La Nuit du carrefour*, 1931 (*The Crossroad Murders*, 1933; also known as *Maigret at the Crossroads*, 1964); *Un Crime en Hollande*, 1931 (*A Crime in Holland*, 1940); *Au rendez-vous des terreneuves*, 1931 (*The Sailors' Rendezvous*, 1940); *La Danseuse du Gai-Moulin*, 1931 (*At the "Gai-Moulin,"* 1940); *La Guinguette à deux sous*, 1931 (*The Guinguette by the Seine*, 1940); *Le Port des brumes*, 1932 (*Death of a Harbour Master*, 1941); *L'Ombre chinoise*, 1932 (*The Shadow in the Courtyard*, 1934; also known as *Maigret Mystified*, 1964); *L'Affaire Saint-Fiacre*, 1932 (*The Saint-Fiacre Affair*, 1940; also known as *Maigret Goes Home*, 1967); *Chez les Flamands*, 1932 (*The Flemish Shop*, 1940); *Le Fou de Bergerac*, 1932 (*The Madman of Bergerac*, 1940); *Liberty Bar*, 1932 (English translation, 1940); *L'écluse numéro un*, 1932 (*The Lock at Charenton*, 1941); *Maigret*, 1934 (*Maigret Returns*, 1941)

1941-1950 • *Cécile est morte*, 1942; *Les Caves du Majestic*, 1942; *La Maison du juge*, 1942; *Signé Picpus*, 1944 (*To Any Lengths*, 1958); *L'Inspecteur cadavre*, 1944; *Les Nouvelles Enquêtes de Maigret*, 1944 (*The Short Cases of Inspector Maigret*, 1959); *Félicie est là*, 1944; *La Pipe de Maigret*, 1947; *Maigret se fâche*, 1947; *Maigret à New York*, 1947 (*Maigret in New York's Underworld*, 1955); *Maigret et l'inspecteur malgraceux*, 1947 (translated in *Maigret's Christmas*, 1951); *Les Vacances de Maigret*, 1948 (*Maigret on Holiday*, 1950; also known as *No Vacation for Maigret*, 1953); *Maigret et son mort*,

1948 (*Maigret's Special Murder*, 1964); *La Première Enquête de Maigret*, 1949 (*Maigret's First Case*, 1958); *Mon Ami Maigret*, 1949 (*My Friend Maigret*, 1956); *Maigret chez le coroner*, 1949 (*Maigret at the Coroner's*, 1980); *Maigret et la vieille dame*, 1950 (*Maigret and the Old Lady*, 1958); *L'Amie de Mme Maigret*, 1950 (*Madame Maigret's Own Case*, 1959; also known as *Madame Maigret's Friend*, 1960)

1951-1955 • *Un Noël de Maigret*, 1951 (*Maigret's Christmas*, 1951); *Les Mémoires de Maigret*, 1951 (*Maigret's Memoirs*, 1963); *Maigret au "Picratt's,"* 1951 (*Maigret in Montmartre*, 1954); *Maigret en meublé*, 1951 (*Maigret Takes a Room*, 1960); *Maigret et la grande perche*, 1951 (*Maigret and the Burglar's Wife*, 1969); *Maigret, Lognon, et les gangsters*, 1952 (*Inspector Maigret and the Killers*, 1954; also known as *Maigret and the Gangsters*, 1974); *Le Révolver de Maigret*, 1952 (*Maigret's Revolver*, 1956); *Maigret et l'homme du banc*, 1953 (*Maigret and the Man on the Bench*, 1975); *Maigret a peur*, 1953 (*Maigret Afraid*, 1961); *Maigret se trompe*, 1953 (*Maigret's Mistake*, 1954); *Maigret à l'école*, 1954 (*Maigret Goes to School*, 1957); *Maigret et la jeune morte*, 1954 (*Maigret and the Dead Girl*, 1955); *Maigret chez le ministre*, 1954 (*Maigret and the Calame Report*, 1969); *Maigret et le corps sans tête*, 1955 (*Maigret and the Headless Corpse*, 1967); *Maigret tend un piège*, 1955 (*Maigret Sets a Trap*, 1965)

1956-1960 • *Un échec de Maigret*, 1956 (*Maigret's Failure*, 1962); *Maigret s'amuse*, 1957 (*Maigret's Little Joke*, 1957); *Maigret voyage*, 1958 (*Maigret and the Millionaires*, 1974); *Les Scrupules de Maigret*, 1958 (*Maigret Has Scruples*, 1959); *Maigret et les témoins récalcitrants*, 1959 (*Maigret and the Reluctant Witnesses*, 1959); *Une Confidence de Maigret*, 1959 (*Maigret Has Doubts*, 1968); *Maigret aux assises*, 1960 (*Maigret in Court*, 1961); *Maigret et les vieillards*, 1960 (*Maigret in Society*, 1962)

1961-1965 • *Maigret et le voleur paresseux*, 1961 (*Maigret and the Lazy Burglar*, 1963); *Maigret et les braves gens*, 1962 (*Maigret and the Black Sheep*, 1976); *Maigret et le client du samedi*, 1962 (*Maigret and the Saturday Caller*, 1964); *Maigret et le clochard*, 1963 (*Maigret and the Bum*, 1973); *La Colère de Maigret*, 1963 (*Maigret Loses His Temper*, 1964); *Maigret et le fantôme*, 1964 (*Maigret and the Apparition*, 1975); *Maigret se défend*, 1964 (*Maigret on the Defensive*, 1966); *La Patience de Maigret*, 1965 (*The Patience of Maigret*, 1966)

1966-1972 • *Maigret et l'affaire Nahour*, 1966 (*Maigret and the Nahour Case*, 1967); *Le Voleur de Maigret*, 1967 (*Maigret's Pickpocket*, 1968); *Maigret à Vichy*, 1968 (*Maigret in Vichy*, 1969); *Maigret hésite*, 1968 (*Maigret Hesitates*, 1970); *L'Ami de l'enfance de Maigret*, 1968 (*Maigret's Boyhood Friend*, 1970); *Maigret et le tueur*, 1969 (*Maigret and the Killer*, 1971); *Maigret et le marchand de vin*, 1970 (*Maigret and the Wine Merchant*, 1971); *La Folle de Maigret*, 1970 (*Maigret and the Madwoman*, 1972); *Maigret et l'homme tout seul*, 1971 (*Maigret and the Loner*, 1975); *Maigret et l'indicateur*, 1971 (*Maigret and the Informer*, 1972); *Maigret et Monsieur Charles*, 1972 (*Maigret and Monsieur Charles*, 1973)

Nonseries novels: 1925-1935 • *L'Orgueil qui meurt*, 1925; *Nox l'insaisissable*, 1926; *Aimer, mourir*, 1928; *Une Femme à tuer*, 1929; *Pour venger son père*, 1931; *Marie-Mystère*, 1931; *Le Rêve qui meurt*, 1931; *Baisers mortels*, 1931; *Le Relais d'Alsace*, 1931 (*The Man from Everywhere*, 1941); *Victime de son fils*, 1931; *Âme de jeune fille*, 1931; *Les Chercheurs de bonheur*, 1931; *L'Épave*, 1932; *La Maison de l'inquiétude*, 1932; *Matricule 12*, 1932; *Le Passager du "Polarlys,"* 1932 (*The Mystery of the "Polarlys,"* 1942; also known as *Danger at Sea*, 1954); *La Figurante*, 1932; *Fièvre*, 1932; *Les Forçats de Paris*, 1932; *La Fiancée du diable*, 1933; *La Femme rousse*, 1933; *Le Château des Sables Rouges*, 1933; *Deuxième Bureau*, 1933; *L'Âne Rouge*, 1933 (*The Night-Club*, 1979); *La Maison du canal*, 1933 (*The House by the Canal*, 1948); *Les Fiançailles de M. Hire*, 1933 (*Mr. Hire's Engagement*, 1956); *Le Coup de lune*, 1933 (*Tropic Moon*, 1942); *Le Haut Mal*, 1933 (*The Woman in the Gray House*, 1942); *L'Homme de Londres*, 1934 (*Newhaven-Dieppe*, 1942); *Le Locataire*, 1934 (*The Lodger*, 1943); *L'Évasion*, 1934; *Les Suicidés*, 1934 (*One Way Out*, 1943); *Les Pitard*, 1935 (*A Wife at Sea*, 1949); *Les Clients d'Avrenos*, 1935; *Quartier Nègre*, 1935

1936-1940 • *Les Demoiselles de Concarneau*, 1936 (*The Breton Sisters*, 1943); *45° à l'ombre*, 1936;

Long Cours, 1936 (*The Long Exile*, 1982; *L'Evadé*, 1936 (*The Disintegration of J. P. G.*, 1937); *L'Île empoisonnée*, 1937; *Seul parmi les gorilles*, 1937; *Faubourg*, 1937 (*Home Town*, 1944); *L'Assassin*, 1937 (*The Murderer*, 1949); *Le Blanc à lunettes*, 1937 (*Talatala*, 1943); *Le Testament Donadieu*, 1937 (*The Shadow Falls*, 1945); *Ceux de la soif*, 1938; *Les Trois Crimes de mes amis*, 1938; *Chemin sans issue*, 1938 (*Blind Alley*, 1946); *L'Homme qui regardait passer les trains*, 1938 (*The Man Who Watched the Trains Go By*, 1945); *Les Rescapés du Télémaque*, 1938 (*The Survivors*, 1965); *Monsieur la Souris*, 1938 (*The Mouse*, 1950); *Touriste de bananes: Ou, Les Dimanches de Tahiti*, 1938 (*Banana Tourist*, 1946); *La Marie du port*, 1938 (*A Chit of a Girl*, 1949; also known as *The Girl in Waiting*); *Le Suspect*, 1938 (*The Green Thermos*, 1944); *Les Sœurs Lacroix*, 1938 (*Poisoned Relations*, 1950); *Le Cheval Blanc*, 1938 (*The White Horse Inn*, 1980); *Chez Krull*, 1939 (English translation, 1966); *Le Bourgemestre de Furnes*, 1939 (*Burgomaster of Furnes*, 1952); *Le Coup de vague*, 1939; *Les Inconnus dans la maison*, 1940 (*Strangers in the House*, 1951); *Malempin*, 1940 (*The Family Life*, 1978)

1941-1945 • *Cour d'assises*, 1941 (*Justice*, 1949); *La Maison des sept jeunes filles*, 1941; *L'Outlaw*, 1941 (*The Outlaw*, 1986); *Bergelon*, 1941 (*The Delivery*, 1981); *Il pleut, bergère . . .* , 1941 (*Black Rain*, 1949); *Le Voyageur de la Toussaint*, 1941 (*Strange Inheritance*, 1950); *Oncle Charles s'est enfermé*, 1942 (*Uncle Charles Has Locked Himself In*, 1987); *La Veuve Couderc*, 1942 (*Ticket of Leave*, 1954; also known as *The Widow*, 1955); *La Vérité sur Bébé Donge*, 1942 (*I Take This Woman*, 1953; also known as *The Trial of Bébé Donge*); *Le Fils Cardinaud*, 1942 (*Young Cardinaud*, 1956); *Le Rapport du gendarme*, 1944 (*The Gendarme's Report*, 1951); *Le Fenêtre des Rouet*, 1945 (*Across the Street*, 1954); *L'Âiné des Ferchaux*, 1945 (*Magnet of Doom*, 1948)

1946-1950 • *Les Noces de Poitiers*, 1946; *Le Cercle des Mahe*, 1946; *La Fuite de Monsieur Monde*, 1945 (*Monsieur Monde Vanishes*, 1967); *Trois Chambres à Manhattan*, 1947 (*Three Beds in Manhattan*, 1964); *Au bout du rouleau*, 1947; *Le Clan des Ostendais*, 1947 (*The Ostenders*, 1952); *Lettre à mon juge*, 1947 (*Act of Passion*, 1952); *Le Destin des Malou*, 1947 (*The Fate of the Malous*, 1962); *Le Passager clandestin*, 1947 (*The Stowaway*, 1957); *Pedigree*, 1948 (English translation, 1962); *Le Bilan Malétras*, 1948; *La Jument perdue*, 1948; *La Neige était sale*, 1948 (*The Snow Was Black*, 1950; also known as *The Stain in the Snow*, 1953); *Le Fond de la bouteille*, 1949 (*The Bottom of the Bottle*, 1954); *Les Fantômes du chapelier*, 1949 (*The Hatter's Ghosts*, 1956); *Les Quatre Jours du pauvre homme*, 1949 (*Four Days in a Lifetime*, 1953); *Un Nouveau dans la ville*, 1950; *Les Volets verts*, 1950 (*The Heart of a Man*, 1951); *L'Enterrement de Monsieur Bouvet*, 1950 (*The Burial of Monsieur Bouvet*, 1955)

1951-1955 • *Tante Jeanne*, 1951 (*Aunt Jeanne*, 1953); *Le Temps d'Anaïs*, 1951 (*The Girl in His Past*, 1952); *Une Vie comme neuve*, 1951 (*A New Lease on Life*, 1963); *Marie qui loche*, 1951 (*The Girl with a Squint*, 1978); *La Mort de Belle*, 1952 (*Belle*, 1967); *Les Frères Rico*, 1952 (*The Brothers Rico*, 1967); *Antoine et Julie*, 1953 (*The Magician*, 1955); *L'Escalier de fer*, 1953 (*The Iron Staircase*, 1963); *Feux rouges*, 1953 (*The Hitchhiker*, 1955); *Crime impuni*, 1954 (*The Fugitive*, 1955); *L'Horloger d'Everton*, 1954 (*The Watchmaker of Everton*, 1955); *Le Grand Bob*, 1954 (*Big Bob*, 1954); *Les Témoins*, 1954 (*The Witnesses*, 1956); *La Boule noire*, 1955; *Les Complices*, 1955 (*The Accomplices*, 1964)

1956-1960 • *En cas de malheur*, 1956 (*In Case of Emergency*, 1958); *Le Petit Homme d'Arkangelsk*, 1956 (*The Little Man from Archangel*, 1966); *Le Fils*, 1957 (*The Son*, 1958); *Le Nègre*, 1957 (*The Negro*, 1959); *Strip-tease*, 1958 (English translation, 1959); *Le Président*, 1958 (*The Premier*, 1966); *Le Passage de la ligne*, 1958; *Dimanche*, 1958 (*Sunday*, 1960); *La Vieille*, 1959 (*The Grandmother*, 1980); *Le Veuf*, 1959 (*The Widower*, 1961); *L'Ours en peluche*, 1960 (*Teddy Bear*, 1971)

1961-1965 • *Betty*, 1961 (English translation, 1975); *Le Train*, 1961 (*The Train*, 1964); *La Porte*, 1962 (*The Door*, 1964); *Les Autres*, 1962 (*The House on the Quai Notre-Dame*, 1975); *Les Anneaux de Bicêtre*, 1963 (*The Patient*, 1963; also known as *The Bells of Bicêtre*, 1964); *La Chambre bleue*, 1964 (*The Blue Room*, 1964); *L'Homme au petit chien*, 1964

(*The Man with the Little Dog*, 1965); *Le Petit Saint*, 1965 (*The Little Saint*, 1965); *Le Train de Venise*, 1965 (*The Venice Train*, 1974)

1966-1972 • *Le Confessional*, 1966 (*The Confessional*, 1968); *La Mort d'Auguste*, 1966 (*The Old Man Dies*, 1967); *Le Chat*, 1967 (*The Cat*, 1967); *Le Déménagement*, 1967 (*The Move*, 1968; also known as *The Neighbors*); *La Prison*, 1968 (*The Prison*, 1969); *La Main*, 1968 (*The Man on the Bench in the Barn*, 1970); *Il y a encore des noisetiers*, 1969; *Novembre*, 1969 (*November*, 1970); *Le Riche Homme*, 1970 (*The Rich Man*, 1971); *La Disparition d'Odile*, 1971 (*The Disappearance of Odile*, 1972); *La Cage de verre*, 1971 (*The Glass Cage*, 1973); *Les Innocents*, 1972 (*The Innocents*, 1973)

Other short fiction: *Les 13 coupables*, 1932 (*The Thirteen Culprits*, 2002); *Les Dossiers de L'Agence O*, 1943; *Nouvelles exotiques*, 1944

Other major works

Novels: *Au pont des arches*, 1921; *Le Roman d'une dactylo*, 1924; *Train de nuit*, 1930

Nonfiction: *Le Roman de l'homme*, 1958 (*The Novel of Man*, 1964); *Quand j'étais vieux*, 1970 (*When I Was Old*, 1971); *Lettre à ma mère*, 1974 (*Letter to My Mother*, 1976); *Mémoires intimes*, 1981 (*Intimate Memoirs*, 1984); *Mes Apprentissages: Reportages, 1931-1946*, 2001

Bibliography

Assouline, Pierre. *Simenon: A Biography*. Translated by Jon Rothschild. New York: Knopf, 1997. A good reference for biographical information on Simenon.

Becker, Lucille Frackman. *Georges Simenon*. Boston: Twayne, 1977. An informative introductory study, with chapters on Simenon's family background, the creation of Maigret, his handling of such basic themes as solitude and alienation, and his understanding of the art of the novel. Includes a chronology, notes, and an annotated bibliography.

_______. *Georges Simenon Revisited*. New York: Twayne, 1999. Further reflections on Simenon, focusing more closely on the novels than did Becker's earlier work.

Bresler, Fenton. *The Mystery of Georges Simenon*. Toronto: General, 1983. A well-written biography that gives a strong sense of Simenon's roots and the development of his career. Includes conversations between Bresler and Simenon.

Carter, David. *The Pocket Essential Georges Simenon*. Harpenden, Hertfordshire, England: Pocket Essentials, 2003. Short book containing a critical analysis of Simenon's work, as well as a bibliography of works by and about him.

Eskin, Stanley. *Simenon: A Critical Biography*. Jefferson, N.C.: McFarland, 1987. Eskin provides a meticulous narrative and analysis of Simenon's work. His notes and bibliography are very detailed and helpful.

Marnham, Patrick. *The Man Who Wasn't Maigret: A Portrait of Georges Simenon*. London: Bloomsbury, 1992. An excellent study of Simenon's life and times. Includes bibliographical references and an index.

Raymond, John. *Simenon in Court*. New York: Harcourt Brace and World, 1968. An excellent overview of Simenon's fiction, as valuable as Becker's introductory study.

Simenon, Georges. "The Art of Fiction IX: Georges Simenon." Interview by Carvel Collins. *The Paris Review* 9 (Summer, 1993): 71-90. A comprehensive interview with the author about his career and his fictional methods.

MAJ SJÖWALL and PER WAHLÖÖ

Maj Sjöwall
Born: Stockholm, Sweden; September 25, 1935

Per Wahlöö
Born: Göteborg, Sweden; August 5, 1926
Died: Malmö, Sweden; June 22, 1975
Type of plot: Police procedural

Principal series

Martin Beck, 1965-1975

Principal series characters

Martin Beck, a member and eventually the head of the Stockholm homicide squad, is tall, reserved, and sometimes melancholy. Fortyish and unhappily married when the series begins, Beck is intelligent, painstaking, patient, and conscientious. He is a skilled police detective who is often troubled by the role that the police play in Swedish society.

Lennart Kollberg, Beck's colleague and closest friend, is good natured, stocky, and a devoted family man. A pacifist by nature, his growing disillusionment with changes in the police system after its nationalization in 1965 eventually leads him to resign.

Gunvald Larsson, a member of the Stockholm homicide squad, is tall, brawny, taciturn, cynical, and often short-tempered. Unmarried and a loner, he is fastidious in his dress and efficient in the performance of his job. He is a hardworking professional with little time for interpersonal relationships.

Fredrik Melander, originally a homicide-squad detective, later transferred to the burglary and violent crimes division. Married and a father, he is valued by his colleagues for his computer-like memory and is notorious for his frequent trips to the men's room.

Einer Rönn, a member of the homicide squad, is an efficient but unremarkable detective. Rarely promoted, he is one of Gunvald Larsson's few friends.

Contribution

The ten novels in the Martin Beck series, written by husband-and-wife team Per Wahlöö and Maj Sjöwall, chronicle the activities of the Stockholm homicide squad from 1965—the year in which the Swedish police force was nationalized—to 1975. Conceived as one epic novel, Beck's story was written and published at the rate of one installment per year—documenting the exact happenings of the years in which they were composed, down to flight numbers and departure times, political events, and the weather.

The books trace the changes in the police force and its relationship to Swedish society as well as the personal lives of the homicide detectives themselves. Marked by dry humor and painstaking attention to detail, they capture both the interplay among the principal characters and the exhaustive amounts of routine research that go into solving a crime. Writing in a detached, clinical style, Sjöwall and Wahlöö paint a portrait of Sweden in the late 1960's and early 1970's as a bourgeois welfare state in which crime is steadily on the rise and the police are seen increasingly by the public as tools of the government rather than as allies of the people. Using the crime novel as a mirror of the ills of the socialist state, Sjöwall and Wahlöö transformed the genre into a vehicle for addressing wrongs, rather than diffusing social anxiety. Until their work, the police procedural had been little appreciated in Sweden; the Beck series influenced Swedish successors such as K. Arne Blom, Olov Svedelid, Kennet Ahl, and Leif G. W. Persson to adopt a similar approach of social awareness.

Biography

Per Wahlöö was born Peter Fredrik Wahlöö on August 5, 1926, in Göteborg, Sweden, the son of Waldemar Wahlöö and Karin Helena Svensson Wahlöö. He attended the University of Lund, from which he was graduated in 1946, and began a career as a journalist. Throughout the 1950's, Wahlöö wrote about criminal and social issues for several Swedish magazines and newspapers before publishing his first novel, *Himmelsgetan*, in 1959. Also deeply involved in left-wing politics, Wahlöö was deported from Francisco Franco's Spain in 1957 for his political activities.

Before his success as coauthor of the Martin Beck books, Wahlöö's published novels were translated into English under the name Peter Wahlöö. Like the Beck books, Wahlöö's other novels are chiefly concerned with philosophical and sociological themes, examining through fiction the relationship of people to the society in which they live. Wahlöö is the author of two detective novels—*Mord paa 31: A vaaningen* (1964; *Murder on the Thirty-first Floor*, 1966; filmed as *Kamikaze 1989* in 1984) and *Staalspraanget* (1968; *The Steel Spring*, 1970)—featuring Chief Inspector Jensen, a police detective in an unnamed, apathetic northern country clearly intended as a bleak projection of Sweden's future. Wahlöö also wrote scripts for radio, television, and film, and translated some of Ed McBain's 87th Precinct novels into Swedish.

Maj Sjöwall (sometimes transliterated as Sjoewall) was born in Stockholm, Sweden, on September 25, 1935, the daughter of Will Sjöwall and Margit Trobaeck Sjöwall. After studying journalism and graphics in Stockholm, she became both a magazine art director and a publishing-house editor.

While working for magazines published by the same company, Sjöwall and Wahlöö met and found their social views closely matched. Married in 1962, they composed a monumental outline for the Beck series, conceived as a single epic three hundred chapters long, divided into ten books for the sake of convenience. Sitting across the dining room table from each other, they simultaneously wrote alternate chapters while their children (Lena, Terz, and Jens) slept.

Perhaps because of journalistic backgrounds that fostered spare, disciplined writing with precise details, their styles meshed seamlessly. The couple shared a desire to use the format of the detective novel to examine deeper issues within Swedish society; Wahlöö said they intended to "use the crime novel as a scalpel cutting open the belly of the ideologically pauperized and morally debatable so-called welfare state of the bourgeois type." The first Martin Beck novel, *Roseanna* (English translation, 1967), appeared in 1965. Sjöwall and Wahlöö collaborated on other projects as well, including a comparison of police methods in the United States and Europe and the editing of the literary magazine *Peripeo*. Maj Sjöwall is also a poet.

The Martin Beck series was published and acclaimed in more than twenty countries, garnering such awards as the Sherlock Award from the Swedish newspaper *Expressen* in 1968, the Edgar from the Mystery Writers of America in 1971, and the Italian Gran Giallo Città di Cattolica Prize in 1973, all for *Den skrattande polisen* (1968; *The Laughing Policeman*, 1970). The novel was filmed in 1973, with its setting transposed to San Francisco. *Den vedervardige mannen fran Saffle* (1971; *The Abominable Man*, 1972) was filmed as *The Man on the Roof* in 1977. Six books were adapted for television in Sweden.

Wahlöö died of pancreatic disease on June 22, 1975. Afterward, Sjöwall wrote one other novel, *Kvinnan som liknade Garbo* (1990), coauthored with Tomas Ross.

Analysis

The ten novels that constitute the Martin Beck series represent a remarkable achievement in the realm of mystery and detective fiction. Begun in 1965 and completed in 1975, the year of Per Wahlöö's death, the books chronicle a decade in the lives of the members of the Stockholm Police homicide squad, focusing primarily on detective Martin Beck, who becomes the head of the squad by the end of the series. The nationalization of the Swedish police force in the early 1960's—an event to which Sjöwall and Wahlöö refer in *Polismordaren* (1974; *Cop Killer*, 1975) as the creation of a state within the state—led the couple to plan a series of ten books that would reflect the changes taking place in Swedish society. Using crime as the basis for their examination, they planned the books as one continuous story told in ten segments, each of which constitutes a separate novel, with characters who recur throughout the series and whose lives change as it progresses.

In choosing the crime novel as the setting for their study, Sjöwall and Wahlöö selected a medium that would allow their characters to interact with all strata of Swedish society, and the cases in the Martin Beck books involve criminals and victims who are drug addicts, sex murderers, industrialists, tourists, welfare recipients, members of the bourgeoisie, and—in a plot that eerily foreshadowed subsequent events—the Swedish prime minister. The police force in most countries, perhaps more than any other group, deals directly with the end result of social problems, both as they affect the social mainstream and as they relate to those who fall through society's cracks, and the crimes that form the plots of the Beck novels are often a direct outgrowth of existing sociological conditions.

Roseanna and The Terrorists

The arc that the series follows moves from fairly straightforward, although horrifying, murders and sex crimes to cases that increasingly reflect the growing violence in most Western societies throughout the 1960's and early 1970's. The first book in the series, *Roseanna*, details the squad's efforts to track down the lone, disturbed murderer of a young American tourist, and the final entry, *Terroristema* (1975; *The Terrorists*, 1976), finds the detectives attempting to thwart the plans of an international assassin during the visit of a right-wing American senator. (The fact that both characters are Americans is almost certainly intentional, as

the books often make mention of the level of crime and the availability of guns in the United States, which is seen as a cautionary model of an excessively violent society.)

The decaying relationship between the police and Swedish society is depicted in the series as an outgrowth of the role the nationalized police force came to play in Sweden's bureaucratic welfare society. This position is outlined in the final pages of *The Terrorists* by Martin Beck's closest friend, Lennart Kollberg, who has left the force: "They made a terrible mistake back then. Putting the police in the vanguard of violence is like putting the cart before the horse." Kollberg's comment puts into words the implied criticism throughout the series of the use of police violence to combat rising social violence.

Murder at the Savoy

The source of that violence is seen by Sjöwall and Wahlöö as a by-product of Western economic systems. In the same book, another character remarks, "For as long as I can remember, large and powerful nations within the capitalist bloc have been ruled by people who according to accepted legal norms are simply criminals." In the series' sixth book *Polis, polis, potatismos!* (1970; *Murder at the Savoy*, 1971), the murder of a wealthy business executive and arms trafficker is traced to a former employee who lost his job, his home, and his family as a result of the executive's ruthless policies. As the story unfolds, it becomes clear that the crime has removed a despicable man from the world, although his "work" will be carried on by his equally unsavory associates. The book ends with Martin Beck unhappy in the knowledge that the man he has caught will spend years in prison for murdering a corrupt man whose callousness Beck despises. As Kollberg notes near the end of *The Terrorists*, "Violence has rushed like an avalanche throughout the whole of the Western world over the last ten years." The book ends with the former police detective playing the letter *X* in a game of Scrabble and declaring, "Then I say X—X as in Marx."

The Laughing Policeman and The Locked Room

The climate of the 1960's, with its antiwar protests and generation-based schisms, also fuels the negative view of the police. In *The Laughing Policeman*,

Beck's teenage daughter, Ingrid, tells him that she had once boasted to her friends that her father was a police officer, but she now rarely admits it. The general mood of the 1960's, combined with the easy availability of drugs and the growing number of citizens living on social welfare rolls, places the police more and more often at odds with ordinary men and women. Sometimes driven by desperation, these citizens commit crimes that were once the province of hardened criminals: A young mother robs a bank in *Det slutna rummet* (1972; *The Locked Room*, 1973); a middle-class teenage boy in *Cop Killer* becomes the object of a manhunt after a crime spree leads to a police officer's death; and a naïve young girl living on the fringes of society shoots the prime minister in *The Terrorists*.

Yet the corruption filtering down through Swedish society from its upper echelons also leaves its peculiar mark on those crimes that have always been associated with the general populace, infecting their modus operandi with a shocking disregard for justice and human life. In *The Laughing Policeman*, a successful businessman who murdered his lover twenty-five years earlier shoots all the passengers on a city bus because two of them have knowledge that might expose him.

Cop Killer

Cop Killer offers a variation on this theme, with its story of a wealthy man who murders his mistress in the manner of a sex crime to throw suspicion on a man once convicted of a similar offense. In both cases, the perpetrators' only thoughts are to protect themselves—and the comfortable lives they have built within their communities—and they do so at a terrible cost to all notions of justice and the sanctity of human life.

Sjöwall and Wahlöö use not only their plots but also their characters in their dramatization of the changes in Swedish society during the period covered by the series. Beck, a tall, reserved, often melancholy man whose years of police work have not impaired his ability to judge each victim and each criminal individually, is the central figure. The moral complexities of his work often trouble Beck—a fact reflected in his sour stomach and slight stoop—yet he carries on in his profession, seeking a philosophical middle road that will allow him to reconcile those aspects of the job that he abhors with those that he believes fulfill a useful social function. Over the course of the series, his marriage worsens, he separates from his wife, his relationship with his daughter strengthens, and he falls in love with Rhea Nielsen, a good-humored earth mother of a woman whose cooking and companionship go a long way toward improving Beck's personal life—and digestion.

Beck's friend and colleague, Lennart Kollberg, also serves as a barometer for the times. Unlike Beck, Kollberg is happily married—he fathers two children during the series—and possessed of a far more effusive personality. The course that Kollberg's professional life will follow is set in motion during *Roseanna*, the series' first book, when he shoots and kills a man. The event has a profound effect on him, and he becomes the most outspoken opponent of the increasing use of police violence throughout the books. In defiance of police regulations, Kollberg afterward refuses to carry a loaded gun, and his growing dissatisfaction with the role of the police in society finally culminates in his resignation at the end of the ninth book, *Cop Killer*. He appears in *The Terrorists* as a fat, contented househusband, minding his children while his wife happily pursues a career.

The remaining recurring characters in the series appear primarily in their professional capacities and are used by Sjöwall and Wahlöö to round out the homicide squad and reflect the interplay of personalities that exists in any working situation. Individuals come and go within the structure of the squad: Fredrik Melander is transferred to another division; an ambitious young detective named Benny Skacke opts for a transfer to Malmö after a mistake that nearly costs Kollberg his life; detective Åke Strenström is among those murdered on the bus in *The Laughing Policeman*; and his girlfriend, Åsa Torell, joins the force as a reflection of the changing role of women during the 1960's and 1970's. (The ebb and flow within the force is also carried over into the outside world, with characters who figured in earlier cases reappearing later in the series.) Beck has an amiable, ongoing association with Per Månsson, his counterpart in Malmö.

The Abominable Man

All these characters serve to illustrate the wide range of personality types who choose police work as a career—a theme that takes a dark turn in *The Abominable Man*, when a former police officer turns murderer and sniper after his wife dies in the custody of a corrupt and sadistic officer. The tragic motive that lies at the heart of *The Abominable Man* has its roots in the psychological makeup of both the killer and his first victim, a crucial point throughout the Martin Beck series. For Sjöwall and Wahlöö, psychological traits are often inextricably bound to sociological forces. In the case of *The Abominable Man*, police corruption perpetuated the career of the sadistic officer whose actions drove his future murderer to the brink of madness. The books delve deeply into the social and psychological factors that set the stage for each crime.

The Martin Beck books fall under the heading of police procedurals, and Sjöwall and Wahlöö's writing style has the clinical, matter-of-fact tone of tough journalistic reporting. The series is characterized by an exceptionally thorough attention to detail that reflects the painstaking process of sifting through vast amounts of information and leaving no lead uninvestigated. Cases often hinge on a remembered shred of evidence or an incorrectly recalled detail, and the role that luck and happenstance sometimes play is never ignored. Sjöwall and Wahlöö frequently present interviews and confessions in the form of typed transcripts, and the books' descriptions are both vivid and utterly unsensationalized.

Given the serious nature of the series' themes and the somber tone of its individual plots, the books' considerable wit and humor come as a pleasant surprise. Droll asides and dryly ironic exchanges of dialogue alleviate the atmosphere of Scandinavian gloom that permeates the novels, with flashes of humor becoming more frequent as the writers progress further into the series and develop a surer grasp of their themes and characters. *The Locked Room* contains a comically executed SWAT-style raid that could easily have been lifted from a Keystone Kops film, and there are sly references throughout the series to the characters' reading preferences, which run to Raymond Chandler and Ed McBain. (In one of the final books, Beck is referred to in a newspaper article as "Sweden's Maigret.") The dour, dismally unphotogenic Gunvald Larsson is also a recurring source of amusement as his picture finds its way into the newspaper several times—with his name always misspelled.

Best among the series' running jokes, however, are two radio patrolmen named Kristiansson and Kvant, memorable solely for their inexhaustible capacity for bungling. They are the bane of Larsson's existence as they mishandle evidence, lose suspects, and even catch a murderer while answering nature's call in the bushes of a city park. Nothing in the lighthearted manner in which they are portrayed prepares the reader for the shock of Kvant's death by sniper fire in *The Abominable Man*. He is replaced in the next book by the equally inept Kvastmo, but the effect of his shooting brings home the degree to which Sjöwall and Wahlöö have successfully created a world that mirrors real life—a world in which crime and violence can alter the course of a human life in an instant. The role that the police should play in such a world is a complex issue, and it constitutes the heart of Sjöwall and Wahlöö's work.

Janet E. Lorenz
Updated by C. A. Gardner

Principal mystery and detective fiction

Chief Inspector Jensen series (by Wahlöö): *Mord paa 31: A vaaningen*, 1964 (*Murder on the Thirty-first Floor*, 1966; also known as *The Thirty-First Floor*); *Staalspraanget*, 1968 (*The Steel Spring*, 1970)

Martin Beck series: *Roseanna*, 1965 (English translation, 1967); *Mannen som gick upp in rök*, 1966 (*The Man Who Went Up in Smoke*, 1969); *Mannen pa balkongen*, 1967 (*The Man on the Balcony*, 1968); *Den skrattande polisen*, 1968 (*The Laughing Policeman*, 1970); *Brandbilen som försvann*, 1969 (*The Fire Engine That Disappeared*, 1970); *Polis, polis, potatismos!*, 1970 (*Murder at the Savoy*, 1971); *Den vedervardige mannen fran Saffle*, 1971 (*The Abominable Man*, 1972); *Det slutna rummet*, 1972 (*The Locked Room*, 1973); *Polismordaren*, 1974 (*Cop Killer*, 1975); *Terroristerna*, 1975 (*The Terrorists*, 1976)

Nonseries novels (by Wahlöö): *Lastbilen*, 1962 (*The Lorry*, 1968; also known as *A Necessary Action*); *Uppdraget*, 1963 (*The Assignment*, 1965); *Generalerna*, 1965 (*The Generals*, 1974)

Other major works

Novels: *Himmelsgeten*, 1959 (by Wahlöö; revised as *Hoevdingen*, 1967); *Vinden och regnet*, 1961 (by Wahlöö); *Kvinnan som liknade Garbo*, 1990 (by Sjöwall, with Tomas Ross)

Short fiction: *Det vaexer inga rosor paa odenplan*, 1964

Bibliography

Benstock, Bernard. "The Education of Martin Beck." In *Art in Crime Writing: Essays on Detective Fiction*, edited by Bernard Benstock. New York: St. Martin's Press, 1983. Critical study of the character of Martin Beck and the role of developing knowledge in his adventures.

Hausladen, Gary. *Places for Dead Bodies*. Austin: University of Texas Press, 2000. This study of the settings of mystery and detective novels includes a section on the Stockholm of Maj Sjöwall and Per Wahlöö.

King, Nina. *Crimes of the Scene: A Mystery Novel Guide for the International Traveler.* New York: St. Martin's Press, 1997. A reading of setting in detective fiction that analyzes the importance and representation of Sweden in Sjöwall and Wahlöö's novels.

Maxfield, James F. "The Collective Detective Hero: The Police Novels of Maj Sjöwall and Per Wahlöö." *Clues: A Journal of Detection* 3 (Spring/Summer, 1982): 70-79. Examination of Sjöwall and Wahlöö's anti-individualist themes and their consequences for the fiction.

Palmer, Jerry. "After the Thriller." *Thrillers: Genesis and Structure of a Popular Genre*. New York: St. Martin's Press, 1979. Traces the origins and conventions of the thriller genre. Sheds light on Sjöwall and Wahlöö's works.

Symons, Julian. *Mortal Consequences: A History, from the Detective Story to the Crime Novel*. London: Faber and Faber, 1972. This history of detective fiction, written by a successful novelist in his own right, places the Martin Beck stories in the context of the evolution of the genre.

Van Dover, J. Kenneth. *Polemical Pulps: The Martin Beck Novels of Maj Sjöwall and Per Wahlöö*. San Bernardino, Calif.: Brownstone Books, 1993. Focused study of the Martin Beck series, comparing the books to the pulps of the 1930's and 1940's.

GILLIAN SLOVO

Born: Johannesburg, South Africa; March 15, 1952
Types of plot: Amateur sleuth; private investigator; courtroom drama

Principal series

Kate Baeier, 1984-

Principal series character

Kate Baeier, a Lithuanian Jew from Portugal, where her father is a leading general, left that country when she was eighteen and moved to London, where she seems perfectly at home. Little is made of her foreign background, except that people have difficulty with her name. She begins the series as a freelance journalist, solving crimes on the side, but she eventually sets up a detective agency, only to return to journalism. Initially, she is seriously involved with a single father, but he dies.

Contribution

In the 1980's, Gillian Slovo became one of a growing number of female mystery novelists writing about young female detectives. However, her detective, Kate Baeier, is rare among these characters because she is not only a feminist but also a socialist. The result is a detective series in which, at least initially, politics comes to the fore and the characters earnestly discuss such things as the relation between the personal and the political. As the series progresses, the politics tend to fade away and even to be renounced at times, creating a somewhat disorienting effect, but what remains constant is the portrayal of Kate as a loner in a hostile universe.

Slovo's most successful crime novel, *Red Dust* (2000), goes beyond the Kate Baeier series by successfully merging political and personal themes. In it Slovo moves away from hard-edged politics to explore the subtleties of South African society. *Red Dust* retains the crime novel form and carries readers along through the deft plotting Slovo learned while producing the Kate Baeier novels, but it aims at deeper things than plot and is more successful than the series novels in attaining them.

Biography

Gillian Slovo was born in Johannesburg, South Africa, on March 15, 1952, to two leading members of the antiapartheid movement: Joe Slovo, leader of the banned South African Communist Party and chief of the military wing of the African National Congress (ANC), and Ruth First, a radical journalist and university lecturer. The family went into exile in London in 1964, and Slovo attended the University of Manchester, graduating in 1974 with a bachelor's degree in the history and philosophy of science. She later worked as a journalist and television producer in England.

In 1982 Slovo's mother, then working in Mozambique, was murdered by agents of the South African government. Slovo later wrote that her novel *Ties of Blood* (1989), her first work set in South Africa, was inspired by thoughts she had while standing at her mother's graveside. Nevertheless, Slovo's first three novels, all in the Kate Baeier series, are set in London, though the initial entry, *Morbid Symptoms* (1984), does focus on characters involved in South African politics. Slovo's attention began to shift more toward Africa in the 1990's. She published *The Betrayal*, a thriller about an ANC member, in 1991, and in 1993 she wrote *Façade*, a novel about a London woman trying to discover the truth about her mother's death, which also mentions Africa. Of the two Kate Baeier series novels published in the 1990's, *Close Call* (1995) contains references to Africa.

In 1997, Slovo published *Every Secret Thing: My Family, My Country*, her best-selling memoir about her parents, their involvement in the antiapartheid movement, and her relationship with them, including the difficulty of having parents whose devotion to a cause reduced the amount of time they could spend with their children. In 2000, Slovo returned to fiction, producing *Red Dust*, a highly acclaimed courtroom drama set in postapartheid South Africa. It won the Radio France International Prize for Literature in 2001 and was made into a film starring Hilary Swank in 2004.

Saying that she might have written her last book about South Africa, Slovo in 2004 published a highly regarded historical epic, *Ice Road*, set in the Soviet Union in the 1930's and 1940's. *Ice Road* was short-listed for England's prestigious Orange Prize in 2004. Also in 2005 Slovo collaborated with Victoria Brittain on *Guantanamo: Honour Bound to Defend Freedom*, a play documenting human rights abuses at the American detention camp in Guantanamo Bay.

Analysis

The very title of Gillian Slovo's first novel, *Morbid Symptoms*, indicates the special nature of her Kate Baeier detective series. As Kate explains, the phrase is a quotation from Antonio Gramsci, the Italian Marxist philosopher, and refers to the minor problems at the end of an era, in this case the capitalist era. Kate is a socialist detective, opposed to capitalism, the rich, the police, and the apartheid leaders of South Africa. She is also a feminist and thus at odds with most of the men she encounters, especially white men and police officers. Kate's feminism is shared by female detectives in other series of the 1980's, notably those by Sue Grafton and Sara Paretsky, but her radical socialism sets her apart.

In the first four books of the series Kate encounters agents of the apartheid South African government; a landlord who violates the fire codes, causing death and injury; oppressed black Londoners who start to organize to overcome their oppression; victims of a fraudulent pension scheme benefiting businessmen and investors; and a host of brutal police officers. On the surface Kate and her author seem left wing and liberated, clearly on the side of the oppressed and against the forces of capitalism. However, as Sally Munt notes in her study of feminism and the crime novel, the Kate Baeier novels pull in conflicting directions and may not be as liberated as they seem. Munt points especially to the position of Kate's black assistant, Carmen, who is very competent and industrious and is portrayed in a positive light but remains, by her own choice, in a subordinate position.

In addition, some of the left-wing politics seems merely tacked on, as when in *Death by Analysis* (1986) Kate approvingly takes note of Irish hunger strikers who have no real role in the plot. Indeed, many of the plots focus on personal rather than political issues, and in *Death by Analysis* the whole issue of the relationship between the personal and the political is uneasily discussed by various characters and is exemplified by the fact that Kate has been in therapy and is not entirely happy that the result of the therapy was to turn her away from changing the world in order to focus on her psyche. A major theme of this novel is the passing of the revolutionary moment. Characters talk nostalgically of the radical 1960's but keep reminding themselves that it is now the 1980's and revolution is out of style. In *Morbid Symptoms*, those who have remained on the radical left are portrayed for the most part as preoccupied with petty infighting among themselves, and in the end the true villain turns out to be not the so-called real enemy, the South African security forces, but a member of one of the left-wing groups.

Although the overt thrust of the novels is to attack authority and privilege and to side with the oppressed and with radical political groups, there is an undercurrent flowing in the opposite direction, so much so that in *Catnap* (1994), Carmen accuses Kate of having switched sides. Even as early as in *Death by Analysis*, Kate feels she is stuck on the black-white divide, not truly able to side with the black victims with whom she sympathizes. She also begins to develop self-doubts. In *Death Comes Staccato* (1987), she twice calls herself a failure as an investigator, and at the end she fingers the wrong suspect for the crime. In *Catnap* she feels incompetent, blames herself for a break-in, and even gets lost in a library.

Kate has lost her boyfriend, Sam, in *Catnap*. Sam was one of the few good men in the novels, gentle and supportive, just the sort of man a feminist might love, but as early as the opening pages of *Morbid Symptoms* Kate seems vaguely dissatisfied with him. In *Death by Analysis* she is leaping out of his arms, and in *Death Comes Staccato* she flirts with someone else and almost lets herself be seduced. Morag Shiach, in her article on female detectives, notes that they often have boyfriends who turn out to be too safe and weak, and she singles out Sam as an example of one who in the end provokes such dissatisfaction that he has to go.

Throughout the Kate Baeier series, Slovo seems to be struggling with the relationship between the personal and the political, and trying to get away from a fairly extreme political viewpoint. In the first three books she seems on one level strongly attached to that viewpoint, but conflicting views somehow emerge as well. In the fourth and fifth books, *Catnap* and *Close Call*, she seems at times to be renouncing her old views, but at other times reasserts them, shuttling back and forth in a confused way. When Slovo leaves Kate Baeier behind and focuses on the politics of South Africa in *Red Dust*, she achieves her greatest success, combining personal and political into one organic whole based on a much more subtle understanding of both politics and human nature.

Catnap

Catnap, which appeared after a seven-year hiatus in the Kate Baeier series, marks a shift in form. After three whodunits in which Kate is hired to solve murders, this time Kate herself is endangered in a Dick Francis-style thriller. Returning to London after five years away as a war correspondent, Kate finds herself almost constantly under attack, first by muggers, then by someone who breaks into her house and seems to be stalking her, and later by several other characters in the book. Much of the politics of the earlier Kate Baeier books disappears in *Catnap*, and surprisingly some of the villains (the muggers) turn out to be black. However, this book resembles the earlier ones in that it depicts Kate as living in a bleak and hostile universe full of angry, violent men.

Close Call

Close Call begins in an unprecedented way for Kate. She is back in journalism interviewing a police officer and discovers that he is sensitive, heroic, and compassionate. She keeps expecting some hidden rage to erupt out of him, which would be typical of the police in the earlier Kate Baeier books, but it never does. The result is that she begins to feel that she is wrong about everything. When she visits this officer's wife, she expects to find a submissive woman oppressed by her husband, but that turns out not to be true either.

In this book Slovo introduces Kate's father, a Portuguese general who, like Slovo's own father at the time, is dying. Kate is estranged from her father, but he keeps on reaching out to her in the friendliest way, and she eventually begins to think she has been wrong about him or that he has changed from the unscrupulous manipulator he used to be.

Kate starts dating a police officer and encounters other apparently friendly police officers. In the first part of the book, the only villains seem to be women. A nasty female police officer threatens her, and an annoying and foolish activist from a rape center pesters her. Kate feels like killing this activist and does smash a vase of hers. Later Kate becomes physically violent with a female police officer. This violence on Kate's part is quite unusual. In the earlier books, Kate does nothing violent; it is the men she encounters who are violent. In this book, however, everything seems turned around. The men are nice, the women are violent, and the message seems to be to reject the viewpoint of the earlier novels.

Everything reverts to normal at the end, however. Some of the nice police officers turn out to be corrupt, Kate's father turns out to be his old manipulative self, and Kate ends up distrusting her police officer boyfriend. The novel's message is therefore ambiguous.

Red Dust

Red Dust is a more complex novel. Instead of being caught in the middle of contradictory feelings, in this novel Slovo seems to be the master of them. She sensitively portrays the attitudes of several of her characters, abandoning the first-person point of view she used throughout the Kate Baeier series to enter the minds of several different characters, including two white South African police officers.

Instead of portraying the police as mindless brutes, Slovo depicts them as complex human beings. She also explores the internal contradictions of two black African characters who in earlier books she might simply have portrayed as heroes. There is also a subtle depiction of the complicated relationship between a young prosecutor and her aging mentor and between the mentor and his wife.

The story focuses on the Truth and Reconciliation Commission in postapartheid South Africa. Black Africans are in control and whites are being held to account for the crimes of apartheid. The Africans are holding a series of amnesty hearings at which whites can be pardoned in return for full confessions.

The heroine of the novel is Sarah Barcant, a white South African who has emigrated to the United States, where she has become a successful and powerful prosecuting attorney in New York. She is summoned back to her hometown in South Africa to help with one of the amnesty hearings, in the course of which she helps solve the mystery of the disappearance of one black activist. The main focus of the hearing, however, is on the torture of another black activist, who is present to confront his old torturer. The novel skillfully presents the intimate relationship between the torturer and his victim, entering the minds of both to depict the psychology of torture.

At the end of the novel some of the old Slovo emerges, with the torturer suddenly denounced as a monster and Sarah making a brief rant against men. For the most part, however, this novel works as both a courtroom drama with a mystery to be solved and the psychology of a crime to be laid bare and as a subtle presentation of the complexities of postapartheid politics and the difficulties inherent in pursuing truth, justice, and reconciliation.

Sheldon Goldfarb

Principal mystery and detective fiction

Kate Baeier series: *Morbid Symptoms*, 1984; *Death by Analysis*, 1986; *Death Comes Staccato*, 1987; *Catnap*, 1994; *Close Call*, 1995

Nonseries novels: *The Betrayal*, 1991; *Red Dust*, 2000

Other major works

Novels: *Ties of Blood*, 1989; *Façade*, 1993; *Ice Road*, 2004

Play: *Guantanamo: Honour Bound to Defend Freedom*, pb. 2005 (with Victoria Brittain)

Nonfiction: *Every Secret Thing: My Family, My Country*, 1997

Bibliography

Eprile, Tony. "Settling Scores." Review of *Red Dust*, by Gillian Slovo. *The New York Times*, April 28, 2002. Finds the novel gripping though at times one-dimensional.

Klein, Kathleen Gregory, ed. *Great Women Mystery Writers: Classic to Contemporary.* Westport, Conn.: Greenwood Press, 1994. Contains an essay on the life and works of Slovo.

Munt, Sally R. *Murder by the Book? Feminism and the Crime Novel.* London: Routledge, 1994. Discusses feminism and socialism in various female crime writers, including Slovo. Focuses on racial issues, including the role of Carmen in the early books in the Kate Baeier series. Indexed.

Shiach, Morag. "Domesticating the Detective." In *Women Voice Men: Gender in European Culture*, edited by Maya Slater. Exeter, England: Intellect, 1997. Discusses the home life of female detectives in fiction, including Kate Baeier's relationship with her boyfriend.

Slovo, Gillian. *Every Secret Thing: My Family, My Country.* Boston: Little, Brown, 1997. Slovo describes growing up in a family where her parents were committed to a greater cause. Provides clues to the ambivalence present in her mysteries and other writings.

Winston, Robert P. "Gillian Slovo." In *Great Women Mystery Writers, Classic to Contemporary*, edited by Kathleen Gregory Klein. Westport, Conn.: Greenwood Press, 1994. Compares Slovo to Sara Paretsky and Sue Grafton. Discusses the political aspects of her early novels. Provides biographical information.

JULIE SMITH

Born: Annapolis, Maryland; November 25, 1944

Types of plot: Police procedural; private investigator; amateur sleuth; cozy

Principal series

Rebecca Schwartz, 1982-
Paul McDonald, 1985-
Skip Langdon, 1990-
Talba Wallis, 2001-

Principal series characters

Rebecca Schwartz is a San Francisco lawyer and an ardent feminist, but she is also the daughter of a prominent lawyer and a woman with some decidedly conventional attitudes about romantic relationships. The conflicts Schwartz faces in trying to succeed in a patriarchal profession allow for the exploration of contemporary social issues within the framework of the mystery novel.

Paul McDonald, Rebecca's friend, works as a journalist and freelance writer in the San Francisco Bay area while strugglng to become a successful mystery novelist.

Skip Langdon, daughter of a prominent New Orleans physician, has turned her back on high society to become a police detective. Partly because her height and weight keep her from fitting the stereotype of the debutante-turned-demure-matron, she feels alienated from the people in the social circles in which she was raised and more at home among the artists and oddballs of the city's French Quarter, where she chooses to live. Not given to following rules or taking orders, she nevertheless manages to parlay her associations with the city's elite to help solve crimes in a city plagued by racism, sexism, hedonism, cronyism, and outdated beliefs involving class structure.

Talba Wallis is a talented computer nerd who moonlights as a poet and entertainer. She has changed her given name, Urethra, to Talba, a shortened version of her stage name, the Baroness de Pontalba. After stumbling into a career as a private investigator, she manages to combine her technological skills with her brash approach to life in a way that lets her solve cases by cutting through individual prejudices and institutional bureaucracy but that often frustrates those who care for her, including her mother, her boss, and her boyfriend.

Contribution

From the publication of her first mystery, *Death Turns a Trick*, in 1982, Julie Smith displayed her ability to create suspenseful narratives while entertaining readers with her tongue-in-cheek assessment of the contemporary social scene. In addition to satisfying the intellectual curiosity of those who enjoy a good "whodunit," the books featuring Rebecca Schwartz and Paul McDonald exposed the vulnerable underside of the supposedly carefree San Francisco singles lifestyle in the 1980's.

Beginning with the publication of *New Orleans Mourning* (1990), the novels set in the Crescent City reflect Smith's development as a literary artist. Like her contemporary James Lee Burke, she makes exceptionally good use of the south Louisiana setting as a means of communicating insights into human character and social relationships. An admirer of William Faulkner and Tennessee Williams, Smith incorporates elements of southern Gothic in her character portraits while maintaining exceptional command over her intricate and well-developed plots. Through the stories of her two female protagonists from New Orleans, one a member of high society who feels alienated from her peers, the other a young African American, Smith is able to examine issues that remain problematic for American society, specifically sexism and racism. Her finest works demonstrate that it is possible to construct a sophisticated novel of social commentary within the framework of the detective thriller.

Biography

Julie Smith was born November 25, 1944, in Annapolis, Maryland, where her father was stationed during World War II. Malberry Smith, a lawyer, and his wife Claire Tanner Smith, a school counselor, moved the family to Savannah, Georgia, after the war. Julie Smith grew up there, leaving in 1962 to attend the University of Mississippi, where she majored in journalism. After graduating in 1965, Smith moved to New Orleans and talked her way into a job as a reporter for the *New Orleans Times-Picayune*. A year later she left for San Francisco, landing a position at the *San Francisco Chronicle*, where she worked for more than a decade. Intent on pursuing a career as a fiction writer, she wrote dozens of stories and drafted several novels while holding down her job as a reporter. In 1979 she and two friends started Invisible Ink, an editorial consulting firm. Smith stayed with the firm for three years until her first novel, *Death Turns a Trick*, was published in 1982.

Buoyed by her success, Smith determined to write full time, and over the next eight years she published five novels set in San Francisco, three featuring feminist lawyer Rebecca Schwartz and two showcasing Schwartz's friend Paul McDonald, a struggling mystery writer. In 1990, Smith chose a new location for her fiction, and for her first novel about New Orleans, *New Orleans Mourning*, she received the 1991 Edgar Award for best novel—the first time this award had gone to a female novelist since 1956. Although Smith published two more novels featuring Rebecca Schwartz, after 1990 the city of New Orleans became her principal métier, and novels about Detective Skip Langdon began appearing regularly. In the eighth Langdon novel, *Eighty-two Desire*, Smith introduced Talba Wallis, a computer whiz turned private detective, who would become the main character in a new series initiated by *Louisiana Hotshot* in 2001.

In the mid-1990's Smith married business entrepreneur Lee Pryor and moved to New Orleans. Intent on assisting other authors who were struggling as she had to establish careers, she created a Web-based course in writing to help them master the basics of their craft. In an example of life following art, after relocating to New Orleans, Smith took the necessary steps to become a licensed private investigator.

Analysis

On first reading, the most notable quality in Julie Smith's novels is the attention she gives to plotting.

Her novels are well-made mysteries, in which information subtly inserted early in the work takes on importance as her detectives draw closer to discovering the perpetrator of the crimes they have set out to solve. Like any good mystery writer, Smith provides a sufficient number of red herrings and false leads to keep her detective busy and her readers guessing about the identity of the murderer. What emerges on careful reading of Smith's novels, however, is an appreciation for her use of setting and characterization. Not only are her descriptions of places deftly drawn, but also in the New Orleans novels especially, they are integral to the larger story she wishes to tell. Smith's major characters—Rebecca Schwartz, Skip Langdon, and Talba Wallis—are multidimensional, evolving slowly through each novel in the series in which they are featured. Through them Smith explores a network of personal and social relationships that offers readers a window on contemporary life that extends beyond the intellectual pleasures derived from solving the mystery around which each novel is organized.

Death Turns a Trick

Smith's first detective novel, *Death Turns a Trick*, introduces readers to Rebecca Schwartz, a self-described Jewish feminist lawyer living in San Francisco. Schwartz is thrust into the role of detective when she discovers a woman dead in her apartment. The young woman is no stranger, however; Schwartz had met her earlier in the evening, at a house of prostitution where Schwartz was attending a risqué party. Because the principal suspect is Schwartz's boyfriend—who is the brother of the victim—complications are manifold as she sets out to defend her lover by finding his sister's killer.

Smith employs a chatty first-person style in presenting the story, allowing her main character to speak directly to readers. She also demonstrates exceptional ability in providing a considerable amount of background information about Schwartz, her family, and her circle of friends. Combining elements of the conventional romance novel with those of the mystery, Smith manages to interest readers not only in the hunt for the killer but also in the personal life of the protagonist. The novel offers a tongue-in-cheek critique of feminism, celebrating its strong points but lampooning its more excessive qualities, which Smith evidently considers to be barriers to healthy relationships between men and women.

Huckleberry Fiend

In *Huckleberry Fiend* (1987), Smith's second novel featuring Paul McDonald, her only male sleuth, the journalist and would-be novelist is called on by a friend to help locate a valuable manuscript: the missing sections of Mark Twain's *Adventures of Huckleberry Finn* (1884). McDonald follows leads that take him to the haunts of several noted collectors, including a famous romance novelist, an enterprising book dealer, and a business tycoon with unusual habits for acquiring unique art objects. Traveling from his native Oakland, California, to Mississippi and Virginia City, Nevada, to track down leads, McDonald ends up endangering not only himself, but also his lover and the friend for whom he is trying to recover the manuscript, as more than one person seems bent on keeping him from discovering what happened to the holograph of Twain's masterpiece. The somewhat surprising denouement allows Smith's amateur sleuth to demonstrate not only his skills at detection and deduction but also his ability to understand and appreciate the vagaries of the publishing business. Although the focus throughout is on McDonald's efforts to locate the manuscript, Smith is able to weave into the tale some interesting literary tidbits about Twain's career and to explore the psyche of collectors, a curious breed of individuals whose love of art and literature drives their actions in strange, often unpredictable ways.

New Orleans Mourning

The event that sets in motion the action of *New Orleans Mourning* is certainly out of the ordinary: Chauncey St. Amant, king of Carnival, is shot as he rides in the Krewe of Rex parade on Mardi Gras day. Because the victim is high profile and high society, the New Orleans police reach outside the detective ranks for help. Officer Skip Langdon, raised among the city's social elite, knows the family and many others who travel in their circle. Though Langdon's family has virtually disowned her for having become a police officer, she is still able to use friendships forged in her youth at exclusive private schools and clubs to help in the search for the killer. She discovers that St. Amant

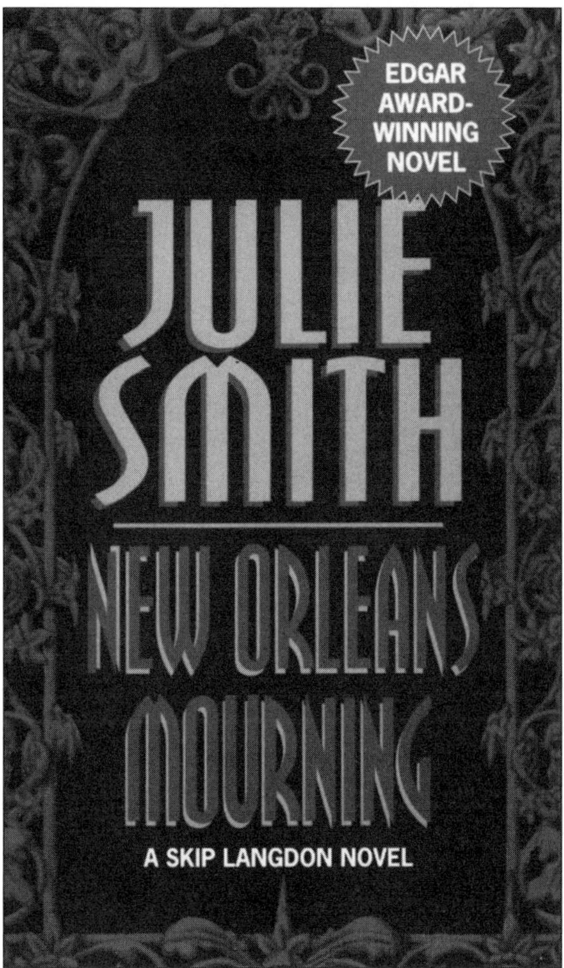

and his immediate family have kept dark secrets for two decades, and as she gets closer to the truth, she finds her own life in danger. Nevertheless, she pursues her leads doggedly, assisted by a California filmmaker in town for the Mardi Gras who takes an amorous interest in her. When she exposes the killer, however, she learns just how influential the rich and powerful are in New Orleans; a convenient lie is accepted by the authorities so that reputations can be preserved.

In this Skip Langdon mystery, Smith demonstrates that she is a master at capturing setting and making it integral to her story. New Orleans comes to life on the pages of her novel, as Langdon's investigation leads her to explore some of the city's storied neighborhoods and interact with a number of the unusual types who make the city unique. Additionally, Smith displays a decided advance in characterization from her previous novels. Not only is Langdon a woman trying to succeed in a profession normally populated by men but, decidedly tall and a bit overweight, she is also presented as someone having to fight against a number of social stereotypes. Similarly, members of the St. Amant family, to all appearances both financially and socially successful, are carefully delineated to illustrate the dysfunctions beneath the veneer of gentility. Smith carefully blends humor and pathos to reveal something about the cronyism, sexism, and racism that underlies the social structure of the metropolis.

Louisiana Bigshot

In *Louisisana Bigshot* (2002), the opening scene of Smith's second novel featuring Talba Wallis, the self-styled poet and computer expert receives her private investigator's license, making her a fully qualified associate in Eddie Valentino's agency. Almost immediately she becomes involved in solving the murder of a friend and fellow poet from a small town outside Baton Rouge. Wallis's discovery regarding her friend's past puts her, her boss, and their families in danger from the henchmen of a powerful Louisiana politician who wants to keep the secrets of the past buried forever.

Like Smith's other Talba Wallis novels, *Louisiana Bigshot* is a study of complex human relationships, revealing depths of character not often associated with detective fiction. For example, while she searches for her friend's killer, Wallis is also working to learn the identity and whereabouts of her half sister, the child of the father who abandoned Wallis and her mother when Talba was a young girl. Smith devotes considerable space to examining Wallis's rocky relationships with her mother and her boyfriend, who is also an estranged father. As an African American woman trying to make a living as a private investigator, Wallis struggles gallantly to overcome longstanding barriers erected on racist and sexist ideologies. The novel also hints at the nature of politics in Louisiana, where cronyism and corruption dominate the political climate and where those in power are not above breaking the law to remain in office.

Mean Woman Blues

In *Mean Woman Blues* (2003), the ninth of her Skip Langdon novels, Smith presents a constantly developing protagonist who has grown in stature within her profession and has matured in her personal life. The novel brings back one of Langdon's recurring nightmares: the sociopath Errol Jacomine, who had disappeared for years but who resurfaces in a rather fantastic way as a televangelist in Dallas. Jacomine is bent on gaining revenge against the woman who destroyed his criminal network, and while Langdon is occupied searching for a ring of thieves stealing cemetery statuary, Jacomine makes his move against her. The complicated plot brings Langdon in contact with Jacomine's younger son Isaac, who has rejected his father's lifestyle and values and takes her to Dallas, where in a showdown with Jacomine she watches as he becomes the victim of revenge at the hands of two of his wives. More a detective thriller than a mystery, *Mean Woman Blues* showcases Smith's ability to analyze her characters' motivations and dramatize a variety of male-female relationships. The novel also explores family bonds, a common theme in Smith's work.

Laurence W. Mazzeno

Principal mystery and detective fiction

Rebecca Schwartz series: *Death Turns a Trick*, 1982; *The Sourdough Wars*, 1984; *Tourist Trap*, 1986; *Dead in the Water*, 1991; *Other People's Skeletons*, 1993

Paul McDonald series: *True-Life Adventure*, 1985; *Huckleberry Fiend*, 1987

Skip Langdon series: *New Orleans Mourning*, 1990; *The Axeman's Jazz*, 1991; *Jazz Funeral*, 1993; *New Orleans Beat*, 1994; *House of Blues*, 1995; *The Kindness of Strangers*, 1996; *Crescent City Kill*, 1997; *82 Desire*, 1998; *Mean Woman Blues*, 2003

Talba Wallis series: *Louisiana Hotshot*, 2001; *Louisiana Bigshot*, 2002; *Louisiana Lament*, 2004; *P.I. on a Hot Tin Roof*, 2005

Other major works

Novel: *I'd Kill for That*, 2004 (coauthor)

Short fiction: *Mean Rooms: A Short Story Collection*, 2000

Edited text: *New Orleans Noir*, 2007

Bibliography

Grafton, Sue, et al., eds. *Writing Mysteries: A Handbook*. Cincinnati: Writer's Digest Books, 2002. Essays by noted mystery writers containing their insights into elements of the genre; includes a contribution by Smith outlining her ideas about the role of background, location, and setting in creating effective mysteries.

Grape, Jan, Dean James, and Ellen Nehr, eds. *Deadly Women: The Woman Mystery Reader's Indispensable Companion*. New York: Carroll & Graf, 1998. Essay by Smith on the importance of receiving the Edgar Award in 1991 is included in this collection of material about women's contributions to detective fiction.

Klein, Kathleen Gregory. *Diversity and Detective Fiction*. Bowling Green, Ohio: Bowling Green State University Popular Press, 1999. Essays by various scholars examine the theme of race and diversity in works by American mystery writers; helps place Smith's work in a larger social context.

_______, ed. *Great Women Mystery Writers: Classic to Contemporary*. Westport, Conn.: Greenwood Press, 1994. Contains an essay on the life and works of Smith.

Pepper, Andrew. *The Contemporary American Crime Novel: Race, Ethnicity, Gender, Class*. Chicago: Fitzroy Dearborn, 2000. Discusses Smith's use of detective fiction as a means of exploring the complex issues of race and gender.

Willett, Ralph. *The Naked City: Urban Crime Fiction in the USA*. New York: Manchester University Press, 1996. Examines Smith's work in chapters exploring fiction set in San Francisco and New Orleans; insightful analysis of the social and racial background of *New Orleans Mourning*.

MARTIN CRUZ SMITH

Born: Reading, Pennsylvania; November 3, 1942
Also wrote as Nick Carter; Jake Logan; Martin Quinn; Simon Quinn
Type of plot: Police procedural

Principal series

Roman Grey, 1971-
Nick Carter, 1972-
The Inquisitor, 1974-
Arkady Renko, 1981-

Principal series characters

ROMAN GREY, a Gypsy antique dealer in his early thirties, lives in New York City. Grey (or Romano Gry—his Gypsy name) walks the line between Gypsy and *gaja* (non-Gypsy). Dating a *gaja* woman and trusted by a *gaja* police officer, he works on criminal cases for Gypsy honor.

FRANCIS XAVIER "THE INQUISITOR" KILLY is a lay brother of the Vatican's Militia Christi and a former Central Intelligence Agency (CIA) agent. A shrewd investigator, he combines physical skill with intellect to maneuver his way through church politics and international crises.

ARKADY RENKO is a dedicated Russian detective who wore his Soviet identity as a badge of honor until the rise of glasnost threw the country into turmoil. Despite personal tragedies and political disorder, Renko is a dogged investigator willing to put his life on the line for duty and honor.

Contribution

Martin Cruz Smith's novel *Gorky Park* (1981), his most important work, showcases his power to create believable characters within the mystery genre. The hero of *Gorky Park*, Arkady Renko, is the prototypical investigator—intelligent, cynical, beleaguered by a cheating wife and cheating superiors—who is proud to be Russian. The villain, American John Osborne, is slippery and homicidal. Smith's ability to make the murderous KGB officer Pribluda more sympathetic than the privileged Osborne proves his skill with plot and characterization. For the most part, Smith's language is compact, page-turner prose. He generally describes the grotesque—such as the dwarf Andreev in *Gorky Park* and the bat caves in *Nightwing* (1977)—without relying on metaphor. Smith is notable as well for his ability to paint a convincing portrait of societies and institutions, such as the bureaucracy in *Gorky Park*, and of the dynamic between a couple, such as the relationship between Anna Weiss and Joe Pena in *Stallion Gate* (1986). He has contributed to an understanding of humans' relationship to other animals with the mythic interaction between man and animal depicted in *Nightwing*, *Gorky Park*, and *Gypsy in Amber* (1971).

Biography

Martin Cruz Smith, born Martin William Smith on November 3, 1942, in Reading, Pennsylvania, is the son of John Calhoun, a musician, and Louise Lopez Smith, an American Indian rights activist. Smith was graduated from the University of Pennsylvania in 1964 with a bachelor of arts degree and then worked as a reporter for the *Philadelphia Daily News* in 1965. He was employed by Magazine Management from 1966 to 1969. On June 15, 1968, he married Emily Arnold, a chef.

In 1970, he published his first novel, *The Indians Won*, which was reviewed in science-fiction journals. From 1970 through 1976, he wrote and published many mystery and adventure novels under various pseudonyms. Written under the name Martin Smith, *Gypsy in Amber* and *Canto for a Gypsy* (1972) indicate his fascination with mismatched partners, a motif that resurfaces in *Gorky Park. Gypsy in Amber* earned a nomination by the Mystery Writers of America as the best first mystery novel of 1971.

In 1973, Smith spent two weeks in the Soviet Union researching a book that was to include a Soviet detective working with an American detective to solve a murder. Refused permission to return to the Soviet Union, he did further research by interviewing Soviet émigrés about life in their homeland.

Smith's Inquisitor series, published in 1974-1975 under the name of Simon Quinn, was received with

Martin Cruz Smith in 1999. (AP/Wide World Photos)

considerable interest. His first substantial success as a writer, however, occurred in 1977 with the publication of *Nightwing*. This book was nominated by the Mystery Writers of America for the 1978 Edgar Allan Poe Award. In 1977, Smith also had his middle name legally changed from William to Cruz, his maternal grandmother's first name.

The success of *Nightwing* allowed Smith to focus on completing his Russian mystery, *Gorky Park*, which was published in 1981. The popularity of *Gorky Park* enabled Smith to spend the next five years researching and writing his novel about the Manhattan Project test site in New Mexico, *Stallion Gate*, published in 1986.

ANALYSIS

Martin Cruz Smith's novels keep the reader turning the pages quickly. His sentences are most often short and emphatic, with repetition and parallelism as important devices. For example, Arkady Renko considers the nature of American John Osborne:

> Arkady felt cold, as if the windows had opened. Osborne was not sane, or not a man. If money could grow bones and flesh it would be Osborne. It would wear the same cashmere suit; it would part its silver hair the same way; it would have the same lean mask with its expression of superior amusement.

Smith achieves success as a writer not through flamboyant style but by placing his protagonists in situations that require them to confront their own codes of ethics. A natural storyteller, he explores people's relationship with their culture. The couples in his books, lovers as well as detective partners, are most real when they are downcast and threatened by the powers that be. Smith's strengths lie in his ability to portray people's responses to crisis—including their frustration, weakness, and cynicism.

Smith works best within the police procedural formula. Smith often uses mismatched partners to investigate a crime. The partners in the Gypsy series are Roman Grey and Harry Isadore, the New York Police Department's expert on Gypsies. Isadore "may still be a sergeant at forty-nine" but can deliver "a lovely lecture on Gypsies at City College." The almost trusting relationship between Grey and Isadore, hindered only by Isadore's occasional unfulfilled threat to arrest Grey, leads the reader to respect the partners in the Gypsy series and see their work as complementary. In *Nightwing*, however, the partners are a bat killer, Hayden Paine, and an Indian deputy, Youngblood Duran, whose relationship is stormy, marked by death threats backed up by loaded guns. Paine has been hired by leaders of a Navajo reservation to locate the source of an outbreak of the plague. Duran is investigating the death of an Indian medicine man who was apparently killed by a wild animal. Both investigations lead to one source: vampire bats that carry bubonic plague. The partners meet for the last time in the middle of the Painted Desert and then seek the bat cave together. The partners' antagonism gives way in the end to Duran's memorializing Paine as a hero for his extermination of the bats.

In *Gorky Park*, Smith was able to create detective partners who are combative and cooperative in a much more satisfying fashion. These investigators, the Russian Arkady Renko and the American James Kirwill, initially threaten each other. Whereas in *Nightwing* the threat begins with tense but quiet accusation, in this novel, Renko and Kirwill first meet at the scene of the murder in Gorky Park, where Kirwill comes close to killing Renko. Their fistfight, which Renko loses, is followed by Kirwill's shooting at Renko:

> When Arkady stepped forward, the hand lowered. He saw a barrel. The man aimed with both hands the way detectives were trained to fire a gun, and Arkady dove. He heard no shot and saw no flash, but something smacked off the ice behind him and, an instant later, rang off stones.

As Renko continues his investigation, he in turn nearly kills the American:

> Arkady wasn't aware of raising the makeshift gun. He found himself aiming the barrel at a point between Kirwill's eyes and pulling the trigger so that the doubled rubber band and plunger started to move smoothly. At the last moment he aimed away. The closet jumped and a hole two centimeters across appeared in the closet door beside Kirwill's ear. Arkady was astonished. He'd never come close to murdering anyone in his life, and when the accuracy of the weapon was considered he could as easily have killed as missed. A white mask of surprise showed where the blood had drained around Kirwill's eyes.

Now the partners are even: Each has nearly shot the other. The symmetry in physical risk between the two culminates in Kirwill's death at John Osborne's hand; just as Renko was stabbed in Moscow, so is Kirwill stabbed in New York. In New York, the partners have been able to overcome their differences and work together to net Osborne.

Smith's partner theme extends from mismatched working partners to mismatched lovers and to a partnership between humans and animals. In his works, Smith creates a universe that places humans in a mythic relationship with animals.

Roman Grey series

Mismatched lovers are sources of conflict in the Roman Grey series. Roman Grey's love for a non-Gypsy, Dany Murray, offends other Gypsies, who often accuse him of being Anglicized by her. His cooperation with Sergeant Isadore further provokes the Gypsies' ire. As a Gypsy colleague says to Grey in *Canto for a Gypsy*, "Each day I see you are more with them than us. First the girl and then the police. Maybe you want to be the first Gypsy in their heaven?"

These mismatched lovers undergo trials by fire in their relationship. Grey envisions his love leaving him because she will not be able to fit in with his Gypsy life, particularly during a trip through Europe:

> She wouldn't break during the first month . . . because she had determination. But determination would only take her so far. Her fascination of Rom would turn to disgust. Their car would carry the stench of sweat and anger. She wouldn't fight, she would just go home. Roman knew it as certainly as he knew at this moment she couldn't believe it would ever happen.

Here Grey's dilemma with a non-Gypsy lover is apparent: Either he gives up his travels as a Gypsy (which is tantamount to giving up life as a Gypsy) or he loses the woman he loves.

In *Gypsy in Amber*, the confrontation between good and evil (Roman Grey and Howard Hale) is mediated by a sacrificed goat. Indeed, the goat strikes the final blow:

> Howie still looked like a broken bust put back, subtly, completely ruined. Roman pulled the goat out of his arms. Its absence left two spongy holes in Howie's chest where its horns had cradled. The animal's gold, gun-slit eyes caught the first light of day as it broke over the pines.
>
> "Howie sacrificed himself," Hillary said.

The goat, which has been tied on Grey's back, for much of the final battle between Howie and Grey, has shielded Grey from death many times and in the end is a sacrificial animal, archetypal figure of early Western mythology.

Nightwing

Suspicion and mistrust between ethnic groups is also evident in *Nightwing*, only this time the protagonist's group is the Hopi Indians. Youngblood Duran must endure racist comments directed toward his white lover, Anne Dillon; other Indians tell him she is interested in him only for sex. The racist preoccupation with "sex with the savage" also figures in *Stallion*

Gate, in which the mismatched couple, like the couple in *Nightwing*, begin with sex and then fall in love. In both instances, Smith portrays the man as the more romantic and vulnerable of the lovers.

Leaving on a trip is central to the plot of *Nightwing* and, as in the Roman Grey book, is a test of love. Early in the novel, Anne Dillon tells Youngblood Duran, the deputy investigating the death of the medicine man, that she will soon be leaving the reservation and that she wants him to come with her; he refuses to leave. After he finds her nearly dead in the desert, however, the only survivor of the group of desert campers, he declares, "My reservation days are over and I'm going to join the living. I finally figured it out. You're my ticket from here because I love you enough to be where you are, wherever that is." The relationship that began as a strong sexual attraction endures and grows, culminating with the pair riding off together at the end of the book, like the lovers in *Canto for a Gypsy.*

The sacrificial relationship between animal and man is further explored in *Nightwing*, only here the man sacrifices himself to the animal. Hayden Paine describes a symbiosis between the vampire bat and Central American Indian civilizations:

> "The vampire lives off large mammals that sleep in herds. It lives off cattle and horses. There weren't any cattle and horses in the New World until the Spanish brought them. What do you think the vampires lived on before then? Name me the one large American mammal that slept together in herds, or villages."
>
> A light-headed sensation came over Anne.
>
> "You mean, people?"
>
> "Yes, that's exactly what I mean. People. Which is why all the old vampire roosts were found next to villages. Of course, we can only speculate on the details of this relationship. Whether one vampire colony would establish territoriality over a particular village and defend its feeding ground against other colonies."

Paine points out that what man gained from this relationship was a god. He speculates on the meaning of religious sacrifice for the Central American Indian tribes. Paine's obsession with the vampire bat reflects the intricacy of humans' relationship with animals; in Paine's case, killing the animals meant killing himself.

Gorky Park

Vulnerability and romance are shared by the mismatched lovers in *Gorky Park*, Irina Asanova and Arkady Renko. The crucial difference between them is that Renko is Russian, but Irina, though born in the Soviet Union, refuses to be Russian. Renko's involvement with Irina is highly dangerous because she is a dissident whose principal goal is to emigrate. Their attraction, like that of Smith's other couples, is intensely physical and develops from sex to love.

In *Gorky Park*, however, though the lovers pass their test, they are not given a happily-ever-after ending. After Renko and Asanova have endured KGB questioning regarding the months during which Renko was recovering from his stab wound, the couple is together in New York City. Asanova has acted as Osborne's lover so that Osborne would bring Renko to New York. The mark of her love for Renko is not, however, prostituting herself for him; she had already prostituted herself to get out of the Soviet Union. The test of her love, instead, is her willingness to go back with him, as she first asserts in New York and reaffirms in their finals words to each other:

> She took a dozen steps. "Will I ever hear from you?" She looked back, her eyes haggard and wet.
>
> "No doubt. Messages get through, right? Times change."
>
> At the gate she stopped again. "How can I leave you?"
>
> "*I* am leaving *you*."

The words "Times change" suggest that there may be for this couple some hope for the future. Most of Smith's mysteries end with some expression of hope of a future together for the mismatched couple.

The relationship between man and animal is further explored in *Gorky Park*, in which the caged sables being smuggled to America become a metaphor for an ironic and perverse sort of freedom. The three murder victims in Gorky Park were caring for and helping to smuggle sables; the victims were living in a shack, their own cage, feeding the other caged victims. Renko considers the pathos in their circumstances as he investigates the crime. In the end, Renko cannot shoot the sables that have been smuggled to America.

Just as he frees Irina Asanova, he ends by freeing the sables, once again meting out justice.

Much loved by readers, Arkady Renko returned in a number of bestselling adventures. Renko is at sea, literally, on a Russian fishing vessel in *Polar Star* (1989), and he explores the seamy underbelly of postcommunist Moscow in *Red Square* (1992). However, the Renko in *Havana Bay* (1999) is a shadow of his former self and intent only on dying. While trying to kill himself, he is attacked and instinctively fights back, only to regret his natural response to self-preservation. When asked to locate an old friend, the reluctant hero travels to Cuba and is immersed in intrigue—enough to keep his suicidal thoughts at bay. The corrupt, burgeoning wealthy class of *Red Square* has fully matured into the uniquely Russian world of oligarchs in *Wolves Eat Dogs* (2004). The apparent suicide of one of these new capitalist princes leads Renko from a pile of salt in the dead man's closet to the dead zone of Chernobyl.

A stickler for research, Smith finds inspiration for his characters and the predicaments in which he sets them in landscapes that resonate with cultural and historical importance. Although Smith has never been at a loss to find ample material in contemporary Russia, he has also set his detectives to work in wartime Japan and Manchuria in *December 6* (2002), in New Mexico for the Manhattan Project in *Stallion Gate*, and in a dismal Victorian mining town in the north of England in *Rose* (1996). Whether writing about a Russian investigator or Gypsy antique dealer, the CIA or the KGB, Los Alamos or Moscow, Smith, dubbed the "master-craftsman of the good read," by Tony Hillerman, continues to deliver in the new millennium.

Janet T. Palmer

Updated by Fiona Kelleghan and Janet Alice Long

Principal mystery and detective fiction

Roman Grey series: *Gypsy in Amber*, 1971; *Canto for a Gypsy*, 1972

Nick Carter series (as Carter): *The Inca Death Squad*, 1972; *The Devil's Dozen*, 1973

Inquisitor series (as Simon Quinn): *The Devil in Kansas*, 1974; *His Eminence, Death*, 1974; *The Last Time I Saw Hell*, 1974; *Nuplex Red*, 1974; *The Human Factor*, 1975; *Last Rites for the Vulture*, 1975; *The Midas Coffin*, 1975

Arkady Renko series: *Gorky Park*, 1981; *Polar Star*, 1989; *Red Square*, 1992; *Havana Bay*, 1999; *Wolves Eat Dogs*, 2004

Nonseries novels: *The Analog Bullet*, 1972; *Code Name: Werewolf*, 1973; *Nightwing*, 1977; *Overture to Death*, 1986; *Stallion Gate*, 1986; *Rose*, 1996; *December 6*, 2002 (also known as *Tokyo Station*)

Other major works

Novels: *The Indians Won*, 1970; *Ride for Revenge*, 1977 (as Logan)

Edited text: *Death by Espionage: Intriguing Stories of Betrayal and Deception*, 1999

Bibliography

"Martin Cruz Smith." *Current Biography* 51 (November, 1990). A well-informed article on Smith as a personality, on the progression of his work, and on the distinctions of his writings.

Ott, Bill. Review of *Stalin's Ghost*, by Martin Cruz Smith. *Booklist* 103, no. 17 (May 1, 2007): 42. Review of Renko series book in which Renko finds himself investigating appearances of Joseph Stalin's ghost in a Moscow subway. Notes that the novels in the series have a theme about the perils of digging.

Smith, Martin Cruz. "Escape: Tales from My Travels—Martin Cruz Smith, Shadows of Chernobyl." Interview by Carl Wilkinson. *The Observer*, April 10, 2005, p. 24. Interview discusses Smith's travels to the Soviet Union in 1973 to research *Gorky Park* and his later visits to Chernobyl.

Wroe, Nicholas. "Saturday Review: Profile—Crime Pays." *The Guardian*, March 26, 2005, p. 20. This substantial profile of Smith looks at his background, how he got started in writing, his early series, his decision to write about the Soviet Union and how his publishers initially were not interested in *Gorky Park*, and his subsequent writing career. Notes how his works about Russia provide a short history of the changes that have taken place in that nation.

STEPHEN SOLOMITA

David Cray

Born: New York, New York; November 29, 1943
Types of plot: Police procedural; private investigator; hard-boiled; thriller; inverted

Principal series

Stanley Moodrow, 1988-
Julia Brennan, 2001-

Principal series characters

Stanley Moodrow is a former New York Police Department officer turned private eye. A large man (six foot six, 250 pounds), Moodrow joined the force during the 1950's and spent thirty-five years as an officer on the Lower East Side before retiring in disgust at the futility of trying to stop crime. A persistent investigator, he still lives in the neighborhood of his former beat with girlfriend Betty Haluka, a feisty Legal Aid lawyer.

Lieutenant Julia Brennan is a detective with Manhattan North Homicide, part of the New York City Police Department. A self-confident, ambitious woman, Julia is essentially a good, proactive person in a tough job, though she acts hardboiled. After dealing all day with mostly male subordinates who are hostile toward a female boss, she often unwinds with her daughter, Corry, and her uncle, Robert Reid.

Contribution

Stephen Solomita has proven to be a prolific and versatile writer since his first mystery novel, *A Twist of the Knife*, featuring police officer (later private eye) Stanley Moodrow, appeared in 1988. His work ranges from the extremely gritty and hard-boiled crime story, such as *Keeplock* (1995), which is told from the point of view of a former convict, to the softer, more traditional mystery, such as *Dead Is Forever* (2004), which concerns the exploits of a wealthy, aristocratic private investigator in the tradition of C. Auguste Dupin or Philo Vance.

A New Yorker through and through, Solomita's particular strength is in depicting the city and its multifarious denizens. He is especially adept at sketching street people—prostitutes, pimps, bums, and other assorted lowlifes—and has an ear well tuned to the rhythm and vocabulary of dialogue as it issues from the mouths of people from the dregs to the pinnacles of society.

A critical favorite among fellow hard-boiled writers, Solomita typically receives positive reviews in both domestic and international venues; however, whether as Solomita or David Cray, he has yet to become a household name among general crime readers. *Forced Entry* (1990), the fourth novel in his Stanley Moodrow series, was selected an Editor's Choice at *Drood Review.* The seventh entry in the series, *Damaged Goods* (1996), was nominated for the Hammett Prize, an award from the North American Branch of the International Association of Crime Writers.

Biography

Stephen E. Solomita was born on November 29, 1943, in New York City and raised with a brother and two sisters in the city's environs. He was the son of auto parts warehouseman Ernest Solomita and commercial artist Evelyn Klein Solomita. An eager reader, during his early teenage years he knew he wanted to be a writer and began publishing essays and stories in the Bayside High School literary magazine and in other periodicals. Following graduation, Solomita attended Queens College in the early 1960's as a literature major but did not graduate. He afterward worked at a variety of jobs, including a stint at his father's warehouse, while occasionally publishing stories and researching subjects of interest that would later figure in his fiction. He was particularly fascinated by the history of the New York Police Department and the criminal justice system.

In 1983, Solomita bought a taxi medallion and drove a cab in New York City for twelve hours per day for several years. This experience allowed him to closely observe passengers, gave him an unparalleled feel for the geography of the city, and provided a plethora of material for his fiction. Fearful that he would end up killing someone or being killed in his dangerous occupation, Solomita quit piloting taxis in favor of the safer, if less secure, task of writing.

Solomita's first mystery was the initial novel in his hard-boiled series focusing on New York City police officer, later private eye, Stanley Moodrow. *A Twist of the Knife* was optioned for a film that was never made. For a number of years, Solomita produced novels in the Moodrow series, the work for which he is probably best known, on an almost yearly basis with such entries as *Force of Nature* (1989), *Bad to the Bone* (1991), and the Hammett Award-nominated *Damaged Goods*. Much of the authentic feel of the series comes from the author's long-standing friendships with active and retired police officers.

In 1995, with the release of the nonseries thriller *Keeplock*—for which Solomita interviewed dozens of former convicts to gain information about the psychology of incarceration—he began publishing novels under the pseudonym David Cray, a pen name intended for work of a slightly less hard-boiled nature, written to accommodate the changing tastes of the reading public. Other novels under the Cray byline include two featuring New York detective Julia Brennan (*Little Girl Blue*, 2002, and *What You Wish For*, 2002), and such nonseries efforts as *Bad Lawyer* (2001) and *Dead Is Forever.*

Solomita has been married twice: His first marriage ended in divorce, and his second wife is deceased. He has one son, now in his thirties. Solomita settled in New York City, near the Lower East Side of Manhattan, an ethnically diverse area with a long and colorful history that figures prominently in much of his fiction.

ANALYSIS

Stephen Solomita knows and obviously has great affection for New York City and its residents. He lovingly describes local landmarks, particularly in his home territory of the Lower East Side, but he is also well versed in the unique qualities of boroughs throughout the sprawling metropolis, from Yonkers to Brooklyn, and from Manhattan to Montauk Point at the eastern extreme of Long Island. Solomita understands the pulse of the city whether detailing rush-hour traffic jams or late-night parties.

Solomita's characters range across the social scale, but he holds a particular fondness for ordinary people: hardworking shopkeepers, cynical bartenders, and crime-weary police officers. His heroes and villains are drawn from all ethnic types—haughty white people, devout Orthodox Jews, rapping African Americans, Italian restaurateurs, Irish toughs, and Russian mobsters. Characters, particularly in Moodrow novels, speak an authentic patois, full of ungrammatical street slang, crude humor, and profanity, sprinkled with colorful expressions in native tongues.

Plots in Solomita's novels cover the full gamut of criminal behavior: rape, murder, kidnapping, drug dealing, and spousal and child abuse. Thematically, the author is an advocate for law and order. Crimes—often shown to be the result of bad upbringing, the pressures of society, unfair happenstance, or just plain evil lurking in the hearts of men and women—typically do not go unpunished.

Stylistically, Solomita writes straightforward prose without much reliance on literary devices; his characters carry the story. While there is occasional humor, mostly in the form of salty exchanges, and now and then a simile to fix an image in the reader's mind, the narrative usually moves forward without many side trips. Most of his works are written in third person. In structure, they typically begin with a dramatic incident or a crisis situation that sets the story in motion, and Solomita is skilled at inventing obstacles for protagonists that increase anxiety and tighten suspense. Although the majority of his work is decidedly hard-boiled, especially the Moodrow series and nonseries novels like *Keeplock*, the author is not afraid to experiment with a lighter tone, as in *Dead Is Forever.* Solomita's best novels are those closest to his own first-hand knowledge—which portray the sights, sounds, and smells of the street while they deal with crimes that affect the reader at gut level.

BAD TO THE BONE

In *Bad to the Bone*, Connie Alamare, a wealthy romance novelist, hires private eye Stanley Moodrow to investigate the circumstances behind the comatose condition of her daughter Florence "Flo" Alamare and to retrieve her grandson. Flo was a bonding mother to children—including her own son, Billy—born at a

Lower East Side pseudo-religious cult and commune called Hanover House. The commune, under the leadership of sinister Davis Craddock, on the surface is an organization that remolds society's misfits into productive citizens. However, it is actually a front for the distribution of a new, potentially lethal designer drug called PURE, which is ten times as addictive as heroin. In the course of setting up and protecting the clandestine drug operation, Craddock and his minions resort to kidnapping, sexual orgies, child abuse, and murder. Once the manufacture and distribution of PURE is under way, Craddock intends to take the millions gained from the sale of the drug and flee to South America.

Using resources from his lifetime of law enforcement and relying on his former partner Jim Tilley for inside information, Moodrow probes for legal weak spots in the commune's defenses and slowly closes in on Craddock. Tension mounts as Moodrow's girlfriend, Betty Haluka, goes underground as a potential commune member at Hanover House, is exposed, and is held for ransom.

Told in third person from several points of view, including that of villain Craddock (who keeps a journal of his misdeeds), *Bad to the Bone* begins slowly as setting, characters, and situation are established. Suspense builds inexorably and the pace quickens to an exciting, white-knuckle finale.

Keeplock

A tough-as-nails nonseries novel, *Keeplock* is a first-person story of career criminal and longtime drug user Peter Frangello, now in his late thirties and newly released on parole from the maximum-security Cortlandt Correctional Facility.

Unwilling to do more time after narrowly avoiding a nasty assassination attempt, Frangello is buffeted between several powerful forces. The parole system places him in a halfway house in a run-down area of New York City, where he is surrounded by criminal temptations. A group of former inmates enlists him to participate in a supposedly foolproof armored car robbery, planned to coincide with the pope's visit so police forces will be preoccupied with security issues. A pair of detectives of questionable morality browbeat the former convict into snitching on his prison buddies so that the lawmen can prevent the planned crime and win accolades. A former girlfriend humiliated by being imprisoned in association with the crime that led to Frangello's most recent incarceration—a robbery during which he stole a ring that he gave to her—still has feelings for her man. Peter himself is torn by contradictory emotions: He wants to go straight, but after a lifetime of crime, fears he is too set in his ways to ever change.

Profane and violent, hard-boiled and unforgiving, *Keeplock* is populated with a cast of well-drawn characters who speak the language of the streets. As complications mount, Peter twists and turns among loyalties to his prison mates, to his girlfriend, and to himself, and the tension ratchets up as the moment for the heist draws closer. Will he go through with the robbery, thereby risking death? Will he betray his buddies and incur their vengeance? Will the police keep their promises? Will Peter survive against impossible odds? A fast-paced thriller that examines many facets of criminal behavior under a microscope, *Keeplock* has the ring of absolute authenticity.

Bad Lawyer

In *Bad Lawyer*, former mob lawyer Sid Kaplan has fallen from the heights, thanks to alcohol and drug addiction, and after a year of rehabilitation is piecing his life and practice together. With the assistance of alcoholic former police officer Caleb Talbot and former prostitute and heroin addict Julia Gill—two people Kaplan rescued on his way up—the lawyer takes on a new case. Priscilla "Prissy" Sweet has been accused of the murder of her abusive, drug-dealing African American husband, Byron, a crime that causes a sensation in the New York media because of its interracial nature and practically guarantees Kaplan new business, if he can get the woman off. However, Kaplan, who despite his past history has a strong moral sense, is not sure Priscilla should be set free, because she has lied about a number of key points. Worse, her lies concerning a suitcase full of drug money set vicious dealers on the people to whom Kaplan is closest, initiating a wave of violence that leaves death and destruction in its wake.

A hard-boiled courtroom procedural in first person, *Bad Lawyer* is populated with Solomita's usual cast of unusual, true-to-life, morally ambiguous characters. The novel provides intriguing, authentic insights into the workings of the justice system and portrays the media as vulturelike, greedy for details to feed to the masses of readers held in thrall by bloody crimes.

Dead Is Forever

Despite its noir-themed title, *Dead Is Forever* is more soft- than hard-boiled. Protagonist Philip Beckett is a wealthy wastrel, the scion of a multimillionaire industrialist, and a product of Choate, Harvard, and the Wharton School of Business. In his early thirties, of average height and weight, and inconspicuous except for the expensive clothing he invariably wears, Philip has turned his back on the family business. Philip, who survives mainly on a trust fund, worked for a security company before becoming a licensed private eye, and for large fees, he performs discreet services for upper-class clients.

In *Dead Is Forever*, Philip's cold-hearted, ambitious sister Regina hires the dilettante private eye to investigate a family affair. Their chubby, homely cousin Audrey is married to a charming but destitute Italian count, Sergio D'Alesse, who has a gambling problem: He is forty thousand dollars in arrears to con man Gaetano Carollo, known as "Gentleman John" Carroll, and the Beckett family refuses to bail him out of debt any longer. Philip investigates, and complications ensue, including the murder of Count D'Alesse, which precipitates several other offstage murders.

Dead Is Forever is an odd novel: too hard-edged to be called a cozy but too rose-tinted, thanks to the hero's book-long affair with corporate lawyer Magdalena "Maggie" Santos, to be categorized as a thriller. Told in first person and populated with Solomita's typical cast of intriguing secondary characters from the seedy side of the street, the novel has few outright action sequences between long, involved scenes in which dialogue dominates. The complicated plot requires some knowledge of the stock market and legal issues. The denouement is reminiscent of traditional mysteries, where the detective gathers primary suspects in the drawing room to eliminate them one by one before naming the culprit. Although Solomita may be credited for his innovation in attempting to blend various subgenres into a unified whole, the ultimate effect is a failed experiment that is neither clue-laden enough to please traditional fans nor tough enough to satisfy noir readers.

Jack Ewing

Principal mystery and detective fiction

Stanley Moodrow series: *A Twist of the Knife*, 1988; *Law According to Moodrow*, 1989; *Force of Nature*, 1989; *Forced Entry*, 1990; *Bad to the Bone*, 1991; *A Piece of the Action*, 1992; *Damaged Goods*, 1996

Julia Brennan series (as Cray): *Little Girl Blue*, 2002; *What You Wish For*, 2002

Other major works

Novels: *A Good Day To Die*, 1993; *Last Chance for Glory*, 1994; *Keeplock*, 1995 (as Cray); *Poster Boy*, 1998; *Trick Me Twice*, 1998; *No Control*, 1999; *Bad Lawyer*, 2001 (as Cray); *Partners*, 2004 (as Cray); *Dead Is Forever*, 2004 (as Cray)

Bibliography

Fletcher, Connie. Review of *Little Girl Blue*, by Stephen Solomita. *Booklist* 98, no. 5 (November 1, 2001): 461. This is a favorable review of a Julia Brennan series novel about child slavery and pedophilia. The critic praises the accuracy of procedural details and plot twists, and Solomita's ability to show the human side of a professional police officer.

Kirkus Reviews. Review of *Bad Lawyer*, by Stephen Solomita. 68, no. 23 (December 1, 2000): 1631. A favorable review in which the critic notes that the story concerning the efforts of fallen lawyer Sid Kaplan and his assistants to defend accused murderer Priscilla Sweet is "refreshing" and "unsentimental."

Needham, George. Review of *Keeplock*, by Stephen Solomita. *Booklist* 91, no. 10 (January 15, 1996): 898. In this favorable review, the critic mentions that the title is a prison term referring to a convict locked in a cell all day and notes that the novel's finale is reminiscent of the ending of the 1932 Paul Muni film *I Am a Fugitive from a Chain Gang*.

Publishers Weekly. Review of *Damaged Goods*, by

Stephen Solomita. 242, no. 47 (November 20, 1995): 68. This is a favorable review of the sixth Moodrow novel, in which the detective, now past sixty years of age, is hired to find a kidnapped four-year-old girl. The critic called the novel "piercing urban melancholy."

Stastio, Marilyn. "Crime: A Twist of the Knife." Review of *A Twist of the Knife*, by Stephen Solomita. *The New York Times Book Review*, December 11, 1988, p. 34. This is a mostly favorable review of Solomita's first published novel, which introduces Stanley Moodrow. While the author is praised for his relentless plot—which involves the detective tracking down terrorists who killed his girlfriend—the critic cautions about the extreme violence.

Wilkins, Mary Frances. Review of *What You Wish For*, by Stephen Solomita. *Booklist* 99, no. 8 (December 15, 2002): 737. This favorable review of *What You Wish For* mentions the plot—a Brennan investigation into the death of an aging, wealthy woman while the lieutenant pursues a relationship with a former police officer—and praises the gritty story in which it is difficult to tell heroes from the villains.

MICKEY SPILLANE

Frank Morrison Spillane

Born: Brooklyn, New York; March 9, 1918
Died: Murrells Inlet, South Carolina; July 17, 2006
Types of plot: Hard-boiled; private investigator

Principal series

Mike Hammer, 1947-1984
Tiger Mann, 1964-1966

Principal series characters

Mike Hammer, a New York City private investigator, is in his mid-twenties and has just returned from World War II as the series opens. Thereafter, he ages gradually to about forty. Irresistible to sexually aggressive women, he remains unmarried. Tough, crusading, and violent, with a simplistic personal sense of justice, he pursues murderers and the organizations shielding them on their own ground and with their own tactics.

Velda, Hammer's sexy secretary, is also a private investigator. She serves as his surrogate mother and mistress and is one of the few people whom he loves and trusts.

Captain Patrick Chambers, a New York City homicide detective, is a foil for Hammer as well as a friend who, though bound to rules and regulations, understands and generally assists him.

Contribution

Mickey Spillane was a phenomenon of popular culture. His twenty-three novels, particularly the Mike Hammer titles, had international sales of more than 225 million copies. Of the top ten best-selling fictional works published between 1920 and 1980, seven were Spillane's, and in the detective-fiction genre few have exceeded his sales. Spillane can attribute part of his popularity to having created in Mike Hammer the quintessential avenger-crusader. Criminal cases in which Hammer becomes involved are personal. Usually the slaying of an old buddy or of a small-timer whom he has encountered and liked prompts him to saddle up, lock, and load. His vengeance is violent, direct, and—compared to that dispensed by the courts—swift. A raw, hangman's justice is realized—illegally, but not without some assistance from the law. Readers are also treated to whole squads of sexually uninhibited women who find Hammer, or his counterparts in other books, Tiger Mann or Gillian Burke, irresistible.

The appeal of Spillane's novels lies in their blunt-force narration, the hero's direct assault on his enemies, and sexual encounters that were, in their time, shocking for their brutishness and frequency. Spillane's loose plotting, scant characterizations, and vio-

Mickey Spillane at his home in 2001. (AP/Wide World Photos)

lent resolutions have a comic book's color and directness, allowing readers to vicariously indulge in personally exacting justice without the niceties of due process. He popularized pulp fiction in a way it had not been popularized previously, in fact almost single-handedly driving the phenomenal growth of the paperback original and gaining an audience that included those who did not generally read books and those who read lots of books—they all read Mickey Spillane.

Biography

Mickey Spillane was born Frank Morrison Spillane on March 9, 1918, in Brooklyn, New York, the son of an Irish bartender. He grew up, by his own report, in one of the tougher neighborhoods of Elizabeth, New Jersey. Little is known about his early schooling. In the mid-1930's he attended Kansas State College, hoping eventually to study law. During the summers, he was captain of the lifeguards at Breezy Point, Long Island.

In 1935, when Spillane was seventeen years of age, he began selling stories to the pulps. He was able to pay his college tuition by writing for radio and by writing comic books. (He claimed to have been one of the originators of the Captain Marvel and Captain America comics, which enjoyed enormous popularity in the 1930's and 1940's.) During World War II, he served in the United States Army Air Force, training cadets and in time flying fighter missions. After the war, he briefly worked as a trampoline artist for Barnum and Bailey's circus.

Spillane's success as a writer really began in 1947, with the publication of what remains his most popular book, *I, the Jury.* In 1952, after publishing half a dozen additional titles, he was converted to the Jehovah's Witnesses. Almost a decade passed before the release of *The Deep* (1961), considered by many to be his finest novel. His last book, *Black Alley* (1996) concluded a half-century-long career. Though Spillane wrote his books in a matter of weeks, or even days, and only when he needed money (a claim intended to deflect criticism with perfect indifference), he could never be accused of "cranking them out"; he wrote fewer than twenty-five novels in fifty years, a relatively modest number for a writer in this genre, and always managed to infuse the formula with the vitality of a righteous and unrestrained rage and a wildly original outcome.

Divorced from his first wife, Spillane married a woman much his junior, Sherri Malinou—a model whom he had met when she posed for the cover of one of his books—in 1965. Along with producer Robert Fellows, Spillane formed an independent film company in Nashville, Tennessee, in 1969 for the filming of features and television productions, while continuing his other writing. Mike Hammer's adventures were depicted in several films of the 1950's, as well as in a television series. Spillane cowrote the screenplay for—and even starred as Mike Hammer in—*The Girl Hunters*, a 1963 film. Later incarnations of Mike Hammer have included a syndicated television series.

Spillane received the lifetime achievement award from the Private Eye Writers of America in 1983 and the Edgar Allan Poe Grand Master award from the Mystery Writers of America in 1995—almost fifty years after the publication of *I, the Jury.* The belated award came near the end of a lifetime of blithely dismissing critics, who for decades had been practically unanimous in disparaging Spillane's artless, primary-palette prose. He routinely neutralized vitriolic reviews by pigeonholing his own work as "chewing gum" fiction and "garbage, but good garbage," and deferring to American taste as evidenced by his royalty checks.

Spillane remarried in 1983, to Jane Rodgers Johnson. He moved to Murrell's Inlet, South Carolina, in 1954. Though his home for more than thirty years was destroyed by Hurricane Hugo in 1989, he remained a resident in that beach town until his death from pancreatic cancer in 2006.

Analysis

Those critics who did not dismiss Mickey Spillane out of hand generally reacted to him caustically. It has been pointed out that his novels debase women, reducing them to sex objects, and frequently evil ones at that. Spillane's handling of sex, stripped of any tenderness, intimacy, or romance, was perceived by many to be pornographic. The violence and gore hurled at the reader have been condemned as gratuitous and revolting. His plots have been deemed shaky, his characterizations thin, his dialogue wooden. In sum, by these criteria, comparisons with the classic writers in his field—Dashiell Hammett, Raymond Chandler, or Ross Macdonald—simply fail.

Nevertheless, Spillane's novels entertain with a frankness and a ferocity that only a literary killjoy could fail to appreciate. They do so without lengthy setups, lyrical embroidery, or brainteasers. They play on basic human instincts and prejudices, the kind of soldier's rage that results in atrocity in the real world but finds its deserving target unfailingly in the unstoppable force of Mike Hammer. What Spillane's novels lack in craftsmanship, they amply make up for in vitality.

The Mike Hammer series

Mike Hammer is a tough private eye, a loner who before the bottom of page 2 in any volume of the series is confronted with a killing that has personal meaning to him. In *I, the Jury*, Hammer's wartime buddy and best friend, Jack Williams, has been shot by a .45 and left to die slowly, crawling before his executioner. In *Vengeance Is Mine!* (1950), Chester Wheeler, Hammer's casual drinking companion, is murdered while he and Hammer, dead drunk, share the same bed. In *Survival . . . Zero!* (1970), Lippy Sullivan, a petty pickpocket whom Hammer knew, calls him while dying with a knife in his back. Such murders invariably launch Hammer's personal crusade to locate the slayer and avenge the death.

The ubiquitous Captain Patrick Chambers, Hammer's detective friend and sometime backup, always warns Hammer to stay off the case, taking the role of society's spokesperson calling for an orderly investigation within the law. The rules are stated, however, only to alert the reader to the fact that they are about to be broken. Soon Pat and Hammer, in leapfrog fashion, are finding and sharing clues. Pat genuinely sympathizes with Hammer and uses him to advance the case in the hope of reaching the culprit before Hammer does, but his actions are implicit acknowledgment that corruption, bureaucratic mismanagement, and public apathy make true justice impossible to attain except outside the law.

As the pursuit progresses, Hammer uncovers (and dispatches) a ring of conspirators—"a meal," Hammer calls it, and the killer "dessert." In *One Lonely Night* (1951), Hammer seeks a killer who is linked to the Communist Party of America; in *Kiss Me, Deadly* (1952), the Mafia lurks, pulling the strings. In *The Girl Hunters* (1962), the killer's shield is an international terrorist organization, as it is also in *Survival . . . Zero!* In *The Big Kill* (1951), Hammer stands against an extensive blackmail ring.

An antiorganizational, antiauthoritarian bias is only one of many prejudices that are expressed by Hammer (or Johnny McBride, Tiger Mann, or Gill Burke). Hammer detests New York City, "fat, greasy" lecherous businessmen, "queers," "Commies," district attorneys, the Federal Bureau of Investigation (FBI), counterespionage agencies, pimps, punks, hoods, drug dealers, modern robber barons, most police officials, and skinny women. He is a bundle of postwar suspicions and hatreds. He is a veteran (one suspects a case of post-traumatic stress, a disorder familiar to but unnamed by Spillane's early readers), with a deep respect for bravery, kindness, and loyalty—qualities that tend to get people killed in Hammer's world.

In pursuit of his enemies, Hammer (and Spillane's other heroes) becomes a one-man war wagon, armed with Old Testament injunctions—particularly "an eye for an eye, a tooth for a tooth." In *One Lonely Night* his urge to kill is so powerful that a terrified woman whom he has rescued from a rapist leaps off a bridge to her death after she sees the lust for killing in his face. Later, in the same book, he butchers a number of political radicals with an FBI machine gun. With his "rod," he lays open the jaw of another enemy, breaks his teeth, and kicks them down his throat. In *My Gun Is Quick* (1950), he takes Feeney Last's head "like a sodden rag and smashed and smashed and smashed and there was no satisfying, solid thump, but a sickening squashing sound that splashed all over me." The greatest cruelties are reserved for prime objects of Hammer's revenge. Unlike the hero avengers in the detective fiction of Chandler and Hammett, who generally leave final vengeance to the cops or to the intervention of fate, Spillane's avengers attend personally to their usually grisly executions. Thus, William Dorn and Renee Talmadge, the principal villains of *Survival . . . Zero!*, their backs against the wall, are persuaded by Hammer that he is going to blow them away with his trademark .45. The prospect terrifies them into swallowing cyanide capsules—only to be shown by a jeering Hammer that his gun is empty. Berin-Grotin, the villainous head of a prostitution ring in *Vengeance Is Mine!*, finally trapped beneath a burning beam and painfully being consumed by the fire, is told that as soon as a fireman comes through the window to rescue him—if he is not already dead by then—Hammer will blow his head off. Hammer's dispatching in *I, the Jury* of Charlotte Manning, the gorgeous psychiatrist turned dope-ring leader and the slayer of his best friend, is classic. Cornered at last, she strips naked to distract him from the murder weapon nearby. Once in love with her, now unmoved, he shoots her in the belly.

> Pain and unbelief.
>
> "How c-could you?" she gasped.
>
> I had only a moment before talking to a corpse, but I got it in.
>
> "It was easy," I said.

Women and sex

The myriad women encountered by Hammer in the course of his crusades are invariably busty, leggy, gorgeous, and sexually well-primed. Though he is described as scarred and ugly, Hammer's wild brown-green Irish eyes and his air of violence and power prove overwhelmingly attractive to a parade of beautiful women. Spillane depicts for his readers a continuous striptease, a procession of women putting on and taking off clothes, lounging in provocative poses, and making themselves utterly available to Hammer. Yet the stereotyping of female sexual displays and the movement of voluptuous women in and out of Hammer's range are less important than Spillane's reliance—as humanist critic John Cawelti suggests—on violence for his chief stimulus. It is the imminent capacity of Spillane's heroes for violence, after all, not

Mickey Spillane was often accused of depicting women as sex objects in his books.

their looks or lines, that attracts women in the first place: the same deadliness that terrifies the villains.

Spillane's crusaders, in any event, are usually ambivalent about women. His female characters are either sex objects—prostitutes, lovers, or temptresses or, like Velda, alternately jealous and tolerant aides-de-camp. There is no way of knowing whether Spillane purposefully pandered to certain audiences with what many critics consider his chauvinism and degradation of women. There is no doubt, however, that the "manly" behavior of his protagonists—and the preening vanity of his villains—reflected one widespread view of men's relations with women.

Period pieces

In comparison to many late twentieth century best sellers, with their anatomization of sex and liberal use of crude, graphic language, Spillane seems almost quaint. Profanity is fairly rare in his works; sex is not comparably explicit. Drugs do not constitute an amusing recreation; indeed, they are treated as debilitating, ultimately deadly (although there is cultural acceptance of drinking and smoking). Written for the adult postwar generation, Spillane's novels are now period pieces. Mike Hammer, for example, is often short of "dough," "jack," or "long green." He "packs" a "rod" and drives a "jalopey." For him and other of Spillane's avengers, the "monikers" assigned to women are "girlie," "sugar pie," "broad," "babe," "kitten," "pet," and "kid." Hard-boiled as they are, they say "wow," "swell," "yup," "bub," "boy oh boy," "okeydoke," "jeez," and "pal." "Punks" get "plugged" or "bumped off" with "slugs" before they are "dumped." In this, he is not so different from Hammett or Chandler. Spillane, however, continued writing into the 1990's with few concessions to the contemporary sense of cultural verisimilitude. In *Black Alley*, Hammer was still calling people "kid."

Black Alley

Time, however, can force certain concessions even from Mike Hammer. The catalyst for action in *Black Alley*, Spillane's last novel, as in *I, the Jury*, his first, is the murder of an old army buddy. Though the formula is essentially the same, the hard-boiled hero has mellowed just a bit: He admits to liking Richard Wagner's music and confesses to Velda that she's the one. In addition, his usual methods are hampered by the fact that he has been seriously wounded. No longer able to beat things out of people, he must actually follow clues. Moreover, on doctor's orders, he cannot consummate his relationship with Velda. Many fans were disappointed that the aging private investigator (a quick finger count puts Mike and Velda in their seventies) was finally slowed by a mere gunshot to the chest.

By the time of Spillane's death, critical reaction to his work was warming. His enormous influence on the genre and on the publishing industry was being recognized, and the taint of "popular taste" was wearing off. Spillane's style, which Hammett and others had perceived as uncraftsmanlike, was in fact perfectly suited to the first-person narration of the brutish, artless Mike Hammer. Sam Spade might have paused for the *mot juste*, but for Mike, "squash," "smash," and "thump" were good enough. The British *Guardian* newspaper (without a whiff of condescension) asserted in its obituary of Spillane that, despite having long lost the ability to shock, he was nevertheless the best-selling novelist of the twentieth century.

Clifton K. Yearley
Updated by Fiona Kelleghan, Jessica Reisman, and Janet Alice Long

Principal mystery and detective fiction

Mike Hammer series: *I, the Jury*, 1947; *My Gun Is Quick*, 1950; *Vengeance Is Mine!*, 1950; *One Lonely Night*, 1951; *The Big Kill*, 1951; *Kiss Me, Deadly*, 1952; *The Girl Hunters*, 1962; *The Snake*, 1964; *The Twisted Thing*, 1966; *The Body Lovers*, 1967; *Survival . . . Zero!*, 1970; *Mike Hammer: The Comic Strip*, 1982-1984; *The Killing Man*, 1989; *Black Alley*, 1996; *The Mike Hammer Collection*, 2001 (2 volumes)

Tiger Mann series: *Day of the Guns*, 1964; *Bloody Sunrise*, 1965; *The Death Dealers*, 1965; *The By-Pass Control*, 1967

Nonseries novels: *The Long Wait*, 1951; *The Deep*, 1961; *The Delta Factor*, 1967; *The Erection Set*, 1972; *The Last Cop Out*, 1973; *Something's Down There*, 2003

Short fiction: *Me, Hood!*, 1963; *Return of the Hood*, 1964; *The Flier*, 1964; *Killer Mine*, 1965; *The Tough Guys*, 1969; *Tomorrow I Die*, 1984; *Together We Kill*, 2001; *Primal Spillane*, 2003

Other major works

Screenplay: *The Girl Hunters*, 1963 (adaptation of his novel; with Roy Rowland and Robert Fellows)

Children's literature: *The Day the Sea Rolled Back*, 1979; *The Ship That Never Was*, 1982

Edited texts: *Murder Is My Business*, 1994 (with Max Allen Collins); *A Century of Noir: Thirty-two Classic Crime Stories*, 2002 (with Collins)

Miscellaneous: *Byline: Mickey Spillane*, 2004 (Max Allan Collins and Lynn F. Myers, Jr., editors)

Bibliography

Collins, Max Allan, and James L. Traylor. *One Lonely Knight: Mickey Spillane's Mike Hammer.* Bowling Green, Ohio: Bowling Green State University Popular Press, 1984. Discusses Hammer's controversial appeal in detail. Collins was an early champion of Spillane and has done much to rehabilitate the author's critical reputation.

Haut, Woody. *Pulp Culture: Hardboiled Fiction and the Cold War.* New York: Serpent's Tail, 1995. Discusses Spillane's antileftist appeal. This somewhat older work supplements the more recent *Gumshoe America*.

Knight, Stephen. *Crime Fiction, 1800-2000: Detection, Death, Diversity.* New York: Palgrave Macmillan, 2004. Spillane receives considerable attention in Knight's chapter "The American Version," in which he describes the influence of the pulps and early hard-boiled detective fiction on the genre.

McCann, Sean. *Gumshoe America: Hard-Boiled Crime Fiction and the Rise and Fall of New Deal Liberalism*. Durham, N.C.: Duke University Press, 2000. Places Spillane amid sociopolitical movements democratizing but degenerating American culture. Hammer is seen as embodying American rugged individualism at a time when patriotism and hard justice were being subverted by liberalism.

McLellan, Dennis. "Mickey Spillane, 1918-2006: A Simple Plot—Violence, Sex, and Royalty Checks." *Los Angeles Times*, July 18, 2006, p. A1. Obituary of Spillane looks at his background and early comic book writing and traces his evolution as a writer. Notes his reported indifference to critics and his devotion to his fans. Although he reportedly was a tough guy when young, Spillane's conversion to the Jehovah's Witness faith made him a much mellower man.

"Mickey Spillane." *The Times*, July 19, 2006, p. 55. This obituary of Spillane discusses his immense popularity and his lack of critical acclaim. Covers his background, his motivation to write, his speed of writing, and his divorces.

Priestman, Martin. *The Cambridge Companion to Crime Fiction*. New York: Cambridge University Press, 2003. Devotes a full chapter to the private eye. Hammer is described as "unidimensional" and a product of Cold War ideology.

Scaggs, John. *Crime Fiction*. New York: Routledge, 2005. Contrasts Mike Hammer with other private eyes of the period, particularly Philip Marlowe. Scaggs calls Hammer one of the "anti-intellectual" private-eye heroes, able to inflict and endure incredible physical punishment, and compares the urban setting of such characters with the lawless frontier of the American West.

Spillane, Mickey. *Byline: Mickey Spillane*. Edited by Max Allan Collins and Lynn F. Myers, Jr. New York: Crippen and Landru, 2005. A collection of very early Spillane short pieces. The critical commentary is by Collins and Myers, both longtime champions of Spillane.

MICHELLE SPRING

Born: Vancouver, British Columbia, Canada; 1951
Also wrote as Michelle Stanworth
Types of plot: Private investigator; psychological

Principal series

Laura Principal, 1994-

Principal series character

Laura Principal is a former academic who has become a skilled private investigator with her professional and personal partner, Sonny Mendlowitz. Principal is a strong, intelligent, and independent heroine, who displays feminist leanings yet shows compassion toward the peculiarities of human nature.

Contribution

Michelle Spring began her writing career with *Every Breath You Take* (1994), which introduces Laura Principal as private investigator, and followed it with four other novels that are concerned with Principal's forays into crimes in and around Cambridge, England. Her sixth book, *The Night Lawyer* (2006), a suspense novel, dispenses with Principal and focuses on the efforts of Eleanor Porter to become strong and independent.

Most readers find Spring's Laura Principal series well crafted, readable, and imbued with a strong sense of place. Spring places Principal, a contemporary woman and a former history professor, confidently in Cambridge, where she moves through an intricate plot realistically searching for answers. Her compelling investigations, which make the most of the English countryside in and around Cambridge, have been compared to those of Colin Dexter's Inspector Morse in Oxford. Like Morse, Principal's investigations frequently uncover the dark side of existence beneath a cultured, refined facade.

For her first novel, Spring was nominated and shortlisted for two awards, but for *In the Midnight Hour* (2001), she was awarded the Arthur Ellis award, given by the Crime Writers of Canada for the best novel of the year. She is one of six novelists who make up the Unusual Suspects, a group of mystery writers who entertain audiences in Britain, Canada, the United States, and Europe with their commentaries on crime fiction. Spring was selected by the London *Times* as one of the twentieth century's one hundred masters of crime.

Biography

Michelle Spring was born Michelle Stanworth in Vancouver, British Columbia, Canada, in 1951. She was raised in Victoria on Vancouver Island and began reading Nancy Drew books at the age of six while she was ill with tuberculosis. While she was quarantined in the hospital, Stanworth's father stole up the fire escape with food and books for her to read. When she was eight, she fainted from the pure excitement of reading a mystery, and was forbidden by her mother to read crime stories. However, as an adolescent, her interest in crime deepened with reading the works of authors such as Sir Arthur Conan Doyle, Daphne du Maurier, Shirley Jackson, Dashiell Hammett, and Patricia Highsmith.

In 1969, Spring moved to England, later becoming a professor of sociology at East Anglia University. In her career in the classroom, which spanned more than twenty-five years, she pioneered the somewhat radical investigation (at that time) into the inequity of teaching based on the gender of students. Her investigation revealed that elementary school teachers were more attached to their male students and were more concerned with them and their abilities than they were with their female students. She discussed the findings and implications of her research in a book on gender and schooling. She later authored feminist books about reproductive technologies and political implications, and coauthored an introductory sociology textbook. Spring has also lectured in the social and political sciences at Cambridge University.

While at East Anglia University, Spring had tried repeatedly to write a more serious book but was unable to get started. However, she was stalked by one of her students, who became violent, and soon after, even as she was about to give up the idea of writing, the first chapter of *Every Breath You Take* fairly wrote itself.

Surprised that she was writing a detective novel, she came to understand her need to write about the traumatic stalking episode and her need to write stories as a means of coping with the violence in the world. She wrote *Every Breath You Take* using the name of Michelle Spring and was pressed by her publisher to write a series.

Analysis

Michelle Spring's private detective novel follows the example of Sue Grafton, whose books feature female private investigator Kinsey Millhone, rather than that of hard-boiled writers such as Dashiell Hammett and Raymond Chandler. Spring's writing is more "soft-boiled," and her series' main character, Laura Principal, a former academic turned private investigator, runs Aardvark Investigations with her professional and personal partner, Sonny Mendlowitz. Mendlowitz is in charge of the London office, while Principal runs the Cambridge branch.

In many ways, Principal is a woman of the 1990's in that she struggles to balance her life between sleuthing and spending time with her long-time friend, librarian Helen Cochrane, and her lover Mendlowitz, who has two young sons. Principal, an intense and thorough investigator, and Cochrane are co-owners of Wildfell Cottage, a remote spot the two visit occasionally on weekends to wind down from work. She shares a flat with Mendlowitz when in London, and he frequently visits her flat in Cambridge. She plays the saxophone, exercises regularly, and is in good condition.

Laura Principal is not based on any individual nor on Spring herself. Principal is athletic, is an excellent driver, and is fairly capable of taking care of herself. Spring has carefully created an admirable female private investigator who is seldom judgmental, is unwilling to jump to conclusions, and whose generous spirit allows her to look for the good in everyone.

Every Breath You Take

Spring's first novel, *Every Breath You Take*, introduces Laura Principal, who investigates the murder of art teacher Monica Harcourt, who had bought a third-part ownership of Wildfell but was bludgeoned to death before she could move in. Principal sifts through possible motivations of those who knew Harcourt and finds none. As she perceives the villain is a man who had stalked Harcourt, she understands the danger she and Cochrane are in because of their friendship with Harcourt. Harcourt was killed by an unstable man who had erroneously presumed her to be a lesbian.

Principal is a well-developed character who lures the reader in to discover her thoughts and inclinations as she conducts her investigation. Essentially an introduction to Principal, the first-person narrative provides insight into Principal's mind, her values, and her past, particularly the protracted painful period during her father's slow death that continues to haunt her.

The story of a stalker, *Every Breath You Take* progresses through Principal's tracking and confronting suspects about histories, alibis, or secrets as she places her own life in danger through her doggedness in following clues or her instincts. Although she ferrets out suspects who appear to be the stalker/killer, the villain turns out to be an unsuspected and unknown person, with the chilling undertone being maintained until the very end.

Running for Shelter

Spring's second novel in the series, *Running for Shelter* (1996), moves between the decadent, London rich and the illegal migrant workers who exist in near forced-slavery conditions. A West End producer who has hired Principal to solve a series of backstage thefts inadvertently introduces her to Maria Flores, a Filipina domestic who asks for Principal's help in collecting money owed her by a former employer. When Flores goes missing and the producer denies any knowledge of her, Principal becomes embroiled in the cruelty and violence dealt the undocumented workers who live in the posh homes of the rich.

Spring's meticulously plotted story carries readers along with Principal's observations and speculations as well as the opportunity to explore treatment of migrant workers afforded her by the search for the missing girl. Principal's character becomes honed with each additional novel; Spring shapes her to be a person whom readers can admire or emulate. Spring is committed to the inclusion of social problems in each book and usually focuses on the dark underside of the lives of privileged persons.

Nights in White Satin

Spring's third detective novel, *Nights in White Satin* (1999), pursues the subject of prostitution at Cambridge and college girls who sometimes become enmeshed in it. The work reflects Spring's knowledge of the history of prostitution in Cambridge in the nineteenth century and the antagonism it generated between the university and the town and more specifically the dark side still present underneath the genteel exterior.

Aardvark Investigations is enlisted to provide security for the May Ball at St. Johns College, and Principal is later hired to find a missing student who was last seen at the ball. The situation is soon complicated by the death of the senior tutor, whose head is shattered by a cricket bat, shortly after he suggests to Principal that the missing student may have been entangled in prostitution.

Nights in White Satin is Spring's most complex book, as it takes many plot twists while sustaining facts about the victim as well as the police investigation and maintaining suspense that keeps readers interested. The book has a layered feel in that it explores relationships between academic and town elements that involve economic standing and generational differences. The book also has a ghostly aspect in that Cambridge's past is interwoven with the plot to ensure connections between the past and present.

In the Midnight Hour

Spring's fifth entry in the series, *In the Midnight Hour,* concerns a famous explorer and his wife who visit Principal's house asking, "Have you ever lost a child?" They proceed to engage her to discover if the sixteen-year-old musician they have befriended is indeed their son, who disappeared on a beach at the age of four. However, Principal is instructed by the father that she should not "heavy" the young man and should only look into his background.

During the course of the investigation, Principal becomes friends with all members of the household, meaning, of course, that they all become suspects at one time or another. The large family provides various plot complications as Spring's menacing undertone reaches a level as distinct as the family's emotional violence. Also, as the bleak landscape of the English north Norfolk coast reflects a pain that has never disappeared, the psychological suspense continues until the last shred of mystery is coaxed out.

In the Midnight Hour explores the unrelieved agony of parents whose child has disappeared and the corrosive secrets each family member has harbored for years. Spring moves toward the discovery of a destructive pattern of abuse with a confidence that belies her own preoccupation with her father's death.

The Night Lawyer

In *The Night Lawyer,* Spring created a nonseries book about the efforts of Eleanor Porter to become a calm, strong, invulnerable person. Recovering from a breakdown because of dependency on her married lover who opted to stay with his wife, she has lost weight, joined a karate club, moved into her own house, and taken a job as a night lawyer who ensures the validity of the articles printed in the paper.

Porter is a petite woman who has turned to karate to keep fear at bay. The fierceness with which she throws herself into fitness training, her work, and her activities is all aimed at quelling painful memories of having accidentally killed her father years ago. However, Porter becomes aware that she is being stalked, is methodically bullied by her neighbor's boyfriend and his thug buddies, and finds herself being drawn back into her married lover's latest ruse—and throughout, she is fighting desperately against her vulnerability.

Spring excels at depicting the creepy feeling of Porter being watched and her private space being violated. She describes Porter's house being broken into, her bed being slept in, her sense of an unseen presence in her garden, and the prickly sensation up her spine when she briefly glimpses her stalker. Spring recounts the deadening fear Porter endures while walking home alone from work late at night. Little by little, Spring escalates the suspense, pushing Porter closer to the edge of insanity until the final showdown.

Mary G. Hurd

Principal mystery and detective fiction

Laura Principal series: *Every Breath You Take*, 1994; *Running for Shelter,* 1996; *Standing in the Shadows*, 1998; *Nights in White Satin*, 1999; *In the Midnight Hour,* 2001

Nonseries novels: *The Night Lawyer,* 2006

Other major works

Nonfiction (as Stanworth):

Gender and Schooling: A Study of Sexual Divisions in the Classroom, 1981; *Women and The Public Sphere: A Critique of Sociology and Politics*, 1984 (with Japanet Siltanen); *Reproductive Technologies: Gender, Motherhood and Medicine (Feminist Perspectives)*, 1987; *Introductory Sociology*, 2002 (with others)

Bibliography

Beard, Mary. Review of *Nights in White Satin*, by Michelle Spring. *Times Literary Supplement*, July 16, 1999, p. 23. Beard compares Spring's novel of Cambridge's scandalous decadence with the depiction of Oxford's "dispassionate" quality by Colin Dexter (creator of Inspector Morse) and finds her lacking.

Block, Allison. Review of *The Night Lawyer*, by Michelle Spring. *Booklist* 103, no. 2 (September 15, 2005): 33. Review praises Spring for her characterization, particularly of Eleanor Porter, but criticizes the lack of suspense.

Dubose, Martha Hailey, with Margaret Caldwell Thomas. *Women of Mystery: The Lives and Works of Notable Women Crime Novelists*. New York: St. Martin's Minotaur, 2000. Provides information on more than one hundred women writers, with especially good coverage of Patricia Highsmith, whom Spring admires.

Klett, Rex E. Review of *Every Breath You Take*, by Michelle Spring. *Library Journal* 199, no. 4 (March 1, 1994): 123. Brief article, interesting because of its sharp criticism of Spring's narrative and faulty plot construction.

Stazio, Marilyn. "Crime." Review of *Nights in White Satin*, by Michelle Spring. *The New York Times Book Review*, July 11, 1999, p. 29. Stazio's review praises Spring's ability to use a beautiful setting that conceals an ugly interior.

Unusual Suspects. The Unusual Suspects. http://www.unusualsuspects.co.uk. Web site maintained by crime writers in the Unusual Suspects, of which Spring is a member. She discusses her beginning as a writer, her main character, Principal, and the development of her plots.

DANA STABENOW

Born: Anchorage, Alaska; March 27, 1952
Types of plot: Police procedural; private investigator; thriller

Principal series

Kate Shugak, 1992-
Liam Campbell, 1998-

Principal series characters

Kate Shugak is a five-foot-tall Aleut who was once an investigator for the Anchorage district attorney's office. When the series starts, she lives in a cabin without electricity or running water on a 160-acre homestead in a fictional national park based on Wrangell-St. Elias National Park in Alaska. She inherited the place from her parents, and her only companion is Mutt, a female half-wolf, half-husky. Her acquaintances, friends, and lovers include miners, hunters, trappers, fishermen, bush pilots, park rangers, police officers, and petty criminals. She has relatives nearby but prefers to avoid them.

Liam Campbell is an Alaska state police officer. Although he was an Air Force brat, he is afraid of flying, much to the disgust of his pilot father, a colonel still on active duty. His life is a mess at the start of the series. His son was killed and wife put in a coma by a drunk driver; he was demoted after an entire family died on his watch; and he feels guilty that, shortly before the auto accident in which his wife was injured, he had fallen in love with another woman.

Contribution

Dana Stabenow won critical and commercial success with her first mystery novel, *A Cold Day for Mur-*

der (1992), which won the 1993 Edgar Allan Poe Award from the Mystery Writers of America for best original paperback. The novel was innovative in two ways. First, it is set in Alaska, which is almost a character in its own right and, as Jack London showed, is almost creative in the many ways its environment can kill people. Although Stabenow is not the first mystery writer to use Alaska as a setting, she is the most popular of a new group of Alaska-based mystery writers, the first of whom was Sean Hanlon, who published *The Cold Front* in 1989.

Second, the main character, Kate Shugak, is both a female detective and a Native American. Neither concept is original. Female detectives are at least as old as Agatha Christie's Miss Marple, and there were Native American detectives even before Tony Hillerman began to write his many books featuring Lieutenant Joe Leaphorn and Sergeant Jim Chee of the Navajo Tribal Police. Along with Jean Hager and her Molly Bearpaw series, Stabenow is one of the first mystery writers to combine the two groups into one detective.

Biography

Dana Helen Stabenow was born in Anchorage, Alaska, on March 27, 1952. Her grandfather was the first DC-3 pilot for Alaska Airlines. She grew up on a seventy-five-foot fish tender named the *Celtic* in Cook Inlet and Prince William Sound and lived with her mother, Joan Perry Barnes, who was a deckhand. Her mother, an avid reader, could bake bread, skin and butcher a moose, pluck and cook ducks, and help maintain and run a fishing boat. Stabenow's earliest memory is of her mother reading the story of Snow White to her, and Stabenow learned to read before entering kindergarten. She read all the Nancy Drew books in the local library's collection in about a month; however, it was Josephine Tey's *The Daughter of Time* (1951) that hooked Stabenow on the mystery genre. She graduated from Seldovia High School in 1969 while working part-time for an air taxi service. Then she put herself through college working as an egg grader, bookkeeper, and expediter for Whitney-Fidalgo Seafoods in Anchorage. She received a bachelor's degree in journalism from the University of Alaska-Fairbanks in 1973.

After graduation, Stabenow backpacked around Europe for four months. After her return, she worked in public relations for Alyeska Pipeline at Galbraith Lake and later for British Petroleum at Prudhoe Bay. In 1982, she enrolled in the University of Alaska-Anchorage's master of fine arts program, from which she graduated in 1985. She began to write seriously at this time. She sold her first novel, *Second Star* (1991), to Ace Science Fiction in 1990. It was the first of three books in her Star Svensdotter series, set in the near future when people are moving off the planet.

In 1991, Laura Anne Gilman, Stabenow's editor at Ace, learned that she had an unsold two-hundred-page mystery novel that she had written two years earlier. After reading the manuscript, Gilman agreed to publish *A Cold Day for Murder* and offered Stabenow a contract for three books featuring Kate Shugak as the main character. When Gilman moved to another publisher, Stabenow started the Liam Campbell series. In 2006, she published her first thriller, *Blindfold Game*. To collect background information, Stabenow spent sixteen days on board the Coast Guard cutter *Alex Haley* on patrol in the Bering Sea. She became president of the Alaska chapter of Sisters in Crime and has written the travel column for *Alaska* magazine.

Analysis

Like Dorothy L. Sayers, Dana Stabenow regards the mystery novel as a kind of fantasy in which good always wins out over evil and all mysteries are solved by the end of the book. This is generally true of Stabenow's fiction. She tends to portray law enforcement officers in a positive light. They have flaws, but with few exceptions, they are honest and always want to do the right thing. She portrays her detectives as loners who often have problems with their relationships.

Kate Shugak series

The Kate Shugak series originated when Stabenow visited an aunt who was moving from Wrangell-St. Elias National Park to take a job elsewhere. Stabenow tried to imagine what kind of person would want to live in the park and decided to write about an Aleut whose family had been displaced by the Japanese occupation of the islands of Kiska and Attu during World War II and forced to move to the interior of Alaska.

She named the female protagonist Kate, after Katherine, an Aleut who was her best friend as a child. She then met a number of people who made negative comments about the National Park Service, which provided her a plot involving the murder of a park ranger.

At the beginning of *A Cold Day for Murder*, the first book in the series, Kate Shugak is angry at the world. She has a severe scar where a child molester stabbed her, and she resigned from her position as an investigator a year before. In one scene, Kate attacks Jack Morgan, her former boss and occasional lover. The series continues for several books before she learns to accept who and what she is. Her relatives regard her as strange for wanting to live in the wilderness rather than with them in the village of Niniltna (population around four hundred) twenty-five miles away, but she is angry at them, too. In *Blood Will Tell* (1996), she is dragged, kicking and screaming, into Native American politics when someone starts to murder the members of the Niniltna Native Association board of directors. In *Breakup* (1997), she becomes a tribal leader. In *The Singing of the Dead* (2001), Shugak is head of security for a political campaign when staff members start to turn up dead.

Liam Campbell series

Stabenow originally considered creating a series around Jim "Chopper Jim" Chopin, a state police officer who is a recurring character in the Kate Shugak series and one of Kate's lovers. However, the publishing rights to the character were held by Berkeley, and Laura Anne Gilman, the editor who had requested the new series, had moved to ROC/Dutton. So Stabenow created a new character, Liam Campbell, based on a state trooper who was responsible for the deaths of three people in one of the national parks. In the first book in the series, *Fire and Ice* (1998), Campbell is demoted and posted to the fishing village of Newenham (population two thousand) as punishment for his negligence in allowing five people to die of exposure.

Shugak and Campbell differ in many ways. The most obvious is their gender. Shugak is an Alaska native who family has been in Alaska for centuries; Campbell moved there as an adult. Campbell tends to becoming involved in more action than Shugak does. For example, in *So Sure of Death* (1999), Campbell jumps out of a Super Cub airplane in flight while chasing a four-wheel all-terrain vehicle driven by the novel's villain. Campbell is also involved in more sexual encounters as he is a good-looking, highly masculine officer who would not be out of place in a genre romance. Although Shugak loves Jack Morgan, their relationship is strictly on her own terms. Campbell, on the other hand, is not in control of his relationship with Wyanet Chouinard, a female bush pilot. Finally, Shugak is more of an outlaw, and Campbell more of a straight arrow. In *Blood Will Tell*, for example, Shugak commits identity theft against Jack Morgan's former wife and breaks into the office of a prominent Anchorage attorney; Campbell would never break the rules like that.

In *Better to Rest* (2002), Campbell has the opportunity to return to Anchorage from his exile and advance up the ranks of the state police but has to decide between Wyanet, who does not want to move from Newenham, and his career. Her family is from the area, and she has an adopted son Tim, whom she would prefer to raise in a small town. In this novel, Stabenow uses multiple points of view, although all of the point-of-view characters live in Newenham.

Blindfold Game

Blindfold Game (2006), a thriller, is not part of either the Shugak or Campbell series. Much of the story is set in Alaska and the surrounding waters, but the action also takes place in Thailand, Hong Kong, North Korea, London, Virginia, Washington, D.C., and Russia. In *Blindfold Game*, terrorists set off a bomb in Thailand and seek to explode a "dirty" nuclear bomb in Anchorage by firing a short-range missile from a hijacked freighter. However, killing thousands of people is only a means to their end, as their ultimate goal is to provoke a war between the United States and North Korea.

The female protagonist is Lieutenant Commander Sara Lange, executive officer on the Coast Guard cutter *Sojourner Truth*. The cutter normally patrols the Northern Pacific and the Bering Sea between Alaska and Siberia looking for Russian trawlers fishing illegally, protecting legal fishing boats from organizations such as Greenpeace, and rescuing victims of storms and other accidents. Lange is married to Hugh Rincon, who was her high school sweetheart in Alaska, but is now an analyst for the Central Intelligence Agency (CIA) in Langley, Virginia. Their long separations have put a strain on their relationship, and they are contemplating divorce.

The villains are two North Korean brothers Ja Yong-bae, aka Smith, and Ja Bae-ho, aka Jones; a half-Norwegian half-Chinese maritime shipping expert named Mr. Noortman; and a Chinese pirate named Fang. Noortman and Fang already have a business relationship in which Noortman identifies ships for Fang to hijack. Hugh discovers their plot from a CIA informer, but his superiors do not believe him, because they are focused on Arab, not Asian, terrorists. Luckily for Hugh, he finds an ally in Kyle Chase, a friend from high school who is now a Federal Bureau of Investigation agent based in Anchorage.

Thomas R. Feller

Principal mystery and detective fiction

Kate Shugak series: *A Cold Day for Murder*, 1992; *A Fatal Thaw*, 1992; *Dead in the Water*, 1993; *A Cold-Blooded Business*, 1994; *Play With Fire*, 1995; *Blood Will Tell*, 1996; *Breakup*, 1997; *Killing Grounds*, 1998; *Hunter's Moon*, 1999; *Midnight Come Again*, 2000; *The Singing of the Dead*, 2001; *A Fine and Bitter Snow*, 2002; *A Grave Denied*, 2003; *A Taint in the Blood*, 2004; *A Deeper Sleep*, 2007

Liam Campbell series: *Fire and Ice*, 1998; *So Sure of Death*, 1999; *Nothing Gold Can Stay*, 2000; *Better to Rest*, 2002

Nonseries novels: *Blindfold Game*, 2006

Other major works

Novels: *Second Star*, 1991; *A Handful of Stars*, 1994; *Red Planet Run*, 1995

Edited texts: *The Mysterious North*, 2002; *Alaska Women Writers*, 2003; *Wild Crimes*, 2004; *Powers of Detection*, 2004

Bibliography

Dahlin, Robert. "Movable Authors, Stationary Backlist." *Publishers Weekly* 245, no. 42. (October 19, 1998): 39. Discusses Stabenow's move from Putnam to St. Martin's Press.

Doran, Leslie. "Dana Doubles the Trouble: Stabenow Busy with Two Series." *Denver Post*, December 12, 2004, p. F12. Profile of Stabenow looks at how she juggles writing two series, her Web site, her writing process, and changes in the series content.

La Plante, Jane. Review of *The Singing of the Dead*, by Dana Stabenow. *Library Journal* 126, no. 8 (May 1, 2001): 132. This review praises the novel, in which Kate protects senatorial candidate Anne Gordaoff, for including a debate about fishing and hunting rights without going overboard and criticizes the novel for its predictability and lack of suspense.

Lindsay, Elizabeth Blakesley. *Great Women Mystery Writers*. 2d ed. Westport, Conn.: Greenwood Press, 2007. Contains an entry on Stabenow that examines her life and writings.

Lindsey, Beth. Review of *Blindfold Game*, by Dana Stabenow. *Library Journal* 131, no. 1 (January,

2006): 102-103. This review praises Stabenow for her skill in evoking a setting, strong characterization, and ability to create suspense in this thriller about Asian terrorists.

O'Brien, Sue. Review of *A Deeper Sleep*, by Dana Stabenow. *Booklist* 103, no. 4 (October 15, 2006): 33. Review of a Kate Shugak novel in which she is determined to find evidence to convict Louis Deem, a dangerous local man. Reviewer praises the plot and characterization as well as the descriptions of the Alaskan wilderness and Native American customs.

Stabenow, Dana. The Official Dana Stabenow Web Site. http://www.stabenow.com. The author's official Web site contains information about her books, upcoming works, blogs, and links for fans.

VINCENT STARRETT

Born: Toronto, Ontario, Canada; October 26, 1886
Died: Chicago, Illinois; January 4, 1974
Types of plot: Amateur sleuth; private investigator

Principal series

Jimmie Lavender, c. 1925-1944
Walter Ghost, 1929-1932
Riley Blackwood, 1935-1936

Principal series characters

James E. "Jimmie" Lavender and his friend Charles "Gilly" Gilruth share many features with another (and much more famous) pair made up of private detective and friend: Sherlock Holmes and Dr. Watson. Like Arthur Conan Doyle's duo, Lavender and Gilly share a suite of rooms, and like Holmes, Lavender is a pipe smoker, extremely confident, generous, and given to logical deductions based on acute observations. A final similarity is that Gilly—like Watson before him—is, more or less, merely the detective's unintelligent but stalwart foil.

Walter Ghost is a New York bibliophile and polyhistor who speaks a dozen languages ("including the Scandinavian"). Ghost is not a detective ("Heaven forbid!"); he is simply good at figuring out mysteries. Otherwise, he is a "great human being, a man like Shakespeare, a grand guy." He is also curiously ugly. Despite this promising introduction, Ghost emerges from the pages of the books of which he is the star as a bland logician.

Dunstan Mollock, his friend and foil, is a mystery writer and the creator of the Lavender stories. He has been described as simply inept.

Riley Blackwood represents Starrett's last attempt at creating a new, American Sherlock Holmes. If Lavender and Ghost are vague, Blackwood is downright washed out.

Contribution

To mystery enthusiasts, Vincent Starrett's main claim to fame is not his own detective fiction. Starrett is known as the "biographer" of Sherlock Holmes. He was a founding member of the Baker Street Irregulars (named for the occasional helpers of Holmes), a member of the Sherlock Holmes Society of England, and the author of the highly acclaimed *The Private Life of Sherlock Holmes* (1933). In this volume, the author examines at leisure, and with a healthy dose of tongue in cheek, various aspects of the life and times of the great (and, so it seems, in the end only barely fictional) English detective and his creator, Sir Arthur Conan Doyle. Starrett's own contributions to the mystery genre are thin and fall squarely into the category of Doyle imitations. He even went so far as to publish a novella featuring the Holmes-Watson team, *The Unique Hamlet: A Hitherto Unchronicled Adventure of Mr. Sherlock Holmes* (1920). Starrett's own greatest gift as a mystery writer was a talent for decent plots.

Biography

Vincent Starrett was born as Charles Vincent Emerson Starrett in Toronto, Canada, on October 26,

1886, the first of four sons born to Robert Starrett and Margaret (née Deniston Young) Starrett. The family moved to Chicago in search of better fortunes when Vincent was only four. Before the move, the boy had already become fascinated with books. This bibliophilism had been fostered in a bookstore managed by his maternal grandfather, John Young. Frequent visits to his native Canada kept the boy in contact with both his beloved grandfather and the books of which Starrett eventually came to be a collector.

Young Starrett attended public schools in Chicago until, at the age of seventeen, he dropped out of his final year of high school. After an aborted trip to the headwaters of the Amazon and brief experience in various menial jobs, he set out for London as a deckhand on a cattle boat. Rescued from starvation by the Salvation Army, he managed eventually to get back to Chicago and settle down to a life of journalism. His dream had been to be a serious writer; practicality suggested the steady income for working for a newspaper. Starrett worked as a cub reporter at the Chicago newspaper *Inter-Ocean* for a year before moving on to the *Chicago Daily News*. Here he became the star crime writer and made some important literary friends, such as Ben Hecht and Carl Sandburg, who were also young striving writers at the time.

In 1909, Starrett was married to Lillian Hartsig, a striking redhead with a talent for the piano and a bent for sociability. Starrett's biographer, Peter A. Ruber, suggests that the marriage was not a very successful one because Lillian did not share Vincent's literary and intellectual tastes. Whatever the truth is, the marriage lasted for fifteen years, until 1924.

During his years at the *Chicago Daily News*, Starrett covered the Mexican-American War for a year, and he began an extracurricular career writing articles about his favorite writers. In 1917, he decided that he was ready to embark on a literary career of his own and left the newspaper. While writing poetry that he had to pay to have published (in a volume uniting the works of five aspiring poets), Starrett made a scant living writing stories for various magazines, including mystery pulps. Economy soon forced him back into journalism. He did another five-year stint coediting the Chicago suburban weekly *The Austinite*.

In 1920, two books by Starrett were published: *The Unique Hamlet: A Hitherto Unchronicled Adventure of Mr. Sherlock Holmes*, a Sherlock Holmes spoof, and *Ambrose Bierce*. In 1924 followed a first collection of short stories, *Coffins for Two*, a mixture of mysteries and black-humor tales. Starrett's first mystery novel was *Murder on "B" Deck*, which was published in 1929. This book was initially planned as a Jimmie Lavender mystery, but problems in the execution led to the elimination of Lavender and the introduction of Walter Ghost. The novel, written in two months, was immediately accepted for publication and was successful, both commercially and critically. This led to a second Ghost-Mollock book, *Dead Man Inside* (1931), which was also moderately successful. Starrett was now established as a mystery writer.

The apogee of Starrett's career was the publication of *The Private Life of Sherlock Holmes* in 1933. This book brought him international fame and such notices as this one from the *New York Herald-Tribune*: "One seems to hear experts on either side of the Atlantic smacking their lips at each sniff at the table of contents."

Starrett received the Mystery Writers of America's Grand Master Award in 1958 and was elected president of that organization in 1961. He died in Chicago in 1974, at the age of eighty-seven.

Analysis

Although Vincent Starrett wrote prolifically in the mystery genre, he spent much of his life wishing that he could afford to do otherwise. He produced hundreds of stories for pulp magazines simply to support himself. His great loves were literary biography and poetry, areas in which he was not very successful. He did, however, have a real admiration for Doyle and his fictional creation Sherlock Holmes and wrote all of his successful mystery fiction in the style of Doyle, featuring Holmes and Watson imitations.

Starrett wrote highly stylized prose, prose that did not even suggest reality. His is a special-purpose prose that creates a special-purpose universe: one in which interesting mysteries can be presented and resolved in a direct—and ever so slightly ironic—way. The characters who inhabit his stories and plots are not living, breathing people; they are fictional people who wear the costumes needed to present an interesting criminal puzzle. The deaths are theater deaths—slightly amusing and unreal. The reader half expects the victims to climb out of the coffins and graves after the denouement to take a bow with the rest of the cast.

"Out There in the Dark"

Starrett is also a very efficient writer. He gets to the point (murder, theft) quickly. The plot is never slowed down by description and psychological intricacies. There are no psychological gradations in the Starrett universe; there are simply good people and bad people. The good are either detectives or victims, the bad are crooks. There are wily crooks and dull-witted crooks, but, basically, a crook is a crook. Such Lavender stories as "Out There in the Dark" and "The Woman in Black" are typical: Good people are threatened and sometimes killed by bad people, yet the reader is not encouraged to feel any real compassion for the murder victim. The servant with the broken skull in "Out There in the Dark" is merely a necessary plot-pawn, not a human being whose life is brutally abrogated. The star is the detective, and the emphasis is on his intellectual contortions to earn the right to receive applause in the end for a job well done.

The focus of Starrett's novels and stories is on plot—and only plot. There is very little characterization. Often, characters are not even described; their appearance and emotions do not matter, for their sole purpose is to carry the plotline, like tin soldiers who fall in the line of duty or move mechanically as the plot dictates. The effect is often entertaining, but never captivating. For the reader, it is difficult to become involved—except as he would in a mathematical problem. Starrett's stories can seem a bit sparse, a bit schematic. Yet Starrett is a deft creator of plots, very satisfying plots of the kind that evolve slowly, adding piece after piece after tiny piece of information until the picture is complete.

The End of Mr. Garment and *The Unique Hamlet*

Most of Starrett's works are set close to home. In *The End of Mr. Garment* (1932), a novelist is murdered en route to a meeting with a group of his peers. In *The Unique Hamlet*, Holmes and Watson are unearthed (although it must be acknowledged that Starrett never thought that they died, as is clear to anyone who has read his Holmes biography) to solve a mystery involving a lost *Hamlet* quarto (dated 1602) with a personal dedication by "Wm. Shakespeare." In this work the *dramatis personae* are book collectors, like Starrett himself, and he pokes good-humored fun at the practitioners of his own beloved hobby. Several of the Lavender stories involve journalists and book collectors. Starrett's detectives are all bibliophiles or literary scholars, and their foils are mystery writers (such as Dunstan Mollock) or recorders of their detective friend's accomplishments (such as Gilly). One has a sense that the author wrote his tales with a wry smile.

From the above, it will be clear that Starrett did not have a social vision, at least not one he cared to express in his mystery fiction. The universe emerging from Starrett's tales is one without a social milieu. Real life never intrudes into the plots.

A comparison of Starrett and his beloved Doyle, which seems natural and obvious, shows the former to be a pale imitation of the latter. Doyle's stories are tantalizingly, sometimes vibrantly full of social reality, a social reality that seeps into the separate universe of Holmes and Watson whenever the door is opened to let in a client. Outside that cozy little nest of male bonding and eccentric tranquillity is a London teeming with people, milling around in the mud and the fog. These people are grouped in social classes, they hate, love, and fight, and they have real blood pumping through (and sometimes out of) their veins. When their problems become unmanageable, when the social rules can no longer contain them, they come to Sherlock Holmes and ask him to solve the problem, restore order, and set the world aright again.

Such is not Starrett's universe. By comparison it is sterile. His nests of male bonding are not pockets of peace that a world in turmoil can come to in an emergency: They are the reason the rest of the world exists. The people and their actions only have the function of presenting the necessary problems for the brilliant detective to solve. The result is that what seemed natural and not in need of explanation in Doyle—the two men who share a suite of rooms—becomes somewhat preposterous in Starrett. One wonders why Jimmie Lavender and Gilly share an apartment. One wonders if there is any reason other than that Holmes and Watson did.

"The Woman in Black"

A key aspect of mystery fiction is the opposition between right and wrong, between society and individual, between law and the lawbreaker. In Starrett's fiction, however, this opposition is never compelling; he merely pays lip service to morality, law, and the restoration of the world to an acceptable order. There are "happy" endings, to be sure—the crime is solved—but the point is not justice, or punishment of the guilty; it is to show off the brainpower of the detective. Starrett's endings are perfunctory, schematic, unimaginative. In the short story "The Woman in Black," for example, the attractive young couple are happy in the end, the villain is beaten up, and the detective moves on to the next case. This is the formula of the oldest tales: young lovers united, the bad guy given a whipping. Starrett's justice is personal and private, not a social matter.

Sometimes Starrett's plots, like those of Doyle before him, verge on the amoral. The crime is solved, but the criminal is not brought to justice. In Doyle the dilemma is resolved satisfactorily: Holmes and his archenemy, the formidable Professor Moriarty, are each other's *raison d'être*. Holmes cannot be happy in a universe that does not include the master of evil, Moriarty. The opposition becomes one between good and evil as human constants. Moriarty is the metaphor for all that is frail and evil in humanity—for the devil himself. The universe created by Doyle is a dualistic one, sharing with the Gnostic universe the idea that light and darkness, good and evil are eternal mutually dependent principles. In Doyle, the two forces merge to create a Hegelian synthesis: Below the level of eternal principles, a form of justice and morality can exist that pertains to the lives of ordinary people. In Starrett's oeuvre the philosophical level is missing. When the two criminals who plan the crime in "Out There in the Dark" escape, never to be found or brought to justice, it seems simply amoral. The simple, stupid worker is caught and fried in the electric chair, while the upscale, educated, white-collar criminals get away.

The absence of justice is not necessarily a sign of an amoral author. It can be a sign of an author commenting negatively on a society that does not value justice highly or values it only selectively. In other words, the fictional criminal's walking away from the crime unscathed could represent a form of social criticism. Starrett, however, is not interested in crime as a social phenomenon, nor in justice as a moral issue. He is interested in crime solely as an intellectual mind game.

In the late twentieth century, Starrett has been forgotten as a mystery writer. The reason could be a combination of the factors outlined above. Great mysteries that live on, those of Doyle and Ross Macdonald, for example, are more than plots in costume; they introduce real people worth caring about and are rich repositories of social history. Starrett was not original enough and did not create characters and situations that were significant enough to transcend their creator and his time. The mysteries he wrote are pleasing but forgettable.

Starrett's one living legacy is the scholarly and entertaining *The Private Life of Sherlock Holmes*, which, despite its excessive hero worship, remains interesting reading as a study of the life and creative processes behind a fictional character who has become part of the symbolic and conceptual universe of readers in the Western world.

Per Schelde

Principal mystery and detective fiction

Jimmie Lavender series: *The Case Book of Jimmie Lavender*, 1944

Walter Ghost series: *Murder on "B" Deck*, 1929; *Dead Man Inside*, 1931; *The End of Mr. Garment*, 1932

Riley Blackwood series: *The Great Hotel Murder*, 1935; *Midnight and Percy Jones*, 1936

Nonseries novels: *The Laughing Buddha*, 1937 (also known as *Murder in Peking*)

Other short fiction: *The Unique Hamlet: A Hitherto Unchronicled Adventure of Mr. Sherlock Holmes*, 1920; *Coffins for Two*, 1924; *The Blue Door*, 1930; *The Quick and the Dead*, 1965

Other major works

Novels: *Seaports in the Moon: A Fantasia on Romantic Themes*, 1928

Short fiction: *Snow for Christmas*, 1935

Poetry: *Rhymes for Collectors*, 1921; *Ebony Flame*, 1922; *Banners in the Dawn*, 1923; *Flames and Dust*, 1924; *Fifteen More Poems*, 1927; *Autolycus in Limbo*, 1943; *Sonnets, and Other Verse*, 1949

Children's literature: *The Great All-Star Animal League Ball Game*, 1957

Nonfiction: *Arthur Machen: A Novelist of Ecstasy and Sin*, 1918; *The Escape of Alice: A Christmas Fantasy*, 1919; *Ambrose Bierce*, 1920; *A Student of Catalogues*, 1921; *Buried Caesars: Essays in Literary Appreciation*, 1923; *Stephen Crane: A Bibliography*, 1923; *Ambrose Bierce: A Bibliography*, 1929; *Penny Wise and Book Foolish*, 1929; *All About Mother Goose*, 1930; *The Private Life of Sherlock Holmes*, 1933 (revised 1960); *Oriental Encounter: Two Essays in Bad Taste*, 1938; *Persons from Porlock*, 1938; *Books Alive*, 1940; *Bookman's Holiday: The Private Satisfactions of an Incurable Collector*, 1942; *Books and Bipeds*, 1947; *Stephen Crane: A Bibliography*, 1948 (with Ames M. Williams); *Best Loved Books of the Twentieth Century*, 1955; *Book Column*, 1958; *Born in a Bookshop: Chapters from the Chicago Renascence*, 1965; *Late, Later, and Possibly Last: Essays*, 1973; *Sincerely, Tony/Faithfully, Vincent: The Correspondence of Anthony Boucher and Vincent Starrett*, 1975

Edited texts: *In Praise of Stevenson*, 1919; *Men, Women, and Boats*, 1921 (by Stephen Crane); *The Shining Pyramids*, 1923 (by Arthur Machen); *Et Cetera: A Collector's Scrap Book*, 1924; *Sins of the Fathers, and Other Tales*, 1924 (by George Gissing); *Fourteen Great Detective Stories*, 1928; *Maggie, a Girl of the Streets, and Other Stories*, 1933 (by Crane); *A Modern Book of Wonders: Amazing Facts in a Remarkable World*, 1938; *221B: Studies in Sherlock Holmes*, 1940 (with others); *The Mystery of Edwin Drood*, 1941 (by Charles Dickens); *World's Great Spy Stories*, 1944; *The Moonstone*, 1959 (by Wilkie Collins)

Bibliography

Honce, Charles. *A Vincent Starrett Library: The Astonishing Results of Twenty-three Years of Literary Activity.* Mount Vernon, N.Y.: Golden Eagle Press, 1941. This bibliography of Starrett's work is accompanied by a complementary essay by Starrett himself.

Murphy, Michael, ed. *Starrett vs. Mahen: A Record of Discovery and Correspondence.* St. Louis, Mo.: Autolycus Press, 1977. Collected letters between Starrett and fellow author Arthur Machen, revealing the personal approach of each man to the craft of writing.

Nieminski, John, and Jon L. Lellenberg, eds. *"Dear Starrett—", "Dear Briggs—": A Compendium of Correspondence Between Vincent Starrett and Gray Chandler Briggs, 1930-1934, Together with Various Appendices, Notes, and Embellishments.* New York: Fordham University Press, 1989. Collects letters between the two men, especially those focused on Sir Arthur Conan Doyle's Sherlock Holmes stories and the Baker Street Irregulars.

Ruber, Peter. *The Last Bookman: A Journey into the Life and Times of Vincent Starrett, Author, Journalist, Bibliophile.* New York: Candlelight Press, 1968. Biography of the author, combined with tributes in various forms—both prose and poetic—by several of Starrett's friends and colleagues.

_______, ed. *Arkham's Masters of Horror: A Sixtieth Anniversary Anthology Retrospective of the First Thirty Years of Arkham House.* Sauk City, Wis.: Arkham House, 2000. Includes a horror tale by Starrett, as well as notes by Ruber on the historical importance of the tale.

Starrett, Vincent. *Born in a Bookshop: Chapters from the Chicago Renascence.* Norman: University of Oklahoma Press, 1965. Autobiographical look at the author's experience of his hometown; provides insight into the influence of Chicago on his life and writing.

ROBERT LOUIS STEVENSON

Born: Edinburgh, Scotland; November 13, 1850
Died: Vailima, near Apia, Samoa; December 3, 1894
Types of plot: Historical; horror; psychological; thriller

Contribution

Robert Louis Stevenson must be seen as an unknowing progenitor of the mystery and detective genre. He was essentially a Romantic writer attempting to be taken seriously in a mainstream literary world caught up in the values of realism and naturalism. As a Romantic writer, he strongly affirmed the preeminent right of incident to capture the reader's attention. He countered Jane Austen's polite cup of tea with Dr. Jekyll's fantastic potion; he left the discreet parsonage to others, while he explored the mysteries of Treasure Island; he eschewed the chronicling of petty domestic strife and struck out instead to write about, not the uneventful daily life of ordinary men, but rather their extraordinary daydreams, hopes, and fears.

Stevenson also insisted on the importance of setting to a narrative. As he writes in "A Gossip on Romance," "Certain dank gardens cry aloud for a murder." The creation of atmosphere has been an important element in mystery fiction since Edgar Allan Poe first had his amateur French sleuth Monsieur Dupin investigate the murders in the Rue Morgue. The rugged Spanish Sierras of Stevenson's "Olalla" are, in their own way, as unforgettable as the Baker Street lodgings of Sherlock Holmes and Dr. Watson.

Stevenson also had a profound interest in psychology. His emphasis on the criminal's motivation, rather than on his identity, clearly presages the method of much modern, post-Freudian, mystery-suspense fiction. In Stevenson's "Markheim," the reader witnesses a murder early in the story and has no doubt about the identity of the murderer; the interest lies in the murderer's motivation, in his emotional and intellectual response to his crime. In terms of plotting, setting, and characterization, Stevenson is a master of all the elements that became so important to the development of the mystery and detective genre.

Biography

Robert Louis Stevenson is one of those intriguing writers, like Oscar Wilde, whose life often competes with his works for the critics' attention. He was born Robert Louis Balfour Stevenson on November 13, 1850, in Edinburgh. He was the only child of Thomas Stevenson and Margaret Isabella (née Balfour) Stevenson. His father, grandfather, and two uncles were harbor and lighthouse engineers who had hopes that Stevenson would follow in their profession. Stevenson, however, was a sickly child whose interest in lighthouses was of the romantic, rather than the structural, sort. Although he studied engineering, and then law, to please his family, it was apparent early that he was destined to become a writer.

Stevenson chose his companions from among the writers and artists of his day, such as William Ernest

Robert Louis Stevenson. (Library of Congress)

Henley, Sidney Colvin, and Charles Baxter. One friend, Leslie Stephen, editor of *Cornhill* magazine, published some of his early essays. His first book, *An Inland Voyage* (1878), was not published until he was twenty-eight years old.

While studying art in France, Stevenson fell in love with Fanny Van de Grift Osborne, who returned reluctantly to her San Franciscan husband, Samuel C. Osborne, in 1878. Stevenson pursued her to the United States, and after her divorce in 1880, they were married. Unfortunately, Stevenson's tubercular condition was a constant difficulty for him; thus, the couple spent the first ten years of their marriage trying to find a congenial climate within easy reach of Edinburgh. That took the Stevensons to the great spa towns of Hyères, Davos, and Bournemouth—places of refuge where he wrote his first novel, *Treasure Island* (1881-1882), as well as *A Child's Garden of Verses* (1885), *Kidnapped* (1886), and his first world-renowned work, *The Strange Case of Dr. Jekyll and Mr. Hyde* (1886).

In 1887, Stevenson's father died, setting him free to search the globe for a safe harbor. First, he went to Saranac Lake in New York for a cure that appeared to arrest his disease, then on to San Francisco, from which he began his South Seas cruise on the *Casco*. His eighteen months on the high seas took him to Tahiti, Australia, Hawaii, and finally his beloved Samoa. In 1889, Stevenson bought property that he named Vailima on a little island called Upolu and settled down to the most creative days of his life. It was there that he composed the compelling fragment *Weir of Hermiston* (1896), which most critics consider to be his most masterful piece of prose. He also fought hard for the political rights of the Samoans, who grieved after his death of a cerebral hemorrhage, on December 3, 1894, as fully as those who understood that the Western world had lost one of its finest writers.

Analysis

Probably the best known of Robert Louis Stevenson's mature works is *The Strange Case of Dr. Jekyll and Mr. Hyde*. It has, in Western culture, somewhat the stature of a number of other supernatural tales with archetypal plots, such as Mary Wollstonecraft Shelley's *Frankenstein: Or, The Modern Prometheus* (1818) and Bram Stoker's *Dracula* (1897). Readers unfamiliar with the novel, or even Stevenson's authorship of it, can still recount in fairly accurate detail the lineaments of the plot. The work's tremendous popularity undoubtedly has much to do with the aspects of action, character, and setting that now characterize so many mystery and detective novels.

The Strange Case of Dr. Jekyll and Mr. Hyde

Mr. Hyde's notorious crimes include trampling an innocent little girl in the street and leaving her to suffer unaided, bludgeoning to death an old man of considerable reputation, supposedly blackmailing the kindly benefactor Dr. Jekyll, and committing a variety of unnameable sins against propriety and morality, the likes of which were best left to the Victorian imagination. Stevenson's Hyde is as dark a character as any who ever stalked the streets of London, and his outward appearance creates disgust wherever he goes. No one could fault *The Strange Case of Dr. Jekyll and Mr. Hyde* for a lack of incident. In describing action, Stevenson is evocative, not explicit. His writing is reminiscent of the somewhat abstract style of Henry James in his psychological thriller *The Turn of the Screw* (1898). That is not really surprising, because the two men had a deep respect for each other's work.

Although there is no detective per se in *The Strange Case of Dr. Jekyll and Mr. Hyde*, there is the lawyer Mr. Utterson, whose curiosity, aroused by the strange stipulations of Dr. Jekyll's will, prompts him to attempt to solve the mystery of Mr. Hyde. Stevenson believed that the reader is most contented when he thoroughly identifies with the characters in a story. It is impossible not to empathize with the rational, but rather pedestrian, Mr. Utterson as he wrestles with a reality too bizarre for him to comprehend. Mr. Utterson serves the essential function, so ably executed by Dr. Watson throughout the Sherlock Homes series, of providing a defective intelligence who moves the story forward, while always keeping the suspense at a nearly unbearable pitch. This thrusting of ordinary people into extraordinary circumstances has also become a mainstay of the modern mystery and detective genre.

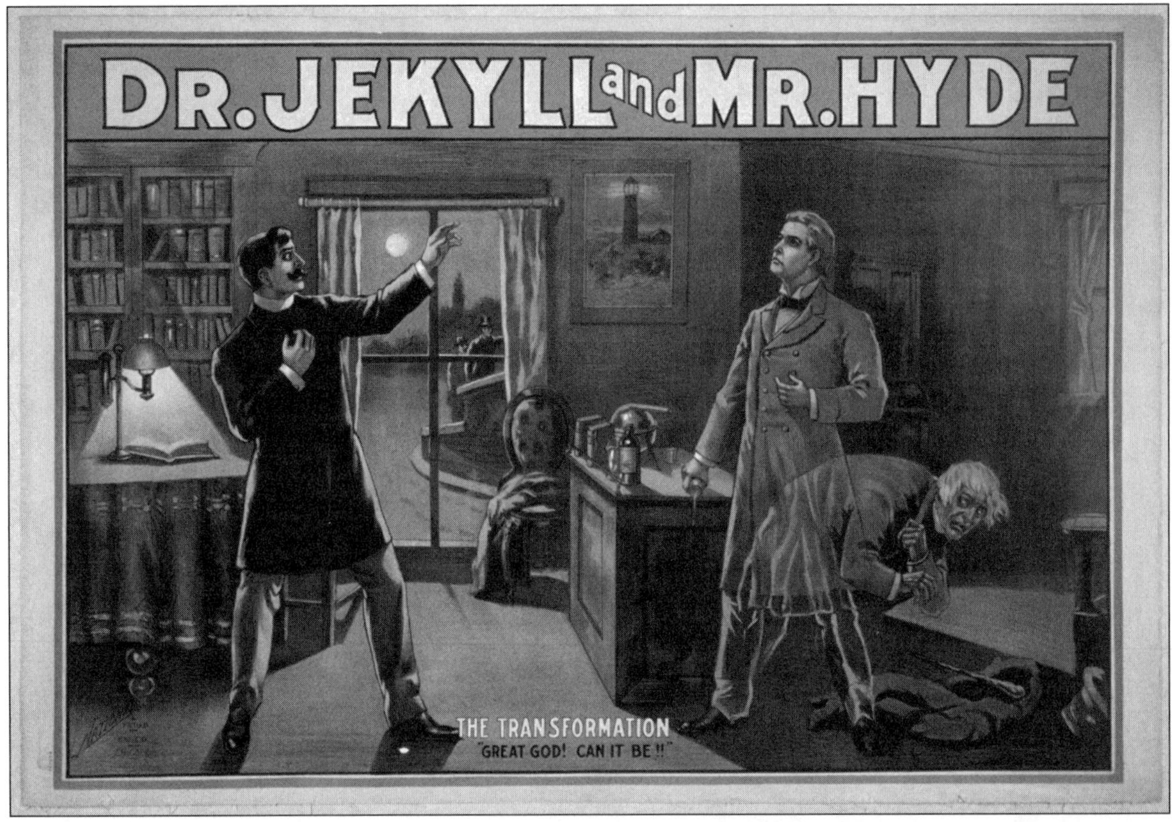

Poster for T. Russell Sullivan's 1887 play, Strange Case of Dr. Jekyll and Mr. Hyde, *showing the transformation of Jekyll into Hyde.* (Library of Congress)

Stevenson's skill in explicating psychological motivation is so strong that the reader even finds himself forcibly identifying with Dr. Jekyll and his evil alter ego, or doppelgänger, Mr. Hyde. It is a well-known hallmark of later mystery fiction to find something noble, or at least exceptional, in the criminal mind, but it was still a novelty in 1886. Writers of the late twentieth century have asked, quite frequently, as Peter Shaffer does in his psychological mystery play *Equus* (pr. 1973), which is more to be admired—a banal normalcy or an exhilarating and unique madness. (Victorians were more likely to see the answer to this question as obvious.)

Although Stevenson was a tremendous Romantic in terms of plot and character, he had a rare gift for the realistic rendering of setting. Just as later mystery writers are scrupulous about forensic detail, Stevenson was a passionate observer and recorder of nature and cityscapes. He even put forth the paradoxical idea, in an essay entitled "The Enjoyment of Unpleasant Place," that given enough time, all settings, even the most inhospitable, could yield a measure of understanding and contentment. A good example of Stevenson's style and attention to salient detail is this short description of the back entrance to Dr. Jekyll's laboratory:

> The door, which was equipped with neither bell nor knocker, was blistered and distained. Tramps slouched into the recess and struck matches on the panels; children kept shop on the steps; the schoolboy had tried his knife on the mouldings; and for close on a generation, no one had appeared to drive away these random visitors or to repair their ravages.

Any number of Stevenson's other works can also be studied as precursors to the mystery and detective genre, because even while he might be working within the rubric of the boys' adventure story or the gothic tale, his fundamental interest in vigorous action, strong character delineation, and detailed settings creates the kind of suspense one associates with mystery and detective fiction.

Treasure Island

For example, *Treasure Island* is full of adventure, which in another setting might be called crime. There are shootings, stabbings, and treachery enough for even the most lurid-minded reader. With the shipwrecks, the malaria, and the harshness of the elements, a tale full of incident emerges. There is also no dearth of mystery: What is the meaning of the black spot? Who is the mysterious blind man? Where is Treasure Island? How do the men aboard the *Hispaniola* find the liquor to get drunk? Who is the "man of the island"? What eventually becomes of Long John Silver?

Long John Silver, the opportunistic but charming pirate, is one of Stevenson's most captivating rogues. Perfectly motivated by enlightened self-interest, his shifts of loyalty almost inevitably move the plot. One identifies with him as surely as one identifies with the spry, touchingly adolescent protagonist. As for setting, one does not even need the supplied treasure map to amble competently, though mentally, around the island. Yet attention must be paid, because without a strong sense of place the mysteries of the island would remain inexplicable.

In *Treasure Island*, as in most of his other works, Stevenson is unusually modern in giving away the ending of the story at the outset, so that the focus of the reader's suspense is not specifically on the denouement but on the nature of the events leading up to it. The reader knows, for example, from the first page, that Jim Hawkins will survive and attain the hidden treasure, because Hawkins is clearly retelling the tale of Treasure Island from the vantage of his secure future. The reader also knows in the short story "Markheim" that Markheim is the man who murdered the antique dealer, although the reader is encouraged to be curious about why he committed the murder. In both cases Stevenson maintains suspense, not around the questions of whether the treasure will be found or whether Markheim is the killer but around the questions of how the treasure will be found and at what human cost and why Markheim kills the antique dealer and at what spiritual price. This preoccupation with process and psychology, rather than brute facts, is a characteristic of much modern mystery and detective writing, as can be seen quite clearly in many of Alfred Hitchcock's films.

Stevenson's works, like those of Edgar Allan Poe, were often dismissed and undervalued in the 1920's and 1930's. Certainly *Treasure Island* suffers if compared with Herman Melville's *Moby Dick: Or, The Whale* (1851), "Markheim" may well seem a poor thing next to Fyodor Dostoevski's *Prestupleniye i nakazaniye* (1866; *Crime and Punishment*, 1886), and "Olalla" pales beside Joseph Sheridan Le Fanu's story "Carmilla." Yet to have written works that bear comparison with all these classics is by no means a small accomplishment. Such has been the plight of many writers in the mystery and detective genre, to have been the beloved of the common reader during their lives and to have their work criticized by academics after their deaths.

"A Lodging for the Night"

Any reader who wants to assure himself of Stevenson's excellent style has only to read a passage of his description, such as this view of Notre Dame on a winter's night in Paris from Stevenson's first published story, "A Lodging for the Night":

> High up overhead the snow settled among the tracery of the cathedral towers. Many a niche was drifted full; many a statue wore a long white bonnet on its grotesque or sainted head. The gargoyles had been transformed into great false noses, drooping towards the point. The crockets were like upright pillows swollen on one side. In the intervals of the wind, there was a dull sound of dripping about the precincts of the church.

There is no question that this is a setting that cries out for a mystery, not for a garden party.

Stevenson's "shilling shockers" and boys' adventures clearly boast intricate and eventful plots, psychologically authentic characterizations, and powerfully observed and conveyed settings. Clearly, Stevenson's fiction was an important precedent to work carried on in the twentieth century by other popular and talented writers in the mystery/detective genre.

Cynthia Lee Katona

Principal mystery and detective fiction

Novels: *Treasure Island*, 1881-1882 (serial; 1883, book); *The Dynamiter*, 1885; *The Strange Case of Dr. Jekyll and Mr. Hyde*, 1886; *The Master of Ballantrae*, 1889; *The Wrong Box*, 1889; *The Wrecker*, 1892 (with Lloyd Osbourne); *The Body Snatcher*, 1895; *The Suicide Club*, 1895

Short fiction: *The New Arabian Nights*, 1882; *More New Arabian Nights*, 1885; *The Merry Men, and Other Tales and Fables*, 1887

Other major works

Novels: *Prince Otto*, 1885; *Kidnapped*, 1886; *The Black Arrow*, 1888; *Catriona*, 1893; *The Ebb-Tide*, 1894 (with Lloyd Osbourne); *Weir of Hermiston*, 1896 (unfinished); *St. Ives*, 1897 (completed by Arthur Quiller-Couch)

Short fiction: *Island Nights' Entertainments*, 1893

Plays: *Deacon Brodie*, pb. 1880 (with William Ernest Henley); *Admiral Guinea*, pb. 1884 (with Henley); *Beau Austin*, pb. 1884 (with Henley); *Macaire*, pb. 1885 (with Henley); *The Hanging Judge*, pb. 1887 (with Fanny Van de Grift Stevenson)

Poetry: *Moral Emblems*, 1882; *A Child's Garden of Verses*, 1885; *Underwoods*, 1887; *Ballads*, 1890; *Songs of Travel, and Other Verses*, 1896

Nonfiction: *An Inland Voyage*, 1878; *Edinburgh: Picturesque Notes*, 1878; *Travels with a Donkey in the Cévennes*, 1879; *Virginibus Puerisque*, 1881; *Familiar Studies of Men and Books*, 1882; *The Silverado Squatters: Sketches from a Californian Mountain*, 1883; *Memories and Portraits*, 1887; *The South Seas: A Record of Three Cruises*, 1890; *A Footnote to History*, 1892; *Across the Plains*, 1892; *Amateur Emigrant*, 1895; *Vailima Letters*, 1895; *In the South Seas*, 1896; *The Letters of Robert Louis Stevenson to His Family and Friends*, 1899 (2 volumes), 1911 (4 volumes); *The Lantern-Bearers, and Other Essays*, 1988

Bibliography

Bathurst, Bella. *The Lighthouse Stevensons*. New York: HarperPerennial, 2000. A history of Stevenson's family, who built fourteen lighthouses along the Scottish coast during the nineteenth century. A fascinating insight into Stevenson's family background.

Bevan, Bryan. "The Versatility of Robert Louis Stevenson." *Contemporary Review* 264 (June, 1994): 316-319. A general discussion of Stevenson's work, focusing on his versatility in a number of genres; discusses early influences on his writing, and comments on his essays and his fiction.

Bloom, Harold, ed. *Robert Louis Stevenson*. Philadelphia, Pa.: Chelsea House, 2005. Compilation of critical essays on Stevenson's fiction, ranging in focus from the dialectic between realism and romance to Stevenson's attitude toward professionalism in authorship.

Callow, Philip. *Louis: A Life of Robert Louis Stevenson*. Chicago: Ivan R. Dee, 2001. An engaging biography that draws on the work of other biographers to present for the general reader a cohesive life of the novelist.

Chesterton, G. K. *Robert Louis Stevenson*. London: Hodder and Stoughton, 1927. An older but distinguished critical study of Stevenson that is still highly regarded for its insights, as well as for its wit and lucidity.

Hammond, J. R. *A Robert Louis Stevenson Companion: A Guide to the Novels, Essays, and Short Stories*. London: Macmillan, 1984. The first three sections cover the life and literary achievements of Stevenson and contain a brief bibliography that lists and describes his short stories, essays, and smaller works. The fourth section critiques his novels and romances, and the fifth is a key to the people and places of Stevenson's novels and stories.

McLynn, Frank. *Robert Louis Stevenson: A Biography*. New York: Random House, 1993. Traces Stevenson's career, noting the malignant influence of his wife and stepson and concluding that Stevenson "is Scotland's greatest writer of English prose."

Reid, Julia. *Robert Louis Stevenson, Science, and the Fin de Siècle*. New York: Palgrave Macmillan, 2006. Study of the role of science, especially the theory of evolution, both in Stevenson's works and in the fin-de-siècle culture that produced them.

Saposnik, Irving S. *Robert Louis Stevenson*. New York: Twayne, 1974. A useful critical survey of

Stevenson's major works. Saposnik's volume is the best starting point for serious study of Stevenson's fiction. Supplemented by a helpful annotated bibliography.

Wright, Daniel L. "'The Prisonhouse of My Disposition': A Study of the Psychology of Addiction in *Dr. Jekyll and Mr. Hyde*." *Studies in the Novel* 26 (Fall, 1994): 254-267. Argues that the story is a portrait of a subject whose aggregate pre-addictive personality disorders reveal a substantial number of risk factors associated with high receptivity to addictive behavior; claims that the story is not just a quaint experiment in gothic terror but Victorian literature's premiere revelation, intended or not, of the etiology, character, and effects of chronic chemical addiction.

MARY STEWART

Mary Florence Elinor Rainbow

Born: Sunderland, Durham, England; September 17, 1916

Type of plot: Thriller

Contribution

Mary Stewart is the preeminent writer of the romantic thriller. She raised the standard of the genre partly by innovations in character, moving beyond the convention of the helpless heroine that dominated romantic fiction in the mid-1950's; she created charming, intelligent, capable young women with whom the reader could identify. She also discarded the convention of the hero's casual and uncaring attitude toward violence. Her heroines and heroes are ordinary people, not especially endowed with courage or heroism, who are thrust into dangerous and challenging situations in which they must make choices. Other qualities of her work that have made her one of the best-selling novelists in the world include an elegant and graceful style and the use of attractive, authentic settings, usually in Europe.

Biography

Mary Stewart was born Mary Florence Elinor Rainbow on September 17, 1916, in Sunderland, County Durham, England. Her father, Frederick A. Rainbow, was a clergyman, and her mother, Mary Edith Rainbow, came from a family of New Zealand missionaries. Stewart was one of three children. When she was seven, the family moved to the mining village of Shotton Colliery in County Durham, and Stewart attended a number of different schools before going to Durham University in 1935. At university, she became president of the Women's Union and of the Literary Society; she was graduated in 1938 with a first-class honors degree in English.

In 1939, she received a diploma in the theory and practice of teaching. She then taught at a school in Middlesborough, in northern England, before becoming head of English and classics at Worcester School, in the Midlands. In 1941, she received an master of arts degree from Durham University and was appointed assistant lecturer in English; during the last years of World War II, she served part-time in the Royal Observer Corps.

In 1945, Stewart married Frederick Henry Stewart, who at the time was a lecturer in geology at Durham University. From 1948 until 1956, she continued her work as lecturer at the university, but on a part-time basis, and she also taught at St. Hild's Teacher Training College in Durham. In 1956, she gave up teaching to concentrate on her writing. She had been writing stories and poems since she was a child, and during her teaching career her poems had been published in the *Durham University Journal*. She started her first novel with no thought of publication, but her husband persuaded her to submit the manuscript to a publisher. *Madam, Will You Talk?* was published in 1955, and Stewart's literary career had begun. The Stewarts then moved from Durham to Edinburgh, where Frederick Stewart had been appointed professor of geology at the university. Between 1955 and 1984, Stewart published nineteen novels, including three for children. In 1960 she was the runner-up for the Crime Writers' Association's Gold Dagger Award. She received the Malice Domestic Award for Lifetime Achievement in 1996.

Analysis

Mary Stewart's comments on her own work in an article published in *The Writer* in 1970 provide an illuminating account of her development and her principal concerns as a novelist. Her first five novels she describes as "exploratory," for she was experimenting with a variety of different forms. *Madam, Will You Talk?* is a chase story with all the traditional elements of the thriller. The plot, which hinged on a series of improbable coincidences, was woven around the theme of a "fate-driven love, self-contained, all-else-excluding." *Wildfire at Midnight* (1956) is a classic detective story, the writing of which, she says, honed certain technical skills. Nevertheless, she was impatient and dissatisfied with the necessary emphasis on plot rather than character and disliked the conventional detective story, in which "pain and murder are taken for granted and used as a parlor game." In *Thunder on the Right* (1957) she experimented for the first and only time with a third-person rather than first-person narrator. In spite of the limitations a first-person narrator imposes in some areas (detailed description can be given, for example, only of events in which the narrator is a direct participant), Stewart came to prefer it because of the "vividness, personal involvement and identification" that it makes possible. Stewart's skillful handling of this form of narration so as to evoke these responses in her readers contributes in no small measure to her popularity.

Perhaps the hallmark of Stewart's fiction can be found in her description of what she was attempting in her first five novels. They were

> a deliberate attempt . . . to discard certain conventions which seemed . . . to remove the novel of action so far from real life that it became a charade or a puzzle in which no reader could involve himself sufficiently really to care. I tried to take conventionally bizarre situations (the car chase, the closed-room murder, the wicked uncle tale) and send real people into them, normal everyday people with normal everyday reactions to violence and fear; people not "heroic" in the conventional sense, but averagely intelligent men and women who could be shocked or outraged into defending, if necessary with great physical bravery, what they held to be right.

Nine Coaches Waiting

These concerns are readily apparent in her fourth and fifth novels, *Nine Coaches Waiting* (1958) and *My Brother Michael* (1960). *Nine Coaches Waiting* is a gothic tale, designed as a variation on the Cinderella story. Young Linda Martin accepts a post as English governess to the nine-year-old Comte Philippe de Valmy, at a remote chateau in High Savoy. She falls in love with the boy's cousin, Raoul de Valmy, but comes to suspect that he is part of a plot against the boy's life. Faced with the choice between love and duty—which Stewart has identified as the main theme of the novel—she puts the boy's welfare first, while hoping against hope that her lover is innocent. Her virtue wins its inevitable reward; in the denouement, the wicked uncle, who is behind the plot, shoots himself, and Cinderella gets her Prince Charming. Although the plot is fragile, Stewart cleverly maintains the suspense with a mix of familiar elements: surprise revelations, sudden and unexpected confrontations, a search—during which the hardly-daring-to-breathe heroine comes within a whisker of being discovered—and a chase. Some ingenious variations include a sleepwalking villainess unconsciously revealing her guilt à la Lady Macbeth, and a romantic red herring in the form of a tall, attractive Englishman who befriends the heroine early in the novel—but who never comes as prominently into the story as the reader, cunningly tricked by Stewart, expects. Linda herself is a typical Stewart heroine. She is modest, tactful, and considerate, possesses integrity but is not a prig (she is capable of some white lies), is vulnerable and understandably frightened at what she has got herself into, but is also resourceful and capable, fully prepared to do what the situation demands of her.

My Brother Michael

A similar description could be applied to Camilla Haven, the heroine of *My Brother Michael*. Her self-deprecating sense of humor, revealed early in the novel by her alarming incompetence behind the wheel of an unfamiliar car in an unfamiliar country, quickly endears her to the reader. Caught up in a series of dangerous events in Delphi, she rises to the occasion not without self-doubt but also with considerable bravery.

Her companion, Simon Lester, is a typical Stewart hero. He first meets Camilla when he takes over the wheel of her car and gets her out of a difficult driving situation (difficult for her, that is—Stewart's men are always superb drivers). Simon possesses an easy, relaxed self-confidence, a quiet strength, competence, and great determination. He stays cool under pressure and rarely betrays much excitement or emotion.

In her article for *The Writer*, Stewart remarks that she had become tired of the convention under which the romantic hero was "unthinkingly at home with violence," and such a description could certainly not be applied to Simon. The violence in which he becomes involved is forced on him; he is a schoolmaster who teaches classics, so that violence is hardly his natural mode of operation. Stewart also comments that she rejected the concept of the hero as a social misfit, a type that was becoming fashionable at the time (she was referring to the literary movement embodied in the so-called Angry Young Men of the 1950's in Great Britain). On the contrary, Simon Lester, like all of her heroes, is unfailingly polite, courteous, and chivalrous, amply possessed, as Stewart put it, of "the civilized good manners that are armour for the naked nerve." He also embodies the common sense and "liberal ideas" that Stewart admires. The latter can be seen, for example, in his reflective comment on the odd ways of the Greek peasantry: "I think that most things can be forgiven to the poor." It is one of the most memorable lines in any of Stewart's novels.

My Brother Michael was inspired by Stewart's first visit to Greece, and a large part of the novel's appeal lies in the richly evoked setting of Delphi. In this passage, for example, Stewart re-creates the landscape around Parnassus in elegant, meandering rhythms and poetic images:

> All along the Pleistus—at this season a dry white serpent of shingle beds that glittered in the sun—all along its course, filling the valley bottom with the tumbling, whispering green-silver of water, flowed the olive woods; themselves a river, a green-and-silver flood of plumy branches as soft as sea spray, over which the ever-present breezes slid, not as they do over corn, in flying shadows, but in whitening breaths, little gasps that lift and toss the olive crests for all the world like breaking spray. Long pale ripples followed one another down the valley.

The setting is not merely adornment; Stewart uses it to create an atmosphere of a land still populated by the ancient gods, whose presence can be felt by those of subtle sense and pulse. Here is Apollo's temple:

> From where we were the pillars seemed hardly real; not stone that had ever felt hand or chisel, but insubstantial, the music-built columns of legend: Olympian building, left floating—warm from the god's hand—between sky and earth. Above, the indescribable sky of Hellas; below, the silver tide of the olives everlastingly rippling down to the sea. No house, no man, no beast. As it was in the beginning.

Classical allusions abound throughout the narrative; Stewart expects her reader to recognize them, and they are an integral part of plot and theme. Indeed, the climax of the plot comes when Camilla discovers a statue of Apollo, untouched and unseen for two thousand years. The theme of the novel has similarities with Aeschylus's *Oresteia* (458 B.C.E.; trilogy translated in 1777 as *Agamemnon*, *Libation Bearers*, and *Eumenides*); the name of Orestes, the avenger of a murdered relative, is invoked on more than one occasion as Simon Lester is forced into avenging the murder of his brother, an event that had taken place fifteen years previously. Violent events in the past cast long shadows over the present, but the Furies are eventually satisfied.

This Rough Magic

The formula that worked so well in *My Brother Michael* was repeated, with different ingredients, in *This Rough Magic* (1964), which has proved to be one of Stewart's most popular novels. Four million copies were sold over the decade following its publication.

Instead of Delphi, the setting is the island of Corfu, and the literary allusions are not to the classics but to William Shakespeare. The opening gambit is familiar: the heroine on holiday in an exotic clime. True to type, Lucy Waring is young and middle-class, modest enough to blush but spirited enough to tackle a villain. Stewart, as always, knows how to lead her reader astray: Once more there is a romantic red herring, a tall English photographer, who this time turns out to be the villain, whereas the likeliest candidate for villain eventually wins the lady's hand.

The strength of the novel lies in the characters, who are well drawn, if not in great depth, a strong plot with plenty of twists and surprises, a careful building of suspense, and the usual exciting (and violent) climax. The novel's charm lies in its setting, its wealth of incidental detail—ranging from the habits of dolphins to local folklore about Corfu's patron saint—and the ingenious way in which Stewart weaves Shakespeare's play *The Tempest* (pr. 1611) into the fabric of the story. The theory of one of the characters, a retired actor famous for his role as Prospero, is that Corfu is the magic island depicted in *The Tempest*, and allusions to the play crop up on every other page. Stewart may be writing popular fiction, but her readers are certainly at an advantage if they are literate; the allusions are not limited to *The Tempest* but include *King Lear* (pr. c. 1605-1606), *Much Ado About Nothing* (pr. c. 1598-1599), and William Congreve's Restoration drama *The Way of the World* (pr., pb. 1700). (An amusing example occurs in the 1965 book *Airs Above the Ground*, in which an ignorant mother prattles about a passage in the Bible, which she cannot quite remember, about a thankless child being sharper than a serpent's tooth—actually an image from *King Lear*.)

Touch Not the Cat

Literary allusions also enrich *Touch Not the Cat* (1976), one of Stewart's best novels, a sophisticated, cleverly plotted gothic mystery that holds its interest until the end and never slackens pace. The action takes place in an old moated grange in the Midlands that belongs to the Ashleys, a venerable English family with a historical pedigree going back to Tudor times and beyond. The plot is set in motion by a cryptic message from a dying man (Stewart employed a similar device in *My Brother Michael*), which leads the heroine, Bryony Ashley, on a trail of clues leading to valuable old books, Roman villas, surprise inheritances, and the unmasking of treacherous cousins. Juxtaposed to the main narrative are a series of brief flashbacks to a tragic love affair involving one of the Ashley ancestors, which eventually turns out to have a vital bearing on the present. The story also includes the novel device of telepathic lovers, a device that Stewart handles convincingly, with subtlety and insight. As usual, she erects a smokescreen to throw the reader off the romantic trail. It is all told with Stewart's customary grace and economy of style.

Later novels

Stewart's later novels, *Thornyhold* (1988), *The Stormy Petrel* (1991), and *Rose Cottage* (1997), are less gripping fare than her fiction of the 1950's and 1960's. Stewart returns to England for her settings, and continues her formula of a young woman encountering a strange new home and stranger family or neighbors, but these are drawn in pastels rather than the vivid colors of the Continent, true cozies and rarely thrilling. Her light, fluent prose is always a pleasure to read, and it is with some justice that her novels have been hailed as "genuine triumphs of a minor art."

Bryan Aubrey
Updated by Fiona Kelleghan

Principal mystery and detective fiction

Novels: *Madam, Will You Talk?*, 1955; *Wildfire at Midnight*, 1956; *Thunder on the Right*, 1957; *Nine Coaches Waiting*, 1958; *My Brother Michael*, 1960; *The Ivy Tree*, 1961; *The Moon-Spinners*, 1962; *This Rough Magic*, 1964; *Airs Above the Ground*, 1965; *The Gabriel Hounds*, 1967; *The Wind off the Small Isles*, 1968; *Touch Not the Cat*, 1976; *Thornyhold*, 1988; *The Stormy Petrel*, 1991; *Rose Cottage*, 1997

Other major works

Novels: *The Crystal Cave*, 1970; *The Hollow Hills*, 1973; *The Last Enchantment*, 1979; *The Wicked Day*, 1983; *The Prince and the Pilgrim*, 1995

Radio plays: *Call Me at Ten-Thirty*, 1957-1958; *Lift from a Stranger*, 1957-1958; *The Crime of Mr. Merry*, 1957-1958; *The Lord of Langdale*, 1957-1958

Poetry: *Frost on the Window, and Other Poems*, 1990

Children's literature: *The Little Broomstick*, 1971; *Ludo and the Star Horse*, 1974; *A Walk in Wolf Wood*, 1980

Bibliography

Friedman, Lenemaja. *Mary Stewart*. Boston: Twayne, 1990. Analysis and criticism of Stewart's Arthurian romances.

Hildebrand, Kristina. *The Female Reader at the Round Table: Religion and Women in Three Contemporary Arthurian Texts*. Uppsala, Sweden: Uppsala University Library, 2001. The published version of the author's dissertation, this study compares Stewart's Arthurian romances with those of Marion Zimmer Bradley and Steve Lawhead.

Huang, Jim, ed. *They Died In Vain: Overlooked, Underappreciated, and Forgotten Mystery Novels*. Carmel, Ind.: Crum Creek Press, 2002. Stewart is among the authors discussed in this book about mystery novels that never found the audience they deserved.

Newquist, Roy. *Counterpoint*. Chicago: Rand McNally, 1964. This book of interviews includes one with Stewart discussing her approach to writing and the significance of her fiction.

Wiggins, Kayla McKinney. "'I'll Never Laugh at a Thriller Again': Fate, Faith, and Folklore in the Mystery Novels of Mary Stewart." *Clues* 21, no. 1 (Spring-Summer, 2000): 49-60. Detailed thematic study of Stewart's thrillers.

FRANK R. STOCKTON

Born: Philadelphia, Pennsylvania; April 5, 1834
Died: Washington, D.C.; April 20, 1902
Also wrote as Paul Fort; John Lewees
Types of plot: Amateur sleuth; private investigator

Contribution

Although Frank R. Stockton is virtually unknown today, he was so greatly esteemed in his own era that American librarians in the 1890's reported only Mark Twain and F. Marion Crawford as more in demand. A 1928 list of great books included Stockton's as among the two hundred best worldwide, an 1899 poll by *Literature* ranked him fifth among the writers of his day (ahead of Henry James and Bret Harte), and noted writers and critics have sung his praises, among them Mark Twain, William Dean Howells, Rudyard Kipling, Arthur Quiller-Couch, Robert Louis Stevenson, Edmund Gosse, Robert Browning, Gertrude Stein, Maurice Sendak, and Edmund Wilson. Stockton's *The Adventures of Captain Horn* (1895) outsold all other American novels the year of its first printing, and his story "The Lady, or the Tiger?" continues to be read.

A prolific popular writer, Stockton paved the way for others in a variety of areas. As Henry L. Golemba notes, his children's stories foreshadowed those of Mark Twain, his fairy tales influenced Maurice Sendak, his experimentation with point-of-view narration inspired Gertrude Stein's technique, and his stories about the complexities and frustrations of ordinary middle-class life anticipated the stories of James Thurber, just as his anti-imperialist and antiwar sketches anticipated Leonard Holton's *The Mouse That Roared* (1955). Some have called him the first American science-fiction novelist, and others have praised his multidimensional depictions of the frustrations of the late nineteenth century woman seeking self-fulfillment. Some of his stories were precursors of the inverted detective story, and his originality in handling ratiocination and in reversing traditional formulas of the genre paved the way for later writers.

Biography

Francis Richard Stockton was born on April 5, 1834, in Philadelphia, the third child of Emily Hepzibeth Drean and William Smith Stockton, one of what would be a family of six children in addition to his father's seven children by a previous marriage. His mother was a school administrator and his father a conservative religious writer. Stockton was born with one leg shorter than the other, an infirmity that kept him out of the Civil War. His family was torn by divided loyalties during the war. Frank sympathized with the South and privately printed "A Northern Voice Calling for the Dissolution of the Union," but his aged father, a fire-and-brimstone Methodist, was an avid abolitionist. Ironically, the father's self-righteousness drove his younger sons to the opposite extreme: They became the community pranksters, and Frank in particular became so disenchanted with his father's stern faith that he turned to an absurdist's view of universal chaos.

Stockton attended public schools in Philadelphia, wrote some juvenile poetry, and won a prize in a story contest. After graduation from high school in 1852, he became a wood engraver and draftsman, though he kept up his literary interests as a member of the Forensic and Literary Circle. He began writing magazine stories for children and then humorous novels, stories, and sketches. During this period, he focused mainly on fairy tales, but eventually he progressed to more realistic stories, yet ones infused with elements of fancy. In September, 1855, his first published story, "The Slight Mistake," appeared in the *Philadelphia American Courier*, and his second, "Kate," in the *Southern Literary Messenger*.

Frank R. Stockton. (Library of Congress)

On April 30, 1860, Stockton was married to Marian (Mary Ann) Edwards Tuttle, a teacher, and he established an engraving office in New York. After his father's death he turned to journalism, freelancing for several newspapers and periodicals. He joined the staff of *Hearth and Home* in 1869, and the editorial staff of *Scribner's Monthly* (later *Century*) in 1872.

Serving as assistant editor for *St. Nicholas* from 1873 to 1881 opened new doors for Stockton, and offered him the chance to reconsider his own efforts. Consequently, he began to write longer works, producing his first novel, *What Might Have Been Expected*, in 1874. When he was struck by blindness in 1876, he began to consider an alternative future. By 1878 it was clear that his vision was permanently impaired, despite recuperative trips to Virginia, Florida, and Nassau, so Stockton retired.

After a two-year stint in Europe, Stockton produced "The Lady, or the Tiger?" the success of which encouraged him to become a full-time author of short stories and novels. Ironically, however, that very success made it more difficult for him to publish for a while, for editors returned manuscripts with the comment that they failed to maintain the high standards the public demanded after "The Lady, or the Tiger?" Nevertheless, three collections of short stories published in 1884 led many to consider Stockton the leading American humorist of the 1880's.

In April, 1902, Stockton was stricken with a cerebral hemorrhage during a National Academy of Sciences banquet in his honor; he died a few days later. Mark Twain was one of the mourners at his funeral.

Analysis

Indifferent to literary movements and unconfined by traditional genre divisions, Frank R. Stockton wrote delightful tales that mix romance, adventure, satire, fairy tale, intrigue, and derring-do. These stories were best when his imagination was not tied down by geographical or historical circumstances (more than half of his tales are set at sea) but could freely range in a mixed world of fantasy and reality. Their basic pattern, no matter what the dominant genre, is parody through inverting convention. Only a handful contain elements of mystery and detection, but because of Stockton's popularity and his innovative tinkering with formulas, these few are significant.

Although he wrote a number of novels, Stockton's forte was the short story, of which he wrote hundreds, and even his novels actually consist of short episodes bound together into longer units. All are characterized by the Stockton formula: what Martin I. J. Griffin calls "the calm, realistic recital of absurdity." Stockton describes the most amazing or ludicrous adventures and the most frightening horrors with a serene objectivity, a plain matter-of-factness, and the most ordinary with such a sense of wonder and intrigue that one's expectations are continually reversed. His fairies enter the human domain like wary strangers in a strange land, so that the real world partakes of the fanciful and the fantastic, while his descriptions of fairyland infuse it with realism. His ghosts are haunted by their human counterparts, and his stolid middle-aged women are drawn into incredible adventures. Mixing the normal and the incongruous, his narrator usually recites events in so detached and distant a manner that the passionate seems dispassionate, the heroic ordinary, the complex simple.

"Struck by a Boomerang"

Stockton's one tale of ratiocination, "Struck by a Boomerang," approaches the murder mystery in a typically skewed fashion. Reuben Farris has been murdered, and the narrator, a reclusive lawyer, sets out to detect the murderer by collecting incontrovertible evidence and presenting it logically. What he discovers is that there is a large amount of circumstantial evidence that indicates that he himself is the murderer. Luckily, he is saved by the timely confession of the true murderer, but he has learned the hard way how misleading circumstances can be. He concludes:

> I have had very good success in the law, but for some years I never pressed an investigation, never endeavored to find out the origin of some evil action, without stopping to consider whether it might not be possible that under some peculiar circumstances, and in some way I did not understand at the time, I might not be the man I was looking for, and that the legal blow I was about to deliver might not be turned, boomerang-like, on my astonished self.

While satirizing the unquestioning self-assurance of a Sherlock Holmes, Stockton questions the legal system and the reliance on circumstantial evidence to win a conviction.

"The Lady, or the Tiger?"

Although Stockton has only one real tale of detection, some of his other works contain intriguing elements of that genre. The most famous of these is "The Lady, or the Tiger?" Persuaded to prepare a story to read at a literary party, Stockton wrote "The King's Arena" but could not complete it to his satisfaction in time. Toying with it, he could not decide how to conclude it; after rewriting the ending five times, he finally left the solution open-ended. He published it as what is now known as his classic riddle story, "The Lady, or the Tiger?" It is the story of a handsome youth whose love for a king's daughter leads the king to condemn him to a choice of two doors, behind one of which lies a ferocious, bloodthirsty tiger that will most certainly eat him, behind the other a beautiful young woman who will be his willing and joyous bride. After a night of anguished consideration, the king's daughter, having bribed a guard for the secret of the doors, firmly directs her beloved to the door on the right, but the reader is left to unravel the psychology of her choice. Would she rather have her handsome young man alive, but in the arms of a rival, or dead, and safely hers for eternity? Stockton spends two sentences on her fears about "the cruel fangs of the tiger" and two paragraphs on her deliberations about the other door, emphasizing her "hot-blooded, semi-barbaric" nature, her gnashing of teeth and tearing of hair, her dreams of her young lover's "start of rapturous delight" on viewing her rival, her "despairing shriek" at the thought of their nuptials.

"The Discourager of Hesitancy"

To thousands of letters begging an answer, Stockton finally replied, "If you decide which it was—the lady, or the tiger—you find out what kind of a person you are yourself." Later, the pleas of readers still desperate for a final answer led to "The Discourager of Hesitancy" in *The Christmas Wreck, and Other Stories* (1886), but therein Stockton merely poses another question: whether the lady who smiles or the lady who frowns at the handsome prince is the king's choice for his bride, a choice he must duplicate or go to his death. The impact of Stockton's "The Lady, or the Tiger?" is clear from the fact that twenty-five thousand copies of it were sold by 1891. Critics still speak of it as "a great link in the development of the short story."

Stockton's story typifies his most intriguing characteristics: the difficulty of labeling his works in traditional ways, the ambiguity that teases and challenges readers, the realistic detail coupled with elements of fantasy, the deep-rooted cynicism beneath a surface idealism. Its concern with the choice between love and jealousy, self-sacrifice and blind possessiveness gives it a universality that has made it endure.

"What I Found in the Sea"

Another tale, involving greed, betrayal, and attempted murder, takes place on the high seas. In "What I Found in the Sea," a former sailor, John Gayther, tells of his near demise. His ship having run aground on some unknown obstacle, Gayther constructs a glass box through which to view the damage, only to discover a Spanish galleon and an English ship, sunk during a sea battle and now forever locked in combat in a watery grave. Curious, Gayther explores the ruined vessels in a diver's suit while his fellow sailors repair their boat. On finding a treasure in sixteenth century gold coins, he makes a secret agreement with the captain for the crew, the captain, and Gayther to mark the location and share the wealth. A passenger, a villainous stockbroker, suspects however, that he is missing out on a treasure; having watched shipboard movements "like a snake watching a bird," he cuts the line and hose on the diver's suit the next time Gayther is underwater. When Gayther finds an ingenious way to survive (breathing "the air of the sixteenth century"), the stockbroker tries to stir the crew against him. Stockton lightens this story of the way greed drives a man to madness, treachery, and murder by focusing on the peculiar psychological transformation wrought in Gayther by the preserved air from more reckless, swashbuckling days.

The Stories of the Three Burglars

The Stories of the Three Burglars (1889), a novelette, portrays three burglars caught by means of wine into which a powerful narcotic has been placed; in an attempt to account for their presence in a strange house, each tells an ingenious but unconvincing tale. Through such stories, Stockton satirizes realists such as Stephen Crane, who insisted that art mirror firsthand experience. At the same time he sets forth a middle-class view of society, with the rich equated with oppressors and socialist attempts to organize the poor denounced as forms of burglary.

The Late Mrs. Null

The Late Mrs. Null (1886), a romance, involves an investigation and disguise, with a cautious young lover, Lawrence Croft, trying to determine the character of his rival, one Junius Keswick, whose previous engagement to Croft's beloved had been broken by his aunt, Mrs. Keswick. Croft hires Annie Peyton, an employee of a New York information agency, to undertake the investigation for him. To facilitate the performance of her job, she disguises herself as "Mrs. Null," for as a married woman she can "go where she pleases and take care of herself." Mrs. Keswick proves to be a terrible, vengeful woman who drove her husband to suicide and unrelentingly harried her childhood lover until he agreed to marry her, only for the pleasure of castigating him mercilessly at the altar and humiliating him in front of family and friends by refusing to continue with the marriage rites. "Mrs. Null," in turn, is full of dash, spirit, and bravery. She cannot reconcile the feuding families, but she does prove fully capable of determining her own fate and fulfilling her contract. She teaches her employer the importance of both emotion and intellect in human relationships. A minor novelty in the book is the introduction of the anti-detective squad, a group of private citizens who have taken it on themselves to counter the efforts of detectives worldwide and who, for an appropriate sum, will undertake to divert and mislead whatever detectives are pursuing the payee.

Five thousand copies of this story sold the first day and more than twenty thousand within five months. In it, Stockton brought together the elements of a potential detective story but avoided using detection as his final approach. Nevertheless, his portrait of a young, active woman, intelligent, perceptive, and capable, paved the way for the modern female detective. Though marriage eventually becomes Annie Peyton's goal, throughout the story she proves her ability to thrive and to conduct her investigations without male assistance. Indeed, in his excellent work on Stockton, Henry Golemba comments, "I know of no American writer who investigates the question of women's liberation in so many permutations who has been as summarily neglected as Stockton."

ARDIS CLAVERDEN

Ardis Claverden (1890), whose plot features a lynching, the burning of a house and a barn, horse theft, a murder, and two hangings, focuses on a woman who beneath a bland, conventional exterior proves somewhat sinister and destructive, driven by dark, overpowering psychological forces. Riding a hot-blooded horse at top speed makes her feel wild and free, especially when she has just stolen back her lover's horse from thieves, and bringing two men to the gallows exhilarates her even more.

"THE KNIFE THAT KILLED PO HANCY"

"The Knife That Killed Po Hancy" further exemplifies Stockton's interest in the darker forces that may possess a human being. Therein an effete, civilized lawyer accidentally cuts himself with a knife stained with the blood of a Burmese robber chieftain, Po Hancy, and finds himself first displaying that long-dead man's uncivilized physical abilities and then his primitive passions. He plots burglaries, considers murder, and finds uncontrollable impulses waging war against his own better self. Humankind's cruel and inhuman designs are examined in other of Stockton's works, particularly in descriptions of the fury of a lynch mob such as that in *Amos Kilbright: His Adscititious Experiences, with Other Stories* (1888) or in tales of ruthless pirates.

Stockton has been praised for his psychological sense, particularly for his understanding of how to depict for children the realities adults must face and how to involve adults in the escapist fantasies of youth, for his treatment of middle-aged women, and for his colorful but sympathetic depiction of southern blacks. In the history of detective fiction he is best known for his competent female investigator, Mrs. Null, for his reversal of Holmesian logic, and for his teasing ending to "The Lady, or the Tiger?"—an ending that forces the reader to play detective.

Gina Macdonald

PRINCIPAL MYSTERY AND DETECTIVE FICTION

NOVELS: *The Late Mrs. Null*, 1886; *The Stories of the Three Burglars*, 1889; *Ardis Claverden*, 1890

OTHER MAJOR WORKS

NOVELS: 1874-1890 • *What Might Have Been Expected*, 1874; *Rudder Grange*, 1879; *A Jolly Fellowship*, 1880; *The Story of Viteau*, 1884; *The Transferred Ghost*, 1884; *The Casting Away of Mrs. Lecks and Mrs. Aleshine*, 1886; *The Hundredth Man*, 1887; *The Dusantes: A Sequel to "The Casting Away of Mrs. Lecks and Mrs. Aleshine,"* 1888; *Personally Conducted*, 1889; *The Great War Syndicate*, 1889

1891-1900 • *The House of Martha*, 1891; *The Squirrel Inn*, 1891; *Pomona's Travels*, 1894; *The Adventures of Captain Horn*, 1895; *Captain Chap: Or, The Rolling Stones*, 1896; *Mrs. Cliff's Yacht*, 1896; *The Buccaneers and Pirates of Our Coasts*, 1898; *The Girl at Cobhurst*, 1898; *The Great Stone of Sardis: A Novel*, 1898; *The Associate Hermits*, 1899; *The Vizier of the Two-Horned Alexander*, 1899; *The Young Master of Hyson Hall*, 1899; *A Bicycle of Cathay: A Novel*, 1900

1901-1927 • *Kate Bonnet: The Romance of a Pirate's Daughter*, 1902; *The Captain's Toll-Gate*, 1903; *The Lost Dryad*, 1912; *The Poor Count's Christmas*, 1927

SHORT FICTION: *The Floating Prince, and Other Fairy Tales*, 1881; *Ting-a-Ling Tales*, 1882; *The Lady, or the Tiger?, and Other Stories*, 1884; *A Christmas Wreck, and Other Stories*, 1886; *Amos Kilbright: His Adscititious Experiences, with Other Stories*, 1888; *The Rudder Grangers Abroad, and Other Stories*, 1891; *The Clock of Rondaine, and Other Stories*, 1892; *The Watchmaker's Wife, and Other Stories*, 1893; *Fanciful Tales*, 1894; *A Chosen Few*, 1895; *New Jersey: From the*

Discovery of the Scheyichbi to Recent Times, 1896; *Stories of New Jersey*, 1896 (also known as *New Jersey*); *A Story-Teller's Pack*, 1897; *Afield and Afloat*, 1900; *John Gayther's Garden and the Stories Told Therein*, 1902; *The Magic Egg, and Other Stories*, 1907; *Stories of the Spanish Main*, 1913; *Best Short Stories*, 1957

Children's literature: *Ting-a-Ling*, 1870; *Roundabout Rambles in Lands of Fact and Fancy*, 1872; *Tales Out of School*, 1875; *The Bee-Man of Orn, and Other Fanciful Tales*, 1887; *The Queen's Museum, and Other Fanciful Tales*, 1906

Nonfiction: *A Northern Voice Calling for the Dissolution of the Union of the United States of America*, 1860; *The Home: Where It Should Be and What to Put in It*, 1872

Miscellaneous: *The Novels and Stories of Frank R. Stockton*, 1899-1904 (23 volumes)

Bibliography

Golemba, Henry L. *Frank R. Stockton*. Boston: Twayne, 1981. Part of Twayne's United States Authors series, this extended examination of Stockton and his art includes an introductory bibliography and chronological investigation of Stockton's works. Golemba also suggests reasons for Stockton's neglect, in relation not only to the works themselves but also to the history of publishing and literary criticism over the last hundred years. Contains a select bibliography of primary and secondary sources.

Griffin, Martin I. J. *Frank R. Stockton*. Philadelphia: University of Pennsylvania Press, 1939. This biography gathers together details of Stockton's life—many taken from original sources—and shows the relationship between his life and his works. In the discussion of Stockton's work, however, plot summary dominates over critical interpretation. Includes a bibliography.

Hall, Ernest Jackson. *The Satirical Element in the American Novel*. Reprint. New York: Haskell House, 1969. Brief monograph on American satire emphasizes Stockton's place in the development of the satirical novel.

Panek, LeRoy Lad. *The Origins of the American Detective Story*. Jefferson, N.C.: McFarland, 2006. Study of the beginnings and establishment of American detective-fiction conventions, focusing especially on the replacement of the police by the private detective and the place of forensic science in the genre. Provides perspective on Stockton's writings.

Vedder, Henry C. *American Writers of Today*. Boston: Silver Burdett, 1894. This analysis of American writers includes a twelve-page chapter on Stockton and his work. Offers interesting insights and a flavor of the times in which Stockton wrote. Vedder gives considerable attention to Stockton's originality and droll humor.

REX STOUT

Born: Noblesville, Indiana; December 1, 1886
Died: Danbury, Connecticut; October 27, 1975
Types of plot: Master sleuth; private investigator

Principal series

Nero Wolfe, 1934-1985
Tecumseh Fox, 1939-1941

Principal series characters

Nero Wolfe is a private detective and recluse who is often goaded into taking on cases by desperate clients. Wolfe is fat (nearly three hundred pounds), intellectual, and something of a romantic. He is a theoretician and tactician; he knows how to manipulate circumstances and make the most of the evidence that his chief assistant hands him.

Archie Goodwin is Wolfe's chief assistant, alter-ego, and narrator of all the Wolfe novels. He is lean, well built, and practical. He and Wolfe make an unbeatable—if often irritable—team. He is a shrewd observer and researcher; he finds the facts.

TECUMSEH FOX, more physically active than Nero Wolfe, operates out of his large farm in Westchester County that his neighbors call the Zoo. He is a daring private detective and breaks the law if he believes that a client's case is at stake.

CONTRIBUTION

Next to Arthur Conan Doyle's Sherlock Holmes and Dr. Watson, Rex Stout's Nero Wolfe and Archie Goodwin may be the most memorable detective team in the history of the murder mystery genre. For more than forty years Stout was able to sustain his series of Nero Wolfe novels and short stories with amazing verve and consistency. Goodwin is the hard-boiled detective, ferreting out facts and collecting information from unusual sources. He brings the world to the contemplative, isolated Wolfe, who rarely leaves his home on business. He is the great mind secluded in his large, three-story brownstone on West Thirty-fifth Street in New York City. Without Goodwin, Wolfe would have to deal with the world much more directly; his mind would be cluttered with minutiae. With Goodwin as his detail man, Wolfe manages to hew his cases into a pleasing, aesthetic shape. When he solves a crime, he has simultaneously unraveled a mystery and tied up many loose ends that have bothered Goodwin and the other characters. As Wolfe suggests in several of the novels, he is an artist. He lives quietly and in virtual solitude, for that is his way of imposing his vision on the world. On those rare occasions when he is forced to leave his house, he as much as admits that sometimes the order he would like to bring to things is threatened by a chaotic and corrupt society he only momentarily manages to subdue.

BIOGRAPHY

Rex Todhunter Stout was born on December 1, 1886, in Noblesville, Indiana, to John Wallace Stout and Lucetta Todhunter Stout. The next year his family moved to Kansas, where he grew up in Wakarusa and Bellview as the sixth of nine children. He lived on a farm, which he remembered fondly in later years, while his father became superintendent of schools in Shawnee County. John Wallace Stout seems to have been a fair-minded parent as well as a great disciplinarian and fearful authority figure. Lucetta Todhunter Stout was a highly intelligent but rather reserved person who did little to encourage her children. As a result, her son Rex learned to rely on his own resources at a very early age.

Rex Stout (standing) at a Mystery Writers of America party in 1960. (Hulton Archive/Getty Images)

John Wallace Stout owned more than one thousand books, all of which his son had read by the age of eleven. Rex Stout was a precocious student, a spelling champion, and an avid reader of poetry with a prodigious memory. His father was involved in politics, which became one of the future novelist's lifelong interests. The Stout family's theatricals, composed and performed at home, made Rex Stout a self-assured speaker and debater. It is not hard to see this background reflected in the duels of wit between the characters in his detective novels.

In his youth, Stout was a great traveler, a sailor, a self-made businessman, and a freelance writer before publishing his first Nero Wolfe novel in 1934. He turned to mystery writing after a respectable but undistinguished effort to write fiction that would compete in seriousness with the work of F. Scott Fitzgerald, William Faulkner, and the other great twentieth century modernist writers. Before the Wolfe series, his modestly successful novels explored complex psychological themes and human characters. Yet through the evolution of the Nero Wolfe series, with its repeating characters and themes, he was able to approach a complex interpretation of human nature.

Very active in World War II as a propagandist for the American government, a controversial supporter of the Vietnam War, and a staunch opponent of J. Edgar Hoover's Federal Bureau of Investigation, Stout was himself a complex man. His fierce interests in politics and society are apparent in the Nero Wolfe series—although his main character is far more aloof from current affairs than Stout ever was. In 1959, he received the Grand Master Award from the Mystery Writers of America. Rex Stout died in October, 1975.

Analysis

In Edgar Allan Poe's short story "The Purloined Letter," the model for much of modern detective fiction, M. Auguste Dupin solves a mystery by cerebration; that is, he persistently thinks through the circumstances of the case, questioning the motives of the culprit and putting himself in the criminal's place so that he can reenact the conditions of the crime. Dupin rarely leaves his room, for he works by ratiocination—Poe's term for the detective's cognitive ability to catch and to outwit the guilty party. Dupin is a man of thought, not a man of action. He is also something of a mystery himself, a remote figure whom his assistant and interlocutor (also the narrator of the story) has trouble fathoming. Dupin, in short, is the cultivated, urban intellectual who prevails in an environment that values strength of mind and mental resourcefulness. "The Purloined Letter," then, is as much about the narrator's fascination with the detective's mind as it is about catching the villain.

Nero Wolfe series

Nero Wolfe is a direct descendant of Dupin. He hates to leave his house on West Thirty-fifth Street in New York City. Except in extremely rare instances, all appointments with clients are in Wolfe's brownstone. The detective has traveled widely—he even owns a house in Egypt—but it is a principle with him not to leave home on business. Archie Goodwin—Wolfe's sidekick, detail man, inquisitor, and protector—is the legman, the detective's link with the outside world. Goodwin prefers to believe that Wolfe is lazy; that is the reason the detective refuses to budge from his lair. Wolfe is sedentary, but his lack of physical exercise is more than a quirk. As his name Nero suggests, he has tyrannically created his own empire out of his towering ego. A man so bent on enjoying his own pleasures (chiefly a greenhouse with three hundred orchids and gourmet meals served by his live-in cook), to the exclusion of all others, has the perfect personality to pit against the egos of criminals, confidence men, and murderers. Wolfe knows what human greed means. He himself works for high fees that support his sybaritic existence.

Wolfe is wedded to his daily routines: breakfast at eight in his bedroom, two hours with his orchids from nine to eleven, office hours from eleven to quarter past one, then lunch and more office hours until four, after which he devotes two more hours to his orchids. Dinner is at half past seven. Goodwin knows better than to disturb the detective when he is working with his flowers, and only emergencies interrupt the other parts of the fixed schedule. This profound sense of order, of instituting a household staff that caters to his habits, is what motivates Wolfe to apprehend murderers—those disrupters of a peaceful and harmonious society. As his last name suggests, he is also a predator. Killers must be caught in Nero Wolfe novels, because they ultimately threaten his own safety; they sometimes intrude into his Manhattan brownstone or violate the lives of others in ways that offend Wolfe's belief (never stated in so many words) that urban man has a right to organize his life in a highly individual, even eccentric, manner. Caring so passionately about his own security, Wolfe is moved to take on cases where another's well-being is menaced.

Although there are significant female characters in

the Nero Wolfe series, their values, characters, and concerns are never central. Wolfe himself is leery of women, especially younger ones. At the conclusion of *In the Best Families* (1950), it is a joke to Goodwin that a woman has finally got close enough to Wolfe to make him smell of perfume. Goodwin is a chauvinist. He can be rather condescending with women. Occasionally, as in *And Be a Villain* (1948), a female character becomes the focal point of the story. In general, however, the power and fascination of Stout's fictional world is male.

Almost every Wolfe novel has this continuing cast of characters: Goodwin (who often has to spur Wolfe into action), Fritz (Wolfe's brilliant, conscientious cook in charge of pleasing his palate every day), Theodore (the orchid nurse), and Saul Panzer, Fred Durkin, and Orrie Cather (Wolfe's operatives, called in to help research and waylay suspects). Inspector Cramer of the New York Police Department is Wolfe's competitor, sometimes his ally, depending on the nature of the case and on whether Wolfe has information that will help the police and encourage them to tolerate his investigations. Wolfe has contact with a newspaperman, Lon Cohen, who passes along tips to Goodwin or plants items in the press at Wolfe's behest. Wolfe's organization of his household and his talent for manipulating the press and the police also speak to his consummate talents as a modern, urban detective.

It is indicative of the strengths of the Nero Wolfe series that the first novel, *Fer-de-Lance* (1934), and the last published before his death, *A Family Affair* (1975), are considered to be among Stout's best work. Every novel is characterized by Goodwin's exasperated familiarity with Wolfe's idiosyncrasies. Somehow Stout is able to create, almost immediately, the illusion of an ongoing world outside the particular novel's plot. Instead of explaining Wolfe's routine with his flowers, for example, Goodwin simply alludes to it as a habit. Gradually, in the course of the novel, brief and recurrent references to the routine are so embedded in the narrative that the presumption of a real world is easily assimilated. Indeed, the solving of a crime becomes inherently fascinating because it is contrasted implicitly with Wolfe's thoroughly regularized agenda. In other words, the detective must settle the case to preserve his deeply domestic order.

And Be a Villain, for example, begins with Goodwin filling out Wolfe's income tax forms: "For the third time I went over the final additions and subtractions on the first page of Form 1040, to make good and sure." It is typical of Stout to start a book in the middle of some action. In this case, the way Goodwin does Wolfe's income tax not only suggests his meticulous technique but also introduces the importance of money in the detective's world. He usually works only when he is forced to replenish the income he spends so extravagantly. "To make good and sure" is also characteristic of Goodwin's clipped speech. He never says more than really needs to be said. He works for Wolfe because he is efficient and accurate. He is by nature a man who wants to get things right—whether it is adding up figures or finding the real murderer.

And Be a Villain is the first novel of the Zeck trilogy—arguably the finest work in the Nero Wolfe series. Certainly the trilogy is representative of the series, and in its depiction of society, human character, and politics it demonstrates some of the most ambitious work ever attempted by a detective story writer. In the Zeck trilogy, Stout exploits and expands the strengths of the murder mystery genre to a point beyond which the genre cannot go without forsaking the conventions of the plot and of the detective's own personality.

And Be a Villain

In *And Be a Villain*, Wolfe is hired to investigate the murder of Cyril Orchard, the publisher of a horse-racing tip sheet, who is murdered in sensational fashion. He is the victim of a poison that is put into a soft drink whose makers sponsor a popular radio show. Nearly all concerned with the show are suspects. Wolfe has to work hard to get them to tell the truth, since they conceal evidence embarrassing to the show's star, Madeleine Fraser. At first, this cover-up obscures the true nature of the case, for what Wolfe learns is that Fraser gets indigestion from her sponsor's beverage. On the live program she has always had a taped bottle filled with cold coffee to simulate the soft drink. Someone switched bottles, however, and Orchard drank what turned out to be the poisoned potion. The suspicion, then, is that Fraser was the true target of the poisoner. Not until Wolfe happens to read a newspaper account of the death of Beulah Poole, publisher of an economic forecasting tip sheet, does he realize that some larger conspiracy is at work and that Orchard was indeed the intended murder victim.

Behind the scenes of the Zeck trilogy is the mastermind, Arnold Zeck, who calls Wolfe to persuade him to drop the case. It seems Wolfe has stumbled on a scam involving blackmail of prominent professionals and businessmen who are forced to take out expensive subscriptions to the tip sheets. Zeck is a very powerful, ruthless, and corrupt figure who buys politicians and poses as a philanthropist. In the event, Wolfe solves the crime and apprehends the murderer without having to confront Zeck. The implication, however, is that Wolfe dreads the day when he will have to battle Zeck. It will mean a revolution in his own life, including his departure from his beloved brownstone to bring his adversary down. Worse than that, Wolfe implies, he may not be successful.

The Second Confession

Each novel in the Zeck trilogy brings Wolfe closer to the confrontation with absolute evil. Striking in all three novels is Wolfe's admission that his triumphs are momentary and local. The very model of the self-sufficient, impregnable detective, Wolfe suddenly seems incredibly vulnerable—really a very insignificant figure when matched against Zeck's crime empire. When one of Zeck's minions, Louis Rony, is murdered and Wolfe refuses to stop his investigation in *The Second Confession* (1949), Zeck has his men machine-gun Wolfe's rooftop orchid greenhouse. That is a shocking invasion of Wolfe's domain. Although it is not the first time that Wolfe has suffered intrusions, Zeck has a societal organization—virtually a government unto itself—that could very well obliterate the detective. For much of the novel Rony has been suspected of being a secret Communist Party member; originally Wolfe was engaged to expose Rony's true political affiliations. Yet, as in *And Be a Villain*, the plot becomes much more complex, more disturbing. Rony, it is learned, was a party member and a Zeck operative, a kind of double agent. Wolfe again escapes a showdown with Zeck once this fact is known, since Zeck apparently believes that Rony betrayed him.

In the Best Families

Finally, in *In the Best Families*, Wolfe is driven underground, for he has come too close to the center of Zeck's operations. In the previous two novels, Zeck has warned Wolfe to be careful, while expressing the highest admiration for Wolfe's techniques. After all, Wolfe has also built up an intricate if much smaller organization. Like Zeck, he is one of a kind. Like Zeck, he is rarely seen outside his headquarters. The difference between the two men is that Zeck wants to penetrate society from within. He wants to control the most important political and financial institutions; he wants to make them perfect extensions of his will. Wolfe, on the other hand, exploits society only to the extent necessary to foster his deeply personal desires. He is as selfish and egotistical as Zeck, but he recognizes the rights and responsibilities of other individuals and organizations. For Zeck there can be only one organization, his own. Wolfe, however, happily pays his income tax and cooperates with the police when they can help him or lies to them when it is necessary to solve a case. Yet he has a sense of limits. His logic of organization turns inward, toward his own appetites, his own home. Zeck, on the other hand, would make the world his oyster if he had a chance.

Wolfe knows all these things about Zeck, so in the final volume of the trilogy he challenges Zeck on his own territory. Wolfe flees his brownstone, surfaces in California, loses more than one hundred pounds, slicks back his hair, grows a beard, talks through his nose, and is unrecognizable as himself. He works up a scam that fits him solidly into Zeck's organization. Like Poe's detective, Wolfe puts himself in the villain's place. Wolfe must make himself over and actually commit crimes to catch a criminal.

The Zeck trilogy is a powerful political and ethical statement, and yet it never loses its focus as detective fiction. Zeck is still the personal symbol of corruption as he would be in a Dashiell Hammett novel—to name another important model for detective fiction. Wolfe immediately gains ten pounds after successfully penetrating Zeck's organization and bringing down its master. He has gone through an agony of self-denial to get Zeck and rejects Goodwin's notion that he should stay in shape. Wolfe must return to fatness, for he has come perilously close to destroying his own identity. In earlier novels it has been enough for Wolfe to outwit his opponents, to absorb their psychology and turn it against them. Here he does that, but much more. In the Zeck trilogy he must follow a policy. He must be political if he is to destroy not only the man but also his empire. David R. Anderson is right. At heart, Wolfe is a romantic who shies away from a society that cannot fulfill his aesthetic and moral craving for perfection. Knowing how decadent life is "out there," he must create a world of his own that is as flawless as he can make it.

The Zeck trilogy represents the middle period of the Nero Wolfe series. As Anderson also notes, the trilogy represents a "rite of passage" for Goodwin and Wolfe. Zeck has been their greatest challenge, and through him they have learned just how dependent they are on each other. When Wolfe flees his home in *In the Best Families* without a word to his partner, Goodwin feels abandoned but easily supports himself as a detective. Yet he continues to wonder whether Wolfe will reappear and is gratified when the detective surfaces and clues Goodwin into his plan to topple Zeck. The fact is that without Wolfe, Goodwin's work would be lucrative but unimaginative. Without Goodwin, Wolfe has been able to plan his plot against Zeck, but he cannot execute it. The loner—and he is incredibly alone during the months he works at penetrating Zeck's organization—cannot ultimately exist alone. The shock of separation, Anderson observes, is what eventually reunites this quarrelsome partnership. Inspector Cramer predicts in *In the Best Families* that Zeck is out of reach. That would be true if Goodwin and Wolfe did not know how to trust each other. In the reconciliation of opposites evil cannot triumph. Zeck has failed to divide and conquer Wolfe's world—although one of the many amusing ironies in this novel occurs when Wolfe (pretending to be Roeder, a Zeck operative) hires Goodwin to do a job for Zeck.

During the mid-1940's, at the height of Rex Stout's popularity, a new mystery magazine was launched to capitalize on his name.

For all the routine of Wolfe's life, there is considerable variety in the series. Although he constantly affirms that he does not leave home on business, for example, there are several instances in the series when he does. In spite of their close, daily association Wolfe still does things that surprise Goodwin. That is perhaps the freshest aspect of the Wolfe novels when they are considered in terms of the murder mystery genre. Each novel repeats the central facts about Wolfe and his entourage without becoming tiresome. In the Nero Wolfe series, invention and convention are complementary qualities. They are what makes the series cohere. A man of the most studied habits, Nero Wolfe knows when it is crucial that he break the pattern.

Carl Rollyson

Principal mystery and detective fiction

Nero Wolfe series: 1934-1940 • *Fer-de-Lance*, 1934 (also known as *Meet Nero Wolfe*); *The League of Frightened Men*, 1935; *The Rubber Band*, 1936 (also known as *To Kill Again*); *The Red Box*, 1937 (also known as *The Case of the Red Box*); *Too Many Cooks*, 1938; *Some Buried Caesar*, 1939 (also known as *The Red Bull*); *Over My Dead Body*, 1940; *Where There's a Will*, 1940

1941-1950 • *Black Orchids*, 1942 (also known as *The Case of the Black Orchids*); *Not Quite Dead Enough*, 1944; *The Silent Speaker*, 1946; *Too Many Women*, 1947; *And Be a Villain*, 1948 (also known as *More Deaths than One*); *The Second Confession*, 1949; *Trouble in Triplicate*, 1949; *In the Best Families*, 1950 (also known as *Even in the Best Families*); *Three Doors to Death*, 1950

1951-1960 • *Curtains for Three*, 1951; *Murder by the Book*, 1951; *Triple Jeopardy*, 1952; *Prisoner's Base*, 1952 (also known as *Out Goes She*); *The Golden Spiders*, 1953; *The Black Mountain*, 1954; *Three Men Out*, 1954; *Before Midnight*, 1955; *Might as Well Be Dead*, 1956; *Three Witnesses*, 1956; *If Death Ever Slept*, 1957; *Three for the Chair*, 1957; *And Four to Go*, 1958 (also known as *Crime and Again*); *Champagne for One*, 1958; *Plot It Yourself*, 1959 (also known as *Murder in Style*); *Three at Wolfe's Door*, 1960; *Too Many Clients*, 1960

1961-1970 • *The Final Deduction*, 1961; *Gambit*, 1962; *Homicide Trinity*, 1962; *The Mother Hunt*, 1963; *A Right to Die*, 1964; *Trio for Blunt Instruments*, 1964; *The Doorbell Rang*, 1965; *Death of a Doxy*, 1966; *The Father Hunt*, 1968; *Death of a Dude*, 1969

1971-1985 • *Please Pass the Guilt*, 1973; *A Family Affair*, 1975; *Death Times Three*, 1985

Tecumseh Fox series: *Double for Death*, 1939; *Bad for Business*, 1940; *The Broken Vase*, 1941

Nonseries novels: *The Hand in the Glove*, 1937 (also known as *Crime on Her Hands*); *Mountain Cat*, 1939; *Red Threads*, 1939; *Alphabet Hicks*, 1941 (also known as *The Sound of Murder*)

Other short fiction: *Justice Ends at Home, and Other Stories*, 1977

Other major works

Novels: *Her Forbidden Knight*, 1913; *A Prize for Princes*, 1914; *Under the Andes*, 1914; *The Great Legend*, 1916; *How Like a God*, 1929; *Seed on the Wind*, 1930; *Golden Remedy*, 1931; *Forest Fire*, 1933; *O Careless Love!*, 1935; *Mr. Cinderella*, 1938

Nonfiction: *The Nero Wolfe Cook Book*, 1973 (with others)

Edited texts: *The Illustrious Dunderheads*, 1942; *Rue Morgue No. 1*, 1946 (with Louis Greenfield); *Eat, Drink, and Be Buried*, 1956 (also known as *For Tomorrow We Die*)

Miscellaneous: *Corsage*, 1977

Bibliography

Anderson, David R. *Rex Stout*. New York: Frederick Ungar, 1984. Critical biography of the author and discussion of the Nero Wolfe series.

Baring-Gould, William S. *Nero Wolfe of West Thirty-Fifth Street*. New York: Viking Press, 1969. The result of Baring-Gould's painstaking research of Rex Stout's Nero Wolfe series provides, in essence, a biography of Stout's fictional characters.

Barzun, Jacques. "Rex Stout." In *A Jacques Barzun Reader: Selections from His Works*, edited and with an introduction by Michael Murray. New York: HarperCollins, 2002. Essay on Stout by a noted philosopher and social theorist.

Bester, Alfred. "Rex Stout." In *Redemolished*. New York: Simon & Schuster, 2004. Essay on Stout and his famous detective by Bester, a skilled essayist in addition to being a successful science-fiction writer.

Darby, Ken. *The Brownstone House of Nero Wolfe, as Told by Archie Goodwin*. Boston: Little, Brown, 1983. Similar to but more detailed than Baring-Gould's effort, this book contains a detailed study of the world of Nero Wolfe, including a blueprint of his brownstone and case files on all of the mysteries he solved.

McAleer, John J. *Rex Stout: A Biography*. 1977. Reprint. Boston: Little, Brown, 1994. McAleer's authorized biography of Rex Stout is considered the definitive and inclusive information source regarding Stout's life.

Murphy, Bruce. *The Encyclopedia of Murder and Mystery*. New York: Saint Martin's Minotaur, 1999. Murphy's short biographical section on Stout provides a crisply written and succinct look at the most important facts of the author's life.

Townsend, Guy M., John J. McAleer, and Boden Clarke, eds. *The Works of Rex Stout: An Annotated Bibliography and Guide*. 2d ed. San Bernardino,

Calif.: Borgo Press, 1995. Useful bibliography of Stout's novels that provides descriptions and analysis of each one.

Van Dover, J. Kenneth. *At Wolfe's Door: The Nero Wolfe Novels of Rex Stout*. San Bernardino, Calif.: Borgo Press, 1991. A book-length study of the Nero Wolfe series, noting the development of the characters over successive novels and the importance of both novels and characters to the detective genre.

EDWARD STRATEMEYER

Born: Elizabeth, New Jersey; October 4, 1862
Died: Newark, New Jersey; May 10, 1930
Also wrote as Horatio Alger, Jr.; Captain Ralph Bonehill; Allen Chapman; Louis Charles (joint pseudonym with Louis Stratemeyer); Oliver Optic; Roy Rockwood; E. Ward Strayer; Arthur M. Winfield
Type of plot: Amateur sleuth

PRINCIPAL SERIES

Rover Boys, 1899-1926
Bobbsey Twins, 1904-1980
Dave Porter, 1905-1919
Tom Swift, 1910-1941
Ruth Fielding, 1913-1934
Hardy Boys, 1927-
Nancy Drew, 1930-

PRINCIPAL SERIES CHARACTERS

THE ROVER BOYS, Dick, Tom, and Sam, are cadets at Putnam Hall military academy. Between classes, activities, and solving mysteries, the boys also spend time with their sweethearts, who attend a nearby girls' school.

THE BOBBSEY TWINS are two sets of fraternal twins: Freddy and Flossie are four years old while Bert and Nan are eight. Because their father travels a great deal, so does the family. The older twins frequently discover mysteries to solve.

DAVE PORTER is a manly youth who is well liked at his boarding school although he is often called away to experience mysterious adventures in different settings.

TOM SWIFT is a young genius and master of inventions. Popular around town, Tom is devoted to his ailing father and Tom's sweetheart, Mary. He must be ever vigilant to guard his inventions from industrial pirates.

RUTH FIELDING is a young orphan in the care of her uncle. She is extremely intelligent and talented at solving mysteries.

THE HARDY BOYS, Frank and Joe, are the sons of internationally famous detective Fenton Hardy. Athletic and intelligent, the boys hope to follow in their father's footsteps.

NANCY DREW is the teenage daughter of prominent attorney, Carson Drew. Nancy is a great help to her father and frequently solves his cases for him.

CONTRIBUTION

Edward Stratemeyer began his writing career as an author of dime novels. He wrote many novels under many different names. His imagination was so vast that he had no time to write every book his mind could conceive. When he left dime novels to write juvenile mystery fiction, he had real success with the Rover Boys series. From his experience with dime novels, Stratemeyer knew that it was important to include a bit of mystery in most books. He also created a template for his juvenile leading characters. The youngsters are usually orphans, semi-orphans, or else the children of extremely hands-off parents. The result is that the boys and girls are independent, responsible, resourceful, and self-possessed, the kind of young person Stratemeyer described as "wide awake." These young people are propelled into the discovery and the solving of mysteries by a series of extraordinary coincidences.

Stratemeyer ensured reader involvement by creating fast-paced action and ending nearly every chapter with a cliffhanger.

When Stratemeyer realized that he would never be able to write all the books that he wanted to write, he created his syndicate sometime around 1910. The syndicate was much like the fiction factory of nineteenth century French novelist Alexandre Dumas, *père*. Stratemeyer would generate an idea for a book or a series, work up relatively detailed outlines, and pay authors to write the books using house names (Carolyn Keene, Franklin W. Dixon, Victor Appleton). The authors were paid a lump sum for each book, signed over the rights, and promised never to reveal that they had written a book as one of the house names.

Stratemeyer also conceived the idea of the breeder set of books. The first three volumes of a new series appeared at the same time. That way the series momentum was established, and readers did not have to wait a year to buy a new volume in a series that they had enjoyed. His sales ideas were based on selling books for fifty cents per book and making his profit on volume rather than price.

Biography

Edward Stratemeyer was born on October 4, 1862, to German émigrés Henry Julius Stratemeyer and Anna Stratemeyer. Anna was the widow of George, Henry's brother, and had three sons with him. After Anna and Henry married, they had three children together; Edward was the youngest. It seems that all the siblings were artistically gifted in some way, but they lived very normal, if slightly privileged, lives. Edward grew up in Elizabeth, New Jersey, where his father owned and operated a tobacco store. The family was comfortable, cultured, and completely apolitical. The Stratemeyer boys worked in their father's store.

Edward Stratemeyer was educated in public schools. He once told a friend that he had known from the age of six that he wanted to be an author. He graduated from Elizabeth High School as valedictorian of his class of three. After high school, he received some private tutoring while working in his brother's tobacco store and writing for story papers. In 1889, with "Victor Horton's Idea," Stratemeyer crossed the bridge from sensationalist literature to a more respectable kind. He moved the family home to Newark, New Jersey, and in 1891, he married Magdalene "Lenna" Van Camp. Though Lenna was an invalid, she helped edit Stratemeyer's books.

Soon after his marriage, Stratemeyer went to work freelancing for Street and Smith Publishers, and from that experience, he learned much about the management and organization of his future syndicate. However, Stratemeyer's greatest accomplishment would prove to be Harriet, his elder daughter, who was born on December 11, 1892. Edna, his second daughter, was born on May 19, 1895.

Sometime around 1905, Stratemeyer began implementing the organization of his syndicate by hiring authors to turn his outlines into complete books under the house names that belonged to the syndicate: Victor Appleton, Franklin W. Dixon, Carolyn Keene, Alice B. Emerson, and Laura Lee Hope. Stratemeyer is generally credited with the writing of the Rover Boys (as Arthur M. Winfield) and the Dave Porter series as well as many other series outside the mystery and detective genre; however, the Bobbsey Twins, Tom Swift, Ruth Fielding, the Hardy Boys, and Nancy Drew series are all series that he created rather than actively wrote. Early on, Stratemeyer hired Lilian Garis, an established newspaper writer who was also writing girls' books. She wrote the Motor and Radio Girls series as Margaret Penrose, and continued to work for the syndicate for many years, alternating that output with books of her own. Howard Garis, her husband, originator of the Uncle Wiggly series, also wrote for the syndicate, penning some of the Bomba books, some of the Tom Swift books, and also some of the Bobbsey Twin books, on which Lilian also worked. Both of the Garis children also wrote for Stratemeyer: Cleo Garis wrote the Arden Blake series and Roger Garis wrote the X Bar X Boys series as James Cody Ferris. In the family biography, Roger Garis later recalled that the family members wrote so many books for so many different series that none of them could remember exactly which ones they had written. Leslie McFarlane, a Canadian newsman and radio writer wrote for several syndicate series before being assigned the Hardy Boys series.

Stratemeyer decided to hire Mildred Wirt Benson, one of the first graduates of the new school of journalism at the University of Iowa and assigned her to the Ruth Fielding series (written as Alice B. Emerson), which was just winding down. He liked her work and assigned Benson to a new girls' series that he was developing. The Nancy Drew breeder set appeared in 1930, just days before Stratemeyer died. It was Benson, writing as Carolyn Keene, who created the character and personality of snappy and slightly sassy Nancy Drew, even though later on, Stratemeyer's daughter Harriet Stratemeyer Adams would insist that she had created Nancy.

Harriet Stratemeyer Adams and Edna Stratemeyer inherited the syndicate when their father died. They intended to sell it, but in the midst of the Great Depression, there was no one to buy it, and there was no one with their father's imagination and foresight. Adams assumed the reins of the organization and wrote outlines for books as her father had. During the 1950's, Harriet undertook the task of rewriting all the titles in the Nancy Drew, Hardy Boys, and Bobbsey Twins series to modernize them. Therefore, in many ways, Harriet did write the Nancy Drew books. After she died in 1982, the syndicate was sold to Simon & Schuster publishers.

Analysis

Edward Stratemeyer used the techniques he developed while writing dime novels to perfect the construction of juvenile mystery fiction. His leading characters were derived from the leading characters in fairy tales and projected a universal appeal because of the essential familiarity of their types (Jung's universal archetype theory). His plots were built on action and strengthened with cliff-hanging suspense with an overabundance of coincidence rather than applied detection, deduction, or induction. In thirty-one years, Stratemeyer managed to create five extremely successful juvenile mystery series that have become embedded in American popular culture. The Rover Boys, Tom Swift, the Bobbsey Twins, the Hardy Boys, and Nancy Drew are cultural icons and centers of controversy, just as Stratemeyer was controversial.

Critics of juvenile fiction have accused Stratemeyer of sensationalism, lack of realism, and the repeated use of similar characters and plots. Teachers, librarians, and the Boy Scouts of America attacked his books. The consensus seemed to be that it was impossible to write as much as Stratemeyer did and still write well. However, Stratemeyer wrote well enough to capture the imaginations of his readers. He chose his syndicate writers based on who best could communicate the excitement he hoped to promote and best express the character he hoped to create. If he, and later, daughter Harriet, found an author to be unsatisfactory, that author was not invited to work for the syndicate again.

The Bobbsey Twins series

Although Howard Garis and Lilian Garis, writing as Laura Lee Hope, worked on the later volumes of this series, the greatest mystery of all about the Bobbseys remains unsolved. The 1904 publication date of the first book in the series is a year or so in advance of estimated dates for the syndicate organization, so who wrote the book? If, as Stratemeyer's daughter said, Stratemeyer, himself, wrote the book, it would be the only book for very young children that he ever attempted, even though he, presumably, outlined succeeding volumes. Because the publishing world was glutted with "tots" series, the syndicate was content with the Bobbsey Twins until 1952 when Harriet introduced the Happy Hollisters series by Jerry West (Andrew Svenson). The idea seemed to be to create an audience for a mystery series by developing an audience for mysteries, and the Bobbsey Twins solved mysteries, beginning with tracking down the identity of a ghost in the first volume. After 1943, the series was devoted to solving mysteries and was popular enough to outlast its competition, and even after it was discontinued in 1979, it went immediately into reprints and a new format. Writers who wrote novels in the series include Elizabeth Ward, Harriet Stratemeyer Adams, Andrew Svenson, Jane Dunn, Grace Grote, Nancy Axelrod, Mary Donahoe, Patricia Doll, Bonnibel Weston, and Margery Howard.

The Tom Swift series

This third volume of the 1910 breeder set, *Tom Swift and His Airship: Or, The Stirring Cruise of the Red Cloud*, demonstrates Stratemeyer's fondness for using names to describe personalities. Tom was quick on the uptake and quick to seize on opportunities. This series by Victor Appleton, a house name, was the syndicate's science series. Authors received anywhere from $75 to $125 to write syndicate volumes. For the first Swift novels, author Howard Garis received $75 each, which seems a small return on volumes that may well have sold 15 million copies. Stratemeyer would insist, however, that the arrangement was only fair, since he, as entrepreneur, took all the risks and every investment came from his own pocket.

Howard Garis was born in Binghamton, New York, in 1873 and was living near the Stratemeyer family in Newark when Stratemeyer approached him about writing the stories. Out of deference to Howard's experience and expertise as a writer, Stratemeyer gave Howard more freedom to create than was usual, and over the next thirty to thirty-five stories (through 1941), Tom Swift invented nearly everything there was to invent. Tom is everything every young man should be: bright, devoted to family, honest, patriotic, and hardworking. Somehow, Tom, who was schooled at home, has absorbed chemistry, physics, higher math, engineering, drafting, and architecture without ever attending college. More important, and by way of a lesson to his readers, Tom never gives up. No matter how bad things are, Tom never says "Uncle," and this positive attitude takes him through the roughest of times.

Garis took the whole concept of inventing very seriously, and so did James Duncan Lawrence, who, from 1954 to 1971, wrote thirty-three volumes of the Tom Swift, Jr., series as Victor Appleton II. In this series, Tom was framed for a bank robbery and forced to track down the robbers to prove his innocence. Still, no matter how wealthy or famous Tom became, he remained essentially the same boyish, eager youngster that everyone admired. Most important, Tom loves what he does and has a wonderful time doing it. The Tom Swift series continued from 1981 to 1984, when the series setting was outer space, then 1991 to 1993, when the series reverted to its science and technology emphasis, which also was the focus of the latest series begun in 2006.

The Hardy Boys series

Although some critics dismissed the Hardy Boys series by Franklin W. Dixon, which began with *The Tower Treasure* (1927), as updated Rover Boys tales, the appearance of the juvenile mystery series coincided with the emergence of American detective fiction for adults. The Philo Vance and Ellery Queen mysteries as well as the classic *Black Mask* pulp magazine helped to confirm an American taste for detection. Sons of famous detective Fenton Hardy, Frank and Joe are ages sixteen and fifteen respectively when they are introduced. Later on, they age appropriately to the point where they can operate vehicles legally but not enough to graduate from high school. (In one volume, they were getting ready for college the next year, but in the succeeding volume, they were back in high school . . . and never left.) It has been said that, of necessity, detective fiction is formulaic in nature, and juvenile detective fiction is no exception. The gimmick for the Hardys is coincidence and regular cliff-hangers. Like Tom Swift and other boy heroes before them, Frank and Joe are tributes to the wide-awake American boy. At the conclusion of each book, the boys receive the congratulations of adults who have been unable to accomplish what the boys did, and many of those congratulating adults are eating a healthy helping of crow. Leslie McFarlane, a popular and well-respected newspaperman, was assigned the Hardy Boys series, and he conceived the characters and his descriptions from scenes of his boyhood. Later on, McFarlane said that he came to dread writing new installments because the series never seemed to go anywhere and the characters did not develop or change.

The Nancy Drew series

When the Nancy Drew series by Carolyn Keene debuted in 1930 with *The Secret of the Old Clock*, there was no pure mystery series featuring a girl in the juvenile market. These books were celebrations of liberated American girlhood before the actual liberation of women. Nancy, depicted on the original dust covers of the books by artist Russell Tandy, is the epitome of the flapper with cloche hat, neck scarf, high-heeled shoes, and shorter skirt. Mildred Wirt Benson was the ideal choice to author the Drew series. Other writers who wrote as Carolyn Keene include Walter Karig, Leslie McFarlane, James Duncan Lawrence, Nancy Axelrod, Priscilla Doll, Charles Strong, Alma Sasse, Wilhelmina Randkin, George Waller, Jr., and Margaret

Schert. Benson was something of an iconoclast and worked as a newspaperwoman. By writing for the syndicate, she was able to support herself, her daughter, and her disabled husband. She brought her own self-assurance, confidence, and no-nonsense attitude to the character of Nancy without diminishing Nancy's own femininity. In the first book of the series, Nancy, convinced that she is in the right, steals an old clock to obtain the will left inside it. From the 1980's on, there have been many testimonies from former Drew readers as to the positive effect that the series had on them, their attitudes, and awareness of being women.

H. Alan Pickrell

Principal mystery and detective fiction

Rover Boys series (as Winfield): 1899-1910 • *The Rover Boys and School: Or, The Cadets of Putnam Hall*, 1899; *The Rover Boys on the Ocean: Or, A Chase for Fortune*, 1899; *The Rover Boys in the Jungle: Or, Stirring Adventures in Africa*, 1899; *The Rover Boys Out West: Or, The Search for a Lost Mine*, 1900; *The Rover Boys on the Great Lakes: Or, The Secret of the Island Cave*, 1901; *The Rover Boys in the Mountains: Or, A Hunt for Fun and Fortune*, 1902; *The Rover Boys on Land and Sea: Or, The Crusoes of Seven Islands*, 1903; *The Rover Boys in Camp: Or, The Rivals of Pine Island*, 1904; *The Rover Boys on the River: Or, The Search for the Missing Houseboat*, 1905; *The Rover Boys on the Plains: Or, The Mystery of Red Rock*, 1906; *The Rover Boys in Southern Waters: Or, The Deserted Steam Yacht*, 1907; *The Rover Boys on the Farm: Or, Last Days at Putnam Hall*, 1908; *The Rover Boys on Treasure Isle: Or, The Strange Cruise of the Steam Yacht*, 1909; *The Rover Boys at College: Or, The Right Road and the Wrong*, 1910

1911-1920 • *The Rover Boys Down East: Or, The Struggle for the Stanhope Fortune*, 1911; *The Rover Boys in the Air: Or, From College Campus to Clouds*, 1912; *The Rover Boys in New York: Or, Saving Their Father's Honor*, 1913; *The Rover Boys in Alaska: Or, Lost in the Fields of Ice*, 1914; *The Rover Boys in Business: Or, The Search for the Missing Bonds*, 1915; *The Rover Boys on a Tour: Or, Last Days at Brill College*, 1916; *The Rover Boys at Colby Hall: Or, The Struggles of the Young Cadets*, 1917; *The Rover Boys on Showshoe Island: Or, The Old Lumberman's Treasure Box*, 1918; *The Rover Boys Under Canvas: Or, The Mystery of the Wrecked Submarine*, 1919; *The Rover Boys on a Hunt: Or, The Mysterious House in the Woods*, 1920

1921-1926 • *The Rover Boys in the Land of Luck: Or, Stirring Adventures in the Oilfields*, 1921; *The Rover Boys at Big Horn Ranch: Or, The Cowboys' Double Roundup*, 1922; *The Rover Boys at Big Bear Lake: Or, The Camps of the Rival Cadets*, 1923; *The Rover Boys Shipwrecked: Or, A Thrilling Hunt for Pirates' Gold*, 1924; *The Rover Boys on Sunset Trail: Or, The Old Miner's Mysterious Message*, 1925; *The Rover Boys Winning a Fortune: Or, Strenuous Days Afloat and Ashore*, 1926

Dave Porter series: *Dave Porter at Oak Hall: Or, The Schooldays of an American Boy*, 1905; *Dave Porter in the South Seas: Or, The Strange Cruise of the Stormy Petrel*, 1906; *Dave Porter's Return to School: Or, Winning the Medal of Honor*, 1907; *Dave Porter in the Far North: Or, The Pluck of an American Schoolboy*, 1908; *Dave Porter and His Classmates: Or, For the Honor of Oak Hall*, 1909; *Dave Porter at Star Ranch: Or, The Cowboy's Secret*, 1910; *Dave Porter and His Rivals: Or, The Chums and Foes of Oak Hall*, 1911; *Dave Porter on Cave Island: Or, A Schoolboy's Mysterious Mission*, 1912; *Dave Porter and the Runaways: Or, Last Days at Oak Hall*, 1913; *Dave Porter in the Gold Fields: Or, The Search for the Landslide Mine*, 1914; *Dave Porter at Bear Camp: Or, The Wild Man of Mirror Lake*, 1915; *Dave Porter and His Double: Or, The Disappearance of the Basswood Fortune*, 1916; *Dave Porter's Great Search: Or, The Perils of a Young Civil Engineer*, 1917; *Dave Porter Under Fire: Or, A Young Army Engineer in France*, 1918; *Dave Porter's War Honors: Or, At the Front with the Flying Engineers*, 1919

Other major works

Bound to Succeed series: *Richard Dare's Venture: Or, Striking Out for Himself*, 1894 (revised 1899); *Oliver Bright's Search: Or, The Mystery of a Mine*, 1895 (revised 1899); *Bound to Be an Electrician: Or, Franklin Bell's Road to Success*, 1897; *To*

Alaska for Gold: Or, The Fortune Hunters of the Yukon, 1899

Ship and Shore series: *The Last Cruise of the Spitfire: Or, Luke Foster's Strange Voyage*, 1894; *Reuben Stone's Discovery: Or, The Young Miller of Torrent Bend*, 1985; *True to Himself: Or, Roger Strong's Struggle for Place*, 1900

Old Glory series: *Under Dewey at Manila: Or, The War Fortunes of a Castaway*, 1898; *A Young Volunteer in Cuba: Or, Fighting for the Single Star*, 1898; *Fighting in Cuban Waters: Or, Under Schley on the Brooklyn*, 1899; *Under Otis in the Philippines: Or, A Young Officer in the Tropics*, 1899; *The Campaign of the Jungle: Or, Under Lawton Through Luzon*, 1900; *Under MacArthur in Luzon: Or, Last Battles in the Philippines*, 1901

Soldiers of Fortune series: *On to Peking: Or, Old Glory in China*, 1900; *Under the Mikado's Flag: Or, Young Soldiers of Fortune*, 1904; *At the Fall of Port Arthur: Or, A Young American in the Japanese Navy*, 1905; *Under Togo for Japan: Or, Three Young Americans on Land and Sea*, 1906

Colonial series: *With Washington in the West: Or, A Soldier Boy's Battles in the Wilderness*, 1901; *Marching on Niagara: Or, the Soldier Boys of the Old Frontier*, 1902; *At the Fall of Montreal: Or, A Soldier Boy's Final Victory*, 1903; *On the Trial of Pontiac: Or, The Pioneer Boys of the Ohio*, 1904; *The Fort in the Wilderness: Or, The Soldier Boys of the Indian Trails*, 1905; *Trail and Trading Post: Or, The Young Hunters of the Ohio*, 1906

Pan-American series: *Lost on the Orinoco: Or, American Boys in Venezuela*, 1902; *The Young Volcano Explorers: Or, American Boys in the West Indies*, 1902; *Young Explorers of the Isthmus: Or, American Boys in Central America*, 1903; *Young Explorers of the Amazon: Or, American Boys in Brazil*, 1904; *Treasure Seekers of the Andes: Or, American Boys in Peru*, 1907; *Chased Across the Pampas: Or, American Boys in Argentina and Homeward Bound*, 1911

Lakeport series: *The Boat Club Boys of Lakeport: Or, The Water Champions*, 1908; *The Football Boys of Lakesport: Or, More Goals Than One*, 1909; *The Automobile Boys of Lakeport: Or, A Run for Fun and Fame*, 1910; *The Aircraft Boys of Lakeport: Or, Rivals of the Clouds*, 1912

Nonseries novels: *Fighting for His Own: Or, The Fortune of a Young Artist*, 1897; *Shorthand Tom: Or, The Exploits of a Young Reporter*, 1897; *The Young Auctioneers: Or the Polishing of a Rolling Stone*, 1897; *The Minute Boys of Lexington*, 1898; *An Undivided Union*, 1899 (as Optic; with William Taylor Adams); *Fortune Hunters of the Philippines: Or , The Treasure of the Burning Mountain*, 1900 (as Charles); *The Land of Fire: Or, Adventures in Underground Africa*, 1900 (as Charles); *Between Boer and Briton: Or, Two Boys' Adventures in South Africa*, 1900 (also known as *The Young Ranchman: Or, Between Boer and Briton*, 1920); *American Boys' Life of William McKinley*, 1901; *Two Young Lumbermen: Or, From Maine to Oregon for Fortune*, 1903; *Joe the Survivor: Or, The Value of a Lost Claim*, 1903; *American Boys' Life of Theodore Roosevelt*, 1904; *Larry, the Wanderer: Or The Rise of a Nobody*, 1904; *Joe the Hotel Boy: Or, Winning Out by Pluck*, 1906 (as Alger); *Ben Logan's Triumph: Or, The Boys of Boxwood Academy*, 1908 (as Alger); *Defending His Flag: Or, A Boy in Blue and a Boy in Gray*, 1907; *First at the North Pole: Or, Two Boys in the Arctic Circle*, 1909 (also known as *The Young Explorers: Or, Adventures Above the Arctic Circle*, 1920); *Making Good with Margaret*, 1918 (as Strayer)

Rise in Life series (as Alger): *Out for Business: Or, Robert Frost's Strange Career*, 1900; *Falling in with Fortune: Or, The Son of a Soldier*, 1901; *Nelson the Newsboy: Or, Afloat in New York*, 1901; *Jerry the Backwoods Boy: Or, The Parkhurst Treasure*, 1904; *Lost at Sea: Or, Robert Roscoe's Strange Cruise*, 1904; *From Farm to Fortune: Or, Nat Nason's Strange Experience*, 1905; *The Young Book Agent: Or, Frank Hardy's Road to Success*, 1905; *Randy of the River: Or, The Adventures of a Young Deck Hand*, 1906

Flag of Freedom series (as Bonehill): *When Santiago Fell: Or, The War Adventures of Two Chums*, 1899 (also known as *For His Country: Or, The Adventures of Two Chums*, 1920); *A Sailor Boy with Dewey: Or, Afloat in the Philippines*, 1899 (also known as *Comrades in Peril: Or, Afloat on a Battleship*, 1920); *Off for Hawaii: Or, The Mystery of a*

Great Volcano, 1899 (also known as *The Young Pearl Hunters: Or, In Hawaiian Waters*, 1920); *The Young Bandmaster: Or, Concert, Stage, and Battlefield*, 1900; *Boys of the Fort: Or, A Young Captain's Pluck*, 1901 (also known as *Boys of the Fort: Or, True Courage Wins*, 1920); *With Custer in the Black Hills: Or, A Young Scout Among the Indians*, 1902 (also known as *On Fortune's Trail: Or, The Heroes of the Black Hills*, 1920)

Mexican War series (as Bonehill): *For the Liberty of Texas*, 1900; *With Taylor on the Rio Grande*, 1901; *Under Scott in Mexico*, 1902

Frontier series (as Bonehill): *With Boone on the Frontier: Or, The Pioneer Boys of Old Kentucky*, 1902 (*Boys of the Wilderness: Or, Down in Old Kentucky*, 1932; *Pioneer Boys of the Great Northwest: Or, With Lewis and Clark Across the Rockies*, 1904 (also known as *Boys of the Great Northwest: Or, Across the Rockies*, 1932); *Pioneer Boys of the Gold Fields: Or, The Nugget Hunters of '49*, 1906 (also known as *Boys of the Gold Fields: Or, The Nugget Hunters*, 1932)

Boy Hunters series (as Bonehill): *Four Boy Hunters: Or, The Outing of the Gun Club*, 1906; *Guns and Snowshoes: Or, The Winter Outing of the Young Hunters*, 1907; *Young Hunters of the Lake: Or, Out with Rod and Gun*, 1908; *Out with Gun and Camera: Or, The Boy Hunters in the Mountains*, 1910

Nonseries novels (as Bonehill): *Gun and Sled: Or the Young Hunters of Snow-Top Island*, 1897; *Young Oarsmen of Lakeview: Or, The Mystery of Hermit Island*, 1897; *The Rival Bicyclists: Or, Fun and Adventures on the Wheel*, 1897; *Leo the Circus Boy: Or, Life Under the Great White Canvas*, 1897; *Young Hunters in Puerto Rico: Or, The Search for a Lost Treasure*, 1900; *Three Young Ranchmen: Or, Daring Adventures in the Great West*, 1901; *The Boyland Boomer: Or, Dick Arbuckle's Adventures in Oklahoma*, 1902; *The Young Naval Captain: Or, the War of All Nations*, 1902; *Neka, the Boy Conjurer: Or, A Mystery of the Stage*, 1902; *Lost in the Land of Ice: Or, Daring Adventures Around the South Pole*, 1902; *The Tour of the Zero Club: Or, Adventures amid Ice and Snow*, 1902; *The Island Camp: Or, The Young Hunters of Lakeport*, 1904 (also known as *The Gun Club Boys of Lakesport: Or, The Island Camp*); *The Winning Run: Or, The Baseball Boys of Lakeport*, 1905 (also known as *The Baseball Boys of Lakeport: Or, The Winning Run*)

Putnam Hall series (as Winfield): *The Putnam Hall Cadets: Or, Good Times in School and Out*, 1901 (also known as *The Cadets of Putnam Hall: Or, Good Times in School and Out*, 1921; *The Putnam Hall Rivals: Or, Fun and Sport Afloat and Ashore*, 1906 (also known as *The Rivals of Putnam Hall: Or, Fun and Sport Afloat and Ashore*, 1921); *The Putnam Hall Champions: Or, Bound to Win Out*, 1908 (also known as *The Champions of Putnam Hall, Or, Bound to Win Out*, 1921); *The Putnam Hall Rebellion: Or, The Rival Runaways*, 1909 (also known as *The Rebellion at Putnam Hall: Or, The Rival Runaways*, 1921); *The Putnam Hall Encampment: Or, The Secret of the Old Mill*, 1910 (also known as *Camping Out Days at Putnam Hall: Or, The Secret of the Old Mill*, 1921); *The Putnam Hall Mystery: Or, The School Chums' Strange Discovery*, 1911 (also known as *The Mystery at Putnam Hall: Or, The School Chums' Strange Discovery*, 1921)

Nonseries novels (as Winfield): *The Schooldays of Fred Harley: Or, Rivals for All Honors*, 1897; *The Missing Tin Box: Or, The Stolen Railroad Bonds*, 1897; *Poor but Plucky: Or, The Mystery of a Flood*, 1897; *By Pluck, not Luck: Or, Dan Granbury's Struggle to Rise*, 1897; *Larry Barlow's Ambition: Or, The Adventures of a Young Fireman*, 1902; *Bob the Photographer: Or, A Hero in Spite of Himself*, 1902; *Mark Dale's Stage Adventures: Or, Bound to Be an Actor*, 1902; *The Young Bank Clerk: Or, Mark Vincent's Strange Discovery*, 1902; *The Young Bridge-Tender: Or, Ralph Nelson's Upward Struggle*, 1902; *A Young Inventor's Pluck: Or, The Mystery of the Wellington Legacy*, 1902

Bibliography

Billman, Carol. *The Secret of the Stratemeyer Syndicate: Nancy Drew, the Hardy Boys, and the Million Dollar Fiction Factory*. New York: Ungar, 1986. A comprehensive analysis of the phenomenon of the Stratemeyer syndicate reviews the origins and impacts of its products.

Caprio, Betsy. *Girl Sleuth on a Couch: The Mystery of Nancy Drew.* Trabuco Canyon, Calif.: Source Books, 1992. A Jungian analysis of the character presented along with a summary of her life, adventures, and character traits.

Dizer, John. *Tom Swift, The Bobbsey Twins, and Other Heroes of American Juvenile Literature.* Lewiston, N.Y.: Edwin Mellon Press, 1997. Everything about juvenile mystery heroes is here.

Dyer, Carolyn Stewart, and Nancy Tillman Romalov, eds. *Rediscovering Nancy Drew.* Iowa City: University of Iowa Press, 1995. The book deals with all things Benson, Adams, Stratemeyer, and Drew.

Neuberg, Victor. *The Popular Press Companion to Popular Literature.* Bowling Green, Ohio: Bowling Green State University Popular Press, 1983. This handy encyclopedic volume defines and exemplifies most aspects of popular literature. Sheds light on the Stratemeyer syndicate's place in society.

Rehak, Melanie. *Girl Sleuth: Nancy Drew and the Women Who Created Her.* Orlando: Harcourt, 2005. Tells the story of how Stratemeyer's daughter Harriet and Mildred Wirt Benson developed the character Nancy Drew.

JEAN STUBBS

Born: Denton, Lancashire, England; October 23, 1926

Types of plot: Historical; private investigator; thriller

Principal series

Inspector John Lintott, 1967-

Principal series character

Inspector John Lintott, retired after forty years at Scotland Yard, is now an occasional private investigator. Wherever he travels, Lintott carries with him the values of his humble origins, including a belief in marital fidelity, a dislike of pretension, and a loathing for those who bully the weak and helpless.

Contribution

Midway in her writing career, Jean Stubbs wrote two historical thrillers; in each of them, retired Scotland Yard inspector John Lintott is persuaded to undertake a private investigation. Although she then left the genre to write a historical saga, Stubbs is notable for her unique mixture of genres in novels that are variously called historical romantic mysteries, historical thrillers, and historical mystery stories. These two books are also memorable in that by placing the conservative, down-to-earth Inspector John Lintott in exotic surroundings, Stubbs uses the private investigator format for ironic social commentary in the tradition of the naïve fictitious foreign observer. The mixture fascinated readers; the fact that Stubbs then abandoned her unique format is a matter for regret.

Biography

Jean Stubbs was born on October 23, 1926, in Denton, Lancashire, England. She was educated at the Manchester High School for Girls and later at the Manchester School of Art, which she attended from 1944 to 1947. A marriage, which ended in divorce, produced two children: a son, Robin, and a daughter, Gretel Sally. Aside from her love of writing, Stubbs also enjoys art, spending time with her family and cooking.

Before settling on a career as a writer, Stubbs was an artist, an actress, and a concert pianist. She published several short stories, reviews, and articles in various periodicals before her career as a novelist. She received the Society of Authors' Tom Gallon Award in 1964 for her short story "A Child's Four Seasons." Stubbs did not gain real literary recognition until the publication of her first novel, *The Rose-Grower* (1962), the first in her historical romance series, the Howarth Chronicles, which she later claimed had been written on the subway. It was not until 1974 that she turned to the mystery format in *The Painted Face*, and after *The Golden Crucible* in 1976, she abandoned that genre for a successful family-saga series.

Analysis

During the twelve years between the publication of her first novel and the publication of *The Painted Face* in 1974, Jean Stubbs developed the interests that in retrospect seem naturally to have led her to the genre of the historical mystery thriller. After three realistic works and a utopian novel, she ventured into a combination of history and crime with *My Grand Enemy* (1967), which tells the story of Mary Blandy, who was hanged in 1752 for poisoning her father and who may well have been merely the tool of the man she loved. Although critics considered that the book had fallen short of high drama, it was praised for its factual accuracy and for its re-creation of the period in which it was set. Although not a conventional mystery and crime writer, Stubbs adjusted the genre to suit her particular interests. Her works have earned wide acclaim for their meticulous historical detail and their imaginative and suspenseful plots.

The Case of Kitty Ogilvie

After a biographical novel about Eleanora Duse, Stubbs once again ventured into the history of crime with *The Case of Kitty Ogilvie* (1970). In this historical novel, Stubbs proves that Ogilvie was indeed cleverly framed, as the supposed murderess had insisted. Stubbs's interpretation is supported by Ogilvie's mysterious escape from prison, which may well have been made possible by respectable friends who knew that she had been wronged but could not prove it. The poignant prison scene in which Ogilvie must bid farewell to her baby, who she senses will not live long in the care of a hired nurse, is one of the most effective pieces of writing that Stubbs has produced. Because by that point in the book she had convinced her readers of Ogilvie's innocence, it is also clear that here, as perhaps in the Blandy story, Stubbs was beginning to explore her concern with feminine vulnerability.

Dear Laura

The theme of vulnerability emerged again in the gothic novel *Dear Laura* (1973) set in the nineteenth century. Although the wife in the novel is foolish, she does not deserve a husband so tyrannical or a life so grim. With this work, Stubbs once again proved that she had learned how to handle intense emotion and to maintain suspense until the last page. These skills were to stand her in good stead when she at last turned to historical mysteries, *The Painted Face* and *The Golden Crucible*.

The Painted Face

Although it is generally agreed that *The Painted Face* lacks the depth of *The Golden Crucible*, the two books share a number of characteristics. In both cases, the setting is the early twentieth century: *The Painted Face* takes place in 1902, *The Golden Crucible* in 1906. Furthermore, in both novels the down-to-earth, meat-and-potatoes Inspector Lintott is removed from his normal surroundings and forced to solve a mystery in an alien, exotic place. To him, the Paris of *The Painted Face* is just as exotic as the San Francisco of the Barbary Coast period to which he travels in *The Golden Crucible*.

Although both books begin with a riddle, only in the first has there been a death, and that is not suspected to have been murder. Twenty years after a railway accident in France, in which his half sister was supposedly killed, a well-to-do English artist wishes to learn more about her fate. The second novel begins with the question of a wealthy American's motivations in attempting to hire the inspector to trick the famous magician Felix Salvador, but the crucial mystery is the disappearance of the magician's sister, Alicia, which occurs almost two weeks later. The injury of Bessie Lintott, which follows, is only briefly a mystery; when the inspector is boldly told that it was designed to intimidate him into dropping his inquiries into Alicia's kidnapping, he acquires a personal reason to follow those responsible—to San Francisco or to the ends of the earth. In both novels, the fact that the victims have been vulnerable females both motivates Lintott to leave his comfortable fireside to take the case and, as far as the structure of the book is concerned, intensifies the suspense inherent in the chase.

If feminine vulnerability is important to the plot, it is also an important theme in both books. The characters can be divided into three groups. First, there are those who are worldly, sophisticated, and corrupt. It is from this group and from their hirelings that the bullies and criminals are drawn. Their antagonist is Inspector Lintott, who has the help both of the person who hired him and of other well-intentioned people who become his friends. The purpose of his efforts is the protection of the third kind of character, the innocent women who are so easily victimized in the male-dominated society of which Stubbs writes.

Stubbs, however, makes her categories somewhat more complex by presenting Lintott himself as a proponent of the ancient pattern of male domination. His argument is clearly stated: Because of the superior physical power of men, women must be protected; that is why they have fathers, brothers, and husbands. In his own case, the system works well; evidently Lintott's wife, Bessie, considers the right to vote far less important than the power she holds in the family, power that arises partly from her husband's respect and concern for her as a woman. Lintott's daughter, however, who appears in both novels, is another matter. Because she has been jailed as a suffragette, her decent but old-fashioned husband has booted her out until she agrees to mend her ways; she has returned to her parents' home, where she is argumentative and unhappy. Although at first Lintott sympathizes in principle with his son-in-law, by the end of *The Golden Crucible* he has seen enough unhappy marriages and tyrannical husbands to be open-minded about his daughter's complaints; finally, he realizes that her rebellion arose from real mistreatment.

If Inspector Lintott is an embodiment of middle-class conservatism, at least he exemplifies the best of his class. Although he is unsophisticated, he is not stupid; although he is restrained and respectful in demeanor, he is not cowardly. It is satisfying to watch as the pretentious and wealthy who have consistently mocked and underrated him at last come to respect him and even to fear him.

The Golden Crucible

The title of Stubbs's second mystery, *The Golden Crucible*, is appropriate both to her plot and to her theme. It is taken from a poem in which America is called a golden crucible, a melting pot, but because most of the action of this story takes place in San Francisco, a city at least partially built by gold, and because the story ends with the fire and earthquake, in which the character of the city's residents is cruelly tested, the title has a very specific application. In personal terms, San Francisco is also the testing place of Inspector Lintott and his daughter, who must pit their virtue against the evil schemes of Bela Barak, whose wealth and power have enabled him to have Bessie Lintott run down, to terrify his own wife, and to kidnap the fragile Alicia, transport her from England to San Francisco, and there hold her hostage.

Despite the luxury that might have tempted another man on the long trip to San Francisco, Lintott holds to his values. He packs cheap linen and stout boots, nothing for show, and on the boat he takes an economy ticket. Although sometimes his dogged frugality is comic, it is this steadfastness that enables him to resist the temptations of Barak, who could buy a lesser man.

Lintott's success lies in finding Alicia and exposing the villains; his daughter's is subtler but not less real. Separated from her stingy husband, she is exposed to the world of fine dresses and first-class hotels. For a time, she fancies herself in love with her employer, the magician Felix Salvador, who has introduced her to high life so that as his supposed assistant she can more effectively help her father. By the end of the novel, she has her own reward, and it is not dependent on the love of Felix or anyone else. Resisting the temptations of riches, adventure, and passion, she has found that she is as brave and strong as any man, and with that discovery, she has banished her querulous, quarrelsome, and secretly uncertain former self forever.

The themes that Stubbs had touched on in the earlier books, such as the vulnerability of women in a male-dominated world, are fully realized in *The Golden Crucible*. In both of the books about historical crimes, the theme of justice is important, and particularly so because there was a strong possibility that the central character had been wrongly condemned. In *The Painted Face*, once it is obvious that the painter's half sister might still be alive, both the painter and the inspector fear that her loss of identity might have condemned her unjustly to a life of ignorance or even to a loss of virtue. In this book, however, there is no real villain; instead, the sister is the victim of understandable human frailties, combined with the element of chance that is a part of every life. In *The Golden Crucible*, the lines of good and evil are clearly drawn. The question is whether the villains will be subject to private revenge, as Salvador would wish, or to the system of public justice to which Lintott has devoted his life. In the end, although Lintott discovers the truth, it is divine retribution, in the form of the earthquake and fire, which destroys the forces of evil, while at the same time it kills the innocent—including the fragile Alicia, whose kidnapping had begun Lintott's quest.

Stubbs has been justly praised for her success in evoking the San Francisco of 1906 in this novel, particularly in her account of the earthquake and fire at the conclusion of the book. Here she abandons the sometimes baroque descriptions and the appropriately formal dialogue of her earlier passages for a slangy, staccato style—full of expostulations, shouts, and warnings—that masterfully captures the atmosphere of the moment.

The historical mystery is a difficult genre because it adds the complexity of a mystery plot to the already exacting demands of a historical novel for factual accuracy and for the believable re-creation of the patterns of thought and dialogue of a past era. Although in her first historical mystery Stubbs was not able to integrate these elements fully and therefore produced a somewhat cerebral work, in her second book in this genre she lived up to all the possibilities of style, plot, and theme of which her earlier works had suggested she was capable. Readers must regret the fact that after *The Golden Crucible*, Stubbs turned away from the genre and instead began to produce her family saga, which though highly praised by reviewers, is not, after all, a mystery.

Rosemary M. Canfield Reisman
Updated by Philip Bader

Principal mystery and detective fiction

Inspector John Lintott series: *My Grand Enemy*, 1967; *The Case of Kitty Ogilvie*, 1970; *Dear Laura*, 1973; *The Painted Face*, 1974; *The Golden Crucible*, 1976

Other major works

Novels: *The Rose-Grower*, 1962; *The Travellers*, 1963; *Hanrahan's Colony*, 1964; *The Straw Crown*, 1966; *The Passing Star*, 1970 (also known as *Eleanora Duse*); *An Unknown Welshman*, 1972; *Kit's Hill*, 1978 (also known as *By Our Beginnings*); *An Imperfect Joy*, 1981 (also known as *The Ironmaster*); *The Vivian Inheritance*, 1982; *The Northern Correspondent*, 1984; *A Lasting Spring*, 1987; *Like We Used to Be*, 1989; *Light in Summer*, 1991 (also known as *Summer Secrets*); *Kelly Park*, 1992; *Family Games*, 1994; *The Witching Time*, 1998; *I'm a Stranger Here Myself*, 2004

Teleplay: *Family Christmas*, 1965

Bibliography

Heilburn, Carolyn G. *Writing a Woman's Life*. New York: W. W. Norton, 1988. This volume describes how writers and biographers artificially reduced the lives of the women about whom they wrote to a narrow, conventional view. Heilburn deals with the struggles of women writers and touches on Stubbs.

Klein, Kathleen Gregory, ed. *Great Women Mystery Writers: Classic to Contemporary*. Westport, Conn.: Greenwood Press, 1994. Contains an entry on Stubbs that examines her life and works.

Scaggs, John. *Crime Fiction*. New York, Routledge, 2005. Contains a chapter on historical crime fiction that sheds light on Stubbs's work.

Stubbs, Jean. Interview. *Books and Bookmen* 18 (April, 1973): 39. A brief interview that includes biographical details about the author and a discussion of themes in her works.

Vasudevan, Aruna, ed. *Twentieth-century Romance and Historical Writers*. 3d ed. Detroit: St. James Press, 1994. Provides an in-depth profile of Stubbs and discussions of her major works, specifically her historical romances.

EUGÈNE SUE

Born: Paris, France; January 20, 1804
Died: Annecy, France; August 3, 1857
Types of plot: Historical; private investigator; thriller

Contribution

Eugène Sue's most famous novels, *Les Mystères de Paris* (1842-1843; *The Mysteries of Paris*, 1843-1846), was the first novel to present a realistic portrait of the criminal underworld of Paris. Modeled on members of a Parisian criminal gang on trial for murder, Sue's characters spoke the slang and displayed the callous attitudes of hardened criminals. Criminal activity was linked to social and economic conditions; Sue argued that many virtuous people became criminals as a result of their unfortunate circumstances. Sue also portrayed crime in more conventional terms, however, because some of his characters were morally vicious while the most virtuous could never be tempted into crime, no matter how desperate their circumstances. Sue's hero, Prince Rodolphe of Gerolstein, displayed characteristics common to latter-day detective heroes. Standing out in sharp contrast to his setting, he roamed the streets of Paris seeking to alleviate the misery that might cause the virtuous poor to fall.

Biography

Eugène Marie-Joseph Sue was born Marie-Joseph Sue on January 20, 1804, in Paris, the son of Jean-Joseph Sue, an eminent medical practitioner, and Marie Sophie Derilly. He was named for his godmother, Josephine Bonaparte, but soon adopted the name of his godfather, Josephine's son, Eugène de Beauharnais. The Sue family was a dynasty of eminent and wealthy physicians. Sue, one of four children, rebelled early in his life against the expectation that he would become a doctor and his father's colleague. He was a miserable student; when apprenticed to his father's hospital in Paris, he devoted much of his time to playing practical jokes. Sue's father found him more distant posts in a hospital in Toulon during a military campaign and in the royal navy for six years. Sue drew on the exotic locales he visited in writing his earliest works.

In 1825, Sue—who did not consider himself a serious writer—wrote his first work, a play, to gain the attention of an attractive actress. Returning to Paris in 1829, he began writing adventure stories for the popular press. After his father's death in 1830, Sue, a confirmed bachelor, lived extravagantly, dissipating his inheritance until he was financially ruined in 1836.

That year marked a turning point in his life, for his friends interested him in the problems of social reform. The publication of *The Mysteries of Paris* made him a best-selling novelist and a hero of the working classes. After the Revolution of 1848, Sue, then a Fourierist, was elected to the National Assembly. He attended conscientiously but spent most of his time writing and correcting the work that totally absorbed him in his last years, *Les Mystères du peuple: Ou, Histoire d'une famille de prolétaires à travers les âges* (1849-1857; *The Mysteries of the People*, 185?, 1867). Arrested in 1851 and released in 1852, Sue went into political exile in Savoy, leaving his property behind and refusing to support the new regime, which continued to harass him.

Sue died on August 3, 1857, in Annecy, Savoy, of nervous disorders exacerbated by stress and fatigue,

Eugène Sue.

leaving behind an enormous corpus of fiction, drama, and political essays.

Analysis

Eugène Sue was one of the most widely read and praised writers of his day, not only in France but also throughout Europe, England, and the United States. His work is no longer read, except for historical interest, because his lack of attention to style—which he believed was unimportant—and the length of his novels make excessive demands on the reader's patience. Yet his development as a writer traced an interesting course. At first, he wrote because literature was amusing and lucrative; later, he became increasingly serious about the importance of his work as a vehicle of social reform, a means to transform the consciousness of all classes. He believed that "if the rich only knew," they would act to correct the injustice and misery that existed in their society. Sue's early reputation was that of a dandy who wrote each new chapter only after putting on a fresh pair of yellow gloves. Most of his novels were first published in installments in the popular press; he drew a large readership for his early historical romances in the manner of Sir Walter Scott and for novels of maritime adventures that earned for him the title "the French Cooper." *Plik et Plok* (1831), *Atar-Gull* (1831; *Atar Gull: A Nautical Tale*, 1846), *La Salamandre* (1832; *The Salamander*, 1844), *La Vigie de Koat-Vën* (1833; *The Temptation; Or, The Watch Tower of Koat-Vën*, 1845), and *La Courcaratcha* (1832-1834) were early successes. These works, although not mystery stories, employed a fantastic realism like that of Charles Dickens, emphasizing the evil and bizarre side of human nature. Sue often investigated the relationship between good and evil, even in a novel of society such as *Mathilde: Mémoires d'une jeune femme* (1841; *Matilda: Or, The Memoirs of a Young Woman*, 1843), which explored one of his favorite themes, the ability of the wicked to manipulate the virtuous.

The Mysteries of Paris

There is no doubt that Sue's reputation as a mystery writer rests on his most famous work, *The Mysteries of Paris*. This novel, published in installments during 1842-1843, took France, Europe, and then the rest of the world by storm. It also makes clear Sue's strengths as a novelist: his ability to create numerous unforgettable characters, to create elaborate but interlocking narratives, and to fashion from so many individual stories a portrait of an entire society. He showed how all lives were interconnected by coincidence, concealed interests, and secrets hidden in the past. The novel was translated as it was being written. The word "mystery" caught the attention of readers; soon, many similarly titled works appeared. Every city had its "mysteries" as writers everywhere capitalized on the appeal of Sue's title.

The Mysteries of Paris was the first novel to use the criminal underworld of a modern urban city as its setting. Sue's dedication to realism turned his novel into an extensive catalog of the crimes and criminals existing in Paris at that time. Sue had read earlier novels presenting brief portrayals of criminal characters, as well as the nonfictional memoirs of François-Eugène Vidocq, former head of the Paris police. Sue, however, was the first writer to present a detailed study of the criminal world in all of its horror, ruthlessness, and poverty. His interest in the criminal class probably stemmed from an interest in poverty as the cause of crime and from the suggestion that he explore social diseases in a manner similar to that of a physician observing physical diseases. Sue was looking for a new subject for a novel, and his attention was drawn to a famous criminal trial of 1839, in which a gang of thieves and prostitutes was tried for the murder of several merchants. Clearly, the accused served as prototypes for Sue's characters, who lived in the same neighborhood, drank in the same taverns, spoke in the same criminal slang, and displayed the same matter-of-fact attitude toward their crimes. Sue warned his readers that they would enter regions as uncivilized and barbaric as the Indian-inhabited forests of North America. The Parisian savages were the former convicts, thieves, and murderers living hidden in the midst of a great city. The reader would "penetrate into horrible and unknown regions"; he would meet "hideous and frightening types, swarming in unclean sewers like reptiles in a swamp." The physical setting of the criminal neighborhood of Paris, "a labyrinth of hidden, narrow, and twisting streets," became a metaphor for the unfathomable secrets of the human soul. Sue used the word "mysteries" in this larger sense of the unknown; he used it in other titles also, but in this novel, the mysteries or secrets often were hidden crimes.

The novel's hero, Prince Rodolphe of Gerolstein, expiates his guilt by attempting to aid worthy individuals whose desperate circumstances might tempt them into crime or make them victims of unscrupulous men and women. He is a secret benefactor who shows how social consciousness and money could improve overall social conditions. To help those in distress, Rodolphe assumes a variety of disguises and gathers information via methods employed by modern operatives.

At the novel's beginning he is disguised as a young artisan. He enters the criminal quarters of Paris in search of François Germain, who has disappeared mysteriously. Germain's father, a member of a gang, placed his son inside a banking house to help with a robbery. After discovering these plans, François fled in desperation. He has apparently gone into hiding, but his mother, a friend of Rodolphe, now fears for his life.

Rodolphe is superior to his adversaries and willing to defend those who need help. In the opening scenes, which introduce many of the novel's main characters, Rodolphe is halted in his mission by a "damsel in distress," a young prostitute who has been nicknamed Fleur de Marie (Mary's Flower) because of her virginal appearance (her name means "virgin" in criminal slang). Le Chourineur (the Stabber) has demanded repayment of money from Fleur de Marie; he threatens to kill her when she cannot pay and tries to defend herself. Rodolphe intervenes, and the ensuing fight with Le Chourineur proves Rodolphe's mettle. He is no coward, never hesitating when threatened with physical violence. His constant companion, Sir Walter Murph, later explains why he is so successful:

> Crabb de Ramsgate taught you boxing, Lacour of Paris taught you the use of the cane and French boxing, and out of curiosity criminal slang; the famous Bertrand taught you fencing, and you often were better than your teachers when matched against them. You kill swallows in flight with a pistol, you have muscles of steel, even though you are slender and elegant.

Rodolphe is clearly a match for all the criminals of Paris. He easily defeats Le Chourineur, and through his generosity and compassion gains the man's undying loyalty. Le Chourineur saves Rodolphe's life on more than one occasion, sacrificing his own life in the end.

After their fight, Rodolphe and Le Chourineur, along with Fleur de Marie, retreat to the tavern of the Ogresse, a spot frequented by criminals and the very poor. Fleur de Marie and Le Chourineur both tell their stories, and Rodolphe resolves to help them. A typical narrative pattern is established here: Numerous flashbacks and inserted narratives prevent the main story from progressing very quickly, even though the main events of the plot span a relatively short period of time.

In the tavern, Rodolphe encounters the Maître d'école (the Schoolmaster), an archcriminal later revealed to be the father of the missing François. He also meets the latter's companion, a hag nicknamed La Chouette (the Owl). La Chouette recognizes Fleur de Marie as a child once left in her care. She swears to take revenge on the beautiful Fleur de Marie, who had fled her abuse. Typically, François, Fleur de Marie, and other characters are constantly threatened with destruction and can continue to survive only through desperate escapes.

These scenes also demonstrate the way in which Sue brings together characters unknowingly related through their pasts. Rodolphe takes Marie to a model farm he has established, placing her in the care of Madam Georges, the mother of François. Here Marie should have been safe from further harm, but she is kidnaped as part of a plot against Rodolphe by Sarah Mac-Grégor. Sarah had once been married to Rodolphe, but his father had had the marriage annulled, and she hopes to gain him back. The child from this marriage, long thought to be dead, turns out to be Fleur de Marie. Most novelists would have made this mystery the center of their plot, but Sue characteristically rejects the simple solution. He reveals the secret to his readers early, because it is only one situation of interest. After seeing its dramatic possibility and its obvious conclusion, he moves on to other narratives and returns to Fleur de Marie's story only periodically, interlacing it with other narrative threads in unexpected ways. Sue's imagination is so fertile that he disdains the obvious and seeks the complex. Fleur de Marie is pursued first by La Chouette and Maître d'école on Sarah's behalf and later by the agents of the hypocritical notary Jacques Ferrand, who had hidden her for Sarah. Ferrand wants to conceal the evidence of his crime. Having declared the child dead, he now attempts to murder the young woman.

Meanwhile, Rodolphe, still seeking François, moves into a boardinghouse at No. 17 rue de Temple, François's last known address. Here Sue introduces another cluster of characters, placing them in the environment of the real criminals of the 1839 trial. Rodolphe believes that one resident, the beautiful and hardworking Rigolette (the Laugher), knows the whereabouts of François—as indeed she does. Rigolette is also a former friend of Fleur de Marie, and she serves to connect many of the characters in the story. The boardinghouse draws together the fates of several characters. The poverty-stricken but honest Morel family, living in the garret, is also persecuted by the hypocritical and miserly Ferrand. Sue uses the Morels' situation to demonstrate his own social theory: Society should eliminate crime by rewarding virtue, a method that would be more effective than punishing crime. "Spies for Virtue" (a phrase and concept he borrows from Napoleon Bonaparte's memoirs) should reward the virtuous poor with money. Sue theorizes that a better standard of living would prevent crime more effectively than the threat of imprisonment and would be less expensive. Rodolphe, whose mission is to spy out virtue, becomes the Morels' secret benefactor.

Besides the criminals of the tavern and the boardinghouse, Sue introduces other members of the criminal class. When Fleur de Marie is incarcerated in Saint-Lazare, a women's prison, Sue paints a detailed picture of several inhabitants and tells their histories. One inmate's lover is the only honest member of a criminal family of several generations. Sue presents a study of this family, the Martials, whose criminality he contrasts with the poverty and the honesty of the Morels. François Germain meets a member of the Martial family when he is imprisoned at the Force, the maximum-security prison for men. Double-crossed by the master criminal of Paris, Nicholas Martial is imprisoned with fellow members of Paris's toughest underworld gang. François also meets the master storyteller Pique-Vinaigre (Sharp Vinegar), whose tale "Coup-en-deux" (Cut-in-Two) resembles Edgar Allan Poe's "The Murders in the Rue Morgue." Because Poe's tale was not published in France until 1846, however, it is unlikely that Sue borrowed from this story.

At the novel's end, the moral order is restored: The wicked die, the virtuous characters are rewarded. The master criminal of Paris turns out to be a police informer. Rodolphe and Fleur de Marie, the latter now a princess, return to Gerolstein. Yet the court of Gerolstein is abstract and unreal when contrasted to the earthy vitality of criminal Paris.

Although Sue's later novels are thematically connected to *The Mysteries of Paris*, he never again focused on the criminal class of Paris or the city's pervasive atmosphere of crime. From his point of view, perhaps, he had thoroughly explored this subject. The highly popular *Le Juif errant* (1844-1845; *The Wandering Jew*, 1868), his next novel, and *The Mysteries of the People*, his final major work, are much more political in their concerns.

In the twentieth century, the melodramatic novels of Sue have fallen out of favor with the reading public. Nevertheless, while reading his best novels, especially *The Mysteries of Paris*, readers will still find themselves caring about his characters. Sue's novels are full of color, drama, and suspense. From his dedicated humanitarian vision and commitment to social change emerges a complete and complex tableau of mid-nineteenth century Paris. His creation of a criminal urban landscape shaped the literary landscapes of many other writers, including Victor Hugo, Honoré de Balzac, Charles Baudelaire, and Fyodor Dostoevski. After Sue, the city was the natural environment of criminal characters.

Marilyn Rye

Principal mystery and detective fiction

Novels: *Les Mystères de Paris*, 1842-1843 (*The Mysteries of Paris*, 1843)

Other major works

Novels: *Plik et Plok*, 1831; *Atar-Gull*, 1831 (*Atar Gull: A Nautical Tale*, 1846); *La Salamandre*, 1832 (*The Salamander*, 1844); *La Courcaratcha*, 1832-

1834; *La Vigie de Koat-Vën*, 1833 (*The Temptation; Or, The Watch Tower of Koat-Vën*, 1845); *Latréaumont*, 1838 (English translation, 1845); *Jean Cavalier*, 1840 (*The Protestant Leader*, 1849); *Mathilde: Mémoires d'une jeune femme*, 1841 (*Matilda: Or, The Memoirs of a Young Woman*, 1843); *Le Juif errant*, 1844-1845 (*The Wandering Jew*, 1868); *Les Mystères du peuple: Ou, Histoire d'une famille de prolétaires à travers les âges*, 1849-1857 (*The Mysteries of the People*, 185?, 1867)

Short fiction: *Les Sept péchés capitaux*, 1848-1852

Bibliography

Cambiaire, Celestine Pierre. "Poe and Gaston Leroux and Eugène Sue." In *The Influence of Edgar Allan Poe in France*. Reprint. New York: Haskell House, 1970. Discusses the reaction to Poe of Sue and Leroux and the influence the American author had on their work.

Chevasco, Berry Palmer. *Mysterymania: The Reception of Eugène Sue in Britain, 1838-1860*. New York: P. Lang, 2003. Important study of the reaction of Victorian England to Sue's mystery and, by extension, the effects of Sue's writing on the development of Victorian crime fiction.

Eco, Umberto. "Rhetoric and Ideology in Sue's *Les Mystères de Paris*." In *The Role of the Reader: Explorations in the Semiotics of Texts*. Bloomington: Indiana University Press, 1984. One of the most famous practitioners of semiotics (the study of signs) applies his distinctive brand of literary analysis to Sue's crime fiction.

Martí-Lopez, Elisa. *Borrowed Words: Translation, Imitation, and the Making of the Nineteenth-Century Novel in Spain*. Lewisburg, Pa.: Bucknell University Press, 2002. Traces the influence—and imitation—of Sue's *The Mysteries of Paris* in nineteenth century Spain.

Morain, Alfred. *The Underworld of Paris: Secrets of the Sûreté*. New York: E. P. Dutton, 1931. Nonfictional study of crime and criminals in Paris; useful background for understanding the reality that Sue fictionalized in *The Mysteries of Paris*.

Pickup, Ian. "Eugène Sue." In *Nineteenth Century French Fiction Writers: Romanticism and Realism, 1800-1860*, edited by Catharine Savage Brosman. Vol. 119 in *Dictionary of Literary Biography*. Detroit: Gale Research, 1992. Places Sue's distinctive realism in relation to that of other nineteenth century French realist authors, as well as to the Romanticism against which they were rebelling.

Prendergast, Christopher. *For the People by the People? Eugène Sue's "Les Mystères de Paris": A Hypothesis in the Sociology of Literature*. Oxford, England: European Humanities Research Centre, 2003. Combines a sociological approach to literature with a close, textual reading of Sue's novel.

JULIAN SYMONS

Born: London, England; May 30, 1912
Died: Kent, England; November 19, 1994
Types of plot: Inverted; psychological

Principal series

Chief Inspector Bland, 1945-1949
Francis Quarles, 1961-1965
Detective Chief Superintendent Hilary Catchpole, 1994-1996

Principal series characters

Chief Inspector Bland is an appropriately named police investigator, who is not impressive or even confidence inspiring at his first appearance. Subsequent appearances, however, prove him to be capable and efficient, even if unimaginative.

Francis Quarles is a private investigator who sets up his practice shortly after World War II. Large of build and flamboyantly dandyish of costume, Quarles masks his efficiency and astuteness behind deceptively languorous behavior.

Detective Chief Superintendent Hilary Catchpole is a virtuous, compassionate, middle-class police investigator. Happily married to a jovial wife, Catchpole represents the stalwart hero of the people, the prototypical "good man."

Contribution

Julian Symons produced a body of crime fiction that moved beyond genre formulas with its emphasis on the artistic representation of a particular worldview, its exploration of the human psyche under stress, and its ironic commentary on a world in which the distinctions between the lawbreaker and the forces of law frequently blur into uselessness. Symons viewed the crime novel as a vehicle for analysis of the effects of societal pressures and repressions on the individual. Symons mainly concentrated on psychological crime novels that delineate what he called "the violence that lives behind the bland faces most of us present to the world." Typically, his characters were ordinary people driven to extreme behavior, average citizens caught in Hitchcockian nightmares; the focus was on the desperate actions prompted by the stresses of everyday life. Symons expanded the limits of the crime novel, proving through his work that a popular genre, like orthodox fiction, can serve as a vehicle for a personal vision of Western society gone awry, of human lives in extremis.

Any assessment of Symons's contribution to crime literature must include mention of his two histories of the genre: *The Detective Story in Britain* (1962) and *Bloody Murder: From the Detective Story to the Crime Novel* (1972, revised 1985; also known as *Mortal Consequences: A History, from the Detective Story to the Crime Novel*). In both of these works, Symons detailed what he perceived to be a shift in both popularity and emphasis in the genre from the elegantly plot-driven classic detective story of the Golden Age of the 1920's and 1930's to the more psychologically oriented crime novel with its emphasis on character and motivation.

Biography

Julian Gustave Symons (the name rhymes with "women's") was born on May 30, 1912, in London, the last child in a family of seven. His parents were Minnie Louise Bull Symons and Morris Albert Symons, but Julian never learned his father's original name or nationality. A seller of secondhand goods until World War I brought him profits as an auctioneer, the elder Symons was a strict Victorian-era father.

As a child, Julian Symons suffered from a stammer that placed him in remedial education despite his intelligence. Although he overcame his speech problems and excelled as a student, Symons nevertheless ended his formal education at the age of fourteen and began an intense program of self-education that encompassed all that was best in literature. Symons worked variously as a shorthand typist, a secretary in an engineering firm, and an advertising copywriter and executive, all in London, before he became established as an important and prolific writer of crime fiction.

At first glance, Symons's literary career appears to fall rather neatly into two distinct and contradictory phases: radical poet in the 1930's and Tory writer of crime fiction. A founder of the important little magazine *Twentieth Century Verse* and its editor from 1937 to 1939, Symons was one of a group of young poets who in the 1930's were the heirs apparent to Stephen Spender and W. H. Auden. Before the outbreak of World War II, Symons was already the author of two volumes of poetry and was acquiring a reputation as an insightful and astute literary critic.

In 1941, Symons married Kathleen Clark; they had two children, Sarah and Maurice. From 1942 to 1944, Symons saw military service in the Royal Armoured Corps of the British army. A major turning point in Symons's career was the publication of his first crime novel, *The Immaterial Murder Case* (1945). Originally written as a spoof of art movements and their followers, this manuscript had languished in a desk drawer for six years until Kathleen encouraged him to sell it to supplement his wages as a copywriter.

The success of this and the novel that followed, *A Man Called Jones* (1947), provided Symons with the financial security he needed to become a full-time writer and spend time on books that required extensive research. With his fourth novel, *The Thirty-first of February* (1950), Symons began to move away from the classic detective forms to more experimental approaches. He supplemented his freelance income with a weekly book review column, inherited from George Orwell, in the *Manchester Evening News* from 1947 to 1956. Through the years, he also wrote reviews for the *London Sunday Times* (1958-1968), served as a member of the council of Westfield College, University of London (1972-1975), and lectured as a visiting professor at Amherst College, Massachusetts (1975-1976).

A cofounder of the Crime Writers' Association, Symons served as its chair from 1958 to 1959. That organization honored him with its Crossed Red Herrings Award for best crime novel in 1957 for *The Colour of Murder*, a special award for *Crime and Detection* in 1966, and the Cartier Diamond Dagger Award for lifetime achievement in 1990. Symons also served on the board of the Society of Authors from 1970 to 1971, succeeded Agatha Christie as president of the Detection Club from 1976 to 1985, and presided over the Conan Doyle Society from 1989 to 1993. The Mystery Writers of America honored him with the Edgar Allan Poe Award for *The Progress of a Crime* in 1961, a Special Edgars Award for *Bloody Murder* in 1973, and the Grand Master Award in 1982. The Swedish Academy of Detection also made him a grand master in 1977; he won the Danish Poe-Kluhben in 1979, and was named a fellow of the Royal Society of Literature in 1975. His final novel, *A Sort of Virtue: A Political Crime Novel*, appeared in 1996—two years after his death.

Analysis

Although Julian Symons's intricately crafted crime novels have their roots in the classic detective tradition, they also represent his lifelong fascination with genre experimentation, with moving beyond the confines of the tightly structured detective story that provides, through a sequence of cleverly revealed clues, an intellectually satisfying solution to a convoluted crime puzzle. In *Bloody Murder*, Symons has made clear the distinctions he draws between the detective story and the crime novel. To Symons, the detective story centers on a great detective in pursuit of a solution to a crime, generally murder. Major emphasis is placed on clues to the identity of the criminal; in fact, much of the power of the detective story derives from the author's clever manipulation of clues and red herrings. Typically, the British detective story is socially conservative, set in a rural England that still reflects the genteel lifestyle of a bygone age. The crime novel, by contrast, generally has no master detective, but rather probes the psychology of individuals who have been driven by their environment—usually urban or suburban—to commit crimes or to become victims. Quite often the crime novel is critical of the social order, especially of the ways in which societal pressures and institutions gradually and inexorably destroy the individual.

Chief Inspector Bland

Although Symons began his career with three formula detective novels featuring Chief Inspector Bland of the slow but adequate methodology, he soon abandoned both the form and the icon for the more ambitious project of using crime literature as social criticism. Nevertheless, these three early novels manifest in embryonic form the themes that dominate Symons's later fiction: the social personas that mask the true identity and motivations of an individual, the games people play to keep their masks in place, and the social pressures that force those masks to fall away, leaving the individual vulnerable and uncontrollable. In fact, masks and game playing are the dominant motifs in Symons's fiction, functioning at times as metaphors for escape from the more unpleasant realities of existence. About his decision to move beyond the series detective, Symons said, "if you want to write a story showing people involved in emotional conflict that leads to crime, a detective of this kind is grit in the machinery."

In Symons's crime novels, the central focus is frequently on individuals who are driven to violent behavior by external forces over which they have—or believe they have—no control. "The private face of violence fascinates me," Symons acknowledged in an interview. More specifically, Symons is intrigued by the violence inherent in suburban dwellers, in respectable middle-class people who commute daily to numbingly dull jobs and return home to stiflingly placid homes and families in cozy English neighborhoods. Not for Symons the placid world of the English village with its hollyhocks and quaint cottages and population of genial eccentrics. His is the world of the ordinary and the average, at home and in the workplace; he delineates the sameness of the workaday routine and the anonymity of the business world that neatly crush the individuality out of all but the most hardy souls, that goad the outwardly sane into irrational and destructive actions. Symons has commented that in his work he consciously uses acts of violence to symbolize the effects of the pressures and frustrations of modern urban living. How these pressures result in bizarre and uncontrollable behavior is sharply described in *The Tigers of Subtopia, and Other Stories* (1982), a collection of stories about the latent tiger buried in the most innocuous of suburban denizens, about submerged cruelty and violence released by seemingly inconsequential everyday occurrences.

Nearly all Symons's characters disguise their true selves with masks, socially acceptable personas that hide the tigers inside themselves, that deny the essential human being. The early work *A Man Called Jones* unravels the mystery surrounding a masked man who calls himself Mr. Jones. Bernard Ross, prominent member of Parliament in *The Detling Murders* (1982), once was Bernie Rosenheim. May Wilkins in *The Colour of Murder*, anxious to hide the existence of a thieving father and an alcoholic mother, takes refuge behind a forged identity as a nice young married woman who gives bridge parties and associates with the right sort of people. Adelaide Bartlett (*Sweet Adelaide*, 1980) plays the part of an adoring and dutiful wife even after she has murdered her husband. In *The Gigantic Shadow* (1958; also known as *The Pipe Dream*), the mask is literal and very public. Disguised as "Mr. X—Personal Investigator," Bill Hunter, a popular television personality, conceals the fact that he is really O'Brien, a onetime prison inmate. When his charade is exposed and he loses his job, he becomes Mr. Smith, with disastrous consequences. False identities are important to *The Paper Chase* (1956; also known as *Bogue's Fortune*), *The Belting Inheritance* (1965), and *The Man Whose Dreams Came True* (1968). Many of Symons's protagonists masquerade behind aliases: Anthony Jones as Anthony Bain-Truscott or Anthony Scott-Williams, Arthur Brownjohn alias Major Easonby Mellon, Paul Vane as Dracula. Each of these characters is forced at some point to come to terms with one of the truths of Symons's world: The person behind the mask cannot—must not—be denied, and role-playing cannot be continued indefinitely. Person and persona must be integrated, or face destruction.

To maintain the fictions of their public personas, Symon's characters often play elaborate games with themselves and with others. Lenore Fetherby *(The Name of Annabel Lee*, 1983), in an effort to acquire irrefutable proof that she is her sister Annabel Lee, sets up a complicated trans-Atlantic charade in which she (as Annabel) has an intense affair with a bookish American professor who can be relied on to remember his only romance. May Wilkins (*The Colour of Murder*) pretends to outsiders that her marriage is the perfect union of two ambitious young people. Determined to make his way in a class-dominated society, Bernard Ross (*The Detling Murders*) disguises his Jewish ancestry by concocting an appealingly down-to-earth background as the son of immigrant farmers in America. For others, games are safety mechanisms that allow people to cope with the tensions and insecurities of urban existence. Mrs. Vane (*The Players and the Game*, 1972), bored and disillusioned by the failure of her marriage, takes refuge in endless bridge games. Bob Lawson works out his frustrations through visits to a prostitute who pretends to be a physician and subjects him to the various indignities of physical examinations.

The Colour of Murder

Frequently, the game playing takes on the more dangerous aspect of fantasy in which a character convinces himself of the truth of some impossible scenario and proceeds to live his life as though the fantasy were reality. Such is John Wilkins's problem in *The Colour of Murder.* Convincing himself, despite all the evidence to the contrary, that Sheila Morton nurses a secret passion for him, Wilkins forces his way into her company, even intruding on her vacation at a seaside resort. Consequently, he is convicted of her murder by a jury that, in an ironic parallel of his refusal to see the obvious vis-à-vis Sheila's feelings about him, chooses to misapprehend the clues and to believe Sheila's murder to be the result of Wilkins's thwarted passion.

Sweet Adelaide and The Players and the Game

For many characters, fantasy has more than one function. Not only does it enable the dreamer to exist comfortably within the mask, but also it becomes an avenue of escape from everyday monotony or an intolerable situation. Immersed from childhood in a fantasy about her aristocratic forebears and her true position in society, Adelaide Bartlett (*Sweet Adelaide*) imagines herself too refined and too delicate for the grocer she is forced to marry. Her dreams of a pure love that permits only celibate relationships between the sexes lead her first to fantasize a chaste affair with a young minister, then to escape to monastic weekends alone at a seaside resort, and finally to murder the man whom she regards as a importunate, oversexed clod of a husband. Paul Vane of *The Players and the Game* has a fully realized fantasy life. As Vane, he is the efficient and respectable director of personnel of Timbals Plastics; as Dracula, he keeps a diary in which he records his alternative life. Ultimately, Dracula intrudes on Vane's life; fantasy and reality collide. The results are tragic for both identities.

Death's Darkest Face

Symons would play on the theme of identity from a different angle in some of his final works. In *Death's Darkest Face* (1990), a fictional version of Symons himself is asked to evaluate the progress of an unsuccessful investigation, and the intersection of the author's life with fiction lends belief to fictional characters who are in reality just so much paper—another series of masks.

Playing Happy Families and A Sort of Virtue

In his final two novels, *Playing Happy Families* (1994) and *A Sort of Virtue: A Political Crime Novel* (1996), Symons once again takes up the series detective, this time with an amused affection that makes Detective Chief Superintendent Hilary Catchpole much more sympathetic to the reader than Symons's earlier investigators. Though Catchpole is a model of the virtuous police officer, his aspirations, foibles, and failings are all too human—he is a hero, but not the elevated supersleuth of Golden Age detective fiction. *A Sort of Virtue* provided Symons a last chance to comment on larger social issues. Catchpole's proffered epitaph, "He had a sort of virtue," stands in for Symons's final comment on human nature—"an ever-surprising mixture of virtue and vice, in which the most realistic aspiration for heroes is simply to do more good than harm."

Throughout many of Symons's novels, his characters live within a stifling, inhibited society in which conformity and bland respectability are prized, and individuality has no place. Progress has created a mechanical world of routine, populated by automatons engaged in the single-minded pursuit of material and social success. Spontaneity, creativity, and play are discouraged by a moralistic society that has room only for those whose behavior is "suitable." The result is the tightly controlled public personas that mask all individual preferences and needs, personas that ultimately become operative not only in the professional life but also at home.

For many of Symons's characters, role-playing or an active fantasy life often begins as a harmless activity that serves to relieve the stresses induced by society's demands and restrictions. In a number of instances, however, the games and the fantasies gradually begin to take precedence over real life, and the individual begins to function as though the imaginary life were real. Tragedy often ensues. Symons has pointed out that all human beings can be broken under too much pressure; his characters—especially those whose energies are devoted to maintaining two separate identities, and who crack under the strain of the effort—prove the truth of that observation. The quiet average neighborhood in a Symons novel seethes with malevolence barely concealed by civilized behavior.

In the Symons crime novel, violence is not an irregularity as it so often is in the classic detective story. Violence—physical, psychological, moral, spiritual—is inherent in the society that suppresses and represses natural actions and desires. Behind the stolid facades of suburban houses, beneath the calm faces of workaday clones, hides the potential for irrationality and violence, denied but not obliterated. "The thing that absorbs me most," says Symons, "is the violence behind respectable faces." In his novels, it is the assistant managers and personnel directors and housewives—good, solid, dependable people—whose carefully designed masks crumple and tear under the pressures of life. Violence erupts from those of whom it is least expected.

In short, the concerns of crime writer Symons were the same concerns addressed by mainstream fiction. Symons portrayed microcosms of Western civilization in decay; he described a world in which the individual has no place, communication is impossible, acceptable behavior is defined by a society determined to eliminate all rebellion against the common standard. He examined the fate of those who will not or cannot conform, and he laid the blame for their tragedies on an environment that shapes and distorts the human psyche into an unrecognizable caricature of humanity.

Like those writers who have earned their reputations in the literary mainstream, Symons created a body of work that embodies a distinctive view of life, a concern with the effects of society on the fragile human psyche, and a realistic portrayal of the alienation and frustration of individuals in late twentieth century England, still struggling to regain a sense of equilibrium decades after World War II. His characters, like so many in twentieth century fiction, are fragmented selves who acknowledge some facets of their identities only in fantasy or role-playing and who otherwise devote all of their energies to repressing their less socially acceptable personas. As a writer of crime fiction, Symons opened up innumerable possibilities for innovation and experimentation in the genre; as a serious writer and critic, he brought to a popular form the serious concerns and issues of the twentieth century novel at its best.

E. D. Huntley
Updated by Fiona Kelleghan and C. A. Gardner

PRINCIPAL MYSTERY AND DETECTIVE FICTION

CHIEF INSPECTOR BLAND SERIES: *The Immaterial Murder Case*, 1945; *A Man Called Jones*, 1947; *Bland Beginning*, 1949

FRANCIS QUARLES SERIES: *Murder! Murder!*, 1961; *Francis Quarles Investigates*, 1965

DETECTIVE CHIEF SUPERINTENDENT HILARY CATCHPOLE SERIES: *Playing Happy Families*, 1994; *A Sort of Virtue: A Political Crime Novel*, 1996

NONSERIES NOVELS: 1950-1960 • *The Thirty-first of February*, 1950; *The Broken Penny*, 1953; *The Narrowing Circle*, 1954; *The Paper Chase*, 1956 (also known as *Bogue's Fortune*); *The Colour of Murder*, 1957; *The Gigantic Shadow*, 1958 (also known as *The Pipe Dream*); *The Progress of a Crime*, 1960

1961-1970 • *The Killing of Francie Lake*, 1962 (also known as *The Plain Man*); *The End of Solomon Grundy*, 1964; *The Belting Inheritance*, 1965; *The Man Who Killed Himself*, 1967; *The Man Whose Dreams Came True*, 1968; *The Man Who Lost His Wife*, 1970

1971-1980 • *The Players and the Game*, 1972; *The Plot Against Roger Rider*, 1973; *A Three-Pipe Problem*, 1975; *The Blackheath Poisonings*, 1978; *Sweet Adelaide*, 1980

1980-1992 • *The Detling Murders*, 1982 (also known as *The Detling Secret*); *The Name of Annabel Lee*, 1983; *The Criminal Comedy of the Contented Couple*, 1985 (also known as *A Criminal Comedy*); *Criminal Acts*, 1987; *Did Sherlock Holmes Meet Hercule . . .* , 1988; *The Kentish Manor Murders*, 1988; *Death's Darkest Face*, 1990; *Portraits of the Missing: Imaginary Biographies*, 1992; *Something Like a Love Affair*, 1992; *The Advertising Murders*, 1992

OTHER SHORT FICTION: *The Julian Symons Omnibus*, 1967; *How to Trap a Crook and Twelve Other Mysteries*, 1977; *The Great Detectives: Seven Original Investigations*, 1981; *The Tigers of Subtopia, and Other Stories*, 1982; *The Man Who Hated Television, and Other Stories*, 1995

OTHER MAJOR WORKS

RADIO PLAYS: *Affection Unlimited*, 1968; *Night Ride to Dover*, 1969; *The Accident*, 1976

SCREENPLAY: *The Narrowing Circle*, 1955

TELEPLAYS: *I Can't Bear Violence*, 1963; *Miranda and a Salesman*, 1963; *The Witnesses*, 1964; *Curtains for Sheila*, 1965; *The Finishing Touch*, 1965; *Tigers of Subtopia*, 1968; *The Pretenders*, 1970; *Whatever's Peter Playing At*, 1974

POETRY: *Confusions About X*, 1939; *The Second Man*, 1943; *A Reflection on Auden*, 1973; *The Object of an Affair, and Other Poems*, 1974; *Seven Poems for Sarah*, 1979

NONFICTION: 1950-1960 • *A. J. A. Symons: His Life and Speculations*, 1950; *Charles Dickens*, 1951; *Thomas Carlyle: The Life and Ideas of a Prophet*, 1952; *Horatio Bottomley*, 1955; *The General Strike:*

A Historical Portrait, 1957; *The One Hundred Best Crime Stories*, 1959; *A Reasonable Doubt: Some Criminal Cases Re-examined*, 1960; *The Thirties: A Dream Revolved*, 1960 (revised 1975)

1961-1970 • *The Detective Story in Britain*, 1962; *Buller's Campaign*, 1963; *England's Pride: The Story of the Gordon Relief Expedition*, 1965; *Crime and Detection: An Illustrated History from 1840*, 1966 (also known as *A Pictorial History of Crime*); *Critical Occasions*, 1966

1971-1980 • *Between the Wars: Britain in Photographs*, 1972; *Bloody Murder: From the Detective Story to the Crime Novel*, 1972 (revised 1985, also known as *Mortal Consequences: A History, from the Detective Story to the Crime Novel*); *Notes from Another Country*, 1972; *The Tell-Tale Heart: The Life and Works of Edgar Allan Poe*, 1978; *Conan Doyle: Portrait of an Artist*, 1979; *The Modern Crime Story*, 1980

1981-1994 • *Critical Observations*, 1981; *Tom Adams' Agatha Christie Cover Story*, 1981 (with Tom Adams; also known as *Agatha Christie: The Art of Her Crimes*); *Crime and Detection Quiz*, 1983; *Dashiell Hammett*, 1985; *Makers of the New: The Revolution in Literature, 1912-1939*, 1987; *Oscar Wilde: A Problem in Biography*, 1988; *The Thirties and the Nineties*, 1990; *Criminal Practices: Symons on Crime Writing 60's to 90's*, 1994

Edited texts: *An Anthology of War Poetry*, 1942; *Selected Writings of Samuel Johnson*, 1949; *Selected Works, Reminiscences, and Letters*, 1956 (by Thomas Carlyle); *Essays and Biographies*, 1969 (by A. J. A. Symons); *The Woman in White*, 1974 (by Wilkie Collins); *Selected Tales*, 1976 (by Edgar Allan Poe); *The Angry Thirties*, 1976; *Verdict of Thirteen: A Detection Club Anthology*, 1979; *The Complete Sherlock Holmes*, 1981 (by Arthur Conan Doyle); *New Poetry 9*, 1983; *The Penguin Classic Crime Omnibus*, 1984; *The Essential Wyndham Lewis, An Introduction to His Work*, 1989

Bibliography

Craig, Patricia, ed. *Julian Symons at Eighty: A Tribute*. Helsinki, Finland: Eurographica, 1992. Collection of essays written in homage to Symons by both novelists and scholars of detective fiction.

Grimes, Larry E. "Julian Symons." In *Twelve English Men of Mystery*, edited by Earl F. Bargainnier. Bowling Green, Ohio: Bowling Green State University Popular Press, 1984. Summary and analysis of Symons's career, comparing him to other important mystery authors.

Herbert, Rosemary. *The Fatal Art of Entertainment: Interviews with Mystery Writers*. New York: G. K. Hall, 1994. Lengthy interview with Symons discusses crime writers from Charles Dickens to modern writers such as Elmore Leonard and Symons's personal history and his writing habits.

Horsley, Lee. *The Noir Thriller*. New York: Palgrave, 2001. Scholarly, theoretically informed study of the thriller genre. Discusses Symons's *The Players and the Game*.

Malmgren, Carl D. *Anatomy of Murder: Mystery, Detective, and Crime Fiction*. Bowling Green, Ohio: Bowling Green States University Popular Press, 2001. Includes analysis of Symons's *The Thirty-first of February*. Bibliographic references and index.

Pritchard, William H. "The Last Man of Letters: Julian Symons." In *Talking Back to Emily Dickinson and Other Essays*. Amherst: University of Massachusetts Press, 1998. An essay in praise of Symons, emphasizing his career as both writer and critic.

Walsdorf, Jack, and Kathleen Symons, eds. *Julian Symons Remembered: Tributes from Friends*. Council Bluffs, Iowa: Yellow Barn Press, 1996. Another homage to Symons, collecting memories of the author from those who knew him personally.

Walsdorf, John J., and Bonnie J. Allen. *Julian Symons: A Bibliography with Commentaries and a Personal Memoir*. New Castle, Del.: Oak Knoll Press, 1996. Combines the tribute form with critical writings on Symons's work and a bibliography of his publications.

T

PACO IGNACIO TAIBO II

Francisco Ignacio Taibo Mahojo

Born: Gijón, Asturias, Spain; January 11, 1949
Types of plot: Hard-boiled; private investigator; historical

Principal series

Héctor Belascoarán Shayne, 1976-

Principal series character

Héctor Belascoarán Shayne, a half-Basque and half-Irish man, gave up his wife, engineering job, and comfortable life to become a private investigator when he was thirty years old. He shares a low-rent Mexico City office with a plumber, a sewage specialist, and an upholsterer. An insomniac, existentialist, and anarchist, Belascoarán has an unhealthy curiosity that leads him into trouble. He doggedly pursues oddball cases that typically connect to shady businessmen, to thuggish law enforcement officers, and ultimately to slimy representatives of the Mexican government. In noir-flavored, surrealistic investigations, Belascoarán sometimes guns down bad guys and seldom comes away unscathed: He loses an eye, gains scars, acquires a limp, and is even apparently killed. However, popular demand brought the detective back to life to carry on in later novels. Like his creator, the antiheroic Belascoarán is a chain-smoker and cola addict.

Contribution

Paco Ignacio Taibo II first captured Mexican readers' imaginations with private detective Héctor Belascoarán Shayne. He then increased his popularity with series and nonseries crime novels that push the boundaries of the genre, using multiple viewpoints, bending reality, drawing mysteries around historical figures and incidents, and exposing the effects of corruption. Taibo's first novel featuring Belascoarán, his iconoclastic investigator, was published in 1976, and he has continued to produce novels in this series. The eighth novel in the series, *Muertos incómodos* (2005; *The Uncomfortable Dead: What's Missing Is Missing*, 2006) represents a true novelty in literature. Featuring Belascoarán in alternating chapters, *The Uncomfortable Dead* is a collaborative effort between Taibo and the masked Chiapas guerrilla known only as Subcomandante Marcos. Serialized in *La Jornada*, the novel prompted a 20 percent rise in the Mexico City leftist newspaper's circulation and cemented Taibo's reputation as one of the world's most inventive, articulate and risk-taking crime writers.

Taibo, a naturalized Mexican citizen since 1980, has become one of Mexico's most popular authors and received many literary awards for both his fiction and nonfiction. He won the 1982 Grijalbo Prize for his creative account of the 1968 massacre, *Heroes convocados: Manual para la toma del poder* (1982; *Calling All Heroes: A Manual for Taking Power*, 1990), and took the National History Prize for his narrative history *Los Bolshevikis*: *Historia narrativa de los origenes del comunismo en México 1919-1925* (1986). Taibo also won Dashiell Hammett Awards for the best crime novel in Spanish for *La vida misma* (1987; *Life Itself*, 1994), *Cuatro Manos* (1990; *Four Hands*, 1994), and *La bicicleta de Leonardo* (1993; *Leonardo's Bicycle*, 1995); the International Planeta Prize for the best historical novel in 1992; and the Bancarella Prize for his fictionalized biography of Che Guevera in 1998. A global best-selling author for more than thirty years—his books are sold in more than twenty countries—Taibo has made inroads into the American mystery community because of translations of a few of his novels beginning in the early 1990's. The majority of his works, however, are not yet available in English.

Paco Ignacio Taibo II in 2004. (AP/Wide World Photos)

Biography

Paco Ignacio Taibo II was born Francisco Ignacio Taibo Mahojo on January 11, 1949, in Gijón, Asturias, Spain, into a family of working-class anarchists. He is the son of late journalist, novelist, and biographer Paco Ignacio Taibo and Maricarmen Taibo. In 1958, the elder Taibo and his family fled from the fascism of Francisco Franco's regime and settled in Mexico.

Inspired by his father, young Taibo—an avid reader who decided as a child to become a writer—studied literature, sociology, and history, immersing himself in the colorful and violent past of his adopted homeland. In the late 1960's, Taibo became caught up in Mexico's latest political upheaval. He was forever after radicalized by the student protest movement of 1968, which ended abruptly just before the start of the 1968 Olympics when police and military forces fired on unarmed demonstrators in Mexico City's Tlatelolco section, killing dozens and wounding hundreds of youths.

In 1969, Taibo started working as a journalist and wrote fiction and nonfiction—especially historical essays—in his spare time. A tireless political activist and union organizer, he served as editor of the newspaper *Revista de la Semana*, and the magazines *Bronca* and *Enigma* and contributed articles to such anthologies as *Nacimento de la memoria* (1971). He married Paloma Saiz in 1971; they had one daughter, Marina. He began teaching in the mid-1970's at the National School of Anthropology and History at the National Independent University of Mexico in Mexico City, and from 1985 to 1989 at the University of Mexico campus in Azcapotzalco.

The prolific Taibo has created a flood of prose, publishing short stories, essays, novels, biographies, and other nonfiction. He gained almost instant recognition in Latin America with his tough, slyly antigovernment Héctor Belascoarán Shayne novels. Most of the entries in the series have made Latin American best-seller lists, and the enthusiasm for his evocative style has spilled over into Taibo's other works.

Taibo has also written, directed, and produced for Mexican television and film, adapting many of his own works—including *Cosa fácil* (1977; *An Easy Thing*, 1990) and *Algunas nubes* (1985; *Some Clouds*, 1992)—for the screen. He directed, edited, and wrote for a comic-book history of Mexico (1981-1982). In the 1990's, Taibo was an official in the administration of radical reformer Cuauhtémoc Cárdenas Solórzano.

Taibo has for many years served as president of the International Association of Writers of Detective Stories. In the early 1990's, he founded the noir fiction and film festival, Semana Negra, in Gijón, Spain, and annually organizes the ten-day event.

Analysis

Historian and novelist Paco Ignacio Taibo II is a rare breed: a critically acclaimed mystery writer who is equally well respected for his staunch political and social commitment. He has embraced the culture of Mexico with the fervor of a native. Much of his work, both fiction and nonfiction, reflects Taibo's love-hate relationship with the sprawling, polluted, crime-ridden—yet ancient, cosmopolitan, and vibrant—megalopolis that is Mexico City. He appreciates the Mexican landscape and climate as well as the history, energy, and diversity of the inhabitants that is the country's soul. However, he abhors the corruption that lies in the heart of the city. The corruption, according to Taibo, is the result of revolutionary turmoil that evolved into a modern civil dictatorship in the form of the Partido Revolucionario Institucional (PRI), a party that, under several names, has exercised political power in Mexico for more than seventy years, sometimes resorting to violence and fraud. This has been part of Taibo's underlying message since 1976, when he began using fiction to illustrate the causes and effects of past and present crimes involving the government.

Independent detective Héctor Belascoarán Shayne, introduced to Mexico in *Días de combate* (1976) and to the English-speaking world in the translation of the second entry of the series, *An Easy Thing*, is Taibo's most famous creation. Inspired by the heroes of American and Latin American hard-boiled novels, Belascoarán has the introspection of Philip Marlowe, the toughness of Mike Hammer, and the detecting skills of Sam Spade. However, this private eye has a distinctively Latino outlook and style as he walks the mean streets of exotic Mexico City. A Don Quixote in a rumpled trench coat, Belascoarán tilts at windmills, knowing it is an impossible task, but hoping to get in a few good charges before he is knocked down for good.

Taibo himself has been a memorable character in several of his novels: He appears as Paco Ignacio in *Some Clouds*. His alter ego, popular crime writer José Daniel Fierro, is a protagonist in *Life Itself* and *Leonardo's Bicycle*. Historical persons from the past—Pancho Villa, Emiliano Zapata Salazar, Leonardo da Vinci—often figure prominently in the stories of Taibo, who manages to make anachronisms plausible as he erases boundaries between supposition and truth and between fiction and fact.

Taibo's mysteries, both series and nonseries, offer considerably more than simple whodunits. His language is concise and economical, with linguistic pyrotechnics used sparingly, yet the tales are rich with allusion and full of quotable observations about the human condition from a fatalist's point of view. His descriptions are as sharp as snapshots. His characters, flawed like real humans, step breathing from the page. Dialogue crackles with authenticity, peppered with slangy street lingo, local references, profanity, and coarse humor. Plots are multilayered, with complications piled on complications. Things are seldom as they seem at first, and there are no tidy solutions at the end of the story. Violence is sudden and brutal, often instigated by minions of the multiple public or private police forces at the beck of the government—and is responded to in kind by protagonists who must react in deadly fashion and without hesitation to stay alive.

The notion of contradiction has informed Taibo's crime fiction from the start and has only become more prevalent over time. Taibo plays off various aspects of contrast: union workers versus capitalists, rich versus poor, comedy versus tragedy, past versus present, gut reaction versus intelligence, tenderness versus violence, and reality versus illusion. A constant theme is waste: human waste, wasted lives, and lost opportunities.

Praised for his fresh, innovative Mexican approach to the mystery genre and for his distinctive voice, the playful, impish, unabashedly antiauthoritarian Taibo is an unpredictable experimenter with style and form. His literate mysteries incorporate mythology, incidents from the past, historical personages, radical politics, extreme violence, and slapstick humor, thereby standing convention, categorization, and reality on their heads.

An Easy Thing

Private detective Héctor Belascoarán Shayne in *An Easy Thing* deals with the death of his mother while simultaneously investigating three separate cases. In the first case, a man in a cantina asks the private eye to look into the rumor that revolutionary Emiliano Zapata Salazar did not die in 1919 but is still, at the age of ninety-seven, alive and living in a cave. The second case involves a former pornographic film star, now a television actress, who hires the detective to prevent her seventeen-year-old daughter from committing suicide. The third case revolves around a murder at a factory, in which union workers are unjustly implicated.

Told from a world-weary, Chandler-like point of view, *An Easy Thing* provides all the elements expected in a hard-boiled mystery novel. There are regular doses of violence, sex, crime, and punishment, plus dabs of low politics and high-flown philosophy that produce a unique brand of hard-boiled noir, Mexican-style.

The Shadow of the Shadow

In *Sombra de la sombra* (1986; *The Shadow of the Shadow*, 1991), which takes place in Mexico City in the 1920's, four domino-playing friends—crime reporter Pioquinto Manterola, seedy lawyer Alberto Verdugo, aspiring poet and advertising jingle-writer Fermin Valencia, and Chinese-Mexican radical and labor organizer Tomás Wong—are ensnared in several complex mysteries that turn violent. The characters individually and collectively untangle various threads of a plot skillfully woven around an actual incident: the secret Mata Redonda Plan, whereby Mexican army officers in collusion with American politicians and oil companies mounted a phony insurrection in exchange for a large cash payoff. The United States responded with Marines to protect American interests, which resulted in American companies controlling the Mexican oil industry until it was nationalized in 1938.

Life Itself

José Daniel Fierro is a popular crime novelist in his fifties who lives in Mexico City, first with his wife, and after his divorce, by himself. In the first of two outings (*Life Itself*), the chain-smoking, cola-guzzling Fierro steps away from the typewriter to accept a job as police chief of fictional Sana Ana—where the last two chiefs were assassinated—on the theory that he is too famous to be killed. Assisted by a corps of deputies with Keystone Cops tendencies, Fierro dodges bullets while investigating two murders: a beautiful blond American found stabbed in a church and an albino felon who is shot at the circus. The cases turn increasingly bizarre as they unfold in a detective story that is by turns ironic, violent, and humorous.

Jack Ewing

Principal mystery and detective fiction

Héctor Belascoarán Shayne series: *Días de combate*, 1976; *Cosa fácil*, 1977 (*An Easy Thing*, 1990); *No habrá final feliz*, 1981 (*No Happy Ending*, 1993); *Irapuato mi amor*, 1984; *Algunas nubes*, 1985 (*Some Clouds*, 1992); *Regreso a la misma ciudad y bajo la lluvia*, 1989 (*Return to the Same City*, 1996); *Sueños de frontera*, 1990 (*Frontier Dreams*, 2002); *Muertos incomodos*, 2005 (*The Uncomfortable Dead: What's Missing Is Missing*, 2006; with Subcomandante Marcos)

Other major works

Novels: 1982-1990 • *Heroes convocados: Manual para la toma del poder*, 1982 (*Calling All Heroes: A Manual for Taking Power*, 1990); *Sombra de la sombra*, 1986 (*The Shadow of the Shadow*, 1991); *De paso*, 1986 (*Just Passing Through*, 2000); *La vida misma*, 1987 (*Life Itself*, 1994); *Palidas banderas*, 1987; *Fantasmas nuestros de cada dia*, 1988; *Sintiendo que el campo de batalla . . .* , 1989; *Amorosos fantasmas*, 1990; *Cuatro Manos*, 1990 (*Four Hands*, 1994)

1991-2006 • *Desvanecidos difuntos*, 1991; *El hombre de los lentes oscuros de llama Domingo y se llama Raul*, 1991; *La lejania del tesoro*, 1992; *De cuerpo entero*, 1992; *Cuevas-Taibo, mano a mano*, 1993; *La bicicleta de Leonardo*, 1993 (*Leonardo's Bicycle*, 1995); *Nomas los muertos estan bien contentos*, 1994; *Que todo es imposible*, 1995; *Ernesto Guevara: Tambien conocido como el Che*, 1996 (*Gue-*

vara, Also Known as Che, 1997); *Máscara Azteca y el Doctor Niebla (después del golpe)*, 1996; *Mi amigo Morán*, 1998; *El camino de María*, 1998; *Primavera pospuesta*, 1999; *Asi es la vida en los pinches Trópicos*, 2000; *Retornamos como sombras*, 2001 (*Returning as Shadows*, 2003); *Fuga, hierro y fuego*, 2006; *Siempre Dolores* (*byblos narrativa*), 2006

SHORT FICTION: *Doña Eustolia blandió el cuchillo cebollero y otras historias*, 1984; *El regreso de la verdadera araña y otras historias que pasaron en algunas fábricas*, 1988

SCREENPLAYS: *Adios, amor*, 1973; *Días de combate*, 1982; *Amorosos fantasmas*, 1994; *Algunas nubes*, 1995

NONFICTION: 1979-1985 • *Historia general de Asturias, tomos 7 & 8, 1978*, 1979; *La huelga de los sombrereros*, 1980; *Asturias 1934*, 1980; *México, historia de un pueblo*, 1980-1982; *La gran huelga del verano de 20 en Monterrey*, 1980; *El primer primero de mayo en México*, 1981; *El primer primero de mayo en el mundo*, 1982; *El socialismo en un solo puerto*, 1983 (also known as *Las dos muertes de Juan Escudero*, 1989); *Memoria roja. Luchas sindicales de los años 20*, 1984 (with Rogelio Viccaíno); *Bajando la frontera*, 1985; *Octubre 1934, cincuenta años para la reflexión*, 1985 (coauthor); *Danzón en Bellas Artes*, 1985; *Pistolero y otras reportajes*, 1985 (with others)

1986-1995 • *Los Bolshevikis*: *Historia narrativa de los origenes del comunismo en México 1919-1925*, 1986; *Ataca Oaxaca*, 1987; *Pascual décimo round*, 1988; *Santa Clara, la batalla del Che*, 1989; *68*, 1991; *El caso Molinet*, 1992; *Adiós, Madrid*, 1993; *Cardenas de cerca: una entrevista biografica*, 1994; *El año en que estuvimos en ninguna parte:* (*La guerrilla Africana de Ernesto Che Guevara*), 1994

1996-2006 • *El general orejón ese*, 1997; *Insurgencia mi amor*, 1997; *Cuentos policiacos mexicanos*, 1997; *Arcángeles: Doce historias de revolucionarios herejes del siglo XX*, 1998; *Olga Forever*, 1998; *Pancho Villa: Una biografia narrativa*, 2006 (*Pancho Villa: A Narrative Biography*, 2007)

BIBLIOGRAPHY

Braham, Persephone. *Crimes Against the State, Crimes Against Persons: Detective Fiction in Cuba and Mexico*. Minneapolis: University of Minnesota Press, 2004. A critical analysis of the differences and similarities between detective fiction in the two countries; includes the works of Taibo.

Ross, John. "One Hundred Days of Solitude." *L.A. Weekly*, March 18, 1998. An article touching on Taibo's investigation into government corruption in Mexico City.

Slivka, Andrey. "Leftist Noir." Review of *The Uncomfortable Dead*, by Paco Ignacio Taibo II. *The New York Times Book Review*, November 19, 2006, p. 27. Reviewer feels that the collaboration with Subcomandante Marcos does not work because the guerrilla's portions are not as well written and do not follow the conventions of fiction but are primarily message oriented.

Stavans, Ilan. *Conversations with Ilan Stavans*. Tucson: University of Arizona Press, 2005. Interviews with Latino artists, writers, entertainers, and intellectuals from both sides of the United States-Mexico border, including Taibo.

Taibo, Paco Ignacio, II. "No Happy Endings." Interview by John F. Baker. *Boston Review*, February/March 2001. An interview with Taibo focusing on his writing techniques.

_______. Paco Ignacio Taibo II: México y Nubes. http://www.vespito.net/taibo/index-es.html. The official Web site of the author contains a biography, bibliography, interview, and other information. In Spanish.

Wyels, Joyce Gregory. "Walking with Mexico City's Private Eye." *Americas* 57, no. 4 (July/August, 2005): 20-27. Wyels strolls through Mexico City with Taibo, who discusses his love-hate relationship with the city and how it affects his writing. Includes discussion of Taibo's home and private life as well as a brief look at his private eye.

AKIMITSU TAKAGI
Seiichi Takagi

Born: Aomori, Japan; September 25, 1920
Died: Tokyo, Japan; September 9, 1995
Types of plot: Police procedural; amateur sleuth; espionage

Principal series

Daiyu Matsushita and Kyōsuke Kamizu, 1948-1960
Saburō Kirishima, 1964-1988

Principal series characters

Chief Inspector Daiyu Matsushita is a highly regarded member of the Tokyo police force. In his inaugural case, Daiyu welcomes his brother Kenzo into his home following the younger man's release from military service.

Kenzo Matsushita is a World War II veteran and amateur sleuth. Frequently he calls on his older brother, an actual detective, for assistance in solving the troubling crimes he encounters, beginning with the death by dismemberment of his tattooed lover. Kenzo is more naïve and trusting than his older brother, on whom he relies for guidance.

Kyōsuke Kamizu is a young genius, a master of six languages, a student at Tokyo University, and an accomplished amateur sleuth who assists the Matsushita brothers in their investigations of mysterious deaths. He is a recurring character in a number of Matsushita novels.

State Prosecutor Saburō Kirishima, an intelligent and discerning man, is respected by his detective colleagues. Most impressively, Kirishima possesses an aptitude for determining with precision the guilt or innocence of a suspect.

Contribution

One of Japan's leading writers of detective and espionage fiction, Akimitsu Takagi garnered both popular success and critical acclaim during his lifetime. His intricate and cleverly plotted police procedurals are favorites of fans of the genre. Critics applaud his creation of psychologically intriguing human beings, whether the characters he presents are the victims, the criminals, or the investigators. Additionally, Takagi expanded the form and focus of the Japanese detective novel to more closely parallel contemporary life. He was among the first Japanese authors to write a novel in the financial-fiction genre. His varied repertoire includes historical thrillers, industrial crime fiction, and courtroom dramas.

Equally important are Takagi's portrayals of Japan and its citizens in the postwar era and in the decades of recovery, the 1950's and 1960's. Takagi's cityscapes provide an image of a culture and a people in transition. In several works featuring State Prosecutor Saburō Kirishima, the courtroom becomes a microcosm of Japanese culture, a place where concerns about changing values and ethics, innovations in business and industry, and tensions between generations and between genders can be voiced, if not necessarily resolved.

The growing appeal of Takagi's novels among English-language readers bodes well for additional translations of his detective novels, which range from police procedurals to accounts of industrial espionage. Critics have compared Takagi's work favorably to that of another master of Japanese detective fiction, Seichō Matsumoto, the popular author of *Ten to sen* (1958; *Points and Lines*, 1970) and *Suna no utsuwa* (1961; *Inspector Imanishi Investigates*, 1989).

Biography

Akimitsu Takagi was born Seiichi Takagi in Aomori, Japan, on September 25, 1920. After completing secondary studies at Daiichi High School, he attended Kyoto Imperial University, majoring in metallurgy. Employed by Nakajima Aircraft, Takagi lost his job because of the ban on military industries imposed by the Allies following their victory over Japan at the end of World War II.

When a fortune-teller revealed to Takagi that his future career was in fiction, not metals, he began to write detective novels. A man of reason even at the age of twenty-eight, he sought expert advice to confirm the seer's prediction. Takagi sent the manuscript of his first novel, *Irezumi satsujin jiken* (1948; *The Tattoo Murder Case*, 1998), to Edogawa Ranpo, a popular and respected Japanese writer of mysteries. On Ranpo's recommendation, the novel was published. As was foretold, Takagi's initial detective novel received positive reviews.

After the success of *The Tattoo Murder Case*, Takagi continued the series featuring Chief Inspector Daiyu Matsushita, a member of the Tokyo police force. These novels are set in the era immediately following World War II, and on occasion, historical incidents (such as the firebombing of Tokyo) feature in the plot. Characters in Takagi's later works, including novels in the Saburō Kirishima series, continue to reflect their creator's personal interest in legal matters. Takagi was a self-educated authority on the law, and most of his protagonists are either detectives (amateur or professional) or public prosecutors.

Recognition of his work arrived early for Takagi. In 1949, while still in his twenties, he won the Mystery Writers of Japan Award for *The Tattoo Murder Case*; however, it was not until the 1965 publication of *Mikkokusha* (1965; *The Informer*, 1971), based on an actual incident of sabotage in Japan's manufacturing sector, that he was elevated to a position among Japan's elite writers of detective fiction. Consequently, his previously published novels, which had been successful in their own right, again found their way to the best-seller lists.

Akimitsu Takagi. (Kamakura Museum of Literature)

Takagi suffered a stroke in 1979 but continued to write and publish works of fiction into the late 1980's. His final years were spent in declining health; by 1990 additional strokes had ended his writing career. He died in Tokyo in 1995.

ANALYSIS

Akimitsu Takagi's writing style is terse, reflecting a Japanese sensibility in both its reserved use of dialogue and its reliance on minimalist description. However, his concise style of writing should not be construed as dispassionate, as certain critics have called it. Takagi's most memorable characters, Kenzo Matsushita in *The Tattoo Murder Case* and Etsuko Ogata in *Zero no mitsugetsu* (1965; *Honeymoon to Nowhere*, 1995), ache with suffering on learning that their lovers have been murdered. The emotions of the bereaved are often conveyed to readers through what is not explicitly expressed. Despite the very modern circumstances of their pain, Takagi's characters are steeped in traditional Japanese behaviors that require them to constrain their words and emotions; their suffering seeps out despite their efforts at containment. The restraint the author exercises in his use of language serves to intensify his characters' miseries even as the objects of their desires are forever removed from their embraces.

A typical Takagi novel intentionally mirrors in its structure and style the tension that existed in Japanese society from the late 1940's through the 1960's. The traditions and social customs associated with a culture as venerable as Japan's inevitably came into conflict with the rapid changes the country faced after its defeat in World War II. First Japan recovered from the devastation the war had wrought; then it rebuilt itself into a modern industrial power. Takagi personalizes this broad conflict between tradition and change by reconfiguring its scale; in his novels it is individual men and women who struggle against imposing societal forces in a more localized venue. Issues of identity within the community emerge as the new men and women of Japan question what it means to be a citizen in the modern era. Depending on the novel in which they appear, those individuals might be on the side of the law or the very criminals the investigator seeks.

A recurring motif in Takagi's novels is the individual's search for romantic fulfillment in a sterile society. Men and women are depicted as equally infused with sexual passions, and erotic subtexts permeate most of the plots. However, there are few fulfilled characters in his novels because their passions frequently get mixed up with their (or others') criminal pursuits, resulting in the loss of the desired object. The prospect of better futures for most of Takagi's characters is bleak, even for those who remain standing at the close of various novels. Neither the resolution of a mystery nor the administration of justice can alleviate the weight of the pessimism that pervades his writing.

Although scholars have commented favorably on Takagi's innovations in style, format, subject, and character, he is not without detractors. Critics cite his overreliance on stock generic devices, such as his fondness for puzzles, coincidences, dead ends, and sensationalistic story lines, as evidence that Takagi is not as original a fabricator of detective fiction as his reputation suggests. Others criticize Takagi's tendency to introduce third parties late in his novels. Typically these characters use extraordinary methods to resolve the mysteries that have frustrated others. The boy genius character in *The Tattoo Murder Case* is a prime example of this particular tendency and yet it is worth noting that this same novel merited its author the Mystery Writers of Japan Award within a year of its publication.

The Tattoo Murder Case

The Tattoo Murder Case is a classic of Japanese fiction and the first of Takagi's novels to be translated into English. Not surprisingly, it is his most popular novel among English-speaking readers. Set in late 1940's Tokyo during the aftermath of the Japanese defeat at the end of the World War II, *The Tattoo Murder Case* features as its chief investigators two recently reunited brothers, Kenzo and Daiyu Matsushita. Newly released from military service, the younger sibling, twenty-nine-year-old Kenzo, joins his older brother, Chief Inspector Daiyu Matsushita, in Tokyo. A criminal investigator with the local precinct, Daiyu allows his younger brother to accompany him on missions.

Kenzo's ambition is to transfer his training as a military medic to a position on the police force, but he is distracted by a beautiful woman. He begins an illicit affair with Kinue Nomura, a tattoo artist's daughter and a mobster's mistress. Kinue is an illustrated woman. Thanks to her father's deft hands, her body displays a one-of-a-kind design that holds numerous men, including Kenzo, enthralled. Among her admirers is Professor Hayakawa, alias Dr. Tattoo, whose macabre collection of ornamented skins retrieved from the bodies of the dead is well known among the investigators. Body art plays a role in this police procedural, which provides a fascinating glimpse into a deviant strain of Japanese art and culture. Though tattooing was illegal and socially taboo in postwar Japan, the practice was continued in secret. Tattoo artists had a loyal clientele, chiefly composed of mob bosses and prostitutes. The tattoos described in the novel are based on symbols drawn from Japanese mythology and provide important clues to the motives and the means of the killer of Kinue.

To resolve the case, the brothers require the skills of a third detective, the hyperintelligent prodigy Kyōsuke Kamizu. In the final section of the novel, Kamizu provides the answer to the riddles posed by this case: How did the limbs and head of Kinue end up locked inside a room with no apparent exit and what became of her tattooed torso? He solves the puzzle in a fastidious and timely manner, one reminiscent of the detective maneuverings of Agatha Christie's Hercule Poirot and his legendary gray matter.

The Informer

Culled from newspaper accounts of an actual case of industrial espionage, *The Informer* became Takagi's most popular novel in Japan. The novel begins from the perspective of Shigeo Segawa, a young Tokyo stockbroker caught making illegal trades, and charts his downward spiral. When Segawa's acquaintance, Mikio Sakai, agrees to hire the young man despite his previous dismissal, the new employee soon finds himself working not as a salesman, the advertised position, but as an industrial spy. Segawa sets aside his initial moral qualms and soon becomes implicated in escalating acts of criminal activity, including sabotage. When his employer's financial target, Shoichi Ogino, is killed, Segawa emerges as the lead suspect in an investigation headed by Saburō Kirishima, a state prosecutor. When Kirishima enters the plot, the novel's point of view shifts from Segawa to that of the prosecutor. *The Informer* offers a compelling case study of a businessman so desperate to attain economic security that he risks things more dear than money. Takagi wrote a number of novels that center on economic crimes, but critics consider *The Informer* the best of them.

Honeymoon to Nowhere

Despite her realization that she is growing older and could become a burden to her family, a lawyer's daughter refuses the suitor her parents offer her in Takagi's *Honeymoon to Nowhere*. Initially, Etsuko Ogata reasons that the man, a junior member of her father's firm, would be a good provider. Though at first she is inclined to acquiesce to her parents' wishes, her heart demands passion and overrules logic. Emboldened, she defies her parents and finds her own prospective mate, Yoshihiro Tsukamoto, an industrial management professor. She fakes a pregnancy to gain her shocked parents' permission to wed Tsukamoto. They wed, but after Tsukamoto receives a telephone call on their wedding night, he flees the nuptial chamber and does not return. When his body is recovered the following day, the mysterious circumstances of his death set the stage for a courtroom drama orchestrated by State Prosecutor Saburō Kirishima. The prosecutor must search through a jumble of evidence and discard several red herrings before he is able to identify the guilty suspect from among a cadre of likely candidates. By novel's end he successfully identifies the killer, whose envy and avarice have arrayed the new bride in the clothes of mourning.

Dorothy Dodge Robbins

Principal mystery and detective fiction

Daiyu Matsushita and Kyōsuke Kamizu series: *Irezumi satsujin jiken*, 1948 (*The Tattoo Murder Case*, 1998); *Nōmen satsujin jiken*, 1949; *Jubaku no ie*, 1949; *Yō no yado*, 1949; *Waga ichi kō jidai no hanzai*, 1951; *Jingisu kan no himitsu*, 1958; *Hitoari*, 1959; *Hakuchū no shikaku*, 1960

Saburō Kirishima series: *Kenji Kirishima Saburō*, 1964; *Mikkokusha*, 1965 (*The Informer*, 1971); *Zero no mitsugetsu*, 1965 (*Honeymoon to Nowhere*, 1995)

Nonseries novels: *Hakai saiban*, 1961; *Yamataikoku no himitsu*, 1973; *Kodai ten'nō no himitsu*, 1986; *Shichifukujin satsujin jiken*, 1987; *Kamen yo saraba*, 1988

Other major works

Nonfiction:

Nihon shisei geijutsu Horiyoshi, 1983 (also known as *Japan's Tattoo Arts: Horiyoshi's World, Vol. 1*); *Shisei yōka 1988 (also known as Japanese Tattoo Ladies)*

Bibliography

Brainard, Dulcy. Review of *The Tattoo Murder Case*, by Akimitsu Takagi. *Publishers Weekly* 244 no. 52 (December 22, 1997): 41. Looks at the novel as a complex tale of obsession set in postwar Japan. Comments on Takagi's emotionless style of writing.

Munger, Katy. Review of *The Informer* and *Honeymoon to Nowhere*, by Akimitsu Takagi. *The Washington Post*, July 25, 1999, p. X08. Examines Japanese morality and social structure through the lens of Takagi's police procedurals. Also critiques the author's techniques and characters.

Williams, Janis. Review of *Honeymoon to Nowhere*, by Akimitsu Takagi. *Library Journal* 124 no. 13 (August, 1999): 147. Classifies the novel as a conventional but ultimately satisfying police procedural.

_______. Review of *The Tattoo Murder Case*, by Akimitsu Takagi. *Library Journal* 123 no. 2 (February, 1998): 113. Enumerates the complicated family relationships that intertwine with Japanese traditions and a complex story line in Takagi's novel.

Zaleski, Jeff. Review of *Honeymoon to Nowhere*, by Akimitsu Takagi. *Publishers Weekly* 246 no. 22 (May 31, 1999): 71. Compares novels written by Takagi to those written by mystery writers Patricia Highsmith and William Irish and identifies their connecting thread: characters entangled in compelling but potentially lethal intrigues.

PHOEBE ATWOOD TAYLOR

Born: Boston, Massachusetts; May 18, 1909
Died: Boston, Massachusetts; January 9, 1976
Also wrote as Freeman Dana; Alice Tilton
Types of plot: Amateur sleuth; cozy

Principal series

Asey Mayo, 1931-1951
Leonidas Witherall, 1937-1944

Principal series characters

Asey Mayo, an amateur sleuth, is a Cape Cod native and an all-around handyman. Of indeterminate age, between thirty-five and seventy years old, he evolves from a handyman in corduroys and a Stetson to the chairman of Porter Motors Company. Known for his physical and mental prowess, Asey charms everyone involved in his cases.

Leonidas Witherall, an amateur sleuth, is a teacher and later a headmaster and the owner of Meredith Academy, a private boys' school. He is a scholarly, witty, and proper old gentleman whose looks earn for him the name "Bill Shakespeare." An author of detective novels, he prefers to be left alone but is always getting involved in the zany escapades of his family and friends.

Contribution

Phoebe Atwood Taylor wrote some thirty detective novels, which have been praised for their historical verisimilitude. Her books about detective Asey Mayo demonstrate her intimate knowledge of the charm and liveliness of Cape Cod communities such as Quanomet, Weesit, and Wellfleet. Taylor does not depict her setting as the famed summer resort it is but rather reveals the Yankee charm of the people of Cape Cod, who live there after the tourists are gone. The dialogue and glimpses of daily life are distinctively Yankee.

Many of Taylor's works move at a brisk pace; there are chases on foot and by motor vehicles, and the detective solves the case in only a day or two. Humor is also a notable element of many of Taylor's mysteries, especially in the stories featuring Leonidas Witherall, the detective-hero of the novels that Taylor wrote under the pseudonym Alice Tilton. The pace of Taylor's novels, combined with a variety of farcical situations, places her mysteries in both the Golden Age of mystery writers, of which Agatha Christie and Ngaio Marsh were a part, and the 1930's era of screwball film comedies.

Biography

Phoebe Atwood Taylor was born in Boston on May 18, 1909. Her parents were natives of Cape Cod and descendants of the Mayflower Pilgrims; her father was a physician. Taylor attended Barnard College, was graduated in 1930, and immediately returned to Boston to live and write. She married a Boston surgeon, also named Taylor, and lived in the Boston surburbs of Newton Highlands and Weston. The Taylors also maintained a summer home in Wellfleet, Cape Cod.

Taylor's literary debut was in 1931, with the publication of *The Cape Cod Mystery*. It sold more than five thousand copies, a huge number of sales for a first mystery. Over the next twenty years, Taylor was to write and publish roughly thirty detective novels, quite an accomplishment considering her harried schedule. She wrote between twelve midnight and three in the morning, "after housekeeping all day." She claims to have written all of her novels "beginning three weeks before the deadline for the novel to be delivered to the New York publishers." Her Leonidas Witherall novels appear to describe the author's own life, as the detective endures a barrage of telegrams from his publisher and struggles to meet his deadlines.

Although Taylor's last detective novel was published in 1951, her popularity with readers did not diminish, and many of her books have been reprinted in both hardback and paperback editions. Taylor died of a heart attack in Boston on January 9, 1976.

Analysis

Phoebe Atwood Taylor has been described as the "essential New England mystery writer," and from her first novel, *The Cape Cod Mystery*, she earned such acclaim. Taylor's novels betray her New England roots in numerous ways. Many of the settings are in Cape Cod towns, usually described as resort areas, such as Wellfleet and Weesit. In the Asey Mayo novels, tourists must constantly be kept away from the scene of the crime. Yet the principal characters are not tourists at all: They are genuine New Englanders, who populate the towns beyond the tourist season. Taylor does not delve intimately into the lives of these individuals; instead, she reveals an intimate knowledge of general life on the Cape. Her characters all speak with a broad *a* (a point she endlessly emphasizes), and they often have Pilgrim or Puritan ancestors. Yet few of her characters boast of "old money"—most either have just managed to survive the Depression or have ingeniously grown rich despite the odds of the time.

THE MYSTERY OF THE CAPE COD PLAYERS

The Depression is but one of the historical interests in Taylor's mystery novels. While she never mentions the Depression directly, she candidly reveals its consequences. In *The Mystery of the Cape Cod Players* (1933), Taylor writes of a troupe composed of actors, a magician, and a puppeteer. This group of rather odd characters have chosen their current roles only because they lost their previous jobs. Taylor never directly mentions the Depression as the cause of their hard luck, but the many intimations of the current difficulties allow the reader to link the poor state of these strolling players to the Depression. In the same novel, a wealthy widow is also affected by the near collapse of the company that her husband left her. The company was all that remained of what must have been a much greater fortune.

Taylor never seems to leave any of her characters untouched by the current state of the country. The best example of this is with the work of her favorite detective, Asa Alden "Asey" Mayo. Asey was involved in both world wars. Although he often says that he spent World War I peeling potatoes on a ship, it is revealed that Asey worked on secret tank plans for the Porter Motors Company. Although the tanks never went into production during World War I, they were later produced during World War II. When Asey was not solving a case during World War II, he spent all of his time living at the Porter plant, developing the tanks. Taylor ultimately reveals to her readers that Asey won a medal for his work on the Porter miracle tank, the Mark XX. Other characters in Taylor's novels contribute to the war effort as well. For example, in *The Perennial Boarder* (1941), Jennie Mayo, the wife of Asey's cousin Sylvanus "Syl" Mayo, busied herself with jujitsu, a commando training course, and target practice with the Women's Defense Corps. Also, Syl joins the navy during World War II.

The narrow focus of many of Taylor's novels heightens their geographic and historical verisimilitude. Xenophobia is a common element throughout Taylor's works, as many of the Cape natives sorely distrust outsiders. In *The Mystery of the Cape Cod Players*, an old hermit, Harm, welcomes to his house only those whom he knows and trusts. When Asey and Syl drive up to Harm's shack, Harm allows only Asey to get out of the car, and he speaks only to him. Syl notes, "Harm'd have made for me if I'd stepped out of this car, but he likes Asey."

THE CRIMSON PATCH

The Crimson Patch (1936) focuses on a problem with outsiders. The natives of Skaket do their best to run a new family out of town by accusing them of being immoral. For the natives, the word "immoral" takes on an unmistakable Puritanical connotation. Taylor's novels also tell of Yankees' occasional racism.

Of all the New England elements in Taylor's novels the most significant are the characterizations of her detectives. Asey Mayo is described through the eyes of an outsider in *The Crimson Patch* as "tall, lean faced, blue eyed, he looked exactly as Myles had fondly imagined all Cape Codders would look, and as, to his intense disappointment, they had not." Indeed, Asey Mayo is the consummate Cape native, with his broad *a* and his New England *r* (pronounced "ah"). Although it is not mentioned in the earlier novels, Asey owns a two-story house on the beach, with its own wharf. His knowledge of the sea is remarkable, and he had spent many years as a sailor before he began his business of solving mysteries.

Asey Mayo is originally introduced by Taylor as what the critics dubbed "the hayseed Sherlock." In the first few novels, Asey is simply Bill Porter's hired hand, a man who can, seemingly, do anything. By *Death*

Lights a Candle (1932), Taylor reveals that Porter has left Asey a large sum of money, even though his appearance speaks otherwise (he was known for his corduroys, flannel shirt, and Stetson hat cocked sideways on his head). By Taylor's last novel, *Diplomatic Corpse* (1951), Asey is chairman of the Board of Porter Motors and sports a business suit and a yachting cap. Yet Asey's wealth never keeps him from doing what he enjoys. He often works odd jobs, as a carpenter, as a cook, and—above all else—as an excellent mechanic. His roadster, given to him by Bill Porter, is the fastest, sleekest car on the Cape. Many times that car is instrumental in solving a mystery. Although Asey may appear as a hayseed detective, it is exactly that quality that enables him to gather so many clues and fit them together to discover the murderer.

Cold Steal

Taylor's other detective, Leonidas Witherall, takes on a totally different New England appearance. He is not at all the small-town Cape Cod native; his home is Boston and its suburbs. His appearance and personality are not at all as charming and comfortable as Asey Mayo's; instead, he is a proper, quaint, and witty old gentleman. Taylor describes Witherall as an odd sort who is first a teacher, then later headmaster and owner of Meredith Academy, a private boys' school. In *Cold Steal* (1939), Taylor tells the reader that Witherall's looks—he is "an elderly man with a small pointed beard"—have earned for him the nickname "Bill Shakespeare," for he resembles Shakespeare so closely "that it seemed as if some library bust or engraved frontispiece had come suddenly to life." Witherall also has a keen mind, never missing the slightest oddity or clue.

Leonidas Witherall was significant for Taylor not so much as a detective—the novels involving him are not as good as those about Asey Mayo—but rather for his transparent character: He was the picture of Taylor in her own stories. Witherall writes detective novels, but he can never measure up to the feats of his heroes. He is often harried by his publishers to meet demands and deadlines. In *Cold Steal*, Witherall notes that "he had written three Haseltine books a year for so many years that he automatically wrote about the daring lieutenant whether he meant to or not." Certainly from 1931 to 1951 Taylor's life paralleled that of her creation, Witherall.

Humor and women

One might consider Taylor's works to be detective comedies, as each novel has numerous farcical aspects. In *The Cape Cod Mystery*, Asey Mayo identifies the murderer of a popular novelist as the three-hundred-pound widow of a Boston minister; she delivered a deathblow to the writer with an advance copy of his own latest book, a sensational account of her husband's life. Often Asey points to the humor in his fellow New Englanders' behavior and thoughts. No one seems to think logically but Asey, adding much to the fun of Taylor's novels. The escapades of Leonidas Witherall are even more ludicrous. He deals with unlikely murder weapons, unlikely murderers, and many friends and family who try to play detective along with him but prove to be of little help. It has been said that Taylor's novels require "a massive suspension of disbelief."

The women in Taylor's novels often appear as strong characters, well able both to witness a murder and to help solve it. Women in Taylor's novels own their own businesses and are successful in a variety of fields. They are sometimes as strong as men physically, and more often than not they are much smarter. Several of Taylor's early novels are narrated by elderly women who help to solve the mysteries they recount. One must credit Taylor for the confidence she demonstrated in the ability of women throughout her novels.

Asey Mayo

Asey Mayo, like many other detectives (excepting the hard-boiled variety), has his share of helpers in solving his mysteries. Besides the variety of bright women who lend their aid, two men in particular stand out as important characters in several novels. In *Death Lights a Candle*, Asey mentions his cousin, but he does not appear until Taylor's next novel, *The Mystery of the Cape Cod Players*, and then he is introduced as Sylvanus Mayo. Syl is a short man with a walrus mustache who always runs and is constantly out of breath. Inevitably, he finds the clue that Asey sends to him to discover, and he claims that any item can be found if one can put oneself in its place and figure out what it would do next. Asey never pretends to understand Syl's style of retrieval, but he attributes Syl's ability to his addiction to detective stories. Syl plays his largest role in *Deathblow Hill* (1935), and from there his character fades until he is only mentioned in the World War II novels as being in the navy.

The other prominent aide to Asey is Doc Cummings, who first appears in *The Tinkling Symbol* (1935). In the early novels, Doc's main tasks are examining the body and attending to fainting women. Later, however, he is given more significant duties by Asey. Doc thoroughly enjoys stalling and leading on Lieutenant Hanson of the state police, and Asey utilizes Doc not only in this way but also to deter others. Occasionally Doc is asked to check out someone's story or to offer his opinion about any possible suspects. Doc's assessment of the suspects, however, is never correct.

Even with all the available help, only Taylor's detectives are capable of piecing together the clues ("clews," as Taylor always writes) and revealing the culprit. They engage in all possible tactics, most of which are common to detective stories, to catch the murderer. The detectives usually find themselves involved in high-speed car or boat chases, mysterious escapades on trains, and chases on foot through backwoods, suburban streets, parking lots, and snow-covered fields. Both detectives have remarkable physical stamina, but Asey is by far the most astounding in physical abilities. As Taylor reveals more and more about Asey throughout her many novels about him, he comes to be somewhat of a superman. He is a superb mechanic and driver, an excellent cook, an expert with guns and knives, a fleet runner, and an able fighter. Although Asey Mayo is endowed with near-superhuman qualities, Leonidas Witherall should not be slighted. He, too, has great stamina for an elderly gentleman, and his endurance through all the circumstances of his investigations is worthy of note.

The style of Taylor's writing matches the breathless style of her detectives. She takes her readers on a race through the one or two days necessary for her detectives to solve the mystery. She rarely leaves time for long descriptions or involved intimate details, and her detectives can summarize events and circumstances usually in less than five minutes. Although Taylor's work has been criticized as mechanical, she is perhaps better described as efficient, even thrifty. She writes what needs to be known and sums up the facts in a tidy manner at the end. Even so, Taylor's novels do not lack the suspense and daring of any good detective novel. Admittedly, the Witherall novels lack the style of the Asey Mayo novels and sometimes seem to gloss over the details necessary for the solution of the mystery, yet even in these books Taylor always manages to maintain the reader's interest. Writers such as Charlotte MacLeod, Lucille Kallen, and Jane Langton trace their roots to Taylor, the quintessential New England mystery writer.

JoAnne C. Juett

Principal mystery and detective fiction

Asey Mayo series: *The Cape Cod Mystery*, 1931; *Death Lights a Candle*, 1932; *The Mystery of the Cape Cod Players*, 1933; *Sandbar Sinister*, 1934; *The Mystery of the Cape Cod Tavern*, 1934; *Deathblow Hill*, 1935; *The Tinkling Symbol*, 1935; *Out of Order*, 1936; *The Crimson Patch*, 1936; *Figure Away*, 1937; *Octagon House*, 1937; *Banbury Bog*, 1938; *Murder at the New York World's Fair*, 1938; *The Annulet of Gilt*, 1938; *Spring Harrowing*, 1939; *The Criminal C.O.D.*, 1940; *The Deadly Sunshade*, 1940; *The Perennial Boarder*, 1941; *The Six Iron Spiders*, 1942; *Three Plots for Asey Mayo*, 1942; *Going, Going, Gone*, 1943; *Proof of the Pudding*, 1945; *Punch with Care*, 1946; *The Asey Mayo Trio*, 1946; *The Iron Clew*, 1947 (also known as *The Iron Hand*); *Diplomatic Corpse*, 1951

Leonidas Witherall series: *Beginning with a Bash*, 1937; *The Cut Direct*, 1938; *Cold Steal*, 1939; *The Left Leg*, 1940; *The Hollow Chest*, 1941; *File for Record*, 1943; *Dead Ernest*, 1944

Bibliography

Dueren, Fred. "Asey Mayo: 'The Hayseed Sherlock.'" *The Armchair Detective* (January, 1977): 21-24, 83. Discussion of the class and seeming lack of sophistication of Taylor's most famous sleuth.

Klein, Kathleen Gregory, ed. *Great Women Mystery Writers: Classic to Contemporary.* Westport, Conn.: Greenwood Press, 1994. Contains an essay on the life and works of Taylor.

Kneeland, Paul F. "Obituary." *Boston Globe*, January 14, 1976, p. 43. Tribute to the author and summary of her career and literary output.

Panek, LeRoy Lad. *The Origins of the American Detective Story.* Jefferson, N.C.: McFarland, 2006. Study of the beginnings and establishment of American detective-fiction conventions that focuses on the replacement of the police by the private detective and the place of forensic science in the genre; provides perspective on Taylor's works.

Pepper, Andrew. *The Contemporary American Crime Novel: Race, Ethnicity, Gender, Class.* Edinburgh: Edinburgh University Press, 2000. Examination of the representation and importance of various categories of identity in mainstream American crime fiction; sheds light on Taylor's works.

DARWIN L. TEILHET

Born: Wyanette, Illinois; May 20, 1904
Died: Palo Alto, California; April 18, 1964
Also wrote as Theo Durrant; William H. Fielding; Cyrus Fisher
Types of plot: Amateur sleuth; espionage; thriller

Principal series

St. Amand, 1931
Baron von Kaz, 1935-1940

Principal series characters

George Talmont Maria St. Amand of the Sûreté, the detective in Teilhet's first book, *Murder in the Air* (1931), is demoniacal in intelligence and appearance. He is tall and has a yellow, cadaverous face with drooping eyelids and a fierce mustache, like cat's whiskers. In *Death Flies High* (1931), St. Amand's given names are changed to Jean Henri, but otherwise he remains the same Satanic investigator.

Baron Franz Maximilian Karagoz und von Kaz, Teilhet's second series detective, once headed the Vienna police department, but because of a failed attempt to restore the Austrian monarchy, he has come to America to make a living as a detective. He is proud of his Habsburg von Kaz heritage and denies the influence of the Gypsy imagination contributed by his Karagoz ancestors. His only weapon is a green umbrella that has a sword concealed in its handle and that is weighted so that the baron can throw it like a club.

Caryl Miquet, a member of a wealthy family in Hawaii, is a major suspect in the first Baron von Kaz book. The remaining books in the series chronicle the baron's courtship of and eventual marriage to Caryl.

Contribution

Darwin L. Teilhet used the classical, fair-play form of the detective story in ways that had rarely been successful with earlier authors. Like some later writers, he based his first books on current events and issues, and thereby produced *The Talking Sparrow Murders* (1934), the greatest detective novel (and one of the most powerful novels in any genre) about the Nazi takeover of Germany. Unlike most mystery writers of the 1930's, who were political and social conservatives, Teilhet throughout his life was a liberal, a fact that adds a special flavor to his books, especially those about Baron von Kaz. In these novels, he includes acute criticisms of overzealous patriotism in the United States as well as attacks on anti-Semitism. The baron, moreover, is probably the most convincing of all humorous detectives. His constant pride lands him in difficulties, but the reader sympathizes with him. The reader understands why he acts as he does, and his foibles are amusing because, though exaggerated, they are human.

Biography

Darwin LeOra Teilhet was born on May 20, 1904, in Wyanette, Illinois, of French Catholic stock. While a teenager, he visited the Correze section of France and worked as a juggler in a French circus. He also worked briefly on the Paris edition of *The New York Herald Tribune*. He was educated at Drake University, the Sorbonne in Paris, and Stanford University, where he met Hildegarde Tolman. They were married on October 28, 1927. His first two books, *Murder in the Air* and *Death Flies High*, had good reviews and good sales, but Teilhet was unsure of his path as a writer. He took a job with the N. W. Ayers Company as a copywriter, and for the next three years he concentrated on writing magazine articles and reviews. In 1934, however, he completed his best book, *The Talking Sparrow Murders*. The same year, James Poling of the Crime Club (Doubleday's mystery imprint) asked Teilhet to write detective novels with a memorable protagonist. The result was Baron von Kaz. Around 1936, Teilhet became executive assistant to the president of Dole Pineapple in Hawaii; the second Baron von Kaz novel, *The Feather Cloak Murders* (1936), has a Hawaiian setting and lists as its authors Darwin and Hildegarde Teilhet. Later Teilhet books might be attributed to either or both Teilhets, but with one or two exceptions they were collaborative efforts.

During World War II, Teilhet was an intelligence officer in Great Britain and the United States. Meanwhile, under his own name he wrote adventure stories, two of which were serialized by *The Saturday Evening Post*. Under Hildegarde's name, the Teilhets wrote espionage thrillers. For a short while in the 1940's, Teilhet taught a journalism course at Stanford and he was a consultant for various film producers. One of his nonmystery novels, *My True Love* (1945), was filmed by Universal in 1952 as *No Room for the Groom*. During the 1950's, he concentrated on historical novels; *The Mission of Jeffery Tolamy* (1951) is a historical espionage story. Teilhet's final book, completed shortly before his death in 1964, was *The Big Runaround*, a thriller based on industrial spying.

Analysis

When Darwin L. Teilhet's first book, *Murder in the Air*, was published, *The New York Herald Tribune* recommended the book "for fans who like their news stories done into fiction." The novel was based on the 1928 disappearance of the Belgian financier Alfred Lowenstein from a small airplane over the English Channel. Though eventually Lowenstein's body was discovered in the channel, Teilhet developed a far more elaborate plot involving the impossible vanishing of a man from a locked plane in midair.

The Talking Sparrow Murders

This interest in current events as sources of fiction led to Teilhet's most important novel, *The Talking Sparrow Murders*, published in 1934. At a time when most novelists, whether writers of mysteries or mainline fiction, looked on Adolf Hitler as merely a German nationalist bent on redressing the inequities of the Treaty of Versailles, Teilhet was almost alone in understanding the terror that the Nazis were creating. He had spent 1928 and 1929 in Heidelberg, and his impressions of what was happening have all the vividness of a young man's views. What he felt was not only the terror of the times but also the sadness of the loss of a great past.

Later, in explaining why he introduced controversial themes into his stories, Teilhet said that a writer must "have something deep in [himself] and . . . the need to express it. They say that applies to the important novels, to the big serious efforts and it may be true, too, I wouldn't know. Perhaps it can apply to anything a man feels he has to write. . . ." Teilhet believed that he had to write about the rape of the Germany he loved, and he did it in a formal detective story.

The Talking Sparrow Murders, which takes place in Heidelberg, begins with an extraordinary mystery. How can a sparrow talk, and why is the man who reported the loquacious bird immediately murdered? Mystery follows mystery, not only of sudden death but also of the man who solemnly bows to a pine tree. Yet, unlike writers who used bizarre events primarily to create interest on the part of the reader, Teilhet writes of talking sparrows and other strange phenomena to introduce the theme of the story: that Heidelberg is a part of a world going mad. The Nazis are consolidating their power, and the left wing responds with equally irrational violence. How can rational detection, indeed how can humane people, exist in such a situation? Herr Polizeidirector Kresch attempts to unravel the mysteries, but one of the major suspects is the head of the local branch of the Nazi Party. Teilhet's point is that people must remain human even if ultimately they cannot control what is happening. Teilhet did not look on fictional murder as merely providing an intellectual puzzle. Witness the opening to the chapter titled "The Live Cat and the Dead Jew," which must be quoted in order to understand the depth of Teilhet's anger:

> It was a dead Jew, all right. . . . Most of the man's body was a pulp of cloth and blood with a great gaping place where the cat had been at him after the Nazis finished. . . . They had thoughtfully burned the swastika sign on the Jew's forehead before finishing with him and tossing him out in the Friedrichsallee as one of their amusing little signs of the cultural revival of Germany.
>
> Except for the mark on the forehead and a bruise below the right eye, the Jew's face had not been touched; it was strong and intelligent, with a sensitive nose and a firm mouth flicked up at the corner by a final frozen grimace of agony or, perhaps, the last physical indication of a refusal to be either humiliated or frightened by torture. . . . From somewhere in the distance a clock struck out mellowly and with a curiously haunting sadness, as if it were a relic of a long forgotten past, two hours in the morning.

Such passages were strong stuff in the detective novel of the 1930's; indeed, they would be strong stuff in novels of any time—not merely because of the repressed brutality of the language but also because, by setting the Nazi murder against a Heidelberg symbolized by the bells of an ancient clock, Teilhet shows that Nazism and fascism are modern evils, evils of propaganda and technology and hatred directed by party and state.

It is remarkable that Teilhet uses such elements to develop the plot of a fair-play detective novel. The incident of the dead Jew foreshadows a later episode in which the narrator reads a newspaper that reports three other murders. Two of the victims are named Rosenkrantz and Jacobson: "You can tell by their names what happened to them. . . . Jews attacked by the righteous Nazis." The third victim however, has the good German name Schmitz, and because he was killed near the site of the talking sparrow, his death proves to be connected with the mystery.

Teilhet's narrative style in *The Talking Sparrow Murders* is unusual. Occasionally the colorfulness of his prose becomes what Bill Pronzini, in reference to a later Teilhet book, calls "overripe," but generally it is vivid and precise. The narrative viewpoint is often unexpected. The book is told in the first person by William Tatson, an American engineer living in Germany. In one scene, Tatson contrasts the unreal gaiety of a nightclub with violence of the Nazi takeover—something that would be done later in the film *Cabaret* (1972). Tatson is attacked by Willi, a homosexual Brownshirt. Playing up to Willi's sexual interest in him, Tatson lures him to an empty room and knocks him out. Instead of describing these events directly, Tatson suddenly tells the reader that he is back in the hall remembering what has happened. No mention is made of the precise occurrences. The result is a feeling of surrealism that contributes to the sense of irrationality of the events.

The Talking Sparrow Murders was a great popular success in 1934. Dorothy L. Sayers described it as having "a queerness and fancifulness which slightly suggest the work of another American mystery writer, John Dickson Carr." Still, the very immediacy of the book meant that its vogue would not last, and it was only in the 1980's, with the interest in the events leading to the Holocaust, that the book had its first paperback printing.

THE TICKING TERROR MURDERS

Teilhet's next mystery novel, *The Ticking Terror Murders* (1935), features Baron Frank Maximilian Karagoz und von Kaz, one of the few successful humorous detectives in fiction. Creating a comic sleuth is not easy, for it is difficult to maintain the balance between the amusing eccentricities of the sleuth and the fundamental seriousness of the detection. Baron von Kaz is different because the reader comes to understand why he acts as he does. The baron is imperfect; he is frequently laughable; but he has the reader's sympathy and, by the final book in the series, the reader's respect and affection.

The baron is not one of the infallible detectives who dominated mystery fiction of the 1930's. His pride in his ancient Habsburg ancestry contrasts with his impecunious situation. He has had to leave Austria after involvement in a failed monarchist coup, and now he has to make a living by his wits in what he considers the uncivilized United States. He tries to impress the unsophisticated Americans by quoting Latin tags, which he has memorized for the occasion. His pride constantly gets him into difficulties, and it is only his imagination—which he distrusts—that helps him solve crimes.

THE FEATHER CLOAK MURDERS

It took Teilhet a while to develop the baron's character. In the first book of the series, the baron is too bumbling to be acceptable as someone who can actually solve crimes. The second book, *The Feather Cloak Murders*, which Teilhet wrote in collaboration with his wife, Hildegarde, is much more successful. The setting, Hawaii in the 1930's, is carefully realized, and the baron is a much more sympathetic character. His love affair with Caryl Miquet makes the reader sympathize with him, and though he still has the foibles and foolish pride of the earlier book, he has become a character with unsuspected depths. For example, when young Billy McKay is badly injured by the murderer, the baron does not try to preserve clues or interview the boy. Instead, he tenderly carries him to the house while soothing him with an old German prayer. Unfortunately, the solution to the mystery is not entirely satisfying. It depends on a suspect's acting in an unconvincing way and on some tiny points of evidence that even the most attentive reader will miss.

THE CRIMSON HAIR MURDERS

The next novel about the baron, *The Crimson Hair Murders* (1936), does not further develop the baron's character, though judged purely as a fair-play detective novel, it is an extraordinary performance. It is full of traps for experienced readers of detective fiction, as Darwin and Hildegarde Teilhet carefully lead them to identify, wrongly, a least likely person as the culprit. The book begins on a ship off the coast of Mexico and ends with a chase across the newly constructed Golden Gate Bridge, two unexpected plot twists, and the baron's fingering the murderer from a hospital bed.

THE BROKEN FACE MURDERS

For a book that in many ways summarizes Teilhet's contributions to the detective novel, the final Baron von Kaz novel, *The Broken Face Murders* (1940), should be examined. The story harks back to the theme of *The Talking Sparrow Murders*. The baron has been in Vienna but was too late to prevent the Nazi takeover of his country or the execution of his friend Solomon Gruenstein, who has been killed "for no other reasons than that his nose was hooked and he worshiped as his ancestors had in the Jewish faith." When the baron returns to America to marry Caryl Miquet, he finds that the town where he plans to spend his honeymoon is dominated by an occult society called the Atlanticians, which is a front for an American anti-Semitic movement. This organization of "real Americans" does not "have much hankering for foreigners. Mostly they're against Jews and Communists." The sheriff warns the baron that "it'd break my heart . . . if some of those fellers got the idea you were a subversive influence or had a lot of Jewish blood in you. You were over there fighting for some of those Jews, I hear." Once again, Teilhet has stretched the usual limits of the fair-play detective novel to include controversial ideas.

Teilhet sugarcoats his message by keeping the comedy in the foreground. Many of the scenes are hilarious, especially when the baron's plans for his wedding night are continually interrupted. Yet, although he is still amusing, the baron has grown as a character. In contrast to the earlier personality, who depends on his self-protecting pride, the baron is no longer sure of himself. To his utter mortification, one of the suspects calls him "Baron von Kazy-Wazy," and a character named Bunny comes to understand the baron better than he does himself. Baron Franz Maximilian Karagoz und von Kaz is, Bunny realizes, "a Harlequin of jests and moods and mercurial changes. . . . This brave baron, this man of steel and sawdust, generous yet cruel, with some wisdom, and overmuch fanfarades, was born out of his time." Thus Bunny and the reader gain "a better comprehension of this man . . . touched more with sympathy and affection than amusement."

Teilhet wrote many books from 1940 until his death in 1964, including romances, spy thrillers, historical novels, and sardonic studies of modern life, and he received all the attention of a successful writer—paperback reprints, book-club editions, film adaptations, and serials in popular magazines. But his major contributions to the detective and mystery story had been made during the 1930's. In Baron von Kaz, he created the only humorous detective whose character has depth and complexity, and he used the fair-play, formal detective novel as a vehicle to protest against what the fascists—both in Germany and in America—were bringing to the world. No other mystery writer had the combination of storytelling ability and political sensitivity to do as well.

Douglas G. Greene

Principal mystery and detective fiction

St. Amand series: *Murder in the Air*, 1931; *Death Flies High*, 1931

Baron von Kaz series: *The Ticking Terror Murders*, 1935; *The Feather Cloak Murders*, 1936 (with Hildegarde Tolman Teilhet); *The Crimson Hair Murders*, 1936 (with Hildegarde Tolman Teilhet); *The Broken Face Murders*, 1940 (with Hildegarde Tolman Teilhet)

Nonseries novels: *The Talking Sparrow Murders*, 1934; *Hero by Proxy*, 1943; *Odd Man Pays*, 1944; *The Double Agent*, 1945; *The Fear Makers*, 1945; *The Rim of Terror*, 1950; *The Marble Forest*, 1951 (with others); *The Mission of Jeffery Tollamy*, 1951; *The Unpossessed*, 1951; *Take Me as I Am*, 1952; *The Big Runaround*, 1964 (also known as *Dangerous Encounter*)

Other major works

Novels: *Bright Destination*, 1935 (also known as *Bells on His Toes*, 1936); *Journey to the West*, 1938 (also known as *Tough Guy, Smart Guy*, 1939); *Trouble Is My Master*, 1942; *Retreat from the Dolphin*, 1943; *My True Love*, 1945; *Something Wonderful to Happen*, 1947; *The Happy Island*, 1950; *Steamboat on the River*, 1952; *Beautiful Humbug*, 1954; *The Lion's Skin*, 1955; *The Road to Glory*, 1956

Children's literature: *Skwee-Gee*, 1940 (with Hildegarde Teilhet); *Ab Carmody's Treasure*, 1948; *The Avion My Uncle Flew*, 1948; *The Hawaiian Sword*, 1956

Bibliography

Greene, Douglas G. "The Demoniacal St. Amand and the Brave Baron von Kaz." *The Armchair Detective* 15 (Summer, 1982): 219-233. Profiles Teilhet's two most memorable sleuths, comparing them to each other as well as to other famous fictional detectives.

_______. Introduction to Teilhet's *The Talking Sparrow Murders*. New York: International Polygonics, 1985. Introduction to a reprint edition of Teilhet's mystery set in Nazi Germany discusses its relationship to history and topical fiction, as well as to the mystery and detective genre.

Horsley, Lee. *Twentieth-Century Crime Fiction*. New York: Oxford University Press, 2005. Very useful overview of the history and parameters of the crime-fiction genre; helps place Teilhet's work within that genre.

Teilhet, Darwin L. "How Some Adventure Stories Are and Are Not Written." *The Writer* 57 (June, 1944): 167-169. Brief piece by Teilhet that provides insight into his writing process and his thoughts about the craft of fiction.

JOSEPHINE TEY

Elizabeth Mackintosh

Born: Inverness, Scotland; June 25, 1896 or 1897
Died: London, England; February 13, 1952
Also wrote as Gordon Daviot
Types of plot: Police procedural; cozy

Principal series

Alan Grant, 1929-1952

Principal series characters

ALAN GRANT, a Scotland Yard police detective, is a shrewd reader of human faces who relies on his "flair," an ingenious, intuitive knack for solving cases. Although he makes mistakes, his intelligence sets him apart from most fictional police detectives, who lack his imagination, initiative, and cosmopolitan outlook.

SERGEANT WILLIAMS, Grant's sidekick, furnishes Grant with detailed information gleaned from his meticulous investigations.

Contribution

Although Alan Grant is a recurring character in Josephine Tey's detective novels, he is not always the main character. As in *To Love and Be Wise* (1950), he may be introduced at the beginning of a novel but not figure prominently until a crime has been committed. In *The Franchise Affair* (1948), he plays only a minor role. Tey is exceptional in not following the conventional plots of mystery and detective stories. She is more interested in human character. Grant is important insofar as he comes into contact with murder victims and suspects, but usually the human scene is fully described before Grant appears. Consequently, Tey's novels never seem driven by a mere "whodunit" psychology. She is interested, rather, in human psychology as it is revealed in the commission of a crime, a disappearance, or a case of imposture. Often readers who do not like the conventions of detective stories like Tey because her novels seem organic; that is, they grow out of what is revealed about the characters. If Tey writes mysteries, it is because human character is a mystery.

Biography

Josephine Tey was born Elizabeth Mackintosh in Inverness, Scotland, where she attended the Royal Academy and studied the humanities. After she was graduated, she continued course work in physical culture at the Anstey Physical College and taught the subject for several years in English schools. She gave up teaching in 1926 to look after her invalid father at their family home. As Gordon Daviot, she wrote novels, short stories, and plays. Her greatest success in the theater came with the production of *Richard of Bordeaux* (pr. 1932), based on the life of Richard III and starring John Gielgud.

In private life, Tey seemed to have few interests besides horse racing and fishing, both of which figure in her fiction. In a letter to a fellow mystery writer, she confessed that she did not read many mysteries. She was a very shy woman with few close friends. She granted no press interviews. It was characteristic of her to have lived with her fatal illness for a year before her death without telling anyone about it. She never married. The strongest women in her fiction are single, and her detective, Alan Grant, is a bachelor who shares many of his creator's interests, including a devotion to the theater.

Analysis

Josephine Tey's first detective novel, *The Man in the Queue* (1929), introduced Alan Grant of Scotland Yard. Grant is a man with considerable style. As later novels indicate, he is regarded as somewhat suspect at the Yard because of his "flair." He might be just a bit too intelligent. His superiors fear that his wit may cause him to be too ingenious, to make too much of certain evidence with his fancy interpretations. Indeed, in *The Man in the Queue*, Grant's brilliance almost does lead him to the wrong conclusion. Some reviewers thought that Tey spent too much time conveying the mental processes of her detective. A greater fault of her first detective novel, however, is the stabbing of the man in the queue—which is done in public

Josephine Tey in 1934. (Hulton Archive/Getty Images)

in a crowded line of people. Reviewers wondered why the man did not cry out. None of Tey's subsequent detective novels depends on gimmickry, however, and with the exception of *The Daughter of Time* (1951), Grant's thoughts are not the focus of the narrative.

The Man in the Queue also introduced Grant's sidekick, Sergeant Williams. As in the classic detective story, Williams plays a kind of Dr. Watson to Grant's Sherlock Holmes. Grant, however, is much more appreciative of Williams, his detail man, than Holmes is of Watson. Grant relies on Williams for meticulous investigations and often goes over the details to be sure that he (Grant) has not missed anything. In other words, Williams is no mere sounding board, even if he worships Grant as his hero.

Brat Farrar

Except for *A Shilling for Candles* (1936), Tey wrote no Alan Grant novels in the 1930's, as though to prevent him from dominating her fiction. *Brat Farrar* (1949) is about an impostor who claims to be the heir to a huge family fortune. The heir is presumed to have committed suicide as a young boy, although the boy's body was never found. In a riveting narrative, Tey achieves the astonishing feat of getting readers to identify with the impostor, Brat Farrar, while deepening the mystery of how the heir actually met his death. As in several other novels, she raises intriguing questions about human identity, about how human beings take on roles that can both obscure and reveal reality.

To Love and Be Wise

Similarly, in *To Love and Be Wise*, an Alan Grant novel, the question at first seems to be what happened to Leslie Searle, an American photographer who has befriended an English family. He disappears on an outing with Walter Whitmore, an English radio personality who is suspected of doing away with Searle because of Searle's involvement with Whitmore's fiancée. By the time Grant becomes deeply involved in the case, the novel is half over and the reader's interest is increasingly focused on exactly who Leslie Searle was. How is it that he insinuated himself into the lives of an English family? What was there about him that made him so appealing? Grant has to pursue these questions before finally realizing that Leslie Searle is not the victim but the perpetrator of a crime.

The Daughter of Time

The most celebrated Alan Grant novel is *The Daughter of Time*. Grant is laid up with an injury in the hospital. He asks his close friend, the actress Martha Hallard (another regular character in the Grant series), to bring him a set of prints. Among other things, Hallard supplies him with a print of the portrait of Richard III that is on display at the National Gallery in London. Grant is stunned that Richard's keenly intelligent and compassionate face is nothing like the villain portrayed by Shakespeare and Sir Thomas More. With the assistance of an American student, Grant engages in a full-scale research project to exonerate Richard III from the charge of murdering the princes in the Tower and of being the most villainous king in English history.

The Daughter of Time has been extravagantly praised as a tour de force, a unique combination of the detective story and a work of history. It has also been disdained as a prejudiced book that libels historians for supposedly blackening Richard's name based on insufficient or biased evidence. It is true that Tey does not offer all the evidence that has been used to confirm Richard's guilt. Worse, the novel has internal flaws. For a novelist who was usually so perceptive about human character, Tey saw only the bright side of Richard's public character and did not make allowances for the brutal age in which he lived, an age in which struggles for the throne often led to bloodshed. In Tey's favor, however, the conventions of the mystery and detective genre may also be held accountable: The form mandates that a criminal be caught. If Richard III is not the villain, then Henry VII must be. Tey's detective amasses a case against Richard's successor. Historians have other options and have conducted much closer studies of Richard III's England than can be permitted in a detective novel. Most readers have found *The Daughter of Time* to be an invigorating work of fiction, particularly appealing for the unusual interpretation of historical events, whatever credence one gives to that interpretation.

The real strength of *The Daughter of Time* lies in Tey's emphasis on Grant as an interpreter of the evidence. Although he attacks historians, his methods are not out of line with what R. G. Collingwood has recommended in *The Idea of History* (1946). In fact, Collingwood invents a detective story to explain how a historian interprets evidence. Even if Grant makes the wrong judgments of history, the important thing is that he is not content to look at secondary sources—that is, other histories of Richard III. Instead, he consults the records and documents produced during Richard's brief reign. Grant tries to use his experience as a detective, his ability to read human faces, to interpret Richard's life and work. Grant asks hard questions. He actively investigates the historical evidence and does not rely on authorities. Tey shrewdly gets readers to identify with Grant by having him slowly discover the evidence and then put it to the test of his formidable skepticism.

The Singing Sands

The Daughter of Time is different from the other Grant novels in that Grant displays more confidence than he does elsewhere. In the other novels he has definite mental and physical weaknesses. Something in the English climate makes him sniffle. In *The Singing Sands* (1952), he retreats to the Scottish highlands to steady himself; in pursuit of a murderer, he is also on the verge of a nervous breakdown. Yet is it his very vulnerability that helps him to identify with others and to see his way through to the solution of his cases.

Much of the beauty of Tey's writing derives from her love of the English and Scottish countryside. When things go awry in this charming, family-oriented world, it is absolutely imperative that the detective restore equilibrium. The scenes in *The Singing Sands* of Grant fishing in Highland streams remain vivid long after the plot of the novel is forgotten. In *Brat Farrar*, which is not part of the Grant series, Tey makes an impostor her main character and makes his identification with an English family and its home such a powerful theme that it becomes imperative that the criminal somehow be able to redeem himself—which he does by discovering the real murderer of the twin whom he has impersonated.

One of the common pitfalls of serial detective fiction is that it can become routinized and thus predictable, the detective employing the same set of gestures and methods that have proved effective and popular in previous novels. This is never so with Tey. Each case confronting Grant is unique, and he must fumble to discover the appropriate technique. Circumstances always influence the way Grant handles a case. In spite of his prodigious mental gifts, he is not presented as a great detective who is the equal of every mystery. He profits from lucky accidents, from the suggestions of others, and from the mistakes of criminals. As a result, the reader's interest is drawn to Grant's character as well as the mysteries he is trying to solve.

It is striking what a clean, highly individualized world Tey presents in her detective fiction. There are relatively few murders and gruesome incidents. The police and the other institutions of society are never seen as corrupt. Rather, it is human character that is crooked or degenerate. In other words, Tey's crimes become moral but never sociological problems. She is a keen observer of society but shies away from generalizations about class and economic structure.

Miss Pym Disposes

Given a sufficient interest in crime, an amateur can become a detective. Such is the case in *Miss Pym Disposes* (1946). Set in a physical education college, this novel draws on Tey's own experience. Miss Lucy Pym is a best-selling author. She has also been a schoolmistress and now finds herself teaching temporarily at a girls' school. When she prevents a girl from cheating on an exam, she is compulsively drawn into a murder and devises an extralegal punishment for the criminal that leads to disaster. The novel is a brilliant attack on the high-and-mighty detectives who dispense their own brand of justice and are contemptuous of the police. Given the destructive way Miss Pym disposes of her case, it is no wonder that Tey did not follow this very popular novel with a sequel. Tey rejected the notion that a detective can solve case after case neatly and efficiently. As a result, she only wrote eight mystery and detective novels; each one had to be unique, and each successive novel was as carefully devised as the previous one.

During Tey's lifetime, two of her works (*A Shilling for Candles*, *The Franchise Affair*) were turned into films. The former served as the basis for Alfred Hitchcock's *Young and Innocent* (1937). *Brat Farrar*, however, was the subject of two adaptations, first as a television movie for the British Broadcasting Corporation, and then as part of the network's perennially popular *Mystery!* series.

Though Tey died in the mid-twentieth century, her works were still in print at the turn of the century. Her crowning achievement, *The Daughter of Time*, which had been recorded for posterity by Derek Jacobi, had been digitally remastered and released in late 2000. Few mystery writers, past or present, have written with such diversity or originality; Tey's small body of work has more than withstood the test of time.

Carl Rollyson
Updated by Fiona Kelleghan and
Taryn Benbow-Pfalzgraf

Principal mystery and detective fiction

Alan Grant series: *The Man in the Queue*, 1929 (as Daviot; also known as *Killer in the Crowd*); *A Shilling for Candles*, 1936; *The Franchise Affair*, 1948; *To Love and Be Wise*, 1950; *The Daughter of Time*, 1951; *The Singing Sands*, 1952

Nonseries novels: *Miss Pym Disposes*, 1946; *Brat Farrar*, 1949 (also known as *Come and Kill Me*)

Other major works

Novels (as Daviot): *Kif: An Unvarnished History*, 1929; *The Expensive Halo*, 1931; *The Privateer*, 1952

Plays (as Daviot): *Richard of Bordeaux*, pr. 1932; *Queen of Scots*, pr., pb. 1934; *The Laughing Woman*, pr., pb. 1934; *The Stars Bow Down*, pr., pb. 1939; *Leith Sands, and Other Short Plays*, pb. 1946; *The Little Dry Thorn*, pr. 1947; *Valerius*, pr. 1948; *Dickon*, pb. 1953; *Plays*, pb. 1953-1954; *Sweet Coz*, pb. 1954

Radio plays (as Daviot): *Leith Sands*, 1941; *Mrs. Fry Has a Visitor*, 1944; *The Three Mrs. Madderleys*, 1944; *Remember Caesar*, 1946; *The Pen of My Aunt*, 1950; *The Pomp of Mr. Pomfret*, 1954; *Cornelia*, 1955

Nonfiction (as Daviot): *Claverhouse*, 1937

Bibliography

Dubose, Martha Hailey, with Margaret Caldwell Thomas. *Women of Mystery: The Lives and Works of Notable Women Crime Novelists*. New York: St. Martin's Minotaur, 2000. Tey is compared to such other novelists as Patricia Highsmith and Dorothy L. Sayers.

Hanson, Gillian Mary. *City and Shore: The Function of Setting in the British Mystery*. Jefferson, N.C.: McFarland, 2004. Analyzes Tey's use of setting in *A Shilling for Candles* and *The Singing Sands*. Bibliographic references and index.

Keen, Suzanne. *Romances of the Archive in Contemporary British Fiction*. Buffalo, N.Y.: University of Toronto Press, 2001. Tey is compared with a variety of other writers, from H. P. Lovecraft and Henry James to Umberto Eco and Edmund Spenser. The point of comparison is each author's representation of the archive and the function of those representations both within and without the text.

Kelly, R. Gordon. "Josephine Tey and Others: The Case of Richard III." In *The Detective as Historian: History and Art in Historical Crime Fiction*, edited by Ray B. Browne and Lawrence A. Kreiser, Jr. Bowling Green, Ohio: Bowling Green State University Popular Press, 2000. Analyzes the use to which Tey and others put history and the ways in which they represent history while exploring and exploiting the life of King Richard III.

Klein, Kathleen Gregory, ed. *Great Women Mystery Writers: Classic to Contemporary.* Westport, Conn.: Greenwood Press, 1994. Contains an essay on the life and works of Tey.

Reynolds, Moira Davison. *Women Authors of Detective Series: Twenty-one American and British Authors, 1900-2000.* Jefferson, N.C.: McFarland, 2001. Examines the life and work of major female mystery writers, including Tey.

Roy, Sandra. *Josephine Tey.* Boston: Twayne, 1980. Biography of Tey combined with literary analysis of her works.

Talburt, Nancy Ellen. *Ten Women of Mystery*, edited by Earl F. Bargainner. Bowling Green, Ohio: Bowling Green State University Popular Press, 1981. Compares Tey to nine other famous female mystery writers.

ROSS THOMAS

Born: Oklahoma City, Oklahoma; February 19, 1926
Died: Santa Monica, California; December 18, 1995
Also wrote as Oliver Bleeck
Types of plot: Espionage; amateur sleuth; thriller

Principal series

Mac McCorkle and Mike Padillo, 1966-1990
Philip St. Ives, 1969-1976
Artie Wu and Quincy Durant, 1978-1992

Principal series characters

Mac McCorkle, the undescribed viewpoint character, is probably in his late thirties as the McCorkle and Padillo series begins. With Mike Padillo, he runs a saloon first in Bonn and then in Washington, D.C. Mac's Place features high prices, low lights, and honest drinks. A typical understated American, Mac was behind the lines in Burma during World War II and can handle himself in a fight when necessary. His bonding to his partner and his commitment to finishing the dirty work so that he can return to drinking motivate his actions.

Mike Padillo, half-Estonian and half-Spanish, with a facility for languages and violence, is blackmailed into military intelligence during World War II and into working for an unnamed Central Intelligence Agency (CIA) competitor after the war. All he wants is to run a good saloon, but Mac's Place provides his cover as well. Cynical and suspicious, he wants to come in out of the cold but is not allowed to do so. His relationship with Mac is a tribute to male bonding.

Philip St. Ives is a former newspaper columnist who has a wide acquaintance with shady characters. He uses that knowledge to act as a go-between in ransoming stolen objects, in the process finding himself obliged to solve the crimes involved, although he is loyal to the criminals until they deceive him in some way.

Myron Greene is St. Ives's attorney and accountant. A corporate lawyer with a taste for flashy clothes and cars, he would not be caught dead trying a case in court but revels in his connection to the seamy life through St. Ives. Cases usually come in through Greene.

Artie Wu is more than six feet tall and weighs nearly 250 pounds. The illegitimate son of the illegitimate daughter of the last Manchu emperor and semiserious claimant to the throne, he met Quincy Durant in an orphanage, and they have been partners in crime ever since. An expert in classical con games, he is the planner of the pair. He is married, with two sets of twins.

Quincy Durant, tall, thin, and nervous as a coiled spring, is the action man, although his talent as a planner of con games is not to be despised either. His love life usually complicates things.

Otherguy Overby is so called because when the gaff is blown, it is always "the other guy" who is left holding the bag. An experienced con man, Otherguy gives the impression he might sell out the partnership, but he never quite does.

Contribution

Ross Thomas made the dark side of the worlds of politics, finance, and espionage as familiar to readers as the headlines in their daily newspapers. Crossing the mean, dark streets lined with executive suites and using the eye of a reporter and the tongue of an adder with a malicious sense of humor, he made the reader feel like an eavesdropper in the halls of power, often using the inside political manipulator as hero. As Oliver Bleeck, Thomas invented a new occupation for amateur sleuth Philip St. Ives. As a professional go-between, St. Ives dabbled in crimes ranging from art theft to Cold War double-crosses.

Biography

Ross Elmore Thomas was born on February 19, 1926 in Oklahoma City, Oklahoma, to J. Edwin Thomas and Laura (née Dean) Thomas. He began his education as a thriller writer while a reporter on the *Daily Oklahoman* in his hometown before serving as a U.S. Army infantryman in the Philippines during World War II. After he graduated from the University of Oklahoma in 1949, he directed public relations for the National Farmers Union and later for the Volunteers in Service to America (VISTA). Thomas managed election campaigns in the United States for two union presidents, for a Republican Senate nominee and for a Democratic governor of Colorado. Interestingly, he also advised an African leader who was running for the post of prime minister in Nigeria, though without success.

Thomas covered Bonn, Germany, for the Armed Forces Network in the late 1950's, and served as a consultant/political mastermind to the United States government from 1964 to 1966 before publishing his first thriller, *The Cold War Swap* (1966), a book that won the Mystery Writers of America's Edgar Allan Poe Award in 1967. In 1974, he married Rosalie Appleton. He always cast a cynical eye on institutions and society at home and abroad, dissecting both with the wit of a morgue attendant and a wiretapper's ear for dialogue. *Briarpatch* (1984) won Thomas another Edgar Award in 1985, and *Chinaman's Chance* (1978) was selected by the Independent Mystery Booksellers Association as one of the One Hundred Favorite Mysteries of the Century. Thomas served a term as president of the Mystery Writers of America. Thomas died in 1995 in Santa Monica, California.

Analysis

If Ross Thomas needed any apprenticeship in writing fiction, he served it during his year as reporter, public relations man, and political manager. His first novel, *The Cold War Swap*, was published three years after John le Carré's pathbreaking *The Spy Who Came in from the Cold* (1963) captured the attention of readers by inverting the morality of the espionage novel. In his first offering, Thomas showed that he was already a master of the Hobbesian world of espionage double-cross, where every man is against every other, the only rule is survival, and the agents from both sides are more sympathetic characters than their masters. His hero, Mike Padillo, is a fully "amortized agent"—the agency's investment in him has long since paid off handsomely. He is to be traded to the Soviets for a pair of gay National Security Agency defectors. His triumph, if it can be called that, is in carrying out his mission without falling into the hands of either side.

Thomas's universe is not the weary world of fallen empire inhabited by Le Carré's neurasthenic heroes but the permanently rotten one invented by the creators of the hard-boiled American detective. In it, few men (and fewer women) are loyal, everything is for sale, and everything is connected—in the worst possible way. His men are professionals whose only pride is in their professionalism and their survival. They survive because a few people have followed E. M. Forster's advice to remain loyal to their friends rather than to their nation, or because they can buy aid from those who have no loyalties. Heroes cannot reform Thomas's world, but the quick or the unprincipled can manipulate it, briefly, in pursuit of the ancient triad of money, power, and sex.

CAST A YELLOW SHADOW AND THE SINGAPORE WINK

Thomas's area of specialization was the world of the double-cross—espionage, politics, and the con game. His viewpoint characters are men of a certain age and experience who can handle themselves in the boardroom, battle, or boudoir. Journalists, former spies, and political insiders, his heroes come in two kinds, those who, like the cowboy, do not go looking for trouble, and those who, like the private eye, do—for money. Those who do not go willingly into trouble have to be blackmailed into doing the job, and their only recompense is money, lots of it, and peace and quiet until the next time. In *Cast a Yellow Shadow* (1967), Mike Padillo agrees to assassinate the prime minister of a white-ruled African nation after Mac's wife is kidnapped. In *The Singapore Wink* (1969), Edward Cauthorne, former Hollywood stuntman and current dealer in vintage cars, agrees to go to Singapore to locate a man for the mob after several of his cars are vandalized. Hoods have also crushed the hands of Sidney Durant, his twenty-year-old body man, by repeatedly slamming a car door on them.

Those who do go willingly into trouble include con men Artie Wu and Quincy Durant, go-between Philip St. Ives, and a miscellaneous crew of journalists and political consultants whose job descriptions cannot be easily distinguished from those of the con men. The professionals cannot be distinguished in their expertise from the amateurs either, and the survival of all depends on quick reflexes fueled by low cunning, inside knowledge, and lashings of untraceable money.

Thomas invents female characters who are as capable of violence, lust, greed, and chicanery as the men; they may be physically weaker, but they make up for it. Although they are usually subsidiary characters in the typical women's roles of secretary or assistant, there are exceptions. Georgia Blue (*Out on the Rim*, 1987) is a former Secret Service agent who has a role equal to the men's in persuading the Filipino revolutionary to retire to Hong Kong, and Wanda Gothar (*The Backup Men*, 1971) is an experienced member of a family that has been involved in espionage since the Napoleonic era. If the women are older, they are capable of the exercise of power, such as Gladys Citron (*Missionary Stew*, 1983), West Coast editor of a *National Enquirer*-type newspaper and former Office of Strategic Services officer decorated personally by Charles de Gaulle for killing three dozen Germans. Realistically, most of the older women exercise power as wives or widows, and they do it by manipulation, at which they are as adept as the men around them. All Thomas's characters like sex the way they like food or drink.

THE SEERSUCKER WHIPSAW

Perhaps because southerners have traditionally had verbal skills that take them into politics, or because Thomas is from the edge of the South, many of his political characters are convincing southern gothics whose careers would enliven the dullest work of academic sociology. The seersucker-suited Clinton Shartelle, hired to manage the political campaign of the African chief Sunday Akomolo in *The Seersucker Whipsaw* (1967), describes his life in Denver to his associate, Peter Upshaw:

> I lived here in a house with my daddy and a lady friend from 1938 to 1939. Not too far from that ball park which is—you might have noticed—a somewhat blighted area. It was a plumb miserable neighborhood even then. I was sixteen-seventeen years old. My daddy and I had come out here from Oklahoma City in the fall driving a big, black 1929 LaSalle convertible sedan. We checked in at the Brown Palace and my daddy got himself a lease on a section of land near Walsenburg, found himself a rig and crew, and drilled three of the deepest dry holes you ever saw.

Shartelle's story goes on for several pages, and before he has finished, Thomas has involved the reader in a three-dimensional character whose childhood has produced a man of flexible morals with a gift of gab that could charm a sheriff bent on eviction or an outraged creditor. He is a man drawn to political manipulation just as naturally as steel filings are drawn to a magnet.

The minor characters Thomas creates are as fully drawn as the major ones. The reader comes to understand them as clearly as he understands his own quirky relatives. The reader can never tell, however, whether the cab driver whose long life story Thomas relates will take his tip and disappear from the pages of the book, or whether he will play a larger part of the story. The characters are so engaging in their frankly seamy humanity that the reader is simply happy to meet them, even if only briefly. Certain minor character types, such as the Village Wise Man or Fixer, reappear in successive books. One of the Fixer types is David "Slippery" Slipper, white-haired and seventy-five, who

> had been, at various times, a New Deal White House aide, or to hear him tell it, "Harry Hopkins's office boy"; a spy of sorts for the wartime Office of Strategic Services; a syndicated columnist (121 daily newspapers); a biographer of the iron-willed Speaker of the House of Representatives, Thomas Brackett (Czar) Reed; an Assistant Secretary of Agriculture (six months); a deputy Undersecretary of the Interior (ninety days); ambassador to Chad (one year, "the longest year of my life," he later said); and for the past fifteen years a political fixer and consultant who charged outrageous fees for his sensible, hardheaded advice.

After several more detailed paragraphs about Slippery, Thomas has him tell the hero to drop his investigation and he disappears forever from *Missionary Stew*. These categories are not exclusively male. Señora Madelena de Romanones plays both the Village Wise Woman and Fixer characters in *Cast a Yellow Shadow*.

The Mordida Man and Out on the Rime

Thomas's spies and spymasters are painted as ridiculous and two-faced. The reader can never tell who is on which side, as even the hero is not always committed to conventional morality. The double-crosses come fast and furious, and the reader will always be wise to expect one more, unless he has just read the last line of the book. Thomas's male characters like fast, expensive cars, exotic weapons, and fast, exotic women. When he is setting up the story, Thomas can "tell the tale" better than any con man alive. His political manipulators are heroes as often as they are villains, and his union officials are simply normal men with a normal lust for power and money, not Working Class Heroes or Red Revolutionaries. In fact, his revolutionaries are normal men with normal lusts. The Libyans in *The Mordida Man* (1981) finally accept revenge when they cannot obtain the return of a kidnapped terrorist, and, in *Out on the Rim*, the aging Filipino rebel Alejandro Espiritu becomes so power-mad that he executes his own nephew without remorse, allowing Wu and Durant to carry out their mission to remove him (and keep a large portion of the money they were supposed to have used to bribe him).

Thomas has a crime reporter's eye for concrete details such as the exact age of a building (and often its history), the number of steps in a flight of stairs, and the number of an airline flight and the precise number of minutes takeoff is delayed. This use of detail creates a sense of reality so palpable that the reader can almost taste the dirt on the cement. Thomas's style, directly descended from the colorful speech of the oral tradition, is so wry and amusing that he makes the reader regret the homogenization of American English by television announcers and bureaucratic memorandum writers. His dialogue is realistic, and conversation between male friends, such as McCorkle and Padillo or Wu and Durant, is as elliptical as the exchange of a couple who have been married for fifty years.

Thomas takes his plots from the front pages of the daily papers, using his experience to invent an inside story that is more treacherous than reality. In *Yellow-Dog Contract* (1976), political campaign manager Harvey Longmore comes out of retirement to investigate the disappearance of a nationally known union leader. *The Porkchoppers* (1972) investigates a crooked, no-holds-barred union election. In *The Mordida Man*, the president's brother, a slick political manager, has been kidnapped by the Libyans. In *Out on the Rim*, Wu and Durant become entangled in the guerrilla war in the Philippines; with an immediacy unmatched by the experts who write for the op-ed pages, Thomas depicts the violence and corruption that plague that former American colony.

The Philip St. Ives books

When Thomas writes as Oliver Bleeck, his voice is more serious, and the Philip St. Ives stories are closer to classical mysteries, but the characters are as closely observed and as colorful as they are in the Ross Thomas books. The crime situations allow him to include overweight, overworked, and underpaid cops, whose lives are as disorderly as they are human, and St. Ives is more nearly a hard-boiled, if amateur, detective, whose own life in a seedy New York residence hotel is not any more orderly than anybody else's. He is as competent and as tricky as Thomas's other heroes, but his soul is darker than the souls of the enthralling manipulators who find real joy—and profit—in the tawdry world around them.

In his books, Thomas has invented a complex world of greed, lust, and chicanery where inside knowledge and money are the only security, a world of betrayal where the quick and flexible may, for a while, stay alive, find a good woman, and come out a bit ahead—and maybe even get in a few licks for the good guys in the process.

Marilynn M. Larew
Updated by Fiona Kelleghan

Principal mystery and detective fiction

Mac McCorkel and Mike Padillo series: *The Cold War Swap*, 1966 (also known as *Spy in the Vodka*); *Cast a Yellow Shadow*, 1967; *The Backup Men*, 1971; *Twilight at Mac's Place*, 1990

Philip St. Ives series: *The Brass Go-Between*, 1969; *Protocol for a Kidnapping*, 1971; *The Procane Chronicle*, 1971 (also known as *The Thief Who Painted Sunlight* and *St. Ives*); *The Highbinders*, 1974; *No Questions Asked*, 1976

Artie Wu and Quincy Durant series: *Chinaman's Chance*, 1978; *Out on the Rim*, 1987; *Voodoo, Ltd.*, 1992

Nonseries novels: *The Seersucker Whipsaw*, 1967; *The Singapore Wink*, 1969; *The Fools in Town Are on Our Side*, 1971; *The Porkchoppers*, 1972; *If You Can't Be Good*, 1973; *The Money Harvest*, 1975; *Yellow-Dog Contract*, 1976; *The Eighth Dwarf*, 1979; *The Mordida Man*, 1981; *Missionary Stew*, 1983; *Briarpatch*, 1984; *Spies, Thumbsuckers, Etc.*, 1989; *The Fourth Durango*, 1989; *Ah, Treachery*, 1994

Other major works

Screenplay: *Hammett*, 1983 (with Dennis O'Flaherty and Thomas Pope)

Nonfiction: *Warriors for the Poor: The Story of VISTA*, 1969 (with William H. Crook); *Cop World: Inside an American Police Force*, 1985

Bibliography

Donovan, Mark. "With Twenty-first Thriller, Writer Ross Thomas Just Might Hit It Big—Not That He Hasn't Been Trying." *People Weekly* 28 (November 30, 1987): 109. A look at Thomas's output and his lack of a breakout hit after twenty-one attempts.

Hiss, Tony. "Remembering Ross Thomas." *The Atlantic Monthly* 278, no. 5 (November, 1996): 117. Tribute to the late author by a writer known for his biographies and social commentary.

Hitz, Frederick P. *The Great Game: The Myth and Reality of Espionage*. New York: Alfred A. Knopf, 2004. Hitz, a former inspector general of the Central Intelligence Agency, compares fictional spies to actual intelligence agents. Gives perspective to Thomas's writing, although he is not directly discussed.

Kelly, R. Gordon. *Mystery Fiction and Modern Life*. Jackson: University Press of Mississippi, 1998. Examines the parallels between real life and detective fiction. Contains brief analysis of Thomas's work.

Roth, Marty. *Foul and Fair Play: Reading Genre in Classic Detective Fiction*. Athens: University of Georgia Press, 1995. A post-structural analysis of the conventions of mystery and detective fiction. Examines 138 short stories and works from the 1840's to the 1960's. Mentions Thomas and helps place him in context.

Scaggs, John. *Crime Fiction*. New York: Routledge, 2005. Contains a chapter on crime thrillers that sheds light on Thomas's work.

JIM THOMPSON

Born: Anadarko, Oklahoma Territory; September 27, 1906
Died: Hollywood, California; April 7, 1977
Types of plot: Inverted; hard-boiled; psychological

Contribution

Jim Thompson brought a level of psychological realism to crime novels seldom achieved by writers in that or any other genre. He explored the criminal mind in chilling and powerful first-person narrations, presenting the ordinary world through the eyes of brutal and brutalized killers to whom commonplace morality and rules of behavior do not apply. Thompson's killers tell their stories and describe their savage behavior without entirely losing the reader's sympathy and understanding, yet Thompson did not justify or excuse his criminals because of their warped environments, nor did he maintain the reader's sympathy by providing his killers with unusually despicable victims. He achieved something much more difficult: He persuasively presented a world that causes readers to suspend their ordinary moral judgments as too simplistic and abstract to apply to the margins of society inhabited by his characters.

Biography

Jim Thompson's childhood was quite unconventional, according to his wife, Alberta. Born James Myers Thompson, he grew up in Oklahoma, Texas, and Nebraska, where his brilliant and charismatic but erratic father first triumphed and then hit the bottom in one career after another, finally going bankrupt in oil after having made millions. Jim Thompson shared his father's brilliance and his inability to establish order in his life. While still in high school, he began his long struggle with alcohol, despairing at the meaninglessness of life and generating a self-destructive rage at the stupidity and parochialism of society around him.

He attended the University of Nebraska for a few years and married Alberta there in 1931. To feed his wife and three children during the Great Depression, he worked in hotels, oil fields, collection agencies, and vegetable fields. He had had his first story published at the age of fifteen and earned extra money by writing true-crime stories, character sketches, and vignettes of his experiences with the down-and-out people around him. His appointment in the late 1930's as director of the Oklahoma Writers Project inspired him to break into the larger publishing world. He wrote two excellent novels, *Now and on Earth* (1942) and *Heed the Thunder* (1946), but despite praise from critics, neither book sold. Thompson worked on several major newspapers and briefly served as editor-in-chief of *Saga* magazine.

In 1949 he wrote his first mystery, *Nothing More than Murder*. It was followed by a string of mysteries, written rapidly and in streaks: Twelve books appeared between 1952 and 1954.

Hindered by alcoholism and never financially secure, Thompson always tapped the writing markets available to him. In the 1950's he collaborated on two screenplays for films directed by Stanley Kubrick, *The Killing* (1956) and *Paths of Glory* (1957), and wrote for several television series. He lived for his writing, Alberta said, and after strokes ended that part of his life, he deliberately starved himself to death, by her account. At the time of his death—April 7, 1977—none of his books was in print in the United States.

Yet Thompson was not forgotten. Several films were made from his books, including *The Killer Inside Me* (1952) in 1976, *The Getaway* (1959) in 1972, *Série Noire* in 1979 (based on the novel *A Hell of a Woman*, 1954), *Coup de Torchon* in 1981 (based on the novel *Pop. 1280*, 1964), *After Dark, My Sweet* (1955) in 1990, *The Grifters* (1963) in 1990, and *Hit Me* in 1996 (based on the novel *A Swell-Looking Babe*, 1954). In the 1980's, publishers began reprinting Thompson's works. They found a market among those who remembered his paperback originals and among members of a new generation who responded to his nihilistic vision of life. Ten years after Thompson's death, most of his novels were back in print, and many of his more famous works remained in print in the twenty-first century.

ANALYSIS

Diversity of themes and settings characterizes Jim Thompson's paperback originals. He wrote fictionalized autobiography, explored the unstable, high-pressure world of confidence rackets, and used the hard-boiled crime style to write black comedy, including a comic masterpiece, *Pop. 1280*.

Thompson's crime novels also take up diverse social themes. As John Steinbeck described the plight of Okies forced off their land and surviving through hard work and strength of character, the Oklahoma-born Thompson portrayed another class of southwestern people, often long detached from the land, living by their wits and luck on the margins of society. In terse paragraphs he described the social and economic impact of soil erosion, the betrayal of the people by railroad corruption, the shenanigans of corrupt politicians, and the human costs of the communist witch-hunt of the 1950's. He explored the constricted lives of sharecroppers and the plight of Indians (*Cropper's Cabin*, 1952), the disease of alcoholism (*The Alcoholics*, 1953), and the source and nature of black rage (*Nothing but a Man*, 1970; *Child of Rage*, 1972).

THE KILLER INSIDE ME

Thompson's reputation and rediscovery rests above all on his unparalleled ability to portray a killer's mind, often in powerful first-person narrations by a disintegrating criminal personality. Deputy Sheriff Lou Ford, who narrates *The Killer Inside Me*, stands out from the people around him only because he is friendlier and nicer. His quiet, smiling exterior masks inner rage:

> I've loafed around the streets sometimes, leaned against a store front with my hat pushed back and one boot hooked back around the other.
>
> Hell, you've probably seen me if you've ever been out this way—I've stood like that, looking nice and friendly and stupid, like I wouldn't piss if my pants were on fire. And all the time I'm laughing myself sick inside. Just watching the people.

Ford, a brilliant young man hiding behind a mask of bland, cliché-spouting stupidity, knows that he is sick. He gently explains to a young delinquent whom he has befriended and is preparing to kill that straight society, while tolerating terrible social injustices, has no place for people like the young man, who commit minor transgressions:

> They don't like you guys, and they crack down on you. And the way it looks to me they're going to be cracking down harder and harder as time goes on. You ask me why I stick around, knowing the score, and it's hard to explain. I guess I kind of got a foot on both fences, Johnnie. I planted 'em there early and now they've taken root, and I can't move either way and I can't jump. All I can do is wait until I split. Right down the middle. That's all I can do.

Ford describes the widening split within him. He does not carry a gun: "People are people, even when they're a little misguided," he says. "You don't hurt them, they won't hurt you. They'll listen to reason." Reason vanishes, however, when he goes to the home of Joyce Lakeland, a pretty young woman engaged in minor prostitution. He tells her to keep her hustling low-key or leave town; she hits him; he beats her unconscious but, once awake, she responds to him sexually, pulling him into a sadomasochistic relationship.

As Ford is drawn to her again and again, he feels "the sickness" returning. He had been sexually abused as a child and had himself molested young girls, for which his brother had been blamed and imprisoned. Now as the sickness returns, he struggles to hold himself together. "I knew she was making me worse; I knew that if I didn't stop soon I'd never to able to. I'd wind up in a cage or the electric chair." He finally (apparently) beats Joyce to death, a crime that sets off a chain of events forcing him to kill person after person, including his longtime sweetheart. The sickness gains increasing control. A drifter threatens to expose him: "I grinned, feeling a little sorry for him. It was funny the way these people kept asking for it. . . . Why'd they all have to come to me to get killed? Why couldn't they kill themselves?" In the end, he deliberately walks into a trap and brings his story to a powerful, fiery climax:

> Yeah, I reckon that's all unless our kind gets another chance in the Next Place. Our kind. Us people.
>
> All of us that started the game with a crooked cue, that wanted so much and got so little, that meant so good and did so bad.

Pop. 1280

Thompson explored the criminal mind in other books. In *Pop. 1280*, Nick Corey, high sheriff of a county in a Southern state, tells his story. The sheriff's job allows him to pursue his favorite activities: eating, sleeping, and bedding women. The voters ask little from him except that he entertain them with his bland ignorance. They enjoy making fun of him, thinking that he is too stupid to understand. As an election approaches, however, some voters want action. Nick begins to clean things up in his own way, first offhandedly shooting a couple of pimps who were making a nuisance of themselves, then engaging in a string of murders to hide his crime. In the end, Nick decides that he is probably Christ, sent by God to "promote" sinners to Glory by killing them.

The disturbing element in Thompson's work comes partly because it rings true; it explains the newspaper stories of bland, quiet people who turn into serial killers. Thompson's world is frightening also because he has a peculiar ability to describe the mind of brutal killers while retaining the reader's sympathy for them. They are victims themselves, sometimes brutalized as children, sometimes racked by alcoholism and poverty, sometimes, as in the case of Lou Ford, losing a desperate struggle to hold onto mental stability. All live in a world that has given little but suffering to them or their victims.

There is no moral center in the world Thompson presents. Concepts of right and wrong are not applicable; platitudes about crime not paying are meaningless. The moral structure that adequately guides most people through life seems shallow and remote in Thompson's world; simple problems of surface morality are not what his characters confront. Psychiatrists cannot understand people such as him, Lou Ford says:

> We might have the disease, the condition; or we might just be cold-blooded and smart as hell; or we might be innocent of what we're supposed to have done. We might be any one of those three things, because the symptoms we show would fit any one of the three.

Insanity, guilt, and innocence dissolve into the same behavior.

After Dark, My Sweet and The Getaway

Thompson does not relieve the reader's fear by bringing in detectives to tidy matters up and reestablish moral norms. Nor does he use love or friendship to lighten the world his characters inhabit. The love that William "Kid" Collins feels for Fay Anderson in *After Dark, My Sweet* (1955) requires him, a mentally unstable former boxer, deliberately to provoke Fay into killing him; only in that way can he save her. In *The Getaway*, Carter "Doc" McCoy and Carol McCoy, who love each other and are married, commit robbery and murder and make a run across the United States for the Mexican border. Their love is eroded by the knowledge that if extreme conditions have pushed them into killing once, they can kill again, even each other. At the end, figuratively, perhaps literally, in Hell, each is trying to kill the other to avoid being killed.

A bleak world

The world sketched by Thompson is bleak, marked by random violence and undeserved suffering. Life reminds Kid Collins of a concrete pasture: "You keep going and going, and it's always the same everywhere. Wherever you've been, wherever you go, everywhere you look. Just grayness and hardness, as far as you can see." Perhaps, Lou Ford hopes, there will be something better in the Next Place, but there seems little promise of that. God is not dead, says the young black man, Allen Smith, in *Child of Rage*:

> Madmen never die. . . . He is still in business on the same old corner. I have seen him there myself, showering riches on rascals, and tendering dung and piss to widows and orphans and stealing pennies from blind men. . . . The Lord . . . is patently as nutty as a goddamned bedbug.

The power of Thompson's writing, whether he is portraying the bleak world of a disintegrating personality or the black comedy of a con man pursuing his swindle, comes from his simple, direct narration. Even in his third-person stories, he keeps the focus so tightly bound to the central character's viewpoint that the external world is warped into a personal vision. Thompson experimented with shifting viewpoints in some novels. In *The Criminal* (1953) and *The Kill-Off* (1957), he uses multiple first-person narrators. In *A Hell of a Woman*, multiple narrative comes from different parts of Frank "Dolly" Dillon's disintegrating personality, with two endings of the novel interchanging line by line, describing Dolly's castration in one and his suicide in another.

Thompson wrote rapidly, polishing page by page as he wrote, and his publisher Arnold Hano recalls that he found it difficult to rewrite. Sometimes he was so drained by the end of a book that he tacked on a hasty conclusion simply to get it over with. If some endings are weak, others are extraordinarily strong: Mafia hit man Charles "Little" Bigger longing for death as his lover hacks him to pieces (*Savage Night*, 1953); the disintegration of Dolly Dillon's life in drugs, alcohol, and insanity; the violent and sad end of Lou Ford, who seeks death to end his sickness; the hell in which Doc and Carol McCoy find themselves; the melancholy of a brooding Nick Corey, who, having come to view himself as Jesus Christ carrying out God's will by killing sinners, confesses, in the last line, "I don't no more know what to do than if I was just another lousy human being!"

William E. Pemberton

Principal mystery and detective fiction

Novels: 1949-1960 • *Nothing More than Murder*, 1949; *Cropper's Cabin*, 1952; *The Killer Inside Me*, 1952; *Bad Boy*, 1953; *Recoil*, 1953; *Savage Night*, 1953; *The Alcoholics*, 1953; *The Criminal*, 1953; *A Hell of a Woman*, 1954; *A Swell-Looking Babe*, 1954; *Roughneck*, 1954; *The Golden Gizmo*, 1954; *The Nothing Man*, 1954; *After Dark, My Sweet*, 1955; *The Kill-Off*, 1957; *Wild Town*, 1957; *The Getaway*, 1959

1961-1988 • *The Transgressors*, 1961; *The Grifters*, 1963; *Pop. 1280*, 1964; *Texas by the Tail*, 1965; *Ironside*, 1967; *South of Heaven*, 1967; *The Undefeated*, 1969; *Nothing but a Man*, 1970; *Child of Rage*, 1972; *King Blood*, 1973; *The Ripoff*, 1985; *Fireworks: The Lost Writings of Jim Thompson*, 1988

Other major works

Novels: *Now and on Earth*, 1942; *Heed the Thunder*, 1946

Screenplays: *The Killing*, 1956 (with Stanley Kubrick); *Paths of Glory*, 1957 (with Kubrick and Calder Willingham)

Bibliography

Brewer, Gay. *Laughing Like Hell: The Harrowing Satires of Jim Thompson*. San Bernardino, Calif.: Borgo Press, 1996. Explores the use of humor in Thompson's work and the relationship between satire and crime fiction.

Collins, Max Allan. *Jim Thompson: The Killers Inside Him*. Cedar Rapids, Iowa: Fedora Press, 1983. Biography of Thompson by an equally famous author of hard-boiled and pulp crime fiction.

Horsley, Lee. *The Noir Thriller*. New York: Palgrave, 2001. Scholarly, theoretically informed study of the thriller genre. Uses Thompson extensively, covering a dozen of his novels, from *Nothing More than Murder* to *Child of Rage*.

McCauley, Michael J. *Jim Thompson: Sleep with the Devil*. New York: Mysterious Press, 1991. McCauley calls Thompson "America's greatest noir writer" and endeavors to explain how he achieved that lofty status.

Pepper, Andrew. *The Contemporary American Crime Novel: Race, Ethnicity, Gender, Class*. Edinburgh: Edinburgh University Press, 2000. Examination of the representation and importance of various categories of identity in mainstream American crime fiction. Sheds light on Thompson's work.

Polito, Robert. "Jim Thompson: Lost Writer." In *Fireworks: The Lost Writings of Jim Thompson*. New York: Donald I. Fine, 1988. Discussion of unpublished and otherwise "lost" manuscripts and what they add to Thompson's oeuvre.

_______. *Savage Art: A Biography of Jim Thompson*. New York: Alfred A. Knopf, 1995. Massive, comprehensive biography of Thompson, his work, and both his public and private lives. Bibliographic references and index.

Sallis, James. *Difficult Lives: Jim Thompson, David Goodis, Chester Himes*. Brooklyn, N.Y.: Gryphon Books, 1993. Brief monograph comparing the works of three hard-boiled writers.

Yarbrough, Trisha. "Jim Thompson's Rural Pulp Fiction." In *Dark Alleys of Noir*, edited by Jack O'Connell. Vashon Island, Wash.: Paradoxa, 2002. Looks at Thompson's relatively unusual choice to set pulp tales outside the big city.

CHARLES TODD

Born: Place and date unknown
Type of plot: Historical

Principal series

Inspector Ian Rutledge, 1996-

Principal series characters

Inspector Ian Rutledge is a haunted, shell-shocked World War I veteran of the western front in France who has returned to his prewar position at Scotland Yard. His senior officer, Superintendent Bowles, keeps dispatching him to cases all over the British Isles.

Superintendent Bowles is an insecure, risen-through-the-ranks police officer who resents the influx of university-trained new blood at Scotland Yard and takes credit for the accomplishments of his subordinates to advance his own career.

Contribution

Even though they are Americans, like Elizabeth George and Martha Grimes, the authors who use the pen name Charles Todd write mysteries set in Great Britain with British police officers and characters. The anonymous mother-and-son team who write as Todd established their credentials beginning with *A Test of Wills* (1996), which follows the series' central character as he restarts his career as an inspector at Scotland Yard. Severely shell-shocked during his tour of duty in France during World War I, Inspector Rutledge suffers from hearing the voice of Hamish MacLeod, a Scottish corporal under his command whom Rutledge had executed for refusing to obey an order, an order Rutledge knew was going to be suicidal to his men. Todd's skill in incorporating MacLeod's monologues into the fabric of Rutledge's suffering and the details of the plots gives this series a psychological dimension often missing in series crime fiction.

The setting—Great Britain in the immediate aftermath of the war—allows Todd to explore the historical period and the changes bought about by the upheaval of the war and its impact on not only the returning soldiers but also the civilian population. The accuracy of the series' historical detail, the nuances of the characters' speech as well as their emotional depth, make the novels remarkable, especially given that they are written by two American authors.

Biography

Charles Todd is the pseudonym of a mother-and-son mystery writing team (Caroline Todd and Charles Todd) who have so closely guarded their privacy they have not revealed their actual names or their residences, except to say that they live on the East Coast. Even their joint authorship was not acknowledged until the year 2000, around the publication of their fourth novel, *Legacy of the Dead.*

The genesis for the series came from their travels throughout England and to the battlefields of France. The character Ian Rutledge came about simply because they wanted to create a character they themselves would like reading about. Rutledge is a little like two other characters who also experienced lingering postwar trauma, Dorothy L. Sayers' Lord Peter Wimsey and Agatha Christie's Captain Hastings. The immediate postwar setting provided an opportunity to examine the past and to make the past and present overlap, reflecting the authors' interest in history. Besides, they have said that they had an uncle/great uncle who flew in World War I, and he aroused an interest in the period. The academic training of the authors who write as Todd also helped to shape the novels. The mother was an undergraduate English and history major and has a graduate degree in international relations, and the son has studied communications and culinary arts and history, especially the American Civil War and both world wars.

The publication of the first Todd novel came about quite by accident when the mother-and-son team sent a copy of *A Test of Wills* to St. Martin's. The publisher accepted the manuscript and the book did well enough for it to solicit another. The team has continued to produce novels in the Ian Rutledge series and also wrote a nonseries novel.

The mother-and-son team's books have garnered an impressive listing of awards and nominations. For example, their first Ian Rutledge novel was nominated for a John Creasey Award, an Edgar, an Anthony, and an Independent Mystery Booksellers Association Dilys Award, and it won the Barry Award from *Deadly Pleasures* magazine. Subsequent novels in the series also have garnered nominations and awards.

Analysis

Ian Rutledge is a university-trained police officer who volunteered for service at the beginning of World War I, referred to as the Great War in Britain. Somewhat miraculously, he survives the horrors of the western front although he loses both his idealism and his will to live. During the Somme offensive in 1916 he is given a routine assignment to destroy a machine gun emplacement, and his corporal, Scot Hamish MacLeod, refuses to lead his men over the top to attack the Germans. A good and loyal soldier until then, MacLeod explains that he can no longer willingly order his men to certain death. Because he refused an order in combat, MacLeod is sentenced to immediate execution by Rutledge, and at dawn the next day a firing squad carries out the order. Rutledge dispatches the coup de grâce. Seconds later he and his men are hit by an artillery shell, burying him alive. When he is dug out, he is suffering from shell shock and is sent home. His sister, Frances, removes him from a military hospital to a private clinic, where through the understanding care of a clinic doctor, Rutledge begins his long road to recovery.

After Rutledge's discharge, he returns to Scotland Yard, the only occupation at which he thinks he is good. There, under the ever-watchful eye of Chief Superintendent Bowles, who both hates him and fears him because of his university education and war service, Rutledge is given a series of risky, potentially career-stalling assignments aiding various murder investigations outside London to induce him to crack under the strain or to embarrass him into resigning because of his incompetence. Bowles's machinations play on Rutledge's insecurities about regaining the prewar detective skills he fears he may have lost because of his precarious mental condition. His recurring memories of the war and its horrors are often triggered by inconsequential daily events or smells or sounds, and more frighteningly by the sound of Hamish MacLeod's voice, which can echo in his mind at any time, frequently at very awkward moments. The voice of MacLeod sometimes serves as a moral guide or as a cautionary reminder and also acts as a foil for Rutledge's intuition.

The mother-and-son team known as Charles Todd set each of the first ten Rutledge novels in a different part of Great Britain, always outside London, usually in a village or small town or some rather remote rural location. Although Todd moves the settings of the novels around in this way, the locales do tend to be rather the same. Hamlets with close-knit inhabitants, often related by blood or marriage; ancient feuds that bring past slights or injuries into the present; and locals who distrust the outsider, the "man from London," who has been sent to interfere in their lives. The distrust of outsiders is usually personified by the local chief constable, who feels Rutledge's presence to be an intrusion into his turf. Also in each of the novels, no matter where it is set, the presence of the war is pervasive in the wounded servicemen, the suffering and loss of those whose loved ones did not return, and in the lingering memories of wartime privations and the scourge of the plaguelike influenza pandemic that followed the war.

The novels in this series are paradigmatic English (and Scottish) village mysteries, all held together by the troubled and likable Scotland Yard Inspector Ian Rutledge, who in spite of his war-induced injuries, struggles to bring order amid murder and to discover the truth of not only the crimes he undertakes to solve but also of the human condition.

A Test of Wills

The Rutledge novels are set a month apart, beginning in June, 1919, when Rutledge returns to Scotland Yard in *A Test of Wills*. Still recovering from months of hospitalization and rejection by his fiancé, Jean, who could not cope with his shattered mind, Rutledge is sent to Upper Streetham in Warwickshire to investigate the shooting death of Colonial Harris, veteran of the Boer and the Great War, who apparently had no enemies in the world. His struggle to keep his madness and claustrophobia under control contend with his gradually strengthening sense of professional competence.

Wings of Fire

In *Wings of Fire* (1998), Rutledge has not only survived his initial test but also managed to solve a tricky mystery, so in July, Bowles sends Rutledge off to Cornwall to examine the death of three members of a distinguished local family, one of whom was a major English poet and wrote understandingly about the war under the pseudonym of O. A. Manning. Quoting her poems becomes a recurring motif in the later novels. By the second book in the series, Todd had established the format of the novels to come. Rutledge arrives as a stranger in a tight-knit community, makes himself unpopular by interrogating everyone, tacking from interview to interview, and casting suspicion widely, only to wrap up the mystery at the very end of the case and book, often arresting someone only tangentially suspected throughout the book.

Search the Dark

In late August, Rutledge is dispatched to Dorset, Thomas Hardy country, in *Search the Dark* (1999), where he conducts an investigation that involves the family of a famous local politician. Putting Rutledge in socially or politically tricky situations is one of Bowles's stratagems for getting him off the force and for freeing himself from the danger of being shown up as a pettifogging bureaucrat. Bowles consistently believes that he is throwing Rutledge to the wolves, only to discover that Rutledge is smarter than he is and has more contacts in high places. This novel begins with a case of murder and some missing children but the initial cause for Rutledge's arrival turns out to be of secondary interest to a broader investigation into a long-buried mystery.

Legacy of the Dead

Legacy of the Dead (2000) might well serve as the title for this entire series as each of the novels resurrects not only Rutledge's dead, MacLeod and the other soldiers who perished in the trenches, but also secrets from the past, most of them believed to be dead and buried. In September, Rutledge finds himself traveling to Scotland in search of Lady Maud Gray's rebellious missing daughter. As he crisscrosses the country, he reopens old scars, especially when MacLeod's fiancé, Fiona MacDonald, who has named her child after Rutledge, becomes one of the suspects for the murder of the missing woman. A bit more of Rutledge's past is revealed through his godfather, David Trevor, whose son was lost in the war. Although the murder investigation is centered in the small town of Duncarrick, Rutledge ranges across Scotland from Edinburgh in the east to Glasgow and Glencoe in the west. As in the other novels, the mystery contains bits of history, this time about Hadrian's Wall and the Battle of Glencoe. At the novel's conclusion, Rutledge is shot and badly wounded.

Watchers of Time

By October, in *The Watchers of Time* (2001), Rutledge is still recovering from his wounds but is feeling confined by his sister's ministrations. "Auld Bowels," as MacLeod calls Bowles, will not let the detective rest. He sees an opportunity to destroy Rutledge in his weakened condition, so he sends him to East Anglia, where Rutledge begins to search for the murderer of the local priest in an ancient seacoast town. In all the novels of the Ian Rutledge series, there are characters who mirror or reflect various of the central character's neuroses. In this case it is a woman who survived the sinking of the *Titanic* and experiences the same survival guilt as does Rutledge. The usual characters abound: Aside from the clergy, both Catholic and Church of England, there is the local gentry, Lord Sedgwick, whose garden contains Egyptian baboon statues called the Watchers of Time, again another apt title for the whole series.

A Fearsome Doubt

A Fearsome Doubt (2002) takes place in Kent in November. Rutledge is sent to look into the death of three former soldiers, all of whom are amputees. He has been reexamining one of his old cases because he suspects he may have gotten it wrong and sent an innocent man to his death. This case, of course, helps resurrect his own guilt about MacLeod and the other men whom he sent to their deaths. All throughout the series MacLeod is a constant presence in Rutledge's consciousness and interrupts his thoughts to question his motives or remind him of his past. The reexamined case is another reminder of Rutledge's remaining uncertainties. The novel also includes a bit of backstory about his wartime experiences, particularly in the immediate aftermath of his shell-shock disorientation when for a brief time he wandered behind German lines. Todd likes to work with multiple story lines, which help to keep the series fresh: the quaint village life and its folk—the vicar, local general practitioner, and the constable—are disrupted by the outsider and are further disrupted by intrusive secondary plots. With multiple plots, the cases can be broadened in more ways.

A Cold Treachery

Cold is the operative word in December in the Lake District in *A Cold Treachery* (2005), when Rutledge, along with the rest of the inhabitants of Urksdale village, becomes trapped by a winter snowstorm. Rutledge, there to investigate the murder of a family of five from which only a single boy escaped, becomes attracted to one of the possible suspects. Half a year and the gradual strengthening of Rutledge's psyche have enabled him to rid himself of his sense of failure over his fiancé's departure; his allowing himself to become attracted is a significant development in his character. Each of the books has an attractive, if often damaged, woman toward whom Rutledge could exhibit some interest, but in this case he admits to being interested. Also by now Rutledge is beginning to catch on to Superintendent Bowles's tactics for getting him to self-destruct.

A Long Shadow

The supernatural appears in *A Long Shadow* (2006) as Rutledge escapes from a séance during a New Year's Eve party to which he has accompanied his sister Frances. Séances, which claim to provide a means of contacting the dead, became fashionable right after the war when so many people were in mourning. Sir Arthur Conan Doyle became one of many who fell under the spell of the séance while searching for a way to contact his dead son. The idea of the haunted follows Rutledge to the small village of Dudlington in Northamptonshire, where the local constable has been shot with an arrow near Frith's Wood, haunted from ancient times by the ghosts of the Saxons slaughtered there by invaders. Something else is happening as well, and Rutledge is being followed by someone who is planting engraved machine-gun shell casings in his rooms, and the stalking turns violent when someone starts shooting at Rutledge. His inspection of the crime by the woods turns into an ancillary case—the search for a girl missing for three years and feared dead in the spirit-infested woods.

A False Mirror

A False Mirror (2007) takes place in late February and early March, 1920. While Rutledge and Scotland Yard are looking for the Green Park murderer in London, former civil servant Matthew Hamilton is nearly beaten to death on the beach near his home along the south coast near Devon. Then former lieutenant Stephen Mallory takes the injured man's wife hostage in their house and requests that former fellow officer Rutledge be sent down to take over the investigation into the assault on Hamilton. The village of Hampton Regis then become the site for another of the murder investigations carried out by Rutledge, the outsider from London, still a fragile war victim haunted by MacLeod, a superior police officer, and the bane of Superintendent Bowles's existence.

Charles L. P. Silet

Principal mystery and detective fiction

Inspector Ian Rutledge series: *A Test of Wills*, 1996; *Wings of Fire*, 1998; *Search the Dark*, 1999; *Legacy of the Dead*, 2000; *Watchers of Time*, 2001; *A Fearsome Doubt*, 2002; *A Cold Treachery*, 2005; *A Long Shadow*, 2006; *A False Mirror*, 2007

Nonseries novels: *The Murder Stone*, 2003

Bibliography

Brinson, Claudia Smith. "Through Murder Investigations, Shell-shocked Veteran Reflects on Aftermath of Death, Conflict in *A False Mirror*." Review of *A False Mirror*, by Charles Todd. *Knight Ridder Tribune News Service*, February 7, 2007, p. 1. Review mentions the history of the series and notes that the mother-and-son team of authors expressed interest in writing about the lasting consequences of war.

Cogdill, Oline H. "Haunted Hero in a Bygone Era." Review of *Legacy of the Dead*, by Charles Todd. *South Florida Sun-Sentinel*, November 5, 2000, p. 13F. Favorable review praises the novel for examining the war's effects on soldiers and for its depiction of the changes that were occurring in England at the time.

Kinsella, Bridget. "A Mystery Behind a Mystery Is Revealed." *Publishers Weekly* 247, no. 37 (September 11, 2000): 24-25. On the publication of the fourth novel in the Rutledge series, it was revealed that Charles Todd was not a single person, but a mother-and-son collaboration. The mother revealed herself to be Caroline Todd, also a pseudonym, but disclosed little else.

Todd, Charles. Charles Todd, Best Selling Mystery Author. http://www.charlestodd.com. Official Web site for mother-and-son team writing as Charles Todd. Provides information on the novels as well as a biography that provides motivation for writing and general biographical details, but no specifics. Identifies the mother as Caroline Todd, but the veracity of the name is in doubt. The pair attend book signings and sign as "Charles Todd." Contains links to Internet interviews.

_______. "Past Mysteries." *The Armchair Detective* 30, no. 2 (Spring, 1997): 176-184. Todd discusses the historical mystery.

Winks, Robin W. "The Historical Mystery." In *Mystery and Suspense Writers: The Literature of Crime, Detection, and Espionage*, edited by Robin W. Winks and Maureen Corrigan. New York: Charles Scribner's Sons, 1998. This comprehensive discussion of the historical mystery was written by a historian and contains a perspective from outside the mystery field. Sheds light on Todd's work.

LILLIAN DE LA TORRE

Lillian de la Torre Bueno McCue

Born: New York, New York; March 15, 1902
Died: Colorado Springs, Colorado; September 13, 1993
Also wrote as Lillian Bueno McCue
Type of plot: Amateur sleuth

Principal series

Dr. Sam Johnson, 1946-1987

Principal series characters

Sam Johnson, detective, is based on the eighteenth century writer and lexicographer of that name. Ungainly, shortsighted, and marked by scrofula, but physically and mentally vital, he outwits the malefactors who cross his path.

James Boswell, "with a swart complection, a long nose, and black hair tied back in the latest mode," records the adventures of Johnson. A lawyer by profession, Boswell exhibits in these stories the same mixture of naïveté, vanity, and curiosity that he displayed in life.

Contribution

Using real crimes and criminals as the basis of fiction is a well-established literary device, as works such as the anonymous *The Tragedy of Mr. Arden of Feversham* (1592), Henry Fielding's *The History of the Life of the Late Mr. Jonathan Wild the Great* (1743, 1754), and Edgar Allan Poe's "The Mystery of Marie Rogêt" demonstrate. No one, however, had considered using a historical figure to solve these crimes before Lillian de la Torre recruited Samuel Johnson as a private investigator. Combining her extensive knowledge of eighteenth century British literature and history with the conventions of the classic detective story, de la Torre produced more than thirty enjoyable short stories. Nevertheless, her purpose went beyond mere entertainment; as a self-described "histo-detector," she solved mysteries that puzzled contemporaries and eluded historians. Although most of her serious histo-detecting was reserved for nonfictional, book-length works, some of her short stories also reveal how actual crimes might have been committed.

Biography

The daughter of José Rollin de la Torre Bueno and Lillian Reinhardt Bueno, Lillian de la Torre was born in New York City on March 15, 1902. After receiving her associate's degree from the College of New Rochelle in 1921, she began teaching high school in New York (1923-1934). At the same time, she pursued graduate studies, specializing in the eighteenth century, and earned master's degrees from Columbia University and Radcliffe College.

After her marriage to George S. McCue in 1932, de la Torre moved to Colorado Springs, Colorado, where her husband began a twenty-seven-year tenure in the English department of Colorado College. De la Torre also taught for a few years at the University of Colorado at Colorado Springs before becoming a full-time histo-detector. Her first published story, "Dr. Sam: Johnson, Detector," later retitled "The Great Seal of England," is based on the actual disappearance of the seal from Lord Chancellor Edward Thurlow's house on March 23, 1784; de la Torre's solution appeared in *Ellery Queen's Mystery Magazine* for November, 1943, and most of her subsequent accounts of Sam Johnson's investigations into the real and imagined crimes of eighteenth century England have first been printed in that periodical. Occasionally, her interest has led to more extensive treatment: *Elizabeth Is Missing* (1945), her first book, suggests what happened to Elizabeth Canning, a servant who disappeared for four weeks in January, 1753. *The Heir of Douglas* (1952) attempts to determine the rightful claimant to the vast Douglas estates and so resolve a case that bedeviled the Scottish courts for seven years in the 1760's, and *The Truth About Belle Gunness* (1955) examines the fate of this notorious murderess, who disappeared in 1908.

De la Torre's interest in amateur theatricals led first to performances as "Mama" in *I Remember Mama* and "Mrs. Cady" in *Beggar on Horseback*, then to plays that extended the scope of her histo-detection to figures such as Lizzie Borden. A pair of biographies (on the Jacobite Flora Macdonald and the actress Sarah Siddons), two cookbooks, a volume of poetry, and various articles round out a career that has earned for her widespread recognition. She received awards from *Ellery Queen Mystery Magazine* (1953) and the Colorado Authors' League (1953-1957), was nominated in the best fact crime category by the Mystery Writers of America in 1956 for "The Truth About Belle Gunness," and served as president of that organization (1979). She also received the Medal of Distinction in the Fine Arts from the Colorado Springs Chamber of Commerce (1980).

Analysis

On the dust jacket of *Elizabeth Is Missing*, Lillian de la Torre commented, "I have been a student of the eighteenth century for seventeen years, and a detective-story fan for longer than that. It was inevitable that the lines would cross." Yet the conjunction occurred by accident. Even as a child she had been fascinated with mystery and detective fiction. Her father, himself a fan of the genre, owned a rich collection that included the works of Émile Gaboriau, Jacques Futrelle, and Arthur Conan Doyle; at the age of nine, de la Torre began devouring these and similar works, and she never stopped. Her husband was far less enthusiastic. As she recalled in a lecture in 1973, "'Boo!' he would say. 'Detectives! What a bunch! Cute brides! Bald Belgians! Quaint old ladies! Roly-poly Chinamen! Next thing you know there'll be a police dog.'" De la Torre defended her reading preferences, arguing that mysteries could be legitimate literary art if the main characters were "solid and three-dimensional, like—like Dr. Samuel Johnson and James Boswell in Boswell's great biography."

Whether the decision to pursue this idea was the inevitable consequence of lifelong interests or the fortuitous outcome of a domestic dispute, the result was a happy one. That most famous of detective duos, Sherlock Holmes and Dr. John Watson, were themselves modeled on the historical Johnson and Boswell, the one a brilliant and eccentric analyst, the other a devoted but often dull-witted recorder. Holmes even refers to Watson as his Boswell. Returning to the originals of this fictional pair was sensible, given de la Torre's knowledge of and interest in their era.

The 1940's were particularly propitious for this undertaking, as Yale University began publishing Boswell's recently discovered manuscripts, thus placing the biographer and his subject in the news. Moreover, the eighteenth century offered a perfect period for detective fiction. The first expert witness appeared in court in 1698. In 1770, footprints in the snow were first matched with the shoes that made them. The first detected use of prussic acid as poison came thirteen years later. The novelist Henry Fielding and his blind half brother, Sir John Fielding, organized a rudimentary police force, the Bow Street Runners, with the means of detecting crimes and their perpetrators.

Samuel Johnson was caught up in these developments. According to Boswell, he spent an entire winter listening to Saunders Welch, Sir John Fielding's assistant, examine suspects. Occasionally, he was more than a spectator. When James Macpherson claimed to have discovered ancient Gaelic verses by Ossian, Johnson correctly declared them forgeries, just as he later recognized that the supposed fifteenth century works of Thomas Rowley were the product of the young Thomas Chatterton. In 1762, he helped investigate the case of the "Cock-Lane Ghost": According to William Parsons, who lived in Cock Lane, Smithfield, Fanny Lynes's ghost was trying to reveal, through Parsons's eleven-year-old daughter, that she had been poisoned by her brother-in-law. In 1762, in "Account of the Detection of the Imposture in Cock-Lane," Johnson exposed the fraud.

De la Torre used such episodes for her stories. "The Manifestations in Mincing Lane," for example, is based on the Cock-Lane Ghost; "The Missing Shakespeare Manuscript" deals with literary forgery. In some instances the mysteries are real: The Great Seal of England actually did disappear from the Lord Chancellor's house; Elizabeth Canning did vanish for four weeks ("The Disappearing Servant Wench"), the Duchess of Kingston was tried for bigamy ("Milady Bigamy"), William Henry Ireland did manufacture a number of Shakespearean manuscripts.

"The Monboddo Ape Boy" and "Prince Charlie's Ruby"

Other tales build on Johnson's experiences and opinions. James Burnett, Lord Monboddo, anticipated Charles Darwin's belief that humans had undergone a process of evolution. Although Johnson disliked both Darwin the man and his theories, Boswell arranged for the two to meet in Scotland. In "The Monboddo Ape Boy," de la Torre creates a pair of confidence men who try to exploit Monboddo's interest in feral children as evidence supporting his assumptions about evolution, and she then shows Johnson foiling the plot during his visit. "Prince Charlie's Ruby" uses Johnson's excursion to the Isle of Skye to see Flora Macdonald, the Jacobite heroine who hid Bonny Prince Charlie after the debacle of Culloden, as the basis of an adventure much like that of Holmes and the six busts of Napoleon Bonaparte.

Attention to history

Still other stories develop from eighteenth century life and customs. "The Tontine Curse" imagines multiple murders committed to collect on a form of life insurance. At the birth of their children, a group of parents would each invest a sum in the funds, the principal and interest to go to the last surviving member of the group. Both the Hosyer tontine and Johnson's involvement in such a case are fictional, but the practice is authentic and invited homicidal thoughts, if not actions. De la Torre's knowledge of eighteenth century stagecraft informs "The Banquo Trap" and "The Resurrection Men." The latter, published in *The Return of Dr. Sam Johnson, Detector* (1984), also reflects the practice of grave robbing to supply cadavers for autopsies, and "The Blackamoor Unchain'd," from the same collection, considers the plight of slaves in England during the age of Johnson.

To help create the atmosphere of the period, de la Torre adopts the spellings and phrases of the day: "cloathes," "pye," "enthusiastick," "topick," "scheaming," "eight-and-twenty days." She uses only words that were extant in the eighteenth century, a practice requiring much checking in the *Oxford English Dictionary.* The real-life Johnson never used a simple word when he could find a hard one, so de la Torre has her character use "mendacious invention" for "lie," "aerostatick globe" for "balloon." Although she reveals an ear and eye for eighteenth century diction and orthography in her re-creation of speech, she makes her language even more authentic by inserting dialogues taken directly from Boswell's *The Life of Samuel Johnson, L.L.D.* (1791) and other sources and by introducing similar period pieces. "The Disappearing Servant Wench," for example, opens by quoting the actual broadside announcing that Elizabeth Canning had vanished. The story also contains excerpts from testimony in the case and contemporary pamphlets relating to it. To heighten verisimilitude, *Elizabeth Is Missing* and *Dr. Sam Johnson, Detector* (1946) are set in modified Caslon, a popular eighteenth century typeface; the title pages present a mixture of italic and roman characters—another characteristic of the period—and, like so many title pages of the time, hers offer a veritable summary of the book's contents.

Like the language and the main characters, the settings are authentic. Mrs. Winwood's boudoir in "The Triple-Lock'd Room" is furnished in Chinese Chippendale, all the vogue in 1775 when the adventure supposedly occurs, and on her marquetry table lies a book printed in black-letter, or Gothic, type, suggesting the beginning of the revival of interest in things medieval. Sally Hosyer ("The Tontine Curse") sleeps with her sister in a canopy bed; both the sharing of sleeping accommodations and the tester are typical of the age.

"The Viotti Stradivarius"

The stories thus offer entertainment as period pieces, but they also adhere to the rules of modern mysteries, observing Emily Dickinson's injunction: "The truth must dazzle gradually." "The Viotti Stradivarius" first creates the setting of the crime, a soiree at the home of the noted eighteenth century musicologist and friend of Johnson, Dr. Charles Burney. Present are the Bettses, father and son, violin makers; Polly Tresilian, Burney's pupil, with her jeweler father and his apprentice, Chinnery; the Italian prodigy Giovanni Battista Viotti; Prince Orloff of Russia and his two Cossack guards; Charles Burney and his novelist daughter, Fanny; and Boswell and Johnson. During the evening, Orloff's diamond, worth 200,000 rubles, and Viotti's priceless violin disappear, and Johnson must deduce the identity of the thief or thieves. Tresilian and Chinnery are logical suspects because of their profession, as are the Bettses because of theirs. Because Viotti is a stranger to the company and refuses to play, he might be a thief masquerading as the virtuoso. Orloff himself might have substituted a piece of glass for the diamond to collect insurance. By dismissing some possibilities as illogical and testing other hypotheses, Johnson finds the missing objects and the culprit.

"Murder Lock'd In"

"Murder Lock'd In," the opening story in *The Return of Dr. Sam Johnson, Detector*, uses another classic device, the homicide—in this case triple homicide—within a locked room. Aware that she is writing for a twentieth century audience familiar with the use of string to lock doors from the outside, de la Torre dismisses this option; when the watchman, Jona Mudge, tries to show how this trick works, it fails. Johnson must then determine how the murderer did effect his (or her) entrance and exit; relying on Holmes's dictum, "when one has eliminated all impossibilities, then what remains, however improbable, must be the truth," he finds the killer. Yet he maintains the suspense by accusing someone he knows is innocent to trick the guilty party into confessing.

Modern, too, is de la Torre's sympathy with the criminal. The killer in "Murder Lock'd In" is sent to Bedlam rather than the gallows. "Milady Bigamy" reverses the court's decision and finds the duchess innocent; the thief in "The Viotti Stradivarius" is never exposed; Johnson pleads for the forger in "The Missing Shakespeare Manuscript." Johnson himself was compassionate, maintaining a household of homeless, impoverished people, and he worked diligently to save the life of the convicted forger William Dodd. Whether Johnson would have been pleased with the insanity defense (not in fact introduced until the next century) is uncertain.

"The Tontine Curse"

More disturbing aesthetically are the limits of the short story, which task even Agatha Christie. Nineteen deaths in about as many pages in "The Tontine Curse" seem excessive and implausible, even though de la Torre kills off groups of children at a time. Suspicion barely has time to build before it is removed when Johnson must quickly sort through a large number of suspects, and there is little time to mislead the reader with red herrings. No one checks on whether Prince Orloff owns the diamond he says he has lost or whether he recently insured it at Lloyd's. Has he recently suffered financial setbacks that might make the theft of the diamond convenient? "The Viotti Stradivarius" hints at Hindu thieves but does little with them for want of space. Even in book-length mysteries, most of the characters remain shadowy; in short stories, they lack the personality that would make them logical or illogical suspects.

De la Torre was therefore most effective when she challenged the reader to discover not who committed a crime but rather where an object has been concealed (as in "Prince Charlie's Ruby") or how a crime has been committed despite careful observation, as in "The Frantic Rebel" or "The Triple-Lock'd Room." Nevertheless as Johnson observed of dictionaries and watches, "the worst is better than none," and de la Torre's best, unlike these other two objects, "go quite true." De la Torre's mysteries provide an excursion into another era. Reading them before a fire with a glass of Johnson's much-loved "poonch" in hand, one may journey back in time. In her writings, the eighteenth century lives, with its elegance, culture, and crime, its Chippendale chairs and open sewers. Perhaps the chief charm of her work, however, lies in discovering not how different the past and its people are but how little the world and human nature have changed.

Joseph Rosenblum

Principal mystery and detective fiction

Dr. Sam Johnson series: *Dr. Sam Johnson, Detector,* 1946; *The Detections of Dr. Sam Johnson,* 1960; *The Return of Dr. Sam Johnson, Detector,* 1984; *The Exploits of Dr. Sam Johnson, Detector,* 1985

Other major works

Plays: *Goodbye, Miss Lizzie Borden*, pr., pb. 1948; *Cheat the Wuddy*, pr. 1948; *Remember Constance Kent*, pr. 1949; *The Sally Cathleen Clain*, pr. 1952; *The Coffee Cup*, pb. 1954; *The Queen's Choristers*, pr. 1961; *The Jester's Apprentice*, pr. 1962; *The Face on the Bar-Room Floor,* pr. 1964; *The Stroller's Girl*, pr. 1966

Poetry: *Stars*, 1982 (as McCue)

Children's literature: *The White Rose of Stuart*, 1954; *The Actress*, 1957

Nonfiction: *Elizabeth Is Missing*, 1945; *The Sixty Minute Chef,* 1947 (as McCue; with Carol Traux); *The Heir of Douglas*, 1952; *The Truth About Belle Gunness*, 1955; *The New Sixty Minute Chef,* 1975 (as McCue; with Carol Traux)

Edited texts: *Villainy Detected*, 1947

Bibliography

Browne, Ray B., and Lawrence A. Kreiser, Jr., eds. *The Detective as Historian: History and Art in Historical Crime Fiction*. Bowling Green, Ohio: Bowling Green State University Popular Press, 2000. Anthology devoted to analysis of the representation of history and the history of representation within historical crime fiction. Provides perspective on de la Torre.

Hoch, Edward D. "A Mirror to Our Crimes." *The Armchair Detective* 12 (Summer, 1979): 282-283. Comments on the use and portrayal of real crimes in detective fiction; sheds light on de la Torre's works.

Johnsen, Rosemary Erickson. *Contemporary Feminist Historical Crime Fiction*. New York: Palgrave Macmillan, 2006. Provides a useful overview of the genre, as well as a detailed analysis of de la Torre's literary descendants.

Peters, Ellis. Foreword to *Historical Whodunits*, edited by Mike Ashley. New York: Barnes & Noble, 1997. The author of the Cadfael mysteries provides commentary on the genre of the historical whodunit and on de la Torre's place in that genre.

Purcell, James Mark. "Lillian de la Torre, Preliminary Bibliography: Blood on the Periwigs." *Mystery Readers Newsletter* 4 (July/August, 1971): 25-27. Bibliography of the author's works through 1971.

LAWRENCE TREAT

Lawrence Arthur Goldstone

Born: New York, New York; December 21, 1903
Died: Oak Bluffs, Massachusetts; January 7, 1998
Also wrote as Lawrence A. Goldstone
Types of plot: Private investigator; police procedural

Principal series

Carl Wayward, 1940-1943
Mitch Taylor, Jub Freeman, and Bill Decker, 1945-1960

Principal series characters

Carl Wayward, a psychology professor specializing in criminology, becomes involved in murder cases as a consultant but quickly takes charge. He is in his thirties, and he is married during the course of the series. An intellectual, he is motivated by the challenge of matching wits with criminals and utilizing his expertise.

Mitch Taylor is a typical big-city cop, mainly interested in avoiding trouble, bucking for promotion, and living simply with his wife and children. He is proud of his uniform and has a sense of duty but is not above minor graft and avoiding work whenever possible.

Jub Freeman, who sometimes teams up with Taylor, is a "new type" of cop whose passion is scientific detection. He is married during the course of the series. In his forays into the field to gather evidence, he displays a certain gaucheness in dealing with the public.

Lieutenant Bill Decker, in charge of the Homicide Division, knows how to handle cops—with a pat on the back and a kick in the pants. He lets his officers break rules and cut corners when necessary. Decker was the prototype of hundreds of tough-talking, hard-driving fictional successors.

Contribution

Lawrence Treat is generally regarded as the father of the police procedural, that subgenre of detective fiction that emphasizes the realistic solution of mysteries through routine police methods, including dogged interrogations, stakeouts, tailings, and utilization of the technology of the police laboratory. Treat established some of the conventions of the police procedural that have appeared almost unfailingly in novels in this category ever since. Among them is the convention of the cop who is unable to maintain a normal family life because his work requires irregular hours and alienates him from everyone except other cops. Another convention is the theme of rivalry and tension within the law enforcement agency, caused by many different personalities trying to win glory and avoid blame. Finally, there is the convention of the police officer being a hated outsider, lied to, ridiculed, maligned, and occasionally made the target of attempted seduction. These conventions have become familiar not only in police procedural novels but also in motion pictures about police officers and in many popular television series.

Biography

Lawrence Treat was born Lawrence Arthur Goldstone on December 21, 1903, in New York City (he changed his name legally in 1940). He had an excellent education, obtaining a bachelor's degree from Dartmouth College in 1924 and a law degree from Columbia University in 1927.

Treat practiced law for only a short time. For many years he had wanted to write, and he was writing poetry while still in law school. He had practiced law for only three months when his firm broke up in 1928, and the partners gave him ten weeks' salary (three hundred dollars). He determined to devote his time to writing. He went to Paris, wrote poetry and worked at odd jobs, and roomed with an old camp counselor and his wife in Brittany. Treat soon came to realize that even if he were a much better poet, he would still be unable to make a living at that craft. A mystery magazine he picked up in a Paris bookstore changed his career. Treat's earliest contributions to mystery fiction were picture puzzles, some of which were collected in *Bringing Sherlock Home* (1930).

After returning to the United States, he married Margery Dallet in June, 1930. During the 1930's, a period of frustration and indecision, he began writing for pulp mystery magazines (he wrote about three hundred short stories and twenty novels during his lifetime). His marriage to Margery ended in divorce in 1939. During a period of frustration and indecision, he discovered the world of detective magazines and reasoned that his legal background and literary interests made him well qualified to succeed in that field. He learned his trade by writing one story per day for a solid month.

Treat's early detective novels featuring the highly intellectual and academically oriented Carl Wayward were well written and received favorable reviews. Yet they were stuck in the conventional mold of the British or classic mystery and did not represent a significant contribution to the genre. During the latter years of World War II, he met two laboratory researchers who stimulated him to take a fresh approach. He also took a seminar in police supervisory work and became acquainted with many working police officers. This experience led to his publication in 1945 of *"V" as in Victim*, the first police procedural ever written.

Treat published hundreds of short stories in such magazines as *Mike Shayne Mystery Magazine*, *Ellery Queen's Mystery Magazine*, and *Alfred Hitchcock's Mystery Magazine*. While living in Yorktown Heights, New York, he taught mystery writing at Columbia University, New York University, and elsewhere. He married Rose Ehrenfreund in 1943; they moved to Martha's Vineyard in 1972.

He received two Edgar Allan Poe Awards, the first in 1965 for "*H* as in Homicide" (1964), and the second in 1978 for *The Mystery Writer's Handbook* (1976) from the Mystery Writers of America, of which he was both a founder and a president.

Analysis

Lawrence Treat received a much better education than the typical mystery writer, and the positive and negative effects of it are evident in his writings. His first mystery novels feature Carl Wayward, a college professor with marked tendencies toward social and intellectual snobbishness. Wayward is not exactly an amateur sleuth, the favored protagonist of the classic school of mystery fiction; he specializes in criminology, which gets him involved in cases as a consultant, not unlike the great Sherlock Holmes. Yet Wayward seems to be perpetually on sabbatical, and his supposed knowledge of criminology rarely surfaces during his investigations. He is indistinguishable from the typical amateur sleuth, who takes up investigations out of idle curiosity or sympathy for someone involved and whose immensely superior intellect enables him to make fools of the bumbling police.

"H" as in Hangman

"H" as in Hangman (1942) is probably the best and most characteristic of the four Carl Wayward novels. It is set in Chautauqua, the famous resort founded in the nineteenth century to bring enlightenment to the masses. Wayward is there to lecture on criminal psychology; his professional contempt for this system of popular adult education is such, however, that it is difficult for the reader to understand why he has chosen to participate at all. Most of the principal characters are American equivalents of the upper- and upper-middle-class types found in typical British mysteries of the classic school, such as those of Agatha Christie. They lounge on porches sipping tea and lemonade, discussing highbrow subjects or gossiping rather viciously about absent acquaintances. The few who are not being supported by relatives or inherited property are vaguely involved in "stocks and bonds" or some other elitist occupation that pays well without demanding much of their attention. Wayward himself is able to spend most of his time leaning against something with his left hand in the side pocket of his tweed jacket. It is a closed environment, the sine qua non of the classic school, which conveniently limits the number of suspects to a manageable handful of known and socially acceptable individuals when the first murder is committed.

The victim, an elderly music professor who has been a leader in the Chautauqua movement for decades, is found hanged in the bell tower shortly after he or his murderer has alerted the whole community that something dastardly was afoot by playing the bells at an ungodly hour. The carillon performer did not choose anything vulgar such as "Pop Goes the

Weasel" but played a portion of "Ase's Death" from Edvard Grieg's *Peer Gynt Suite* (1867). Instead of a rope, the dead man was hanged with a cello string. Such "smart aleck kills," which Raymond Chandler reviled, are characteristic of the classic school of detective fiction. The leisure-class characters, the circumscribed setting in which the soon-to-be suspects are almost formally introduced, the tidbits of culture and arcane information, the gothic overtones of the modus operandi, and the incompetent sheriff who begs Wayward for help are some of the features that mark the Wayward novels as derivative ventures. They also strike the reader as an excessive display of knowledge.

Treat's Wayward novels show intelligence and literary talent. He had started with aspirations to write poetry and quality mainstream novels and, like Ross Macdonald in later years, had had to step down in class for pragmatic reasons. Critics recognized the quality of his writing and praised his Wayward novels.

In addition to his mystery novels, Treat also wrote several books for children in which readers are challenged interpret clues in pictures to solve mysteries.

Nevertheless, he dropped his intellectual hero unceremoniously in 1943; two years later, he produced a mystery novel that not only represented a quantum leap forward in his writing career but also became a landmark in the genre.

"V" as in Victim

"V" as in Victim, published in 1945, is regarded as the first police procedural. It is such a dramatic departure from the Wayward novels that it seems not to have been written by the same person. Set in the heart of Manhattan, it conveys a feeling not unlike that of the noir literature and films that had been flourishing during the war years. As in many of the novels by Cornell Woolrich, the people in *"V "as in Victim* seem dwarfed and intimidated by their towering, dehumanized environment. Treat's language, too, departed radically from the gracefully turned phrases in the Wayward books: His police procedurals sound American rather than Anglophilic. A few elitist characters remain, but now they seem to be living on borrowed time. They have discovered adultery and dry martinis.

It is interesting to speculate on what factors could have caused such a remarkable change in the whole approach of a writer. Treat has not discussed this subject in print, but clues can be garnered from his books, facts of his personal life, and the period during which he matured as a writer. He went through a divorce; then there was the war. He was not personally involved, but there are many indications in his books, notably in *"H" as in Hunted* (1946), that as a sensitive, artistic person he was strongly affected by reports of the atrocities that were perpetrated in Europe and Asia during those fateful years. Treat was undoubtedly influenced by the Black Mask school of writers, including Dashiell Hammett. Motion pictures must have been another influence: They became more proletarian and less elitist during the war years and have remained so ever since. There was the beginning of the so-called white flight from the big cities that would undermine the tax base and result in physical and moral deterioration. There was the influx of minorities, all suspicious, hostile, and alienated in the minds of many white Americans. Big cities in the United States were becoming sinister places. All these undercurrents of change can be felt in *"V" as in Victim*, published in that historic year of 1945, when Germany surrendered and atom bombs were dropped on Japan.

One of the positive effects of Treat's extensive formal education was his intellectual discipline. When he decided to write a realistic novel about working police officers, he went about it with a thoroughness worthy of another lawyer-mystery writer, Erle Stanley Gardner. Treat's exposure to real hard-nosed officers in the precinct station, in the laboratories, in the field, and after hours in the taprooms undoubtedly had a strong influence on his writing. He also did much academic-type research. In his preface to *The Mystery Writer's Handbook* (1976), he reveals his wide knowledge of the literature covering various aspects of the crime field, including law, forensic medicine, ballistics, and fingerprinting. Carl Wayward may have been a criminologist in name, but his creator actually became one. Because *"V "as in Victim* was to have such an important influence, it was fortunate for the development of this subgenre that Treat was a learned and conscientious practitioner of his craft.

There was an inherent contradiction within the police procedural from its very beginnings. Treat wanted to create realistic officers going about their work in a realistic manner, but at the same time he wanted to retain the traditional element of mystery—that is, the process of discovering who among a limited cast of clearly established characters committed a particular crime. In reality, many crimes are never solved or even investigated but merely documented; the records are then held in open files until someone informs or confesses. Police officers do not have the luxury of working on only one case at a time, like the private eye or amateur sleuth. They are often yanked off one case and assigned to another because there are too many murderers and not enough detectives. In the process of tailing a suspect or questioning informants, police officers may come on a different crime that will lead them off on a tangent. Furthermore, there is no such thing as a limited cast of interrelated suspects in a city of millions of strangers. Any attempt to impose artificial boundaries around an urban crime would only lead to absurdity.

"H" as in Hunted and Lady, Drop Dead

Treat recognized these problems and tried various means to get around them without giving up the traditional mystery. In *"H" as in Hunted*, for example, his focal character is a man who was imprisoned and tortured by the Nazis and who has come back to New York to confront the coward who betrayed him. Jub Freeman becomes involved because he is a boyhood friend of the protagonist, but by focusing on a civilian, Treat is able to limit his story to a single mystery and a single cast of suspects.

Unfortunately, this approach weakens the book as a police procedural and makes it more like a Cornell Woolrich-type novel of private vengeance. In *Lady, Drop Dead* (1960), the feckless Mitch Taylor is involved in the story, but the protagonist is a private detective, which makes this police procedural veer dangerously close to being a private-eye novel reminiscent of Raymond Chandler.

Eventually, Treat moved his three sustaining characters, Taylor, Freeman, and Decker, out of New York, evidently hoping that the traditional mystery element in his plots would seem less incongruous in a smaller city. Yet though you can take a writer out of New York, you cannot always take New York out of a writer. Treat's unidentified city seems like an older and less hectic New York but is still too big and impersonal to provide a comfortable home for the apparatus of the traditional British mystery yarn. *Lady, Drop Dead*, the last of the Taylor/Freeman/Decker series, still reads like a set piece. Its limited cast of suspects is assembled in a classic finale so that the real murderer—who is the one the reader most suspected simply because he is the one who seemed least likely—can break down and unburden his conscience with a detailed confession.

The police procedural has evolved and proliferated since *Lady, Drop Dead* was published in 1960, but Treat did not participate in its development. His formal education may have saddled him with too much esteem for tradition and thus been an inhibiting factor. His police procedurals, like his Carl Wayward novels, seem to belong to an older, safer, much slower-moving world, but he deserves great credit for having originated this fascinating form of mystery fiction.

Bill Delaney

Updated by Fiona Kelleghan

Principal mystery and detective fiction

Carl Wayward series: *"B" as in Banshee*, 1940 (also known as *Wail for the Corpses*); *"D" as in Dead*, 1941; *"H" as in Hangman*, 1942; *"O" as in Omen*, 1943

Mitch Taylor, Jub Freeman, and Bill Decker series: *"V" as in Victim*, 1945; *"H" as in Hunted*, 1946; *"Q" as in Quicksand*, 1947 (also known as *Step into Quicksand*); *"T" as in Trapped*, 1947; *"F" as in Flight*, 1948; *Over the Edge*, 1948; *Big Shot*, 1951; *Weep for a Wanton*, 1956; *Lady, Drop Dead*, 1960

Nonseries novels: *Run Far, Run Fast*, 1937 (as Goldstone); *The Leather Man*, 1944; *Trial and Terror*, 1949; *Venus Unarmed*, 1961

Other short fiction: *"P" as in Police*, 1970

Other major works

Children's literature: *You're the Detective!*, 1983

Nonfiction: *Bringing Sherlock Home*, 1930; *Crime and Puzzlement: Twenty-four Solve-Them-Yourself Picture Mysteries*, 1981-1982, 1988, 1991, 1993; *The Clue Armchair Detective: Can You Solve the Mysteries of Tudor Close?*, 1983 (with George Hardie); *Crimes to Unravel*, 1988

Edited texts: *Murder in Mind: An Anthology of Mystery Stories by the Mystery Writers of America*, 1967; *The Mystery Writer's Handbook*, 1976 (with Herbert Brean); *A Special Kind of Crime*, 1982

Bibliography

Dove, George N. *The Police Procedural*. Bowling Green, Ohio: Bowling Green State University Popular Press, 1982. One of the first major studies of the subgenre pioneered by Lawrence Treat.

"Lawrence Treat, Ninety-four, Prolific Mystery Writer." *The New York Times*, January 16, 1998, p. B11. Obituary of Treat details his contributions to mystery and detective fiction.

Panek, LeRoy Lad. *The American Police Novel: A History*. Jefferson, N.C.: McFarland, 2003. Traces the evolution of the police procedural and Treat's influence on the subgenre. Bibliographic references and index.

Reitz, Caroline. *Detecting the Nation: Fictions of Detection and the Imperial Venture*. Columbus: Ohio State University Press, 2004. This study of Victorian crime fiction should be read as a prehistory of the American police procedural; shows the state of narrative conventions inherited by Treat and throws his contribution into greater relief.

Vicarel, Jo Ann. *A Reader's Guide to the Police Procedural*. New York: G. K. Hall, 1995. Geared to the mainstream reader, this study introduces and analyzes the police procedural form. Provides a perspective on Treat's work.

Washer, Robert. Review of *"P" as in Police*, by Lawrence Treat. *The Queen Canon Bibliophile* 3 (April, 1971): 18. Review of Treat's collection of short crime fiction.

PETER TREMAYNE

Peter Berresford Ellis

Born: Coventry, Warwickshire, England; March 10, 1943

Also wrote as Peter Berresford Ellis; Peter MacAlan

Types of plot: Historical; amateur sleuth

Principal series

Sister Fidelma, 1993-

Principal series characters

Sister Fidelma is a seventh century Irish nun, daughter of a former king of Cashel and sister to the current ruler. A *dálaigh*, or advocate of the Irish law courts, she has the power to gather evidence, ascertain whether a crime has been committed, and identify the criminal. She is a highly educated and strong-willed individual capable of answering the call to investigate mysteries at home and abroad.

Brother Eadulf, a young Saxon monk, begins a professional collaboration with Fidelma early in the series. As the series progresses, he and Fidelma develop a close friendship and finally a love relationship that leads to marriage and parenthood. The relationship, which Fidelma has trouble balancing with her professional life, causes turbulence throughout the series.

Colgú, the brother of Sister Fidelma and son of former Muman king Faílbe Fland mac Aedo, ascends to the throne of Cashel, seat of Muman. At times he is nothing more than part of Fidelma's background; in other books he plays an important role within the plot, either as an active participant or in his role as king, initiating or being the object of actions that ultimately involve his sister.

Contribution

Before turning to the mystery genre as Peter Tremayne, Peter Berresford Ellis had written dozens of books, primarily biographical and critical works under his own name or fiction (principally war and fantasy novels) under pseudonyms. Although respected as a scholar in England and Ireland, he did not win wide international popularity until he embarked on his Sister Fidelma series in 1993 with four short stories introducing the Irish nun.

The Fidelma stories introduced the author, as Peter Tremayne, to an international audience. The Fidelma series proved especially popular in the United States, where the International Sister Fidelma Society was established in 2001. The society publishes a magazine, *The Brehon*, about the author and Fidelma-related matters. In September, 2006, Féile Fidelma, the first international conference on the Sister Fidelma stories, was held at Cashel, Ireland.

The Sister Fidelma stories occupy a unique position in mystery writing with their seventh century Irish setting, detailed historical context, reflections of early Irish Christianity, and a protagonist who seems both historically credible and engagingly modern in her attitudes and attributes.

An occasional reviewer has complained that Tremayne idealizes early Celtic society, but most critical responses have been positive. On the whole, the historical dimensions of the stories have been viewed as accurate and important to the success of the series.

Biography

Peter Tremayne was born Peter Berresford Ellis on March 10, 1943, in Coventry, Warwickshire, England, to Alan J. Ellis and Eva Daisy Randell Ellis. Peter most likely inherited his interest in writing from his father, a journalist who began his career writing for the Cork *Examiner* and also wrote for the pulp market. The family's extensive Celtic ancestry may have contributed to Ellis's lifelong interest in Celtic history and culture.

Ellis earned a bachelor's degree with first-class honors and a master's degree, both in Celtic studies, at the Brighton College of Art and University of East London. He initially chose a career in journalism, starting as a junior reporter for the weekly *Brighton Herald* in 1960. He became deputy editor of the *Irish Post* in 1970 and editor of *Newsagent & Bookshop* in 1974. In 1966, he married Dorothea P. Cheesmur.

Ellis published his first book, *Wales—A Nation Again! The Nationalist Struggle for Freedom*, in 1968. The book, which recounts Wales's struggles for freedom, previewed its author's lifelong interest in Celtic political, historical, and cultural matters. Those interests continued to appear in several books that he wrote in the 1970's.

By 1975, Ellis had established himself as primarily a professional writer rather than a journalist. He continued to write extensively on Celtic culture, including *Celtic Women: Women in Celtic Society and Literature* (1996), which reflects the scholarship on Celtic women that Ellis would also draw on for his Sister Fidelma mysteries. Biographical works, including accounts of the lives of the British adventurers and popular writers Henry Rider Haggard, Captain W. E. Johns, and Talbot Mundy (William Gribbon), undoubtedly helped him learn how to create a fully realized character who could retain the readers' interest.

Ellis began his career as a novelist in the 1970's, writing principally horror and fantasy novels and short stories under the pseudonym Peter Tremayne. These forays into popular literature included three Dracula novels and the Lan-Kern trilogy. In addition to other novels in the horror and fantasy genres, Ellis, under the pseudonym Peter MacAlan, published eight adventure novels primarily set in World War II, beginning with *The Judas Battalion* (1983) and concluding with *The Windsor Protocol* (1993).

By 1993, Ellis, as Peter Tremayne, was ready to embark on still another genre, the mystery novel, which would bring him to a far larger audience than had his previous writings. He published four short stories featuring Sister Fidelma. The London publisher Headline then offered a three-book contract for novels starring the mystery-solving nun. The first book of the series, *Absolution by Murder: A Sister Fidelma Mystery*, appeared in 1994. Since 1994, his writing has primarily consisted of scholarly studies of Celtic culture and the Sister Fidelma stories.

Analysis

Peter Tremayne's Sister Fidelma stories depend for their success on several elements: a fully realized heroine, a historical context that permits her to function as both a religious person and a detective, and mysteries that engage the reader as they attract the interest of Fidelma. The Sister Fidelma stories typically integrate these elements effectively.

Tremayne persuasively depicts the substantial rights accorded Irish women in the seventh century. Fidelma's education at the bardic school at Tara to the level of *anruth*, one degree below the highest level possible, and her profession as a *dálaigh*, or advocate, of the Brehon Court thus appear convincing within the narratives and also give her access to the world of crime. Contributing to Fidelma's ability to move freely at the highest levels of Irish society is her royal status as a sister to the Muman king, Colgú.

Although a nun, Fidelma is sexually experienced, acknowledging in *Shroud for the Archbishop: A Sister Fidelma Mystery* (1995) a number of earlier affairs. In *Act of Mercy: A Celtic Mystery* (1999), she encounters her first lover, and throughout the series, she progresses in her relationship with Brother Eadulf from partner in solving crimes to friend, lover, wife, and mother of Eadulf's child. All of this is possible for Fidelma because the seventh century Celtic church, as the stories often remind readers, did not require celibacy for religious vocations.

In an age not far removed from the pre-Christian world of Druids and in which many remnants of the old ways still persisted, Fidelma is very much a transitional woman. In at least two novels (*Shroud for the Archbishop* and *Suffer Little Children: A Sister Fidelma Mystery*, 1995), for example, she practices *dercad*, the ancient Druidic form of meditation. In addition, she eschews the type of individual confession to a priest favored by the Roman church, instead taking a soul-friend, or *anamchara*, who serves as her confidant, spiritual guide, and personal confessor.

Tremayne's use of historical events, including the Synod of Whitby (664), and depiction of such seventh century cultural artifacts as beehive huts, the clepsydra (a water clock), hanging leather satchels used for storing manuscripts in monastery libraries, and texts written in the Ogham alphabet add to the appeal of the Fidelma stories.

The mysteries confronting Sister Fidelma challenge her intellectually and often place her in physical danger. Brother Eadulf assists Fidelma but inevitably proves far less perceptive than she. Fidelma's recognition of the uncomfortable position in which her superior talents place Eadulf contributes to the psychological realism that characterizes the account of their relationship. Once Fidelma and Eadulf have a son, she also recognizes her ambivalence toward the maternal role, which gets in the way of her original love, the law. These internal conflicts help readers to see in Fidelma not only as a seventh century woman but also as a woman of their own time.

Absolution by Murder

The first Sister Fidelma novel, *Absolution by Murder*, is set during the Synod of Whitby that Oswy, king of Northumbria, called in 664 to settle disputes between the Roman and Celtic churches. Several murders occur during the gathering, and Fidelma, a member of the Celtic delegation, answers Oswy's request to solve them. She reluctantly agrees to Oswy's suggestion that she work with the Saxon Brother Eadulf to give a greater sense of impartiality to the investigation, beginning a relationship that continued throughout the series.

Fidelma carries out her sleuthing amid a number of other historical personages who, along with the synod itself, create a pattern of historical context and verisimilitude that Tremayne followed throughout the series.

The novel also established Tremayne's practice of linkage between novels. The immediate plot of a specific novel is brought to a definitive resolution through Fidelma's investigative efforts, but typically the conclusion also leads the reader to anticipate what will come next. In this first novel, Brother Wighard appears as the designated successor to the current archbishop of Canterbury, but in the second novel, *Shroud for the Archbishop*, Wighard is murdered. At the end of the first book, Fidelma receives word that she is to go to Rome on behalf of her religious order, therefore making her available to be called on to solve the mystery when Wighard is killed.

SUFFER LITTLE CHILDREN

Suffer Little Children moves the personal story of Sister Fidelma forward at the same time that she solves yet another crime, in this case the murder of a highly respected scholar named Dacán, which could embroil her home kingdom of Muman in a serious dispute with the kingdom of Laigin. The king of Muman is dying of the yellow plague (later known as yellow fever) and has instructed Fidelma's brother, Colgú, his successor, to send for her to investigate the murder.

The novel continues Tremayne's practice of informing the reader about life in Celtic Ireland, including an explanation of how a king as well as his successor, known as the *tánaiste*, was chosen. Fidelma's investigation at the abbey of Ros Ailithir, site of the murder, leads her to the library where Dacán had spent much of his time and provides readers with information on the making and storing of books as well as on the Ogham alphabet in which texts were written on wooden wands.

The novel establishes the close bond between brother and sister that will be evident throughout the series. The absence of Brother Eadulf from the book allows readers to focus on the sibling relationship, although Eadulf returns to Fidelma's life in the next novel, *The Subtle Serpent: A Sister Fidelma Mystery* (1996).

ACT OF MERCY

Act of Mercy finds Fidelma in a period of uncertainty. She is questioning her feelings about Eadulf and her role as a nun. To sort out her feelings, she goes on a pilgrimage to the Shrine of Saint James in present-day Spain.

Onboard the ship carrying Fidelma to the continent, she discovers that a murder has been committed, one that she resolutely sets out to solve. Also on the voyage is Cian, who years before had seduced the young Fidelma and then abandoned her. As a psychological exploration of Fidelma, the novel is especially interesting and marks a critical juncture in her life. She is able to see Cian for what he now is and bring closure to that period of her life. As she acknowledges to herself that Cian no longer has any hold on her, she thinks of Eadulf and realizes that in some way he has been with her on her entire voyage.

At that moment, Fidelma reads a message that has

come from her brother urging her quick return to Cashel. Eadulf has been arrested and charged with murder. Fidelma does hurry back in the next novel, *Our Lady of Darkness: A Novel of Ancient Ireland* (2000). Her rescue of Eadulf will propel the two together, although Fidelma will still have many moments of uncertainty regarding their relationship.

Edward J. Rielly

Principal mystery and detective fiction

Sister Fidelma series: *Absolution by Murder: A Sister Fidelma Mystery*, 1994; *Shroud for the Archbishop: A Sister Fidelma Mystery*, 1995; *Suffer Little Children: A Sister Fidelma Mystery*, 1995; *The Subtle Serpent: A Sister Fidelma Mystery*, 1996; *The Spider's Web: A Sister Fidelma Mystery*, 1997; *Valley of the Shadow: A Sister Fidelma Mystery*, 1998; *The Monk Who Vanished: A Celtic Mystery*, 1999; *Act of Mercy: A Celtic Mystery*, 1999; *Our Lady of Darkness: A Novel of Ancient Ireland*, 2000; *Hemlock at Vespers: Fifteen Sister Fidelma Mysteries*, 2000; *Smoke in the Wind*, 2001; *The Haunted Abbot*, 2002; *Badger's Moon*, 2003; *Whispers of the Dead: Fifteen Sister Fidelma Mysteries*, 2004; *The Leper's Bell: A Novel of Ancient Ireland*, 2004; *Master of Souls*, 2006; *A Prayer for the Damned*, 2006; *An Ensuing Evil and Others: Fourteen Historical Mystery Stories*, 2006

Other major works

Novels: 1977-1985 • *Dracula Unborn*, 1977 (also known as *Bloodright: Memoirs of Mirceas, Son of Dracula*); *The Hound of Frankenstein*, 1977; *The Revenge of Dracula*, 1978; *The Vengeance of She*, 1978; *The Ants*, 1979; *The Curse of Loch Ness*, 1979; *The Fires of Lan-Kern*, 1980; *Dracula, My Love*, 1980; *Zombie!*, 1981; *The Return of Raffles*, 1981; *The Morgow Rises!*, 1982; *The Destroyers of Lan-Kern*, 1982; *The Buccaneers of Lan-Kern*, 1983; *Snowbeast!*, 1983; *The Judas Battalion*, 1983 (as MacAlan); *Raven of Destiny*, 1984; *Kiss of the Cobra*, 1984; *Airship*, 1984 (as MacAlan); *Swamp!*, 1985; *Angelus!*, 1985

1986-1993 • *Kitchener's Gold*, 1986 (as MacAlan); *Trollnight!*, 1987; *Nicor!*, 1987; *The Rising of the Moon: A Novel of the Fenian Invasion of Canada*, 1987 (as Ellis); *The Valkyrie Directive*, 1987 (as MacAlan); *The Doomsday Decree*, 1988 (as MacAlan); *Ravenmoon*, 1988 (also known as *Bloodmist*); *Island of Shadows*, 1991; *The Windsor Protocol*, 1993 (as MacAlan); *Dracula Lives!*, 1993

Short fiction: *My Lady of Hy-Brasil, and Other Stories*, 1987; *Aisling, and Other Irish Tales of Terror*, 1992

Nonfiction (as Ellis): 1968-1980 • *Wales—A Nation Again! The Nationalist Struggle for Freedom*, 1968; *The Creed of the Celtic Revolution*, 1969; *The Scottish Insurrection of 1820*, 1970 (with Seumas Mac a'Ghobhainn); *The Problem of Language Revival*, 1971 (with Mac a'Ghobhainn); *A History of the Irish Working Class*, 1972; *The Cornish Language and Its Literature*, 1974; *The Boyne Water: The Battle of the Boyne, 1690*, 1976; *The Un-Dead: The Legend of Bram Stoker and Dracula*, 1977 (with Peter Haining); *A Voice from the Infinite: The Life of Sir Henry Rider Haggard, 1856-1925*, 1978

1981-1990 • *By Jove, Biggles! The Life of Captain W. E. Johns*, 1981 (with Piers Williams); *The Last Adventurer: The Life of Talbot Mundy, 1879-1940*, 1984; *A Dictionary of Irish Mythology*, 1987; *The Celtic Empire: The First Millennium of Celtic History, c. 1000 B.C.-51 A.D.*, 1990

1991-1999 • *A Guide to Early Celtic Remains in Britain*, 1991; *A Dictionary of Celtic Mythology*, 1992; *Celt and Saxon: The Struggle for Britain, A.D. 410-937*, 1993; *The Celtic Dawn: A History of Pan Celticism*, 1993; *The Druids*, 1994; *Celtic Women: Women in Celtic Society and Literature*, 1996; *Celt and Greek: Celts in the Hellenic World*, 1997; *The Ancient World of the Celts*, 1998; *Celt and Roman: The Celts of Italy*, 1998; *The Chronicles of the Celts: New Tellings of Their Myths and Legends*, 1999; *Erin's Blood Royal: The Gaelic Noble Dynasties of Ireland*, 1999

Edited text: *Irish Masters of Fantasy*, 1979 (also known as *The Wondersmith, and Other Macabre Tales*)

Bibliography

Chadwick, Nora. *The Celts*. Rev. ed. New York: Penguin Books, 1997. A study of the history and culture of the Celts by one of the greatest Celtic scholars; originally published in 1971, the book is still considered a masterpiece of Celtic history. Useful for background information on the Sister Fidelma stories.

The International Sister Fidelma Society. http://sister fidelma.com. Contains considerable information about Tremayne, Sister Fidelma, and the historical setting for the stories, as well as in-depth interviews.

Luehrs, Christiane W., and Robert B. Luehrs. "Peter Tremayne: Sister Fidelma and the Triumph of Truth." In *The Detective as Historian: History and Art in Historical Crime Fiction*, edited by Ray B. Browne and Lawrence A. Kreiser, Jr. Bowling Green, Ohio: Bowling Green State University Popular Press, 2000. Examines the Sister Fidelma stories within their historical setting and is more critical of Tremayne than are most critics and reviewers, seeing him as too partisan an advocate for Celtic culture. Illustrations, indexed.

Mathews, Caitlín. *The Elements of the Celtic Tradition.* Boston: Element Books, 1991. Includes readable and succinct accounts of elements of Celtic culture, including many depicted in the Fidelma stories, such as the Ogham alphabet, Celtic Christianity, and the concept of the soul-friend. Illustrations, indexed.

Rielly, Edward J. "Sister Fidelma: A Woman for All Seasons." *The Brehon: Journal of the International Sister Fidelma Society* 3, 2 (May 2004): 3-13. An analysis of Sister Fidelma as both a credible seventh century heroine and a twenty-first century woman.

ELLESTON TREVOR

Trevor Dudley-Smith

Born: Bromley, Kent, England; February 17, 1920
Died: Cave Creek, Arizona; July 21, 1995
Also wrote as Mansell Black; Trevor Burgess; T. Dudley-Smith; Trevor Dudley-Smith; Roger Fitzalan; Adam Hall; Howard North; Simon Rattray; Warwick Scott; Caesar Smith; Leslie Stone
Types of plot: Espionage; hard-boiled; psychological; private investigator; historical

Principal series

Hugo Bishop, 1951-1957
Quiller, 1965-1996

Principal series characters

Hugo Bishop, lay analyst, gentleman detective, and chess enthusiast, plays a fast game of life and death among the beautiful, the rich, and the decadent, assisted by his secretary Miss Gorringe. Bishop studies people and relationships as closely as he studies the moves on his chessboard. His detached yet inquisitive nature elicits confidences, but Bishop is wise enough to realize that the truth lies hidden. Where others see the crowd with a floodlight, he claims to "use a spotlight" to "see the individual in clear focus." As a consequence, he is quick to note the out-of-character, a clue to hidden realities. Under the pen name H. B. Ripton, he writes exhaustive theses on human behavior.

Quiller is a British "shadow executive," employed by a secret government bureau to handle situations so sensitive that they do not exist officially. An infiltrator who, after refusing military service, helped European Jews escape Nazi concentration camps, Quiller is an adept troubleshooter. He is also a formidable linguist, a karate expert, a practitioner of Zen mind control, a jet pilot, and a paranoid cynic (he has to be to survive). A loner who avoids the risks of associates, Quiller is sharp-tongued, suspicious, and abusive of all but the true professional. In effect, Quiller is defined only in terms of his work and needs danger and challenge to confirm his identity and to make life endurable.

Contribution

Elleston Trevor wrote approximately one novel per year from 1943 to the late 1980's, under many pseudonyms. It was, however, the best seller *The Berlin Memorandum* (as Adam Hall, 1965; also known as *The Quiller Memorandum*) that brought him international acclaim. It won for him the Mystery Writers of America's Edgar Allan Poe Award in 1966 and the French Grand Prix Littérature Policière, was filmed by Twentieth Century Fox (1966), and was later made into a British Broadcasting Corporation television series; it has been cited as a definitive example of the realistic Cold War espionage novel. Trevor made psychoanalysis a central concern of his detective and espionage fiction, and he explored deep-seated motives, needs, and compulsions that compel action at odds with the rational and conscious mind. He preferred to investigate people under pressure, driven by external and internal forces, and to focus on the animal instincts of the pursued.

The espionage novels, in the tradition of John le Carré and Len Deighton, explore double agentry—the motives, the tensions, the psychological complexities, and the fears of the clandestine life. They focus on the professional agent as a highly competent expert at survival, a tough-minded antihero beset by secret conspiracies within his own organization. At its best, the detail in Trevor's novels creates the illusion of documentary, while the attitudes of the heroes—at times flippant, at times downright bitter and irreverent toward authority—reflect the Weltanschauung of the Cold War period.

Biography

Elleston Trevor was born Trevor Dudley-Smith on February 17, 1920, in Bromley, Kent, the son of Walter Smith and Florence (née Elleston) Smith. Educated at Yardley Court Preparatory School and Sevenoaks School, Kent, Trevor was an apprentice race car driver from 1937 to 1938, but with the outbreak of World War II joined the Royal Air Force and served as a flight engineer from 1939 to 1945. He turned to full-time writing in 1946, and in 1947 married Jonquil Burgess, with whom he had one son, Peregrine Scott, who would serve as his literary manager. Before turning to the genre that made him famous, Trevor initially focused on wartime stories about Dunkirk and other key historical events.

Trevor and his family lived in Spain for a time and then in France from 1958 to 1973. In 1973 they moved to the United States, where they lived in Fountain Hills, Arizona. Trevor's interests included chess, travel, designing model airplanes, and astronomy, with the latter helping him "to keep a sense of perspective." Trevor published novels for adults and adolescents as well as plays and stories. When asked his reason for writing, he first replied, "Complete inability to do anything else," later adding, "I don't know." Finally, he answered that it certainly was not to escape life, which he found "too darned interesting," but maybe it was to "escape some imprisoning memory of infancy . . . such as we all have deep in the subconscious." The Mugar Memorial Library, Boston University, houses an Elleston and Jonquil Trevor Collection, but post-1980 materials are located at Arizona State University.

Analysis

Elleston Trevor was intrigued with the psychology of a mind under pressure, of men forced to the edge physically, emotionally, and intellectually. Trevor's early works frequently include Freudian psychoanalysis of everything from male-female driving patterns and responses to war-induced stress syndrome. *A Blaze of Roses* (1952), for example, sensitively traces the roots of psychosis: how the private horror of a long-term fantasy romance exposed as illusion drives a meek and mild man to turn arsonist and embark on a wild flight to Tangiers with police in hot pursuit. *The Billboard Madonna* (1960), in turn, is typical in its compelling analysis of the effects of guilt on a hit-and-run driver, who pushes himself to the brink of total nervous collapse in his attempt to expiate his guilt.

The Theta Syndrome and *The Sibling*

All Trevor's work questions the human reponse to shock and trauma and the psyche that provokes the response. In *The Theta Syndrome* (1977), the victim of one murderous attack is so terrified that she literally cannot breathe and, while in a coma, develops telekinetic and telepathic abilities to project her fears, while in *The Sibling* (1979), a story of sibling rivalry and reincarnation, an innocent youth must face the reality of her brother's insanity and his incestuous and murderous intent. Trevor's detective Hugo Bishop argues,

> Human beings are never straight. . . . Our minds are spirals, curves, zigzags, circles—because before we can get anything straight in them, something gets in the way: a prejudice, a principle, a fear, a doubt, an inhibition. . . . Most of the time we don't even realize why we do things, and say things.

Quiller

Trevor's Quiller series observes Quiller in extreme situations: flying a Russian MiG into a trap behind Soviet lines; being attacked by a cocaine-crazed murderer; and parachuting into the Libyan desert with a small nuclear device that he must detonate to destroy British-manufactured nerve gas. In every case Quiller continually analyzes his own neurophysiology, receiving instant feedback from his various body parts under stress and sending internal commands to control their function ("shuddup stomach," "hands grip like claws"). He tries to separate his mind from the pain and to remain objective in the most subjective of circumstances, as he feeds his internal computer the complex information necessary to make the intuitive leap in decision making that will mean the difference between life and death. Trevor relishes including physiological explanations of the functioning of brain and body under stress and using terms such as "retrogressive amnesia," "isolation factors," "alpha waves," and "guilt-transference."

To delve into this psyche, Trevor depended on either a first-person narrative or a third-person omniscient narrative that focuses on the inner thoughts or reactions of two or three main characters. The first-person narrators often engage in a stream-of-consciousness internal dialogue that reveals to the reader what the speaker hides even from himself, while the third-person narrators are as terse and controlled as an Ernest Hemingway hero.

Dialogue and imagery

Trevor reveled in including lengthy passages of dialogue in foreign languages, particularly German, to give the reader a sense of realism, of alien culture, and of competence. He skips about in time as one would if following the memories of a fallible narrator and frequently speeds up or telescopes time in accordance with the psychological situation of his characters. Often he takes one step back for every two steps forward. Sometimes the action seems to occur in slow motion, with several pages devoted to the passage of seconds, and other times, as in the following example from *The Sinkiang Executive* (1978), it races forward to its inescapable outcome:

> The gun had slid across one of the Chinese rugs and she wrenched herself free and got halfway there before I caught her again and threw her against the settee and went for the gun myself and got it and hit the magazine out and slipped it into my pocket and kicked the gun hard and send it spinning across the floorboards . . . as she came at me with her nails.

Trevor's imagery grows out of a Darwinian view of nature, tooth and claw. The cat that toys coquettishly with men at the beginning of a Hugo Bishop story proves a lethal cheetah at the end. Quiller is the ferret, put down the hole to initiate a chase that will expose the enemy but that might cost Quiller his life: "An agent is sent like a ferret into a hole and he is not told if there is a dog at the other end." Trevor records actions he finds "natural for a hunted creature," such as instinctively making for the middle of a field or for the deeper cover of the furrows. Trevor's narrators inevitably explore the way instinct interacts with reason to give a desperate man the same edge as a wild animal—a wild figuring of the odds and then a sudden rush based on instinct alone.

Trevor's depiction of the police varies. In the espionage novels the police are often incompetent, unable to deal with the competition of trained assassins and competent operatives. In the pursuit novels the police are relentless, organized, methodical; their patterns are mechanical and hence often inescapable. In fact, at times they prove overzealous and jump to an erroneous interpretation of the facts, mistaking arson committed for personal reasons for carefully calculated sabotage and limited blackmail for political kidnapping.

The Berlin Memorandum

Trevor usually included arresting studies of the inner workings of a large organization: a major advertising firm that depends on the strengths and weaknesses of a handful of men to keep it solvent, a scientific project with carefully constructed safeguards that a single member can undermine, a think tank that leaks word of a nonexistent ultimate weapon and then must bear the earth-shattering consequences, a government bureau whose members reflect the cold, calculated policies necessitated by its prime directive. The description of "The Bureau" in *The Berlin Memorandum* is typical: "a government department" whose "nihilistic status" casts a "creeping blight over the people who work here, . . . rootless souls." The directors are all cold-hearted and ruthless, characterized by "the noncommittal eyes, the sharp nose, the lopsided jaw and the go-to-hell line of the mouth."

Through his focus on governments and organizations, Trevor explored how far governments and individuals are willing to go to defend their political or social views and how easily conflicting motives and failures of understanding can lead to catastrophe. In *Deathwatch* (1984), a Moscow-produced lethal genetic virus used by a Kremlin power broker to make the world safe for communism leads to a countdown to nuclear destruction.

Trevor's depiction of the truly hard-boiled hero focuses on his ability to inflict and receive superhuman punishment and is directly related to the author's interest in human psychology and in the interaction of animal instinct and rational logic. Quiller might be exposed to cyanide fumes, crash in a high-speed chase, be ejected from an exploding jet, be concussed by a grenade, or be shot with a dart gun, but he forges ahead, transforming the assignment from a single impossible act to a full-scale impossible operation. The minds of Trevor's heroes, whether hard-boiled supermen or average nonentities, grow clinically detached under pressure, calculate risks and potential actions at incredible speeds (three-second decisions), and then respond instinctively despite the calculations. As Quiller says, "By the time you'd been a few years at it you could handle pretty well anything because your mind turned into a computer, scanning the data and keeping you out of trouble."

Violence

Part of what creates the hard-boiled effect is Trevor's close focus. A description of a physical confrontation might involve as many as nine pages of meticulous detail of characters gouging, punching, and hammering—for example, of Quiller barely hanging on to the undercarriage of a speeding car or inching up a narrow broom closet to escape detection. Even in the more gentlemanly Bishop series the details of a fistfight or of a brutal crash are enumerated meticulously. As LeRoy Panek writes in *The Special Branch: The British Spy Novel, 1890-1980* (1981), Trevor's goal is "to bring violence home to his readers." Whether he is describing the mutilated body of an accident victim or a fight to the death between operatives, the images of violence are intensely vivid:

> Fingers at his face, scrambling blindly, live things, live weapons, *move faster*, digging, clawing in the night, in the dark, *this is the way*, feeling the soft flesh, hooking down, hooking down deep, his body shifting, *yes*, his arm lifting to—*don't let him*—lifting to stop my fingers. . . . I . . . brought a series of eye-darts against his face and felt him jerk and swung a wedge-hand across his throat. . . . I paralysed the nerves in the bicep with a centre-knuckle . . . and drove the wedge-hand down with all the strength that was in me and felt the vertebrae snap and the head come forward . . . He didn't move.

The effect of such detail is that the reader shares the terror, the paranoia, and the physical discomfort of being set up, being up on the run, being hunted, being interrogated, being physically abused. In other words, such explicit violence creates suspense, tension, and the illusion of realism.

The Ninth Directive

The detail may also be technical. For example, consider the description of a 561 Husqvarna in *The Ninth Directive* (1966):

> . . . a .358 Magnum center-fire, with a three-shot magazine, 25½ inch barrel, hand-checkered walnut stock, corrugated butt-plate and sling swivels. The fore-end and pistol grip are tipped with rosewood. The total weight is 7¾ pounds and the breech pressure is in the region of 20 tons p.s.i., giving a high muzzle velocity and an almost flat trajectory with a 150-grain bullet.

Panek believes that such technical detail and the focus on "humanistic psychology" do not fuse well with an adventure tale of what he calls "a cybernetic man," but it is exactly this fusion that creates a typical Trevor novel. When it works well, it is stunning, as in *The Sinkiang Executive*'s terse but fascinating technical description of a military briefing session on how to cross Soviet airspace.

Despite the predictability of the pattern in Trevor's work, there is always enough variety to keep the reader guessing. The changes in setting, with their well-defined topicality (Bangkok, Cambodia, the Sino-Russian border, Germany, the Amazon, the Sahara), create new situations of terrain and culture; so too do the individual natures of the assignments. The suspense always builds and the action overwhelms: car, boat, and submarine chases, the running of blockades, narrow escapes on or under water, aerial combat, and threats from individuals, groups, and machines. Pursuit is vital to a Trevor plot. It is the combination of fast action, psychological analysis, and Cold War cynicism that has earned for Trevor a permanent place in detective and espionage fiction.

Gina Macdonald

Principal mystery and detective fiction

Hugo Bishop series (as Hall in United States, as Rattray in Great Britain): *Knight Sinister*, 1951; *Queen in Danger*, 1952; *Bishop in Check*, 1953; *Dead Silence*, 1954 (also known as *Pawn in Jeopardy*); *Dead Circuit*, 1955 (also known as *Rook's Gambit*); *Dead Sequence*, 1957

Quiller series (as Hall): *The Berlin Memorandum*, 1965 (also known as *The Quiller Memorandum*); *The Ninth Directive*, 1966; *The Striker Portfolio*, 1968; *The Warsaw Document*, 1970; *The Tango Briefing*, 1973; *The Mandarin Cypher*, 1975; *The Kobra Manifesto*, 1976; *The Sinkiang Executive*, 1978; *The Scorpion Signal*, 1979; *The Sibling*, 1979; *The Peking Target*, 1981; *Quiller*, 1985; *Quiller's Run*, 1988

Nonseries novels: 1943-1950 • *Over the Wall*, 1943 (as T. Dudley-Smith); *Double Who Double Crossed*, 1944 (as T. Dudley-Smith); *The Immortal Error*, 1946; *Escape to Fear*, 1948 (as T. Dudley-Smith); *Now Try the Morgue*, 1948 (as T. Dudley-Smith); *Chorus of Echoes*, 1950; *The Mystery of the Missing Book*, 1950 (as Burgess)

1951-1960 • *Dead on Course*, 1951 (as Black); *Image in the Dust*, 1951 (as Scott; also known as *Cockpit*); *Redfern's Miracle*, 1951; *Sinister Cargo*, 1951 (as Black); *Tiger Street*, 1951; *A Blaze of Roses*, 1952 (also known as *The Fire-Raiser*); *The Domesday Story*, 1952 (as Scott); *Shadow of Evil*, 1953 (as Black); *The Passion and the Pity*, 1953; *Naked Canvas*, 1954 (as Scott); *Steps in the Dark*, 1954 (as Black); *The Big Pick-Up*, 1955; *The Gale Force*, 1956; *The Killing Ground*, 1956; *Heat Wave*, 1957 (as Caesar Smith); *The Pillars of Midnight*, 1957; *Dream of Death*, 1958; *Silhouette*, 1959; *The V.I.P.*, 1959; *Murder by All Means*, 1960; *The Billboard Madonna*, 1960; *The Mind of Max Duvine*, 1960

1961-1970 • *The Burning Shore*, 1961 (also known as *The Pasang Run*); *The Volcanoes of San Domingo*, 1963 (as Hall); *The Flight of the Phoenix*, 1964; *The Second Chance*, 1965; *Weave a Rope of Sand*, 1965; *The Shoot*, 1966; *A Blaze of Arms*, 1967 (as Fitzalan); *A Place for the Wicked*, 1967; *The Freebooters*, 1967; *Bury Him Among the Kings*, 1970

1971-1985 • *Expressway*, 1973 (as North); *The Paragon*, 1975 (also known as *Night Stop*); *Blue Jay Summer*, 1977; *Seven Witnesses*, 1977; *The Theta Syndrome*, 1977; *The Damocles Sword*, 1981; *The Penthouse*, 1983; *Deathwatch*, 1984; *Northlight*, 1985 (as Hall)

Other major works

Short fiction: *Elleston Trevor Miscellany*, 1944

Plays: *The Last of the Daylight*, pr. 1959; *A Pinch of Purple*, pr. 1971; *A Touch of Purple*, pr. 1972; *Just Before Dawn*, pr. 1972

Screenplay: *Wings of Danger*, 1952 (with John Gilling and Peckham Webb)

Children's literature: *Animal Life Stories: Rippleswim the Otter, Scamper-Foot the Pine Marten, Shadow the Fox*, 1943-1945; *Into the Happy Glade*, 1943 (as T. Dudley-Smith); *By a Silver Stream*, 1944 (as T. Dudley-Smith); *Deep Wood*, 1945; *Wumpus*, 1945; *Heather Hill*, 1946; *More About Wumpus*, 1947; *Badger's Beech*, 1948; *The Island of the Pines*, 1948; *The Secret Travellers*, 1948; *The Wizard of the Wood*, 1948; *Where's Wumpus?*, 1948; *A Spy at Monk's Court*, 1949 (as Burgess); *Badger's Moon*,

1949; *Ants' Castle*, 1949; *Challenge of the Firebrand*, 1951; *Mole's Castle*, 1951; *Secret Arena*, 1951; *Sweethallow Valley*, 1951; *The Racing Wraith*, 1953 (as Burgess); *Forbidden Kingdom*, 1955; *Badger's Wood*, 1958; *Green Glades*, 1959; *The Crystal City*, 1959; *Squirrel's Island*, 1963

Bibliography

Cawelti, John G., and Bruce A. Rosenberg. *The Spy Story.* Chicago: University of Chicago Press, 1987. Scholarly study of British espionage fiction; sheds light on Trevor's works.

East, Andy. *The Cold War File.* Metuchen, N.J.: Scarecrow Press, 1983. Examines the representations of espionage in Cold War fiction and of the Cold War in espionage stories; provides context for understanding Trevor's novels.

Hitz, Frederick P. *The Great Game: The Myth and Reality of Espionage.* New York: Alfred A. Knopf, 2004. Hitz, the former inspector general of the Central Intelligence Agency, compares famous fictional spies and spy stories to real espionage agents and case studies to demonstrate that truth is stranger than fiction. Helps place Trevor's work within the genre.

Panek, LeRoy. "Adam Hall." In *The Special Branch: The British Spy Novel, 1890-1980.* Bowling Green, Ohio: Bowling Green University Popular Press, 1981. Scholarly study of British espionage thrillers written by a major critic in the academic study of mystery and detective fiction look at Trevor, writing as Adam Hall.

Penzler, Otto, ed. "Quiller." In *The Great Detectives.* Boston: Little, Brown, 1978. Argues for including Trevor's mysterious Quiller among the espionage genre's "great detectives."

MARGARET TRUMAN

Mary Margaret Truman

Born: Independence, Missouri; February 17, 1924
Types of plot: Psychological; police procedural

Principal series

Capital Crimes, 1980-

Principal series characters

MACKENZIE "MAC" SMITH and ANNABEL SMITH are a pleasant, urbane, and sophisticated lawyer couple. Mac, a former criminal attorney, is now a George Washington University law professor. Annabel, a former divorce attorney, now owns an upscale art gallery in the fashionable Georgetown district of Washington, D.C. The couple try to fathom some of the crimes that cross their paths and thereby become amateur sleuths.

Contribution

In her mystery novels, Margaret Truman has given the world a close and private look into the sleaze of Washington Beltway politics. Her Capital Crimes mystery novels are set mostly in Washington, D.C., often at familiar sites, such as the White House, the Kennedy Center, agencies such as the Central Intelligence Agency (CIA), and major parks. Truman also uses sites of historic significance such as Ford's Theatre and Union Station. For more than a quarter of a century, at a pace of about a book per year, she has been producing these tales of violence and mayhem, mostly involving individuals in high places or those connected with them. Truman highlights the wheelings and dealings of politicians and other powerful people and explores their secret agendas.

Biography

Margaret Truman, also known by her married name, Margaret Truman Daniel, was born Mary Margaret Truman on February 17, 1924, in the heart of the Midwest, in Independence, Missouri. Her father,

Harry S. Truman, a Democrat, became the thirty-third president of the United States on the death of Franklin Delano Roosevelt on April 12, 1945. Her mother was Elizabeth "Bess" Virginia Wallace Truman. Margaret attended public school in her hometown but also Gunston Hall, a girls' boarding school in Washington, D.C., winning prizes for her mastery of English and Spanish. She majored in history and international relations and earned a bachelor's degree from George Washington University in 1946, studying piano and voice on the side. Her father was also an amateur pianist and would often accompany her singing.

From 1947 to 1954, Margaret Truman performed as a coloratura in programs featuring operatic arias and light classics on the stage, radio, and television. Her reviews were mixed. She also did some summer stock acting. On April 21, 1956, she married *New York Times* reporter and later editor E. Clifton Daniel, Jr., at Trinity Episcopal Church in Independence, becoming Mary Truman Daniel. Her husband died in 2000. The couple had four sons—Clifton, William, Harrison, and Thomas—born between 1957 and 1966.

Truman became fairly well known in the literary world by publishing some girlhood recollections in 1956 but especially because of the biographies of her father in 1972 and her mother in 1986. Eventually, she wrote books on White House First Ladies, pets, and the history of 1600 Pennsylvania Avenue and its inhabitants. Although she had long been an avid reader of mystery novels, her initiation into the genre was the result of a casual conversation with her publisher.

Truman launched her Capital Crimes series mystery novels in 1980 with the best-selling *Murder in the White House* and followed it with many other volumes. Considering that she once remarked that writing was the hardest and most exacting career she had ever had, her literary output has been remarkable. Her honors include honorary degrees from Wake Forest University (1972), from her alma mater George Washington University (1975), and Rockhurst College (1976). She is a trustee of the Harry S. Truman Institute and of George Washington University and has held various directorships. She has also won other forms of recognition such as the selection of her *Murder in Georgetown* (1986) by the Mystery Guild.

Analysis

Margaret Truman's inside knowledge of life in the corridors of power and privilege are evidenced in many of her books. Such familiarity gives her stories of misdeeds in high places crucial realism, at times making the reader wonder if her writing is indeed totally fiction. This is especially true in the age of investigative reporting, when disclosures of scandals among those in power are commonplace. Truman understands Washington and its players and how in their political lives, which can make for strange bedfellows, these powerful people can cut deals even—or especially—in the midst of mayhem. Truman's distaste of chicanery and hypocrisy and moral dishonesty sounds genuine. Her strength lies in her attention to detail, especially about local landmarks and legends in Washington. She depicts these with precision, providing her readers with a sense of space that many recognize. For instance, in *Murder in the White House*, to guarantee authenticity, Truman scrutinized the floor plans of the White House where she had spent seven years of her life. Such attention to detail, however, has also been criticized as overkill. Some critics have wondered why it is necessary to describe so many meals and drinks at specific restaurants and bars visited by some of the characters in her novels when these details are irrelevant to the story line.

The plots engaging Truman's characters are often complicated and at times fast-moving. In this way, Truman's style is reminiscent of that of Agatha Christie. There are usually false leads pointing to the wrong suspect, and the issue is often confused among the usually large cast of characters. Although Truman's nonfictional biographies are generally considered by her critics to be graceful, simple, warm, genuine, and modest, suggesting an author from middle America barely affected by the rest of the world, some of her writing in the mystery novels has been characterized as lacking polish. She views the political leaders, bureaucrats, diplomats, and others in high places with a cynical eye, and this, together with her emphasis on authenticity, may redeem any stylistic shortcomings she may have.

Murder in the White House

Murder in the White House, the initial novel in Truman's Capital Crimes series, was financially successful and has more than a million copies in print. The story, set in Truman's onetime home, is about the murder of Lansard Blaine, the corrupt secretary of state who is found strangled to death in the family quarters of the White House. Because Blaine had been a shady businessman, a powerful politician, and a womanizer, there are many suspects. Blaine may have been removed from circulation by one of his known lady friends, by an agent of a foreign power, or even by someone highly placed in the White House given the personal and political scandals involving presidential family members and staff in the book. The ending holds a surprise for the readers.

Murder at Ford's Theatre

The setting of *Murder at Ford's Theatre* (2002) is the theater where President Abraham Lincoln was assassinated in 1865. In an alley behind the theater, the body of Nadia Zarinski, an attractive woman who worked for Virginia senator Bruce Lerner and a part-time volunteer intern at the theater, is discovered. On digging into her life, two detectives find a growing cast of suspects, beginning with the senator himself. The rumor is that he—among many others—had had sexual encounters with Nadia. The senator's former wife is Clarise Emerson, producer/director at Ford's, whose nomination to head the National Endowment for the Arts is threatened by the scandal. Jeremiah Lerner, the aimless hot-headed son of the Lerners, was also one of Nadia's lovers. When Jeremiah is arrested for the murder, his mother, Clarise, enlists her friend Mackenzie Smith and his law partner to defend her son. As usual, several of the characters had good reason to murder the victim. Again, Truman provides a surprise ending.

Murder at Union Station

In *Murder at Union Station* (2004), the twentieth mystery novel in Truman's Capital Crimes series, an aging former New York City mafioso, Louis Russo, has just returned from a witness protection program that had initially led him to Mexico and then to Israel. He boards a train from Newark International Airport to Washington, where he is to testify at a hearing chaired by arch-conservative Senator Karl Widmer of Alaska. Russo was allegedly the hit man turned government informer whom the former head of the CIA, now United States president Adam Parmele, had contracted to assassinate a Central American head of state. Widmer intensely dislikes the liberal Parmele.

Russo's defense lawyer, Frank Marienthal, had introduced the Mafia man to his son, Richard Marienthal, an aspiring writer working on a book based on Russo's life. Senator Widmer intends to use the draft of this book—as well as the interview tapes in the writer's possession—at the impending hearing. The senator's objective is to derail the president's plan for a second term. However, Russo is gunned down immediately on arrival at the railroad station in Washington. The killer, a well-dressed biracial man, soon turns up dead in a Washington park.

Before it is all over, the Washington Metropolitan Police, the CIA, the Federal Bureau of Investigation, and the White House, as well as Senator Widmer and his adviser in Congress, all get involved in the unfolding of the two crimes. The complicated plot involves many characters, many scenes, and many venues before it draws to a conclusion.

MURDER AT THE OPERA

In *Murder at the Opera* (2006), Charise Lee, a young Asian Canadian soprano at the Washington National Opera, is barely known to the public until the aspiring singer is found stabbed backstage during a rehearsal. Truman's sleuths, Mackenzie Smith and Annabel Smith, are strongly urged by the opera's board to unmask the killer. They are assisted by a former homicide detective and an opera fan. Soon they find themselves among a cast of suspects with all sorts of scores to settle. What they uncover is an increasingly complex case reaching beyond Washington to a shady world of informers and terrorists. The climax occurs on a fateful night at the opera attended by the president of the Untied States.

Peter B. Heller

PRINCIPAL MYSTERY AND DETECTIVE FICTION

CAPITAL CRIMES SERIES: *Murder in the White House*, 1980; *Murder on Capitol Hill*, 1981; *Murder in the Supreme Court*, 1982; *Murder in the Smithsonian*, 1983; *Murder on Embassy Row*, 1984; *Murder at the FBI*, 1985; *Murder in Georgetown*, 1986; *Murder in the CIA*, 1987; *Murder at the Kennedy Center*, 1989; *Murder at the National Cathedral*, 1990; *Murder at the Pentagon*, 1992; *Murder on the Potomac*, 1994; *Murder at the National Gallery*, 1996; *Murder in the House*, 1997; *Murder at the Watergate*, 1998; *Murder at the Library of Congress*, 1999; *Murder in Foggy Bottom*, 2000; *Murder in Havana*, 2001; *Murder at Ford's Theatre*, 2002; *Murder at Union Station*, 2004; *Murder at the Washington Tribune*, 2005; *Murder at the Opera*, 2006; *Murder on K Street*, 2007

OTHER MAJOR WORKS

SHORT FICTION: *Margaret Truman: Three Complete Mysteries*, 1994

NONFICTION: *Souvenir: Margaret Truman's Own Story* (with Margaret Cousins), 1956; *White House Pets*, 1969; *Harry S. Truman*, 1972; *Women of Courage*, 1976 (with Thomas Fleming); *Bess W. Truman*, 1986; *First Ladies: An Intimate Group Portrait of White House Wives*, 1995; *The Presidents's House: A President's Daughter Shares the History and Secrets of the World's Most Famous Home*, 2003

EDITED TEXTS: *Letters from Father: The Truman Family's Personal Correspondence*, 1981; *Where the Buck Stops: The Personal and Private Writings of Harry S. Truman*, 1989

BIBLIOGRAPHY

Broyard, Anatole. "Books of The Times." Review of *Murder in the Smithsonian*, by Margaret Truman. *The New York Times*, June 24, 1983, p. C26. Considers Truman's *Murder in the Smithsonian* as reminiscent of the work of Helen McInnes, both being attractive to readers seeking escape from reality.

Cannon, Peter. Review of *Murder at Ford's Theatre*, by Margaret Truman. *Publishers Weekly* 249, no. 42 (October 21, 2002): 58. Describes how this historic national landmark is used by the author to contrive her drama.

Klein, Kathleen Gregory, ed. *Great Women Mystery Writers: Classic to Contemporary.* Westport, Conn.: Greenwood Press, 1994. Contains an essay on the life and works of Truman.

Quinn-Musgrove, Sandra L., and Sanford Kanter. *America's Royalty: All the President's Children.* Rev. ed. Westport, Conn.: Greenwood Press, 1995. Explains the positives of being President Harry S. Truman's daughter (such as being his personal representative abroad) but also its negatives (such as the Secret Service's presence limiting Margaret's romantic opportunities). With illustrations, appendix, bibliography, and index.

Salzberg, Charles. "Books in Brief: Fiction." Review of *Murder at the Watergate*, by Margaret Truman. *The New York Times*, August 16, 1998, p. BR 17. In this case involving the famed apartment complex, the reviewer suggests that Truman's masterly description of Washington, of the trappings of power, and of the various attractive but irrelevant menus do not redeem the weak plot and the obvious resolution of the mystery.

Williams, Nick B. "A Skunk Tips the Scales of Justice: Margaret Truman Makes Her Best Case." Review of *Murder in the Supreme Court*, by Margaret Truman. *Los Angeles Times Book Review*, January 30,

1983, p. 2. Review provides a sociological and moralistic spin, speculating on whether the bad people in the story are typical of the age and consequently are where the country may be heading.

Zvirin, Stephanie. Review of *Murder at the Washington Tribune*, by Margaret Truman. *Booklist* 102, no. 1 (September 1, 2005): 71-72. This reviewer says that Truman's twenty-first mystery involving the death of a *Tribune* reporter found strangled in a closet in the newsroom falls flat but offers a strong portrait of a middle-aged veteran police reporter forced to face the fact that his life is unraveling.

SCOTT TUROW

Born: Chicago, Illinois; April 12, 1949
Also wrote as L. Scott Turow; Scott F. Turow
Types of plot: Thriller; police procedural; courtroom drama

Contribution

Scott Turow has drawn extensively on his experience as a practicing attorney in Chicago to create mystery and suspense novels that meet the standards of serious fiction. His dramatic and gripping plots incorporate the profound meditations of an insider on the incongruities of the American legal system, while presenting human nature in all its complexity. Though many novels in this genre have aimed primarily to entertain, Turow insists that his works abide by the Aristotelian dictum to instruct as well as entertain. Besides the law, Turow's main source of artistic inspiration has been great literature that follows this dictum. Although justice may or may not be served in his legal thrillers, in a broader sense the works portray the search for individual redemption and collective healing.

An amalgam of the practical, the gritty, and the philosophical, Turow's work has influenced contemporaries such as Steve Martini and relative newcomers such as Kermit Roosevelt. As an attorney, he served on a commission that reviewed the administration of capital punishment in Illinois, leading Governor George Ryan to declare a moratorium on executions in that state. Turow recorded the evolution of his own thought on the issue in a nonfiction work, *Ultimate Punishment: A Lawyer's Reflections on Dealing with the Death Penalty* (2003).

Biography

Scott Turow was born in Chicago on April 12, 1949, to David D. Turow, a physician, and Rita Pastron Turow, a writer. He grew up in Chicago and later in the affluent suburb of Winnetka, Illinois. From both parents he inherited a strong work ethic and powerful ambition. They expected him to become a physician like his father, but from a very early age he dreamed of being a writer. He edited his school newspaper and avidly read the authors who were to influence his own thought and work: Charles Dickens, James Joyce, Ernest Hemingway, William Faulkner, and Saul Bellow, whom he considered the voice of his parents' generation. After high school, he enrolled as an English major at Amherst College. He began writing fiction, publishing short stories in literary periodicals such as the *Transatlantic Review*. After earning a bachelor's degree from Amherst in 1970, Turow attended the Stanford University Creative Writing Center for two years on an Edith Mirrielees Fellowship. On April 4, 1971, he married Annette Weisberg, an artist; the couple has three children.

While enrolled at Stanford, Turow worked on a novel about Chicago to be called *The Way Things Are*. However, one publisher after another rejected the manuscript, leading Turow to doubt his prospects as an author. He decided to pursue a legal career, entering Harvard Law School in 1975. However, he never abandoned writing, even temporarily, though at this point he saw it as a "private passion" rather than a career. He later recounted his law school experiences in a nonfiction book published in 1977 as *One L: An Inside*

Scott Turow.

Account of Life in the First Year at Harvard Law School. While capturing the manic quality of life in law school, the book also assesses how well law school actually prepares its students for issues encountered in the practice of law. In time, many law professors would recommend the book to young people considering a legal career.

Turow received a juris doctor degree in 1978 and worked as an assistant United States attorney in Chicago until 1986. While in Chicago, he prosecuted several widely publicized corruption cases, including a tax-fraud indictment against the state attorney general. Turow also was lead prosecutor in a federal case known as Operation Greylord, initiated to combat judicial corruption in Illinois.

All the while, Turow kept notebooks of ideas for the fiction he was writing on the side. Increasingly, these notebooks described corrupt officials and backbiting lawyers. He shelved a literary manuscript he had begun in favor of a story about an attorney in a bribery case. He had to borrow time from other endeavors to work on his fiction, until his wife, Annette, persuaded him in 1986 to resign from the U.S. Attorney's Office and focus on the book. First, however, he joined the Chicago law firm of Sonnenschein, Carlin, Nath & Rosenthal as a partner and immediately went on leave to complete his manuscript.

The resulting novel, *Presumed Innocent*, was published in 1987 by Farrar, Straus after a furious bidding war. Turow signed with Farrar in part because it was the only firm that had encouraged him as a writer in his days at Amherst. *Presumed Innocent* received the Silver Dagger Award from the Crime Writers' Association in 1988 and remained a best seller for forty-three weeks, selling four million paperback copies. A 1990 film adaptation was among the ten top-grossing films of that year. That year, Turow published his second novel, *The Burden of Proof*, and his photograph was featured on the cover of *Time* magazine, which described him as the "Bard of the Litigious Age." In 1999, *Time* named Turow's *Personal Injuries* Best Fiction Novel. Turow received the Heartland Prize in 2003 for *Reversible Errors* (2002) and the Robert F. Kennedy Book Award in 2004 for *Ultimate Punishment*.

Although many of his books have become best sellers and several have won literary awards, Turow has continued the practice of law, setting aside mornings to write at home. He has worked pro bono in many cases, including one in 1995 in which he obtained the release of Alejandro Hernandez, who had spent eleven years on death row for a murder he did not commit.

Analysis

Scott Turow has said that he found much popular literature "just plain dumb," while literary fiction was either inaccessible or uninteresting. He wrote *Presumed Innocent* in the belief that he could make the book "an island in between." In his view of human nature, he has also sought a middle ground. The 1960's were instrumental in shaping his initial idealism and making him aware of crushing social problems. The eight years he spent as a prosecutor further shaped his view of the law and of human nature. No longer totally a child of the Aquarian age, he confronted the truth that "there are some people who are incorrigibly evil." However, he does not believe in Original Sin, holding instead that humans are maimed by early experience. As one defense attorney in *Reversible Errors* declares, "There's just no point in giving up on a human being."

A consistent theme in Turow's work is that a human being has many sides and many motives. A criminal, like Robbie Feaver in *Personal Injuries* (1999), may commit crimes to provide for a troubled family. Prosecutors, like Stan Sennett in the same novel, may have admirable goals along with overbearing zeal. The tension between opposing traits in single characters is a large factor in the believability of Turow's stories.

When Turow began writing, he saw himself as a writer who practices law, but he has come to see himself as a lawyer who writes books. He notes that his legal experience has provided him with material for fiction even as it has required him to become adept at a kind of courtroom storytelling. He contends that prosecutors in particular, because they bear the burden of proof, must present a case through various witnesses just as an author tells a story through characters. Like a traditional story, the prosecutor's case must have a moral—the verdict requested of the jury.

Turow believes that, like himself, the American populace underwent a disillusioning experience in the 1970's. It was the Watergate scandal that engendered close scrutiny of the legal profession (and incidentally increased public interest in the genre of legal thrillers). President Richard Nixon's administration included many officials who, though trained in the law, faced indictment and prison terms as a result of the break-in and subsequent cover-up. Paradoxically, although individual attorneys and judges were no longer seen as models of integrity, it was in the courts that major questions of ethical and moral value were being decided.

Turow's works are the products of a discerning mind, trained in law and literature, at pains to sift out various orders of truth. Generally, though certainly not always, the truth revealed in court serves justice in the strictest sense, but the truth of the system's human participants cannot be contained in this frame of reference. With a perspective gained from eight years as a prosecutor, Turow has said that everyone in his stories is guilty of something, making the court system an "awkward" device for finding the whole truth. He adds, "It's the inability of the laws and institutions to accommodate these fine differences in people that has always provided a theme for me."

Presumed Innocent

Turow's first novel, *Presumed Innocent*, is a strong statement about the varieties of truth. In a large midwestern city, prosecuting attorney Carolyn Polhemus has been brutally murdered, and deputy prosecutor Rusty Sabich is assigned to investigate. With his boss, the district attorney, campaigning feverishly for reelection, the pressure is on to solve the case before voting day—and before Rusty's adulterous affair with the victim is exposed. Suddenly, however, Rusty is taken off the case and is himself charged with the murder. Through the long, bitter trial that ensues, prosecution and defense distort the meaning of evidence to win the case, until the reader wonders whether public institutions have any real interest in, or are capable of, finding the truth. Ultimately, long after Rusty has been exonerated, the real culprit is revealed by extralegal means—someone whose identity throws an ironic light on the title *Presumed Innocent*. Rusty believes it imperative to conceal the culprit's identity to protect his loved ones, and he lives with the guilty knowledge that his own actions triggered the events leading to the murder.

The Burden of Proof

Although Turow has not used series characters, he does feature some characters in more than one story, as might be expected from his consistent use of a fictitious midwestern locale, Kindle County, as his setting. The action in *The Burden of Proof* begins when Sandy Stern (the brilliant defense attorney from *Presumed Innocent*) finds his beloved wife dead by her own hand. His agonized search for the reasons leads him into a tangled web of circumstance and guilt. Meanwhile, Sandy's chief client, Dixon Hartnell, an unscrupulous commodities trader, is targeted for federal indictment. Sandy has shielded the man—but added to his own torment—out of family loyalty, for Dixon is married to Sandy's sister. As he struggles with new revelations of family intrigue and insider stock trading, Sandy realizes the extent of the secret existence his wife had led. Spectacular courtroom scenes, a mark of the legal thriller, are contrasted with the profound private tragedy that Sandy uncovers, making this novel an excellent example of the middle ground Turow has sought between entertaining fiction and serious, meditative literature.

The Laws of Our Fathers

Turow has said that 1960's produced both an idealized sense of human nature and the gang-ridden housing projects of later decades. His visits to the projects in the late 1980's while doing pro bono legal work shocked him profoundly as he encountered firsthand the desperation of the black urban poor. The plot of *The Laws of Our Fathers* (1996) weaves together two legacies from the 1960's: the projects and the common pasts of several Kindle County figures, including Judge Sonia "Sonny" Klonsky, a major character from *The Burden of Proof.*

A seemingly random drive-by shooting near a housing project takes the life of a state senator's former wife. The senator has long been acquainted with Judge Klonsky, who is assigned to preside over the murder case. Soon, questions of justice and equity appear to be made moot by the extraordinary animosity focused on the judge by her enemies, who are determined to cause her downfall. As the case develops, more acquaintances from the years of Vietnam-era protests—including an old boyfriend of Sonia's and a prominent and vocal black defense attorney—become involved, and the characters relive that era in their thoughts while the story reveals what, individually and collectively, they have since become.

The black defense attorney, Hobie Tuttle, has a nearly archetypal backstory: He had a somewhat privileged childhood and young manhood (like Turow), later participated in the Black Power movement, and still later achieved an uneasy success as a defense attorney. Turow describes Hobie as one of his favorite characters, combining basic decency with outstanding ingenuity. A scene that combines riveting courtroom drama with deep meditation on the social issues underlying the story is Hobie's cross-examination of another compelling black character, "Hardcore" Trent, a dope dealer and leader of a housing-project gang, who is a key prosecution witness. With understatement, Turow notes that Hardcore is "not a nice guy," yet in the author's hands, Hardcore is not just a simplistically drawn villain. A common 1960's complaint was that government institutions were an inadequate response to the complexities of human life, and in this novel Turow strongly suggests that the complaint still applies.

Personal Injuries

Critics and lawyers alike have praised the authentic tone of *Personal Injuries*, inspired by Turow's experience in Operation Greylord, the judicial bribery case. The central character is Robbie Feaver, a prominent personal-injury attorney who bribes judges with funds from a secret bank account. The Federal Bureau of Investigation discovers Robbie's crimes and induces him to entrap corrupt officials via a concealed microphone while arranging more payoffs. Robbie is a con artist with a heart of gold, devoted to his dying wife; he commits his crimes partly to foot her medical bills. He is also a philanderer, but the female undercover agent supervising his case is unreceptive to his charms. Much of the story's drama is in the mutual probing of these two complex and enigmatic personalities.

Though more of a procedural story than a legal thriller, *Personal Injuries* avoids the flat characterizations of a predictable genre novel. Turow accomplishes this by showing the characters in all their complexity and frailty, arousing compassion even for the troubles they have brought on themselves.

Thomas Rankin

Principal mystery and detective fiction

Novels: *Presumed Innocent*, 1987; *The Burden of Proof*, 1990; *Pleading Guilty*, 1993; *The Laws of Our Fathers*, 1996; *Personal Injuries*, 1999; *Reversible Errors*, 2002; *Limitations*, 2006

Other major works

Novel: *Ordinary Heroes*, 2005

Nonfiction: *One L: An Inside Account of Life in the First Year at Harvard Law School*, 1977; *Ultimate Punishment: A Lawyer's Reflections on Dealing with the Death Penalty*, 2003

Edited texts: *Guilty as Charged: A Mystery Writers of America Anthology*, 1996 (also known as *Guilty as Charged: The Penguin Book of New American Crime Writing*, 1996); *The Best American Mystery Stories*, 2006

Bibliography

Ahley, Mark. *Modern Crime Fiction: The Authors, Their Works, and Their Most Famous Creations*. New York: Carroll & Graf, 2002. Contains a short essay on legal thrillers and courtroom dramas. Describes Turow as a major practitioner of the genre.

D'Amato, Barbara. "Chicago as a Mystery Setting." In *The Fine Art of Murder: The Mystery Reader's Indispensable Companion*, edited by Ed Gorman, Martin H. Greenberg, Larry Segriff, and Jon L. Breen. New York: Carroll & Graf, 1993. Discusses Chicago as a city with high winds, a corrupt image, and social conditions providing motives for murder. Sheds light on Turow's writings.

Macdonald, Andrew F., and Gina Macdonald. *Scott Turow: A Critical Companion*. Westport, Conn.: Greenwood Press, 2005. A well-researched chronicle of Turow's progress from struggling writer to widely read and respected author of legal thrillers. Provides plot analysis and character descriptions for Turow's books through *Reversible Errors*. Includes a bibliography of his works and books and articles written about him.

Murphy, Stephen M. *Their Word Is Law: Bestselling Lawyer-Novelists Talk About Their Craft*. New York: Berkley Books, 2002. Includes an interview with Turow that provides firsthand information about his development as a writer, his experiences in the practice of law, and the relationship between his legal and authorial practices.

MARK TWAIN

Samuel Langhorne Clemens

Born: Florida, Missouri; November 30, 1835
Died: Redding, Connecticut; April 21, 1910
Types of plot: Amateur sleuth; inverted

Contribution

Mark Twain is best known as the author of the quintessentially American novel *Adventures of Huckleberry Finn* (1884), the work from which, in Ernest Hemingway's judgment, all modern American writing derives and in which neither mystery nor detection plays any significant role. Of the novel's two murders, one, Pap Finn's, is quickly disposed of in the final page and the other, Huck's feigning his own death, is, for all the brilliance of the plan and the psychological resonance of the symbolic act of self-destruction, little more than the means by which Twain keeps his plot moving.

Because *Adventures of Huckleberry Finn* is in many ways not only Twain's finest work but also his most representative, it may appear that he holds little claim to a place in the history of mystery and detective fiction. Twain, however, demonstrated a deep interest in these particular literary forms over the course of his entire career. From the inquest in "Petrified Man" to his purest and most complete venture into the field, *Tom Sawyer, Detective* (1896), he adapted the conventions of these literary subgenres to his own purposes, aesthetic, and financial needs. His forays into mystery and detective fiction may therefore best be classified according to form and function: satirizing the forms themselves and certain social conditions, capitalizing on already popular (and therefore potentially profitable) literary formulas, and finding an appropriate vehicle for those melodramatic climaxes of which he was perhaps overfond. Not surprisingly for a writer who generally wrote without any plan in mind and whose episodic works often appear innocent of both plot and structure, the formal constraints of detective and mystery writing often proved too confining for Twain. However, for a writer obsessed with the question of mistaken identity, mystery and detective fiction held a certain attraction. Indeed, mistaken identity plays a central role in his posthumously published short story *A Murder, a Mystery, and a Marriage* (2001), which might be best seen as a parody of detective fiction.

Biography

Mark Twain was born Samuel Langhorne Clemens on November 30, 1835, in Florida, Missouri. Four years later, his family moved to Hannibal, Missouri, the fictionalized St. Petersburg of *Adventures of Huckleberry Finn* and Dawson's Landing of *The Tragedy of Pudd'nhead Wilson* (1894). As a youth, Twain learned the printer's trade, but in 1857 he fulfilled his boyhood dream of becoming a steamboat pilot, which he describes in "Old Times on the Mississippi" (1876) and *Life on the Mississippi* (1883). After the Civil War (1861-1865) ended commercial steamboat traffic on the Lower Mississippi River, he spent the next five years (1861-1866) as a miner and journalist in California and the Nevada Territory, an experience he later recounted in the highly fictionalized *Roughing It* (1872). It was during this period that he first used the pseudonym Mark Twain (a nautical term for two fathoms of water).

With the publication of "Jim Smiley and His Frog" (later republished as "The Celebrated Jumping Frog of Calaveras County") in New York's *The Saturday Press* in 1865, Twain came to national attention, not as a serious, respectable writer, however, but as a southwestern humorist. He traveled to the Sandwich Islands (Hawaii), lectured widely, and in 1867 he toured the Mediterranean and Holy Land, culling material for his masterwork of American-style humorous irreverence, *The Innocents Abroad* (1869).

Twain's marriage to Olivia Langdon, the daughter of a New York coal baron, in 1870, had a double effect. It not only provided him with the emotional and social stability he craved but also further accentuated the division in his own personality, the split between the frontier humorist whose work and person were not tolerated in polite company and the serious writer who longed for literary and social acceptance. Continuing to mine his own experiences for literary material, Twain produced his two best-known works, *The Adventures of Tom Sawyer* (1876) and *Adventures of Huckleberry Finn*. His business ventures during the 1880's and early 1890's, such as the formation of his own publishing firm, Charles L. Webster and Company, and his obsession with new inventions, especially the Paige automatic typesetter, brought about his bankruptcy in 1894.

Mark Twain. (Library of Congress)

From mid-1895 to mid-1896, Twain went on a lecture tour around the world in order to pay off his creditors in full. His behavior was a matter of personal obligation rather than legal necessity. Although by 1904 he was once again prosperous and celebrated, the memory of the earlier bankruptcy and the deaths of his wife and daughter darkened his final years and caused him to accentuate the pessimistic strain that had never been very far from the surface of even his most humorous work. His gloom, in particular his growing belief that human life was entirely determined and as entirely devoid of meaning, led him to suppress certain works that he believed were too shocking for publication and to leave others, including his "mysterious stranger" manuscripts, unfinished. "The Lincoln of our literature," as his friend William Dean Howells called him, died on April 21, 1910.

Analysis

As Mark Twain explains in his essay "How to Tell a Story," the art of the humorous tale relies more on how a story is told than what it tells, on its manner rather than its matter. Nowhere is this distinction clearer than in those Twain stories that depend heavily on mystery and detection, in which these literary forms meet Twain's particular use of southwestern humor and the oral tradition. In "A Ghost Story," for example, the particularly clumsy ghost of a petrified man known as the Cardiff Giant learns from the tale's narrator that he has been mistakenly haunting a plaster cast of himself on display in New York rather than the actual petrified figure on exhibit in Albany.

"The Great Landslide Case"

In another short piece, "The Great Landslide Case," a tall tale in *Roughing It*, Twain works a variation on the familiar squatter-and-the-tenderfoot plot. The tenderfoot in this instance is General Buncombe, the recently appointed United States attorney general to the Nevada Territory. Buncombe readily agrees to represent Dick Hyde, who seeks to "evict" Tom Morgan, whose farm has slid from the side of the mountain and now lies atop Hyde's farm to a depth of thirty-eight feet. The judge rules against Hyde, claiming that he has been deprived of his farm by a "visitation of God! And from this decision there is no appeal." Although Hyde may dig his farm out, if he so chooses, Buncombe is furious. His anger is so intense that it takes two months for him to realize that he has been the butt of the town's vast joke.

"A Dying Man's Confession"

Similarly structured but more intricately involved in its telling and less obvious in its humor, "A Dying Man's Confession," a story in *Life on the Mississippi*, is a tale-within-a-tale. The long inside narrative takes the form of a dying man's confession. Ritter, nightwatchman in a German charnel house, recounts to the frame tale's narrator the murder of his wife and child and how he tracked down the murderer and his accomplice (using the then-new science of fingerprinting) and took his revenge, only to discover years later that he has murdered the wrong man. As nightwatchman, Ritter has the satisfaction of seeing the right man die after having twice risen from the dead—once as a result of Ritter's mistake and again in the charnel house where the bodies of the dead are briefly kept to ensure that no one is buried alive. Against this grisly background, Twain sets the additional tale of Ritter's efforts to locate the murderer's secret loot and give it to the son of the man he mistakenly killed so many years ago. Ritter succeeds in finding where the money has been hidden—in Napoleon, Arkansas—and charges the frame tale's narrator with securing it for the murdered man's son.

Only as this "double-barreled" story draws to its close does the reader learn that he is Twain's victim. Aboard a Mississippi steamboat, the narrator finishes telling Ritter's tale to his two listeners; together they decide to split the money among themselves and, after much thought, to send the son "a chromo" (that is, a chromolithograph, an inexpensive colored picture). At this point, they (and the reader) learn that the town they seek has been swept away by one of the river's sudden shifts. The story's joke—or its "nub," as Twain termed it—is on them and, naturally, the reader.

"The Stolen White Elephant"

Twain's overturning or inverting of the conventions of mystery and detective fiction to suit the needs of his comic style and vision reaches a more satiric pitch in

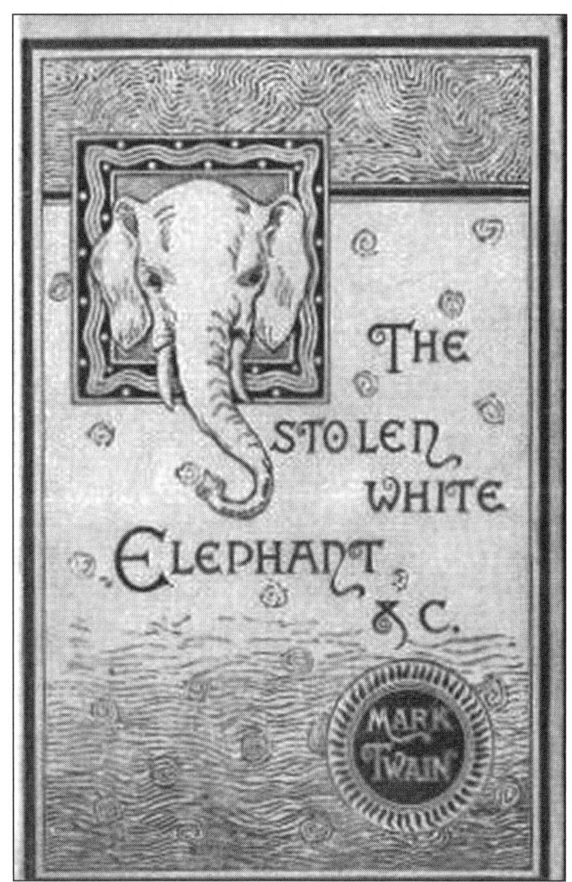

(Arkent Archive)

works such as "The Stolen White Elephant" and *A Double-Barrelled Detective Story* (1902). Like "The Great Landslide Case," the former story quickly telegraphs its comic intentions and settles down to the task at hand: ridiculing detective fiction in general and police detectives in particular. The police inspector's "instinct" triumphs over all the facts, including the discovery of the elephant, now dead, in the basement of police headquarters.

A Double-Barrelled Detective Story

First published in 1902, *A Double-Barrelled Detective Story* is a more intricately written burlesque. Far from being "probably the worst story Mark Twain ever wrote," as Everett Emerson has claimed, it provides some of the best evidence of Twain's parodic mastery of late nineteenth century detective fiction as practiced by Sir Arthur Conan Doyle. Especially noteworthy is the fact that Twain does not merely switch from the serious to the ludicrous, from convention to parody, or from mimetic illusion to the reader's disillusionment but oddly switches back and forth, repeatedly winning back the gullible reader's credence despite repeated flights into parodic absurdity. What begins as a rather compelling tale of offense taken and revenge given is soon doubled, with the second story quickly turning into farce. The vehicle of the wife's revenge on her husband is a son who literally rather than metaphorically embodies the traits of a bloodhound and who eventually discovers that he has been "hounding" the wrong man. Twain adds story to story, mystery to mystery until the original—and by this point virtually forgotten—narrative of the wife's revenge is at last resolved, with no thanks due either to the bloodhound son or Sherlock Holmes, whose arrival in a Nevada mining camp is simply one of the story's absurd givens. That Holmes becomes an accessory to murder at one point and at another accuses an innocent man of the deed on the basis that he is left-handed makes clear Twain's attitude toward Doyle's "pompous sentimental 'extraordinary man' and his cheap and ineffectual ingenuities."

As a committed realist, Twain had as little patience for the implausibilities of Doyle's stories and the posturings of that sham genius, Sherlock Holmes, as he had for the narrative inconsistencies he found in James Fenimore Cooper's fiction. He preferred the competence and common sense displayed by Tom Sawyer—not the character in *Adventures of Huckleberry Finn*, who prefers romance to reality, but the title character of his own earlier *The Adventures of Tom Sawyer* and of the later *Tom Sawyer, Detective*. The contrast in the structure of these two works and the relative greatness of the one coupled with the general obscurity of the other show the difficulty that a writer of Twain's temperament and writing habits might have in attempting to write a detective story. In *The Adventures of Tom Sawyer*, nearly one-third of the novel goes by before Tom and Huck witness the event that evokes most of the novel's most interesting action: Injun Joe's murder of Dr. Robinson and his blaming an unsuspecting Muff Potter. The internal conflict between the boys' fear of Injun Joe and their pangs of conscience as they witness the wrong man on trial culminates in Tom's heroic courtroom testimony (immediately followed by Injun Joe's escape). Another third of the novel then transpires before Twain resumes this narrative line and ends his novel on a note of high adventure that, like the plots of many of Twain's longer works, is as contrived as those discoveries of Sherlock Holmes that Twain loved to pillory.

Tom Sawyer, Detective

As *A Double-Barrelled Detective Story* constitutes one side of Twain's double-barreled response to the Holmes mania, *Tom Sawyer, Detective* represents the other. It is Twain's fullest and most serious attempt to capitalize on Holmes's popularity while managing to restrain both his satiric impulse and his own wayward imagination. It is, with "The Man That Corrupted Hadleyburg" (another of his longer though still not novel-length works), one of Twain's most tightly plotted and narrowly focused works, and perhaps for that reason one of his least successful and in many ways least representative. Read in the context of *Adventures of Huckleberry Finn* or *The Adventures of Tom Sawyer*, it seems slight; read as detective fiction, however, it takes on considerable power.

The narrator of *Tom Sawyer, Detective* is Huck Finn, not the Huck Finn who narrated his own earlier adventures and whose vernacular language and perspective play such an important role in that book, but a boy version of Dr. Watson to Tom Sawyer's Sherlock Holmes. Although the setting is that of the end of *Adventures of Huckleberry Finn*—the Phelps farm in Arkansas, about one year later—the plot is drawn from Steen Steenson Blicher's Danish murder mystery *Praesten i Vejlbye* (1829; *The Parson at Vejlby*). As Blicher weaves together his American materials and his Danish source, Twain weaves two stories of theft, murder, and revenge into a single mystery that points all too clearly to Tom's gentle but recently deranged Uncle Silas Phelps, whose delusions cause him to become his own worst accuser. Silas's lawyer is, like Wilhelm Meidling in Twain's later "The Chronicle of Young Satan" thoroughly incompetent. Proving Silas's innocence falls therefore entirely on Tom, whose legal status in the trial Twain takes pains to authenticate according to Arkansas law. Twain proves equally determined to demonstrate that the proof of Silas's innocence and therefore the solution to the mystery depends on nothing more than Tom's ability to see what is before him and to draw the simple conclusions that anyone (not simply a Sherlock Holmes) can draw—that, for example, a certain gesture may identify a man better than his clothing, hairstyle, or other physical description. What characterizes Tom Sawyer, detective, is therefore not any supernatural powers or intellectual genius but his native intelligence coupled with a very human desire for attention and fame and, like his creator, his love of melodrama.

Like the arrival of mysterious strangers in many of Twain's novels and stories, melodramatic courtroom scenes play an important role in several of his works: *The Adventures of Tom Sawyer*; *Tom Sawyer, Detective*; "The Chronicle of Young Satan"; *Personal Recollections of Joan of Arc* (1896); "The Great Landslide Case," in which the judicial process is burlesqued; *The Gilded Age* (1873), where it is made the vehicle for scathing social satire; and most significant, *The Tragedy of Pudd'nhead Wilson*.

The Tragedy of Pudd'nhead Wilson

If *Tom Sawyer, Detective* stands as Twain's most complete and most consistent work of detective fiction, then *The Tragedy of Pudd'nhead Wilson* stands as the work in which Twain makes the most interesting use of mystery and detection. In it, Twain transfers his own interest in scientific and pseudoscientific theories and inventions to David Wilson, a lawyer, whose intelligence, irony, and interest in palmistry and the new science of fingerprinting mark his distance from the other citizens of Dawson's Landing, where the shams and superstitions of the Cavalier South continue to reign. Thematically, the novel concerns the triumph of science over superstition, the modern over the medieval. More specifically, Twain uses fingerprinting not merely to expose the real murderer, but, more important, to expose the baselessness of the southern myth of the inherent supremacy of the white race.

Throughout his career, and in his later writings in particular, Twain makes clear his belief that no human trait is inherent, that everything is the result of training. Thus, in the novel's climactic courtroom scene, Wilson demonstrates not only that the murderer is Tom Driscoll but also that Tom is not the heir of the First Families of Virginia tradition. He is rather a black slave reared, which is to say trained, as a white man after being switched in the cradle with the child who is the rightful heir but who is now an illiterate black slave, again a result of training. (As for any difference in color, Twain points to the reality of miscegenation in southern life.) After suffering the town's jokes for twenty years, Wilson triumphs, as does the scientific spirit he represents. There is, however, little reason for the reader to rejoice, as there is in "Tom Sawyer, Detective," for while evil does not triumph, neither does good. What emerges is that sense of irony and cynicism that Wilson shares not only with his maker, Twain, but also with his progeny: the hard-boiled detectives of a later literary generation.

Robert A. Morace

Principal mystery and detective fiction

Novels: *The Tragedy of Pudd'nhead Wilson*, 1894; *Tom Sawyer, Detective*, 1896; *A Double-Barrelled Detective Story*, 1902; *Simon Wheeler, Detective*, 1963 (Franklin R. Rogers, editor); *A Murder, a Mystery, and a Marriage*, 2001 (Roy Blount, Jr., editor)

Short fiction: *The Stolen White Elephant, and Other Stories*, 1882

Other major works

Novels: *The Gilded Age*, 1873 (with Charles Dudley Warner); *The Adventures of Tom Sawyer*, 1876; *The Prince and the Pauper*, 1881; *Adventures of Huckleberry Finn*, 1884; *A Connecticut Yankee in King Arthur's Court*, 1889; *The American Claimant*, 1892; *Tom Sawyer Abroad*, 1894; *Personal Recollections of Joan of Arc*, 1896; *Extracts from Adam's Diary*, 1904; *A Horse's Tale*, 1906; *Eve's Diary, Translated from the Original Ms*, 1906; *Extract from Captain Stormfield's Visit to Heaven*, 1909; *The Mysterious Stranger*, 1916 (revised as *The Chronicle of Young Satan*, 1969, by Albert Bigelow Paine and Frederick A. Duneka); *Report from Paradise*, 1952 (Dixon Wecter, editor); *Mark Twain's Mysterious Stranger Manuscripts*, 1969 (William M. Gibson, editor)

Short fiction: *The Celebrated Jumping Frog of Calaveras County, and Other Sketches*, 1867; *Mark Twain's (Burlesque) Autobiography and First Romance*, 1871; *Mark Twain's Sketches: New and Old*, 1875; *Punch, Brothers, Punch! and Other Sketches*, 1878; *Merry Tales*, 1892; *The £1,000,000 Bank-Note, and Other New Stories*, 1893; *The Man That Corrupted Hadleyburg, and Other Stories and Essays*, 1900; *King Leopold's Soliloquy: A Defense of His Congo Rule*, 1905; *The $30,000 Bequest, and Other Stories*, 1906; *The Curious Republic of Gondour, and Other Whimsical Sketches*, 1919; *The Complete Short Stories of Mark Twain*, 1957 (Charles Neider, editor); *Letters from the Earth*, 1962; *Selected Shorter Writings of Mark Twain*, 1962; *Mark Twain's Satires and Burlesques*, 1967 (Franklin R. Rogers, editor); *Mark Twains's Which Was the Dream? and Other Symbolic Writings of the Later Years*, 1967 (John S. Tuckey, editor); *Mark Twain's Hannibal, Huck and Tom*, 1969 (Walter Blair, editor); *Mark Twain's Fables of Man*, 1972 (Tuckey, editor); *Life as I Find It*, 1977 (Neider, editor); *Early Tales and Sketches*, 1979-1981 (2 volumes; Edgar Marquess Branch and Robert H. Hirst, editors)

Plays: *Colonel Sellers*, pr., pb. 1874 (adaptation of his novel *The Gilded Age*); *Ah Sin*, pr. 1877 (with Bret Harte); *Is He Dead? A Comedy in Three Acts*, pb. 2003 (Shelley Fisher Fishkin, editor)

Nonfiction: *The Innocents Abroad*, 1869; *Roughing It*, 1872; *A Tramp Abroad*, 1880; *Life on the Mississippi*, 1883; *Following the Equator*, 1897 (also known as *More Tramp Abroad*); *How to Tell a Story, and Other Essays*, 1897; *My Début as a Literary Person*, 1903; *What Is Man?*, 1906; *Christian Science*, 1907; *Is Shakespeare Dead?*, 1909; *Mark Twain's Speeches*, 1910 (Albert Bigelow Paine, editor); *Europe and Elsewhere*, 1923 (Paine, editor); *Mark Twain's Autobiography*, 1924 (2 volumes; Paine, editor); *Mark Twain's Notebook*, 1935 (Paine, editor); *Letters from the Sandwich Islands, Written for the Sacramento Union*, 1937 (G. Ezra Dane, editor); *Mark Twain in Eruption*, 1940 (Bernard DeVoto, editor); *Mark Twain's Travels with Mr. Brown*, 1940 (Franklin Walker and G. Ezra Dane, editors); *Mark Twain to Mrs. Fairbanks*, 1949 (Wecter, editor); *The Love Letters of Mark Twain*, 1949 (Dixon Wecter, editor); *Mark Twain of the Enterprise: Newspaper Articles and Other Documents, 1862-1864*, 1957 (Henry Nash Smith and Frederick Anderson, editors); *Traveling with the Innocents Abroad: Mark Twain's Original Reports from Europe and the Holy Land*, 1958 (Daniel Morley McKeithan, editor; letters); *Mark Twain-Howells Letters: The Correspondence of Samuel L. Clemens and William D. Howells, 1872-1910*, 1960 (Smith and William M. Gibson, editors); *The Autobiography of Mark Twain*, 1961 (Neider, editor); *Mark Twain's Letters to His Publishers, 1867-1894*, 1967 (Hamlin Hill, editor); *Clemens of the Call: Mark Twain in San Francisco*, 1969 (Edgar M. Branch, editor); *Mark Twain's Correspondence with Henry Huttleston Rogers, 1893-1909*, 1969 (Lewis Leary, editor); *A Pen Warmed-Up in Hell: Mark Twain in Protest*, 1972; *Mark Twain's Notebooks and Journals*, 1975-1979 (3 volumes); *Mark Twain Speaking*, 1976 (Paul Fatout, editor); *Mark Twain Speaks for Himself*, 1978 (Fatout, editor); *Mark Twain's Letters*, 1988-2002 (6 volumes; Edgar Marquess Branch, et al, editors); *Mark Twain's Own Autobiography: The Chapters from the "North American Review,"* 1990 (Michael J. Kiskis, editor); *Mark Twain's Aquarium: The Samuel Clemens Angelfish Correspondence, 1905-1910*, 1991 (John Cooley, editor); *Mark Twain: The Complete Interviews*, 2006 (Gary Scharnhorst, editor)

Miscellaneous: *The Writings of Mark Twain*, 1922-1925 (37 volumes); *The Portable Mark Twain*,

1946 (Bernard De Voto, editor); *Collected Tales, Sketches, Speeches, and Essays, 1853-1891*, 1992 (Louis J. Budd, editor); *Collected Tales, Sketches, Speeches, and Essays, 1891-1910*, 1992 (Budd, editor)

Bibliography

Camfield, Gregg. *The Oxford Companion to Mark Twain*. New York: Oxford University Press, 2003. Collection of essays, including several by other scholars, on diverse aspects of Twain's life and writing, with encyclopedia reference features. Includes a three-page entry on detective stories. Indexed.

Emerson, Everett. *Mark Twain: A Literary Life*. Philadelphia: University of Pennsylvania Press, 2000. Complete revision of Emerson's *The Authentic Mark Twain* (1984), this masterful study traces the development of Twain's writing against the events in his life and provides illuminating discussions of many individual works, including the mystery and detective stories discussed here. Indexed.

Horn, Jason Gary. *Mark Twain: A Descriptive Guide to Biographical Sources*. Lanham, Md.: Scarecrow Press, 1999. Richly annotated bibliography of nearly three hundred books and other sources on Mark Twain, including many works of criticism.

LeMaster, J. R., and James D. Wilson, eds. *The Mark Twain Encyclopedia*. New York: Garland, 1993. Comprehensive reference work broadly similar in organization to Rasmussen's *Critical Companion to Mark Twain*, differing in devoting most of its space to literary analysis. Includes a long entry by Don L. F. Nilsen on detective fiction.

Messent, Peter B. *Mark Twain*. New York: St. Martin's Press, 1997. A standard introduction to Twain's life and works. Provides bibliographical references and an index.

Rasmussen, R. Kent. *Bloom's How to Write About Mark Twain*. New York: Chelsea House, 2008. Practical guide to writing student essays on Mark Twain, with numerous general and specific suggestions on his major novels. Contains a general introduction to writing on Mark Twain and chapters on ten individual works, including *Pudd'n head Wilson*. Each chapter has a lengthy bibliography.

________. *Critical Companion to Mark Twain*. New York: Facts On File, 2007. Revised and much expanded edition of *Mark Twain A to Z* (1995), which covered virtually every character, theme, place, and biographical fact relating to Mark Twain and contained the most complete chronology ever compiled. Among new features in this retitled edition are lengthy critical essays on Twain's major works, including all the mystery and detective stories discussed here; an extensive, annotated bibliography; and a glossary of unusual words in Mark Twain's writings. Indexed.

Twain, Mark. *The Stolen White Elephant, and Other Detective Stories*, edited by Shelley Fisher Fishkin. New York: Oxford University Press, 1996. Omnibus volume containing facsimile reprints of the first American editions of *The Stolen White Elephant, and Other Stories* (1882), *Tom Sawyer, Detective* (1896), and *A Double-Barrelled Detective Story* (1902). Part of the twenty-nine-volume Oxford Mark Twain edition, this volume also includes a new introduction by mystery writer Walter Mosley and an analytical afterword by scholar Lillian S. Robinson.

U

ARTHUR W. UPFIELD

Born: Gosport, Hampshire, England; September 1, 1888
Died: Bowral, New South Wales, Australia; February 13, 1964
Type of plot: Police procedural

Principal series

Napoleon "Bony" Bonaparte, 1929-1966

Principal series character

Detective Inspector Napoleon "Bony" Bonaparte of the Queensland Police is half white and half Aborigine. Bony has a master's degree from Brisbane University; he combines Western intelligence with an Aboriginal instinct. Married to a half-caste, Marie, he has three sons. Handsome and a fine dresser, he can assume various identities to solve a mystery. Bony is respectful of the police, as he is of his suspects. He is characteristically patient, working at a snail's pace to unravel the most difficult of crimes.

Contribution

Arthur W. Upfield's originality comes mainly from two sources. One is his firsthand acquaintance with the whole of the Australian landscape, not only the towns, lakes, deserts, and mountains but also the infinite variety of fauna and flora that populate the continent. His readers can draw a map of Australia and place a particular crime. Upfield had Ernest Hemingway's eye for detail and could bring alive the smallest incident peculiar to a certain area. Second is his vivid, totally believable characterization of Napoleon Bonaparte, who appears in most of his more than thirty novels. Bony can assume various characters, from swagman to deep-sea fisherman, depending on the place, to "get his man." He also understands the different cultures in Australia and can mediate between them to restore order. Critics see the Americans James Fenimore Cooper and Herman Melville as models for Upfield's humanism, symbolism, and rhetorical skills.

Biography

Arthur William Upfield was born on September 1, 1888, in Gosport, England, to James Oliver Upfield and Annie Barmore Upfield, who ran a drapery business. The eldest of five sons, he was reared largely by his grandmother and her two sisters. Suffering from bronchitis, he was often confined to bed, where he learned to read voraciously, and at sixteen he had written the first of three novels.

Upfield's father wanted his son to be a real estate surveyor, but when Arthur failed the test, he sent the boy to Australia. Though he started working on a farm, and then as a hotel cook, Upfield finally achieved his dream as a boundary rider along the fences of a huge sheep farm in Momba, Victoria, an experience that gave him firsthand knowledge of Australia's bush country and its abundant wildlife.

Overcome by loneliness, the young man returned by bike with his dog to New South Wales, where he exchanged his bike for a boat to pursue an idyllic existence on the Darling River. His traveling, as well as his experiences as a cattle drover, rabbit trapper, and horse trainer, enabled him to meet many of the strange characters he would describe in his novels.

In 1915, Upfield was married to a nurse, Anne Douglas, and had a son, Arthur Douglas, though his marriage soon failed. He joined the Australian Imperial Force in 1924, serving for five years in Gallipoli, the Egyptian desert, and France. Again he returned to Australia to trap and mine, concluding, "my life was influenced by sheep, cattle, riding camels, war, women, gold, opals, delirium tremens, and, fortunately, Mary."

Mary and Angus owned a sheep farm, and virtually

became Upfield's parents. They encouraged him to write what eventually became his first "Bony" novel, *The Barrakee Mystery* (1929). Most important, however, was Leon Wood, a trapper who, according to Upfield, "taught me to read the Book of the Bush. He revealed the eternal war within himself, as an example to me."

Apart from his novels, Upfield wrote articles on the topography and history of Australia, publishing some before World War I in the London *Daily Mail*. In the 1920's he also wrote stories for *Novel Magazine* and various articles for *Wide World Magazine*. He was elected justice of the peace in 1935, and in 1948 headed a party of experts on a six-thousand-mile expedition to northern and western Australia for the Australian Geographic Society.

Upfield died in Bowral, New South Wales, on February 13, 1964, at the age of seventy-five. Between 1929 and his death in 1964 he completed more than thirty novels. J. L. Price and Dorothy Strange completed and revised his final work, *The Lake Frome Monster* (1966).

Arthur W. Upfield.

Analysis

As an adolescent living with his grandmother in England, Arthur W. Upfield, under the name "Arker-William" Upfield, wrote several lengthy manuscripts—his unpublished Yellow Peril series. After his father sent him to Australia, he wandered the continent for twenty years doing odd jobs before attempting his first serious novel, *The Barrakee Mystery*, at the instigation of friends. The book lacked focus, however, so Upfield attempted a straight thriller, *The House of Cain* (1928), but his characters were still flat and the theme melodramatic. Then, while working as a cook at Wheeler's Well in New South Wales, Upfield stopped to talk to Leon Wood, a tracker with whom he had spent five months patrolling hundreds of miles of fence as a boundary rider. This incident enabled Upfield to give focus and direction to his life as a crime and mystery writer.

The Barrakee Mystery

Wood's father was white and his mother Aborigine. Intelligent and widely read, he gave Upfield a copy of a biography of Napoleon Bonaparte. Using Leon as a model, Upfield then created the main protagonist for most of his thirty-odd novels, Detective Inspector Napoleon "Bony" Bonaparte of the Queensland Police. Upfield then rewrote *The Barrakee Mystery* around Bony, and his career as a mystery writer began. Bony would be his detective hero, and the Australian landscape he knew so well would constitute the background for his entire fictional world.

Upfield, who claimed Hemingway as his favorite author, was fascinated by everything he saw, and he saw the whole of Australia. In *Bony and the White Savage* (1961) and *The Widows of Broome* (1950), he wrote about western Australia; he wrote about an area near the Northern Territory in *The Will of the Tribe* (1962), Queensland in *The Bone Is Pointed* (1938), and many sites in and around New South Wales, including the ocean off the southeastern coast in *The Mystery of Swordfish Reef* (1939). Upfield's style reflects Hemingway's simple vocabulary and sense of the concrete world. Of Upfield Betty Donaldson says, "When he describes a forest fire we can feel the heat, hear the crackle of the flames and sense the terror and desperation of the fleeing animals."

Though he works within the conventions of the classical detective story, which require certain presuppositions about society, law, and morality that are distinctively English, Upfield introduces a certain originality into the genre by examining the relationship between different cultures. In Australia these are the modern, urban culture of the coastal regions, the white culture of the Outback (diverse in national backgrounds), and the ancient Aboriginal culture in various stages of assimilation into the dominant white culture.

In Upfield's novels, Detective Napoleon Bonaparte mediates the interaction of these cultures. Himself a half-caste, he is able to represent the customs, beliefs, and powers of Aboriginal culture. Yet as the agent of a national police authority, Bony also represents the thrust of modernization with its centralized authority, bureaucratic administration, and hierarchy of educated expertise. He uses his Aboriginal intuition and civilized authority to penetrate the truth of crime and restore the harmony of society disrupted by violence.

As a detective writer, Upfield is less a social novelist than one rooted in nature, and critics compare his literary skills to those of Cooper and Melville because the natural world, so vast and powerful, must somehow be transcended or overcome. Like Cooper's Natty Bumppo, Bony represents the best in the primitive and civilized worlds, but unlike Cooper's mythic hero, Bony is real, down-to-earth, as arrogant as he is sensitive to others. Upfield lacks the full epic range of Melville, but he approaches such a scope through his use of the Australian terrain, and, like Ishmael, Bony is a humanist in his knowledge of and respect for all peoples. Upfield's rhetorical skills are not unlike Melville's in *Moby Dick* (1851), for his taste for similes and extended metaphors gives his work unmistakable intensity and depth. Like Melville, Upfield is also a symbolist, applying symbolism to both the civilized world, through the airplane in *Bushranger of the Skies* (1940), and the natural landscape, in novels such as *The Beach of Atonement* (1930), *Death of a Lake* (1954), and *The Mountains Have a Secret* (1948).

Bony Buys a Woman

Among Upfield's novels, one of the most successful is *Bony Buys a Woman* (1957), set in the very heart of Australia near Lake Eyre, sixty miles wide and one hundred miles long. The book centers on the murder of a white woman, Mrs. Bell, and the abduction of her daughter Linda, who is taken to the center of the dried-up lake by Ole Fren Yorky. It begins:

> The day was the 7th of February, and it was just another day to Linda Bell. Of course, the sun was blazing hot at six in the morning, another morning when the wind sprang up long before six and was a half-gale when the sun rose. It sang when crossing the sandy ground, roared farewell as it sped through the line of pine trees guarding the Mount Eden homestead from the sprawling giant called Lake Eyre.

Here the writing, with the introduction of a child and the music of the wind near a small city in the outback, is (like Hemingway's) simple and direct. Yet through personification and metaphor—the wind "sprang up" and "roared" as the trees guard the supposedly paradisaical town from a "sprawling giant"—the author also hints at the terror to come. Before long Upfield will bring that dead lake alive, personifying local windstorms, called "willi-willies," as a way of populating this desert area; then he makes the area the center of the action symbolic of the tenuous condition of humankind.

Yorky, who retreats with Linda to an island in the middle of dried-up Lake Eyre, called "The Sea That Was," is unaware that he has been framed and remains loyal to the murderer. The Aborigines under King Canute will not pursue Yorky because of their loyalty to him, a "white blackfeller," and their regard for the child. Bony in detective-like fashion examines all the clues (such as artificial footprints) and asks pertinent questions to determine that Yorky is not guilty, but his true genius comes from his ability to represent the white notion of justice while relating to all races, thus penetrating the complex of loyalities that shield the murderer. Old King Canute, with his childlike dialogue, attitude, and storytelling, is an interesting parallel to the young Linda Bell, whose presence pervades the novel. Bony, himself part Aborigine, identifies with Canute as Natty Bumppo does with the Indians in Cooper's Leatherstocking Tales; he speaks Canute's simple language, negotiating forty plugs of tobacco for Yorky's daughter as his gift to her lover, Charlie.

She, in turn, helps Bony communicate with Yorky on the island. Then the ground begins to move under their feet, and they are "pinned like specimens" by the real murderer about to erase all the evidence of his guilt.

In the tradition of Melville, Upfield is able to turn that ground into a metaphor for life itself, and the lake bottom takes on the significance of Melville's sea. Says Yorky:

> Yair, that's it. I've never seen it before, but the abos have a name for it. It's a low sort of swell and the sun's glinting on it along one slope, like a water wave. Old Canute told me about it. The water keeps pushing into the mud, and instead of running over the top of the mud, it comes up from under.

With crows and swooping eagles overhead, the whole situation resembles a Greek play—Euripides torn by the Furies, but Bony, never losing control, maintains his identity with others as well as his individual optimism:

> You and I are merely animated shells crammed with fears, inhibitions, humility and pride. What white people might name courage is in us instinctive revolt against the abyss for ever opening at our feet. We must not fail. We dare not think of failure. So we must go on, even if we have to travel right across this abominable lake.

Here Upfield gives the terrain semiepic scope, while Bony, again instinctively in tune with the environment and the Aboriginal temperament, uses his modern psychological skills and characteristic determination to move forward.

The lake, therefore, is central to the drama, and takes on moral and mythical significance integrated with the movement of the story. It is a landscape, however, that is always related to the ingenuity of the central character—a character who never acts alone. Presently, Charlie (who made dolls for Linda) appears to help Bony "bonk" the murderer, much as Yorky's daughter helped him relate to Yorky; the marriage of these two "abos" signals the restoration of order in the end. Thus Bony, loving yet firm, understanding yet decisive, is able to mediate between the races, expose the criminal, and restore the fragile fabric of society threatened by the murder. Indeed, through this half-caste detective, Upfield balances the old with the young, the primitive with the modern, and communal living with individual action in a moving and convincing story of the Australian Outback—far removed from civilization, but somehow symbolic of life in the twentieth century.

Thomas Matchie

Principal mystery and detective fiction

Napoleon Bonaparte series: *The Barrakee Mystery*, 1929 (also known as *The Lure of the Bush*); *The Sands of Windee*, 1931; *Wings Above the Diamantina*, 1936 (also known as *Winged Mystery* and *Wings Above the Claypan*); *Mr. Jelly's Business*, 1937 (also known as *Murder Down Under*); *Wind of Evil*, 1937; *The Bone Is Pointed*, 1938; *The Mystery of Swordfish Reef*, 1939; *Bushranger of the Skies*, 1940 (also known as *No Footprints in the Bush*); *Death of a Swagman*, 1945; *The Devil's Steps*, 1946; *An Author Bites the Dust*, 1948; *The Mountains Have a Secret*, 1948; *The Bachelors of Broken Hill*, 1950; *The Widows of Broome*, 1950; *The New Shoe*, 1951; *Venom House*, 1952; *Murder Must Wait*, 1953; *Death of a Lake*, 1954; *Cake in a Hat Box*, 1954 (also known as *Sinister Stones*); *The Battling Prophet*, 1956; *The Man of Two Tribes*, 1956; *Bony Buys a Woman*, 1957 (also known as *The Bushman Who Came Back*); *Bony and the Black Virgin*, 1959; *Bony and the Mouse*, 1959 (also known as *Journey to the Hangman*); *Bony and the Kelly Gang*, 1960 (also known as *Valley of Smugglers*); *Bony and the White Savage*, 1961 (also known as *The White Savage*); *The Will of the Tribe*, 1962; *Madman's Bend*, 1963 (also known as *The Body at Madman's Bend*); *The Lake Frome Monster*, 1966 (with J. L. Price and Dorothy Strange)

Nonseries novels: *The House of Cain*, 1928; *The Beach of Atonement*, 1930; *A Royal Abduction*, 1932; *Gripped by Drought*, 1932

Bibliography

Asdell, Philip T. *A Provisional Descriptive Bibliography of First Editions of the Works of Arthur W. Upfield*. Frederick, Md.: P. T. Asdell, 1984. Attempts to list all first editions of Upfield's work in the United States, England, and Australia.

Browne, Ray B. "The Frontier Heroism of Arthur W. Upfield." *Clues: A Journal of Detection* 7 (Spring/Summer, 1986): 127-145. Detailed article focused on the setting (both social and geographic) of Upfield's mysteries.

_______. *The Spirit of Australia: The Crime Fiction of Arthur W. Upfield*. Bowling Green, Ohio: Bowling Green State University Popular Press, 1988. Reads Upfield's fiction as distinctively Australian and expressive of the essential spirit of the author's adopted nation.

Donaldson, Betty. "Arthur William Upfield: September 1, 1888-February 13, 1964." *The Armchair Detective* 8, no. 1 (November, 1974): 1-11. Memorial tribute to Upfield and evaluation of his work.

Hausladen, Gary. *Places for Dead Bodies*. Austin: University of Texas Press, 2000. This study of the settings of mystery and detective novels includes a section on the Australian Outback of Upfield.

Hawke, Jessica. *Follow My Dust! A Biography of Arthur Upfield*. London: Heinemann, 1957. Hawke's biography begins with an introduction written from the point of view of Inspector Bonaparte.

Knight, Stephen. *Continent of Mystery: A Thematic History of Australian Crime Fiction*. Melbourne, Vic.: Melbourne University Press, 1997. Study of the dominant themes and concerns distinctive to the crime fiction of Australia. Sheds light on Upfield's work. Bibliographic references and index.

Nile, Richard. *The Making of the Australian Literary Imagination*. St. Lucia: University of Queensland Press, 2002. Discussion of prevalent features of Australian writing and the cultural and geographic influences on the continent's literary history. Provides background for understanding Upfield's work.

JONATHAN VALIN

Born: Cincinnati, Ohio; November 23, 1948
Types of plot: Hard-boiled; private investigator

Principal series

Harry Stoner, 1980-

Principal series character

Harry Stoner, a private investigator, is a Vietnam War veteran and a lifelong resident of Cincinnati, where he was for a time attached to the office of the district attorney. At the beginning of the series, he is thirty-seven years old and single. While he is often annoyed by the smugness of what he calls the Cincinnati Puritans, he admits that he is a moralist, so angered by the drug-ridden, brutal society of the 1980's that he often runs deadly risks to protect its victims.

Contribution

Like his predecessors Dashiell Hammett and Raymond Chandler, Jonathan Valin has created a hard-living, wisecracking, but essentially admirable private investigator. Valin's Harry Stoner solves mysteries that the police are unable or reluctant to handle, often because the wrongdoers—though not always wealthy or influential themselves—have links to the rich and powerful. In the tradition of Hammett and Chandler, Valin writes in a straightforward, colloquial style. Like the earlier writers of the hard-boiled school, he is compassionate toward characters who despite their human frailties, occasionally rise to heights of courage and concern. Valin differs from the earlier writers of this school in his greater emphasis on sexual perversion, drug addiction, and graphic, sadistic violence. Clearly, he sees these elements as characteristic of the decadent, corrupt American society of the 1980's and 1990's, in which Harry Stoner must wage his lonely wars. Popularly and critically acclaimed for his fiction—winning a Shamus Award for *Extenuating Circumstances* (1989), garnering a Shamus nomination for *Second Chance* (1991), and named top vote-getter in an informal 2006 *Rap Sheet* poll asking which series readers would most like to see continued—Jonathan Valin has since 1995 eschewed fiction for nonfiction. Currently a contributing editor to *The Absolute Sound*, an audiophile periodical, Valin is considered an authority on contemporary upper-range stereo equipment and on classical musical recordings.

Biography

Jonathan Louis Valin was born on November 23, 1948, in Cincinnati, where he has spent most of his life. His parents were Sigmund Valin and Marcella Fink Valin. Valin married poet Katherine Brockhaus in 1971. He was educated at the University of Chicago, where he received a masters of arts in 1974. Following two years as a lecturer in English at the University of Cincinnati (1974-1976), he pursued doctoral studies and taught creative writing at Washington University in St. Louis (1976-1979).

After winning the 1978 Norma Lowry Memorial Fund Prize for his short story, "Replay," Valin became a full-time writer. He published his first two mystery novels—*The Lime Pit* and *Final Notice*—in 1980. Both books, like all of Valin's novels, concerned former police officer turned private detective Harry Stoner. Modeled on such hard-boiled private eyes as Sam Spade, Philip Marlowe, and Lew Archer, Stoner is based in Cincinnati. More than simply a wisecracking tough guy, Stoner is a sensitive music-loving loner who typically takes on cases involving missing persons or suspicious deaths, often becoming entangled in middle-class family relationships that have fragmented.

The Stoner novels, thanks to their action-packed, often violent plots, complex characters, and well-drawn settings in and around Cincinnati, gained a loyal readership. Valin responded by adding to the series on a regular basis, releasing *Dead Letter* (1981), *Day of Wrath* (1982), and *Natural Causes* (1983). After a hiatus of several years, the author again continued the series with *Life's Work* (1986), and added five more entries, including the Shamus Award-winning *Extenuating Circumstances*, the Shamus-nominated *Second Chance*, and *Missing* (1995). During the same time period, Valin also contributed "Malibu Tag Team" to the anthology *Raymond Chandler's Philip Marlowe* (1988) and "Loser Takes All" to *The Armchair Detective* (1991).

In the early 1990's, Valin began moving away from the detective novel—he felt he had begun to repeat himself and had nothing new to add to the private investigator genre—and toward a different longtime interest, music. This is reflected in *The Music Lovers* (1993) and in the nonfictional book he released in the same year: *Living Stereo: The RCA Bible, a Compendium of Opinion on RCA Living Stereo Records*, considered the definitive guide to the Living Stereo classical recordings made between 1958 and 1964.

In the mid-1990's, Valin fully committed to his new fascination by cofounding a magazine devoted to music criticism and stereo equipment reviews, *Fi* (short for hi-fi). The magazine lasted four years, then Valin became senior writer and executive editor for *The Absolute Sound*, frequently contributing reviews of high-end audio equipment for that magazine and reviews of sophisticated video equipment for its companion publication, *The Perfect Vision*. He also occasionally writes for "Cincinnati CityBeat" a column describing attractions in the Queen City, and wrote the foreword for Thomas R. Schiff's *Panoramic Cincinnati* (1999), describing 360-degree photos of the city taken with a Hulcherama panoramic camera. Valin has stated that he does not plan to return to detective Harry Stoner, despite winning a *Rap Sheet* online poll as the mystery writer readers would most like to continue an established series.

Analysis

Unlike more leisurely traditional mysteries, Jonathan Valin's hard-hitting mystery-adventure stories do not begin with the exploration of character or the creation of atmosphere. Instead, they jump into action almost immediately when private investigator Harry Stoner is hired for a specific task, usually finding a missing person or investigating a death.

Although Stoner accepts whatever case is offered, he is often suspicious of the person who hired him, and his suspicions often prove to be justified. In *The Lime Pit*, for example, Hugo Cratz telephones to ask Stoner to look for his little girl. Charitably, Stoner agrees, but instead of a child, the missing girl proves to be a prostitute with dangerous associates. In *Final Notice*, *Dead Letter*, *Natural Causes*, and *Life's Work*, it is prosperous, respectable individuals who hire Stoner: a librarian, a scientist, a corporate representative, and a professional football executive. As Stoner soon discovers, however, none of these clients has told him the complete truth; one, the scientist in *Dead Letter*, is a Machiavellian villain who intends to use Stoner to cover up past misdeeds and to facilitate future murders.

Realizing that even his employers have not leveled with him, Stoner remains skeptical of everyone he interviews, because he is intent on deducing the truth and because his own survival depends on it. If he trusts the wrong person, he may be led into a trap. In *Fire Lake* (1987), Stoner trusts and helps a former college roommate, Lonnie "Jack" Jackowski—now a psychologically unstable drug addict, with criminal connections—and nearly loses his life.

In all Valin's mysteries, his detective's relationship with a woman helps build and sustain suspense. By nature, Stoner is chivalrous. Sometimes he is called a male chauvinist by liberated women such as young Kate Davis (*Final Notice*), who eventually must admit that she can use Stoner's help and that her brown belt in karate may not be enough to protect her from a well-armed psychopathic killer. Stoner worries about her, and he worries even more because she is impulsive, inexperienced, and unlikely to spot a trap. In *Dead Letter*, much of the suspense involves Sarah Lovingwell, whose insistence that her scientist father is a murderer naturally arouses Stoner's protective instincts. However, he cannot believe both Sarah's story and the well-respected professor's plausible account of Sarah's emotional instability. To arrive at the truth, Stoner must suppress his own chivalric instincts. At the end of the book, although he has exposed the vil-

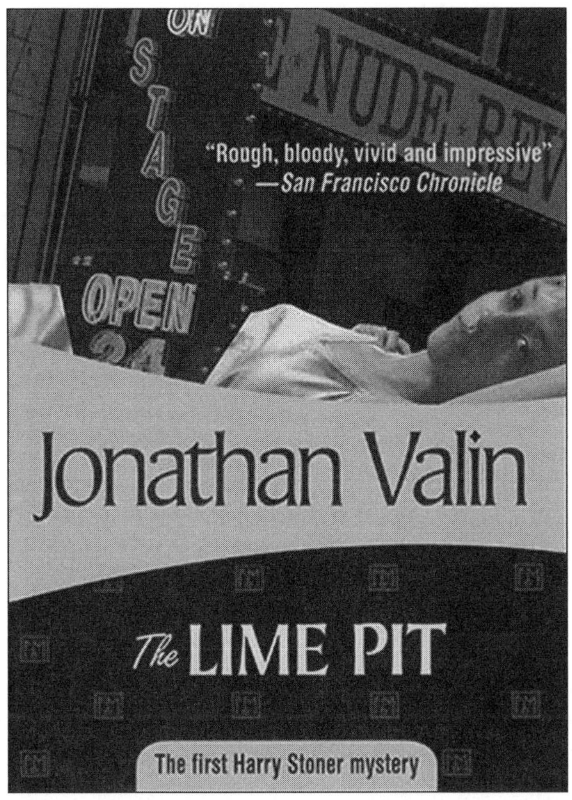

lainous professor, Stonger has lingering doubts about Sarah—he is certain she outsmarted him.

Valin's readers and critics praise the realism of his settings. Although all of his novels are set partially or wholly in Cincinnati, in each Valin creates a different environment, varying from the library setting of *Final Notice* and the football locker rooms and bars of *Life's Work* to the sordid haunts of pimps, prostitutes, and addicts in *The Lime Pit* and *Fire Lake*.

When Valin takes his detective from the slums to the luxurious homes and offices of his employers and their friends, the description of setting becomes ironic, since some of the rich and powerful are deeply involved in criminal activities, often drug related. The furniture may be different, but the corruption is the same. To discover the secret of that corruption and with it the secret of the murder, Stoner must resist the trappings of wealth, just as he must resist the blandishments of beautiful but evil women.

Though Stoner is a large, imposing specimen, there is a David-and-Goliath element in all his adventures: He must always face superior forces—officials, police officers, businessmen, drug lords, and their minions. When such Goliaths arrange the elimination of the little people who get in their way, Stoner must avenge the victims. In *The Lime Pit*, it is a young girl casually killed in a sexual orgy; in *Natural Causes*, it is a Mexican mother and child tortured and knifed. Whenever someone defenseless suffers, Stoner becomes a killing machine.

Most of Valin's characters, however, are ordinary people, neither all good nor all bad. Although Jackowski of *Fire Lake* is a junkie and a thief, even the wife who kicked him out knows that he is too gentle to have committed murder. In *Life's Work*, a hostile, brutal football player becomes Stoner's friend and dies in a heroic attempt to rescue a fellow player. Although one police officer in that novel is evil, recurring character Lieutenant Al Foster is a decent man; George DeVries, of the district attorney's office, though corrupt, is often helpful to Stoner.

Much as Stoner loathes the sadistic characters he encounters—whom he kills without compunction—he reserves hatred for the manipulators behind the sadists. When he confronts them, Stoner is capable of a merciless execution, as when he shoots Red Bannion and lets him burn in the dramatic finale of *The Lime Pit*.

The graphic descriptions of violence in Valin's novels may prove too much for squeamish readers. Yet Valin has a sense of humor—in *Life's Work*, he describes a preacher: "Like most evangelists, he looked as if he'd been dressed by his mother." Because all the novels are written in first person, it is the sensitive, observant Stoner who comments on society, who notices, for example, that the relatively innocent drug-sharing friendships of the 1960's no longer exist. Drug lords of the 1980's have their addicts trained to kill on command, Stoner muses in *Fire Lake*. There are no friendships in the biggest business in the United States.

In the corrupt society of Valin's novels, Stoner constantly tries to resist evil, both in his violent world and within himself. His code is simple: He will protect the weak; he will be true to friends; and he will seek the truth and conceal it only when telling it would harm the innocent. Although he has no objection to casual sex, he never treats partners with contempt, and it is clear that he continues to hope for a permanent relationship. Against the background of decadence, greed, and violence, Stoner carries Valin's central theme: Even in modern society, good people can and must defy the evil that surrounds them.

Natural Causes

Natural Causes is Valin at his best. Like his other novels, it begins in Cincinnati when Jack Moon, a representative of a soap company that sponsors television shows, hires Stoner. In the initial scene, a major Valin theme is suggested. Although the soap company emphasizes the purity of its product and its image, its sponsored television show deals with alcoholics, drug addicts, and nymphomaniacs. Stoner is hired to look into the death of the chief writer of the popular serial *Phoenix*—a death that occurred, ironically, when the victim, Quentin Dover, was taking a shower.

As Stoner investigates, he finds things are not squeaky clean in the kingdom of soap. Dover's wife is a brainless, promiscuous alcoholic, who sold her self-respect for a luxurious lifestyle. A brilliant writer, Dover was addicted to alcohol and drugs, and there are rumors he had become incapable of writing and was facing termination. Dover's business associates in Los Angeles, apparently concerned and compassionate, testify against one another in their greed and ruthless pursuit of power.

If illusion is the stuff of soap operas, lies are the tool of their makers, indeed, of everyone in Southern California, Valin suggests. Police officer Sy Goldblum is typical. He looks like a film-star version of a police officer, but he is not who he seems to be. He started life as Seymour Wattle from Butte, Montana, and took a Jewish name hoping it would help him in Los Angeles. Sy is helpful to Stoner, but only when the fee is set in advance; as Sy's callous description of the dead body indicates, he has neither compassion nor interest in justice. His only motivation for finding the person responsible for Dover's death is the money he can make by helping Stoner.

Another reflection of the theme of illusion and deception is the fact that Dover always lied about his past—he never told the same story twice. To the detective, trying to arrive at the truth, Dover's habit of making his own history as fictional as the scripts he outlined makes the investigation difficult: Dover's deliberate concealment of the activities of his final weekend only makes it harder for Stoner to solve the mystery of his death.

In this novel, Valin again dramatizes his belief that cold-blooded, prosperous leaders of society are willing to victimize the poor and unknown. Dover became involved in large-scale drug operations because he had gone dry as a writer and preferred to risk the lives of unimportant people than reduce his own standard of living. He was willing to join the drug trade to get a manuscript he could pretend to have written. As a result of his actions, one Hispanic family is murdered, and a ranch foreman faces imprisonment. At the end of the novel, the evil deeds of the wealthy hypocrites have been exposed, with Stoner acting as the instrument of justice; as in other Valin novels, they have been killed, committed suicide, or face prison terms.

Nevertheless, there is only an approximation of justice. Too many innocent people, such as Maria Sanchez and her child, have died along the way, and too many individuals who are basically decent, such as the ranch foreman and Jack Moon, are punished out of proportion to their offenses.

Finally, even Stoner himself must live with guilt, for in *Natural Causes* many of the deaths that occur are a direct result of his investigations. In an imperfect world, Valin believes, the burden of evil falls on the innocent and the helpless, on the well meaning and the bumbling, as well as on the evildoers themselves. Burdened with guilt, Stoner can only reiterate his belief that hidden evil breeds more evil than exposed evil and that he is the agent of truth, no matter the risk, no matter the loneliness, no matter the grimness of his later recollections. Within the conventions of the hard-boiled private investigator novel, Valin has constructed works that have a tragic dimension.

Missing

In *Missing*, Valin returns to familiar themes: a missing person with a past and secrets that must be uncovered to reveal the truth. In this case, it is Mason Greenleaf who has disappeared, and his lover, Cindy Dorn, hires the detective to find him. Greenleaf is a well-respected teacher who happens to be bisexual, and his history is tainted by a disputed soliciting charge and littered with gay former partners. When Greenleaf turns up dead in a sleazy hotel several days later, an apparent suicide, Stoner embarks on an investigation that leads him into the twilight world of closeted homosexuals, corrupt homophobic police officers, and the plague of acquired immunodeficiency syndrome (AIDS). In the course of his work, Stoner bonds with Cindy, and though the results of the case are ultimately inconclusive, the detective finds redemption for his own past misdeeds—and possibly love—in the arms of a good woman.

Rosemary M. Canfield Reisman
Updated by Jack Ewing

Principal mystery and detective fiction

Harry Stoner series: *The Lime Pit*, 1980; *Final Notice*, 1980; *Dead Letter*, 1981; *Day of Wrath*, 1982; *Natural Causes*, 1983; *Life's Work*, 1986; *Fire Lake*, 1987; *Extenuating Circumstances*, 1989; *Second Chance*, 1991; *The Music Lovers*, 1993; *Missing*, 1995

Other major works

Nonfiction: *Living Stereo: The RCA Bible, a Compendium of Opinion on RCA Living Stereo Records* (1993)

Bibliography

Callendar, Newgate. "Crime." Review of *Dead Letter*, by Jonathan Valin. *The New York Times Book Review*, January 17, 1982, p. 29. This reviewer criticizes *Dead Letter*, calling protagonist Harry Stoner "predictable" and "boring," an investigator who wears his introspection on his sleeve while dealing with a college professor and his alienated daughter. The reviewer labels the novel "laborious and contrived," while deploring the author's careless use of language.

_______. "Crime." Review of *Natural Causes*, by Jonathan Valin. *The New York Times Book Review*, September 4, 1983, p. 20. A mixed review of *Natural Causes* in which the novel—concerning the detective's investigation into the death of an employee at a large corporation—while praised for its many passages of realistic and biting dialogue, is criticized for its lack of flow and labored effort.

DeAndrea, William L. *Encyclopedia Mysteriosa: A Comprehensive Guide to the Art of Detection in Print, Film, Radio, and Television*. New York: Prentice Hall, 1994. Provides brief entries on Jonathan Valin and his best-known creation, private detective Harry Stoner.

Moore, Lewis D. *Cracking the Hard-boiled Detective: A Critical History from the 1920s to the Present*. Jefferson, N.C.: McFarland, 2006. This examination of the development of the hard-boiled detective provides background for understanding Valin's Harry Stoner.

Pronzini, Bill, and Marcia Muller, eds. *1001 Midnights: The Aficionado's Guide to Mystery and Detective Fiction*. New York: Arbor House, 1986. Contains a favorable review of *Natural Causes*, a novel that demonstrates why Valin is considered one of the best of the contemporary private eye writers.

Publishers Weekly. Review of *Missing*, by Jonathan Valin. 241, no. 49 (December 5, 1994): 69. The reviewer praises the work for its unexpected solution and particularly evocative portrait of the victim and the circumstances of his life but takes Valin to task for his writing, which is sometimes plodding.

Publishers Weekly. Review of *The Music Lover*, by Jonathan Valin. 240, no. 6 (February 8, 1993): 79. A favorable review that centers on the author's interests in rare recordings and high-end stereo systems; the fast-paced plot contains a wealth of audio lore for aficionados and offers a powerful conclusion.

JANWILLEM VAN DE WETERING

Born: Rotterdam, the Netherlands; February 12, 1931
Type of plot: Police procedural

Principal series

Amsterdam Police, 1975-

Principal series characters

Henk Grijpstra, an adjutant in the Amsterdam homicide division, is married but unhappy with his nagging wife, who has become fatter and fatter in their many years of marriage. An experienced big-city cop, he manages to get his suspects to reveal information. Polite but persistent, he looks on himself not only as a detective who protects the innocent but also as a public servant.

Rinus de Gier, a detective sergeant and Grijpstra's partner, is younger and unmarried. In his well-tailored blue denim suit, he represents the rising generation in the Amsterdam police department. Although he is a romantic who loves music and is susceptible to the charms of young women, he prefers to live alone with his cat.

The Commissaris, or inspector, the oldest member of the group, is a highly experienced and kindly detective. He suffers from very painful arthritis, but this does not prevent him from flying off to Italy to question a suspect when he considers it necessary.

Contribution

Janwillem van de Wetering is far more interested in character than in plot, and his perception of the criminals and the life around him is tempered by his Zen Buddhist experience. Thus, he brings a new dimension to the fiction of crime and detection. More than other writers in this genre, he also has a sense of place, and he conveys to the reader a feeling for Amsterdam. At the same time, he is a realist, and if he admires the beauties of the city's canals, he makes no secret of the fact that there often is garbage and filth floating in them. In keeping with his interest in the mental, rather than the physical, excitement of the mystery story, he has a keen sense of psychology and an understanding of dreams.

Biography

Janwillem van de Wetering was born on February 12, 1931, in Rotterdam, Netherlands, the son of Jan Cornelius van de Wetering, a businessman, and Catherine van de Wetering. He studied at the Delft Institute of Technology, the College for Service Abroad, Cambridge University, and the University of London. In 1954, he was married to Edyth Stewart-Wynne, from whom he was later divorced. He was married to Juanita Levy in December of 1960; a daughter, Thera, was born to them.

Van de Wetering spent more than fifteen years of his life as a businessman, beginning as a salesperson for Dutch companies in South Africa in 1952. Then, in 1958, he became a layperson in a Zen monastery in Kyoto, Japan, for a year. This put an end to what he has described as the "beatnik sort of life" that he had earlier led. In 1959, he returned to his business career, serving as the manager of a company in Bogotá, Colombia, until 1962; later he worked in Lima, Peru. He also worked as a real estate salesperson in Brisbane, Australia. After returning to the Netherlands in 1965, he became manager of the family textile business, which had been failing, and restored it to profitability. As an alternative to military service, he joined the Amsterdam Reserve Police, where he rose from the rank of patrol officer to sergeant. Van de Wetering has made very good use of his Amsterdam police experience. Almost all of his novels are set in Amsterdam, and as he has admitted, "All my novels are built on police reports."

In 1975, van de Wetering left Amsterdam for Maine. He joined a Buddhist group in New England, remaining a member until 1980. He has contributed to several magazines in the United States and the Netherlands and has also written plays for Dutch television. Both *Tumbleweed* (1976) and *Outsider in Amsterdam* (1975) have been produced as films.

Analysis

Janwillem van de Wetering launched his literary career with two autobiographical nonfictional books, written in Dutch and published in Amsterdam. Both were later translated into English and were published in Boston by Houghton Mifflin, which eventually produced the American editions of almost all of his books. *De lege spiegel: Ervaringen in een Japans Zenklooster* (1971; *The Empty Mirror: Experiences in a Japanese Zen Monastery*, 1973) and *Het dagende niets* (1973; *A Glimpse of Nothingness: Experiences in an American Zen Community*, 1975) are accounts of van de Wetering's study of Zen.

Outsider in Amsterdam

In 1975, he began his Amsterdam police series with *Outsider in Amsterdam*, one of his best novels. Sergeant de Gier and Adjutant Grijpstra are summoned to one of the seventeenth century gabled houses that line the canals of central Amsterdam and give the city so much of its charm and beauty. De Gier admires the graceful old architecture and deplores the ugly buildings of a later period. The house to which they have been summoned was once owned by a respectable gentleman of the merchant class. Now, however, it has a body hanging in it.

As the detectives get to work, their characters are revealed, and even the secondary characters come to life. Unlike some writers of detective fiction, van de Wetering does not use much violence. His characters can cope with it when they must, but they do not go out of their way to seek it. Although dogged and relentless, like most of their counterparts in the genre, these detectives are also very human, with distinctive personalities. According to one critic, who quotes from an interview with van de Wetering,

> They're comfortable people to be around, these policemen, all of them readier to discuss life than to pull the trigger, but each with distinctive traits of character. De Gier, a sensitive fellow with a passion for music and cats, is, says de Wetering, "What I would like to be." The less imaginative Grijpstra? "Me again—my solid Dutch side."

Van de Wetering is also an observant critic of society, though not a solemn one, for wit, irony, and humor enliven his style. The house ostensibly belongs to a quasi-religious group, a kind of commune, but the manager of it, now dead, had turned it into a profitable drug-distribution center. As the murder investigation proceeds, van de Wetering hurls barbs at drugs and drug dealers, the underground economy and businessmen who declare only part of their income, and hippies and the founders of communes and new societies. De Gier, for example, is angered by the discovery of young addicts who have been pushed into degradation and self-destruction. Lured by easy profits, a bright university student has set up an "antiques" business, which de Gier correctly identifies as a front for a drug-wholesaling operation. Sneering at de Gier's low salary, the former student offers him a job. In their exchange, van de Wetering portrays two very different worlds in conflict. After the drug wholesaler offers a percentage of the profits, saying, "You could make more on one deal, a deal taking a few weeks, than you are now making in a year," de Gier rejects the entire idea. He responds, "Drugs mean the end of everything. . . . It was the end of China before the communists solved the problem. Drugs mean dry earth, dust storms, famine, slaves, bandit wars."

Early in their investigation, Grijpstra and de Gier find out that the dead manager, who was a stingy man, had been exploiting the young people who lived and worked in the house and were members of his religious society. His financial adviser, who was also lending him the money for his drug operations, is an elegant, prosperous, and respected certified public accountant. Both detectives are aware of the privileged position of such a professional in modern society: "He is a man trusted by the establishment. Whatever he says is believed and the tax inspectors talk to him as equal to equal." Another brushstroke completes the ironic portrait:

> His smile glinted in the dark room. Grijpstra studied the smile for a moment. Expensive teeth. Eight thousand guilders perhaps? Or ten thousand? The false teeth looked very natural, each individual tooth a work of art, and the back teeth all of solid gold.

Aside from the three Amsterdam detectives, the most interesting character in the novel is the actual outsider in Amsterdam, the black man who opens the door for Grijpstra and de Gier when they first respond to the call for police assistance. He is a Papuan, and his name is Jan Karel van Meteren; the assonance with the name of his creator is probably no coincidence. Near the end of the book, van Meteren is identified as the killer. A loyal Dutch soldier and a police officer, he was also a victim of post-World War II political changes:

> Here you laugh about the royal family perhaps, the crown is a symbol, a symbol of the past they say, but to us in New Guinea the queen was holy. We saluted every time we passed her portrait. Religion and the law are very close. I still think the queen is a sort of saint. I cried when I saw her in the street. She was all I had when I left my island. But nobody wanted me when I came to the Hague to ask for the queen's orders. I showed them my medals and my papers. They were polite and patient, but they had no time for me. I was a strange black fellow from far away. With a Dutch passport.

In the end, van Meteren escapes, but nobody is really upset about it. In the words of the commissaris, "Van Meteren is a policeman, a real policeman. I kept on having the idea that he was one of us, even after he had been arrested. . . . And if you think that someone belongs to you, that he is part of the same group, you don't pay special attention to him." Van Meteren is an honest and very competent man, proud of having been both a soldier and a police officer. The real scoundrels have all been arrested, and even the dead man had been a scoundrel. This is not the only mystery by van de Wetering in which a killer is allowed to go unpunished. It is all tied up with the author's study of Zen and his view of the world. The commissaris, oldest and highest ranking of the three detectives and a wise and kindhearted man, suggests that van Meteren may find a little island where he can spend his life in meditation.

The Blond Baboon

The Amsterdam detectives are part of a paramilitary organization and a hierarchical social group—as is evident in many of the things they do and in the customs they observe. When they meet in the office of the commissaris in *The Blond Baboon* (1978), for example, Grijpstra sits in the "chair of honor, a heavy piece of furniture capped by wooden lions' heads." Cardozo, a young new detective, sits "on a hard-backed chair"; he is the lowest-ranking member of the group. During the conference, the commissaris asks his more senior men for their ideas on the case, then says, "I am not asking you, Cardozo, I will ask you in a few years' time. That doesn't mean I don't value your opinion but it has to be formed first."

There is intraservice rivalry as well as cooperation. When de Gier takes a flying leap into the Amstel River while pursuing a suspect attempting to escape in a boat, Grijpstra radios the water police, who soon pick them up; the water police even have spare dry clothes, which they keep for such emergencies. The water sergeant and Grijpstra admire de Gier in his new uniform. Grijpstra says, "I prefer the gold trim to our silver. Why do the water police have gold trim anyway?" The water sergeant responds, "Because gold is noble and so are we. . . . The water may be polluted these days, but it can never be as dirty as the shore."

Although most of van de Wetering's novels are set in the Netherlands, specifically in Amsterdam, many international influences can be felt and seen. Many Asians, New Guineans, and Middle Easterners have settled in the country, and American dropouts and hippies hang around the squares and canals. Indeed, the adventurous spirit of the seventeenth century merchants can still be found in the neighborhood where the South American streetbird (actually a type of vulture) belonging to a black witch doctor flies undisturbed, accompanied by a small, domestic cat.

The Maine Massacre and The Japanese Corpse

Not all the books are confined to the Netherlands. Part of *The Blond Baboon* takes place in Italy, and *The Maine Massacre* (1979) is set in the United States, where the commissaris has gone to help his widowed sister dispose of her husband's estate so that she can return to Amsterdam. Although the commissaris does not wish to admit his frailties, his men are worried; de Gier accompanies his superior to protect him. Once there, they discover that several people living on an isolated peninsula have died, leaving their homes to be destroyed by fire and the weather. *The Japanese Corpse* (1977) takes place mainly in Amsterdam, but part of it has a Japanese setting, and much of the background material "came from Tokyo police files." There is a scene in the novel in which the head of a Japanese gang, the daimyo, gives a party for the commissaris who, he believes, is the leader of a rival gang. The party leads not to a confrontation but to a discussion of *jin-gi*, an ancient Chinese idea "that two men can only truly meet after they've destroyed their own desires." The commissaris, who is a seeker of truth, both physical and philosophical, enjoys his encounter with the daimyo.

Van de Wetering's cops and crooks are not simply "good guys" and "bad guys"; they are ordinary men drawn from the world of reality. They work hard but enjoy having dinner together in inexpensive Chinese restaurants. Aware of the beauties of the city of Amsterdam and of nature, they are also sensitive to one another's feelings. Yet they do not take themselves too seriously, for they are aware that they are servants of the Dutch people.

The commissaris sums it up for de Gier in *The Blond Baboon*:

> "The turtle is fine. I saw him trying to plow through the rubbish in the garden this morning. The garden is covered with broken branches and glass and the garden chairs of the neighbors, but the turtle just plows on. He looked quite cheerful, I thought."
>
> "Maybe he'll be reincarnated as a police detective."
>
> The commissaris touched de Gier's sleeve. "He has the right character."

Seymour L. Flaxman

Principal mystery and detective fiction

Amsterdam Police series: *Outsider in Amsterdam*, 1975; *The Corpse on the Dike*, 1976; *Tumbleweed*, 1976; *Death of a Hawker*, 1977; *The Japanese Corpse*, 1977; *The Blond Baboon*, 1978; *The Maine Massacre*, 1979; *The Mind-Murders*, 1981; *De Kat van Brigadier de Gier*, 1983 (*The Sergeant's Cat, and Other Stories*, 1987); *The Streetbird*, 1983; *De ratelrat*, 1984 (*The Rattle-Rat*, 1985); *De zaak Ijsbreker*, 1985 (*Hard Rain*, 1986); *Just a Corpse at Twilight*, 1994; *The Hollow-Eyed Angel*, 1996; *The Perfidious Parrot*, 1997; *The Amsterdam Cops: Collected Stories*, 1999

Nonseries novels: *The Butterfly Hunter*, 1982; *Murder by Remote Control*, 1984 (with Paul Kirchner); *Seesaw Millions*, 1988; *Judge Dee Plays His Lute: A Play and Selected Mystery Stories*, 1997

Other short fiction: *Inspector Saito's Small Satori*, 1985

Other major works

Children's literature: *Little Owl: An Eightfold Buddhist Admonition*, 1978; *Hugh Pine*, 1980; *Bliss and Bluster: Or, How to Crack a Nut*, 1982; *Hugh Pine and the Good Place*, 1986; *Hugh Pine and Something Else*, 1989

Nonfiction: *De lege spiegel: Ervaringen in een Japans Zenklooster*, 1971 (*The Empty Mirror: Experiences in a Japanese Zen Monastery*, 1973); *Het dagende niets*, 1973 (*A Glimpse of Nothingness: Experiences in an American Zen Community*, 1975); *Robert van Gulik: His Life, His Work*, 1998; *Afterzen: Experiences of a Zen Student out on His Ear*, 1999

Bibliography

Cooper-Clark, Diana. *Designs of Darkness: Interviews with Detective Novelists*. Bowling Green, Ohio: Bowling Green State University Popular Press, 1983. Van de Wetering is one of the novelists interviewed in this study of the craft of crime fiction in Canada, England, and the United States.

Genberg, Kjell E. "Hollandska mord (Dutch Murder)." *Jury* 9, no. 3 (1980): 21-23. Brief profile of van de Wetering and his fiction.

Hausladen, Gary. *Places for Dead Bodies*. Austin: University of Texas Press, 2000. This study of the settings of mystery and detective novels includes a section on the Stockholm of van de Wetering.

Van de Wetering, Janwillem. *Hard Rain*. New York: Pantheon Books, 1986. A manuscript edition of van de Wetering's novel, revealing the history of its composition and the author's creative process.

_______. "Reality in a Zen Monastery." In *Adventures with the Buddha: A Personal Buddhism Reader*, edited by Jeffery Paine. New York: W. W. Norton, 2005. Autobiographical reflections on author's experience of the nature of the real; provides insights into his attitude toward literary representation.

White, Jean M. "Murder by Zen: Janwillem van de Wetering." *The New Republic* 179 (July 22, 1978): 34-35. Brief study of the role played by van de Wetering's Zen Buddhism in his crime fiction.

S. S. VAN DINE

Willard Huntington Wright

Born: Charlottesville, Virginia; October 15, 1888
Died: New York, New York; April 11, 1939
Type of plot: Master sleuth

Principal series

Philo Vance, 1926-1939

Principal series characters

Philo Vance, a debonair, aristocratic, brilliant amateur sleuth is a dilettante whose one passion is art. He is also well versed in psychology, skilled at sports and games, and the author of studies on polo, hieroglyphics, physics, criminology, Florentine and Chinese art, Greek drama, and Norwegian fishing. A handsome bachelor, he is thirty-two years old at the beginning of the series. In personality he is reserved, cynical, and whimsical.

S. S. Van Dine, is a Harvard classmate, attorney, manager of financial and personal affairs, and friend and constant companion of Philo Vance. Like Sherlock Holmes's friend Dr. Watson, Van Dine, self-described as "a commonplace fellow, possessed of a conservative and rather conventional mind," serves as a foil to the brilliant and fascinating Vance, and as narrator of his murder cases.

John F. X. Markham, district attorney of New York, is a longtime friend of Vance, on whom he depends for help in solving difficult cases. His personality is in contrast to Vance's; he is "sternly aggressive, brusque, forthright, and almost ponderously serious." An "indefatigable worker" and "utterly incorruptible," he holds Vance's respect.

Ernest Heath, sergeant of the Homicide Bureau, is the man officially in charge of Vance's cases. At first he resents Vance's participation and often he is irritated by his mannerisms, but he comes to respect and admire his abilities. Heath is unimaginative but diligent.

Contribution

S. S. Van Dine is a significant figure in the history of detective fiction, both as a theorist and as a practitioner of the genre. As a theorist, he articulated a strict code of "fairness" in the plotting of the detective novel and enunciated important ideas about the nature of the genre's appeal. *The Benson Murder Case* (1926) and *The Canary Murder Case* (1927) attracted a new audience for detective fiction in the United States, bringing it to the attention and serious consideration of intellectual and sophisticated readers and initiating what has come to be known as the Golden Age of American detective fiction. In the 1920's and 1930's, Van Dine's Philo Vance novels were the most widely read detective stories in the United States. They inspired thirty-one motion pictures, filmed between 1929 and 1947, and a popular weekly radio series, *Philo Vance*, during the 1940's.

Biography

S. S. Van Dine was born Willard Huntington Wright on October 15, 1888, in Charlottesville, Virginia, the son of Archibald Davenport Wright and Annie Van Vranken Wright. (Wright adopted his pen name, based on Van Dyne—an old family name—and the abbreviation of "steamship," when he turned to writing detective fiction.) Van Dine attended St. Vincent College, Pomona College, and Harvard University and also studied art in Munich and Paris. In 1907, he became a literary and art critic for the *Los Angeles Times*. During his distinguished career in this field, Van Dine published books on art, literature, philosophy, and culture. Also in 1907, he married Katharine Belle Boynton; they had one daughter and were divorced in 1930. He later married Eleanor Pulapaugh.

From 1912 to 1914, Van Dine edited *The Smart Set*, a sophisticated New York literary magazine, to which he attracted important new authors. He continued his career as critic and journalist until 1923, when a demanding work schedule caused his health to deteriorate. Confined to bed with a heart ailment for more than two years and forbidden by his physician to do any serious work, he spent his convalescence assembling and analyzing a two-thousand-volume collection of detective fiction and criminology. These activities inspired him to write a detective novel of his own. As S. S. Van Dine, he submitted to a publisher thirty thousand words of synopsized plans for three novels. The expanded draft of the first plan appeared in 1926 as *The Benson Murder Case.* This novel introduces Philo Vance, the hero of the most popular American detective series in its day. Van Dine also wrote several short detective films for Warner Bros. from 1931 to 1932 (their titles and exact dates are not known).

The twelve Philo Vance novels brought wealth to their heretofore debt-ridden author, enabling him to cultivate a luxurious lifestyle comparable to that of his fictional hero. Van Dine lived in a penthouse, delighted in witty and erudite conversation, fine cuisine, costly wines, and elegant clothes, and spent his very large income rapidly; he left an estate of only thirteen thousand dollars when he died on April 11, 1939.

Analysis

The development of S. S. Van Dine's theory and the composition of his early detective novels occurred at the same time—during his two-year convalescence beginning in 1923. Writing under his real name, Van Dine articulated his theory of detective fiction in a detailed historical introduction to his anthology *The Great Detective Stories: A Chronological Anthology* (1927). Van Dine's theory underlies "Twenty Rules for Writing Detective Stories" (1928), his acerbically witty credo, which, as he affirmed, was "based partly on the practice of all the great writers of detective stories, and partly on the promptings of the honest author's inner conscience." Van Dine's theory is important in its own right as well as in the context of detective writers' concerns about the integrity of the genre during this period. His theory is also borne out to a large degree in the Philo Vance novels, although significant departures from it may be observed.

The rules of detective fiction

In his 1927 introduction, Van Dine begins by distinguishing detective fiction from all other categories of fiction. "Popular" rather than "literary," it is unlike other kinds of popular fiction—romance, adventure, and mystery (that is, novels of international intrigue and suspense)—in that it provides not a passive emotional thrill but an engaging intellectual challenge. Rather than merely awaiting "the author's unraveling of the tangled skein of events," the reader of a detective novel experiences "the swift and exhilarating participation in the succeeding steps that lead to the solution." Van Dine sees the detective novel as unlike "fiction in the ordinary sense." It is an "intellectual game, . . . a complicated and extended puzzle cast in fictional form," and puzzles, he avers, have been humankind's "chief toy throughout the ages." Van Dine likens the detective novel to the crossword puzzle:

> In each there is a problem to be solved; and the solution depends wholly on mental processes—on analysis, on the fitting together of apparently unrelated parts, on a knowledge of the ingredients, and, in some measure, on guessing. Each is supplied with a series of overlapping clues to guide the solver; and these clues, when fitted into place, blaze the path for future progress. In each, when the final solution is achieved, all the details are found to be woven into a complete, interrelated, and closely knitted fabric.

All the Philo Vance novels are intricately plotted; several underscore the puzzle element. In *The Bishop Murder Case* (1929), for example, clues to a series of murders include allusions to Mother Goose rhymes, mathematical theories, and chess moves. Vance himself approaches his cases as if they were puzzles or mathematical problems; he is an adherent of "cold, logical exactness in his mental processes."

The solution to be sought in a detective novel, according to Van Dine, is ideally that of a murder: "Crime has always exerted a profound fascination over humanity, and the more serious the crime the greater has been that appeal." He once said that he considered "murder" the strongest word in the English language, and he used it in the title of each of his Philo Vance novels.

For a puzzle to be enjoyable—and solvable—it must be logical and fair. Many of Van Dine's twenty rules address the issue of fairness. For example, "The reader must have equal opportunity with the detective for solving the mystery. All clues must be plainly stated and described" (rule 1); "No willful tricks or deceptions may be placed on the reader other than those played legitimately by the criminal on the detective himself" (rule 2); "The detective himself, or one of the official investigators, should never turn out to be the culprit . . . " (rule 4); "The culprit must be determined by logical deductions—not by accident or coincidence or unmotivated confession . . . "(rule 5).

Van Dine stresses that the detective writer must be ingenious but never implausible: "A sense of reality is essential to the detective novel." The ideal material for the plot is commonplace, not exotic; the detective writer's task is "the working of familiar materials into a difficult riddle" that, if the reader should go back over the book after reading it the first time "he would find that the solution had been there all the time if he had had sufficient shrewdness to grasp it." The Philo Vance novels meet this criterion, for the most part. Vance typically solves his cases by a process of elimination and through his knowledge, both academic and intuitive, of human psychology.

Although, unlike romances or adventure novels, the detective novel, according to Van Dine, must have only enough atmosphere to establish the "pseudo-actuality" of its plot, setting, as opposed to atmosphere, is crucial:

> The plot must appear to be an actual record of events springing from the terrain of its operations; and the plans and diagrams so often encountered in detective stories aid considerably in the achievement of this effect. A familiarity with the terrain and a belief in its existence are what give the reader his feeling of ease and freedom in manipulating the factors of the plot to his own (which are also the author's) ends.

Accordingly, the Philo Vance novels usually feature maps and room diagrams. They also present a fascinatingly detailed picture of upper-class life in New York City in the 1920's and 1930's.

The style of a detective story, according to Van Dine, must aid in creating the sense of reality and verisimilitude; it "must be direct, simple, smooth, and unencumbered." It must be unemotional as well, and thus contribute to what is for Van Dine "perhaps the outstanding characteristic of the detective novel"—unity of mood, a mood conducive to "mental analysis and the overcoming of difficulties." In the Philo Vance novels, accordingly, the author presents himself through the narratorial persona of S. S. Van Dine, the protagonist's lawyer and companion. The narrator's status as an attorney serves to underscore the importance of logical analysis and objectivity, but his style, especially in the later novels, is frequently mannered and elaborate, and he digresses frequently into lengthy disquisitions, complete with footnotes, about such matters as art, archaeology, music, mathematics, criminology, and religion—typically in their most esoteric manifestations.

Van Dine's recommendations about characterization suggests that he thinks of characters—excluding the detective hero himself—primarily as pieces in a puzzle. Although they must not be "too neutral and colorless" (which would spoil the effect of verisimilitude), the detective writer should avoid delineating them "too fully and intimately." Characters should "merely fulfill the requirements of plausibility, so that their actions will not appear to spring entirely from the author's preconceived scheme." They are not to fall in love, since "the business at hand is to bring a criminal to the bar of justice, not to bring a lovelorn couple to the hymeneal altar" (rule 3); nor are they to belong to "secret societies, camorras, mafias" (rule 13), or, it appears, to be professional criminals, who are the con-

Van Dine's debonair amateur sleuth, Philo Vance.

cern of police departments, "not of authors and brilliant amateur detectives" (rule 17).

Story materials, plot, atmosphere, setting, style, narration, mood, characterization—according to Van Dine's theory all of these are strictly functional parts of a puzzle to be solved, counters in an exciting mental game. The primary player in this game is the detective hero and, vicariously, the reader. Van Dine's ideal detective hero stands in contrast to his world. He is singular. In fact, Van Dine rules that "There must be but one detective—that is, but one protagonist of deduction—one deus ex machina." To have more than one detective would be to confuse the reader: "It's like making the reader run a race with a relay team" (rule 9). The detective is singular, not only in number but, more important, in kind. His brilliance sets him above others, especially the police. Preferably, he is an amateur, and this status divorces him from mundane considerations such as earning a living or gaining a promotion. In Van Dine's view he is at once godlike, heroic (like Oedipus), wise ("the Greek chorus of the drama"), and fascinating:

> All good detective novels have had for their protagonist a character of attractiveness and interest, of high and fascinating attainments—a man at once human and unusual, colorful and gifted.

The Benson Murder Case

Philo Vance meets these criteria. The opening chapter of the first volume of the series, *The Benson Murder Case*, provides a detailed character portrait of Vance. He is described as "a man of unusual culture and brilliance." He is learned in psychology and criminology, enjoys music, and has a passion for art; he is an authority on it as well as "one of those rare human beings, a collector with a definite philosophic point of view." "Unusually good-looking" and in dress "always fashionable—scrupulously correct to the smallest detail—yet unobtrusive," Vance is skilled in various sports and games: He is an expert fencer, his golf handicap is only three, he is a champion at polo and an "unerring" poker player. An "aristocrat by birth and instinct, he held himself severely aloof from the common world of men." Vance is a snob both intellectually and socially: "He detested stupidity even more, I believe, than he did vulgarity or bad taste."

Reactions to Vance over the years have differed widely and range from fascination and adulation to the bemused annoyance of Ogden Nash's famous lines, "Philo Vance/ Needs a kick in the pance." In the later novels his mannerisms sometimes seem self-parodic. Although he did not always avoid them, it is evident in the following passage from *The Benson Murder Case* that Van Dine knew the risks he was taking with his characterizations of Vance:

> Perhaps he may best be described as a bored and supercilious, but highly conscious and penetrating, spectator of life. He was keenly interested in all human reactions; but it was the interest of the scientist, not the humanitarian. Withal he was a man of rare personal charm. Even people who found it difficult to admire him found it equally difficult not to like him. His somewhat quixotic mannerisms and his slightly English accent and inflection—a heritage of his postgraduate days at Oxford—impressed those who did not know him well as affectations. But the truth is, there was very little of the *poseur* about him.

The Bishop Murder Case

Van Dine was very interested in the philosophy of Friedrich Nietzsche; in 1915, in fact, he published a book titled *What Nietzsche Taught*. His ideal detective hero bears significant resemblance to the Nietzschean *Übermensch* (literally, "overman"), who, unlike common human beings, has managed to overcome his passions, has genuine style, is creative, and is above ordinary morality. Van Dine's Philo Vance is a self-professed disciple of Nietzschean philosophy, and in *The Bishop Murder Case* he plays the part of an *Übermensch* when he avoids being murdered by switching poisoned drinks with Professor Bertrand Dillard, the killer he has been investigating. Reproached by the district attorney for taking the law into his own hands, Vance says,

> " . . . I felt no more compunction in aiding a monster like Dillard into the Beyond than I would have in crushing out a poisonous reptile in the act of striking."
>
> "But it was murder!" exclaimed Markham in horrified indignation.
>
> "Oh, doubtless," said Vance cheerfully. "Yes—of course. Most reprehensible. . . . I say, am I by any chance under arrest?"

Here Vance does what the author or reader would, perhaps, like to do—deliver justice, not merely to facilitate it through his detection.

Van Dine's theory posits the detective as an alter ego for both author and reader. The detective is

> at one and the same time, the outstanding personality of the story, . . . the projection of the author, the embodiment of the reader, . . . the propounder of the problem, the supplier of the clues, and the eventual solver of the mystery.

For Van Dine, then, the detective hero serves the function not only of entertainment but also of wish fulfillment: He satisfies a fantasy about intellectual and moral power. Ultimately and paradoxically, therefore, fictional realism and strict logic serve in Van Dine's theory of detective fiction a compelling fantasy that cannot be satisfied in the real world of human society.

Eileen Tess Tyler

Principal mystery and detective fiction

Philo Vance series: *The Benson Murder Case*, 1926; *The Canary Murder Case*, 1927; *The Greene Murder Case*, 1928; *The Bishop Murder Case*, 1929; *The Scarab Murder Case*, 1930; *The Kennel Murder Case*, 1933; *The Casino Murder Case*, 1934; *The Dragon Murder Case*, 1934; *The Garden Murder Case*, 1935; *Philo Vance Murder Cases*, 1936; *The Kidnap Murder Case*, 1936; *The Gracie Allen Murder Case*, 1938 (also known as *The Smell of Murder*); *The Winter Murder Case*, 1939

Nonseries novel: *The President's Mystery Story*, 1935 (with others)

Other major works

Novels: *The Man of Promise*, 1916 (as Wright)

Screenplay: *The Canary Murder Case*, 1929 (as Wright, with others)

Nonfiction (as Wright): *Europe After 8:15*, 1914 (with H. L. Mencken and George Jean Nathan); *Modern Painting: Its Tendency and Meaning*, 1915; *What Nietzsche Taught*, 1915; *The Creative Will: Studies in the Philosophy and Syntax of Aesthetics*, 1916; *The Forum Exhibition of Modern American Painters, March Thirteenth to March Twenty-fifth, 1916*, 1916; *Informing a Nation*, 1917; *Misinforming a Nation*, 1917; *The Future of Painting*, 1923; *I Used to Be a Highbrow but Look at Me Now*, 1929

Edited texts (as Wright): *The Great Modern French Stories*, 1917; *The Great Detective Stories: A Chronological Anthology*, 1927

Bibliography

Braithwaite, William Stanley. "S. S. Van Dine—Willard Huntington Wright." In *Philo Vance Murder Cases*. New York: Charles Scribner's Sons, 1936. Biography of the author of the Philo Vance series and of his fictional alter ego.

Crawford, Walter B. "The Writings of Willard Huntington Wright." *Bulletin of Bibliography* 24 (May-August, 1963): 11-16. Checklist of Wright's writings, both as himself and as S. S. Van Dine.

Garden, Y. B. "Philo Vance: An Impressionistic Biography." In *Philo Vance Murder Cases*. New York: Charles Scribner's Sons, 1936. Fictional biography of Van Dine's master sleuth, based on clues to the character's past dropped over the course of his adventures.

Loughery, John. *Alias S. S. Van Dine*. New York: Scribner, 1992. Combined biography of Wright and critical examination of Van Dine's novels. Bibliographic references and index.

Panek, LeRoy Lad. *The Origins of the American Detective Story*. Jefferson, N.C.: McFarland, 2006. Study of the beginnings and establishment of American detective-fiction conventions, focusing especially on the replacement of the police by the private detective and the place of forensic science in the genre. Provides context for understanding Van Dine's work.

Penzler, Otto. *S. S. Van Dine*. New York: Mysterious Bookshop, 1999. Literary biography of Van Dine by the owner of the Mysterious Bookshop, who was also the editor of *The Armchair Detective*.

Roth, Marty. *Foul and Fair Play: Reading Genre in Classic Detective Fiction*. Athens: University of Georgia Press, 1995. A post-structural analysis of the conventions of mystery and detective fiction. Examines 138 short stories and works from the 1840's to the 1960's. Contains some discussion of Van Dine's rules for writing mysteries.

ROBERT H. VAN GULIK

Born: Zutphen, the Netherlands; August 9, 1910
Died: The Hague, the Netherlands; September 24, 1967
Type of plot: Historical

Principal series

Judge Dee, 1949-1968

Principal series characters

Judge Dee, a Chinese district magistrate, is married, with three wives who live together harmoniously, providing the perfect team for his favorite game, dominoes. A fervent Confucian, he administers his many official responsibilities justly, seeking to maintain social order and respect for justice.

Ma Joong, the son of a junk cargo owner, is trained in boxing and intended for a career in the army. Having accidentally killed a cruel magistrate, he is forced to live as a bandit. Fond of women and drink, he is physically fearless but somewhat superstitious.

Hoong Liang is a servant in the household of Judge Dee's father. He insists on following the judge to the provinces. Completely loyal, he in turn has the complete trust of the judge.

Chiao Tai, from a good family, was also forced to become a highwayman because of a corrupt official. He offers his services to the judge, stipulating only that he be allowed to resign if he finds the man responsible for the death of his comrades. Intelligent, thoughtful, and shy, he is unlucky in love.

Tao Gan, seeking revenge on the world for the base behavior of his beloved wife, becomes an itinerant swindler. His familiarity with the criminal underworld and his skill with disguises make him an effective fourth assistant. Parsimonious to the extreme, he will scheme for free meals whenever possible.

Contribution

Robert H. van Gulik's stories of Judge Dee are fine examples of the historical mystery novel, which recaptures a bygone era even as it tells a good story. Though his stories are fiction, his training as a scholar and a diplomat enabled him to draw on a vast store of historical material to enrich his mystery novels.

During his diplomatic service in Asian countries, van Gulik noted that even poor translations of Western detective stories were enthusiastically received by Japanese and Chinese readers, so he decided to demonstrate the strong tradition of Chinese detective stories that already existed. He started with a translation of an anonymous eighteenth century novel about Judge Dee, then went on to write several more of his own. He originally wrote them in English, then translated some for serial publication in Japanese journals. Western audiences found them so interesting that he decided to continue writing in English, and he translated his own work. He was thus responsible for introducing the classical Chinese detective story to the West, while the minutiae of the novels and his scholarly notes appended to the novels provide glimpses of the ancient Chinese way of life.

Biography

Born in Zutphen, the Netherlands, on August 9, 1910, to Willem Jacabus van Gulik, a physician, and his wife, Bertha de Ruiter, Robert Hans van Gulik displayed an interest in Asian language and culture as a boy. The Chinese inscriptions on his father's collection of porcelain intrigued him, and he started studying Chinese in the Chinatown section of Batavia, Java, where his father was serving in the Dutch army. Back in the Netherlands for his college education, van Gulik took up law and languages at the University of Leiden, adding Japanese, Tibetan, Sanskrit, and Russian to his list of languages. His thesis, *Hayagriva: The Mantrayanic Aspect of Horse-Cult in China and Japan*, won for him a doctoral degree with honors from the University of Utrecht in 1935. His entry into the Netherlands Foreign Service led to postings in China, India, and Japan. In Chung-king, China, in 1943 he met and married Shui Shih-Fang, with whom he had three sons and a daughter.

Van Gulik's career as a diplomat flourished, bringing him many awards and honors. Despite the constant moves—which took him to Washington, D.C., the Middle East, Malaysia, Japan, and Korea—van Gulik continued his scholarly activities, researching, translating, editing, and writing. He was a skilled calligrapher—a rare talent for a Westerner—and had some of the other preoccupations of a traditional Chinese gentleman, collecting rare books, scroll paintings, musical instruments, and art objects. Of the breed of scholars who found meaning in small, esoteric subjects, he wrote, for example, two monographs on the ancient Chinese lute, which he himself played, and translated a famous text on ink stones. A talented linguist, historian, and connoisseur, van Gulik published scholarly articles on a variety of topics about traditional Chinese life, ranging from Chinese classical antiquity (c. 1200 B.C.E.-200 C.E.) to the end of the Ching Dynasty (1644-1911 C.E.). It was through his mysteries about Judge Dee that van Gulik popularized the specialized knowledge of Chinese life he had gained. Having finally obtained the post of ambassador from the Netherlands to Japan in 1965, he died two years later of cancer in his homeland, on September 24, 1967.

Analysis

In his brief notes explaining the origins of his collection of short stories, *Judge Dee at Work* (1967), Robert H. van Gulik mused on the importance of each of his three careers: As a diplomat, he dealt with matters of temporary significance; as a scholar, he confined himself to facts of permanent significance; as a mystery writer, he could be completely in control of the facts and give free play to his imagination. It is the interplay of these separate experiences that give van Gulik's Judge Dee novels a distinct position in the genre of historical mystery novels.

Dee Goong An

A real historical figure who was politically important during the Tang Dynasty (618-907), Judge Dee was more popularly remembered as a folk figure, not unlike the Robin Hood of English folk history. The first appearance in English of the famed detective-magistrate Di Renjie (630-700), was in van Gulik's translation of an anonymous novel of the eighteenth century, *Wu Zetian si da qi an*, published as *Dee Goong An: Three Murder Cases Solved by Judge Dee* (1949). The success of his translation led van Gulik to write his own stories. Though he drew on his scholarly background and interest in China to find stories, create accurate details, and provide illustrations, the Judge Dee stories are fictional, based on the Chinese form but adapted to Western audiences.

In his translator's preface, van Gulik points out five distinct features of Chinese detective stories. Rather than the cumulative suspense that characterizes Western whodunits, Chinese stories introduce the criminal at the beginning, explaining the history of and the motive for the crime. The pleasure for the reader lies in the intellectual excitement of following the chase. Nor are the stories bound to the realistic: Supernatural elements abound, animals and household items give evidence in court, and the detective might pop into the netherworld for information. Other characteristics have to do with the Chinese love and patience for voluminous detail: long poems, philosophical lectures, and official documents pad the purely narrative, resulting in novels of several hundred chapters; then too, each novel may be populated with two hundred or more characters. Finally, the Chinese sense of justice demands that the punishment meted out to the criminal be described in gruesome detail, sometimes including a description of the punishment the executed criminal receives in the afterlife.

The Chinese Lake Murders

These elements are toned down considerably or eliminated entirely in the stories that van Gulik wrote. In *The Chinese Lake Murders* (1960), for example, the first, short chapter is a diary entry by an official who has fallen in love with the woman who is to be a murder victim. It appears to be a confession of sorts, but one that is so intensely brooding, vague, and mystical that its purport becomes clear only toward the end of the story. Van Gulik thus neatly manages to include a convention while adapting it. Similarly, Judge Dee is often confronted with tales of haunted monasteries, temples invaded by phantoms, mysterious shadowy figures flitting in deserted houses, and other supernatural elements. A sensitive person, the judge is also often overcome by an inexplicable sense of evil in certain locations, which prove to be the sites of brutal torture or murder or burial—information revealed only after the judge has determined the mysteries' solutions. Although his assistants are sometimes spooked by tales of ghosts and spirits, van Gulik portrays his judge primarily as a rational man suspicious of tales of the supernatural, and indeed most of these otherworldly elements prove to be concoctions fashioned by the criminals for their own convenience.

The van Gulik narrative flow is interrupted only by his own maps and illustrations, which are based on but not exact reproductions of Chinese woodblock prints; though a short poem or an official account may occasionally appear, they are strictly related to the story. Van Gulik retains the characteristic of the anonymous eighteenth century Judge Dee novel in telling three separate stories that prove to be related. Though he borrowed freely from his historical research, combining stories from disparate sources, van Gulik's considerable inventiveness and storytelling ability are evident in the way he can maintain the reader's interest in three separate stories. The list of dramatic personae, grouping the characters by story, is provided as a guide and numbers only a dozen or so.

Although the traditional form is skillfully adapted to modern audiences, what remains completely faithful to the original Chinese detective story is the position of the detective figure, who was always a judge. In the precommunist social structure, the district magistrate had so many responsibilities over the affairs of the citizens in his jurisdiction that his title meant "the father-and-mother official." The term "judge" may therefore sound slightly misleading, for not only did the district magistrate receive reports of crimes, but also he was in charge of investigating them, questioning suspects, making a decision, and sentencing. The wide powers that he wielded are fully delineated in van Gulik's novels. Judge Dee is regularly portrayed presiding over the daily sessions, resplendent in his official dark green robe with a black winged hat, his constabulary with whips and truncheons ready at his command. The habit, startling to twentieth century readers, was to treat anyone who came to the tribunal, defendant and complainant, the same way. Both had to kneel, hands behind them, in front of the judge, who could command his constables to whip or otherwise torture any recalcitrant suppliant. Particularly stubborn or arrogant people, such as the artist in *The Chinese Maze Murders* (1956), could be beaten into unconsciousness. The Chinese system of justice also required that criminals confess their crimes, even if they had to be tortured into confession, and the forms of death were gruesome. Judge Dee's way of cutting a deal with a criminal sometimes is to offer a more merciful form of death in return for cooperation. People who bore false witness could also be severely punished.

Though he will resort to such powers of his authority when necessary, Judge Dee solves cases because of his careful sifting of evidence, his powers of observation, and his experience and understanding of human nature. A firm upholder of traditional Chinese values, Judge Dee exercises his power wisely. It is the higher purpose of justice that rules his decisions: The main purpose of the law, he realizes, is to restore the pattern disrupted by the crime, to repair the damage as much as possible. So it is that Judge Dee will sometimes start his tenure in a remote district that is in disarray, ruling over a populace made cynical by previous weak or corrupt officials or in the grip of evil men. The process of solving the murder mysteries is intrinsically linked to the process of restoring order and respect for the law and the imperial court.

The Chinese Gold Murders

Also typical of the Chinese detective story are the four assistants to the judge, often recruited from the "brothers of the green woods"—that is, bandits. Though his first and most trusted assistant, Sergeant Hoong Liang, is a faithful family retainer who follows the judge to the various outlying provinces in which the judge wants to work, the other three are reformed men. Ma Joong and Chiao Tai are typical of their ilk in that they are honest men who have been forced by circumstances into a life of crime. They meet Judge Dee when they attempt to rob him on the highway (*The Chinese Gold Murders*, 1959). Delighted by this rare opportunity to practice his swordsmanship, Judge Dee pulls out a family heirloom, the legendary sword Rain Dance, and is so annoyed when a group of officers comes to his rescue that he claims the highwaymen as his assistants. The two bandits are so impressed that they ask to be taken into his service. The fourth assistant, Tao Gan, also volunteers to join the judge. In contrast to the corrupt officials who caused honest men to become criminals, Judge Dee is thus neatly shown as a just and admirable man. The assistants are very useful in gathering evidence among the populace for the cases, and Judge Dee himself will take to the streets incognito. These reconnoitering missions provide little touches of ribald humor in the novels but also give readers a sense of the very hard life of common people, scrambling for their daily bowl of rice, subject to invasions from the northern borders. After the first five novels, van Gulik decided to simplify the pattern, for a "new" Judge Dee series; he dropped all but one assistant and focused more on character development. In response to popular demand, he brought back Sergeant Hoong, who had been killed in a previous novel.

Other historically accurate characteristics tend to simplify the narrative in predictable ways. Van Gulik toned down the vehement xenophobia of the truly devout Confucianist judge; even so, Judge Dee is openly contemptuous of foreign influences such as Buddhism or Daoism; even when Tatars, Indians, or Koreans are not actually criminals, they are suspect and considered dangerous. He prefers didactic poetry to love songs, and while he may say, in a tolerant spirit, that what people do in the privacy of their own homes is their business, any character who deviates from the norm in his sexual preference or social behavior is suspect.

The author's scholarly training and interest are evident in other ways. His interest in art is manifest in the number of illustrations that enliven the novels; one, *The Phantom of the Temple* (1966), is based on the Judge Dee strips he created for Dutch and Scandinavian newspapers. One incident reveals the connection between van Gulik's scholarship and mystery writing. The Japanese publisher of *The Chinese Maze Murders* insisted on an image of a female nude for the cover. Seeking to verify his view that the prudish Confucianist tradition precluded the art of drawing nude human bodies, van Gulik discovered instead that an antique dealer had a set of printing blocks of an erotic album from the Ming period, which in turn led him to publish two scholarly books on the subject of erotic art and sexual life in ancient China. Beyond the care for historical accuracy, however, van Gulik's interest in art is integrally important in the mystery novels. Paintings are important as clues; two contrasting pictures of a pet cat and Judge Dee's careful observation of the position of the sun in each lead him to a solution in *The Haunted Monastery* (1962), for example.

In the context of the Western mystery novel tradition, such features as maps, lists, and illustrations are typical of puzzle-plots. Some of the motifs in the Judge Dee novels may be more familiar to the devotee of the tougher kind of hard-boiled novels, however, such as the distinct misogyny that permeates the novels. The custom of poor families selling daughters to brothels and the reverence for sons over daughters are undoubted, if sad, historical facts. Still, the number of beautiful young women who are kidnapped, locked up, beaten, and otherwise tortured and killed in the course of the novels is cumulatively oppressive. By extension, incestuous and sadomasochist characters appear often.

The Chinese Nail Murders

As a detective figure, even with the vast powers he has, Judge Dee is not portrayed solely as the great detective, the brilliantly intuitive crime solver who never falters. In *The Chinese Nail Murders* (1961), he comes perilously close to losing both his job and his head when he orders that a grave be dug up and then cannot find any evidence of murder. In deep despair, he prepares himself for disgrace, saved only by the help of a beautiful woman he has come to admire very much, wistfully recalling his father's words, that it is very lonely at the top. Such touches of psychological individuality are lightly done. The emphasis on the social role rather than the individual characterizes van Gulik's style: Phrases such as "the judge barked" and a liberal use of exclamation marks in dialogue suggest the peremptory nature of the detective's task.

Ever the scholar, van Gulik included a postscript, detailing the origins of his stories, with remarks on relevant Chinese customs. Even without these aids, his Judge Dee stories provide a generalized picture of ancient Chinese life and have repopularized the Chinese equivalent of Sherlock Holmes.

Shakuntala Jayaswal

Principal mystery and detective fiction

Judge Dee series: *Dee Goong An: Three Murder Cases Solved by Judge Dee*, 1949 (translation of portions of an anonymous eighteenth century Chinese novel; *Celebrated Cases of Judge Dee*, 1976); *The Chinese Maze Murders*, 1956; *New Year's Eve in Lan-Fang*, 1958; *The Chinese Bell Murders*, 1958; *The Chinese Gold Murders*, 1959; *The Chinese Lake Murders*, 1960; *The Chinese Nail Murders*, 1961; *The Red Pavilion*, 1961; *The Haunted Monastery*, 1962; *The Emperor's Pearl*, 1963; *The Lacquer Screen*, 1963; *The Monkey and the Tiger*, 1965; *The Willow Pattern*, 1965; *Murder in Canton*, 1966; *The Phantom of the Temple*, 1966; *Judge Dee at Work*, 1967; *Necklace and Calabash*, 1967; *Poets and Murder*, 1968 (also known as *The Fox-Magic Murders*)

Nonseries novel: *Een gegeven dag*, 1963 (*The Given Day*, 1964)

Other major works

Novels: *De nacht van de tijger: Een rechter tie verhaal*, 1963; *Vier vingers: Een rechter tie verhaal*, 1964

Nonfiction: *Hayagriva: The Mantrayanic Aspect of Horse-Cult in China and Japan*, 1935; *The Lore of the Chinese Lute*, 1940; *Hsi K'ang and His Poetical Essay on the Lute*, 1941; *Pi-Hsi-T' u-K' ao, Erotic Colour Prints of the Ming Period*, 1951; *De Boek Illustratie in Het Ming Tijdperk*, 1955; *Chinese Pictorial Art as Viewed by the Connoisseur*, 1958; *Sexual Life in Ancient China*, 1961; *The Gibbon in China*, 1967

Edited text: *Ming-Mo I-Seng Tung-Kao-Chan-Shih Chi-K' an*, 1944

Translations: *Urvaci*, 1932; *Mi Fu on Ink-stones*, 1938; *T' ang-Yin-Pi-Shih (Parallel Cases from Under the Peartree)*, 1956

Miscellaneous: *The English-Blackfoot Vocabulary*, 1930 (with C. C. Uhlenbeck); *The Blackfoot-English Vocabulary*, 1934 (with C. C. Uhlenbeck); *Ch' un-Meng-So-Yen, Trifling Tale of a Spring Dream*, 1950

Bibliography

Hausladen, Gary. *Places for Dead Bodies*. Austin: University of Texas Press, 2000. This study of the settings of mystery and detective novels includes a section on van Gulik's representation and use of seventh century China.

King, Nina. *Crimes of the Scene: A Mystery Novel Guide for the International Traveler.* New York: St. Martin's Press, 1997. Another reading of setting in detective fiction that analyzes van Gulik's representation of China.

Lach, Donald F. Introduction to *The Chinese Gold Murders*, by Robert H. van Gulik. Chicago: University of Chicago Press, 1977. This introduction to a reissue of van Gulik's fourth original Judge Dee tale looks back at the author's career and his most famous character.

Mugar Memorial Library. *Bibliography of Dr. R. H. van Gulik (D.Litt.)*. Boston: Boston University, 1968. Complete bibliography of van Gulik's writings, published the year after his death.

Peters, Ellis. Foreword to *Historical Whodunits*, edited by Mike Ashley. New York: Barnes & Noble, 1997. This discussion of the subgenre by a well-known practitioner treats van Gulik's work; the collection includes van Gulik's "He Came with the Rain."

Sarjeant, William Antony S. "A Detective in Seventh-Century China: Robert van Gulik and the Cases of Judge Dee." *The Armchair Detective* 15, no. 4 (1982): 292-303. Overview of the Judge Dee stories and the importance of their historical setting.

Van de Wetering, Janwillem. *Robert van Gulik: His Life, His Work*. 1987. Reprint. New York: Soho Press, 1998. Biography and critical study that gives equal time to van Gulik's writing and the personal experiences informing that writing.

MANUEL VÁZQUEZ MONTALBÁN

Born: Barcelona, Spain; June 14, 1939
Died: Bangkok, Thailand; October 18, 2003
Types of plot: Private investigator; hard-boiled

Principal series

Pepe Carvalho, 1972-2004

Principal series character

Pepe Carvalho is in many respects the alter ego of Manuel Vázquez Montalbán, as becomes evident in the course of the series. Although Pepe's biography is sketchy and not always consistent, the reader learns that he has participated in the clandestine resistance against General Francisco Franco, has served a traumatic jail term during the dictatorship, and has worked for the Central Intelligence Agency for four years. Like the author, he was a member of the Catalan Communist Party who later became disillusioned with the role of the party in the democratic reconstruction of Spain. Pepe ages and matures in the course of the series; he becomes more disillusioned and cynical, and he begins to worry about supporting himself in retirement.

Contribution

Manuel Vázquez Montalbán was one of the leading Spanish authors and intellectuals of the second half of the twentieth century. He was not only a keen observer of Spanish society, particularly during the period of transition from the Franco dictatorship to a modern European democracy, but also a severe critic of modern global politics, economics, and popular culture. His detective series around his alter ego, the private investigator Pepe Carvalho, therefore serves both as a stepping-stone in the development of detective fiction in Spain, more or less nonexistent during the Franco regime, and as an appropriate device for the investigation of modern Spanish social history.

Not surprising considering Vázquez Montalbán's family background, his investigation into Spanish social history was somewhat slanted to the left of the political spectrum, focusing on the mainly clandestine, Franco-fascist pockets still not only in existence but also very influential in Spanish business and politics during and after the transition. In this respect, the Carvalho series offers a perspective very similar to that of the German detective novel immediately after World War II. In his later works in the Carvalho series, Vázquez Montalbán widened the scope of his detective's investigations, both geographically and thematically, from Spain to all of Europe, until in his last, posthumously published work, *Milenio Carvalho* (2004; the Carvalho millennium), his critical purview included global famine, international terrorism, and the economic devastation of developing countries.

The Carvalho series is thus a fortuitous combination of the best of hard-boiled detective fiction in the mold of Raymond Chandler's Philip Marlowe novels with mainstream political fiction. After brief experimentations, Vázquez Montalbán rejected postmodernist metafictional prose techniques for a neorealist approach.

Biography

Manuel Vázquez Montalbán was born on June 14, 1939, in a poor neighborhood of Barcelona, shortly after Francisco Franco's victory in the Spanish Civil War. His father, an opponent of Franco, was arrested and sentenced to death when he returned from exile for the birth of his son; this verdict was commuted to a twenty-year sentence in prison, of which he served five years.

During his years at the University of Barcelona, Vázquez Montalbán participated in leftist student organizations and, after transferring to the School of Journalism, joined the Catalan branch of the Spanish Communist Party. After getting married and working as a journalist, he was fired because he did not have the right party affiliation; in 1962 he was arrested for participating in an anti-Franco demonstration in support of striking miners and sentenced to three years in jail, of which he served some eighteen months. During his time in prison, Vázquez Montalbán began to write and to develop his theory of subnormal literature. In the 1960's he worked as an editor for the Larousse encyclopedia and published his first collections of poetry.

In 1969 Vázquez Montalbán became a lecturer in the School of Journalism at the University of Barcelona and published his first collection of short stories. The following year, he published his *Manifesto subnormal* (subnormal manifesto), which stands at the beginning of what critics have called his subnormal period, characterized by highly experimental prose and poems. His first two Carvalho novels, *Yo maté a Kennedy: Impresiones, observaciones y memorias de un guardaespaldas* (1972; I killed J. F. Kennedy) and *Tatuaje* (1974; tattoos), fall into this category, although the latter is a first step toward a more realistic, popular detective novel modeled on the hard-boiled detective novel and the French roman noir.

After the death of Franco in 1975 and through 1985, Vázquez Montalbán dedicated himself to the development of the Carvalho series, turning it into a portrait of post-Franco Spain from the perspective of a jaded leftist intellectual. Though he continued to write novels and stories about his most popular character, he also worked in several other genres, producing plays, screenplays, lyric poetry, and a prodigious amount of nonfiction, dealing with such topics as critical theory, urban planning, cooking, art history, and globalization. In 1981, he won the Grand Prix de Littérature Policière for *Los mares del sur* (1979; *Southern Seas*, 1986).

Vázquez Montalbán died unexpectedly of a heart attack in the transit lounge of the Bangkok airport on October 18, 2003; he was mourned in Spain and abroad. His last work involving his most famous literary character, Pepe Carvalho, a two-volume novel entitled *Milenio Carvalho*, appeared posthumously, although it had been announced at the end of *El hombre de mi vida* (2000; *The Man of My Life*, 2005). In it, the detective and Biscuter, his longtime secretary, go global in their critical observation of the modern world, with obvious allusions to both Jules Verne's *Le tour du monde en quatre-vingts jours* (1873; *Around the World in Eighty Days*, 1873) and Miguel de Cervantes's *El ingenioso hidalgo don Quixote de la Mancha*(1605, 1615; *The History of the Valorous and Wittie Knight-Errant, Don Quixote of the Mancha*, 1612-1620; better known as *Don Quixote de la Mancha*).

Analysis

The beginning of Manuel Vázquez Montalbán's Carvalho series coincides with the beginning of the modern Spanish detective novel and plays a large part in its history. The first novel in the series, *Yo maté a Kennedy*, was not originally intended as the first novel of a series. It was one of the last works of Vázquez Montalbán's so-called subnormal period, characterized by neorealist, postmodernist fiction, which takes its name from the author's *Manifesto subnormal*, in which he finds that the writer has the subnormal task, particularly in a dictatorial society, of providing a counterbalance to social stability and harmony, which leads to a sense of alienation. This sense of alienation of Vázquez Montalbán's detective hero is very similar to that found in the American hard-boiled detective novels of Raymond Chandler and others. Vázquez Montalbán freely admits to having been inspired by Chandler and his protagonist Philip Marlowe in the creation of Pepe Carvalho and the moral landscape of the series.

While his second novel, *Tatuaje*, still retains some features such as the collage and intertextuality of *Yo maté a Kennedy*, the third novel in the series is the first of what Vázquez Montalbán has called his chronicle novels, a term designed to define his detective's investigations into a historical era—initially that of the transition of Spain from Franquism to democracy and in the later novels the transition from national and regional cultures to the advent of globalization.

Vázquez Montalbán's detective, Pepe Carvalho—his full name is José Carvalho Tourón—was born, like the author's father, in the northwestern Spanish province of Galicia in the little village of Souto and later moved to Barcelona. Pepe is a passionate and expert gourmet cook, and he used to be a voracious reader with a large library, which he now burns book by book in his fireplace. He has frequent love affairs, in addition to his relationship with Charo, his longtime girlfriend, but finds it impossible to commit himself to any stable attachment.

To underline his role as an outsider, Pepe surrounds himself with a group of people who are from the margins of modern Spanish society. His girlfriend Charo is a prostitute; his general factotum and cook is the eccentric Biscuter, who was his cell neighbor during his time in jail. He also associates with Francisco Melgar, known as Bromuro, a shoeshine man and his main informer, who got his name because he paranoically maintains that the government puts bromide into the public water supply to sedate any urges and desires in the population. Another frequently recurring figure is Inspector Contreras, a Franquist police officer and enemy of Carvalho.

The Angst-Ridden Executive

In *La soledad del manager* (1977; *The Angst-Ridden Executive*, 1990), Pepe Carvalho is hired by the widow of Antonio Jauma to investigate the murder of her husband. The police quickly deduce from some underwear found in his pocket that Jauma was the victim of a sordid love affair; however, Pepe determines that Jauma was silenced because he had discovered financial malfeasance in the multinational company for which he worked. The company had helped finance the 1973 coup in Chile and is diverting funds to neofascist groups during Spain's transition.

The investigation of Jauma's murder is also a journey into Pepe's own past as he visits a number of the victim's friends from their time together in the underground struggle at the university fifteen years before. Pepe finds that many of them have left behind their youthful idealism and betrayed their comrades who perished in the fight against tyranny.

This scrutinizing of the past, particularly from the perspective of Pepe's and Vázquez Montalbán's leftist origins, is a constant ingredient in most of the novels in the series. The detective shares much of the author's history as well as his political convictions and his hobbies. Pepe is a gourmet cook and loves wine, sex, and conversations with anyone who interests him. The disillusionment with the betrayal of the working classes in post-Franco Spain has outwardly made him a cynic. However, there is a romantic hidden behind Pepe's cynical exterior; like Chandler's Marlowe he is given to quixotic behavior despite claiming to believe only in his stomach, early in *The Angst-Ridden Executive.* Still, when the murderer offers Pepe a fine and rare bottle of wine, Pepe pours the expensive wine on the equally luxurious carpet. Though not a saint, he is the most trustworthy man on the mean streets of Barcelona.

Southern Seas

Southern Seas, the fourth novel in the series, is considered by most readers and critics to be Vázquez Montalbán's best novel in the series. It combines a well-constructed detective plot with a thinly veiled critique of modern Spanish society and still contains many of the more self-consciously literary elements, particularly intertextuality, that are a trademark of the author's early literary output.

In *Southern Seas*, a wealthy Spanish industrialist, who had ostensibly become disillusioned with his life and wanted to move to the South Pacific for spiritual regeneration, is found dead at a construction site. When the police fail to find the murderer, the widow hires Pepe to find out what the dead man had done during his last year, not so much out of love for her dead husband but to protect her inheritance. As usual the investigation of the crime is subordinate to Pepe's wanderings through an urban moral wasteland against the background of a municipal election. His search, aided by some pieces of poetry found on the corpse, takes him to San Magín, a working-class district in the south of Barcelona that the murdered man made a fortune developing years before. To atone for his exploitation of the San Magín district, he had worked incognito as an accountant there and begun a love affair with a working-class girl. He was killed by her stepbrother and dumped in another part of the city. The widow, no longer worried about any danger to her inheritance, keeps the true circumstances of her husband's death from the police and goes on the same trip to the South Pacific that her husband had planned before his murder. Pepe, angry and saddened by her callousness, refuses her invitation to accompany her.

As one would expect from a long series, the later novels become more self-referential and intertextual, reusing characters from previous novels, such as the daughter of the victim in *Southern Seas*, who reappears in *The Man of My Life*.

Franz G. Blaha

Principal mystery and detective fiction

Pepe Carvalho series: 1972-1980 • *Yo maté a Kennedy: Impresiones, observaciones y memorias de un guardaespaldas*, 1972; *Tatuaje*, 1974; *La soledad* *del manager*, 1977 (*The Angst-Ridden Executive*, 1990); *Los mares del sur*, 1979 (*Southern Seas*, 1986)

1981-1990 • *Asesinato en el Comité Central*, 1981 (*Murder in the Central Committee*, 1984); *Los pájaros de Bangkok*, 1983; *A rosa de Alejandría*, 1984; *El balneario*, 1986; *Jordi Anfruns, sociólogo*, 1986; *Aquel 23 de febrero*, 1986; *Desde de los tejados*, 1986; *Cenizas de Laura*, 1986; *Historias de padres e hijos*, 1987; *Historias de fantasmas*, 1987; *Tres historias de amor*, 1987; *Historias de política ficción*, 1987; *Asesinato en Prado del Rey y otras historias sórdidas*, 1987; *El delantero centro fue asesinado al atardecer*, 1988 (*Off Side*, 1996)

1991-2004 • *El laberinto griego*, 1991 (*An Olympic Death*, 1992); *Sabotaje olímpico*, 1993; *El hermano pequeño*, 1994; *Roldán, ni vivo ni muerto*, 1994; *El premio*, 1996; *Quinteto de Buenos Aires*, 1997 (*The Buenos Aires Quintet*, 2003); *El hombre de mi vida*, 2000 (*The Man of My Life*, 2005); *Milenio Carvalho*, 2004 (2 volumes)

Other major works

Novels: *El pianista*, 1985 (*The Pianist*, 1989); *Galíndez*, 1990 (*Galíndez*, 1992); *Autobiografia del general Franco*, 1992; *El estrangulador*, 1994; *O César o nada*, 1998

Short fiction: *Recordando a Dardé y otros relatos*, 1969; *El matarife*, 1986; *Cuarteto*, 1988

Play: *Guillermota en el país de las Guillerminas*, 1973

Poetry: *Una educacíon sentimental*, 1967; *Movimientos sin éxito*, 1969; *Coplas a la muerte de mia tiá Daniela*,1973; *A la sombra de las muchachas sin flor: Poemas del amor y del terror*, 1973; *Praga*, 1982; *Memoria y deseo: Obra poética (1963-1990)*, 1986; *Los alegres muchachos de Atzavara*, 1987; *Pero el viajero que huye*, 1991

Nonfiction: *Informe sobre la informacíon*, 1963; *Manifesto subnormal*, 1970; *Croníca sentimental de España*, 1971; *¿Qué es el imperialismo?*, 1976; *Barcelonas*, 1987 (revised in 1992); *La literatura en la construcción de la ciudad democrática*, 1998

Bibliography

Bayo Belenguer, Susana. *Theory, Genre, and Memory in the Carvalho Series of Manuel Vázquez Montalbán*. Lewiston, N.Y.: Edwin Mellen Press, 2001. A thorough study of the Carvalho series, based mainly on critical and narrative theory.

Cate-Arriès, Francie. "Lost in the Language of Culture: Manuel Vázquez Montalbán's Novel of Detection." *Revista de estudios hispánicos* 22, no. 3 (1988): 47-56. A brief survey of Vázquez Montalbán's detective fiction to around 1988, including the author's most distinguished novels in the Carvalho series.

Colmeiro, José F. "The Hispanic (Dis)Connection: Some Leads and a Few Missing Links." *Journal of Popular Culture* 34, no. 4 (Spring, 2001): 49-64. Prompted by the celebrations of the twenty-fifth anniversary of the Carvalho series, Colmeiro points out the disconnection of Spanish detective fiction from the British and French models, and the idiosyncratic development of the genre in Spain and Latin America.

_______. "The Spanish Connection: Detective Fiction After Franco." *Journal of Popular Culture* 28, no. 1 (Summer, 1994): 151-161. A concise, informative article on detective fiction in Spain after the death of Franco, devoting substantial attention to Vázquez Montalbán.

Hart, Patricia, ed. *The Spanish Sleuth: The Detective in Spanish Fiction*. Rutherford, N.J.: Fairleigh Dickinson University Press, 1987. A collection of historical/critical essays on Spanish detective fiction and individual authors, including Hart's essay on Vázquez Montalbán.

Puvogel, Sandra. "Pepe Carvalho and Spain: A Look at Manuel Vázquez Montalbán's Detective Fiction." *Monographic Review/Revista Monográfica* 3, nos. 1-2 (1987): 261-267. A brief essay on the author in the context of Spanish history and culture.

FRANÇOIS-EUGÈNE VIDOCQ

Born: Arras, France; July 24, 1775
Died: Paris, France; May 11, 1857
Type of plot: Police procedural

Contribution

François-Eugène Vidocq was the first official detective in the Western world. Having led the life of a vagabond, strolling actor, soldier, robber, gambler, dealer in illicit goods, and convict, he offered his services to the préfect of the brigade of the Sûreté in 1809. Hired as a police spy, he became by 1811 the chief of the detective bureau of the Sûreté that he had organized. Phenomenally successful in his investigations, by the time *Mémoires de Vidocq, chef de la police de Sûreté jusqu'en 1827* (1828-1829; *Memoirs of Vidocq, Principal Agent of the French Police Until 1827*, 1828-1829) appeared, he had become a legend not only in France but also in England and Germany. His fame spread to the United States. An American edition of his memoirs was published simultaneously in Philadelphia and Baltimore in 1834. Excerpts from the memoirs ran from September to December, 1838, in *Burton's Gentleman's Magazine*, a Philadelphia periodical.

Vidocq's memoirs proved an important stimulus to the development of detective and mystery fiction. They inspired the American writer Edgar Allan Poe to become the "father of the detective story"; it is no accident that Poe set the first bona fide story of this genre, "The Murders in the Rue Morgue," in Paris. In this story, Poe refers to Vidocq as "a good guesser" but one who "impaired his vision by holding the object too close." Poe's detective hero C. Auguste Dupin is not modeled on Vidocq but is a mask for Poe himself. Vidocq is represented by the bourgeois, philistine, bureaucratic Préfect G—, the antithesis of Dupin, the titled aristocrat, poet, mathematician, and amateur detective.

Vidocq's success as a detective did not depend on any great power of ratiocination. Instead, it depended on his intimate knowledge of the criminal class. He was also a master of disguise and gifted at extracting information from unsuspecting persons. In his memoirs, he describes his methods of investigation swiftly and forcefully, sometimes using the argot of the underworld. In addition to Poe's work, Vidocq's influence may be seen in the work of Honoré de Balzac, Victor Hugo, Eugène Sue, Charles Dickens, Wilkie Collins, Émile Gaboriau, Arthur Conan Doyle, Maurice Leblanc, E. W. Hornung, G. K. Chesterton, and Leslie Charteris. The "gentleman-crook" hero of mystery fiction—Leblanc's Arsène Lupin, Hornung's A. J. Raffles, and Charteris's Simon Templar—derived from Vidocq's memoirs.

Biography

François-Eugène Vidocq was born in Arras, France, on July 24, 1775, the son of a baker and his wife. At thirteen, he began learning the baker's trade from his father, starting by delivering bread to customers in the city. A wild youth who loved to indulge himself, he began to steal from his parents. Finally, he absconded with the family savings, planning to flee to the New World. Ironically, he himself was robbed. After suffering a series of misadventures, he returned home to Arras. There, he easily obtained his mother's forgiveness and his father's permission to join the army. He enlisted and served in engagements at Valmy and Jammapes. Returning to Arras in 1794, he married Marie-Anne-Louise Chevalier but soon abandoned her on learning that she was having an affair with another man.

Going to Belgium, Vidocq accepted an officer's commission in the army. Following a quarrel with a fellow officer, he was imprisoned at Lille. In 1796, he was sentenced to eight years of forced labor for complicity in forging an order to release a laborer from imprisonment during the Terror. Vidocq was imprisoned in Bicêtre in 1797. In 1798, he was removed to Brest, from which he soon escaped. Recaptured in 1799, he was incarcerated anew at Bicêtre. Later he was transferred to Toulon, from which he escaped in 1800. There followed a series of adventures, imprisonments, and escapes. When free, Vidocq continued to live among the thieves of Arras, Paris, and the provinces. In 1805, he was divorced from his first wife.

In 1809, Vidocq decided to offer his services to the police. In a report to the chief of the brigade of the

Sûreté, in which he discussed the prevalence of crime in Paris, Vidocq suggested that no one knew criminals so well as one who had been a criminal himself, hinting at his own usefulness at criminal investigation. Neither the préfect of the Parisian police nor the minister of the Police General rejected Vidocq's idea. It was agreed that Vidocq be employed as an undercover agent for the Sûreté. By 1810, he escaped from prison, with the approval of the new préfect, who remained in this post until 1814 and particularly befriended Vidocq. In 1811, Vidocq was officially invested with police powers and appointed chief of the detective division of the Sûreté. By 1817, he had seventeen agents under him and had made 772 arrests, setting a police record. In 1824, the brigade numbered thirty-one agents, including five women. In 1820, Vidocq had married Jeanne-Victoire Guérin; she died in 1824. Shortly thereafter, he married his cousin, Fleuride Maniez.

In 2003, France honored François-Eugène Vidocq with a postage stamp.

By 1827, Vidocq's success and power had gained for him political enemies, forcing him to resign. He bought a paper factory in Saint-Mandé, at which he employed former convicts. This business soon failed, and he turned to writing; his memoirs were published in 1828-1829 and proved to be an immense success. Taking advantage of political turmoil, he returned to his police work in 1831, and he is said to have played an important role in saving Louis-Philippe's throne. The new préfect of the Parisian police proved hostile to Vidocq, however, and faced with this new enmity, he resigned once again from the Sûreté.

During his career, Vidocq formed close friendships with some of the most prominent figures of French literature. By 1832, he had become a friend of Honoré de Balzac and inspired him to create his great fictional character Vaudrin, the master criminal who figures in several volumes of *La Comédie humaine* (*The Comedy of Human Life*, 1885-1893, 1896; best known as *The Human Comedy*, 1895-1896, 1911). Vidocq wrote additional works as well, including *Le Paravoleur: Ou, L'Art de se conduire prudemment en tout pays, notamment à Paris* (1830) and *Les Voleurs: Physiologie de leurs mœurs et de leur langage* (1836). In 1844, he published *Les Vrais Mystères de Paris* and *Quelques mots sur une question à l'ordre du jour: Réflexions sur les moyens propres à diminuer les crimes et les récidives*. In 1845-1846, he published *Les Chauffeurs du nord*, a novel about bandits who terrorized Picardy during the eighteenth and first half of the nineteenth centuries. During this period, Vidocq made trips to Belgium and England. In 1847, his third wife died. In 1848, Vidocq became well acquainted with the poet Alphonse Lamartine and had an interview with Prince Louis-Napoléon, who was to become Napoléon III. In 1849, Vidocq renewed his friendship with Victor Hugo, who began to write *Les Misérables* (English translation, 1862), which was published in 1862. Vidocq died in Paris on May 11, 1857.

Analysis

François-Eugène Vidocq's memoirs may be considered a novelistic autobiography. The central character, Vidocq himself, appears simply as the narrator, "I." The narrator is the only character who appears throughout the work, and his narrative takes him from his birth in Arras, France, in 1775 to his resignation in 1827 as the chief of the detective division of the Sûreté in Paris. For the most part, secondary characters appear only in short scenes, but their significance is always clear. The most important secondary character in the book is the chief of the brigade of the Sûreté when Vidocq joins the force. A model police officer, this man becomes Vidocq's mentor, teacher, and friend.

Memoirs of Vidocq, Principal Agent of the French Police Until 1827

As his story unfolds, the narrator experiences, at about the age of thirty-five, a complete reversal of character. His many years of imprisonment and association with criminals have finally disgusted him, and he believes that his life up to this point has been wasted. Believing that he must do something to make up for the past, both for himself and for society, he offers his services to the Paris police. When given the opportunity to serve in the Sûreté, he develops a new social consciousness and becomes society's protector.

This transformation of the central character is paralleled by a change in the plot structure. Vidocq's vagabond adventures follow in the tradition of such picaresque novels as *Lazarillo de Tormes* (1554; English translation, 1576), Alain-René Lesage's *Histoire de Gil Blas de Santillane* (1715-1735; *The History of Gil Blas of Santillane*, 1716, 1735; better known as *Gil Blas*), and Tobias Smollett's *The Adventures of Peregrine Pickle* (1751). After the narrator's transformation, however, the plan of action is something entirely new to narrative; it represents the birth of the police procedural—the kind of plot that Poe would satirize when he opposed his amateur detective Dupin to the official préfect of the Paris police. Given the opportunity to play pursuer rather than pursued, Vidocq zealously attempts to limit crime and contribute to the public welfare, using his past experience.

The most important legacy of Vidocq's memoirs has been the image they have presented of him as the great detective. By 1825, Vidocq had been the chief of the detectives of the Sûreté for fourteen years. During this period, he had established an amazing record as an indefatigable and unbribable crime fighter. Vigorous, broad-shouldered, powerfully built, of medium height, with tousled blond hair and penetrating steel-blue eyes, this man is built for action, whether it be prowling the Paris streets, visiting resorts of ill fame, listening to reports from police spies, or using various names and disguises during his rounds. Gifted with rare intelligence, prodigious memory, keen perception, and no mean acting abilities, he has through experience acquired a comprehensive knowledge of criminal behavior—argot, specialties, and modi operandi. A master reader of expressions and body language, he maintains files on criminals and their past

Fanciful depiction of Vidocq's fleeing from a brothel to escape capture by the police from an English edition of Vidocq's memoirs published in 1841.

histories, uses scientific graphology to distinguish forged writing from the authentic, and believes that fingerprints can be used for the identification of people. He possesses an uncanny instinct for ferreting out criminal activities. Altogether, he is a dedicated, relentless, courageous crime fighter. Once he has made an arrest, however, he is not lacking in compassion. He firmly believes that if society would cooperate, most criminals could be rehabilitated. (In real life, Vidocq was often generous in helping former prisoners.)

Because of the fuzzy publication history of Vidocq's memoirs, it is hard to say anything definitive about his style or technique. The text that the world has known is the four-volume edition prepared by editors Émile Morice and Louis L'Héritier de l'Ain, based in turn on the work of the original editor to whom Vidocq had unfortunately entrusted his manuscript. All three editors were unscrupulous. By the time Vidocq realized what they had perpetrated, it was too late: The work was in print in France and translations of it had been published simultaneously in England and Germany. Nevertheless, Vidocq at once engaged Froment, who had been the chief of the brigade of the special cabinet of the préfect of the Parisian police, to prepare for him an edition that would conform to his original intentions. Froment's edition was issued in Paris in 1829 as *Histoire de Vidocq, chef de la police de Sûreté: Écrite d'après lui-même* (the story of Vidocq, chief of the Sûreté, as told by himself). This edition essentially contains the contents of the original manuscript. Yet as Edwin Rich, the English translator of the memoirs, has stated:

> Whether the *Memoirs* of Vidocq are genuine or 'spurious' has been a question that has disturbed many critics, who appear to overlook the fact that their value and importance remain exactly the same. . . . The importance of the book . . . depends in no degree on who was the actual author. Ever since this material appeared in print, it has been a source of inspiration.

The memoirs generally contain antiquated references, interpolated passages, and indulgences in verbosity. Nevertheless, the emphasis is placed on descriptions of actions. These descriptions are concerned primarily with the activities of the central character, Vidocq. They are speedy and effective, often developing a rhythm of suspense and excitement until resolved to the satisfaction of the reader. A typical example occurs when Vidocq is seeking to capture the counterfeiter Watrin. Having learned Watrin's address, Vidocq has hurried to the place and has arrived

> just as someone was going out. Persuaded that it was Watrin, I tried to seize him. He escaped me; I dashed after him up the staircase, but, just as I was reaching for him, a kick in my chest sent me down twenty steps. I dashed after him again and with such speed that, to get rid of my pursuit, he was obliged to get into his quarters through a window on the landing. I then knocked on his door and summoned him to open. He refused.
>
> Annette [Vidocq's assistant, an agent of the Sûreté] had followed me. I ordered her to go in search of the police, and, while she went to obey, I imitated the noise of a man going downstairs. Watrin was deceived by this feint, and wanted to assure himself that I had really gone. He put his head out of the window.
>
> That was what I wanted, and I at once grabbed him by the hair. He seized me in the same way, and a fight started. . . . I gathered my strength for a last jerk; already he had only his feet left in the room; another effort and he was mine. I pulled him out vigorously and he fell into the corridor. To deprive him of the shoemaker's knife with which he was armed and drag him outside was the work of a moment.

The development of Vidocq's narrative is essentially ironic. An unprincipled social nonconformist becomes a consistent lawbreaker. He is punished by society, becoming a long-term convict. His failure produces within him a change of attitude toward himself and society. Thus, when given the opportunity, he becomes a lawman and a renowned detective. He transforms his antisocial behavior into something socially productive, exchanges rags for riches, and changes failure into success. The effect of the narrative is the exaltation of the detective as police officer and crime fighter.

Perhaps the greatest of ironies in both the work and the life of Vidocq was that the more successful he became as a detective, the greater was the envy of his colleagues in the police department. They engaged in intrigues against him, even attempting to incriminate him falsely and trying to return him to his former criminal status. Thus, occasionally Vidocq found that he had more to fear from his lawman peers than from criminals. Inspired by Vidocq, Poe made his detective French and placed him in the city of Paris. In 1841, Paris was the only city in the Western world to have a detective-police organization. Indeed, for thirty years the Sûreté had enjoyed renown for its skill and efficiency in solving crimes and capturing its perpetrators. Yet Poe did not see Vidocq's memoirs as a model for the kind of detective story he envisioned, nor did he consider Vidocq a proper model for his detective. His composition was not to be a loose series of episodes but a tense, concise, unified narrative of detection whose solution was to be reserved for the end. His detective, C. Auguste Dupin, is not a vulgar, middle-class bureaucrat, an unthinking man of action, but a cultured aristocrat, a scholarly recluse, an amateur solver of mysteries, to whom crime is not a social problem but a problem in philosophy and aesthetics. Dupin's cognitive powers make the solution of a murder not only an exercise in the relationship of intuition to logical demonstration but also a creative act whose formal perfection amounts to a fine art. If Poe refrained from exploring the possibilities of the detective-story genre any further, that challenge was taken up by Gaboriau—nevertheless, he remained closer than Poe to Vidocq—and then by Doyle, who extended the work of both Poe and Gaboriau, putting the detective story on the map of popular literature.

Richard P. Benton

Principal mystery and detective fiction

Novels: *Les Vrais Mystères de Paris*, 1844; *Les Chauffeurs du nord*, 1845-1846

Other major works

Nonfiction: *Mémoires de Vidocq, chef de la police de Sûreté jusqu'en 1827*, 1828-1829 (*Memoirs of Vidocq, Principal Agent of the French Police Until 1827*, 1828-1829; revised as *Histoire de Vodocq, chef de la police de Sûreté: écrite d'après lui-même*, 1829); *Le Paravoleur: Ou, L'Art de se conduire prudemment en tout pays, notamment à Paris*, 1830; *Les Voleurs: Physiologie de leurs mœurs et de leur langage*, 1836; *Quelques mots sur une question à l'ordre du jour: Réflexions sur les moyens propres à diminuer les crimes et les récidives*, 1844

Bibliography

Edwards, Samuel. *The Vidocq Dossier: The Story of the World's First Detective*. Boston: Houghton Mifflin, 1977. Biography of Vidocq, emphasizing his role in creating Paris's detective bureau.

Morton, James. *The First Detective: The Life and Revolutionary Times of Eugène Vidocq, Criminal, Spy and Private Eye*. London: Ebury, 2004. Comprehensive biography of Vidocq, discussing his sometimes ambiguous position in the Paris underworld and the role played by that ambiguity in the invention of the police detective.

Murch, Alma E. *The Development of the Detective Novel: From the Detective Story to the Crime Novel*. New York: Philosophical Library, 1958. This broad overview of the detective story gives Vidocq his due as the first detective author, as well as the first real-life detective.

Porter, Dennis. *The Pursuit of Crime: Art and Ideology in Detective Fiction*. New Haven, Conn.: Yale University Press, 1981. Study of the ideological and aesthetic effects of stylistic choices made by mystery and detective writers; sheds light on Vidocq's works.

Sayers, Dorothy L. *Les Origines du Roman Policier: A Wartime Wireless Talk to the French*. Translated by Suzanne Bray. Hurstpierpoint, West Sussex, England: Dorothy L. Sayers Society, 2003. Address to the French by the famous English mystery author, discussing the history of French detective fiction and its relation to the English version of the genre; provides perspective on Vidocq's writings.

Stead, J. P. *The Police of Paris*. London: Staples Press, 1957. Useful study of the Paris police department, its history, administration, and methodology. Helps readers understand Vidocq's novels. Includes bibliography.

Vidocq, François Eugène. *Memoirs of Vidocq: Master of Crime*. Translated and edited by Edwin Gile Rich. Reprint. Oakland, Calif.: AK Press, 2003. Vidocq's own account of his life in the Paris underworld, which influenced most great detective-fiction authors of the nineteenth century.

VOLTAIRE

François-Marie Arouet de Voltaire

Born: Paris, France; November 21, 1694
Died: Paris, France; May 30, 1778
Type of plot: Amateur sleuth

Contribution

Although Voltaire wrote in several different genres, including theater, poetry, and letters, he has remained most famous for the philosophical tales (*contes philosophiques*) that he composed during the last four decades of his lengthy literary career. In such well-structured works as *Zadig: Ou, La Destinée, Histoire orientale* (1748; *Zadig: Or, The Book of Fate*, 1749), *Le Micromégas* (1752; *Micromegas*, 1753), and *Candide: Ou, L'Optimisme* (1759; *Candide: Or, All for the Best*, 1759; also known as *Candide: Or, The Optimist*, 1762; also known as *Candide: Or, Optimism*, 1947), Voltaire described the pernicious effects of social injustice and religious intolerance. Yet these philosophical tales also illustrate the power and limits of both logical and intuitive reasoning. Several critics have properly judged Voltaire to be a precursor to later detective novelists. *Zadig* contains his most significant contribution to the detective genre. In the third chapter, Zadig uses deductive reasoning and explains convincingly that tracings left on the sand reveal the recent passing of a limping spaniel bitch and a galloping horse. According to Theodore Besterman in his book on Voltaire, "Sherlock Holmes must have read attentively" this chapter, which demonstrates the usefulness of deductive reasoning in interpreting physical evidence.

Biography

On November 21, 1694, Voltaire was born François-Marie Arouet in Paris, the son of François Arouet and Marie-Marguerite Arouet. ("Voltaire" was a pseudonym first used in 1717.) From 1704 until 1711, he studied in Paris at the Jesuit secondary school of Louis-le-Grand, where he developed a keen interest in the classics and an intense distrust of organized religions. During his literary career, which lasted more than six decades, Voltaire remained a freethinker who never hesitated to denounce social injustice. His criticism was acerbic and frequently caused problems for him. In 1726, he offended an influential French nobleman, the Chevalier de Rohan, and was imprisoned in the Bastille. He obtained his freedom only by promising to leave France for England, where he would live for almost three years. Following his return to France, he lived with his mistress, Émilie du Châtelet, on her country estate at Cirey in northern Champagne.

After her death in 1749, the disconsolate Voltaire accepted an offer from King Frederick the Great of Prussia that he move to the royal court at Potsdam, just outside Berlin. By 1753, Voltaire had tired of Frederick's benevolent despotism and decided to move to Geneva, where he admired the religious tolerance of this French-speaking city. In 1758, Voltaire purchased a country estate in Ferney, just across the French border from Geneva. Voltaire spent much of the last two decades of his life in Ferney, where he enjoyed his life as a "gentleman farmer" and the companionship of his niece, Mme Denis. During this very creative period, Voltaire wrote several important philosophical tales as well as his influential *Dictionnaire philosophique portatif* (1764; also known as *La Raison par alphabet* and *Dictionnaire philosophique*; *A Philosophical Dictionary for the Pocket*, 1765; also known as *Philosophical Dictionary*, 1945, enlarged 1962). In February, 1778, Voltaire made a triumphal return to Paris, where he died on May 30, 1778, at the age of eighty-three.

Analysis

A first reading of *Zadig* may suggest that it is inappropriate to consider this "philosophical tale" an early detective novel. Like most of Voltaire's major works, however, *Zadig* can be interpreted from several different perspectives, and each critical approach enriches the understanding of Voltaire's artistry. Readers who favor sociocriticism have analyzed Voltaire's effective denunciation in *Zadig* of social exploitation, religious hypocrisy, and intolerance. Although Voltaire called *Zadig* an "Oriental story" whose action takes place in

Voltaire. (Library of Congress)

fifteenth century Babylon, in it, he discusses the social problems of his own era, not those of medieval Babylon, about which he and his contemporaries knew very little. In eighteenth century France, true censorship existed; Voltaire himself had been imprisoned twice in the 1720's because of his criticism. The pseudo-Babylonian elements in *Zadig* made it easier for Voltaire to avoid problems with the French police.

Zadig

The many levels of irony and the refined style in *Zadig* have attracted much critical attention since the eighteenth century, and several scholars have noted that Voltaire's style combines formal eloquence with subtle wit. His arguments are presented in such an aesthetically pleasing and yet unpretentious manner that it seems inappropriate to question his sincerity. His very style creates a favorable impression on his readers. In addition, his consistent understatement and the aesthetic distance that he maintains between his third-person narrative and his fictional characters make his philosophical tale appear objective and thus worthy of serious attention. Moreover, his well-balanced sentences permit and even encourage diverse interpretations. Readers of *Zadig* conclude that Voltaire respects all intellectual freedom; this interpretation leads them to respond favorably to Voltaire's perception of reality.

In the development of the detective genre, *Zadig* is important not because of its well-constructed plot and refined style but rather because it illustrates appropriate ways of explaining perplexing situations. In his influential work *Les Pensées* (1670; *Monsieur Pascal's Thoughts, Meditations, and Prayers*, 1688), Blaise Pascal argued that there existed two major ways of perceiving the world. Those who use purely deductive and logical reasoning practice "l'esprit de géométrie" (the spirit of geometry), whereas those who discover truth intuitively practice "l'esprit de finesse" (the spirit of finesse). Voltaire frequently referred to Pascal's distinction. According to Pascal, each individual uses a unique blend of these two major types of reasoning, and neither "the spirit of geometry" nor "the spirit of finesse" suffices in itself to explain reality. Each person must sense intuitively when it is necessary to resort to deductive reasoning to discover a specific truth. *Zadig* illustrates the usefulness of both "the spirit of geometry" and "the spirit of finesse." Later detective writers could learn from *Zadig*, if not directly from Pascal, that both deductive and intuitive reasoning are essential to any search for truth.

Like such amateur sleuths as G. K. Chesterton's Father Brown and Agatha Christie's Miss Marple, Zadig does not seek out opportunities to solve crimes. He is not a professional detective who seeks monetary gain. No one ever questions the sincerity of Zadig's motives. If, by chance, someone asks questions about specific crimes, he willingly works to explain logically how things actually happened.

In chapter 2, Voltaire states that Zadig's marriage to Azora has serious problems. Zadig decides to divorce his wife; this act leaves him with much free time, which he spends studying "the properties of animals and plants." Zadig soon acquires objective knowledge, and he is able to recognize "a thousand differences" in nature "where others would see everything as uniform"—he has become an expert in zoology and botany.

Near the palace one day, the queen's eunuch asks Zadig if he has seen the royal dog. In reply, Zadig observes that the dog is a small spaniel bitch that limps and has recently given birth to puppies. Although the eunuch assumes that Zadig has seen the animal, Zadig denies it. A few minutes later, court officials come by and inquire about the king's missing horse, which Zadig also describes. Although Zadig states that he has seen neither animal, his audience is unconvinced; he is arrested for stealing both spaniel and stallion.

During his trial, Zadig ably defends himself, explaining that specific tracings on the sand and broken branches in the trees enabled him to determine the physical characteristics of the missing animals. The judges are convinced; because there is no proof that he stole either creature, he is acquitted. This chapter in *Zadig* has influenced later detective writers because it demonstrates that the objective analysis of physical clues can prove innocence or guilt beyond a reasonable doubt. Detective writers after Voltaire would strive to develop equally creative and totally logical explanations for perplexing cases.

Not all the characters in this philosophical tale reason as effectively as Zadig. Near the end of the piece, he meets a hermit who practices "the spirit of finesse" in a strange and unpersuasive manner. (The hermit is the antithesis of the reasonable Zadig.) After Zadig and the hermit have spent a pleasant night as guests of a kindly widow, the hermit repays her hospitality by drowning her fourteen-year-old nephew. The hermit justifies this murder by claiming that if this adolescent had lived, he would have strangled his aunt and Zadig within two years. Even after the hermit transforms himself into a winged angel, Zadig refuses to accept the hermit's questionable defense, noting that there was a simple alternative to this murder: "Would it not have been better to have corrected this child and rendered him virtuous rather than drowning him?" Thus, logic discredits all attempts to justify murder.

Although the hermit acted with the purest of intentions, his action is nevertheless criminal. Zadig, like later detectives, understands that people are to be judged by their actions and not by the ingenious explanations they may present in defense of their crimes. Unless the absolute value of each life is accepted, society will soon fall into chaos. Zadig realizes that the hermit is basically a well-intentioned murderer who used specious reasoning to justify murder.

In his 1972 book *Bloody Murder: From the Detective Story to the Crime Novel*, Julian Symons perceptively states that although *Zadig* does contain an "ingenious piece of analytical deduction," it is not merely "a crime story." In *Zadig*, Voltaire wrote primarily about the search for happiness in an imperfect world. Zadig, however, is a detective in two ways: He uses deductive reasoning to solve a perplexing case and also recognizes the faulty reasoning of a criminal.

Edmund J. Campion

PRINCIPAL MYSTERY AND DETECTIVE FICTION

NOVEL: *Zadig: Ou, La Destinée, Histoire orientale*, 1748 (originally as *Memnon: Histoire orientale*, 1747; *Zadig: Or, The Book of Fate*, 1749)

OTHER MAJOR WORKS

NOVELS: *Le Micromégas*, 1752 (*Micromegas*, 1753); *Histoire des voyages de Scarmentado*, 1756 (*The History of the Voyages of Scarmentado*, 1757; also known as *History of Scarmentado's Travels*, 1961); *Candide: Ou, L'Optimisme*, 1759 (*Candide: Or, All for the Best*, 1759; also known as *Candide: Or, The Optimist*, 1762; also known as *Candide: Or, Optimism*, 1947); *L'Ingénu*, 1767 (*The Pupil of Nature*, 1771; also known as *Ingenuous*, 1961); *L'Homme aux quarante écus*, 1768 (*The Man of Forty Crowns*, 1768); *La Princesse de Babylone*, 1768 (*The Princess of Babylon*, 1769)

SHORT FICTION: *Le Monde comme il va*, 1748 (revised as *Babouc: Ou, Le Monde comme il va*, 1749; *Babouc: Or, The World as It Goes*, 1754; also known as *The World as It Is: Or, Babouc's Vision*, 1929); *Memnon: Ou, La Sagesse humaine*, 1749 (*Memnon: Or, Human Wisdom*, 1961); *La Lettre d'un Turc*, 1750; *Jeannot et Colin*, 1764 (*Jeannot and Colin*, 1929); *Le Blanc et le noir*, 1764 (*The Two Genies*, 1895); *L'Histoire de Jenni*, 1775; *Les Oreilles du Comte de Chesterfield*, 1775 (*The Ears of Lord Chesterfield and Parson Goodman*, 1826)

PLAYS: 1718-1740 • *Œdipe*, pr. 1718, pb. 1719 (*Oedipus*, 1761); *Artémire*, pr. 1720; *Mariamne*, pr. 1724, pb. 1725 (English translation, 1761); *L'Indiscret*, pr., pb. 1725 (verse play); *Brutus*, pr. 1730, pb.

1731 (English translation, 1761); *Ériphyle*, pr. 1732, pb. 1779; *Zaïre*, pr. 1732, pb. 1733 (English translation, 1736); *La Mort de César*, pr. 1733, pb. 1735; *Adélaïde du Guesclin*, pr. 1734; *L'Échange*, pr. 1734, pb. 1761; *Alzire*, pr., pb. 1736 (English translation, 1763); *L'Enfant prodigue*, pr. 1736, pb. 1738 (verse play; prose translation; *The Prodigal*, 1750?); *La Prude: Ou, La Grandeuse de Cassette*, wr. 1740, pr., pb. 1747 (verse play; adaptation of William Wycherley's play *The Plain Dealer*); *Zulime*, pr. 1740, pb. 1761

1741-1750 • *Mahomet*, pr., pb. 1742 (*Mahomet the Prophet*, 1744); *Mérope*, pr. 1743, pb. 1744 (English translation, 1744, 1749); *La Princesse de Navarre*, pr., pb. 1745 (verse play; music by Jean-Philippe Rameau); *Sémiramis*, pr. 1748, pb. 1749 (*Semiramis*, 1760); *Nanine*, pr., pb. 1749 (English translation, 1927); *Oreste*, pr., pb. 1750

1751-1779 • *Rome sauvée*, pr., pb. 1752; *L'Orphelin de la Chine*, pr., pb. 1755 (*The Orphan of China*, 1756); *Socrate*, pb. 1759 (*Socrates*, 1760); *L'Écossaise*, pr., pb. 1760 (*The Highland Girl*, 1760); *Tancrède*, pr. 1760, pb. 1761; *Don Pèdre*, wr. 1761, pb. 1775; *Olympie*, pb. 1763, pr. 1764; *Le Triumvirat*, pr. 1764, pb. 1767; *Les Scythes*, pr., pb. 1767; *Les Guèbres: Ou, La Tolérance*, pb. 1769; *Sophonisbe*, pb. 1770, pr. 1774 (revision of Jean Mairet's play); *Les Pélopides: Ou, Atrée et Thyeste*, pb. 1772; *Les Lois de Minos*, pb. 1773; *Irène*, pr. 1778, pb. 1779; *Agathocle*, pr. 1779

Poetry: *Poème sur la religion naturelle*, 1722; *La Ligue*, 1723; *La Henriade*, 1728 (a revision of *La Ligue*; *Henriade*, 1732); *Le Mondain*, 1736 (*The Man of the World*, 1764); *Discours en vers sur l'homme*, 1738 (*Discourses in Verse on Man*, 1764); *Poème de Fontenoy*, 1745; *Poème sur la loi naturelle*, 1752 (*On Natural Law*, 1764); *La Pucelle d'Orléans*, 1755, 1762 (*The Maid of Orleans*, 1758; also known as *La Pucelle: Or, the Maid of Orleans*, 1758-1786); *Poème sur la désastre de Lisbonne*, 1756 (*Poem on the Lisbon Earthquake*, 1764); *Le Pauvre Diable*, 1758; *Épître à Horace*, 1772

Nonfiction: *An Essay upon the Civil Wars of France. . . , and Also upon the Epick Poetry of the European Nations from Homer Down to Milton*, 1727; *La Henriade*, 1728 (*Henriade*, 1732); *Histoire de Charles XII*, 1731 (*The History of Charles XII*, 1732); *Le Temple du goût*, 1733 (*The Temple of Taste*, 1734); *Letters Concerning the English Nation*, 1733; *Lettres philosophiques*, 1734 (originally published in English as *Letters Concerning the English Nation*, 1733; also known as *Philosophical Letters*, 1961); *Discours de métaphysique*, 1736; *Éléments de la philosophie de Newton*, 1738 (*The Elements of Sir Isaac Newton's Philosophy*, 1738); *Discours en vers sur l'homme*, 1738-1752 (*Discourses in Verse on Man*, 1764); *Vie de Molière*, 1739; *Le Siècle de Louis XIV*, 1751 (*The Age of Louis XIV*, 1752); *Essai sur les mœurs et l'esprit des nations*, 1756, 1763 (*The General History and State of Europe*, 1754, 1759); *Traité sur la tolérance*, 1763 (*A Treatise on Religious Toleration*, 1764); *Commentaires sur le théâtre de Pierre Corneille*, 1764; *Dictionnaire philosophique portatif*, 1764, enlarged 1769 (also known as *La Raison par alphabet* and *Dictionnaire philosophique*; *A Philosophical Dictionary for the Pocket*, 1765; also known as *Philosophical Dictionary*, 1945, enlarged 1962); *Avis au public sur les parracides imputés aux calas et aux Sirven*, 1775; *Correspondence*, 1953-1965 (102 volumes)

Miscellaneous: *The Works of M. de Voltaire*, 1761-1765 (35 volumes), 1761-1781 (38 volumes); *Candide, and Other Writings*, 1945; *The Portable Voltaire*, 1949; *Candide, Zadig, and Selected Stories*, 1961; *The Complete Works of Voltaire*, 1968-1977 (135 volumes; in French)

Bibliography

Aldridge, A. Owen. *Voltaire and the Century of Light*. Princeton, N.J.: Princeton University Press, 1975. A teacher of comparative literature, Aldridge reexamines the life and career of Voltaire within the context of European intellectual and political history, providing useful insights in a style equally suited to the specialist as to the general reader.

Bird, Stephen. *Reinventing Voltaire: The Politics of Commemoration in Nineteenth Century France*. Oxford, England: Voltaire Foundation, 2000. An examination of the critical response to Voltaire, particularly in the nineteenth century. Includes bibliography and indexes.

Braun, Theodore E. D. "Voltaire, *Zadig*, *Candide*, and Chaos." In *Studies on Voltaire and the Eighteenth Century*, edited by Anthony Strugnell. Oxford, England: Voltaire Foundation, 1997. Discusses the importance of social disorder in *Zadig*, as well as in *Candide*. Bibliographic references.

Davidson, Ian. *Voltaire in Exile*. New York: Grove Press, 2005. A biography focusing on Voltaire's life after being banished from France. Includes analysis of much of Voltaire's personal correspondence.

Gray, John. *Voltaire*. New York: Routledge, 1999. A biography of Voltaire that covers his life and works, while concentrating on his philosophy. Includes bibliography.

Knapp, Bettina Liebowitz. *Voltaire Revisited*. New York: Twayne, 2000. A basic biography of Voltaire that describes his life and works. Includes bibliography and index.

Mason, Haydn Trevor. *Voltaire: A Biography*. Baltimore: The Johns Hopkins University Press, 1981. Concise but lively survey of Voltaire's life that clearly relates the major works to their context. Closely documented, useful both as biography and as criticism, this volume is recommended to the student and to the general reader alike.

Pearson, Roger. *Voltaire Almighty: A Life in Pursuit of Freedom*. London: Bloomsbury, 2005. A readable, compelling account of Voltaire's life. Includes bibliography and index.

Vartanian, Aram. "*Zadig:* Theme and Counter-theme." In *Dilemmas du roman*, edited by Catherine Lafarge. Saratoga, Calif.: Anima Libri, 1990. Argues that the philosophic theme of impersonal fate is counterpoised against a background theme which creates a contrapuntal movement of the narrative structure. Asserts the story is told in such a way that its overall meaning emerges from a network of tensions felt among its various elements.

C. E. VULLIAMY

Born: Wales; June 20, 1886
Died: England; September 4, 1971
Also wrote as Anthony Rolls
Type of plot: Inverted

Contribution

C. E. Vulliamy is best known for his novels and biographies of the Johnsonian era (the most controversial being a portrait of James Boswell as an opportunist in his friendship with Samuel Johnson), for his Voltaire, Jean-Jacques Rousseau, John Wesley, and George Gordon, Lord Byron, and for his articles in *The Spectator*. His mysteries are not as widely known. In the main they are novels of academia (*Don Among the Dead Men*, 1952) or of clergy (*The Vicar's Experiments*, 1932; *Tea at the Abbey*, 1961), though the protagonist may be merely a headmaster or a rector. In Vulliamy's novels, the mystery plot actually serves as the backdrop for mildly satiric treatments of British society and consequently depends on the techniques that dominate more traditional satiric forms. There is a sense of *reductio ad absurdum* in the portraits of foolish and fallible humanity. Vulliamy's virtue is his vice, with the satiric at its best adding an extra dimension to the mystery genre, but at its worst detracting to such a degree that neither satire nor mystery convinces. Vulliamy employs the conventions of detective fiction but turns them on end, mocking them and, through his reversals and exaggerations, mocking the weaknesses of humanity that necessitate such conventions.

Biography

C. E. Vulliamy, born Colwyn Edward Vullimay in Wales on June 20, 1886, studied art under Stanhope Forbes in Newlyn, Cornwall, from 1910 to 1913. During World War I, he served in the King's Shropshire Light Infantry and was stationed in France, Macedonia, and Turkey; he joined the Royal Welch Fusiliers in 1918, becoming camp commandant of the Twenty-eighth Division Headquarters and later education officer of the division, with a rank of captain. He was married to Eileen Hynes in 1916, and they had a son and a daughter.

After the war, Vulliamy pursued a full-time literary career. He was active in field archaeology, contributed regularly to *The Spectator*, and was a respected historical biographer. He was a fellow of the Royal Society of Literature and an active member of the Royal Anthropological Society. His wife died in 1943; he survived her by almost thirty years, dying on September 4, 1971.

Analysis

C. E. Vulliamy's mysteries are all to some degree inverted, and they follow the same general pattern. They begin with a grudge against another person (usually a social parasite who tends toward malicious gossip), a search for a perfect murder method, and a murder attempt (sometimes successful and sometimes not), followed by plans for further crimes, a deterioration of character involving a movement toward insanity, outside intervention, apprehension, a trial scene, a questionable verdict, and an ironic conclusion. This pattern varies slightly from tale to tale—sometimes the trial scene is excluded, sometimes the focus on madness is diminished—but the basic ingredients tend to remain consistent.

The stories reflect a pessimistic view of human nature and a deep-seated contempt for the foolishness of many social types, from Panglossian rectors to pretentious social climbers, from the limited products of public schools to the dim-witted, eccentric lords of the manor. Their characters and style partake of the artificial and exaggerated speech, manners, and sensibilities of some turn-of-the-century works, yet their negative, sometimes black-humor interpretations of human motivations and human behavior seem more modern. In other words, despite their strong sense of place—the English village—these works seem out of time, neither fully Edwardian nor fully modern. Although the narrative voice focuses particularly on the perspective of the villains, the murderers and would-be murderers, the effect is not that of the typical inverted form, in which the reader shares the perspective and the sensibilities of a first-person narrator. Instead, Vulliamy relies on a third-person omniscient narrative voice, which is distanced from characters and action, as if a superior judge, amused by the comic antics of his inferiors, retold them in such a way as to call attention to their limitations and to prove their inferiority. At his best, Vulliamy's wit is keen and his tales ironic; at his worst, his characterizations are shallow and his narrative is overwrought.

The Vicar's Experiments and Cakes for Your Birthday

Some consider *The Vicar's Experiments*, an imitation of Francis Iles's mysteries, a "minor masterpiece," for it is written with discipline, the satire and negativism more carefully controlled than in Vulliamy's other works. Usually, however, his plots are only contrived frames on which to hang satire, and as a consequence they sometimes verge on the silly. In *Cakes for Your Birthday* (1959), for example, after a foiled first attempt, the would-be murderers mail arsenic-coated cakes to their intended victim, who passes them on to an aunt who has just informed her of a will leaving her a considerable amount of money. The aunt dies; the intended victim is accused and tried, all the while reveling in her notoriety. Meanwhile, the main engineer of the plot goes slowly mad because he firmly believes that hanging the wrong person would be a miscarriage of justice. No one believes his confession, but a professional criminal, outraged by the ungentlemanly behavior of the accomplices, forces them to confess. The victim, who deserves punishment for her other deeds, though not for murder, is acquitted, but soon thereafter is thrown over a cliff by some unknown party. In *Body in the Boudoir* (1956), there is a coroner's inquest before the results of the autopsy are known, a murder investigation before there is clearly a murder, and a murder weapon (a West African Calabar bean) that boggles the imagination. Clearly, one does not read Vulliamy for plot. Instead it is for what one critic has called "verbal coruscation" and "its glitter of style, now broadly funny, now keenly acidulous."

Vulliamy's pet peeves

As in *Don Among the Dead Men*, the story of a chemist who discovers a poison that leaves no traces,

Vulliamy uses his plots as excuses to expostulate on his pet peeves. Everyone is subject to attack (sometimes most heavy-handedly), from the all-too-innocent clergyman to the self-made "Carbon King," from the narrow-minded and befuddled academician to the malicious small-town gossip. It is gossip that disturbs Vulliamy most and is the subject of his most damning attacks in all of his works. In fact, he is highly suspicious of any village organization, from the Red Cross to "Scouts for louts" and "Guides for girlies," believing that they are all dedicated to the propagation of gossip as if it were a duty required by their association. Male-female relationships also come under heavy attack, with all marriages depicted as a balancing act and all "love" relationships unnatural and exploitative. Lady Ruggerbrace, a minor character in *Body in the Boudoir*, sums up the Vulliamy attitude: "I am never surprised when I hear that a man has made a fool of himself: that is a phenomenon which I observe every day of my life."

Vulliamy is also highly critical of bad taste, particularly in clothing and in architecture. In many works there is some description of what Vulliamy terms "giving rein to the Free Philistine." This might involve, for example, wearing a bright yellow tie with polka dots or developing "desirable residences," made most undesirable by "their pebble-dashed impudence, their green and red tiles, their doubly-damnable sham antiquity and their preposterous gables," all of which would fill "an intelligent observer with dismay." It might also involve a delight in the grotesque styles of eighteenth and nineteenth century "antiquities": "the painted ceilings where tumbling nudities clustered on swagging clouds . . . the state beds (nurses of nightmares or couches for corpses), the wanton vagaries of rococo stucco . . . the picture galleries—cows by Cuyp, ladies by Lely, doubtful Rembrandts and undoubted Landseers . . . the rowdy-dowdies of Rubens." A Mr. Foggery, who mistrusts any intelligence not associated with money-making and has a face "red and yellow in patches like the brickwork of his preposterous villa," is typical of such philistine taste.

The police and professional criminals equally merit attack. Both groups deride bungling amateurs, but in doing so expose their own limitations. The professional robbers and murderers often are graduates of public schools or even of the University of Oxford, have a set of inviolate principles and inflationary fees, and alternate between rather contrived street talk and informed discussions of dahlias and Pythagorean laws of mathematics. Still, they are hardened criminals and think nothing of murdering for a fee or robbing for pleasure. In turn, the police in a Vulliamy mystery often long for a nice little corpse from a real professional. In *Cakes for Your Birthday*, they rather regret a failed murder, because they consider the would-be victim a "wicked slanderer" whose "obscene repulsive scandals" bring "misery and suspicion into a dozen innocent families" and, worst of all, mix "abominable lies with abominable truth." Furthermore, they admit that legal remedies often do no good because of "a notable army of liars, fools, and idiots" who cloud the issues and leave the slandered forever tainted. "Cultivate suspicion," says Inspector Fishbox to Sergeant Applecot, but that motto proves the undoing of many of Vulliamy's detectives, who suspect far too many for far too little reason.

BODY IN THE BOUDOIR

The inspector in *Body in the Boudoir* is typical. A cheerful cynic, he is a man with a system: Fearful that setting up a theory will lead one to reject all that does not fit, "even to the extent of twisting or fabricating evidence," he instead considers all possibilities, working out dozens of possible solutions, even the most absurd. The result is much meaningless and nonproductive busywork and interminable interviews. He continually dreams up untenable theories about witnesses and draws conclusions on the flimsiest of evidence, all the while calling for neutrality. There is an Inspector Clouseau quality to the bungling. Harboyle metaphorically trips over his feet throughout his investigation. For example, he carries around morgue photographs of a dead girl and then overreacts, suspecting a guilty conscience, when someone shows distress and shock. His ideal is a detective chief superintendent who "wears glasses, quotes poetry, and looks peculiarly innocent," a man who can move comfortably among the landed gentry as a police spy and hence has "more kills to his credit than anyone else in the whole perishing Force." Ironically, it is this detective who solves the mystery, not Harboyle, by sketching out a working hypothesis based on the probability of the improbable and pursuing it to its fantastic but correct conclusions. In other words, though using the standard ploys of the detective mystery genre, Vulliamy reduces all to the absurd.

Word play and comedy

Stylistically, Vulliamy's works tend toward the stilted, being at times overly euphuistic, with balanced phrasing, contrived sound combinations, and elaborate sentence construction—a bit too strained, a bit too arch. The result is characters whose speech and acts seem incredible. There are mock sermons, with inflated phraseology and hidebound clichés, sentences of more than two hundred words, and exhortations to action or nonaction, as the case may be. Phrases such as "brittle tinkle of icy drops" and "so furry in winter, so flimsy in summer," with their heavy assonance, alliteration, and balance, abound, along with aphorisms such as "The dead shot shoots dead." The better-educated characters quote Homer in Greek and Seneca in Latin; an angry lord towers "in red Homeric wrath among his myrmidons" in *Body in the Boudoir*, and a police dandy lectures from John Dryden's translation of Persius and muses on "the terrible torture of thirst for the naphthaline waters of passion accurst."

There are comic catalogs, including lists of murder methods and murder weapons: ingestion, penetration, puncture, "deadly dose . . . whiff or prick . . . stealthy stiletto . . . a blow in the bark or a stab in the back," "a short though heavy bludgeon, truncheon, cudgel, or cosh." Doctors roll out absurd lists of symptoms: "torticollis, kypchosis, scoliosis, and lordosis." Characters' names, too, are comically suggestive: Inspector Belching, the Reverend Theophilus Pogge, Sir Bedwith Bathwedder, Millie Peasewillow, Arthur Packett Lollesworth, William Edward Ripsguard, Ethel Meatring Peelyard, Agnes Farrier-Sludge, and Samuel Johnson, the butcher. Miss Wasp, Miss Bickerslow, Mrs. Pigge, and Lily Loveylove behave in accordance with their names, as do the "Old Rotters" of the Rotting Hill public school or the "Coddlers" from Coddlebury College for Women. The marquis of Ruggerbrace has an imposingly majestic figure but suffers from a remarkable "mental torpidity," while Detective Inspector Harboyle is not as hard-boiled as his name might suggest. Mr. Pukey, of the *Daily Whatnot*, is determinedly obnoxious in his pursuit of a story, while the hateful Misses Waddleboy are "grim images of human decay and of mouldy frustration," Victorian in sensibilities and social attitudes.

Vulliamy delights in calling attention to phrases that reflect one's values or psychology, as when a mild-mannered gentleman, angered at his daughter's murderer, repeats unhappily, "I would like to flay the bastard alive," or when a detective talks about getting the murderer "safely to the gallows." The "grim adverb" makes another's heart turn cold at the thought of describing the entrapment of a suspect "just as a fisherman would speak of bringing a salmon to the gaff or a trout to the net." There is deflation: "She was a Pardol of Stoke Ampersand, a family at least moderately famous for eleven centuries in the history of Great Britain, if only in footnotes and appendices"; there are mild satiric jibes: "He had learnt many things during his service in the Colonial Office and a truculent indecision was one of them." Classic British understatement is another favorite comic device; for example, on being told that there is a body in the boudoir and a police inspector at the door, the marchioness of Ruggerbrace remarks, "There seems to be something wrong." Literary and historical allusions similarly partake of the satiric, as in the comparison of a Captain Bashe to William of Ockham, for both "lived and thought (if that is the word) on the principle of rejecting unnecessary ideas," a process in which Bashe "succeeded so admirably that he had scarcely any ideas at all." After a long string of witnesses can remember almost nothing about a murder victim except her melancholy, the lengthy description given by a Miss Bleat is comic in its wealth and precision of detail, from the red agate brooch and unusual blue eyes to the fingernails varnished a pale pink, the lightly penciled eyebrows, and the hair the color of weak tea. Comic, too, is Vulliamy's reliance on the hyperbolic, whereby the trivial acts of trivial minds are blown up out of proportion. Curiosity seekers visiting a castle the day after a murder are described as a highly destructive invading army and their various skirmishes with the residents and staff as full-blown battles.

Vulliamy will delight those who enjoy a heavy dose of debunking, but there is a superficiality to his attacks, for he ignores the deep-seated horrors of human nature and is content to mock its surface forms: manners, attire, diction, pretension. He is best at a comedy of manners of the sort one finds in *The Vicar's Experiments* and *Don Among the Dead Men*.

Gina Macdonald

Principal mystery and detective fiction

Novels: *Clerical Error*, 1932; *Lobelia Grove*, 1932; *The Vicar's Experiments*, 1932; *Family Matters*, 1933; *Scarweather*, 1934; *Don Among the Dead Men*, 1952; *Body in the Boudoir*, 1956; *Cakes for Your Birthday*, 1959; *Justice for Judy*, 1960; *Tea at the Abbey*, 1961; *Floral Tribute*, 1963

Other major works

Novels: *Fusilier Bluf: The Experiences of an Unprofessional Soldier in the Near East, 1918-1919*, 1934; *Edwin and Eleanor: Family Documents, 1854-56*, 1945; *Henry Plumdew: His Memoirs, Experiences, and Opinions, 1938-1948*, 1950; *Jones: A Gentleman of Wales*, 1954; *The Proud Walkers*, 1955

Nonfiction: 1914-1930 • *Charles Kingsley and Christian Socialism*, 1914; *Our Prehistoric Forerunners*, 1925; *Unknown Cornwall*, 1925; *Immortal Man: A Study of Funeral Customs and of Beliefs in Regard to the Nature and Fate of the Soul*, 1926; *The Archaeology of Middlesex and London*, 1930; *Voltaire*, 1930

1931-1940 • *John Wesley*, 1931; *Rousseau*, 1931; *James Boswell*, 1932; *William Penn*, 1933; *Judas Maccabaeus: A Study Based on Dr. Quarto Karadyne's Translation of the Ararat Codex*, 1934; *Aspasia: The Life and Letters of Mary Granville, Mrs. Delany (1700-1788)*, 1935; *Mrs. Thrale of Streatham: Her Place in the Life of Dr. Samuel Johnson and in the Society of Her Time, Her Character and Family Affairs*, 1936; *Royal George: A Study of King George III*, 1937; *Outlanders: A Study of Imperial Expansion in South Africa, 1877-1902*, 1938; *Crimea: The Campaign of 1854-56, with an Outline of Politics and a Study of the Royal Quartet*, 1939; *Calico Pie: An Autobiography*, 1940

1941-1960 • *A Short History of the Montagu-Puffins*, 1941; *The Polderoy Papers*, 1943; *Doctor Philligo: His Journal and Opinions*, 1944; *English Letter Writers*, 1945; *Ursa Major: A Study of Dr. Johnson and His Friends*, 1946; *Man and the Atom: A Brief Account of the Human Dilemma*, 1947; *Byron, with a View of the Kingdom of Cant and a Dissertation of the Byronic Ego*, 1948; *Prodwit's Guide to Writing*, 1949; *Rocking Horse Journey: Some Views of the British Character*, 1952; *The Onslow Family, 1528-1874, with Some Account of Their Times*, 1953; *Little Arthur's Guide to Humbug*, 1960

Edited texts: *The Letters of the Tsar to the Tsaritsa, 1914-1917*, 1929 (translated by A. L. Hynes); *The Red Archives: Russian State Papers, and Other Documents, 1915-1918*, 1929 (translated by A. L. Hynes); *The Anatomy of Satire: An Exhibition of Satirical Writing*, 1950

Translation: *"The White Bull," with "Saul" and Various Short Pieces*, 1929 (by Voltaire)

Bibliography

Breen, Jon L., and Martin H. Greenberg, eds. *Synod of Sleuths: Essays on Judeo-Christian Detective Fiction*. Metuchen, N.J.: Scarecrow Press, 1990. Discusses important Jewish and Christian religious figures in detective fiction; sheds light on Vulliamy's works.

Erb, Peter C. *Murder, Manners, and Mystery: Reflections on Faith in Contemporary Detective Fiction—The John Albert Hall Lectures, 2004*. London: SCM Press, 2007. Collected lectures on the role and representation of religion in detective fiction; provides perspective on Vulliamy's writings.

Nover, Peter, ed. *The Great Good Place? A Collection of Essays on American and British College Mystery Novels*. New York: P. Lang, 1999. Compilation of essays focused on crime fiction set at college campuses or featuring academic characters; helps readers understand Vulliamy's novels.

Shibuk, Charles. "Notes on C. E. Vulliamy." *The Armchair Detective* 3, 5 (April, 1970; April, 1972): 161, 145. Contains information about the writing of Vulliamy.

_______. Review of *Tea at the Abbey*, by C. E. Vulliamy. *The Armchair Detective* 7 (November, 1973): 55. Review by a fan of the author looks at this novel of the clergy.

HENRY WADE

Henry Lancelot Aubrey-Fletcher

Born: Leigh, Surrey, England; September 10, 1887
Died: London, England; May 30, 1969
Types of plot: Police procedural; inverted

Principal series

Chief Inspector Poole, 1929-1954

Principal series character

John Poole, chief inspector, Criminal Investigation Department, New Scotland Yard, belongs to the new breed of police officers, college-educated and police academy-trained. Poole rises through the ranks to become the youngest inspector in the Criminal Investigation Department and eventually its chief. Personally charming and politically radical, Poole is clever, competent, and witty.

Contribution

Henry Wade, who has been described as a "staunch advocate of the classical detective story in its purest form," produced a total of twenty-one novels, some of them in the inverted rather than the classic form. Wade is often compared to Freeman Wills Crofts, but his novels have deeper characterizations and their depiction of police procedure is more realistic. Wade's novels frequently raise questions about the British legal system, and his strongly developed sense of irony, which seasons most of his work, finds its fullest expression in his criticism of the legal procedure. In his exposure of flaws in the legal system Wade anticipated and influenced a number of later writers. Many of Wade's novels intersperse social commentary with clues, motives, and suspects, but his novels written between 1947 and 1957 take a particularly close look at the changing values in post-World War II England.

Biography

Henry Wade was born Henry Lancelot Aubrey-Fletcher on September 10, 1887, in Leigh, Surrey, England, the eldest son of Sir Lancelot Aubrey-Fletcher and Emily Harriett Wade Aubrey-Fletcher. ("Henry Wade" was a pen name that he adopted in 1926.) Educated at Eton College and New College, University of Oxford, Wade joined the Grenadier Guards in 1908, serving in the First Battalion until his retirement in 1920. He returned to active duty during World War II (1940-1945). Wade was wounded twice during World War I and was awarded both the Distinguished Service Order and the French Croix de Guerre.

In 1911, Wade was married to Mary Augusta Chilton. They had four sons and one daughter. Mary Augusta died in 1963; in 1965, Wade was married to Nancy Cecil Reynolds.

After retiring from the Grenadier Guards, Wade held a number of positions in Buckinghamshire, including justice of the peace, alderman, and high sheriff. He served as lord lieutenant of Buckinghamshire (the queen's representative in the county) from 1954 until 1961 and was a lieutenant in the Body Guard of the Honourable Corps of Gentlemen-at-Arms (1956-1957). Wade succeeded to the baronetcy after his father's death in 1937.

Wade began his career as a writer in 1926 with the publication of *The Verdict of You All*. His 1929 novel, *The Duke of York's Steps*, introduced Detective Inspector Poole. During a writing career that stretched from 1926 until 1957, Wade produced a total of twenty-one novels (seven featuring Poole) and two collections of short stories, plus one nonfictional work, *A History of the Foot Guards to 1856* (published in 1927 under his own name). Wade's novels and short stories reflect his extensive experience with police business, as well as his dissatisfaction with the British legal system and its traditions. Wade's work as a writer was interrupted by World War II, but he resumed writing in 1947 and produced seven novels following the war. He died on May 30, 1969.

Analysis

The Verdict of You All, Henry Wade's first novel, and *The Missing Partners* (1928), his second, have been compared to novels written by Freeman Wills Crofts. Crofts, who is notable for having created one of literature's least colorful detectives, the plodding Inspector French, has been called "the master of timetables and alibis" because of his frequent use of railway timetables—provided as frontispieces in his novels—and seemingly unbreakable alibis that could be broken by clues hidden in the timetables. Wade's emulation of Crofts is most evident in his second novel, *The Missing Partners*, but both this novel and *The Verdict of You All* involve railways and clues in timetables.

Although comparisons between Wade and Crofts are inevitable, there are discernible differences, even in Wade's earliest novels. For one thing, Wade's novels have an authentic ring that is absent from the novels written by Crofts. Unlike Crofts, who knew little about police procedure, Wade could call on his own experiences as high sheriff and justice of the peace for Buckinghamshire when describing police procedure. This expertise gives an authenticity to his accounts of police work that sets him apart, even in his earliest novels. Another thing that sets Wade apart not only from Crofts but also from other writers of detective novels is the manner in which he uses irony in his criticism of the British legal system. Both *The Verdict of You All*, with its trial scene that ends in a questionable verdict, and *The Missing Partners*, in which justice nearly miscarries, raise questions about the entire legal system.

The Duke of York's Steps

Although Wade's subsequent works reveal his continued indebtedess to Crofts (as well as to other writers in the classic tradition), Wade began to find his own voice in his third novel, *The Duke of York's Steps*. Considered by many to be Wade's best, this novel introduces readers to Inspector John Poole, who would become Wade's most frequently used character.

The Hanging Captain

Wade followed *The Duke of York's Steps* with *The Dying Alderman* (1930) and *No Friendly Drop* (1931). *The Hanging Captain* (1932) is the most important novel of this period, not only because it marks the end of what some have called Wade's apprentice period but also because it marks the full flowering of his sense of irony. In *The Hanging Captain* Wade is able to give clear expression to the ironic criticism of the legal system that was latent in his earliest novels. Such criticism became a hallmark of Wade's writing, and it anticipated and influenced the work of writers such as Richard Hull, Cyril Hare, Henry Cecil, Raymond Postgate, Michael Underwood, and Roderic Jeffries.

The Hanging Captain deals with the problem of whether a certain captain has died by his own hand or whether he has been murdered. Once it has been determined that the captain has, in fact, been murdered, Superintendent Dawle, a thorough police officer, suggests to his chief constable, Major Threngood, that the high sheriff should be questioned as a suspect. Like many of the police officials in Wade's novels, Threngood is chief constable purely by virtue of his military rank. Scandalized by Dawle's suggestion, and fearing the uproar that would ensue if it became known that the high sheriff was a suspect, Threngood forbids the questioning. Superintendent Dawle defers to the constable but makes it clear that, in the interest of justice, the sheriff should be questioned. Wade concludes the conversation between Threngood and Dawle with an ironic comment that suggests trenchant questions regarding his country's legal system:

> The significant note in the Superintendent's voice brought home to Threngood the responsibility of his position. For the first time since his appointment he realized that his office was something more than an interesting, well-paid job. It might carry with it the difference between life and death, justice and injustice; it was a terrible responsibility.

Wade's censure of certain aspects of the British practice of law and justice is also implicit in the manner in which he brings the *The Hanging Captain* to its conclusion. When it becomes obvious that the questioning of the high sheriff cannot be avoided, Threngood decides to steer clear of responsibility for any scandal: He calls in Scotland Yard. In response, the Yard sends one of its most brilliant young men, Detective Inspector Lott. Lott, who has a low opinion of the rural constabulary, brings to the investigation the best of modern police methods. The reader expects that this representative of all that is modern will solve the case, but in the end it is the careful, rather undramatic work of the uninspired, old-fashioned Superintendent Dawle that brings the killer to justice.

This type of reversal is one of the characteristics of Wade's best novels. In *Mist on the Saltings* (1933), for example, another chief constable with a military title, Major Fennel, describes the sound theorizing of Inspector Lamming as "special pleading" (that is, contrived). Lamming, as it turns out, is right. Similarly, in *A Dying Fall* (1955), the chief constable, Colonel Netterly, responds condescendingly to Detective-Superintendent Hant's theory, based on solid police work, that Charles Rathlyn has murdered his wife. The irony of this rebuff is revealed in the last sentence of the novel—a sentence that, coming as it does at the end of Wade's next-to-last novel, may express both Wade's frustration with the British legal system and his own answer to the questions raised in his first two books.

After the success of *The Hanging Captain*, Wade turned from straight detective stories to experimentation with other genres. Some critics have commented that Wade liked to challenge himself with new difficulties as he planned each new work. Wade's experimentation led to two collections of short stories: *Policeman's Lot: Stories of Detection* (1933) and *Here Comes the Copper* (1938). It also led him to attempt a project that may have been too great a challenge.

Mist on the Saltings

Mist on the Saltings, which followed his first collection of short stories, is the result of Wade's attempt to write a novel that would include elements of crime and detection yet would focus on the development of character. The attempt is something of a failure, primarily because Wade lacked the ability to sustain the suspense and develop the novel's numerous subthemes at the same time. Each time he deals with the novel's marital triangle, for example, suspense evaporates and the pace of the novel slows. The pace is also slowed by Wade's style, which is sometimes forced, stilted, and artificial.

A Dying Fall

This problem with an unwieldy style plagued Wade throughout his career. *A Dying Fall*, for example, is marred by the kind of labored prose illustrated by the following passage:

> In the meantime Charles and Anne Rathlyn were in that seventh heaven that is reserved for lovers from whose path insuperable obstacles have suddenly melted away. . . . Further than that, the nebulous plans that they had discussed on that afternoon when they had met in the woods and realised their mutual love had now developed into firm intention.

Wade's best novels are those in which he was able to practice an economy of narration, avoiding the long descriptions that gave him so much trouble. *Mist on the Saltings* fails to achieve that economy and must therefore be judged as one of Wade's least successful works.

Constable, Guard Thyself!

After *Mist on the Saltings*, Wade returned to the straight detective story with *Constable, Guard Thyself!* (1934). This novel, which features Inspector Poole, is a model of the classic detective story. Beginning with the standard accessory, a frontispiece showing the scene of the crime, it moves forward through a jumble of clues and possible motives to a conclusion in the detective-novel tradition. This is not to suggest, however, that the novel is merely a mechanical exercise in detective-story writing. Characteristically, Wade gives *Constable, Guard Thyself!* an added dimension by paying careful attention to characterization and by seasoning his narrative with social commentary.

Heir Presumptive

Perhaps to give himself another challenge, Wade made a dramatic departure from the classic tradition by following *Constable, Guard Thyself!* with an inverted story, *Heir Presumptive* (1935). Inversion is a difficult technique, but Wade masters it in this story of extermination for inheritance. Wade, whose strongly developed sense of irony has been noted, gives the story a wry twist at the end, but one of the outstanding features of *Heir Presumptive* is the way in which he is able to convey the irony involved in the murderous scheming of the heir. This is one of Wade's best novels, even if there is some murkiness surrounding the explanation of the difference between "tail male" and "general entail," two legal terms that are important to the plot.

Postwar novels

Wade's writing career was interrupted when he returned to military service at the beginning of World War II. When he resumed writing, it was to revise his last prewar novel, *Lonely Magdalen* (1940), for a 1946 edition. His first postwar novel, *New Graves at Great Norne* (1947), was followed by six more, concluding with *The Litmore Snatch* (1957). Only two novels of this period, *Too Soon to Die* (1953) and *A Dying Fall*, rank with the best of Wade's prewar writing. *New Graves at Great Norne* is bloodier than most of Wade's novels, and *Diplomat's Folly* (1951), which features no detection, is reminiscent of Crofts. Social commentary, which is always present in Wade's early novels, plays an even greater role in the postwar novels. *A Dying Fall*, in particular, takes a very close look at the changing values, especially among the "horsey set," in postwar England. Many critics believe that Wade's treatment of these changing values may be the best of that of any writer in the field.

Wade retired from writing after publishing his somewhat disappointing last novel, *The Litmore Snatch*, ending a productive career that has earned for him a place among the great writers of detective fiction. Innovative and willing to attempt a variety of genres, Wade produced a body of work distinguished by its plotting, its characterization, its situations, its social commentary, its questioning of the British legal system, and—most of all—its subtle undertones of irony. It is not surprising that *The Times* (London) called Henry Wade "the greatest English writer of detective fiction."

Chandice M. Johnson, Jr.

Principal mystery and detective fiction

Chief Inspector John Poole series: *The Duke of York's Steps*, 1929; *No Friendly Drop*, 1931 (revised 1932); *Constable, Guard Thyself!*, 1934; *Bury Him Darkly*, 1936; *Lonely Magdalen*, 1940 (revised 1946); *Too Soon to Die*, 1953; *Gold Was Our Grave*, 1954

Nonseries novels: *The Verdict of You All*, 1926; *The Missing Partners*, 1928; *The Dying Alderman*, 1930; *The Floating Admiral*, 1931 (with others); *The Hanging Captain*, 1932; *Mist on the Saltings*, 1933; *Heir Presumptive*, 1935; *The High Sheriff*, 1937; *Released for Death*, 1938; *New Graves at Great Norne*, 1947; *Diplomat's Folly*, 1951; *Be Kind to the Killer*, 1952; *A Dying Fall*, 1955; *The Litmore Snatch*, 1957

Other short fiction: *Policeman's Lot: Stories of Detection*, 1933; *Here Comes the Copper*, 1938

Other major works

Nonfiction: *A History of the Foot Guards to 1856*, 1927

Bibliography

Barzun, Jacques, and Wendell Hertig Taylor. "Preface to *The Dying Alderman*." In *A Book of Prefaces to Fifty Classics of Crime Fiction, 1900-1950*. New York: Garland, 1976. Preface by two preeminent scholars of mystery and detective fiction, arguing for Wade's novel's place in the annals of the genre.

Hausladen, Gary. *Places for Dead Bodies*. Austin: University of Texas Press, 2000. This study of the settings of mystery and detective novels includes extended discussions of the police procedural subgenre and the specific importance of setting within police procedurals; provides background for understanding the works of Wade.

Horsley, Lee. *Twentieth-Century Crime Fiction*. New York: Oxford University Press, 2005. Very useful overview of the history and parameters of the crime-fiction genre; helps place Wade's work within that genre.

Shibuk, Charles. "Henry Wade." In *The Mystery Writer's Art*, edited by Francis M. Nevins, Jr. Bowling Green, Ohio: Bowling Green University Popular Press, 1970. Essay devoted to Wade's particular craft, his distinctive style, and their consequences for detective fiction.

Vicarel, Jo Ann. *A Reader's Guide to the Police Procedural*. New York: G. K. Hall, 1995. Geared to the mainstream reader, this study introduces and analyzes the police procedural form, which Wade uses in his novels.

MARTYN WAITES

Born: Newcastle upon Tyne, England; 1963

Types of plot: Hard-boiled; private investigator; thriller

Principal series

Stephen Larkin, 1997-

Joe Donovan, 2006-

Principal series characters

Stephen Larkin is a dispirited, world-weary journalist working for a sleazy London tabloid. Given to bouts of self-pity because of his own actions, which cost him his wife and son, he returns at the orders of his boss to his hometown, Newcastle, to report on a series of crimes and their consequences—a mob-style murder and subsequent trial, a pedophilia ring, and child prostitution. He reenters the human race and is redeemed through his work, which often involves physical danger. Though he has different qualities, traits, and motivations, Larkin, who has a strong sense of right and wrong, may be seen as a precursor to investigator Joe Donovan.

Detective Inspector Henry Moir of Newcastle and formerly of Edinburgh, Scotland, like Larkin, has his own demons, the result of witnessing too much violence and because of a personal loss: His sixteen-year-old daughter, Karen, ran away from home and is lost in the gritty underworld of London.

Joe Donovan is a former hotshot investigative reporter for the London *Herald*. Devastated by the disappearance of his six-year-old son, David, during a birthday shopping spree two years earlier, Joe quit his job to search for his boy. Divorced from his wife, Annie, and neglectful of his surviving daughter Abigail, who resents his obsession with her brother, Joe has turned to alcohol to ease the pain of his loss and has suicidal tendencies—until he is revived through the investigative work that is his strength. He is in his thirties, with graying hair and haggard features, and usually dresses casually, in jeans and old T-shirts. He lives alone in a rural area in the north of England in an old house, where he devotes a room to photographs of and clippings relating to his missing son.

Contribution

Martyn Waites has become a leading figure in British neo-noir since the publication of his first novel, *Mary's Prayer*, in 1997. This subgenre consists of extremely dark, ultraviolent crime fiction influenced by such American writers as James Ellroy, Andrew Vachss, Elmore Leonard, and Walter Mosley; however, the British version of this subgenre is not without faint rays of hope.

Waites has staked out the city of his birth, Newcastle, as his fictional territory. Newcastle, in the northeast of the country in the enclave of Tyne and Wear County, is neither quite English nor quite Scottish and has both a contemporary face and a hidden past. Once a heavy-industrial area, it has become a modern service and call center with many new buildings, yet it retains a shadowy, seedy quayside district full of despair, desolation, and abandoned warehouses. Waites populates that milieu with a cast of colorful characters—criminal perpetrators, victims, crime fighters, and witnesses—whose qualities are neither all good nor all bad. He deals with disturbing social issues in a uniformly blunt and unflinching manner, and his depictions of horrific acts are not for the faint of heart.

Initially a writer with a cult status among cognoscenti, Waites has slowly achieved greater recognition for his work. Reviews of his novels have been overwhelmingly favorable. His *Born Under Punches* (2003) was listed among *January Magazine*'s best crime novels of the year. For his body of work, Waites was nominated for the Crime Writers' Association's Dagger in the Library Award. His first entry in the Joe Donovan series, *The Mercy Seat* (2006), was selected as the initial title released by the publisher Pegasus and was nominated for the Ian Fleming Steel Dagger Award.

Biography

Martyn Waites was born in 1963 in Newcastle upon Tyne, England, where he was raised. He grew up reading comic books, particularly enjoying the exploits of Batman, and developed a fondness for crime novels, especially the work of Graham Greene. Following high school, he worked at a variety of occupations—barman, market trader, leather-coat salesman, stand-up comedian, and stagehand at the Playhouse. During his late teens and early twenties, Waites played bass, sang, and wrote songs in several obscure local bands, including Dennis, Pin Up, Tractors Are Go, and the Fire Escape. In the early 1980's, on behalf of the National Association for Charitable Recycling Organizations (NACRO), he taught drama to teenagers who had broken the law. After two years of service with NACRO at Huntercombe Young Offenders Institution, Waites left for London to study acting. He later served as writer-in-residence at Her Majesty's Prison in Chelmsford.

As an actor, Waites landed a few small roles in such television series as *Spender* (1991-1993), *The New Adventures of Robin Hood* (1997-1998), *Badger* (1999), and *Close and True* (2000). He began writing in the early 1990's and contributed short stories and articles to both print and online publications, including *Bizarre*, *The Big Issue*, and *The Bookseller.* His fiction has appeared in such anthologies as *The Adventure of the Missing Detective: Nineteen of the Year's Finest Mystery and Crime Stories* (2005) and *London Noir* (2006). Waites's first novel, *Mary's Prayer,* a dark-edged thriller involving mobs and featuring tabloid reporter Stephen Larkin, appeared in 1997. Two additional entries in the Larkin series, *Little Triggers* (1998) and *Candleland* (2000), quickly followed.

In 2003, Waites released the first of a pair of dark thriller novels dealing with Britain's "secret history," *Born Under Punches*, a literary crime thriller that shows Stephen Larkin—just one of several central characters—as a young, idealistic journalist investigating an actual historical event, the long, drawn-out miners' strike of 1984. The second, *The White Room* (2004), named one of *The Guardian*'s books of the year, also deals with history, focusing on 1960's Newcastle child-killer Mary Bell.

Waites began a new gritty, noir-flavored series, built around psychologically damaged investigative reporter Joe Donovan, in 2006 with the publication of the critically acclaimed *The Mercy Seat*, which was nominated for several major awards. He followed up with *Bone Machine* (2007).

Though writing is now the primary emphasis of Waites's career, drama and acting still consume part of his life. He participated in the 2003 National Film Theater Events: Crime Scene with workshops on "Rogues and Vagabonds" and "Snobbery, Assault, and Battery." He has also given dramatic readings for audio versions of other authors' works. Waites has overseen arts-based workshops for socially excluded teenagers and adults in South London and in Essex, where he was a fellow at the University of Essex (2006-2007).

Analysis

As Martyn Waites is a product of culturally distinct Newcastle, England, it is not surprising that he writes with a strong sense of place. In all of his books, Newcastle assumes a brooding presence that affects each of the key elements of his fictional work: plot, characterization, dialogue, atmosphere, pace, theme, language, and style.

Waites's plots, which verge on melodrama in their striking contrasts between the heights of good and the depths of evil, typically revolve around the examination of social issues—government and police corruption, unemployment, drugs, the huge chasm between the wealthy and the poor, or the exploitation of mine workers—and their effects on a select group of individuals. Waites does not preach; rather, he demonstrates in shudder-inducing closeups and cringeworthy vividness how the corrosive influence of poverty breeds crimes and how violence begets violence. Pacing is frequently breathtakingly fast, with disturbing but memorable images piled one on another.

Characterization, reinforced by dialogue that is blunt, brutal, and profane, is a particular Waites strength, thanks in part to his background in acting, a profession in which one must slip into someone else's skin to be believable. His many years of work with both teenage and adult offenders has undoubtedly also given him considerable insight into the workings of criminal minds. Waites is adept at drawing subtly shaded characters across a wide range of behavior. Heroes are severely flawed, often as the result of a traumatic past event, but are redeemed through their all-consuming drive toward a specific goal: the solution of a problem. Villains, no matter how perverted, violent, or nasty, have some small quality that makes them at least slightly sympathetic. It is through the confrontation of these damaged and unpredictable characters that Waites creates tension, conflict, and suspense.

Stylistically, Waites is a study in contrasts. Playing off his pithy, pungent dialogue are descriptive passages that, while lyrical, are nonetheless lean and stark, with no wasted words. Stories are told in the third person, past tense, often with shifting viewpoints from chapter to chapter and a dearth of gimmicks or literary pyrotechnics to clutter the narrative.

Paying homage to his lifelong love of music and to his brief career as a performing musician, Waites often includes comments on the current pop music scene. The titles of all his fictional works are taken from songs: "Mary's Prayer," for example, was composed by the 1980's Scottish band Danny Wilson; "Little Triggers" is from a Waites favorite, Elvis Costello; "Candleland" is courtesy of Ian MacCulloch; "Born Under Punches" comes from the Talking Heads album *Remain in Light* (1980); and "The White Room" is a 1960's hit by Cream.

Born Under Punches

Born Under Punches describes a real-life 1984 miners' strike in the northeast of Great Britain and the nearly two decades that had passed by the book's publication in 2003. The book focuses on a group of interrelated characters, each somehow connected to the strike: Tony Woodhouse, a professional soccer player with a shady past; thuglike debt collector Tommy Jobson; miner Mick Hutton, who as the strike lengthens grows ever more desperate in his attempts to support his family; young journalist Stephen Larkin, looking to make a name for himself in the news world with an exposé of the conditions that caused the strike; and Stephen's sister, Louise, who is infatuated with Tony. Moving back and forth between 1984 and the present, *Born Under Punches* examines not only the immediate effects of a debilitating work stoppage but also the long-lasting repercussions on those involved.

The Mercy Seat

The first in a series of novels featuring Joe Donovan, former investigative reporter for the London *Herald*, *The Mercy Seat* is set in modern Newcastle upon Tyne, Waites's birthplace. The city plays an important role in the novel, serving as both a backdrop for much of the action and as a symbol of the deterioration of modern society. After Joe's six-year-old son, David, disappeared from a department store two years earlier, the reporter began an obsessive search that cost him his job and marriage and left him in despair. He is pulled out of his depression through the visit of former colleague Maria Bennett, the attractive young editor of the *Herald*, and the newspaper's slimy lawyer, Francis Sharkey. Maria enlists Joe's aid to help find reporter Gary Myers, who has gone missing in the course of investigating a story. If Joe assists, all the newspaper's resources will be placed at his disposal in determining what happened to his son.

Joe accepts the deal and is plunged into a convoluted and deadly game of predator and prey. Gary was working with a corporate scientist, Colin Huntley, who is also missing. A key piece of information, the missing reporter's computer mini-disc, which contains incriminating evidence, is likewise gone, stolen by a slippery fourteen-year-old half-African London street hustler and prostitute, Jamal Jenkins. Jamal, hoping to sell his prize, flees with the disc to Newcastle, pursued by a professional killer called Hammer, a large, muscular man with a shaved head and a tooth into which a sapphire has been set, who can pound nails using just his fist. Hammer is in the employ of Alan Keenyside, a corrupt police officer with a thriving drug trade who perpetrated the incident that propels the story: the brutalization of a band of Travelers (a nomadic group) in exchange for a supposed secret scientific formula that Keenyside hopes to sell to a foreign power. Exposure of Keenyside's illegal activities would cost him his career and all his ill-gained possessions, and the crooked police officer will do anything—including kidnap and murder—to prevent that from happening.

In Newcastle, Jamal falls into the clutches of Father Jack, a grossly obese man who pretends to shelter runaway juveniles but is in reality nothing more than a peddler of their young flesh. Father Jack is being observed and photographed by a pair of private investigators, former police officer Peta Knight and her gay Asian partner, Amar Miah, who hope to gather enough evidence to put Father Jack out of business and gain publicity for their failing private eye business. When Donovan turns up, following Jamal's trail in the course of resurrecting his lost investigative skills, the private investigators form an alliance with him: Joe will help them put Father Jack out of business if they will help him corner Jamal long enough to extract the information he holds that will locate the missing reporter and scientist.

Played out against a nightmarish urban wasteland of derelict cars, abandoned homes, and rat-infested warehouses, *The Mercy Seat* is a brutal, violent, noir-flavored thriller. Narration, pared to the bone, is crisp, fragmented, and harsh. Dialogue is rough and profane but realistic, spoken by characters who could exist. The story is disturbing, a glimpse of horrific and distasteful things hidden among decay, but necessary. Only through exposure to the full light of day, Waites seems to be saying, does humankind have the chance to end all the nastiness that lurks in the darkness.

Jack Ewing

PRINCIPAL MYSTERY AND DETECTIVE FICTION

STEPHEN LARKIN SERIES: *Mary's Prayer*, 1997; *Little Triggers*, 1998; *Candleland*, 2000

JOE DONOVAN SERIES: *The Mercy Seat*, 2006; *Bone Machine*, 2007

NONSERIES NOVELS: *Born Under Punches*, 2003; *The White Room*, 2004

BIBLIOGRAPHY

Cannon, Peter. "A Flying Start for Pegasus." *Publishers Weekly* 253, no. 31 (August 7, 2006): 20. This is a brief article about the new American publisher Pegasus, which chose Waites's *The Mercy Seat* for its initial release.

Douglass, Dave. "Miners Then and Now." Review of *Born Under Punches*, by Martyn Waites. *The Weekly Worker* 487 (July 3, 2003). A mostly favorable review, which praises the author's skill in creating an atmosphere of menace but finds fault with the inconsistency in tone, particularly in sections dealing with the past, which lack the immediacy of those dealing with the present.

Penzler, Otto. "The Mean Streets of Anytown." *The New York Sun*, April 19, 2006. An overview of recent hard-boiled and noir fiction, with particular attention paid to Waites's *The Mercy Seat*.

Publishers Weekly. Review of *The Mercy Seat*, by Martyn Waites. 253, no. 8 (February 20, 2006): 135. This is a starred review of *The Mercy Seat*, which is termed a "beautifully written and constructed thriller" and deemed an outstanding accomplishment, particularly for the first entry in a new series.

Stasio, Marilyn. "Crime." Review of *Candleland*, by Martyn Waites. *The New York Times Book Review*, June 11, 2000, p. 32. In this mostly favorable review, Stasio takes the author to task for the unrelenting violence but praises the novel for its characterizations, dialogue, and the consistency of its dark tone.

Stone, Andrew. "Our Friends in the North." Review of *Born Under Punches*, by Martyn Waites. *Socialist Review*, April 2003. A mostly positive review, crediting the work for its realism, particularly in scenes in which strikers combat the police, but faulting it for its frequent references to contemporary music and for Waites's gratuitous use of sex as a catch-all metaphor for everything from drug addiction to exploitation.

Williams, Wilda W. "Dark Is the New Cozy: Crime in Translation, the Dominance of Noir, and Conjuring the Paranormal." *Library Journal* 131, no. 6 (April 1, 2006): 36-39. A broad discussion of new entries in the noir genre from around the world, which highlights Waites's *The Mercy Seat*, predicts a bright future for the author, and includes a brief question-and-answer session.

ANN WALDRON

Born: Birmingham, Alabama; December 14, 1924
Types of plot: Amateur sleuth; cozy

Principal series

McLeod Dulaney, 2003-

Principal series characters

McLeod Dulaney is a Pulitzer Prize-winning journalist who is invited to teach a course once a year at Princeton University. Trained as an investigative reporter, she feels compelled to solve mysterious crimes that baffle the police and disrupt the placid life on the Princeton campus.

Lieutenant Nick Perry is a Princeton detective who is called on to investigate cases in which Dulaney becomes involved. Although he objects to her meddling in crime scenes, he also relies on her inquisitive nature and her ability to elicit testimony from witnesses and suspects.

George Bridges, the assistant to the president of Princeton University, provides Dulaney with inside information concerning the crimes that occur on or near campus. Initially involved with Dulaney romantically, he later becomes a friend and sounding board for her speculations about the guilt and innocence of criminal suspects.

Contribution

Ann Waldron admits to being inspired by the detective novels of Agatha Christie and Rex Stout. Like Christie's amateur detective Miss Marple, Waldron's McLeod Dulaney has an advantage over professional detectives and police officers in that she can simply follow her intuitions and curiosity. The crimes committed in her community interest her precisely because they touch on her relationships with friends and colleagues. Dulaney differs from Miss Marple in that she is a trained journalist with a tough hide who does not mind being rebuffed by those she wants to interview. Like Stout's Nero Wolfe, Dulaney works best in conversation with others, especially George Bridges, assistant to the president of Princeton, and Lieutenant Nick Perry, both of whom challenge her surmises and also build on her understanding of the cases she is determined to solve.

Dulaney may be an amateur sleuth situated in the comfortable—indeed self-congratulatory—ambiance of an Ivy League institution, but her southern take on her surroundings and years of experience at the *Tallahassee Star* make her a highly alert and shrewd observer of the criminal behavior lurking under the genteel veneer of university life. In other words, she does not take her environment for granted.

Biography

Ann Waldron was born on December 14, 1924, in Birmingham, Alabama, to Eric Watson Waldron, a bookkeeper, and Elizabeth Roberts Wood. Waldron's parents and older sister lived three blocks from the Vine Street Presbyterian Church, where they attended services every Sunday and prayer meetings on Wednesdays. Waldron, still a member of the Presbyterian Church, is a lifelong Democrat whose southern roots are reflected in much of her writing.

Waldron's interest in journalism began when she became coeditor of her high school newspaper and then editor of the *Crimson-White*, the student newspaper at the University of Alabama. After graduating from college in 1945, she worked as a reporter for the *Atlanta Constitution*, where she met Martin Waldron, whom she married on October 18, 1947. The couple raised four children while working on newspapers in Florida and Texas.

When Martin Waldron accepted a *New York Times* offer, the couple settled in Princeton, where Ann Waldron concentrated on raising her family and writing children's books. Soon Waldron was attending classes at Princeton University and working for the school's publications. She interviewed professors and reported on life in Princeton, a valuable experience reflected in her rich evocation of the Princeton milieu in her mystery novels.

When Martin Waldron died in 1981, Ann began working full time for the Princeton *Campaign Bulletin*. An understanding boss allowed her to do library research that led to the publication of her first biography, *Close Connections: Caroline Gordon and the Southern Renaissance* (1987). Acclaim for this biography and another of southern newspaper editor Hodding Carter established Waldron's credentials as a researcher and investigator of lives—not unlike her heroine McLeod Dulaney.

Waldron's work on an unauthorized biography of Eudora Welty perhaps sharpened her sense of the reporter/biographer/crime solver who often has to go against accepted opinion and deal with hostility and rebuffs from establishment figures. Despite her established reputation as a writer on southern subjects, Waldron faced considerable opposition from Welty and her supporters who wished to nurture a certain myth of the writer. Like Dulaney, whose ability to solve crimes is based on both her empathy for others and her innate inquisitiveness, Waldron persevered, investigating the roots of Welty's personality and creativity.

After writing the Welty book, Waldron wanted a change of pace and turned to mystery writing. Although her turn to mystery novels may seem to mark a departure from her other writings, in fact it represents a return to a first love. She grew up reading the novels of Agatha Christie and Rex Stout, and in 1965 she wrote a mystery novel that she could not get published. In 2003, she published the first novel in the McLeod Dulaney series, *The Princeton Murders*. She has continued to produce novels in this series at the pace of one per year.

Analysis

Ann Waldron's career as a journalist and long association with Princeton has helped her create a remarkable mystery series surrounding McLeod Dulaney, a Pulitzer Prize-winning investigative journalist who teaches at Princeton University. The Dulaney series bears some resemblance to Agatha Christie's Miss Marple series. However, Dulaney is a harder, tougher version of Miss Marple, partly because of her training as a reporter, and the series departs from the conventions of the cozy mystery in that Dulaney's work, in her unabashed but sometimes clumsy quest to learn the truth about crime, is not always superior to that of Lieutenant Nick Perry. Dulaney can be fooled, be seriously misled, and in one case be downright wrong about the perpetrator of a murder. However, even when she does not solve the crime—and she sometimes puts herself in harm's way because she does not realize who the real murderer is—she creates the conditions that make it possible to solve the murder cases. Dulaney's law-enforcement partner, Nick Perry, seems credible not only as a detective but also as a person with whom Waldron is deeply familiar, probably because the author learned a good deal from talking to police officers while she was a reporter and later in life. Waldron's Princeton experience is most visible in her large cast of supporting characters, including a writer-in-residence, a university president, professors from various departments, members of the press, and the staff (principally women) who keep the departments running smoothly.

Waldron's personal history is apparent in southerner Dulaney's acute observations on the northern climate and mentality. Another element brought into the novels from Waldron's personal life is her obvious relish for good meals. One of her editors suggested that she append to each novel recipes of the dishes in the meals that Dulaney prepares. These are all dishes, tried and true, that Waldron has made herself. In sum, Waldron has created a series of novels that provide both a cultural and a culinary delight while creating precise evocations of characters and locales that harbor unsuspected opportunities for murder.

The Princeton Murders

The first novel in the McLeod Dulaney series, *The Princeton Murders*, has Ann Waldron's amateur sleuth/journalist teaching her first writing course as a visiting professor. New to academia, Dulaney finds the array of characters: a radical feminist, a prickly pan-African studies scholar, a Marxist, a queer theorist—just to mention a few of the memorable members of the supporting cast—almost stupefying in their feuding and preening behaviors. When does eccentricity lead to murder? she wonders. There is no shortage of suspects when Professor Archibald Alexander is found dead, and Dulaney (to the consternation of her academic colleagues) resists the notion that his demise is the result of natural causes.

Waldron makes clear at the beginning of this novel that this is not a roman à clef; that is, she has not created characters who are only thinly disguised versions of real people. Instead, she has exploited the Princeton setting itself, the institution's pride in its probity and high standards, to introduce events that challenge the community's belief in its own rectitude. Certainly the world of academic politics is exposed in this novel, but not in a malicious way. Dulaney is bemused with the quirky professors and even develops a certain affection for them. She loves the Princeton milieu, which is palpably evoked in descriptions of restaurants, university buildings, and environs.

In Waldron's mystery series, one murder always begets another, a pattern that is introduced in *The Princeton Murders*.

Death of a Princeton President

When the president of Princeton goes missing in *Death of a Princeton President*, no one expects foul play, but leave it to McLeod Dulaney, who finds President Melissa Faircloth dead in a closet in her office. The Princeton provost would prefer to prevent this ghastly turn of events from becoming a huge news story, but Dulaney, a tireless quester after the truth, keeps both the Princeton administration and the police hard at work. As usual, she runs up against Lieutenant Nick Perry, who is conflicted about her efforts. On one hand, he warns her not to interfere with his investigation; on the other, he cannot help but rely on the valuable testimony she is able to elicit from the people she interviews.

Dulaney's life is complicated by a romance with George Bridges, assistant to the president. Although

he admires Dulaney, he also tends to discount her theories about murder and is surprised when her hard work exposes the unseemly side of university life. Indeed, Dulaney puts herself in harm's way by refusing to stop her investigation.

Clarence Brown, a Princeton professor emeritus of classics, observed in the *Trenton Times* that Waldron's evocation of Princeton is one of the great pleasures of the novel even as her believable characters create the sense of intrigue indispensable to a work of mystery fiction. Her deft handling of the plot kept him guessing about the identity of the murderer, spreading "suspicion around in the very best tradition of the whodunit."

Unholy Death in Princeton

In *Unholy Death in Princeton*, McLeod Dulaney is in Princeton not only to teach a writing course but also to research the life of an abolitionist newspaperman, Elijah P. Lovejoy. While walking along the tow path beside the Delaware and Raritan Canal, she stumbles across a naked corpse in a garment bag. Because she is the one who finds the body, Dulaney becomes a suspect.

The setting for this novel, perhaps the most fascinating of all Waldron's works, is the Princeton Theological Seminary, which Lovejoy attended and where his personal papers are now housed. Waldron recreates the seminary in enticing detail. The personalities of the students and their teachers, the debates over doctrine (how to view the historical Jesus, for example), and the tensions between faith, belief, and scholarship are deftly dramatized.

Waldron, however, does not base her work on actual events or characters, preferring to explore the nexus between individuals and institutions by creating her own characters. The murder victim—in this case a fundamentalist type who angered many of his contemporaries—provides Waldron's detective with a perfect opportunity to explore how issues such as the roles of gays and women in the church might have not only affected merely the life of the institution but also have influenced the motives for murder.

A Rare Murder in Princeton

In *A Rare Murder in Princeton*, visiting professor McLeod Dulaney is working in the university's rare book collection—a serendipitous result of her meeting Nathaniel Ledbetter, director of Rare Books and Special Collections.

McLeod is staying with George Bridges, and although their romance is over, they have become fast friends. When Ledbetter comes over for dinner with George and McLeod, he suggests she might be interested in the papers of Henry Van Dyke, a nineteenth century clergyman, novelist, and political figure. Now that she has completed her biography of Lovejoy, she needs a new subject.

Just as McLeod is beginning to work with the 179 boxes of Van Dyke material, however, one of the prime benefactors of Rare Books and Special Collections, Philip Sheridan, is found dead—right in the department. Having met and liked Sheridan, McLeod has trouble understanding why anyone would want to kill him. Even more troubling, the police cannot find a murder weapon or come up with credible suspects.

Lurking in the background is the fact that George Bridges lives in what Ledbetter calls the "murder house." The house used to be owned by longtime Princeton resident Jill Murray, whose murder has never been solved. Although Dulaney does not tie the two murders together, her natural inquisitiveness leads her to explore both the past and present crimes simultaneously.

This time Dulaney makes some rather costly blunders that almost end her life, and yet her very openness—she is far less focused than the professional detective, Nick Perry—ultimately means that she gathers a comprehensive group of suspects and evidence that helps Perry put together a solution to crimes past and present.

The Princeton Imposter

In *The Princeton Imposter*, one of McLeod Dulaney's brightest students, Greg Pierre, is suddenly arrested right before all the students in her class. The stunned visiting professor learns that he is an imposter—a parole breaker whose real name is Bob Billings and who has been convicted of a drug charge in Wyoming.

In spite of much evidence to the contrary and the skepticism of Nick Perry and George Bridges, McLeod sets out to vindicate her student, who tells her he was framed. In surprisingly quick order, she is able to contact one of her former students, who discovers that Greg is indeed telling the truth. Then a student is murdered on campus, and Greg becomes a suspect because the victim was a student from Wyoming who alerted Princeton authorities that Greg was an imposter.

Still believing in her student's innocence, Dulaney forges ahead into the world of chemistry labs and graduate students, the environment in which the murder has been committed. The plot becomes even more complicated when a second student is murdered off campus, and Dulaney begins to suspect that one of the chemistry professors is the culprit.

Believing too strongly in her own surmises, Dulaney almost makes a fatal mistake. In the end, she has to be rescued by a professional. Thus Waldron neatly balances the strengths and weaknesses of the amateur sleuth while paying her respects to the law enforcement personnel she has come to admire while doing her own journalism.

Carl Rollyson

Principal mystery and detective fiction

McLeod Dulaney series: *The Princeton Murders*, 2003; *Death of a Princeton President*, 2004; *Unholy Death in Princeton*, 2005; *A Rare Murder in Princeton*, 2006; *The Princeton Imposter*, 2007

Other major works

Children's literature: *The House on Pendleton Block*, 1975; *The Integration of Mary Larkin-Thornhill*, 1975; *The Luckie Star*, 1977; *Scaredy Cat*, 1978; *The French Detection*, 1979; *The Bluebury Collection*, 1981; *Claude Monet*, 1991; *Francisco Goya*, 1992

Nonfiction: *Your Florida Government*, 1965 (with Allen Morris); *True or False? Amazing Art Forgeries*, 1981; *Close Connections: Caroline Gordon and the Southern Renaissance*, 1987; *Hodding Carter: The Reconstruction of a Racist*, 1993; *Eudora: A Writer's Life*, 1998

Bibliography

Brown, Clarence. Review of *Death of a Princeton President*, by Ann Waldron. *The Times of Trenton*, April 25, 2004. A book review by a former Princeton resident discusses Waldron's fiction in terms of its real-life setting.

Cotterell, Bill. "Princeton Mystery Is a Tasty Mix of Food, Fun." Review of *The Princeton Murders*, by Ann Waldron. *Tallahassee Democrat*, August 10, 2003. Notes the recipes at the end of book and praises the novel for its entertainment value.

Waldron, Ann. Ann Waldron. http://www.annwaldron.com. An excellent author's Web site, including an extensive biography, summaries of Waldron's books, a comprehensive interview with the author, and links to other sites.

_______. "Murder, She Wrote." Interview by Sharon Krengel. *New Brunswick Home News*, March 10, 2004, pp. 6-7. An excellent interview with Waldron, exploring her interest in writing mystery stories, her experience as a journalist and biographer, her work at Princeton University, and how she chooses the settings for her crime novels.

_______. "Whodunits? Whydoits? Princeton's Ann Waldron Turns, Belatedly, to Mystery Writing." Interview by Clara Pierre Reeves. *The Times of Trenton*, June 5, 2005. An interview focusing on Waldron's decision to write mysteries and set them in Princeton.

EDGAR WALLACE

Born: Greenwich, England; April 1, 1875
Died: Beverly Hills, California; February 10, 1932
Types of plot: Private investigator; police procedural; thriller

PRINCIPAL SERIES

Four Just Men, 1905-1928
J. G. Reeder, 1925-1932

PRINCIPAL SERIES CHARACTERS

LEON GONZALEZ, RAYMOND POICCART, GEORGE MANFRED, and MIQUEL THERY constitute the group in the original 1905 work *The Four Just Men*, and three of them reappear in later Four Just Men books. These characters are determined, like the Three Musketeers, to take justice into their own hands.

J. G. REEDER is a more traditional English detective. With his square derby, muttonchop whiskers, tightly furled umbrella, spectacles, large old-fashioned cravat, and square-toed shoes, this elderly gentleman carries a Browning automatic and fears no one, despite a feigned apologetic habit. Claiming that he has a criminal mind and using his power of recollection (and a great collection of newspaper clippings), Reeder has the goods on everyone involved in his specialty—financial-related murder.

CONTRIBUTION

Edgar Wallace's publication of more than 170 books, an impressive list of short stories, comedies, plays, and screenplays—as well as his lifetime career as journalist, correspondent, and editor—marks him as the best-selling English author of his generation and one of the most prolific. Howard Haycraft declared that Wallace's "vast audience gave him an influence, in popularizing the genre, out of all proportion to the actual merit of his writing." He made the thriller popular in book form and on stage and screen, throughout the English-speaking world. Only John Creasey, with his more than five hundred novels, wrote more than Wallace, and perhaps Agatha Christie was the only mystery and detective writer whose novels attracted more readers.

The best of Wallace's detective fiction recounts the cases of Mr. J. G. Reeder, a very British sleuth of valiant courage whose triumphs are won by both chance and deduction. Critics Stefan Benvenuti and Gianni Rizzoni observe that Wallace "concentrated on the extravagant, the exotic, and the freely fantastic, all interpreted in a style derived from the Gothic novel." He steered clear of sex or controversy, but he often challenged the system of justice of his era and pointed to errors in police practices.

BIOGRAPHY

Edgar Wallace was born as Richard Horatio Edgar Wallace on April 1, 1875, in Greenwich, England, the son of Polly Richards and Richard Edgar, unwed members of an acting company. As an illegitimate child, Wallace was placed in the home of George and Millie Freeman in Norway Court, London, where he spent his boyhood as Dick Freeman until he ran away to join the army at the age of eighteen. Like his mother and grandmother, he loved the theater and, without much formal education, learned to read primarily from public library books. He soon was writing verses of his own.

Wallace joined the Royal West Kent Regiment as an enlisted private; in July, 1896, he sailed on a troopship to South Africa. After six years of military service as a hospital orderly, he bought his own discharge and became a celebrated war correspondent in the Boer Wars. Wallace was named to the staff of the London *Daily Mail* and covered the end of the war in South Africa. He married a minister's daughter, Ivy Caldecott, in April, 1901, in Cape Town and at the end of the war returned to make his home in England. The couple had three children before they were divorced in 1919. Soon after, Wallace married his secretary of five years, Violet "Jim" King; in 1923, they had a daughter, Penelope.

Plagued by debts left unpaid in South Africa and new bills accumulating in London, Wallace began writing plays and short stories while serving as correspondent or editor for various newspapers. His lifelong love of gambling at horse racing led him to write

Edgar Wallace. (AP/Wide World Photos)

and edit several racing sheets, but his losses at the tracks continually added to his debts. Blessed with an indomitable sense of optimism and self-confidence, he drove himself as a writer and established his name as an author. In 1905, Wallace wrote and published his first great novel, *The Four Just Men*. After a series of lawsuits forced the *Daily Mail* to drop him as a reporter, he was able to draw on his experience in the Boer Wars and his assignments in the Belgian Congo, Canada, Morocco, Spain, and London slums, which provided rich material for short stories and novels.

On the advice of Isabel Thorne, fiction editor for Shurey's Publications, Wallace began a series for the *Weekly Tale-Teller* called "Sanders of the River," based on his experiences in the Congo. He was editor of *Town Topics*, a sports weekly, when World War I broke out in 1914. From the second day of the war until the Armistice, for twelve guineas a week, he wrote six daily articles for the *Birmingham Post*, summarizing the war news, which were published in nine volumes under the title *The War of the Nations: A History of the Great European Conflict* (1914-1919). Using dictation, he increased his writing speed, producing a series of paperback war novels. He also wrote his first motion-picture script, on the life of Edith Cavell, the English nurse who, in 1915, was executed in German-occupied Belgium for aiding the escape of Allied soldiers.

The last ten years of Wallace's life were the most rewarding. Success as a playwright came with the 1926 production of *The Ringer* in London. Numerous plays were produced, many more novels were published, and he continued to edit a Sunday newspaper and write a daily racing column. In 1931, he sailed to the United States to write for film studios in California; there, he collaborated with other writers on a horror film that later became *King Kong* (1933). Suddenly taken ill, he died on February 10, 1932, at the age of fifty-six.

Analysis

Edgar Wallace carved a permanent niche in the early twentieth century development of the mystery and detective novel. His books featured heroes and villains who were accessible to the reading public of his generation. Wallace patriotically upheld the British flag in his own life and in the fictional lives of his detectives. In his novels and stories, those who commit murder die for their crimes.

The Four Just Men

The protagonists of *The Four Just Men* (and others in that series) go above the law when justice is not properly meted out by the courts or when the criminal escapes unpunished. These just men are heroes who redress wrongs and often succeed after the authorities have failed. When Wallace capitalized on this theme, his characters were do-gooders of a romantic cut: Right and wrong were clearly distinguished in these works, the heroes of which persevered until good triumphed over evil.

Within the English-speaking world of the 1920's, Wallace became a widely read author; even in postwar Germany, he was hailed for his enormous popularity. Most scholars of detective fiction agree that he was instrumental in popularizing the detective story and the thriller. Libraries had to stock dozens of copies of each of his best works for decades. Somehow, Wallace was closely in tune with his times and his readers, as Margaret Lane makes clear in her biography of the writer:

> "Edgar Wallace," wrote Arnold Bennett in 1928, "has a very grave defect, and I will not hide it. He is content with society as it is. He parades no subversive opinions. He is 'correct.'" This was a shrewd observation and was never more plainly demonstrated than by Edgar's newspaper work during the war. It was not that he feared to cross swords with public opinion; he always, most fully and sincerely, shared it.

Wallace shifted from newspaper writing to writing short stories, novels, and plays after his war experiences in South Africa. His natural ability to describe graphically events for readers of daily papers led to longer feature articles that reflected popular opinion. Thrilled with the sight of his own words in print, driven by debt, and born with a sense of ambition and self-confidence, Wallace struggled to find his literary identity. Overly eager to cash in on his first great mystery thriller, *The Four Just Men*, he published and advertised it himself, offering a reward for the proper solution (which consumed all the income from the novel's successful sales). By the time *The Four Just Men* appeared, Wallace had developed the technique that would become the hallmark of much of his mystery and detective fiction. His editor had honed his short stories into very salable copy, and his characters had become real people in the minds of British readers. His biographer Margaret Lane summarizes his maturity in style:

> He realised, too, that these stories were the best work he had ever done, and that at last he was mastering the difficult technique of the short story. He evolved a favourite pattern and fitted the adventures of his characters to the neat design. He would outline a chain of incidents to a certain point, break off, and begin an apparently independent story; then another, and another; at the crucial point the several threads would meet and become one, and the tale would end swiftly, tied in a neat knot of either comedy or drama.

In 1910, while Wallace wrote and edited racing sheets, he observed legal and illegal activities by the best and the worst characters of the racetrack crowd, activities that eventually emerged in his mystery fiction. *Grey Timothy* (1913), a crime novel about racing, paralleled two of his mystery books, *The Fourth Plague* (1913) and *The River of Stars* (1913). His more famous *Captain Tatham of Tatham Island* (1909; revised as *The Island of Galloping Gold*, 1916; also known as *Eve's Island*) also had a racing theme.

Wallace scoffed at critics who declared that his characters were paper-thin; others from more literary and academic circles denounced him for not writing more carefully, with greater depth to his plots and characters. In spite of these criticisms, before World War I Wallace had found his place as a mystery writer: "That is where I feel at home; I like actions, murderings, abductions, dark passages and secret trapdoors and the dull, slimy waters of the moat, pallid in the moonlight."

ON THE SPOT

Many editors and readers believed that Wallace had close ties with the criminal world and that his characters were taken from real life, but according to his daughter-in-law that was not so. Perhaps Al Capone of Chicago (whose home Wallace visited in 1929) came the closest to his vision of the supercriminal. He promptly wrote one of his best plays, *On the Spot* (pr. 1930), about the American gangster. Yet in *People: A Short Autobiography* (1926), Wallace devotes a chapter to his knowledge of criminals and the reasons for their lawbreaking. He declared:

> To understand the criminal you must know him and have or affect a sympathy with him in his delinquencies. You have to reach a stage of confidence when he is not showing off or lying to impress you. In fact, it is necessary that he should believe you to be criminally minded.

Whether it was Detective Surefoot Smith, Educated Evans, Carl Rennett, Timothy Jordan, Superintendent Bliss, Inspector Bradley, or Mr. Reeder, Wallace spun his yarns with equal knowledge about the skills, habits, and frailties of both murderers and their detectors.

Various efforts to classify Wallace's works of mystery and detective fiction have failed, but certain series and types of plot do emerge. The Four Just Men series was published between 1905 and 1928. There are the police novels—including his famous *The Ringer* (1926), *The Terror* (1929), and *The Clue of the Silver Key* (1930)—and the thrillers, such as *The Green Archer* (1923), *The India-Rubber Men* (1929), and the classic *The Man from Morocco* (1926; also known as *The Black*). The J. G. Reeder series, begun in 1925 with *The Mind of Mr. J. G. Reeder* (also known as *The Murder Book of J. G. Reeder)*, was brought to its height with the popular *Red Aces* (1929). Yet many of Wallace's detective stories were short stories that overlapped such categories or were not collected until after his death.

Many of Wallace's works reflect his generation's reluctance to accept the authority of "science." Although other authors after 1910 were incorporating scientific equipment such as lie detectors into their detective works, his London crime fighters used old-fashioned wits instead of newfangled widgets. Although many authors turned to more modern, psychological solutions for murder mysteries, Wallace believed that his readers would be lost in such heavy character analysis; he did not let such new devices spoil the fun. Mr. Reeder relies on his own phenomenal memory (buttressed by musty scrapbooks of murder cases), his incriminating evidence often coming from unsuspecting sources. When he astonishes his superiors of Scotland Yard, his conclusions are based on information found outside the criminal labs. Wallace's haste to write his stories led him to depend on his own fertile mind; seldom did he leave his study to search for more documentary detail.

His readers loved his fantastic and scary secret passages, hiding places, trapdoors, and mechanical death-dealing devices. (He let his imagination roam like that of a science-fiction writer.) The setting for many of his novels was London, which provided a wide variety of suburbs, railroads, and steamship docks through which the underworld characters prowled and detectives searched. Although his work is sometimes marred by sloppy writing, the fast pace of Wallace's stories thrilled his readers to their sudden conclusions—the culprit revealed, arrested, or killed all within the last few pages.

Paul F. Erwin

Principal mystery and detective fiction

Four Just Men series: *The Four Just Men*, 1905 (revised 1906, 1908); *The Council of Justice*, 1908; *The Just Men of Cordova*, 1917; *Jack o' Judgment*, 1920; *The Law of the Four Just Men*, 1921 (also known as *Again the Three Just Men*); *The Three Just Men*, 1925; *Again the Three Just Men*, 1928 (also known as *The Law of the Three Just Men* and *Again the Three*)

J. G. Reeder series: *The Mind of Mr. J. G. Reeder*, 1925 (also known as *The Murder Book of J. G. Reeder*); *Terror Keep*, 1927; *Red Aces*, 1929; *Mr. Reeder Returns*, 1932 (also known as *The Guv'nor, and Other Stories*)

Nonseries novels: 1908-1920 • *Angel Esquire*, 1908; *Captain Tatham of Tatham Island*, 1909 (revised as *The Island of Galloping Gold*, 1916; also known as *Eve's Island*); *The Nine Bears*, 1910 (also known as *The Other Man, Silinski, Master Criminal*, and *The Cheaters*); *Grey Timothy*, 1913 (also known as *Pallard the Punter*); *The Fourth Plague*, 1913; *The River of Stars*, 1913; *The Man Who Bought London*, 1915; *The Melody of Death*, 1915; *The Clue of the Twisted Candle*, 1916; *The Debt Discharged*, 1916; *The Tomb of Ts'in*, 1916; *Kate Plus Ten*, 1917; *The Secret House*, 1917; *Down Under Donovan*, 1918; *The Man Who Knew*, 1918; *The Green Rust*, 1919; *The Daffodil Mystery*, 1920

1921-1925 • *The Book of All Power*, 1921; *Captains of Souls*, 1922; *Mr. Justice Maxwell*, 1922; *The Angel of Terror*, 1922 (also known as *The Destroying Angel*); *The Crimson Circle*, 1922; *The Flying Fifty-five*, 1922; *The Valley of Ghosts*, 1922; *The Clue of the New Pin*, 1923; *The Green Archer*, 1923; *The Missing Million*, 1923; *Room 13*, 1924; *Double Dan*, 1924 (also known as *Diana of Kara-Kara*); *Flat 2*, 1924 (revised 1927); *The Dark Eyes of London*, 1924; *The Face in the Night*, 1924; *The Sinister Man*, 1924; *The Three Oaks Mystery*, 1924; *A King by Night*, 1925; *Blue Hand*, 1925; *The Daughters of the Night*, 1925; *The Fellowship of the Frog*, 1925; *The Gaunt Stranger*, 1925 (also known as *The Ringer*); *The Hairy Arm*, 1925 (also known as *The Avenger*); *The Strange Countess*, 1925

1926-1930 • *Barbara on Her Own*, 1926; *Penelope of the Polyantha*, 1926; *The Black Abbot*, 1926;

The Day of Uniting, 1926; *The Door with Seven Locks*, 1926; *The Joker*, 1926 (also known as *The Colossus*); *The Man from Morocco*, 1926 (also known as *The Black*); *The Million Dollar Story*, 1926; *The Northing Tramp*, 1926 (also known as *The Tramp*); *The Ringer*, 1926; *The Square Emerald*, 1926 (also known as *The Girl from Scotland Yard*); *The Terrible People*, 1926; *The Yellow Snake*, 1926; *We Shall See!*, 1926 (also known as *The Gaol Breaker*); *Big Foot*, 1927; *Number Six*, 1927; *The Feathered Serpent*, 1927; *The Forger*, 1927 (also known as *The Clever One*); *The Hand of Power*, 1927; *The Man Who Was Nobody*, 1927; *The Squeaker*, 1927 (also known as *The Squealer*); *The Traitor's Gate*, 1927; *The Double*, 1928; *The Flying Squad*, 1928; *The Gunner*, 1928 (also known as *Gunman's Bluff*); *The Thief in the Night*, 1928; *The Twister*, 1928; *The Golden Hades*, 1929; *The Green Ribbon*, 1929; *The India-Rubber Men*, 1929; *The Terror*, 1929; *The Calendar*, 1930; *The Clue of the Silver Key*, 1930; *The Lady of Ascot*, 1930; *White Face*, 1930

1931-1932 • *On the Spot*, 1931; *The Coat of Arms*, 1931 (also known as *The Arranways Mystery*); *The Devil Man*, 1931 (also known as *The Life and Death of Charles Peace*); *The Man at the Carlton*, 1931; *The Frightened Lady*, 1932; *When the Gangs Came to London*, 1932

Other short fiction: 1911-1920 • *Sanders of the River*, 1911; *The People of the River*, 1912; *Bosambo of the River*, 1914; *The Admirable Carfew*, 1914; *Bones, Being Further Adventures in Mr. Commissioner Sanders' Country*, 1915; *The Keepers of the King's Peace*, 1917; *Lieutenant Bones*, 1918; *The Adventures of Heine*, 1919

1921-1925 • *Bones in London*, 1921; *Sandi, The King-Maker*, 1922; *Bones of the River*, 1923; *Chick*, 1923; *Educated Evans*, 1924

1926-1930 • *More Educated Evans*, 1926; *Sanders*, 1926 (also known as *Mr. Commissioner Sanders*); *Good Evans!*, 1927 (also known as *The Educated Man—Good Evans!*); *The Brigand*, 1927; *The Mixer*, 1927; *Again Sanders*, 1928; *Elegant Edward*, 1928; *The Orator*, 1928; *Again the Ringer*, 1929 (also known as *The Ringer Returns*); *Circumstantial Evidence*, 1929; *Fighting Snub Reilly*, 1929; *For Information Received*, 1929; *Forty-eight Short Stories*, 1929; *Four Square Jane*, 1929; *Planetoid 127*, 1929; *The Big Four*, 1929; *The Black*, 1929 (revised 1962); *The Cat Burglar*, 1929; *The Ghost of Down Hill*, 1929; *The Governor of Chi-Foo*, 1929; *The Iron Grip*, 1929; *The Lady of Little Hell*, 1929; *The Little Green Men*, 1929; *The Lone House Mystery*, 1929; *The Prison-Breakers*, 1929; *The Reporter*, 1929; *Killer Kay*, 1930; *Mrs. William Jones and Bill*, 1930; *The Lady Called Nita*, 1930

1931-1984 • *Sergeant Sir Peter*, 1932; *The Steward*, 1932; *The Last Adventure*, 1934; *The Undisclosed Client*, 1962; *The Man Who Married His Cook, and Other Stories*, 1976; *Two Stories, and the Seventh Man*, 1981; *The Sooper and Others*, 1984

Other major works

Novels: *The Duke in the Suburbs*, 1909; *Private Selby*, 1912; *1925: The Story of a Fatal Peace*, 1915; *Those Folks of Bulboro*, 1918; *The Books of Bart*, 1923; *The Black Avons*, 1925 (also known as *How They Fared in the Times of the Tudors*, *Roundhead and Cavalier*, *From Waterloo to the Mutiny*, and *Europe in the Melting Pot*)

Short fiction: *Smithy*, 1905 (revised as *Smithy, Not to Mention Nobby Clark and Spud Murphy*, 1914); *Smithy Abroad: Barrack Room Sketches*, 1909; *Smithy's Friend Nobby*, 1914 (also known as *Nobby*); *Smithy and the Hun*, 1915; *Tam o' the Scouts*, 1918; *The Fighting Scouts*, 1919

Plays: *An African Millionaire*, pr. 1904; *The Forest of Happy Dreams*, pr. 1910; *Dolly Cutting Herself*, pr. 1911; *Hello, Exchange!*, pr. 1913 (also known as *The Switchboard*); *The Manager's Dream*, pr. 1913; *Whirligig*, pr. 1919 (with Wal Pink and Albert de Courville; also known as *Pins and Needles*); *M'Lady*, pr. 1921; *The Looking Glass*, pr. 1924 (with de Courville); *The Whirl of the World*, pr. 1924 (with de Courville and William K. Wells); *Double Dan*, pb., pr. 1926; *The Mystery of Room 45*, pr. 1926; *The Ringer*, pb. 1926; *A Perfect Gentleman*, pr. 1927; *The Terror*, pb. 1927; *The Yellow Mask*, pr. 1927; *The Flying Squad*, pr. 1928; *The Lad*, pr. 1928; *The Man Who Changed His Name*, pr. 1928; *The Squeaker*, pb. 1928 (also known as *Sign of the Leopard*); *Persons*

Unknown, pr. 1929; *The Calendar*, pr. 1929; *On the Spot*, pr. 1930; *Smoky Cell*, pr. 1930; *The Mouthpiece*, pr. 1930; *Charles III*, pr. 1931; *The Case of the Frightened Lady*, pr. 1931 (also known as *Criminal at Large*); *The Old Man*, pr. 1931; *The Green Pack*, pr. 1932

Screenplays: *Nurse and Martyr*, 1915; *The Forger*, 1928; *The Ringer*, 1928; *Valley of the Ghosts*, 1928; *Red Aces*, 1929; *Should a Doctor Tell?*, 1930; *The Squeaker*, 1930; *The Hound of the Baskervilles*, 1931 (with V. Gareth Gundrey); *The Old Man*, 1931; *King Kong*, 1933 (with others)

Poetry: *The Mission That Failed! A Tale of the Raid, and Other Poems*, 1898; *Nicholson's Nek*, 1900; *War!, and Other Poems*, 1900; *Writ in Barracks*, 1900

Nonfiction: *Unofficial Dispatches*, 1901; *Famous Scottish Regiments*, 1914; *Fieldmarshall Sir John French and His Campaigns*, 1914; *Heroes All: Gallant Deeds of War*, 1914; *The Standard History of the War*, 1914-1916; *The War of the Nations: A History of the Great European Conflict*, 1914-1919; *Kitchener's Army and the Territorial Forces: The Full Story of a Great Achievement*, 1915; *People: A Short Autobiography*, 1926; *This England*, 1927; *My Hollywood Diary*, 1932

Bibliography

Bergfelder, Tim. "Extraterritorial Fantasies: Edgar Wallace and the German Crime Film." In *The German Cinema Book*, edited by Tim Bergfelder, Erica Carter, and Deniz Gokturk. London: British Film Institute, 2002. Study of the adaptations of Wallace's stories to the German screen and their effects on the evolution of German cinema.

Croydon, John. "A Gaggle of Wallaces: On the Set with Edgar Wallace." *The Armchair Detective* 18, no. 1 (Winter, 1985): 64-68. Brief discussion of Wallace's role in the adaptation of his stories to the screen.

Dixon, Wheeler Winston. "The Colonial Vision of Edgar Wallace." *Journal of Popular Culture* 32, no. 1 (Summer, 1998): 121-139. Discusses the role of imperialist and colonial ideology in Wallace's novels.

Gardner, Martin. "Edgar Wallace and *The Green Archer*." In *Are Universes Thicker than Blackberries? Discourses on Gödel, Magic Hexagrams, Little Red Riding Hood, and Other Mathematical and Pseudoscientific Topics*. New York: W. W. Norton, 2003. Discussion of Wallace's representation of mathematics and science in *The Green Archer* and its relation to the solution of the mystery.

Kestner, Joseph A. *The Edwardian Detective, 1901-1915*. Brookfield, Vt.: Ashgate, 2000. This narrowly focused reading of British detective fiction compares Wallace to his fellow Edwardians.

Lane, Margaret. *Edgar Wallace: The Biography of a Phenomenon*. New York: Doubleday, Doran, 1939. Detailed biography of Wallace emphasizing the popularity of his work and the factors contributing to and consequences arising from that popularity.

Wallace, Ethel, and Haydon Talbot. *Edgar Wallace by His Wife*. London: Hutchinson, 1932. This biography of the author includes details of his life that only a wife could know.

Watson, Colin. "King Edgar, and How He Got His Crown." In *Snobbery with Violence: Crime Stories and Their Audience*. New York: Mysterious, 1990. Attempts to account for Wallace's popularity among Edwardian and later audiences as part of a general study of the appeal of crime fiction.

MINETTE WALTERS

Born: Bishop's Stortford, Hertfordshire, England; September 26, 1949
Types of plot: Psychological; thriller

CONTRIBUTION

Minette Walters's psychological thrillers have been compared with those of Agatha Christie, P. D. James, and Ruth Rendell, placing her in the tradition of the English crime novel. Walters is not a series mystery writer; each book stands alone and her novels can be read in any order. Her literary work combines elements of the first-person hard-boiled detective style, the gothic mystery, the feminist desire for strong female characters in the detective tradition, and the epistolary novel. Her novels are character driven, with an emphasis on the character of the victim as well as of the murder suspects and investigator. Motives become more complex as characters' backgrounds are slowly revealed. Readers are kept guessing as the multiple possibilities of who murdered the victim and why emerge through plot twists until the last pages. Walters has been called a master of ambiguity; the motives of the characters are never simple or predictable, and sometimes questions remain even after the end of the book. The dark side of human nature is explored through Walters's characters and plots; readers are uncomfortably aware that murder can be a possible solution to an array of situations. The literary quality of Walters's work has been recognized by a remarkable number of awards in the United States and Great Britain, including the Crime Writers' Association's Gold Dagger Award for *Fox Evil* (2002) in 2003, and the number of best sellers she has written evidences the appeal of her work to readers.

BIOGRAPHY

Minette Walters was born Minette Caroline Mary Jebb on September 26, 1949, in Bishop's Stortford, Hertfordshire, north of London. Her father died when she was young. Her mother supplemented his small pension by painting miniature portraits from photographs and managed to send her three children to good boarding schools. Walters attended the Godolphin School in Salisbury, a university preparatory school. She spent six months in a volunteer service program in Israel, then attended Durham University, where she majored in French and German literature.

After earning her degree, Walters worked as a magazine journalist and later as an editor of romance fiction. Unhappy with the quality of the manuscripts she was reading, she began to write short romance novels herself, eventually writing more than thirty of them under a pseudonym that she has never revealed. This romance fiction, written to strict guidelines, served as her apprenticeship.

In 1978, Minette married Alexander Walters, a businessman. Their first son, Roland, was born in late 1979, followed by Philip in 1982. Walters was a full-

Minette Walters. (Courtesy, Allen & Unwin)

time homemaker and mother until her youngest son was in school. During this time, she was active in volunteer work and ran for local public office. She also renovated three houses with her husband and has written that do-it-yourself tasks are one of her favorite forms of relaxation.

When Walters returned to writing, she shifted from romance to mystery fiction, a genre she had always enjoyed. She has stated that she admired Agatha Christie, Patricia Highsmith, and Graham Greene, whose characters struggle with eternal truths. From Greene she learned that fiction can be both literary and entertaining. The influence of true crime books also can be seen in her work, reflected in her interests in psychology and criminology

The Ice House (1992), Walters's first published crime novel, was a popular and critical success, winning the British Crime Writers' Association's John Creasey Award for best first crime novel. *The Sculptress* followed in 1993, based on an idea from her experience as a prison visitor. *The Sculptress* won the Edgar Allan Poe Award from the Mystery Writers of America. Walters's third novel, *The Scold's Bridle* (1994), won the Crime Writers' Association's Gold Dagger Award. Since then, Walters has been writing at the rate of nearly a book per year, and many of her works have won awards and been on best-seller lists. Her books have been published in thirty-five countries around the world, and her first five books have been adapted for television by the British Broadcasting Corporation. In addition to her full-length crime novels, Walters has published features articles in magazines, short stories, and two novellas.

Walters moved into an eighteenth century manor in the Dorset countryside with her family. *The Breaker* (1998) and *The Shape of Snakes* (2000) are both set in Dorset, and *The Shape of Snakes* features an eighteenth century farmhouse in need of renovation, reflecting her interest in renovations. Walters continues to be active in volunteer and charitable organizations.

Analysis

Minette Walters's psychological suspense and crime fiction is character driven. In each case, a body is discovered in the first pages of the novel, and the rest of the novel is spent uncovering the background and circumstances of the murder. The character of the victim is explored along with the character of the suspects and investigators. Motivation, why the murder was committed, is as important as who did it. A long list of possible suspects is revealed through the twists, turns, and revelations of the plot. Walters stated in an interview that she does not necessarily know the identity of the murderer when she begins writing the novel; a number of characters have a motive for the crime. One of the questions Walters explores is why one character was driven to murder as a solution, while other equally motivated characters did not resort to murder.

Other characteristics of a Walters mystery include gruesome, graphic descriptions of the crime scene; themes of prejudice, bigotry, and giving the victim a voice; a love element that explores the fragility of relationships, the struggle for love, and the hard work involved in maintaining a stable relationship; the enclosed and claustrophobic nature of life in the family, the village, or neighborhood, where all involved, not only the victim, may be traumatized by a crime; and the dark side of human nature, the idea that the capability for murder may rest within anyone. Walters also explores form in the crime novel. In addition to traditional narrative, Walters involves the reader in the investigation by including maps, letters, e-mails, records of police interviews, newspaper clippings, and photos without narrative commentary, allowing the reader to interpret the evidence along with the investigator.

The Ice House

Walters's first novel, *The Ice House*, has elements of the gothic in its setting, a manor house called Streech Grange. The Grange is owned by Phoebe Maybury, who lives there in isolation with two eccentric female companions. The novel opens with three newspaper clippings referring to the unsolved disappearance of David Maybury ten years earlier. Although a body was never found, the local villagers as well as Detective Chief Inspector George Walsh believe that Phoebe killed her husband. The opening scenes of the narrative focus on a graphic description of a decomposed body found in the cryptlike ice house on the property. The immediate assumption is that the body in the ice house is the missing

David Maybury, but soon the investigation is complicated by the revelation of another missing person, a man whose business failure has cost Phoebe's friend Diana Goode a small fortune. As more possible motivations for murder are revealed, it becomes essential to determine the identity of the body in the ice house. Walsh's determination to prove that Phoebe is guilty of her husband's murder hinders the investigation from the start, so it falls to the moody misogynist Detective Sergeant McLoughlin to probe other possibilities. The idea that police investigations may be flawed runs through several of Walters's books. Two stories unfold simultaneously: the story of what really happened ten years earlier, and the story of the police investigation in the present time.

The claustrophobic, enclosed nature of village life is another theme that first appears in *The Ice House* and reappears in later Walters novels. The locals not only assume that Phoebe killed her husband, generally acknowledged to be a cruel and violent man, but also suspect the three women of being lesbians or witches. Ultimately the identity of the body is revealed, as is the solution to the disappearance of Maybury. The novel ends with the beginning of a love affair between the gruff McLoughlin and suspected lesbian Ann Cattrell.

By the end of the gripping novel, with its twists and turns of plot, the reader has been involved in the psychology of vengeance and the nature of loneliness and of friendship and loyalty among the three women, who are protecting Phoebe and her daughter from a secret darker than the possible murder of an abusive husband and father.

The Sculptress

Minette Walters's second novel, *The Sculptress*, also opens with a crime that has already been committed. A newspaper clipping refers to the murder conviction of Olive Martin, a young woman who has been sentenced to life imprisonment for the brutal murders of her mother and sister. Rosalind "Roz" Leigh, the amateur investigator, is a journalist who has been assigned to write a book about the case. Olive, a grotesquely obese woman, has confessed to the murders but refuses to speak about her motive. Roz, who has recently suffered a great loss followed by depression, must gain Olive's confidence through a series of prison visits and give the murderer a voice. As the visits proceed, the tables are sometimes turned, and it is Olive who asks the questions, causing Roz to open up and begin to talk about her own life and its disappointments. The psychology of both murderer and investigator are explored.

Themes of loneliness, trust and distrust, truth and lies, and the claustrophobic nature and secrets of family life are woven into the plot as Roz discovers that there was little police investigation surrounding the murders. Thorough police and defense work was neglected because it was a foregone conclusion that Olive was guilty. As Roz begins to unravel Olive's past in an attempt to discover why a young woman who appears sane and intelligent though odd would commit the brutal murder of her mother and sister, she becomes convinced that Olive is innocent. Therefore Roz must find the true murderer, and Olive's motive for confessing to the crime. In the course of her investigation, she interviews a growing number of characters and becomes involved in a relationship with Hal Hawksley, a retired police officer who was the investigator at the scene of the crime. The reader's imagination is engaged as the cast of possible suspects becomes more and more complex.

The ending of the novel is the source of Walters's reputation as a master of ambiguity. Where does fact end and fiction begin? Olive is a skilled manipulator, and while Roz is convinced that Olive is innocent and is able to prove that the police investigation was flawed, she is never able to definitively prove who the true killer is. In the end, Olive is freed, and as she is leaving the prison, there is a look of gloating triumph on her face that causes doubt. Did Olive kill her mother and sister or not?

The Breaker

The Breaker is set in Dorset, where Walters makes her home. As the novel opens, the body of a naked woman is found on an isolated beach. The woman has been raped, strangled, and drowned. Her identity must be established and her murderer found. Constable Nick Ingram is the hero of the mystery, a local police officer who knows the people of the community and the tides and waters of the area. Suspects include the drowned woman's husband and a handsome, rather sleazy, young actor. The cast of characters includes a pair of lonely women, Maggie Jenner and her mother, who have lost their money to the confidence man Maggie married; several police detectives; the severely withdrawn young daughter of the murdered woman; and a number of local characters and suspects. Records of police interviews and psychologists' reports punctuate the traditional narrative. Who murdered the woman and why are not revealed until the last pages of the novel. Themes include loneliness, date-rape drugs, and child abuse as well as psychology and possible motives for the murder, while plot and action are never sacrificed in this best-selling, page-turning thriller.

THE SHAPE OF SNAKES

The Shape of Snakes opens with a twenty-year-old crime. On a rainy night in a London neighborhood, an African Caribbean woman with Tourette's syndrome, known as Mad Annie, died in the gutter. The police dismissed the death as an accident; they concluded that Annie had wandered into the road and was hit by a truck. The first-person narrator, M, was convinced that Annie was murdered and that racism and indifference by the police led to a cover-up of the crime. M's accusations of racism caused the neighbors to harass her into silence, and she and her husband moved abroad shortly after the crime.

Twenty years later, M and her husband have returned to England, and M is determined to seek justice for the murdered woman. Her own motives, however, are complicated. Although she seems to be driven by a desire for justice for Annie, her investigation is just as likely to be motivated by a desire for revenge for how she was treated and her subsequent isolation and depression. The nature of life in an urban neighborhood where everyone knows everyone else's business is painfully probed. Revelations are made about the affairs of a vivid and varied cast of characters through letters, police reports, newspaper clippings, photos, and e-mails in addition to traditional narrative. Themes of silence and isolation are explored until readers hear the voice of the victim at last in the moving letter on the final page. The ending of this original, emotional, and literary mystery is revealing, yet questions remain.

Susan Butterworth

PRINCIPAL MYSTERY AND DETECTIVE FICTION

NOVELS: *The Ice House*, 1992; *The Sculptress*, 1993; *The Scold's Bridle*, 1994; *The Dark Room*, 1995; *The Echo*, 1997; *The Breaker*, 1998; *The Shape of Snakes*, 2000; *Acid Row*, 2001; *Fox Evil*, 2002; *Disordered Minds*, 2003; *The Devil's Feather*, 2005; *Chickenfeed*, 2006; *The Chameleon's Shadow*, 2007

BIBLIOGRAPHY

Dubose, Martha Hailey, with Margaret Caldwell Thomas. *Women of Mystery: The Lives and Works of Notable Women Crime Novelists*. New York: St. Martin's Minotaur, 2000. Contains essays combining biography and literary criticism of female writers, including Walters. The article on Walters offers biography and background along with an analysis of a number of Walters's themes and some critical reactions to her work.

Forselius, Tilda Maria. "The Impenetrable M and the Mysteries of Narration: Narrative in Minette Walters's *The Shape of Snakes*." *Clues: A Journal of Detection* 24, no. 2 (Winter, 2006): 47-61. Scholarly article focusing on problems of memory, justice, and truth in *The Shape of Snakes*. Also discusses the narrative complexity of the novel and the ambiguous motivation of the narrator.

James, Dean. "Interview with Minette Walters." In *Deadly Women: The Woman Mystery Reader's Indispensable Companion*, edited by Jan Grape, Dean James, and Ellen Nehr. New York: Carroll & Graf, 1998. Covers many female mystery authors and a wide cross section of styles and genres. Includes Louisa May Alcott, Agatha Christie, Dorothy L. Sayers, P. D. James, Donna Leon, and Patricia Cornwell. The format is wide-ranging and accessible but not in-depth. The engaging interview with Walters reveals her influences and interests.

Lebihan, Jill. "Tearing the Heart Out of Secrets: Inside and Outside a Murder Mystery." *Journal of Gender Studies* 10, no. 3 (November, 2001): 287-295. This scholarly article presents a psychoanalytical and feminist analysis of *The Ice House* as an example of the narrative process of identification in the murder mystery. Lebihan's thesis is based on the premise that the male police detectives cannot solve the murder because they cannot identify with a female killer and her secrets.

Muller, Adrian. "Minette Walters." In *Speaking of Murder: Interviews with the Masters of Mystery and Suspense*, edited by Ed Gorman and Martin H. Greenberg. New York: Berkley Prime Crime, 1998. A two-volume set of entertaining and enlightening interviews with a wide range of mystery writers. The well-written profile of Walters discusses themes and settings of her novels.

Walters, Minette. Minette Walters Official Website. http://www.minettewalters.co.uk. Comprehensive and up-to-date information on Walters and her work, including a biography, news, profiles, video clips, and an interactive question-and-answer page. An excellent resource.

JOSEPH WAMBAUGH

Born: East Pittsburgh, Pennsylvania; January 22, 1937

Types of plot: Police procedural; historical

CONTRIBUTION

Joseph Wambaugh, the Los Angeles police officer who became a best-selling novelist, began writing out of a need to describe the Watts riots of the 1960's from the perspective of the police officers assigned to restore order there. He wanted to describe "what it was like for young men, young policemen, to grow up, on the streets, in that dreadful and fascinating era." The body of his work concerns American police procedure and the lives of those who belong to what has been called the "maligned profession." It is a world of frustrating, counterproductive rules and regulations drawn up by police administrators who have not been on the streets for years, a world where brutality mixes with courage, corruption with dedication, and evil with honor.

Although occasionally criticized for lengthy philosophical discourses and an undeveloped style, Wambaugh is more often praised for thoughtful and realistic storytelling, and he has been regarded as one of the "few really knowledgeable men who try to tell the public what a cop's life is like." Beginning with his first novel, *The New Centurions* (1970), positive popular response has led to the reproduction of Wambaugh's stories in other media such as film, television, and audio cassettes. His police officers were violent, afraid, foulmouthed, and fallible. "Do you like cops? Read *The New Centurions*," a *New York Times* reviewer wrote. "Do you hate cops? Read *The New Centurions*."

Critical acclaim for his writing began in 1974, when he received the Herbert Brean Memorial Award for *The Onion Field* (1973), which, according to *The New York Times* reviewer James Conaway, is equal to Truman Capote's *In Cold Blood* (1966) and placed Wambaugh in the tradition of Theodore Dreiser and James T. Farrell.

Wambaugh's books, gritty, hyperrealistic, and nonlinear, typically interweave several story lines at once. His characters are composites of real-life cops and criminals; his dialogue is praised and reviled as "outrageously colorful." What Wambaugh brought to detective fiction was actual life on the beat from a cop's perspective: the gallows humor, the ugliness, the drugs and booze, the boredom and the raw fear. "I didn't realize what I was doing, but I was turning the procedural around," Wambaugh told an interviewer. "The procedural is a genre that describes how a cop acts on the job; I was showing how the job might act on the cop . . . how it worked on his head."

Wambaugh shows that investigations can be mishandled and that police officers, who can be bigots, alcoholics, and hard cases, make bad errors of judgment. However, he believes that most Americans are unwilling to grasp the reality, the human cost, of police work. Wambaugh's books are enormously popular among cops as well as civilian readers because of their accuracy. "Police work is still, in my opinion, the most emotionally hazardous job on earth," he said in 2000. "Not the most physically dangerous, but the most emotionally dangerous."

Biography

The only child of Anne Malloy and Joseph Aloysius Wambaugh, Joseph Aloysius Wambaugh, Jr., was born on January 22, 1937, in East Pittsburgh, Pennsylvania. The German surname accounts for one-quarter of his ethnic heritage; the other three-quarters is Roman Catholic Irish. His was a family of hard workers, many of whom labored in the Pittsburgh steel mills.

Wambaugh's California settings originate in his personal experience. His father had been police chief in East Pittsburgh before the family moved to California in 1951. Three years later, Wambaugh left high school to enlist in the United States Marine Corps. During his service time, in 1956, he and Dee Allsup, his high school sweetheart, were married. They had three children; their son Mark would later die at the age of twenty-one. On Wambaugh's discharge from the Marines in 1957, the couple returned to California, where Wambaugh worked at different jobs while earning an associate degree in English from Chaffey College in 1958.

Joseph Wambaugh. (Library of Congress)

In 1960, Wambaugh graduated from California State College, Los Angeles, with a bachelor's degree and joined the Los Angeles Police Department (LAPD) as a burglary detective. However casually he came to police work (he once told an interviewer that he joined the police department because he had "nothing better to do" and because the money was more than he had ever earned), he soon found himself deeply involved. He was a solid, commonsense investigator who cracked more than his share of tough cases. He has said that police work relaxed him and soothed his soul.

Wambaugh began writing after he became involved in helping to control the Watts riot. On August 11, 1965, six days of rioting began in the Watts section of South Central Los Angeles following a routine traffic stop. African Americans were tired of abusive treatment from white police officers in the cities, which included the use of water cannons, clubs, and cattle prods. In the ensuring violence, thirty-four people were killed and 856 injured. Nearly four thousand people were arrested and 209 buildings were destroyed. It was a difficult time for citizens and police alike.

Wambaugh intended to maintain both careers, as writer and police officer, but his status as a "celebrity cop" would not permit that option. In 1973, for example, he was presented with California State University's first outstanding-alumnus award. Interrupting police calls and visits at the Hollenbeck Station were one problem, but great tension developed from the changed relationships inside the department: "The other cops were starting to treat me differently—sort of like a star—and I couldn't bear being different." On March 1, 1974, he left the force.

As production consultant for the television series adapted from his novel *The Blue Knight* (1972), Wambaugh fought to maintain authenticity in the scripts. Indeed, his insistence has become legendary. He filed and won a lawsuit over violations committed against the text when *The Choirboys* (1975) was made into a film. Indeed, his literary career has been plagued with litigation. "I've been under continuous litigation for my writing since 1974," Wambaugh once told an interviewer. "There's a million ambulance chasers who say, 'Let's sue him!'"

The most famous case concerned the murders forming the basis of Wambaugh's *Echoes in the Darkness* (1987). On September 14, 1994, Philadelphia's Upper Merion High School principal Jay C. Smith, convicted of the murders of a schoolteacher and her two children, filed suit against Wambaugh, claiming that he had conspired with police investigators to conceal exculpatory evidence and to fabricate evidence linking Smith to the murders, in order to make money from the book and a television miniseries. Smith lost the case, although his conviction was overturned.

After being sued over *The Onion Field*, *Lines and Shadows*, and *Echoes in the Darkness*, Wambaugh swore off writing nonfiction. *The Blooding* (1989) was the only true-crime book he wrote that was not the subject of a defamation lawsuit. Wambaugh attributed this to the fact that it dealt not with Americans but with an English murder case.

Wambaugh eventually left Los Angeles for a house in Palm Springs and an estate overlooking the San Diego harbor and Coronado Island when he made his fortune with best seller after best seller. In 2004, Wambaugh received the Grand Master Award from the Mystery Writers of America.

Analysis

It is not the subject matter (crime and police work) or the types of characters (police officers, criminals, and victims) that distinguish Joseph Wambaugh's books: It is the intimacy he develops between the reader and the police officers. Like a trusted partner, the reader is privy to others' baser qualities—including vulgarity, bigotry, and cruelty. Yet the reader also comes to know human beings, and that knowledge allows for affection, sometimes admiration, and always a shared fatalism about police work: It is an after-the-fact effort—after the robbery, after the rape, after the child abuse, after the murder.

This fatalistic outlook does not develop from book to book; it is present in full measure from Wambaugh's first novel:

> It is the natural tendency of things toward chaos. . . . It's a very basic natural law Kilvinsky always said, and only the order makers could temporarily halt its march, but eventually there will be darkness and chaos. . . .

The point is convincingly dramatized through the police confrontations during the 1965 Watts riots.

Even the survivors—those police officers who finish enough shifts to reach retirement and the prized pension—pay with a piece of their souls. The wise Kilvinsky in *The New Centurions* learns all the natural laws and then shoots himself. Bumper Morgan, the blue knight in the book of that title, is the kind of police officer who radicals had in mind when shouting "pig." He is a fat, freeloading womanizer (teenage belly dancers preferred), and the reader would probably turn away in disgust if, beneath the crudity, loneliness and depression were not detectable.

The Onion Field

Victimization of police officers is one of Wambaugh's recurring themes. They are victimized by the dislike of those they swear to protect and by the justice system they swear to uphold. Two of his books make this premise particularly convincing. Writing for the first time in the genre of the nonfiction, or documentary, novel, Wambaugh in *The Onion Field* painstakingly reconstructed the 1963 kidnapping of two fellow officers, the murder of one, and the trial that followed. During that trial, the surviving officer became as much a defendant as the two killers.

To Wambaugh's credit, however, he stays out of the story. Here, for example, are none of the intrusions found in *The New Centurions*. Nowhere does one officer turn to another and inquire about psychological-sociological implications, such as "Gus, do you think policemen are in a better position to understand criminality than, say, penologists or parole officers or other behavioral scientists?" The questions and answers have not disappeared, however. They are simply left either for the reader to ask and answer in the course of reading the book or for one of the force to understand as an integral part of the story. "I don't fudge or try to make it [a true-crime story] better by editorializing or dramatizing," Wambaugh said, "I try to be a real investigative reporter and write it as it happened as best I can."

Lines and Shadows

The realization of Dick Snider in *Lines and Shadows* (1984) is a case in point. After watching San Diego cops chase illegal aliens through the city's San Ysidro section, Snider knows that the crime of illegal entry and the various authorities' efforts to stop it are simply shadows hiding the truth. Illegal entry is, in fact, only about money: "*There is not a significant line between two countries. It's between two economies*."

In studying so closely the ruined careers, marriages, and lives of the Border Alien Robbery Force, the BARF Squad, as it became known, Wambaugh also provides an explicit answer to a puzzle within all of his books—indeed, to a puzzle about police inside or outside the covers of a book. Why would they want such a job? Wambaugh's answer is that they are caught up as the players in a national myth:

> They gave their nightly performance and almost everyone applauded. They did it the only way they knew—not ingeniously, merely instinctively—by trying to resurrect in the late twentieth century a mythic hero who never was, not even in the nineteenth century. A myth nevertheless cherished by Americans beyond the memory of philosophers, statesmen, artists and scientists who really lived: the quintessentially American myth and legend of the Gunslinger, who with only a six-shooter and star dares venture beyond the badlands.

The Glitter Dome

Those who recognize the myth and how they have been used by it clearly have great difficulty continuing to play their parts. Yet these are the most likable and most interesting police officers in Wambaugh's fiction—Martin Welborn, for example (*The Glitter Dome*, 1981). He is a ploddingly thorough detective, with a penchant for orderliness in his police work and in his personal life. Glasses in his kitchen cupboard rest "in a specifically assigned position." Drawers display dinner and cocktail napkins "stacked and arranged by size and color." Neither can he leave "out of place" an unsolved case or the memory of a mutilated child. He depends on two universals: People always lie and, with less certainty, the devil exists (because "life would be unbearable if we didn't have the devil, now wouldn't it?"). What happens, then, when one of the universals is taken away? Yes, people always lie, but there is no evil and, consequently, no good. All that happens happens accidentally. With that realization, detecting who committed a crime and bringing the criminal to justice loses significance. So, too, does life, and Marty Welborn ends his by driving over a mountain cliff as he recalls the one perfect moment in his life. At the time, he had been a young, uniformed police officer, and he had just heard an old cardinal deliver a solemn High Mass. As he kneeled to kiss the cardinal's ring, Welborn saw, in one perfect moment, the old priest's "*lovely crimson slippers*."

The Black Marble

Although Martin Welborn is the totally professional police officer, a winner who nevertheless takes his life, Andrei Milhailovich Valnikov (*The Black Marble*, 1978) is a loser, a "black marble" who endures. Like Welborn, he has his reveries, usually drunken ones, of past-perfect moments. Yet they come from a czarist Russia Valnikov never personally experienced. Such an absence of reality works perfectly with the constant losses in the detective's work. He cannot, for example, find his handcuffs; he gets lost on the streets of Los Angeles; and he is all the more touchingly comical for both the reveries and the misadventures. In Valnikov, Wambaugh demonstrates his ability to develop a memorable character.

The Choirboys

As good as Wambaugh is at occasional character development, he is even better at telling amusing stories, as in *The Blue Knight* and *The Black Marble. The Glitter Dome, The Delta Star* (1983)—which was described by one reviewer as "Donald Westlake meets Ed McBain"—and *The Secrets of Harry Bright* (1985) are also amusing. None of these novels, however, measures up to the humor in *The Choirboys*. All that has been said about Wambaugh's humor in this book is true: It is "sarcastic and filled with scrofulous expletives"; it is "scabrous"; and it is often "intentionally ugly." Indeed, the reader may believe that laughing at *The Choirboys* is giving in to an adolescence long outgrown.

Wambaugh would be offended by none of this. He lists among his literary influences both Joseph Heller and Truman Capote, on one hand, and humorists P. J. O'Rourke and Dave Barry, the Pulitzer-winning humor columnist, on the other. "I wanted to use the tools of gallows humor, satire, hyperbole, all of that, to make people laugh in an embarrassed way," Wambaugh told an interviewer. "I reread [Heller's] *Catch-22* and [Kurt Vonnegut's] *Slaughterhouse-Five* to see how it was done in war novels. . . . I couldn't find anybody who'd done it in a police novel."

Typical of Wambaugh's humor is Officer Francis Tanaguchi's impression of Bela Lugosi in *The Choirboys*:

> For three weeks, which was about as long as one of Francis's whims lasted, he was called the Nisei Nipper by the policemen at Wilshire Station. He sulked around the station with two blood dripping fangs slipped over his incisors, attacking the throat of everyone below the rank of sergeant.

The jokes in *The Choirboys* are sandwiched between a prologue, three concluding chapters, and an epilogue filled with terror and insanity. Wambaugh's novel illustrates well an idea popularized by Sigmund Freud: Beneath a joke lies the most horrific of human fears.

However, Wambaugh's works became more lighthearted following *The Secrets of Harry Bright* (1985). "As I mellowed with age, or got farther from day-to-day police work, I wrote books that were more consciously entertaining," he said. "*Harry Bright* was the exception. I happen to like that book better than any of the other novels, but that one was so dark, I think I had to lighten up, it was all about fathers and sons and death."

His novels of the 1990's were broadly comical—*The Golden Orange* (1990), a tale of an alcoholic cop among the millionaires of the Gold Coast of Orange County; *Fugitive Nights* (1992), in which another alcoholic cop teams up with a female private eye to handle a drug-smuggling case, depending, as one reviewer said, "mostly on vulgar police humor for its laughs;" *Finnegan's Week* (1993), a funny and witty thriller about toxic waste comparable to the works of Carl Hiaasen; and *Floaters* (1996), a romp concerning racing spies, saboteurs, scam artists, and hookers swarming around San Diego Bay, the site of the America's Cup international sailing regatta, into which two Mission Bay patrol-boat cops of the "Club Harbor Unit" get dragged out of their depth.

Several of Wambaugh's novels were adapted to film. *The New Centurions* (1972) starred George C. Scott; more successful was *The Black Marble*, directed by Harold Becker as a romantic comedy and produced by Frank Capra, Jr., and starring James Woods and Harry Dean Stanton. *The Choirboys* (1977) was disappointingly directed by Robert Aldrich; it is understandable why Wambaugh filed suit when he saw the results. *The Blue Knight* was filmed as a television miniseries of four one-hour installments in 1973; lead actor William Holden and director Robert Butler both received Emmy Awards for their work.

A second *Blue Knight* television movie, filmed in 1975 and starring George Kennedy as seasoned cop Bumper Morgan, served as the pilot for a short-lived television series (1975-1976). *The Glitter Dome* (1985) was filmed for cable television and starred James Garner, John Lithgow, and Margot Kidder. *Fugitive Nights: Danger in the Desert* aired on television in 1993, with Teri Garr as leading lady. The nonfictional novels *The Onion Field* (motion picture) and *Echoes in the Darkness* (made-for-television miniseries re-released as video) were also filmed in 1979 and 1987, respectively. Wambaugh's fast-paced, violent, and funny writing continues to attract the attention of Hollywood.

Wambaugh, however, was dissatisfied with these adaptation projects—except for ones to which he contributed. Television's regular series *Police Story* (1973-1980) was "based on his memoirs" and focused on the LAPD. A particularly interesting project was The Learning Channel's series *Case Reopened*, in which Lawrence Block, Ed McBain, and Wambaugh were asked to host hour-long segments about notorious unsolved crimes. Wambaugh's turn came with "The Black Dahlia," which aired October 10, 1999. The murder of Elizabeth Short had occurred when Wambaugh was ten, and during his rookie years on the beat he heard many anecdotes about the sensational manhunt. Despite his vow not to return to true-crime writing, Wambaugh reviewed the evidence and offered his own solution.

Of the crime committed as documented in *Echoes in the Darkness*, Wambaugh wrote, "Perhaps it had nothing to do with sin and everything to do with sociopathy, that most incurable of human disorders because all so afflicted consider themselves *blessed* rather than cursed." The fate of a police officer who becomes a best-selling author as a representative of the police to the rest of the human species might be considered both a blessing and a curse. Certainly Wambaugh's insights into the follies and struggles of humanity have proved a blessing for crime fiction.

Alice MacDonald
Updated by Fiona Kelleghan

Principal mystery and detective fiction

Novels: *The New Centurions*, 1970; *The Blue Knight*, 1972; *The Choirboys*, 1975; *The Black Marble*, 1978; *The Glitter Dome*, 1981; *The Delta Star*, 1983; *The Secrets of Harry Bright*, 1985; *The Golden Orange*, 1990; *Fugitive Nights*, 1992; *Finnegan's Week*, 1993; *Floaters*, 1996; *Hollywood Station*, 2006

Other major works

Screenplays: *The Onion Field*, 1979 (adaptation of his book); *The Black Marble*, 1980 (adaptation of his novel)

Teleplay: *Echoes in the Darkness*, 1987 (adaptation of his book)

Nonfiction: *The Onion Field*, 1973; *Lines and Shadows*, 1984; *Echoes in the Darkness*, 1987; *The Blooding*, 1989; *Fire Lover: A True Story*, 2002

Edited texts: *The Best American Crime Writing, 2004*, 2004

Bibliography

Donahue, Deirdre. "Wambaugh, Veteran of the Cop Beat." *USA Today*, May 8, 1996, p. 1D. This article discusses the popularity, due to their accuracy, of Wambaugh's books among police officers. Wambaugh also is described as being more mellow in his later works and injecting more humor into them.

Dunn, Adam. "Burning Down the House." *Book* 22 (May/June, 2002): 19. Background of Wambaugh's first book after a six-year hiatus.

Hitt, Jack. "Did the Writer Do It?" *GQ* 68, no. 7 (July, 1998): 172. Detailed yet highly readable explanation of a lawsuit against Wambaugh stemming from his writing of *Echoes in the Darkness*.

Jeffrey, David K. "Joseph Wambaugh: Overview." In *St. James Guide to Crime and Mystery Writers*, edited by Jay P. Pederson. 4th ed. Detroit: St. James Press, 1996. This article leans heavily toward literary criticism, with intermittent biographical information.

"Joseph Aloysius Wambaugh, Jr." In *Current Biography Yearbook: 1980*, edited by Charles Moritz. New York: H. H. Wilson, 1981. In addition to a brief biography, this article contains excerpts of press interviews with Wambaugh and critical evaluations of his works.

Kaminsky, Stuart. *Behind the Mystery: Top Mystery Writers*. Cohasset, Mass.: Hot House Press, 2005. Wambaugh is one of eighteen mystery writers interviewed in this collection who reveals the creative process that goes into producing best-selling mystery fiction.

Malmgren, Carl D. *Anatomy of Murder: Mystery, Detective, and Crime Fiction*. Bowling Green, Ohio: Bowling Green State University Popular Press, 2001. Malmgren discusses Wambaugh's *The Secrets of Harry Bright*, alongside many other entries in the mystery and detective genre. Bibliographic references and index.

Meisler, Andy. "Paranoid Among the Palms." *The New York Times*, June 13, 1996, p. C1. In this interview, Wambaugh offers his observations on what he considers the erosion of the American judicial system in the late twentieth century. He also provides an overview of his own career as a Los Angeles detective and novelist.

Van Dover, J. Kenneth. *Centurions, Knights, and Other Cops: The Police Novels of Joseph Wambaugh*. San Bernardino, Calif.: Brownstone Books, 1995. A critical study of Wambaugh's first fourteen books. Includes an excellent chronology of his life.

Wambaugh, Joseph. "Ship to Shore with Joseph Wambaugh: Still a Bit Paranoid Among the Palms." Interview by Andy Meisler. *The New York Times*, June 13, 1996, p. C1. An interview with Wambaugh on his boat, *Bookworm*, near the San Diego harbor. The article explores some of Wambaugh's views and gives a brief description of his career.

HILLARY WAUGH

Born: New Haven, Connecticut; June 22, 1920
Also wrote as Elissa Grandower; H. Baldwin Taylor; Harry Walker
Types of plot: Hard-boiled, police procedural; private investigator; thriller

PRINCIPAL SERIES

Sheridan Wesley, 1947-
Fred Fellows, 1959-
David Halliday, 1964-
Frank Sessions, 1968-
Simon Kaye, 1981-

PRINCIPAL SERIES CHARACTERS

FRED FELLOWS, the chief of police in Stockford, Connecticut, is married, with four children. At first glance, Fellows is the stereotypical small-town police officer—the overweight, tobacco-chewing storyteller. As criminals who choose to commit a crime in Stockford quickly learn, however, the truth of the matter is that Fellows is an extraordinarily good detective, solving his cases with a combination of solid police work and imaginative thinking. Fellows is fifty-three years old in his first novel (1959), and he ages slightly over the course of the eleven novels in which he appears.

FRANK SESSIONS, a detective second grade in the homicide squad, Manhattan North, is divorced. A tough and capable detective, Sessions originally became a detective because his father was a police officer. Quick to dispel any idealistic notions about his job, Sessions is a veteran of more than sixteen years on the force who nevertheless remains passionate about justice. This passion is often tested in his brutal cases.

SIMON KAYE, a private investigator, is single. A former cop, Kaye is a resourceful private eye who works in the same unnamed city in which he grew up. Around thirty years old, Kaye is a very physical investigator who is capable of inflicting as well as absorbing much physical damage. Often cynical and sarcastic, Kaye works as a detective to help people as individuals, not out of some overblown Don Quixote/Sir Galahad complex.

CONTRIBUTION

One of the true pioneers of the police procedural, Hillary Waugh was not the first writer to use police officers as detectives, but he was one of the first to present a realistic portrait of police officers and police work, emphasizing all the details of the case from start to finish, including the dull legwork that is often ignored. This emphasis was picked up later by other writers such as Ed McBain and Dell Shannon. According to Julian Symons and others, Waugh's first police procedural, *Last Seen Wearing . . .* (1952), is one of he classics of detective fiction. Waugh's later police novels involving Fred Fellows and Frank Sessions are praised for their realism and polish. In his less-known works as well as in these police procedurals, Waugh is a master craftsman who knows how to tell a good story and construct a tight and suspenseful plot. His prolific and enduring career is a testament to his ability and innovation.

BIOGRAPHY

Hillary Baldwin Waugh was born on June 22, 1920, in New Haven, Connecticut. He remained in that city until he received his bachelor's degree from Yale University in 1942. Straight from graduation, he entered the navy and became a pilot in the Naval Air Corps in May, 1943. He remained in the navy until January, 1946, achieving the rank of lieutenant. It was in the navy that he began to write his first mystery, which was published in 1947 as *Madam Will Not Dine Tonight.*

After his discharge from the navy, Waugh returned to New England. With the exception of some time in New York and Europe, Waugh has mostly lived in Connecticut. In 1951, he married Diana Taylor, with whom he had two daughters and one son. After a divorce in 1981, he married Shannon O'Cork. He has worked as a teacher (1956-1957), has edited a weekly newspaper (1961-1962), and has been involved in local politics, serving as First Selectman of Guilford, Connecticut (1971-1973). These vocations have always been secondary, though, to his writing.

A prolific writer, Waugh published more than forty novels in the forty-two-year span between 1947 and 1989. Waugh is a past president of the Mystery Writers of America and received that organization's Grand Master Award in 1989.

Analysis

One of the most interesting aspects of the detective story is the vast variety of forms it has taken in its history. The police procedural, one major variation of the detective novel, got its start in the 1940's and 1950's with the work of writers such as Lawrence Treat and Hillary Waugh and has since become one of the most popular forms of the genre. This particular type of story follows the efforts of a police officer or a police force (not a gifted amateur or a private eye) working toward solving a case. Waugh himself explains this emphasis in an essay, "The Police Procedural," in John Ball's *The Mystery Story* (1976):

> The police procedural thrusts the detective into the middle of a working police force, full of rules and regulations. Instead of bypassing the police, as did its predecessors, the procedural takes the reader inside the department and shows how it operates.
>
> These are stories, not just about policemen, but about the world of the policeman. Police Inspector Charlie Chan doesn't belong. (There're no police.) Nor does Inspector Maigret. (There are police, but Maigret, like Chan, remains his own man.)

Thus, the police procedural presents a realistic milieu to the reader; the emphasis is on ordinary police officers who solve cases through a combination of diligence, intelligence, and luck. Waugh helped pioneer this particular form and remains one of its masters.

Waugh began to write while he was a pilot in the navy, and he began his career with three fairly standard private eye novels: *Madam Will Not Dine Tonight, Hope to Die* (1948), and *The Odds Run Out* (1949). He returned to the private eye form in the early 1980's with his Simon Kaye novels, a series of entertaining mysteries. It was in 1950, however, that Waugh began a work that would become an influential classic, a work that would help define the emerging type of detective novel known as the police procedural. In writing that novel, Waugh found himself influenced by an unlikely source. In 1949, he had read a book by Charles M. Boswell titled *They All Died Young: A Case Book of True and Unusual Murders* (1949). The book, a true-crime collection of ten stories about murders of young girls, had a tremendous impact on Waugh. "I went through those stories, one by one, and was never the same thereafter." Waugh resolved to write a detective story in the same matter-of-fact style as that of Boswell, a detective story that would show how the police of a small town would solve the case of the disappearance and murder of a college girl. That novel, which appeared in 1952 as *Last Seen Wearing . . .*, is still considered by many to be one of the best detective stories ever written.

Last Seen Wearing . . .

That novel, which appeared in 1952 as *Last Seen Wearing . . .* , is still considered by many to be one of the best detective stories ever written. The detectives in the story are Frank Ford and his sergeant, Burton Cameron, two ordinary police officers who are well-drawn and realistic characters. In fact, they were so realistic that the rough, grouchy Ford seemed to take over the work as the novel progressed. Waugh had originally intended the two to be modeled on the rather nondescript detectives of the true-crime stories—solid professionals with no outstanding features. Instead, the realistic, complex portrayal of the detectives became an important part of the story and was to become an important part of later successful police procedurals. Like the classic puzzle story or the private eye story, the successful police procedural depends on and revolves around the detectives. Ford and Cameron lack the genius of Sherlock Holmes or the guile of Sam Spade, but they make up for that by being admirably professional police officers and believable, engaging characters.

Sleep Long, My Love

Waugh had clearly hit on a successful formula. In 1959, he returned to the idea of a small-town police force in *Sleep Long, My Love*. That novel featured a slightly overweight, folksy gentleman named Fred Fellows, the chief of police of Stockford, Connecticut. Over the next nine years, Fellows appeared in eleven novels, and it is these novels that show Waugh in full mastery of the form.

In the creation of Fellows, Waugh transformed a stereotype into a complex, three-dimensional character. Police officers in small towns have often been portrayed as inept and bumbling, if not incompetent and corrupt. Stockford is definitely a typical small town (except for its extraordinarily high crime rate), and Fellows is, on the surface, the typical small-town police chief. He is fifty-three at the beginning of the series, and he is married, father to four children—a devoted family man. He is slightly overweight, a source of anxiety for him. He chews tobacco and has nude pinups on the wall of his office. Deliberate and methodical, he has a penchant for telling stories in the manner of parables, using them to illustrate his thought processes.

Road Block

In Fellows's second adventure, *Road Block* (1960), one of the crooks planning a payroll holdup in Stockford dismisses Fellows and his force as "a bunch of hick cops." As that criminal and many others discover, the truth of the matter is that Fellows and his coworkers are a group of very talented police officers. In *Road Block*, Fellows tracks down the criminals by using the mileage on the odometer of a car and catches them by feeding them false reports over the police radio. Behind Fellows's genial, folksy manner, the reader discovers a complex individual—a police officer who is not bound by his office, but instead brings to it shrewdness and imaginative thinking.

Fellows series

In addition to introducing a realistic detective, Waugh set a precedent in the Fellows series by giving attention to the actual nuts and bolts of a police investigation. Rather than dismissing the details—the endless interviewing of suspects and witnesses, the tracking down of leads that prove to be false as well as those that are valuable, the combing of neighborhoods, the searching through all types of records—Waugh relishes them, utilizing them to create suspense. For an organized police force, bound by the legal system, cases are built piece by piece. Information comes in as bits and pieces—some useful, some worthless. Detection for Fellows and his men is pure work—work that sometimes leads nowhere, yet work that ultimately pays off.In Waugh's deft hands, the step-by-step, repetitive legwork of a case is never dull. By allowing the reader to focus on the detectives as they sort out the details of the case, Waugh builds suspense the same way his detectives build their cases, moving step by step. As he says, "The tension should build to an explosion, not a let-down."

All the novels in the Fellows series exhibit another strength of Waugh's writing—his tight, believable plots. Waugh does not use the multiple-case approach of later writers; each novel focuses on a single case, following it from beginning to end. *Road Block*, for example, begins with the crooks planning the holdup, and their plans are revealed in great detail. As the robbery unfolds and the plans go awry, the story moves swiftly. Time is of the essence for Fellows, and the novel reflects that. There is no time for subplots, and there are none. Every detail of the novel builds the suspense of the case, propelling it toward the climax.

The Missing Man

Another example is *The Missing Man* (1964), which begins with the discovery of the body of a young woman on the beach of a lake near Stockford. The case is a frustrating one for Fellows and his men as they struggle to identify both the victim and her murderer; although it takes them weeks to solve the case, there are no extraneous subplots. This deliberate focus is a skillful way of building tension in the work, forcing the reader to continue turning pages. There are simply no lulls in the action.

Frank Sessions series

After leaving Fred Fellows, Waugh turned his attention to another police officer, Detective Second Grade Frank Sessions of the homicide squad, Manhattan North. Sessions first appeared in *30 Manhattan East* (1968), which appeared the same year as the last Fellows novel, *The Con Game*; he also appeared in *The Young Prey* (1969) and *Finish Me Off* (1970). With this trio of brutal and gritty novels, Waugh left the small-town locale of Fellows and Ford for the big city, but he did not abandon the strengths and innovations of his earlier works. As a central character, Sessions is complex enough to sustain the reader's interest. A sixteen-year veteran of the force, Sessions, like Fellows and Ford, is a true professional. On one hand, he sees police work for the demanding job that it is; on the other, he remains dedicated to that difficult job.

In the three Sessions novels, Waugh pays even

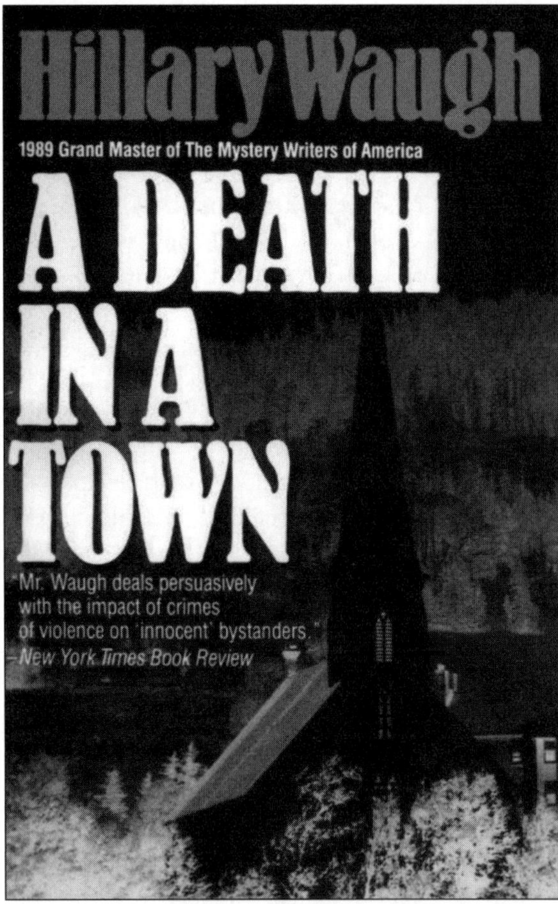

Waugh's A Death in a Town *(1989), concerns the rape and murder of a teenager in a quiet New England town.*

more attention to the detailed legwork of the cases. The everyday workings of a police department are once again the primary focus, and the manner in which the homicide squad of Manhattan North goes about solving a case is examined very closely. The urban setting amplifies the importance of the tedious, repetitive legwork, for here it is even more difficult to reach a solution to a case. The late 1960's were an uneasy time in the history of America, and Waugh captures the uneasiness and unrest perfectly. It was an especially difficult time to be an urban police officer, and the Sessions novels reflect that. Like his other works, these novels demonstrate Waugh's mastery of the procedural; the three Sessions novels are textbook examples of tight, controlled plotting and masterful storytelling.

The police procedural form owes much to Waugh; that is apparent. Yet, for all of his pioneering and innovation, Waugh's greatest claim to fame is the simple fact that he is an excellent storyteller. All of his works—be they police procedurals, private eye novels, or other types of works—show this ability. His long career attests the fact that, above all, Waugh tells a story that people take great pleasure in reading.

Stephen Wood

Principal mystery and detective fiction

Sheridan Wesley series: *Madam Will Not Dine Tonight*, 1947 (also known as *If I Live to Dine*); *Hope to Die*, 1948; *The Odds Run Out*, 1949

Fred Fellows series: *Sleep Long, My Love*, 1959 (also known as *Jigsaw*); *Road Block*, 1960; *That Night It Rained*, 1961; *Born Victim*, 1962; *The Late Mrs. D*, 1962; *Death and Circumstances*, 1963; *Prisoner's Plea*, 1963; *The Missing Man*, 1964; *End of a Party*, 1965; *Pure Poison*, 1966; *The Con Game*, 1968

David Halliday series: *The Duplicate*, 1964 (as Taylor); *The Triumvirate*, 1966 (as Taylor)

Frank Sessions series: *30 Manhattan East*, 1968; *The Young Prey*, 1969; *Finish Me Off*, 1970

Simon Kaye series: *The Doria Rafe Case*, 1980; *The Glenna Powers Case*, 1980; *The Billy Cantrell Case*, 1981; *The Nerissa Claire Case*, 1983; *The Veronica Dean Case*, 1984; *The Priscilla Copperwaite Case*, 1986

Nonseries novels: *Last Seen Wearing . . .*, 1952; *A Rag and a Bone*, 1954; *The Case of the Missing Gardener*, 1954; *Rich Man, Dead Man*, 1956 (also known as *Rich Man, Murder* and *The Case of the Brunette Bombshell*); *The Eighth Mrs. Bluebeard*, 1958; *The Girl Who Cried Wolf*, 1958; *Murder on the Terrace*, 1961; *Girl on the Run*, 1965; *The Trouble with Tycoons*, 1967 (as Taylor); *Run When I Say Go*, 1969; *The Shadow Guest*, 1971; *Parrish for the Defense*, 1974 (also known as *Doctor on Trial*); *A Bride for Hampton House*, 1975; *Seaview Manor*, 1976; *The Summer at Raven's Roost*, 1976 (as Grandower); *The Secret Room of Morgate House*, 1977 (as Grandower); *Madman at My Door*, 1978; *Blackbourne Hall*, 1979 (as Grandower); *Rivergate House*, 1980 (as Grandower); *Murder on Safari*, 1987; *A Death in a Town*, 1989

Other major works

Nonfiction: *Hillary Waugh's Guide to Mysteries and Mystery Writing*, 1991

Edited text: *Merchants of Menace*, 1969

Bibliography

Ball, John, ed. *The Mystery Story*. San Diego: University Extension, University of California, 1976. Collection of essays about the mystery genre, its conventions, and its authors. Includes an essay on the form by Waugh himself.

Dove, George N. "Hillary Waugh." In *The Police Procedural*. Bowling Green, Ohio: Bowling Green State University Popular Press, 1982. Examines Waugh's relationship to the genre of police procedural.

_______. Introduction to *Last Seen Wearing . . .* New York: Carroll and Graf, 1990. Critical analysis of Waugh's novel, arguing for its central place in the history of detective fiction.

Malmgren, Carl D. *Anatomy of Murder: Mystery, Detective, and Crime Fiction*. Bowling Green, Ohio: Bowling Green State University Popular Press, 2001. Discusses Waugh's *Last Seen Wearing . . .* Bibliographic references and index.

Penzler, Otto, ed. *The Great Detectives*. London: Little, Brown, 1978. Waugh's characters are among those afforded the status of "great" fictional detectives in this study of the most important and memorable characters in detective fiction.

Waugh, Hillary. *Hillary Waugh's Guide to Mysteries and Mystery Writing*. Cincinnati, Ohio: Writer's Digest Books, 1991. Waugh's handbook for aspiring writers and critical analysis of the genre provides crucial insight into his own creative process and investments.

JACK WEBB

Born: Los Angeles, California; January 13, 1916
Also wrote as John Farr; Tex Grady
Types of plot: Amateur sleuth; hard-boiled; police procedural; private investigator

Principal series

Father Shanley and Sammy Golden, 1952-
Cy Clements, 1955-

Principal series characters

Father Joseph Shanley is the priest of a Catholic parish in a poor section of Los Angeles, where he suspects or encounters crimes and seeks the help of the police in solving them.

Sammy Golden, a Jewish police detective sergeant, is a friend of Father Shanley and takes charge of the cases brought by the priest, often getting himself into more trouble than expected.

Red Adams, Sammy's partner on the police force, figures in a number of the Shanley-Golden adventures, as do Bill Cantrell, the detectives' boss; Tom Meigs, a reporter who assists the pair with research and publicity; and Liz Songer, one of Sammy's girlfriends.

Cy Clements is a zookeeper who uses his knowledge of animals to solve several murder cases involving animals.

Contribution

Jack Webb's principal series of mystery novels, the Father Shanley and Sammy Golden books, features a Catholic priest with a church in a Hispanic neighborhood of Los Angeles who teams up with a Jewish police detective. As a result, Webb places heavy emphasis on ethnic characters and their attitudes and problems, an unusual approach that ran against the grain of the culturally cautious 1950's, when all but the last book in the series appeared. Even more unusual than the characters who appear in Webb's novels are his warm approach to human problems (even criminals are sometimes sympathetically viewed as victims of forces beyond their control), his emphasis on higher moral issues (usually raised by Father Shanley), and his frequent references to music, art, and literature.

Biography

Jack Webb was born as John Alfred Webb on January 13, 1916, in Los Angeles and has lived most of his life there, except for military service and a period of residence in Phoenix, Arizona, from 1957 to 1966. He attended Occidental College in Los Angeles and was graduated with a degree in English literature in 1937. For the next two years, he worked at the San Diego Zoo and developed an interest in animals. During World War II, he served as a lieutenant with the Office of Strategic Services as part of a Signal Corps unit stationed near Chungking, China.

Webb was married to his wife, Nell, in 1950, and they have two children and a large collection of animals. During his time in Arizona, he established an aviary and a natural history library. He was most active as a writer during the 1950's, when the majority of his work appeared. He worked at a series of jobs, including a position at an advertising agency, before becoming manager of the Technical Information Unit of the General Electric Company. Although he retired from that company in 1986, he continued to work as a consultant.

Analysis

Although mystery writer Jack Webb is often confused with Jack Randolph Webb (1920-1982), who produced and starred in the popular television series *Dragnet*, it is difficult to see how the mystery novels of Webb could be considered the work of the television star. *Dragnet* and other series produced by television's Jack Webb are noted for a tough, no-nonsense approach to crime that emphasizes the boring and tedious elements of daily police work, debunks the conventions of detective fiction, and makes direct and simple, sometimes simplistic, moral judgments. By contrast, the mystery novels of the Jack Webb discussed here make heavy use of the conventions of detective fiction (unusual characters, elaborate plots, and abundant violence) but are also remarkable for their humor and frequent literary allusions, qualities for which the other Jack Webb is not noted.

The Big Sin

The unlikely pair of Father Shanley and Sammy Golden was introduced in *The Big Sin* (1952). Father Shanley, a rose-growing, pipe-smoking priest in his thirties, asks for the help of the police in solving the case of the death of one of his parishioners, Rose Mendez, who was ruled by the police to have committed suicide in the office of a nightclub owner. As a suicide (the "big sin" of the title), Rose may not receive the sacraments of the Church and may not be buried in consecrated ground. Father Shanley is at first attracted by a moral problem. Although Rose was a dancer in the club and lived on the fringes of the gangster world, the priest does not believe that she was a corrupt person or that she would kill herself. At the police station, he tries to arouse the interest of Sammy Golden, a plumpish Jewish detective in his thirties. Not only has Sammy been around the streets of Los Angeles, but he has also been action in World War II in North Africa, Salerno, and Anzio. Although he at first regards the priest's request as motivated by naïve sentimentality, he soon becomes interested in the case; indeed, his sense of morality is as intense as that of the priest, although the detective tries to mask his humanity under a hard shell. When someone attempts to cover up certain aspects of the case, Sammy becomes fully committed to helping Father Shanley. The priest and the detective eventually solve the case, save the reputation of the girl, and uncover a scandal that reaches to the highest level of the city's government. All the while, Father Shanley remains faithful to his priestly obligations; he says a prayer aloud, for example, as he and Sammy do some breaking and entering during their investigations.

The main weakness of the Webb mysteries is their elaborate and sometimes confusing plots. *The Big Sin*, Webb's first book, has a labyrinthine structure that suggests that its author was unsure whether there was enough mystery and so kept adding plot twists. Webb's later entries in the series are sparer and more effective.

The Naked Angel

The moral problems that Father Shanley encounters are interesting not only from the perspective of a priest but also from that of an ordinary reader. In *The Naked Angel* (1953), the priest hears police detective Mike Shannon call one of his parishioners a "greaser" and learns of his roughing up Mexican American suspects. Father Shanley believes that he must fight the detective to defend the honor of his flock and teach Shannon a lesson; the priest is good with his fists, an important skill to have considering the trouble that he and Sammy encounter. Father Shanley teaches the neighborhood boys to box and reminds Shannon that a priest started the Golden Gloves tournament. The priest lands some punches, but Shannon knocks him down, though not without regret. Later, confronting in an alley one of the Latin suspects in the naked angel case, Shannon remembers what he did to the priest, hesitates, and in that unguarded moment receives a knife in the belly. In the hospital, he asks to see the priest and dies cursing him, unrepentant, leaving Shanley to consider the practical difficulties of maintaining Christian civility in a fallen world.

The love interests in these mysteries are left for Sammy Golden to handle. (Father Shanley is so genuinely righteous that if he is ever attracted to a woman, the reader never discovers it.) Sammy's work does not allow him to meet many law-abiding people, so the women with whom he becomes involved are usually on the wrong side of the law or tramps with hearts of gold. When a "good" woman does come along, such as Barbara Mendez, the sister of the murder victim in *The Big Sin*, Sammy considers her out of his league. Even so, Sammy usually becomes fond of one of the women involved in the mystery and by the end of the novel has become very close to her. Nell Wharton, a high-class lady of the evening who appears in *The Big Sin*, falls in love with the detective, and there is talk of marriage between them at its close. When *The Naked Angel* begins, however, Nell is footloose again, and Sammy is carrying the torch for her. In that book, Sammy becomes involved with Myra Merrick, who proves to be part of a scheme to compromise him. Webb finally gave Sammy a more permanent liaison in *The Damned Lovely* (1954), where he meets Elizabeth Songer (with whom he is saved from death by Father Shanley), who becomes a regular girlfriend and appears in several other cases until she departs to get married. Sammy's activities beyond normal police procedure sometimes get him in trouble: At the end of *The Naked Angel*, he is demoted to patrolman, and in *The Deadly Sex* (1959), he seriously considers joining a beautiful female thief and fleeing to the Caribbean.

Webb does not stress Sammy's ethnic background as strongly as that of the priest, although the reader finds in *The Naked Angel* that the detective's mother and father operate a delicatessen. At the end of *The Brass Halo* (1957), when Father Shanley says that God will listen to the prayers of the murderer caught by the detective team, Sammy remarks, "Your God is a kinder one than mine."

One for My Dame and Make My Bed Soon

Webb gave the priest and detective a rest at the end of the 1950's before bringing them back for a final appearance in *The Gilded Witch* (1963). Each of the two books between *The Deadly Sex* and *The Gilded Witch, One for My Dame* (1961) and *Make My Bed Soon* (1963), concerns different characters, and each allows Webb to explore two of his favorite interests, animals and literature. Rick Jackson, the protagonist of *One for My Dame*, runs a pet shop and has three pets who figure in the plot (a Great Dane, a mynah, and a squirrel monkey). When Rick becomes involved with the kidnapped daughter of a Mafia chieftain, he is able to withstand a considerable amount of punishment by the mob because he had been a prisoner of war in Korea and had already been tortured by experts. Rick is beaten so frequently in this novel that the effect is finally comic, and Webb's intent may be satiric.

Make My Bed Soon also has a main character who is knowledgeable about animals, Al Duffey. He presents a theory about the crime with which he is involved as part of a discussion of the mating ritual of the Argus pheasant in relation to the theory of evolution as developed by Charles Darwin from his observation of the finches found on the Galápagos Islands. *Make My Bed Soon* is also the most strongly literary of Webb's books; the title comes from the English ballad "Lord Randal," and there are references to William Shakespeare, John Milton, John Keats, Thomas Wolfe, Ernest Hemingway, William Blake, and Omar Khayyám. The most literary book before this work had been *The Delicate Darling* (1959), which featured

Juan Delicado, a Cuban poet and revolutionary who was clearly modeled on José Marti; this book not only gave Webb an opportunity to indulge his penchant for Latin characters but also allowed him to smuggle some poetry into a mystery novel. In *One for My Dame*, the kidnapped girl compares Rick Jackson to Don Quixote, whom he greatly resembles, for after he frees the two of them from her captors, she drops back and is recaptured so that he may escape, but he returns to free her again. The emphasis on animals in these two books parallels that in an earlier series of three books, written under the pen name of John Farr, about a zookeeper who is called in to solve crimes apparently committed by animals. Another John Farr book is Webb's only essay in the hard-boiled detective field: In *The Deadly Combo* (1958), a seedy private eye tries to track down the murderer of a jazz trumpet player.

One for My Dame and *Make My Bed Soon* not only suffer from overly elaborate plots but also present another problem—strangers who appear at just the right time to help the hero. In *One for My Dame*, Rick Jackson takes refuge in a model tract house and finds it inhabited by a television actor who helps him and, coincidentally, holds a grudge against the criminals Jackson is chasing. Al Duffey, the hero of *Make My Bed Soon*, is befriended by a Mexican shoeshine boy who knows all about the people trying to kill Duffey and leads him to a boat where the crooks are hiding. Later, Duffey is fished out of the Gulf of California by a man who happens to be from Duffey's army unit in Korea. Furthermore, the plot of *Make My Bed Soon*, which involves a double-crossing woman who helps thieves smuggle cars into Mexico and smuggle drugs out, and which ends in that country, is quite similar to the plot of *The Naked Angel*, which involves a deceptive woman and a used-car dealer who smuggles drugs from Mexico, where that book's climactic scenes occur.

Humor

Webb's mysteries are often enlivened by humor. The highlight of *The Deadly Sex* is a fight at a bar: A diamond thief, a corrupt bar owner, Sammy Golden operating undercover, a widow who is trying to get information about the men who killed her police-officer husband, members of a Chicano motorcycle gang, another undercover police officer, and Father Shanley all arrive at the bar at the same time, with hilarious consequences. In addition to the usual banter between the characters, there are inside jokes that suggest that the author does not take himself too seriously. In *The Naked Angel*, people are watching a film titled *High Mesa*—the title of Webb's only Western novel, published in 1952 and issued under the name Tex Grady because his publishers thought that readers would be skeptical of a Western written by Webb. *The Broken Doll* (1955) has a joke about Sergeant Joe Friday, and in *The Delicate Darling*, Sammy describes a character as "overcome by her Thursday night television." Thursday was the night when *Dragnet* appeared.

Fans of pure mystery are sometimes alienated by the blend of humor, literature, and philosophy that gives the Webb books their distinctive character. Like Raymond Chandler and Ross Macdonald, Webb regarded the mystery as merely an instrument for evoking an atmosphere or making a psychological or philosophical point.

James Baird

Principal mystery and detective fiction

Father Shanley and Sammy Golden series: *The Big Sin*, 1952; *The Naked Angel*, 1953 (also known as *Such Women Are Dangerous*); *The Damned Lovely*, 1954; *The Broken Doll*, 1955; *The Bad Blonde*, 1956; *The Brass Halo*, 1957; *The Deadly Sex*, 1959; *The Delicate Darling*, 1959; *The Gilded Witch*, 1963

Cy Clements series (as Farr): *Don't Feed the Animals*, 1955 (also known as *The Zoo Murders* and *Naked Fear*); *She Shark*, 1956; *The Lady and the Snake*, 1957

Nonseries novels: *The Deadly Combo*, 1958 (as Farr); *One for My Dame*, 1961; *Make My Bed Soon*, 1963

Other major works

Novels: *High Mesa*, 1952 (as Grady)

Bibliography

Brean, Herbert, ed. *The Mystery Writer's Handbook*. New York: Harper, 1956. Guide to writing mysteries with examples of successful writers, including Webb.

Breen, Jon L., and Martin H. Greenberg, eds. *Synod of Sleuths: Essays on Judeo-Christian Detective Fiction*. Metuchen, N.J.: Scarecrow Press, 1990. Discusses important Jewish and Christian religious figures in detective fiction; provides perspective from which to understand Webb's works.

Erb, Peter C. *Murder, Manners, and Mystery: Reflections on Faith in Contemporary Detective Fiction—The John Albert Hall Lectures, 2004*. London: SCM Press, 2007. Collected lectures on the role and representation of religion in detective fiction; sheds light on Webb.

Keating, H. R. F. *Whodunit? A Guide to Crime, Suspense, and Spy Fiction*. New York: Van Nostrand Reinhold, 1982. General overview of the conventions and practitioners of British and American crime fiction; provides background for understanding Webb.

Penzler, Otto, et al., eds. *Detectionary: A Biographical Dictionary of Leading Characters in Detective and Mystery Fiction*. Woodstock, N.Y.: Overlook Press, 1977. Reference work by detective-fiction editor contains information on Webb's Father Shanley.

PATRICIA WENTWORTH

Dora Amy Elles Dillon Turnbull

Born: Mussoorie, India; 1878

Died: Camberley, Surrey, England; January 28, 1961

Types of plot: Private investigator; cozy

Principal series

Maud Silver, 1928-1961

Principal series characters

Maud Silver, a professional private investigator, unmarried, operates her detective agency from her drawing room after her retirement from a position as governess. Her clients are usually young females who are friends or have been referred by friends. Seemingly acquainted with people throughout England, including the police, she works carefully and efficiently, not only proving the innocence of her clients but also reinstating their inevitable social respectability.

Ernest Lamb is the woolly and not entirely skillful chief investigator who often works with Miss Silver. His three daughters are all named after flowers.

Ethel Burkett is Miss Silver's favorite niece, whose four young children receive most of the bounty from Miss Silver's perpetual knitting.

Gladys Robinson is Miss Silver's other niece. Her complaints about her husband make her less than pleasant both to Miss Silver and to the reader.

Randal March is the chief constable in the county where many of Miss Silver's cases occur. When she worked as a governess, Randal was her favorite child, and their devotion to each other remains.

Contribution

The more than seventy novels of Patricia Wentworth, more than half of which feature Miss Silver, Inspector Lamb, or both, have been variously judged anodyne, dependable, and engaging—solid praise for such an extensive canon. Often compared to Jane Marple, Wentworth's heroine, Miss Silver, is enriched with much detail, making her one of the most successfully and clearly drawn private detectives in the genre. She inevitably brings a happy solution to varied maidens-in-distress who have been wrongly accused of crime and stripped of their good names and reputations. Wentworth's style, though in no way poetic or memorable, is sufficient to tell the story, and is, at times, mildly witty. Her plots play fair with the reader, even though they are at times highly unrealistic. They are successful, however, because they create considerable suspense by placing ordinary, decent people from comfortable English settings into extreme danger, a plot device that Wentworth helped to initiate. Like other prolific mystery writers, notably Agatha Christie, Wentworth wrote novels that are uneven in quality, with the least successful written at the end of her career. Yet her charming, rational heroine, Miss Silver, and her skill in creating suspense ensure Wentworth's lasting popularity as a writer of detective fiction.

Biography

Patricia Wentworth was born Dora Amy Elles in Mussoorie, India, in 1878. She was the daughter of a British army officer. She received a high school education at the Blackheath High School in London, where she and her two brothers had been sent to live with their grandmother. When she completed her education, she returned to India, where she married Colonel George Dillon in 1906. He died soon after, leaving her with three stepsons and a young daughter. She returned to England with the four children and established a successful writing career, publishing six well-received novels of historical fiction between 1910 and 1915.

In 1920, Wentworth (then Dillon) married another British army officer, Lieutenant George Oliver Turnbull, and moved to Surrey. He encouraged and assisted her in her writing and served as a scribe while she dictated her stories, the two of them working only during the winter months between 5:00 and 7:00 P.M. In 1923, she began writing mystery novels with *The Astonishing Adventure of Jane Smith*; in 1928, she introduced Miss Silver in *Grey Mask*. Then, after an interim of nine years and fifteen mystery novels, she revived the Maud Silver character in 1937 and used her exclusively in her books written between 1945 and 1961. She died on January 28, 1961.

Analysis

Like many other prolific mystery novelists, Patricia Wentworth began her professional career writing in another genre, historical fiction. Unlike her peers, however, she earned a solid reputation as such a writer, with her first novel, *A Marriage Under the Terror* (1910), appearing in ten editions and winning a literary prize. She wrote five more historical novels, which were published annually through 1915. Although technically unremarkable, these early volumes helped her develop style, plotting technique, and the extensive use of detail in characterization.

When Wentworth began writing mysteries in 1923, she was a polished writer already showing the traits that would become the hallmarks of her entire body of work. In her first novel of detection, *The Astonishing Adventure of Jane Smith*, while using generic mystery plot elements, she conjured up considerable suspense and intrigue. In many of her books, the typical English settings of pastoral country village or urban London gain deadly and suspenseful qualities with the emphasis on secret passageways and gangs of disguised criminals who have mysterious though entirely mortal power. Such plot elements are saved from becoming silly and absurd throughout her work because of the suspense they consistently generate.

Wentworth's settings offer the orderly, romanticized views of England that the reader of English mystery novels has come to expect. The small English village, made most famous by Christie, contains within itself all the plot and character requirements. The village green is surrounded by a few small cottages with their requisite gardens, fewer still larger homes built in the Georgian style and filled with unpretentious furniture that, though worn, is very good indeed, a group of small shops containing collections of innocuous items for sale, and the necessary official places, a vicarage and a solicitor's office. Such exaggerated peace in the setting is stressed to create a strong contrast to the strange and nearly diabolical evil that enters and temporarily cankers the village. It is also the peace to which the village returns after Miss Silver has excised the evil. Thus, Wentworth uses setting in a traditional mystery fashion.

On the surface, too, Wentworth's characters resemble those of Christie. First among them is Maud Silver herself, an elderly female whose powers of knitting and detection seem unbounded. Often compared to Jane Marple, she is only superficially similar. Interestingly, Miss Silver's appearance in *Grey Mask* predates that of Miss Marple in *Murder in the Vicarage* (1930) by two years. Wentworth's creation of Miss Silver is highly detailed, perhaps more than that of any other detective hero. These details function to make her comfortably familiar to the reader and often stunningly unpredictable to her foes. Nearly everything about her is misleadingly soft, pastel, and chintz, from her light blue dressing gown and pale smooth skin to her little fur tie and ribbon-and-flower-bedecked hat. She is not a fussy elderly lady, however, and, it is important to note, not an amateur. With her detective agency she has established a professional reputation, and her skills are acknowledged both financially and socially.

Other characters in the books, particularly the dozens of damsels in distress, may be fit into categories. This placement must be made with caution, however, to avoid the mistaken conclusion that they are similar, interchangeable, or two-dimensional. The damsels' behavior is a result of more than beauty and virtue; each has her own consistent weaknesses and idiosyncrasies that are not extraneous but instead primary sources for the movement of the plot. The characters who reappear from book to book are also endowed with their own traits, but they gain their entertainment value from the pleasant familiarity the reader soon establishes with them. A newly introduced character may suddenly realize that he or she knows one of Miss Silver's longtime favorites, a niece or a student perhaps, and the requisite order of social class, inherent in the world of the English detective story, is underscored.

Such order is clearly seen in Wentworth's plots. Although plot conflicts range from the unlikely to the downright silly, they succeed because the characters who are placed in outlandish predicaments are themselves down to earth. Hence, manmade monsters threateningly lying in wait for realistic victims are not entirely foolish. Even when the threat seems to be an ordinary person using no mechanical monsters, that person is horrible within; the individual's evil becomes diabolical, almost unmotivated. It is comforting to purge such characters from the ordered society. Considered a pioneer in the use of artful suspense, Wentworth has been compared to Charlotte Armstrong, the most successful writer of suspenseful detective fiction. It is Wentworth's own method, however, to juxtapose the everyday and the horrible in order to sustain suspense and bring consistently satisfying conclusions.

The style of Wentworth's novels, while often pedestrian, serves the plots well, particularly as a result of its nonintrusiveness. Readers pause neither to admire its brilliance and wit nor to shake their heads over the jarring clichés. In a chatty, second-person style, the nearly omniscient narrator briefs readers on the personalities and motivations of the various characters and also allows them to hear their ongoing thoughts. Short lines of light wit also color the descriptions so that Wentworth's books become something other than reportage.

MISS SILVER COMES TO STAY

In *Miss Silver Comes to Stay* (1949), Wentworth presents a story typical of many of her successful novels. The closed setting of the small village of Melling provides the predictable scenes of a manor house library with doors leading to the garden, cottage parlors, a solicitor's office, and a general store. The proximity and the small number of these scenes enables the reader to imagine easily their location; further, it allows characters to socialize and to be aware of one another's business. The setting also functions as a presentation of the order to which this little village of Melling will return after Miss Silver removes the chaotic element.

The cast of characters, too, is pleasant and predictable. Miss Silver has come to Melling to visit her friend, appropriately named Cecilia Voycey. Acting as a foil to Miss Silver, she is an old school chum who chatters and gossips, while Miss Silver, on the other hand, quietly and methodically solves the murders. The heroine, Rietta Cray, is the damsel in distress, the leading suspect; for variation, however, she is forty-three years old, has big feet, and is often compared to Pallas Athene. In this volume, she becomes the wife of Chief Constable Randal March, the recurring character who is Miss Silver's favorite student from her governess days. He is attractive both in his admiration and affection for Miss Silver and in his common sense and wisdom. His subordinate, Inspector Drake, impetuous and imprecise, acts as his foil. The victim, James Lessiter, a wealthy lord of the manor, is amoral and unscrupulous, thereby arousing sufficient numbers of enemies who become suspects to puzzle the police. Both he and the second victim, Catherine Welby, are unlikable, which ensures that their deaths raise no grief in the other characters or in the reader. A final important suspect is Carr Robertson, Rietta Cray's twenty-eight-year-old nephew, whom she reared. He and his aunt are the chief victims of misplaced accusations; they are also both involved in their own star-crossed love affairs and are unable to marry their lovers. Thus Miss Silver not only purges the village of evil but also opens the path to love for four deserving people. She herself is drawn with no new strokes. A first-time reader is easily introduced to her knitting, good sense, and prim appearance, while the longtime reader of Miss Silver is seduced with the pleasure of familiarity.

The plot is not outlandish and depends on only one scene of outrageous coincidence, the fact that Marjory Robertson, Carr's first wife, happens to have run away with Lessiter. Otherwise, the plot contains no twists that are not acceptable in the detective-story genre. A weakness of this particular story, however, is the lack of a sufficient number of suspects, and a few more lively red herrings are needed. The murder of Lessiter in his library is accomplished by bashing in his head with a fireplace poker. Ordinarily, men and not women commit murder using such means; still, only four men are possible suspects, one of whom is the loving and loyal Carr. The others are two minor characters, who are not involved enough to have committed the crime, and the real murderer himself. His means, motive, and opportunity for murdering Lessiter are logical but not overwhelming, and the solution is not one that completes a splendid puzzle. The pacing of the plot is classic, with the cast of characters being introduced as future suspects in the first few chapters and the murder scene being described in detail with the curtain drawn on the reader at the necessary moment. It is during this scene that Wentworth creates her standard suspense scene when the evil Lessiter acts as both the aggressor with Rietta and as the victim with the unknown murderer. Following this scene comes the questioning of suspects, the second murder, the discovery of secrets in everyone's closet, and the final revelation. The latter, however, is somewhat carelessly revealed too soon. The finger of blame seems not to point falsely at successive suspects; it simply appears and aims at the real killer. Clearly this work follows a formula plot and utilizes formula characters. Nevertheless, it is ordinarily with the expectation of such formula writing that the reader takes up such a book in the first place.

Although language and style are appropriate, the dialogue is stilted and mannered. Descriptions of the physical are clear but often repetitious. The bloodied sleeve of Carr's raincoat, for example, the most gruesome image in the story, is noted an extraordinary number of times, considering that it is unimportant in the solution to the crime. In a similarly repetitive manner, lovers kiss, embrace, and kneel beside the beloved so many times that a pervasive tone of romance is cast over the entire story. Murder—romanticized, unregretted, and evil—suspensefully committed and covered up, with several pairs of happy lovers united in the end, thanks to Maud Silver: Such is the formula for the entire canon of Wentworth.

Vicki K. Robinson

Principal mystery and detective fiction

Maud Silver series: 1928-1945 • *Grey Mask*, 1928; *The Case Is Closed*, 1937; *Lonesome Road*, 1939; *In the Balance*, 1941 (also known as *Danger Point*); *Miss Silver Deals with Death*, 1943 (also known as *Miss Silver Intervenes*); *The Chinese Shawl*, 1943; *The Clock Strikes Twelve*, 1944; *The Key*, 1944; *She Came Back*, 1945 (also known as *The Traveller Returns*)

1946-1950 • *Pilgrim's Rest*, 1946 (also known as *Dark Threat*); *Latter End*, 1947; *Wicked Uncle*, 1947 (also known as *Spotlight*); *Eternity Ring*, 1948; *The Case of William Smith*, 1948; *Miss Silver Comes to Stay*, 1949; *The Catherine Wheel*, 1949; *The Brading Collection*, 1950; *Through the Wall*, 1950

1951-1961 • *Anna, Where Are You?*, 1951 (also known as *Death at Deep End*); *The Ivory Dagger*, 1951; *The Watersplash*, 1951; *Ladies' Bane*, 1952; *Out of the Past*, 1953; *Vanishing Point*, 1953; *The Benevent Treasure*, 1954; *The Silent Pool*, 1954; *Poison in the Pen*, 1955; *The Listening Eye*, 1955; *The Fingerprint*, 1956; *The Gazebo*, 1956 (also known as *The Summerhouse*); *The Alington Inheritance*, 1958; *The Girl in the Cellar*, 1961

Ernest Lamb series: *The Blind Side*, 1939; *Who Pays the Piper?*, 1940 (also known as *Account Rendered*); *Pursuit of a Parcel*, 1942

Nonseries novels: 1923-1930 • *The Astonishing Adventure of Jane Smith*, 1923; *The Annam Jewel*,

1924; *The Red Lacquer Case*, 1924; *The Black Cabinet*, 1925; *The Dower House Mystery*, 1925; *The Amazing Chance*, 1926; *Anne Belinda*, 1927; *Hue and Cry*, 1927; *Will-o'-the-Wisp*, 1928; *Fool Errant*, 1929; *Beggar's Choice*, 1930 (also known as *Kingdom Lost*, 1930); *The Coldstone*, 1930

1931-1945 • *Danger Calling*, 1931; *Nothing Venture*, 1932; *Red Danger*, 1932 (also known as *Red Shadow*); *Seven Green Stones*, 1933 (also known as *Outrageous Fortune*); *Walk with Care*, 1933; *Devil-in-the-Dark*, 1934 (also known as *Touch and Go*); *Fear by Night*, 1934; *Blindfold*, 1935; *Red Stefan*, 1935; *Dead or Alive*, 1936; *Hole and Corner*, 1936; *Down Under*, 1937; *Mr. Zero*, 1938; *Run!*, 1938; *Rolling Stone*, 1940; *Unlawful Occasions*, 1941 (also known as *Weekend with Death*); *Silence in Court*, 1945

Other major works

Novels: *A Marriage Under the Terror*, 1910; *A Little More than Kin*, 1911 (also known as *More than Kin*); *The Devil's Wind*, 1912; *The Fire Within*, 1913; *Simon Heriot*, 1914; *Queen Anne Is Dead*, 1915

Poetry: *A Child's Rhyme Book*, 1910; *Beneath the Hunter's Moon: Poems*, 1945; *The Pool of Dreams: Poems*, 1953

Nonfiction: *Earl or Chieftain? The Romance of Hugh O'Neill*, 1919

Bibliography

Amelin, Michael. "Patricia Wentworth." *Enigmatika* 25 (November, 1983): 3-9. Brief but useful discussion of Wentworth's career and her contribution to detective fiction.

Dresner, Lisa M. *The Female Investigator in Literature, Film, and Popular Culture*. Jefferson, N.C.: McFarland, 2007. Study of the figure of the female detective and her role in popular culture. Provides context for understanding Wentworth's writings. Bibliographic references and index.

Klein, Kathleen Gregory. *Great Women Mystery Writers: Classic to Contemporary*. Westport, Conn.: Greenwood Press, 1994. Wentworth is compared with other successful and notable female writers of detective fiction.

Kungl, Carla T. *Creating the Fictional Female Detective: The Sleuth Heroines of British Women Writers, 1890-1940*. Jefferson, N.C.: McFarland, 2006. Study of the fifty years immediately preceding the primary beginning of Wentworth's career; details the evolution of the conventions that Wentworth worked with and the state of the female detective subgenre when she inherited it.

Malmgren, Carl D. *Anatomy of Murder: Mystery, Detective, and Crime Fiction*. Bowling Green, Ohio: Bowling Green State University Popular Press, 2001. Includes analysis of Wentworth's *The Gazebo*. Bibliographic references and index.

Reynolds, Moira Davison. *Women Authors of Detective Series: Twenty-one American and British Authors, 1900-2000*. Jefferson, N.C.: McFarland, 2001. Examines the life and work of major female mystery writers, including Wentworth.

DONALD E. WESTLAKE

Born: Brooklyn, New York; July 12, 1933
Also wrote as John B. Allan; Curt Clark; Tucker Coe; Timothy J. Culver; J. Morgan Cunningham; Samuel Holt; Richard Stark; Edwin West
Types of plot: Inverted; comedy caper

Principal series

Parker, 1962-1974, 1997-
Alan Grofield, 1964-
Mitch Tobin, 1966-
John Dortmunder, 1970-

Principal series characters

Parker is a ruthless, brilliant master thief with no first name. Through an elaborate underground criminal network, Parker is recruited or sometimes recruits others for daring thefts: an army payroll, an entire North Dakota town. Meticulous and coldly efficient, he will kill without compunction but abhors needless violence.

Alan Grofield is an aspiring actor, thief, and sometimes associate of Parker. Grofield is more charming, human, and humorous than Parker but equally conscienceless in perpetrating the thefts and scams by which he subsidizes his acting career.

Mitch Tobin, an embittered former police officer, is guilt-ridden because his partner was killed while Tobin was sleeping with a burglar's wife. Though he tries to hibernate in his Queens home, Tobin grows progressively more involved with other people by reluctantly solving several baffling murders. Eventually, he becomes a licensed private detective.

John Dortmunder is a likable two-time loser who lives a quiet domestic life with May, a grocery checker and shoplifter, when not pursuing his chosen career as a thief. Often lured into crimes against his will by Andy Kelp, Dortmunder designs brilliant capers that always go wrong somehow.

Andy Kelp, an incurable optimist, is a car thief who steals only doctors' cars. He is a sucker for gadgets and Dortmunder's longtime associate and jinx.

Stan Murch is a gifted getaway driver who monomaniacally discusses roads, routes, detours, and traffic jams, often with his mother, a cabdriver usually referred to as Murch's mom.

Tiny Bulcher, a cretinous human mountain, leg breaker, and threat to the peace, is often called "the beast from forty fathoms."

Contribution

By combining the intricate plotting characteristic of mystery writing with the deconstructive energies of comedy and satire, Donald E. Westlake invented his own form of crime fiction, the comic caper. Comedy was a significant element in the fiction Westlake published under his own name during the late 1960's, beginning with *The Fugitive Pigeon* (1965). In those novels, harried protagonists bumblingly encounter the frustrations of everyday life while sidestepping dangerous enemies. Somehow, all the negative forces are rendered harmless in the end, as is usual in comedy. In the same period, Westlake, writing as Richard Stark, produced novels featuring master thief Parker, which developed increasingly more complex capers, or "scores."

With *The Hot Rock* (1970), Westlake united these two creative forces in a single work and found his perfect hero/foil, John Archibald Dortmunder. In the series of novels that followed, Dortmunder designs capers as brilliant as Parker's. His compulsive associates follow through meticulously, but these capers never quite succeed. The reader, hypnotized by the intricacy and daring of Dortmunder's planning, watches in shocked disbelief as the brilliant caper inexorably unravels. The laughter that inevitably follows testifies to Westlake's mastery of this unique subgenre.

Some of Westlake's novels have been made into American, English, and French films starring actors as varied as Lee Marvin (*Point Blank*, 1967), Sid Caesar (*The Busy Body*, 1967), Robert Redford (*The Hot Rock*, 1972), Robert Duvall (*The Outfit*, 1973), George C. Scott (*Bank Shot*, 1974), Dom DeLuise (*Hot Stuff*, 1979), Gary Coleman (*Jimmy the Kid*, 1983), Christopher Lambert (*Why Me?*, 1990), Antonio Banderas and

Melanie Griffith (*Two Much*, 1996), and Mel Gibson (*Payback*, 1999). Westlake has also scripted several films, most famously his Academy Award-winning screenplay for *The Grifters* (1990, based on Jim Thompson's novel, directed by Stephen Frears and starring John Cusack, Angelica Huston, and Annette Bening).

Westlake was thrice awarded the Edgar. The first was for his novel *God Save the Mark* (1967); the second for his short story "Too Many Crooks" (1989), which appeared in the August issue of *Playboy. The Grifters* won an Edgar for best motion picture screenplay in 1991. The Mystery Writers of America named Westlake a Grand Master in 1993. He received lifetime achievement awards in 1997 from the Bouchercon Mystery Convention and in 2004 from the Private Eye Writers of America.

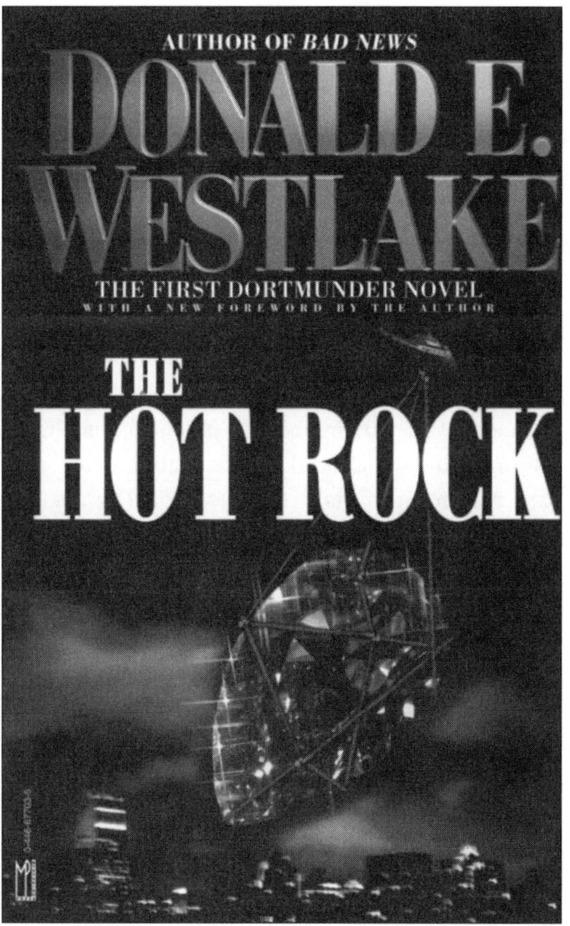

Biography

Donald Edwin Westlake was born July 12, 1933, in Brooklyn, New York, the son of Albert Joseph Westlake and Lillian Bounds Westlake. He was educated at Champlain College and the State University of New York at Binghamton and served in the United States Air Force from 1954 to 1956. Westlake married Nedra Henderson in 1957, and they were divorced in 1966. He married Sandra Foley in 1967; they were divorced in 1975. These marriages brought Westlake four sons: Sean Alan, Steven Albert, Tod David, and Paul Edwin. In 1979, he married writer Abigail Adams, with whom he collaborated on two novels, *Transylvania Station* (1987) and *High Jinx* (1987).

After a series of jobs, including six months during 1958-1959 at the Scott Meredith literary agency, Westlake committed himself to becoming a full-time writer in 1959. He quickly became one of the most versatile and prolific figures in American popular literature. His first novel, *The Mercenaries*, published in 1960, was followed by more than sixty other titles, some published under Westlake's own name, some under the pen names Richard Stark, Tucker Coe, Curt Clark, and Timothy J. Culver. During 1967, for example, as Richard Stark he published *The Rare Coin Score* and *The Green Eagle Score*, both featuring the ruthless thief Parker, and *The Damsel*, starring the more charming Alan Grofield. In the same year, *Anarchaos*, a work of science fiction, appeared under the pseudonym Curt Clark; Westlake's name was on the cover of *Philip*, a story for children, and the comic crime novel *God Save the Mark*. The latter received the Edgar Allan Poe Award from the Mystery Writers of America, demonstrating that Westlake's writing was distinguished as well as prolific.

In an interview with *Publishers Weekly* in 1970, Westlake credited his experience in a literary agency for his understanding of the practical aspects of the literary life. His books have enjoyed good sales not only in the United States but also abroad, especially in England.

Analysis

Donald E. Westlake's earliest novels were praised by the influential Anthony Boucher of *The New York*

Times as highly polished examples of hard-boiled crime fiction. Although Westlake wrote only five novels exclusively in this idiom, concluding with the extremely violent *Pity Him Afterwards* in 1964, he did not entirely abandon the mode. The novels he wrote under the pen names Richard Stark and Tucker Coe all display elements of hard-boiled detective fiction. In fact, much of this work invites comparisons to that of Dashiell Hammett and Raymond Chandler. The resemblances, however, are much more a matter of tone than of character or structure. Although Tucker Coe's hero, Mitch Tobin, solves murder mysteries, he does so as a discredited police officer rather than as a private detective. The two Richard Stark series are even less traditional, since their protagonists are thieves and murderers. Illustrating the inverted mode of crime fiction, these novels draw the reader into sympathy with, or at least suspended judgment toward, Parker and Alan Grofield. Whether attributed to Stark or Coe, all these novels present a professionally controlled hard edge.

Parker series

Parker, the master thief, is a remarkable creation in himself: calculating, meticulous, highly inventive, and totally lacking in normal human feelings. In some respects he resembles characters in the earlier novels published under Westlake's own name, but Parker elevates these qualities through exaggeration. For example, murder is easy for Parker, but small talk is difficult, as are most human relations, because Parker sees no practical advantage to such transactions. When involved in a caper, Parker is all business, so much so that he feels no sexual desire until the current heist is completed. Then he makes up for lost time. The purely instrumental nature of this character is further evident in the fact that he has only a surname. According to Francis M. Nevins, Jr., the first novel in the series, *The Hunter* (1962), came so easily to Westlake that he had written more than half the book before he noticed that Parker had no first name. By then, it was too late to add one unobtrusively. Because Parker normally operates under an alias in the series, this lack causes few problems. Parker was scheduled to wind up in the hands of the police at the end of *The Hunter*, and it was Westlake's editor at Pocket Books who recognized the potential for a series. Westlake easily arranged for Parker to escape and to pursue a successful criminal career.

The basic plot in the Parker novels and in the Grofield series is an elaborate robbery, a heist, caper, or score. In *The Seventh* (1966), for example, the booty is the cash receipts of a college football game; in *The Green Eagle Score*, the payroll of an army base; in *The Score* (1964), all the negotiable assets in the town of Copper Canyon, North Dakota. Daring robberies on this scale require sophisticated planning and criminal associates with highly varied skills, weapons, transportation, electronic equipment, explosives, and perhaps uniforms, false identification, or other forms of disguise. Engaged by the detailed planning and execution of the caper, readers temporarily suspend the disapproval that such an immoral enterprise would normally elicit. Thus, readers experience the release of vicarious participation in antisocial behavior.

Westlake cleverly facilitates this participation through elements of characterization. For example, Parker would unemotionally kill in pursuit of a score, and he can spend half a book exacting bloody revenge for a double cross, but he will not tolerate needless cruelty on the part of his colleagues. Furthermore, he maintains a rigid sense of fair play toward those criminals who behave honestly toward him. His conscientiousness is another winning attribute. In the same way, Grofield appeals to readers because he is fundamentally an actor, not a thief. He steals only to support his unprofitable commitment to serious drama. In addition, although Grofield often collaborates with Parker on a caper, his wit and theatrical charm give him more in common with the comic protagonists of Westlake's *The Spy in the Ointment* (1966) and *High Adventure* (1985) than with the emotionless Parker. Thus, despite being far from rounded characters, both Parker and Grofield offer readers the opportunity to relish guilty behavior without guilt.

Westlake left off writing the Parker series with *Butcher's Moon* (1974), telling interviewers, "Parker just wasn't alive for me." He had wearied of the noir voice. So Parker fans were delighted when, after twenty-three years, he returned in *Comeback* (1997) to steal nearly half a million dollars from a smarmy televangelist, only to find that a co-conspirator means to kill Parker and keep the loot for himself. A *New York Times* notable book of the year, the novel found a reception so hot that Westlake quickly followed up with a string of Parker best sellers, including *Backflash* (1998), *Flashfire* (2000), and *Breakout* (2002). In *Nobody Runs Forever* (2004), Parker's perfect bank heist disintegrates spectacularly and leaves the more than usually frustrated thief running before the bloodhounds, apparently without possible escape. Refuge does, however, present itself in the opening pages of *Ask the Parrot* (2006), in the person of Tom Lindahl, an embittered whistle-blower who has been quietly plotting revenge. The titular bird is the cause of an uncharacteristcally comic episode in this otherwise noir novel.

Mitch Tobin series

Mitch Tobin comes much closer to filling the prescription for a rounded fictional character, largely because of his human vulnerabilities and his burden of guilt. After eighteen years as a New York City police officer, Tobin was expelled from the force because his partner, Jock Sheehan, was killed in the line of duty while the married Tobin was in bed with Linda Campbell, the wife of an imprisoned burglar. Afterward, consumed by guilt but supported by his understanding wife, Kate, Tobin tries to shut out the world by devoting all his time and energy to building a high brick wall around his house in Queens. The world keeps encroaching, however, in the persons of desperate individuals needing help—usually to investigate a murder—but unable to turn to the police. A crime kingpin, a distant relative's daughter, the operator of a psychiatric halfway house, the homosexual owner of a chic boutique—all seek Tobin's aid. Partly in response to Kate's urging, partly because of his own residual sense of decency, Tobin takes the cases, suffers the resentment and hostility of the police, and solves the murders.

Although Tobin returns to his wall after every foray into the outside world, with each case he clearly takes another step toward reassuming his life, thereby jeopardizing his utility as a series character. In fact, Westlake wrote in the introduction to *Levine* (1984) that Tobin's character development inevitably led to the expiration of the series. In the final novel, *Don't Lie to Me* (1972), Tobin has a private investigator's license and is regularly working outside his home as night watchman at a graphics museum. Linda Campbell reappears, several murders take place, and a hostile police officer threatens and beats Tobin, but he copes with it all effectively and without excessive guilt—that is to say, he comes dangerously close to becoming the conventional protagonist of crime fiction. At this point, Westlake wisely abandoned the pen name Tucker Coe and turned to more promising subjects.

Nonseries novels

By 1972, the year of Mitch Tobin's disappearance, Westlake had already published, under his own name, a number of comic novels about crime. Thus, Westlake was already well on his way toward establishing his unique reputation in the field. Appearing at the rate of about one per year, beginning with *The Fugitive Pigeon* in 1965, these novels usually featured a down-to-earth, young, unheroic male hero, suddenly and involuntarily caught in a tangled web of dangerous, often mob-related, circumstances. Charlie Poole, Aloysius Engle, J. Eugene Raxford, and Chester Conway are representative of the group. Though beset by mobsters, police, and occasionally foreign agents, these protagonists emerge, according to comic convention, largely unscathed and usually better off than when the action commenced, especially in their relations with women. In this respect they resemble Alan Grofield, as they do also in their personal charm and their sometimes witty comments on contemporary society. Westlake's achievement in these novels was demonstrated by their continuing favorable reception by reviewers such as Boucher and by the recognition conveyed by the Edgar Allan Poe Award for *God Save the Mark*.

Dortmunder series

The novels in the Dortmunder series depart from these patterns in various ways. For one thing, John A. Dortmunder is not young or particularly witty. Nor is he an innocent bystander: He is a professional thief. Furthermore, he is seldom much better off at the end of the novel than he was at the beginning, and his only romantic attachment is a long-standing arrangement with May, a food market checker, who fell in love with Dortmunder when she caught him shoplifting. Finally, Dortmunder is not a lone wolf, despite his frequently expressed wish to be one, but only one member of what is probably the least successful criminal gang of all time.

In the course of the novels making up the series, the membership of this gang varies somewhat, depending on the caper at hand. Andy Kelp steals cars for a living, usually doctors' cars because they come with outstanding optional equipment and can be parked anywhere. Another regular gang member is Stan Murch, a getaway driver who talks obsessively about the shortest drive between two points. He is often accompanied by his mother, a cynical New York cabbie who is usually referred to as Murch's mom. She and May sometimes act as a sort of ladies' auxiliary, making curtains in *Bank Shot* (1972) and taking care of the kidnap victim in *Jimmy the Kid* (1974). The mammoth and very dangerous Tiny Bulcher is also frequently on hand. Sullen, ignorant, and violent, he often frightens his fellow crooks, but he is strong enough to lift or carry anything. Fictional criminals who can be categorized in this way according to their obsessions and character defects seem to belong more to the world of conventional Jonsonian comedy than to the frightening world of contemporary urban America. This disparity permits Westlake to approach disturbing subject matter in these novels without upsetting his readers.

Among the early members of Dortmunder's gang are Roger Chefwick, expert on locks and safes and an obsessive model-train hobbyist; Wilbur Howey, who served forty-eight years in prison on a ten-year sentence because he could not resist the temptation to escape; and Herman X, whose criminal activities support both black activist political causes and a sybaritic lifestyle. As the series developed, extra hired hands became less frequent, although the regular planning sessions of Dortmunder, Kelp, Stan, and Tiny in the back room of Rollo's beloved and atmospheric bar remained de rigeur.

Dortmunder does the planning, even though the original idea for the crime is usually brought to him by someone else, often his old pal and nemesis, Andy Kelp. In *What's So Funny?* (2007), Dortmunder is presented with a heist he cannot refuse. An unscrupulous former cop named Eppick has the ability to put Dortmunder in prison but instead chooses to use his leverage to acquire a valuable chess set through the unwilling services of Dortmunder and his associates. Westlake thoroughly milks the comic irony of Eppick's choice of this singularly unlucky thief to pull off a nearly impossible theft.

Comedy and mystery

In *Adventure, Mystery, and Romance: Formula Stories as Art and Popular Culture* (1976), John G. Cawelti argues that detective fiction generally functions as a comic genre because it subdues the threatening elements of life through the powers of mind and structure. Overly elaborate plotting, that is, inevitably triggers some sort of comic reader response. Even before discovering Dortmunder in 1970, Westlake showed evidence of a similar conviction in the incredibly complex kidnap caper he created for *Who Stole Sassi Manoon?* (1968). Later, *Help I Am Being Held Prisoner* (1974) develops another non-Dortmunder caper of Byzantine complexity, a double bank robbery conducted by prison inmates who have a secret passage to the outside world. In these novels, as in the Dortmunder and Parker series, the intricacy of the caper both enthralls readers and distracts them from the negative judgments they would make in real life.

The fundamental difference between the comic and the chilling capers lies in the degree to which Westlake permits realistic circumstances to undermine the design. Paradoxically, the comic variety entails a greater degree of realism. Though Parker must sometimes settle for a fraction of his anticipated haul, Dortmunder gets even less. Moreover, the antagonistic forces subverting Dortmunder's plans are rarely the sorts of dangerous assassins whom Parker encounters but more mundane elements such as weather, illness, time, and coincidence—in other words, real life. The distinction of Westlake's comic caper novels, therefore, arises from his combining the coherence available only in elaborately constructed fiction with the comic incoherence familar to readers in their everyday lives. Such comedy, though often howlingly hilarious, is ultimately a serious, highly moral form of literature.

Humans and Smoke

Westlake's *Humans* (1992) showed just how seriously he intends his comedy. In the 1990's he undertook a number of novels that are neither comedy capers (though they are occasionally highly comedic) nor hard-boiled. In *Smoke* (1995), Freddie Noon, a burglar, breaks into a secret tobacco research laboratory, swallows some experimental solutions, and finds himself invisible. *Humans*, however, is narrated by an angel, Ananayel, who has been sent by God to arrange the end of the world. "He" encounters obstacles not only from the resident devils, who will do anything to thwart God's will, but also from his growing love for a human woman.

The Ax

The Ax (1997) addressed the phenomenon of the increasing, one might say hasty, layoffs and downsizing in the name of the corporate bottom line that ruined hundreds of thousands of American lives during the period of greatest prosperity that America had ever known. The protagonist, Burke Devore, gets fired from his middle-management position at a paper mill, and his rage drives him to commit murder—in fact to commit mass murder.

Kahawa

The 1995 republication of 1982's *Kahawa* by Mysterious Press includes an introduction by Westlake that signaled how strongly he indicts the kind of crime about which he writes so (apparently) casually. It also showed that by comparison, even in the Parker novels there were lengths to which he would not go, a barrier beyond which lies soul-blanching horror. *Kahawa* is based on a true story: In Idi Amin's Uganda, a group of white mercenaries stole a coffee-payload railroad train a mile long and made it disappear. Of Uganda after Amin fled, Westlake writes in his introduction, "Five hundred thousand dead; bodies hacked and mutilated and tortured and debased and destroyed; corridors running with blood. . . ." His research, he reported, "changed the character of the story I would tell. As I told my wife at the time, 'I can't dance on all those graves.'" One is reminded of Joseph Conrad's Marlow, in *Heart of Darkness* (1899), who murmurs as he looks upon civilized England, "And this also has been one of the dark places of the earth."

After spending considerable time in those dark places, many a writer turns to absurdism. Westlake's blessing is that, though his outrage seems to grow by the year, he has never lost his sense of humor. Although he documents the atrocities of Uganda, he also creates lovable characters over whom a reader might well weep. Although he plans the end of the world, he dramatizes how precious and valuable are human follies and foible-filled lives. Westlake, after the 1990's, is no longer the madcap he pretends, who remarks, "It probably says something discreditable about me that I put the serious work under a pseudonym and the comic under my own name." Westlake's ever-evolving career has proven that he is not merely a "genius of comedy" or a "heistmeister." He has become one of the truly significant writers of the twentieth century.

Michael Dunne

Updated by Fiona Kelleghan and Janet Alice Long

Principal mystery and detective fiction

Parker series (as Stark): *The Hunter*, 1962 (also known as *Point Blank* and *Payback*); *The Man with the Getaway Face*, 1963 (also known as *The Steel Hit*); *The Mourner*, 1963; *The Outfit*, 1963; *The Score*, 1964 (also known as *Killtown*); *The Jugger*, 1965; *The Handle*, 1966 (also known as *Run Lethal*); *The Seventh*, 1966 (also known as *The Split*); *The Green Eagle Score*, 1967; *The Rare Coin Score*, 1967; *The Black Ice Score*, 1968; *The Sour Lemon Score*, 1969; *Deadly Edge*, 1971; *Slayground*, 1971; *Plunder Squad*, 1972; *Child Heist*, 1974; *Butcher's Moon*, 1974; *Comeback*, 1997; *Backflash*, 1998; *Flashfire*, 2000; *Firebreak*, 2001; *Breakout*, 2002; *Nobody Runs Forever*, 2004; *Ask the Parrot*, 2006

Alan Grofield series (as Stark): *The Damsel*, 1967; *The Blackbird*, 1969; *The Dame*, 1969; *Lemons Never Lie*, 1971

Mitch Tobin series (as Coe): *Kinds of Love, Kinds of Death*, 1966; *Murder Among Children*, 1968; *Wax Apple*, 1970; *A Jade in Aries*, 1971; *Don't Lie to Me*, 1972

John Dortmunder series: *The Hot Rock*, 1970; *Bank Shot*, 1972; *Jimmy the Kid*, 1974; *Nobody's Perfect*, 1977; *Why Me?*, 1983; *Good Behavior*, 1986; *Drowned Hopes*, 1990; *Don't Ask*, 1993; *What's the Worst That Could Happen?*, 1996; *Bad News*, 2001; *The Road to Ruin*, 2004; *Thieves' Dozen*, 2004; *Watch Your Back!*, 2005; *What's So Funny?*, 2007

NONSERIES NOVELS: 1960-1970 • *The Mercenaries*, 1960 (also as *The Smashers*); *Killing Time*, 1961 (also as *The Operator*); *Brother and Sister*, 1961 (as West); *Campus Doll*, 1961 (as West); *Young and Innocent*, 1961 (as West); *Strange Affair*, 1962 (as West); *361*, 1962; *Killy*, 1963; *Pity Him Afterwards*, 1964; *The Fugitive Pigeon*, 1965; *The Busy Body*, 1966; *The Spy in the Ointment*, 1966; *God Save the Mark*, 1967; *Who Stole Sassi Manoon?*, 1968; *Somebody Owes Me Money*, 1969; *Comfort Station*, 1970 (as J. Morgan Cunningham); *Ex Officio*, 1970 (as Timothy J. Culver; also known as *Power Play*)

1971-1980 • *I Gave at the Office*, 1971; *Cops and Robbers*, 1972; *Gangway*, 1973 (with Brian Garfield); *Help I Am Being Held Prisoner*, 1974; *Brothers Keepers*, 1975; *Two Much*, 1975; *Dancing Aztecs*, 1976 (also as *A New York Dance*); *Enough*, 1977; *Castle in the Air*, 1980

1981-1990 • *Kahawa*, 1982; *High Adventure*, 1985; *One of Us Is Wrong*, 1986 (as Holt); *I Know a Trick Worth Two of That*, 1986 (as Holt); *High Jinx*, 1987 (with Abby Westlake); *What I Tell You Three Times Is False*, 1987 (as Holt); *Transylvania Station*, 1987 (with Abby Westlake); *Trust Me on This*, 1988; *The Fourth Dimension Is Death*, 1989 (as Holt)

1991-2003 • *Smoke*, 1995; *The Ax*, 1997; *Corkscrew*, 2000; *The Hook*, 2000; *Put a Lid on It*, 2002; *Money for Nothing*, 2003; *The Scared Stiff*, 2003

SHORT FICTION: *The Curious Facts Preceding My Execution, and Other Fictions*, 1968; *Levine*, 1984; *Tomorrow's Crimes*, 1989; *Horse Laugh, and Other Stories*, 1991; *A Good Story, and Other Stories*, 1999

OTHER MAJOR WORKS

NOVELS: *Anarchaos*, 1967 (as Clark); *Up Your Banners*, 1969; *Adios, Scheherezade*, 1970; *A Likely Story*, 1984; *Sacred Monster*, 1989; *Humans*, 1992; *Baby, Would I Lie? A Romance of the Ozarks*, 1994

SCREENPLAYS: *Cops and Robbers*, 1972; *Hot Stuff*, 1975 (with Michael Kane); *The Stepfather*, 1987; *The Grifters*, 1990; *Why Me?*, 1990 (adaptation of his novel; with Leonard Mass, Jr.)

TELEPLAYS: *Supertrain*, 1979; *Fatal Confession: A Father Dowling Mystery*, 1987; *Flypaper*, 1993

CHILDREN'S LITERATURE: *Philip*, 1967

NONFICTION: *Elizabeth Taylor*, 1962 (as John B. Allan); *Under an English Heaven*, 1972

EDITED TEXTS: *Once Against the Law*, 1968 (with William Tenn); *Murderous Schemes: An Anthology of Classic Detective Stories*, 1996; *The Best American Mystery Stories*, 2000

BIBLIOGRAPHY

Banville, John, and Donald Westlake. "Lives of Crime: Novelists John Banville and Donald Westlake Compare Notes on the Seedy Worlds That Inspire Their Fiction." Interview by Malcolm Jones. *Newsweek* 149, no. 15 (April 23, 2007): 56. Banville and Westlake talk about using pseudonyms and creating different sorts of novels.

Cannon, Peter. "A Comic Crime Writer." *Publishers Weekly* 254, no. 6 (February 5, 2007): 25. Profile of Westlake traces his history and notes that Westlake writes six days a week on an old Smith-Corona typewriter.

Knight, Stephen. *Crime Fiction, 1800-2000: Detection, Death, Diversity*. New York: Palgrave Macmillan, 2004. Knight sees Westlake as a transitional writer, one whose characters derive from the traditions of earlier fictional private eyes but who live and work in a modern America, with all its broadened understanding of race, gender, and psychology.

Priestman, Martin. *The Cambridge Companion to Crime Fiction*. New York: Cambridge University Press, 2003. An excellent, all-around trove of information for the reader. Priestman discusses paid assassins, such as Parker, who are a mainstay of the thriller.

Taylor, Charles. "Talking with Donald E. Westlake, Grand Master of Crime." *Newsday*, March 18, 2001, p. B11. Profile focuses on the career of Westlake and his longevity as a writer. Westlake says that he does not use outlines and writes for his readers.

DENNIS WHEATLEY

Born: London, England; January 8, 1897
Died: London, England; November 10, 1977
Types of plot: Espionage; historical; thriller

PRINCIPAL SERIES

Duke de Richleau, 1933-1970
Gregory Sallust, 1934-1968
Julian Day, 1939-1964
Roger Brook, 1947-1974

PRINCIPAL SERIES CHARACTERS

DUKE DE RICHLEAU, patterned after Athos in *Les Trois Mousquetaires* (1844; *The Three Musketeers*, 1846), was one of Dennis Wheatley's favorite characters. A vivid and colorful figure, the duke is involved with many significant historical events during his long life (in his first appearance, it is 1894 and he is eighteen; he dies in 1960 at the age of eighty-five).

GREGORY SALLUST is a British agent during World War II. Sent behind German lines to assist those in Germany who do not support Adolf Hitler, he attempts to bring about the latter's defeat by various means, including, finally, use of the occult. At the end of the war, Sallust is married to Erika von Epp, his beautiful assistant.

JULIAN DAY has a flair for languages, and during World War II he is assigned to the Interpreter Corps in Cairo; he participates in Great Britain's winning campaigns in North Africa and witnesses his country's losses to the Nazis in Greece.

ROGER BROOK is a special agent for Prime Minister William Pitt. During the period covered by Brook's activities (1783-1815), he participates in espionage involving every important historical event and plays a role in the lives of significant figures such as the Dauphin Louis XVII and Napoleon Bonaparte. He is in love with Georgina Thursby; although married to another, he has an affair with Georgina throughout the series.

CONTRIBUTION

As a very young man, Dennis Wheatley wrote for his own pleasure; his career as a writer began only when financial need demanded it. Once he found an audience for his writing and saw the possibility for a comfortable income, he became involved in the advertising and marketing of his work. He was both a writer and a businessman, and once he recognized a new market, he adjusted for it.

During World War II, Wheatley's reputation as a writer gained for him the opportunity to serve his country in an official capacity by using his imagination to assist military leaders in devising plans for defeating the enemy. His experiences in this capacity are related in *Stranger than Fiction* (1959).

Wheatley's novels of crime, mystery, and espionage brought enjoyment to many people over a number of years. His attitude about producing fiction for the sake of the readers' pleasure was expressed when he wrote, "From the beginning, I had always believed that the vast majority of my readers wanted to read about people of wealth or beauty, such as they never met in their own lives." Wheatley succeeded as a writer because of his recognition of the needs and desires of those of his period who sought entertainment through reading.

BIOGRAPHY

Dennis Yeats Wheatley, the son of Albert David Wheatley and Florence Baker Wheatley, was born in London on January 8, 1897. In 1908, he was sent for a time to Dulwich College, a private school near where his family lived. From 1909 to 1913 he was a cadet aboard H.M.S. *Worcester*, chosen for him because of its reputation for producing young men of discipline. At the age of sixteen, Wheatley was escorted by his father to Germany, where at Traben-Trarbach he was expected to learn wine making from a local family. In less than a year, he was back in London, where he was put to work in his father's wine shop on South Audley Street, in the Mayfair section of London.

As a boy of seventeen, Wheatley was extremely eager to join the army that was being formed in preparation for war with Germany. He was finally accepted in 1914 in the Royal Field Artillery, City of London Brigade. From 1917 until 1919, he served in France with the Thirty-sixth Ulster Division. His release from service was the result of his having developed bronchitis, having been exposed to the chlorine gas released by the Germans at the front.

Wheatley, after recuperating, went back to work in the family wine business. His first marriage, to Nancy Madelaine Leslie Robinson, lasted for just over nine years and produced a son, Anthony Marius. Wheatley's second wife was Joan Gwendoline Johnstone.

Wheatley began writing as a way of earning a living. His first novel, *Three Inquisitive People*, though written in 1932, was not published until 1940. His second novel, *The Forbidden Territory*, published in 1933, was so well accepted that it set him on a career that was to give him great satisfaction both monetarily and artistically.

During World War II, Wheatley was the only civilian directly commissioned to serve on the Joint Planning Staff of the War Cabinet. For three years during the war, he served as one of Sir Winston Churchill's staff officers. These positions came about because in 1940 and 1941, Wheatley had written a number of papers in which he had explained how the British might transport supplies from the United States via convoys of wooden rafts and how best to confuse the enemy should it invade and occupy England. Wheatley died in London on November 10, 1977.

Analysis

A small tombstone beneath which lie Dennis Wheatley's ashes is inscribed:

> Dennis Wheatley
> 8.1.97-10.11.77
> "Prince of Thriller Writers"
> RIP

"Prince of Thriller Writers" would have pleased Wheatley—indeed, he may have requested the inscription himself. It was in the pursuit of a life full of those things that princes might take for granted that Wheatley discovered and made use of a talent placing him among the "royalty" of British authors of action-oriented crime, mystery, and spy fiction during and since World War II.

Wheatley began writing seriously when business failures had left him in debt and without prospect for financial recovery. He was in his early thirties when he lost the wine business that had been given him by his dying father. Encouraged by his wife, who had read some of the short stories he had written years before for his own pleasure, he wrote his first novel. About his reaction to his wife's suggestion that he write, Wheatley said in his memoirs:

> I had little faith in my ability to do so and even if I did, and succeeded in getting a publisher to take it, I could not hope to make out of it more than about fifty pounds. But having a shot at it would at least take my mind off my worries; so I bought some paper and sat down to write a thriller.

From that beginning, Wheatley made of himself a successful writer, having more than seventy published works to his credit when he died at the age of eighty. He noted in his memoirs that his books had been published in thirty-one languages. He was especially proud of the many letters he had received from people who had enjoyed reading his books while bedridden.

Because he was dependent on the income from his writing, it was very important to Wheatley that his books have wide distribution. He took a serious interest in the demand for books, in the trends in what people were reading, and in the way in which his books were marketed. From the beginning of his writing career, he participated in the plans for advertising. To market his first book, he says:

> I had 2000 postcards printed; on one side they had the pictorial end-papers of the book, on the other, alongside the space for the address, simply the title, date of publication and a request that the recipient, if he enjoyed adventure stories, should ask for the book at his library.

This book became a best seller and was reprinted seven times in seven weeks.

Wheatley's first novels were historical thrillers, full of color and drama. As a young man, he had enjoyed reading historical novels; among his favorites were those of Alexandre Dumas, *père*. Wheatley does not, however, share the reputation of Dumas for altering historical fact to suit his fictional purposes. Wheatley, a lifetime student of history, insisted that the historical information in his novels be absolutely accurate. Not only did he receive critical praise for his novels' historical accuracy, but also he was gratified to learn that his books were used successfully by teachers as a means to encourage their pupils to study history.

THE SCARLET IMPOSTER

In the late 1930's, Wheatley decided that spy stories would be well received, now that there was a war on, and he wrote *The Scarlet Imposter* (1940). Of it, he said:

> It was the longest book that I had so far written—172,000 words—and highly topical, as it covered the events of the war during the autumn and even, by remarkable good fortune, a forecast of the conspiracy to assassinate Hitler. Moreover, during that first winter of the black-out people were reading as never before.

People were indeed reading more escapist fiction. With England engaged in an all-out defense effort, other popular forms of entertainment were less and less available.

The Scarlet Imposter features Wheatley's Gregory Sallust. For fear that he might find himself stuck with one character and a limited following, as perhaps Sapper had with Bulldog Drummond and Leslie Charteris with the Saint, Wheatley inserted a message at the back of *Faked Passports* (1940), inviting readers to write to him and indicate whether they would prefer more of Sallust or a choice of other fiction subjects. The response favored Sallust; as a result, Wheatley continued his stories featuring the British agent.

OTHER WORKS

Four very popular novels that proved too expensive to continue in production were the so-called crime dossiers. Wheatley was given the idea by his friend Joe Links of including in a mystery novel photographs of real people and clues such as bits of hair, fabric, telegrams, and handwritten letters. The pages that revealed the solution to the mystery were sealed. Inclusion of the physical clues required special packaging, making the product unsuitable for use in lending and subscription libraries. The novels were rather expensive to buy, as well. They serve as evidence, however, of Wheatley's interest in the marketing aspects of publishing. These "detective games" were *Murder off Miami* (1936), *Who Killed Robert Prentice?* (1937), *The Malinsay Massacre* (1938), and *Herewith the Clues!* (1939).

After the end of World War II, Wheatley was not sure whether he should continue writing espionage stories, because he had had access to secrets, knew the way in which the intelligence system worked, and feared that he would be accused of revealing classified information. The solution was to write espionage stories in a historical setting. Wheatley chose the Napoleonic Wars because they were so different from the most recent one, and Roger Brook became the new hero of espionage fiction.

Wheatley described himself as a hard worker, putting in thirteen or more hours per day, six or seven days a week. Encouraging aspiring young writers, he wrote that anyone willing to work very hard could achieve and maintain the same degree of success that he had enjoyed. He further maintained that he had succeeded in writing many best sellers, in spite of his serious difficulty with spelling and grammar, because of his determination and his understanding of what it took to satisfy the reader. He believed that he had mastered the ability to combine fiction and fact in such a way as to appeal to both emotion and intellect.

Paula Lannert

PRINCIPAL MYSTERY AND DETECTIVE FICTION

DUKE DE RICHLEAU SERIES: *The Forbidden Territory*, 1933; *The Devil Rides Out*, 1934; *The Golden Spaniard*, 1938; *Three Inquisitive People*, 1940; *Strange Conflict*, 1941; *Codeword—Golden Fleece*, 1946; *The Second Seal*, 1950; *The Prisoner in the Mask*, 1957; *Vendetta in Spain*, 1961; *Dangerous Inheritance*, 1965; *Gateway to Hell*, 1970

GREGORY SALLUST SERIES: *Black August*, 1934; *Contraband*, 1936; *Faked Passports*, 1940; *The Black Baroness*, 1940; *The Scarlet Imposter*, 1940; *"V" for Vengeance*, 1942; *Come into My Parlor*, 1946; *The Island Where Time Stands Still*, 1954; *Traitor's Gate*, 1958; *They Used Dark Forces*, 1964; *The White Witch of the South Seas*, 1968

JULIAN DAY SERIES: *The Quest of Julian Day*,

1939; *The Sword of Fate*, 1941; *Bill for the Use of a Body*, 1964

Roger Brook series: *The Launching of Roger Brook*, 1947; *The Shadow of Tyburn Tree*, 1948; *The Rising Storm*, 1949; *The Man Who Killed the King*, 1951; *The Dark Secret of Josephine*, 1955; *The Rape of Venice*, 1959; *The Sultan's Daughter*, 1963; *The Wanton Princess*, 1966; *Evil in a Mask*, 1969; *The Ravishing of Lady Mary Ware*, 1971; *The Irish Witch*, 1973; *Desperate Measures*, 1974

Nonseries novels: *Such Power Is Dangerous*, 1933; *The Fabulous Valley*, 1934; *The Eunuch of Stamboul*, 1935; *Murder off Miami*, 1936 (also known as *File on Bolitho Blane*); *They Found Atlantis*, 1936; *The Secret War*, 1937; *Who Killed Robert Prentice?*, 1937 (also known as *File on Robert Prentice*); *The Malinsay Massacre*, 1938; *Uncharted Seas*, 1938; *Herewith the Clues!*, 1939; *Sixty Days to Live*, 1939; *The Man Who Missed the War*, 1945; *The Haunting of Toby Jugg*, 1948; *Star of Ill-Omen*, 1952; *Curtain of Fear*, 1953; *To the Devil—a Daughter*, 1953; *The Ka of Gifford Hillary*, 1956; *The Satanist*, 1960; *Mayhem in Greece*, 1962; *Unholy Crusade*, 1967; *The Strange Story of Linda Lee*, 1972

Other short fiction: *Mediterranean Nights*, 1942 (revised 1963); *Gunmen, Gallants, and Ghosts*, 1943 (revised 1963)

Other major works

Screenplay: *An Englishman's Home (Madmen of Europe)*, 1939 (with others)

Nonfiction: *Old Rowley: A Private Life of Charles II*, 1933 (also known as *A Private Life of Charles II*); *Red Eagle: A Life of Marshall Voroshilov*, 1937; *Invasion*, 1938; *Blockade*, 1939; *Total War*, 1941; *The Seven Ages of Justerini's*, 1949 (revised as *1749-1965: The Eight Ages of Justerini's*, 1965); *Alibi*, 1951; *Stranger than Fiction*, 1959; *Saturdays with Bricks and Other Days Under Shell-Fire*, 1961; *The Devil and All His Works*, 1971; *The Time Has Come: The Memoirs of Dennis Wheatley—The Young Man Said, 1897-1914*, 1977; *The Time Has Come: The Memoirs of Dennis Wheatley—Officer and Temporary Gentleman, 1914-1919*, 1978; *The Time Has Come: The Memoirs of Dennis Wheatley—Drink and Ink, 1919-1977*, 1979; *The Deception Planners: My Secret War*, 1980

Edited texts: *A Century of Horror Stories*, 1935; *A Century of Spy Stories*, 1938; *Uncanny Tales*, 1974

Bibliography

Cabell, Craig. *Dennis Wheatley: Churchill's Storyteller.* Staplehurst, Kent, England: Spellmount, 2006. Tells the story of Wheatley's experiences during World War II, when he worked for the British Joint Planning Staff, writing fake official documents that would then be fed to Nazi spies.

Hedman, Iwan. "Dennis Wheatley: A Biographical Sketch and Bibliography." *The Armchair Detective* 2 (April, 1969): 227-236. Lists Wheatley's novels alongside a discussion of his life and work.

Symons, Julian. *Bloody Murder: From the Detective Story to the Crime Novel—A History.* 3d ed. New York: Mysterious Press, 1993. Symons, a successful mystery author in his own right, argues that mystery fiction evolved over time from being concerned with the figure of the detective and the methods of detection to a primary focus on the nature of crime and criminality. Sheds light on Wheatley's work.

Wheatley, Dennis. *The Time Has Come: The Memoirs of Dennis Wheatley.* 3 vols. London: Hutchinson, 1977-1979. Primarily focused on Wheatley's childhood and youth: The first two volumes of this three-volume memoir cover the first twenty-two years of the author's life, while the remaining years are relegated to the third volume.

VICTOR WHITECHURCH

Born: Norham, England; March 12, 1868
Died: England; May 25, 1933
Types of plot: Amateur sleuth; police procedural

Contribution

Victor Whitechurch's crime novels were written when England was not at war and when the prospect of war seemed remote. During this welcomed peace, the detective story form no doubt provided amusement and stimulation for Whitechurch as well as for his readers, yet his bucolic settings and the sturdy country folk about whom he wrote with such grace seemed hardly suited to violent crime. Perhaps having no taste for tales of brutal injury, he chose to dispense with the horror in the first chapter, in which he always revealed the crime's occurrence. From that point he could proceed, in the remaining chapters, with the less emotional work of bringing the guilty to justice.

Whitechurch's method of plot development, confided to the reader in the foreword of the novel, no doubt made writing each all the more pleasurable and challenging. By revealing his method, Whitechurch gives the reader a special participation in the work and a more intense interest in each turn of events.

Biography

Victor Lorenzo Whitechurch was born in Norham, England, on March 12, 1868. His parents were William Frederick Whitechurch and Matilda Cornwall Whitechurch. As a youth, he attended Chichester Grammar School in Sussex, England, and received his licentiate of theology from Chichester Theological College, an affiliate of Durham University. In October, 1896, he was married to Florence Partridge. They had one daughter.

Whitechurch spent most of his life in rural England, primarily in towns and villages to the west and northwest of London in the counties of Berkshire and Buckinghamshire. As an Anglican churchman, he served with varying church titles, first as curate (parson), then as senior curate, vicar, dean, and rector, in various country parishes. Late in his life, he was named Honorary Canon of Christ Church, Oxford. His home was Stone Vicarage, Aylesbury, Buckinghamshire, England. Whitechurch died May 25, 1933.

Analysis

Who is better qualified than a rural Anglican churchman to write novels of crime detection whose settings are quaint English villages? There surely can be no one with more experience in the observation of behavior and with more intimate knowledge of the secret pain of his contemporaries than the sympathetic parson of a country church. During the latter part of his thirty-year avocation as a writer, Victor Whitechurch became fascinated with crime fiction. His service and experience in the church no doubt provided his imagination with abundant material for character development, and once his first crime novel was published, his work of this type soon became well accepted by readers and critics alike.

The Crime at Diana's Pool

Whitechurch had an unusual approach to plot development, one that he was not in the least hesitant to share with his readers. In the foreword to *The Crime at Diana's Pool* (1927), he confides that his method was to write the first chapter without knowing "why the crime had been committed, who had done it, or how it was done." He set himself this task, he says, because in a true crime those in charge of investigation are in the same position and must work their way through the clues as they are uncovered or as they appear. Whitechurch suggested that after reading the first chapter, the reader might close the book and devise his own plot, then compare the result with that of the author. One can assume, however, that very few of Whitechurch's readers would be willing to forgo the pleasure of proceeding through the novel, once begun, in favor of working out a separate plot. In the first chapter of *The Crime at Diana's Pool*, the host of a summer garden party is found dead in his own pool, a knife having penetrated his green coat, which had originally been worn by a musician hired for the party. After such a beginning, one would find it difficult to put the novel aside.

Whitechurch was obviously familiar with life in English villages and thoroughly knowledgeable regarding the people of whom he wrote. Included in each novel is a police investigator who is intelligent, cautious, and conscientious. There is often a vicar, who may serve as the amateur sleuth. (In *The Crime at Diana's Pool*, the vicar, through careful, reasoned study, deduces the identity of the murderer and provides the proof necessary to arrest him.) An attractive couple provides the token wearisome romance. Other characters often present are the village doctor, a lawyer or two, town tradesmen, members of the propertied class, and their gardeners and other servants (in one novel, the butler is the culprit). Men are in the positions of authority, and women stay in their places. Diana Garforth, in *The Crime at Diana's Pool*, is described as follows:

> Diana was four-and-twenty, essentially a type of the English country girl. She played a good game of golf and tennis, rode to hounds, drove a car, and was game for a tenmile walk over the hills when the mood took her. Added to this she was a first-rate housekeeper, and "ran" "Beechcroft" admirably. Also she was, if not exactly brilliant, a well-informed girl, and had had the advantage of being educated at a school modeled on the lines of a public school, with nothing "finicky" in its atmosphere. She was good company, frank and natural and without affectation.

By and large, all the characters are unpretentious and are described sympathetically and with humor. Their habits of life and mind would not have been atypical, surely, of those living out their lives in a small English village of the period.

After the crime is described in chapter 1, the story moves quietly and without haste. The reader is kept well abreast of the investigation as it proceeds toward the solution, which is achieved through the accumulation of evidence. Questions arise and are answered one by one, as a chain of connections is exposed. Predictably, the first and perhaps the second party arrested will not prove to be guilty, for at the time of arrest there is still too far to go in the novel. Plenty of time remains for the suspect(s) to be cleared, and the reader knows from the start the fruitlessness of pursuing a solution based on evidence incriminating those so early arrested.

Shot on the Downs

The end is not too predictable, except that the solution will be highly moral, but it is not always satisfactory to the reader. The reader of *Shot on the Downs* (1927) would prefer that almost any character other than the one chosen by the author would have committed the crime. The murderer is perhaps the most sympathetic and most vulnerable character in the novel, and the reader is left with a sense of loss, even though, technically, justice has been served. Whitechurch's more typical final chapters are more satisfying: In most cases, the crime has been committed by a recent comer to the town, one whose background and character are not known and whose values prove to be not at all similar to those of the villagers.

Whitechurch takes the opportunity, when he considers it appropriate, to insert a bit of instruction into his stories. Although this practice dates his novels, it adds a certain charm, if one does not view these passages as pedantry. In *The Crime at Diana's Pool*, Vicar Westerham is used as a means to give the reader in-

Victor Whitechurch also wrote stories about a railway detective named Thorpe Hazell; this picture by Alfred Paget illustrated "A Station Master's Story," which Whitechurch published in The Strand Magazine *in 1899.*

sight into the professional life of a parish parson. This passage may have served also to appease Whitechurch's own congregation, who may have found fault with the time and attention he devoted to his writing, believing that it was done at their expense:

> The next morning the Vicar was busy in his study over the forthcoming fête and sale of work. He had settled down to a full morning's work. Many people, because they only come across the parson on Sundays, imagine that his profession only entails one day per week of real work, but in this they are greatly mistaken. Often the work on a week day is much more exacting than the taking of services or preaching on Sundays. And the parson is rarely given credit for the many hours he spends in his study over a variety of matters that would puzzle many a business man.

The Floating Admiral

For *The Floating Admiral* (1931), Whitechurch wrote only the first of the twelve chapters. The remaining eleven, along with the introduction, prologue, and appendixes, were written by fellow members of the Detection Club. The method of construction of the novel was described by Dorothy L. Sayers in the introduction: "Each contributor tackled the mystery presented to him in the preceding chapters without having the slightest idea what solution or solutions the previous authors had in mind." Each of the participants, who included Agatha Christie, Henry Wade, and John Rhode, was required to have a definite solution in mind and to present it, along with the manuscript for his or her assigned chapter, for publication. All the solutions (except that of Whitechurch and the author of the second chapter) are provided in an appendix to the novel. The project provided amusement for the participants and afforded them exposure among readers who might not previously have known the work of them all.

Whitechurch's crime novels are gracefully written and are among the better mysteries of their time. His respect for the reader's intelligence makes his novels satisfying to read, interest being heightened by his admittedly unorthodox method of plot development.

Paula Lannert

Principal mystery and detective fiction

Novels: *The Templeton Case*, 1924; *Shot on the Downs*, 1927; *The Crime at Diana's Pool*, 1927; *The Robbery at Rudwick House*, 1929; *Murder at the Pageant*, 1930; *The Floating Admiral*, 1931 (with others); *Murder at the College*, 1932 (also known as *Murder at Exbridge*)

Short fiction: *Thrilling Stories of the Railway*, 1912 (also known as *Stories of the Railway*); *The Adventures of Captain Ivan Koravitch*, 1925

Other major works

Novels: *The Course of Justice*, 1903; *The Canon in Residence*, 1904; *The Locum Tenens*, 1906; *Concerning Himself: The Story of an Ordinary Man*, 1909; *Off the Main Road: A Village Comedy*, 1911; *A Downland Corner*, 1912; *Left in Charge*, 1912; *Three Summers: A Romance*, 1915; *If Riches Increase*, 1923; *A Bishop out of Residence*, 1924; *Downland Echoes*, 1924; *The Dean and Jecinora*, 1926; *Mixed Relations*, 1928; *First and Last*, 1929; *Mute Witnesses: Being Certain Annals of a Downland Village*, 1933

Short fiction: *The Canon's Dilemma, and Other Stories*, 1909

Nonfiction: *Parochial Processions: Their Value and Organization*, 1917; *Concerning Right and Wrong: A Plain Man's Creed*, 1925; *The Truth in Christ Jesus*, 1927

Bibliography

Barzun, Jacques, and Wendell Hertig Taylor. *A Catalogue of Crime*. Rev. ed. New York: Harper & Row, 1989. List, with commentary, of the authors' choices for the best or most influential examples of crime fiction. Whitechurch's work is included and evaluated.

Cox, Michael. Introduction to *Victorian Tales of Mystery and Detection: An Oxford Anthology*. New York: Oxford University Press, 1992. Relates Whitechurch's fiction to the preceding Victorian culture from which it emerged.

Keating, H. R. F., ed. *Whodunit? A Guide to Crime, Suspense, and Spy Fiction*. New York: Van Nostrand Reinhold, 1982. General overview of the conventions and practitioners of British and American crime fiction; sheds light on Whitechurch's works.

Kestner, Joseph A. *The Edwardian Detective, 1901-1915*. Brookfield, Vt.: Ashgate, 2000. Reads Whitechurch as emerging from and continuing the Edwardian tradition in detective fiction.

Steinbrunner, Chris, and Otto Penzler, eds. *Encyclopedia of Mystery and Detection*. New York: McGraw-Hill, 1976. Analyzes Whitechurch's distinctive contributions to British detective fiction between the wars.

Whitechurch, Victor. Foreword to *The Crime at Diana's Pool*. New York: Duffield, 1927. The author reveals his method to his readers in this foreword, allowing them a glimpse behind the curtain before the novel has even begun.

PHYLLIS A. WHITNEY

Born: Yokohama, Japan; September 9, 1903
Types of plot: Psychological; cozy; amateur sleuth; historical

Contribution

Phyllis A. Whitney is one of the few mystery writers to excel in both adult and juvenile mysteries. In the sixty years after her first book appeared, she published seventy-six novels, twenty of them young-adult mysteries and thirty-nine of them adult mysteries. There is no incongruity in the Virginia State Reading Association presenting its Young Readers Award for 1997 to Whitney's adult novel *Daughter of the Stars* (1994), as her mysteries can be read by every member of the family. Neither the romance nor the crime is graphic, and her characters inhabit a moral universe. Often an unsolved murder turns out to be a crime of passion or an accidental death, not a premeditated murder or a killing in cold blood. Keeping secrets has upset the balance of the universe. Once those involved give up their secrets, remorse rights the balance between right and wrong.

Whitney holds her readers by telling a good story. She spins a plot full of action and unexpected developments while allowing her heroine to grow emotionally and psychologically. Whitney is known for using a location as if it were a character. Her thorough research of a location and its history provides not only a colorful background but also important clues to the solution of the mystery. Whitney's novels have been consistently ranked as best sellers throughout her career and have been published in twenty-four languages.

Biography

Phyllis Ayame Whitney was born on September 9, 1903, to Charles Joseph Whitney and Mary Lillian Mandeville. Her American-born parents had been living in Asia. When their daughter was born in Yokohama, they gave her a middle name that means "iris" in Japanese. After her father died in 1918, Whitney and her mother returned to the United States and lived in California and Texas until her mother's death in San Antonio in 1922. Whitney lived with her aunt in Chicago, where she graduated from high school in 1924. She married George Garner a year later. In 1928, she sold her first short story to the *Chicago Daily News*. She wrote in her spare time while she worked in the children's room of the Chicago Public Library and later in area bookstores. Her daughter, Georgia, was born in 1934. Whitney had published more than one hundred short stories before her first book, the young-adult novel *A Place for Ann* (1941), was published.

Although in 1943 Whitney published an adult mystery, *Red Is for Murder* (later reissued as *The Red Carnelion*), in her early career she was primarily a writer of young-adult novels and mysteries. In three of her earliest books, *A Star for Ginny* (1942), *Ever After* (1943), and *The Silver Inkwell* (1945), her young female protagonists work toward a career in publishing, two as illustrators of children's books and one as an author. In 1942, Whitney began a four-year stint as a children's book editor for the *Chicago Sun*. She held the same position on *The Philadelphia Inquirer* from 1947 to 1948. In 1945, she taught children's fiction writing at Northwestern University. Two years later, she produced a nonfictional book, *Writing Juvenile Fiction*, which she updated in 1976. She taught a similar course for ten years at New York University between 1947 and 1958.

In 1945, Whitney and Garner divorced. Two years later, she published the most prescient of her young-adult novels, *Willow Hill*. The book explores the reaction of a young white girl and her friends to the integration of a neighborhood housing project. The topic was so controversial that Whitney had to search for a publisher, but the book won a Youth Today contest as well as Book World's Spring Book Festival Award. Seven years later, she tackled a similar subject in *A Long Time Coming* (1954), when her young heroine attempts to heal the rift between Hispanic migrant workers and the residents of the Midwest farm town that employs them.

Whitney married Lovell F. Jahnke in 1950. The couple lived on Staten Island, New York, for twenty years, and until Jahnke's death in 1973, they traveled together to places that became locations in Whitney's books. By 1950, Whitney had begun alternating between young-adult novels and young-adult mysteries, publishing approximately one per year. With the publication of *The Quicksilver Pool* (1955), Whitney added adult mysteries to this rotation, and by 1960, she was primarily alternating between adult and young-adult mysteries, often using a similar setting for each. For example, the young-adult mystery *Secret of the Samurai Sword* (1958) and the adult mystery *The Moonflower* (1958) both take place in Kyoto, Japan; *The Secret of the Tiger's Eye* (1961) and *Blue Fire* (1961) take place in South Africa; *The Secret of the Spotted Shell* (1967) and *Columbella* (1966) take place in the Virgin Islands.

In 1961, *The Mystery of the Haunted Pool* (1960) won the Edgar Allan Poe Award for best juvenile mystery. Three years later *The Mystery of the Hidden Hand* (1963) won the same award as well as the 1963 Sequoia Children's Book Award. By 1975, when Whitney was elected president of the Mystery Writers of America, she had published twenty adult mysteries and nineteen young-adult mysteries. In 1988, the Mystery Writers of America designated Whitney a Grand Master of the genre. Two years later, she received the Malice Domestic Award for lifetime achievement. In 1995, the Society of Midland Authors presented her with a lifetime achievement award.

Analysis

In the essentially moral and virtuous worlds of Phyllis A. Whitney's adult and young-adult mysteries, secrets, thefts, or murders are temporary departures from the norm. Once the air is cleared, the characters can live in peace. For example, in the *Mystery of the Hidden Hand*, Grandfather Thanos confesses his crime and returns the stolen artifact to the museum authorities. In *Amethyst Dreams* (1997), the housekeeper and daughter-in-law confess to Hallie Knight and the murdered girl's father that they covered up what was actually an accidental drowning. Whitney's books are as much *Bildungsrcmane* as they are clever, fast-paced mysteries. Whitney's final young-adult mystery appeared in 1977, and the young-adult worlds she created seem dated: The young people dress for dinner and respect their elders, and their elders never miss a chance to teach them a life lesson. However, like the adult mysteries, the characters reflect the four decades of change in the roles available for women in the United States and abroad that Whitney witnessed. Her early heroines might wear kid gloves, but they are as independent as the later heroines. The heroines in both the adult and young-adult novels are determined to find themselves as well as save a family, a marriage, or a home whose harmony is threatened by secrets.

Mystery of the Haunted Pool

Mystery of the Haunted Pool (1960) is Whitney's seventh young-adult mystery and the first to win an Edgar Award. It typifies Whitney's young-adult mysteries. Most of these mysteries are narrated in the third person from the point of view of the protagonist, a teenage girl who has been separated from her family. In this story, Susan Price moves to upstate New York from New York City to live with her aunt for a month. Her mother, her ailing father, and her three brothers will follow if she can help her aunt persuade a former Hudson River boat captain to rent his family's mansion to them. The mansion, like the spotted shell or golden horn of later mysteries, holds the clue to a family secret. In this story, the secret is the fate of priceless jewels supposedly lost at sea a century ago by the family patriarch who had been hired to deliver them. Repaying the debt impoverished the family for generations; therefore, when the captain's grandson is hit by a car, the captain must give up his home to pay the medical bills. Susan is the touchstone. She hears the bumps in the night, sees the face in the pool, and recovers the beads that provide clues to the location of the treasure. She is also the glue that holds the families together. She befriends the captain and his grandson as well as the mysterious neighbor who is also bent on discovering the family secret and perhaps destroying the fragile bond between generations. Her older brother arrives in time to help her, but she is the one who solves the mystery, reunites her family, and brings the captain and his grandson closer.

Mystery of the Hidden Hand

Mystery of the Hidden Hand is Whitney's tenth young-adult mystery and the second to win an Edgar Award. It typifies Whitney's use of exotic locations and pacing that keeps the reader guessing. An American teenager, Gale Tyler, her mother, and her brother Warren visit an aunt and cousins they have never met who live on the Island of Rhodes. Gale is the lightning rod. She sees a caped figure, discovers a guest with a grudge against their cousin's family, and helps reconcile her cousins with their grandfather and owner of the family business, Pegasus Pottery. Gale's new cousins and their grandfather keep secrets from each other, the deepest being the ancient marble hand hidden in Grandfather Thanos's study. Whitney sets up the question of antiquities theft with descriptions of the beauty of the landscape, the villages, and the island's history as well as the ruins at Camiros and Lindos that help the reader sympathize with Grandfather Thanos's desire to keep the exquisite object he discovered in his youth during an archaeological dig. Through Gail, Whitney reveals her character's secrets bit by bit. For example, Gale discovers that one of her new cousins is the caped figure, but she does not discover until much later who signaled the figure from the house below the hotel. Once she finds out the identity of the signaler, she must work harder to find out why he was signaling.

Seven Tears for Apollo

Seven Tears for Apollo (1963) is the adult companion book to *Mystery of the Hidden Hand*. It is also set in Rhodes and deals with antiquities theft. Dorcas Brandt is an American of Greek descent whose manipulative husband had grown up in Rhodes. Dorcas suspects him of antiquities theft. When she believes he has died in a plane crash, she takes their four-year-old daughter and returns to Rhodes to find the truth. Dorcas is terrorized by her husband, who ransacks her rooms, scrawls eyes on walls and mirrors, and leaves cryptic messages. She teeters on the brink of mental collapse as her friends doubt her suspicions, but she is also strong enough to persist. Again, Whitney reveals bit by bit how secrets distort and corrupt relationships. Whitney uses Dorcas's status as a stranger to present the reader with stunning descriptions of the scenery as well as the ancient and contemporary history behind the locations and the art treasures. Whitney draws on every mother's fear for her child's safety to heighten the suspense. History and kidnapping converge when Dorcas discovers that her husband has been stealing ancient sculptures and replacing them with copies. Finally, all parties involved in the theft have the opportunity to confess before poetic justice ends the tale as Dorcas's husband is killed by one of the sculptures he was stealing, freeing Dorcas to begin a new life with a new man. This book is a particularly striking example of how integral Whitney's research is to the mystery. For example, Dorcas cannot solve the riddle of the scrawled eyes without knowing about the owl as the symbol of the goddess Athena.

Amethyst Dreams

Amethyst Dreams is Whitney's seventy-sixth adult novel and follows a well-established pattern. The narrator is a woman who is young, but not too young. She is summoned to a place where she has never been before, and her presence sets off a chain of events that compel her to solve a mystery. In this story, Hallie Knight is summoned by the ailing father of her college friend to the family mansion on Topsail Island to discover the truth about his daughter's mysterious disappearance from her bedroom two years before. Like many of Whitney's heroines, Hallie is in emotional turmoil: She is fleeing the breakup of her marriage. Throughout the novel, she measures her own situation against that of the broken marriages of the characters

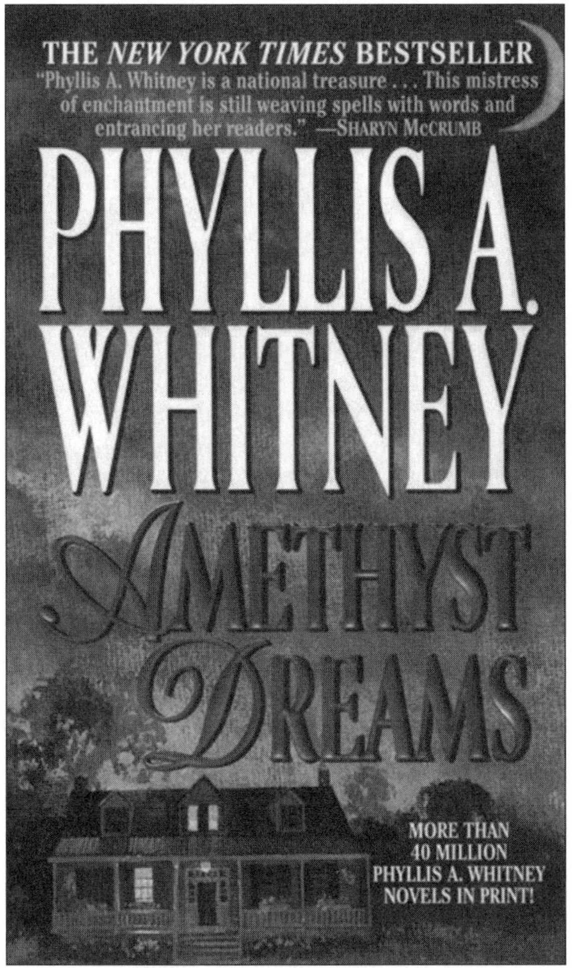

around her. Without being clairvoyant, like many of the heroines of Whitney's later novels, she is the psychic touchstone. She can sense the negative energy of the pool, later revealed as the murdered girl's final resting place, as well as that of the housekeeper, later revealed as complicit in covering up the murder. Readers are attracted as much by the heroine scaring herself with her feelings of impending doom as they are by the knowledge that all will be resolved in the end.

Cecile Mazzucco-Than

Principal mystery and detective fiction

Novels: 1943-1960 • *Red Is for Murder*, 1943 (reissued as *The Red Carnelian*, 1965); *The Quicksilver Pool*, 1955; *The Trembling Hills*, 1956; *Skye Cameron*, 1957; *The Moonflower*, 1958; *Thunder Heights*, 1960

1961-1970 • *Blue Fire*, 1961; *Window on the Square*, 1962; *Seven Tears for Apollo*, 1963; *Black Amber*, 1964; *Sea Jade*, 1965; *Columbella*, 1966; *Silverhill*, 1967; *Hunter's Green*, 1968; *The Winter People*, 1969; *Lost Island*, 1970

1971-1980 • *Listen for the Whisperer*, 1972; *Snowfire*, 1973; *The Turquoise Mask*, 1974; *Spindrift*, 1975; *The Golden Unicorn*, 1976; *The Stone Bull*, 1977; *The Glass Flame*, 1978; *Domino*, 1979; *Poinciana*, 1980

1981-1990 • *Vermillion*, 1981; *Emerald*, 1983; *Rainsong*, 1984; *Dream of Orchids*, 1985; *Flaming Tree*, 1986; *Silversword*, 1987; *Feather on the Moon*, 1988; *Rainbow in the Mist*, 1989; *The Singing Stones*, 1990

1991-1997 • *Woman Without a Past*, 1991; *The Ebony Swan*, 1992; *Star Flight*, 1993; *Daughter of the Stars*, 1994; *Amethyst Dreams*, 1997

Children's literature: *The Mystery of the Gulls*, 1949; *The Island of Dark Woods*, 1951 (reissued as *Mystery of the Strange Traveler*, 1967); *Mystery of the Black Diamonds*, 1954; *Mystery on the Isle of Skye*, 1955; *Mystery of the Green Cat*, 1957; *Secret of the Samurai Sword*, 1958; *Mystery of the Haunted Pool*, 1960; *Secret of the Tiger's Eye*, 1961; *Mystery of the Golden Horn*, 1962; *Mystery of the Hidden Hand*, 1963; *Secret of the Emerald Star*, 1964; *Mystery of the Angry Idol*, 1965; *Secret of the Spotted Shell*, 1967; *Secret of Goblin Glen*, 1968; *The Mystery of the Crimson Ghost*, 1969; *Secret of the Missing Footprint*, 1969; *The Vanishing Scarecrow*, 1971; *Mystery of the Scowling Boy*, 1973; *Secret of Haunted Mesa*, 1975; *Secret of the Stone Face*, 1977

Other major works

Children's literature: *A Place for Ann*, 1941; *A Star for Ginny*, 1942; *A Window for Julie*, 1943; *The Silver Inkwell*, 1945; *Willow Hill*, 1947; *Ever After*, 1948; *Linda's Homecoming*, 1950; *Love Me, Love Me Not*, 1952; *Step to the Music*, 1953; *A Long Time Coming*, 1954; *The Fire and the Gold*, 1956; *Creole Holiday*, 1959; *Nobody Likes Trina*, 1972

Nonfiction: *Writing Juvenile Fiction*, 1947; *Writing Juvenile Stories and Novels*, 1976; *Guide to Fiction Writing*, 1982

Bibliography

DuBose, Martha Hailey, with Margaret Caldwell Thomas. *Women of Mystery: The Lives and Works of Notable Women Crime Novelists*. New York: St. Martin's Minotaur, 2000. These essays look at the lives and works of early writers such as Mary Robert Rinehart, Golden Age writers such as Agatha Christie, and modern writers such as Mary Higgins Clark. While Whitney is not covered, the biographies of women of her generation shed light on her work.

Klein, Kathleen Gregory, ed. *Women Times Three: Writers, Detectives, Readers*. Bowling Green, Ohio: Bowling Green State University Popular Press, 1995. These essays on books about female detectives authored by women, while not discussing Phyllis Whitney directly, shed light on her fiction, as they cover both older and newer masters of the genre.

Whitney, Phyllis. *Guide to Fiction Writing*. Boston: The Writer, 1982. Whitney's guide, intended to instruct would-be authors, reveals a great deal about her motivations for writing and her process.

_______. "Letter to a Young Writer." *Writer* 120, no. 2 (February, 2007): 38-39. In her letter to a young writer, she urges the writer not to be too self-critical and to produce that first novel, whether great or not.

_______. Phyllis A. Whitney: The Official Web Site. http://www.phyllisawhitney.com. The official Web site for Phyllis Whitney. Contains synopses of all of her books as well as information about the author.

CHARLES WILLEFORD

Born: Little Rock, Arkansas; January 2, 1919
Died: Miami, Florida; March 27, 1988
Also wrote as Will Charles; W. Franklin Sanders
Types of plot: Hard-boiled; comedy caper

Principal series

Hoke Moseley, 1984-1988

Principal series character

Hoke Moseley is a cynical, grizzled Miami police detective who smokes Kool cigarettes and drives a battered 1973 Pontiac LeMans. A Vietnam veteran, toothless and prematurely aging, Hoke is the divorced father of two teenage daughters. As a police officer, he is hard-boiled and has his own code of honor but is not above scrounging free drinks when he can.

Contribution

Charles Willeford's colorful career, which included military service, university teaching, journalism, and writing, crested during the 1980's, when his Hoke Moseley crime novels, set in Miami, gained both critical and popular acclaim. However, success came late to Willeford, and he died only days after the release of *The Way We Die Now*, the fourth and last novel in the Moseley series. Known as the father of the south Florida crime novel, Willeford captured the sun, sleaze, and violence of the Miami region, inspiring other writers such as Carl Hiaasen and James W. Hall as well as film director Quentin Tarentino, who compared his film *Pulp Fiction* (1994) to Willeford's work.

Willeford's unique style combined black humor, satire, and touches of the absurd with startlingly real and abrupt acts of violence. His characters, whether heroes, antiheroes, or villains, offer the reader a skewed yet oddly convincing worldview. Willeford readers learn to expect the unexpected. In the first chapter of *Wild Wives* (1956), one of Willeford's early pulp novels, private eye Jacob Blake fends off a surprise attack in his office—but the attacker is a teenage girl and the weapon is a water pistol. In *High Priest of California* (1953), another early pulp novel, a car salesman enters a bar, sizes up a stranger, and knocks him cold. "I felt a little better," he comments as he walks out. The protagonist of *Cockfighter* (1962), a novel that was filmed in 1974, communicates with written notes, having taken a vow of silence that he will break only when he wins the Cockfighter of the Year award. Hoke Moseley, though closer to the mainstream than many Willeford protagonists, has his eccentric side, as seen in *Sideswipe* (1987), the third book in the series, when a semi-retired Hoke decides to pare his wardrobe down to only two costumes, both of them bright yellow jumpsuits.

Willeford himself had a quirky, iconoclastic approach to life. After *Miami Blues* (1984) became a success, his publishers asked him to continue the Hoke Moseley character in a series. Despite years of financial struggle, Willeford's first response was to write a violent, nihilistic black comedy in which the detective kills his daughters to avoid having to take custody of them. His agent refused to submit it, and Willeford eventually wrote *New Hope for the Dead* (1985), in which Hoke stays mainly on the side of the law. A versatile writer, Willeford wrote everything from Westerns (*The Hombre from Sonora*, 1971) to a strange little medical memoir (*A Guide for the Undehemorrhoided*, 1977), but he is best known for bridging the gap from postwar noir to modern crime fiction.

Biography

Charles Ray Willeford III was born in Arkansas in 1919. In *The Burnt Orange Heresy* (1971), a crime caper about an art critic who schemes to steal a painting from a secretive artist, the hero muses that men who grow up without fathers never develop a superego. Willeford echoed the thought in *I Was Looking for a Street* (1988), a memoir of his youth, in a free-verse poem musing on the father who died in 1921 when Willeford was two, a father he knew only from faded photographs and family stories. Willeford's mother died six years later, and he lived with his grandmother until he was thirteen. Worried that she could no longer support him after losing her job, he left home and took to the road, riding freight trains and taking odd jobs to survive. In 1935, he enlisted in the U.S. Army, where he served on and off until 1956, including service in World War II, for which he earned the Silver Star, Bronze Star, Purple Heart, and Luxembourg War Cross.

Between army hitches, Willeford studied art and art history in Peru and published a book of poetry, *Proletarian Laughter* (1948). In 1953, he published his first novel, *High Priest of California*. Like most of Willeford's early work, it was published as a paperback original in a cheap pulp edition. Willeford's publishers had a tendency to illustrate his work with scantily clad women, to use misleading cover teasers, and to change his titles without notice—for example, *The Director* became *The Woman Chaser* (1960). In one case, the publishers even spelled his name wrong. Disillusionment with the publishing industry may have been one reason for the gap between the publication of *Cockfighter* in 1962 and his next novel, *The Burnt Orange Heresy*, in 1971, his first hardcover publication. During his hiatus from fiction writing, Willeford earned his bachelor's and master's degrees at the University of Miami and

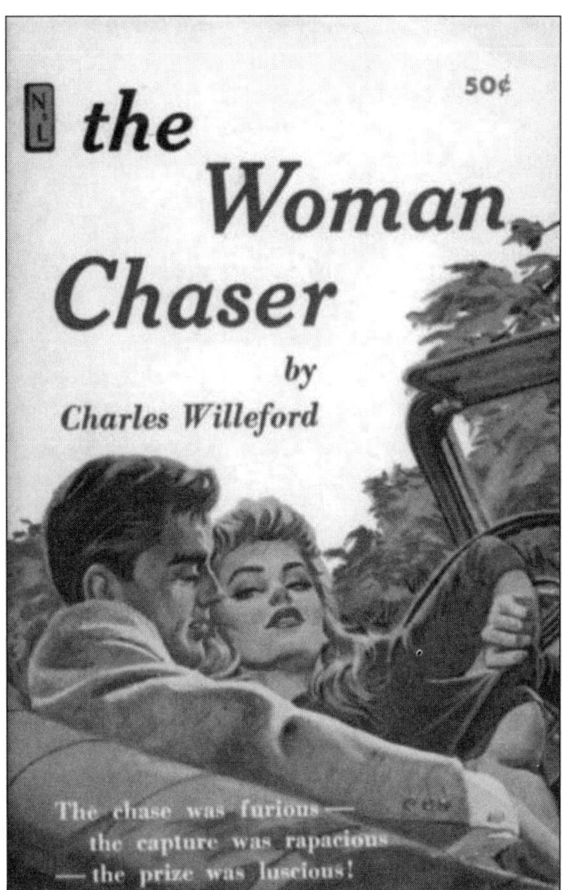

Despite its title, Charles Willeford's The Woman Chaser *is actually about a vicious used-car salesman who wants to make a movie. Willeford's own title for the book was* The Director.

later taught there and at Miami-Dade Junior College. He also wrote for a Miami newspaper and edited *Alfred Hitchcock's Mystery Magazine*. A longer, revised version of *Cockfighter* was published in hardcover in 1972, earning good reviews and the attention of director Roger Corman, who bought the film rights. The film version of *Cockfighter*, released in 1974 under various titles, featured a strong performance by Warren Oates and received some critical attention but was not a box-office success. Willeford again took a break from fiction writing, only to come back in 1984 with his greatest success, *Miami Blues*, published in hardcover by a mainstream publisher. The character of Hoke Moseley proved the perfect vehicle for Willeford's dark, ironic voice. Suddenly, after more than thirty years as a writer, Willeford was in the world of six-figure book deals, praised by critics for his wry, atmospheric depiction of a seedy and violent world.

Willeford, however, had only a few years left to enjoy his success. In 1988, he died of congestive heart failure, leaving behind his third wife, Betsy Pollar, and a lifetime of writings, some of which were collected and published after his death. Willeford has become something of a cult figure, and many of his early works have been reprinted in stylish new editions.

Analysis

As a crime writer, Charles Willeford is difficult to categorize. Not only did he work in different subgenres, but his writing broke the boundaries of genre as well. His early work can best be described as pulp noir, in the tradition of James M. Cain and Jim Thompson, but with a comic twist. *Wild Wives*, for example, seems almost an absurdist parody of a private eye novel, until the intrusion of a brutally realistic murder. Marshall Jon Fisher, writing in *The Atlantic Monthly*, noted that Willeford never found humor and violence mutually exclusive. The doomed romanticism of writers like Cain and Cornell Woolrich is absent in Willeford's work; instead, there is a self-contained, confident pragmatism and an eye for the quirky details of everyday life. Whether his heroes are smooth-talking car salesmen, silent cockfighters, pretentious art critics, or middle-aged, chain-smoking detectives, Willeford takes the reader fully into their world. Readers know Willeford's characters: how they speak; what they eat, and, more important, what they drink; the cars they drive; how they dress (often eccentrically, as with Hoke's yellow jumpsuit); and the routine of their work, whether that work involves solving crimes or committing them.

Pick-Up

Pick-Up (1955) is representative of Willeford's early pulp period, the bleakest and perhaps the best of his 1950's paperback novels. It was collected in the Library of America's prestigious series *Crime Novels: American Noir of the 1950s*, together with the work of Jim Thompson, Patricia Highsmith, and other classic noir authors. This short novel tells the story of Harry Jordan and Helen Meredith, lovers who share a weakness for alcohol and an inability to live in the world. Dark, nihilistic, and disturbing, *Pick-Up* is one of Willeford's most serious works, with only flashes of the black humor that infused his later novels.

When Harry Jordan, a failed artist and unemployed art teacher working in a diner, meets beautiful and reckless Helen Meredith, a woman from an upper-class background who prefers to lose herself in drink, they form an instant connection. However, Helen's love for Harry is not enough to end her self-destructive behavior. When Harry finds her in a bar, helplessly drunk and being fondled by a sailor, he erupts in a jealous rage and beats the man, slashing his face with a broken bottle. The lovers decide that death is their only way to attain peace, so Harry strangles Helen and tries to gas himself to death. Ironically, he fails even at suicide, having left a window open. He confesses to Helen's murder and eagerly awaits execution, but in a final ironic twist, an autopsy reveals that Helen actually died of natural causes, and he is free to resume his hopeless existence, a "tall, lonely Negro" walking the rainy streets.

Willeford's use of the theme of interracial romance, a motif also used in *Honey Gal* (1958, originally titled *The Black Mass of Brother Springer)*, was daring for 1955, an era when segregation, Jim Crow laws, and open racism were very much present. At one point, Harry compares himself to a car without a driver, a machine functioning without feeling or desire. Viewed in the context of his race—a detail not revealed until the novel's end—Harry's alienation and despair may be seen not as madness but as a rational response to a brutal society.

The Burnt Orange Heresy

The Burnt Orange Heresy stands alone among Willeford's novels. In this comic novel, Willeford uses the plot device of a crime caper to satirize modern art, art collectors, and critics who look for "movements" to praise or condemn. Willeford introduces James Figueras, a writer trying to make his name as an art critic. Figueras is proud that his article on Jacques Debierue, the "Grand Old Man of Modern Art," is featured in a recently released art encyclopedia, and he writes a regular column for an art journal, but his finances are less impressive than his education. In the monied world of Florida's Palm Beach, he is a self-described freeloader, living on the fringe of several social groups. When Figueras meets Joseph Cassidy, a wealthy art collector, he is easily persuaded to steal a picture from the reclusive Debierue, who never sells and rarely shows his work. Debierue, the founder of an art movement known as Nihilistic Surrealism, is most famous for his *No. One*, an empty picture frame placed over a crack in a wall.

Although the tale involves deception, arson, and eventually murder, the tone remains essentially light. Willeford, who had studied art history, uses his background to good effect as he describes Debierue's role in the art community of Paris between the world wars. The critical world's worship of an artist who is most famous for a painting he did not paint gives Willeford an opportunity to satirize art, criticism, and celebrity. *The Burnt Orange Heresy* is also notable for its dapper, cheerfully amoral narrator, James Figueras, a cad in a red silk dinner jacket, whose treatment of his long-suffering girlfriend, Berenice, is both horrific and hilarious.

Miami Blues

Willeford's first Hoke Moseley novel, *Miami Blues*, is notable not only for its hero, veteran police detective Hoke Moseley, but also for its villain, Freddy Frenger, a murderer and psychopath who explains to his former prostitute girlfriend that he just wants to live a normal, suburban married life. However, Freddy has left a few corpses behind, including a Hare Krishna follower whose finger Freddy broke when the man asked him for money at the airport. (The man later dies of shock.) Hoke is called in to investigate the bizarre case of murder-by-finger, and the parallel stories of detective and killer begin. Hoke—overweight, morose, rumpled, and old beyond his years—is the antithesis of the glamorous Hollywood detective hero, while Freddy, despite his penchant for random violence, comes across as the more competent and certainly the more cheerful of the two. Jon A. Jackson, in his introduction to *Miami Blues*, comments on Willeford's remarkable ability to invert the usual roles of hero and villain.

Miami Blues, like *The Burnt Orange Heresy*, has a south Florida setting, but the difference in the two Floridas depicted is remarkable. *The Burnt Orange Heresy* depicts the Florida of the 1960's and 1970's, still mainly a sleepy retiree's haven except during "the season," when society visitors arrive from the north. It is a community of rules, where homogeneous social groups seldom intermingle. By the time of the later novel, set in the mid-1980's, south Florida is a much faster, more diverse, and more dangerous world. Foreign tourists, Cuban refugees, middle-American vacationers, and hustlers of every variety crowd this new Florida of strip malls and theme parks. Willeford's writing evokes this world in all its energy, vulgarity, flashes of beauty, and underlying violence.

*Miami Blue*s is filled with what can only be called Willeford moments, as when Hoke Moseley has his gun, badge, and false teeth stolen, and when Freddy Frenger returns from a trip to the convenience store covered in blood, an eyebrow hanging from his face by a thread, and tells his girlfriend that he was run over by a car. Unfazed, she replies that she thought it was something like that. *Publishers Weekly* praised *Miami Blues* for expertly combining elements of a satire and a thriller, and crime writer Elmore Leonard paid homage to Willeford, calling him the best writer in the field.

Kathryn Kulpa

Principal mystery and detective fiction

Hoke Moseley series: *Miami Blues*, 1984; *New Hope for the Dead*, 1985; *Sideswipe*, 1987; *The Way We Die Now*, 1988

Nonseries novels: *Pick-Up*, 1955; *Wild Wives*, 1956 (also known as *Until I Am Dead*); *The Burnt Orange Heresy*, 1971

Other major works

Novels: *High Priest of California*, 1953; *Honey Gal*, 1958; *Lust Is a Woman*, 1958; *The Woman Chaser*, 1960; *Understudy for Love*, 1961; *No Experience Necessary*, 1962; *Cockfighter*, 1962 (revised 1972); *The Shark-Infested Custard*, 1993; *Deliver Me from Dallas*, 2001

Short fiction: *The Machine in Ward Eleven*, 1963; *Everybody's Metamorphosis*, 1988; *The Difference*, 1999; *The Second Half of the Double Feature*, 2003

Poetry: *Proletarian Laughter*, 1948; *Poontang, and Other Poems*, 1967

Nonfiction: *The Whip Hand*, 1961 (as Sanders); *The Hombre from Sonora*, 1971 (as Charles); *A Guide for the Undehemorrhoided*, 1977; *Off the Wall*, 1980; *Something About a Soldier*, 1986; *New Forms of Ugly: The Immobilized Hero in Modern Fiction*, 1987; *I Was Looking for a Street*, 1988; *Cockfighter Journal*, 1989; *Writing and Other Blood Sports*, 2000

Bibliography

Brannon, Julie. "The Rules Are Different Here: South Florida Noir and the Grotesque." In *Crime Fiction and Film in the Sunshine State: Florida Noir*, edited by Steve Glassman and Maurice O'Sullivan. Bowling Green, Ohio: Bowling Green State University Popular Press, 1997. This chapter in a genre study looks at depictions of south Florida in the fiction of Willeford and Carl Hiaasen.

Fisher, Marshall Jon. "The Unlikely Father of Miami Crime Fiction." *Atlantic Monthly* 285, no. 5 (May, 2000): 117-121. A profile of Willeford by a writer who knew him in Miami, with discussion of his works and publishing career.

Herron, Don. *Willeford*. Tucson, Ariz.: Dennis McMillan Publications, 1997. A biography of the author, with transcripts of interviews, descriptions of his works, and a complete bibliography.

Oder, Norman. "Willeford Returns Darkly, Via Dell." *Publishers Weekly* 243, no. 1 (January 1, 1996): 36. Discusses the republication of the four Hoke Moseley books as well as the release of the formerly unpublished *The Shark-Infested Custard*.

Sublett, Jesse. "Doing Right by a Poet of the Pulp Novel." *The New York Times*, June 18, 2000. Discusses the filming of *The Woman Chaser*, an adaptation of a 1960 Willeford novel, with commentary on other film adaptations of the author's work.

Willeford, Charles. *I Was Looking for a Street*. Woodstock, Vt.: Countryman Press, 1988. This memoir of the author's youth describes his early life and its influences on his work.

_______. *Something About a Soldier*. New York: Random House, 1986. Willeford describes his days and antics as an enlisted man in the Depression army. Sheds light on his later life as a writer.

DON WINSLOW

Born: New York, New York; October 31, 1953
Also wrote as McDonald Lloyd
Types of plot: Private investigator; comedy caper; thriller; inverted; espionage

Principal series

Neal Carey, 1991-

Principal series characters

Neal Carey is a part-time, reluctant investigator for a confidential organization known as Friends of the Family, operated by the Bank in Providence, Rhode Island, which provides clandestine services for wealthy depositors. Neal, the son of a heroin-addicted prostitute, never knew his father (one of his mother's customers) and was orphaned at the age of twelve. Neal seldom uses guns because he is a lousy shot and is even more inept as a fistfighter. A frustrated scholar with a peculiar sense of humor and a jaded attitude, Neal transferred credits from Columbia University to Nevada, where he lives in the desert village of Austin.

Joe Graham is Neal's adopted father: They met when Neal attempted to pick Joe's pocket, and thereafter Joe raised the youngster, teaching him tricks of the investigative trade, such as lock picking, surveillance, and tracing missing persons. He also serves as Neal's boss, handing out assignments for Friends of the Family. A short, almost dwarfish man with an artificial hand, Joe is not afraid to mix it up with the bad guys with whom his son's assignments invariably bring him in contact, and often he has to bail the younger man out of trouble.

Karen Hawley is an occasional elementary schoolteacher, an attractive, no-nonsense woman, and Neal's live-in girlfriend. She often becomes unwittingly entangled in Neal's assignments. Keenly aware of her biological clock, Karen wants to marry Neal and have children.

Contribution

Don Winslow, like many writers, has converted significant autobiographical events into fiction. Winslow's life encompasses considerable occupational and geographical territory. His interesting, if checkered, earlier career has provided a wealth of material related to crimes of domestic and international scope, has given him an expanded worldview, and has lent him a dry, sardonic wit that informs much of his work. His stints as undercover agent, private investigator, hostage simulator, fraud and arson analyst, safari leader, and freelance consultant have brought him into contact with a wide range of criminal and law enforcement types that he delineates with unerring accuracy, and he writes about the work involved with unquestioned authority.

Not yet a household name, Winslow has elicited an enviable degree of critical acclaim for his novels and a collaborative nonfictional work. His first novel, *A Cool Breeze on the Underground* (1991), which introduced private investigator Neal Carey, gained an Edgar Award nomination. *California Fire and Life* (1999) garnered a Shamus Award for best novel. *The Power of the Dog* (2004) was nominated for a Macavity Award and for *Deadly Pleasure* magazine's Barry Award. His nonfictional collaborative effort *Looking for a Hero: Staff Sergeant Ronnie Hooper and the Vietnam War* (2004) attracted considerable attention for its unflinching portrait of the tempestuous life of a real soldier. His *The Death and Life of Bobby Z* (1997) was made into a feature film in 2007, and his *The Winter of Frankie Machine* (2006) has been optioned.

Biography

Don Winslow was born on October 31, 1953, in New York City, the son of U.S. Navy noncommissioned officer Don Winslow, Sr., and librarian Ottis Schevrmann Winslow. Because of his father's occupation, Winslow moved frequently when he was a child. He grew up primarily in Warwick, near Providence, and in South Kingstown, Rhode Island. As a youngster, he performed in theater and voiced radio commercials.

In the early 1970's, Winslow attended the University of Nebraska-Lincoln, majoring first in journalism and later in African history, and directed a theater company. During his junior year in college, he worked as a researcher at the University of Cape Town, South Africa, and freelanced as a newspaper reporter. Winslow also surreptitiously brought in funds for TEACH—an educational organization in Soweto banned by the apartheid government—an action that led to his arrest and deportation. He afterward traveled around southern Africa for a time before returning home to complete his bachelor's degree.

Following graduation, Winslow directed a theater company for two years, then moved to rural Idaho, where he herded cattle. Winslow relocated to New York City, where he managed movie theaters for three years then worked at a detective agency as an undercover operative investigating theft at a chain of theaters. For the same agency, he was also engaged in operations in London and Amsterdam. The work led to employment with the Institute for International Studies, where—through simulated kidnappings—he helped train representatives from the national government, law enforcement, and the media in terrorist situations and hostage negotiations.

Winslow returned to school, earning a master's degree in military history while freelancing as a private investigator. He aspired to join the U.S. Foreign Service but instead joined a firm specializing in safaris and spent five years planning, selling, and leading treks into China and Kenya. In Kenya in 1985, he met and proposed to his wife, designer Jean Enstrom; the couple had a son, Thomas, born in 1989. After a term designing overseas educational programs for high school students, Winslow was briefly employed with Forensic Anthropology as an arson and fraud analyst. When the company folded, he continued working as a freelance investigator and consultant to law firms, assisting witnesses preparing to give testimony.

Drawing on his colorful history for inspiration, Winslow published his first novel, *A Cool Breeze on the Underground*, in 1991. The first in a series of novels centering on private investigator Neal Carey, it was nominated for an Edgar Award. Later nonseries novels have garnered Winslow similar critical acclaim and comparisons to Elmore Leonard and Carl Hiaasen for his unique amalgamation of hard-boiled action and humor. He has also written short stories, stage plays, screenplays, and television scripts, and he has collaborated on a nonfictional book about a troubled American Medal of Honor winner, *Looking for a Hero: Staff Sergeant Ronnie Hooper and the Vietnam War.*

Analysis

As important as Don Winslow's convoluted plots are to his work, his novels are first and foremost studies of intriguing characters from both sides of the law and from all gradations in between. His well-trained (and somewhat jaundiced) eye has the ability to spot telling physical clues that help reveal personality, and his ear catches subtle nuances and rhythms of conversation. Winslow is particularly adept at portraying a character's angst and giving voice to innermost thoughts, often tinged with terse, ironic, self-deprecating understatement. Even the best characters are severely flawed, and the worst have redeeming features.

Winslow's early novels (beginning with *A Cool Breeze on the Underground*) all concern freelance private investigator Neal Carey and the bizarre cases he is enlisted to undertake. These are told in the third person rather than the usual first person used for detective novels, giving the author the ability to jump from character to character as necessary to present information the protagonist alone would not know, thus increasing suspense. Though violence plays a role in these books, it takes a backseat to the generally lighthearted presentation of madcap adventures fraught with multiple, humorous complications and of an assortment of types of usually believable people who either want something or want to prevent others from achieving something. Winslow's growing maturity as a writer is evident from book to book, as characters become more sharply drawn, dialogue grows terser, and the prose style becomes leaner—all of which combine to make pacing more consistent, resulting in increased tension throughout.

Later nonseries novels take a darker tone while keeping Winslow's strengths—character portrayal, dialogue, and twisty plots—intact. Protagonists in these novels, unlike Neal Carey, who though laid-back is nonetheless heroic, are more complex and contradictory. For example, Walter Withers, an alcoholic private eye of questionable morality in *A Long Walk Up the Water Slide* (1994), commits various dubious acts while battling both the Central Intelligence Agency (CIA) and the KGB in the course of protecting an ambitious politician in *Isle of Joy* (1996), a thriller set in the 1950's against the paranoia of the Cold War. The central character in *The Death and Life of Bobby Z* (1997) is born loser Tim Kearney—sentenced to life for killing a member of the Hell's Angels and surrounded by vengeful imprisoned bikers—who is given the chance to win his freedom by impersonating a missing drug kingpin named Bobby Zacharias ("Bobby Z"). Crack arson investigator Jack Wade from *California Fire and Life* lost his job as a police officer for beating a confession out of a felon. Former CIA operative and Drug Enforcement Agency (DEA) agent Art Keller in *The Power of the Dog* constantly breaks rules in his pursuit of justice and is especially unconcerned about legal issues in his devotion to the destruction of Mexican drug lord Tio Barrea, a former police officer whose ascent Keller unwittingly aided by eliminating his rivals. Protagonist Frank Machianno, in *The Winter of Frankie Machine*, is a never-miss mob hit man, now retired and running a bait shop in Southern California, who is reluctantly lured back into his former profession.

Though another Winslow trademark, humor, is not entirely absent in his tales of espionage, drug deals gone wrong, horrible deaths by immolation, and wholesale mob assassinations, the laughs are somewhat downplayed, because they would be inappropriate given the more serious nature of the subject matter. People lie and cheat and die and kill—such things are not the usual stuff of comedy, except for the morbidly inclined. Thus, Winslow transforms the ridiculous to the sublime, in the form of wry and truthful observations concerning human nature, and plot complications farfetched enough to be believable—operating on the "truth is stranger than fiction" principle—provoke sad smiles of recognition rather than hearty guffaws. Winslow, though he shows violence close up and in Technicolor, does not glorify it. Graphic scenes are presented matter-of-factly, as the logical progression of evil deeds that cannot help but adversely affect the good, the bad, and the in-between alike.

A Long Walk Up the Water Slide

The fourth novel in the Neal Carey mystery series, *A Long Walk Up the Water Slide*, begins as a routine assignment for Neal and quickly deteriorates into a farcical romp, perhaps inspired by the Jimmy Swaggert and Jim Bakker sex scandals. Brooklyn-born Polly Paget, a secretary for the wholesome television show the *Jack and Candy Family Hour*, has been having an affair with Jackson "Jack" Landis, costar of the show and founder, president, and majority owner of the Family Cable Network. Polly publicly claims that after ending their affair, Jack raped her, but her heavy New York accent and bimbo-like appearance prevent her from presenting herself credibly before the media. Therefore, Neal is to hide her at his Nevada home while, like Henry Higgins, he grooms her linguistically so she will be more believable and more likely to be awarded a large settlement.

There are many forces at work throughout the story, because in addition to the fate of the network in the wake of a scandal, there is much at stake, including Candyland, a planned family resort under construction outside San Antonio, Texas, featuring condominiums and a gigantic water slide. Antagonists include tabloid reporters eager for a scoop, an alcoholic private detective sent by a pornography publisher to offer Polly a small fortune to appear in a magazine spread, mobsters and their minions raking off money from the construction of Candyland, lawyers for various factions within the network who have their own agendas, and a professional assassin sent to make sure Polly does not survive to jeopardize the whole television empire.

A Long Walk Up the Water Slide is a complex, fast-paced satirical thriller told in snapshot scenes from divergent viewpoints across the whole cast of participants. Winslow performs a masterful balancing act, veering from slapstick to extreme violence but never losing sight of his objective: the demonstration that large issues consist of small acts. The novel has a manic feel, with numerous plot reversals and unexpected twists. Characters, who often begin as stereotypes, reveal hidden depths that make them fully rounded. Dialogue, a particular Winslow strength, is full of insight and irony, sparked throughout with humorous throwaway lines that provide comic relief in tense situations.

While Drowning in the Desert

The fifth Neal Carey novel, *While Drowning in the Desert* (1996), presents the detective with a seemingly straightforward errand: elderly Nathan Silverstein, supposedly in the first stages of Alzheimer's, has wandered away from his California condominium. He is currently in Las Vegas, and it is Carey's task to collect him and fly with him back to his home.

As usual, the simple job becomes complicated. Nathan Silverstein turns out to be an old-time stand-up comedian known in his Catskills heyday as Natty Silver. Far from having Alzheimer's, Natty is still sharp: He has an inexhaustible supply of jokes and one-liners that he is not shy about airing. The octogenarian also has an active libido, which comes into play when he runs into an old flame in Las Vegas, former showgirl and current piano bar chanteuse Hope White. Natty refuses to fly, so Neal must rent a car for the long drive to California. During the trip, it is revealed that Natty witnessed a crime and that is why he fled. Reluctant to return to the scene of the crime, Natty steals Neal's rental car and sets off across the desert, pursued by the criminals who wish to eliminate the only witness to their misdeeds while Neal scrambles to catch up.

A fast-paced page-turner with a relatively small cast of well-drawn characters, the novel features hallmarks of Winslow's popular series: sparkling dialogue, wry observations about life in general and aging in particular, and gently satirical humor.

Jack Ewing

Principal mystery and detective fiction

Neal Carey series: *A Cool Breeze on the Underground*, 1991; *The Trail to Buddha's Mirror*, 1992; *Way Down on the High Lonely*, 1993; *A Long Walk Up the Water Slide*, 1994; *While Drowning in the Desert*, 1996

Nonseries novels: *Isle of Joy* (1996; also known as *A Winter Spy*, 1977, as Lloyd); *The Death and Life of Bobby Z*, 1997; *California Fire and Life*, 1999; *The Power of the Dog*, 2004; *The Winter of Frankie Machine*, 2006

Other major works

Play: *Alexander Hamilton: In Worlds Unknown*, pr. 2004

Screenplays: *Alexander Hamilton: In Worlds Unknown*, 2004; *The Full Ride*, 2002 (with George Mills)

Nonfiction: *Looking for a Hero: Staff Sergeant Ronnie Hooper and the Vietnam War*, 2004 (with Pete Maslowski)

Bibliography

Mobilio, Albert. "An Insurance-Business Thriller? Actually, Yes." Reviw of *California Fire and Life*, by Don Winslow. *Fortune* 144, no. 4 (August 16, 1999): 44. A highly favorable review in which the critic notes that Winslow spent many years working with arson investigators, giving the story—dealing with former police officer and claims adjuster Jack Wade—the ring of authenticity. The author is praised for his skill in presenting factual information, his smooth style, and his many plot turns that keep readers guessing.

Publishers Weekly. Review of *A Cool Breeze on the Underground*, by Don Winslow. 238, no. 2 (January 11, 1991): 94. A mixed review of the author's first novel. Though praised for its colorful characters, the novel is criticized for its lack of technical sophistication, particularly for its plodding early pace.

_______. Review of *The Trail to Buddha's Mirror*, by Don Winslow. 239, no. 6 (January 27, 1992): 91. A highly favorable review, demonstrating that Winslow learned from his mistakes to produce a tale of a routine missing-persons case—a brilliant scientist has fallen in love with a beautiful Chinese woman—that turns into a complicated morass on an international scale. Called a "superb mystery," loaded with vivid details.

_______. Review of *Way Down on the High Lonely*, by Don Winslow. 240, no. 40 (October 4, 1993): 67. A starred review showing Winslow's progress as a storyteller in a novel dealing with Neal Carey's efforts to recover a two-year-old boy snatched by his divorced father, a member of a white supremacist group who has fled into the wilds of Nevada. The reviewer especially notes the author's skillful blend of action, well-drawn characters, wry humor, and sharp prose.

Winslow, Don. Don Winslow's Official Website. http://www.donwinslow.com. The author's Web site, containing a brief biography; summaries and cover shots of Winslow's most recent books; news of signings, appearances, and other events; links, and contact information.

STUART WOODS

Stuart Lee

Born: Manchester, Georgia; January 9, 1938

Types of plot: Police procedural; private investigator; hard-boiled

Principal series

Will Lee, 1982-
Stone Barrington, 1991-
Holly Barker, 1998-
Rick Barron, 2004-

Principal series characters

Will Lee is Stuart Woods's most developed character. Readers come to understand his family's political background and witness him grow into a man. After serving as a lawyer, a chief aide to a U.S. senator, and a U.S. senator, Lee becomes the president of the United States. Weathered by everyday problems, Lee becomes a leader who does not allow lies and manipulation to encroach on his obligations, mostly because of his keen instinct about the strengths and weaknesses of those around him.

Stone Barrington begins as a New York City homicide detective and leaves the department to begin a law practice. However, his curiosity, personal connections, and lifelong commitment to solving crime constantly place him in the role of private investigator. Barrington is familiar with the dark side of humanity but has not let that destroy him. Instead, he remains gallant and loyal to his lifelong calling, as if he were a modern-day knight.

Holly Barker, a friend of Barrington and a former army major and military police officer, is the police chief in the fictional town of Orchid Beach, Florida. In battling drug traffickers, organized crime, and crooked real estate developers, Barker uses her knowledge of human greed, lust, and hubris to succeed. She later is depicted working for the government. Her beauty, wit, and sense of humor make her successful as a fictional character. The most fun-loving, courageous, and independent of Woods's characters, she is often obligated to put her life on the line with little or no help from others.

Contribution

Stuart Woods began his career in mystery and detective fiction with the critically acclaimed novel *Chiefs* in 1981. Woods used stories from his hometown and family history to create a critically acclaimed thriller lauded for its realistic portrayal of a small town's political dynamics and its critical dissection of a seemingly peaceful American community, themes that Woods has revisited occasionally throughout his career. *Chiefs* won the Edgar Allan Poe Award from the Mystery Writers of America and gave rise to the possibility that Woods could become one of the premier mystery writers of his day. Woods's novel *Palindrome* (1991) was nominated for the Edgar Award, and his *Imperfect Strangers* (1995)

was awarded France's Prix de Littérature Policière. He has written more than thirty-five novels, most of which have become best sellers because he has gained a strong American and international readership.

With a few exceptions, rather than offering a deep analysis of his characters, Woods focuses on the systems in which the characters function. These are typically the bureaucracies of politics, criminal justice, and law. His protagonists are those who willingly accept the consequences of breaking normal protocol to solve a problem for the greater good of the system, community, or nation in which they live and work. His protagonists' ability to overcome bureaucratic obstacles makes them modern-day heroes and makes their experiences relevant to contemporary American civilization.

Biography

Stuart Woods was born Stuart Lee in Manchester, Georgia, in 1938. A pivotal event in his adolescence was finding a chief-of-police badge in his grandmother's closet. According to Woods, it was dented by buckshot and spattered with dried blood. It belonged to his grandfather, who was wearing it when he was shot to death on duty ten years before Woods was born. The story of his grandfather influenced the premise of the novel *Chiefs* and provided the framework for the character William Henry Lee, Sr. Georgia, his home state, has been the setting for many of his novels and is mentioned in most of them. His hometown provided the setting of the fictional town Delano.

Woods majored in sociology at the University of Georgia and served in the Air National Guard in the early 1960's. He spent ten months of his year of service in Mannheim, Germany, during the Berlin Wall Crisis. During the rest of the 1960's, he worked as an advertising agent in New York, and at the end of that decade, he moved to London, where he worked quite successfully in advertising and copy writing. Despite his career choices up to that point, he had not forgotten about the chief-of-police badge and the novel that had been brewing inside him, so in 1973 he decided to move to Ireland to write his novel. It is not clear why he chose to move to Ireland, but he found a peaceful place to begin writing while working part-time at an ad agency.

Although he was in a position to write, he was distracted for a time by sailing. It became such a passion that he had a boat built in Cork and raced it in the 1976 Observer Singlehanded Transatlantic Race (OSTAR) from Plymouth, England, to Newport, Rhode Island. He returned to Georgia and wrote two nonfictional books: a travel book about England and Ireland and a memoir about his time in Ireland and the OSTAR race. The British publisher of the latter, *Blue Water, Green Skipper* (1977), sold the rights to W. W. Norton. Based on an outline and two hundred completed pages, W. W. Norton gave Woods a contract for the novel he had begun in 1973 and advanced him seventy-five hundred dollars, which gave him the incentive to finish *Chiefs*, the first Will Lee series novel, and diligently to pursue his fiction-writing career. He has continued to write in the Will Lee series and written novels in the Stone Barrington, Ed Eagle, Holly Barker, and Rick Barron series as well as nonseries novels.

Woods has established homes on the Treasure Coast of Florida, on an island off the coast of Maine, and in New York City. In addition to being an accomplished sailor, he is also an experienced small-aircraft pilot, both of which factor heavily into his novels.

Analysis

Stuart Woods, like many writers, is influenced and inspired by his childhood and personal experiences. His writing shows an antipathy to bureaucracy, military protocol, authority, and blind obedience to orders that may partially be the result of his time in the Air National Guard during the Berlin Wall Crisis. Though he was certainly not on a combat mission, he has hinted that he still does not thoroughly understand why the government sent him to Mannheim. His attitude may also stem from being a young American in the 1960's and early 1970's. In addition, he may have moved to London in the late 1960's as an act of protest against the political situation in the United States. All of Woods's protagonists are people who will listen to and carefully consider orders from superiors and advisers, but they ultimately will make their own decisions. Though it is important for his protagonists to work with the system to improve it, their competence and courage in the face of mortal danger often supersede the guidelines set forth by those sitting behind desks. Some of the government officials in his novels—such as Will Lee, Katherine Rule Lee, and Lance Cabot in *Dark Harbor* (2006) and *Iron Orchid* (2005) and Robert Kinney in *Capital Crimes* (2003)—are talented people, but Woods does not let readers forget the fact that officials' incompetence can endanger ordinary people. In creating intuitive, talented, versatile, and ethical heroes, he appeals to the ideals of American independence and individuality and the frustrations of those who are not satisfied with the political status quo.

Woods's childhood in Manchester, Georgia, clearly influenced his fiction. He has often experimented with the ways deep-rooted, small-town problems can have universal consequences. For example, the plots of *Chiefs* and *Under the Lake* (1987) are based on the premise that a few divulged secrets, pertaining to perversion, racism, fraud, and other sins, can shake the foundations of a small town. In these and the Holly Barker novels, if no one is interested in the truth, or if the root problems of the community are micromanaged, then the conflicts can and will reach beyond the township limits, affecting a state or even a nation. This is also how Woods's background in sociology comes into play in the world of his fiction.

Woods's experience in navigation and travel have helped him create dynamic characters and plots. In preparation for his novel *White Cargo* (1988), for example, he spent a lot of time flying over Columbia. His geographic knowledge of Florida helped to fuel the plots of *Orchid Beach* (1998), *Orchid Blues* (2001), and *Blood Orchid* (2002). His time in Maine helped him conceive of places for fugitives to hide and small airstrips suitable for dramatic landings and pursuits in novels such as *Capital Crimes* and *Dark Harbor*. Furthermore, his knowledge of London gave him an intriguing setting for the Stone Barrington novel *The Short Forever* (2002). His knowledge of boats, sailing, and aviation allows him to place extra barriers in the protagonists' way, thereby generating more suspense, and to create chases in which protagonists pursue wealthy criminals escaping by water or air.

In creating a suspenseful novel, Woods immediately sets up a murder mystery for the protagonist to solve, then he methodically creates several red herrings, disincentives, and obstacles for that character to overcome. These obstacles are often caused by or manifested in the following character types: derelict leaders trying to serve a large bureaucracy instead of the general public, egotistical leaders who micromanage because of fear or lack of faith in others, irresponsible journalists (as in the novel *Dirt*, 1996), organized criminals who are eternally flawed because they take sex and money more seriously than their own collective success, and technologically savvy criminals who strive for some semblance of control in a postmodern world (Teddy Fay in *Capital Crimes* and *Shoot Him if He Runs*, 2007). To complement the fast pace and suspense, Woods uses a clear and concise style of dialogue that very rarely strays from standard English. He seldom uses jargon, slang, idioms, or clichés that would detract from the credibility of the characters or, more important, the reader's understanding of what has transpired.

Capital Crimes

Little attention has been paid to Woods's understanding of the positive and negative dynamics of social groups. Although one person often takes the leadership role in solving the murder in Woods's novels, many of the solutions occur through the work of several individuals, often working as a team toward one common goal, as in *Dark Harbor* and *Capital Crimes*.

In *Capital Crimes*, Will Lee has settled into his first term as president of the United States, and he has enough experience in Washington, D.C., to know what to expect from those around him. He knows his enemies and allies, and he and his wife, Katherine Rule Lee , director of the Central Intelligence Agency (CIA), can safely delegate some of their problems to the expertise of others, in this case, Federal Bureau of Investigation (FBI) deputy director Robert Kinney. The problem is that someone as intelligent and skilled as any FBI agent is killing conservative leaders: First, Republican senator Frederick Wallace was killed, then a right-wing radio personality. Next, a powerful figure in the religious right was nearly killed. It takes Katherine's finesse, Kinney's leadership and diligence, and a tip from a traitor and former CIA agent, Ed Rawls, to locate the man responsible. In addition, several people have to put their differences aside to stop these murders.

Woods wrote this book shortly after the September 11, 2001, attacks on New York City, which makes the themes of political dichotomy, postmodern isolation, and blame-seeking more relevant to his readers.

Dark Harbor

As in *Capital Crimes*, the solution to the murders in *Dark Harbor*, an island village in Maine, requires the work of a group whose members trust one another. The primary murders, those of Stone Barrington's cousin Dick Stone, his wife, and their daughter, occur shortly before Barrington reads a will sent to him by Dick. The will grants Barrington the Dick Stone estate, which is peculiar considering the timing and the fact that Dick's brother Caleb would be the most likely beneficiary. After learning that Dick, also a lawyer, had been working covertly as a CIA operative, Barrington gains an ally in CIA agent Lance Cabot, who informs him that there are other retired agents living on Islesboro Island, including Ed Rawls. As the case becomes life-threatening, Barrington calls in his friend and former New York Police Department colleague Dino Bacchetti, along with Holly Barker and her father, Ham. Barrington's group, which includes Sergeant Young of the Maine State Police, bonds to pursue a solution when one of the CIA retirees and his granddaughter are murdered.

Because the reader initially suspects that Caleb is the murderer, *Dark Harbor* seems to be about the consequences of greed; however, it is about the hubris of individuals who have an exaggerated vision of their power in a small community and no knowledge of the truth of their own existence in the broad spectrum of society. This relates to most of Woods's novels in that the truth is exposed by a group of people who will put their professional reputations and lives on the line to solve a problem. While others are pointing fingers and hacking at the branches of the problem, Woods's heroes are busy digging for the roots.

Troy Place

Principal mystery and detective fiction

Will Lee series: *Chiefs*, 1981; *Run Before the Wind*, 1983; *Deep Lie*, 1986; *Grass Roots*, 1989; *The Run*, 2000; *Capital Crimes*, 2003

Stone Barrington series: *New York Dead*, 1991; *Dirt*, 1996; *Dead in the Water*, 1997; *Swimming to Catalina*, 1998; *Worst Fears Realized*, 1999; *L.A. Dead*, 2000; *Cold Paradise*, 2001; *The Short Forever*, 2002; *Dirty Work*, 2003; *Reckless Abandon*, 2004; *Two Dollar Bill*, 2005; *Dark Harbor*, 2006; *Fresh Disasters*, 2007; *Shoot Him if He Runs*, 2007

Ed Eagle series: *Santa Fe Rules*, 1992; *Short Straw*, 2006

Holly Barker series: *Orchid Beach*, 1998; *Orchid Blues*, 2001; *Blood Orchid*, 2002; *Iron Orchid*, 2005

Rick Barron series: *The Prince of Beverly Hills*, 2004

Nonseries novels: *Under the Lake*, 1987; *White Cargo*, 1988; *Palindrome*, 1991; *L.A. Times*, 1993; *Dead Eyes*, 1994; *Heat*, 1994; *Imperfect Strangers*, 1995; *Choke*, 1995

Other major works

Nonfiction: *Blue Water, Green Skipper*, 1977; *A Romantic's Guide to the Country Inns of Britain and Ireland*, 1979

Bibliography

Abbot, Jillian. "Three Writers on Plot." *The Writer* 117, no. 5 (May, 2004): 16. A question-and-answer interview with three consistently best-selling authors: Dennis Lehane, Gayle Lynds, and Stuart Woods. Includes Woods's typical concise and unambiguous comments about plot, setting, and literary background. Also provides a short biography.

Huntley, Kristine. Review of *Capital Crimes*. *The Booklist* 100, no. 1 (September 1, 2003): 9. This favorable review summarizes the plot of this Will Lee series novel and recommends it to Woods's fans.

_______. Review of *Dark Harbor*. *The Booklist* 102, no. 12 (February 15, 2006): 7. This favorable review provides a plot summary and praises the pairing of Barrington and Barker.

St. Martin, Tiffany. "Stuart Woods Coming to Sarasota: Novelist Brings Back Popular Protagonist." *Knight Ridder Tribune Business News*, October 15, 2006, p. 1. This short profile written on the author's appearance in Sarasota to promote *Short Straw* looks at Woods's motivations to write, the difference in his pace and dedication now versus when he started, and the return of a series character, lawyer Ed Eagle.

Woods, Stuart. Stuart Woods Official Website. http://www.stuartwoods.com. Includes the most insightful and thoroughly compiled information on Woods's life and philosophy toward writing, plus a bibliography and plot summaries.

CORNELL WOOLRICH

Born: New York, New York; December 4, 1903
Died: New York, New York; September 25, 1968
Also wrote as George Hopley; William Irish
Types of plot: Psychological; thriller; police procedural; inverted; historical

Principal series

Black series, 1940-1948

Contribution

Cornell Woolrich's highly suspenseful plots are often recounted from the standpoint of leading characters who, however ordinary they may seem at the outset, become embroiled in strange and terrifying situations. Woolrich was particularly adept at handling questions of betrayal and suspicion, arousing doubts about characters' backgrounds and intentions. Works dealing with amnesia or other unknowing states of mind produce genuine tension, though in other hands such themes might seem forced and overused.

Woolrich rarely made use of master detectives or other agents committed to bringing criminals to justice. His police officers attempt as best they can to grapple with apparently inexplicable occurrences; some of them are willful and corrupt. When they reach solutions, often it is with the help of individuals who themselves have been suspected of or charged with criminal acts. One of Woolrich's strengths is the vivid depiction of stark emotional reactions; the thoughts and feelings of leading characters are communicated directly, often in sharply individual tones. Some of his plots revolve about methods of crime or detection that might seem ingenious in some instances and implausible in others. Taken as a whole, his work may appear uneven; his best tales, however, produce somber and deeply felt varieties of apprehension, plunging the reader into the grim, enigmatic struggles of his protagonists.

Biography

The dark forebodings that affected the author's works may have originated in his early life. Cornell Woolrich was born Cornell George Hopley-Woolrich in New York City on December 4, 1903. His father was a civil engineer and his mother was a socialite; as a boy, Woolrich was often in Latin America. At about the age of eight, after seeing a production of Giacomo Puccini's *Madame Butterfly* (1904), he was overwhelmed with a profound sense of fatalism. When revolutions broke out in Mexico, he was fascinated by the fighting and collected spent cartridges that could be found on the street. It would appear that he was badly shaken by the eventual breakup of his parents' marriage, which left him unusually dependent on his mother.

In 1921, Woolrich entered Columbia University in New York, where courses in English may have spurred his interest in creative writing. One of his classmates, Jacques Barzun, later recalled that Woolrich was an amiable if somewhat distant individual. On one occasion, he was immobilized by a foot infection, an experience that may be reflected in the theme of enforced immobility that would appear in some of his later writings. During that time, however, under the name Cornell Woolrich he composed his first novel, *Cover Charge* (1926); this romantic work was favorably received. His *Children of the Ritz* (1927) won a prize offered jointly by *College Humor* magazine and a motion-pciture company; Woolrich went to Hollywood to adapt a film script from that book. In 1930, he married Gloria Blackton, a film producer's daughter, but she left him after a few weeks. Woolrich may have had homosexual inclinations. After he returned to New York, he wrote other sentimental novels, the last of which was *Manhattan Love Song* (1932), before devoting his efforts entirely to mystery writing.

In 1934, Woolrich's first crime and suspense stories were published in detective magazines. Even with the success of *The Bride Wore Black* (1940) and other full-length works, Woolrich remained a reclusive figure; frequently he would remain in his room at a residential hotel for long periods, venturing outside only when necessary. Success and public esteem apparently meant little to him, even when his works were widely distributed and had become known through films and other adaptations. In 1950, he won the Edgar Allan Poe Award of the Mystery Writers of America for the motion picture *The Window*, based on his story "The Boy Who Cried Murder." His mother, to whom he remained inordinately devoted, died in 1957, and he dedicated the stories in *Hotel Room* (1958) to her. His ensuing despondency seemed to diminish his creative output. In addition to bouts of alcoholism, he developed diabetes, yet he ignored the progressive deterioration of his health. Gangrene affected one leg, but he left this condition untreated until it became necessary for doctors to amputate the limb. He finally suffered a stroke and died in his native city on September 25, 1968. Very few people attended his funeral. His will established a trust fund, dedicated to his mother's memory, in support of scholarships for the study of creative writing at Columbia.

Analysis

The stories that marked Cornell Woolrich's debut as a mystery writer display a fatalism that lends added weight to surprise endings and ironic twists. Almost invariably, seemingly innocuous situations become fraught with dangerous possibilities. Outwardly ordinary people prove to harbor devious and malign intentions; the innocent, by the odd machinations of fate, often find themselves enmeshed in the schemes of the guilty. Frequently, the outcome of these dark, troubled struggles remains in doubt, and Woolrich was not averse to letting characters perish or be undone by their own devices. Many of his works are set in New York or other large urban areas during the Depression and depict people who, already impoverished and often desperate, are drawn relentlessly into yet more serious and threatening circumstances.

In Woolrich's first suspense work, "Death Sits in the Dentist's Chair," the mysterious demise of a man who has recently had his teeth filled leads to some frantic searching for the murderer. An unusual murder method is uncovered, and the protagonist is nearly poisoned during his efforts to show the culprit's mode of operation. In "Preview of Death," when an actress costumed in an old-fashioned hoop skirt is burned to death, a police detective shows how the fire could have been produced by one of her cohorts. "Murder at the Automat" leads to some anxious investigations when a man dies after eating a poisoned sandwich obtained from a machine; actually, the trick seems remarkably simple once the murderer's likely whereabouts have been reviewed. Other deadly devices, some outwardly improbable, appear in various stories.

In "Kiss of the Cobra," death from snake poison cannot easily be explained until it is learned how a strange Indian woman could have transferred venom to common articles used by her victims. Suggestions of supernatural agencies are developed more fully in "Dark Melody of Madness" (also known as "Papa Benjamin" and "Music from the Dark"), in which a musician all too insistently attempts to learn the secrets of voodoo from some practitioners of that dark religion. Although he can compel them to divulge the incantations that seemingly will summon malevolent spirits, such forces are not content to be used in the man's stage performances. Eventually, whether from the intervention of unearthly powers or from sheer fright, he collapses and dies. "Speak to Me of Death," which eventually was incorporated into another work, concerns a seemingly prophetic warning: When a wealthy old man is told that he will die at midnight, other interested parties take note of the means specified and gather to prevent harm from coming to him. In the end he falls victim not to any human agency or to anxiety and apprehension; rather, the original design is carried through in a wholly unexpected way. In Woolrich's stories, the distinction between known operations of the physical world and his characters' subjective beliefs is often left shadowy and uncertain; when improbable events take place, it is not always clear whether individual susceptibilities or the actual workings of malignant powers are responsible. Similarly, when protagonists are introduced in an intoxicated state, sometimes it cannot easily be determined whether they are actually responsible for deeds that were perpetrated when they were inebriated. In other stories, certain individuals are under the sway of narcotics, such as marijuana or cocaine.

At times, Woolrich's protagonists find themselves implicated in grim plots that begin with apparently incriminating situations and end with unusual resolutions. In "And So to Death" (better known as "Nightmare"), a man who has been found at the scene of a murder has some difficulty in convincing even himself that he is innocent, and only with the intervention of others can the facts in the case be established. Police procedures are often portrayed as arbitrary and brutal. A marathon dance contest furnishes the background for "Dead on Her Feet," a macabre study of a killing in an unusual pose. When a girl is found rigid, not exhausted but actually murdered, a ruthless police officer forces a young man, weary and frightened, to dance with his dead partner; though soon afterward he is absolved, he breaks down under the strain and falls prey to uncontrollable mad laughter. In "The Body Upstairs," police torment a man with lighted cigarettes in an attempt to make him confess; all the while, another man on the force has tracked down the real killer.

"The Death of Me" and "Three O'Clock"

If the innocent generally suffer in Woolrich's stories, it is also true that crime often fails to achieve its ends. Well-laid plans tend to go awry in strange or unanticipated ways. In "The Death of Me," a man determines to stage his own death to defraud his insurance company. He exchanges personal effects with someone who was killed at a railroad crossing, but this other man proves to have been a criminal who had stolen a large sum of money; thus, the protagonist is pursued both by the man's cohorts and by an insurance investigator. When he turns on his company's agent and kills him, he realizes that he will be subject to criminal charges under whichever name he uses. In "Three O'Clock," a man decides to eliminate his wife and her lover. He builds a time bomb that he installs in the basement of his house; once the mechanism is in place, however, he is accosted by burglars, who tie him up and leave him behind as the fateful countdown begins. After the man has abandoned all hope of rescue, it is discovered that the device had inadvertently been deactivated beforehand, but by then he has been driven hopelessly mad by his ordeal.

"It Had to Be Murder"

In other cases, those who in one way or another are confronted with crime are able to confound lawbreakers. In "Murder in Wax," a woman uses a concealed phonograph machine to record the testimony that is required to save her husband from murder charges. "After-Dinner Story" has the host at a social gathering use the threat of poison to elicit a vital admission from one of the guests. The notable story "It Had to Be Murder" (also known as "Rear Window") begins with a man with a cast on his leg casually observing others in his vicinity; some mysterious movements by a man at the window across from him attract his attention, and he arrives at the inference that his neighbor's wife has been murdered. Although at first the police are inclined to dismiss this theory, these suppositions prove to be correct, and an encounter at close quarters with the killer takes place before the matter is settled.

Woolrich's crime novels, notably those that came to be grouped together because of their common "color scheme"—the word "black" figures in the titles of six Woolrich novels—deal with more complex issues of anxiety and violence. Multiple killings, for example, raise questions about how apparently unrelated persons and occurrences may have become part of a larger web of havoc and destruction; the pattern is eventually explained by reference to previous events that have left the perpetrators permanently embittered and changed. In some cases, the murderer's actions and the efforts at detection are shown in alternating sequences, so that the overarching question becomes which side will prevail in the end. Although clues and testimony figure prominently in some works, the reader rarely is challenged directly by such means; assessments of character and intentions often are equally significant. Problems of love frustrated or gone wrong frequently account for the single-minded intensity and twisted, circuitous logic underlying murderous deeds; some characters are driven by an anguished loneliness that has turned ordinary emotional impulses inside out.

THE BRIDE WORE BLACK AND RENDEZVOUS IN BLACK

The pursuit of revenge is a common motivation for crime in Woolrich's novels. In *The Bride Wore Black*, various murders seem to implicate a mysterious woman; it is learned that years ago her husband was killed on the church steps immediately after their wedding ceremony, and she has vowed to eliminate those responsible. In some respects *Rendezvous in Black* (1948) is a haunting, bittersweet study in love denied. After the death of his fiancé, a man sets forth to inflict similar anguish on others who may have been involved; killing those whom each of them loved most, he leaves a trail of bodies that can be explained only when his original design is uncovered. All the while tangled, turbulent feelings have welled up within the killer; when a woman is hired by the police to lure him into the open, she creates the illusion that his beloved has returned to him.

THE BLACK CURTAIN AND THE BLACK ANGEL

Woolrich was adept at portraying the lonely desperation of those who must struggle against the most unfavorable odds to prove their innocence or to save loved ones. Sometimes it appears that sheer willpower and determination can triumph over the most imposing obstacles; even the most unlikely forms of evidence can be instrumental in efforts to find the real culprits. *The Black Curtain* (1941) concerns a man who has suffered a blow to the head that has effaced the memories of three years; uneasily, he sorts out the bits of information that may cast some light on the missing period of his life. It emerges that under another identity he was falsely implicated in a murder, and the actual perpetrators have been trying to do away with him once and for all. The protagonist's groping, agonizing attempts to learn about his own past, despite his fear that some terrible secret lies at the end of his quest, makes this work a highly compelling one. *The Black Angel* (1943) begins with a man's sentence to death for the murder of his presumed mistress; his wife believes in him implicitly, however, and as the date for the execution draws near she sets off on her own to clear him. Beginning only with a monogrammed matchbook and some entries in the victim's notebook, she succeeds finally in confronting the real killer. Along the way there are a number of unsettling encounters in the murky night world of call girls and criminal operators. A man who fled to Havana with a gangster's wife is implicated in her murder, in *The Black Path of Fear* (1944); dodging threats from several sides, he receives aid from some unexpected quarters, and eventually some bizarre and vicious criminals are brought to justice.

PHANTOM LADY AND DEADLINE AT DAWN

In many of Woolrich's works, time itself becomes an enemy. This motif is utilized most powerfully in *Phantom Lady* (1942), which begins 150 days before a man's scheduled execution. The time remaining, down to the final hour, is announced at the beginning of each chapter. The protagonist has been found guilty of murdering his wife, after no one would believe that he had actually been with another woman on the night in question. Even he has begun to doubt that she ever existed. Finally, after much fruitless searching, the mystery woman is located. The evidence used to bring her into the open is no more substantial than an old theater program. In the end, the real culprit turns out to be an individual who had been close to the condemned man. In *Deadline at Dawn* (1944), a man and a woman who happened to be at the scene of a killing must find the actual murderer within a matter of hours; chapter headings consist simply of clock faces showing how much closer the protagonists have come to freedom, or to disaster, at each turn.

Waltz into Darkness

Suspicion and conflict at close quarters also appears in Woolrich's works; while husbands and wives, and for that matter lovers of various sorts, often act on behalf of each other, when differences arise the results can be frightful and unsettling. In *Waltz into Darkness* (as William Irish; 1947), set in New Orleans in 1880, a man seeks a mail-order bride, but he discovers that the woman he has married is not quite the one he had expected. His new wife appropriates his money, and he discovers that she probably had a hand in the death of his original betrothed. Yet she exercises a fatal sway over him, and though she mocks him for his apparent weakness, he believes that the signs of her deep underlying love for him are unmistakable. This curious polarity seems to enervate him and leave him without a will of his own; he commits murder for her sake, and even when he learns that she is slowly poisoning him, his devotion to her is so strong that he cannot save himself.

Woolrich frequently employed first-person narratives. Those works in which accounts of crime and detection follow each other on parallel courses utilize an omniscient narrator, who appears, however, never to be far from the thoughts, hopes, and fears of the leading characters. In some of his stories he adopts a lilting, sentimental tone for the recounting of romantic aspirations; the shock of disillusionment and distrust is conveyed in a jarring, somber fashion. In some of his later offerings such tendencies took on maudlin qualities, but at his best Woolrich could create an acute and well-drawn contrast between lofty ideals and close encounters with danger. Reactions to impending threats are expressed in a crisp, staccato tempo; blunt, numbing statements, either in direct discourse or in narration, generally bring matters to a head. Often situations are not so much described as depicted through the uneasy perspective of characters who must regard people and objects from the standpoint of their own struggles with imminent danger. Odd metaphors for frenzied and violent action sometimes lend ironic touches. In much of Woolrich's writing, action and atmosphere cannot readily be separated. Indeed, quite apart from the original conceptions that are realized in his leading works, the dark and penetrating power of his studies in mystery and fear entitle his efforts to be considered among the most important psychological thrillers to appear during the twentieth century.

J. R. Broadus

Principal mystery and detective fiction

Black series: *The Bride Wore Black*, 1940 (also known as *Beware the Lady*); *The Black Curtain*, 1941; *Black Alibi*, 1942; *The Black Angel*, 1943; *The Black Path of Fear*, 1944; *Rendezvous in Black*, 1948

Nonseries novels: *Phantom Lady*, 1942 (as Irish); *Deadline at Dawn*, 1944 (as Irish); *Night Has a Thousand Eyes*, 1945 (as Hopley); *Waltz into Darkness*, 1947 (as Irish); *I Married a Dead Man*, 1948 (as Irish); *Fright*, 1950 (as Hopley); *Savage Bride*, 1950; *Strangler's Serenade*, 1951 (as Irish); *You'll Never See Me Again*, 1951 (as Irish); *Death Is My Dancing Partner*, 1959; *The Doom Stone*, 1960; *Into the Night*, 1987

Other short fiction: 1943-1950 • *I Wouldn't Be in Your Shoes*, 1943 (as Irish; also known as *And So to Death* and *Nightmare*); *After-Dinner Story*, 1944 (as Irish; also known as *Six Times Death*); *If I Should Die Before I Wake*, 1945 (as Irish); *Borrowed Crimes*, 1946 (as Irish); *The Dancing Detective*, 1946 (as Irish); *Dead Man Blues*, 1947 (as Irish); *The Blue Ribbon*, 1949 (as Irish; also known as *Dilemma of the Dead Lady*); *Six Nights of Mystery*, 1950 (as Irish); *Somebody on the Phone*, 1950 (as Irish; also known as *The Night I Died* and *Deadly Night Call*)

1951-1960 • *Bluebeard's Seventh Wife*, 1952 (as Irish); *Eyes That Watch You*, 1952 (as Irish); *Night-*

mare, 1956; *Violence*, 1958; *Beyond the Night*, 1959; *The Best of William Irish*, 1960 (as Irish)

1961-1986 • *The Dark Side of Love*, 1965; *The Ten Faces of Cornell Woolrich*, 1965; *Nightwebs*, 1971; *Angels of Darkness*, 1978; *The Fantastic Stories of Cornell Woolrich*, 1981; *Darkness at Dawn*, 1985; *Vampire's Honeymoon*, 1985; *Blind Date with Death*, 1986

Other major works

Novels: *Cover Charge*, 1926; *Children of the Ritz*, 1927; *Times Square*, 1929; *A Young Man's Heart*, 1930; *The Time of Her Life*, 1931; *Manhattan Love Song*, 1932

Short fiction: *Hotel Room*, 1958

Screenplay: *The Return of the Whistler*, 1948 (with Edward Bock and Maurice Tombragel)

Bibliography

Haining, Peter. *The Classic Era of American Pulp Magazines*. Chicago: Chicago Review Press, 2000. Looks at Woolrich's contribution to the pulps and the relationship of pulp fiction to its more respectable literary cousins.

Horsley, Lee. *The Noir Thriller.* New York: Palgrave, 2001. Scholarly, theoretically informed study of the thriller genre. Examines a half dozen of Woolrich's novels, from *The Bride Wore Black* to *I Married a Dead Man*.

Lee, A. Robert. "The View from the Rear Window: The Fiction of Cornell Woolrich." In *Twentieth-Century Suspense: The Thriller Comes of Age*, edited by Clive Bloom. New York: St. Martin's Press, 1990. Analysis of Woolrich's contributions to the suspense thriller genre, centering on Alfred Hitchcock's adaptation, *Rear Window* (1954).

Nevins, Francis M., Jr. *Cornell Woolrich: First You Dream, Then You Die*. New York: Mysterious, 1988. This comprehensive study of Woolrich's lengthy career also serves as a history of the pulp and mystery publishing industries.

Renzi, Thomas C. *Cornell Woolrich: From Pulp Noir to Film Noir.* Jefferson, N.C.: McFarland, 2006. Comprehensive study of twenty-two Woolrich novels and short stories and twenty-nine film and television adaptations of his work. Bibliographic references and index.

Roth, Marty. *Foul and Fair Play: Reading Genre in Classic Detective Fiction*. Athens: University of Georgia Press, 1995. A poststructural analysis of the conventions of mystery and detective fiction. Examines 138 short stories and works from the 1840's to the 1960's. Contains discussion of Woolrich's work.

Woolrich, Cornell. *Blues of a Lifetime: The Autobiography of Cornell Woolrich*. Bowling Green, Ohio: Bowling Green State University Popular Press, 1991. Woolrich provides a series of vignettes, rather than a single coherent narrative, detailing moments and episodes from his life and career.

Z

ISRAEL ZANGWILL

Born: London, England; February 14, 1864
Died: Midhurst, West Sussex, England; August 1, 1926
Type of plot: Police procedural

Contribution

Israel Zangwill, hailed in his time as "the [Charles] Dickens of the ghetto" and praised as a peer of classic writers such as Thomas Hardy, Henry James, Rudyard Kipling, and George Bernard Shaw, made his single outstanding contribution to the realm of mystery fiction when he was twenty-seven years old. Serialized in 1891 and published in book form in 1892, *The Big Bow Mystery*, Zangwill's unique crime novel, has been termed the first full-length treatment of the locked-room motif in detective literature. Zangwill has thus come to be proclaimed the father of this challenging mystery genre, and properly so. On the fictional trail to the solution of the Big Bow murder, the author's professional sleuths, along with a number of amateur newspaper theorists and assorted curbstone philosophers, offer a number of ingenious alternate explanations of the puzzle, possible hypotheses that through the years have inspired other literary craftsmen involved in constructing and disentangling locked-room mysteries. In addition, *The Big Bow Mystery* offers a graphic picture of late Victorian life in a seething London working-class neighborhood. Zangwill effectively combined social realism of the streets with a realistic depiction of the criminal investigative process.

Biography

Israel Zangwill was born in the ghetto of London's East End. His father, an itinerant peddler, was an immigrant from Latvia; his mother, a refugee from Poland. Part of Zangwill's childhood was spent in Bristol, but by the time he was twelve, the family had returned to London, where young Israel attended the Jews' Free School in Whitechapel, becoming at the age of fourteen a "pupil-teacher" there.

By the time he was eighteen, Zangwill had manifested extraordinary talent for writing, winning first prize for a humorous tale brought out serially in *Society* and publishing a comic ballad. He showed, too, an early interest in social realism by collaborating on a pamphlet describing market days in the East End Jewish ghetto. In 1884, Zangwill was graduated from London University with honors in three areas: English, French, and mental and moral sciences. He continued teaching at the Jews' Free School until 1888, when he resigned to devote all of his considerable energy to a career in letters.

Subsequently, the writings of Zangwill were indeed prolific: In addition to twenty-five collected volumes of drama and fiction, Zangwill wrote hundreds of essays for popular and esoteric journals and gave as many speeches. He worked efficiently and rapidly, and editors quickly recognized and rewarded his talent. Zangwill once observed that he had never written a line that had not been purchased before it was written. His plays were produced in London and New York; his final drama, staged on Broadway, provided Helen Hayes with one of her first starring roles.

Zangwill's range of interests was remarkably extensive: art, economics, pacifism, politics, racial assimilation, World War I, and Zionism and the Jewish homeland. Around these themes he composed romances and satires, entertainments and polemics. Though he continued his strenuous habits of composition right up to his death, Zangwill's most effective period of fiction writing came, so the consensus records, during the 1890's, the era he had ushered in with *The Big Bow Mystery.* Critics of fiction regard *Children of the Ghetto* (1892), *The King of Schnor-*

Israel Zangwill. (Library of Congress)

rers: Grotesques and Fantasies (1894), and *Dreamers of the Ghetto* (1898) as his most provocative and enduring contributions to socio-ethnic literature. His most famous drama, *The Melting-Pot* (pr., pb. 1909)—"That's a great play, Mr. Zangwill," declared President Theodore Roosevelt on opening night—presented for the first time the now-clichéd metaphor of America as a crucible for uniting into a single people the disinherited of the Old World.

Zangwill soon focused his work on social and political issues, bringing to modern problems a sensibility at once idealistic in its hopes and realistic in its proposed solutions. His ideas were given wide publicity in both England and America; he was always a popular attraction as an orator. Late in his life, Zangwill suffered a nervous breakdown, brought on by the stresses of his work for the theater as dramatist and theater manager. He died in the summer of 1926 in Sussex.

Analysis

In the lore of mystery and detective fiction, Israel Zangwill's reputation, based on one classic work, is secure. He is the father of the locked-room mystery tale, a subgenre launched by Edgar Allan Poe in short-story format but made especially attractive by Zangwill's versatile, full-length rendering. Written in 1891, when Zangwill was at the virtual beginning of his career, *The Big Bow Mystery* was serialized in the *London Star*, published a year later in book form, and finally collected in *The Grey Wig: Stories and Novelettes* (1903). More than a whodunit cipher or a pure exercise in inductive reasoning, Poe's "ratiocination," Zangwill's novel brings together the intellectual acumen of the scientific sleuth with the inventive imagination of a poet. At the same time, the novel offers a perceptive and sociologically valid picture of working-class life in late Victorian England, replete with well-defined portraits of fin de siècle London characters. Many of the issues and ideas distinguishing the turbulent 1890's are mentioned or explored in the novel.

The Big Bow Mystery

As a writer with roots in the ghetto, Zangwill theorized that it was essential to reveal the mystery, romance, and absurdity of everyday life. In *The Big Bow Mystery* he employs a photographic realism to render the human comedy. With vivid attention to detail, he depicts the truths inherent in class relationships, the tensions in political realities, and the passions in reformist clamor. Influenced himself by the pulp novels or "penny dreadfuls" of the time, Zangwill was perhaps paying homage to them through loving parody. In the main, however, the literary sources of the novel are Edgar Allan Poe, Charles Dickens, and Robert Louis Stevenson, whose romances of the modern and the bizarre, particularly *The Strange Case of Dr. Jekyll and Mr. Hyde* (1886), had caught Zangwill's attention.

The characters in *The Big Bow Mystery* are Dickensian in name as well as behavior: Mrs. Drabdump, a hysterical widowed landlady who, with retired Inspector Grodman, discovers the body of the victim; Edward Wimp, the highly visible inspector from Scotland Yard who undertakes the well-publicized investigation; Denzil Cantercot—poet, pre-Raphaelite devotee of the beautiful, professional aesthete—who has ghostwritten Grodman's best-selling memoirs, *Criminals I Have Caught*; Tom Mortlake—union organizer, "hero of a hundred strikes," veritable saint to all workingmen of Bow—who is arrested for the murder of Arthur Constant—idealist, much-loved philanthropist, believer in the true. The ideas of the philosopher Arthur Schopenhauer, particularly those set forth in his essay on suicide, had become important to Constant; so, too, had the visions of Madame Helena Petrovna Blavatsky, one of the founders of Theosophy, who claimed power over superphysical forces and whose cult during the 1890's attracted serious thinkers, dabbling dilettantes, and crackpots. Fascinated by the confluence of these intellectual and spiritual forces, Zangwill juxtaposed esoteric discussions of astral bodies to pragmatic reviews of trade unionism. *The Big Bow Mystery* presents an almost encyclopedic view, sometimes satiric but always accurate, of polarized British thought patterns of the age.

Constant's dead body is discovered in a room sealed as effectively as a vault, with no instrument of death found on the premises. As Grodman and Wimp, experienced Scotland Yard detectives, endeavor to solve the mystery, the popular *Pell Mell Gazette* prints numerous ingenious theories mailed in by interested amateurs. With a sly twist, Zangwill even brings Poe directly into the story by having a newspaper correspondent assert that Nature, like the monkey she is, has been plagiarizing from "The Murders in the Rue Morgue" and that Poe's publisher should apply for an injunction. Another would-be investigator suggests that a small organ-grinder's monkey might have slid down the chimney and with its master's razor slit poor Constant's throat. Thus Zangwill pays his debt to Poe and serves notice that he intends to embellish the genre.

As the true and the useful, the aesthetic and the utilitarian collide, as the tenets of Oscar Wilde and Algernon Charles Swinburne challenge the ideas of John Stuart Mill and Jeremy Bentham, Zangwill graphically sustains the brooding, gaslit Victorian atmosphere. His characters trudge through London mists, take tea in musty, gray boardinghouses, and slink through bleak working-class neighborhoods. Zangwill possessed a strong awareness of environmental factors and their effect on people's lives. Before he begins to unravel the complexities of this tale, however, even Prime Minister William Ewart Gladstone and the home secretary appear as actors in the drama. The ultimate revelations come as a shocking series of twists, yet no clues have been denied the reader; the solution is honest, intricate, and logical. Zangwill has remained in total control of his material.

"The Memory Clearing House" and "Cheating the Gallows"

The King of Schnorrers contains two mystery tales: "The Memory Clearing House" and "Cheating the Gallows." Again, Poe is the inspiration behind both. "The Memory Clearing House" has as its basis a theory of supernatural thought transference, with people selling unwanted and superfluous memories to a memory broker, who catalogs these unique materials and sells them. He runs a "pathological institution." When an author purchases a murderer's memory for use in a realistic novel he has in progress, the complications begin. The climax occurs when the published novel is damned for its tameness and improbability. Zangwill's inventiveness is again evident in "Cheating the Gallows." In this story, an odd pair who happen to live together—a respectable bank manager and a seedy, pipe-smoking journalist—become involved with the same woman. A murder, a suicide, and a phantasmic dream bring about several stunning revelations. A few other grotesques and fantasies from the volume—"A Double-Barrelled Ghost," "Vagaries of a Viscount," and "An Odd Life"—also capture Zangwill's art in the area of mystery; each has a balanced dose of humor and pathos.

As much an interpreter of life's vicissitudes and problems as he was an entertainer in his mystery writings, Israel Zangwill—and his famed locked room in *The Big Bow Mystery*—will continue to occupy a prestigious position in the annals of detective fiction.

Abe C. Ravitz

Principal mystery and detective fiction

Novel: *The Big Bow Mystery*, 1892

Short fiction: *The King of Schnorrers: Grotesques and Fantasies*, 1894; *The Grey Wig: Stories and Novelettes*, 1903

Other major works

Novels: *The Premier and the Painter: A Fantastic Romance*, 1888 (with Louis Cowen); *Children of the Ghetto*, 1892; *Joseph the Dreamer*, 1895; *The Master*, 1895; *The Mantle of Elijah*, 1900; *Jinny the Carrier: A Folk Comedy of Rural England*, 1919

Short fiction: *The Bachelor's Club*, 1891; *The Old Maid's Club*, 1892; *Ghetto Tragedies*, 1893; *Merely Mary Ann*, 1893; *Dreamers of the Ghetto*, 1898; *The Celibate's Club: Being the United Stories of the Bachelors' Club and the Old Maids' Club*, 1898; *Ghetto Comedies*, 1907

Plays: *The Great Demonstration*, pr. 1892; *Aladdin at Sea*, pr. 1893; *Six Persons*, pr. 1893; *The Lady Journalist*, pr. 1893; *Threepenny Bits*, pr. 1895; *Children of the Ghetto*, pr. 1899 (adaptation of his novel); *The Monument of Death*, pr. 1900; *The Revolted Daughter*, pr. 1901; *Merely Mary Ann*, pr., pb. 1903 (adaptation of his short story); *The Serio-Comic Governess*, pr., pb. 1904; *Nurse Marjorie*, pr., pb. 1906; *The Melting-Pot*, pr., pb. 1909; *The War God*, pr., pb. 1911; *The Next Religion*, pr., pb. 1912; *Plaster Saints*, pr., pb. 1914; *The Moment Before*, pr. 1916; *Too Much Money*, pr. 1918, pb. 1924; *The Cockpit*, pr., pb. 1921; *The Forcing House: Or, The Cockpit Continued*, pb. 1922; *We Moderns*, pr. 1923; *The King of Schnorrers*, pr. 1925 (adaptation of his novella)

Poetry: *The Ballad of Moses*, 1892; *Blind Children*, 1903

Nonfiction: 1882-1900 • *Motza Kleis*, 1882 (with Cowen); *"A Doll's House" Repaired*, 1891 (with Eleanor Marx Aveling); *Hebrew, Jew, Israelite*, 1892; *The Position of Judaism*, 1895; *Without Prejudice*, 1896; *The People's Saviour*, 1898

1901-1910 • *The East African Question: Zionism and England's Offer*, 1904; *What Is the ITO?*, 1905; *A Land of Refuge*, 1907; *One and One Are Two*, 1907; *Talked Out!*, 1907; *Be Fruitful and Multiply*, 1909; *Old Fogeys and Old Bogeys*, 1909; *Report on the Purpose of Jewish Settlement in Cyrenaica*, 1909; *The Lock on the Ladies*, 1909; *Italian Fantasies*, 1910; *Sword and Spirit*, 1910

1911-1920 • *The Hithertos*, 1912; *The Problem of the Jewish Race*, 1912; *Report on the Jewish Settlement in Angora*, 1913; *The War and the Women*, 1915; *The War for the World*, 1916; *The Principle of Nationalities*, 1917; *The Service of the Synagogue*, 1917 (with Nina Davis Salaman and Elsie Davis); *Chosen Peoples: The Hebraic Ideal Versus the Teutonic*, 1918; *Hands Off Russia*, 1919; *The Jewish Pogroms in the Ukraine*, 1919 (with others); *The Voice of Jerusalem*, 1920

1921-1937 • *Watchman, What of the Night?*, 1923; *Is the Ku Klux Klan Constructive or Destructive? A Debate Between Imperial Wizard Evans, Israel Zangwill, and Others*, 1924; *Now and Forever: A Conversation with Mr. Israel Zangwill on the Jew and the Future*, 1925 (with Samuel Roth); *Our Own*, 1926; *Speeches, Articles, and Letters*, 1937; *Zangwill in the Melting-Pot: Selections*, n.d.

Translation: *Selected Religious Poems of Ibn Gabirol, Solomon ben Judah, Known as Avicebron, 1020?-1070?*, 1923

Bibliography

Adams, Elsie Bonita. *Israel Zangwill*. New York: Twayne, 1971. Along with a thorough critical analysis of Zangwill's literary works, Adams provides a brief biography, a chronology, and an annotated bibliography.

Gilman, Sander L. *Multiculturalism and the Jews*. New York: Routledge, 2006. Study of the representation of Jewish identity and multiculturalism in literature by a preeminent scholar; includes a chapter on Zangwill's notion of the "melting pot."

Kahn-Paycha, Danièle. *Popular Jewish Literature and Its Role in the Making of an Identity*. Lewiston, N.Y.: E. Mellen Press, 2000. Zangwill and Philip Roth are the two major subjects of this study.

Roth, Laurence. *Inspecting Jews: American Jewish Detective Stories*. New Brunswick, N.J.: Rutgers University Press, 2004. Detailed examination of the figure of the Jewish American detective and of the Jewish American authors who write about him.

Udelson, Joseph H. *Dreamer of the Ghetto: The Life and Works of Israel Zangwill*. Tuscaloosa: University of Alabama Press, 1990. Udelson views Zangwill's works as a series of meditations on the nature of Jewish identity. He analyzes the contradictory positions Zangwill entertained from time to time.